All round perfection, beyond expectation

Address all your financial requirements, under one roof.

- Bank Transfers
- Instant Bank Transfers
- Instant Money Transfers
- Online Money Transfers
- Foreign Exchange

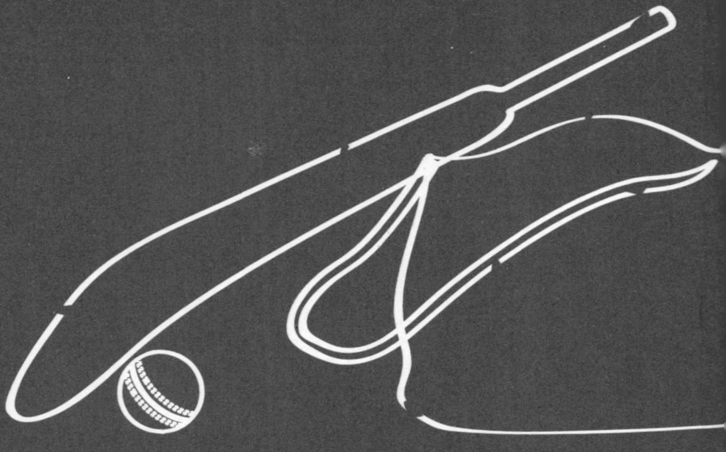

Customer Service: 600 555 550 | www.uaeexchange.com

Reviews of the 2016 Edition

There are gems in this 800-pager by some great writers and players.
It kept me enthralled.
— The Cricketer, UK

Wisden India gives more attention to the IPL... the editor speaks for
tradition (too)...
— The New Statesman, UK

The Wisden India Almanack offers an old-world pleasure involving the
tactile feel of leafing through a big book, the joy of stumbling upon a lovely
phrase, the marrying of a beloved past and a frenetic present that is often
considered the spine of following sport, and above all, a recap of
cricket's last season.
— The Hindu

Wisden India Almanack gives the also rans something to cherish that
somewhere their names and achievements are recorded in
the history of the game.
— Sanjay Bangar

Wisden India Almanack 2016 traverses both a cricketing year, several
decades and many ideas... Much of modern cricket writing, as reflected in
the Comment section, covers a vast range of topics and theories.
— ESPNcricinfo

I look forward to *Wisden India Almanack* always. There's plenty of thought-
provoking cricket reading and joyous essays on 'cricket, lovely cricket.'
— Bishan Bedi

This edition is a must read... (it) is a purist's delight, offering the reader
a variety blending tradition with modernity, the orthodox with the
unorthodox.
— Deccan Chronicle

WISDEN
INDIA ALMANACK
2017

EDITED BY SURESH MENON

WISDEN
INDIA

ALMANACK
2017

5th Edition

John Wisden & Co.

BLOOMSBURY
NEW DELHI • LONDON • OXFORD • NEW YORK • SYDNEY

JOHN WISDEN & CO.
An imprint of Bloomsbury Publishing Plc.
50 Bedford Square, London WC1B 3DP

Copyright © John Wisden & Company Limited 2017

WISDEN INDIA ALMANACK

Editor **Suresh Menon**
Senior copy editor **Karunya Keshav**
Senior staff writer **Sidhanta Patnaik**
Sub-editor **Shubham Malaviya**
Lead designer **Ashish Mohanty**

Reader feedback: suresh@wisdenindia.com

www.wisdenindia.com; www.wisden.com
Follow Wisden India on Twitter @wisdenindia and on Facebook at Wisden India

Wisden, Wisden India and the device/logo of two cricketers in top hats are trademarks of John Wisden and Company Ltd, a fully owned subsidiary of Bloomsbury Publishing Plc

Published in India by Bloomsbury India

All rights reserved. No part of this publication may be reproduced or transmitted in any form or by any means, electronic or mechanical, including photocopying, recording, or any information storage or retrieval system, without prior permission in writing from the publishers

No responsibility for loss caused to any individual or organisation acting on or refraining from action as result of the material in this publication can be accepted by Bloomsbury India or the author/editor

General legal notice: Wisden India is a collaboration between
John Wisden and Company Ltd,
a fully owned subsidiary of Bloomsbury Publishing Plc and FW Sports and Media India Private Limited, an affiliate of FidelisWorld, FZ LLC

Published by Bloomsbury Publishing India Pvt Ltd
Second Floor, LSC Building No. 4
Pocket C – 6 & 7, Vasant Kunj
New Delhi 110 070

Printed by Thomson Press India Ltd.

Hard cover ISBN 978-93-85936-48-7
Soft cover ISBN 978-93-85936-47-0
Leatherbound ISBN 978-93-85936-49-4
eBook ISBN 978-93-85936-50-0

A Taste of Wisden India 2017

The point is that cricket has a meaning that has nothing to do with profit and loss… the only people who don't know that are those who actually run the game.
Simon Barnes, Page 35

* * *

I carried no baggage whatsoever and had no idea who I was kicking out of the changing room. It is the reason, I'm told, I don't get too many Christmas cards.
John Wright, Page 40

* * *

Cricket can be an instrument for diplomacy, not an alternative to it.
Shashi Tharoor, Page 45

* * *

What are you here for? The love of the game or the clout it brings? Take away the clout and will the love remain?
Sharda Ugra, Page 58

* * *

"What god wants is a heart – any old turnip will do as a head".
Ray Monk, Page 85

* * *

The foundation of this possibility of harmony is intentionality.
TM Krishna, Page 87

* * *

Cricket for me is like a wondrous Russian novel with plots and subplots played out over the course of multiple acts.
Satya Nadella, Page 102

* * *

Sourav the captain tended to overshadow Sourav the batsman.
VVS Laxman, Page 126

The 2016-17 India-England series was the first five-Test series in India after 1986-87. Detailed reports of the series in the next edition of *Wisden India Almanack*. – *BCCI*

PREFACE

When the CEO of Microsoft, Satya Nadella says in these pages, "I am haunted by cricket," he speaks for a few million people. Not all of them actually play the game or even played it at one time, not all watch every ball of an international match, not all believe that to fully enjoy the game you should understand every aspect of it.

While putting together five editions of *Wisden India*, we have been conscious of this; our aim has been to "haunt" everybody from the stats-obsessed to the philosophically-inclined and those in-between. While writing his only essay on cricket for us, the great essayist and travel writer Pico Iyer said, "I know about 1500 words on the game, and now you have all of it." Prashant Kidambi, scholar and cricket enthusiast added a significant chapter to the history of Indian cricket in these pages, David Papineau gave us a perspective on cheating. In this issue we have Ray Monk dispelling one myth about the great philosopher Wittgenstein while adding another legend to his story. We've had the actor Naseeruddin Shah telling us about his obsession. Justice Mukul Mudgal, Ramachandra Guha, Tariq Ali and even the late Jack Hobbs have appeared here. Mike Marqusee's final piece before he succumbed to multiple myeloma asked the fundamental question: Why cricket?

The players and writers who have contributed are the best in the business (see list on page 860). It has been our pleasure to host them just as it has been our practice to introduce new writers.

In this edition, we break a convention by naming Virat Kohli Cricketer of the Year for the second time. Traditionally, you could be named for the honour just once. But Virat's transformation from a misunderstood "brat" to a dignified captain, his incredible all-round record and the manner in which he is shaping the Indian team in his own image just could not be ignored. "I wish Virat all the best to handle the extra bit of pressure that will surely come his way having received this honour," his skipper Mahendra Singh Dhoni had said on the first occasion. Kohli certainly has handled the pressure well!

No compendium can ever be the credited to a single individual. My thanks go to Karunya Keshav and Sidhanta Patnaik, the two pillars of this publication, to Shamya Dasgupta, Shubham Malaviya and to the designer Ashish Mohanty. Thanks to statisticians Mohandas Menon and P Jayapal.

Thanks to Bloomsbury, Rajiv Beri and Arvind Booni in India and in the UK, Richard Charkin, Charlotte Atyeo, Hugh Chevalier, Christopher Lane and Lawrence Booth. To *Wisden India* friends, a big thank you to Dileep Premachandran, Anand Vasu, R Kaushik.

Special thanks to my wife Dimpy, who might be "haunted" by cricket yet, and to our son Tushar, who already is.

SURESH MENON
Bangalore, November 2016

CONTENTS

Part 1 – Comment

Wisden India Honours	18
Notes by the Editor	19
A remarkable journey *by Harsha Bhogle*	28
They don't get it *by Simon Barnes*	34
The toughest job *by John Wright*	39
Cricket's burden of diplomacy *by Shashi Tharoor*	44
Legend of the oak *by Ayaz Memon*	50
BCCI feels force of Butterfly Effect *by Sharda Ugra*	55
Wittgenstein: An old turnip for cricket *by Ray Monk*	81
Aesthetics of cricket *by TM Krishna*	87
Yours sincerely *by Haresh Pandya*	94
Boardroom pitch *by Satya Nadella*	101
Finding Crowe *by Greg Chappell*	104
Evolution theory *by Sidharth Monga*	108
The gavel sounds on parity *by Saurabh Somani*	114

WISDEN INDIA HALL OF FAME

Vinoo Mankad *by Nari Contractor*	119
Sourav Ganguly *by VVS Laxman*	124
Changing laws for changing times *by Fraser Stewart*	129
Awayitis *by Karthik Lakshmanan*	132

SIX CRICKETERS OF THE YEAR

Virat Kohli *by Suresh Menon*	140
Shreyas Iyer *by Sidhanta Patnaik*	143
Yasir Shah *by Ahmer Naqvi*	146
Kusal Mendis *by Shanaka Amarasinghe*	150
Mustafizur Rahman *by A T M Sayeeduzzaman*	154
David Warner *by Ian Chappell*	157

PERSON OF THE YEAR

Justice RM Lodha *by Sandeep Dwivedi*	161
Press pass *by Raju Bharatan*	166
Pressed for trust *by R Kaushik*	172
About a boy *by Clayton Murzello*	177
Complex solutions in Bangladesh *by Shamya Dasgupta*	180
Buying into new cricket *by Vidya Subramanian*	185
It began with shattered glass in Ranchi *by Siddhartha Vaidyanathan*	190

FAREWELL

Leaders bow out *by Clayton Murzello*	193

Part 2 – Misses and hits

Into the fifth decade	200
If we had failed, it'd have gone kaput *by Shantha Rangaswamy*	201

From a history of shared kits *by Shubhangi Kulkarni*	208
The rail road *by Snehal Pradhan*	211
A record fashioned by inexperience *by Mithali Raj*	216
Homecoming *by Lisa Sthalekar*	219
Watching, waiting *by Shashank Kishore*	223
Stumbling blocks as stepping stones *by Ananya Upendran*	227
For joy, for respect *by Karunya Keshav*	231
India Women All-time XI *by Purnima Rau*	234
Statistics	240

Part 3 – Domestic review

INDIAN CRICKET

Changing times *by Sidhanta Patnaik*	246
Ghost stories and champions' lore *by Abhishek Nayar*	250
Mumbaikars make most of practice	254
Ranji Trophy	256
Irani Cup *by Sidhanta Patnaik*	319
Vijay Hazare Trophy *by Manoj Narayan*	321
Deodhar Trophy *by Himanish Bhattacharjee*	336
Syed Mushtaq Ali Trophy *by Shubham Malaviya*	338
Indian Premier League *by Karthik Lakshmanan*	350
Bista's season of opening *by Himanish Bhattacharjee*	371
Under-23 CK Nayudu Trophy *by Nisha Shetty*	373
Under-19 Vinoo Mankad Tournament *by Sidhanta Patnaik*	384
Under-19 Challenger Trophy *by Ajay Suresh*	392
Under-19 Cooch Behar Trophy *by Ajay Suresh*	393
Under-16 Vijay Merchant Trophy *by Shubham Malaviya*	405
Vizzy Trophy (Inter-Zonal University) *by Sidhanta Patnaik*	413

WOMEN'S CRICKET *by Ananya Upendran*

Inter-State One-day Competition	415
Inter-State T20 Competition	422
Inter-Zonal Three-day Competition	429
Inter-State Under-23 One-day Competition	431
Inter-Zonal Under-23 One-day Competition	436
Inter-Sate Under-19 One-day Competition	438
Inter-Zonal Under-19 Two-day Competition	446
BCCI Awards 2015-16 (Winners of 2014-15 season)	448

Pakistan Cricket *by Mazher Arshad*	450
Sri Lanka Cricket *by Andrew Fernando*	455
Bangladesh Cricket *by Quazi Zulquarnain Islam*	458
The United Arab Emirates Cricket *by Paul Radley*	460
Winners around the globe	462

Part 4 – International series

High-impact Ashwin raises the bar *by Impact Index*	476
International series scoreline	480
Debutants	481
Some shine in the rough *by Vaneisa Baksh*	484
Big boys play at night *by Dileep Premachandran*	487

INDIA INTERNATIONALS
South Africa in India *by Saurabh Somani*	491
India in Australia *by Saurabh Somani*	513
Sri Lanka in India *by Karthik Lakshmanan*	519
India in Zimbabwe *by Bharat Sundaresan*	522
India in West Indies and USA *by Anand Vasu*	528

GLOBAL TOURNAMENTS
Asia Cup *by Shamya Dasgupta*	547
ICC World T20 *by Tim Wigmore*	556

INDIA'S OTHER INTERNATIONALS
Under-19 Triangular Series in Kolkata *by Disha Shetty*	583
Under-19 Triangular Series in Colombo *by Disha Shetty*	584
ICC Under-19 World Cup *by Manoj Narayan*	586
India A in Australia *by Manoj Narayan*	595

OTHER INTERNATIONALS
Pakistan v England in UAE *by John Etheridge*	600
Ireland in Zimbabwe	610
Afghanistan in Zimbabwe	611
West Indies in Sri Lanka *by Sa'adi Thawfeeq*	614
New Zealand in Australia *by Geoff Lemon*	620
Zimbabwe in Bangladesh *by Neil Manthorp*	628
West Indies in Australia *by Adam Collins*	630
Sri Lanka in New Zealand *by Mark Geenty*	635
England in South Africa *by Stephen Brenkley*	642
Afghanistan v Zimbabwe in UAE	651
Pakistan in New Zealand	653
Zimbabwe in Bangladesh	655
Australia in New Zealand *by Geoff Lemon*	657
Australia in South Africa	663
Sri Lanka in England and Ireland *by Gary Naylor*	665
Tri-nation series in West Indies *by Ajay Suresh*	676
Pakistan in England and Ireland *by Lawrence Booth*	679
Australia in Sri Lanka *by Geoff Lemon*	692
New Zealand in Zimbabwe	702

New Zealand in South Africa	704
Afghanistan in Bangladesh	706
Ireland and Australia in South Africa	708
Beyond the Test nations	711

WOMEN'S CRICKET

INDIA INTERNATIONALS

Much promise, yet much ground to cover *by Shashank Kishore*	719
India in Australia *by Saurabh Somani*	721
Sri Lanka in India *by Ananya Upendran*	724

GLOBAL TOURNAMENTS

ICC Women's World T20 Qualifier *by Karunya Keshav*	726
ICC Women's World T20 *by Karunya Keshav*	727

OTHER INTERNATIONALS

Pakistan in West Indies	736
Sri Lanka in New Zealand	738
Zimbabwe in Bangladesh	739
England in South Africa	740
Australia in New Zealand	742
West Indies in South Africa	743
Pakistan in England	745
South Africa in Ireland	747
Bangladesh in Ireland	748
Australia in Sri Lanka	750
ICC Women's Championship 2014-2017	752

Part 5 – Reviews and Records

Cricket books *by Zenodotus*	755
Film review *by Rakesh Ramamoorthy*	768
Obituaries	771
Voice in the Windies *by Vaneisa Baksh*	776
Chronicles	806
Records	813
Selection from *Wisden India* website	853
Wisden India Almanack honours board	859
Contributors over five editions	**860**

SYMBOLS AND ABBREVIATIONS

*	In full scorecards signifies captain.
*	In short scorecards, records, signify not out.
*	In other places signifies notes.
†	In full scorecards signifies the designated wicketkeeper.
MoM/PoM	In full and short scorecards signifies Man/Player of the Match.
MoS/PoS	In full and short scorecards signifies Man/Player of the Series.
DLS	Signifies where a result has been decided under the Duckworth/Lewis/Stern method for curtailed matches.
VJD	Signifies where a result has been decided under the V Jayadevan method for curtailed matches.
	Matches abandoned or postponed are either because of rain or bad weather, unless otherwise mentioned.
(Numbers besides dismissal)	In full scorecards of first-class and Test matches signifies the batting order of a batsman in the second innings.
Economy Rate	The figure at the end of each bowler's analysis in full scorecards is the economy rate.

All statistics are valid through November 9, 2016.

FIRST-CLASS MATCHES

Men's matches of three or more days' duration are first-class unless otherwise stated. All other matches are not first-class, including one-day and Twenty20 internationals.

SCORECARDS AND RECORDS

Where full scorecards are not provided in this book, they can be found at Cricket Archive (cricketarchive.com), Wisden India (wisdenindia.com), Wisden (wisdenrecords.com) or ESPNcricinfo (espncricinfo.com).

More records can be found at www.wisdenrecords.com. The online records database is regularly updated and, in many instances, more detailed than in *Wisden India Almanack 2017*.

Cover: *Virat Kohli (BCCI);* ***Back cover:*** *Bangladesh after their win over England in the Second Test at Mirpur, October 2016. (Getty Images)*

Wisden India Honours

WISDEN INDIA HALL OF FAME

We honour sportspersons in various ways; by naming streets, roundabouts and stadiums after them, by instituting trophies in their memory, by turning them into adjectives ('Bradmansque'), by arguing, generation after generation, over the relative merits of our heroes. The most enduring and dignified method in recent years has been to induct the best into the Hall of Fame. It is the concept – often a virtual 'hall' – that is the honour, not the bricks-and-mortar building.

In its fifth year, *Wisden India* is happy to announce the names of two players inducted into the Wisden India Hall of Fame:

> Vinoo Mankad (Page 119)
> Sourav Ganguly (Page 124)

This, along with the Six Cricketers of the Year (see below) is a Wisden India annual feature.

SIX CRICKETERS OF THE YEAR

Wisden's Cricketers of the Year – a tradition dating back to 1899 in the original Almanack – is given a subcontinental flavour in *Wisden India Almanack*. The six cricketers are picked by the editor, the selection based on the players' positive impact on the season under review. It is necessary to highlight the distinction since in recent years, some players who have made an impact have done so for the wrong reasons. Negative impact does not count.

This year the list includes two Indians, and one player each from Pakistan, Sri Lanka and Bangladesh. The sixth player is from outside the subcontinent.

> Virat Kohli (page 140)
> Shreyas Iyer (page 143)
> Yasir Shah (page 146)
> Kusal Mendis (page 150)
> Mustafizur Rahman (page 154)
> David Warner (page 157)

BEYOND THE BOUNDARY
Rajendra Mal Lodha (page 161)

WISDEN INDIA BOOK OF THE YEAR

Stroke of Genius: Victor Trumper and the Shot that Changed Cricket
by Gideon Haigh (page 756)

Notes by the Editor

In recent years, the men who have had the greatest impact on Indian cricket have not been players but judges of the country's top courts. What the Board of Control for Cricket in India should have done but didn't was left to two men of integrity and wit: Justice Mukul Mudgal and Justice Rajendra Mal Lodha. Together they might have changed the face of Indian cricket by dragging the feudalistic BCCI kicking and screaming into the 21st century.

First, Justice Mudgal established that there had been spot-fixing in the IPL, and affixed responsibility. As suspected, two team owners had bet on matches. Then Justice Lodha spelt out the punishments, including bans for the owners and a two-year suspension of the two teams involved, Rajasthan Royals and Chennai Super Kings. He tempered justice with mercy, however, by not scratching the teams altogether. Two years ago, the Supreme Court had asked: Why can't the Chennai Super Kings be disqualified?

By the time the Supreme Court, tired of the BCCI's intransigent ways, its delaying tactics and woolly responses, asked Justice Lodha to put in place systems that would guarantee transparency and accountability, the BCCI had painted itself into a corner.

The climax of that saga has not played out yet. Perhaps by the time you read this there will be clarity. The BCCI, upset about the "cooling off" period recommended by Justice Lodha's committee (the recommendations were given the force of rulings by the Supreme Court), upset about the age-limit of 70 years for office-bearers and upset about a dozen other matters, chose the path of hubris rather than humility by kicking its heels in and doing nothing.

All this while the team moved steadily towards the No. 1 ranking in Tests, a feat achieved briefly in the West Indies and for a longer period during the home series against New Zealand.

Amazingly, these two major events unfolded on parallel tracks without the one affecting the other, although when the lines sometimes almost met, there was the threat of everything blowing up in the face of Indian cricket. At least the BCCI strove to give that impression, speaking of the New Zealand tour being in jeopardy, there being no money to run domestic cricket and so on.

The new BCCI, post-Narayanaswami Srinivasan, post-Shashank Manohar, steadily became indistinguishable from the old, as it ignored the Supreme Court deadlines with an arrant disregard for propriety or legality. There was a hint that the BCCI was merely part of a larger battle between the executive and the judiciary of the land. Arun Jaitley, senior minister of the government and president of the scandal-hit Delhi and Districts Cricket Association (DDCA) had said in another context that the judiciary was "destroying the edifice of India's legislature step by step, brick by brick".

By getting into the nuts of bolts of administration, the Supreme Court, however, did lay itself open to charges of judicial overreach. On the other hand, without its involvement, the extent of corruption in some of the state associations – Delhi, Jammu & Kashmir, Goa and Hyderabad to name some – might not have been exposed. Nor might the public perception have begun to change from "these things happen" to "they can't get away". Corruption is an end in itself as well as a path to garnering votes and support.

However, whatever the merits of a three-man selection committee, the matter is best left to the governing body. The 15-day break after the IPL meant that the Champions Trophy in England this year might suffer. That is a call the BCCI should make in consultation with the players' association. While the focus on Northeast cricket is welcome, justice must be tempered with pragmatism. It is too early for individual states that lack proper systems to play in the Ranji Trophy. A solution might be to have a combined Northeast team initially.

It is useful to remember, though, that the BCCI had actually invited the Supreme Court in to spring clean. It had begun in 2013 with the spot-fixing case in the IPL, and the court had given the cricket body enough time to regulate itself. But the then president, Srinivasan, was more keen on protecting his son-in-law Gurunathan Meiyappan, accused of betting on IPL matches, and decided to brazen it out, a tactic laden with peril.

The BCCI had abdicated its responsibility even before the Supreme Court came into the picture.

With Anurag Thakur, the incumbent president, following Srinivasan's tactics of delay and distraction, the reforms when Manohar took over after Srinivasan was forced to leave seemed like an aberration. Manohar quit to take over as chairman of the International Cricket Council, leaving a new generation to sort out the problems created by his own and others before them. In his brief period in charge, Manohar revealed a remarkable to-do list, considering the BCCI's traditional allergy to reform. His decisions to appoint an ombudsman to handle conflict-of-interest cases, to place the BCCI's balance sheet online and call for financial accountability from the state associations were nothing short of revolutionary.

Sometimes, when you merely do what should have been done, it can appear revolutionary. The BCCI, rich, arrogant, opaque, feudalistic, known as an international bully, operating with a remarkable lack of accountability over the years, is still the best run and most efficient sports body in the country. Which means that the rulings affecting it have the force to change the face of Indian sport itself.

Justice Lodha and his team had clearly listened to the cricketing fraternity and read the enormous amount of writing available on the matter of reforming the BCCI. Aspects of the National Sports Development Bill were seen in the report, as were elements of the ICC's Woolf report that was summarily rejected by India. Lord Woolf had said then, "The ICC acts as though it is primarily a members club. Its interest in enhancing the development of the global game is secondary."

Replace "global" with "national" and the criticism held good for the BCCI too as social clubs with little interest in cricket voted in office-bearers at state associations. Lodha did away with the proxy votes that kept the undeserving in power for decades in some associations; a clear distinction was made between the cricketing and social aspects of clubs.

The formation of a players' association, the three-member selection committee, the registration of players' agents, separate bodies for the BCCI and the IPL, the manner of dealing with conflicts of interest, bringing in the RTI Act had all been progressive ideas in the air for a long time. Had the BCCI been so inclined, it could have plucked any or all and implemented them. It didn't, and the Supreme Court had to make things clear when it said, "Fall in line, or else we will make you fall in line."

At the time of writing, the BCCI has been given more time to fall in line. If it doesn't – perhaps as part of a larger battle – the parallel tracks are in danger of meeting. And not at infinity, as our school geometry taught us, but somewhere just around the corner.

Preparing for the night

The Duleep Trophy, played under lights, may have been only a qualified success, but night Test cricket will arrive in India soon. It has made its debut in Australia already; in August this year, England take on West Indies in a day-night Test at Edgbaston.

The nay-sayers at the Duleep had a grocery list of complaints: the durability of the ball, the difficulty of seeing the seam, the artificiality of the turf which had to be 'doctored' to reduce the wear and tear on the ball, the late finish every day and more. Abhinav Mukund, a centurion in the inaugural match, said when the ball was scuffed up its colour went from pink to grey. Cheteshwar Pujara, who made 256 in the final, said he had difficulty with the seam and couldn't pick the googly.

These are genuine problems, but in waiting for perfect conditions, cricket has often lost out. Day-night Tests add an extra degree of difficulty to the sport. As Dale Steyn has said, "You want to test your skills against all that," meaning the unfamiliar conditions: the ball, the pitch, the atmosphere.

Yet something that the managing director of Kookaburra, the ball manufacturers, said in an interview to *Cricinfo* must give us pause. "The biggest challenge is the variation of pitch and playing conditions around the world. And not just from one country to the next, but even so much as one ground to the next." The implication is that the pink ball will work best around the world when pitch and ground conditions are identical. This is inimical to the idea of competition where conditions differ from Barbados to Chennai to Lord's to MCG. Homogeneity is anathema to the game, a forced one even more so. Administrators should not exchange one set of problems for another.

But if the ball is the biggest problem, surely the manufacturers can improve its quality and strength. Sometimes cricket is excessively conservative, and prefers the status quo. Familiarity breeds contempt for the new.

The game has evolved continually. Nearly every change was met with resistance; then the wheel turned again, and yet another generation resisted changes in the mistaken notion that they were protecting the integrity of the game. Night cricket, coloured clothing, the third umpire, use of technology, code of conduct, the match referee, placement of advertisement on the ground, electronic boundary hoardings, Danny Morrison – any one of these we recognise as part of the game today might have caused earlier generations apoplexy.

In India, there will be other challenges – the dew, for one. It may not be all good initially, but things will settle down, making the transition interesting. Uncertainty is the basis of competitive sport. Cricket has adapted before.

Duleep deserves better

The occasional IPL-isation of first-class cricket in the country is disturbing. When you play a national tournament for teams named after the colours of the rainbow – as those contesting the Duleep Trophy did – then it is a sign that the authorities are converting a team sport into an individual one. It is difficult to retain loyalty to entities like "red" and "green", which is why players decided to place themselves above the team. After all, no one will remember which colour won, so centuries and double-centuries alone matter. Officially sanctioned selfishness is now part of our domestic policy.

A tournament named after Duleepsinhji deserves better. Duleep, nephew of the more famous Ranji, did not play for India, but he did represent the country, as the High Commissioner to Australia. The original concept was a tournament involving five zones; it was a stepping stone to Test cricket. Now it is played merely to test out how the pink ball behaves. Last season it was called off because it was World T20 year, and the focus was on the shortest format.

DRS is here

India's cautious welcome to the Decision Review System is significant, and ensures uniformity in the one area of the game where it is called for – in decision-making. Increasingly, it has become evident over the years that India's reluctance following the 2008 series in Sri Lanka was justified. Skipper Mahendra Singh Dhoni alone gave a reason, but it wasn't the right or the logical one. He wanted the system to be 100% perfect, which, given the physics of projectiles, is impossible. The BCCI didn't explain its stand.

Yet, in hindsight, the BCCI was right to stick to it. Had India relented early, there might not have been the need or the urgency to research further. The ICC finally had DRS tested by an independent body at the Massachusetts Institute of Technology.

Paul Hawkins, who developed Hawk-Eye, once made a startling statement. "What cricket hasn't done," he said, "is test anything." By then the ball-tracking system had been in use in international cricket for five years!

An inclusive World Cup

The World T20 in India succeeded in converting many traditionalists and T20 cynics. It was a marvellous tournament, full of character and characters, none more so than Virat Kohli, who showed that runs could be made and victories launched without having to attempt big sixes all the time. With remarkable awareness, he knew precisely where the fielders were, and thus importantly, where they were not. He was master of the unoccupied areas.

On the other hand, West Indies' Carlos Brathwaite showed why six-hitting was so important, his four big ones in the final over of the tournament deciding the destination of the trophy. In trying to build a bridge between these two extremes will lie much of T20 cricket's charm and excitement in the near future.

This was a most inclusive World Cup, with enough in it for all age groups as well as for fans across formats.

West Indies were the first great team in one-day internationals, winning the World Cup twice (1975, 1979). Now they are the first great team in T20 cricket. Their cricket board might be in a shambles, but West Indies won the women's tournament at the T20 as well as the Under-19 World Cup to raise hopes for the future whatever their current status.

But spare a thought for Ben Stokes, who bowled that last over demonstrating once again that cricket is a game of centimetres. The difference between a run-choking yorker and an invitation to send the ball into the crowd is almost negligible. Almost, but not quite. In the end, Stokes sat clutching his face, his aspect that of a man who had accidentally blown up the bridge carrying his mates across a river. It wasn't just disappointment, there was horror.

One team, Afghanistan, beat the champions. And for many, the story of the tournament is the story of Afghanistan, whose entry into the main draw had all the romance and fantasy connected with sport. A collection of enthusiastic amateurs had earned the right to sup at the high table with the best in the world. No team celebrated with greater abandon, not even West Indies, no team could have inspired their beaten rivals to join them in celebrations as they did. T20 suddenly seemed to be the upholder of the spirit of cricket.

It was the English poet George Herbert who said the best revenge is living well. For Darren Sammy and his men, the best revenge was playing well, and winning the Cup.

Ashwin makes a point

Not since Erapalli Prasanna in the 1960s has an off-spinner been the spearhead of India's bowling attack, a role played with enthusiasm and intelligence by Ravichandran Ashwin. He became the quickest bowler to 200 Test wickets in 80 years, and has kept the craft alive despite regular obituaries written about it in recent years, most involving the quality of bats and T20 cricket.

Leg-spin is sexy in a manner off-spin is not. It is difficult, those who succeed at it are always seen as special. Left-arm spin is somehow associated with either grace (Bishan Bedi) or cussedness (Ashley Giles). But off-spin is seen as the journeyman's specialty; throw a ball to a non-bowler, ask him to bowl, and chances are that he will send down an off-break. Yet, in its very commonness lies the clue to its challenges. Batsmen are more likely to swing to leg, which means the offie's stock ball is in constant danger of landing up among the crowd at midwicket or long on.

There is an argument, therefore, for elevating off-spin to higher reaches of the degree-of-difficulty chart. If it is easy to bowl and easy to hit, then the bowler who is successful at it must be extra special.

Ashwin's four successive Man of the Series awards, his haul of 151 wickets in 21 Test wins, his average while claiming 110 top-five wickets (30.51) are all records. Add to that his four Test centuries and the hint of VVS Laxman in his batting, and the Tamil Nadu player can be seen as very very special too.

In a home season with 13 Tests (to be reviewed in *Wisden India Almanack* 2018), India's fortunes depend heavily on Ashwin exploiting the conditions. In recent years, the moral dilemma (if there was one) over preparing home wickets having dissipated, Indian spinners welcome teams with an understandable smacking of the lips and twinkle in the eyes.

Good news

As women's cricket enters its fifth decade in India (the first national championship was held in 1973), there is good news all around. Despite the initial scepticism after the BCCI takeover of the administration, there has been a casual switch to the kind of professionalism that raises the standard of competitive sport. The BCCI's decision to award central contracts to the players, with those in the 'A' grade receiving Rs15 lakh per year is aimed at providing security and establishing a base for regular rise in pay in future. The decision to allow the women to participate in leagues abroad should see a jump in standards.

Harmanpreet Kaur and Smriti Mandhana have signed up for Sydney Thunder and Brisbane Heat respectively in the Women's Big Bash League in Australia, the first Indians – men or women – to be involved in a foreign T20 league. India had beaten England in a one-off Test in Wormsley in 2014; then last season they beat world champions Australia 2-1 in a T20 series to stake a claim to being spoken of in the same breath as the best teams in the world. As Shantha Rangaswamy, one of the first superstars of the game says in these pages, "Things can only improve."

From Don to David

I was once allowed to handle a bat used by Don Bradman. I was amazed at its flimsiness. Nearly as flat as a pancake and with a thin handle to boot, it was a museum piece – indeed, it was at a museum that I found it! Using that bat and others like it, Bradman made his double and triple centuries (and even a quadruple). It is frightening to imagine how many runs he would have scored with today's bats.

For, to compare that bat with the ones used by the likes of David Warner would be to understand the difference between a match stick and a baseball bat. The modern batsman is fitter, stronger and supremely confident that the extended 'sweet spot' on his weapon will often carry the ball over the boundary ropes. And that's the problem.

It is an issue that is exercising the game's law-makers. The balance between bat and ball is heavily tilted in favour of the former. The bat's length and weight are defined by law, but not the areas that cause the maximum damage to bowlers (and fielders) today: the depth and the size of the edge.

The depth has increased from an average of 18mm to around 80mm today; the edges have ballooned to 55mm. One of the recommendations of the MCC Laws sub-committee is that the former be reduced to between 60 and 65mm and the latter 35 and 40mm. To use big bats that are light seems unfair to the bowler, as Ricky Ponting, among others, has pointed out.

There is also talk of a gauge through which the bat must pass for it to be deemed legal. These are some of the changes to the Code of Laws that are being contemplated before they are introduced in October this year. Fraser Stewart, the MCC Laws Manager at Lord's, has given us in this edition a "flavour of the areas of the game that are under consideration", from player behaviour to how a non-striker backing up can be run out. There was some discussion on introducing yellow and red cards, but it was felt that it is "inappropriate for cricket at this time". The key phrase there is "at this time", so a relook is possible.

Let's keep the cards out, then. I suspect that the sporting gesture – recalling a batsman, not bowling bouncers to tailenders, pointing out that a catch hasn't been taken cleanly – is in decline. But that does not mean that the opposite is on the rise. No international captain is likely to recall a batsman the way Gundappa Viswanath did during the Mumbai Test of 1980. But no captain is likely to suggest that his opposite number take him on in a wrestling bout to decide which team bats first either. That happened more than a century ago. Times change.

My country, right or left

Garry Sobers was batting on 364, the then world record of Len Hutton's, when the occasional off-spinner bowling to him, the batsman Hanif Mohammad, switched to left-arm spin. It was the third ball of the over. "Hanif, not a bowler of note," Sobers is quoted as saying in Osman Samiuddin's *The Unquiet Ones,* "asked the umpire if he could bowl left handed as I needed just one run for the record. I said it was all right and he could bowl with both hands if he wished."

Sobers pushed to cover and ran the single for the highest individual score in a Test innings – a record that stood for 36 years before Brian Lara broke it.

At the turn of the century, John Buchanan, coach of the Australian team, said the next big thing would be the bowler who could deliver off either hand. In a first-class match in 1982, Sussex opening batsman Charles Rowe bowled Geoff Arnold with off-spin, then switched to left-arm spin next ball and dismissed the No. 11 off a rank long hop.

In India, Vidarbha's Akshay Karnewar, Kerala's Mohammed Sanuth, and Gujarat's Pradip Champawat have all been known to bowl off either hand. Most coaches would advise such bowlers to focus on the style they are more comfortable with. There are too many adjustments that a bowler has to make – from getting his feet, his trunk, head, eyes in alignment – to suddenly be able to do all that with the other side of the body. Most people have a stronger eye, a stronger shoulder and a stronger side; bowling at the highest level off either hand will require both sides of the body to be of equal strength.

But with cricket – especially the shorter variety – constantly searching for the all-rounder (in various senses of the term), might not a combination of nature and nurture work in the favour of the 'freak'? The thought is exciting. After all, who believed that the reverse swing or the doosra were possible till someone actually bowled these deliveries?

Rain rules

There are few things more frustrating in cricket than to have no play while the ground is bathed in sunshine. Test cricket must ensure that an already diminishing audience is not further diminished because of administrative apathy. The ICC must carry out periodic checks to ensure that grounds are equipped to handle international matches, handing the hosts a detailed 'must-do' list before the start of a series. If matches do not take place owing to human agency, then such hosts bring the game into disrepute, and ought to be pulled up.

But there's another side to it. Umpires and players look for perfect conditions before an interrupted game can resume. The balance ought to be weighted in favour of play in less-than-perfect conditions so long as there is no physical danger to the players. I think the benefit of the doubt should go to the spectator.

Modern cricketers make too much fuss. "The elements are cricket's presiding geniuses," wrote Cardus. Players who conquer the elements dine at the high table, admired for their technique and all-round ability. Cardus worked for the print media, not television.

Wittgenstein and cricket

"Ah had no confidence in Maister Stood, sur," is a quote that immediately evokes The Oval Test of 1882 and the start of the Ashes legend. CT Studd ("Stood") was the batsman expected to take England to a win, but he could only watch from the non-striker's end as Ted Peate swung and missed and was bowled, handing Australia an improbable victory. Peate's excuse for doing so was laid out in that startling sentence.

"Whereof one cannot speak, thereof one must be silent," is the most famous statement by another philosopher, the Austrian Ludwig Wittgenstein.

What does a 19th century Yorkshire wit have in common with 20th century's greatest philosopher?

Well, nothing actually. But there is a link with the unbeaten batsman in these pages, discovered by Ray Monk, the philosopher and biographer of Wittgenstein. In his Cambridge days, Wittgenstein was a great fan of cricket, goes the legend. Ahem…, says Monk here, explaining how that misunderstanding arose. The Studd story is more fascinating.

Fantasy cricket

Everybody has his fantasy match. Jim Laker's involves Bishan Bedi and Ray Lindwall bowling at Lord's. More recently, Scyld Berry has written, "Let Michael Holding and Ted McDonald measure out their run-ups to bowl against Saeed Anwar and Wally Hammond." My own – at the moment; these things change – has Victor Trumper and David Gower taking on Dennis Lillee and Bhagwat Chandrasekhar.

A remarkable journey

HARSHA BHOGLE

Starry eyed, uncertain and, I suspect, a bit in awe of the land they were travelling to, a group of cricketers got on a boat bound for England in 1932. I have often tried to imagine being one of them; tried to travel back and live the situation. India wasn't yet independent but here was the opportunity to become 'India's' first Test cricketers. It must have been wonderful, uplifting.

Eighty-four years later, in a world beset by greater danger and uncertainty, India play 13 home Tests. It is an aberration and an examination. Can the format that is so part of us, so witness to deeds both stirring and capable of producing despair, which has produced literature and broadcasts worthy of the performances on the field, survive our era? The celebration of a landmark at the First Test against New Zealand in Kanpur was also a reminder that in a world of short attention spans, of 400-word match reports, of 140-character news sources, a five-day sporting encounter is so amazingly anachronistic.

From being one of the homes of Test cricket, where crowds snaked around stadiums and where a ticket was a trophy, India is one of the outposts. Nobody calls to ask for passes, schoolchildren are let in free to help create some 'atmosphere' and, while people still follow the Test and know what is happening, viewership, the new index of success, has recently plummeted. Yet, encouragingly, the new cricketers are happy to say that Test cricket remains the ultimate form of the game for them and still believe that respect, if not necessarily box-office value, comes from being a successful Test cricketer.

Eighty-four years and 500 Tests have been quite a journey. England remained the destination either side of the war, with Australia allowing a solitary visit soon after Partition when a land enfeebled by violence and separation sent as many players as it could to try and match Bradman's team. But cricket had long since taken root in India and players of the calibre of Vijay Merchant, Vijay Hazare, Vinoo Mankad, Polly Umrigar and Subhash Gupte had begun arriving. There were wins at home in 1952 and 1959,

Badges of history: 1932 Lord's, 1971 The Oval and 2001 Eden Gardens. – *Getty Images*

a world-record opening partnership arrived in 1956 and an away series win in New Zealand in 1967-68 (after a tour to Australia, only the second and 20 years after the first!). But 1971 remains a turning point for it coincided with the arrival of the first genuine great in Sunil Gavaskar and series wins, hitherto considered impossible, in the West Indies and, rather stunningly so, in England.

And so, I attempted to put together a team that would capture the essence of Indian cricket pre-1971. While it is beset with the inadequacies of such an effort, this is what I came up with: Merchant, Mankad, Hazare, Umrigar, Vijay Manjrekar, MAK Pataudi, Farokh Engineer, Dattu Phadkar, Erapalli Prasanna, Gupte and Mohammad Nissar, with an allowance for the great Bishan Singh Bedi somewhere and room for argument for the likes of Chandu Borde, Dilip Sardesai, BS Chandrasekhar and Salim Durrani.

Till Gavaskar came along, only two batsmen of sufficient longevity, Hazare and Umrigar, had averages in excess of 40. Only Borde, Manjrekar and Umrigar had more than 3000 runs. Gavaskar averaged 51 and made more than 10,000. He was a pioneer and seven years after him, another would arrive.

Before Kapil Dev, India's leading wicket-taker among those bowling the new ball (and often that didn't mean being a 'fast' bowler) was Ramakant Desai with 74 wickets. Phadkar had 62 and Syed Abid Ali had 47. Kapil got 434 and showed how an Indian could become among the best in his business. After him, India produced Javagal Srinath, Zaheer Khan, Irfan Pathan and Ishant Sharma in the 100-wicket club and while that isn't earth shattering, it is indicative of change. Kapil broke many stereotypes and Indian cricket has much to thank him for.

As Kapil started to wane towards the late eighties, he passed the baton to the brightest star Indian cricket has produced. The arrival of Sachin Tendulkar in 1989 coincided with an extraordinary collection of talents. In the next ten years arrived Rahul Dravid (13,265 runs), VVS Laxman (8781 runs) and Sourav Ganguly (7212 runs). Virender Sehwag with 8503 was round the corner. A year after the landmark Tendulkar debut, a young man from Bangalore carried on a tradition of engineering graduates-turned-spin bowlers (one that R Ashwin continues). Anil Kumble took 619 wickets, but the decade also saw the arrival of Harbhajan Singh with 417 and Srinath with 236. Zaheer with 311 was already in the wings. Even as one-day cricket struck roots and flowered and, indeed, bore fruit, India was to have its most fertile phase of Test cricketers.

The expression 'Golden Era' is often bandied about to speak of a time that none of us has seen. But I dare say, in years to come, this will be seen as just that. It was also an era of extraordinary gentlemen and it was their integrity and personality, as much as their glittering cricket, that saw India through a phase that was deeply painful to its devoted followers. Ganguly's Indian team erased the wounds of match-fixing quickly and brought joy back to the fans, who, by now, had become the greatest asset world cricket had.

The presence of the Fab Four allowed for the unique talents of Sehwag to burst forth. He batted like no Indian had in Test cricket and the bastion of orthodoxy, as symbolised by the batting cultures of Mumbai and the south, was revolutionised by his blazing style. Sehwag's style seemed fraught with danger, his footwork occasionally non-existent, but his approach, a perfect extension of his personality, was breathtaking, and a player who seemed to play too many shots has the three highest scores by an Indian in Test cricket.

There were some great Test matches in this phase and maybe it was befitting that so many of those came in Chennai, a land where Test cricket had firm roots. In 1998, 1999, 2001 and 2008 we got four fabulous games and India won three of those. But there were matching games and none as dramatic as the landmark Test at Eden Gardens in 2001, by any yardstick the greatest in India's history (with Laxman's 281 the finest innings played by an Indian). But much joy came in Leeds in 2002, Adelaide in 2003, Multan and Rawalpindi in 2004, Johannesburg in 2006, Nottingham in 2007 and Perth in 2008. And, you could argue, in the West Indies in 2006 and in Durban and Mohali in 2010.

There were unforgettable bowling moments. In 2001, a very young Harbhajan took 32 wickets in three Tests, a number lent greater significance by the fact that the next highest Indian wicket-taker had three! Harbhajan drew much strength from the enormous character of Kumble, who, only two years earlier, had taken all ten against Pakistan in Delhi.

But as the decade wound to an end, twin challenges appeared for Test cricket in India. First Ganguly and Kumble left, then Dravid and Laxman. Sehwag and Harbhajan faced decline and in November 2013, Tendulkar had India spellbound and teary-eyed with a moving farewell speech. Off the field, in 2008, the Indian Premier League made its debut and in captivating a generation, emerged as a rival, within the game, to the venerable but increasingly threatened Test match.

I find a lot of people looking down at T20 cricket, but they do so because they look at it through the eyes of Test cricket and miss, within it, the setting up of a batsman, the rhythm of Test cricket and the many challenges it imposes on its players; the front foot seems to go away from the pitch of the ball rather than towards it and wagon-wheels increasingly show the 'V' between third man and fine leg rather than between cover and midwicket. It is like searching for a cut of a suit in an off-the-rack T-shirt. For the future of Test cricket, we must acquire different sets of eyes for different forms of the game.

Sometimes it seems so much has changed. Fitness standards, the contours of cricket bats and, maybe in the near future, the colour of the ball. Big bats are affecting technique and defence is getting more porous. We live in an era where patience, tenacity and resilience are lower down the pecking order to style, flair and living for the day. And so, not just India, but every nation is struggling to play Test cricket in even slightly adverse conditions.

As 500 ticks over, we are lucky that the pillars of Test cricket in India, Virat Kohli, Ajinkya Rahane and Ashwin are thoughtful people. They need to play all forms but they respect Test cricket. Hopefully, they can continue to hold people's interest in the format and hand over a good product to the next generation.

I hope India plays a 1000th Test. I don't know if anyone reading this would be around. And I certainly don't know whether articles like this one would still be written. But what I do know is that if a generation emerges that doesn't know what Test cricket is, they will have missed a lot.

Harsha Bhogle (@bhogleharsha) is a cricket journalist and commentator.

Peaks and landmarks: A win over New Zealand in India's 502nd Test in Indore took the Virat Kohli-led side to the top of the ICC Test rankings. — *BCCI*

They don't get it

SIMON BARNES

What is the principal duty of an adult human being? Is it to make money at the expense of all else? To dedicate every aspect of mind, body and soul to the pursuit of riches? Or are there also duties of love? Is there also a requirement to seek beauty, truth and wisdom? Should you seek to do good? Or only to do well?

Let's look at that another way. Say you were running a sport. Let's say, for the sake of argument, you were running cricket. Is it your job to see that the sport makes as much money as possible? Or are there other considerations?

Take the chief executive's wicket. This is a recently coined term for a Test match wicket designed to last for a good five days. The idea is to maximise income: the more days, the more dollars. So you have a match in which 600 runs plays 550 runs by the fourth day, the bowlers run themselves into the ground and the batsmen score cheap centuries.

Such wickets are designed to produce bad cricket. They keep getting made because they make more money. In the short term anyway – but if you keep supplying a shoddy product then people tend to stop buying. And people are buying Test cricket less and less.

Or another relatively small point: electronic advertising boards. Here are devices specially designed to distract spectators from what they're watching. They clamour for attention in direct competition with the action. They have been deliberately introduced to decrease the enjoyment of spectators. But they make money, so they have become part of the fixtures of international cricket.

No one asks the question: Is it good for cricket? They ask instead: Will we make money from it? In other words, cricket is a business: neither more nor less. And by the harsh principles that govern such things, if it makes money it's good and survives; if it doesn't, it gets killed off.

It seems to have been agreed that the most exciting thing in cricket is the six-hit. A six was considered a special thing because it was very difficult and therefore very rare. So to make cricket more pop-

Hopes and heroes: Cricket is about the maidan and the village green. It's about caring far too much about something that doesn't really matter at all. — *Getty Images*

ular and therefore a bigger earner, the game has done everything it can to encourage sixes. The grounds are made smaller by means of boundary ropes covered by a sponsored daft-excluder. In the shorter formats, you aren't allowed to have fielders protecting the boundary, or not very many, anyway. Wickets have become roads on which bowlers can only tee it up for the sloggers. Bat technology has leapt ahead, so that mishits routinely go for six. Ball technology is static, or even retrograde: they use two white balls in 50-over cricket to keep the advantage with the batsman.

The result is that sixes have become routine. No longer worth getting excited about: Oh look, here comes another. That's the sort of thing that happens when you look at cricket entirely as a business. Goals are the most exciting things in football, but if we doubled the size of the goals, would football become instantly twice as exciting, twice as wealthy?

I am not an opponent of T20, or the IPL. Nor am I saying that we need to return to colonial values; they were also profoundly flawed in sporting as well as in other ways. That's not the argument here.

The heart of the matter is that cricket isn't an entertainment or a brand or a commodity. It's not Coca-Cola or McDonald's; for that matter it's not Krug or Beluga. The point is that cricket has a mean-

Oh look, here comes another: To make cricket more popular and therefore a bigger earner, the game has done everything to encourage sixes. — *Getty Images*

ing that has nothing to do with profit and loss.

You know that, I know that, the players know that. It seems that the only people who don't know that are those who actually run the game. And that is the most terrible thing.

Cricket is about the maidan and the village green. It's about hopes and heroes. It's about caring far too much about something that doesn't really matter at all. It's about what Albert Camus, when talking of football, described as "the stupid desire to cry on evenings when we had lost".

It's about impossible deeds and impossible results. It's about the way cricket is a dialogue between bowler and batsman, parent and child, stranger and stranger, friend and friend. It's about discussing reverse swing in a bar, or borrowing an orange to demonstrate the doosra.

It's about the place you belong to and the places you travel to. It's a little bit about being the sort of person you happen to be. It's a licensed craziness; it's a glorious way of feeling quite dreadful about a triviality. It's a way of experiencing love, truth, beauty, wisdom, hope, despair, dismay, hilarity, joy.

But you can't explain that to the people who run cricket because they don't get it. They just see us all as customers.

Why this blindness? It comes about because people in positions of serious power tend to put power first and everything else a rather distant second. And it's a fact of life that the more money you control the more power you have.

People who run cricket don't necessarily want the money for themselves. They want the power it gives. They want to control things, make decisions, have people do what they say, and, as a bonus, revel in the cosmetic side of power: the private jets and presidential suites and unsolicited gifts and the fawning of one and all.

And so cricket is being run in order to maximise the power of those who run it – rather than to make cricket a better game.

Here's a question: What do you need for good sport? Answer: A good contest with good contestants. In other words, every leading cricket nation has a vested interest in the rude health of all the other nations.

If Coca-Cola put every other soft drink company out of business, then so much the better for them. If Manchester United put every other Premier League team out of business, they would cease to exist themselves. That's because sport is not the same thing as business.

But the governing bodies of cricket in India have allied with those of England and Australia to take control of the game and to squeeze the rest. Cricket would be a much lesser thing without West Indies or poor homeless Pakistan. The ICC should be doing everything possible to help them. Instead, the policy of the ICC seems to be to nudge them gently towards extinction.

Sport is also about the pursuit of excellence. At the Olympic Games you see many sports that are not, on the face of it, entertaining, certainly not in the manner of the IPL. In the rowing events six crews row along a lake 2000 metres long and, er, that's it. It's short on cheap thrills, but it's a superb exhibition of trained-in excellence. The International Olympic Committee is not trying to drop rowing in case people with short attention spans fail to cope with its demands. It's part of the Olympic programme.

Most cricketers agree that Test match cricket is the ultimate form of the game: the one on which excellence most profoundly resides. The one that counts. The shorter forms are great, sure, but they lack the epic resonance of Test match cricket.

A sporting body's duty, then, is to do all it can to promote sporting excellence. It's not a matter of what fills the coffers and what people with short attention spans like best. A sporting administrator has a duty to excellence before finance. But that duty is not being fulfilled. In fact, they are not even trying. Test match cricket is dying before our eyes because business has triumphed over excellence – over sport itself – in a manner that is not so much a victory as a rout.

You can see the same sort of thing happen with charities. There comes a point in the life of a charity when you can make a jump into a bigger league, generally by making an alliance with a commercial partner with its own agenda. You can become more important, employ more people and wield more power. All you lose is your original mission.

You can kid yourself that it's a mature compromise from which everybody benefits – or you can say no, damn it, what matters here is the integrity of our original mission.

What matters in cricket is balance. It starts with the balance between bat and ball – and these days that's grotesquely skewed towards the batters. It continues with the balance between one cricketing country and another. After that you must strike a balance between the pursuit of money and the pursuit of excellence.

It's all about soul. We follow cricket because the game has a soul. Sell it to the corporates and you will end up with no soul and no game and no opponents and no spectators and no one raiding the fruit-bowl to bowl a doosra and the maidans and the village greens will become luxury housing developments – because that's the way to make money and money is after all the only thing in life that maters, is it not?

Unless you happen to have a soul.

Simon Barnes (@simonbarneswild) has written about cricket and wildlife in a career that has spanned over three decades.

Maximum impact: Someone like Anil Kumble, who has played at the highest level, can bring with him a rare but precious trait: empathy. — *BCCI*

The toughest job

JOHN WRIGHT

A few days after his appointment as India coach, when I read that Anil Kumble brought my name up when talking about how he would go about the job, I thought maybe something all those years ago had rubbed off, but I knew he would do it his way.

From a distance, it appeared that the Indian team had come full circle; the cycle that began with the appointment of its first foreign coach in 2000 had ended with one of the strongest cricketers and tacticians I have worked with in charge of a team with an ambitious captain and exciting players. For this young Indian team, it appeared a very good fit. Anil would be like he was as a cricketer, quietly going about his business: minimum fuss, maximum impact.

Many years after I left the India job, Anil and I were to work again with Mumbai Indians. He was mentor and called me in to be head coach and it was an easy and enjoyable partnership. To experience and succeed in the tough IPL environment was very satisfying. At work in the dugout, Anil was impressive, his analysis of batting opposition outstanding and meticulous; but then he had been doing that for years. It's not like we talked about coaching; he's seen enough coaches over the years, is a good observer and has a fair idea of what works and what doesn't.

It has been a long time, more than ten years, since my stint with the Indian team – a lifetime really – and I can only try to imagine what doing the job would be like today. Much has changed and more than birds now twitter. In 2000, being an outsider and the first foreign coach for the Indian team had its advantages. I carried no baggage whatsoever and had no idea whom I was kicking out of the changing room. It is the reason, I'm told, I don't get too many gilt-edged Christmas cards. Being a foreign coach in India was not expected to work and that perhaps was my single biggest motivation.

Coaching, if you can last, is similar to most professions. The more you do it the more you learn about the job and yourself. In tough situations experience can be an asset. Prior to the Indian job I had the advantage of a four-year coaching stint with Kent on the county circuit. Invaluable. You learn from your experiences and it is funny some of the things you remember. George Sharp, the ex-Northamptonshire wicketkeeper who later went on to become a top umpire, offered this when I began working in county cricket: If you can keep them happy, you'll beat half of them.

In the county set-up, that's not far from the truth.

And as a player I have never forgotten my old Derbyshire scorer who pulled me into line over a pint of bitter when I chose to wax lyrical about my innings of the day. The old man said, "Aye, lad, you did play well. But if you die tonight, we'll manage." Or the groundsman to whom I cribbed about a wicket being particularly green, to which he abruptly replied, "Grass is always bloody green."

Undoubtedly, one or two in India unhappy with the decision to appoint a foreign coach would have definitely managed without me. What I was to learn in coaching and in India was this: You have to have the confidence and strength of mind to be yourself while respecting others and their opinions. From there the group has to decide what is best for the team and move on with it. If everyone can put everything else aside – theories, notions, assumptions, egos – and answer the question of what is best for the team, it's a good start. You fix the things you can fix – fitness, punctuality, the right support staff – and the cricket in the cricketers will take over.

In a coach's early days, like with me, one of the most important factors is whether the players stand up for you and your efforts. Players are not silly, they have to believe the person or the systems in place are actually helping them as individuals and as a team. Then differences in language, culture and approach are duly respected and quickly fade into the background. All the greats have a strong sense of self-awareness and the boys I worked with did. I was fortunate to coach an outstanding group of players, exceptionally gifted, who wanted to learn and above all else to perform, particularly outside India.

Anil was part of that original engine room, and we were able to make things move. Over the next decade, from 2000 to 2011, with different set-ups and personnel, I was pleased to see the group I'd first worked with and the next generation that came though – Bhajji, Viru, Yuvi, Zak, Ash Nehra, Kaif – make the Indian team stamp their mark on the world game. In that first decade, they began winning Tests overseas, reached the No. 1 ranking in all forms of the game and were part of World Cup-winning teams in two formats. Their generation will always be counted among the great Indian teams, remembered with pride by Indian fans. As a fighting team, which I always said the fans deserved. It was a simpler message in simpler times.

Some parts of the India job were unforgiving, others tested me to my limit. The job never felt particularly secure, it hinged on results. Just before the team left for the 2003 World Cup, Jagmohan Dalmiya, then BCCI president, a demanding but fair boss, had me over to his office for a chat. He wished me well and said, "If you don't come first or second, we might not be meeting again."

In hindsight, at the highest level, it is only fair everyone should be on their toes, including the coach. Ever since then, I have never bought into the jargon of team rebuilding, etc. It is what it is – not cathedral construction, but winning matches.

Anil's familiarity with the environment and his stature among the players meant he could get directly to the heart of the business. A successful coach doesn't have to necessarily "have played" at the highest level. In some cases, not being a player from the top can allow a more objective assessment, but only if the coach does not think of himself as the man in charge of reinventing the wheel. On the other hand, a coach who has played at the highest level can bring with him a rare but precious trait: empathy. His own playing career would have taught him the hard lessons of failure, how to pick him-

John Wright: 'Parts of the India job were unforgiving, others tested me to my limit.' – *Getty Images*

self up, the reasons for action and tactics – if a second slip is worth having then perhaps a first is as well – and how to identify and tackle doubt weighing down a player.

To get things to work inside a team, a deep knowledge of the game is helpful, an understanding of who is responsible for what is necessary, and being able to trust each other is critical. As head coach, I favoured a small tight support group because sometimes getting out of the way is more important than getting involved. A busload of helpers becomes problematic.

Besides, a modern-day coach must work over three formats. While basics of the game remain the same, there are subtleties in tactics and approach and the coach must switch between them, deal with a wider turnover of players and handle a varying range of skill levels.

Coaches often look at players and go: "Wow, this kid could really be something!" Then their job begins. To help shortcut the development of that player so he doesn't repeat the mistakes you have seen or even made yourself. You can't do their bowling or batting for them, but you can help individual players mature. You need to let the player arrive at the point where he knows what works for him and who he is as a player. You can save him some time in getting there or lead him in the direction of fellow players whose messages and conversations are often more contemporary or powerful than from the coaching staff. In that sense, for a long time, alongside my work, Anil was also coaching the younger members of the Indian team, as were other senior peers.

Anil implicitly understands his environment. As a captain, he was known as a man of utter fairness; senior, junior, superstar, debutant makes no difference to him and he doesn't suffer fools gladly. Having effectively been appointed by his ex-playing peers, he understands that he will be judged by them, the media and the fans. It is also a lonely job, as it means a lot of time away from family. He invited on himself again the kind of pressure that he went through as a player.

That's what made it a big and a brave call, for an ex-cricketer to put himself up to coach his national team. Ravi Shastri also did that for a short period and while Anil and he are very different personalities, they are both passionate and care about Indian cricket. Anil could have stood back and taken the easy option, not had a go at coaching India. That means sitting back and making blanket judgements from a safe distance.

It is only wise to tap into the knowledge of outstanding home players. When I look back at the group that I worked with and, in a sense belonged to, it had some outstanding people and cricket minds. Along with Anil there were Sourav, Rahul, Sachin, Laxman, Srinath, Viru and Zak and it is good to see them involved in some capacity, which is healthy for Indian cricket. In some countries, the game has been hijacked by administrators who like to keep ex-players at arm's length and that is a great waste of knowledge. Fortunately, India have gone down a different road. I couldn't be happier.

From an old Indian coach to a new one, I say only this: Enjoy the job, I certainly did. Life was never dull.

A former New Zealand captain, John Wright coached India to success between 2000 and 2005.

Cricket's burden of diplomacy

SHASHI THAROOR

Consider the evidence. In Mumbai, the powerful Shiv Sena party says it will object to any bilateral cricketing engagement with Pakistan, and it trashes the offices of the Board of Control for Cricket in India when the Pakistani cricket board chief is visiting his counterpart there. A T20 match has to be shifted from the Himachal Pradesh town of Dharamsala because the chief minister there felt the families of Indian soldiers from his state would not welcome a game with the enemy. And when rumours float in the media of a possible resumption of Test series, a ruling party legislator, himself a former home secretary, rises to condemn the very thought of playing cricket with a country whose terrorists continue to attack India with impunity.

What are the prospects for normal cricketing relations with Pakistan in these circumstances? Since the horrors of the attack on Mumbai in November 2008 (known to many as 26/11), India and Pakistan have not played a bilateral Test series against each other, though they have clashed in one-day and T20 tournaments, including three World Cups. There was a three-match bilateral one-day series in India in 2011, but that turned out to be an aberration: resistance to bilateral cricketing contact remains high in India.

The irony is that there is a good argument to be made for the healing capabilities of sport, and the United Nations has made it. Cricket, like all international sport, embodies the values of co-existence transcending political differences – a key United Nations principle, which is why the UN, since Kofi Annan's time, has promoted Sports for Development and Peace. Cricket, as a global game, features people with different ethnicities, colours, religions and creeds striving towards the same goals. Cricket is also dedicated to the notion of 'playing by the rules'; strict adherence to the laws of cricket includes honouring the spirit of those laws, so that, for instance, the mildest show of dissent against an umpiring decision is severely sanctioned. The phrase "it's not cricket" has come to be used whenever any conduct is palpably unfair, or – to recall a deplorably sexist but irreplaceable word – ungentlemanly. With all of these elements, cricket can arguably be a valuable force for the promotion of the values and

Plank for peace: Cricket is a sport; a cricket team represents a country, it does not symbolise it. – *Getty Images*

principles of peace and co-existence between any two countries – India and Pakistan surely not excepted.

And yet, the question of whether, amid all the strife that besets the two countries' cricketing relations, a mere sport can bring India and Pakistan together, is at one level easy to answer: No. Sport can sublimate many emotions, but it cannot be a substitute for geopolitics. Cricket can be an instrument for diplomacy, not an alternative to it.

After all, six decades of cricketing relations have done little to promote good relations between the two antagonists. If anything, the game has been a victim of politics, as proved by the 18-year gap in cricketing relations between the two countries from 1960 to 1978, the dozen-year hiatus in Pakistani Test tours of India between 1987 and 1999, and the current stalemate, brought about by the Pakistani terrorist assault on Mumbai on 26/11 and sustained by subsequent incidents.

The basic challenge to 'normal' cricketing relations lies in the nature of Partition, which carved a Muslim state out of India. In Pakistan, cricket is expected to bear a particularly heavy burden as the embodiment of national pride against the larger (and more powerful) neighbour from which it seceded. From the 1950s, Pakistan acquired its own distinctive characteristics marked by increasing militarisation and growing Islamicisation. Soon after its first military coup,

Pakistan's new president, the rather grandly titled Field Marshal Mohammed Ayub Khan, also named himself the president of the Board of Control for Cricket in Pakistan (as the Pakistan Cricket Board was known then) and consciously sought to use cricket as an expression of Pakistani national identity. Ayub's dual roles highlighted for the first time two vital features that would come to be fundamentally important to an appreciation of Pakistan cricket: the increasing militarisation of Pakistani society, including its sport; and the growing identification of Pakistani cricket with Pakistani nationalism.

The instrumentalisation of cricket in the service of a militarised nationalism, especially against India, is a feature of Pakistani cricket. So are explicit evocations of a religious mission (as when Pakistan's then captain, Shoaib Malik, publicly thanked "Muslims all over the world" for their presumed support to his team in the 2007 T20 World Cup, the kind of bigoted remark that would have had an Indian captain sacked within minutes). The contrast with India's multi-religious, multi-ethnic and commercially driven cricketing culture is striking, and significant.

These are two countries whose soldiers have frequently shot at each other, where border tensions have erupted into war, and where the result of a cricket match can prompt a soldier to unleash a volley of celebratory or intimidatory fire on the Line of Control. Above all, this is a region where the fomenting of terrorism in India by Pakistan and (in Pakistani eyes) the 'sufferings' of Muslims in India creates in each side a 'moral obligation' to teach the perpetrators a lesson on the cricket field. No other cricketing rivalry in the world has to contend with such a perverse mixture of elements sharpening the keen edge of competition between them.

It is striking that, even when 'normal' cricketing contacts and frequent bilateral series flourished between 1978 and 1989, they provided a jarring contrast to the tensions prevailing off the field. During this very period, Pakistan regimes sought to bleed India through militancy sponsored by Islamabad, while maintaining seemingly bonhomous cricketing relations. For all his professions of good neighbourliness, the Pakistani dictator at the time, General Zia-ul-Haq, who even attended a Test match in Jaipur amidst much fanfare and talk of 'cricket diplomacy', provided more than moral support to two groups of rebels active in India, the Khalistani terrorists and the Kashmiri mujahideen. There was of course something utterly cynical about an exercise in which General Zia visited India to watch a Test match to defuse tensions being stoked by his own intelligence services' sponsorship of terror in India, which is why the slogan "cricket for peace" had a hollow ring in New Delhi. Many across the Indian political spectrum questioned the wisdom of playing cricket as usual with a country that was systematically seeking to undermine India at the same time. The hiatus in mutual tours, which followed, was thus inevitable.

Against such a background, it is expecting too much for cricket matches between India and Pakistan to remain mere sporting spectacles. As CLR James has so memorably written, "What do they know of cricket who only cricket know?" The two sides once played each other in the 1999 World Cup in England while the Pakistani-instigated war over Kargil in Kashmir was going on. On the very day of India's 47-run victory, six Pakistani soldiers and three Indian officers were killed.

And yet there is a good argument to be made for the healing capabilities of cricket. When India embarked on a peace offensive with its 2003-04 tour of Pakistan, the Pakistan government, for the first time in five decades, allowed thousands of Indians to cross the border on 'cricket visas'. They were greeted effusively by ordinary Pakistanis; to be an Indian in Lahore or Karachi those days was to be offered free rides, discounted meals and purchases, and overwhelming hospitality. It was said, not entirely in jest, that large numbers of Pakistanis were going about pretending to be Indians to avail of these benefits for themselves.

But, less than five years later, came the horrors of 26/11. The first cricketing casualty (aside from the Champions League scheduled in Mumbai itself the week after the attacks) was the planned Indian tour of Pakistan in January 2009. As MS Gill, India's then sports minister, remarked in calling off the government's permission, "You can't have one team coming from Pakistan to kill people in our country and another team going from India to play cricket there." Since then, the two countries have hardly played each other, except in international tournaments like the World Cup, a single charity game and one solitary one-day series in 2011; and Pakistani players have not participated in subsequent editions of the IPL, initially because of a Pakistani ban on their cricketers playing in India, and subsequently because no IPL team seemed willing to bid for Pakistanis. Politics has clearly again trumped cricket.

So where does this leave the prospects for cricket promoting peace between these sibling nations entwined together by history with bonds of paradox?

For many years now, the talk has been of war, militancy, terrorism and even nuclear threat. (Both the Kargil War in 1999 and the attack on India's Parliament in 2001 occurred just a few years after both countries had exploded nuclear devices. A military rivalry that had once been described by an ignorant critic as "a communal riot with machine guns" had now escalated into the threat of mutual annihilation.) Indian politicians routinely ask how India could play cricket with a country that supports terrorism against us and has not punished the perpetrators of 26/11 or reined in those who vow to conduct more such attacks on India. Many ruling party MPs object to any sporting relations with Pakistan; even Anurag Thakur, then secretary and now president of the BCCI, himself a BJP MP, found himself undermining his own cause by questioning whether cricket was possible as long as Pakistan did not change.

When a thaw occurs, cricket matches will instantly follow. But there's the rub: Cricket will follow diplomacy, not precede it. Even the warmth of 2003-04 was not a cause for better relations between the countries, but a reflection of it. And when things are unpleasant between the governments, matches that take place at times of tension, as with the World Cup encounter during Kargil, mirror the antagonism; they do not cause it.

Yet the tendency to see these matches as warfare by proxy is also unfortunate. Cricket is a sport; a cricket team represents a country, it does not symbolise it. To ask cricket to bear a larger burden than any other national endeavour is palpably unfair. Yet cricket is selectively being made to pay the price of Indian anger against Pakistan. We have not imposed sanctions on that country, withdrawn ambassadors or stopped trade with them. But the one activity being singled out for opprobrium is the playing of cricket.

That's unfair. I happen to believe that we need to engage Pakistan across a variety of fronts, and I am strongly in favour of people-to-people contacts with regular Pakistanis to balance the malign influence of the military and the mullahs. Cricket affords one of the best ways of getting the two countries to engage with each other constructively, and the two peoples to think about each other's talents and not their prejudices. Cricket has been, and can be, an instrument of policy-makers determined to send a broader message to the general public. But the policy issues remain unresolved, and till they are, cricket remains above all a sport, not "war minus the artillery".

There is too much at stake for both the governments of India and Pakistan in their political relations for any serious breakthrough to be prompted by the interests of cricket. But when leaders wish to make a breakthrough, sending a cricket team can be a highly effective way of doing so. Cricket has been, and can be, an instrument of policy-makers determined to send a broader message to the general public. But if political interests can drive cricket tours, the interests of cricket will never determine national policy.

Just as there is no certitude that periods of peace will ever last, so too it is to be hoped that the period of tension we have experienced for over eight years will also ebb. If normality comes, cricket might gradually achieve a more reasonable place in the national discourse between the two countries. Many liberals on both sides of the border hope that one day India and Pakistan will enjoy relations comparable to those between the United States and Canada – with open borders, shared culture and entertainment, free trade, even frequent migration. Healthy sporting competition would then be part of a healthy overall relationship; cricket matches between the two countries, followed with good-natured partisanship rather than religiously-inspired passion, could be the centrepiece of such a new era. It is not too much to hope for – one day.

Shashi Tharoor (@ShashiTharoor) is an Indian Member of Parliament, former United Nations diplomat and author. A version of this essay appeared on the Wisden India website.

Legend of the oak

AYAZ MEMON

"Legends are material to be moulded, and not facts to be recorded," wrote the American author Hervey Allen somewhere. This flies in the face of the first primer of journalism, that accuracy is everything. But there are stories where some license in imagination is not such a bad thing. In fact, it may actually take us closer to the truth.

Facts are sacrosanct, but oftentimes in sport they can be terribly mundane. Legends and myths breathe life into personalities, circumstances and achievements. They add a dimension that can help understand the core value of a proposition or person better.

Cricket buffs growing up in Mumbai in the 1960s and '70s frequently heard of Colonel CK Nayudu's exploits: of how he once hoicked the ball out of the Bombay Gymkhana onto Dadabhoy Naoroji Road, about 150 yards away. And on another occasion, hit the clock in Rajabai Tower when playing at Oval Maidan.

Neither of these incidents is true. What is fact is that Nayudu hit 11 sixes in an innings (of 153) playing for Hindus against Arthur Gilligan's MCC at Bombay Gymkhana in 1926-27, and that one of them landed on the roof of the club house.

But it is the folklore surrounding his big hitting that paints a more riveting picture of Nayudu's power and the grip he had on the Indian cricket follower's psyche: something that made him the most idolised cricketer in the country (long after his death too!) till the arrival of Sachin Tendulkar.

The most absorbing legend I heard growing up in Mumbai is about Hanif Mohammad, the dapper opening batsman from Karachi who died on August 11, 2016, and specifically the 160 he scored at Brabourne Stadium during the First Test of the 1960-61 series against India.

"So solid was his defence, you could hear the ball hitting the middle of his bat even at Churchgate Station," an old-timer told me a number of times. His eyes would light up each time he related this, as if overwhelmed by his own description. And each time he would follow up with a loud "*Tok!*" to highlight the impact of

Hanif Mohammad, the Little Master: A game built on superb technique, mastery over opponents and respect among anyone who watched him. — *Popperfoto/Getty Images*

ball on Hanif's bat. This offbeat imagery and melodramatic sound effect spoke of not just Hanif's superb technique and mastery over opponents but, more pertinently, the respect he evoked. Remember, this was being said of a Pakistani batsman. Given the peculiar and volatile socio-political fabric of the subcontinent, this would ordinarily have been anathema.

It was not just cricket fans who could get hyperbolic about Hanif. "He had the broadest bat I have seen in any batsman," India's Madhav Mantri, wicketkeeper-batsman for a few Tests in the 1950s, told me a few years ago. "Once he was set, he was unshakeable, like an oak tree."

Mantri was from the Bombay school of batsmanship, which boasts of arguably the richest legacy in the cricket universe. He had played alongside Vijay Merchant, was Sunil Gavaskar's uncle, and had seen Tendulkar grow from a prodigy into a full-blown genius. For Hanif to be spoken of in the same vein was extraordinary praise.

But then Hanif was no ordinary cricketer. A child prodigy, he was weaned on cricket, with his mother the driving force. Four of her five boys (Wazir, Mushtaq and Sadiq being the others) were to play Tests, making them a unique cricketing family; the only one to miss out was Raees.

The Mohammad family migrated from Junagadh to Karachi during Partition and initially found refuge in a temple before settling down among the *mohajirs* (migrants). Hanif's talent was evident from a young age and he found a mentor in Master Aziz, father of Salim Durrani, the mercurial all-rounder who was to play with some distinction for India.

"In Hanif *bhai*, my father found everything that he himself wanted to be," Durrani once told me. The precocious youngster loved to bat for hours on end and also showed wicketkeeping and bowling skills. "He wanted him to be a great all-rounder, but Hanif *bhai* lost interest in bowling as his batting flowered," said Durrani.

At 18, Hanif made his Test debut against India in Delhi, scoring a half-century in the first innings of the First Test of the first series between the two new countries. It was the start of something that was to give him cult status.

The aftermath of Partition loomed over the subcontinent. Cricket between India and Pakistan then was played amid much tumult, mutual suspicion and an anything-but-lose approach. Fans in both countries were unforgiving of failure. The burden on players was enormous. Only the most capable – technically and temperamentally – could take the strain.

I have dwelt at length on Indo-Pak cricket because in many ways this defined Hanif's stature in the game; perhaps even more than his monumental 337 against West Indies, or 499 playing for Karachi versus Bahawalpur in a first-class match, an innings that earned him international renown and the sobriquet of 'Little Master'.

His overall record against India is not earthshattering: 970 runs in 15 Tests at 40.41. Without context, this would pass off as modest, but it, in fact, was the most made by any batsman from either country in the first decade (1952-62) of Indo-Pak bilateral cricket.

Hanif was soon the bulwark of his side, playing out long hours, frustrating bowlers and being the biggest obstacle for India. While this earned him the grudging respect of fans and rivals in India, there were some unsavoury events too: Just before the Bombay Test in 1961-62, he had his hand slashed by a blade-wielding man. Fortunately, it was no more than a gash.

By the time I became conscious of Indo-Pak cricket and its heroes, this bilateral contest had come to a standstill as political relations between the two countries nosedived. There were no Tests played between 1961 and 1978 when, finally, India hopped across the border for a three-Test series.

Hanif had long retired by then, but his legend hadn't faded, so when I was on my first overseas assignment, to Pakistan in 1982-83, he was the player I was most keen to meet. When I got a chance to go to his house in Karachi, tagging along with Lala Amarnath, I was overjoyed.

In his fifties then, Hanif still moved with grace, gliding along the floor with minimum effort. He chain-smoked through a cigarette holder, and in between puffs, spoke softly but with clarity. I thought the feisty Lala, who had had several run-ins with Pakistani players in his time, would not get along with Hanif beyond the formalities of the visit. But the two were soon like a house on fire, reminiscing about the old days.

The conversation was littered with choice Punjabi expletives (mainly from Lala), particularly when discussing captaincy. Both seemed to believe they were victims of board and dressing room politics. But what I remember most from that memorable evening was Hanif's views on batting.

While talent was undoubtedly needed, he said, batsmanship centred on balance, concentration and conservation of energy (he had, remember, scored 337 and 499), without which bowlers could sort you out soon enough.

It's important to read the ball from the bowler's hand. For that you need absolute and constant attention. It's also equally important to know which ball to play and which to leave. That's learned through hours of net practice, not in a match. He found all these qualities in Gavaskar, he said – who, as an opener, was a kindred soul.

He remembered many of those he had played against, making special mention of Ramakant Desai, who had subdued him with short-pitched stuff in 1960-61. "I enjoyed the hook shot, but had to cut it out because of the demands of the team," he said, confessing that the small-built Desai had surprised him with his pace and bounce.

Hanif was delighted that Indo-Pak cricket had resumed. "My biggest regret is that we (India and Pakistan) stopped playing in 1961, when I was at my peak," he said. To which the irascible Lala countered: "*Tumne jitna pareshan kiya woh kya kam tha?* (Didn't you trouble us enough?)"

But just how good was Hanif? A Test career batting average of 43.98 would pale against the game's best. In Pakistan cricket itself, Javed Miandad, Zaheer Abbas, Mohammad Yousuf, Inzamam-ul-Haq, Saeed Anwar, Younis Khan and Misbah-ul-Haq boast of more impressive figures.

Hanif, though, ticks all boxes that validate greatness: Test centuries in every country he played in, and 12 overall in just 55 matches, including a double and a triple. His first-class average from 238 matches is 52.32.

For most of his career, he opened the batting, and when you look at the performances of players from all countries in the 1950s, it marks him out as special – perhaps the best opener of his era.

But while statistics give very good insight into the prowess of a cricketer, they do not necessarily tell the true story. The era and circumstances the runs were scored in, the quality of the opposition and the strength of his own team have a significance that can't be found in scorecards.

Hanif's career coincided with the infancy of his country and the socio-psychological impact he had on his people was immense. When Hanif was at the crease, Pakistan felt secure, so to speak. That can never be adequately explained by batting average, runs scored and centuries, but '*Tok!*' says it all.

Ayaz Memon (@cricketwallah) has over 30 years of experience in writing on sport.

BCCI feels force of Butterfly Effect

SHARDA UGRA

If the Board of Control for Cricket in India had the time or energy to look back from where it found itself at the tail end of 2016, it would have grasped the full meaning of the Butterfly Effect. The richest governing body in Indian sport had its financial freedom clipped, its biggest rights deal slowed to a standstill and its leading officer-bearers under pressure to respond to directives of the Supreme Court.

How did it get there? Call it the Butterfly Effect, which belongs to chaos theory in mathematics and was once used to create the most attractive metaphor around weather systems. A butterfly flapping its wings in one part of the world, we were told, could lead to a hurricane or tornado elsewhere. In the more certain sciences, the Butterfly Effect is about understanding how microscopic changes can lead to mammoth consequences.

In the BCCI's case, what began as a single decision in a Mumbai courtroom three years ago has led to a chain of events that could have a profound effect on how Indian sports will be run.

The tornado in this case is a document called the Report of the Supreme Court Committee on Reforms in Cricket. Or, more commonly, the Lodha report. The BCCI's refusal to comply with its recommendations in totality when ordered to do so by the Supreme Court on July 18, 2016, stretched into a months-long wrestle and spectacular displays of brinkmanship.

It involved two parties – the BCCI and the committee behind the creation of the report – and took place through a series of emails, media leaks and obfuscation. Between the BCCI's drive to retain some of its most precious elements of status quo and the panel's desire to see its recommendations implemented, Indian cricket administration was put on the rack.

At the heart of the debate, the document: the Report of the Supreme Court Committee on Reforms in Cricket covers 189 pages. The first 84 examine the BCCI's established practices, take apart its functioning and suggest remedies across the board. The remaining 105 pages helpfully lay down a newly minted BCCI constitution.

BCCI's top brass, with Anurag Thakur as president, remained defiant in the face of court directives to implement the Lodha report. — *Getty Images*

The report is supported by 146 pages of annexures and reference material, models of sports governance around regulation, recognition, and ethics codes of member bodies and professional franchises.

The report was the result of one of two major tasks given to a Supreme Court-appointed panel, led by a former Chief Justice of India, Rajindra Mal Lodha, 67, and with two former Supreme Court judges, Ashok Bhan, 73, and RV Raveendran, 70, as members. Their first task, detailed by the Supreme Court on January 22, 2015, was more high profile: to decide the quantum of punishment for entities caught in the 2013 IPL corruption scandal.

The second task appeared amorphous: The same panel was asked to suggest amendments to the BCCI's rules and regulations "with a view to preventing sporting frauds, conflict of interest, streamlining the working of BCCI to make it more responsive to the expectations of the public at large and to bring transparency in practices and procedures followed by BCCI." When the court issued its order, the task appeared doomed for the category called One of Those – a judicial committee report that would find its way into the Supreme Court's basement cupboard of much-ignored court committee recommendations.

It was a fate that had befallen recommendations in India on far more important issues – like investigations into communal riots or labour and police reforms. This was Indian cricket, the stuff of bread and circuses, involving the BCCI, which contained in its ranks many political heavies and enormous financial weight. In January 2015, no one would have offered attractive odds on the Lodha panel report making any impact.

It was only the chaos theorists who could have read the signs and given the BCCI a warning. The two-year suspensions handed out to Rajasthan Royals and Chennai Super Kings, and life bans for two key franchise officials Gurunath Meiyappan and Raj Kundra would become mere footnotes in the jumbled history of cricketing corruption in India. What was happening on the ground beyond it was more significant.

The judges in the Supreme Court who ran into the 2013 IPL corruption case were in their 60s and 70s, cricket fans to a man, it appeared, from the Sunil Gavaskar era. One of them on the bench that had followed on the case from July 2014 onwards was next in line to become the Chief Justice of India. When Tirath Singh Thakur took over the highest job in the Indian judiciary, he was to challenge and confront the new government, pitting the judiciary against the executive. It was part of an environment referred to by political commentator Pratap Bhanu Mehta as "judicial exasperation". When the singular former Chief Justice RM Lodha was named to head the three-man panel appointed by Thakur and FMI Kalifullah, the Butterfly Effect had gone into play. A hurricane was coming.

In July 2015, the Lodha committee announced its quantum of punishment to the parties concerned in the IPL scandal and set upon its more complex task: exploring the nuts and bolts of the BCCI's functioning, identifying its governance and ethical loopholes, and finding and suggesting a way to rectify them. It wasn't exactly needle in haystack stuff. It was discovering what lay under the haystack and why it couldn't be moved.

In early April 2015, the committee sent out a questionnaire to the BCCI – 135 questions under eight heads – which covered the extent of the organisational structure and asked questions about its membership, its election process, finances, dispute resolution mechanisms, transparency and conflict of interest issues. The exhaustive examination in the questionnaire should have given the BCCI an indication of the seriousness of the Lodha committee.

The panel then travelled around the country interviewing 74 individuals who worked in and around Indian cricket – administrators, players and selectors, club owners operating at national, state and club level, journalists, commentators, and others including fans and lawyers. It examined Indian cricket through microscope and telescope – from the president's office to a Test match ticket counter.

In less than a year since its formation, on January 4, 2016, the report was presented to the Supreme Court. It recommended a virtual overhaul of the BCCI from the very top – focusing not on daily cricketing operations, but shredding the fabric of its power. The game's governors and policy makers India were asked a central question: What are you here for? The love of the game or the clout it brings? Take away the clout and will the love remain?

The Lodha committee said it had sought solutions by asking two questions: "Will this benefit the game of cricket?" and "What does the Indian cricket fan want?" The recommendations separated the business of Indian cricket governance from that of daily management, to trim and streamline the BCCI's functioning, professionalise its operations. The BCCI, it said, needed not cosmetic but fundamental changes and it was the fundamental that the Lodha report set about taking apart and then reassembling.

The most controversial of the Lodha recommendations was changing the very composition of the BCCI's 'house' and the creation of a one-state-one-vote electoral college. It meant taking away the vote of governmental institutions and private cricket clubs – like the CCI, which is a real institution in brick and mortar, and Kolkata's National Cricket Club, which is not – as well as an end to multiple associations in several states – three each to Maharashtra and Gujarat. It struck out the BCCI's zonal approach, distilled its five zonal vice-presidents into a single vice-presidential post and five selectors for three, banished multiple meaningless committees, and pushed for the mandatory creation and involvement of player associations for both men's and women's cricket. The 14-member working committee was trimmed down to a tight nine-member Apex Council made up of five BCCI officials (president, vice-president, secretary, treasurer and joint secretary), one elected member from the general body, two players' representatives (one each from the men's and women's player associations) and a nominated representative from Comptroller and Auditor General's office.

In September 2015, a few months before the report was to emerge, Shashank Manohar, who was tipped to be elected BCCI president within a few days, met with the committee. He agreed with much of the committee's conclusions: negligence of financial malpractices by state associations, the lack of transparency in the BCCI's processes, the absence of a conflict of interest policy, the need for an ombudsman. A few days after he was made president, the BCCI went into a flurry of activity. An ombudsman and ethics officer was appointed, the board constitution, until then a hard-to-access document, was uploaded on their website, and a conflict of interest policy was put in place.

Such rapid changes may have signalled the dawn of a new age in the BCCI's operations, yet they did not win the board enough brownie points when the Lodha committee was writing up its report.

The Lodha report had recommended a selection panel of three, but BCCI went ahead with the original five when it was time to constitute a new committee. – BCCI

The steps taken were "in the right direction" but the Lodha report found them, "not comprehensive and substantive". "Comprehensive" and "substantive" became bywords for the heaviest blows that the Lodha report sought to inflict upon the BCCI's existing structures. The change it demanded was fundamental and went right to the top, to the highest offices in the board. The report's focus was on strengthening the larger institution and minimising the control exerted by select individuals and "forces from politics and business" who "see cricket administration as a stepping stone to recognition and publicity".

It began by recommending that the BCCI's five leading office-bearers – the president, the single vice-president, the secretary, the treasurer and the joint secretary – not hold two simultaneous posts in state associations and the BCCI. It recommended an age limit for officials (70) as well limited tenures for board and state association posts: three terms of three years each only, with a "cooling off period" between two positions in the same body. The cooling off period was not specified, but it was interpreted as three years.

In practical terms, it meant that an administrator could hold office in a state association for three years, then stand down and become eligible for a position in the BCCI for the next three years. Once his BCCI term was up he could return to the state association and stand for election for a different post there should he so wish. In all, a cricket official could spend 18 years switching between BCCI and

Highlights of the Lodha panel report

One state, one member, one vote: Only one association from a state (such as Gujarat and Maharashtra, which are home to multiple bodies) can have voting rights at a time. The others will be Associate Members, and will continue getting BCCI grants and can host teams. Services, Railways, National Universities, Cricket Club of India and NCC will become Associate Members.

Age and tenure limits: No person over the age of 70 can contest or hold a post. A candidate can hold a post for three three-year terms, with a cooling off period of three years, but can alternate between national and state bodies.

Eligibility: Ministers or government servants are not eligible to be office-bearers, nor is a member who holds any post of another sports body in the country.

New structure: The working committee will be replaced by a governing body called the Apex Council. Of this nine-member body, five would be elected office-bearers of BCCI (president, vice-president, secretary, joint secretary, treasurer), two (one male and one female) would be nominated by players' associations, one elected by BCCI Full Members and one nominated by Comptroller & Auditor General of India.

IPL governance: IPL governing council will be reconstituted with more autonomy. Of its nine members, three will be ex-officio members (secretary, treasurer and CEO of BCCI), two elected by the general body, two nominees of the franchisees, one nominee of the C&AG and one nominee of the players' association. Thus, four of the nine members will be independent of the BCCI.

Management: Non-cricketing matters will be handled by a team headed by a CEO, whose primary mandate is to cater to fans and players. Cricketing matters of selection, coaching, umpiring and performance evaluation is left exclusively to ex-players.

Conflict of interest: Within 15 days of taking up a post, an individual must disclose in writing to the Apex Council any existing or potential event that may be deemed to cause a conflict of interest. To resolve such matters, the following will be appointed: ombudsman to resolve internal conflicts independent of the BCCI, ethics officer to administer the principles governing conflict of interest and electoral officer to ensure that the process of selecting office-bearers is clean and transparent.

Oversight: An independent auditor will verify how the Full Members have expended the grants given to them by the BCCI. State associations should restrict the tenures of office-bearers, prescribe disqualifications, do away with proxy voting, provide transparency in functioning and be open to scrutiny and audit.

Selection panel: It will be a three-member committee, rather than five.

Schedule: BCCI should ensure a 15-day gap between the IPL season and the national calendar.

Transparency: All rules and regulations, details of meetings, expenditure, balance sheets, reports and orders of authorities are to be uploaded on the BCCI website.

state association posts and eventually he would not be eligible to stand for office again.

Once the report was out, and a slew of arguments began in CJI Thakur's court, the BCCI chose to adopt a single line of argument. Rather than debate key cricketing issues – *a CEO selects a coach?* – the BCCI's tack remained that as a private body registered under the Tamil Nadu Societies Registration Act, they could not be spoken to in this manner. Even if it was by a Supreme Court-appointed committee.

The Lodha panel had an entire range of recommendations that were controversial and contentious – limiting advertising during live television coverage of matches, legalising betting, having franchise officials serve on committees in the IPL, three selectors instead of five – but as time passed, one of two things happened to them. Either the Supreme Court struck them down on advice from their *amicus curae* Gopal Subramaniam – legalising betting, restricting television advertisements, the franchise owners' involvement as well as recommending the board come under the RTI Act – or the BCCI lost interest in arguing over them.

As the matter dragged on, cursory murmurs about the government's interference in the BCCI in the form of the CAG nominee also began to fade because of the office-bearers' focus on the key flashpoints that affected them directly: dual roles, age and tenure limits, and the cooling off period.

On July 18, 2016, the court accepted a majority of the Lodha recommendations and gave the BCCI between four and six months to implement them, with the Lodha panel asked to oversee the implementation process. The BCCI's influence, strength and financial muscle was known, felt and understood all over world cricket and its obstinate devotion to opaqueness reflexively kicked in.

Its first response was to file a review petition and then carry on with business as usual: holding its annual general meeting, appointing five selectors instead of three, transferring a large tranche of funds to state associations and, according to ICC CEO David Richardson in a TV interview, BCCI president Anurag Thakur asking the ICC to send a letter stating that accepting the Lodha reforms would amount to 'government interference', which was contrary to the ICC's own statutes. It was a claim Thakur was to deny ever being made.

The first set of timelines being set by the Lodha panel were ignored, emails went unanswered, and while a few state associations decided to refrain from elections to prevent themselves being found in contempt, the BCCI's top brass remained defiant. When the Lodha committee's status report was presented in court on September 28, it asked for the court to replace the office-bearers who had caused "serious impediments" to reforms with a panel of administrators. The court froze the BCCI's funding to state associations, ordered the panel to appoint an independent auditor to oversee the BCCI's financial operations and sought affidavits of compliance from the most recalcitrant.

The arm-wrestle played itself out in public while New Zealand and England toured with doomsday scenarios proffered in the press at regular intervals. About how the tours could be called off, how with accounts frozen state associations did not have funding to organise games, how practice matches for the touring teams were in jeopardy. The decoy of the state associations refusing to comply with the recommendations marked a fresh front opened in the game of obstruction with only Tripura and Vidarbha having accepted the Lodha reforms. The fact that the key office-bearers of the BCCI also headed or occupied key positions in their home state associations and could, if they so intended, get their state associations to fall in line and put pressure on the rest, was ignored. The idea itself was outrageous because it would have meant the officials relinquishing one of two honorary positions.

Their intention was to dig in the heels until CJI Thakur's term ended, out at the onset of the new year. In the interim, the process for awarding IPL rights for 2018 onwards was delayed. Both Anurag Thakur and Ajay Shirke, the BCCI secretary, who were ordered by the court to meet with the panel inside two weeks from October 21, refused to do so. The Lodha panel would not engage with them until it received letters of compliance. The Lodha report became the Timeless Test played out in the minds of resentful BCCI officials and annoyed judges.

That the BCCI is in this position is ironic. In comparison to other Indian sports associations, the BCCI from the outside could well advertise itself as a self-sustaining model for Indian sports governance. Early on in its piece, the Lodha report actually says so, commending the BCCI's efficiency in organising and staging matches and harvesting talent, without any dependence on regular government grants. "The committee has therefore consciously ensured that no measures are recommended that would interfere or limit the good work being done on behalf of the BCCI."

The reason the BCCI had come under the court's scrutiny was the 2013 IPL corruption case. That became a case study in exposing, one after another, the institutional flaws of an organisation that had operated with impunity due to political involvement across party lines and dictated terms to world cricket on the strength of its financial power, which in turn arose from the size of the game's audience in India and its playing numbers. Governance principles finding their way into international sports bodies and leagues were staunchly resisted on the strength of 'autonomy.' In sports where there is far less public scrutiny and pressure, the scale of misconduct and financial improprieties is considerable. The National Sports Bill has been resisted by India's cross-party political class because they have fingers in many sports federation pies and do not want to be questioned nor have those fingers forcibly extricated. The BCCI is the biggest domino at the top of the line in the battle to rein in Indian sports administration, particularly those who seek taxpayer funding: If the BCCI falls, the rest will be made to tumble.

When, you may wonder, did the butterfly begin to flap its wings? There's a time and date on it. On August 5, 2013, the BCCI filed a Special Leave Petition in the Supreme Court seeking a stay on the Bombay High Court order of July 30, which declared that the IPL's own probe panel investigating the May 2013 arrests was constituted "illegally". Within three years, the BCCI was looking far beyond the 2013 IPL scandal. It was fighting for the survival of its freemasonry of fiefdom.

Sharda Ugra is senior editor at ESPNcricinfo.

HALL OF FAME: Vinoo Mankad

HALL OF FAME: Sourav Ganguly – *Getty Images*

CRICKETER OF THE YEAR: Virat Kohli – *Getty Images*

CRICKETER OF THE YEAR: Shreyas Iyer – *Joshua Veeranathan*

CRICKETER OF THE YEAR: Yasir Shah — *Getty Images*

CRICKETER OF THE YEAR: Mustafizur Rahman – *ICC*

CRICKETER OF THE YEAR: Kusal Mendis – *Getty Images*

CRICKETER OF THE YEAR: David Warner – *Getty Images*

Indian cricketers and officials pitched in to clean Eden Gardens to mark Gandhi Jayanti. — BCCI

There was no let up on the glamour quotient of the IPL, and Dwayne Bravo got in on the act as his fledgling music career took off. — BCCI

Faf du Plessis made a few new friends when in India for the ICC World T20. — *ICC*

Even when playing holi while in India for the ICC World T20, Glenn Maxwell stuck to Australian colours. — *ICC*

The Adelaide evening sky was painted the perfect shade for the first ever day-night Test using pink balls, between Australia and New Zealand. — *Getty Images*

Caribbean celebrations lit up Eden Gardens after Darren Sammy's men and Stafanie Taylor's women made it an ICC World T20 double for West Indies. — *Getty Images*

David Warner led Sunrisers Hyderabad to the IPL 2016 title at the M Chinnaswamy Stadium in Bangalore. — *BCCI*

Mumbai found heroes at every stage as a young side added a 41st Ranji Trophy title to the domestic giant's cabinet. — *Joshua Veeranathan*

Former Test captains of the Indian teams came together to mark the 500th Test played by the men's team, in Kanpur against New Zealand.
– *BCCI*

Langza, Spiti, in Himachal Pradesh, at an altitude of 14,500ft above sea level, becomes ground zero for an afternoon game of cricket.
— *Mukunda R*

It wasn't quite like old times when the likes of Sachin Tendulkar and Virender Sehwag dusted off their cricket gear, but audiences for the All Stars in the US weren't complaining. — *Getty Images*

Wittgenstein: An old turnip for cricket

RAY MONK

When the editor of *Wisden India Almanack* got in touch to ask me to write something on 'Wittgenstein's love for cricket', I felt honoured and excited. I have been a cricket fan all my life, and I have also devoted much of my life to the study of Ludwig Wittgenstein, one of the 20th century's most influential philosophers, so the subject could not have suited me better. There was only one problem: I didn't know anything about Wittgenstein's love for cricket. I didn't, indeed, even know that he had any interest in cricket at all, which was rather surprising, since it was, surely, the sort of thing that I, of all people, should have known about. How had it passed me by?

After a bit of Googling, I discovered to my surprise that it was fairly widely accepted as a fact that Wittgenstein did indeed love cricket. In the summer of 2015, *The Guardian* published an article by James Gingell that took Wittgenstein's love of the game for granted, and sought not to prove it but to explain it. The thing about cricket that most likely drew Wittgenstein's interest, according to Gingell, was its complex and often arcane language. "Cricket, with its dense and extraordinary quilt of gorgeous words and phrases," he reasoned, "must have utterly captivated him." In fact, Gingell was prepared to go further and make what he acknowledged to be the very bold claim that one of Wittgenstein's most celebrated contributions to philosophy – the notion of language games that he developed in *Philosophical Investigations* – had grown out of his fascination with the language of cricket.

But now, hold on a minute. If cricket was *that* important to Wittgenstein, if his interest in it and its language inspired him to develop one of the seminal ideas of modern thought, shouldn't we investigate more closely the details of that interest? Shouldn't we see what evidence there is in the historical record of his love of the game? What games did he watch? With whom did he discuss it? Where in his writings are there mentions of particular matches or reflections on the game's specialised vocabulary? Did he follow a particular team? Was he a fan of particular players? As far as I know (and I have searched longer and harder than most people), the

The two things that mattered to Wittgenstein: thinking clearly and being a morally decent man...

historical record is *entirely silent* on these questions. Wittgenstein, it seems, *never* mentions cricket in any of his philosophical works, in any of his letters, or in any of his recorded conversations, and there are no records (in, say, the many memoirs of him written by his friends) of him ever watching cricket. In short, there is no evidence that he had even the remotest interest in the game, still less that he 'loved' it.

In private exchanges, Gingell has admitted to me that he himself has never seen any evidence of Wittgenstein's love for cricket. Apparently, he never thought it needed any evidence; he assumed it was an uncontested fact. The reason for this, I think, is the appearance a year before Gingell's piece of an article, 'Ludwig Wittgenstein: Cricket connections of the great philosopher', by Arunabha Sengupta, the cricket historian. There, Sengupta describes Wittgenstein as a "keen cricket fan" and, like Gingell, links Wittgenstein's supposed interest in cricket with his concept of a language game. As for where Sengupta got that idea from, it seems to have originated in his misinterpretation of a remark in Brian Clack's *Introduction to Wittgenstein's Philosophy of Religion*, in which Clack expounds Wittgenstein's later philosophy using a cricket analogy in a way that might be taken to suggest that Wittgenstein himself had used that same analogy. So, it seems, the widespread acceptance of the 'fact' that Wittgenstein loved cricket has its roots in a slight ambiguity in a secondary text. From little acorns ....

Discovering that something widely believed is in fact a myth has its satisfactions, but tracing the origins of this particular myth has had for me an unexpected and positive outcome. For it led me to an intriguing connection between Wittgenstein and cricket that *does* have a solid basis in the documentary record, one that I had known nothing about before and which I find extremely interesting. While I was digging around Wittgenstein sources, looking for something, *anything*, to link him with cricket, my friend and fellow Wittgenstein scholar, James Klagge, drew my attention to a comment by Wittgenstein's close friend and literary executor, Elizabeth Anscombe, in her paper, 'The Simplicity of the Tractatus'. Wittgenstein, Anscombe writes there, "loved the utterance of a certain cricketer who had become a missionary and said in his preaching: 'What god wants is a heart – any old turnip will do as a head'".

... Which is why CT Studd, England cricketer turned missionary, would have appealed to him.

The cricketer in question – and it gives me a frisson of excitement to discover that Wittgenstein had even so much as heard of this man – is the English all-rounder, CT Studd, who had a short but illustrious cricket career in the 1880s, playing for England, Cambridge University, Middlesex and the MCC. Studd's greatest claim to fame is that he played in the original Ashes Test in the summer of 1882. He was then just 21 and still an undergraduate student at Trinity College, Cambridge (which, of course, was also Wittgenstein's college), but he was already regarded (this was the time of WG Grace) as the second-best batsman in England, having already scored two centuries against the Australians earlier in the summer. In the famous match in question, Studd was expected by almost everybody present to score the winning runs. Australia had never won a Test in England, and no one expected them to win this one either, even though England's batting order had collapsed calamitously. Despite his reputation as a batsman, Studd had come in at No. 8 and such was the rapidity of England's batting collapse that he had still not faced a ball when England's last man, the Yorkshire slow left-arm bowler Ted Peate, came to the crease. Things weren't going particularly well, but England needed just ten runs to win and few doubted that Studd, when at last he faced the bowling, would get them. All it needed was for Peate to play safe, survive a few balls and allow Studd at the other end to win the match. Inexplicably, Peate had other ideas. He hit out, scoring two flukey runs before being bowled. When asked by an irate WG to explain himself, Peate famously replied cheekily: "Ah had no confidence in Maister Stood, sur." A few days later, *Sporting Times* published its famous obituary, "In affectionate remembrance of English cricket, which died at The Oval on 29 August 1882," and announced that "The body will be cremated and the ashes taken to Australia." Thus was a glorious tradition born.

But Studd's immortalisation in Ashes history does not end there. The following year, when England travelled to Australia to, in the words of Ivo Bligh, their captain, "recover those ashes", Studd was a key member of the team. When England won the series 2-1, the now famous urn, supposedly containing the ashes, was presented to Bligh. On it was pasted the following verse, ensuring that Studd's name would live on forever in cricketing folklore:

> When Ivo goes back with the urn, the urn;
> Studds, Steel, Read and Tylecote return, return;
> The welkin will ring loud,
> The great crowd will feel proud,
> Seeing Barlow and Bates with the urn, the urn;
> And the rest coming home with the urn.

When the team arrived back in England, they were indeed greeted as heroes, and for the rest of his life, wherever he went, Studd was asked for his autograph. He died at the age of 70 in 1931. Two years later, his biography written by his son-in-law, Norman Grubb, titled *CT Studd: Cricketer and Pioneer*, was released. The biography became extremely popular, and it seems fairly safe to assume that it was the source of Wittgenstein's knowledge of Studd and where he first came across the remark mentioned by Anscombe.

The book tells the story of Studd's cricketing career, but for the most part it is concerned with Studd not as a sportsman but a religious figure, chronicling his work as a missionary in China, India and Africa. And it is not difficult to see why the figure that emerges from this book would have appealed to Wittgenstein. One of the things about Wittgenstein that exercises the fascination of many is his determination to strip his life down to the basics, so as to leave him free to dedicate himself to the two things that really mattered to him: thinking clearly and being a morally decent man. In this respect, he was a kind of modern-day saint. And the people for whom he had the deepest respect – St Augustine, St Francis, Leo Tolstoy – shared the same determination to let *nothing* stand in the way of, so to speak, the good life. "What shall it profit a man if he gain the whole world and lose his soul?" was an inspirational text for Wittgenstein and for many of those he most admired. So moved was Wittgenstein by the emphasis in the gospels on the value of poverty and spiritual dangers of wealth that he gave away the huge fortune that he inherited from his immensely rich father. Interestingly, CT Studd did exactly the same thing. In his biography, Grubb devotes a chapter to detailing how Studd, inspired by the text "Lay not up for yourselves treasures on earth", gave away his inheritance of about £30,000 (a fortune, equivalent to about £4 million today) to various religious organisations.

"All god wants is a heart, any old turnip will do for a head." The phrase of Studd's that Wittgenstein admired so much came in an appeal that he wrote in 1915 for Christian evangelists to devote themselves not to the affluent and comfortable British, but to the poor, uneducated and destitute people around the world. It was a plea for action, not words, for practical help, not sermons, for emotional engagement rather than intellectual contemplation. As such, it chimes perfectly with Wittgenstein's own outlook on religion. He once said: "I am not a religious man but I cannot help seeing every problem from a religious point of view." The point of view in question is that which comes with a certain attitude, namely a devout *seriousness*. It is the attitude that rejects everything easy, comfortable and frivolous, that insists on, to use a phrase Wittgenstein was very fond of, "going the bloody hard way". It is the attitude that Studd was urging evangelists to take, and the one that led him to give his money away and to travel to remote places of the world to live in poverty while he attempted to save people's souls. It is also the attitude required to resist temptation, to write great philosophy – and to be a great cricketer.

For readily intelligible reasons, Gingell and Sengupta tried to find links between Wittgenstein's supposed love of cricket and his philosophy of language, but Wittgenstein's admiration of Studd takes us to another, deeper place; not to particular views about the nature of language, but to fundamental attitudes to life. It takes us, in fact, to the heart, not the head. After all, any old turnip will do for *that*.

Ray Monk is a professor of philosophy at the University of Southampton and biographer of Ludwig Wittgenstein, Bertrand Russell and J Robert Oppenheimer.

Aesthetics of cricket

TM KRISHNA

The mathematician's patterns, like the painter's or the poet's, must be beautiful; the ideas like the colours or the words, must fit together in a harmonious way. Beauty is the first test: there is no permanent place in the world for ugly mathematics.

– GH Hardy in A Mathematician's Apology

Three words from this excerpt compel attention: beautiful, harmonious, permanent. Beauty is most elusive and can only be felt. No description can capture its presence. Yet, the idea of beauty is constantly put down to subjectivity and taste. As an artiste, I have to ask this question: Is there a beauty that eludes, even transcends, individual and collective limitations, one that can be experienced in a dispassionate intensity that allows us to be in a state of utter and unprecedented wonderment? In essence, can there be beauty that is not constricted by 'me'?

If we say, for the sake of argument, that there is such a thing, then another question emerges: How do we perceive it? For this, we turn to that second word, 'harmonious', a musical expression. It brings another musical term to mind: 'concert', which refers to a union; 'to strive', as in concerted effort – an underlying current that brings together the various elements within a frame for a purpose. And they fit together using form, structure, shape, skill and thought. In coming together in harmony, they merge and absorb each other until they are experienced as 'one'. This oneness is what Hardy refers to as beauty. And in that one word he has injected complex ideas of form and nature.

The foundation of this possibility of harmony is intentionality. Going beyond styles and interpretations, this unquantifiable yet distinct beauty, as Hardy puts it, is the first test.

The paradox lies in the fact that it is possible to recognise this beauty even through the haze of conditioned responses. There are moments in art when we are transported by a non-articulated, un-nostalgic experience that contradicts our taste. But it is also true that we come running back to the security of entrenched opinions – our identifying markers.

The experiencing of sport, whether as active participant or engaged spectator, is a complex bundle of such possibilities. For example, in cricket, we meditate upon the inside-out lofted cover-drive even after the ball has rolled over the rope. Of course, we may also lustily cheer a terrible mis-hit over the keeper's head. I am not judging either of those, but it is necessary for us to recognise this jugglery.

All this is about moments, even extended moments. What, then, acquires permanence – that slippery object of all artistic endeavours?

This is where I come to the artistic term 'aesthetics'. Aesthetics links three essentials 'intention-form-experience', which lead to the permanence of art. These three are facets of the same (aesthetics) and any disturbance in one will affect the whole. For example, the urge in a concert musician to titillate the audience warps the intentionality of the form, directly impacting its experience. Similarly, if the music in a film, however pleasing it might be, ignores its primary intention of being a part of the visual narration, it will affect the experience of the film. And Hardy, in his magnificent essay, is discussing the aesthetics of mathematics. This may sound vague and abstract, but I wonder whether this feeling comes more from the constant need for empirical proof (Hardy would have wanted it!) when the answer actually lies in the intangibles – experience and the constant questioning of that experience.

It is essential at this stage to understand that this discussion is not about what you or I may find nice, pleasant or even beautiful (in the colloquial sense of prettiness). We hope to understand form in greater depth, and detachment provides awareness.

But how does all this connect with cricket and its vagaries? While it is not my contention that cricket, music and math all inhabit the same orbit, I will, with confidence, use aesthetics as a mechanism to understand cricket.

What is the endeavour of cricket? Recreation and entertainment? What then of the magnificence of its structure, play and intellect. Can I write it off as a battle for supremacy resulting in victors and vanquished? In fact, the score is not in the numbers; it is in the music that flows from partnerships that evolve from the plans, positions, actions, manoeuvrings, stratagems, athleticism, skill,

Symphony: Whether the batsman plays a drive or a defensive shot, everyone on and off the field feels the life in cricket. – *BCCI*

patience, stability and silence that every participant sharing vertical and horizontal space summons. All this may result in numerous runs or many wickets, but the harmony is in the process and not the end. Which is why an over that results in no runs or wickets might have us spellbound.

Is there an intention to the game, a reason to play it that is more intricate than just the result? I believe cricket is a game of relationships, elegantly bringing countless factors into its playing matrix. Every player is both an individual and a part of various clusters of association. These groupings are not just made up of human beings; they include elements of nature – wind, moisture, sun and soil. And at every stage, the elements impact the individuals, each sub-group, the team and even tools of the game, such as the cricket ball. Let us not forget the effect of human beings on nature. Even among the players, the sporting relationship is not just a single. Strategy alters individual and group roles. A spin bowler works with the captain and every member of the team to find a way to dislodge the batsman.

This can happen in many ways, from the sheer ability of the bowler to use the ball and the environment – a classic example is Shane Warne's first ball to Mike Gatting in the Ashes of 1993 – to the bowler creating an illusion of comprehension in the batsman, like Bishan Singh Bedi used to do by altering the length of the flighted delivery, convincing the batsman that all is well. Every fielder's position and

In the moment: Every ball delivered is an opportunity to understand the batsman, the pitch, the weather and every player on the field. – *BCCI*

commitment also contributed to the batsman's attitude. They were part of the mind play. It could also be just a mistake by the batsman – a lofted drive lands in the hands of the long-on fielder. In every one of these probabilities – and there are multitudes of others between and beyond these examples – the players and the environment have evolving roles, transforming from one to the other without a change in title.

The batsman, though facing the music alone, is playing with the non-striker and in his subconscious he holds the events and positions of his colleagues and opponents on the field at the moment and in the past. Cricket is a game of ongoing experiential understanding. It is a game of individuals, groups and teams, with the composition, strength and effect shifting constantly and delicately.

Cricket is also an abstraction of life and all that we face as its active participants. Is it a replication of the things we do at home, work and on the road? That it certainly is not, but it distils in some essential way the experience of living. Cricket operates within a framework that imitates socio-political scaffoldings, allowing it an exploration of human possibilities. Which automatically means that ambiguity is part of the form.

Cricket is played to win, but, more importantly, to work with oneself and other human beings, within the boundary that society has thrown around us, using the tools at hand, exploring possibilities of understanding. Every ball delivered by a pace bowler is an opportunity, a chance to understand the batsman, different areas of the pitch, weather and every single player on the field. This changes from moment to moment, which is why the unexpected, however subtle, is always at play. And 'chance' is, of course, the unnamed member of the team.

There is something else extraordinary taking place that we tend to miss. Even when the ball is driven through extra-cover by the batsman, the fine-leg fielder is active. Everyone on and off the field feels the life in cricket even when the ball is played down in stern defence at the feet of the batsman. Nothingness in cricket is itself a happening, a profound experience that convinces me that this is much more than a battle between bat and ball.

I recall something the sculptor Anish Kapoor said to me about cinema. He said with regret that boredom is no more a part of cinema. It is an intriguing insight. Boredom to him is not empty; it is full to the brim, providing movies another shape of emotion. Is not the nothingness that I write of also the boredom that Anish seeks in cinema? And, importantly, has cricket also lost this facet?

The harmony of cricket has exploration at its heart. And the beauty is that the framework of cricket allows – even forces – everyone to experience this intentionality. It seems to me that many of the rules of the game evolved in such a manner that it facilitated this process, at times providing more areas of uncertainty. The lbw is one such fascinating condition. It is not just about disallowing the batsman from obstructing the ball. This rule brings into the game components of length, height, pitch, speed and forethought, coming together at the point of observation. The lbw thrives only because it is, in a weird way, Schrodinger's cat.

This kind of uncertainty is not to be equated with human error of judgement or a simple decision of whether the ball crossed the rope on one bounce or not. Here it is about a built-in nicety. Continuing with lbw, look at how the way a ball pitching outside the leg stump trapping the batsman in front used to be viewed as opposed to one that came in from outside the off stump. The physiological and psychological combine in these unsaid rules.

What about graceful strokeplay and bowling actions that commentators often call beautiful? This to me seems like only a reiteration of beauty that is structured from what we have come to believe as elegance or prettiness. Beauty in cricket exists not in the perception of habit but in being able to understand thought-action in context – in other words, its aesthetics. The beauty of a stroke, for instance, emanates from the macro of the game situation and every micro-influencing factor, including the field placement, the abilities of the fielders in the respective positions, the bowler, the specific ball, its movement in the air and off the pitch. All this and more consciously and subconsciously influence the batsman into playing the said stroke. It is in this whole experience that the aesthetics of batting exists.

Within cricket's aesthetics, technique and sophistication are in unison. Therefore, Mohammad Azharuddin's flick is an aesthetic stroke, and so is MS Dhoni's 'inelegant' back-foot thump. This is not a judgement of effectiveness; it is technical affectivity that creates the experience. We feel this and hence smile or gasp reflexively when these moments occur, when the cricketing whole is encapsulated in one delivery or stroke. The opposite is equally true: a flick could be aesthetically ugly even if it is visually appealing.

Where is the spectator in all this? There is no doubt that the pressure of millions of fans is part of every cricketer's mind space and some even say it 'pumps them up'. But even the most excitable player will concede that when really 'in cricket', the spectators vanish, the scoreboard disappears; all they are doing is playing a symphony. In these phases, the aesthetics of cricket is complete. I am certain this is also true of the fielders or the captains. Being intensely participatory is as much an emotional investment as it is in the expertise of the craft itself – both for the cricketers and the spectator.

Permanence is, therefore, in the experience derived from the intention and form working in tandem. Cricket's intention of simultaneously creating obvious and shaded relationships has led to the form becoming an elaborate labyrinth. As I had suggested in my initial arguments, the aesthetics of cricket lies not in what I perceive as self-satisfying, but what I can attempt to observe in dispassionate intensity. This separation is essential if we want to seriously investigate the game.

One could argue, and correctly so, that all sports have similar qualities. But it is only in cricket that I find a larger umbrella of human experience at play, and the conscious intent of the makers of the game down the ages to bring it within the sport's gambit.

So what then of the newer formats of one-day cricket and T20? Have we tampered with the intention of the game, reducing it to that one extra run or that last wicket? Even the tightest of contests attain permanence only when the layers of cricketing depth that the whole game steadily built itself on, is felt even in that very last ball bowled. If you rub off the various shades of colour from the foundations of the game-structure, you will find the resultant contest thrilling but ephemeral.

One could argue that these questions are only important for aestheticians, but I would counter that by saying that the effective direction the sport is taking will finally carry off cricket itself to a point where we would have linearised what is intrinsically a complex organic structure. This has a direct impact on the cricketing experience.

What I am interested in is understanding how changes in conditions, rules, format came into being. Can we actually differentiate between those that were part of an internal process of the game's movement, adding another degree of experience, and those that flatten it? The administrators, sponsors and spectators have argued that the game must be made exciting and action-packed, presumably to draw a new set of viewers to the game. But these qualities, when imposed forcefully, achieve nothing aesthetically. It is pointless to attempt to discuss this in terms of skill sets and technique, which are, after all, inherent to a sport, any sport. And therefore any shift in the intention of the game will unmistakably change the required abilities. It would be naïve to use newer cricketing strokes to justify a fundamental structural change. This is as relevant to Test cricket as it is to T20s.

Cricket has been a serious part of who I am. To me, life is a musical experience and hence, maybe, I am interpreting cricket in a manner that another cricketing fan finds unnecessary. But I have found within cricket's formations the possibility of living experiences that are usually attributed to purely abstractive preoccupations such as art, mathematics and philosophy. Although it might be incorrect to depict cricket as an art form, I do think that an aesthetic perspective provides us a channel of enquiry, one that urges all those engaged with the game to step back and question.

TM Krishna is a Carnatic music vocalist and author who won the 2016 Magsaysay award for his commitment as artist and advocate of art's power to heal India's deep social divisions.

Yours sincerely

HARESH PANDYA

"Thank you for your inquiry about my health," Sir Donald Bradman wrote to me. "At my age (82), the No. 1 priority is to stay alive. I still manage the occasional round of golf and am able to keep my garden reasonably tidy, but not much else," he added. "The sadness in growing old is the loss of marvellous friends, which seems to happen all too often. Plus the inability to hit the right key on the typewriter, for which I apologise."

The 1980s and early 1990s, when the world was not yet wonderstruck by the miracles of the internet, were ideal for writing letters for a fan growing up in an India basking in the 1983 World Cup triumph. My hero Gundappa Viswanath was the first cricketer I wrote to. I did not receive a reply.

One day my mother handed me a letter when I returned from college. It was from Vijay Merchant, concisely composed and neatly typed, carrying his views on Viswanath. It was the first letter I ever received from an international cricketer. I put the original in a safe place and proudly showed off the photocopy.

I felt encouraged by Merchant's prompt reply. I wrote about a dozen letters initially. My budget was limited – decent stationery and postage stamps for overseas letters were expensive.

Gradually, the replies started coming in. Erapalli Prasanna, Ajit Wadekar, Sunil Gavaskar, Polly Umrigar, Dattu Phadkar, Ken McEwan, Eddie Barlow, Michael Brearley all wrote back. Gavaskar had taken my letter with him to Bahrain and sent me a warm reply from there. "I was very touched by your great admiration for Viswanath. You know I rate him as the best batsman of the decade 1970-80 and there certainly will not be another like him. When I meet him, I will convey your feelings," he wrote.

The postman began to assume an important role in my life. He recognised my excitement and would either nod or shake his head depending on whether there was a letter for me or not. At times I would rush to the post office and get there while the sorting was being done. How I hated Sundays and national holidays! Later, I took the postman out for dinner a couple of times.

Finally, the day arrived when the postman handed me the most eagerly awaited letter. "I did not write to you earlier for the simple reason that I did not receive your earlier letters," Viswanath wrote. I was ecstatic.

Like Merchant and Gavaskar, many cricketers were meticulous in their replies. Keith Miller, MJ Gopalan, Ramnath Kenny, Dennis Amiss, Geoffrey Boycott, Aunshuman Gaekwad, Derek Underwood, Dilip Doshi, Rajinder Goel, Alan Knott, Bob Taylor, Syed Kirmani and David Richardson, to name some.

"Dennis Lillee and Jeff Thomson bowled against us on perfect bowling wickets in Australia – hard, green, fast and bouncy. They were nearly unplayable. I felt I was never going to score a run against Lillee," wrote Amiss, who had a torrid time down under in the 1974-75 Ashes series.

I had published a quiz in *The Sunday Observer* on Gavaskar's 45th birthday and sent a copy to him. "Though it was nice of you to have given a quiz on my birthday, I would have preferred if you had not, for when I am trying to keep a low profile, you go and announce to the world that it is my birthday. Fortunately, I was out of Bombay," he wrote back. "I was indeed privileged to have played with Viswanath and, of course, doubly blessed that he is my brother-in-law. You may perhaps be aware that they have got a son, who is five months old, and is named Daivik."

In 1992, the 19-year-old Sachin Tendulkar became the first overseas player to play for Yorkshire. "I am hoping for a good season from Mr Tendulkar, who is one of the best players I have ever seen. I am sure he will make a great contribution to Yorkshire," wrote Colin Cowdrey.

"I must say it is always good to hear from friends in India, where I was fortunate enough to tour on three occasions. I enjoyed greatly my career. I don't particularly miss the playing side but I certainly miss the way of life and the fellowship that the game of cricket engenders... To me, Bishan [BS Bedi] and Chandra [BS Chandrasekhar] were two of the greatest exponents of the art of spin bowling. I will never forget Chandra's bowling on my first trip to India. He never bowled a bad ball and somehow created extra bounce and turn from nowhere... I have been fortunate to play against the best batsmen in the world and, of course, have suffered on many occasions from the bats of the Soberses, the Richardses, the Gavaskars and the Viswanaths," wrote Underwood in his affectionate letter.

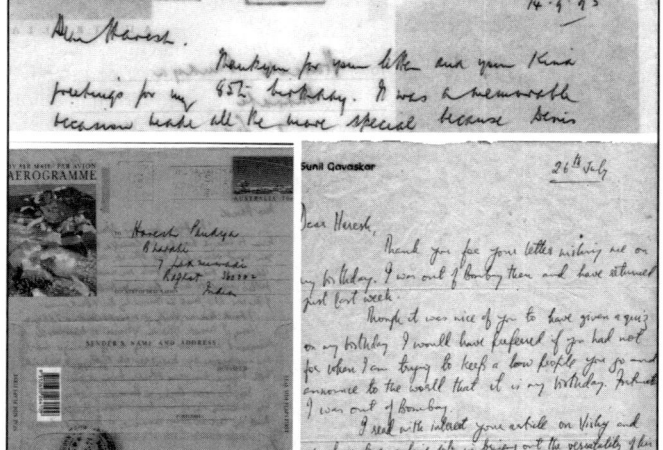

"Thank you for your letter and your kind greetings for my 85th birthday. It was memorable," wrote Bradman in one letter. Said Gavaskar: "I read with interest your article on Vishy and you have done a fine job in bringing out the versatality of his cricket."

When I communicated with Miller, I was pursuing my MA in American, English and European classics. "I was most interested in your letter regarding your academic life. You hope to soon become a Professor of English. You should come out here and teach a lot of Aussies English. It's a language becoming bastardised with Australian slang," wrote the dashing all-rounder in his reply dated October 27, 1989.

Mushtaq Ali was always gracious. "I am guilty of not having acknowledged your most charming letter, from the land of Ranjitsinhji and Duleepsinhji. Since even the period within which an apology could be offered with grace has elapsed, I can only depend upon your generosity to forgive me," he wrote. "A batsman's approach should be bold. He should not play for himself. He should give something to the people. I mean he should play bright cricket. I played cricket for the joy of it and for the people. I believe in quality," he emphasised in another letter.

When I wrote to Doshi, he had been dropped from the Indian team. "It seems you know quite a bit of what goes on in Indian cricket. I have no comments to offer except that I know I am still good enough to play for India and win a few games," he replied in his beautiful handwriting. "I felt great when I played my first Test but was rather very keen to prove that I am an international bowler."

Similarly, when I wrote to Kirmani after he was dropped for good, he replied in his equally good handwriting and in no uncertain terms: "I appreciate your enthusiasm on the cricketing rigmarole. We as cricketers have no say into the whims, fancies and policies of the board; we are at their mercies."

"You have mentioned that I am a bad fielder, which in my opinion is wrong as I see myself as a safe fielder than an acrobatic or overcharged fielder!" Prasanna corrected me.

"I got bypassed by the selectors since the comparison of opening batsmen was with Sunil [Gavaskar]. Moreover, the instructions given to me by the selectors and managers were to play a second fiddle to Sunil. The golden rule was: 'Just stay at the wicket and Sunil will do the rest.' Well, as a gentleman I obeyed the orders. As a result I used to bat for two or three hours and score just 20-30 runs. This was not good enough for me to stay in the team. So the pressure of being dropped was always there. Under this fear no one can really perform freely," revealed Gaekwad in his 13-page handwritten letter when I wrote to him immediately after he retired in 1991.

"My biggest drawback was I was too straightforward and believed in obeying orders. As a result I got stamped as a slow batsman. I think I should have used my discretion to play once I was in the middle and surely the picture would have been different. Maybe at times I should have been selfish and got my runs as the others did, and do. I was very keen on playing my shots, particularly the cover-drive and square-cut, which gave me lot of runs."

Although Wadekar has written in detail in *My Cricketing Years* about the history made at The Oval in 1971, I wanted to hear from him personally. So I wrote to him, asking what kind of atmosphere prevailed in the dressing room when India were chasing a seemingly small target of 173 on a difficult wicket with only a few wickets left. "Tense," he replied. "But I was asleep as I was sure of winning."

One of the finest letters I ever received was from Richardson: "During our years of isolation I was well aware of the reasons behind the sporting and cultural boycotts imposed on my country by the international community. I understood such reasons and found them most justifiable in the circumstances," he wrote. "Now that South Africa is back in international sport, I would hope to remain its first choice wicketkeeper until at least 1994, when we undergo *[sic]* a tour of the United Kingdom. I am sure it is every cricketer's ambition to play in a Test match at Lord's, the home of cricket."

I was in correspondence with many distinguished cricket writers, including Peter Roebuck, whose long letters, composed in his woefully illegible handwriting, were often as much a challenge to decipher as the news and views they carried were a perpetual delight. "Somerset is rather like California. Your IQ drops one point every year you stay here. It is a farming land, and things are slow and gentle, mostly," he once wrote.

"The secret of good writing is, I suppose, first a real affection for the game, second a detailed knowledge of it and its history, and third a clear and simple style. I often used to think when writing and broadcasting that I was just writing or talking to a friend. After all, you may be communicating with a large audience, but only one at a time, if you follow me," wrote Jim Swanton.

It was with Bradman that I had the most cherished experience of my life as a correspondent. I did not approach him until 1989. I was in for a surprise when he replied to my maiden letter only minutes after he received it. Nearly two years later I sent another, seeking his views on Sobers. This would be the start of a correspondence between us for a couple of years. "I do not normally respond to questions of the kind you pose about Sobers but am doing so briefly on the strict understanding that my reply is solely for your private use and not for publication, as per the promise in your letter," he emphasised in his typed reply. While describing Sobers's batting as "impressive in every way", Bradman said he "would not differentiate between his work as a speedster or a spinner" simply because "his value would depend on the state of the pitch", adding that "there is no doubt he was worth a place in a Test side as a bowler of either type." He ranked Sobers as "the greatest" all-rounder he ever saw.

Overwhelmed with joy, I replied expressing my gratitude. "Let me be honest and tell you that I get hundreds of letters every year from Indians and that only a handful get answered," he wrote back. "Firstly, the cost of answering them all would be prohibitive and, secondly, I sense that so many of them have the ulterior motive of personal aggrandizement and/or publicity. In your case I backed my intuition that you were a genuine cricket lover and had nothing but a sincere private and personal motive."

Bradman would share with me his views on players, issues, cricket writers, broadcasters, books and discuss his personal life, too, sometimes. Never have I breached Bradman's trust, not even 16 years after his death. This is the first time I am sharing something from Bradman's letters because of the nature and theme of this essay. Savour the following pearls of wisdom from the great man's handwritten letter of June 5, 1992:

- "I am impressed by Tendulkar, who displayed a maturity well beyond his years and should become a great batsman."
- "That little boy [Mushtaq] Ahmed bowled very well out here. One-day games, which place such a premium on accuracy, are very difficult for leg-spinners, but his control was splendid. I would like to see him in a Test match."
- "I have read *Beyond a Boundary*, a fine book. He [CLR James] was certainly one of the best writers, though I don't think he had the same command of English as Cardus. Many thought Cardus a bit 'flowery', but he never failed to pick up the crucial points in a game. Another marvellous writer was Ronald Mason. An article by him in *Barclays World of Cricket* is probably the best piece of cricket writing I have read."
- "Actually I had a difficult summer due to the continuing illness of my wife and I saw very little cricket except on TV. The simple

truth is that my wife and I are old and subject to all the problems of age. But last week we happily celebrated our 60th wedding anniversary that was really a milestone."

Times have changed. Life itself has changed. Priorities have changed. I have long ceased to write to cricketers. But I often read and reread many of the letters I received.

So what if I have not received replies from Sobers, Botham and others? I have the Bradman letters, addressed to me personally in my collection. Nine in all, they are my most prized possessions.

The writer is a freelance journalist published in leading Indian and foreign publications.

Boardroom pitch

SATYA NADELLA

I am haunted by cricket. No matter where I am, cricket is always there. The joy, the memories, the drama, the complexities and the ups and downs – the infinite possibilities. Like most south Asians, I somehow fell in love with this most English of games on the dusty matting wickets of the Deccan plateau.

This is an article about that obsession and the lessons learnt from dreaming and reflecting on all things cricket, more than playing it.

The early years of my life surrounded my father's work as a civil servant in the district headquarters of Andhra Pradesh and the hills of Mussorie in what is now Uttarakhand. Cricket was not the phenomenon it is now, especially in those more rural parts of India. But it became a phenomenon for me when I landed in Hyderabad at the age of eight.

We stayed in a rented house in Somaji Guda, and our landlord, Mr Ali, was a gracious and proud Hyderabadi who wore his Osmania University cricket cap while working in his auto shop. He was full of stories about the great Hyderabadi cricketers of the 1960s. He once took me to watch a first-class match between Hyderabad and Bombay. It was my first time at Fateh Maidan. I was completely smitten that day with all the glamour of cricket in India. ML Jaisimha, Abbas Ali Baig, Syed Abid Ali and Mumtaz Hussain became my heroes. The Bombay side had Sunil Gavaskar and Ashok Mankad among other stars. I don't recall any of them making much of an impression, even though they beat Hyderabad handily. I was in awe of Jaisimha's on-field presence – his fashionable upturned collar and distinctive gait. To this day I remember Mr Ali's descriptions of Hussain's mystery ball, and watching Abid Ali charging down the wicket to a medium-pacer.

Soon my dad was again transferred, and I moved to Delhi. There I watched my first Test match at Feroz Shah Kotla. It was a match between India and England. Watching these two sides play left an indelible impression. I remember the English batsman Dennis Amiss and bowler John Lever combined to destroy India by an innings, leaving me distraught for weeks. Amiss hit a century and Lever, playing in his first Test match, bowled medium pace through that long afternoon. The ball was swinging for him like I'd never seen before. Suddenly all the Indian players were back in the hut.

As a ten-year-old I returned again to Hyderabad, and for the next six years I truly and surely fell in love with cricket as a player for Hyderabad Public School. In fact, Jaisimha's two children attended my school; as a result, we were surrounded by cricket glamour, tradition and obsession. In those days, everyone was talking about the two India school players from HPS. One of them, Saad Bin Jung (who also happened to be Tiger Pataudi's nephew), still in school, went on to smash a hundred against a touring West Indies side while playing for South Zone. I began playing on the B team and graduated to the senior team, which played in the A leagues of Hyderabad. We were the only school team to play in the A leagues as the other teams were sponsored by banks and corporates. Ranji players would turn up in these league games, and all that intrigue made for intense competition.

What excited me then about cricket is what excites me even today, even in living in a non-cricketing country (though, the United States over a hundred years ago did regularly host Australian and English sides). Cricket for me is like a wondrous Russian novel with plots and subplots played out over the course of multiple acts. In the end, one brilliant knock or three deftly bowled balls can change the complexion of a game.

There are three stories from my all too brief cricketing past that speak directly to business and leadership principles I use even today as a CEO.

The first principle is to compete vigorously and with passion in the face of uncertainty and intimidation. In my school cricketing days, we played a team one summer that had several Australian players. During the match, our PE teacher, who acted as a sort of general manager for the team, noticed that we were admiring the Aussies play. In fact, we were more than a little intimidated by them. We had never competed against foreign players, and Australia of course loomed large in the national cricketing psyche. I now recognise our teacher and general manager as very much like an American football coach: loud and very competitive. He was having none of our admiration and intimidation. He began by yelling at the captain to get more aggressive. I was a bowler and a terrible fielder but he positioned me at forward short leg, right beside the powerful Australian batsmen. I would have been happy standing far off at long on, but he put me right next to the action. In time, with new energy and new focus, we transformed into a competitive team. It showed me that, as in business, you must always have respect for your competitor, but don't be in awe. Go and compete.

A second principle is simply the importance of putting your team first, ahead of your personal statistics and recognition. One of my teams had a brilliant fast bowler. He was one of the most promising young cricketers in the land. He became better after attending an Under-19 South Zone coaching clinic. His pace and accuracy were just brilliant. As a tail-end batsman myself, being in the nets against this guy was tough. But he had a self-destructive mindset. During one game, our captain decided to replace him with another bowler. Soon, the new bowler coaxed the opposing batsman to shoot a ball skyward, an easy catch for our cantankerous teammate now at mid-off. Rather than take a simple catch, he plunged both hands deep into his pockets and watched passively as the ball fell right in front of him. He was a star player, and we looked on in complete disbelief. The lesson? One brilliant character who does not put the team first can destroy the team.

There are, of course, many lessons one can take from cricket, but for me, a third is the central importance of leadership. There was one match in which my off-spin bowling was getting hammered. I was serving up very ordinary stuff. Our team captain, in retrospect, showed me what real leadership looks like. When my over had ended, he replaced me, and quickly got a wicket. Immediately he gave the ball back to me and I took seven wickets of my own. Why did he do it? I surmised he wanted me to get my confidence back. He was an empathetic leader, and he knew that if I lost my confidence it would be hard to get it back. That is what leadership is about: bringing out the best in everyone. It was a subtle, important lesson about when to intervene and when to build the confidence of an individual and a team. That team captain went on to play many years of Ranji Trophy competition, and he taught me a very valuable lesson.

Satya Nadella is the CEO of Microsoft Corporation, and an admirer of all things cricket.

Finding Crowe

GREG CHAPPELL

The greatest challenge in life is discovering who you are. The second greatest is being happy with what you find.

– Unknown

The above quote perfectly sums up the life journey of Martin David Crowe (1962-2016).

Martin was a cricket prodigy who, despite his internal battles, became one of the great batsmen of his generation. A sensitive soul, the abrasiveness of top-level sport and the element of failure that it embodied nearly claimed him before he got started.

Plucked straight out of school to play for his country at 19, against an experienced Australian team in Wellington in February 1982, his doubts and fears were intensified as he struggled to cope with the sharp lift in standard.

Despite his lack of comfort in the environment, he was aware enough to seek out the more experienced members of the opposition to try to understand what it took to succeed in such illustrious company.

I played in his debut Test match in Wellington and, despite his stuttering nine runs in the first innings, saw something that others must have seen to select such a callow young man to be thrown in at the deep end.

Despite being overwhelmed by the pace of Dennis Lillee and Jeff Thomson – not the first batsman to have been – and the guile of Terry Alderman, Martin looked to be well organised and very well balanced before running himself out in a moment of confusion.

My immediate thought at the end of that Test was that it may have been sensible to have given him a less daunting initiation.

His two runs in the Second Test highlighted how discombobulated he had become in the ten days between games as it dawned upon him how far out of his depth he was. He looked on edge and decidedly uncomfortable for his brief stay, but as New Zealand won the Test match, he was retained for the final Test.

His third Test was less encouraging than his first two.

Martin had every reason to be relieved that the series was over, but I was impressed that every evening after play he continued to front up for a drink and a chat and that he kept asking intelligent questions of those who had played successfully at the top level.

The likeable young fellow had made quite an impression on me off the field with his intelligence and his thirst for knowledge, so I followed his career with interest.

The New Zealand selectors showed admirable foresight when they selected him to tour England in the northern summer of 1983 and while not setting the world alight, Martin slowly began to find his feet and, more importantly, some confidence and belief.

It didn't surprise me when, back at Basin Reserve in early 1984, he notched up his first Test century against the touring England team, which included Bob Willis and Ian Botham in the pace attack. The youngster had finally broken through and went on to establish himself as the pre-eminent New Zealand batsman of his era and, arguably, the best ever produced by them.

I believe that had Martin played anywhere else but New Zealand, his record would have been even better. Conditions for batting in New Zealand in those days were as challenging as anywhere with damp pitches always offering some seam movement to the pace bowlers. Even if he had played in the current era with better drained grounds and drier pitches that are less bowler-friendly and the modern, more forgiving bats, I believe his record would have better reflected his talent.

Martin was a classical batsman. He stood tall and still at the crease, was well balanced and relaxed, and played with an efficiency of movement that is the hallmark of all of the best players.

At ball release, Martin had a slight movement on to the ball of the back foot to ready himself to push forward if the ball was full, but he quickly picked up length and if he saw it was short, he planted the front foot to push back to cut, force off the back foot or pull the short ball.

His takeaway was the essence of economy. He didn't have the high flourish of Garry Sobers or Brian Lara; the hands hardly went back, but the strength in his forearms cocked the bat back to load the arms and the bat with all the power needed to hit the ball hard through the off side or, to the ball that angled in to him, through or over the leg-side field with effortless ease.

Classical cricketer: When Martin Crowe returned to club cricket in his forties, it was as if he still had much to prove. — *Getty Images*

I always marvelled that, with his minimalist take away, his front leg appeared to be getting to the pitch of the ball before the bat, which, almost as an afterthought, whipped into action to get there first. It is something that I have never seen with any other batsman.

Despite a knee problem that dogged him for much of his career, Martin eventually played 77 Tests for New Zealand and racked up 17 Test centuries at a credible average of 45.36. He, along with Richard Hadlee, was the mainstay of the New Zealand teams.

Tellingly, Martin averaged 55 in the 16 Test victories he was involved in and that, to me, is a much better reflection of his true worth.

Because of his knee problem, Martin was forced to retire earlier than he would have liked. Despite the success he had in his post-cricket career in sports television, during which he created Cricket Max, which proved hugely popular with players and audiences alike, he felt there was some unfinished business.

It did not come as any surprise to me when, in his forties, he decided to make a comeback to club cricket to prove to himself that he could still make runs. He felt that his more mature self would handle things better than he did the first time around and that he would make up for any physical decline with a more advanced mental game.

Once again, his body let him down and his short – but thoroughly enjoyable – return to the game was consigned to posterity.

Martin and I had kept in contact with each other over the years and when he invited me to come to play in a Cricket Max Masters game I reluctantly agreed on the basis that Trevor Chappell and I would go over to New Zealand early to meet Martin and his brother Jeff near Lake Taupo for a relaxed weekend Crowe-Chappell challenge of golf, fishing and skeet shooting.

Martin and Jeff were both accomplished golfers so Trevor and I lost the first Test. We then boarded a boat to go onto Lake Taupo for the second Test of fishing, at which they were both much more experienced than Trevor and me.

As luck would have it, with the Chappells on one side of the boat and the Crowes on the other, all the fish were in a school under our side of the boat. At one stage I looked up to see Jeff silently beseeching the captain to swing the boat around, but despite the home-ground advantage, Australia evened the series.

Skeet shooting was foreign to both Trevor and me so the Crowes were quietly confident of winning the third Test, but Trevor exceeded all expectations, not the least of all his, to propel us to one of the more satisfying victories of our sporting lives.

Nothing other than bragging rights were on the line, but we all competed as though our lives depended upon it.

All the while, Martin had been working on himself. His early cricket career had been dogged by self-doubt and feelings that confused him, but he was as relaxed as I had ever seen him.

Ironically, it took a diagnosis of lymphoma for him to explore his inner-self more deeply than before. By truly facing and unmasking his emotions he had begun to live fully for the first time.

Cruelly, just as he found the true Martin Crowe and was starting to live to his potential, the great umpire in the sky signalled the end of his innings. Thankfully, not before he had met the second of life's great challenges and discovered that he was truly happy with what he had found.

Greg Chappell is a former Australian captain, who turned out for them in 87 Tests – bringing up a hundred in his first and last – and 74 ODIs.

Evolution theory

SIDHARTH MONGA

Samuel Badree is not likely to be recognised in an airport queue if he is not wearing his cricket kit. He is a legspinner from Trinidad who plays T20 internationals for West Indies. He doesn't turn the ball much, he doesn't play international cricket in any other format, but he is a true pioneer in T20 cricket. Take the 2016 World T20, played in India, for example. Amid all the flamboyant big hitters in the champion side, Badree quietly played a key role, invariably bowling in the powerplay and going for just 5.39 runs an over in his 23 overs in six matches.

There is a reason why Badree is so unremarkable. He is the opposite of what we were taught a good spinner was. He doesn't flight the ball, he doesn't turn it. His trajectory is lower than what we were told of good spinners, his length shorter. Therein lies his success. Badree is arguably the first spinner to have realised that in T20 cricket the first thing that needed to go out was cricket vocabulary. That a good ball in T20 is one that goes to a fielder at the boundary. That hitting aerial shots is easier off the front foot. So if you keep the batsman on the back foot, have the field for it, and don't give them pace to time it, you will not be hit for boundaries.

In the World T20, for example, 25.36% of the deliveries bowled by Badree were either short or short of a length. All the other spinners pitched short only 11.88% of the time. While the commentators keep repeating, "Oh he is lucky to get away with this!"

Redefining spin: Samuel Badree doesn't turn the ball and bowls shorter lengths. – *BCCI/Spotzpics*

when a spinner dropped short, it is a legitimate strategy for spinners now. Only in two of the 35 times that Badree didn't bowl the traditional spinner's length was he hit for boundaries; in all, the short balls he bowled went for just 4.45 an over. Badree quietly managed to keep the trick to himself, but other spinners are catching up. In an interview with *ESPNcricinfo*, R Ashwin, who seems destined for unbelievable numbers in Test cricket, broke rank with the secretive cricket society and admitted bowling short for a spinner is the new good delivery. Except that Badree has been using it for years now.

This is just one example of how T20 cricket has left behind its followers: fans, commentators, cricket writers. Some people call T20 the greatest revolution in cricket since over-arm bowling. There has been reverse swing, the doosra, the switch hit, but they were all isolated innovations. T20 is a collective explosion. It moves so fast that by the time we identify a tactic or a strategy, others have countered it and moved on to the next.

The bottom line is the result. You cannot look at an event independently. You cannot say it was a bad ball that got a wicket or a good ball that went for six. Nobody cares for the niceties. And because this is the most contemporary format of what is considered an almost intimidatingly anachronistic sport, there is no shortage of money or effort to achieve these results.

In such a short match, the value of each ball has gone up massively. One of the biggest changes is the amount of planning that goes into a single ball. Gujarat Lions' Ravindra Jadeja didn't bowl a single over in their 2016 IPL match against Sunrisers Hyderabad. Aaron Finch explained that they just couldn't get the match-up right for him. Either David Warner, a left-hander, would be on strike at the start of an over or the over would have to be bowled from the end not considered good for Jadeja keeping in mind the size of the boundary. This amount of deliberation over a bowling change was unheard of before T20. At times, captains go to the extent of trying to bowl the last ball in a certain fashion so that a certain batsman is on strike first ball of the next over so that a certain bowler can be introduced.

Man-to-man marking and set plays are terms introduced to cricket by T20. Analysis nowadays tells bowlers where a certain batsman is likely to hit out if he has been bogged down, based on his history in such scenarios. Batsmen know where a bowler is likely to bowl immediately after being hit for a six. It is not nearly enough, though. One coach says these stats are useless in a live match. He wants live

Hawk-Eye stats, but they haven't been able to arrange that with the broadcasters yet. They want to know, for instance, on a given day, how many runs per ball the bowler has conceded if he has pitched the ball in the range of six to nine metres from the stumps. They could start paying broadcasters to share the data, they could even pay Hawk-Eye to work just for them during matches. They don't want perceptions, they want exact numbers.

It's all nerdy stuff, though. If anything, it is a response to the biggest change T20 cricket has brought. The luxury of ten wickets in hand in 20 overs has freed up the batsman's mind to explore the true limits of batting. Batting is one of the more psychological pursuits in sports. You know if you make one mistake, you can be out of the rest of the game. You can spend hours waiting your turn, and then be asked to score six off one ball. There is doubt and insecurity that bowlers have historically preyed on, that has allowed bowlers to compete on even terms. The doubt is gone because in order to adjust their games to having the same number of wickets in such a short time, the batsmen have let go of the fear of getting out. The foundation of this sport has been turned upside down.

It is lamented bats have improved beyond recognition, grounds have become smaller, regulations have empowered batsmen. They are all contributing factors all right, but nothing without a free mind. Watch on YouTube the highlights of Ian Botham's legendary 149 not out at Headingley. When he came in to bat in the second innings, England needed 122 to make Australia bat. Soon he saw two more wickets fall. He told the No. 9 batsman Graham Dilley they were going to give it some humpty. Botham had nothing to lose now. In other words he had no fear of getting out. With that toothpick of a bat he hit a six into the confectionary stall, which remains one of the biggest ever hit at Headingley.

Amid the blue seats in the Great Southern Stand of MCG, way up on level three, is a yellow seat that commemorates the biggest six hit at the historic ground. Simon O'Donnell played that shot in a Sheffield Shield game with the puny little bat you used to get back in 1993.

Of course the bats have given the modern batsmen a bigger sweet spot, but the distance the ball travels is a function of the weight not the thickness. Also, compared to the tennis racket or the golf club, the material used for the cricket bat at least remains the same. Most of those involved closely with the game believe bigger sixes are

New vocabulary: The switch hit, embraced by the likes of Glenn Maxwell, has opened up the field for batsmen. — *Getty Images*

being hit because the batsmen are trying to hit them, practising for them. T20 training involves drills where the batsman just aims for a clean swing, hitting gentle lobs into the stands. They work on their strength so that they are able to impart optimum power. T20 batting coaches tell batsmen not to worry about getting caught when they play a shot because now they know even half-hits travel for sixes in most grounds.

It's almost as if batsmen didn't know these avenues existed in the past. Look at all the new shots that have entered the game. When he used to play with his brother in the backyard as a kid, Kevin Pietersen had to bat left-handed if he got out first ball. He was strong batting the "wrong way". When he was an international player, looking for scoring areas, especially after he had been frustrated by Shane Warne bowling into the rough from round the wicket, he toyed with the idea of opening up the other side of the field. Away from the media's eyes, in the nets, he would go on a knee, bat left-handed, and ask for lobs that he could hit and feel comfortable with. Then he went to step two, holding the bat incredibly loose when in his stance, then switching hands and feet, dropping his back leg and then playing a shot he was already comfortable playing. When he first tried it, in a Test against the bowling of Muttiah Muralitharan, he did so after he had reached 60-70, having made sure he was playing the next match. He had got rid of that fear of getting out.

This switch hit has opened up avenues for batsmen with a different batting grammar. I once asked Glenn Maxwell how he perceived risk vis-à-vis his innovative shots, especially the ones where he plays the reverse flick against a fast bowler. This was after he had scored a match-winning 95 at the WACA Ground. "When you are playing in a place like this where the boundaries are so short straight and when the fielders are up inside the circle, I feel all you need to do is get it a little bit above them and it is four," said Maxwell. "To me, it seems less of a risk than try and go against the pace and try and go over mid-off and mid-on. I find it so much easier using the pace to get it over the guys behind me than it is to go straight. They were bowling slower balls into the wicket so I felt like I could sort of scoop it over myself which might seem unorthodox, but when you practise it a lot, when you have trained against the guys in the nets who are bowling slower balls, slower-ball bouncers and that sort of thing, you get used to it. You hit more than you miss."

What the bowlers have been doing – analysis, slower balls, slower bouncers, wide yorkers, carrom balls, knuckle balls – has all been in reaction to batting's ascent to the next level. Such is the confidence of a free mind that in the nets AB de Villiers spends some time batting with a stump. He wants to play the ball late; the single-stump drill helps him do so. He wants to play late so he can make better choices, have a cleaner swing, have the time to recover to off-pace balls, and with the knowledge that he is not going to be too late on the shot because if he hits the ball hard enough, it is going to go.

Bowling, unfortunately, didn't have that much scope of improvement while staying within the limits of legality. The increase in technology has only meant less reverse swing and fewer dodgy actions. Unless there is a seismic shift in the landscape of the sport, bowling is doomed to play catch-up, which is ironic because as a sport it is the batsmen who react to bowlers who start the play. Now the poor bowlers are consigned to second-guessing what the batsman is going to do and react to it.

There is some consolatory help for the bowlers, though, through the fielding. Because of the shorter duration and because of the significance of each ball, the fielders have started to give their all to each ball. There is no question of conserving your energy now. Every ball is chased down, every throw is fired in, relay catches at the boundary line do not leave mouths agape. There are fielding drills for all of this.

There is a downside to every change, though. For every sensational relay catch at the boundary there is a slip catch dropped in a Test because slip catching requires a whole different temperament, which doesn't go well with the hyper T20 game. Rahul Dravid, one of the greatest Test batsmen ever, has made a post-retirement career out of coaching T20 teams. He knows both worlds. When he came back to coaching junior India sides over multi-day cricket, he made a pertinent observation, which is a direct impact of T20. He was awed with the young batsmen's striking ability, but he observed that they struggled to keep taking singles when presented with in-and-out fields, and the corollary that young spinners didn't know how to work towards taking wickets if the batsmen started taking singles and stopped going after them.

The value of the single, for a long time the blood stream of limited-overs batting, has diminished because the batsmen know they can make up for the dot balls with a six any time, as demonstrated by West Indies in the semi-final of the World T20. They played 50 dot balls to India's 27, but still gunned down India's 192 with ease thanks to 146 runs in boundaries as against India's 92. Which is what raises the question: Is it more desirable to have a Virat Kohli who seeks perfection, reduces risk, tries to play long or have three big bad hitters who might take risks and get out but are likelier to go faster than Kohli? After all you have got ten wickets to lose in 20 overs.

Well, there is a price to pay for everything.

Sidharth Monga is assistant editor at ESPNcricinfo.

Game of chess: There is no room for questionable decision making – not on the field, not in the auction room. – *BCCI/Sportzpics*

The gavel sounds on parity

SAURABH SOMANI

The single largest fact in the cricketing universe for the past decade has been the Indian Premier League.

That is neither something to be proud of nor to be sneered at – it simply is. But while nine iterations of the tournament have had analyses running deep and wide, covering the spectrum from Virat Kohli's run-machine avatar to Gabriella Pasqualotto's blog, the chamber where it all begins has remained something of a Ballroom of Befuddlement.

Every year, before the teams line up on the field to face each other one at a time, they assemble for the IPL auctions with eight facing eight simultaneously. It's a game of multi-dimensional chess: You're playing seven opponents at the same time, while they're all playing one another. Each must plan several moves in advance and keep track of the others' strategies. Each must arrive fully prepared, because if you don't, the results, on the field or your bottom-line, won't be pretty.

It didn't begin that way. In 2008 and 2009, it was teams largely feeling their way into the world of franchise T20 cricket. The focus was on getting 'star' players, a fact franchise officials across the board admit to. They also point out that in those initial years they didn't have hard data. After all, how would you judge the calibre of a player in such a nascent format? But even in this imperfect world, the decision-making was questionable: Witness the furious bidding war between Kolkata Knight Riders and Kings XI Punjab that jacked up Mashrafe Mortaza's price to $US 600,000 in 2009, a figure even the cricketer's most ardent fans wouldn't have believed possible from a base price of $US 50,000. Besides, the owners had, as one former official put it, the tendency to pull a Vijay Mallya, to "just turn around and pick whom he wanted to, very often to the consternation of his team, who had done a lot of research."

The first major churn came in 2011, but it needed 2014, and the biggest auction the league had seen, to level the playing field. On the field, players had grasped the fundamentals of T20 cricket; in the bidding room, a similar understanding took effect only then, seven seasons on. Teams by then were more professional and, for the most part, men who understood cricket and statistics had the power to make decisions. Crucially, with uncapped Indian cricketers finally part of the auction, they had a canvas large enough for each team to build a potentially title-winning squad. It's the nature of competition that one team will win, and one will lose, but IPL 2014 was the first one in which you felt before the tournament that every team had the wherewithal to go all the way.

How did this change come about? Data. To twist a phrase allegedly beloved of a former England coach, the data was worth looking at. And there was lots of it to analyse thanks to the T20 explosion around the world.

Today's strategy is far advanced beyond bland batting strike-rates and bowling economy-rates. "The trend now is to look at specific roles and see if a player fits into those roles," says Hemant Dua, the Delhi Daredevils chief executive. "It could be death bowling, as an example, so then you try to look at data that is in and around death bowling. Similarly, if someone has to be a floater as a batsman, you try to look at how that person performs across various batting positions."

Joy Bhattacharjya, who worked with Kolkata Knight Riders as team director, explains: "We would see the number of fours and sixes hit after the first six overs, because clearing the in-field up front with the harder ball and the field in is easier. It's different to get boundaries when the ball is softer and you have a lot of boundary riders. Even when I look at economy rate, if someone is bowling the eighth, tenth and 12th overs, you won't compare him to someone who bowls up front and at the death. It's now literally, 'Are you a slog-overs economy bowler?' And if you give me an economy-rate of 8.5 in the slog overs, you're doing a darned good job."

Refining data is one part. Another is the finances available with each team. In 2008, it made sense to have the marquee Indian players as 'icons' for their home teams. But with T20 still such a new quantity, teams ended up being of uneven strengths. In principle, retention was a good idea in 2011 to build each franchise's brand. In practice, it was a travesty, with Chennai Super Kings and Mumbai Indians the main beneficiaries.

That a franchise could pay what it liked to a retained player while losing only an arbitrarily fixed amount from its auction purse skewed one of the fundamental tenets that made IPL a level playing field: the fixed budget each team had. Mumbai retained Sachin Tendulkar, Lasith Malinga, Harbhajan Singh and Kieron Pollard. Chennai went with MS Dhoni, Suresh Raina, M Vijay and Albie Morkel. Each franchise lost only $US 4.5 million out of their $US 9 million budget. How absurd that amount was, was proved within the first half hour of that year's auction, with Kolkata spending $US 4.5 million on just Gautam Gambhir and Yusuf Pathan.

In 2014, the effects of retention were thinner. It helped, too, that retention budgets were made steeper, and a 'right to match' option was introduced. In an ideal world, each franchise would have only had right to match cards and no retention option, with market value rather than an arbitrary fixed amount determining what was lost from their budget. But, on the whole, with uncapped players in the auction, heftier cuts for retaining players and better analysis to rely on, 2014 afforded more financial parity than before.

It's still not entirely the same for all, as any real-world situation is, because budgets mean different things to different franchises. For example, Mumbai, whose owner is Mukesh Ambani, India's richest man, would likely have no qualms spending every bit of their allotted Rs 60 crore (approximately $US 9 million; from 2014 the auction was held in INR). For some other franchises, the given figure is separated from what they are willing to spend. One celebrated coach, when asked why franchise X spent Y on player Z, when better options were available, explained the sums being done at each table. At the dynamic setting of an IPL auction table, things are not linear. Several franchises come with pre-fixed budgets.

Data is worth looking at: Teams wade through analytics to find a particular kind of player who can fit into a particular role. – *Getty Images*

Rajasthan Royals were a famous example of that: They might have Rs 20 crore left to spend, but their owners set them with an upper limit of Rs 12 crore, say, so that's the budget they operated within. Pre-fixed budgets mean identifying exactly what roles you need filled in your squad and in what order of priority.

This also explains why bidding wars are often not two-team affairs, even if they start off as such. Some teams have a price-point at which they have to drop out; if that point is within the range of a third team, they enter the bidding then. Bidding itself can be used strategically, to artificially pump up the price of a player if you are certain that a rival franchise is willing to spend big on him. More money spent by a rival leaves you that much more bargaining power when a player you *really* want comes under the hammer. That is also why some players appear in the accelerated auction but find no bids. A player can only come under the hammer for the accelerated auction if at least one franchise indicates an interest in bidding for him, but franchises indicating interest only means that they want the player to come under the hammer, not that they mean to buy him. Sometimes, they are hoping that another franchise picks him up, thereby either filling up their overseas quota or depleting their budget, leaving the field clearer for someone else the franchise in question *does* want to buy.

It all comes together in a sort of ordered chaos in the modern auction room. Yet, no franchise relies only on refined statistics or Excel sheets of budgets, strengths and weaknesses. This being cricket, there is still room for the gut-call. An analyst for an IPL-winning franchise revealed that rather than stats, he initially looks at the shape of a batsman and his temperament – the unquantifiables. Another official from a winning team spoke of how the auction room resembled a start-up convention – people betting on a lot of new ventures, confident that enough will come good to recoup the investments – or a stock market, with prices rising and falling based on past performance and current mood.

Auction rooms acquire a logic of their own, which someone on the outside might not get. Evolution dictates that as the grammar of T20 cricket is understood better, there will be a truly even contest inside the auction room, with greater depth of analysis and variety of players negating any imbalance in spending power. Perfect symmetry inside, the asymmetry of the real world outside. The vagaries of form and conditions the only deciding factors in who wins, not deeper pockets. Cricket's glorious uncertainties; in other words, equalising fortunes in the IPL.

Saurabh Somani (@saurabh_42) is assistant editor at Wisden India.

HALL OF FAME

Vinoo Mankad

NARI CONTRACTOR

To most cricketers of my generation, Mulvantrai Himmatlal Mankad is the greatest all-rounder produced by India. And for those who are not convinced, let me say that only Kapil Dev would even figure in a debate.

When I think of Vinoo, I think about his achievement of taking only 23 Tests to score 1000 runs and claim 100 wickets; the 27 consecutive matches he played on India's 1946 tour of England; the two Test hundreds in the Australian summer of 1947-48 against Ray Lindwall and Keith Miller; the 1952 Lord's Test, which came to be known as Mankad's Test. But watching him in the Test against England at the Brabourne Stadium as a collegian in 1951 gave me the biggest thrill of all.

It's 65 years after that first sighting and I am honoured to write an appreciation in Vinoo's birth centenary year.

Cricket in India has benefited greatly from patrons and when we talk about Vinoo, we must mention the Jamsaheb of Nawanagar Digvijaysinhji. It was he who provided him the opportunities to grow as a cricketer. There were two more benefactors and Vinoo never forgot to credit them: Albert Wensley for his bowling, Duleepsinhji for his batting, although he was taught the basics of the game at school in Jamnagar by SHM Colah. However, India would never have had a cricketer of the stature of Mankad had it not been for the Jamsaheb.

At home he was called Minu. At school, they called him Vinoo. Although Arthur Gilligan, the former MCC captain, told Wensley he was convinced that Vinoo would go on to become a world-class all-rounder, Vinoo's start in the Ranji Trophy was far from spectacular. He went wicketless on debut for Western India and ended with an unbeaten zero at No. 11 in December 1935. Vinoo was transformed into a spinner from a medium pacer on the insistence of Wensley.

Nawanagar made an entry in the 1936-37 edition of the Ranji Trophy and won it on debut under Wensley. Vinoo performed well enough (185 in the final against Bengal) to be part of the Indian team in the unofficial Tests against Lord Tennyson's XI in 1937-38. Jamsaheb, then president of the Board of Control for Cricket in India, was surprised to see Vinoo's name missing from the original list, however. The president said he wouldn't interfere, but insisted the selectors were making a big mistake. Playing for Jamsaheb of Nawanagar XI, Vinoo showed how wrong the selectors were by scoring 62 and 67 not out against Tennyson's team. And when it came to picking the team for the second match in Bombay, the 20-year-old was not ignored. With scores of 38 and 88 and the wicket of Tennyson and AW Wellard, Vinoo Mankad had arrived.

Even before I played a little cricket with him and came to know him, I could tell from afar where Vinoo was on the field when I watched him. He didn't have to bowl to stand out. It was his demeanour, his neat attire and, most of all, his alertness that you just couldn't miss. I have never seen a player so watchful, so agile. You can call it cricketing radiance.

He was never known to drop a catch but I saw him drop one at Brabourne Stadium in the 1951-52 Test. Tom Graveney went on to score 175. Even a schoolboy would have taken that edge, but that is cricket. It also showed that Vinoo was human. He was a brilliant fielder, especially off his own bowling. If a batsman pushed one to mid-off, he would be there to stop it. He knew exactly where the batsman was going to play. And if he thought the ball would go straight, he would swiftly move there. His bowling and fielding movements were in sync with each other. When Vinoo bowled he didn't need a mid-off fielder. For us, in those days, Vinoo and Alf Valentine were the best left-arm spinners.

Every plaudit he received for his batting was well deserved. After all, he and Pankaj Roy shared a record opening stand of 413 against New Zealand in Madras in 1955-56. That partnership was amazing and to us sitting in the dressing room, Pankaj and Vinoo never looked like getting out.

I enjoyed watching him bowl. Accuracy, length, spin ... he had everything. He had a good arm ball, but his most prominent art was the flight. Vinoo never relied on turning tracks. It was his flight that got him his wickets. Often, today's so-called top-class spinners don't reap rich rewards when they encounter flat tracks. On spinning wickets, his spin could be devastating, and on good tracks, he got batsmen befuddled by his flight.

An all-rounder: Vinoo Mankad seen here with his family - despite his feats he was a simple man. – *Photo courtesy Raju Bharatan*

Vinoo was the ultimate professional in Indian cricket. England was home away from home. The story of him being summoned from Haslingden club in the Lancashire League to join the Indian team, and performing with bat and ball in the Lord's Test of 1952 is straight out a fairy-tale book.

Despite helping India win the Madras Test of the 1951-52 series – India's first ever victory – with 12 wickets, the selectors/board could not guarantee him a place in the England-bound team. That's how the establishment functioned in those times. Luckily, the Indian team had the venerable Pankaj Gupta as manager, who, I learnt, played a key role in convincing Haslingden that Vinoo would be better off playing for India.

Scores of 72 and 184 along with a five-wicket haul – no Indian has ever matched this performance at the headquarters of cricket. We followed it over the radio. I remember young Fred Trueman hitting Vinoo on his right finger. The bowler refused to go near the injured batsman and Vinoo didn't like it. He hit 17 off Trueman's next over. Vinoo had bravado written all over him.

I was fortunate to have played in the same Indian team as Vinoo for a few Tests. He swore by discipline although he didn't say much in terms of advice to players new to the Indian team. Among the very few things he emphasised on was practising well. He was the first to land up at the nets and the last to leave. "Be prepared to bat at any number so practise accordingly," he used to say. He didn't speak much, but in those days, no one really was forthcoming with advice. "You are doing fine, just carry on," was the standard line.

In fact, he said the same thing while I was batting with him on my Test debut (against New Zealand in Bombay in 1955-56) when he had completed his double-century. "Don't worry, you are doing fine," he said. There were no coaches to tell us what to do.

Let me give you another example of how things were in our days: The dressing room at Eden Gardens had a partition. The seniors sat on one side and juniors on the other. When I became captain I insisted on team meetings. In fact, I was the first Indian captain to hold team meetings and I encouraged even junior players to speak out.

Vinoo had a dry sense of humour. He once asked Ray Lindwall what he was doing wrong when it came to tackling his yorker the night before batting against him in Melbourne in 1947-48. After he gained from Lindwall's advice, Vinoo is believed to have asked him, "Ray, my bat is coming down well now?"

He could tease you; at times his vocabulary was colourful. An interviewer asked him in the evening of his life whether he believed that luck plays an important part in cricket. Vinoo just said, "I didn't believe in bad luck."

I don't have to mention Vinoo's Test statistics to endorse his greatness, but I can tell you, his career figures would have been far more impressive if not for the Second World War coming in the way of his playing years. Like Don Bradman, Vinoo missed out too.

Vinoo, like the great Australian, had two 200-plus scores in a series (v New Zealand in 1955-56). Bradman had a lot of time for

Vinoo, who treasured a signed photograph Bradman had presented him with the words, "Well bowled, Mankad."

Bradman rightly supported him in the controversy over the Bill Brown run-out (after warning the batsman several times) in the Sydney Test of 1947-48. The term 'Mankaded' is still used, but Vinoo shouldn't be remembered by the cricketing world for that incident alone. Those two hands did a lot more, like shaking the hand of the Queen of England, who not only congratulated him for his performance at Lord's in 1952, but also stated that she had watched and enjoyed his exploits on television.

Despite his great feats, he was a simple man. Even after retiring from first-class cricket, he worked tirelessly at the LR Tairsee Memorial nets at Bombay's PJ Hindu Gymkhana where he nurtured an array of first-class cricketers including Eknath Solkar, who went on to play for India. His three sons, Ashok, Atul and Rahul, played first-class cricket too.

The term all-rounder is used very loosely nowadays, but only a few cricketers have done full justice to it. And if I were to compile my dream team of all-rounders, MH Mankad would be the first on the list because no regular opening batsman had such a great variety of cricketing skills.

Career stats

	M	R	HS	Ave	50s	100s	W	BBI	5wI	10wM
Tests	44	2109	231	31.47	6	5	162	8/52	8	2
First-class	233	11591	231	34.70	52	26	782	8/35	38	9

Nari Contractor is a former India captain and left-hand batsman who returned to first-class cricket after recovering from a near-fatal injury on the field.

Sourav Ganguly

VVS LAXMAN

The first words that come to mind as I sit down to write about Sourav Ganguly are 'remarkable transformation'.

Sourav the India cricketer was a quiet, shy, unassuming, reticent character who largely kept his own counsel, seldom spoke at team meetings and would have been largely anonymous had it not been for the vast legion of journalists from Bengal travelling with the Indian team. Sourav the India captain was the exact opposite: charged up, aggressive, ready with a sledge and wearing his heart on his sleeve, even if he was still more of a listener at team meetings.

Having shared the Indian dressing room with him for the better part of 12 years, I was well placed to watch this fascinating cricketer's journey in international cricket.

We had played together for India A in Sharjah in 1995, and after a very good Wills Trophy that season, he broke into the Test team for the tour of England in 1996. There were a few murmurs over his selection, but Sourav silenced the naysayers with centuries in his first two Test matches. That was to be a recurring phenomenon over the next dozen years: Every time Sourav was cornered, he fought back with a tiger's resolve.

My Test debut came in the same year, at home against South Africa in Ahmedabad, and that was because Sourav missed the match through injury. From then on, we were constant companions in the Indian dressing room, part of an emerging young brigade that enjoyed and fed off one another's company and success.

The standout feature of Sourav's character has to be his resilience, and his whole-hearted commitment to every responsibility he embraced. He took charge of the Indian team at a difficult time, not long after the 3-0 pounding in Australia in 1999-2000 and immediately after losing 2-0 at home to South Africa. Not just on the field, it was a difficult time for India off it too with the match-fixing saga exploding. It was important not just to win matches but also to restore the faith of the fans. Sourav proved to be the ideal leader at that stage, helped by the fact that he had at his command players who already were or would go on to become legends of the game.

As it always does with success, several things fell in place at the start of Sourav's tenure. In John Wright, we had our first foreign coach, and his thought process was remarkably aligned to Sourav's. John was a strong advocate of discipline and work ethic, and both he and Sourav placed greater emphasis on contributions to the team's cause rather than individual milestones. If tough calls had to be made, then they were made, but players were always kept informed about why certain decisions had been taken because Sourav realised early on that his captaincy legacy would depend entirely on getting the team to understand and buy into his line of thinking.

It was 2001, and Sourav had been captain for less than a year, when Steve Waugh's Australia arrived in India chasing a record winning streak in Tests. For the first time, an Indian captain was willing to give as good as he got. Tiger Pataudi and Sunil Gavaskar, among others, had stood up for causes in the past, but they were never in your face; they never deliberately tried to rile the opposition. Sourav believed that as players, we were second to none, and therefore if he had to give the opponents back in the same coin, then so be it.

That 2001 series win was to have massive repercussions on the way we approached the game. Suddenly, there was this belief that we could win from any situation, in any condition, against any opposition.

Sourav placed particular emphasis on winning overseas because he felt that was the hallmark of a good team. India were historically not successful overseas and it was a tag he was desperate to erase. He also realised that for India to be successful abroad, we needed to play to our strengths. In England in 2002, for instance, our pace bowlers hadn't troubled the home side in the first two Tests, so going into the Headingley Test, we decided that our best chance of victory was to play both our frontline spinners. Having picked two spinners, we would have to bowl last if the option presented itself, which meant we had to bat first in somewhat tricky conditions. The batting group was up for the challenge. We knew that we would encounter an uncomfortable few hours, but we also knew that as a team, this was our best chance for victory. As it transpired, Rahul (Dravid), Sachin (Tendulkar) and Sourav made hundreds, and Anil (Kumble) and Harbhajan (Singh) played their parts in our innings victory.

This is but one instance of Sourav empowering the playing group, and especially the bowlers. As a captain, when the team is batting, the most you have to do from time to time is to decide whether to

One for posterity: 141 made against a pacy Pakistan attack in Adelaide, 2000. – *Getty Images*

shake up the batting order or when to declare. When you are on the field, though, you need to make many more decisions. With Sourav, the decision-making was pretty much left to the bowlers. After all, they were the ones doing the executing, so it made sense that they do the planning as well. That way, they would also be more responsible and take ownership of their actions.

Sourav the captain tended to overshadow Sourav the batsman, but I have seen few better timers of the cricket ball or few clearing the straight boundaries with greater ease. The way he leaned into his drives on the off side was a visual delight and the envy of batsmen the world over. He was brilliant at hitting in the air down the ground, not just while dancing down the track to the spinners, but while also using the depth of the crease against the faster bowlers, especially in one-day cricket where he was clearly one of the finest openers of all time.

His first Test tour, to England in 1996, provided the world with a fair idea of what to expect when Sourav was at the batting crease. During those first two centuries, he showed no signs of nerves and demonstrated a composure that doesn't come to everyone; I don't remember seeing a single shot hit in anger or haste.

His timing through the off side was extraordinary. It was as if he was merely putting bat to ball, and there the little cherry would speed away to thud into the boundary boards. I have always believed his best Test innings was the 144 against Australia on a bouncy, quick Gabba surface in 2003. It was the First Test, and Sourav came out all guns blazing, his positivity and attacking nature letting the Australians know that we were not there just to make up the numbers. That counter-attacking knock from 62 for 3 was a big factor that series as we dominated the Tests, narrowly missing out on our first series win on Australian soil.

In one-day internationals, he seldom batted under Sachin's giant shadow, always more than holding his own, fearless and with an innate understanding of which bowler to go after and whom to treat with respect. His annihilation of Sri Lanka in the World Cup game in Taunton in 1999 was breath-taking – he made the County Ground appear far smaller than it was – though I am partial to the pair of 141s against a Pakistan attack comprising Wasim Akram, Shoaib Akhtar and Saqlain Mushtaq in Adelaide in 2000, and against a South Africa side that included Allan Donald, Shaun Pollock, Jacques Kallis and Lance Klusener in the ICC Knockout Trophy in Nairobi later that year.

He did have his problems against the short ball, and with word travelling, it wasn't long before teams got their fast bowlers to bang the ball in and angle it at his ribs. Sourav found a way to tackle that challenge too, like he did during that darkest phase in his career from the 2005 tour of Zimbabwe onwards.

Considered superfluous by coach Greg Chappell, whose approach was diametrically opposite to Sourav's even if their mindsets in some ways were similar, he rediscovered his batting and stormed back into the Test side, enjoying a purple patch between the end of 2006 and his retirement in November 2008. It was another example of Sourav's ability to put mind over matter, and to make his point when he felt it needed to be made.

Sourav, while not being the swiftest mover, was smart at practice, knowing exactly what he wanted from each session. His reading of the game was outstanding, and I always felt that he was a couple of steps ahead of the game.

It came as no surprise when he made his foray into cricket administration. He has always been excellent at managing situations and people. I have often told him, and only half in jest, that he is cut out for a life in politics to serve people because not only does he know what needs to be done, he also knows how to get it done. Having seen first-hand the proactive steps he has taken as president of Cricket Association of Bengal, I am sure he has plenty to offer not just for Indian cricket, but to the nation as a whole if and when he does take the plunge into politics.

There is that burning desire to excel in whatever he does that has been a glowing Sourav trait. He showed fortitude to return to the Indian team in 1996 after nearly five years in the wilderness, he took exceptionally well to captaincy, he reorganised his game whenever questions were asked, he bounced back from his ouster during the

Chappell era. He has already proved himself to be an able administrator, he has been a sharp, insightful television commentator who is not afraid to speak his mind, and hosts a massively successful reality show on Bengali television. There is very little he has embraced that he hasn't been successful at, and that comes from strong, powerful and aggressive willpower and the skill to remain in his own bubble even in the midst of hundreds of people.

From time to time, Sourav still fancies a game in the middle, the cricketer in him refuses to go away. He is still competitive, but while the mind is willing, the body doesn't always respond. That ship has most definitely sailed, Sourav, but there are plenty of other ports of call waiting for you.

Career stats

	M	R	HS	Ave	50s	100s	W	BBI	5wI
Tests	113	7212	239	42.17	35	16	32	3-28	0
ODIs	311	11363	183	41.02	72	22	100	5-16	2
First-class	254	15687	239	44.18	89	33	167	6-46	4
List A	437	15622	183	41.32	97	31	171	5-16	2
T20	77	1726	91	25.01	8	0	29	3-27	0

VVS Laxman (@VVSLaxman281) scored 8781 runs in 134 Tests for India, with his highest of 281 at Eden Gardens considered one of the best Test knocks by an Indian.

Changing laws for changing times

FRASER STEWART

Following a global consultation with players, umpires and administrators in 2015, the Marylebone Cricket Club (MCC) worked on a review of the Laws of Cricket. The new Code of Laws comes into force in October 2017. At the time of writing, the changes are still to be approved by the MCC committee; so the details below are designed to give a flavour of the areas of the game that are under consideration, rather than to be taken as guaranteed changes.

An area of concern to many in recent years has been the seemingly ever-increasing dominance of bat over ball. There is incontrovertible evidence that the balance between bat and ball has changed, favouring the former, over recent years. There are many factors that have caused this, such as smaller boundaries in some places, more stringent fielding restrictions, batsman-friendly pitches, more attacking batting and fitter and stronger batsmen, but there is little doubt that one of the most significant factors is the development of the size and shape of the bat.

One approach to redress the balance would be to limit the bat's dimensions using a gauge through which a bat would have to pass; another would be to consider using balls that spin, seam or swing more and which retain their hardness and shape for longer. Consultations were held with both bat and ball manufacturers by MCC, while scientific and statistical research was commissioned too.

MCC's world cricket committee recommended in July 2016 that limits be placed on the thickness of the bat's edges and the overall depth of the bat, which followed a similar plea from the International Cricket Council's (ICC) cricket committee. Scientific research showed that limiting the thickness of the edge would be the best way to prevent mis-hits from near or off the edge of the bat from going for sixes. Such shots are at the heart of MCC's concerns, rather than well-timed shots off the middle of the bat. Consultations with bat manufacturers are continuing, and a decision will be taken early in 2017.

Another area of the game under review is player behaviour. The 2015 global consultation confirmed MCC's suspicions wherein a

Player behaviour under review: Cricket is one of the few sports where punishment for poor behaviour is administered after the match. Seen here are Mitchell Starc and Ben Stokes testing the spirit of the game. — *Getty Images*

strong majority felt that standards of behaviour had slipped and that umpires should be given more powers to provide an on-field remedy. In 2015, five games in the UK had to be abandoned due to violence on the field, while the number of post-match reports for behavioural breaches is increasing. Cricket is one of the few sports where punishment is administered after the match, rather than as an in-match punishment. As many as 70% favoured a system where sanction was immediate and would have a consequence on that particular match.

In 2016, certain UK competitions trialled a system in which breaches were codified to mirror the England and Wales Cricket Board's (ECB) code of conduct: four levels of contravention, with Level 4 the most severe. A Level 1 breach brought on a warning, with a repetition resulting in a five-run penalty. Level 2 breaches cost five runs, while Level 3 breaches called for the offender to be suspended from play for a prescribed period, usually ten overs, in addition to the five-run penalty. A Level 4 breach resulted in a player being removed from the field for the remainder of the match, plus the five-run penalty. Initial reports have suggested that the system has improved behaviour. Based on feedback, MCC will decide on introducing such a system.

The bowler running out the non-striker is an area of the Laws surrounded by confusion and controversy. Some of the confusion stems from the difference between the Laws and ICC's playing conditions, the latter requiring the non-striker to remain in his ground for slightly longer. It is likely MCC will seek to align the relevant rule with ICC's, meaning the non-striker is only safe to leave his ground at the expected moment of the ball's release from the bowler's hand. Other methods to deter the non-striker from leaving the crease early were considered, but it was felt that the batsman losing his wicket is the ultimate deterrent. There needed to be a shift in emphasis over who is in the wrong: In such a dismissal, the bowler is often cast as the villain, yet he is doing something the Laws allow, while the batsman who tries to gain an unfair advantage receives sympathy.

Another area under scrutiny is when a batsman should be deemed to be out of his ground, notably when he has already made his ground, but – often because he has dived – his bat subsequently bounces up. Slow-motion television replays have brought this area into focus, with respondents in MCC's consultation process feeling the batsman should be protected in these situations. In 2010, MCC changed the Laws to protect a running batsman whose foot had landed beyond the popping crease and who had continued running towards the stumps and beyond. This was because, in the action of running, both feet can be airborne at the same time. Some people see the bouncing bat as an extension of this principle, while others hold that the batsman is charged with ensuring he has something grounded behind the popping crease and that it is simply unlucky if his bat bounces up. Both ICC's cricket committee and MCC's world cricket committee have expressed sympathy for the batsman when the bat inadvertently bounces up and MCC is now trying to see if a Law can offer suitable protection for the bouncing bat in a run-out situation while not compromising a stumping scenario.

Fraser Stewart (@FraserStewart27) is MCC Laws manager.

Awayitis

KARTHIK LAKSHMANAN

"Come to India, we'll show you."

This was Gautam Gambhir's threat to the Australians midway through India's disastrous Test series down under in 2011-12. Similar lines were spouted by Virat Kohli and Ishant Sharma, and possibly others in the side, despite the Indians slipping to an embarrassing 4-0 whitewash.

To be fair to Gambhir et al, the Indians did *show* as promised when Australia came visiting a year later, returning the favour with an equally convincing 4-0 scoreline. Gambhir's words weren't just a manifestation of his confidence, but also the perfect reflection of Test cricket in the current generation.

Come home, we'll show you.

Sports fans will insist home advantage counts for something. Ice hockey and baseball are among those sports to have minor rule advantages for home sides, and football sometimes rewards away goals, but, largely, with rising professionalism, 'home' and 'away' are more psychological concepts than direct on-field influences. The real challenge for away teams is to play in front of hostile crowds. It might sound simple, but the pressure of countering thousands of partisan fans is anything but. The pressure is not only said to affect players, but also referees. Yes there is the effect of climatic and ground conditions, tedious travel and time zones, but home advantage is often the intangible things.

Cricket is unique in that there is a crucial factor in addition to all these: the pitch. Nearly every aspect of the on-field game changes with the 22-yard strip, which often varies drastically across venues.

Teams visiting the Indian subcontinent will have to adjust to the dry, abrasive pitches apart from the life-sucking heat and loud crowds in many parts of the country. In Australia and South Africa – and once the West Indies – it's all about tackling bounce and pace. England and New Zealand challenge you with their chill and swing. All this, while living out of your suitcase at various hotels.

Home advantage – or away disadvantage, which is perhaps more apt usage – is more prominent in cricket because the sport is unique in another way: It is played in multiple formats, all largely different from the other.

A cricketer thus has to go through gruelling, packed schedules, constantly making rapid adjustments to venues and formats. He doesn't have the time to work on his skills to counter his inherent away disadvantage. On long tours, there is little time to acclimatise for players who feature in more than one format.

And featuring in multiple formats is vital for modern cricketers. No cricketer will want to miss out on the money that T20 brings in and thus most players try to adjust to all formats. Unfortunately, it's the Test performances that take a beating.

More than 2200 Test matches have been played in the sport's 139-year history, but very few teams have managed to conquer all conditions. Barring the West Indians during their heyday in the 1980s and the Australians in the 1990s and early 2000s, no team can boast of succeeding consistently across the world. Away disadvantage is more prominent in this era. An analysis of numbers by dividing the cricket world into two broad categories – Asia and outside Asia – tells the story.

Almost all teams have struggled *(see tables)* – the magnitudes varying – outside their comfort zones, while being increasingly stronger at home. Post 2000, Sri Lanka have lost more than 60% of Tests outside Asia. The once mighty Australia lost close to 50% of their games in Asia in the same period. Compare that with the previous 30 years, when their loss percentage was significantly lower.

There have been occasional displays of brilliance in totally alien conditions: England's 2-1 win in India in 2012 came in the toughest of conditions, as did India's 2014 Lord's win and Sri Lanka's victory over South Africa in Durban, 2011. All those, however, were exceptions to the norm.

The only team to break the trend were South Africa, who remained unbeaten away from home since 2006 before India ended the dream streak with a 3-0 thrashing in the four-Test series last year.

"I haven't seen any great teams (in this era)," says Michael Holding, who was part of the invincible West Indians of the 1970s and '80s. "I have seen some very good teams, and I would think that's the reason why you don't have teams winning that much away from home these days.

"The reason for not having great teams these days is there is so much cricket being played. People are finding it difficult to keep

India Test post 2000

	Home	Away	Outside Subcontinent
Matches	73	96	70
Won	39	29	16
Lost	11	37	29
Draw	23	30	25
Loss %	**15.06**	**38.54**	**41.42**
No. of Series	26	33	22
Series Won	18	12	6
Series Lost	3	15	12
Series Draw	5	6	4

Pakistan Test post 2000

	Home	Away	Outside Subcontinent
Matches	60	78	52
Won	28	26	16
Lost	15	36	29
Draw	17	16	7
Loss %	**25**	**46.15**	**55.76**
No. of Series	24	30	20
Series Won	11	10	4
Series Lost	6	12	8
Series Draw	7	8	8

Sri Lanka Test post 2000

	Home	Away	Outside Subcontinent
Matches	86	63	43
Won	45	16	7
Lost	20	32	26
Draw	21	15	10
Loss %	**23.25**	**50.79**	**60.46**
No. of Series	34	27	18
Series Won	22	7	2
Series Lost	6	15	13
Series Draw	6	5	3

Australia Test post 2000

	Home	Away	In Subcontinent
Matches	93	89	33
Won	67	45	12
Lost	10	30	16
Draw	16	14	5
Loss %	**10.75**	**33.70**	**48.48**
No. of Series	30	27	11
Series Won	3	17	5
Series Lost	24	9	6
Series Draw	3	1	0

England Test post 2000

	Home	Away	In Subcontinent
Matches	117	89	39
Won	66	28	11
Lost	25	33	15
Draw	26	28	13
Loss %	**21.36**	**37.07**	**38.46**
No. of Series	34	26	12
Series Won	5	10	5
Series Lost	23	10	5
Series Draw	6	6	2

South Africa Test post 2000

	Home	Away	In Subcontinent
Matches	83	77	32
Won	48	30	11
Lost	21	22	11
Draw	14	25	10
Loss %	**25.30**	**28.57**	**34.37**
No. of Series	30	28	14
Series Won	21	15	5
Series Lost	6	7	5
Series Draw	3	6	4

New Zealand Test post 2000

	Home	Away	In Subcontinent
Matches	65	68	25
Won	24	16	5
Lost	20	34	10
Draw	21	18	10
Loss %	**30.76**	**50**	**40**
No. of Series	28	31	10
Series Won	11	8	2
Series Lost	9	16	4
Series Draw	8	7	4

West Indies Test post 2000

	Home	Away	In Subcontinent
Matches	80	81	29
Won	21	9	5
Lost	32	52	17
Draw	27	20	7
Loss %	**40**	**64.19**	**58.62**
No. of Series	27	28	12
Series Won	9	5	3
Series Lost	14	21	8
Series Draw	4	2	1

1970 to 2000
Loss % outside comfort (worst to best): NZ: 53.12; India 39.28; Pakistan 37.20; Australia 34.28; England 28.20; WI: 25

Post-2000
Loss % outside comfort (worst to best): Sri Lanka: 60.46, West Indies: 58.62, Pakistan: 55.76, Australia: 48.48, India: 41.42, New Zealand: 40, England: 38.46, South Africa: 34.37

Post-2000 home-away difference:
Tiger at home, lamb abroad - Aus: 37.73; SL: 37.21; Pak: 30.76; India: 26.36
Bad everywhere - WI: 18.62
Good everywhere - SA: 9.07, Eng: 8.94
Decent everywhere - NZ: 4.24

a team on the field for an extended period of time. You constantly have to change teams – either because people need rest or because of injury. And when you're constantly having changes like that, you're not going to have a truly great team. It's not because the cricketers aren't as good, it's because of the pressure and strain they have to go through with the amount of cricket they play.

"In our days, we had loads of time with us. We always had gaps between tours, and we always went on tours in such a way that we had enough time to acclimatise to the country we were in. These days, teams go away and arrive perhaps a week before they play the first international game. So they're ill-prepared. I don't think teams today are getting that time required to acclimatise, making it a lot more difficult to win abroad as much as they should, or could."

It's easy to understand Holding's point. The absence of acclimatisation-time makes it tough for teams to begin well. By the time you're acclimatised, the series is perhaps already lost. And once you lose, the already long tour only becomes longer, the mind already yearning for family and dog and home.

Modern cricketers are workhorses and have workloads that none of their predecessors ever experienced. There have been nearly the same number of Tests played since 2000 as they were in the 30 years before. Ironically, this is also the era where Test cricket is supposedly dying. This, apart from the numerous ODIs, T20Is and the IPLs, BBLs and the CPLs across the world.

It is not just coincidence that the current situation ran parallel to cricket's power-centre shifting to India. With BCCI extending control well beyond Indian borders, T20 became the most preferred format for administrators across the world and IPL-type tournaments popped up across the globe. The spread of T20 leagues led to players experiencing different conditions more frequently, but clearly, the experiences counted for little when it came to Test cricket. David Warner, for example, averages more in IPL than in Tests in Asia. The packed schedule means players no longer spend time in county cricket, as they used to before.

The number of Test matches, particularly involving the Big Three of India, England and Australia, have increased, but how has that affected the quality of the cricket?

"I've been talking about this but the administrators don't hear," laments Holding. "All they want to do is play as much cricket as they can because they make as much television contracts and money

All at sea: The visiting South African batsmen had their work cut out on turning pitches against India's best tweakers. — *BCCI*

as they can. That's all they're interested in. They are not interested in seeing the development of the game or maintaining a particular standard of the game.

"Administrators throughout the world have become very short-sighted. When you question them about it, all they talk about is [that] the cricketers want more and more money, so we have to earn more and more money. It's the tail that's wagging the dog, and not the dog wagging the tail."

The shift of power also meant subcontinent teams, led by India, became less shy about making use of home advantage, making life difficult for the likes of Australia and England. In earlier times, while the Asian teams' struggles abroad were scrutinised, the reverse was often condoned. Now, with the non-Asian teams' inability to tackle spin exposed, the subcontinent teams are no longer reluctant to prepare pitches that assist turn from the outset. MS Dhoni, for example, has often asked for pitches that turned from the first day, as opposed to the traditional Indian tracks on which Tests meandered for three days before jumping to life in the last two.

It was a high-risk approach and backfired against England in 2012, but worked well more often than not. India won series against Australia (2013), South Africa (2015) and New Zealand (2016), while

Sri Lanka whitewashed Australia for the first time ever (2016). Pakistan, too, enjoyed success in UAE, where they didn't lose a single series after adopting it as their new home.

Ironically, the Indian board decided to play all domestic first-class matches in the 2016-17 season at neutral venues as teams were increasingly misusing home advantage. England too did away with the toss for their County Championship, giving the away captain the option of fielding first to safeguard against one-sided pitches.

The consequence is that nearly all the teams are increasingly inclined to stretch 'home advantage' to the maximum permissible limits, thus creating a cycle where teams are almost content winning at home.

"For a champion, there is no home ground," said Erland Kops, the former All England badminton winner. It seems now that there are no champion sides in Test cricket.

Will the cycle be broken? Pakistan took an important step in that direction by drawing their four-Test series in England 2-2. There is always hope, but for now, Gambhir's words have become the mantra of teams all over.

Karthik Lakshmanan (@lk_karthik) is senior staff writer at Wisden India.

CRICKETERS OF THE YEAR

Virat Kohli

SURESH MENON

Indian captains fall into two broad categories: those who aim merely to avoid defeat, and those who play for victory. In Virat Kohli's first Test as captain, India were set 364 to make on the final day in Adelaide. The skipper's two centuries in the match ought to have been crowned by victory if only as reward for boldness and imaginative strokeplay, but India fell short by 48 runs. Kohli showed, however, on which side of the divide his captaincy fell. Not since Tiger Pataudi has an Indian captain been willing to risk defeat in pursuit of victory.

Since then, Kohli has taken ownership of Indian cricket. He believes he has a world-class team, with players who will be spoken of in the same breath as the legends of the recent past. Victory against New Zealand in the Kolkata Test gave statistical solidity to that belief – India became the No. 1 Test team under a captain whose age then, 27, was roughly the average age of the team.

"We are all good friends," he said of his team-mates. "We visit when we are in one another's city. We laugh together a lot."

Captaincy by friendship has seldom been the Indian way; if anything it has been the reverse. Traditionally, there are always three or four players in a team who feel they should be captain instead. And no captain has been a hero to his vice-captain.

There is something happening in the Indian team that goes beyond cricket, and it is being authored by Kohli. The obsession with fitness, for one. The fixation with eating right, for another. The confidence that the core of a world-beating team is in place. "I will not ask anyone to do anything I am not willing to do myself," he has said; it is the basis of all leadership. He is shaping the national side in his own image: tough, uncompromising, and with a profound respect for the game.

We had breakfast together one morning as selfie-seekers and autograph-hunters kept interrupting. He obliged nearly everybody – but after our conversation. This was not merely old-fashioned good manners. "Fans have made us what we are," he said, adding, "Many come from great distances and we need to give them good memories to take back with them."

During the home series, Kohli kept playing the crowd, getting them involved, keeping them in good humour. This is clearly Kohli 2.0, enjoying his game and communicating that enjoyment.

How did the change come about? How did a brash, much-maligned youngster who often let it all hang out on the field – the good, the bad and the ugly – become a respected captain and one of the finest all-round batsmen in the game?

Kohli still plays with a passion and an intensity that seems foreign to Indian fans brought up on the quiet certitudes of a Sunil Gavaskar or a Rahul Dravid. Critics predicted a burnout. Kohli proved them wrong.

There was a time when his career teetered on the verge of disappointment. It wasn't so long ago, but Kohli has gone so far beyond the bad old days that it might even feel like they never happened at all.

The Adelaide Test changed everything. Kohli seemed to shine a light on his inner self, throwing into sharp focus his discipline, his temperament and the meditative quality he brings to his strokemaking. Self-awareness replaced self-indulgence. Responsibility was clearly a catalyst.

Kohli himself sees the Adelaide Test as a turning point. He recalled in an interview: "The thing that gave me belief that I can lead this young team was on the fourth day of the Adelaide Test when Australia were still batting. We had a brief chat in the dressing room [and agreed] that whatever target they give us, we would go for it no matter what. I asked, 'Do all the players buy into it and agree?' And all 11 players said yes. Although we lost the game, that showed to me trust and courage from the whole bunch. To be able to do one thing together till the end was something very important to understand who we are. It was a standout evening in terms of knowing that we can go places as a Test team, but [that] will take sustained effort over a long period of time."

In his formative years, as Kohli grew under the shadow of India's greatest batting line-up, he picked up elements of the craft unique to the best. From Virender Sehwag, he absorbed the ability to put the best deliveries away to the boundary, from Rahul Dravid the focus to play the long innings, from Sachin Tendulkar the ability to carry an entire team's batting on his shoulders, from VVS Laxman the ability to flick the wrist and send a ball screaming between fielders on the leg side. He may not do this consistently, nor does it make him a better batsman than the others, but the influences are apparent.

But in one area – the shortest format of the game – he has overtaken them all. At the World T20 in India, he was a star, with three fifties in five matches, an average of 137 with a strike rate of 147.

Against Australia, there were four boundaries in the 19th over of the chase, each fit to be preserved in a cricket museum for its textbook precision and grace under pressure. His 51-ball 82 sealed the game for India.

That innings didn't just bring victory, it stamped the format with the seal of acceptance. Here was a young man at the peak of his powers demonstrating the classical underlying the innovative, and the essential grammar upon which all batsmanship is built. It was as if Kohli was saying: Hey, we haven't fully explored the possibilities in traditional strokeplay yet. He was returning the sport to its basics.

He carried that form and style into the IPL that followed, scoring four centuries and striking 38 sixes (having earlier said he was forced to find gaps in the field since he was not much of a six-hitter!). His record 973 runs in the tournament came at a strike-rate of 152 and average of 81. All this before he became the first India captain to make two double-centuries in Tests.

It is not often that the best batsman in the Indian side is acknowledged as the best captain too, as Kohli is. CK Nayudu, India's first captain, was one such. A case could be made for Vijay Hazare, too. Later there was Sunil Gavaskar, although he belonged to the defeat-avoidance category.

Kohli is a work in progress, both as captain and player. That should make Indian cricket exciting viewing for some years to come. His influence over the team, already considerable, will grow. His focus on victories – he has won ten of the 17 Tests he has led in by the end of the New Zealand series – and his manner of shaping the team philosophy as an extension of his own suggests he might finish his career as one of the great captains.

Few players have shaken off the inessentials in their life and game with the single-mindedness of Virat Kohli, whose journey from gifted but flawed to complete and mature is already one of the more fascinating ones in Indian cricket.

Shreyas Iyer

SIDHANTA PATNAIK

On the day his 117 against Saurashtra put Mumbai in a strong position to win their 41st Ranji Trophy title, Shreyas Iyer was asked if he had received any tips from Sachin Tendulkar and Rahul Dravid. Iyer admitted to having benefitted from the legends, before adding, "A majority of the credit goes to me because I have worked hard."

Iyer may be labelled arrogant for a fair remark, but his is a pleasant deviation from a surfeit of vanilla quotes. He epitomises the social media generation: colourfully opinionated and unfussy about political correctness.

He is witty, speaking unprovoked about the favourable tilt in his equation with the fairer sex post stardom, and proclaims the media's dull questions bore him. A believer in god, he is inspired by books, music, movies like *Kung Fu Panda* and *Pele: Birth of a Legend*, and the cheek of Zlatan Ibrahimovic and Usain Bolt. He jokes he is a better footballer than cricketer, declares his love for his pet white retriever, prefers the company of friends rather than a phone screen, and confesses to not going to bed early. His spirit is like that of any other PlayStation-loving youngster. But at 22, his innocence and maturity go hand in hand.

Based on his early exploits, it is tempting to club Iyer with those who could shape the game's future. It is a dangerous estimation considering the sport's stories of failed promises, but Iyer's confidence convinces you he is here to create an identity for himself.

At the age of 21, he made 1321 runs in only his second Ranji season in 2015-16 – the second-most in a season behind VVS Laxman's 1415 for Hyderabad in 1999-2000. His strike-rate of 92.70 was way better than that of the other 15 to have crossed the 1000-run mark in a season, and allowed Mumbai enough time to dismiss teams twice in six matches of their 11-match undefeated streak. The third cricketer, after Vijay Bharadwaj and Abhishek Nayar, to register 11 fifty-plus scores in one Ranji edition, he was also the first Mumbai batsman since Wasim Jaffer in 2008-09 to top the competition's batting charts.

The absence of a Mumbaikar from the top of the run-getters list for six successive seasons marked a big dip in the standards of the famed Mumbai school of batsmanship. Outside of Ajinkya Rahane and Rohit Sharma, no other Mumbai batsman has come close to breaking into the Indian team in the recent past. The emergence of Iyer, who is comfortable against both pace and spin across three formats, has revived hope for the city's rich batting lineage.

Iyer's technique is still evolving, and he is susceptible outside the off stump early in his innings. He is yet to be tested in seaming conditions, patience is not his biggest virtue and his head is not always in positions prescribed by traditionalists. With time, he will address these issues, but, for now, his attacking intent that dictates the pace of the game excites you the way Virender Sehwag used to.

A risk-taker, he believes scoring runs in long-form cricket is easier as "fielders are in an attacking mode and one can easily pierce the gaps". His technical foundation is not the one Vijay Merchant or Sunil Gavaskar had, but in the T20 age, Iyer's is a skill necessary in every line-up.

Iyer's spectacular debut in 2014-15 earned him instant promotion to No. 3 in the batting order and held together a factious dressing room. Mumbai, desperate to reclaim the title they last won in 2012-13, had tried 25 players, including six debutants. Iyer's aggressive 75 from No. 7 against Uttar Pradesh – made wearing Shardul Thakur's clothes as he had left his kit in the hotel – after his team were 57 for 6 helped Mumbai recover from a shocking loss against Jammu & Kashmir. It put them on track for a semi-final finish.

Iyer's strike-rate was the best among that season's top six batsmen and helped make him the most expensive uncapped buy in the Indian Premier League 2015 at Rs 2.6 crore. He used his good form to overcome the nerves on IPL debut for Delhi Daredevils. His 809 runs exemplified his temperament and he won the award for emerging player of the year.

A tally of 1548 runs across formats was a good start, and Iyer then shifted his focus towards avoiding the second-season blues.

His maiden double-century, in 175 balls against Punjab – the third-fastest in Ranji history – was a career-defining moment. He got a first taste of the benefits of spending time at the crease, and it triggered a spree of sprightly knocks that built a reputation and assured him of a regular India A berth.

Before the dominance, there were failures against Andhra in the season-opener and for Board President's XI against the visiting South Africans. Pravin Amre intervened, asking Iyer to stay side-on, keep his head in line and bring the left shoulder down slightly. Amre also suggested finding a routine between deliveries for the mind to function cyclically. Their *guru-sishya* bond had started when Amre took the 13-year-old under his wing at Shivaji Park Gymkhana.

Shreyas Santosh Iyer, born on December 6, 1994, to Rohini and Santosh Iyer in Mumbai, belongs to a south Indian Brahmin family, who have started boiling eggs in the kitchen only recently due to their son's diet plan. His father first spotted his talent while bowling to him in the living room. Space constraints in the locality and regular complaints from neighbours forced Iyer at 11 to shift to Worli Sports Club opposite his house. A 40-ball century by the age of 12 earned him the complete support of his parents.

The essence of Iyer is not so much the early success, but the perceptions he has altered at every stage of his career. A positive outlook when he had few backers – his parents, Amre and Vinod Raghavan, the popular Mumbai age-group coach – formed the crux of his journey.

Iyer's first moment of truth arrived at 16 when his father asked him to give up cricket and focus on studies after he failed to make it to a Mumbai Cricket Association camp. Hit hard, he channelled his self-belief to prove a point.

Selected for the 2012-13 Under-19 Cooch Behar Trophy as a leg-spinning all-rounder, Iyer, sent as a nightwatchman against Himachal Pradesh after Mumbai followed on, saved the game by remaining unbeaten for 93.5 overs. His maiden century for Mumbai at any level helped the team make it to the final. That competition, which he says was the turning point of his career, liberated Iyer and helped him ease his way into the Indian team for the 2014 Under-19 World Cup in the United Arab Emirates.

Ignored till India crashed out in the quarter-finals, he redeemed himself with consecutive half-centuries in the play-off games. The snub made him determined. He signed up with Clifton Village in the Nottinghamshire League in England where he batted with the singular objective of being so good that the club would not be able to afford him the next time. His first long stint away from home also expanded his horizon. The shift in the mindset was visible in his maiden first-class season. Unsurprisingly, Iyer has left most of his Under-19 batchmates behind in the race.

A poor show in his second IPL, partly due to the inability to shift from a successful red-ball season to white-ball cricket, possibly contributed to Iyer being overlooked for the Zimbabwe tour. He sees the exclusion as a pattern in his career graph, but remains confident. Iyer, if his short history of bouncing back is anything to go by, will make any chance he gets count.

Sidhanta Patnaik (@sidhpat) is a senior staff writer at Wisden India.

Yasir Shah

AHMER NAQVI

The bowler is running in full flight, but it is not to deliver a ball. Instead, he is racing towards the edge of the inner circle, his team-mates chasing him. Most times, he ends by sliding into a dive, though sometimes a team-mate trips him by mistake. Either way, he ends with his head cradled in his arms, stomach flat on the ground and the cameras zooming in on his magnificent smile. In a short career, Yasir Shah has played out this scene a few times already.

Yasir, born May 2, 1986, was the central cog of the Pakistan team that ascended – for the first time in its history – to the No. 1 spot on the ICC Test rankings. His captain, Misbah-ul-Haq, had achieved that peak in the very country where Pakistan's last Test tour had ended in shame, humiliation and criminal proceedings. After his team won the First Test of their England tour, Misbah had stood with Yasir as they watched their names go up on the Lord's honours board. Having led his team for six years since that disaster, it was poetic justice to see Misbah at the helm with his team at the top. But that journey had only seen Yasir accompany him near the end.

Like a good film or novel, the story of Team Misbah's rise to the top splits quite neatly into three acts. The first began after the 2010 spot-fixing series, when Misbah led his team to squeeze out a draw against the world's best side, South Africa. It kicked off a string of defiant performances from a limited side, as they won Test series away in New Zealand and Bangladesh, drew in the West Indies and beat Sri Lanka at home. That glorious first act ended with a stunning whitewash of the then No. 1 side, England.

The second act was the exact opposite, as Pakistan's Test side descended into a disastrous spiral for the next two years. Despite some isolated moments of hope, things were generally bleak. By the end of that act, Pakistan had just three wins and nine losses in 15 Tests. And right after, just to compound the horror, the ICC started a clampdown on bowling actions, leading to bans for Mohammad Hafeez and Saeed Ajmal. A side in free fall had just lost its main weapon and its best all-rounder.

The third act began with the arrival of the Australians to the UAE, and Pakistan playing with a brand new bowling attack. That Test series set up a new template for Pakistan's side, which would carry it all the way to The Oval two years later. That formula built on Misbah's previous tactic of using spin to strangle the opposition on slow, flat tracks and added a layer of heavy batting totals on it. This meant that unlike the helter-skelter, collapse-riddled whitewash of England, Pakistan now dominated sides. Over three home series, Pakistan would win five Tests, draw two and lose just one.

It was in this arc of Team Misbah's rise that Yasir emerged as a star.

It began due to the evangelism of Shane Warne, the high priest of leg-spin who patronises the art for his own legacy as much as the skill itself. A member of the commentary side in the Australian series, Warne raved about the promise in the man from Swabi in Khyber Pakhtunkhwa. It also helped that Yasir revealed how he had grown up trying to imitate videos of Warne sent over by a relative who lived abroad. And then the other Australians also helped out by being absolutely hopeless against spin, and Yasir picked up 12 wickets at 17 in his first series.

Next up were New Zealand, perhaps the best recent visitors to the UAE, who offered a stiffer challenge to Yasir and gave him 15 wickets at 33. Bangladesh were similarly difficult, but then Sri Lanka and England had Yasir picking up bags of wickets again. By the time he arrived in England, he had a genuine chance of beating one of cricket's oldest records: George Lohmann's for fastest to 100 wickets.

When Yasir, aged 30, picked up ten wickets in the First Test in England, the world was in raptures. After all, as Pakistan and other teams know all too well, global appreciation in cricket only arrives after performing away at one of the Big Three. With Warne as his publicist and English batsmen having seen him do to them what he did in the UAE, everyone seemed unanimous in agreeing with his ascension to the world's top-ranked bowler. So when Old Trafford happened, it seemed strange to see how many people claimed that Yasir had been 'found out'. Bowling in the first innings against two great batsmen, Yasir had a horror Test. Given how young his career was, the same people who had been feting him a week earlier now dismissed his previous efforts as lucky efforts on 'spin-friendly' UAE wickets (a description that revealed how few people understood those tracks). When he returned from the Third Test with modest figures, many were ready to hammer nails in his career's coffin.

Why has Yasir been the recipient of such wildly disparate reactions? The answer lies in the embracing of two narratives that are far larger than the bowler himself, yet his enigmatic presence has meant that he has often been held up as the exemplar of both. The first is the one held in the game about leg-spin, which is often seen as the most exotic and difficult of all bowling skills. Leggies like Warne and Abdul Qadir played up this idea, and created the stereotype of the leg-spinner as the wiliest, most devious type of bowler.

The second narrative has to do with the desire to see Pakistan as inherently mercurial. Despite six years of Misbah, the fickle nature of his white-ball teams as well as the fragility of its Test batting (for the first two acts at least) meant that the reputation stuck. Yet Misbah had been constructing a team that bowled dry, focused on spin not pace, and batted heavy – the opposite of what one expected from Pakistan. His players had no flashy hairstyles or scandals, and they were all as unmercurial as it could get.

The addition of Yasir to this team, however, added that irrepressible glamour associated with Pakistan. A leg-spinner prone to taking big wickets and wild celebrations was the type of Pakistani bowler the world wanted to see. Yasir was seen both as the heir to Warne as well as the rockstar bowlers Pakistan was known for.

Yet, the truth was that Yasir the bowler was far closer to the Team Misbah ideal than Warne or his Pakistani predecessors. Unlike Warne, he is permanently ebullient, with little appetite for mind games and posturing. And unlike previous Pakistani bowlers, Yasir's modus operandi is bowling with control and forcing mistakes, rather than blowing batsmen away with magic balls. He is also far from accomplished in white-ball cricket, where he struggles to find the control he needs. Consequently, whenever Yasir has had a Test where he can't find his control, it seems like he is a terribly inferior bowler, and those unrealistic expectations seem to become just that.

At the same time, this has also meant that Yasir is still not appreciated for what he is genuinely good at. Unlike most leg-spinners, he is excellent at finding and maintaining his lengths very quickly. Unlike Pakistani leggies like Danish Kaneria, Mushtaq Ahmed or even Imran Tahir, he lacks an addiction to the googly, and has far subtler variations. Most Yasir wickets involve a series of tidy deliveries, punctuated by one that turns a lot, before picking up the wicket next ball with one that doesn't move much. As a result, both the English and Australians in particular have often complained that they gave away their wickets to Yasir off straight deliveries – an assessment that reveals how oblivious they are to how he sets them up.

What all this means is that Yasir ends up being celebrated for the idea he represents, rather than who he truly is – but even that is not a bad thing. While Misbah's side has always been solid, the addition of Yasir adds much sparkle to it. His batting bolsters a terrible tail, while he is electric in the field for a side that can barely perform that skill. And, most importantly, he adds that mystique that is central to Pakistani cricket, the joy and delight that its fans crave, but which they don't often find in their current side's wins. He brings together all these great expectations in his bubbly self, and even when they get too much, they never break him.

Crucially, he has brought exuberance to this side. His trademark celebrations, where he runs at full pelt chased by his team-mates, has now graced several Test wins. I have little doubt that the confidence and joy displayed in Pakistan's celebratory push-ups in England owed a lot to the attitude Yasir has brought to this side.

Having spent so many years toiling away in the domestic circuits, it is heartwarming to see Yasir finally arrive and immediately fill the Saeed Ajmal-shaped hole in the side. The discrepancy between his actual abilities and those he is hyped for will mean he will always has a legion of doubters. But what no one can deny is that just like when he picks a crucial wicket, Yasir has been leading this team in a mad, joyous rush. He has raced fearlessly to the top, and has forced his chasing team-mates to join him there.

Ahmer Naqvi (@karachikhatmal) is a journalist and teacher. He hosts the online cricket show Pace is Pace Yaar.

Kusal Mendis

SHANAKA AMARASINGHE

"I'll meet you by the cemetery," Kusal had said, in a scene resembling one from a Bond movie, except starring the members of Monty Python. I wait by the cemetery and call him again. He realises the guy on the phone is not calling about the interview he's in the middle of already. He thinks quickly, apologises and sends his 13-year-old brother, on a bicycle, to escort me to their residence, down winding, narrow residential lanes. I'd have been a little stressed, but it's 9am on a Monday morning and the lad is 13.

Kusal Mendis is already double-booked for interviews and it's only the first working day since the Australians have departed after three Tests, five one-day internationals and two T20 internationals. His defiant 176 in the second innings of the First Test in Kandy was the catalyst for what is probably Sri Lanka's greatest series victory.

In an extended period of unbroken mediocrity, Angelo Mathews's men hosted the No. 1 Test side with the expectations of fans incredibly low. The lack of 'big names', injuries, off-field politicking and just general on-field ineptitude had made the Sri Lankan team uninteresting to its own. When Mitchell Starc triggered a Sri Lankan collapse ending in 117 in the first innings, the most optimistic fans shook their heads, turned off their televisions and went back to work, or whatever else it was they were doing. They can be forgiven then for missing some of what was probably the most important century by a young Sri Lankan batsman in decades – not only for its spirit and panache, but also as a reminder of a cricket nation that punches above its weight. As the folk tales would have us believe about Hans from the Netherlands, all it needs sometimes, is for one youngster to plug the leak with his finger to prevent the entire dyke collapsing.

Kusal drags the mike under his T-shirt and clips it to his collar with the practised art of one who has been doing this all his life. He hasn't. Until Pallekele, nobody cared to find out who this chap walking in at No. 3 was. Even though he was easily the most promising batsman on a dismal England tour. One series later, he needs a secretary and gopher to coordinate his interviews.

Kusal lives in the Colombo suburb of Moratuwa. He's not even the most famous cricketer from the area. Duleep Mendis, former captain, was the first of the famous Mendises (none of whom are related). Ajantha Mendis, bamboozler of Indian batsmen, winner of Asia Cups and bowler of the carrom ball was next. Recent evidence indicates that Kusal just may make his way up the hierarchy into third, surpassing Jeevan Mendis. My 13-year-old guide is playing Under-13 cricket at Prince of Wales College, alma mater of Somachandra de Silva, Lahiru Thirimanne and Shehan Jayasuriya.

Moratuwa is credited with unleashing the irrepressibly popular baila music. A remnant from Portuguese times, the music emboldens the denizens of Moratuwa in much the same way as falling into the cauldron of potion made Obelix freakishly strong. They have an aura about them that makes them unafraid to fail. It is what allows a 13-year-old on a bicycle to meet a stranger in a cemetery. Here in Moratuwa, they get trained to play what's in front of them.

Balapuwaduge Kusal Gimhan Mendis, born February 2, 1995, has the calm assuredness of someone much older and much bigger than him. His neo Vanilla Ice hair adds a few inches to his 5' 5" frame.

"He's always had it in him," says Dinesh Mendis, Kusal's father and mentor. "I knew it from the day he picked up a bat as a three year old. Even then he never hit across the line." A former cricketer and athlete in the previous generation of Mendis boys studying at Prince of Wales, Dinesh took his son to the nets as early as possible. "People passing by used to tell me not to bowl like I did at a small boy, but he never shied away, and always played everything straight."

Kusal's teenage years were not easy ones for Dinesh, working half a day in carpentry and timber, which Moratuwa is famous for, and driving a tuk tuk the other half to take Kusal to practice and make some money along the way.

"I was playing Under-13 when I was about nine," says Kusal of his appearance for the Jayalath Aponso Cricket Academy in the Nelson Mendis Trophy in 2004. He scored his first hundred at ten playing against bigger boys. "He hit 16 fours and one six," chimes in Dinesh, who remembers the innings like it was yesterday.

"Whether in the national team or not, we've never been afraid to fail," says Kusal of his early days. He speaks highly of captain 'Angelo *aiya*' and the culture of the dressing room under coach Graham Ford – "No innings is deemed a failure ... He doesn't put any pressure on us." No stranger to captaincy himself, Kusal skippered the Sri Lanka Under-19s at the World Cup in a disappointing 2014 campaign where they finished eighth. So he wasn't touted as the Next Big Thing as previous successful junior skippers Mathews and Dinesh Chandimal were.

Kusal was plucked out of relative obscurity by the selection panel led by Kapila Wijegunawardene, the former national fast bowler, to debut against West Indies in 2015, with hardly any first-class preparation. After the Kumar Sangakkara-Mahela Jayawardene departure, the new selectors had to dig deep, and found the Development Squad the most promising. This squad included Dhananjaya de Silva – who, with Kusal, looks like forming the axis of Sri Lanka's future batting order – promising leggie Jeffrey Vandersay and fast bowler Vishwa Fernando.

"We chatted to the players and told them they were within touching distance of the national side," explains Wijegunawardene. "We gave them opportunities in the side games and then, based on those performances, in the A team and emerging team." Kusal grabbed every opportunity. After a breakout Moin-ud-Dowlah Gold Cup in India where he scored a big century and two half-centuries, the selectors were convinced they had "unearthed a special talent". Their unanimity and decisiveness was rare, and he was given a steady run.

Suranga Wijenaike, the Under-19 coach who coached Kusal for three years at Prince of Wales as well, sings off the same hymn sheet as everyone who had been exposed to his career prior to the national debut. "He can get things done on the field. And he's always very positive. He won't hesitate to declare an innings and try to turn a game on its head. He knows how to handle the team and also knows how to build an innings."

"I think playing with bigger boys from the time I was small helped me," says the youngster. "My coach Jayalath Aponso used to play me even against the foreign schoolboys who used to come on cricket tours ... Nobody held my hand, I just had to do it. I guess they played me because they thought I was good enough." While others start off on simulator, he was getting his flying hours under his belt early on, developing the instinct that top players struggle to articulate.

Kusal's uncle, Dilruk Mendis, played first-class cricket and is now a coach at the Jayasuriya Foundation. Uncle and nephew argue about technique sometimes, but the youngster's technique doesn't need a lot of tweaking. Dilruk is trying to get him not to hide his bat behind his right hip too much. "Watch as many of the innings you can where you batted well" is the mantra, "and try to replicate that."

Kusal is, for now, keeping it simple.

The Jayawardene parallels are already flowing in. From the tight back-foot defence, to the expansive bottom-hand-off-the-bat drives that see him caught at second slip, the resemblance is easy to see, especially given both players' slight build. However, his induction against 15-year-old English public school boys at the stump-high age of ten has held him in good stead for when he stands chest high to Starc glaring down the pitch at him.

"I can do both," is his response to whether he sees himself as an aggressive player or a patient one. He clearly doesn't see the need for labels. He is happy to bat wherever the team needs him. Both the cockiness of youth and its exaggerated silence are non-existent. A smile and the glint of determination, though, are never far.

Kusal is quick to acknowledge the lengths his father went to, to give him the best opportunity. "This is my profession now," he says. "I never went to class much even in school" – across the room, his family members shake their heads amused. It seems unlikely that he will throw it away, or forget his roots. This is underscored by the surfeit of Catholic imagery in the living room. Interspersed with a number of framed family pictures are posters of the Virgin Mary and paintings of Biblical scenes. The gold crucifixes worn by almost the entire family show that Kusal's grounding is one of restraint and discipline, those foundational Catholic building blocks.

When Kusal had just celebrated his first birthday, his father, in a rare un-Christian display, snuck off to India to watch Sri Lanka play against the home side in that infamous World Cup semi-final of 1996. "I lied to my wife and somehow made it to the match," says Dinesh, without pride, but also without regret. Kusal comes from determined and resilient stock. His environment seems to have bred a desire to succeed but without the disproportionate consequences of failure. The Mendis clan, like most of its Moratuwa brethren, is a happy, secure unit.

Kusal seems pleasantly surprised by the attention on him. But he is not in the least bit overawed. No doubt he will quickly rise up the Mendis hierarchy in Moratuwa's cricketing pantheon.

Shanaka Amarasinghe (@ShanakaScore) is a lawyer by day and sports journalist some afternoons. He hosts Sri Lanka's only English radio sports show.

Mustafizur Rahman

A T M SAYEEDUZZAMAN

It's a nation of 160 million, and counting. On the roads, in the buses or the trains, everywhere, there are so many young men, one as unmemorable as the next. A cynic might even say there is no need to bother with any of them.

But, on April 24, 2015, a young man no different from scores of others appeared on the Bangladesh cricket horizon. It took barely a handful of matches for him to create an impact, make a place for himself in the national consciousness. Within days, everyone knew everything about the young man from Satkhira in south-western Bangladesh. They even knew his shoe size: 12. A country of millions, but size 12 is rare. But, then again, that wasn't the only thing extraordinary about Mustafizur Rahman.

At the time of writing, Mustafizur, who is still only 21, has played top-flight cricket for only a year and a half since that first T20 international against Pakistan in Mirpur. He has 52 wickets in 24 internationals across formats.

Is that really so spectacular? Not really. But the numbers don't show how he has left batsmen in a tangle on so many occasions, how he has humbled them, humiliated them.

What is the solution to the Mustafizur puzzle – just play him out, leave as many deliveries as possible, or try to smash him out of the attack? Whether it's a bilateral series or in the Indian Premier League with its constellation of T20 stars, he remains an enigma.

As for the man himself, he just laughs at everything. It's a laugh that showcases his simplicity; it's not put on to fool the batsmen, or even rub it in after he has left them in knots one more time.

Soon after Mustafizur made his international debut, Bangladeshi journalists looked up his childhood coach, Mufassirul Ahmed, who was quick to tell us, "The boy is from a village, he is very simple and humble. He doesn't have any polish. He can't always express himself. You shouldn't misunderstand him." No one took too long to understand Mustafizur. We have had the chance to interact with him in the past year or so; his answers are monosyllabic, but that smile, sometimes a laugh, is always just a breath away.

I hear he is quite different in the team bus or dressing room, though. Apparently he talks nineteen to the dozen and can be a bit of a prankster too. There's no chance of being misquoted there, after all. But you seat him in front of a mike and, "Not much, I just try to bowl well, what else ..." is usually what we get. The words come after a smile, and they end with a smile. It falls on us to create a response with the stray words he has sent our way. It's a bit like for the batsmen he bowls to: If you don't understand Mustafizur, you are likely to be bowled.

I don't know if there are too many others like him, bowlers whom batsmen try hard to dissect. Within the Bangladesh team too there is a lot of analysis around him, led by Tamim Iqbal. Unfortunately for Tamim & co., Mustafizur is as difficult to face in the nets as he is during a match. He primarily bowls length deliveries in the nets. The off-cutters and other tricks are reserved for the tail-enders. It has to do with the domestic circuit: Mustafizur prefers not to let the batsmen – like Tamim – face too many of his off-cutters. He has to play against Tamim too, after all. He told me after returning from the 2016 IPL that he followed the same practice when with Sunrisers Hyderabad as well.

No one asked the shy and polite Mustafizur, the youngest son of Abul Qasem Gazi, born on September 6, 1995, in Satkhira near Khulna, to do any of this. It's what he decided himself, much like that off-cutter he developed on his own.

When he was growing up, and being invited to different *paras* (neighbourhoods) and adjoining villages to bowl with 'tape-balls', the off-cutter hadn't yet made an appearance. It came much later, when he was a net bowler to the national team, and Enamul Haque, the Bangladesh opener at the time, urged him to bowl cutters. Mustafizur had no idea what to expect, but he found himself beating Enamul again and again. Out of nowhere, he had stumbled onto the secret that would make him unplayable. He is grateful to Enamul for it, and so is Bangladesh cricket.

But it's not just about bowling the off-cutter. As Mashrafe Mortaza, his captain, says, "There's nothing new about bowling cutters – we all do it. But, with Mustafiz, it's a physiological thing. His shoulder is such that it rotates at the point of release. If I try to do the same thing, I will end up bending my elbow. Now, you have to call it a gift from god then, won't you?"

No one is contesting that. Especially not Mustafizur: "It's what

Allah wants," he says, and switches on that thousand-watt smile.

But is all of it a gift from above? What about the ability to read a batsman quickly, even if the batsman is AB de Villiers? I say de Villiers because of the tremendous success Mustafizur has had against him, and there aren't many better batsmen in the world. But it's not just the South African virtuoso. If you go through the list of batsmen Mustafizur has sent back in his short international career so far, you'll find some big names. Like Shahid Afridi. Mustafizur dismissed Afridi in only his third over in international cricket; it was his first wicket at the highest level.

Does picking up the wickets of the most prolific batsmen excite him more than the others, I ask. "A wicket is a wicket ... I like all of them. Actually, when I bowl, the best batsmen are batting, maybe that's why ..."

And he's correct. Mustafizur is always handed the ball at the most crucial times. Like in that international debut, when Mortaza pushed himself and Taskin Ahmed behind and asked the youngster to bowl first up. If there's a strong partnership developing in the middle overs of a short-format match, who does the captain turn to? Mustafizur again. The captain wants him in the death overs as well. There's no difference in the demands, whether it is Mortaza or David Warner, the Hyderabad captain.

Such a young boy, how does he deal with the immense pressure of expectation? "He is very professional," says Mortaza. "I could see that soon after I met him. You know how? The day after his first match, when we were all resting, he was in the gym working on his recovery. I could see that he knew how to preserve his body for the long haul."

Refusing to play in the Pakistan Premier League or delaying saying yes to Sussex were both with an eye on the future. He doesn't want to put too much pressure on his body, he has said more than once. In Bangladesh cricket circles, refusing to follow the instructions of the trainer while in the off-season is the done thing. Mustafizur is probably the only prominent player who doesn't do that. He actually imposes curfews on himself. While on tour, whether with the national team or at the IPL or with Sussex, he prefers staying in his room: "I like spending time alone, playing on my phone."

But, then, why does he keep getting injured? The answer is simple: It's the busy schedule in modern-day cricket. Throw in travel and training sessions, and injuries become a big part of the game, especially for pace bowlers. And if it is someone like Mustafizur, slight of built anyway, then it can get worse. "Any captain who has Mustafiz will ask him to bowl all the time," explains Mortaza.

It's the lot of the strike bowler, always has been. It's a matter of pride for them, and worry too.

These days, there's another part to the story, otherwise why would Mustafizur, such a good strike bowler, say: "I always try to bowl as many dot balls as possible"? A wicket-taker saying that his priority is to bowl dot balls – a purist might fall off his chair if he hears that. Oh, what a waste of talent!

But that's what players in this T20 age have to do. If you want to be a part of the T20 wave, you must focus on dot balls. That's just how it is. He has only 52 wickets in his international career so far, but it's fair to say that if he had been trying to get edges and not trying to beat batsmen, that number could have been higher.

It's just the beginning for him. Where will he stop? It's not the sort of question that worries him yet. "Yes, I am trying to make sure my body goes on for at least ten years," he says. For Mustafizur, that's the extent of his dreams, a dream he dreams with that shy smile of his.

ATM Sayeeduzzaman is sports editor of Bangladesh's Daily Kaler Kantho. *This piece has been translated from Bangla by Shamya Dasgupta.*

David Warner

IAN CHAPPELL

In early 2009, I watched with growing interest as a spirited young Australian left-hander thrashed a South African ODI attack that included Dale Steyn, Makhaya Ntini, Albie Morkel and Jacques Kallis.

"This kid David Warner can bat," I said to my wife Barbara-Ann as dinner was being served. "What do you mean?" she enquired. "All the fours and sixes?"

"No, not just that," I answered. "He can bat, not just hit."

Warner had caught my attention for the ease with which he'd adjusted to a couple of testing deliveries from Steyn. This wasn't the response of a T20 specialist; Warner was a batsman, not a hitter.

Warner has subsequently proved this to be the case, though, for an extended period after that 2009 breakthrough innings, he was pigeonholed as a T20 batsman. Even when he made the Test side and then outshone 'traditional' Australian batsmen like Ricky Ponting, Michael Clarke and Michael Hussey by carrying his bat for 123 in a losing total of 233 in the Second Test against New Zealand, he was described as a T20 batsman who made it to Test cricket.

In an innings of controlled defiance he struck 14 fours but no sixes on a tricky Bellerive Oval surface. He regularly adjusted to testing deliveries on that day, as he fought in vain to bring Australia victory against a determined New Zealand attack.

Barbara-Ann isn't an avid cricket fan but I'd piqued her interest in this blonde dasher, David Andrew Warner, who was born on October 27, 1986, in Paddington and grew up in the working-class area of Matraville. When Warner was dismissed cheaply at the Gabba in his first Test innings, I received a text in the commentary box, simply saying: "Bugger".

When Warner completed his maiden century at Bellerive, I received another succinct text: "Beauty"; the kid was on his way.

And what an incredible success story he has been; a mountain of Test runs on varying surfaces, including a blitz unleashed on the Indian attack at the WACA, when he sprinted Usain Bolt style to a century off just 69 balls. Here was a T20 player all right: a batsman capable of scoring a Test century inside twenty overs.

He hit 13 fours and three sixes in romping to his WACA century, the last of that trio bringing up the three figures. This was batting Virender Sehwag style, ironic when you consider the advice Warner received when Virender was a team-mate at Delhi Daredevils. "You'll be a better Test cricketer than you will be a T20 player," Sehwag told Warner. Then, by way of explanation, he added, "All the fielders are around the bat, if the ball is in your zone you're going to hit it. You're going to have ample opportunity to score runs."

A prescient prediction when you think that at the time, Warner hadn't even played a first-class game for New South Wales (NSW). This was a selection blunder, as Warner had scored 165 not out opening for NSW in a 2008 fifty-over game.

He should've been given the opportunity to open in Shield cricket that season to determine if he could repeat his success in the longer version. His match-winning style of batting needed to be encouraged but NSW responded by saying he wasn't making enough runs in club cricket to warrant selection. The ability to slaughter first-class and international bowlers should override any lack of success at club level.

Warner's eventual international success has led to fame and fortune; lucrative IPL and Big Bash League contracts, as well as being highly paid as an invaluable Australian player and, probably the most personally rewarding, the vice-captaincy.

Despite all the money and glory, Warner has kept things in perspective by recalling his roots. When he first earned big money from cricket, he purchased an apartment in Matraville for his parents Howard and Lorraine. And in an article outlining his elevator rise to fame, he talked about keeping his feet on the ground by regularly recalling that as a young bloke he was stacking shelves in a Woolworths supermarket.

This grounded approach tallies with his thought process on cricket. An aggressive player, his philosophy is based around keeping it simple and attacking.

When he received a broken thumb in September 2015 from a steepling Steven Finn delivery, he was unable to take his place a few weeks later in the NSW fifty-overs side. While he sat out the tournament he did some television commentary for Channel Nine. His on-air comments were thoughtful and enunciated with authority and off-air it was enlightening to hear about his approach to the game. His assessment of his own batting during the 2015 England tour was full of interesting insights and his overall summation of the series was an indication of a cricketer who thought deeply about the game.

Not surprising then that he was rewarded with the vice-captaincy, and, at the age of nearly 30, stood in for Steve Smith in Sri Lanka.

The elevation to a leadership position coincided with a reduction in his role as the on-field 'mouthpiece' for the Australian side. As a young player, he was encouraged by the team hierarchy to unnerve opponents with his comments. This is a worrying trend because with large contracts now available to young players, they probably feel it's not in their best interests to disobey orders.

Warner is to be admired for the fact that he now desists from such practice and hopefully, if he ever captains Australia full time, he won't place a young player in that invidious position.

His elevation to status of senior player has also coincided with a change of direction off the field. In 2013, he was disciplined for an altercation with England's Joe Root in a Birmingham bar. To his credit, he accepted his punishment – a demotion to the touring Australian A side – and scored heavily, earning a quick recall to the senior team. Even earlier in his career, there were concerns about the direction in which he was heading when late-night card-playing seemed to hold more interest than club cricket.

However, his relationship with Australian iron woman Candice Falzon has not only led to marriage but also the birth of two daughters and a fitter, more focused cricketer. He's now regularly seen cradling a daughter in his arms and acting like the archetypal doting father.

Lately, he's also abstained from alcohol on the basis that "things can be misconstrued if you're seen in the bar drinking late at night".

This gives the lie to a bathroom door cartoon that I was exposed to regularly when I was growing up. It stated: "Drink, the curse of the working class."

The working-class Warner is doing just fine the way he is. He's become a very valuable member of any Australian team; his fast scoring intimidates opponents and his athletic fielding is always a likely wicket-taking resource.

His skills and competitive nature have made him a very popular cricketer and he draws more young fans to the game than any other Australian cricketer. He also possesses an exceptional skill as an ambidextrous batsman who can hit sixes with either hand. This is the result of a coach urging him to become a right-hander for a short while in his formative years. While I don't believe the switch hit should be legal because it's unfair to the bowling side, it's an exceptional skill and no one employs it better than Warner.

Despite his aggressive instincts, Warner shouldn't be seen as purely a 'damn the torpedoes' type of cricketer; he is a think-first-and-then-act player. Which is one of the reasons why he was always destined to be much more than just a T20 batsman.

One of Australia's great captains, Ian Chappell brought up 5345 runs in 75 Tests before going on to build a career as a commentator.

PERSON OF THE YEAR

Justice RM Lodha

SANDEEP DWIVEDI

A single mother of two stood helplessly in front of a Bombay High Court division bench while the two judges whispered the limitations of law to each other. More than a decade later, one of the judges, Justice Rajendra Mal Lodha, recalls that moment. "She was a Bombay Municipal Corporation peon and she wore her work clothes, that cotton sky-blue sari. Her only desire was to give her boy English-medium education, but the school had rejected her application," he says.

Lodha's brother judge wanted to throw the case out, citing the autonomy of the private school, which superseded the court's jurisdiction. But, not swayed by the bookish counsel, the man who would one day be Chief Justice of India, pushed the envelope like so often during his 21 years as a judge.

He wasn't going against the legal system or over-reaching. Lodha simply didn't have the heart to kill the woman's trust in the law of the land by throwing the rulebook at her. He sent the school a notice, asking for their reasons for rejection. The school lined up top lawyers. Those mighty men listed their client's flawless administration and reminded the court of its powerlessness in such cases. Lodha's masterstroke was to ask for their accounts for the three previous years to verify the claims made in court. The next hearing started, or rather ended, with the senior-most among the school's legal brigade making a barely audible opening statement: "My Lord, the boy has been given admission."

At his modest first-floor rented house in New Delhi, Lodha, despite the post-chikungunya trauma of swollen joints and crippling pain in the soles of the feet, narrates the low-profile case with John Grisham-like drama. "These are the cases that give you satisfaction, not those 'coal-gate' cases involving crores of rupees. Those, of course, are cases of constitutional importance, but don't have the same flavour," he says.

Lodha was referring to the high-profile case he heard as CJI about irregularity in allowing companies to mine coal. It ended with the Supreme Court quashing the allocations, exposing interference of

Pushing the envelope: Justice RM Lodha's role in cleaning cricket administration in India has made him a household name. — *India Today/Getty Images*

top politicians, inviting fresh bids and snubbing the Central Bureau of Investigation by calling it a "caged parrot". It wasn't a one-off: Lodha has even rejected an army chief's age claims.

Ironically, it's his post-retirement assignment of reforming cricket that has made Lodha the most uttered name on the cricket circuit after Kohli and Dhoni.

By rewriting the Board of Control for Cricket in India constitution, the Lodha committee, on the court's instruction, weeded out Indian cricket's ad interim approach and planted institutional decision-making. Lodha tried to end the long reign of Indian cricket's imperishables: the powerful politicians, influential bureaucrats, and cricket officials who have seen Sunil Gavaskar's debut, Sachin Tendulkar's retirement and are well into the Virat Kohli era.

Lodha acknowledges that his cricket report has overshadowed other landmark judgments. Yet, his most gratifying case remains the one about the lady in the sky-blue sari.

His early days in Jodhpur help explain why he still remembers the aspirational mother. Lodha comes from a middle-class family that received high-class education. His father and uncles were toppers and judges of repute. He describes his mother as a "woman with robust common sense" and rooted in Jainism. He grew up listening to his parents talk about religion and discourses of Jain monks. Naturally inquisitive and a compulsive debater, he would get lost in thought about the three principles that are the bedrock of Jainism: *ahimsa* (non-violence), *anekantavada* (non-absolutism) and *aparigraha* (non-possessiveness).

"I wasn't deep into religion, but non-absolutism impressed me. Everybody talks about non-violence and about being non-materialistic, but this was new. *Anekantavada* means no statement is absolutely right and no statement is absolutely wrong. What you see, what you feel, what you read, everything has a bit of deception. There is always something that is unexplored, something that is beyond ..." he trails off.

This open-minded and objective approach came in handy when he heard complex cases. "Even if someone is dishonest or a liar, I would find something that he says that could be right. Everything is multi-faceted. Everyone says a coin has two sides but actually it has many," he shares this deeply philosophical thought with a hearty laugh, almost suggesting you switch to lighter questions.

There is an intensity and rigour common to all his pursuits – from his philosophy to his two biggest stress-busters, walking and cooking. There is nothing about Lodha that is casual. His crisp dressing and even his punctuality. Word from the courts is that people adjust their clocks when he enters the premises. Discipline is a way of life. All his life he has been a 4am walker, covering 10km daily. "These days I take it easy," he says. "Nine?" you ask. "Five," he replies with the same hearty laugh.

Lodha *saab*'s walks figure in a few jokes on the judges' circuit. He was once a regular at Lodhi Gardens, but used to leave the park before the place turned into a networking haven with gossip from Delhi's Lutyens striding in sync with the capital's heavyweights.

If walking gives the busy judge 'me time', cooking is something he shares with his family. Early in life, he decided that to be neutral in court he needed to avoid extended family members, not-too-close friends and social events. With evenings spent at home, the family cooked and ate together. "The aroma of Indian spices gives you tremendous relaxation. The *hing ka chhonk*, the crackling of cumin ..." he closes his eyes expecting the whiff to travel to him.

His two daughters, both married, still request for his special potato-less *pav bhaji*. Talking about *gatte ki subzi,* a Rajasthani dish of steamed gram flour dumplings in a spicy curd gravy, he sounds like Tendulkar about a complicated flick to square leg. "The *gatte* (dumplings) shouldn't be too hard or too soft. When you serve them on the plate they should break and once you place them on your tongue they should melt," he explains. He shares the secret he learnt by observing his mother: "You need to brush the gram dough with ghee."

It's these small pleasures that make Lodha's world. His family house in Jodhpur is locked, but the beliefs drilled into him by his mother are alive. He lives in an up-market area of New Delhi, but it isn't exclusive real estate. His is what property dealers in the city call a 'builder's floor': a floor of your own in a three- or four-storeyed building where twice a day you need to pick a fight to park your car. "When my daughter comes to my place she parks the car 200m away from home," he says. The daughters have other complaints too. They went to a modest, typically Gujarati neighbourhood school, as Lodha describes it. "Other judges sent their kids to these big schools, but I told my wife we will admit our girls to a neighbourhood school. Actually, everything depends on the children, not the school," he says.

His belief in simplicity got validation while on a walk to Badrinath, on the foothills of the Himalayas. "Looking at those majestic mountains around me, I felt very small. You are nothing in the context of this world. You hear people boasting ... just see these mountains. Many CJIs have come, how many have gone, tomorrow you will also go. When you go to the Himalayas, you realise all this 'me, me, me' talk is nothing. What you are? You are nothing," the philosopher judge falls silent.

His interest in sports enlivens the conversation. Lodha isn't a sports nut, but he recalls the India-Pakistan five-Test drawn series of the early 1960s. He remembers a visit to Eden Gardens with cousins to watch Salim Durrani hit sixes on demand. Apart from cricket, he enjoys tennis. There's a pattern to his favourite tennis players: He wasn't a Ramanathan Krishnan fan, he loved Premjit Lall. Not Pete Sampras, it was Andre Agassi for him. And, you guessed it, it isn't Roger Federer, he is a Rafael Nadal fan. Silken touch, sophistication and lazy elegance don't impress him. He prefers the hard-working grinders.

From Jodhpur to New Delhi, Lodha too has run the hard yards. He speaks about selling his Jaipur house, the one bought when he was a lawyer there, to buy one in New Delhi. It certainly isn't a conversation you would expect from a man who decides the fate of powerful men. That's when Lodha reminds you of *aparigraha* (non-possessiveness). That's when you feel that like the lady in the sky-blue sari, the boys in blue, too, are in safe hands. Lodha has again pushed the envelope.

Sandeep Dwivedi is sports editor of the Indian Express.

Press pass

RAJU BHARATAN

Opener Dennis Brookes had just gone past an elegant 150 against the 1952 touring Indians when *Wisden* editor Norman Preston entered the press box. "What's a bright young man like you doing in this stuffy box, intently watching a routine game?" he sought to know. "Go out and find a girl and enjoy yourself."

Mr Preston had taken to me but he now shocked my sensibilities. But how was I, a 17-year-old, even on such a momentous tour of England? My father AS Bharatan, influential as the first general manager of *Press Trust of India* (tying up with *Reuters* in the UK), had worked it for me. Each day after play I was to send a 600-word special report done "from the Indian point of view".

Play in England ended at 11pm (Indian time) and I had to finish my typed dispatch in 15-20 minutes after that. I soon discovered that the only way to meet this deadline was to dictate my report. This involved urgently dialling the *Reuters* office in London and saying: "Reverse charges." The typist would have trouble picking up what she called my "Injun" accent, but we managed.

To be in England then was to be in cricketing wonderland. Everything was green – literally – on their side of the fence. The small grounds with their convivial surroundings; the weather fluctuating as unpredictably as Pankaj Roy's form; my first glimpse of Lord's as the ultimate destination of the cricketing pilgrim; free mingling of the sexes antithetical to Indian values; the average Englishman's blissful ignorance of the fact that the British, not too long ago, had ruled India – all this came as an eye-opener on my first tour.

To be at the Parks with the Oxford University lads my age was to be told that you could glimpse every single tree in England at that ground. Then to be at Canterbury as the Indians played Kent was to find that cricket ground no less pretty. Polly Umrigar's hard-hitting 204 came there; later, it would be a reminder that 636 of his tour averages-heading 1688 runs came from three double-hundreds against moderate attacks. Umrigar's nervy showing (43 from seven Test innings) against Fred Trueman was the letdown of the series.

Two seasoned reporters from India were with me on that tour of

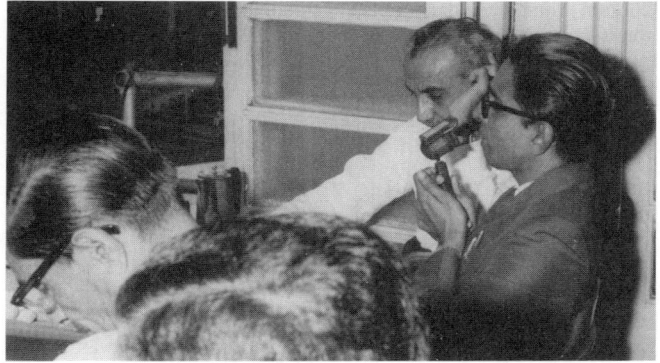

Raju Bharatan (right) began a long career in cricket writing and broadcasting as a 17-year-old. Seen with Vijay Merchant in the commentary box.

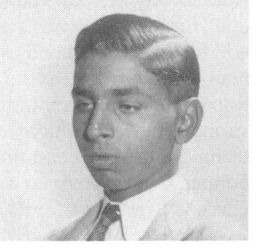

1952: SK Gurunathan (*The Hindu*) and Berry Sarbadhikari (*Hindustan Times* and *Amrita Bazar Patrika*). Neither took kindly to one of my youth being in the box they graced. The end of the first two hours of play would see them taking off to be with the Indian team for lunch. I was left to fend for myself. Upon identifying myself as vegetarian, I would be offered fish and chips.

Then the ball rolled my way. Pankaj Gupta, the Indian team manager, came into the Leicestershire press box for player feedback from Bill Ferguson, the scorer. Nearly 72, Ferguson had trouble with his eyesight. Thus did 'Fergie', with Guru and Berry away, direct Gupta to me as "the one pressman watching each ball of the tour through his binoculars". Astonished, Gupta, exclaiming "What! Our Raju?" turned to me for the lowdown on our players' performance. After he heard me out, Gupta said: "From today, you are one of us, Raju. In an hour from now, join the team for lunch. You shall be in the same hotel as the boys."

Gupta treated me like a protégé. From county to county I travelled with our players in the team bus. I grew close to Dattu Phadkar and Madhav Mantri and went out for dinner with them. The soft-spoken

Ghulam Ahmed regularly exchanged song notes with me as a connoisseur of vintage film music. Umrigar spoke to me only in Gujarati – a Gujarati laced with expletives peculiarly Parsi. CD Gopinath – 'Charlie' to me – I had often to awaken to the fact that our bus had reached its destination.

Where travel had been an ordeal, it became a near picnic. Vijay Manjrekar was the one to entertain the team with the finest in Hindi film music on the bus. He sang well and I was there to furnish the lyrics if he faltered. That made me indispensable.

I was frequently approached for my autograph as a player. "Not a player!" became my signature tune. I did, on occasion, bowl my donkey drops at the nets. Nets in which Ramesh Divecha was Buck, Mantri was George, Roy was Ghatla, Manjrekar was Tat (so named for imitating Roy Tattersall's bowling action), Ahmed was Nizam (for the way he shaped up in the field) and Hemu Adhikari was London (for the frequency with which he visited his wife there). GS 'I will hit you' Ramchand, who struck some brave blows against Trueman – felt outraged as the English press identified him as 'Gopinath' Ramchand. Gopinath himself took the *faux pas* lightly. Ramchand, strong as an ox, demonstrated what sheer guts could accomplish in technique-testing conditions. His 134 v Cambridge University at the Fenner's was a study in rugged grandeur against the electric pace of Cuan McCarthy (5 for 60).

You missed the bus if you were even five minutes late. The signal to get going was Ferguson's emissary calling to collect our baggage from outside the hotel room.

The opening match of the tour was a two-day friendly against Indian Gymkhana at Osterley. Jim Swanton offered me a lift to the ground. I felt flattered that Swanton had felt drawn to that match, but I was swiftly disillusioned. It was not that *the Daily Telegraph* stalwart had wanted to watch the touring Indians; he had driven down to see (playing for Indian Gymkhana) BB Nimbalkar. This following Nimbalkar's record-breaking 443 not out for Maharashtra v Kathiawar in the December 1948 Ranji Trophy encounter in Pune. On a rain-affected wicket, he hit an impressive 60 (in 104 for 5) against the Indians.

Swanton's lack of attention to the visiting Indians was to be the pattern of the tour. There was the landmark press conference called after Len Hutton had been appointed the first professional to captain England against Vijay Hazare's India. In vain did I wait through that

The visiting Indians were consistently showed up during a doleful four-month tour. Seen here is GS Ramchand. — *Photo courtesy Raju Bharatan*

press meet for a question to be put about the touring Indians, only to discover that Hazare and his men virtually did not exist for the British press. Its focus was on the 1953 Ashes series to follow our tour. To a query on England's Ashes prospects, Hutton had the British press in titters with his retort: "I see no reason why, under me, we should not be winning all five Tests against Australia!"

India's tour take-off did nothing to dispel the British estimation of our worth. Indeed I was a hapless onlooker as we nosedived to 0 for 4 in the First Test at Headingley, Leeds. It all but obliterated the memory of 20-year-old Manjrekar's first-innings century. Tour moments to treasure were rare for the Indians, looking lost from the instant they took the field. Hazare's poor form through the tour was lifted only by his herculean performance in the Tests: 89 and 56 at Headingley, 69 not out and 49 at Lord's, 16 and 16 at Old Trafford, plus an India-highest 38 at The Oval on a rain-freshened wicket that had India shot out for 98.

It was no joke watching India's being bowled out twice in a day (for 58 and 82) at Old Trafford on "a beast of a wicket". And the 0 for 4 was followed by 5 for 6 at The Oval. I was a glum eyewitness to India's tendency to cave in when up against the fast ball rising from short of length. Some of our batsmen genuinely believed that such Trueman bowling could not be played.

Alec 'Big Fella' Bedser's partnership with Trueman was a treat; Godfrey Evans standing up to Bedser was a revelation. Watching Hutton's 150 at Lord's, 104 at Old Trafford and 86 at The Oval was to wonder if Vijay Merchant really would have been a technical match as opener, if he had come on tour.

Among the Indians, Hazare alone displayed a semblance of Hutton's defensive skills. But, as captain, he never looked the part. My personal equation with Hazare – as with others in the team – was good. But the man never seemed to complete a sentence he started. The only thing that I heard him clearly say was "play for a draw" on the eve of a Test match. I could see Hazare smiling only as the tour neared its doleful four-month end. A 0-4 whitewash it would have been but for the weather intervening at The Oval.

But yes, there was the Vinoo Mankad star turn in the Lord's Test that came to be acclaimed as "Mankad's Test". His daredevil 72 and 184, allied to his 73-24-196-5 and 24-12-35-0, turned him into a personality. Mankad's wife, Manorama, too was present with their five-year-old son, Ashok, later an India batsman. This contest was the only one where India looked Test class.

The press box buzzed as Vinoo hit out. For the first time, the British press wanted to know something about someone in the Indian team. Recurring interaction on tour made John Woodcock, then with *the Manchester Guardian*, an esteemed colleague. What I discerned was that the bigger the name, the easier the approach. I found myself seated next to RC Robertson-Glasgow in the Lord's press box. Highly witty, 'Crusoe' was warm and friendly. No less forthcoming was football icon Geoffrey Green, writing rivetingly on cricket for *The Times*, London.

Neville Cardus was pointed out to me from a distance; I never dared get near him, I wish I had tried. John Arlott I had walked up to with many misgivings, only to discover him to be very interested in Indian cricket. To get to watch Arlott doing the commentary – sitting on a ledge – was an experience. Brian Johnston was refreshingly easy-going. Michael Melford (*the Daily Telegraph*) already appeared a writer headed for the big time. Only Rex Alston (*BBC*) remained aloof. Alex Bannister (*Daily Mail*) I found engaging. SC Griffith, there to write for *the Sunday Times*, I ran into but once a week, but he was always pleasant in conversation. Bill Bowes (*the Yorkshire Post*) towered over me like the imposing bowler he was for England, yet there were no airs about him. It was in the Canterbury press box that I met up with the charming wife of Bruce Harris, the *Evening Standard* 'sturdy'. I was told to keep away from EM Wellings (*Evening News*) and Charles Bray (*Daily Herald*) but, ultimately, I cut through even here. It did not take much to get Wally Hammond going on Don Bradman. One who often sidled up to me for a story was Vivian Jenkins (*News of the World*).

The British press, by and large, was avuncular in its attitude to me. Maybe because it could always get something out of me as one close to the Indian team.

Reg Hayter (*Press Association*) was one to whom I always looked up. His PA colleague, Leslie Smith, was a familiar reporting figure from the time I debuted by covering all five Tests v Nigel Howard's MCC during England's 1951-52 tour of India. My first day as a Test cricket reporter was in November 1951 at the Feroz Shah Kotla, the start of the five-Test series, Hazare's India v Howard's England.

It was by boat – 14 days on the SS *Chitral* – that I had sailed for England on 14 April, 1952. I returned with the Indian team by the SS *Stratheden* after a 133-day tour seasoning me for the job. On the 12-day journey back, I wrote my first book, a survey of the 1952 tour of England. Immaturely did I title it *Rivals in the Sun*. I was quite ashamed of the effort until KN Prabhu, the esteemed cricket correspondent of *The Times*, began commending the book to fellow pressmen for my eye for out-of-the-way tour detail.

Raju Bharatan was assistant editor of the Times Group's long-running Illustrated Weekly of India, *and author of* Indian Cricket: The Vital Phase *(1976).*

Pressed for trust

R KAUSHIK

It was an early October afternoon in 1998, at the scenic Harare Sports Club, with India battling for survival in the one-off Test against Zimbabwe. Chasing 235 for a rare away victory, India's top had been blown away by Zimbabwe's four-pronged pace attack. At 37 for 4 with Sachin Tendulkar and Mohammad Azharuddin among those dismissed, the writing was pretty much on the wall, even though Rahul Dravid and Sourav Ganguly were engaged in a stirring duel with Messrs Streak, Olonga, Johnson and Mbangwa.

There was no concrete press box, no air-conditioned structure to protect us from the vagaries of the elements, no fabulous view from right behind the bowler's arm, which would allow us to track the path of the ball when it left the hand. Instead, we were housed inside a heavy, white, plastic tent, sweat pouring down despite the whirring pedestal fans. We were helpfully placed at fine-leg from one end and long-off from the other to the right-hand batsman, in perfect position to make out absolutely nothing of how the ball behaved, to start with.

'We' were a bunch of travelling Indian journalists. Three to chronicle events in words, two to click them for posterity. The three of us print journalists were just reconciling ourselves to another overseas Test defeat when a familiar figure burst into the tent, pulled up a chair and slid into it with a long sigh.

It was Azharuddin, the skipper – still in his whites, pads and gloves and inner protective wear discarded, collar upturned, mood pensive. For a while after hellos and hard lucks were exchanged, there was silence. The few non-Indian journalists, a couple of them from neighbouring South Africa, were a little in awe: 'Azhar in our mix. But what's he doing here?'

After a few minutes, with Dravid and Ganguly still stonewalling, the mood lightened a little. Then, in the midst of a couple of familiar faces with whom he was extremely comfortable and shared a Hyderabadi thread, Azhar came into his own, using nostalgia to dissipate the pervasive tension in the middle.

At one point, after a particularly hilarious narrative, Azhar led a chorus of booming laughter from the tent, actually stopping play momentarily as everyone on the field – the two young Indian batsmen, the 11 Zimbabweans and the two umpires – wondered what on earth was going on. Angry stares only softened when they spotted Azhar among us; aware that the timing wasn't great, what with a Test match on the line, the skipper gently bade us adieu and headed for the dressing room, still chuckling and leaving us still clutching our stomachs.

Is something like that even imaginable today? Is any of that, really, even imaginable today? Just five travelling Indian cricket journalists? Not a single one of them from the television media? No press box? And, the Indian captain coming across to hobnob with the journos in the middle of play?

It's hard to state with any certainty when, and why, the relationship between the Indian cricketers and the Indian media reached the pass that it has today. It is not a bad pass, mind, it is just different. No more than a cursory exchange of pleasantries when you run into each other at practice or at the airport, press conferences full of clichés and platitudes and political correctness, an air of general wariness if not suspicion, couched in indifference.

Quite obviously, the number of journalists who write/talk on cricket in India has mushroomed enormously since 1998. Since 2005 even, when no more than a handful of us were at hand to witness the breakdown of relationships between Ganguly and Greg Chappell, again in Zimbabwe. The huge numbers make it almost impossible for players and journalists to strike a personal rapport, unless you hail from the same region and therefore both speak the same language and have interacted with each other at the junior or first-class levels. From the players' perspective, increasingly, the media is a necessary evil, probing and prying and looking for stories that may or may not be true, but which are bound to grab eyeballs. From the journalists' perspective, it is more about cricketer and less about cricket, the action an excuse to be there as you try to one-up your colleague, your competitor.

Is this how it is going to be? That players will be players and journalists will be journalists, the two sets united by the string that is cricket but divided by their different outlooks, different pressures and different requirements that make it all but impossible to be friends? Perhaps it is, given the ground realities, but that will be a shame. A real shame.

Across the divide: With the proliferation of news outlets and greater scrutiny on players, there grew a wariness in player-press relations. — *ICC/Getty Images*

Over many a cup of coffee, the occasional meal and the far less frequent drink, I have benefitted immensely as a person and as a journalist with my interactions with cricketers of my generation, as well as those of generations gone by who I have grown up admiring, revering and sometimes envying. Just as those get-togethers have allowed me to understand a little bit the psyche of a top-notch performer who has not only one of the highest profiles but also the pressure of maximum expectations on a consistent basis of an Indian sportsperson, I know that the players too have enjoyed a sneak peek into the mind of a journalist, and of how we look at situations and individuals.

In many ways, and definitely without intending to be, ML Jaisimha was my cricketing mentor. I had seen him from afar, a dashing figure with a deep voice and a walk that minimised contact between feet and ground. His older son Vivek, himself a stylish right-hand batsman, was playing for Hyderabad when I started my career in journalism. Vivek and the rest of the team, among them Azhar and Venkatapathi Raju, made an outsider feel welcome and I will always remember that with great fondness, but it was Vivek's father who furthered my cricketing education with technical and tactical analyses on the game and on how I should think about it.

At that time, the international calendar wasn't half as packed as it is now, so most of India's top players were available and willing to play in the Ranji Trophy. With the tournament played on an intra-zonal basis at the league stage and teams playing home and away alternately, and with the Moin-ud-Dowla Gold Cup still a prestigious stop in the domestic calendar, contemporary players such as Anil Kumble, Javagal Srinath and Rahul Dravid, and WV Raman and VB Chandrasekhar and Robin Singh, would play in Hyderabad almost every year, just as past masters Syed Kirmani, Karsan Ghavri and Roger Binny would. The informal, laidback setting of Hyderabad cricket and the towering, influential presence of Jaisimha opened doors as one got to meet with stars and stars-in-the-making away from the bustle of action, but with cricket as the unifying factor. It is a schooling I will forever be grateful for.

Today's ultra-busy, ultra-competitive, multiple-demand era almost inevitably, and sadly, rules out camaraderie across the board. Most interviews are pretty much a story, a byline, a notch in the CV, and that is not said with either cynicism or condescension. It is the reality as it exists because the stately pace of the past has given way to the frenetic hustle-and-bustle from which there is no getting away, however much you might want to.

With the onus increasingly on headlines – and for some reason, negative news is considered a greater headline-grabber than focusing on the vast goodness that exists – there is a tangible line of wariness that exists between the media on the one side and everyone else associated with cricket that is on the other side. Especially from the players' point of view, that is understandable because they don't have the time or the inclination to read/see/hear what is said of them, and they often rely on word of mouth to keep themselves informed. Since the tours are packed, the numbers of the travelling media contingent are huge and there are not many who travel on a consistent basis, the players tend to paint everyone with the same brush, so they would rather err on the side of caution than invest time and effort into getting to know the ones cut from a different cloth. Trust is a commodity that takes more time to eventuate in the modern era than it did in the past, and that is another unfortunate fallout of the passage of time and the changing milieu of cricket journalism, particularly in India.

Throw in the additional policing and the immense strictures that the Anti-Corruption and Security Unit of the International Cricket Council has been forced to put in place because of several unsavoury incidents, and the picture of a distinct demarcation of boundaries emerges instantaneously. It is well nigh impossible to go out for a meal from Sharjah to Dubai with the Indian captain, and even more difficult to meet up in the Adelaide hotel room of another Indian captain at the conclusion of a fractious Test series that threatened to sour relationships between nations. Or to sit on the floor in a hotel room in Rawalpindi, listening to words of wisdom from the double-centurion who was to set up India's first Test series win in Pakistan.

Even given that one of the few constants is change, the changing face of the Indian media is as remarkable as it is dramatic. Most of the changes are for the better, as they must be, though change always comes at a cost.

R Kaushik is managing editor of Wisden India.

About a boy

CLAYTON MURZELLO

If there is a schoolboy cricketer who can claim to be the first to trend on social media, it is Pranav Dhanawade.

Five days into the new year, 15-year-old Dhanawade smashed his way into the record books by scoring an unbeaten 1009 off 327 deliveries (129x4, 59x6) to break a 117-year-old minor cricket record.

The school to profit from Dhanawade's punitive blade was Smt KC Gandhi School, Kalyan, who declared at 1465 for 3 before bowling out Arya Gurukul for 31 and 52 at Wayle Maidan, Kalyan. The innings-and-1382-run margin was far less publicised than the boy's

Long road ahead: 15-year-old Pranav Dhanawade channelled his determination into a record-breaking 1009 not out. — *Wisden India*

1009. Aakash Singh (173) and Siddhesh Patil (137) were the other principal scorers.

The nearly unheard-of HT Bhandari Cup inter-school tournament was suddenly part of reports in Mumbai newspapers and the international media. The famous Harris and Giles Shield tournaments for Mumbai city schools were put in the shade for a few days.

Dhanawade, the opening batsman and wicketkeeper, was incredible on the first day of the two-day tie when he plundered 652 not out, a score that displaced Arthur Collins's unbeaten 628 in a junior house match at Clifton College in 1899 and fellow Indian Prithvi Shaw's 546 in the 2013-14 Harris Shield.

Indeed, Dhanawade, who idolises Australia's Brad Haddin, put Kalyan, 40km from Mumbai, on the international cricket map. Already exhausted from his 396-minute epic, he had to face a bunch of television cameras and a flock of print and website journalists. Apart from Harish Sharma, his school coach, and Mobin Shaikh, his mentor, a well-known former cricketer on Mumbai's club scene, even the scorer was interviewed.

The human-interest element to the boy's heroics was not missed: "Son of a rickshaw driver bats his way into cricket record books". Sachin Tendulkar and Mahendra Singh Dhoni tweeting their congratulations added to the festivities and his friends were kicked when they heard that even a *BBC* correspondent was on his way to cover the feat.

Of course, there were the nay-sayers. The opposition bowling was deemed poor. One report pointed out that 25 catches were dropped and the fielders were knackered on a very small ground where boundaries came easy. But to score 1000 runs in any class of cricket and against any type of bowling is no mean feat. End of argument.

There was a certain kind of determination that led Dhanawade to score big. Performers in his area were seldom rewarded with selection in Under-16 teams. It was drilled into him that unless he came up with a massive score, he wouldn't get noticed.

His mentor told *Mid-Day* that Dhanawade had taken the game for granted. He hadn't seemed serious at the Modern Cricket Club nets. Things had reached boiling point when he laughed about the way he got out in an all-India tournament when his dismissal was shown on the big screen. Shaikh, a former A division club cricketer who represented Rajasthan Sports Club for 25 years, pulled the boy aside and issued him an ultimatum: Get serious or pack up.

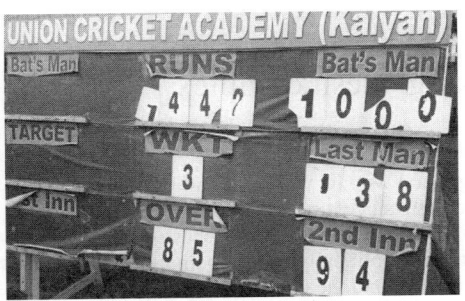

Final score 1465 for 3 dec.: The nearly unheard-of HT Bhandari Cup inter-school tournament was suddenly in the limelight. — *Wisden India*

The youngster got back on track, trained hard and realised that he could make something of himself if he did full justice to his talent. A month later came that 1009.

Since then, he has had his share of felicitations. Tendulkar even presented him with a bat. In his first couple of competitive games he didn't get another three-figure score. The opposition was not as feeble and the pressure of expectation couldn't be ignored. He also had to prepare for his Secondary School Certificate examinations. He got through with 60% and joined Ramniranjan Jhunjhunwala college, where his coach and several Mumbai first-class players, including Balwinder Singh Sandhu, studied.

There are several examples of big scorers not living up to expectations. In 2006, Mumbai's Yash Gandhi scored 365 for Don Bosco (Matunga) to go past Tendulkar's record 364 in the Harris Shield. He shifted to Gujarat for better prospects but couldn't play first-class cricket. He bid goodbye to the game.

Dhanawade will look to play with a straight bat for quality runs and the sooner he uses his quantitative school-level effort as an inspiration and not as a pressure builder, he will find his feet in the tough world of Mumbai cricket. At a felicitation function where Mumbai Cricket Association announced a monthly scholarship of Rs 10,000 for five years, Madhav Apte, the former Mumbai captain and India batsman, told Dhanawade, as reported by *The Hindu*: "Cricket is not always a game of success. But it will reward cricketers who make an effort. You have talent. You have to keep your head on your shoulders."

Clayton Murzello (@ ClaytonMurzello) is Mid-Day's *group sports editor.*

Bangladesh complex

SHAMYA DASGUPTA

East Pakistan fought and won its war of liberation from West Pakistan in 1971. In the years since the partition of India in 1947, huge cracks had appeared between East and West because of West's dominance – socially, culturally, politically and economically – over East, and it all came to a head around the late 1960s and early 1970s.

The political stories of 1947 and 1971 are long, meandering and bloody. The impact on cricket is less easy to assess. The Quaid-e-Azam Trophy was the main first-class tournament at the time in West, and a team from East was allowed to take part in it. The corresponding tournament in the East, the Sher-e-Bangla Cup, didn't have any West teams, but players from there did take part. In the 24 years of this arrangement, before Bangladesh's liberation, Pakistan had made a name for itself as a cricketing nation, but no one from East ever got a chance to play for the team, apart from Roquibul Hasan, an opening batsman, who played one four-day 'Test' against 'International XI', led by Mickey Stewart. This was in 1971, and was widely seen as a peace offering from West, not so much a comment on Hasan's abilities

Was no East cricketer good enough? Names like Abdul Latif and Javed Masood, both middle-order batsmen, and Sukumar Guha, an all-rounder, are still spoken with reverence in Bangladeshi circles. Whether they were good enough to play Test cricket is another matter. Fact remains they didn't. And, seeing the overall climate – one of feeling persecuted in every walk of life – in what later became Bangladesh, it's easy to see why Bangladeshi players of that era felt hard done by.

Surprisingly, passion for cricket remained undiminished in the country. Limited-overs cricket is most popular, and when it is something like a Bangladesh v India/Pakistan game, Sher-e-Bangla Stadium not only lets in around 30,000 people in its 26,000-seater facility, but approximately the same number of people have an all-evening party on the street just outside the stadium. Cricket bats and tennis balls are brought out, noise from drums and bugles fill the air, vendors of savouries and snacks make a killing, and, well, you wonder

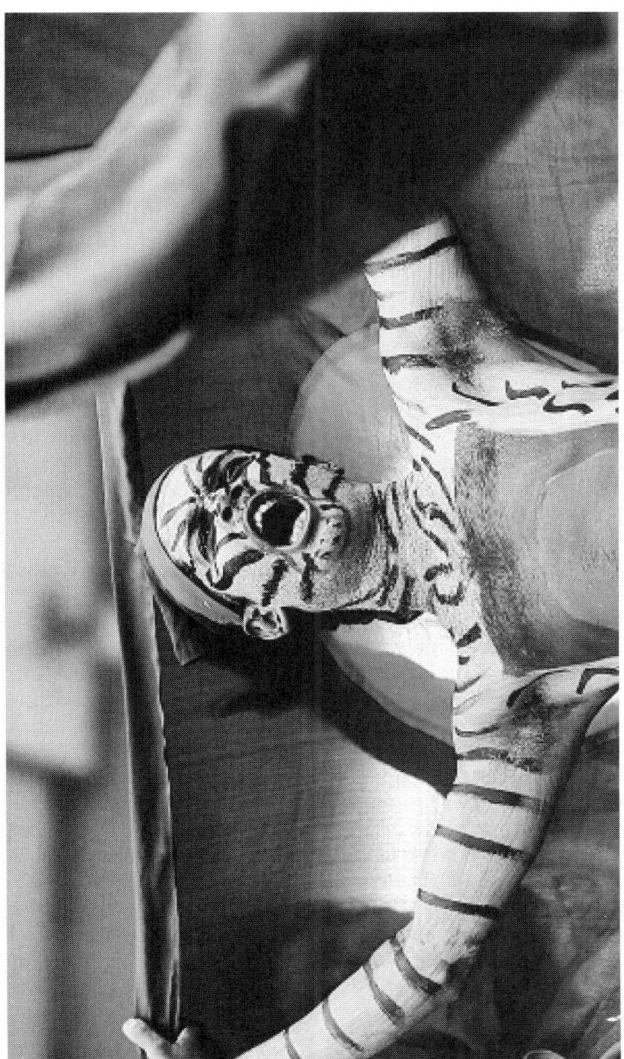

National passion: Indians call cricket a religion, but they cannot match the Bangladeshi fan's sheer fervour for the sport. – *Wisden India*

which lot is having more fun – the lucky ones who have tickets to the game, or the ones who don't. Indians call cricket a religion, but they cannot match Bangladeshis for sheer fervour.

What about the country's players then? Those who have played these 16 years in Test cricket and some more in limited-overs international cricket – do they actually vindicate the zeal of their fans? If one leaves out the recent run – mainly at home and mainly in 50-over games, and the one momentous Test win over England late in 2016 – and the rare win of note, the answer has to be 'no'.

Why, though?

To start with, while the average Bangladeshi will most likely punch you in the nose if you say this, the country's elevation to Test status was little more than a Jagmohan Dalmiya power call. Therefore, when Bangladesh played their first Test in 2000, against India, they were not ready for it: a truth belied by their first-innings total – 400, with Aminul Islam scoring 145 – but evidenced in their second-innings effort – 91. Perhaps their real worth lay somewhere in the middle – 245 or thereabouts.

In all these years, that's not gone up too much. For the longest time after the 2000 debut, Bangladesh cricket was a fledgling, wobbling fallacy: flattering here and there but largely deceiving, feting cricketers who would struggle to make the playing XI in an English county or a premier Ranji Trophy team.

There was no first-class system to speak of, infrastructure outside of Dhaka was in a shambles (where it existed at all), administration was a mess; hardly a handful of talented players were emerging. Truly, they could not be expected to do more than that so early on. Crucially, most Test-playing nations (bar Zimbabwe, who have their own woes) hardly invited or visited Bangladesh for a full series.

Bangladesh play a Test in India for the first time in February 2017.

In this context, there is another, more difficult aspect of cricket in Bangladesh that needs discussing: the persecution complex that exists at all levels in the system. There's no kind way of saying this, but it needs to be said. There is a lot of anger, among fans and sections of the media in Bangladesh and, though it isn't expressed the same way, among cricketers too. Once upon a time, the target of this ire, the cause of the persecution, was (West) Pakistan. That, by all accounts, was justified. Of late, it's a more general angst, with India the main target. But that could well be incidental – it really is Bangladesh v the World.

Bangladesh have traditionally invited and not visited India. There are very good reasons for this – the Bangladesh board needs the money more than its Indian counterpart – but the general feeling is that India don't think Bangladesh worthy of calling over for bilateral series. Now, there is truth in that too; they have not always been good enough opponents, no contest that would excite sponsors or spectators; they still are not at the Test level. And only recently has the Bangladesh team made a splash serious enough in limited-overs cricket.

The last time I saw delusion on quite this scale was during the Sourav Ganguly era in Calcutta. The sports pages of the city's newspapers between 1992 and 1996 raged about Ganguly's absence from the Indian national team. It was largely reported as a massive conspiracy to keep 'Maharaj' out. Through the Greg Chappell years, Ganguly could well have been Che Guevara if the Kolkata dailies were anything to go by; fighting against the system, against the bad foreigner.

In Bangladesh, after the no-ball controversy at the 2015 World Cup against India in the quarter-final, Mustafa Kamal, then ICC president, came up with: "It seemed as if they (the umpires) had gone into the match with something in mind." Similarly, when Taskin Ahmed was suspended for a faulty action in early 2016, rare was the Bangladeshi cricket fan who didn't holler conspiracy on India's part. Forget not that social media nonsense about Taskin holding MS Dhoni's head. Thankfully, there are some voices in Bangladesh who keep the balance, call their bluff. But one wonders which side is more populated.

But, through it all, as they say about the lotus that grows in the muck, emerged Habibul Bashar, Mashrafe bin Mortaza, Mohammad Rafique and Mohammad Ashraful first, and then Aftab Ahmed, Mushfiqur Rahim and Shakib Al Hasan. It's the classic pattern: First comes a period of struggle, then along come the role models, who show the others what possibilities there are, and then, slowly, the maturation. Once Bangladesh had attained Test status, and cricket emerged as a viable career option, the stars emerged.

That's happening now, headlined by young Mustafizur Rahman and the even younger Mehehi Hasan. Mustafizur is one of the few true world-class cricketers to have come out from the small, politically and socially disturbed, poor, heavily populated, chaotic country with the most amazing fish in the world. And Mehedi – well, not many teenagers have started out in top-flight cricket with quite the same bang.

Still, how threatening have they managed to be outside their Mirpur backyard?

Not very. But things are better. Sponsors, big-ticket cricket at home, results, stars, coaching staff that isn't inferior to that of any premier cricket country – you see the signs. Despite Bangladesh being one of 50 poorest nations in the world (according to 2015 International Monetary Fund data), cricket in the country lacks for little by way of money and, needless to say, public support.

Us against the world: India and ICC were the target of the fans' ire after Bangladesh lost their 2015 World Cup quarter-final match. – *AFP/Getty Images*

Tigers at home and lambs abroad they still are, but think: How many years – leave out 1971 and 1983-1986 – did it take for India to become a team oppositions feared? Didn't it take till India's golden generation of the 2000s to make the team a true force to reckon with while on tour? And have India really been consistent enough, or have the results come frequently enough, for them to still be considered a big threat when they travel? If we are honest, no. Only once in a way.

So, perhaps, Bangladesh haven't done as well as anyone, let alone their fans, would have expected them to. It's quite the one-sport country, so the disappointment is fair.

Part of the why lies in the complex logic of the international calendar, part of it in the reality that everything apart from Usain Bolt takes time. But the most crucial problem is the refusal to look within. And junk the persecution complex. Address those, and the Bangladesh cricket riddle could well be solved, which, in turn, would be grand for world cricket.

Shamya Dasgupta (@shamyad) is senior editor at Wisden India.

Buying into new cricket

VIDYA SUBRAMANIAN

PG Wodehouse in one of his comic masterpieces, *The Mating Season*, places his blundering protagonist Bertie Wooster in a crowd at a village carnival where his friend Esmond Haddock has just rendered a hunting song. The performance that follows Haddock's, the audience finds, leaves something to be desired. At a pause in action on stage, writes Wodehouse, in his inimitable style:

"We want Haddock," he said. "We want Haddock, we want Haddock, we want Haddock, we want HADDOCK!"

He uttered the words in a loud, clear, penetrating voice, not unlike that of a costermonger informing the public that he has blood oranges for sale, and the sentiment expressed evidently chimed in with the views of those standing near him. It was not long before perhaps twenty or more discriminating concert-goers were also chanting:

"We want Haddock, we want Haddock, we want Haddock, we want Haddock, we want HADDOCK!"

And it just shows you how catching this sort of thing is. It wasn't more than about five seconds later that I heard another voice intoning.

"We want Haddock, we want Haddock, we want Haddock, we want Haddock, we want HADDOCK!" and discovered with a mild surprise that it was mine. And as the remainder of the standees, some thirty in number, also adopted the slogan, this made us unanimous.

It is an easy illustration of the effect that runs through crowds, and how one single sentiment becomes the voice of a mass of people. As Gustave LeBon pointed out in *The Crowd: A Study of the Popular Mind* in 1895, a "psychological crowd" is a "provisional being" created in certain moments and made up of "heterogeneous elements, which for a moment are combined" to produce, he suggests, a being different from each individual that forms it.

The crowd is the thing that exists at the core of all spectacle. The audience is the reason there is theatre and cinema and art shows and indeed, sporting events. The IPL is one of these massive, audience-heavy events, making it an effective platform for seekers of publicity. As advertisers and publicists have discovered, the sporting arena is one of the most effective ways of 'grabbing eyeballs' in the modern world. Piggybacking on the popularity of the spectacle of sport, in exchange for financial support to organisers and players, advertisers have managed to successfully convert the sporting 'arena' into a 'platform'.

The crowd at Bertie Wooster's village carnival is quite different from the crowd at a modern sporting event. The chief 'audience' of such a contest now is absent from the site of the spectacle. The manner in which an event, sporting or otherwise, is broadcast live to millions of people around the world changes the notion of the 'crowd' that exists at the heart of a spectacle. The 'crowd' now is all of those people watching the show on television, on the internet and in public spaces, all put together. This fragmented, non-unified, and yet seemingly all-powerful crowd belongs to what French theorist Paul Virilio has called the "city of the instant". This 'city' is a virtual space in which almost everyone, everywhere in the world can be watching an event 'live' on screens – on computers, TV, mobile phones – separately and individually.

Steve Redhead, in 2007, quoted Virilio from an interview in the early 1980s as having said, "Those absent from the stadium are always right." For, it is those who watch the spectacle of the event on television and the internet for whom the event is 'produced'. Virilio said:

> "The billion people who watch the Olympic Games in Moscow, or the soccer championship in Argentina, impose their power at the expense of those present, who are already superfluous. The latter are practically no more than bodies filling the stadium so that it won't look empty. But their physical presence is completely alienated by the absence of the television viewer, and that's what interests me in this situation. Once, the stadiums were full. It was a magnificent popular explosion. There were 100,000 people in the grandstands, singing and shouting. It was a vision from an ancient society, from the agora, from paganism. Now when you watch the Olympics or the soccer championship on television, you notice there aren't that many people. And even they, in a certain way, aren't the ones who make the World Cup. The ones who make the World Cup are the ra-

dios and televisions that buy and – by favouring a billion and a half television viewers – 'produce' the championship. Those absent from the stadium are always right, economically and massively. They have the power. The participants are always wrong."

Further, Redhead argues that spectators at home are "treated to the spectacle of spectators within the grounds, watching not only the replays of incidents on giant screens but also the game live on screens on their mobile phones". So they are, in effect, watching people watch the event. Even those at the stadium end up watching the game and replays on the giant screens within the stadium. Thus, the entire 'watching' experience of the sport becomes mediated through various screens.

Cricket in India is as much sport as entertainment. There are more than five television channels in India that telecast cricket related content 24 hours a day, seven days a week. The IPL is one of the most popular televised sporting events in the country.

Yet, many observers feel there is a lack of technical, in-depth engagement with the nuances of the game. One television sports director that I interviewed believed fans care only about the glitz and glamour surrounding the sport, understanding only the easy binary of win-loss.

The sports fan has been recast as a spectator-consumer, who not only watches the sport on TV but also 'consumes' the programming, the advertisements and the celebrity 'brands'. The connoisseur gave way to the boisterous fan who just watched matches in which India played, hoping for victory and to enjoy the carnival that cricket became precisely to attract this kind of audience. Writes Satadru Sen: "Those who participate in online polls on 'Will India win the World Cup?' or 'Should Ganguly be sacked as captain?' probably do not assume that the question poses a worthwhile intellectual challenge or requires a deep technical knowledge of the game." This new fan, one who seeks to merely enjoy the moment of the match, is perhaps what Richard Giullianotti refers to as a "post-fandom", where fans as consumers use sport to seem 'cool'.

In 2009, Brian Lara, while calling cricket a "dying sport" and "welcoming" the new T20 form of the game, said this new spectator is "one who just wants to go to the game and doesn't even know what happens". The lack of knowledge about the longer version or the nuances and intensity of the sport seems not to bother these fans.

Some fans have argued that television has created a more engaged audience than ever before. Hawk-Eye and spidercams and umpire-vision cameras make for a better viewing experience. Add-ons such as super slow motion replays and ultra motion cameras makes this generation of fans the most knowledgeable.

This generation of fans is knowledgeable about cricket, but also embraces the sport for the 'celebrity' it involves. Seen here are fans with Steve Smith. — *Getty Images*

But, while the viewership, the money invested in broadcast rights and the unceasing coverage might indicate an increase in the number of people watching cricket, there is no way to know whether these are informed fans or those simply watching for the entertainment.

One of the issues raised before the IPL was created was how the viewership for cricket on TV was dwindling. According to Rohit Gupta, president of Sony Entertainment Television, television ratings for one-day matches had tapered off from above ten in 2003 to three in 2008. "It clearly showed that viewers didn't have the eight hours to watch a one-day international. It meant that youngsters were moving away from cricket," he said. It was at this juncture that Lalit Modi created the IPL.

The attempt was to lure the spectator in the periphery. Modi admitted as much in a 2008 interview to *Outlook Business* when he said: "We are not pitching IPL against cricket; we are pitching it against the prime time (7 to 11pm) of general entertainment channels... To make a show a hit, one needs star attraction. We have cherry-picked the best players from across the world... We have added a lot of music to the games. I think it provides entertainment to the crowds and between breaks. People are able to lap it up and enjoy it – it's an evening out. A Bollywood movie is three hours. This is a three-hour function. A lot of good food and catering and popcorn and ice cream for the kids."

It would appear that in place of creating a more discerning fan, new cricket is more about finding new and more entertainable audiences, not just those who don't have the patience for a day-long game but also those who may only be interested in the allied industries of celebrity and entertainment.

Cricket is one of several treats on offer to the spectator. With a package that boasts of Bollywood stars, industrialists and their celebrity scions, and cricketing celebrities from around the world, the IPL is a crucial moment in the understanding of sport and television in present day India.

This Sporting-Entertainment Complex – so painstakingly put together by those in the allied industries of sports, marketing, broadcast, and industry – is at once a sporting arena for modern-day gladiators, an evening out for young people after a day's work, a treasure trove of 'eyeballs' for advertisers, brand recognition for businesses, an image makeover for business people and film stars, and for the board a means to put on a cricket show in which India could never lose.

The target audience for the IPL is the urban middle-class consumer with a fairly large disposable income and immense purchasing power. The IPL sells to this audience a lifestyle that is in tune with ideas of global brands and exotic vacations. With the emergence of such a league, this cosmopolitan Indian cricket fan appears to be embracing more fully his other identity of a consumer, switching easily between brands, commodities and IPL teams as the fortunes of one overtake another on the sporting, and indeed, advertising field.

Vidya Sumbramanian is a doctoral candidate at the Centre of Science and Policy at Jawaharlal Nehru University.

It began with shattered glass in Ranchi

SIDDHARTHA VAIDYANATHAN

MS Dhoni is many things. Batsman. Wicketkeeper. Captain. Legend. Magician. Energizer Bunny. Expert chaser. Media baiter. He is also a peerless striker of sixes, has always been, serving up never-to-be-forgotten sixes in an era of frequent big hits. This is the side of Dhoni that goes back to his emergence as a cricketer, before the World Cup win and the superstardom, before the last-ball finishes and the rabbit-out-of-hat captaincy, before his Test, ODI and first-class debuts, before the world had heard of MS Dhoni. It goes back to a row of shattered glass in Ranchi.

The story goes, as a local college student told *India Today* in 2005, that schoolboy Dhoni smashed the windowpanes that flanked DAV Shyamali School by thundering sixes from a nearby MECON ground. That is quite an image especially because the distance he supposedly cleared was an incredible 250 metres. And it added to the growing legend around his ability to hit monster sixes. Most young batsmen catch the eye by piling on a mountain of runs. Dhoni's arrival was accompanied by a sizeable folklore around his breathtaking hitting. Launching a ball not too far from a selector (after he wasn't picked for an Under-19 World Cup camp). Losing eight balls during a Ranji Trophy game at Sector 16 Stadium in Chandigarh. Firing three balls outside M Chinnaswamy Stadium in Bangalore.

Soon it was the turn of international teams to suffer. Mane flowing and bat twirling at unorthodox angles, Dhoni made a mess of Pakistan (148, four sixes), Zimbabwe (56 and 67 not out, seven sixes) and Sri Lanka (183 not out, ten sixes) in ODIs. In the seventh ball of his fifth Test, in Faisalabad, with India in trouble and Shoaib Akhtar pounding it in short, Dhoni rocked back, wound up his bat, met the ball on the rise and, torso tilted, hooked a six over square leg. Bang! Oozing swagger. Jump-starting a frenetic counter-attack.

So we knew Dhoni could hit big. We knew he could get audacious. Yet, few anticipated the 'helicopter' he let fly against England in an ODI in Margao in 2006: a shot that extended the limits of death-overs batting. Up until then, James Anderson's full ball outside off may have been pushed for a single down the ground. A glide or

It began with shattered glass in Ranchi

Six appeal: The sweet crunch of bat on ball, the power, the elevation, the focus, the unmistakable swagger. — *Getty Images*

scoop may have brought two. A handful of batsmen may have picked off a four. Dhoni was having none of it. He opened up his stance, brought his bat down from a great height, whipped the ball high over midwicket and followed through with a 360-degree swing that was so glorious it could have been cricket's answer to flamboyant actor Rajinikanth annihilating an army of bad men in one furious stroke.

Now bowlers had nowhere to hide. Short ball, good length, yorker length, fast ball, slow ball, dart on the pads: Dhoni cleared the boundary irrespective. He would disrupt length by charging and disrupt lines with short-arm thumps. He wasn't content with merely clearing the ropes. His mission, it seemed, was to demoralise. To go so high, so far as to drain bowlers of all hope.

The shots themselves were only one part of the story. What was becoming apparent was Dhoni's keen sense of timing, targeting certain bowlers, strategically releasing pressure, taking the game to the final over and then backing himself to pull off the big hits. There are umpteen clips online of Dhoni belting last-over sixes but equally vital are his cat-and-mouse tactics in the lead-up, declining singles, raising the stakes, unruffled by the steep asking rate. Few innings captured this better than his 29-ball 54 for Chennai Super Kings in a vital game against Kings XI Punjab in the 2010 IPL. Dhoni walked in in the tenth over. The required rate was over ten. At the end of the 18th over, with 29 still needed, he was on 24 off 20, with two fours and 13 singles – nothing to suggest his team was in a hole. Then came the explosion. Two fours, a two, a single, another single, a four, a two, a six and another six: 30 runs with the game on the line, guiding his team to the semi-final.

Such last-over finishes became Dhoni's trademark. He hit eight off the last over (with seven needed) to beat England in an ODI in Mohali in 2011, seven of the eight required to tie with Sri Lanka in the 2012 CB Series, 11 of 13 to beat Australia in the same tournament and 16 (15 needed) to beat Sri Lanka in the final of a tri-series in the West Indies in 2013. The last of these was the most arresting, when an injured Dhoni added 21 with No. 11 Ishant Sharma, sealing the title with a sequence that read 6, 4, 6. Those may have been his only sixes all innings but the threat loomed large. Bowlers knew they couldn't afford to err. Fielders stood deep – allowing easy twos. And Sri Lanka knew no field setting could stop him. Even when the game was up for grabs, for many watching, Dhoni had already won.

All of which made it wholly fitting that on the night of April 2, 2011, it was Dhoni who put a seal on India's World Cup triumph. And with such style! The bat tracing a beautiful swing, the sweet crunch of bat on ball, the awesome power, the elevation, the unwavering focus and the delectable twirl in the follow-through. The game was ready for a defining image. India was ready for a cathartic release. And Dhoni being Dhoni swung for the fences.

Siddhartha Vaidyanathan (@sidvee) is a US-based journalist.

FAREWELL

Leaders bow out

CLAYTON MURZELLO

"Thanks for the memories, Brendon." The placard at **Brendon McCullum**'s international farewell at Hagley Oval on his final day as a Test cricketer on February 24, 2016, didn't win a prize for wit or innovation, but it wasn't far from the truth. McCullum's very name conjures up images of a dazzling strokeplayer, a rampaging destroyer of bowling attacks and, in his own assessment, someone who always chose an attacking option under duress.

There was nothing passive about his decision to quit the international scene at 34, a call that would have found favour with batting greats of another era: England's Patsy Hendren and India's Vijay Merchant, the first preachers of the 'quit when they ask why and why not' credo. Indeed, followers of the game had good reason to ask 'why' when New Zealand's finest wicketkeeper-batsman hung up his black cap. Only the previous year had he led the Kiwis to their first World Cup final. And 24 months before his retirement, he scored a Test triple-century against the touring Indians in Wellington. However, there is no denying that his back worried him.

"The time's right. And now I walk away comfortable with my decision and looking forward to the next stage of my life. You walk away knowing that you've been able to front up and try to go out there and get a performance on the board and I guess now you're a little bit relieved," he said.

The best tribute came from New Zealand's greatest all-rounder, Richard Hadlee. Writing in the *Wisden India Almanack 2016*, Hadlee had described McCullum as "a special person, player and a leader of men", who was "thoughtful, clever and innovative on the field". "Brendon McCullum has led the Black Caps renaissance. He is the face of the side and to young, aspiring cricketers in New Zealand, he is a national hero," he wrote. After the younger man's retirement, he said: "Brendon, it is an end to your career, the end of an era. You've been an inspirational captain. As the great Viv Richards said, you're the type of player that puts bums on seats, people will come down to watch you, and I think that's a tremendous tribute."

McCullum scored 6453 runs in 101 Tests, with 12 hundreds and

Trailblazer: Charlotte Edwards retired with 5992 ODI runs, the most among women, and 2605 runs in T20Is, the most in the format, among men or women. — *Getty Images*

31 fifties, 6083 runs in 260 ODIs and 2140 runs in 71 T20 internationals.

Elder brother and off-spinning all-rounder **Nathan MCullum** too quit in the 2015-16 season and he did so without fuss. "I don't want to make a big song and dance about it, but it's time to start thinking about the next phase of my life," McCullum told *New Zealand Herald* in December 2015 while announcing his decision. Nathan, who didn't figure in Test cricket, claimed 63 wickets in 84 ODIs. In 63 T20 internationals, he captured 58 wickets.

Had it not been for the Masters Champions League, a T20 tournament for retired players, West Indies' most enduring batsman (1994 to 2015) **Shivnarine Chanderpaul** would probably not have informed the West Indies Cricket Board not to consider him for international cricket.

Signals that he was no longer needed had been sent out the previous year. He refused to throw in the towel, though, when the Clive Lloyd-led selection committee dropped him after he averaged 15.33 in six innings during the three-Test home series against England in 2015.

The left-handed battler ended up 86 runs short of Brian Lara's Test run tally of 11,953 and Lara was not pleased. "I was very disappointed that Shiv was not allowed a couple of more Test matches, not necessarily to break the record, but to have a proper send-off. He has been a great servant for West Indies cricket and has done some tremendous things throughout his career. Credit must be given to the man for how he has played," said Lara of the player who was at the other end when he broke Garry Sobers's 365-run mark at Antigua Recreation Ground against the Englishmen in 1994.

Apart from Chanderpaul, the WICB granted no-objection certificates to pacers **Tino Best**, **Fidel Edwards** and **Krishmar Santokie** for the MCL, which pushed them into the retired category.

Sri Lanka's **Thillakaratne Dilshan** too was persuaded to retire and make way for a new generation. Three years after he gave up Test cricket in 2013, the innovater of the 'Dilscoop' bid adieu to the limited formats, aged 39 and placed second on the all-time list of T20I run-getters. Age had done little to dull his form or figures: Since 2013, he averaged 49.18 and made 1207 runs from 25 matches in 2015, the third-best numbers for that year, and was a good fielder.

"I started the series thinking that I'll play for another year - at least in T20 cricket. But when I woke up on the 25th I felt that it was time to go... I could easily play for another year or two. But we have to look to the future," he told *ESPNcricinfo*. "Since I started opening six years ago, we haven't found a permanent partner for me. I've opened with about 10 people - so that's a problematic area for us. If I keep playing we won't be able to get two batsmen settled in that place."

He finished with 5492 runs and 39 wickets from 87 Tests, and 1889 runs from 80 T20Is. In ODIs, he was one of the few to have crossed 10,000 runs, his 10,290 coming from 330 games, while his off-spin netted him 106 wickets with a best of 4 for 4 against Zimbabwe in 2011.

Having quit Test cricket the previous year after Australia's failure to win yet another Ashes series in England, **Shane Watson**, the all-rounder, ended his international career after Australia's World T20 campaign in India. A win would have been the icing on the cake for a player who performed better in limited-overs cricket as against the traditional form, but it was not to be. "I've really enjoyed my time being back in the Australian squad. But it is quite different, none of the other guys I played with growing up are here any more. I've made the right decision. I couldn't really see the light with all the injuries I had," he said to *ESPNcricinfo*. Watson probably deserved better from the game, but he can find solace in the fact that he was part of two World Cup-winning teams: in 2007 in the Caribbean and at home in 2015.

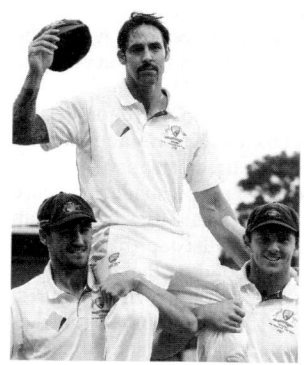

Mitchell Johnson had all the pace and aggression that makes for a fearsome fast bowler. – *Getty Images*

Ricky Ponting, who led him in two World Cups, backed Watson during a particularly difficult time in 2013, when the all-rounder was one of four players suspended during the India tour over what was described as a breach in discipline. "Shane worked as hard as anybody around his cricket, there's no doubt about that. I've never known him to be anything other than a very good team player and a great bloke to have around your team," said Ponting then.

Mitchell Johnson, also among the four who got into trouble that tour for not returning the assignment asked of them, put a full stop to his international career in the 2015-16 season too. Confirmation of his retirement came after the Perth Test against New Zealand in which he claimed 1 for 157 in the first innings with Ross Taylor scoring 290 and Kane Williamson cracking 166, although he claimed both the New Zealand wickets to fall in the second innings during the drawn Test. Ironically, he played his last Test at a venue synonymous with pace, a ground on which he claimed 45 of his 313 Test scalps. But, at age 34, he lost the drive and had no qualms in admitting it: "I'm really happy with my decision and I just lost that hunger in the end to play out on those tough days, that's where my decision came. That's something I used to really enjoy about Test cricket, the challenge of those really difficult days and I just wasn't enjoying it out there." Johnson's tally from 73 Tests for Australia is only behind that of Shane Warne, Glenn McGrath and Dennis Lillee.

Ben Hilfenhaus was another Australian pacer who called it quits. He said goodbye to first-class cricket at 32 after having to cope with a troublesome hamstring. He played his last Test in 2012 and ended with 99 wickets in only 27 Tests.

English cricket lost a run machine in Kent's **Robert Key** when he announced his retirement from all forms of cricket in April. He played 15 Tests for England in a five-year span and lit up Lord's with 221 against West Indies in 2004. The right-hander scored 19,419 first-class runs garnished with 54 centuries.

However, the biggest career closure in English cricket last season was of **Charlotte Edwards**, who brought the curtains down on her 20-year career in May. She broke down at her retirement press conference, which left many of her supporters echoing the words, "Hey, that's no way to say goodbye." 'Lottie', England's top scorer at the World T20, was told she had no place in a side that sought to go in a new direction. "There was a real hunger to carry on as a player. But it's not to be. It has come as a big shock to me," she said. The most capped female cricketer in the world, Edwards played 23 Tests, 191 ODIs and 95 T20Is. Her 5992 ODI runs is the most among women, while her 2605 runs in T20Is is the most in the format, for men or women. She is aware of just how much she changed the game – and its rules. "I did not have a female role model as a cricketer growing up so to think I have done that is really special to me. I started playing in skirts and had to pay for my own blazer ... It's been an unbelievable journey."

She was followed into retirement by team-mate **Lydia Greenway**, a fantastic fielder who ended a 13-year run in England with 121 catches to go with 362 Test runs, 4081 ODI runs and 1240 runs in T20Is.

As shocking was the premature retirement of **James Taylor**, whose promising career was cut short at 26 with a serious heart condition. The outpouring of sympathy was immediate, the conviction that the young batsman could bounce back as strong. "My world is upside down. But I'm here to stay and I'm battling on!" said Taylor on his Twitter account, which would become a heart-warming window into his determined fight and remarkable positivity.

James Taylor: A promising career cut short by illness. – *Getty Images*

Next door, **John Mooney**, the all-rounder who represented Ireland 182 times over a decade and some, stepped back from cricket at 33 to concentrate on his business ventures. William Porterfield, his captain, hailed the "passion, fighting qualities and enthusiasm" that made Mooney an integral part of three World Cup sides, including memorably in their 2011 win over England. "Of course he'll always be remembered for the game against England in Bangalore, but for me his bowling display in the Intercontinental Cup win over Afghanistan summed up for me what he was all about. He led the attack after Trent Johnston went off injured and took 10 for 81 on a batting paradise in difficult conditions," he said.

PART TWO
Misses and hits

Into the fifth decade

In *Skirting the Boundary – A History of Women's Cricket*, Isabelle Duncan argues that despite cricket's rich literature, there is very little known about the women's game. Christine Willes was the first to bowl overarm in a backyard game with her brother in the 19th century, and the maiden Women's World Cup in 1973 was two years ahead of the men's version. Barring a collection of facts, however, Duncan's contention is relevant even in the age of e-journalism, Women's Big Bash League and double-headers.

The media's lack of interest in the women's sport stands out in India, cricket's largest market. As Shashank Kishore, who has reported on three Women's World T20s and one World Cup since 2012, writes in these pages, "At several tournaments, the press box was used by scribes to download music and movies."

Wisden India has attempted to cover the gap over the years, and this special section, which features voices of four captains, celebrates 40 years of India Women's internationals.

The celebration acknowledges pioneers – from those who fought for the first Test win in Patna (witnessed by a big crowd) to those who hasseled the Railways minister for jobs. The stalwarts are here, like Mithali Raj, maker of India's only Test double-century, and so is the future, the Smritis and Harmanpreets who are reaching for new shores.

The 2015-16 season was a significant one as BCCI introduced central contracts and the team recorded its first series win over Australia. But the dominance of Railways, an institution where the best gravitate because of job security, has not helped senior domestic standards. The board started Under-23 tournaments to bridge the skills gap, but what about those lost to the game in the teens?

India's early exit from the 2016 World T20 at home was a missed opportunity, but that is a blip. As the women go into an important World Cup year, the media can no longer ignore them. And as much as this section is a celebration of four decades of achievement, it is also an addition to much-needed literature on the women's game.

Passion on the field, in the stands: Unlike these days, women's cricket in India once attracted large, enthusiastic crowds. — *Getty Images*

If we had failed, it'd have gone kaput

SHANTHA RANGASWAMY

India played their first Test match against West Indies Women at the M Chinnaswamy Stadium in Bangalore on October 31, 1976, but the story of women's cricket in India started much earlier, in 1973.

The first senior national women's championship was played among Mumbai, Maharashtra and Uttar Pradesh in Pune in April that year. Uttar Pradesh did not have enough players, so some of the Maharashtra juniors made up their playing XI. Mumbai beat Maharashtra by ten wickets in the final. The next nationals were held in Varanasi a few months later in November. That is where I made my Karnataka debut, and we beat Maharashtra to play Bengal in the final.

Initially, many thought women's cricket was a passing trend. They came to watch us out of curiosity, but found the standards were pretty good. The publicity we got from print media back then is more than what the current lot gets.

Australia Under-25 were the first 'international' team to visit India in February 1975. They played four warm-up matches against the zonal sides before taking on the Indians in a three-day game in Pune. The second game in Delhi was an interesting one. I made 92 in the first innings, and Australia needed 121 in their second innings for a win. Most of our teammates were young, so Diana Edulji and I bowled all but seven overs in that innings. In fact, I bowled unchanged for 16 overs and it boiled down to them needing five runs with three wickets in hand in the final over. Lynette Smith, the No.3 batter, was at the non-striker's end. I conceded two runs in the first ball – Shirin Kiash, who represented India in basketball and hockey, misfielded at square-leg – but I got a wicket the next ball, and then beat Cecilia Wilson, their wicketkeeper-captain, for three balls before dismissing her off the final delivery. I finished with 5 for 54 as we almost pulled off a victory. That game was almost like a T20, with so much 'masala'. Everyone was thrilled.

The third game was in Kolkata and I was made vice-captain. We were chasing 198 and were told to pull down the shutters. We were 61 for 2 when I joined Fowzieh Khalili in the middle and we decided to play deaf to that advice, and go for the shots as the target was gettable on that pitch. We had a 74-run partnership, but she was run out for 45 and I for 55. After that, they pulled the shutters down again and we ended on 186 for 5, just 12 runs short of a memorable win!

New Zealand then came down for a five-match series in early 1976, but the matches were still not considered official 'Tests'. Ironically, when we went to New Zealand in 1977, they fielded almost the same team, and that Test was official. I still wonder why the Women's Cricket Association of India (WCAI) didn't get official status for the games in India. I scored a century in Pune – for which I got a Luna moped (a two-wheeler)! – but with none of those eight matches granted Test status, that obliterated the 575 runs I made and 33 wickets that Diana took. We have moved on, of course. Fortunately for me, I got a century in Dunedin or else I may have never made it to the record books.

The first of many

Credit for our Test debut in 1976 goes to Mahendra Kumar Sharma, the force behind WCAI. I remember Chinnaswamy was almost houseful for the First Test. People had paid to come and watch us! I was captaining the side, and I was keen for a win. After Shubhangi Kulkarni took five wickets to dismiss West Indies for 274 on the first

A newspaper clipping from India's 1986 tour of England.
— Photo courtesy Sunil Yash Kalra

day and the top three batters gave us a good start, we were more determined. I made a quick-fire 74 and hit India's first recorded six in international cricket. Lala Amarnath, who was the chairman of our selection committee, was doing radio commentary. He did not like that I went for my strokes straightaway. We declared five runs short of West Indies' first-innings total of 274, and then they declared their second innings on 175 for 7. We were chasing 181, but rain washed out most of the third and final day.

I must acknowledge the influence of Lala Amarnath. He took a lot of interest in our development and held camps. He shared some of the finer points about the technicalities of the game and captaincy with us, which are still fresh in my memory.

Our first win came in the Fourth Test at the Moin-ul-Haq Stadium in Patna, where Shubhangi took four wickets in the second innings and we chased down 55 with five wickets in hand. There were more than 25,000 people at the ground and a lot of them lined up to be a part of the impromptu celebration from the ground to the hotel. We too were dancing – Rajeshwari Dholakia and a few others who were good in traditional dances were leading the way! We were taken to a women's college for the celebration and the auditorium was packed.

We carried that form to New Zealand. We played all the state sides and remained unbeaten before playing the one-off Test in Dunedin, where I got 108 and we drew the game.

Another game I cherish is the 1982 World Cup win against England in Wanganui. We made 178, thanks mainly to a heroic knock by Fowzieh Khaleeli and her partnership with Rajeswari Dholokia, and then relied on our spinners to bowl out a star-studded line-up that had the likes of Rachael Heyhoe-Flint and Enid Bakewell for 131.

Those days we had to raise funds to finance parts of our travelling expenses, but it was good fun. Going by statistics, the founding members of Indian women's cricket may not stand anywhere near the current lot, but we derived satisfaction from laying a solid foundation. Had we failed in those initial years, it would have gone kaput. No one can take that satisfaction away from us.

The administrative battle

Cricket suffered after the ouster of MK Sharma not long after we hosted the World Cup in January 1978. By the time we played our next Test, it was 1984. We got back on track only in 1991 when Anuradha Dutt became de facto WCAI secretary. She was there for almost a decade. Things really improved when Shubhangi took over. She got team sponsorships and organised more games. The national team had its best run between 2002 and 2006, when Shubhangi was in charge.

We made it to the 2005 World Cup final, and won a Test series in England when I was chairperson of the selection committee. BCCI, when Sharad Pawar was president, sponsored that tour and it was a great boost. After that, BCCI took over WCAI and things became smooth as we got access to the best facilities. Indian women's cricket owes a lot to Pawar for taking the game under BCCI despite opposition.

The golden period: India made it to the final of the World Cup in 2005, their best performance at the event to date. — *Getty Images*

Of course, things could have moved faster in the last decade. After Anurag Thakur became secretary, BCCI went all out to support us. He was very receptive to our suggestions and the biggest example of that are the central contracts handed out to some players. Earlier, the BCCI's women's committee barely met, but now there are more women in the panel and the board has asked them to submit a vision document.

There were a lot of challenges when we were not under BCCI. We had to travel unreserved in second class in trains, probably spending the entire journey sitting near the toilet! Those days are gone.

The jobs dilemma

By the time a state association stabilises its domestic team, two or three key players leave them for a job with the Railways, and it is back to square one. As Railways are the only institution now providing female cricketers jobs and some stability, most aim for that.

The BCCI should use its clout and get corporates to form teams and give jobs to female cricketers. That will not only help more than 500 cricketers be financially secure, but also make the domestic competition more balanced. Don't get me wrong: It is very important that Railways continue to recruit cricketers, but it is not enough. BCCI have to amend the constitution and facilitate this. You don't have to give the new institutions voting rights, but allow corporates to play tournaments.

Looking at the grass roots

The start of the Under-23 inter-state and inter-zonal competition is a wonderful initiative. For many of the Indian cricketers, there is a vacuum after Under-19, as they don't immediately graduate to the national team. They get frustrated and give up.

Critics of the Under-23s point out that those playing for Railways Under-23 have to be content with just one competition in the season, as it is difficult for them to break into the senior squad and India Women lose out. But the way I look at it, perhaps 20 players cannot play, but 400 girls have got another platform to push their case. Railways can perhaps decide they don't want to play in the competition, and allow the girls to play for their state teams.

One area where the board is dithering is at the Under-16 level. BCCI asked the respective zones to organise their own tournaments, but most have not followed the directive. Only South Zone have been religiously holding this tournament. Indian women have a short career span in sports – they shine at Under-19, and just when they are peaking they get married, have kids and give up the game – so we must start earlier so that we get around four to five years of their peak.

It's not a big deal to organise an IPL-like tournament for women. It is, however, a big deal to have a wide base to pick from and that you will get if your Under-16 and schools structure is strong.

Support for the support staff

There is a trend internationally to have male coaches for the women's team. But some of Indian cricket's best moments have come when Sudha Shah was the coach: the 2005 World Cup final and the 2014 Test win in England, for example. She doesn't take risks and keeps things simple. Some senior players have recently spoken about the need for a male coach. It's not wrong, but it should not be at the cost of female coaches. Instead, the BCCI should ensure female coaches learn by watching their male counterparts go about their work. That way, you are grooming a new set of coaches and over a period of time they will become independent. It will widen the pool. It's just like what happened with the men's team: When John Wright took over, there were hardly any quality home-grown coaches. Now we have so many of them.

A team of world beaters

Had we made it to the finals of the 2016 World T20 at home, BCCI's outlook towards women's cricket would have changed completely. While the new regime has been proactive, there continue to be some reservations in certain quarters. The team, though, buckled. Unlike our generation of cricketers, who played before packed stands, they are not used to such home pressure. The batting did not click, there was lack of match awareness in crunch moments and the game-by-game approach could have been different.

But that's now in the past. The 2017 World Cup in England offers another opportunity. India will have to play the qualifiers to make it to the main tournament, but you can rest assured that away from home pressure, the team will do wonders. This is a team that can win the World Cup. Indian cricket – and its future – is in safe hands. It is time to exhort Mithali Raj and Team India to catapult the game to a high level by winning the 2017 World Cup.

Arjuna Award winner and India's first captain, Shantha Rangaswamy led in 12 Tests and 16 ODIs.

From a history of shared kits

SHUBHANGI KULKARNI

It was 1973. Over 40 years since our fellow cricket enthusiasts began playing in England, Australia and New Zealand. The excitement in the air was palpable. The first whiff of leather against willow was sensed by a motley crew of women. I was one of them. We had picked up the five ounces of leather and started what would become the women's version of the game that was to become religion in our country.

We played the game just like the men did, despite all the gender-specific odds we faced: societal, financial, infrastructural and organisational. We played for one thing alone: the love of the game. The naysayers, doubters and wondering passers-by were many. "Are the girls playing in skirts?" "Do they wear saris?" "Are they playing with a rubber ball?" "Are the boundaries the same distance?" – questions that could have served as inspiration to Gloria Steinem, or today's millennials. Of course, there were the men too, in true feminist form, who came out in support – the dynamic MK Sharma, for example, who formed the Women's Cricket Association of India (WCAI), in Lucknow that year.

A rag-tag assembly of women of various sporting backgrounds, appearances and character, we quickly graduated to playing our first 'international' match, against a visiting Australian side in 1975, in front of a crowd of 15,000-20,000. We had arrived! Of course, it wasn't easy. Not then, and not for long after then.

We challenged societal mores in the 1970s and '80s. Parents refused to allow their girls to play fearing they would get injured with the hard ball. They needed convincing to let girls travel on tours with unknown people. Financial pressures were many: Cricket kits were expensive, so players had to use a common kit. When a new batter walked into the middle, she'd take the bat from the player who was on her way out. Sponsorships were not easy. When we weren't playing, we were knocking on doors of corporates and individuals to garner support.

Infrastructure was conspicuous by its absence. Our domestic games were played on club and college grounds with bumpy un-

Trailblazers: Shubhangi Kulkarni (right), during her stint as manager of the team at the 2009 World Cup, with (L-R) Sudha Shah, coach, captain Jhulan Goswami and vice-captain Amita Sharma. — *Getty Images*

even outfields and barren patches. Fielding was a huge challenge and it was a wonder we avoided major injuries. Facilities provided by perpetually cash-strapped organisers were sub-par. We travelled unreserved in trains, standing for long distances or sitting on our bags when there simply weren't enough seats available. The whole team shared one large room and sometimes two teams shared one room with a divider. Needless to say, the toilets and bathrooms were appalling.

But we endured every challenge, overcame every obstacle and answered every naysayer the only way we knew how: by showing up every single time and playing the game the best we could. We survived and we thrived! There was nothing in it for us – just all for the love of the game. Some took time away from other careers to play, others took time off the field to have families. But the sum total of every woman who has played cricket since 1973 is the foundation of the sport in India today.

When some of us meet now, as we did during the 500th (men's) Test celebrations in Kanpur, there is nary a negative thought about the hardships we endured. The joy of our collective achievement binds us together.

As one generation gave way to another, some of us took it upon ourselves to be better administrators than the ones we had. When I was voted WCAI secretary in 2003, we had a single goal in mind: the 2005 International Women's Cricket Council (IWCC) World Cup in South Africa. We put a strategy in motion. We asked corporates like Infosys to come on board, not for money but for facilities. The Infosys campus with its well-manicured grounds was where we shaped our players mentally and physically, replete with athlete diet plans, team-building workshops and personality development sessions.

And it paid off: Team India reached the finals of that edition.

Today, parents encourage their daughters to take up the sport, provide them with the equipment, spend on personalised coaching, change holiday plans to ensure that their daughters don't miss crucial events and even agree to allow them to drop out of school or college to pursue the sport!

On the international front, in 2005, the International Cricket Council merged with the IWCC to ensure that women had access to the same set of resources that the men did. This has meant playing and training facilities, travel and accommodation; match allowances and prize monies have improved. The top eight nations have introduced contracts for their players. With rankings taking into account all three formats of the game, every international match is more meaningful. At home, the BCCI have extended the pension scheme and medical benefits to former India Women cricketers as well.

Women now also have a seat at the high table: The ICC women's committee chairperson also sits on the chief executives' committee. It is great to see female commentators, coaches, physiotherapists, match referees, scorers and umpires. The game that was originally played only in England, Australia and New Zealand has now spread far and wide. We have indeed come a long way from the dust bowls, shared gear and unreserved train coaches of 1973.

A recipient of the Arjuna Award, Shubhangi Kulkarni is a former India captain, who turned to administration after her retirement in 1991.

The rail road

SNEHAL PRADHAN

Badhwar Park is a residential complex for officers of Central and Western Railway, the two lifelines that share the burden of transporting the millions of Mumbai. Nestled between the slums that dot the coast and the south Bombay or 'SoBo' opulence further inland, the colony is a misfit; demure, despite being among the best railway colonies in the city. Few know that Badhwar Park itself used to once be a railway station – for trams, though. It was where Ajmal Kasab and his ill-intentioned team landed in 2008 to wreak havoc that November 26. It is also the place where the first female Railways cricketer was raised.

As a child, Diana Fram Edulji played cricket with the boys at Badhwar Park, where her father, an officer in Western Railway, had been allotted quarters. "Those games sparked my interest in sports," recounts Edulji. "And at the same time, they kept me connected to the railways family."

The games at Badhwar Park led her to join Albee's in 1971, the first club for women cricketers in Mumbai, named after Aloo Bamjee, its founder. Women's cricket was taking root in India, and in 1974, the Women's Cricket Association of India (WCAI) was formed. Edulji rose through the ranks, and in 1976, when India played their first official Test against West Indies, she was the cornerstone of the spin attack.

For the Third Test in Delhi, Kamlapati Tripathi, then the railways minister, was in attendance. (His daughter-in-law, Chandra Tripathi, was president of WCAI. The WCAI would later name its junior competition after her.) Edulji handed the minister an application for a job in the railways; her father was due to retire the same year. She thus became the first female cricketer to be employed by the railways.

"All of us should be indebted to her for taking that initiative," says Anjali Pendharkar, a middle-order bat in the first Indian Railways women's team. "Diana took things further single-handedly."

Today, the railways exerts an influence on women's cricket that dwarfs even SoBo's tallest buildings.

Former India Women captains at the celebration of 500 men's Tests. Diana Edulji (right) was the first cricketer to be employed by the railways, while the likes of Anjum Chopra (second from right) was with Air India. Also seen are (L-R) Shantha Rangaswamy, Nilima Joglekar and Shubhangi Kulkarni. – *BCCI*

Of the 15 members of the Indian squad for the World T20 2016, nine worked with the railways. The number was as high as 12 in the last 50-over World Cup. Since 2006, when the BCCI took over the women's game too, Railways have won 18 of the 19 senior domestic titles across all formats. Central Zone, in which Railways play, have won nine out of ten inter-zonal titles. In all, the Railways team has been defeated only five times since 2006, across all competitions. Such is their domination.

Back in Edulji's early working years, though, things moved less emphatically. Only eight full years after she was hired did the women's team take shape, and again credit went to another railways minister. In 1984, a group of players attending a national camp in Delhi reached out to Madhavrao Scindia through Edulji, requesting jobs. Scindia, a sports lover himself, commissioned the creation of women's cricket teams in the zones where the players were based. Three teams, Western Railway, Southern Railway and Eastern Railway, played the first inter-railways women's cricket tournament that year. The first Railways side was picked in 1985.

The players were given time off to train, as with all sportspersons hired by the railways. They worked in offices till 3pm and trained in the evenings. They were the first semi-professional female cricketers, perhaps in the world. While others paid to play, the Railways players were salaried. While others travelled across the country second class, often unreserved, Railways players travelled in air-conditioned coaches. They were the envy of the domestic circuit.

Legends like Edulji, Sandhya Agarwal, Rajani Venugopal, Sreerupa Bose and Gargi Banerji formed the spine of the early sides. Edulji recalls how if Railways won the toss and chose to bat, the match (three-day matches in the 'first innings to finish' format, with both teams needing to complete their first innings for a result) would often stretch into the fourth day, much to the chagrin of the organisers. "We would bat three days and not declare. It was the only way our middle order, who otherwise got no chances to impress the selectors, would get to bat. Then we would bundle [the opposition] out on the fourth morning!"

They could never take their position at the top for granted, though, for the minister took a personal interest in their progress. "Once we (Railways players representing Institutional Zone) lost an inter-zonal match to South Zone," recounts Edulji. "We got a call from Mr Scindia himself. And that summer, we had a punishment camp in the heat of Delhi."

Cut to the present and both the work schedules and the winning culture of the team remain unchanged. Players enjoy permanent employment, even after they step away from the game (although they must then work regular timings). They get paid leave for all official BCCI tournaments and training camps. Trophies translate into increments and out-of-turn promotions. The team itself is chosen from the hundred-odd players employed with the eight zones, thus giving them a deep talent pool to pick from.

"The Railways team is filled with players who have the 'India player' tag. So the expectation to win is built up. We have a culture of performance that creates an aura around this team," says Mithali Raj, India captain and skipper of Railways for more than a decade.

"Be it match referees, selectors or coaches, the railways has given us leave for BCCI tournaments, even when we aren't active players," says Pendharkar, who is now a national selector. Purnima Rau, India coach, echoes the sentiment. "I remember being granted 30 days leave to recover from a broken finger … it was good to have the organisation behind us."

However, the dominance of Railways, as a team and an employer, turned the power structure of women's cricket on its head. The railways absorbed the best talent. While once teams like Bombay, Maharashtra, Karnataka and Bengal would offer stiff competition for the title, Railways railroaded the national tournaments. It was a juggernaut that rolled merrily on until Air India came into the picture. But more on that later.

There are also instances of players losing international places soon after being picked for Railways. Automatic selections for their state teams, once they joined railways they faced fierce competition for spots, and the lack of opportunity cost them. Frustrated, some have braved sanctions from the behemoth to turn out for their state teams instead.

Recently, Under-23 players faced the brunt of this. Railways fielded a team in the U-23 tournament, which meant that young employees, who would have otherwise turned out for state teams, were duty bound to register with Railways for the year. But with little chance of breaking into the senior team, they played just one tournament that year at what was a crucial time in their development.

Air India provided some much needed balance – and resistance – when they entered the fray in 1991. While they did not routinely offer permanent employment, they hired players, very often Under-19s, on annual contracts. With the likes of Pramila Bhatt, Smita Harikrishna, and later Rau, Anju Jain and Anjum Chopra, they offered healthy competition in the domestic circuit. "A fierce rivalry was born. Each side, while playing against the other, had a special kind of *khunnakh* (determination)," says Jhulan Goswami, who was one of the few to whom the airline offered a permanent job.

The effects of a healthy domestic rivalry were felt internationally as India enjoyed a period of unprecedented success. They won the New Zealand Women's Centenary Tournament in 1994-95, a tri-series featuring the hosts and Australia. "The Railways-Air India domestic rivalry helped us win that," insists Rau, who was captain then and starred in the final with 48 runs and three wickets. "The rivalry created so much pressure that we had a pool of 30 players simulating the pressures of international cricket."

India won six of the eight ODI bilateral series they played between 1994 and 2005 (the travesty is that so few were played), including a 2-1 away win over England in 1999. A Test win over South Africa was only their second in the format. Then came the 2005 Women's World Cup, where India reached their first – and till date only – final before losing out to Australia. Of the XI that played in that World Cup final, eight belonged to Railways and three were from Air India.

In 2006, when the BCCI took over women's cricket, Railways retained their place in the domestic set up, since they were playing in the Ranji Trophy. Air India, however, didn't. "The same rules that applied to the men were applied to the women. So the Air India team was disbanded," says Pendharkar. Those willing and able were picked up by Railways. It meant stable jobs for the cricketers, but also a great osmosis of talent back into Railways. Again, through no fault of their own, the railways created a domestic structure that was incredibly lopsided.

It is no surprise then that since 2006, when Railways have been largely unchallenged, the graph of the Indian women's team has been on the downturn. Finalists in 2005, India have failed to make the semi-finals of a world event since 2012. While there are multiple factors at play here, a one-sided domestic competition hasn't helped. "It is very important that the best players are challenged, or we stagnate as a team and as players," says Raj. "Then when we play internationals, it is a big upgrade we need to make."

On January 31, 2016, Edulji retired from Western Railway as the senior sports officer, one of the highest positions that an employee in the sports cadre can achieve. She followed in a family tradition of sorts, but no other Edulji has joined the state employer since her. "Now that's over," she says, wistful but proud. But for another generation of female cricketers, the relationship is unlikely to be over anytime soon.

The BCCI may have offered the women their first retainers, advertisers are out with their own contracts, and with avenues opening up in foreign leagues, the top female players are more financially secure than ever before. Yet, the railways connection with women's cricket is stronger than ever. What started with three teams now is eight. What began as employment has become a phenomenon. What was a means of livelihood is now a way of life.

A former India and Maharashtra bowler, Snehal Pradhan (@SnehalPradhan) now writes about the game from the sidelines.

A record fashioned by inexperience

MITHALI RAJ

More than 14 years have passed by since I made 214 – the highest individual score in Women's Test history at that time – against England in the Second and final Test in Taunton during the 2002 series, but, honestly, as a 19-year-old girl then I was too naïve to understand the significance of being a world-record holder. It was only much later that I realised what I had achieved.

We had failed to make it to the final of the triangular series and the First Test in Shenley was abandoned due to rain. Forced to stay indoors, Nooshin Al Khadeer, my best friend and roommate, and I watched on television Michael Vaughan's 197 against India at Trent Bridge. I wondered how he must have felt to spend so many hours at the crease and yet fall three runs short of a double-century. A week later, I found myself in a similar position.

It was our last game on the tour, and we wanted to end it on a high after losing almost everything. There was a big discussion before we played four frontline batters in the XI. When I walked out to bat on the second afternoon – India's Independence Day – we were 45 for 2 after England had made 329 in 128 overs. Thankfully, I was not the wicketkeeper! I was quite fresh when I took strike, and my immediate focus was to occupy the crease. We knew that the longer we batted, the easier it would be for us to control the game.

It was just my third Test, but the responsibility was huge because of the circumstances. It helped that I had good partnerships with Anjum (Chopra, the captain), Hemlata Kala and Jhulan (Goswami).

I can hardly remember how I got those runs, but I know I was wearing a black floppy hat and played with a BDM bat that weighed around 1.5kg – heavier than the bats of some of the male cricketers. I still have that bat. I did not know the mechanics of pacing an innings in Tests, and my entire focus was on the team's goal of batting for as long as possible.

I was unbeaten on 43 at stumps on the second day, but we lost three quick wickets next day and were 297 for 6. That is when Jhulan joined me in the middle, and played a big role in pushing me.

Mithali Raj during her 214 at Taunton, 2002: "When I felt tired, Jhulan made me look at the India flag and pushed me: 'We have to do it for the country.'" — *Getty Images*

Those days, the set-up was very amateurish, and there was hardly any money involved. We were all very raw, but the India flag at the ground was a big motivation. When I felt tired, Jhulan made me look at the flag and said, "We have to do it for the country."

I was not nervous in the 190s, and that's because I was unaware of the statistics. I did not know then that Sandhya Agarwal was India's highest individual scorer, having made 190 against England on the 1986 tour, but when I was on 208, Jyoti Joshi, our coach, sent a message through the twelfth man that I was two short of surpassing Karen Rolton's 209 not out made for Australia against England in 2001. I told myself, 'If I have reached so far, why can't I make two more runs?'

If I find myself in a similar situation today, there'll be so much running through my head that I may get out for 199. The irony of maturity! That I was new to international cricket and the opponents did not know much about my game also helped me.

Like the century on my ODI debut against Ireland in 1999, this knock, too, was an important one in my career. But, when you play such an innings so early on, you don't get to soak it in because your primary focus is on securing a spot in the team. Suddenly, the expectations increased.

My record stood till March 2004 when Pakistan's Kiran Baluch made 242 against West Indies in Karachi. No other batter, however, has scored a double-century after that. We are an elite club of six, and that's because there is hardly any Test cricket played. Since Baluch's knock, there have been only 16 Tests in over 12 years, and most of them have been one-off affairs. You need to give batters a few games in a row to get into the groove before expecting them to make double-centuries.

When I broke the record, I was too shy to lift my bat properly. I don't remember celebrating the achievement even though I was happy. I returned to the hotel, and called my father. Like always, he shifted my focus to the next goal. After that, I was too exhausted and just crashed on my bed. It was only when I returned to India that I felt I had done something special.

Mithali Raj (@M_Raj03) is India's most successful captain, and was Wisden India Cricketer of the Year 2015.

Homecoming

LISA STHALEKAR

Over the course of my international career, I have been fortunate enough to travel the world, meet amazing people and do the thing that I love best: play cricket.

Cricket is a global game, but there is one place where the following is fanatical. I had to wait three years after my debut for Australia before I was able to represent my country in India.

In December 2004, the Southern Stars had a seven-match one-day international series against India. It was the first time in 20 years that the Australian team had toured India and as soon as I walked out of the plane, India hit me right between the eyeballs.

Immediately, the smell of Indian spices, the warmth of the air and the choking humidity of Bangalore greeted me, yet there was a real sense of coming home. As someone born in India and having visited my grandmother in Mumbai throughout my childhood, India conjured happy memories for me. Arriving as part of the Australian team fulfilled one of my childhood dreams.

Back in 2004, the Indian Women's Cricket Association was not integrated with the BCCI, so our series ran on a shoestring budget compared to what players would receive now if they were to tour India – although Lisa Keightley did win a car once as Player of the Match.

The tour was extremely special as Belinda Clark became the first Australian female player to win 100 ODI caps and we won 4-3. The series will also be remembered for Leonie Coleman, our wicketkeeper, shattering her eye socket with a ricochet off the stumps. Of all my five tours to India, this was by far the most memorable. With all those milestones achieved on the subcontinent and the mishaps of the trip, including being caught up in the tsunami aftermath in Chennai, as a group we saw India in all its glory.

Apart from the smell of India that hits you, the other noticeable part is the incessant honking. Back home the sound of a car horn was to alert other drivers that they had done something wrong. Yet here in India it was a reminder to other cars or big trucks that you were close by so watch out as we come through. We got to witness

Special title: Lisa Sthalekar won the World Cup with Australia Women in 2013 in India. — *Getty Images*

all of that first hand, as we travelled by bus to all our locations. Both teams were on the same bus, which meant we watched Hindi movies the whole time.

Unlike my teammates over the years, I looked forward to the food. The curries, *dal*, *rotis* and *parathas*, *masala dosa*, *dahi puri*, *shrikhand* and *pedas*, just to name a small portion of the things I love. It certainly got my salivary glands in overdrive, in anticipation of the smorgasbord that awaited me every time I visited India. Most thought India was a great opportunity to lose weight, whereas I was resigned to the fact that I was going to put some on and enjoy what India had to offer me. Over time, I started to expose my friends to my favourite meals and while they will never get to the level of enjoyment I experience as the spices hit my mouth, they can at least have more than *naan* with vegemite.

Everyone else's suitcase was filled with food from home, whereas I had an empty bag: My other favourite pastime is shopping. There isn't anything that you can't get in India, and I have bought it all. I picked up jewellery, bed linen, pillow cases, traditional Indian clothes and even a coffee table that fit perfectly into my cricket coffin.

I love the colours splashed around, from the fabrics to the food, all delivered to you with a smile on the hosts' faces as they make your stay the most enjoyable experience.

While the food, the people and shopping excited me about India, as a cricketer, there was no other place in the world that challenged me more. Not only are you taken out of your comfort zone, in terms of food, sounds, crowds and your normal routine, the cricket too is fought on wickets that take some getting used to.

They say that Test cricket is the hardest format of the game because it 'tests' you physically and mentally. Given that only a very small portion of cricketers are honoured with that opportunity, the next best challenge for most is touring India.

As a spinner, I was licking my lips at the prospect of being able to turn the ball square on the subcontinent surfaces. However, the expectation that I put on myself to perform in the country of my birth probably wasn't the wisest to have on my first tour.

It wasn't until our next tour in 2007 that I was finally able to feel at home on the field. It was a quadrangular ODI series featuring the top four international teams. Funnily enough, the pitches in Chennai weren't the dust bowls we expected; they were fast bouncing tracks and while my bowling didn't stand out, I had one of my most successful tours with the willow.

The heat and humidity in Chennai was something that I never had experienced before, nor was I prepared for the monkeys gracing our field as they stalked the table that kept our snacks and lunch. During this series I got into the strange ritual of sleeping before I was required to bat. I would lie down on the physiotherapist's bed and would only wake up when I had to go in to bat. I guess I was trying to conserve energy in that heat and it seemed to work as I averaged 98.50 while top-scoring with 394 runs.

Following her retirement, Lisa Sthalekar is a part of IPL's commentary team. – *BCCI*

My final tour of India, which would also be my last for Australia, was the Women's World Cup in 2013. I couldn't have asked for a better ending. Not only were we based in the Taj Hotel in

Mumbai, my favourite hotel in the world, we beat West Indies in the final to win the trophy. The Southern Stars were again No. 1 in the world in all formats.

Personally there was something very gratifying, almost cyclical. Mumbai had been a place of very happy memories for me, almost my second home, and I was able to close a huge chapter of my life with World Cup glory in that same city.

India has always been a place that I have loved both on and off the field. To be able to share it with my teammates, friends and family is special.

The most exciting part is that there is still so much of India that I haven't explored and I look forward to discovering the hidden gems.

Since her international retirement after eight Tests, 125 ODIs and 54 T20Is for Australia and the unique ODI double of 1000 runs and 100 wickets, Lisa Sthalekar (@sthalekar93) has put her experience to use in the commentary box.

Watching, waiting

SHASHANK KISHORE

The 2012 Women's World T20 in Sri Lanka was tough on India. They extended their winless streak in the group stage with a one-run loss to Pakistan, who defended 98 to win their first match in the tournament's history. A crestfallen Mithali Raj fronted up to the press, but there was nobody listening. She was instructed by the lone cameraperson present to look left and right as if to suggest she was answering questions from different sections of the media. In truth, she was looking at empty seats, but for one journalist (this writer) and the cameraperson.

It was a sight she would have been used to – and I was to get familiar with. Ahead of that World T20 2012 campaign, MS Dhoni had been asked to address a hastily arranged pre-departure press conference hours before the men's flight from Chennai. Every seat was taken. In Bangalore, Raj, the women's team captain, turned up for a scheduled press meet after a month-long preparatory camp for India's Sri Lankan campaign. The media briefing room echoed her spikes. There couldn't have been a more glaring sign of the disparity between men's and women's cricket in the country.

It was shortly before the team's departure that I interviewed Raj for the first time. There was some apprehension, not because of the risk of courting controversy, but because the BCCI could create a problem. Permission had to be sought from the board to publish the interview, a harmless one that attempted to report on a team that was also competing for glory, that had made the semi-final of the two previous World T20s.

The board was in a state of flux in 2012. The absence of a travelling media manager with the women's team made it near impossible to speak to players unless you knew them personally. If you were a first-time journalist covering women's cricket, the chances of speaking to India's female cricketers were not very good.

When the team crashed out winless, Raj, subdued and guarded until then, suggested they needed a better mindset and approach, more matches and television coverage.

There have been at least 30 recorded press conferences and several

The spotlight's on them: Away from the limelight, India Women completed a historic Test win against England in 2014. Since then, the attention and scrutiny have only increased. — *Getty Images*

other informal media sessions addressed by her from then till the end of 2015. In most of those, variations of the question of what needed to be done to popularise women's cricket in India were put to her. Her response each time was the same: more opportunities and match-time. This was not because she isn't articulate, but because there wasn't anything new to talk about.

Then, in January 2016, ahead of India's tour of Australia, Raj was asked the same question. "An IPL-like league for women would go a long way in promoting the game in the country," she said. Her answer exuded optimism – and was a drastic change from the cliché of "more opportunities".

What triggered the change in tone? The overwhelming success of the inaugural Women's Big Bash League in Australia may have played a part, but the clincher might have been the introduction of annual retainers for top female cricketers, a decade after the Women's Cricket Association of India merged with the BCCI. The new dispensation led by Anurag Thakur, who inaugurated the first full-fledged women's academy in Dharamsala during his time as Himachal Pradesh Cricket Association chief, spelt out the need to chart a roadmap. To his credit, Thakur walked the talk within six months of assuming charge at the BCCI.

The mood in the team, too, was so different to the pall of gloom that hung over them in 2012, where Raj seemed burdened by the responsibility she carried not just as a captain but as a player.

At the time, the T20 format was not even pencilled into the domestic calendar – that happened only in 2015. Players found out about their inclusion at national camps only a day before they started.

The World Cup in 2013 promised bigger things. Sadly, things fell flat even before the tournament started. The team was made to stay at a budget hotel along Marine Drive in Mumbai, even as the other sides checked into luxury hotels. A television journalist spotted a group that "faintly resembled" India's women's team because of the blue jerseys, chatting with Diana Edulji, the former captain, by the road side. Soon after, the team was shifted to a five-star hotel.

If haggling for hotels wasn't enough, Wankhede Stadium was pronounced a no-go zone as preparations were on to host the Ranji Trophy final between Mumbai and Saurashtra. That meant the women had to train at the Police Gymkhana, a venue that can get slippery, particularly when it rains, and with patches of brown scattered amid dead grass. The prospect of the country's best female cricketers getting injured in the run-up to a world event was a real one.

If the players were offended, they didn't show it. They brushed off the issue, insisting they were focused on the tournament. One nonchalantly pointed out that they had seen worse.

Official apathy was one thing, but as problematic was the attitude of the media, which went beyond no-shows at press conferences. The team's issue with the hotel, for instance, went unreported even on the national news channel that employed that same journalist. Apparently, "women's cricket had no takers, and therefore no TRPs". At several tournaments, the press box was used by scribes to download music and movies while they waited for the men's games that followed.

In 2015, Raj was pleasantly surprised at being recognised as one of the *Wisden India Almanack*'s Cricketers of the Year. At the felicitation, she chose to put her team over herself. She was particularly vocal about how the treatment meted out to women's cricket would affect the younger generation coming through.

The big question a few years ago was: Who after Mithali and Jhulan Goswami? And that defined much of their performances as well. A little more than 24 hours after crashing out of the 2013 World Cup main draw, Raj came out and blasted Pakistan's bowlers in their seventh-place play-off game. Her century was a purist's delight, but it sent out a message to her team-mates that she still had to carry the batting even after all these years.

Now, thanks to a proactive BCCI, a more involved media and fan base, and of course the cricketers who are prepared to push their limits, there is optimism for the future. Most members of the current squad – many of them, noticeably from the outposts – believe the Test win over England in 2014, their first four-day game in eight years, was the game-changer. As memorable for me was the first ODI against New Zealand in Bangalore in 2015, when they choked their opponents with spin, backed by unorthodox field placements, to clinch a low-scoring thriller. A historic T20I series win in Australia in 2016, their first-ever of any kind against the defending World T20 champions, furthered hope for the players. Importantly, through it all, they managed to find women for a crisis during the tough times.

Two of those are Harmanpreet Kaur and Smriti Mandhana, the first Indians to feature in the Women's Big Bash League for Sydney Thunder and Brisbane Heat respectively. The warmth with which their path-breaking deals were received within the community was telling. An extension perhaps of the attention from the fans and the media from the World T20. If social media was any indication of sporting frenzy, India Women received as much backing as the men did. Nearly 9000 people trooped into Feroz Shah Kotla to watch India take on Pakistan. There were requests for selfies everywhere.

Harmanpreet summed it up superbly when she said, "For the first time at an ad shoot, I didn't have to introduce myself." The shoot in question was for an ad conceptualised by a leading sports apparel brand to promote women's empowerment by bringing together the top female athletes in the country. That, indeed, speaks volumes of how the sport has grown.

With the likes of Dipa Karmarkar, Sakshi Malik and PV Sindhu doing the country proud at the Rio Olympics, parents are slowly moving from wanting their girls to be 'fair and lovely' to taking up sport – cricket, fortunately, is one of these sports.

Shashank Kishore (@captainshanky) is a senior sub-editor with ESPNcricinfo.

A rallying belief: Old hands and youthful spirit came together as India Women completed their first series victory against Australia. — *Getty Images*

Stumbling blocks as stepping stones

ANANYA UPENDRAN

January 26, 2016. India's first international as a 'professional' team. They were chasing 141 against Australia at Adelaide Oval. They had not beaten the hosts in a T20 international since March 2012. They had never successfully chased over 127 against any opposition. The odds were stacked against them. Two years earlier, they might have folded under the pressure of chasing a sizeable total against the world champions. But there was something in the air that day. This Indian team believed.

When Mithali Raj was dismissed early in the chase, they did not panic, for they believed. When Smriti Mandhana smashed Jess Jonassen for a six over long on, they believed. When Veda Krishnamurthy swiped at every ball she faced to assert herself, they believed. When Harmanpreet Kaur carefully chose the moments to unleash her power, they believed. Even when Australia clawed their way back, they continued to believe.

As Anuja Patil faced Sarah Coyte with India needing three runs to beat Australia only for the second time in T20Is, the team fell into a huddle at the boundary. They were on the cusp of something great. When Patil stroked a half-volley through the covers and Rene Farrell failed to chase it down, the camera panned to the Indian dugout. It was pure elation. There were hugs, laughter, tears, singing and even some dancing, led by the ever enthusiastic Niranjana Nagarajan. Raj, who barely ever shows emotion on a cricket field, was beaming with pride. She had finally got this Indian team to believe.

India had, for at least six years, relied almost solely on the efforts of Raj and Jhulan Goswami. The two tirelessly carried the team on their shoulders, never complaining, never giving up. They absorbed all the pressure and allowed the younger players to blossom around them, cajoling them, inspiring them. This victory over the three-time World T20 champions, built on some special performances from the youngsters, was particularly heartening. It seemed a weight had been lifted: young India had finally arrived.

How had the team turned it around? After a disastrous 2013 World Cup campaign where they were knocked out in the first round, the team underwent a facelift. Having fallen behind the likes of even Sri Lanka and South Africa in development of talent and fitness, India were in need of a major shake up. Old hands bid adieu, promising youngsters took their places.

Over the next 12-15 months, results were inconsistent, but there were glimpses of growth and potential. Test match victories over England and South Africa (2014) helped build confidence, and the come-from-behind ODI series win against New Zealand (2015) could have only added to that.

Going into the tour of Australia, Raj's team certainly looked like the most stable unit to don the blue jersey in three years. The players had clearly defined roles, which allowed them to prepare appropriately, and competition for spots in the XI pushed them to improve. Their first contracts meant they had something to prove. And as they warmed up for the World T20 at home with limited-overs series whitewashes over Sri Lanka, it seemed the tournament was India's to win. For the first time, the women stood shoulder to shoulder with MS Dhoni's men in advertisements and promotions as the global extravaganza came to India.

But, after all the hype and expectation, it was something of an anti-climax as the hosts crashed out in the group stage after managing only one win. Against Pakistan, they were in a race against the elements, against England, they needed two wickets, against West Indies, they needed ten runs in the last over. When they were looking down the barrel you could see they held on to that self-belief, but it would be eroded by a lack of exposure to pressure situations.

Now, as the team faces another stern climb, they will have to believe again.

In the wake of India's exit, many questions were asked. There was greater media scrutiny than ever before. It seemed as though the country had finally opened its eyes to the women's team. As their Australian sojourn had been celebrated, so was their Indian summer derided – but even that criticism was a reflection of the great strides taken in the past year.

The year, in general, has shown that women's cricket in India is on its way up, not only in terms of results, but administration too. By introducing player contracts, increasing women's domestic match fees, telecasting the women's domestic T20 Super League matches and opening the doors for players to participate in foreign T20 leagues, the BCCI is taking steps in the right direction.

Playing in foreign leagues especially will allow Indian women valuable exposure to different playing environments, larger crowds and the weight of expectation. Some of West Indies' World T20 stars attributed their success to the experience of having played Australia's Women's Big Bash League, and that's precisely the boost India needs too.

The team has showed it is no longer scared of the big names. There is a fearlessness in the group that makes them exciting and unpredictable, but they must now learn to turn the surprises into consistency.

There is new-found professionalism, along with emphasis on raising fitness levels and fielding standards. The players take time off from work to train throughout the year instead of only two months before the season. They realise they are playing catch up to Australia, England, New Zealand, West Indies and even South Africa.

There is a stability stemming from clearly defined roles, which has come with consistency in selection. The players have been around for a while and not only do they understand their own game, but one another's as well.

Mandhana's rise as one of the best young batters in the world has been heartening; Veda's successful return to international cricket is another happy story; MD Thirushkamini's technique is strong; Harmanpreet has the skill, experience and aggression to take the Indian team forward – the batting is in good hands. The spin department, as is always the case with India, is rich with Poonam Yadav, Rajeshwari Gayakwad and Ekta Bisht at the top of their game, Deepti Sharma finding her feet in international cricket, and Gouher Sultana and Preeti Bose waiting in the wings. Shikha Pandey's performance in Australia and Nagarajan's success in England before that have shown that the country's pace bowling cabinet is not bare: there is hope after Goswami. Patil has probably been one of India's best finds. She can bowl, bat and field and has brought with her a cheekiness and inventiveness that the team desperately needs.

The rise of Sharma and R Kalpana is also testament to the talent flow from the junior circuit. Devika Vaidya, Meghana Sabbineni, Tanusree Sarkar and Sushree Pradhan have lit up age-group and senior tournaments with their all-round displays. Meanwhile, the old guard of Sultana, Karuna Jain, Mamtha Kanojia and Kavita Patil continue to stay solid in the senior circuit.

The standard of the domestic circuit has also improved. Although Railways still find a way to take home the silverware, they have had to survive recent scares, especially in T20s. Goa, Andhra and Baroda are making the right noises, while Hyderabad, Mumbai and Maharashtra have continued to improve.

2015-16 has shown that India have the ingredients in place to make a champion team. What they need is time, patience and support from their parent body. One hopes the World T20 was merely a stumbling block that becomes a stepping stone to bigger things. With the BCCI putting together a 'vision document' towards making India a champion team by 2020, the goal seems realistic.

As Harmanpreet says in that TV ad that seems to capture much of the present excitement, let's go!

Ananya Upendran (@a_upendran11) is an India A and Hyderabad all-rounder.

For joy, for respect

KARUNYA KESHAV

As far as playground insults go these days, "play like a girl" is in Trumpian territory.

Its absurdity as a slight lay exposed by the Sanias and Sainas, the Sindhus and Sakshis, who in 2016 India showed exactly what it meant to play like a girl.

The injustice of it was challenged at the senior national squash championship, where Deepika Pallikal ended her five-year boycott of the event to win the title and take home equal prize money as the men for the first time. "If I wanted [money], I would have played some other sport. It's all about respect," she had said.

The stereotypes and condescension those words carry were discredited at the Women's Kabaddi Challenge, the first two games of which, according to the Broadcast Audience Research Council of India, had more viewership than the 45 Euro 2016 football matches together. Two months later, PV Sindhu raised the bar, her Rio Olympics final against Carolina Marin becoming the most-watched non-cricket sporting event on Indian television ever.

Away on foreign shores, on and off the 22-yard strip, similar battles were won.

The kid gloves were off when coach Mark Robinson exchanged sentiment for fitness, and encouraged in England a fearlessness and freedom and awareness that dragged the women's game into this decade. And, he was clear: "It isn't the same as men's cricket … it is a different game."

The inaugural Women's Big Bash League had already helped in acquiring a taste for a different game. Record crowds – and television coverage that hit six times the projected average – added fuel to Cricket Australia's argument for a stand-alone Women's World T20 in 2020. "Having the ICC Women's World Twenty20 as a stand-alone event means we can hold it in stadiums that we can fill, put on TV at prime-time and ensure it has the space to be promoted as the main event, away from the shadow of the men's game," said David Peever, chairman of Cricket Australia.

Competition from other sports for gaining and retaining tal-

Catch 'em young: Give every wide-eyed cricket-crazy girl more female role models.
— *ICC/Getty Images*

ent meant improved contracts and better-than-ever funding. NSW Breakers secured landmark sponsorship to become the first fully professional women's domestic cricket team. ICC took on board criticism and promised the same stay and travel for men and women at global events.

All this – the techniques, the crowds, the approval – had been the future dreamed of for the Indian women's cricket team in the 40-odd years since its inception. The future is here; but, it would seem, the Indian team isn't quite on board yet.

Since their appearance in the Women's World Cup 2005 final, the ladies in blue have been playing catch up. Every year offers more to celebrate – but players and fans are still kept waiting: for a future in which there are big-ticket wins and an environment to enable it.

India need a domestic set-up that is robust: a schools cricket pathway that throws up a steady stream of contenders for the higher levels; Under-16 competitions at the state level that are obligatory rather than advised; more stable jobs for sportspersons so that Railways aren't the only viable employer and their win at the senior tournaments is not a given; more matches, so a national aspirant doesn't have to wait months between chances to prove herself; more days games, so technique withstands the test of time and slam-bang cricket; a busier A or academy set-up to make the jump from domestic to international less stark; bigger audiences, so the inexperience isn't debilitating on the global stage; and access to well-trained support staff with the skills and professionalism to guide them there. Players, past and present, agree: India needs more girls playing more competitive cricket. The drain that occurs when young women in their mid-20s quit the game, just as they're reaching their cricketing peak, must be reversed.

The glass half-full says it is a matter of time, it will come. At the time of writing, BCCI have set the women's committee the task of putting together a vision document. And, historically, vision isn't something the pioneers of women's cricket in the country have lacked – they, after all, brought the World Cup carnival to large crowds in India five years before the men won theirs.

But in the half-empty portion is a reflection of society and the work to be done. It's an administrative issue to ensure for women a livelihood in cricket – it's everyone's job to show them it's an acceptable one.

Tell a girl she can pick cricket over studies, and you might get a Smriti Mandhana. Definitely don't tell her her training shorts are too short, or that she'll get dark playing in the sun – if she listens, she may never be a Mithali Raj. Give every wide-eyed cricket-crazy girl more female role models – it worked for Jhulan Goswami, who saw Belinda Clark do a lap of honour at her beloved Eden Gardens. In these pages, Shantha Rangaswamy speaks of the 25,000-odd people who came to watch India's first win – be one making up those kinds of numbers at the next match.

Dismissing sexism as 'locker-room talk' and 'just a joke' tells a girl she doesn't belong. A certain Jamaican with his 'big bats' innuendo, 'I named my baby Blush' trolling and 'Sorry if you're offended' non-apology is a symptom, not the sole problem.

Cricket is about joy. It is also about respect. The future of Indian women's cricket is only worth talking about if it has both.

Karunya Keshav (@kuks) is senior copy editor at Wisden India.

INDIA WOMEN ALL-TIME XI

Raj to lead Edulji, David et al

PURNIMA RAU

Picking an all-time India XI is an exhausting experience. It hasn't been done in print before, and there were a lot of gifted cricketers I had to put aside during this introspection.

Since India have played only 36 Tests so far, I combined the three formats to come up with what would be my best all-time XI. Anju Jain and Smriti Mandhana open the batting, and the middle order comprises Mithali Raj, Shubhangi Kulkarni, Rumeli Dhar and Harmanpreet Kaur. Dhar along with Jhulan Goswami and Shantha Rangaswamy are my pacers. Pramila Bhatt, Diana Edulji and Neetu David handle the spin department alongside Kulkarni and Harmanpreet. The biggest strength of this side is its all-round ability. Kulkarni, Rangaswamy and Kaur are among the most versatile cricketers of their respective eras, and Goswami has a reputation for her big-hitting abilities. The very popular Chanderkanta Aheer will be the twelfth woman of the side. Raj leads the team featuring eight captains.

Anju Jain (wicketkeeper)
(2170 runs, 104 dismissals in 73 matches. HS: 110)
Diminutive, quiet and letting her gloves speak very often, Jain is the ideal wicketkeeper-opener. Highly experienced with four World Cup appearances, her work ethic and humility are the secret to an international career that lasted eight years. More than a decade after her last game, she remains among the top ten wicketkeepers the world has seen in both Tests and ODIs.
Off the field: She loves to watch horror films at night.

Smriti Mandhana
(1047 runs in 42 matches. HS: 102)
The unassuming Mandhana is a hugely talented southpaw who burst into the scene with a match-winning 51 on her Test debut against England in 2014. Having been on a few tours with her, I noticed that aggression mixed with caution is her approach. She has a mature

104 dismissals in 73 matches: Anju Jain was the ideal wicketkeeper-opener.
— *Getty Images*

head on her young shoulders, as was displayed when she made a double-century for Maharashtra Under-19 in a domestic game a few years ago. There are still areas like strike rotation that she needs to work on, but Mandhana will be the workhorse around whom India's success will be built in the future.
Off the field: She loves to cook and watch cookery shows.

Mithali Raj (captain)
(7452 runs in 233 matches. HS: 214)
The best batter in the history of Indian women's cricket, Raj is an automatic choice at No. 3. Her grace, exquisite timing and subtle aggression make Raj a purist's delight. The only Indian to have made a double-century in Tests, her staggering statistics will put any opposition on the back foot. She remains one of two players, along with Charlotte Edwards, with a tally of more than 5000 ODI runs. Very open minded, she embraces new ideas and is never afraid of taking a risk. She will lead this team with flair and panache. In a career spread over 17 years, Raj has been an excellent role model.
Off the field: She is a voracious reader.

Shubhangi Kulkarni

(1047 runs and 98 wickets in 46 matches. HS: 118, BBM: 7-57)

Kulkarni is a stylish all-rounder. Her gentle, compassionate ways on and off the field, and her uncanny knack of accumulating runs and picking up wickets with her slow leg-spin makes her a perfect fit in any team. She recorded a five-wicket haul in India's maiden Test against West Indies in Bangalore in 1976, and then marked her captaincy debut with 118 against England in Wetherby in 1986. The only Indian with a double of 700 runs and 60 wickets in Tests, Kulkarni's influence as an administrator has also been significant.

Off the field: Her talk on visualisation and the book *The Inner Game of Golf* she gifted me when I was young made a huge impact on me.

Perfect all-rounder: Rumeli Dhar bowled medium-pace, was an elegant batter and a great fielder. – *Getty Images*

Rumeli Dhar

(1328 runs and 81 wickets in 97 matches. HS: 92, BBM: 4-19)*

At her peak, Dhar was a gifted all-rounder who could play all the shots in the book. The field was her stage. She bowled medium-pace with a fluid action, batted with consummate ease and was a great fielder in all positions, especially in the slips. Her 37 catches is the third most by an Indian in ODIs, and she remains among the country's top ten bowlers. Dhar's medium-pace will be the ideal foil for the new-ball pair of Goswami and Rangaswamy.

Off the field: Rumi, as she is fondly called, is my favourite poet.

Harmanpreet Kaur

(2512 runs and 33 wickets in 118 matches. HS: 107, BBM: 9-85)*

A dynamo, Harmanpreet's game awareness makes it a delight to watch her when in flow. Controlled aggression and dominance in all three departments are the hallmarks of her game. A bridge between two generations of cricketers, she can effortlessly turn a game around from any position. She is one of only three Indians with two or more ODI centuries against her name, and she was in the forefront when India recorded their first-ever series win over Australia in the T20Is in 2016. As a bowler, she can switch her style depending on the team's requirement.

Off the field: Her love for dancing is infectious in the dressing room. She has contributed in improving Goswami's moves.

Shantha Rangaswamy
(1037 runs and 33 wickets in 35 matches. HS: 108, BBM: 6-114)

Rangaswamy was a legend, very clever in the way she changed gears according to the situation. She was India's first Test captain, and led the team to victory in only their fourth game, against West Indies in Patna in 1976. Her gentle inswingers and massive hits to the fence drew crowds to the stadium. She became the first Indian to score a Test century, against New Zealand in Dunedin in 1977. The intelligence of Rangaswamy, still the joint second-most capped Test captain, played a big role in establishing India's credentials on the world stage.

Off the field: She has a keen interest in astrology.

Jhulan Goswami
(260 wickets and 1540 runs in 211 matches. BBM: 10-78, HS: 69)

The sight of Goswami, the only Indian to have taken ten wickets in a Test, tearing into bowl gets the hearts of batters and spectators alike racing. Among the fastest on the circuit, her height and accuracy have taken her to the second spot in the list of wicket-takers in ODIs. Her genuine match-winning abilities, both with bat and ball in all conditions, make her a potent force. By pursuing her craft passionately for 14 years now at the highest level, Goswami has motivated many young girls in India to become pace bowlers.

Off the field: Jhulu, as she is addressed popularly, makes the best cardamom tea ever.

Pramila Bhatt
(37 wickets in 27 matches. BBM: 5-60)

Bhatt is one of the best off-spinners of all time, though often underrated. Her ability to hold one end up allowed bowlers like me to take wickets from the other end. She infused a lot of energy and incisive-

ness in the team, and was the poster girl of Indian cricket during her time. She always played within the spirit of the game. She was a good batter and a fielder too. In my first Test as captain against New Zealand in Nelson in 1995, she came out to bat at No. 8 and dug in for 168 minutes to make 42 and take us to a comfortable position.
Off the field: Pammi loved her music, her fitness, not to forget her comb and mirror – a pleasurable pain for a roommate like me.

Diana Edulji
(109 wickets in 54 matches. BBM: 6-64)
Edulji is a legend with a never-say-die attitude, who hated to lose. A left-arm spinner who could land the ball consistently at the same spot, she is still the third-highest wicket-taker in Tests, behind only England's Mary Duggan and Australia's Betty Wilson. In fact she is one of only six bowlers with 60 or more Test wickets. Edulji was the go-to bowler everytime India needed a breakthrough. Her knowledge about the rules and laws of the game make her invaluable to any team. She hit the winning runs in India's maiden Test triumph.
Off the field: She loves eating tandoori chicken and kebabs.

Neetu David
(182 wickets in 107 matches. BBM: 9-90)
Neetu was god's gift to Indian cricket. Her mesmerising left-arm spin wove a web around the batters. A tormentor of all opponents, her orthodox action was poetry in motion. She was at her best in the 1995 Test against England in Jamshedpur. Her spell of 8 for 53 in the second innings meant that India were left to chase only 128. But we lost by two runs in what was my last assignment as captain.
Off the field: Neetu's plaits were her trademark, and she could have umpteen cups of masala chai any time of the day.

Twelfth woman: Chanderkanta Aheer
(934 runs and 4 catches in 36 matches)
Aheer was a specialist cover-point fielder who could break the stumps at will. A fantastic runner, she had a wonderful arm. It resulted in many run-outs from the boundary. Sadly, statistics don't record those occurrences. A team person to the core, she was quiet and unruffled.
Off the field: Like me, Chander was the only cricketer to use an RNS Larsons kit throughout her playing career.

India Women all-time XI

Record within reach: Jhulan Goswami has her sights set on becoming the leading wicket-taker in women's ODIs. — *Getty Images*

*Records of the current players – Smriti Mandhana, Mithali Raj, Harmanpreet Kaur and Jhulan Goswami – are as on November 9, 2016.

India coach and a former captain, Purnima Rau is among the finest all-rounders of the game.

STATISTICS

Tests

Span	Matches	Won	Drawn	Lost
1976-2014	36	5	25	6

Against	Span	Matches	Won	Drawn	Lost
Australia	1977-2006	9	0	5	4
England	1986-2014	13	2	10	1
New Zealand	1977-2003	6	0	6	0
South Africa	2002-2014	2	2	0	0
West Indies	1976-1976	6	1	4	1

Highest total: 467 against England (Taunton, August 2002)
Lowest total: 65 against West Indies (Jammu, November 1976)
Largest victory (wickets): By ten wickets against South Africa (Paarl, March 2002)
Largest victory (innings): By an innings and 34 runs against South Africa (Mysore, November 2014)

Most runs: Sandhya Agarwal – 1110 in 13 matches
Highest individual score: Mithali Raj – 214 against England (Taunton, August 2002)
Most hundreds: Sandhya Agarwal – 4
Most runs in a series: Shantha Rangaswamy – 381 against West Indies (1976-77)

Most wickets: Diana Edulji – 63 in 20 matches
Best bowling (innings): Neetu David – 8-53 against England (Jamshedpur, November 1995)
Best bowling (match): Jhulan Goswami – 10-78 against England (Taunton, August 2006)
Most five-wicket hauls (innings): Shubhangi Kulkarni – 5
Most wickets in a series: Shubhangi Kulkarni – 23 against West Indies (1976-77)

Most dismissals (wicketkeeper): Anju Jain – 23 in 8 matches
Most dismissals (innings): Fowzieh Khalili – 5 against Australia (Perth, January 1977) and Anju Jain – 5 against England (Shenley, July 1999)
Most dismissals (match): Anju Jain – 7 against England (Shenley, July 1999)
Most dismissals in a series: Nilima Jogalekar – 10 against Australia (1983-84)
Most catches (fielder): Sudha Shah – 21 in 21 matches
Most catches in a series: Sudha Shah – 9 against West Indies (1976-77)

Highest partnership: 275 by Thirush Kamini and Poonam Raut for 2nd wicket against South Africa (Mysore, November 2014)

Most-capped player: Sudha Shah – 21
Most matches as captain: Shantha Rangaswamy – 12
Most successful captain: Mithali Raj – 3 wins in 6 matches

Caps (82): Sandhya Mazumdar, Shobha Pandit, Sudha Shah, **Shantha Rangaswamy**, **Shubhangi Kulkarni**, Susan Itticheria, Sharmilla Chakraborty, Fowzieh Khalili, Ujwala Nikam, **Diana Edulji**, Behroze Edulji, Runa Basu, Jyotsna Patel, Rajeshwari Dholakia, Uthpala Chakraborty, Gargi Banerji, Vrinda Bhagat, Shashi Gupta, **Nilima Jogalekar**, Anjali Pendharker, Sujata Sridhar, **Sandhya Agarwal**, Arundhati Ghosh, Rita Dey, Sandra Braganza, Mithu Mukherjee, Lopamudra Bhattacharj, Rajani Venugopal, Neeta Kadam, Minoti Desai, V Kalpana, Rekha Punekar, Manimala Singhal, **Pramila Bhatt**, Seema Desai, Sangita Dabir, Neetu David, Laya Francis, Anju Jain, Chanderkanta Aheer, Renu Margrate, Rishijae Mudgel, **Purnima Rau**, Arati Vaidya, **Anjum Chopra**, Shyama Shaw, Kalyani Dhokarikar, Hemlata Kala, Deepa Marathe, Rupanjali Shastri, Jhulan Goswami, Bindeshwari Goyal, Arundhati Kirkire, **Mamatha Maben**, **Mithali Raj**, Amrita Shinde, Jaya Sharma, Sunita Singh, Sulakshana Naik, Sunetra Paranjpe, Nooshin Al Khadeer, Amita Sharma, Rumeli Dhar, Karuna Jain, Sravanthi Naidu, Asha Rawat, Monica Sumra, Devika Palshikar, Nidhi Buley, Preeti Dimri, Reema Malhotra, Ekta Bisht, Thirush Kamini, Harmanpreet Kaur, Smriti Mandhana, N Niranjana, Shikha Pandey, Poonam Raut, Shubhlakshmi Sharma, Rajeshwari Gayakwad, Poonam Yadav, Sushma Verma.

Test wins

India beat West Indies by five wickets, 1976
Moin-ul-Haq Stadium, Patna, November 17-19: West Indies 127 in 60.2 overs (Yolande Geddes-Hall 32*, Vivalyn Latty-Scott; Diana Edulji 3-24, Shubhangi Kulkarni 3-43) and 88 in 76.3 overs (Gloria Gill 34; S Kulkarni 4-14, Sharmila Chakraborty 3-17) lost to **India** 161/9 dec in 100.5 overs (Fowzieh Khalili 58, Shantha Rangaswamy 32; V Latty-Scott 3-65, Pat Whittaker 2-13) and 55/5 in 26 overs (D Edulji 20*; Nora St Rose 3-21) by five wickets.

India beat South Africa by ten wickets, 2002
Boland Bank Park, Paarl, March 19-22: India 404/9 dec in 168 overs (Anjum Chopra 80, Hemlata Kala 64; Cindy Eksteen 2-64, Crizelda Brits 2-91) and 13/0 in 1.3 overs beat **South Africa** 150 in 83.3 overs (Josephine Barnard 31, Magdalena Terblanche 25; Deepa Marathe 3-14, Neetu David 2-41) and 266 in 142.2 overs (f/o) (Alison Hodgkinson 77, Sunnette Viljoen 71; Hemlata Kala 3-18, Jhulan Goswami 3-63) by ten wickets.

India beat England by five wickets, 2006
County Ground, Taunton, August 29-September 1: India 307 in 148.1 overs (Anjum Chopra 98, Mithali Raj 65; Isa Guha 4-61. Holly Colvin 2-52) and 98/5 in 29.2 overs (Karu Jain34, M Raj 22*; H Colvin 2-26) beat **England** 99 in 51 overs (Charlotte Edwards 26; Jhulan Goswami 5-33, Rumeli Dhar 2-16) and 305 in 160.2 overs (f/o) (C Edwards 105, Caroline Atkins 68; J Goswami 5-45, Nooshin Al Khader 3-58) by five wickets.

India beat England by six wickets, 2014
Sir Paul Getty's Ground, Wormsley, August 13-16: England 92 in 41.2 overs (Sarah Taylor 30; Nagarajan Niranjana 4-19, Shubhalakhshmi Sharma 2-12) and 202 in 96.3 overs (Jennifer Gunn 62*, S Taylor 40; Jhulan Goswami 4-48, Shikha Pandey 2-33, Ekta Bisht 2-33) lost to **India** 114 in 64.2 overs (N Niranjana 27, Smriti Mandhana 22; Jenny Gunn 5-19, Kate Cross 3-29) and 183/4 in 95.3 overs (S Mandhana 51, Mithali Raj 50*; Kate Cross 3-42) by six wickets.

India beat South Africa by an inning and 34 runs, 2014
Gangothri Glades Cricket Ground, Mysore, November 17-19: India 400/6 in 148.4 overs

(Thirush Kamini 192, Punam Raut 130; Sunette Laubser 3-90) beat **South Africa** 234 in 110 overs (Mignon du Preez 102, Trisha Chetty 56; Harmanpreet Kaur 5-44, Rajeshwari Gayakwad 4-54) and 132 in 78.2 overs (f/o) (T Chetty 35, Chloe-Lesleigh Tryon 30*; H Kaur 4-41, Jhulam Goswami 2-21) by an inning and 34 runs.

ODIs

Span	Matches	Won	Lost	Tied	No result
1978-2016	225	117	103	1	4

Against	Span	Matches	Won	Lost	Tied	No result
Australia	1978-2016	41	8	33	0	0
Bangladesh	2013-2013	3	3	0	0	0
Denmark	1993-1993	1	1	0	0	0
England	1978-2014	61	25	34	0	2
International XI	1982-1982	3	3	0	0	0
Ireland	1993-2012	9	9	0	0	0
Netherlands	1993-2000	3	3	0	0	0
New Zealand	1978-2015	44	16	27	1	0
Pakistan	2005-2013	8	8	0	0	0
South Africa	1997-2014	10	5	4	0	1
Sri Lanka	2000-2016	24	22	1	0	1
West Indies	1993-2013	18	14	4	0	0

Highest total: 298/2 against West Indies (Dhanbad, February 2004)
Lowest total: 26 against New Zealand (St Saviour, July 2002)
Largest victory: By 207 runs against Pakistan (Dambulla, May 2008)

Most runs: Mithali Raj – 5301 in 164 matches
Highest individual score: Jaya Sharma – 138* against Pakistan (Karachi, December 2005)
Most hundreds: Mithali Raj – 5

Most wickets: Jhulan Goswami – 175 in 148 matches
Best bowling: Mamatha Maben – 6-10 against Sri Lanka (Kandy, April 2004) ,
Most five-wicket hauls: Neetu David & Jhulan Goswami – 2

Most dismissals (wicketkeeper): Anju Jain – 81 in 62 matches
Most dismissals (innings): V Kalpana – 6 against Denmark (Slough, July 1993)
Most catches (fielder): Jhulan Goswami – 51 in 148 matches
Highest partnership: 258* by Reshma Gandhi and Mithali Raj for 1st wicket against Ireland (Milton Keynes, June 1999)

Most-capped player: Mithali Raj – 164
Most matches as captain: Mithali Raj – 87

Most successful captain: Mithali Raj – 49 wins in 87 matches

Caps (116): Gargi Banerji, Runa Basu, Lopamudra Bhattacharj, Sharmilla Chakraborty, **Diana Edulji**, Nilima Jogalekar, Fowzieh Khalili, Sandhya Mazumdar, Shobha Pandit, Kalpan Paropkari, Anjali Sharma, Susan Itticheria, **Shubhangi Kulkarni**, Ujwala Nikam, Sudha Shah, Rajeshwari Dholakia, Vrinda Bhagat, Anjali Pendharker, **Shantha Rangaswamy**, Sujata Sridhar, Rita Dey, Arundhati Ghosh, Shashi Gupta, Rekha Godbole, Sandra Braganza, Sandhya Agarwal, Sirupa Bose, Manimala Singhal, Rita Patel, Neeta Kadam, Rajani Venugopal, Minoti Desai, Rekha Punekar, V Kalpana, **Pramila Bhatt**, Laya Francis, **Anju Jain**, **Chanderkanta Aheer**, **Mamatha Maben**, **Purnima Rau**, Sangita Dabir, **Anjum Chopra**, Neetu David, Smitha Harikrishna, Renu Margrate, Rishijae Mudgel, Arati Vaidya, Kalyani Dhokarikar, Manju Nadgoda, Shyama Shaw, Lissy Samuel, Purnima Choudhary, Deepa Marathe, Reshma Gandhi, Hemlata Kala, **Mithali Raj**, Rupanjali Shastri, Sunita Singh, Arundhati Kirkire, Kavita Roy, **Jhulan Goswami**, Jaya Sharma, Nooshin Al Khadeer, Amrita Shinde, Bindeshwari Goyal, Sulakshana Naik, Sunetra Paranjpe, Amita Sharma, **Rumeli Dhar**, Reema Malhotra, Babita Mandlik, Mamatha Kanojia, Beas Sarkar, Diana David, Karuna Jain, Varsha Raffel, Monica Sumra, Asha Rawat, Sravanthi Naidu, Devika Palshikar, Preeti Dimri, Nidhi Buley, Thirush Kamini, Rajeshwari Goyal, Seema Pujare, Priyanka Roy, Gouher Sultana, Anagha Deshpande, Snehal Pradhan, N Niranjana, **Harmanpreet Kaur**, Poonam Raut, Soniya Dabir, Samantha Lobatto, Neha Tanwar, Veda Krishnamurthy, Ekta Bisht, Shilpa Gupta, Archana Das, Madhuri Mehta, Shubhlakshmi Sharma, Mona Meshram, Rasanara Parwin, Ritu Dhrub, Swagatika Rath, Smriti Mandhana, Poonam Yadav, V Sneha Deepthi, Rajeshwari Gayakwad, Sneh Rana, VR Vanitha, Shikha Pandey, Sushma Verma, Deepti Sharma, RV Kalpana, Preeti Bose.

T20Is

Span	Matches	Won	Lost	Tied	No result
2006-2016	66	33	33	0	0

Against	Span	Matches	Won	Lost	Tied	No result
Australia	2008-2016	12	3	9	0	0
Bangladesh	2013-2016	8	8	0	0	0
England	2006-2016	11	2	9	0	0
New Zealand	2009-2015	7	2	5	0	0
Pakistan	2009-2016	7	5	2	0	0
South Africa	2014-2014	1	1	0	0	0
Sri Lanka	2009-2016	10	7	3	0	0
West Indies	2011-2016	10	5	5	0	0

Highest total: 163/5 against Bangladesh (Bangalore, March 2016)
Lowest total: 62 against Australia (Billericay, June 2011)
Largest victory: By 79 runs Bangladesh (Sylhet, March 2014)

Most runs: Mithali Raj – 1488 in 59 matches
Highest individual score: Harmanpreet Kaur – 77 against Bangladesh (Sylhet, March 2014)

Most fifty-plus scores: Mithali Raj – 8

Most wickets: Jhulan Goswami – 45 in 53 matches
Best bowling: Jhulan Goswami – 5-11 against Australia (Visakhapatnam, March 2012)
Most five-wicket hauls: Jhulan Goswami & Priyanka Roy – 1

Most dismissals (wicketkeeper): Sulakshana Naik – 31 in 31 matches
Most dismissals (innings): Sulakshana Naik (twice), Karuna Jain, Sushma Verma – 4
Most catches (fielder): Harmanpreet Kaur – 22 in 61 matches

Highest partnership: 130 by Poonam Raut and Thirush Kamini for 1st wicket against Bangladesh (Vadodara, April 2013)

Most-capped player: Harmanpreet Kaur – 61
Most matches as captain: Mithali Raj – 32
Most successful captain: Mithali Raj – 17 wins in 32 matches

Caps (50): Anjum Chopra, Rumeli Dhar, **Jhulan Goswami**, Hemlata Kala, Reema Malhotra, Sulakshana Naik, **Mithali Raj**, Amita Sharma, Noor Al Khadeer, Preeti Dimri, Monica Sumra, Thirush Kamini, Jaya Sharma, Gouher Sultana, Seema Pujare, **Harmanpreet Kaur**, Latika Kumari, Priyanka Roy, Poonam Raut, Soniya Dabir, Babita Mandlik, Diana David, Samantha Lobatto, Ekta Bisht, Anagha Deshpande, Veda Krishnamurthy, Snehal Pradhan, Neha Tanwar, Archana Das, Mamatha Kanojia, Shubhlakshmi Sharma, Madhuri Mehta, Mona Meshram, N Niranjana, Anuja Patil, Rasanara Parwin, Ritu Dhrub, V Sneha Deepthi, Swagatika Rath, Smriti Mandhana, Poonam Yadav, Sushma Verma, Rajeshwari Gayakwad, VR Vanitha, Sneh Rana, Karuna Jain, Sravanthi Naidu, Shikha Pandey, Devika Vaidya, Deepti Sharma.

* The names of those who have captained India are in bold
*Records as on November 9, 2016

PART THREE
Domestic review

Ranji giants on the prowl: Mumbai's march to their 41st Ranji Trophy title was the story of an inspired team and a combined effort. — *Joshua Veernathan*

INDIAN CRICKET

Changing times

SIDHANTA PATNAIK

The swiftness with which the Board of Control for Cricket in India conducted more than 900 matches, resulting in 2100 play days over six months across senior and age-group levels for both men and women was remarkable considering the turmoil in Indian cricket ahead of the domestic season.

More than four months after Anil Kumble's technical committee – in their last responsibility before Sourav Ganguly's team took charge – recommended a revamped points structure in Ranji Trophy to encourage more outright results, the proposal remained undiscussed as BCCI's working committee meeting in Kolkata on August 28 had to be adjourned. N Srinivasan's presence at the meeting, as president of Tamil Nadu Cricket Association, was the point of contention. Srinivasan had been ordered by the Supreme Court in March 2014 to step aside as BCCI president because of the 2013 Indian Premier League spot-fixing scandal.

After 51 of the 108 Ranji league matches in 2014-15 had ended in a draw, the technical committee felt that instead of awarding three points to the team that took the first-innings lead, bonus points for sides that made 300 runs or picked up eight wickets in 85 overs would make the games more interesting. It would have been a radical step towards creating a 'win-first' culture, forced teams to think outside their comfort zone and made games more competitive.

BCCI also had to indirectly police power fights in Jammu & Kashmir Cricket Association, Rajasthan Cricket Association and Delhi and Districts Cricket Association. Then, the incumbent president, Jagmohan Dalmiya, passed away just 11 days before the start of the season. Fortunately, BCCI, as always, was in autopilot mode before the first ball was bowled.

The board presented a pragmatic picture and designed the season to aid India's preparations for the Under-19 World Cup in Bangladesh and the World T20 (men's and women's) at home. The Ranji schedule was split into two, each played on either side of the winter, so that bad weather did not hamper prospects in north India. The Duleep Trophy was shelved for a season and the focus was on limited-overs contests to give India regulars more practice and a fair chance for fringe cricketers to state their case in a busy T20 season. For the first time, the Deodhar Trophy was not played on a zonal basis. India A beat India B – both teams picked by the national selectors – in the final, with Gujarat, the Vijay Hazare Trophy champions, making up the third side.

Similarly, an Under-19 Challenger Trophy to facilitate selection for the Youth World Cup, a three-day senior inter-zonal, and Under-23 inter-state and inter-zonal women's 50-over tournaments were held for the first time. Then, the Super League stage of the inter-state women's T20 tournament was televised.

The Vijay Hazare Trophy and Syed Mushtaq Ali Trophy were pencilled in before the IPL auctions to give players a chance to impress franchises. As in the Ranji Trophy, states were divided into groups for the league phase based on seeding and not zones. For the first time since BCCI started conducting domestic tournaments in 1934-35, there was no zonal event at the senior men's level. It was a sweeping change in every sense, and could potentially free up youngsters from 'zonal politics'.

The board announced the fixtures almost three months ahead of the season. It was a pleasant change.

In such transformational times, it was only fitting that a youngster, in only his second season, was the biggest talking point. His 1414 first-class runs, a strike-rate of 92.70 in 11 Ranji matches for Mumbai, including a match-winning century in the final against Saurashtra on a seaming track in Pune, made Shreyas Iyer hot property. His tally of 1321 runs, which had four centuries and seven fifties, put him second on the list of highest run-getters in a Ranji season, behind VVS Laxman's 1415 for Hyderabad in 1999-2000, and made him one of *Wisden India Almanack*'s Cricketer of the Year.

Mumbai's 41st Ranji title, coming after Karnataka's dominance for two seasons, had other contributors too. Akhil Herwadkar (879) and Suryakumar Yadav (788) were among the top four run-getters, Siddesh Lad made an impressive 88 after they were 268 for 9 in the final, Shardul Thakur crossed the 40-wicket mark for the second successive season, and Dhawal Kulkarni exploited the conditions intelligently. The leadership unit of Chandrakant Pandit, who returned as the side's coach after 12 seasons, Aditya Tare, the captain, and seniors like Abhishek Nayar looked after the team atmosphere, and Sachin Tendulkar's occasional inputs pepped up the boys.

Assam's first-ever Ranji semi-final appearance, achieved on the back of Arun Karthik's 802 runs, and a combined tally of 85 wickets for Krishna Das and Arup Das, was the season's other major story. They beat Rajasthan, Haryana, who along with Andhra were relegated to Group C, Delhi and Punjab, and took the first-innings lead in the season-opener against Karnataka, who struggled to find the right composition after defending an unprecedented treble of Ranji, Vijay Hazare and Irani Cup last season.

Mumbai, who won six of their 11 matches and remained undefeated, and Assam were refreshing to watch as they built their game on flair and attack, but many other teams depended on rank turners at home to propel their case.

In fact, a total of seven league matches ended within two days, 17 finished in three days and teams were bowled out within 100 on 14 occasions, with Odisha's 37 against Bengal in Kalyani on a pitch described as a "paddy field" being the lowest. A total of four spinners were among the top five wicket-takers, a change from 2014-15 when only one spinner was in the top ten after BCCI's unofficial directive to state associations to leave 3-8mm grass on pitches.

The desperation among state associations to make ends meet is not new in domestic cricket, but sharp criticism, most notably from Rahul Dravid, the coach of India A and Under-19, left BCCI with little option but to host all 2016-17 Ranji games at neutral venues.

Ravindra Jadeja benefitted from the conditions to finish with 38 wickets in the first four matches, putting Saurashtra on track for a knockout berth from Group C and hastening his successful return to the Indian team for the Test series against South Africa. Jalaj Saxena fell short by a scalp to become the second player with a season-record of 500 runs and 50 wickets while guiding Madhya Pradesh to the semi-final. Shahbaz Nadeem was the first bowler since 2006-07 to take 50 wickets in a season, as

Wasim Jaffer, seen here in a 2008 match for India, became the first player to cross 10,000 Ranji runs. – *Getty Images*

Jharkhand became the second team from Group C to earn promotion.

In between all this, Wasim Jaffer, in his maiden season as a professional with Vidarbha, became the first player to cross the 10,000-run mark in Ranji history.

Curtains were drawn on a gripping season of first-class cricket on the final day of the Irani Cup when Faiz Fazal, Sudip Chatterjee, Karun Nair, Sheldon Jackson and Stuart Binny scripted Rest of India's successful record chase of 480 against Mumbai.

In white-ball cricket, MS Dhoni, Shikhar Dhawan, R Ashwin, Ishant Sharma and Yuvraj Singh added colour to the Vijay Hazare Trophy. Jasprit Bumrah's accurate yorkers gave Gujarat the title and hastened his international debut. Hardik Pandya and Suresh Raina stood out in the Syed Mushtaq Ali Trophy where Uttar Pradesh beat Baroda in the final.

Railways dominated the women's circuit although Andhra's Meghana Sabbineni, who chose cricket over badminton, made a splash in different tournaments.

Jay Bista hogged the headlines for becoming the first player to score 1000-plus runs in one season of Under-23 CK Nayudu Trophy during Mumbai's successful outing. Abhishek Sharma's 1200 runs and 57 wickets in seven matches gave Punjab the Under-16 Vijay Merchant Trophy.

After Iyer set the tone in the first half, Virat Kohli's breathtaking batting in the IPL during Royal Challengers Bangalore's journey to the final, where they lost to Sunrisers Hyderabad, kept everyone hooked till the end of the season.

Kohli, the first player to be the Cricketer of the Year twice, is at the centre of an exciting phase in Indian cricket and is backed by a receptive BCCI. The Duleep Trophy, on its return to the calendar in 2016-17, was played between India Blue, the winners, India Red and India Green with the pink ball under lights at Greater Noida, and all the four games attracted decent crowds. It was, however, the appetizer. No matter what the verdict is regarding the feasibility of neutral venues in Ranji Trophy, both logistically and cricket wise, critics cannot point fingers at BCCI for not wanting to experiment.

See round-wise reviews page 282.

Ghost stories and champions' lore

ABHISHEK NAYAR

When Aditya Tare lifted the 2015-16 pre-season Buchi Babu Trophy in Chennai, I had a sinking feeling. Mumbai had never won the Buchi Babu and the Ranji Trophy in the same year. I reminded Adu about this trivia and he said, "Nayaree, we will make it happen this time and lift the Ranji Trophy as well." This young team did it with an innings win over Saurashtra in the final in Pune, and we finally broke the jinx.

We were going through a tough period when Adu took over the captaincy in the middle of the 2014-15 season. With a little luck on our side and a first-innings lead over Karnataka, the eventual champions, we entered the knockout. We beat Delhi convincingly after conceding the first-innings lead in the quarter-final, and then lost to Karnataka in the semi-final because of one bad session. But, the manner in which we came back gave us hope and belief. Pravin Amre, the coach that season, said that finally we had got a team that could win the Ranji Trophy again. He was not there in the dressing room when we finally lifted the trophy, with Chandrakant Pandit the new coach, but a lot of credit goes to Amre and Tare for shepherding the team through a tricky phase, and to the selectors, who kept faith in a young side.

We have always believed that a team is built much before entering the field of play, and effort was put in that direction. Pandit and Tare gave me the responsibility of keeping the team together, and I would like to believe that my efforts counted towards building a sense of brotherhood and fun. From going to hill stations and pushing cars up the hill, to unwieldy dancing competitions and rolling the dice at casino nights, we did it all. The most important outing was perhaps to Khandala before the season. We came back as not just 15 players but a close-knit team of 30 ready to take on the world. We learnt a lot about one another. A painting relay showed us there was serious scarcity of talent and sharing ghost stories told us who the *darpoks* or scaredy-cats were, and suddenly the house became haunted only for them! The football and golf were fun experiences, and daring people to do crazy stuff broke the barriers.

You expect most players to do well in any champion team and that was exactly the case with this Mumbai unit. But, the big differentiator was the remarkable and aggressive batting of Shreyas Iyer. We were confident of his ability since he made his Mumbai debut last season, but what gave our campaign a real push and left us delighted were his 1321 runs at an average of 73.38 – the most by a Mumbai batsman in a season, and only behind VVS Laxman's 1415 in the 82-year history of Ranji Trophy.

The numbers speak highly of his talent and mental toughness, but I am also privy to his high level of commitment. I remember once we went to Zaheer

Diet of fun and hard work: Team dinners and unconventional training routines did their bit in bringing together the Mumbai side. — *Photos courtesy Abhishek Nayar*

Khan's fitness studio after a session of yoga and a sumptuous meal of *poha* for another tough workout. We were in our third and final set of hard-core circuit training, and Shreyas was on the treadmill. He was panting hard, and something did not seem right. He threw up as soon as he finished the set. Concerned, I asked him why he did not stop the treadmill beforehand. His reply: "I couldn't as I hadn't finished my set." That to me was an example of how far he was willing to push himself to achieve his goals.

Yet, Mumbai was not just about one guy. I once heard that if you want your team to play like lions on the field, make sure you treat them the same off it. It may be clichéd, but most of us went about expressing ourselves on the pitch like we do off it. That for me reiterates the fact that the work we put in during the offseason brought out the best during the season. Akhil Herwadkar's well-crafted innings were gritty, just like his personality, Suryakumar Yadav was at his flamboyant best with some swashbuckling knocks, Siddhesh Lad was Mumbai's man of crisis, stepping up when others failed, and Tare himself played responsibly, always putting the team first.

Our bowlers stepped up too. Last year, we had analysed that our bowling needed to be strengthened, so Onkar Salvi, our bowling coach, put in hours with them and the efforts paid off. Dhawal Kulkarni, Shardul Thakur, Vishal Dabholkar, Iqbal Abdulla and Balwinder Singh Sandhu Jr all got wickets at important junctures. They clicked beautifully as a unit.

Dhawal had been going through a lean phase. He was bowling in great areas but neither was the ball moving as much as he'd liked, nor was he picking up wickets. The bowling coach, along with Sachin Tendulkar – we were lucky to have the master in our corner – worked on Dhawal's wrist position while running in to bowl and loading. It took only one game for things to fall in place for DK: the next game, he picked up five against Baroda with some great seam bowling. He then did not let go of the good length spot and was like a real estate tycoon who had purchased that bit of turf.

Shardul went after the batsmen like a bull, and Ballu, like the musician he is, got the batsmen dancing to his tunes when the surface offered some assistance. When the pitch turned, Vishal and Iqbal too chipped in.

With everyone making their contribution, the unit gelled game after game. When Siddhesh and Ballu put on that match-changing 103-run stand for the tenth-wicket in the second innings of the final, it was like an opera singer hitting a high note.

What everyone saw on the field was only one side of the story. Pandit wanted us to be more disciplined because he thought that would help the team tighten up its game and be focused when it came to seizing key moments. To achieve that, we meditated every morning of a match for ten minutes to develop a calm mind and facilitate clarity in thinking. Initially, it was tough, but within a week it became a habit that we did not want to let go of.

Pandit's renewed approach since becoming the coach is also noteworthy. Having worked with him at the Under-19 level many years ago, I saw a huge change in how he handled this team with calm and a composed demeanour. It was refreshing and the boys responded well. It also helped that Tendulkar kept track of our progress and spent hours with the players at the nets. Rohit Sharma too came along for team-building activities even though there was no guarantee he would play a game in the season. It showed us how every player, big or small, cared for the team.

And then there was Tare's leadership skills. Leading a Mumbai team filled with big names is never easy, especially when you haven't won a title for two seasons. But, Tare did it like a seasoned pro. He never seemed to get affected by how the team fared and kept his composure in circumstances where most would have lost their cool. Despite the injury that forced him to miss the quarter-final against Jharkhand, he insisted on travelling with the team. He earned everyone's respect, and that made things easier.

We went through a gamut of emotions on and off the field, but when Shardul knocked the stump off the ground and we got the Ranji Trophy in our hands we felt nothing but happiness and pride. A fifth Ranji Trophy for me and a first for eight blokes in the dressing room.

Even as we bathed in the glory and celebration of Mumbai's 41st Ranji title, we realised that it was yet another start. We have to go out there again and prove to everyone that this is not a young team anymore, but a seasoned champion side that is here to represent Mumbai for a long time and counter challenges together.

An all-rounder, Abhishek Nayar (@abhisheknayar1) has won the Ranji Trophy five times with Mumbai.

Mumbaikars make most of practice

Suryakumar Yadav's 248 and Vishal Dabholkar's 6 for 48 in the league stages of the Buchi Babu Memorial Tournament stood out as Mumbai Cricket Association XI lost just one game on their way to the championship. In Bangalore, Iqbal Abdulla topped the bowling charts with 28 wickets to give Dr DY Patil Sports Academy the Dr (Capt) K Thimmappiah Memorial Cricket Tournament title. The pre-season forms of Mumbai cricketers held them in good stead throughout their successful Ranji campaign.

Dr (Capt) K Thimmappiah Memorial Tournament
Final: M Chinnaswamy Stadium, Bangalore, August 14-16: Karnataka State Cricket Association XI 184 in 73.5 overs (J Suchith 30, Pavan Deshpande 25; Iqbal Abdulla 4-42, Swapnil Singh 3-63) and 92 in 33 overs (Vinay Kumar 25, S Aravind 24; I Abdulla 5-39, Swapnil 4-33) lost to **Dr DY Patil Sports Academy** 307 in 72.1 overs (Yogesh Takawale 110, Shubham Ranjane 44; Vinay 2-44, S Aravind 2-54) by an innings and 31 runs.

Winners: Dr DY Patil Sports Academy

Dr DY Patil Sports Academy with the Dr (Capt) K Thimmappiah Memorial Tournament trophy in Bangalore. — *KSCA*

Buchi Babu Invitational Tournament
Final: MA Chidambaram Stadium, Chepauk, Chennai, August 31-September 1: Tamil Nadu Districts XI 163 in 74 overs (NS Chaturvedi 60, Xavier Sargunam 28, Antony Dhas 28;

Vishal Dabholkar 6-46, Abhishek Nayar 2-24) lost to **Mumbai Cricket Association XI** 166/6 in 45.2 overs (Aditya Tare 53, Akhil Herwadkar 46; P Sakthi 3-76) by four wickets.

Winners: Mumbai Cricket Association XI

Moin-ud-Dowlah Gold Cup

Final: Rajiv Gandhi International Stadium, Uppal, Hyderabad, September 14-16: India Cements 299 in 84.5 overs (Abhinav Mukund 154, Dinesh Karthik 82; Sudeep Tyagi 3-42, Chama Milind 2-54) and 37/1 in 20 overs drew with **Hyderabad Cricket Association XI** 207 in 71.2 overs (Akshath Reddy 101; L Balaji 3-39, L Vignesh 3-83). India Cements won on the basis of first-innings lead.

Winners: India Cements

Ranji Trophy

Young blood takes domestic giants to 41

Group A

Vidarbha

Akshay Wakhare enjoyed a landmark season, his off-spin netting him 49 wickets. — *Wisden India*

It was a season of progress for S Badrinath's men, who topped the heavyweight group. Faiz Fazal stood out with two centuries and three fifties, and Wasim Jaffer became the first batsman to score 10,000 runs in the history of the competition, but it was their spinners who were the trump cards. Off-spinner Akshay Wakhare finished as the season's joint-third highest wicket-taker, while Aditya Sarwate, the left-arm spinner, was next with 33 scalps. The bowling group took all 20 wickets in four matches, finishing with the most outright wins in the group. Vidarbha were able to skate by despite four totals below 200 in the group stages, but a two-month break before the quarter-final didn't do them any favours as Saurashtra drubbed them inside three days. Badrinath did not renew his contract for 2016-17, and Baroda signed up Ambati Rayudu as their third professional. *Nisha Shetty*

Results: Took first-innings lead against Odisha (home), lost to Delhi by ten wickets (away), conceded first-innings lead to Karnataka (away), beat Assam by three wickets (home), beat Maharashtra by 82 runs (home), lost to Bengal by 105 runs (away), beat Rajasthan by eight wickets (home), beat Haryana by an innings and 31 runs (home), lost to Saurashtra by an innings and 85 runs in the quarter-final (neutral).
Best batsman: Faiz Fazal (559 runs, 8 matches)
Best bowler: Akshay Wakhare (49 wickets, 9 matches)
Debutants (3): Aditya Shanware, Jitesh Sharma, Aditya Sarwate.

*** Overall first-class records ***
(P 251, W 39, L 87, D 125)
Maiden match: Drew with Uttar Pardesh (December 14-16, 1957, Nagpur)
Highest team total: 583/9 dec v Saurashtra (Nagpur, 2014-15)
Lowest team total: 40 v Rajasthan (Jaipur, 1977-78)
Highest run-getter: Faiz Fazal – 4263 in 59 matches

Highest individual score: 221 by Samir Gujar v Madhya Pradesh (Nagpur, 1991-92)
Most 100s: Faiz Fazal – 9
Highest wicket-taker: Pritam Gandhe – 314 in 85 matches
Best bowling (innings): 8-39 by Arun Ogiral v Madhya Pradesh (Nagpur, 1967-68)
Best bowling (match): 13-162 by Akshay Wakhare v Gujarat (Surat, 2014-15)
Most dismissals (wicketkeeper): Amit Deshpande – 113 (102ct+11st) in 45 matches
Most dismissals (wicketkeeper/innings): 7 by Sadashiv Iyer v Uttar Pradesh (Allahabad, 1997-98)
Most catches (fielder): Faiz Fazal – 66
Highest partnership: Samir Gujar/Suhas Phadkar – 315 for fifth wicket v Uttar Pradesh (Nagpur, 1988-89)
Most capped player: Pritam Gandhe – 85

Bengal

After avoiding relegation by a whisker in 2014-15, Bengal, without the experienced duo of Laxmi Ratan Shukla and Saurasish Lahiri, qualified for the knockouts. Sudip Chatterjee – one of three batsmen with four centuries in the season – was their best performer, with his 351-minute 145 against Karnataka standing out. Manoj Tiwary, who was involved in an ugly altercation with Gautam Gambhir, made two hundreds, four fifties and led the side to two outright wins. A pre-season camp in Colombo, time with VV Laxman and Muttiah Muralitharan, and the hiring of Pragyan Ojha as a professional boosted their prospects. Eager to resurrect his international career, Ojha took 36 wickets, his highest in a Ranji season. His partnership with Ashok Dinda was best showcased in a must-win game on an underprepared pitch at Kalyani. On what their opponents called a "paddy field", they bowled unchanged for 19.2 overs to dismiss Odisha for 37. On the same track, Abhimanyu Eashwaran made a gritty 88 and 39 and put Bengal in command.
Himanish Bhattacharjee

Results: Conceded first-innings lead to Karnataka (away), took first-innings lead against Rajasthan (home), took first-innings lead against Delhi (away), took first-innings lead against Haryana (away), beat Vidarbha by 105 runs (home), took first-innings lead against Maharashtra (away), beat Odisha by 133 runs (home), took first-innings lead against Assam (away), lost to Madhya Pradesh by 355 runs in the quarter-final (neutral).
Best batsman: Sudip Chatterjee (735 runs, 9 matches)
Best bowler: Ashok Dinda, Pragyan Ojha (36 wickets, 9 matches)
Debutants (7): Naved Ahmed, Aamir Gani, Pankaj Shaw, Pramod Chandila, Mukesh Kumar, Sayan Ghosh, Anurag Tiwari.

*** Overall first-class records ***

(P 395, W 149, L 67, D 179)
Maiden match: Lost to Australians by nine wickets (December 27-29, 1935, Calcutta)
Ranji wins (2): 1938-39, 1989-90
Highest team total: 760 v Assam (Calcutta, 1951-52)
Lowest team total: 58 v Haryana (Rai, 1976-77)
Highest run-getter: Arun Lal – 5823 in 65 matches
Highest individual score: 323 by Devang Gandhi v Assam (Guwahati, 1998-99)
Most 100s: Pankaj Roy – 21

Highest wicket-taker: Utpal Chatterjee - 403 in 95 matches
Best bowling (innings): 10-20 by Premangsu Chatterjee v Assam (Jorhat, 1956-57)
Best bowling (match): 15-109 by Premangsu Chatterjee v Madhya Pradesh (Calcutta, 1955-56)
Most dismissals (wicketkeeper): Sambaran Banerjee – 154 (126ct+28st) in 58 matches
Most dismissals (wicketkeeper/innings): 6 by Sambaran Banerjee v Punjab (Calcutta, 1988-89)
Most catches (fielder): Manoj Tiwary – 71
Highest partnership: Wriddhiman Saha/Laxmi Ratan Shukla – 417 for sixth wicket v Assam (Kolkata, 2010-11)
Most capped player: Laxmi Ratan Shukla – 115

Assam

Their resilience and poor weather on the final day of the league stages gave Assam a draw against Bengal after following on, and took them to the knockouts. Then, Arup Das and Syed Mohammad, egged on by the team's special centre-pitch practice in Vapi to get reacquainted with the red ball after two months of limited-overs matches, produced career-best performances for an outright win over Punjab. Assam had made it to their maiden semi-final.

Right at the start of the season, Sanath Kumar, the coach before Sunil Joshi replaced him for 2016-17, aimed to take the first-innings lead over defending champions Karnataka. Once Syed, Amit Verma and Arun Karthik, who batted with maturity on difficult pitches to be the season's third-highest run-getter, made that possible, Assam recorded many firsts, like a win against Delhi and Krishna Das's 50-wicket haul. *Sidhanta Patnaik*

Results: Took first-innings lead against Karnataka (home), beat Rajasthan by an innings and 152 runs (home), lost to Odisha by eight wickets (away), lost to Vidarbha by three wickets (away), beat Haryana by six wickets (away), beat Delhi by five wickets (home), took first-innings lead against Maharashtra (away), conceded first-innings lead to Bengal (home), beat Punjab by 51 runs in the quarter-final (neutral), lost to Saurashtra by ten wickets in the semi-final (neutral).
Best batsman: Arun Karthik (802 runs, 10 matches)
Best bowler: Krishna Das (50 wickets, 10 matches)
Debutants (2): Rahul Hazarika, Wasiqur Rahman.

*** Overall first-class records ***

(P 257, W 44, L 125, D 88)
Maiden match: Lost to United Provinces by an innings and 97 runs (December 17-19, 1948, Shillong)
Highest team total: 684/7 dec v Tripura (Guwahati, 1991-92)
Lowest team total: 32 v Bihar (Patna, 1971-72)
Highest run-getter: Dheeraj Jadhav – 3256 in 44 matches
Highest individual score: 257 by Zahir Alam v Tripura (Guwahati, 1991-92)
Most 100s: Dheeraj Jadhav – 12
Highest wicket-taker: Arlan Konwar - 204 in 66 matches
Best bowling (innings): 9-52 by Gautam Dutta v Tripura (Guwahati, 1991-92)
Best bowling (match): 14-96 by Gautam Dutta v Tripura (Guwahati, 1991-92)
Most dismissals (wicketkeeper): Kunal Saikia – 121 (105ct+16st) in 44 matches

Season of firsts: Assam's win over Delhi, their first over the seven-time champions, triggered frenetic celebrations. — *Special arrangement*

Most dismissals (wicketkeeper/innings): 8 by Samarjit Nath v Tripura (Guwahati, 2001-02)
Most catches (fielder): Tarjinder Singh – 63
Highest partnership: Zahir Alam/Lalchand Rajput – 475 for second wicket v Tripura (Guwahati, 1991-92)
Most capped player: Arlen Konwar – 66

Delhi

Delhi crumbled at the business end of the season for the second consecutive time. Table-toppers before their last league game, they conceded first-innings lead to Karnataka and were knocked out after Vidarbha, Bengal and Assam did what they had to do to qualify. Even then, Gautam Gambhir and Vijay Dahiya did a good job of holding the team together and grooming youngsters. Dahiya had been reappointed as coach after Ajay Jadeja made himself unavailable for the first match and then quit following differences of opinion with DDCA members. The departure of Virender Sehwag, Mithun Manhas and Rajat Bhatia, who had a combined tally of 256 matches for Delhi, added to the drama – as did the selectors dropping Ishant Sharma from the initial squad because he "did not respond to calls", before doing a volte-face. Despite DDCA's well-documented administrative apathy, Delhi reached the Vijay Hazare Trophy final. They started 2016-17 on a fresh note with KP Bhaskar's appointment as coach. *Himanish Bhattacharjee*

Results: Conceded first-innings lead to Rajasthan (away), beat Vidarbha by ten wickets (home), beat Haryana by four wickets (home), conceded first-innings lead to Bengal (home), took first-innings lead against Odisha (away), beat Maharashtra by nine wickets (home), lost to Assam by five wickets (away), conceded first-innings lead to Karnataka (away).
Best batsman: Nitish Rana (557 runs, 8 matches)
Best bowler: Manan Sharma (35 wickets, 8 matches)
Debutants (7): Mohit Ahlawat, Nitish Rana, Sarang Rawat, Rishabh Pant, Suboth Bhati, Pulkit Narang, Dhruv Shorey.

*** Overall first-class records ***

(P 436, W 180, L 60, D 196)
Maiden match: Lost to United Provinces by an innings and 99 runs (December 8-9, 1934, Agra)
Ranji wins (7): 1978-79, 1979-80, 1981-82, 1985-86, 1988-89, 1991-92, 2007-08
Irani wins (3): 1979-80 (shared), 1980-81, 1989-90
Highest team total: 721 v Bengal (Delhi, 1988-89)
Lowest team total: 37 v United Provinces (Agra, 1934-35)
Highest run-getter: Mithun Manhas – 7986 in 127 matches
Highest individual score: 312 by Raman Lamba v Himachal Pradesh (Delhi, 1994-95)
Most 100s: Ajay Sharma – 31
Highest wicket-taker: Madan Lal – 313 in 97 matches
Best bowling (innings): 9-31 by Madan Lal v Haryana (Delhi, 1979-80)
Best bowling (match): 14-122 by Maninder Singh v Punjab (Patiala, 1981-82)
Most dismissals (wicketkeeper): Puneet Bisht – 216 (209ct+7st) in 63 matches
Most dismissals (wicketkeeper/innings): 7 by Puneet Bisht v Baroda (Vadodara, 2009-10)
Most catches (fielder): Aakash Chopra – 102
Highest partnership: Ravi Sehgal/Raman Lamba – 464 for first wicket v Himachal Pradesh (Delhi, 1994-95)
Most capped player: Mithun Manhas – 127

Karnataka

After a rare treble defence in 2014-15, Karnataka failed to find the right composition and ended empty-handed. Robin Uthappa shared wicketkeeping responsibilities with CM Gautam in matches, eyeing a national comeback, and this hampered the team spirit. KL Rahul and Stuart Binny, away on India duty, were unavailable for most of the season, Manish Pandey was laid low by a finger injury and the pacers couldn't make an impact, barring HS Sharath's hat-trick against Haryana. Unfortunately, none of the youngsters seized their chances. Uthappa made 160, 148 and 148 in three consecutive games, equalling Rahul Dravid's tally of 17 centuries to go joint-second on the list for the state. This brightened Karnataka's chances, but a loss to Maharashtra when they needed at least a first-innings lead halted their three-year streak of 37 first-class matches without a loss.

Roshan Thyagarajan

Best batsman: Robin Uthappa (759 runs, 8 matches)
Best bowler: Vinay Kumar (24 wickets, 8 matches)
Results: Conceded first-innings lead to Assam (away), took first-innings lead against Bengal (home), took first-innings lead against Vidarbha (home), conceded first-innings lead to Haryana (home), beat Rajasthan by 92 runs (away), beat Odisha by an innings and 64 runs (home), took first-innings lead against Delhi (home), lost to Maharashtra by 53 runs (away).
Debutant (1): David Mathias

*** Overall first-class records ***

(P 427, W 190, L 64, D 173)
Maiden match: Lost to Madras by an innings and 23 runs (November 4, 1934, Madras)
Ranji wins (8): 1973-74, 1977-78, 1982-83, 1995-96, 1997-98, 1998-99, 2013-14, 2014-15
Irani wins (6): 1974-75, 1983-84, 1996-97, 1998-99, 2013-14, 2014-15
Highest team total: 791/6 dec v Bengal (Calcutta, 1990-91)

Lowest team total: 28 v Bombay (Bangalore, 1951-52)
Highest run-getter: Brijesh Patel – 6635 in 88 matches
Highest individual score: 337 by KL Rahul v Uttar Pradesh (Bangalore, 2014-15)
Most 100s: Brijesh Patel – 26
Highest wicket-taker: Sunil Joshi – 489 in 119 matches
Best bowling (innings): 9-72 by BS Chandrasekhar v Kerala (Bijapur, 1969-70)
Best bowling (match): 16-99 by Anil Kumble v Kerala (Thalassery, 1994-95)
Most dismissals (wicketkeeper): CM Gautam – 226 (215ct+11st) in 66 matches
Most dismissals (wicketkeeper/innings): 6 by Thilak Naidu v Andhra (Mysore, 2008-09)
Most catches (fielder): Manish Pandey – 94
Highest partnership: Sanjay Desai/Roger Binny – 451* for first wicket v Kerala (Chikmagalur, 1977-78)
Most capped player: Sunil Joshi – 119

Rajasthan

Questions over the legality of Lalit Modi's status as RCA president forced BCCI to form an ad-hoc committee and run the show for the second consecutive season. Unsure of things, Robin Bist, the team's most dependable batsman, left for Himachal Pradesh. The void was partly filled by Rajat Bhatia, who joined as a professional from the fourth game and finished with 290 runs and ten wickets. Pankaj Singh took 16 wickets in Rajasthan's wins in the last two games to help avoid relegation, but injury kept him out for the rest of the season. Aniket Choudhary, the left-arm seamer first spotted by Greg Chappell, led the attack well in Pankaj's absence, but Nathu Singh's emergence was Rajasthan's biggest positive. Impressed by his pace after he took 7 for 87 against Delhi on debut, the selectors named him in India Board President's XI against the touring South Africans.

7-87 on debut: Nathu Singh's pace caught the eye of national selectors and Mumbai Indians. – *RCA*

Sidhanta Patnaik

Results: Took first-innings lead against Delhi (home), lost to Assam by an innings and 152 runs (away), conceded first-innings lead to Bengal (away), conceded first-innings lead to Maharashtra (home), lost to Karnataka by 92 runs (home), lost to Vidarbha by eight wickets (away), beat Haryana by nine wickets (away), beat Odisha by two wickets (home).
Best batsman: Ashok Menaria (612 runs, 8 matches)
Best bowler: Aniket Choudhary (25 wickets, 7 matches)
Debutants (4): Nathu Singh, Ajay Singh, Siddharth Dobal, Manender Singh.

*** Overall first-class records ***

(P 316, W 87, L 86, D 143)
Maiden match: Lost to Services by an innings and 173 runs (December 8-10, 1951, Ajmer)
Ranji wins (2): 2010-11, 2011-12
Highest team total: 641/7 dec v Maharashtra (Nasik, 2010-11)
Lowest team total: 51 v Orissa (Jaipur, 2015-16)
Highest run-getter: Vineet Saxena – 6371 in 101 matches
Highest individual score: 301* by Aakash Chopra v Maharashtra (Nasik, 2010-11)
Most 100s: Hanumant Singh/Vineet Saxena – 15
Highest wicket-taker: Pankaj Singh – 310 in 72 matches
Best bowling (innings): 10-78 by Pradeep Sunderam v Vidarbha (Jodhpur, 1985-86)
Best bowling (match): 16-154 by Pradeep Sunderam v Vidarbha (Jodhpur, 1985-86)
Most dismissals (wicketkeeper): Rohit Jhalani – 204 (188ct+16st) in 64 matches
Most dismissals (wicketkeeper/innings): 7, Dishant Yagnik v Saurashtra (Rajkot, 2005-06)
Most catches (fielder): Vineet Saxena – 81
Highest partnership: Robin Bist/Ashok Menaria – 398 for third wicket v Railways (Delhi, 2011-12)
Most capped player: Vineet Saxena – 101

Maharashtra

After two good seasons where they played the final and semi-final, Maharashtra finished seventh on the table. A monumental batting effort against Haryana and the win against Karnataka in the last league game, built on half-centuries from Ankit Bawne and Rahul Tripathi and a disciplined bowling effort, were interspersed with collapses against Vidarbha and Delhi. The pace trio of Anupam Sanklecha, Samad Fallah and Shrikant Mundhe, protagonists in 2013-14 and 2014-15, did not strike regularly, with only Mundhe touching the 30-wicket mark. Akshay Darekar, their lead spinner, played just two games because of injury and Kedar Jadhav failed to convert starts and had an average of 29.40. Maharashtra signed up Shrikant Kalyani as their new coach for 2016-17 in place of David Andrews, the Australian who had success in different roles over the last few seasons. *Himanish Bhattacharjee*

Results: Took first-innings lead against Haryana (home), took first-innings lead against Odisha (away), took first-innings lead against Rajasthan (away), lost to Vidarbha by 82 runs (away), lost to Delhi by nine wickets (away), conceded first-innings lead to Bengal (home), conceded first-innings lead to Assam (home), beat Karnataka by 53 runs (home).
Best batsman: Ankit Bawne (505 runs, 8 matches)
Best bowler: Shrikant Munde (30 wickets, 8 matches)

*** Overall first-class records ***

(P 374, W 89, L 66, D 219)
Maiden match: Drew with Bombay (September 28-30, 1934, Poona)
Ranji wins (2): 1939-40, 1940-41
Highest team total: 826/4 v Kathiawar (Poona, 1948-49)
Lowest team total: 39 v Nawanagar (Jamnagar, 1941-42)
Highest run-getter: Surendra Bhave – 6543 in 79 matches
Highest individual score: 443* by Bhausaheb Nimbalkar v Kathiawar (Poona, 1948-49)
Most 100s: Surendra Bhave – 26

Highest wicket-taker: Iqbal Siddiqui – 259 in 64 matches
Best bowling (innings): 9-35 by Vasant Ranjane v Saurashtra (Khadakvasla, 1956-57)
Best bowling (match): 13-58 by Sayajirao Dhanawade v United Provinces (Kanpur, 1948-49)
Most dismissals (wicketkeeper): Rohit Motwani – 179 (167ct+12st) in 61 matches
Most dismissals (wicketkeeper/innings): 6 by Vishant More v Mumbai (Mumbai, 2007-08)
Most catches (fielder): Surendra Bhave – 107
Highest partnership: Kamal Bhandarkar/Bhausaheb Nimbalkar – 455 for second wicket v Kathiawar (Poona, 1948-49)
Most capped player: Surendra Bhave – 79

Odisha

Natraj Behera marked his return to captaincy with an unbeaten 255 against Haryana as Odisha posted a total in excess of 500 for the first time since 2006-07. Govinda Poddar made three centuries, and Basant Mohanty crossed the 40-wicket mark for the second consecutive season. As a team though, Odisha swung between extremes to just avoid relegation. The win against Assam in a low-scoring thriller after conceding the lead proved crucial in the final analysis. Odisha ended their campaign after being bowled out for their second-lowest score of 37 against Bengal on an underprepared pitch in Kalyani, which their coach called a "paddy field", and a loss against Rajasthan after dismissing them for 51 for a 100-run lead. The team's fickle temperament came under scrutiny with various past players speaking off record about the urgent need to revamp the system. *Karthik Lakshmanan*

Results: Conceded first-innings lead to Vidarbha (away), conceded first-innings lead to Maharashtra (home), beat Assam by eight wickets (home), conceded first-innings lead to Delhi (home), lost to Karnataka by an innings and 64 runs (away), took first-innings lead against Haryana (away), lost to Bengal by 133 runs (away), lost to Rajasthan by two wickets (away).
Best batsman: Govinda Poddar (555 runs, 8 matches)
Best bowler: Basant Mohanty (41 wickets, 8 matches)
Debutants (3): Rajesh Dhuper, Amit Das, Ranjit Singh.

*** Overall first-class records ***
(P 281, W 62, L 103, D 116)
Maiden match: Lost to Bihar by 356 runs (December 10-12, 1949, Jamshedpur)
Highest team total: 671/6 dec v Bengal (Baripada, 2001-02)
Lowest team total: 35 v Bihar (Patna, 1958-59)
Highest run-getter: Shiv Sundar Das – 6105 in 88 matches
Highest individual score: 300* by Shiv Sundar Das v Jammu & Kashmir (Cuttak, 2006-07)
Most 100s: Pravanjan Mullick – 18
Highest wicket-taker: Debasis Mohanty – 337 in 82 matches
Best bowling (innings): 9-52 by Sushil Kumar Prasad v Tripura (Agartala, 1990-91)
Best bowling (match): 15-89 by Sushil Kumar Prasad v Tripura (Agartala, 1990-91)
Most dismissals (wicketkeeper): Haladhar Das – 140 (130ct+10st) in 43 matches
Most dismissals (wicketkeeper/match): 9 by Gautam Gopal v Assam (Cuttack, 1997-98)
Most catches (fielder): Rashmi Ranjan Parida - 75
Highest partnership: Shiv Sundar Das/Sanjay Raul - 436 for third wicket v Bengal (Cuttack, 1997-98)
Most capped player: Shiv Sundar Das – 88

Vintage display: Virender Sehwag, who moved from Delhi to Haryana, was a favourite of local crowds. — *Special arrangement*

Haryana

Aniruddh Chaudhary's tweet about the appointment of Virender Sehwág as Haryana's captain after his move from Delhi generated some buzz. There was a 92 against Maharashtra on his state debut and 136 against Karnataka during a 206-run stand with Jayant Yadav – according to Jayant, the partnership included Sehwag needing help humming the tune '*Tu Jaane Na*' from '*Ajab Prem Ki Gazab Kahani*' – in front of a big crowd in Mysore. Haryana were prevented from an outright win against Karnataka by just two wickets, but the team looked set for a resurgence under their new leader. Sehwag made 467 runs at 51.88, but played only five matches before he left for the All Stars in the US, and then retired. That exposed his domestic side. Except for Nitin Saini, no other batsman made it count as they managed just two century stands outside of Sehwag's involvement. On the bowling front, injury to Amit Mishra, and Mohit Sharma missing some matches nullified the efforts of Ashish Hooda, Harshal Patel and Jayant. *Karthik Lakshmanan*

Results: Conceded first-innings lead to Maharashtra (away), lost to Delhi by four wickets (away), took first-innings lead against Karnataka (away), conceded first-innings lead to Bengal (home), lost to Assam by six wickets (home), conceded first-innings lead to Odisha (home), lost to Rajasthan by nine wickets (home), lost to Vidarbha by an innings and 31 runs (away).
Best batsman: Nitin Saini (542 runs in 8 matches)
Best bowler: Ashish Hooda (24 wickets in 8 matches)
Debutants (5): Rahul Dagar, Sanjay Pahal, Rohit Sharma, Mohit Hooda, Shamsher Yadav.

*** **Overall first-class records** ***

(P 288, W 100, L 73, D 115)
Maiden match: Lost to Delhi by 74 runs (November 13-15, 1970, Chandigarh)
Ranji win (1): 1990-91
Irani win (1): 1991-92
Highest team total: 673/9 dec v Maharashtra (Pune, 1991-92)
Lowest team total: 55 v Vidarbha (Rohtak, 2012-13)
Highest run-getter: Amarjit Kaypee – 6625 runs in 89 matches
Highest individual score: 312 by Sunny Singh v Madhya Pradesh (Indore, 2009-10)
Most 100s: Amarjit Kaypee – 24 centuries
Highest wicket-taker: Rajinder Goel – 391 in 61 matches
Best bowling (innings): 8-24 by Joginder Sharma v Vidarbha (Nagpur, 2004-05)
Best bowling (match): 15-140 by Pradeep Jain v Himachal Pradesh (Bhiwani, 1993-94)
Most dismissals (wicketkeeper): Vijay Yadav – 212 (180ct+32st) in 68 matches
Most dismissals (wicketkeeper/innings): 6 by Salim Ahmed v Services (Delhi, 1984-85)
Most catches (fielder): Ravinder Chadha – 92
Highest partnership: Ajay Jadeja/Amarjit Kaypee – 405 for third wicket v Services (Faridabad, 1991-92)
Most capped player: Sarkar Talwar – 97

Group B

Mumbai

A young Mumbai rebuilt their team – the seeds had been sown in 2014-15 – in a spectacular fashion, remaining undefeated on the way to their 41st Ranji title. Aditya Tare's astute leadership, Chandrakant Pandit's return as coach after 12 years, Abhishek Nayar's role as everyone's elder brother, and the economical bowling of Dhawal Kulkarni and Balwinder Singh Sandhu were sideshows to Shreyas Iyer. Iyer's 1321 runs was the second-highest ever in Ranji history after VVS Laxman's 1415 in 1999-2000 and came at a strike-rate of 92.70. His 11 fifty-plus scores equalled Vijay Bharadwaj (1998-99) and Nayar (2012-13) for the most in a season. Shardul Thakur crossed the 40-wicket mark for the second consecutive season, Akhil Herwadkar and Suryakumar Yadav provided stability at the top to finish among the season's top-four run-getters, Vishal Dabholkar picked up 27 wickets before his action came under scrutiny, and Siddhesh Lad got the best out of the tail-enders, especially during his tenth-wicket stand of 103 runs with Sandhu against Saurashtra in the final.

Disha Shetty

Results: Conceded first-innings lead to Andhra (away), beat Punjab by an innings and 12 runs (home), beat Tamil Nadu by one wicket (home), took first-innings lead against Baroda (away), took first-innings lead against Uttar Pradesh (home), beat Railways by six wickets (home), beat Madhya Pradesh by three wickets (away), took first-innings lead against Gujarat (home), beat Jharkhand by 395 runs in the quarter-final (neutral), took first-innings lead against Madhya Pradesh in the semi-final (neutral), beat Saurashtra by an innings and 21 runs in the final (neutral).
Best batsman: Shreyas Iyer (1321 runs in 11 matches)
Best bowler: Shardul Thakur (41 wickets in 11 matches)
Debutants (3): Jay Bista, Ankush Jaiswal, Sufiyan Shaikh.

Domestic review

*** Overall first-class records ***

(P 538, W 244, L 39, D 255)
Maiden match: Lost to Lord Hawke's XI by eight wickets (December 26-28, 1892, Bombay)
Ranji wins (41): 1934-35, 1935-36, 1941-42, 1944-45, 1948-49, 1951-52, 1953-54, 1955-56, 1956-57, 1958-59-1972-73, 1974-75-1976-77, 1980-81, 1983-84, 1984-85, 1993-94, 1994-95, 1996-97, 1999-00, 2002-03, 2003-04, 2006-07, 2008-09, 2009-10, 2012-13, 2015-16
Irani wins (15): 1959-60-1963-64, 1965-66 (shared), 1967-68, 1969-70, 1970-71, 1972-73, 1975-76, 1976-77, 1981-82, 1985-86, 1994-95, 1995-96, 1997-98,
Highest team total: 855/6 dec v Hyderabad (Bombay, 1990-91)
Lowest team total: 42 v Gujarat (Bulsar, 1977-78)
Highest run-getter: Wasim Jaffer – 10585 in 130 matches
Highest individual score: 377 by Sanjay Manjrekar v Hyderabad (Bombay, 1990-91)
Most 100s: Wasim Jaffer –36
Highest wicket-taker: Padmakar Shivalkar – 421 in 86 matches
Best bowling (innings): 10-78 by Subhas Gupte v Pakistan Combined Services and Bahawalpur XI (Bombay, 1954-55)
Best bowling(match): 13-34 by Padmakar Shivalkar v Tamil Nadu (Madras, 1972-73)
Most dismissals (wicketkeeper): Vinayak Samant – 254 (225ct+29st) in 69 matches
Most dismissals (wicketkeeper/innings): 6 by Zulfiqar Parkar v Maharashtra (Bombay, 1981-82)
Most catches (fielder): Wasim Jaffer – 161
Highest partnership: Wasim Jaffer/Sulakshan Kulkarni – 459 for first wicket v Saurashtra (Rajkot, 1996-97)
Most capped player: Wasim Jaffer – 130

Punjab

In a must-win last league game for both teams at Dindigul, Punjab's spin trio of Harbhajan Singh, Rajwinder Singh and Sarabjit Ladda picked up all 20 wickets for a two-day finish on a poor strip prepared by Tamil Nadu. The good times were short-lived as Punjab lost to Assam in the quarter-final, conceding their third non-final knockout game in four seasons. Punjab's campaign started with Gurkeerat Singh Mann's unbeaten double-century and his unbroken 306-stand with Gitansh Khera – the season's highest – in an innings win over Railways, but two big defeats pegged them back. Despite Harbhajan and Yuvraj, who missed the quarter-final because of back spasm, being available for most part of the season, Punjab lacked consistency. Only Uday Kaul stood out with three centuries while Barinder Sran did enough to earn an India call-up. Sandeep Sharma's absence because of a shoulder surgery proved costly in the final analysis. *Roshan Thyagarajan*

Results: Beat Railways by an innings and 126 runs (home), lost to Mumbai by an innings and 12 runs (away), took first-innings lead against Gujarat (home), conceded first-innings lead to Madhya Pradesh (home), beat Andhra by seven wickets (home), lost to Baroda by an innings and 116 runs (away), took first-innings lead against Uttar Pradesh (away), beat Tamil Nadu by 243 runs (away), lost to Assam by 51 runs in the quarter-final (neutral).
Best batsman: Uday Kaul (636 runs, 9 matches)
Best bowler: Sarabjit Ladda (25 wickets, 5 matches)
Debutants (2): Pargat Singh, Deepak Bansal.

*** Overall first-class records ***
(P 303, W 105, L 50, D 148)
Maiden match: Beat Jammu & Kashmir by an innings and 255 runs (November 23-24, 1968, Jammu)
Ranji win (1): 1992-93
Highest team total: 780/8 v Delhi (Delhi, 1994-95)
Lowest team total: 42 v Haryana (Amritsar, 1978-79)
Highest run-getter: Pankaj Dharmani – 7621 in 117 matches
Highest individual score: 308* by Dinesh Mongia v Jammu & Kashmir (Jalandhar, 2000-01)
Most 100s: Pankaj Dharmani – 23
Highest wicket-taker: Bharati Vij – 265 in 61 matches
Best bowling (innings): 8-37 by Umesh Kumar v Delhi (Delhi, 1974-75)
Best bowling (match): 14-84 by Deepak Chopra v Jammu & Kashmir (Srinagar, 1982-83)
Most dismissals (wicketkeeper): Arun Kumar Sharma – 200 (163ct+37st) in 71 matches
Most dismissals (wicketkeeper/innings): 6 by Uday Kaul v Uttar Pradesh (Meerut, 2010-11)
Most catches (fielder): Dinesh Mongia - 95
Highest partnership: Bhupinder Singh/Pankaj Dharmani – 460 for seventh wicket v Delhi (Delhi, 1994-95)
Most capped player: Pankaj Dharmani – 117

Madhya Pradesh

Denied a knockout berth on the last day of the league stages in 2014-15 by a defiant Bengal, Madhya Pradesh recorded their biggest win in terms of run-margin against the same opponent in the quarter-final this season for their first semi-final appearance since 1998-99. Ankit Sharma's 13-wicket haul gave Madhya Pradesh a bonus-point win over Andhra in their last league game and tied them with Gujarat on the points table, but a better net run-rate of -0.059 took them to the knockouts. Jalaj Saxena recorded the joint-second-best match returns, along with Rajasthan's P Sunderam in 1985-86, with 16 for 154 against Railways, but fell a scalp short of becoming only the second player in the history of the competition to achieve a season double of 500 runs and 50 wickets. Madhya Pradesh made nine hundreds and 30 fifties, of which two by Devendra Bundela, their captain, in the quarter-final took him past the 9000-run mark in first-class cricket. *Roshan Thyagarajan*

Results: Drew with Uttar Pradesh (away), conceded first-innings lead to Tamil Nadu (home), took first-innings lead against Punjab (away), beat Baroda by 87 runs (away), beat Railways by nine wickets (home), lost to Gujarat by 153 runs (away), lost to Mumbai by three wickets (home), beat Andhra by an innings and nine runs (home), beat Bengal by 355 runs in the quarter-final (neutral), conceded first-innings lead to Mumbai in the semi-final (neutral).
Best batsman: Harpreet Singh (750 runs, 9 matches)
Best bowler: Jalaj Saxena (49 wickets, 10 matches)
Debutants (4): Ankit Dane, Rajat Patidar, Chandrakant Sakure, Jagdeep Baweja.

*** Overall first-class records ***
(P 302, W 69, L 62, D 171)
Maiden match: Lost to Hyderabad by three wickets (December 22-25, 1950, Nagpur)
Highest team total: 619/8 dec v Saurashtra (Indore, 2013-14)
Lowest team total: 60 v Baroda (Vadodara, 2013-14)

Highest run-getter: Devendra Bundela – 8296 in 130 matches
Highest individual score: 265 by Jai Prakash Yadav v Railways (Indore, 1999-00)
Most 100s: Devendra Bundela – 23
Highest wicket-taker: Narendra Hirwani – 412 in 86 matches
Best bowling (innings): 8-52 by Narendra Hirwani v Vidarbha (Nagpur, 1993-94)
Best bowling (match): 16-154 by Jalaj Saxena v Railways (Gwalior, 2015-16)
Most dismissals (wicketkeeper): Naman Ojha – 303 (268ct+35st) in 94 matches
Most dismissals (wicketkeeper/innings): 6 by Naman Ojha v Gujarat (Delhi, 2007-08)
Most catches (fielder): Syed Abbas Ali – 90
Highest partnership: Syed Abbas Ali/Prashant Dwivedi - 436 for fourth wicket v Railways (Indore, 1997-98)
Most capped player: Devendra Bundela – 130

Gujarat

Gujarat were left ruing their luck when their penultimate game against Tamil Nadu was washed out in Tirunelveli, leaving them with a solitary point. They were primed to seal a quarter-final spot, but when Mumbai claimed the first-innings lead in their final league clash, despite Bhargav Merai's 166, Gujarat were pipped to the third spot by Madhya Pradesh, who recorded a bonus-point win over Andhra, by a net run-rate difference of 0.033. They finished with exactly the same position and points (24) in 2014-15. It hastened the end of Ramesh Powar's long career; in a quirk of fate, Powar was a part of the visitors' dressing room at the Wankhede in his last first-class game, having represented Mumbai for all but three seasons. Priyank Panchal was one of the positives again, but the bowlers – Jasprit Bumrah, RP Singh and Axar Patel, all of whom played a key role in them winning the Vijay Hazare Trophy – did not perform as expected. *Manoj Narayan*

Results: Conceded first-innings lead against Andhra (away), conceded first-innings lead against Punjab (away), beat Railways by an innings and 36 runs (away), lost to Uttar Pradesh by 155 runs (home), beat Baroda by an innings and 46 runs (home), beat Madhya Pradesh by 153 runs (home), drew against Tamil Nadu (away), conceded first-innings lead against Mumbai (away).
Best batsman: Priyank Panchal (665 runs, 8 matches)
Best bowler: Rujul Bhatt (24 wickets, 8 matches)
Debutant (1): Alshaaz Pathan

*** Overall first-class records ***

(P 319, W 54, L 108, D 157)
Maiden match: Drew with Bombay (February 2-4, 1935, Ahmedabad)
Highest team total: 640 v Maharashtra (Ahmedabad, 1995-96)
Lowest team total: 43 v Bombay (Bombay, 1958-59)
Highest run-getter: Mukund Parmar – 6644 in 79 matches
Highest individual score: 283 by Mukund Parmar v Maharashtra (Ahmedabad, 1995-96)
Most 100s: Mukund Parmar – 20
Highest wicket-taker: Ashok Joshi – 227 in 66 matches
Best bowling (innings): 8-21 by Jasu Patel v Saurashtra (Surat, 1960-61)
Best bowling (match): 14-96 by Rakesh Dhruve v Rajasthan (Ahmedabad, 2012-13)
Most dismissals (wicketkeeper): Parthiv Patel – 227 (201ct+26st) in 78 matches

Most dismissals (wicketkeeper/innings): 6 by Nilesh Modi v Karnataka (Ahmedabad, 2005-06)
Most catches (fielder): Nilesh Modi - 57
Highest partnership: Polly Umrigar/G Kishenchand - 293 for fourth wicket v Maharashtra (Kolhapur, 1951-52)
Most capped player: Niraj Patel –82

Uttar Pradesh

For a side that won the Syed Mushtaq Ali Trophy and reached the Vijay Hazare Trophy quarter-final, falling four points clear of a knockout berth in the Ranji Trophy was a downer. Uttar Pradesh had only five centurions; among them were Suresh Raina, who played in four games, and Sarfaraz Khan, who made 155 on his state debut against Madhya Pradesh after his move from Mumbai, but was available for only three matches because of India Under-19 commitments. Umang Sharma hit a double-century against Baroda in the last league game and was the team's best batsman, but lacked the impetus that the teenaged-trio of Mohammad Saif, Sarfaraz and Almas Shaukat had provided in the opening fixture against Madhya Pradesh. Also, being dismissed for 58 against Railways and only 23 wickets for Piyush Chawla and Kuldeep Yadav did not help the team. *Nisha Shetty*

Results: Drew with Madhya Pradesh (home), lost to Railways by 282 runs (home), beat Andhra by 56 runs (away), beat Gujarat by 155 runs (away), conceded first-innings lead to Mumbai (away), took first-innings lead against Tamil Nadu (home), conceded first-innings lead to Punjab (home), took first-innings lead against Baroda (home).
Best batsman: Umang Sharma (607 runs, 6 matches)
Best bowler: Praveen Kumar (28 wickets, 8 matches)
Debutants (2): Almas Shaukat, Israr Azim.

*** Overall first-class records ***

(P 355, W 88, L 84, D 183)
Maiden match: Lost to Bihar by 47 runs (February 4-7, 1950, Jamshedpur)
Ranji win (1): 2005-06
Highest team total: 686/7 dec v Madhya Pradesh (Moradabad, 2015-16)
Lowest team total: 53 v Holkar (Indore, 1952-53)
Highest run-getter: Rizwan Shamshad – 5892 in 90 matches
Highest individual score: 261* by Shashikant Khandkar v Railways (Moradabad, 1984-85)
Most 100s: Rahul Sapru – 16
Highest wicket-taker: Ashish Zaidi – 348 in 94 matches
Best bowling (innings): 9-45 by Ashish Zaidi v Vidarbha (Kanpur, 1990-2000)
Best bowling (match): 15-192 by Ashish Zaidi v Vidarbha (Kanpur, 1990-2000)
Most dismissals (wicketkeeper): Mohammad Amir Khan – 213 (196st+17st) in 65 matches
Most dismissals (wicketkeeper/innings): 6 by Anil Bhanot v Vidarbha (Agra, 1973-74)
Most catches (fielder): Mohammad Kaif – 73
Highest partnership: Krishna Tiwari/Vijay Manjrekar – 315 for third wicket v Madhya Pradesh (Indore, 1957-58)
Most capped player: Gyanendra Pandey – 97

Tamil Nadu

A combination of insipid performances and incessant monsoon rain in the state meant Tamil Nadu failed to qualify for the knockouts after playing in the 2014-15 final. A one-wicket loss to Mumbai in their third game, despite a 140-run lead, pushed them back, and they banked on home advantage to get back on track. But, with rain affecting two games – against Andhra in Chennai and Gujarat in Tirunelveli – their qualification chances dipped. In a must-win situation in their last league game against Punjab, Tamil Nadu opted for a spin-friendly track but the ploy backfired as they were dismissed for 68 and 69 in a two-day loss. With L Balaji not playing a single game despite being with the team as a bowling coach-cum-player, the bowling lacked depth as only Rahil Shah and Malolan Rangarajan took more than 20 wickets. That only Baba Indrajith, Dinesh Karthik, Rangarajan and J Kousik scored a century each exposed the batting. Eager to get on track, Tamil Nadu roped in Hrishikesh Kantikar as coach for 2016-17. *Karthik Lakshmanan*

Results: Beat Baroda by seven runs (home), took first-innings lead against Madhya Pradesh (away), lost to Mumbai by one wicket (away), beat Railways by eight wickets (away), drew with Andhra (home), conceded first-innings lead to Uttar Pradesh (away), drew with Gujarat (home), lost to Punjab by 243 runs (home).
Best batsman: Baba Indrajith (360 runs, 8 matches)
Best bowler: Rahil Shah (25 wickets, 6 matches)
Debutants (3): DT Chandrasekar, J Kousik, L Vignesh.

*** Overall first-class records ***

(P 459, W 162, L 81, D 216)
Maiden match: Lost to Marylebone Cricket Club by 211 runs (January 23-25, 1927, Madras)
Ranji wins (2): 1954-55, 1987-88
Irani win (1): 1988-89
Highest team total: 912/6 dec v Goa (Panaji, 1988-89)
Lowest team total: 56 v Ceylon Cricket Association (Colombo, 1956-57)
Highest run-getter: S Sharath – 6720 in 105 matches
Highest individual score: 313 by WV Raman v Goa (Panaji, 1988-89)
Most 100s: S Sharath – 23
Highest wicket-taker: S Venkataraghavan – 609 in 106 matches
Best bowling (innings): 9-50 by KS Kannan v Hyderabad (Secunderabad, 1947-48)
Best bowling (match): 14-118 by Sunil Subramaniam v Assam (Chennai, 1992-93)
Most dismissals (wicketkeeper): Dinesh Karthik – 242 (213st+29st) in 91 matches
Most dismissals (wicketkeeper/innings): 6 by Bharath Reddy v Kerala (Palakkad, 1982-83)
Most catches (fielder): S Venkataraghavan – 105
Highest partnership: M Vijay/Abhinav Mukund – 462 for first wicket v Maharashtra (Nasik, 2008-09)
Most capped player: S Venkataraghavan – 106

Baroda

Despite recording two bonus-point wins, Baroda found it impossible to salvage their campaign because of three outright losses and their inability to take the first-innings lead in another three games. Against both Tamil Nadu and Madhya Pradesh, Baroda claimed the lead but then allowed the opposition to fight back for an outright win. There was the demoralising innings defeat to Gujarat as well, and though that was followed by a big win against Punjab, the momentum fizzled out and they finished third from bottom. Things would have been different had Ambati Rayudu, in what would be his last season for Baroda, Irfan Pathan and Munaf Patel found more playing time. The batting was in the relatively good hands of Kedar Devdhar and Aditya Waghmode, but none of the bowlers who featured regularly could touch the 20-wicket mark. To put things in perspective, Irfan, in his three outings, claimed 14 scalps.

Manoj Narayan

Results: Lost to Tamil Nadu by seven runs (away), beat Railways by an innings and 113 runs (home), conceded first-innings lead to Andhra (away), conceded first-innings lead to Mumbai (home), lost by 87 runs to Madhya Pradesh (home), lost by an innings and 46 runs to Gujarat (away), beat Punjab by an innings and 116 runs (home), conceded first-innings lead to Uttar Pradesh (away).
Best batsman: Kedar Devdhar (659 runs, 8 matches)
Best bowler: Swapnil Singh (19 wickets, 8 matches)
Debutants (4): Hitesh Solanki, Monil Patel, Rishi Arothe, Atit Sheth.

*** Overall first-class records ***
(P 377, W 100, T 1, L 87, D 189)
Maiden match: Lost to Nawanagar by an innings & 275 runs (October 30-31, 1937, Jamnagar)
Ranji wins (5): 1942-43, 1946-47, 1949-50, 1957-58, 2000-01
Highest team total: 784 v Holkar (Baroda, 1946-47)
Lowest team total: 37 v Nawanagar (Jamnagar, 1937-38)
Highest run-getter: Jacob Martin – 6877 in 94 matches
Highest individual score: 319 by Gul Mohammad v Holkar (Baroda, 1946-47)
Most 100s: Jacob Martin – 20
Highest wicket-taker: Vijay Hazare –250 in 59 matches
Best bowling (innings): 8-17 by Dashrat Pardeshi v Gujarat (Vadodara, 1981-82)
Best bowling (match): 13-66 by Ranga Sohoni v Hyderabad (Secunderabad, 1948-49)
Most dismissals (wicketkeeper): Pinal Shah – 278 (244ct+34st) in 77 matches
Most dismissals (wicketkeeper/innings): 6 by Nayan Mongia v Punjab (Vadodara, 2003-04)
Most catches (fielder): Jacob Martin – 88
Highest partnership: Vijay Hazare/Gul Mohammad – 577 for fifth wicket v Holkar (Baroda, 1946-47)
Most capped player: Connor Williams – 108

Railways

Railways were the punching bag in the group for much of the season, losing six games (three of them by an innings) – the most by any side in the league phase. They won their remaining two games, the same number as those achieved by higher placed sides such as Baroda, Tamil Nadu and Uttar Pradesh, hence not being a part of a single draw in the season – a rarity in Ranji Trophy. Their 282-run victory against Uttar Pradesh was a comprehensive one where Anureet Singh and Krishnakant Upadhyay took nine wickets between them to shred the opposition for 58. The other win, in the last match against Andhra, was also thanks to the bowling heroics of Anureet and Karn Sharma, and it helped the side avoid relegation. It was scant consolation, however, for what was a disappointing season, especially after the highs of 2013-14 where they topped Group B. Part of the disappointing outing was due to the 60-plus strike-rates of three of the team's top four bowlers.

Nisha Shetty

Results: Lost to Punjab by an innings and 126 runs (away), lost to Baroda by an innings and 113 runs (away), beat Uttar Pradesh by 282 runs (away), lost to Gujarat by an innings and 36 runs (home), lost to Tamil Nadu by eight wickets (home), lost to Madhya Pradesh by nine wickets (away), lost to Mumbai by six wickets (away), beat Andhra by 148 runs (home).
Best batsman: Saurabh Wakaskar (649 runs, 8 matches)
Best bowler: Anureet Singh (36 wickets, 7 matches)
Debutants (7): Ashish Singh, Hitesh Kadam, Faiz Ahmed, Bhima Rao, Sagar Mishra, Akshat Pandey, Vivek Singh.

*** Overall first-class records ***

(P 330, W 95, L 61, D 174)
Maiden first-class match: Drew with Eastern Punjab (December 19-21, 1958, Jalandhar)
Ranji wins (2): 2001-02, 2004-05
Irani wins (2): 2002-03, 2005-06
Highest team total: 656/5 v Maharashtra (Pune, 2000-01)
Lowest team total: 33 v Services (Delhi, 1958-59)
Highest run-getter: Sanjay Bangar – 6980 in 126 matches
Highest individual score: 233 by Yusuf Ali Khan v Vidarbha (Nagpur, 1989-90)
Most 100s: Sanjay Bangar – 12
Highest wicket-taker: S Hyder Ali – 299 in 85 matches
Best bowling (innings): 9-25 by Hyder Ali v Jammu & Kashmir (Delhi, 1969-70)
Best bowling (match): 13-77 by Gunwant Desai v Services (Delhi, 1974-75)
Most dismissals (wicketkeeper): Mahesh Rawat – 204 (189ct+15ct) in 64 matches
Most catches (fielder): Sanjay Bangar – 127
Highest partnership: Tejinder Singh/Raja Ali – 326 for fourth wicket v Madhya Pradesh (Indore, 2001-02)
Most capped player: Sanjay Bangar – 126

Andhra

Having jumped from Group C after a year of hard toil, Andhra struggled to cope, not least in the final league game against Madhya Pradesh. Needing at least three points to avoid relegation, they were dismissed for 56 in their first innings to lose in three days. "Our average age must be 21 – I am the only old man and will turn 35 tomorrow!" Mohammad Kaif, the captain whose services were terminated after the loss, had remarked in the build up to the final league clash, adding that it was all a learning curve on pressure management for the young side. And, so it was. KS Bharat had another good season with the bat, but Ricky Bhui's services were missed towards the latter stages because of India Under-19 duty. The qualities of a pedigreed spinner was also missed, all of which led them to manage just ten points, despite starting the season with a first-innings lead over Mumbai. Having fallen from grace, Andhra got Hanuma Vihari, Ravi Teja and Bhargav Bhatt to play for them in 2016-17 and signed up Sanath Kumar as coach.

Manoj Narayan

KS Bharat had a good season, leading the run charts for Andhra with 541 runs. – *Wisden India*

Results: Took first-innings lead against Mumbai (home), took first-innings lead against Gujarat (home), took first-innings lead against Baroda (home), lost to Uttar Pradesh by 56 runs (home), lost to Punjab by seven wickets (away), drew with Tamil Nadu (away), lost to Railways by 148 runs (away), lost to Madhya Pradesh by an innings and nine runs (away).
Best batsman: KS Bharat (541 runs, 8 matches)
Best bowler: B Ayappa (26 wickets, 8 matches)
Debutants (5): KV Sasikanth, H Shivraj, Jyothi Sai Krishna, K Sreekanth, Sneha Kishore

*** Overall first-class records ***
(P 294, W 41, L 127, D 126)
Maiden match: Lost to Mysore by eight wickets (November 28-30, 1953, Bangalore)
Highest team total: 593/9 dec v Tamil Nadu (Vizianagaram, 1985-86)
Lowest team total: 29 v Tamil Nadu (Coimbatore, 1978-79)
Highest run-getter: Amit Pathak – 4564 in 73 matches
Highest individual score: 308 by KS Bharat v Goa (Ongole, 2014-15)
Most 100s: Amit Pathak – 11
Highest wicket-taker: Syed Sahabuddin – 242 in 75 matches
Best bowling (innings): 8-46 by B Mahendra Kumar v Kerala (Trivandrum, 1967-68)
Best bowling (match): D Sivakumar – 12-120 v Maharashtra at Rohtak, 2014/15
Most dismissals (wicketkeeper): MSK Prasad – 190 (175ct+15st) in 63 matches
Most dismissals (wicketkeeper/innings): 6 by Srikar Bharat v Assam (Anantpur, 2013-14)
Most catches (fielder): A Ganga Pradeep – 64
Highest partnership: Prasad Reddy/Amit Pathak – 380 for first wicket v Bengal (Margao, 2000-01)
Most capped player: Syed Sahabuddin – 75

Group C

Saurashtra

Relegated to Group C in 2014-15, Saurashtra stormed into the knockouts with five outright wins – the most by any team in the league phase. It included a successful chase of 302 against Services. In all, they won seven games on their way to the final. Ravindra Jadeja's 38 wickets in the first four matches gave Saurashtra the impetus. Jaydev Unadkat benefitted from it, finding a new stride in his bowling for 24 wickets in three knockout games. Sheldon Jackson made two centuries and three fifties to gain a spot in the Rest of India team for Irani Cup. Had Arpit Vasavada and Cheteshwar Pujara not dropped

Finishing what Jadeja started: Jaydev Unadkat, seen here batting in the Ranji Trophy final against Mumbai, took 24 wickets in Saurashtra's knockout games after Ravindra Jadeja's star turn in the early rounds. — *Joshua Veeranathan*

sitters at slip in the final against Mumbai, Saurashtra could have fancied being second time lucky, having lost to the domestic giants in their maiden final appearance in 2012-13. Jaydev Shah became the most-capped Ranji captain in the game against Himachal Pradesh, going past Ravinder Chadha, who led Haryana in 87 matches.

Sidhanta Patnaik

Results: Beat Tripura by an innings and 118 runs (home), beat Jharkhand by eight wickets (home), beat Hyderabad by 35 runs (home), beat Services by four wickets (away), took first-innings lead against Goa (home), conceded first-innings lead to Himachal Pradesh (home), lost to Kerala by 45 runs (away), beat Jammu & Kashmir by an innings and 63 runs (away), beat Vidarbha by an innings and 85 runs in the quarter-final (neutral), beat Assam by ten wickets in the semi-final (neutral), lost to Mumbai by an innings and 21 runs in the final (neutral).
Best batsman: Sheldon Jackson (538 runs, 10 matches)
Best bowler: Jaydev Unadkat (40 wickets, 11 matches)
Debutants (4): Mohsin Dodia, Vandit Jivrajani, Samarth Vyas, Prerak Mankad

*** Overall first-class records ***

(P 312, W 50, L 108, D 154)
Maiden match: Lost to Commonwealth XI by nine wickets (October 10-11, 1950, Rajkot)
Highest team total: 718/9 dec v Karnataka (Rajkot, 2012-13)
Lowest team total: 25 v Bombay (1951-52)
Highest run-getter: Sitanshu Kotak – 7607 in 121 matches
Highest individual score: 352 by Cheteshwar Pujara v Karnataka (Rajkot, 2012-13)
Most 100s: Cheteshwar Pujara – 17
Highest wicket-taker: Kamlesh Makvana – 202 in 77 matches
Best bowling (innings): 8-55 by Surjuram Girdhari v Gujarat (Ahmedabad, 1947-48)
Best bowling (match): 13-126 by Ravindra Jadeja v Jharkhand (Rajkot, 2015-16)
Most dismissals (wicketkeeper): Sagar Jogiyani – 287 (251ct+36st) in 91 matches

Most dismissals (wicketkeeper/innings): 6 by Sagar Jogiyani v Jammu & Kashmir (Jammu, 2015-16)
Most catches (fielder): Sitanshu Kotak – 98
Highest partnership: Sagar Jogiyani/Ravindra Jadeja – 539 for third wicket v Gujarat (Surat, 2012-13)
Most capped player: Sitanshu Kotak – 121

Jharkhand

Jharkhand put their game face on to recover from being dismissed for 45 in their first innings against Services to record four outright wins – the most by them in a season – and earn a promotion for 2016-17. The innings wins against Tripura and Himachal Pradesh, where Shahbaz Nadeem took 11 wickets on a turning track at home, gave them the momentum to carry into their must-win clash in Hyderabad. A bonus-point win, set up by Saurabh Tiwary's unbeaten 209, put them ahead of Himachal Pradesh in the race by just a point for their second quarter-final appearance in four seasons. They benefitted from MS Dhoni's time and expertise during the two-month break before the knockout stages, but then missed Varun Aaron, who played just two games in the season, in the quarter-final against Mumbai. Nadeem became the first bowler since Ranadeb Bose in 2006-07 to take 50 wickets in a season.
Disha Shetty

Results: Lost to Services by nine wickets (away), lost to Saurashtra by eight wickets (away), beat Kerala by 133 runs (away), conceded first-innings lead to Goa (home), took first-innings lead against Jammu & Kashmir (home), beat Tripura by an innings and 67 runs (away), beat Himacal Pradesh by an innings and 71 runs (home), beat Hyderabad by ten wickets (away), lost to Mumbai by 395 runs in the quarter-final (neutral).
Best batsman: Saurabh Tiwary (698 runs, 9 matches)
Best Bowler: Shahbaz Nadeem (51 wickets, 9 matches)
Debutants (2): Vinayak Vikram, Sonu Singh.

*** Overall first-class records ***
(P 310, W 94, L 79, D 137 *Includes Bihar's record till 2003-04)
Maiden match: Drew with Saurashtra (November 16-19, 2004, Rajkot)
Highest team total: 556/9 dec v Hyderabad (Ranchi, 2014-15)
Lowest team total: 45 v Services (Delhi, 2015-16)
Highest run-getter: Saurabh Tiwary – 4469 in 57 matches
Highest individual score: 238 by Saurabh Tiwary v Mumbai (Mumbai, 2013-14)

Shahbaz Nadeem, seen here in action for Delhi Daredevils, took 51 wickets in nine Ranji matches.
– *Wisden India*

Most 100s: Saurabh Tiwary – 13
Highest wicket-taker: Shahbaz Nadeem – 220 in 60 matches
Best bowling (innings): 7-45 by Shahbaz Nadeem v Himachal Pradesh (Ranchi, 2015-16)
Best bowling (match): Ajay Yadav – 11/73 v Services (Delhi, 2012-13)
Most dismissals (wicketkeeper): Shiv Gautam – 78 (71ct+7st) in 35 matches
Most dismissals (wicketkeeper/innings): 7 by Shiv Gautam v Maharashtra (Nasik, 2011-12)
Most catches (fielder): Saurabh Tiwary – 44
Highest partnership: Ishank Jaggi/Shiv Gautam – 253* for fifth wicket v Hyderabad (Ranchi, 2010-11)
Most capped player: Shahbaz Nadeem – 60

Himachal Pradesh

For the third season in a row Himachal Pradesh fumbled at the business end of the league stages and missed out on a quarter-final berth by a whisker. A three-day innings defeat to Jharkhand broke their flow, and losing six wickets in a chase of 24 against Kerala, in a game that lasted for just 483 minutes, denied them a bonus point and further progress. Their dominance for the first five games was engineered by Paras Dogra, who equalled Ajay Sharma's competition tally of seven double-centuries, and Robin Bist, who made an unbeaten 220 in his second game for the state during their 707 for 8 declared against Hyderabad – the highest innings total of the season. The young Nikhil Gangta continued to impress, making 203 against Jammu & Kashmir. Rishi Dhawan's average form meant that he did not take 40 wickets for the first time in three seasons, and Ronit More, the professional from Karnataka, managed only four wickets in three matches. *Disha Shetty*

Results: Beat Jammu & Kashmir by ten wickets (home), took first-innings lead against Hyderabad (home), took first-innings lead against Goa (home), beat Tripura by an innings and six runs (home), drew with Services (home), took first-innings lead against Saurashtra (away), lost by an innings and 71 runs against Jharkhand (away), beat Kerala by six wickets (away).
Best batsman: Paras Dogra (703 runs, 8 matches)
Best bowler: Rishi Dhawan (28 wickets, 8 matches)
Debutant (1): Shresth Nirmohi.

*** Overall first-class records ***
(P 179, W 30, L 82, D 67)
Maiden match: Lost to Jammu & Kashmir by an innings and 66 runs (September 30-October 2, 1985, Srinagar)
Highest team total: 707/8 dec v Hyderabad (Dharamsala, 2015-16)
Lowest team total: 64 v Services (Una, 1986-87)
Highest run-getter: Rajeev Nayyar – 6113 in 86 matches
Highest individual score: 271 by Rajeev Nayyar v Jammu & Kashmir (Chamba, 1999-2000)
Most 100s: Paras Dogra – 19
Highest wicket-taker: Vikramjeet Malik – 292 in 76 matches
Best bowling (innings): 7-29 by Vikramjeet Malik v Haryana (Rohtak, 2008-09)
Best bowling (match): 13-72 by Vikramjeet Malik v Haryana (Rohtak, 2008-09)
Most dismissals (wicketkeeper): Manvinder Singh Bisla – 106 (94ct+12st) in 49 matches
Most dismissals (wicketkeeper/innings): 6 by Ravikant Sharma v Delhi (Bilaspur, 2001-02)

Most catches (fielder): Paras Dogra – 88
Highest partnership: Sangram Singh/Bhavin Thakkar – 353 for second wicket v Jharkhand (Ranchi, 2008-09)
Most capped player: Rajiv Nayyar – 86

Services

Services lost ground after two wins in their first three games. Missing out on bonus points against Jharkhand and Jammu & Kashmir, conceding a three-run lead to Kerala and allowing Saurashtra to chase 302 meant that a bonus-point win in their last game served only academic interest. Their bright start against Jharkhand, where they dismissed the opposition for 45 on the first morning, was because of debutant Diwesh Pathania becoming the fourth Services bowler to take 13 or more wickets in a match. Rajat Paliwal, one of the three players in the season to make four hundreds, became the first Services batsman to make twin centuries in a match. Yashpal Singh, in what would be his farewell season for Services before moving to Tripura, marked his 100th first-class match with a century. The duo lacked support as all other batsmen made less than 500 runs.

Shubham Malaviya

Results: Beat Jharkhand by nine wickets (home), took first-innings lead against Goa (away), beat Jammu & Kashmir by nine wickets (away), conceded first-innings lead to Kerala (home), lost to Saurashtra by four wickets (home), drew with Himachal Pradesh (away), took first-innings lead against Hyderabad (home), beat Tripura by an innings and 62 runs (away).
Best batsman: Rajat Paliwal (753 runs, 8 matches)
Best bowler: Diwesh Pathania (37 wickets, 8 matches)
Debutants (9): Diwesh Pathania, Poonam Poonia, Raushan Raj, Ravi Chauhan, Shashank Sharma, Sufiyan Alam, Vikas Hathwala, Kamal Passi, Amit Pachhara

*** Overall first-class records ***

(P 314, W 82, L 109, D 123)
Maiden match: Lost to Commonwealth XI by ten wickets (November 5-7, 1949, Delhi)
Highest team total: 567 v Delhi (Delhi, 1952-53)
Lowest team total: 31 v Baroda (Vadodara, 2013-14)
Highest run-getter: Yashpal Singh – 6461 in 87 matches
Highest individual score: 250* by Yashpal Singh v Tripura (Agartala, 2012-13)
Most 100s: Yashpal Singh – 18
Highest wicket-taker: Gokul Inder Dev – 206 in 52 matches
Best bowling (innings): 8-37 by Gokul Inder Dev v Jammu & Kashmir (Jammu, 1968-69)
Best bowling (match): 14-104 by Iqbal Karan v Eastern Punjab (Amritsar, 1950-51)
Most dismissals (wicketkeeper): Sarabjit Singh – 192 (166ct+26st) in 80 matches
Most dismissals (wicketkeeper/innings): 6 by Dinkar Deshpande v Haryana (Delhi, 1972-73)
Most catches (fielder): Yashpal Singh – 77
Highest partnership: Hemu Adhikari/AK Khanna – 315* for sixth wicket v Rajasthan (Ajmer, 1951-52)
Most capped player: Yashpal Singh – 87

Kerala

Kerala finished in Group C's mid-table for the third year in a row. They had two outright wins and claimed the first-innings lead on four occasions, but in a group where only the top two progressed, Kerala were guilty of not converting some of those leads into outright wins. They needed a bonus-point win against Himachal Pradesh in their last league game at Malappuram and prepared a rank turner, but it backfired as they lost the game in just 483 minutes. KS Monish, the left-arm spinner, had a breakthrough season to end as the third-highest wicket-taker, but Sandeep Warrier was the team's next best bowler with only 28 wickets. Though Rohan Prem finished 11th on season's batting charts, no other batsman touched the 500-run mark and Sanju Samson averaged only 16.00 in 13 innings. They signed up Iqbal Abdulla, Jalaj Saxena and Bhavin Thakkar as their three professionals for the 2016-17 season.

Manoj Narayan

Results: Took the first-innings lead against Jammu & Kashmir (away), took the first-innings lead against Hyderabad (away), lost to Jharkhand by 133 runs (home), took the first-innings lead against Services (away), took the first-innings lead against Tripura (home), beat Goa by an innings and 83 runs (away), beat Saurashtra by 45 runs (home), lost to Himachal Pradesh by six wickets (home).
Best batsman: Rohan Prem (705 runs, 8 matches)
Best bowler: KS Monish (49 wickets, 8 matches)
Debutants (3): Ahmed Farzeen, Fabid Ahmed, Mohammed Azharuddeen

*** Overall first-class records ***

(P 293, W 45, L 139, D 109)
Maiden match: Lost to Madras by seven wickets (November 9-11, 1957, Madurai)
Highest team total: 566/6 dec v Services (Palakkad, 2007-08)
Lowest team total: 27 v Mysore (Bangalore, 1963-64)
Highest run-getter: Sunil Oasis - 3906 in 74 matches
Highest individual score: 306* by Sreekumar Nair v Services (Palakkad, 2007-08)
Most 100s: Rohan Prem – 10
Highest wicket-taker: KN Ananthapadmanabhan - 310 in 88 matches
Best bowling (innings): 9-45 by Amarjith Singh v Andhra (Kannur, 1971-72)
Best bowling (match): 14-77 by Bhaskaran Ramprakash v Karnataka (Palakkad, 1996-97)
Most dismissals (wicketkeeper): V Kamaruddin – 93 (77ct+16st) in 44 matches
Most dismissals (wicketkeeper/innings): 6 by Ranjith Thomas v Tamil Nadu (Madras, 1981-82)
Most catches (fielder): Sunil Oasis – 88
Highest partnership: George Abraham/Balan Pandit – 410 for fourth wicket v Andhra (Palakkad, 1959-60)
Most capped player: KN Ananathapadmanabhan – 88

Goa

Hrishikesh Kanitkar was appointed coach and Prashant Parameswaran, Rituraj Singh and Dheeraj Jadhav, the captain, were signed up as professionals to boost Goa's chances of earning a promotion. It was not be, as except for Swapnil Asnodkar and Sagun Kamat, who made three centuries each, none of the other batsmen clicked. The bowling lacked bite as only the spin pair of Shadab Jakati and Amit Yadav took 25 or more wickets. It did not help matters that there were only four five-wicket hauls in the season. In the game against Jammu & Kashmir, Asnodkar became the first cricketer from the state to make three double-centuries, and it was also the first time that three Goan batsman scored hundreds in an innings. But they lacked the same kind of application in other games, especially against Kerala where they were bowled out below 200 twice for an innings defeat. *Shubham Malaviya*

Results: Took first-innings lead against Hyderabad (home), conceded first-innings lead to Services (home), beat Tripura by nine wickets (home), conceded first-innings lead to Himachal Pradesh (away), took first-innings lead against Jharkhand (away), conceded first-innings lead to Saurashtra (away), lost to Kerala by an innings and 83 runs (home), took first-innings lead against Jammu & Kashmir (away).
Best batsman: Swapnil Asnodkar (762 runs, 8 matches)
Best bowler: Shadab Jakati (26 wickets, 8 matches)

*** Overall first-class records ***

(P 168, W 18, L 77, D 73)
Maiden match: Lost to Kerala by six wickets (November 30-December 2, 1985, Vasco Da Gama)
Highest team total: 583 v Jharkhand (Porvorium, 2010-11)
Lowest team total: 28 v Kerala (Thalassery 1998-99)
Highest run-getter: Swapnil Asnodkar – 5052 in 70 matches
Highest individual score: 254* by Swapnil Asnodkar v Railways (Margao, 2007-08)
Most 100s: Swapnil Asnodkar – 13
Highest wicket-taker: Shadab Jakati - 223 in 78 matches
Best bowling (innings): 9-29 by Faizal Shaikh v Services (Delhi, 2002-03)
Best bowling (match): J Gokulakrishnan – 11-114 v Karnataka at Panaji, 1996/97
Most dismissals (wicketkeeper): Ajay Ratra – 56 (50ct+6st) in 21 matches
Most dismissals (wicketkeeper/innings): 6 by Amitabh Velaskar v Karnataka (Bangalore, 2001-02)
Most catches (fielder): Sagun Kamat – 59
Highest partnership: Ajay Ratra/Rahul Keni – 310 for fourth wicket v Rajasthan (Jaipur, 2010-11)
Most capped player: Shadab Jakati –78

Jammu & Kashmir

Returning home after floods forced them to play all their matches away in 2014-15, Jammu & Kashmir failed to take advantage, partly because of two factions claiming rights to run affairs and hampering pre-season preparations. Ian Dev Singh, the season's fifth-highest run-getter who was selected in the Rest of India squad for the Irani Cup, Parveez Rasool and Mithun Manhas, who moved from Delhi after 18 seasons to be his birth state's coach and captain, made seven centuries between them, but lacked

Ian Dev Singh: 773 runs, eight matches. – *Wisden India*

support from others. The seamers – the team's biggest strength – were ordinary, and only three of the 23 players fielded featured in all the games. Among individual milestones, Manhas became the fourth batsman to cross the 8000-run mark in Ranji history, and Bandeep Singh's 16-ball 51 against Himachal Pradesh is now the fastest fifty, bettering 18-ball efforts of Shakti Singh in 1990-91and Yusuf Pathan in 2012-13. *Sidhanta Patnaik*

Results: Conceded first-innings lead to Kerala (home), lost to Himachal Pradesh by ten wickets (away), lost to Services by nine wickets (home), took first-innings lead against Tripura (away), took first-innings lead against Hyderabad (away), conceded first-innings lead to Jharkhand (away), conceded first-innings lead to Goa (home), lost to Saurashtra by an innings and 63 runs (home).
Best batsman: Ian Dev Singh (773 runs, 8 matches)
Best bowler: Ram Dayal (20 wickets, 7 matches)
Debutants (8): Samad Bhat, Rohit Sharma, Deepak Manhas, Abhinav Puri, Aamir Sofi, Pranav Gupta, Vijay Dogra, Umar Nissar.

*** Overall first-class records ***

(P 267, W 21, L 185, D 61)
Maiden match: Lost to Eastern Punjab by an innings and 78 runs (January 15-17, 1960, Jullundur)
Highest team total: 579/5 v Himachal Pradesh (Una, 1994-95)
Lowest team total: 23 v Delhi (Srinagar, 1960-61)
Highest run-getter: Kavaljit Singh – 4455 in 69 matches
Highest individual score: 210* by Ashwani Gupta v Himachal Pradesh (Una, 1994-95)
Most 100s: Ian Dev Singh – 11
Highest wicket-taker: Abdul Qayoom - 152 in 47 matches
Best bowling (innings): 8-23 by Ravinder Pandit v Services (Srinagar, 1986-87)
Best bowling (match): 13-81 by Ravinder Pandit v Services (Srinagar, 1986-87)
Most dismissals (wicketkeeper): Arshad Bhatt – 82 (71ct+11st) in 32 matches
Most dismissals (wicketkeeper/innings): 6 by Sanjeeva Chowdhury v Haryana (Srinagar, 1988-89)
Most catches (fielder): Ashwani Gupta – 48
Highest partnership: Ashwani Gupta/Vidya Bhaskar – 279 for fourth wicket v Himachal Pradesh (Una, 1994-95)
Most capped player: Kavaljit Singh – 69

Hyderabad

The absence of Pragyan Ojha, who moved to Bengal to improve his chances of an international return, was felt in Hyderabad's bowling as no one took 20 wickets. The strike-rate of the top three bowlers was more than 65, and Sudeep Tyagi, the professional, claimed just four scalps in four matches. While conceding the first-innings lead to Himachal Pradesh after putting up 434 showcased bowling woes, the failed chase of 170 against a Ravindra Jadeja-inspired Saurashtra on a turning pitch exhibited the batting troubles. Hanuma Vihari, in his last season for Hyderabad before shifting to Andhra, continued to show promise, but did not feature among the top 20 run-getters. In a bid to resurrect their lost charm, Hyderabad appointed B Arun as their coach and got S Badrinath to lead them in 2016-17. *Sidhanta Patnaik*

Results: Conceded first-innings to Goa (away), conceded first-innings lead to Kerala (home), conceded first-innings lead to Himachal Pradesh (away), lost to Saurashtra by 35 runs (away), conceded first-innings to Jammu & Kashmir (home), conceded first-innings lead to Services (away), took first-innings lead against Tripura (home), lost to Jharkhand by ten wickets (home).
Best batsman: Hanuma Vihari (626 runs, 8 matches)
Best bowler: Vishal Sharma (17 wickets, 5 matches)
Debutant (1): Mohammed Siraj.

*** Overall first-class records ***

(P 405, W 136, L 77, D 192)
Maiden match: Drew with Maharaj Kumar of Vizianagram's XI (January 11-13, 1931, Secunderabad)
Ranji wins (2): 1937-38, 1986-87
Irani win (1): 1987-88
Highest team total: 944/6 dec v Andhra (Secunderabad, 1993-94)
Lowest team total: 21 v Rajasthan (Jaipur, 2010-11)
Highest run-getter: MV Sridhar – 6056 in 84 matches
Highest individual score: 366 by MV Sridhar v Andhra (Secunderabad, 1993-94)
Most 100s: VV Laxman – 23
Highest wicket-taker: Venkatapathy Raju – 367 in 102 matches
Best bowling (innings): 9-53 by Ghulam Ahmed v Madras (Secunderabad, 1947-48)
Best bowling (match): 14-81 by Ghulam Ahmed v Madras (Secunderabad, 1947-48)
Most dismissals (wicketkeeper): Ibrahim Khaleel - 206 (182ct+24st) in 56 matches
Most dismissals (wicketkeeper/innings): 7 by Ibrahim Khaleel v Assam (Guwahati, 2011-12)
Most catches (fielder): A Nanda Kishore – 89
Highest partnership: Akshath Reddy/Hanuma Vihari – 386 for second wicket v Mumbai (Hyderabad, 2012-13)
Most capped player: Venkatapathy Raju – 102

Tripura

The experienced quartet of Parvinder Singh, Virag Awate, Arindam Das and Rakesh Solanki could not do much to change Tripura's fortune. They went back to the bottom of the table, having finished seventh in the 2014-15 season. On an individual note, Parvinder had a decent season, hitting two centuries and three fifties, but Manisankar Murasingh and Udiyan Bose were the only two players to make more than 400 runs. Rana Dutta waged a lone battle in the bowling department, with no one else recording a five-wicket haul. They lost four games by an innings, and the widening gap between Tripura and the other sides was best captured in the season-opener against Saurashtra where Ravindra Jadeja made 91 and took 11 wickets without being challenged.

Shubham Malaviya

Results: Lost to Saurashtra by an innings and 118 runs (away), lost to Goa by nine wickets (away), conceded first-innings lead to Jammu & Kashmir (home), lost to Himachal Pradesh by an innings and six runs (away), conceded first-innings lead to Kerala (away), lost to Jharkhand by an innings and 67 runs (home), conceded first-innings lead to Hyderabad (away), lost to Services by an innings and 62 runs (home).
Best batsman: Parvinder Singh (499 runs, 8 matches)

Best bowler: Rana Dutta (23 wickets, 8 matches)
Debutants (2): Tapash Mandal, Subash Chakraborty

*** Overall first-class records ***

(P 151, W 7, L 98, D 46)
Maiden match: Lost to Bengal by an innings & 221 runs (December 28-30, 1985, Kolkata)
Highest team total: 650/8 dec v Hyderabad (Hyderabad, 2013-14)
Lowest team total: 42 v Bengal (Agartala, 1995-96)
Highest run-getter: Timir Chanda – 2366 in 71 matches
Highest individual score: 212 by Yogesh Takawale v Hyderabad (Hyderabad, 2013-14)
Most 100s: Nishit Shetty – 5
Highest wicket-taker: Timir Chanda – 136 in 71 matches
Best bowling (innings): 8-133 by Timir Chanda v Himachal Pradesh (Agartala, 2011-12)
Most dismissals (wicketkeeper): Rajib Dutta – 94 (79st+15st) in 48 matches
Most dismissals (wicketkeeper/innings): 6 by Karthik Iyer v Vidarbha (Nagpur, 2004-05)
Most catches (fielder): Subal Chowdhury – 44
Highest partnership: Rajarshi Chaudhuri/Arshad Baig – 233* for second wicket v Bengal (Kolkata, 1989-90)
Most capped player: Timir Chanda – 71

Round-wise review by KARUNYA KESHAV and SIDHANTA PATNAIK

Round 1: Saurashtra, Punjab pocket bonus points

Karnataka extended their unbeaten run in the Ranji Trophy to 31, but a draw against Assam while conceding first-innings points was not how they would have liked to do it. For Assam, promoted to Group A from C, it was payback for the quarter-final defeat at the hands of the same opposition the previous year. As they took another step in their development, Arun Karthik's century, his first of three for the season, was portentous.

Of the 12 games, four provided outright results, with Saurashtra and Punjab pocketing bonus points.

Gurkeerat Singh extended his match-winning form with the India A side to post the season's first double-hundred. He was one of four Punjab batsmen to polish his career stats with a ton against Railways, with Varun Khanna, the left-arm spinner, unravelling what was left of the hapless side.

There were run-fests aplenty; even Umesh Yadav found himself among the highest scorers, with a 106-ball hundred for Vidarbha from No. 9.

Diwesh Pathania, on debut, bundled Jharkhand out for their lowest score of 45 with his medium-pace in a low-scoring game. Also swimming against the tide of bat speaking louder than ball in the first round was Ravindra Jadeja. His third ten-wicket haul in first-class cricket bode well for an India comeback.

The controversies that dogged Delhi in the pre-season with high-profile transfers and administrative issues continued as Ajay Jadeja, the new coach, missed their first game and stepped down.

Group A

Barsapara Cricket Stadium, Guwahati, October 1-4: Karnataka 187 in 75.2 overs (Shishir Bhavane 65, Mayank Agarwal 36; Syed Mohammad 7-44, Amit Verma 2-16) and 394/8 dec in 94 overs (R Samarth 131, M Agarwal 47; Swarupam Purkayastha 3-78, Syed 2-91) drew with **Assam** 194 in 78.5 overs (A Verma 57, Pallavkumar Das 55; Vinay Kumar 2-20, Karun Nair 2-11) and 259/5 in 102 overs (Arun Karthik 115*, Gokul Sharma 55; Vinay 2-41, J Suchith 2-60). Assam won on the basis of first-innings lead. *MoM*: Syed Mohammad.

MCA Stadium, Pune, October 1-4: Haryana 335 in 106.1 overs (Himanshu Rana 157, Virender Sehwag 82; Nikit Dhumal 3-55, Samad Fallah 3-78) drew with **Maharashtra** 570/6 in 150 overs (Ankit Bawne 172, Chirag Khurana 136*; Ashish Hooda 2-75, Jayant Yadav 2-175). Maharashtra won on the basis of first-innings lead. *MoM*: Ankit Bawne.

Sawai Mansingh Stadium, Jaipur, October 1-4: Delhi 138 in 47 overs (Sumit Narwal 25, Gautam Gambhir 24; Deepak Chahar 5-60, Aniket Chaudhary 3-26) and 437/9 dec in 124.5 overs (S Narwal 106*, G Gambhir 93; Nathu Singh 7-87, Puneet Yadav 2-42) drew with **Rajasthan** 240 in 75.4 overs (D Chahar 50, Puneet 46; S Narwal 3-47, Manan Sharma 3-59) and 186/3 in 91 overs (Vineet Saxena 80*, Puneet 75*; Pawan Suyal 2-23). Rajasthan won on the basis of first-innings lead. *MoM*: Deepak Chahar.

VCA Stadium, Jamtha, Nagpur, October 1-4: Vidarbha 467 in 143.4 overs (Umesh Yadav 128*, Aditya Shanware 119; Basant Mohanty 3-65, Suryakant Pradhan 3-76) drew with **Odisha** 274 in 94.3 overs (Govinda Poddar 148*, Anurag Sarangi 35; Akshay Wakhare 4-84, Ravikumar Thakur 3-34) and 230/6 in 105 overs (f/o) (A Sarangi 92, Pratik Das 39*; A Wakhare 5-77). Vidarbha won on the basis of first-innings lead. *MoM*: Akshay Wakhare.

Group B

Dr PVG Raju ACA Sports Complex, Vizianagaram, October 1-4: Andhra 244 in 123.2 overs (Ricky Bhui 103, Mohammad Kaif 90; Balwinder Sandhu 5-53, Shardul Thakur 3-47) and 176/3 in 65 overs (Prasanth Kumar 59, M Kaif 49*; Vishal Dabholkar 2-26) drew with **Mumbai** 237 in 91.5 overs (Siddhesh Lad 86, Akhil Herwadkar 33; B Ayyappa 6-71, CV Stephen 2-61). Andhra won on the basis of first-innings lead. *MoM*: B Ayyappa.

PCA Stadium, Mohali, October 1-4: Punjab 604/5 in 171.1 overs (Gurkeerat Singh Mann 201*, Uday Kaul 112, Mandeep Singh 109, Gitansh Khera 102*) beat **Railways** 196 in 56 overs (Ashish Singh 90, Saurabh Wakaskar 69; Barinder Sran 6-61, Siddarth Kaul 4-53) and 282 in 68 overs (Arindam Gosh 98*, Prashant Awasthi 44; Varun Khanna 8-97) by an innings and 126 runs. *MoM*: Barinder Sran.

MA Chidambaram Stadium, Chepauk, Chennai, October 1-3: Tamil Nadu 125 in 57.4 overs (Baba Aparajith 44, Bharath Shankar 28; Yusuf Pathan 4-29, Bhargav Bhatt 4-32) and 155 in 59.4 overs (B Aparajith 39, Baba Indrajith 35; B Bhatt 6-58, Swapnil Singh 2-56) beat **Baroda** 159 in 49.2 overs (Y Pathan 41, Kedar Devdhar 40; Rahil Shah 4-38, DT Chandrasekar 4-50) and 114 in 35.4 overs (Deepak Hooda 32, K Devdhar 23; Rahil Shah 5-43, Malolan Rangarajan 3-38) by seven runs. *MoM*: Rahil Shah.

Teerthanker Mahaveer University Ground, Moradabad, October 1-4: Uttar Pradesh 686/7 dec in 185.1 overs (Mohammad Saif 198, Sarfaraz Khan 155, Almas Shaukat 128; Ishwar Pandey 3-75, Jalaj Saxena 3-194) drew with **Madhya Pradesh** 531/7 in 172 overs (Aditya Shrivastava 169, Harpreet Singh 88*; Ankit Rajpoot 4-87, Kuldeep Yadav 3-152). No result. *MoM*: Mohammad Saif.

Group C

GCA Academy Ground, Porvorim, October 1-4: Hyderabad 325 in 101 overs (Hanuma Vihari 82, Akshath Reddy 61; Rituraj Singh 3-74, Shadab Jakati 2-29) drew with **Goa** 425/7 in 140.4 overs (Sagun Kamat 109, Darshan Misal 67; Vishal Sharma 3-93, Akash Bhandari 2-81). Goa won on the basis of first-innings lead. *MoM*: Sagun Kamat.

Sher-i-Kashmir Stadiium, Srinagar, October 1-4: Jammu & Kashmir 330 in 106.5 overs (Bandeep Singh 82, Waseem Raza 73; KS Monish 3-63, Raiphi Gomez 2-33) and 225 in 82.5 overs (Adil Reshi 54, Ian Dev Singh 50; R Gomez 3-8, Rohan Prem 3-48) drew with **Kerala** 485/8 dec in 161 overs (Sachin Baby 151, Sanju Samson 101; Ram Dayal 3-79, Parveez Rasool 2-92) and 44/4 in 8 overs (R Dayal 2-15, Mohammad Mudhasir 2-20). Kerala won on the basis of first-innings lead. *MoM*: Sachin Baby.

Madhavrao Scindia Cricket Ground, Rajkot, October 1-4: Saurashtra 307 in 106 overs (Sheldon Jackson 97, Ravindra Jadeja 91; Tushar Saha 4-72, Abhijit Dey 4-118) beat **Tripura** 103 in 59.1 overs (Arindam Das 24; R Jadeja 6-27, Kamlesh Makvana 3-32) and 86 in 53 overs (f/o) (Manisankar Maurasingh 36; R Jadeja 5-45, Dharmendrasinh Jadeja 4-12) by an innings and 118 runs. *MoM*: Ravindra Jadeja.

Palam A Ground, Model Sports Complex, Delhi, October 1-3: Jharkhand 45 in 37.5 overs (Diwesh Pathania 6-19, Raushan Raj 3-14) and 192 in 74 overs (Saurabh Tiwary 56, Virat Singh 51; D Pathania 7-64) lost to **Services** 161 in 51 overs (Rajat Paliwal 26, Poonam Poonia 24; Rahul Shukla 3-61, Jaskaran Singh 2-24) and 78/1 in 29.5 overs (Soumik Chatterjee 37, Anshul Gupta 34*) by nine wickets. *MoM*: Diwesh Pathania.

Round 2: Jadeja to the fore

Ravindra Jadeja bowled long, threatening spells to take his tally in two matches to 24, a career-best 13 for 126 against Jharkhand helping Saurashtra wrap up a win within two days. And as if to prove there were no demons on a dry pitch, he backed it up with his second fifty in as many matches.

It was a good week for India internationals and those knocking on national doors: Ishant Sharma, who had been left out of the initial Delhi squad because the selectors claimed they couldn't reach him on the phone to confirm his availability, returned for the second match and gave Vidarbha a taste of his intimidating Test form. Hardik Pandya built on his stellar IPL run with five wickets, while Shreyas Iyer reached his maiden 200.

Krishna Das, seen here with Assam coach Sanath Kumar, took his side to the top of Group A. — *Special arrangement*

Krishna Das, who nine years previously had been left doubting himself after an accident nearly signalled the end of his cricket dreams, picked up ten wickets as Assam shot to the top of Group A. Krishna formed a formidable lead partnership with Arup Das, bowling out Rajasthan for 84 in their second hit, while Arun Karthik did his bit with a 151.

Karnataka's struggles continued, a freakish dismissal of Bengal's Shreevats Goswami winning them no fans. R Vinay Kumar threw the ball back at the batsman's end after it had been straight-batted; Goswami could ground his bat, but the throw not only ricocheted off his willow onto the stumps, but also caused the bat to jump upon impact; Goswami was given out.

Group A

Barsapara Cricket Stadium, Guwahati, October 8-11: Rajasthan 186 in 83.4 overs (Vineet Saxena 42, Dishant Yagnik 36*; Krishna Das 5-32, Arup Das 2-26) and 84 in 28.4 overs (Ashok Menaria 21; Krishna 5-23, Arup 5-39) lost to **Assam** 422/9 dec in 151 overs (Arun Karthik 151, Kunal Saikia 50; Ajay Singh 5-116, Nathu Singh 2-77) by an innings and 152 runs. *MoM*: Krishna Das.

Feroz Shah Kotla, Delhi, October 8-11: Vidarbha 298 in 117 overs (Faiz Fazal 56, S Badrinath 44; Ishant Sharma 6-36, Pradeep Sangwan 3-53) and 98 in 55.1 overs (Aditya Shanware 25, Wasim Jaffer 21; Ishant 3-11, P Sangwan 3-30, Manan Sharma 3-31) lost to **Delhi** 302 in 123.3 overs (Gautam Gambhir 96, Nitesh Rana 61; Akshay Wakhare 5-113, Swapnil Bandiwar 2-48) and 96/0 in 14.1 (Unmukt Chand 51*, G Gambhir 45*) by ten wickets. *MoM*: Manan Sharma.

M Chinnaswamy Stadium, Bangalore, October 8-11: Bengal 312 in 88.2 overs (Sudip Chatterjee 145, Wriddhiman Saha 90; Vinay Kumar 4-80, HS Sharath 3-47) and 248/4 in 86 overs (Manoj Tiwary 102*, Naved Ahmed 95) drew with **Karnataka** 537/9 dec in 150.4 overs (Shreyas Gopal 139, Karun Nair 126, Shishir Bhavane 119; Veer Pratap Singh 4-86, Ashok Dinda 2-115). Karnataka won on the basis of first-innings lead. *MoM*: Manoj Tiwary.

Barabati Stadium, Cuttak, October 8-11: Maharashtra 281 in 101.2 overs (Harshad Khadiwale 74, Ankit Bawne 60; Suryakant Pradhan 4-90, Biplab Samantray 3-31) and 289/4 dec in 92.1 overs (Kedar Jadhav 100*, Swapnil Gugale 71; Basant Mohanty 2-58) drew with **Odisha** 267 in 103.5 overs (Govinda Poddar 100, Pratik Das 62; Shrikant Mundhe 6-62, Anupam Sanklecha 2-58) and 129/5 in 55 overs (Girija Rout 31, Anurag Sarangi 28; Anupam Sanklecha 2-11). Maharashtra won on the basis of first-innings lead. *MoM*: Shrikant Mundhe.

Group B

Dr PVG Raju ACA Sports Complex, Vizianagaram, October 8-11: Gujarat 308 in 100.3 overs (Parthiv Patel 122, Venugopal Rao 39; D Siva Kumar 3-44, P Vijaykumar 3-61, CV Stephen 3-99) and 254/4 in 90 overs (Priyank Panchal 72, Bhargav Merai 54) drew with **Andhra** 421 in 127.2 overs (Srikar Bharat 127, Mohammad Kaif 76; Rush Kalaria 5-55, Niraj Patel 3-39). Andhra won on the basis of first-innings lead. *MoM*: Srikar Bharat.

Moti Bagh Stadium, Vadodara, October 8-10: Railways 166 in 48 overs (Karn Sharma 51, Krishnakant Upadhyay 26; Hardik Pandya 5-61, Swapnil Singh 4-31) and 221 in 61.3 (Prashant Awasthi 67, Karn 51; H Pandya 3-30, Bhargav Bhatt 2-40) lost to **Baroda** 500/8 dec in 142 overs (Deepak Hooda 122, Kedar Devdhar 88, Anureet Singh 5-111) by an innings and 113 runs. *MoM*: Hardik Pandya.

Emerald High School Ground, Indore, October 8-11: Tamil Nadu 596/9 dec in 202.2 overs (J Kousik 151, Malolan Rangarajan 131; Udit Birla 3-52, Ishwar Pandey 3-145) drew with **Madhya Pradesh** 407 in 141.3 overs (Jalaj Saxena 124, Aditya Shrivastava 90; Aswin Crist 4-88, L Vignesh 2-81). Tamil Nadu won on the basis of first-innings lead. *MoM*: J Kousik.

Wankhede Stadium, Mumbai, October 8-11: Punjab 154 in 57 overs (Manan Vohra 34, Gitansh Khera 32; Balwinder Sandhu 4-31, Shardul Thakur 4-47) and 403 in 127.3 overs (Mandeep Singh 116, Jiwanjot Singh 91; Akhil Herwadkar 6-52) lost to **Mumbai** 569/8 dec in 124 overs (Shreyas Iyer 200, Aditya Tare 137*; Barinder Sran 3-87, Siddarth Kaul 2-103) by an innings and 12 runs. *MoM*: Shreyas Iyer.

Group C

GCA Academy Ground, Porvorim, October 8-11: Services 402 in 137.1 overs (Rajat Paliwal 92, Anshul Gupta 89; Shadab Jakati 3-80, Rituraj Singh 3-88) and 217/7 dec in 65.5 overs (Soumik Chatterjee 64, Yashpal Singh 59; Amit Yadav 3-40) drew with **Goa** 285 in 134.3 overs (Swapnil Asnodkar 139, Rahul Keni 29; Poonam Poonia 5-60, Diwesh Pathania 3-87) and 3/0 in 6 overs. Services won on the basis of first-innings lead. *MoM*: Poonam Poonia.

HPCA Stadium, Dharamsala, October 8-11: Jammu & Kashmir 293 in 94.5 overs (Parveez Rasool 114*, Ian Dev Singh 47; Rishi Dhawan 4-107, Akash Vasisht 2-59) and 276 in 107.5 overs (Shubham Khajuria 73, Paras Sharma 43; A Vasisht 4-71, Bipul Sharma 3-50) lost to **Himachal Pradesh** 554 in 142.4 overs (Nikhil Gangta 203, Bipul 117*; Parveez Rasool 3-140, Umar Nazir 2-90) and 16/0 in 5 overs by ten wickets. *MoM*: Nikhil Gangta.

Rajiv Gandhi International Stadium, Uppal, Hyderabad, October 8-11: Kerala 401 in 160.2 overs (Rohan Prem 208, VA Jagadesh 42; Akash Bhandari 5-72, Mehdi Hasan 3-97) drew with **Hyderabad** 218 in 113 overs (Akshath Reddy 73, B Anirudh 57*; KS Monish 6-91, Sandeep Warrier 2-24) and 176/7 in 77 overs (f/o) (Tanmay Agarwal 64, Akshath Reddy 43; KS Monish 5-73). Kerala won on the basis of first-innings lead. *MoM*: Rohan Prem.

Madhavrao Scindia Cricket Ground, Rajkot, October 8-9: Jharkhand 168 in 43.5 overs (Ishan Kishan 87, Saurabh Tiwary 25*; Ravindra Jadeja 6-71, Kamlesh Makvana 4-46) and 122 in 52 overs (Ishank Jaggi 31; R Jadeja 7-55, K Makvana 3-34) lost to **Saurashtra** 205 in 50 overs (R Jadeja 58, Cheteshwar Pujara 27; Shahbaz Nadeem 4-38, Samar Quadri 2-54) and 86/2 in 28.5 overs (Sagar Jogiyani 46, C Pujara 23*) by eight wickets. *MoM*: Ravindra Jadeja.

Round 3: Mumbai find answers at every step

The appearance of new names every week along with the regulars in Mumbai's column of match-winners was perhaps an early indicator of a team clicking on multiple levels. A last-wicket come-from-behind victory against Tamil Nadu found stars in Vishal Dhabolkar, the left-arm spinner, and Siddesh Lad, with Iyer and Suryakumar Yadav doing their bit to top Group B.

Another left-arm spinner, Shahbaz Nadeem, picked up seven Kerala wickets, a career highlight for him, to turn around Jharkhand's campaign with their first win of the season from Group C.

Himachal posted 707 for 8, the highest total of the season, thanks to Robin Bist's double-hundred, Rishi Dhawan's own completed double of 2000 runs and 200 wickets, and Ankush Bains's 161.

Parthiv Patel's second century in as many matches signalled a timely return to consistency, but Gujarat were trumped in the batting stakes by a fiery Yuvraj Singh, who too had much to prove.

Virender Sehwag's homecoming to the Feroz Shah Kotla was a disappointment, for him personally

Mumbai's soldier: Suryakumar Yadav finished among the season's top-four run-getters. — *Joshua Veeranathan*

and for Haryana. Delhi, putting their off-field troubles behind them, rose to the top of Group A as Unmukt Chand, falling agonisingly short of a ton, helmed a tough chase.

Assam were handed a reality check in a low-scoring game in Cuttack. Seamers were in the thick of action as 15 wickets fell on the first day, then 13 on the second, before Govinda Poddar's run-a-ball 77 sealed a win for Odisha.

Group A

Eden Gardens, Kolkata, October 15-18: Rajasthan 198 in 95.5 overs (Vineet Saxena 66*, Ashok Menaria 40; Pragyan Ojha 4-49, Ashok Dinda 2-44) and 146/5 in 57 overs (A Menaria 69*, Puneet Yadav 33; A Dinda 2-21) drew with **Bengal** 282 in 90.3 overs (Manoj Tiwary 83; Pankaj Shaw 52; Ajay Singh 3-72, Aniket Choudhary 2-32). Bengal won on the basis of first-innings lead. *MoM*: Manoj Tiwary.

Feroj Shah Kotla, Delhi, October 15-18: Haryana 195 in 78.1 overs (Jayant Yadav 41, Virender Sehwag 37; Manan Sharma 5-57, Ishant Sharma 2-29) and 265 in 93.4 overs (V Sehwag 51, Sachin Rana 46; Manan 6-105, Pradeep Sangwan 2-53) lost to **Delhi** 237 in 73.4 overs (Unmukt Chand 68, Nitish Rana 48; Jayant 4-78, Ashish Hooda 3-33, Harshal Patel 3-61) and 225/6 in 68 overs (U Chand 99, Milind Kumar 44*; Harshal 4-76, A Hooda 2-46) by four wickets. *MoM*: Unmukt Chand.

M Chinnaswamy Stadium, Bangalore, October 15-18: Karnataka 350 in 102.4 overs (Manish Pandey 104, Robin Uthappa 59; Ravikumar Thakur 4-50, Swapnil Bandiwar 2-74) and 331/3 dec in 112 overs (R Samarth 121*, Karun Nair 101*; S Bandiwar 2-50) drew with **Vidarbha** 310 in 118.4 overs (S Badrinath 92, Ganesh Satish 81; S Aravind 4-46, J Suchith 4-51) and 17/0 in 11 overs. Karnataka won on the basis of first-innings lead. *MoM*: Manish Pandey.

Barabati Stadium, Cuttak, October 15-17: Assam 92 in 52.4 overs (Amit Verma 20; Basant Mohanty 5-24, Alok Sahoo 2-18) and 137 in 75.3 overs (Syed Mohammad 42*, Tarjinder Singh 27; Suryakant Pradhan 5-27, B Mohanty 3-29) lost to **Odisha** 88 in 41 overs (Anurag Sarangi 27, Natraj Behera 23; Krishna Das 7-21, Arup Das 3-45) and 142/2 in 35 (Govinda Poddar 77*, A Sarangi 29*) by eight wickets. *MoM*: Basant Mohanty.

Group B

Dr PVG Raju ACA Sports Complex, Vizianagaram, October 15-18: Baroda 302 in 107.2 overs (Kedar Devdhar 97, Swapnil Singh 74; CV Stephen 4-72, B Ayyappa 2-52) and 60/2 in 17 overs (K Devdhar 30*, Deepak Hooda 29*; B Ayyappa 2-18) drew with **Andhra** 474/6 dec in 195.4 overs (Srikar Bharat 144, Ricky Bhui 116, AG Pradeep 100; Ketan Panchal 2-23, Sagar Mangalorkar 2-97). Andhra won on the basis of first-innings lead. *MoM*: Srikar Bharat.

Bandra Kurla Complex, Mumbai, October 15-18: Tamil Nadu 434 in 144.4 overs (Dinesh Karthik 167, Baba Aparajith 62; Vishal Dabholkar 5-122, Shardul Thakur 2-73) and 95 in 36 overs (Malolan Rangarajan 33, M Vijay 29; V Dabholkar 7-53, S Thakur 2-19) lost to **Mumbai** 294 in 93 overs (Siddhesh Lad 150, Dhawal Kulkarni 39; M Mohammed 5-86, Rahil Shah 3-78) and 236/9 in 60.4 overs (Shreyas Iyer 83, Surykumar Yadav 58; R Shah 4-78, M Rangarajan 3-44) by one wicket. *MoM*: Vishal Dabholkar.

PCA Stadium, Mohali, October 15-18: Gujarat 467 in 139.1 overs (Parthiv Patel 113, Priyank Panchal 105; Sarabjit Ladda 5-133, Barinder Sran 2-96) and 135/4 in 43 overs (Bhargav Merai 56, Rujul Bhatt 32; S Ladda 2-60) drew with **Punjab** 608 in 159.3 overs (Yuvraj Singh 187, Manan Vohra 104; R Bhatt 8-151). Punjab won on the basis of first-innings lead. *MoM*: Yuvraj Singh.

Jawaharlal Nehru Stadium, Ghaziabad, October 15-18: Railways 375 in 101.3 overs (Ashish Singh 101, Faiz Ahmed 74; Kuldeep Yadav 3-64, Piyush Chawla 2-53) and 229/4 dec in 70 overs (F Ahmed 80, Ashish 60; Ankit Rajpoot 2-53) beat **Uttar Pradesh** 264 in 103.5 overs (Tanmay Srivastava 93, Almas Shaukat 76; Ranjit Mali 5-88, Anureet Singh 3-67) and 58 in 42 overs (Anureet 5-15, Krishnakant Upadhyay 4-32) by 282 runs. *MoM*: Anureet Singh.

Group C

GCA Academy Ground, Porvorim, October 15-17: Tripura 61 in 31.5 overs (Kaushal Acharjee 20; Rituraj Singh 3-17, Darshan Misal 2-1) and 245 in 75.1 overs (Manisankar Murasingh 104, Arindam Das 41; Shadab Jakati 5-54, Amit Yadav 2-53) lost to **Goa** 257 in 90.1 overs (D Misal 62, Sagun Kamat 45; Rana Dutta 4-44, Manisankar Murasingh 2-42) and 50/1 in 25.1 overs (S Kamat 28*, Amogh Desai 20*) by nine wickets. *MoM*: Shadab Jakati.

HPCA Stadium, Dharamsala, October 15-18: Hyderabad 434 in 146.3 overs (Tanmay Agarwal 118, Hanuma Vihari 101; Ronit More 4-84, Rishi Dhawan 3-138) and 2/0 in 13 overs drew with **Himachal Pradesh** 707/8 dec in 195 overs (Robin Bist 220*, Ankush Bains 161, R Dhawan 114; B Sandeep 3-163, Chama Milind 3-161). Himachal Pradesh won on the basis of first-innings lead. *MoM*: Robin Bist.

Gandhi Memorial Science College Ground, Jammu, October 15-16: Jammu & Kashmir 85 in 43 overs (Parveez Rasool 24*, Shubham Khajuria 24; Raushan Raj 7-38, Diwesh Pathania 3-37) and 161 in 53.5 overs (S Khajuria 51, P Rasool 32; Muzzaffaruddin Khalid 7-61) lost to **Services** 229 in 66.4 overs (Rajat Paliwal 70, Yashpal Singh 66; Rohit Sharma 4-55, Umar Nazir 4-75) and 18/1 in 3.3 overs by nine wickets. *MoM*: Rajat Paliwal.

Perintalmanna Cricket Stadium, Malappuram, October 15-18: Jharkhand 202 in 76 overs (Saurabh Tiwary 75, Prakash Munda 54; Sandeep Warrier 4-56, Rohan Prem 2-2) and 262 in 88.4 overs (Ishan Kishan 58, S Tiwary 46; KS Monish 5-66, Raiphi Gomez 2-27) beat **Kerala** 148 in 65.4 overs (R Prem 52, VA Jagadeesh 44; Varun Aaron 5-23, Kaushal Singh 2-11) and 183 in 63.5 overs (Akshay Kodoth 72, VA Jagadeesh 21; Shahbaz Nadeem 7-64, Kaushal 2-34) by 133 runs. *MoM*: Shahbaz Nadeem.

Round 4: Sehwag adds to Mysore's Dasara festivities

Having announced his retirement from the IPL and international cricket just two days previously, Sehwag treated a vocal group of fans in Mysore to a vintage, carefree game, his 42nd first-class century adding to the city's Dasara festivities. With an all-round Jayant Yadav backing him every step of the way, Karnataka found little relief, not even in HS Sharath's first-innings hat-trick. Robin Uthappa was not pleased with the 'local' support: The heckling was "appalling" and "disappointing", he said. And when Haryana needed just two wickets in the final half hour of the game, it took a valiant effort by Manish Pandey, who batted 28 minutes with a stitched-up finger, to stave off a loss for another game.

Mumbai's batsmen continued to pile on the runs, Akhil Herwadkar coming into his own at the top, Iyer and Suryakumar extending their dominance, while Dhawal Kulkarni and Shardul Thakur formed an incisive and relentless wicket-taking pair.

Jadeja again drove Saurashtra's fortunes, his 13-wicket haul – and sixth straight five-for – scripting their third consecutive win in a match where spinners spoke loudest. Jammu & Kashmir's Bandeep Singh entered the record books with a 16-ball 51, while Uttar Pradesh overcame a first-innings deficit against Andhra to pull off their season's first win.

Virender Sehwag's 42nd first-class century: The Haryana captain, having announced his international retirement, enthralled the Mysore crowd. — *Special arrangement*

Delhi were in the news again for the wrong reasons as Gautam Gambhir and Manoj Tiwary nearly came to blows during an ill-tempered Delhi-Bengal game.

Group A

Feroz Shah Kotla, Delhi, October 22-25: Bengal 357 in 135.5 overs (Sudip Chatterjee 116, Wriddhiman Saha 72; Pradeep Sangwan 4-48, Manan Sharma 2-108) and 217/5 dec in 73.2 overs (Manoj Tiwary 97, Aamir Gani 62; Sumit Narwal 2-37, Manan 2-88) drew with **Delhi** 249 in 101.2 overs (Milind Kumar 77, Nitish Rana 43; Pragyan Ojha 4-77, Ashok Dinda 3-59) and 161/4 in 37 overs (Rishabh Pant 57, N Rana 49; A Gani 3-47). Bengal won on the basis of first-innings lead. *MoM*: Sudip Chatterjee.

Srikantadatta Narasimha Raja Wadeyar Ground, Mysore, October 22-25: Haryana 331 in 90.1 overs (Virender Sehwag 136, Jayant Yadav 100; HS Sharath 5-48, David Mathias 2-48) and 262/9 dec in 91 overs (Nitin Saini 52, V Sehwag 40; Shreyas Gopal 4-53, Vinay Kumar 2-56) drew with **Karnataka** 221 in 75.4 overs (KL Rahul 63, CM Gautam 41*; Rahul Dagar 3-10, Jayant 2-75) and 202/8 in 98 overs (Robin Uthappa 66, R Samarth 32; Jayant 6-65). Haryana won on the basis of first-innings lead. *MoM*: Jayant Yadav.

Sawai Mansingh Stadium, Jaipur, October 22-25: Rajasthan 318 in 102.1 overs (Ashok Menaria 84, Rajat Bhatia 59; Samad Fallah 3-77, Shrikant Mundhe 3-94) and 334/5 dec in 115.3 overs (Ashok Menaria 150*, Rajat Bhatia 64; S Mundhe 2-51) drew with **Maharashtra** 409 in 120.5 overs (Rahul Tripathi 119, Chirag Khurana 77; Ajay Singh 4-87, Deepak Chahar 3-94) and 23/0 in 6 overs (Swapnil Gugale 20). Maharashtra won on the basis of first-innings lead. *MoM*: Rahul Tripathi.

VCA Stadium, Jamtha, Nagpur, October 22-25: Assam 206 in 87 overs (Syed Mohammad 69, Amit Verma 57; Akshay Wakhare 4-47, Umesh Yadav 4-49) and 160 in 81.3 overs (Swarupam Purkayastha 35, A Verma 28; Aditya Sarwate 6-64, A Wakhare 4-37) lost to **Vidarbha** 154 in 74 overs (Ganesh Satish 67, Wasim Jaffer 40; S Purkayastha 4-50, A Verma 3-24) and 215/7 in 74 overs (W Jaffer 71, Faiz Fazal 63; A Verma 3-55, S Purkayastha 3-90) by three wickets. *MoM*: Wasim Jaffer.

Group B

CSR Sharma College Ground, Ongole, October 22-25: Uttar Pradesh 170 in 61.5 overs (Praveen Kumar 47, Tanmay Srivastava 42; D Siva Kumar 3-29, CV Stephen 3-41) and 309 in 88.5 overs (Eklavya Dwivedi 72, Mohammad Saif 56; P Vijaykumar 4-68, D Siva Kumar 2-34) beat **Andhra** 297 in 95.3 overs (Prasanth Kumar 67, Srikar Bharat 62; Praveen 4-86, Piyush Chawla 2-35) and 126 in 47.3 overs (P Vijaykumar 28; Ankit Rajpoot 5-35, Kuldeep Yadav 2-15) by 56 runs. *MoM*: Praveen Kumar.

Reliance Stadium, Vadodara, October 22-25: Mumbai 447 in 127.1 overs (Shreyas Iyer 173, Abhishek Nayar 89; Ajitesh Argal 4-67, Hardik Pandya 2-50) and 202/5 in 61.3 overs (Suryakumar Yadav 100*, Akhil Herwadkar 58; Swapnil Singh 3-70) drew with **Baroda** 397 in 158.5 overs (Kedar Devdhar 95, Murtuja Vahora 57*; Dhawal Kulkarni 5-82, Abhishek Raut 2-82). Mumbai won on the basis of first-innings lead. *MoM*: Shreyas Iyer.

Dhruve Pandove Stadium, Patiala, October 22-25: Madhya Pradesh 370 in 125.1 overs (Aditya Shrivastava 131, Jalaj Saxena 70; Sarbjit Ladda 5-110, Pargat Singh 3-108) and 314/6 in 107 overs (J Saxena 95, Devendra Bundela 55*; S Ladda 3-52, Pargat 2-88) drew with **Punjab** 358 in 113.5 overs (Uday Kaul 139, Jiwanjot Singh 64; Ankit Sharma 5-122, J Saxena 3-111). Madhya Pradesh won on the basis of first-innings lead. *MoM*: Jalaj Saxena.

Karnail Singh Stadium, Delhi, October 22-24: Gujarat 387 in 127.4 overs (Priyank Panchal 141, Rush Kalaria 80*; Anureet Singh 4-91, Arnab Nandi 2-42) beat **Railways** 234 in 83.5 overs (Saurabh Wakaskar 93, Ashish Singh 36; Jasprit Bumrah 4-47, RP Singh 4-55) and 117 in 39.4 overs (Arindam Ghosh 25*, Ashish 23; Mehul Patel 3-25, J Bumrah 3-37) by an innings and 36 runs. *MoM*: Priyank Panchal.

Group C

HPCA Stadium, Dharamsala, October 22-25: Goa 324 in 104.4 overs (Sagun Kamat 163, Snehal Kauthankar 74; Rishi Dhawan 6-108, Akshay Chauhan 3-77) and 367/6 dec in 118 overs (S Kauthankar 101, Swapnil Asnodkar 72; R Dhawan 2-58, Akshy Vasisht 2-96) drew with **Himachal Pradesh** 376 in 89.2 overs (Paras Dogra 167, Nikhil Gangta 47; Prasanth Parameswaran 5-82, Rituraj Singh 3-95) and 125/2 in 30 overs (Prashant Chopra 60, Ankush Bains 49). Himachal Pradesh won on the basis of first-innings lead. *MoM*: Sagun Kamat.

SCA Stadium, Rajkot, October 22-23: Saurashtra 102 in 42 overs (Sagar Jogiyani 51; Mehdi Hasan 5-43, Vishl Sharma 4-30) and 215 in 67 overs (Chirag Jani 65, Avi Barot 25; M Hasan 5-69, Vishal 4-92) beat **Hyderabad** 148 in 42.2 overs (K Sumanth 41, B Sandeep 24; Ravindra Jadeja 6-75, Kamlesh Makvana 4-23) and 134 in 40 overs (B Sandeep 46, Akshath Reddy 26; R Jadeja 7-60, K Makvana 2-28) by 35 runs. *MoM*: Ravindra Jadeja.

Palam A Ground, Model Sports Complex, Delhi, October 22-25: Kerala 322 in 151 overs (Rohan Prem 101, VA Jagadeesh 59; Rajat Paliwal 3-33, Muzzaffaruddin Khalid 2-72) and 176/3 dec in 57.1 overs (Akshay Kodoth 72, VA Jagadeesh 43; Anshul Gupta 2-23) drew with **Services** 319 in 129.4 overs (A Gupta 68, Ravi Chauhan 56; R Prem 4-44, KS Monish 4-105) and 43/4 in 18 overs (Sachin Baby 3-24). Kerala won on the basis of first-innings lead. *MoM*: Rohan Prem.

Tripura Institute Of Technology Ground, Agartala, October 22-25: Jammu & Kashmir 428 in 121.2 overs (Parveez Rasool 130, Mithun Manhas 96; Abhijit Sarkar 3-66, Rana Dutta 3-86, Manisankar Murasingh 3-91) and 163/3 dec in 30 overs (Bandeep Singh 51*, Ian Dev Singh 40*; R Dutta 2-24) drew with **Tripura** 224 in 91.3 overs (Parvinder Singh 60,

Drama behind the wicket: After their record-breaking 2014-15 season, Karnataka looked a side in disarray. — *Special arrangement*

Udiyan Bose 40; Ram Dayal 4-51, Umar Nazir 2-52) and 244/2 in 91.3 overs (Arindam Das 106*, Parvinder Singh 100*). Jammu & Kashmir won on the basis of first-innings lead. *MoM*: Parveez Rasool.

Round 5: Uthappa's answer to critics

Even as he was criticised for wanting to share Karnataka's wicketkeeping duties with CM Gautam in alternating innings to boost his chances of an international comeback, Uthappa made 160 from No.4 against Rajasthan to set up the first win of the season for the defending champions.

While Karnataka were slow to hit their stride, Saurashtra went a step closer towards booking their place in the knockouts by chasing down 302 against Services. Jaydev Unadkat's first five-wicket haul since November 2013 meant that Yashpal Singh's unbeaten 115 in his 100th first-class match and Rajat Paliwal's record of becoming the first Services batsman to score twin centuries went in vain.

Meanwhile, Devendra Bundela became the fifth batsman to score 8000 runs in the history of the competition, and Mihir Hirwani's maiden five-wicket haul helped Madhya Pradesh celebrate the milestone with their first win of the season.

Paras Dogra's 209 against Tripura made him Himachal Pradesh's most prolific centurion, surpassing Rajiv Nayyar's tally of 17. Happily, it also facilitated a big win.

Basant Mohanty became the third Odisha bowler to take a hat-trick to mark the maiden first-class match at the KIIT Stadium, but Pradeep Sangwan's career-best figures of 7 for 38 gave Delhi the first-innings lead.

Strong performances by Uttar Pradesh, Vidarbha, Tamil Nadu and Punjab, on Gurkeerat Singh Mann's captaincy debut, also stood out as eight of the 12 matches produced outright results.

Group A

CH Bansi Lal Cricket Stadium, Lahli, Rohtak, October 30-November 2: Bengal 329 in 103.3 overs (Pramod Chandila 65, Pankaj Shaw 54; Sachin Rana 5-46, Ashish Hooda 2-49) and 211/8 dec 93.5 overs (P Shaw 61, Sudip Chatterjee 49; A Hooda 4-65) drew with **Haryana** 225 in 83.4 overs (Rohit Sharma 78, Yuzvendra Chahal 42; Mukesh Kumar 4-53, Veer Pratap Singh 2-49) and 195/6 in 62 overs (Rohit 50, S Rana 50; Ashok Dinda 3-52). Bengal won on the basis of first-innings lead. *MoM*: Pankaj Shaw.

KIIT Stadium, Bhubaneswar, October 30-November 2: Delhi 311 in 136.1 overs (Milind Kumar 59, Dhruv Shorey 42; Suryakant Pradhan 4-119, Deepak Behera 3-46, Basant Mohanty 3-80) and 193/9 dec in 31.3 overs (D Shorey 62, Gautam Gambhir 54; B Mohanty 6-39, Dhiraj Singh 2-62) drew with **Odisha** 217 in 75.5 overs (Anurag Sarangi 76, Natraj Behera 62; Pradeep Sangwan 7-38) and 88/3 in 38 overs (N Behera 35, Rajesh Dhuper 26; Pulkit Narang 2-29). Delhi won on the basis of first-innings lead. *MoM*: Pradeep Sangwan.

Sawai Mansigh Stadium, Jaipur, October 30-November 2: Karnataka 281 in 94 overs (Mayank Agarwal 66, R Samarth 65; Aniket Choudhary 5-77, Ajay Singh 2-34) and 318/5 dec in 63 overs (Robin Uthappa 160, Abhishek Reddy 69; Rajat Bhatia 2-44) beat **Rajasthan** 242 in 91.4 overs (R Bhatia 99, Puneet Yadav 28; S Aravind 3-42, Vinay Kumar 3-42) and 265 in 82.2 overs (Pranay Sharma 114, Dishant Yagnik 71*; David Mathias 3-53, Stuart Binny 2-24) by 92 runs. *MoM*: Robin Uthappa.

VCA Ground, Nagpur, October 30-November 2: Vidarbha 332 in 125 overs (Faiz Fazal 120, Shalabh Shrivastava 63; Anupam Sanklecha 3-60, Shrikant Mundhe 3-60) and 149 in 48 overs (Amol Ubarhande 47, Wasim Jaffer 33; Akshay Darekar 5-78, Bharatkumar Solanki 2-21) beat **Maharashtra** 237 in 90.1 overs (Chirag Khurana 74, Swapnil Gugale 42; Aditya Sarwate 3-41, Ravikumar Thakur 2-28) and 162 in 46.3 overs (Harshad Khadiwale 55, Kedar Jadhav 28; Akshay Wakhare 6-58, A Sarwate 4-74) by 82 runs. *MoM*: Faiz Fazal.

Group B

Moti Bagh Stadium, Vadodara, October 30-November 2: Madhya Pradesh 269 in 111.2 overs (Rajat Patidar 60, Harpreet Singh 51; Swapnil Singh 4-61, Bhargav Bhatt 2-30) and 288/6 dec in 68 overs (R Patidar 101, Harpreet 53; Swapnil 4-94) beat **Baroda** 296 in 113.2 overs (Aditya Waghmode 68, Yusuf Pathan 55; Mihir Hirwani 5-60, Jalaj Saxena 2-63) and 174 in 48.4 overs (Y Pathan 86, Swapnil 47; Puneet Datey 4-20, M Hirwani 4-41) by 87 runs. *MoM*: Mihir Hirwani.

Sardar Vallabhbhai Patel Stadium, Valsad, October 30-November 1: Uttar Pradesh 273 in 90.5 overs (Himanshu Asnora 57*, Eklavya Dwivedi 50; Jasprit Bumrah 3-35, Rush Kalaria 3-51) and 257 in 75.2 overs (Umang Sharma 66, Piyush Chawla 62*; Axar Patel 5-90, Jasprit Bumrah 2-33) beat **Gujarat** 100 in 31.4 overs (Parthiv Patel 39, Manpreet Juneja 21; Praveen Kumar 5-16, Saurabh Kumar 5-37) and 275 in 59.4 overs (M Juneja 91, Axar 80; Saurabh 5-106, Ali Murtazza 3-38) by 155 runs. *MoM*: Saurabh Kumar.

Dhruve Pandove Stadium, Patiala, October 30-31: Andhra 80 in 45 overs (Prasanth Kumar 33; Gurkeerat Singh Mann 4-14, Siddarth Kaul 2-11) and 133 in 41.4 overs (Srikar Bharat 39, Prasanth 29; Gurkeerat 5-38, Rajwinder Singh 3-33) lost to **Punjab** 147 in 55 overs (Jiwanjot Singh 59, Uday Kaul 27; Prasanth 4-14, B Ayyappa 2-25) and 67/3 in 19.3 overs (Mandeep Singh 22*) by seven wickets. *MoM*: Gurkeerat Singh Mann.

Dhruve Pandove Stadium, Patiala, October 30-November 2: Tamil Nadu 328 in 111.2 overs (Baba Indrajith 151, Abhinav Mukund 49; Anureet Singh 5-104, Krishnakant Upadhyay 2-93) and 77/2 in 23.2 overs (Dinesh Karthik 43; Anureet 2-43) beat **Railways** 164 in 65.5 overs (V Cheluvaraj 66, Arindam Ghosh 48; Aswin Crist 6-60, J Kousik 3-9) and 240 in 88.2 overs (f/o) (V Cheluvaraj 88, Mahesh Rawat 78; Rahil Shah 4-38, J Kousik 2-45) by eight wickets. *MoM*: Baba Indrajith.

Group C

HPCA Stadium, Dharamsala, October 30-November 2: Tripura 285 in 107.4 overs (Udiyan Bose 95, Manisankar Murasingh 44; Akshay Chauhan 3-55, Bipul Sharma 2-30) and 270 in 84.5 overs (Nirupam Sen Chowdhary 66*, Udiyan Bose 60; Ankush Bedi 3-50, Akash Vasisht 3-63) lost to **Himachal Pradesh** 561/5 dec in 130 overs (Paras Dogra 209*, Ankush Bains 114, Prashant Chopra 101; Rana Dutta 3-79) by an innings and 6 runs. *MoM*: Paras Dogra.

Rajiv Gandhi International Stadium, Uppal, Hyderabad, October 30-November 2: Jammu & Kashmir 460 in 131.2 overs (Mithun Manhas 150, Ian Dev Singh 83; Anwar Ahmed 5-92, Sudeep Tyagi 2-112) and 56/2 in 17 overs (Ian Dev 26*, P Rasool 25*) drew with **Hyderabad** 280 in 92 overs (Tanmay Agarwal 71, B Anirudh 68*; Zahoor Sofi 4-37, Rohit Sharma 4-78) and 329 in 113.1 overs (f/o) (K Sumanth 78, Hanuma Vihari 65; Ram Dayal 5-55, Umar Nazir 3-63). Jammu & Kashmir won on the basis of first-innings lead. *MoM*: Mithun Manhas.

Keenan Stadium, Jamshedpur, October 30-November 2: Goa 302 in 98.4 overs (Swapnil Asnodkar 71, Dheeraj Jadhav 63; Samar Quadri 6-97, Shahbaz Nadeem 3-63) and 102/5 dec in 37 overs (Darshan Misal 39*, S Asnodkar 28; Rahul Shukla 2-7, S Nadeem 2-32) drew with **Jharkhand** 209 in 72.4 overs (Sumit Kumar 51, Kumar Deobrat 49; Shadab Jakati 5-72, Amit Yadav 3-59) and 105/6 in 34 overs (Shiv Gautam 41, K Deobrat 25*; Amit 3-47). Goa won on the basis of first-innings lead. *MoM*: Swapnil Asnodkar.

Palam A Ground, Model Sports Complex, Delhi, October 30-November 2: Services 254 in 69 overs (Rajat Paliwal 121, Yashpal Singh 55*; Jaydev Unadkat 6-80, Shaurya Sanandia 3-62) and 311/6 dec in 76 overs (Yashpal 115, R Paliwal 103; S Sanandia 3-54, Jaydev Unadkat 2-78) lost to **Saurashtra** 264 in 92.4 overs (Avi Barot 66, Chirag Jani 47; Muzzaffaruddin Khalid 5-74, Diwesh Pathania 4-72) and 302/6 in 80.3 overs (Mohsin Dodia 65, Arpit Vasavada 57; M Khalid 4-147) by four wickets. *MoM*: Rajat Paliwal.

Round 6: Jaffer's foray into 10,000 territory

Wasim Jaffer became the first batsman to score 10,000 runs in the history of the competition. "To get these many runs feels really good. I was lucky that I got the opportunity to play for Mumbai for that long," he told *Wisden India*, reflecting on his achievement. "Obviously to have scored these many runs is something I will cherish for the rest of my life."

Vidarbha though could not gift Jaffer with a win as Bengal's Pragyan Ojha took his first ten-wicket haul since his last Test appearance in November 2013. With his 227, Paras Dogra equalled Ajay Sharma's tally of seven double-centuries – the most in Ranji history.

Saxena provided the other highlight of this round with 16 for 154 in Madhya Pradesh's three-day win over Railways in Gwalior. It is now the joint-second-best returns in the competition, along with Pradeep Sunderam's effort for Rajasthan against Vidarbha in 1985. "Mr Narendra Hirwani asked me to bowl with a bit more side-on action. I tried it in the nets, and it worked," explained Saxena. Released by the Indian team, Rohit Sharma made 113 against Uttar Pradesh, even as Iyer hit his third century. Baroda's Irfan Pathan and Munaf Patel returned from injuries for their first match of the season, but could not stop six Gujarat batsmen from making fifty-plus scores.

Group A

Jadavpur University Campus 2nd Ground, Kolkata, November 7-10: Bengal 334 in 115.4 overs (Sudip Chatterjee 116, Abhimanyu Easwaran 58; Akshay Wakhare 4-85, Shrikant Wagh 3-53) and 164 in 62.5 overs (Manoj Tiwary 63, Abhimanyu 26; A Wakhare 5-61, S Wagh 3-27) beat **Vidarbha** 202 in 69.1 overs (Faiz Fazal 63, S Wagh 60*; Pragyan Ojha 7-58, Sayan Ghosh 2-46) and 191 in 91.1 overs (Ganesh Satish 96, S Badrinath 31; P Ojha 4-60, Veer Pratap Singh 3-23) by 105 runs. *MoM*: Pragyan Ojha.

Feroz Shah Kotla, Delhi, November 7-8: Maharashtra 80 in 25.4 overs (Harshad Khadiwale 21; Navdeep Saini 6-32, Pradeep Sangwan 2-19) and 176 in 56 overs (Sangram Atitkar 30, Rohit Motwani 27*; Manan Sharma 4-47, Pawan Negi 2-12) lost to **Delhi** 230 in 68.1 overs (Dhruv Shorey 104*, Nitish Rana 59; Samad Fallah 5-45, Shrikant Mundhe 4-10) and 30/1 in 14 overs by nine wickets. *MoM*: Dhruv Shorey.

CH Bansi Lal Cricket Stadium, Lahli, Rohtak, November 7-10: Haryana 168 in 70.5 overs (Himanshu Rana 56, Rohit Sharma 45; Krishna Das 6-56, Dhiraj Goswami 4-38) and 111 in 50.3 overs (H Rana 27; Arup Das 6-39, Krishna 4-48) lost to **Assam** 120 in 52.2 overs (Gokul Sharma 43, Rahul Hazarika 23; Ashish Hooda 4-27, Harshal Patel 3-37) and 160/4 in 54.1 overs (Amit Verma 51*, Arun Karthik 48; A Hooda 2-62) by six wickets. *MoM*: Krishna Das.

Srikantadatta Narasimha Raja Wadeyar Ground, Mysore, November 7-10: Odisha 232 in 84.1 overs (Govinda Poddar 153, Pratik Das 40; Shreyas Gopal 4-75, J Suchith 3-56) and 104 in 36.1 overs (Anurag Sarangi 44; Stuart Binny 4-34, Shreyas 3-43) lost to **Karnataka** 400/9 dec in 128 overs (Robin Uthappa 148, Mayank Agarwal 78; Suryakant Pradhan 3-94, Dhiraj Singh 3-156) by an innings and 64 runs. *MoM*: Robin Uthappa.

Group B

Sardar Vallabhbhai Patel Stadium, Valsad, November 7-10: Gujarat 505 in 148.2 overs (Priyank Panchal 128, Axar Patel 81; Irfan Pathan 6-47, Hardik Pandya 2-102) beat **Baroda** 252 in 82.3 overs (I Pathan 58, Ambati Raydu 47; Axar 3-81, Jesal Karia 2-21) and 207 in 73.4 overs (f/o) (H Pandya 43, A Raydu 43; Rujul Bhatt 4-48, Axar 4-71) by an innings and 46 runs. *MoM*: Axar Patel.

Captain Roop Singh Stadium, Gwalior, November 7-9: Railways 256 in 82.4 overs (Saurabh Wakaskar 73, V Cheluvaraj 50; Jalaj Saxena 8-96, Ankit Sharma 2-58) and 131 in 51.1 (S Wakakar 26, V Cheluvaraj 25; J Saxena 8-58, Mihir Hirwani 2-22) lost to **Madhya Pradesh** 276 in 90.2 overs (Rajat Patidar 113, Rameez Khan 53; Karn Sharma 5-105, Anureet Singh 3-40) and 112/1 in 19.1 overs (J Saxena 47*, R Patidar 40) by nine wickets. *MoM*: Jalaj Saxena.

Wankhede Stadium, Mumbai, November 7-10: Mumbai 610/9 dec in 153 overs (Shreyas Iyer 137, Rohit Sharma 113; Bhuvneshwar Kumar 2-99, Ankit Rajpoot 2-112) drew with **Uttar Pradesh** 440 in 151 overs (Himanshu Asnora 92, Piyush Chawla 84; Abhishek Nayar 4-63, Vishal Dabholkar 4-116) and 140/1 in 45 overs (f/o) (H Asnora 68*, Umang Sharma 62*). Mumbai won on the basis of first-innings lead. *MoM*: Shreyas Iyer.

MA Chidambaram Stadium, Chepauk, Chennai, November 7-10: Andhra 203 in 77.2 overs (AG Pradeep 78, Srikar Bharat 56; DT Chandrasekar 4-41, Malolan Rangarajan 3-72) drew with **Tamil Nadu** 164/7 in 37 overs (Baba Indrajith 43, R Sathish 33; B Sudhakar 2-44). Andhra won on the basis of first-innings lead. *MoM*: AG Pradeep.

Group C

HPCA Stadium, Dharamsala, November 7-10: Himachal Pradesh 531 in 138.3 overs (Paras Dogra 227, Nikhil Gangta 98; Diwesh Pathania 3-108, Anshul Gupta 2-16) drew with **Services** 448/8 in 170 overs (Yashpal Singh 115, Rajat Paliwal 107; Shresth Nirmohi 3-62, Akshay Chauhan 3-101). No result. *MoM*: Paras Dogra.

Keenan Stadium, Jamshedpur, November 7-10: Jharkhand 551/8 dec in 171.2 overs (Anand Singh 124, Ishan Kishan 109; Parveez Rasool 3-127, Ram Dayal 2-124) drew with **Jammu & Kashmir** 309 in 90.2 overs (Mithun Manhas 98, P Rasool 55; Kaushal Singh 4-38, Shahbaz Nadeem 4-107) and 265/4 in 81.2 overs (f/o) (Ian Dev Singh 126, Shubham Khajuria 77; Jaskaran Singh 2-38). Jharkhand won on the basis of first-innings lead. *MoM*: Kaushal Singh.

Perintalmanna Cricket Stadium, Malappuram, November 7-10: Kerala 347 in 129.5 overs (Rohan Prem 118, Sachin Baby 70; Rana Dutta 5-50, Swapan Das 3-103) and 117/4 dec in 19.3 overs (R Prem 72*; Manisankar Murasingh 3-57) drew with **Tripura** 236 in 98.2 overs (Udiyan Bose 62, Rakesh Solanki 43; Sandeep Warrier 6-69) and 53/0 in 17 overs (U Bose 32*). Kerala won on the basis of first-innings lead. *MoM*: Rohan Prem.

SCA Stadium, Rajkot, November 7-10: Goa 239 in 84 overs (Darshan Misal 106*, Rituraj Singh 45; Dharmendrasinh Jadeja 3-41, Shaurya Sanandia 3-51) and 299/7 dec in 89 overs (Swapnil Asnodkar 104, Snehal Kauthankar 58; Kamlesh Makvana 3-85, S Sanandia 2-38) drew with **Saurashtra** 258 in 101.3 overs (Avi Barot 56, K Makvana 39; Rituraj 5-70, Amit Yadav 4-61) and 223/5 in 76.1 overs (A Barot 93, Sheldon Jackson 55; Amit 3-52). Saurashtra won on the basis of first-innings lead. *MoM*: Avi Barot.

Round 7: Mumbai and Assam head upwards

Dinesh Karthik (8000), Suresh Raina (6000), and Faiz Fazal and Robin Bist (5000) crossed significant milestones in their first-class careers, but Mumbai produced the story of the seventh round with their highest successful fourth-innings chase of 295. After Railways declared on 408 for 4, Mumbai rode on half-centuries from Herwadkar, Iyer and Tare, and an unbroken fifth-wicket partnership of 95 between Tare and Siddesh Lad (41*) to score at 4.60 runs per over.

Arun Karthik's twin half-centuries and Krishna Das's 100th first-class wicket – Gautam Gambhir was the batsman – gave Assam a historic win over Delhi and put them in a strong position for successive quarter-final berths.

Haryana's Jayant Yadav too got his 100th victim in a game where Natraj Behera made an unbeaten 255 – the highest individual score of the season, but Odisha could not push for an outright win on a placid track.

Sudip Chatterjee became the first batsman to score four centuries in the season. Jaydev Shah, the most-capped captain in Ranji Trophy history, marked his 100th first-class match with a knock of 142 against Himachal Pradesh, but that was not enough for Saurashtra to take the first-innings lead.

Umesh Yadav took a hat-trick as Vidarbha recorded another win on their way to a quarter-final spot.

Ambati Rayudu, Baroda's captain, got into a confrontation with the crowd at the Moti Bagh Stadium during their game against Punjab. The police had to be deployed and play was stopped for some time.

Group A

Barsapara Cricket Stadium, Guwahati, November 15-18: Delhi 149 in 59.4 overs (Manan Sharma 46*, Milind Kumar 45; Krishna Das 4-38, Arup Das 3-49) and 172 in 83.2 overs (Unmukt Chand 44, Dhuv Shorey 38; Amit Verma 3-42, Syed Mohammad 3-42) lost to **Assam** 157 in 64.1 overs (Arun Karthik 81, Gokul Sharma 24; Manan 4-41, Pradeep Sangwan 3-33) and 168/5 in 56 overs (Rahul Hazarika 59, A Karthik 55; Manan 2-51) by five wickets. *MoM*: Arun Karthik.

CH Bansi Lal Cricket Stadium, Lahli, Rohtak, November 15-18: Odisha 529/6 dec in 163 overs (Natraj Behera 255*, Ranjit Singh 112; Harshal Patel 2-94, Jayant Yadav 2-164) drew with **Haryana** 216 in 85.5 overs (Nitin Saini 51, Jayant 46; Basant Mohanty 3-51, Suryakant Pradhan 3-53) and 250/4 in 103 overs (f/o) (Chaitanya Bishnoi 86*, N Saini 64; Dhiraj Singh 2-56, Suryakant Pradhan 2-56). Odisha won on the basis of first-innings lead. *MoM*: Natraj Behera.

Haryana beneftted from all-round performances by Jayant Yadav throughout the season. – *Special arrangement*

MCA Stadium, Pune, November 15-18: Bengal 528/8 dec in 180 overs (Sudip Chatterjee 147, Abhimanyu Easwaran 65; Chirag Khurana 4-141, Samad Fallah 2-102) and 100/1 in 33 (Abhimanyu 56*, Sayan Mondal 36) drew with **Maharashtra** 406 in 129.2 overs (Rahul Tripathi 132, Sangram Atitkar 69; Pragyan Ojha 3-71, Mukesh Kumar 2-41). Bengal won on the basis of first-innings lead. *MoM*: Sudip Chatterjee.

VCA Ground, Nagpur, November 15-18: Rajasthan 216 in 88.4 overs (Puneet Yadav 67, Siddharth Dobal 51*; Umesh Yadav 4-45, Akshay Wakhare 3-78) and 226 in 79.1 (Ashok Menaria 76, Vineet Saxena 54; Aditya Sarwate 5-58, Ravi Jangid 3-31) lost to **Vidarbha** 247 in 99.3 overs (A Sarwate 50, Faiz Fazal 40; Tanvir-ul-Haq 4-60, Rajat Bhatia 3-21) and 199/2 in 61.4 overs (S Badrinath 70*, Ganesh Satish 61*) by eight wickets. *MoM*: Aditya Sarwate.

Group B

Moti Bagh Stadium, Vadodara, November 15-17: Baroda 475 in 130.5 overs (Kedar Devdhar 186, Aditya Waghmode 96; Deepak Bansal 3-57, Gurkeerat Singh Mann 2-76) beat **Punjab** 212 in 65.5 overs (Uday Kaul 58, Yuvraj Singh 43; Hardik Pandya 3-50, Munaf Patel 3-54, Irfan Pathan 3-61) and 147 in 38.4 overs (f/o) (Siddarth Kaul 40*, Jiwanjot Singh 27; Munaf 3-19, I Pathan 3-19) by an innings and 116 runs. *MoM*: Kedar Devdhar.

Lalabhai Contractor Stadium, Surat, November 15-18: Gujarat 311 in 106.1 overs (Manpreet Juneja 61, Axar Patel 55; Jalaj Saxena 3-56, Puneet Datey 2-56) and 202/9 dec in 74.3 overs (M Juneja 41, Priyank Panchal 38; J Saxena 6-60, Ankit Sharma 2-72) beat **Madhya Pradesh** 200 in 80.2 overs (Naman Ojha 56, Harpreet Singh 34; Jasprit Bumrah 3-46, Axar 2-39) and 160 in 49.5 overs (Ankit 55, Ankit Kushwah 29; RP Singh 5-33, J Bumrah 2-44) by 153 runs. *MoM*: RP Singh.

Wankhede Stadium, Mumbai, November 15-18: Railways 217 in 84.4 overs (Arindam Ghosh 67, Sagar Mishra 46; Shardul Thakur 4-38, Dhawal Kulkarni 2-40) and 408/4 dec in 104 overs (Saurabh Wakaskar 185, V Cheluvaraj 133*; Vishal Dabholkar 3-115) lost to **Mumbai** 331 in 95.4 overs (Akhil Herwadkar 145, Nikhil Patil 83; Karn Sharma 7-91) and 295/4 in 64 overs (Shreyas Iyer 91, A Herwadkar 75; S Mishra 2-53) by six wickets. *MoM*: Akhil Herwadkar.

Green Park, Kanpur, November 15-18: Uttar Pradesh 348 in 107.1 overs (Almas Shaukat 88, Umang Sharma 73; Malolan Rangarajan 3-51, Aswin Crist 3-86) and 273/5 dec in 62 overs (Suresh Raina 145*, A Shaukat 75; Baba Aprajith 2-73) drew with **Tamil Nadu** 231 in 88 overs (Vijay Shankar 92, M Rangarajan 45; Praveen Kumar 4-65, Saurabh Kumar 2-11) and 212/4 in 84 overs (Abhinav Mukund 71, Baba Aprajith 71; Saurabh 2-30). Uttar Pradesh won on the basis of first-innings lead. *MoM*: Suresh Raina.

Group C

GCA Academy Ground, Povorim, November 15-17: Kerala 441 in 143.4 overs (Robert Fernandez 109, Fabid Ahmed 106; Amit Yadav 4-119, Prasanth Parameswaran 2-51) beat **Goa** 191 in 68.4 overs (Amogh Desai 38, Darshan Misal 37; Sandeep Warrier 6-44, F Ahmed 2-50) and 167 in 52.4 overs (f/o) (P Parameswaran 38, Amit 36; S Warrier 3-31, F Ahmed 2-28) by an innings and 83 runs. *MoM*: Fabid Ahmed.

SCA Stadium, Rajkot, November 15-18: Himachal Pradesh 551 168.1 overs (Prashant Chopra 187, Robin Bist 101; Jaydev Unadkat 4-69, Shaurya Sanandia 2-65) drew with **Saurashtra** 437 in 172 overs (Jaydev Shah 142, Chirag Jani 56; Akash Vasisht 3-101, P Chopra 2-33). Himachal Pradesh won on the basis of first-innings lead. *MoM*: Prashant Chopra.

Palam A Ground, Model Sports Complex, Delhi, November 15-18: Services 353 in 124 overs (Soumik Chatterjee 156, Yashpal Singh 51; Ravi Kiran 4-65, Chama Milind 3-78) and 217/7 dec in 57 overs (Diwesh Pathania 42*, Yashpal 41; C Milind 2-42, R Kiran 2-72) drew with **Hyderabad** 272 in 118.5 overs (Akshath Reddy 125, Tanmay Agarwal 50; D Pathania 3-63, Muzzaffaruddin Khalid 2-43) and 140/3 in 43 overs (A Reddy 72*, K Sumanth 28*; Kamal Passi 2-34). Services won on the basis of first-innings lead. *MoM*: Soumik Chatterjee.

Tripura Institute of Technology Ground, Agartala, November 15-18: Tripura 166 in 55 overs (Parvinder Singh 66, Virag Awate 31; Rahul Shukla 6-40, Jaskaran Singh 2-33) and 161 in 52.5 overs (Manisankar Murasingh 52, Abhijit Sarkar 35; Shahbaz Nadeem 6-50, Jaskaran 2-29) lost to **Jharkhand** 394/4 dec in 113 overs (Ishank Jaggi 102*, Saurabh Tiwary 94; M Murasingh 2-89) by an innings and 67 runs. *MoM*: Rahul Shukla.

Round 8: Turners draw flak

In a thrilling encounter against Madhya Pradesh, Jay Bista's 74 and an unbroken eighth-wicket partnership of 68 between Iqbal Abdulla and Shardul Thakur helped Mumbai chase 280 and become the first team to make it to the knockouts.

Karnataka's prospects received a severe dent when they could not beat Delhi despite Robin Uthappa's third century in a row, during which he hit Dhruv Shorey for 32 runs in one over. It is now the second-most expensive over in the competition history. The draw also left Delhi's fortune in the hands of Vidarbha, Bengal and Assam, who secured a crucial first-innings lead over Maharashtra on a dangerous pitch in Pune.

Eager to secure outright wins to propel their chances, Jharkhand and Bengal produced rank turners for their home games against Himachal Pradesh and Odisha respectively. The pitches came in for scrunity; especially the one

Mayank Agarwal and Robin Uthappa hit centuries, but Karnataka could only draw with Delhi. – *Wisden India, Joshua Veeranathan*

at Kalyani where Odisha were dismissed for 37, even as 26 wickets fell on the second day in Ranchi.

Virender Sehwag returned from the All-Stars series in the US for what would be his last first-class game, but could not arrest Haryana's slide. In the same game, Pankaj Singh, playing his first game of the season after recovering from a spinal injury, took nine wickets as Rajasthan almost avoided relegation.

A rained-out game between Tamil Nadu and Gujarat on first-class cricket's return to Tirunelveli after a decade hampered the chances of both teams. Mohammad Kaif recorded his fourth successive duck as Andhra's relegation fears came close to reality.

Group A

Bengal Cricket Academy Ground, Kalyani, November 23-24: Bengal 142 in 47.3 overs (Abhimanyu Easwaran 88; Dhiraj Singh 5-58, Suryakant Pradhan 3-15) and 135 in 55.2 (Abhimanyu 39, Sudip Chatterjee 37; Basant Mohanty 5-16, Dhiraj Singh 2-47) beat **Odisha** 107 in 29 overs (Arabind Singh 21, Ranjit Singh 20; Aamir Gani 6-34, Pragyan Ojha 2-25) and 37 in 19.2 overs (Ashok Dinda 7-19, P Ojha 3-14) by 133 runs. *MoM*: Abhimanyu Easwaran.
CH Bansi Lal Cricket Stadium, Lahli, Rohtak, November 23-26: Haryana 112 in 52.2 overs (Virender Sehwag 29, Mohit Sharma 23; Pankaj Singh 4-10, Rajat Bhatia 3-41) and 324 in 121.5 (Nitin Saini 146, Mohit Hooda 56; Pankaj 5-85, Tanvir-ul-Haq 3-92) lost to **Rajasthan** 279 in 88.3 overs (Ashok Menaria 47, Puneet Yadav 46; Mohit 5-56, Ashish Hooda 3-62) and 161/1 in 38.5 overs (Puneet 107*, Manender Singh 41*) by nine wickets. *MoM*: Pankaj Singh and Puneet Yadav.

KSCA Rajnagar Stadium, Hubli, November 23-26: Karnataka 542 in 149 overs (Robin Uthappa 148, Mayank Agarwal 118; Navdeep Saini 3-85, Pradeep Sangwan 3-102) drew with **Delhi** 301 in 104.1 overs (Gautam Gambhir 75, Manan Sharma 56; S Aravind 2-41, HS Sharath 2-46) and 290/2 in 92 overs (f/o) (Nitish Rana 132*, Dhruv Shorey 107*; S Aravind 2-39). Karnataka won on the basis of first-innings lead. *MoM*: Mayank Agarwal.

MCA Stadium, Pune, November 23-26: Assam 298 in 105 overs (Arun Karthik 130, Gokul Sharma 76; Shrikant Mundhe 4-67, Anupam Sanklecha 2-55) and 135 in 48.2 (Rahul Hazarika 31; Domnic Muthuswami 4-21, A Sanklecha 3-42) drew with **Maharashtra** 196 in 69 overs (Rahul Tripathi 52, Kedar Jadhav 36; Krishna Das 6-73, Abu Nechim 2-26) and 82/3 in 15 overs (Sangram Atitkar 40*, Swapnil Gugale 30). Assam won on the basis of first-innings lead. *MoM*: Arun Karthik.

Group B

Holkar Cricket Stadium, Indore, November 23-25: Madhya Pradesh 240 in 75.1 overs (Harpreet Singh 59, Ishwar Pandey 35; Ankush Jaiswal 4-63, Shardul Thakur 2-42) and 201 in 71.2 overs (Jalaj Saxena 79, Devendra Bundela 42; S Thakur 3-33, Iqbal Abdulla 3-53) lost to **Mumbai** 162 in 38.1 overs (Jay Bista 27, I Abdulla 21; J Saxena 5-66, Ankit Sharma 5-80) and 283/7 in 73.3 overs (J Bista 74, Aditya Tare 45; J Saxena 4-89) by three wickets. *MoM*: Ankush Jaiswal.

Karnail Singh Stadium, Delhi, November 23-25: Railways 182 in 64.4 overs (Saurabh Wakaskar 43, V Cheluvaraj 42; Sneha Kishore 5-76, B Ayyappa 4-27) and 204 in 69.2 overs (Ashish Yadav 62, S Wakaskar 38; B Sudhakar 5-49; Prasanth Kumar 2-29) beat **Andhra** 114 in 50 overs (Prasanth 49; Karn Sharma 5-30, Anureet Singh 3-25) and 124 in 64.2 overs (Srikar Bharat 32, Ashwin Hebbar 30*; Anureet 4-32, Ashish 3-36) by 148 runs. *MoM*: Ashish Yadav.

Indian Cement Company Ground, Tirunelveli, November 23-26: Gujarat 165/2 dec in 63 overs (Priyank Panchal 90, Bhargav Merai 68*) drew with **Tamil Nadu**. *MoM*: Priyank Panchal.

Green Park, Kanpur, November 23-26: Punjab 272 in 90.3 overs (Mayank Sidhana 85, Gitansh Khera 74; Praveen Kumar 4-81, Ankit Rajpoot 3-60) and 295/7 dec in 80 overs (Uday Kaul 109*, Mandeep Singh 84; A Rajpoot 3-67, Praveen 2-90) drew with **Uttar Pradesh** 226 in 77.4 overs (Umang Sharma 49, Akshdeep Nath 35; Siddarth Kaul 4-82, Harbhajan Singh 3-31) and 204/6 in 72 overs (A Nath 76*, Piyush Chawla 58; Harbhajan 2-57, Barinder Sran 2-59). Punjab won on the basis of first-innings lead. *MoM*: Mayank Sidhana.

Group C

Rajiv Gandhi International Stadium, Uppal, Hyderabad, November 23-26: Hyderabad 548/5 dec in 173 overs (Hanuma Vihari 219, B Sandeep 93; Manisankar Murasingh 2-82, Tushar Saha 2-159) drew with **Tripura** 237 in 82.4 overs (Arindam Das 73, M Murasingh 51; Ravi Kiran 3-45, Chama Milind 3-50) and 294/5 in 88 overs (f/o) (Parvinder Singh 104*, M Murasingh 49; Himalay Agarwal 2-21). Hyderabad won on the basis of first-innings lead. *MoM*: Hanuma Vihari.

Gandhi Memorial Science College Ground, Jammu, November 23-26: Goa 552/5 dec in 162 overs (Swapnil Asnodkar 232, Amogh Desai 106, Sagun Kamat 105; Parveez Rasool 4-169) and 82/1 in 19 overs (Darshan Misal 41, S Kamat 23*) drew with **Jammu & Kashmir** 501 in 140.5 overs (Mithun Manhas 135, Ian Dev Singh 115; Shadab Jakati 4-103, Rituraj Singh 4-118). Goa won on the basis of first-innings lead. *MoM*: Swapnil Asnodkar.

JSCA International Stadium Complex, Ranchi, November 23-24: Jharkhand 337 in 103 overs (Shiv Gautam 122, Saurabh Tiwary 79; Bipul Sharma 6-59, Rishi Dhawan 2-67) beat **Himachal Pradesh** 133 in 36.2 overs (Ankit Kalsi 53, Paras Dogra 22; Shahbaz Nadeem 7-45, Samar Quadri 2-48) and 133 in 32.1 overs (f/o) (Nikhil Gangta 38, Prashant Chopra 32; S Nadeem 4-45, Kaushal Singh 3-10) by an innings and 71 runs. *MoM*: Shiv Gautam.

Perintalmanna Cricket Stadium, Malappuram, November 23-25: Kerala 166 in 62.2 overs (VA Jagadeesh 59, Fabid Ahmed 25; Dharmendrasinh Jadeja 5-44, Vandit Jivrajani 4-61) and 105 in 41 overs (Akshay Chandran 32, Mohammed Azharuddeen 23; D Jadeja 6-59, V Jivrajani 4-31) beat **Saurashtra** 157 in 60.4 overs (Samarth Vyas 54*, Chirag Jani 34; KS Monish 6-81, Rohan Prem 2-22, Fabid Ahmed 2-22) and 69 in 33.1 overs (KS Monish 5-46, A Chandran 2-3) by 45 runs. *MoM*: KS Monish.

Round 9: End of Karnataka's dominance

With knockout spots up for grabs, nine teams secured outright wins even as Karnataka crashed out after a defeat to Maharashtra. They needed a first-innings lead to keep their title defence alive, but the batting disappointed and their unbeaten streak of 37 games, stretching back to three years and eight days, came to a halt.

Aided by bad weather, Assam held on for a draw by just two wickets against Bengal, and Vidarbha beat Haryana as the three teams progressed to the quarter-final at Delhi's expense.

Over in Group B, Harbhajan Singh ran past a feeble Tamil Nadu line-up on an underprepared pitch in Dindigul for his first ten-wicket haul since 2008 and took Punjab to the quarter-finals. Madhya Pradesh secured a bonus point over Andhra and edged ahead of Gujarat in the race.

Even though Himachal Pradesh beat Kerala in just 483 minutes – the shortest game in Ranji history, it was not enough as Jharkhand, through Saurabh Tiwary's double-century, put up a decisive show against Hyderabad.

Even if they were out of contention, Rajasthan's spirited comeback for a two-wicket win over Odisha after being dismissed for 51 in the first-innings gave them enough breathing space.

Ramesh Powar and Yashpal Singh were the two prominent veterans to bid adieu after the last round. The other talking point was the injury to

This shot from Barinder Sran struck umpire John Ward, who had to be rushed to hospital. — *Wisden India*

John Ward, the Australian umpire, when he was hit on his head by Punjab's Barinder Sran. He was taken to hospital 30km away from Dindigul, and was declared safe after scans. C Gururaj, a local umpire, filled in for Ward for the rest of the game.

Group A

Barsapara Cricket Stadium, Guwahati, December 1-4: Bengal 444/6 dec in 158 overs (Shreevats Goswami 112*, Pankaj Shaw 99; Gokul Sharma 2-39, Krishna Das 2-94) drew with **Assam** 143 in 54.4 overs (Tarjinder Singh 50, Syed Mohammad 31; Ashok Dinda 4-39, Mukesh Kumar 3-20, Pragyan Ojha 3-33) and 143/8 in 84 overs (Pallavkumar Das 55; Aamir Gani 5-62). Bengal won on the basis of first-innings lead. *MoM*: Shreevats Goswami.

MCA Stadium, Pune, December 1-4: Maharashtra 212 in 62.4 overs (Ankit Bawne 87, Swapnil Gugale 30; S Aravind 3-35, Vinay Kumar 2-44) and 260 in 93 overs (Shrikant Mundhe 81, Rahul Tripathi 78; Vinay 4-71, S Aravind 3-59) beat **Karnataka** 180 in 67.4 overs (Mayank Agarwal 33, Robin Uthappa 23; Anupam Sanklecha 4-58, Nikit Dhumal 3-46, S Mundhe 3-54) and 239 in 72 overs (CM Gautam 65*, R Uthappa 61; N Dhumal 5-78, A Sanklecha 4-65) by 53 runs. *MoM*: Nikit Dhumal.

Sawai Mansingh Stadium, Jaipur, December 1-3: Odisha 151 in 52.2 overs (Anurag Sarangi 43; Aniket Choudhary 6-27, Pankaj Singh 3-53) and 129 in 39.2 overs (Alok Sahoo 31, Ranjit Singh 30; A Choudhary 4-31, Pankaj 4-43) lost to **Rajasthan** 51 in 27.2 overs (A Sahoo 6-33, Basant Mohanty 4-17) and 231/8 in 65.5 overs (Puneet Yadav 59, Siddharth Dobal 52; B Mohanty 3-65, Alok Mangaraj 2-53) by two wickets. *MoM*: Aniket Choudhary.

VCA Ground, Nagpur, December 1-4: Vidarbha 504/7 in 155 overs (Faiz Fazal 126, Ravi Jangid 110, Aditya Sarwate 103*; Harshal Patel 2-70, Jayant Yadav 2-189) beat **Haryana** 241 in 99.3 overs (Nitin Saini 67, Shamsher Yadav 50; R Jangid 4-44, A Sarwate 4-50) and 232 in 103.1 overs (f/o) (Rohit Sharma 107, Nitin Saini 42; R Jangid 7-59, Akshay Wakhare 2-105) by an innings and 31 runs. *MoM*: Ravi Jangid.

Group B

Holkar Cricket Stadium, December 1-3: Madhya Pradesh 279 in 92.5 overs (Rameez Khan 89, Harpreet Singh 81; B Ayyappa 5-66, Sneha Kishore 4-86) beat **Andhra** 56 in 38.2 overs (Ankit Sharma 6-17, Saransh Jain 2-7) and 214 in 78.3 overs (f/o) (AG Pradeep 62, Mohammad Kaif 51; Ånkit 7-91) by an innings and nine runs. *MoM*: Ankit Sharma.

Wankede Stadium, Mumbai, December 1-4: Mumbai 531 in 141.2 overs (Akhil Herwadkar 192, Suryakumar Yadav 104; Axar Patel 3-99, RP Singh 2-74) and 227/6 in 65 overs (Nikhil Patil 44*, A Herwadkar 41; Rujul Bhatt 4-76, Axar 2-85) drew with **Gujarat** 421 in 139.4 overs (Bhargav Merai 166, Axar 88; Shardul Thakur 6-107, Badre Alam 2-93). Mumbai won on the basis of first-innings lead. *MoM*: Akhil Herwadkar.

NPR College Ground, Dindigul, December 1-2: Punjab 206 in 57 overs (Yuvraj Singh 49, Barinder Sran 31; DT Chandrasekar 3-43; Malolan Rangarajan 2-67) and 174 in 42.5 overs (Gitansh Khera 43*; M Rangarajan 4-53, DT Chandrasekar 4-56) beat **Tamil Nadu** 68 in 23.4 overs (J Kousik 30; Rajwinder Singh 6-29, Harbhajan Singh 3-30) and 69 in 22 overs (Baba Aprajith 32*; Harbhajan 7-37, Sarabjit Ladda 3-16) by 243 runs. *MoM*: Harbhajan Singh.

Greater Noida Sports Complex Ground, December 1-4: Baroda 321 in 113.5 overs (Ambati Raydu 70, Aditya Waghmode 56; Piyush Chawla 3-41, Praveen Kumar 2-50) and 258/3 in 68.4 overs (A Waghmode 100*, Deepak Hooda 86) drew with **Uttar Pradesh** 524 in 152.1 overs (Umang Sharma 215, Eklavya Dwivedi 90; Munaf Patel 2-42, Irfan Pathan 2-62). Uttar Pradesh won on the basis of first-innings lead. *MoM*: Umang Sharma.

Group C

Rajiv Gandhi International Stadium, Uppal, Hyderabad, December 1-4: Hyderbad 145 in 76.1 overs (B Sandeep 39, Tanmay Agarwal 23; Jaskaran Singh 3-32, Shahbaz Nadeem 3-33, Kaushal Singh 3-35) and 269 in 101.4 overs (B Anirudh 79*, B Sandeep 58; Rahul Shukla 5-89, Jaskaran 2-53) lost to **Jharkhand** 388/8 dec in 104.4 overs (Saurabh Tiwary 209*, Kaushal 54; Chama Milind 3-77, Ravi Kiran 3-94) and 29/0 in 3.4 overs (Anand Singh 22*) by ten wickets. *MoM*: Saurabh Tiwary.

Gandhi Memorial Science College Stadium, Jammu, December 1-4: Jammu & Kashmir 138 in 49.1 overs (Amir Sofi 32, Ian Dev Singh 29; Shaurya Sanandia 5-53, Dharmendrasinh Jadeja 2-7) and 296 in 86.4 overs (Ian Dev 127, Pranav Gupta 39; Kamlesh Makvana 7-100, D Jadeja 2-113) lost to **Saurashtra** 497 in 126.2 overs (Sheldon Jackson 121, Jaydev Unadkat 92; Zahoor Ali 3-51, Vijay Dogra 3-137) by an innings and 63 runs. *MoM*: Kamlesh Makvana.

Perintalmanna Cricket Stadium, Malappuram, December 1-2: Kerala 103 in 47.4 overs (Sanju Samson 25; Rahul Singh 6-19, Rishi Dhawan 3-24) and 83 in 25.2 overs (Bipul Sharma 6-33) lost to **Himachal Pradesh** 163 in 37.5 overs (Prashant Chopra 40, Ankush Bains 23; Fabid Ahmed 3-12, KS Monish 3-60) and 24/4 in 4.3 overs (KS Monish 4-0) by six wickets. *MoM*: Prashant Chopra.

Maharaja Bir Bikram College Stadium, Agartala, December 1-4: Services 512 in 136.3 overs (Rajat Paliwal 203, Devendra Lochab 95; Rana Dutta 4-104, Tushar Saha 3-98) beat **Tripura** 230 in 84 overs (Saurabh Das 53, Rajesh Banik 46; Diwesh Pathania 3-49, Anshul Gupta 2-11) and 220 in 94.5 overs (f/o) (Parvinder Singh 58, R Banik 56; Raushan Raj 3-37, D Pathania 2-49) by an innings and 62 runs. *MoM*: Rajat Paliwal.

Group A Points Table

Teams	M	W	L	D	T	A	Pts	NRR
Vidarbha	8	4	2	2	0	0	29	+0.047
Bengal	8	2	0	6	0	0	28	+.0110
Assam	8	3	2	3	0	0	26	-0.304
Delhi	8	3	1	4	0	0	25	+0.215
Karnataka	8	2	1	5	0	0	24	+0.336
Rajasthan	8	2	3	3	0	0	17	-0.313
Maharashtra	8	1	2	5	0	0	17	+0.301
Odisha	8	1	3	4	0	0	12	+0.016
Haryana	8	0	4	0	0	0	6	-0.406

Vidarbha, Bengal and Assam qualified for the quarter-finals

Group B Points Table

Teams	M	W	L	D	T	A	Pts	NRR
Mumbai	8	4	0	4	0	0	35	+0.851
Punjab	8	3	2	3	0	0	26	+0.045
Madhya Pradesh	8	3	2	3	0	0	24	-0.059
Gujarat	8	3	1	4	0	0	24	-0.092
Uttar Pradesh	8	2	1	5	0	0	21	-0.117
Tamil Nadu	8	2	2	4	0	0	18	-0.322
Baroda	8	2	3	3	0	0	17	-0.045
Andhra	8	2	6	0	0	0	12	+0.039
Railways	8	0	4	4	0	0	10	-0.459

Mumbai, Punjab and Madhya Pradesh qualified for the quarter-finals

Group C Points Table

Teams	M	W	L	D	T	A	Pts	NRR
Saurashtra	8	5	1	2	0	0	36	-0.061
Jharkhand	8	4	2	2	0	0	31	+0.088
Himachal Pradesh	8	3	1	4	0	0	30	+1.013
Services	8	3	1	4	0	0	27	+0.472
Kerala	8	2	2	4	0	0	25	+0.084
Goa	8	1	1	6	0	0	18	-0.210
J&K	8	0	3	5	0	0	9	-0.053
Hyderabad	8	0	2	6	0	0	8	-0.467
Tripura	8	0	5	3	0	0	3	-0.760

Saurashtra and Jharkhand qualified for the quarter-finals

1st quarter-final: Saurashtra beat Vidarbha by an innings and 85 runs

Vidarbha were one of only two teams to qualify for the knockouts in all three formats of the domestic competition, but their Ranji campaign came to an end when they ran into a well-oiled Saurashtra outfit in Vizianagaram.

Unadkat picked up nine wickets while Sagar Jogiyani and Sheldon Jackson hit centuries and put on a fourth-wicket stand of 206 runs.

Saurashtra opted to bowl and set the tone in just the second ball of the match as Unadkat had Jitesh Sharma for nought. The rest of Vidarbha's top order too crumbled against pacers Hardik Rathod and Chirag Jani, while Unadkat took care of the lower order. Wasim Jaffer was the only batsman to show some resistance scoring 41 of the 151.

Saurashtra lost Avi Barot (5), Cheteshwar Pujara (47) and Arpit Vasavada (1) but the pair of Jackson and Jogiyani deflated Vidarbha. While Jogiyani, the opener, was solid taking 261 balls for his effort, Jackson was more attacking and took just 175 balls for his 122. He also smashed six sixes and 13 fours before being bowled by Umesh Yadav, playing his 50th first-class match.

Jackson's departure led to a collapse of sorts as Saurashtra went from 288 for 3 to 375 all out in a space of 17 overs, with Yadav ending with five wickets and Aditya Sarwate, the left-arm spinner, picking up four.

The lead of 224 runs was, however, too much for Vidarbha, who were skittled out for a paltry 139, with Unadkat taking four wickets. Only the 44-run fifth-wicket stand between Ravi Jangid and Jaffer, who again waged a lone battle, offered some defence. Deepak Punia bagged three wickets, ending the game shortly after tea on the third day. *Karthik Lakshmanan*

Dr PVG Raju ACA Sports Complex, Vizianagaram, February 3-5: Vidarbha 151 in 50.4 overs (Wasim Jaffer 41, Umesh Yadav 25; Jaydev Unadkat 5-70, Hardik Rathod 2-28) and 139 in 68.1 overs (W Jaffer 48, Faiz Fazal 36; J Unadkat 4-35, Deepak Punia 3-32) lost to **Saurashtra** 375 in 112.4 overs (Sagar Jogiyani 130, Sheldon Jackson 122; Umesh 5-81, Aditya Sarwate 4-63) by an innings and 85 runs. *MoM*: Jaydev Unadkat.

2nd quarter-final: Assam beat Punjab by 51 runs

Having prepared through a special camp at Vapi to readjust to red-ball cricket after two months of white-ball matches, Assam found many heroes to earn their first semi-final berth.

Syed Mohammad's battling century in the first innings after they were 115 for 5 set the tone, and Arup Das's career-best 8 for 83 in the second when Punjab were chasing 288 closed the game late on the penultimate day. Arup had earlier made 31 from No.10 to take Assam past the 100-run mark in their second innings.

Put in, Assam's top order yielded to the seam-trio of Siddarth Kaul, Barinder Sran and Deepak Bansal. Harbhajan Singh, captaining in the absence of an injured Yuvraj Singh, accounted for Pallavkumar Das for the only wicket off a spinner in the innings. Siddarth removed Karthik, Assam's best batsman, and Tarjinder Singh in quick succession before Amit Verma and Syed rebuilt the innings with a 66-run stand for the sixth wicket. However, with Siddarth dismissing Verma for 42, Assam limped to 223 for 8 at stumps on the first day.

Next morning, Syed batted aggressively to add 100 runs for the last two wickets in 20 overs, his contribution being 71.

Arup and Krishna reduced Punjab to 13 for 4 in five overs. Uday Kaul and

Mayank Sidhana added 73 before Pallavkumar, the part-time medium pacer, had Uday caught behind. Sidhana remained unbeaten on 80, but Punjab batted for only 47.2 overs as Assam took a lead of 186.

When Assam too became 13 for 4, 16 wickets had fallen on the second day. And they continued to do so the next morning. Arup was the top scorer with three fours and two sixes.

Chasing 288, Punjab were 26 for 3 before Mandeep Singh and Gurkeerat Singh Mann put on 70. Once Dhiraj Goswami accounted for both of them, Sidhana (43) and Gitansh Khera (35) tried hard, but Arup reduced them to 224 for 8 by the end of the third day. Assam then needed just 1.2 overs on the fourth morning to create history. *Manoj Narayan*

Sardar Vallabhbhai Patel Stadium, Valsad, February 3-6: Assam 323 in 308 overs (Syed Mohammad 121, Pallavkumar Das 46; Siddarth Kaul 4-99, Deepak Bansal 3-75) and 101 in 35.5 overs (Arup Das 31; Barinder Sran 5-43, S Kaul 4-25) beat **Punjab** 137 in 47.2 overs (Mayank Sidhana 80*, Uday Kaul 25; Arup 3-41, Krishna Das 3-54) and 236 in 63.2 overs (Gurkeerat Singh Mann 64, Mayank Sidhana 43; Arup 8-83, Dhiraj Goswami 2-38) by 51 runs. *MoM*: Arup Das.

3rd quarter-final: Madhya Pradesh beat Bengal by 355 runs

The Brabourne pitch was a good batting surface and both captains said as much ahead of the game. But the dampness in the wicket on the morning of the match convinced Manoj Tiwary, the Bengal captain, to have a bowl first.

There was movement off the pitch, but Madhya Pradesh wore the bowlers down with their wait-and-watch approach in the morning session, Aditya Shrivastava and Rajat Patidar taking 17.2 overs for their second-wicket stand of 31. The pace picked up once Naman Ojha joined Shrivastava in the middle. Their hundred-run partnership laid a solid foundation for Devendra Bundela, the captain, and Harpreet Singh to capitalise.

The eventual total of 348 might have seemed like a bit of a let-down, but Ishwar Pandey, Puneet Datey and Chandrakant Sakure, the debutant, gave Bengal bowling lessons, frustrating batsmen with tight lengths. Only Abhishek Easwaran showed some application while eight batsmen fell for single-digit scores.

Rajat Patidar's third hundred came in just his fifth game. – *Joshua Veeranathan*

The 22-year-old Patidar's third hundred in just his fifth game, and his 141-run stand with Naman (52) and 114-run association with Bundela (72) shut the door on Bengal. When Patidar was finally dismissed for 137, succumbing to Tiwary's part-time off-spin in the last hour of the third day, he had put his side in pole position at 338 for 5.

Harpreet then extended Madhya Pradesh's dominance with a century of his own, finding good support from Ankit Dane and Ankit Sharma.

Madhya Pradesh declared shortly after Harpreet's dismissal, giving Bengal an improbable target of 788. After being 156 for 5, Tiwary and Pankaj Shaw made centuries, and had a stand of 108 for the sixth wicket. Shaw then added 58 and 78 with Pragyan Ojha and Ashok Dinda. He was the last wicket to fall, as Madhya Pradesh completed a resounding win on the final afternoon for their first semi-final appearance since 1998-99. *Nisha Shetty*

Brabourne Stadium, Mumbai, February 3-7: Madhya Pradesh 348 in 114.5 overs (Aditya Shrivastava 65, Naman Ojha 64; Veer Pratap Singh 5-76, Ashok Dinda 3-85) and 560/9 dec in 160.3 overs (Harpreet Singh 139, Rajat Patidar 137; A Dinda 2-92, Veer Pratap 2-94) beat **Bengal** 121 in 45.2 overs (Abhimanyu Easwaran 48, Shreevats Goswami 22; Ishwar Pandey 4-45, Puneet Datey 3-30, Chandrakant Sakure 3-38) and 432 in 91.4 overs (Manoj Tiwary 124, Pankaj Shaw 118; I Pandey 4-93, C Sakure 3-114) by 355 runs. *MoM*: Ishwar Pandey.

4th quarter-final: Mumbai beat Jharkhand by 395 runs

Mumbai reached Mysore five days in advance to kick off their preparations, and stayed at their 'lucky' hotel, the same one they had camped at when Wasim Jaffer's side had beaten Karnataka in a thrilling 2009-10 Ranji final to win their 39th title. Luck may have played its part, but Mumbai, led by Abhishek Nayar in place of an injured Aditya Tare, found heroes at every turn to hand Jharkhand their largest defeat.

Mumbai opted to bat on a track that aided spin bowlers considerably from the opening day, and Herwadkar laid the foundation with his fourth first-class ton. Half-centuries from Suryakumar and Nayar lifted Mumbai to 416 even though Shabhaz Nadeem took five wickets to become the first bowler since Bengal's Ranadeb Bose in 2006-07 to pick up 50 scalps in a season.

Nayar made some canny bowling changes as Mumbai gained control of the game. Herwadkar, who was

Mumbai's Akhil Herwadkar backed up his first-innings century in Mysore with three wickets. – *Wisden India*

cleared to bowl his off spin after being reported during the league game against Madhya Pradesh, and Iqbal Abdulla made the most of the responsive surface with three wickets each.

Despite a 244-run lead, Nayar didn't enforce the follow-on, preferring to give his bowlers a break. In Mumbai's second dig, Iyer's 81 took him past the 1000-run mark. Nayar's 43 was the next-best score in the innings, but everyone went for their shots to set Jharkhand a 490-run target. On a deteriorating pitch that had a few rough patches, Jharkhand's batsmen did not apply themselves. Only Shiv Gautam and Virat Singh crossed 25, and seven batsmen made single-digit scores. Both Abdulla and Jay Bista finished with five-wicket hauls to end the game with a day to spare, as Jharkhand were dismissed for less than 100 for the second time in the season. *Disha Shetty*

Srikantadatta Narasimha Raja Wadeyar Ground, Mysore, February 3-6: Mumbai 416 in 114.4 overs (Akhil Herwadkar 107, Suryakumar Yadav 75; Shahbaz Nadeem 5-140, Jaskaran Singh 2-73) and 245 in 63.1 overs (Shreyas Iyer 81, Abhishek Nayar 43; Samar Quadri 5-62, Kaushal Singh 2-15) beat **Jharkhand** 172 in 71.5 overs (Kaushal 43, Anand Singh 39; A Herwadkar 3-26, Shardul Thakur 3-37, Iqbal Abdulla 3-50) and 94 in 42.4 overs (Shiv Gautam 27, Virat Singh 26; Jay Bista 5-16, I Abdulla 5-35) by 395 runs. *MoM*: Akhil Herwadkar.

Saurashtra, Assam, Madhya Pradesh and Mumbai qualified for the semi-finals

1st semi-final: Saurashtra beat Assam by ten wickets

For most of the Assam players, it was their first televised match and it showed in their body language. Pujara (126) and Unadkat (11 wickets) had no such issue, playing stellar roles in taking Saurashtra to their second final in four seasons.

After Saurastra won the toss on a fair pitch, Hardik Rathod induced an outside edge off Rahul Hazarika in the fourth over of the match, and Unadkat bowled Gokul Sharma. Even when Verma and Karthik, Assam's best bets, were going about their 127-run stand for the fourth wicket, Saurashtra were in control. The partnership in 48.2 overs was aimed at stopping the rut rather than pushing the pace of the game. Predictably, once Rathod got one to come back and uproot Karthik's stumps for his third wicket, there was a collapse. Assam were 180 for 7 in no time, with Unadkat too hot to handle.

Verma, a key member of the Karnataka team that won the Ranji Trophy in 2013-14, was defiant, rallying with Dhiraj Goswami in a 54-run stand for the eighth wicket. But, it was always going to be a matter of time. After spending 393 minutes at the crease, he mistimed a pull shot to be caught by Dharmendrasinh Jadeja at square leg two runs short of what would have been his 11th first-class century.

With the pitch having eased out, Assam's biggest strength, their seamers, was blunted. It gave Pujara, who couldn't convert a start in the quarter-final, a good chance to bed down for a big one. At 85 for 3, Assam would have hoped to pull things back, but Pujara, Arpit Vasavada and Chirag Jani never lost sight of the goal. By the time Pujara was caught at cover, he had spent 377 minutes in the middle and taken the fight out of Assam. Deepak Punia, in his first season for Saurashtra after moving from Services, hit three sixes and three fours for an unbeaten 42, giving Saurashtra a lead of 119.

Barring Syed Mohammad's 39, there was little resistance in Assam's second innings. Unadkat had another five-wicket haul. Saurashtra's openers chased down 21 in a jiffy to finish the game in three days. *Sidhanta Patnaik*

Reliance Stadium, Vadodara, February 13-15: Assam 234 in 87 overs (Amit Verma 98, Arun Karthik 59; Jaydev Unadkat 6-77, Hardik Rathod 3-56) and 139 in 39.1 overs (Syed Mohammad 39; J Unadkat 5-45, H Rathod 3-26) lost to **Saurashtra** 353 in 113.5 overs (Cheteshwar Pujara 126, Sheldon Jackson 47; Krishna Das 3-80, Arup Das 3-105) and 24/0 in 3.1 overs (Sagar Jogiyani 23*) by ten wickets. *MoM*: Jaydev Unadkat.

2nd semi-final: Mumbai beat Madhya Pradesh on first-innings lead

Iyer's legend had grown with the 1173 runs he had compiled before this game, and it only went upwards as his 104-ball 90 was the base for Mumbai's 144-run lead over Madhya Pradesh.

In their league clash, Madhya Pradesh had put up a spirited show on a turning track in Indore to take a significant lead, but then Mumbai had chased down 280 for a thrilling three-wicket win. So, the background was set for this knockout affair.

Apart from Iyer's twin half-centuries, Tare and Lad also made fifties, and Balwinder Singh Sandhu took five wickets to hand them the lead. In the second innings, Suryakumar and Tare made centuries, and shared a 217-run stand to rescue Mumbai from 95 for 3.

Put in, Mumbai started cautiously. Madhya Pradesh sensed an opening at 113 for 3 in 34.2 overs, but Iyer was seeing the ball better than the rest. And so the dominance began. He looked loose outside the off stump with his feet not getting to the pitch as much as purists would have liked, but his Virender Sewhag-esque hand-eye coordination let him meet the ball right off the middle of the bat every time he brought his blade down from a high backlift. His movements were a haze, as was his scoring.

Iyer belted everything Madhya Pradesh threw at him before Sakure made him his third of five scalps in the innings. Tare (68), Lad (60) and Abhishek Nayar (43) compounded Madhya Pradesh's misery.

The Madhya Pradesh batsmen had little answer to Sandhu and Nayar, who picked up eight wickets between them.

Right through the league phase, Mumbai had shown that they were better in the second innings, possibly because their young batsmen got a better understanding of the pitch. They made 426 runs from 125.1 overs, with Iyer's 46-ball 58, studded with nine fours and a six.

Pursuing 571 after fielding for 228 overs across two innings was going to be a stretch. Surprisingly, the batting stood up to the test on a dying strip with

Mumbai march continues: Naman Ojha's century, which raised hopes of an improbable Madhya Pradesh win, was in vain. – *Joshua Veeranathan*

Naman Ojha and Harpeet compiling pleasing hundreds after Shrivastava's measured 68. The fourth-wicket association of Ojha and Harpreet raised fleeting hopes of an improbable Madhya Pradesh win, but there was never enough time.

Roshan Thyagarajan

DRIEMS Ground, Tangi, Cuttack, February 13-17: Mumbai 371 in 102.5 overs (Shreyas Iyer 90, Aditya Tare 68; Chandrakant Sakure 5-137, Ishwar Pandey 2-34) and 426 in 125.1 overs (Suryakumar Yadav 115, A Tare 109; Harpreet Singh 3-55, I Pandey 3-103) drew with-**Madhya Pradesh** 227 in 92.1overs (Naman Ojha 79, Ankit Dane 44; Balwinder Sandhu 5-43, Abhishek Nayar 3-56) and 361/5 in 109 overs (N Ojha 113, Harpreet 105). Mumbai won on the basis of first-innings lead. *MoM*: Aditya Tare.

Saurashtra and Mumbai qualified for the final

Final: Mumbai beat Saurashtra by an innings and 21 runs

Few teams have dominated any competition in any sport anywhere in the world like Bombay/Mumbai have the Ranji Trophy. An extraordinary 41 titles in 82 tilts – the next most successful team, Karnataka, have won the tournament eight times – and an unprecedented 15 straight triumphs between 1958-59 and 1972-73. A domestic behemoth, a unit that knows what it takes to win and how to get the job done, no matter the personnel at its disposal, Mumbai are the yardstick against which other teams are judged.

They don't always play the prettiest cricket, but when it comes to efficiency and effectiveness, they have no parallel. Successive generations have embraced the rich legacy of champions of eras gone by. As if wearing the Mumbai cap isn't motivation enough, the dressing room is visited from time to time by some of the biggest names in Indian cricket who have played starring roles in previous title fights.

It was this irresistible force, fired up and smarting from not having laid their hands on the trophy for two years in a row, that confronted Saurashtra in the final of the 2015-16 season at the MCA International Stadium in Pune. It was classic David v Goliath, but there was no mythmaking as Goliath bore down inexorably on a tame, insipid Saurashtra team gripped by stage fright and blown away by the intensity of the Mumbai juggernaut.

Saurashtra were the first team to seal a place in the knockouts, largely thanks to homespun surfaces in Rajkot brilliantly exploited by the left-arm spin of Ravindra Jadeja. Once Jadeja was weaned away by the national team, Unadkat came to the party with his left-arm pace, taking 20 wickets in the quarterfinal and semifinal combined. Consequently, Saurashtra stormed into the title round with seven outright wins in ten games.

Mumbai haven't always placed overwhelming emphasis on outright wins. Especially in knockout games, they are happy going through on first-innings lead, like they did in the semifinal against Madhya Pradesh. Where Saurashtra had banked on their bowlers to get the job done, Mumbai's charge was spearheaded by the batsmen, Iyer and Herwadkar the principal run-getters, with Thakur providing the incisiveness with the ball.

A generous coating of live grass greeted the teams in Pune, making the toss a crucial if not decisive factor. Tare, who had turned Mumbai's fortunes around after taking charge midway through the previous season when the team was in the doldrums under Suryakumar, promptly stuck Saurashtra in, and watched Dhawal Kulkarni run riot against batsmen both technically and temperamentally wanting against the moving ball.

Pujara was understandably expected to shore up Saurashtra, but he managed just 4 and 27, looking horribly out of sorts in the second innings even though much of the life had seeped out of the surface. It was left to Vasavada and Prerak Mankad, the debutant, to haul their side to 235. Kulkarni's 5 for 42 was his third five-wicket haul in a Ranji final.

In a furious but unsupported opening burst, Unadkat fired out the Mumbai openers, but Iyer set stall with some of the most majestic strokeplay seen all season. He nonchalantly flicked the first ball he faced, from Unadkat, through midwicket and lit up the second day with a truly special knock. Decisive in his footwork and possessing that little extra fraction of a second that separates the gifted players from the rest, he pulverised Saurashtra, who didn't help their cause by grassing him on 37 and Lad on 24. Lad was involved in a Ranji record last-wicket stand of 103 with Sandhu. Having suffered a mini-collapse in the immediacy of Iyer's dismissal, Mumbai rode on the late heroics to open up a 136-run lead. It was to be more than enough.

Saurashtra's second innings was less edifying than their modest first-in-

Kulkarni's third five-wicket haul in a final: With Dhawal Kulkarni (top) razing the Saurashtra batting to finish with seven wickets for the match, only Arpit Vasavada offered a semblance of resistance. — *Joshua Veeranathan*

nings outing. At least on day one, there was some assistance for the quicker bowlers. On a far better surface for batting, they lasted no more than 48.2 overs, finding the four-pronged Mumbai pace attack too hot to handle. Pujara's laboured 98-ball 27 was the highest individual contribution as they keeled over by an innings and 21 runs, well inside three days. Thakur did the most damage, ending the mismatch by cleaning up Hardik Rathod for his 41st wicket this competition.

It was the second time in four years that Saurashtra had been humbled in the final by Mumbai. In their first entry into the title round in 2012-13, they had been battered out of sight, by an innings and 25 runs, at the Wankhede Stadium by a team that included Sachin Tendulkar, Jaffer and Ajit Agarkar. This Mumbai side obviously didn't have quite that same glittering star cast, but they showed throughout the season that as a team, their aura is very much intact. Their mastery of the opponent and the occasion in the final was no more than the icing on the cake. *R Kaushik*

Venue: Maharashtra Cricket Association Stadium, Pune, India, February 24, 2016
Toss: Mumbai won the toss and elected to bowl
Result: Mumbai won by an innings and 21 runs
MoM: Shreyas Iyer (Mumbai)

Saurashtra

		R		*R*
Avi Barot	c Iyer b Kulkarni	14	LBW b Sandhu	4
Sagar Jogiyani †	c Tare b Thakur	8	c Thakkar b Kulkarni	9
Cheteshwar Pujara	c Yadav b Kulkarni	4	c Herwadkar b Thakur	27
Aarpit Vasavada	c Yadav b Kulkarni	77	c Herwadkar b Sandhu	3
Sheldon Jackson	c Herwadkar b Sandhu	0	c † Tare b Nayar	13
Jaydev Shah*	c † Tare b Kulkarni	13	c † Tare b Thakur	17
Chirag Jani	c † Tare b Thakur	13	c † Tare b Thakur	11
Deepak Punia	c Yadav b Nayar	6	c † Tare b Thakur	3
Prerak Mankad	c Yadav b Kulkarni	66	c Abdulla b Kulkarni	1
Jaydev Unadkat	c Herwadkar b Thakur	31	Not out	16
Hardik Rathod	Not out	0	b Thakur	2
Extras	(0b,2lb,0nb,1w)	3	(2b,7lb,0nb,1w)	10
Total	(all out, 93.2 overs, 2.52 runs per over)	235	(all out, 48.2 overs, 2.38 runs per over)	115

Fall of wickets: 1st Innings: 22-1 (Avi Barot, 6.4 ov), 22-2 (Sagar Jogiyani, 7.1 ov), 36-3 (Cheteshwar Pujara, 10.5 ov), 42-4 (Sheldon Jackson, 20.2 ov), 77-5 (Jaydev Shah, 35.3 ov), 95-6 (Chirag Jani, 48.6 ov), 108-7 (Deepak Punia, 51.6 ov), 192-8 (Aarpit Vasavada, 84.4 ov), 235-9 (Prerak Mankad, 92.3 ov), 235-10 (Jaydev Unadkat, 93.2 ov)
2nd Innings: 13-1 (Avi Barot, 3.4 ov), 15-2 (Sagar Jogiyani, 6.2 ov), 24-3 (Aarpit Vasavada, 13.4 ov), 48-4 (Sheldon Jackson, 25.6 ov), 67-5 (Cheteshwar Pujara, 34.1 ov), 86-6 (Jaydev Shah, 38.6 ov), 91-7 (Prerak Mankad, 41.6 ov), 91-8 (Chirag Jani, 42.1 ov), 102-9 (Deepak Punia, 44.4 ov), 115-10 (Hardik Rathod, 48.2 ov)

Bowling: 1st Innings: Dhawal Kulkarni 23-6-42-5-1.83, Shardul Thakur 21.2-4-89-3-4.17

(1 wd), Abhishek Nayar 24-11-42-1-1.75, Balwinder Sandhu 19-6-41-1-2.16, Iqbal Abdulla 4-1-11-0-2.75, Akhil Herwadkar 1-0-5-0-5.00, Suryakumar Yadav 1-0-3-0-3.00
2nd Innings: Dhawal Kulkarni 16-2-34-2-2.13, Balwinder Sandhu 11-3-21-2-1.91, Shardul Thakur 13.2-1-26-5-1.95 (1 wd), Abhishek Nayar 8-1-26-1-3.25

Mumbai

		R
Akhil Herwadkar	c Jackson b Unadkat	0
Bhavin Thakkar	b Unadkat	6
Shreyas Iyer	c Shah b Jani	117
Suryakumar Yadav	c Pujara b Punia	48
Aditya Tare* †	c Vasavada b Jani	19
Siddhesh Lad	c Jackson b Unadkat	88
Abhishek Nayar	LBW b Rathod	19
Dhawal Kulkarni	b Rathod	1
Iqbal Abdulla	b Unadkat	15
Shardul Thakur	c Pujara b Rathod	0
Balwinder Sandhu	Not out	34
Extras	(4b,3lb,13nb,4w)	24
Total	(all out, 82.2 overs, 4.51 runs per over)	371

Fall of wickets: 1st Innings: 0-1 (Akhil Herwadkar, 0.2 ov), 23-2 (Bhavin Thakkar, 6.2 ov), 175-3 (Shreyas Iyer, 41.6 ov), 195-4 (Aditya Tare, 45.6 ov), 205-5 (Suryakumar Yadav, 48.2 ov), 235-6 (Abhishek Nayar, 59.5 ov), 250-7 (Dhawal Kulkarni, 63.3 ov), 250-8 (Shardul Thakur, 63.4 ov), 268-9 (Iqbal Abdulla, 66.6 ov), 371-10 (Siddhesh Lad, 82.2 ov)
2nd Innings: Shardul Thakur, Shreyas Iyer, Suryakumar Yadav, Balwinder Sandhu, Siddhesh Lad, Aditya Tare, Abhishek Nayar, Dhawal Kulkarni, Iqbal Abdulla, Akhil Herwadkar, Bhavin Thakkar
Bowling: 1st Innings: Jaydev Unadkat 25.2-3-118-4-4.66 (2 wd), Hardik Rathod 15-2-73-3-4.87, Prerak Mankad 3-0-18-0-6.00 (1 nb), Deepak Punia 24-4-107-1-4.46 (9 nb), Chirag Jani 15-2-48-2-3.20 (2 wd, 3 nb)

Umpires: CK Nandan and Chettithody Shamsuddin
TV umpire: KN Ananthapadmanabhan
Referee: Sanjay Verma

Season statistics

Batting

Most runs

Player	R	M	Inn	NO	HS	Ave	100s/50s
Shreyas Iyer (Mumbai)	1321	11	18	0	200	73.38	4/7
Akhil Herwadkar (Mumbai)	879	11	18	0	192	48.83	3/4
Arun Karthik (Assam)	802	10	19	2	151	47.17	3/3

Highest individual scores

Runs	Player	For/Against	Venue
255*	Natraj Behera	Odisha v Haryana	Rohtak
232	Swapnil Asnodkar	Goa v Jammu & Kashmir	Jammu
227	Paras Dogra	Himachal Pradesh v Services	Dharamsala

Most centuries

100s	Players
4	Rajat Paliwal (Services), Sudip Chatterjee (Bengal), Shreyas Iyer (Mumbai)

Highest partnership for each wicket

Wicket	Runs	Players	For/Against	Venue
1st	245	Kedar Devdhar, Aditya Waghmode	Baroda v Punjab	Vadodara
2nd	282	Natraj Behera, Ranjit Singh	Odisha v Haryana	Rohtak
3rd	240*	Dhruv Shorey, Nitish Rana	Delhi v Karnataka	Hubballi
4th	287	Mohammad Saif, Sarfaraz Khan	Uttar Pradesh v Madhya Pradesh	Moradabad
5th	217	Paras Dogra, Nikhil Gangta	Himachal Pradesh v Services	Dharamsala

6th	306*	Gurkeerat Singh, Gitansh Khera	Punjab v Railways	Mohali
7th	212	Ravi Jangid, Aditya Sarwate	Vidarbha v Haryana	Nagpur
8th	132	Umang Sharma, Praveen Kumar	Uttar Pradesh v Baroda	Greater Noida
9th	105	Rohit Sharma, Yuzvendra Chahal	Haryana v Bengal	Rohtak
10th	119	Jaydev Unadkat, Dharmendrasinh Jadeja	Saurashtra v Jammu & Kashmir	Jammu

Bowling

Most wickets

Bowler	W	M	BBI	BBM	Ave	5wI/10wM
Shahbaz Nadeem (Jharkhand)	51	9	7/45	11/90	19.62	4/1
Krishna Das (Assam)	50	10	7/21	10/55	16.06	5/2
KS Monish (Kerala)	49	8	6/81	11/127	17.91	5/2
Jalaj Saxena (Madhya Pradesh)	49	10	8/58	16/154	22.55	4/1
Akshay Wakhare (Vidarbha)	49	9	6/58	9/146	26.63	4/0

Best bowling in an innings

Figures	Player	For/Against	Venue
8-58	Jalaj Saxena	Madhya Pradesh v Railways	Gwalior
8-83	Arup Das	Assam v Punjab	Valsad
8-96	Jalaj Saxena	Madhya Pradesh v Railways	Gwalior

Best bowling in a match

Figures	Player	For/Against	Venue
16-154	Jalaj Saxena	Madhya Pradesh v Railways	Gwalior
13-83	Diwesh Pathania	Services v Jharkhand	Delhi
13-108	Ankit Sharma	Madhya Pradesh v Andhra	Indore

Hat-tricks

Player	For/Against	Victims	Venue
HS Sharath	Karnataka v Haryana	Sachin Rana, Rahul Dagar, Nitin Saini	Mysore
Basant Mohanty	Odisha v Delhi	Punit Bisht, Suboth Bhati, Pulkit Narang	Bhubaneswar
Umesh Yadav	Vidarbha v Rajasthan	Ajay Singh, Aniket Choudhary, Nathu Singh	Nagpur

Wicketkeeping

Most dismissals

Player	M	D	Ct.	St.
Aditya Tare (Mumbai)	10	48	45	3
Sagar Jogiyani (Saurahtra)	11	35	30	5
CM Gautam (Karnataka)	8	33	32	1

Most dismissals in a match

Player	D	Ct.	St.	For/Against	Venue
Amol Ubarhande	9	7	2	Vidarbha v Bengal	Kolkata
Sanju Samson	8	6	2	Kerala v Jharkhand	Malappuram
Sagar Jogiyani	8	7	1	Saurashtra v Jammu & Kashmir	Jammu
Naman Ojha	8	8	0	Madhya Pradesh v Mumbai	Cuttack

Fielding

Most catches

Catches	Players
20	Suryakumar Yadav (Mumbai, 11 matches)
19	Wasim Jaffer (Vidarbha, 9 matches)
16	Sheldon Jackson (Saurashtra, 10 matches); Akhil Herwadkar (Mumbai, 11 matches)

Most catches in a match

Player	Catches	For/Against	Venue
Cheteshwar Pujara	5	Saurashtra v Tripura	Rajkot
Sagun Kamat	5	Goa v Tripura	Porvorim
Rajat Paliwal	5	Services v Kerala	Delhi
R Samarth	5	Karnataka v Rajasthan	Jaipur
Gokul Sharma	5	Assam v Haryana	Rohtak

Team

Highest team total

Score	For/Against	Venue
707/8 dec	Himachal Pradesh v Hyderabad	Dharamsala
686/7 dec	Uttar Pradesh v Madhya Pradesh	Moradabad
610/9 dec	Mumbai v Uttar Pradesh	Mumbai

Lowest team total

Score	For/Against	Venue
37	Odisha v Bengal	Kalyani
45	Jharkhand v Services	Delhi
51	Rajasthan v Odisha	Jaipur

Largest victory by innings

Margin	Teams	Venue
Innings and 152 runs	Assam beat Rajasthan	Guwahati

Largest victory by runs

Margin	Teams	Venue
395 runs	Mumbai beat Jharkhand	Mysore

Victories by ten wickets

Teams	Venue
Delhi beat Vidarbha	Delhi
Himachal Pradesh beat Jammu & Kashmir	Dharamsala
Jharkhand beat Hyderabad	Hyderabad
Saurashtra beat Assam	Vadodara

Victories by lowest run margin

Margin	Teams	Venue
7 runs	Tamil Nadu beat Baroda	Chennai

Victories by lowest wicket margin

Margin	Teams	Venue
One wicket	Mumbai beat Tamil Nadu	Mumbai

Debutants (93)

Andhra (5): KV Sasikanth, H Shivraj, Jyothi Sai Krishna, K Sreekanth, Sneha Kishore; **Assam (2):** Rahul Hazarika, Wasiqur Rahman; **Baroda (4):** Hitesh Solanki, Monil Patel, Rishi Arothe, Atit Sheth; **Bengal (7):** Naved Ahmed, Aamir Gani, Pankaj Shaw, Pramod Chandila, Mukesh Kumar, Sayan Ghosh, Anurag Tiwari; **Delhi (7):** Mohit Ahlawat, Nitish Rana, Sarang Rawat, Rishabh Pant, Suboth Bhati, Pulkit Narang, Dhruv Shorey; **Gujarat (1):** Alshaaz Pathan; **Haryana (5):** Rahul Dagar, Sanjay Pahal, Rohit Sharma, Mohit Hooda, Shamsher Yadav; **Himachal Pradesh (1):** Shresth Nirmohi; **Hyderabad (1):** Mohammed Siraj; **Jammu & Kashmir (8):** Samad Bhat, Rohit Sharma, Deepak Manhas, Abhinav Puri, Aamir Sofi, Pranav Gupta, Vijay Dogra, Umar Nissar; **Jharkhand (2):** Vinayak Vikram, Sonu Singh; **Karnataka (1):** David Mathias; **Kerala (3):** Ahmed Farzeen, Fabid Ahmed, Mohammed Azharuddeen; **Madhya Pradesh (4):** Ankit Dane, Rajat Patidar, Chandrakant Sakure, Jagdeep Baweja; **Mumbai (3):** Jay Bista, Ankush Jaiswal, Sufiyan Shaikh; **Odisha (3):** Rajesh Dhuper, Amit Das, Ranjit Singh; **Punjab (2):** Pargat Singh, Deepak Bansal; **Railways (7):** Ashish Singh, Hitesh Kadam, Faiz Ahmed, Bhima Rao, Sagar Mishra, Akshat Pandey, Vivek Singh; **Rajasthan (4):** Nathu Singh, Ajay Singh, Siddharth Dobal, Manender Singh; **Saurashtra (4):** Mohsin Dodia, Vandit Jivrajani, Samarth Vyas, Prerak Mankad; **Services (9):** Diwesh Pathania, Poonam Poonia, Raushan Raj, Ravi Chauhan, Shashank Sharma, Sufiyan Alam, Vikas Hathwala, Kamal Passi, Amit Pachhara; **Tamil Nadu (3):** DT Chandrasekar, J Kousik, L Vignesh; **Tripura (2):** Tapash Mandal, Subash Chakraborty; **Uttar Pradesh (2):** Almas Shaukat, Israr Azim; **Vidarbha (3):** Aditya Shanware, Jitesh Sharma, Aditya Sarwate.

Fifth-day action: Rest of India scripted the highest chase in the history of the Irani Cup to deny Mumbai the title. — *BCCI*

Irani Cup

Rest rally around Fazal, Nair in epic chase

SIDHANTA PATNAIK

It was the kind of a game that makes you appreciate the ebbs and flow of cricket. For the most part of five days, after Mumbai chose to bat on a Brabourne pitch that became lifeless early, the match looked to be meandering towards a draw, with the winner set to be decided on the basis of first-innings lead.

Centuries from Jay Bista and Suryakumar Yadav set the tone for Mumbai's massive 297-run lead, but Aditya Tare did not enforce the follow-on. It looked like the home team was in a mood to enjoy the last two days of a first-class season where they remained undefeated for 11 games spread across five months to reclaim the Ranji Trophy after two years.

Even after Mumbai were dismissed for 182 in their second dig and Rest of India reached 100 for 1 at stumps on the fourth day, a successful fourth innings chase of 480 looked a stretch. Only nine times previously had a team won chasing 480 or more; of these, only West Zone's 541 for 7 against South Zone in the 2009-10 Duleep Trophy – the highest ever – had happened in India. All the cynicism fell by the wayside on the final day as Faiz Fazal and Karun Nair played lead roles to script the highest successful chase in the history of Irani Cup and give RoI the silverware after Karnataka's two-season dominance.

Having conceded the first-innings lead, RoI had nothing to lose on the final morning, and it showed in the positive intent with which Fazal and

Sudip Chatterjee, who had put on 34 the previous evening, resumed. Iqbal Abdulla, in what would be his last game for Mumbai, had Chatterjee caught and bowled for 54 in the 25th over of the morning. It brought Fazal and Nair together for their 130-run stand, which came at a fair pace of 4.08 – the second-best rate among the four century partnerships in the match.

With the pitch assisting neither spinners nor pacers, and 304 runs still to play with, Mumbai went on the defensive. Tare set a field to avoid the sweep shot, but left too many open spaces in front. Fazal and Nair milked the gaps.

Fazal, who spent 420 minutes at the crease and later became the first Indian since Sameer Dighe in 2001 to make his international debut after turning 30, Nair, who now has five half-centuries in three Irani Cups, and Naman Ojha, the captain, fell with 127 still needed.

By then, Mumbai's strategy and spirit had slipped behind. Sheldon Jackson and Stuart Binny's sixth-wicket stand of 92 in 16.5 overs shifted the chase to fifth gear. Fittingly, Jackson, who made a brisk 59, hit the winning boundary to complete the formalities in the company of Jayant Yadav.

Jayant's role in the victory was as crucial, as he was the only bowler to adapt to the conditions for match returns of eight wickets. He and Jaydev Unadkat picked up seven scalps between them in the second innings to not only dismiss Mumbai in just 51.2 overs, but also give RoI a little more than four sessions to have a go.

After conceding the lead, RoI bowlers reduced Mumbai to 62 for 4, which included the scalp of Shreyas Iyer for his first duck after making 1414 runs in only his second first-class season.

Iyer had made an attractive half-century – his 12th 50-plus score in 13 matches – in the first innings, but it was Bista who stood out for his maiden century. His 90-ball knock, and an opening partnership of 193 with Akhil Herwadkar (90) allowed the middle-order to bat around Suryakumar. Tare and Siddhesh Lad too made half-centuries. Mumbai had been 386 for 3 at stumps on the first day, and would have planned to bat RoI out of the game. But, some careless shot selection and intelligent bowling meant they added only another 399 runs across two innings. It was just the window RoI needed.

"It was really disappointing. We never thought they would chase it down so easily. I think we went into a defensive mode in the last day, which was not us," Iyer told *Wisden India*. "Throughout the Ranji season, we were attacking and suddenly in the last game we went defensive. That change of tactic really didn't help us. We took it lightly in the second innings as we had a 297-run lead and thought we had won the game. It was a good lesson, and now we will come back stronger in the next season."

Brabourne Stadium, Mumbai, March 6-10: Mumbai 603 in 158.2 overs (Suryakumar Yadav 156, Jay Bista 104; Jayant Yadav 4-132, Jaydev Unadkat 2-128) and 182 in 51.2 overs (Siddhesh Lad 60, Suryakumar 49; Jayant 4-93, J Unadkat 3-16) lost to **Rest of India** 306 in 99.5 overs (Karun Nair 94, J Unadkat 48; Abhishek Nayar 3-35, Jay Bista 2-52) and 482/6 in 129.4 overs (Faiz Fazal 127, K Nair 92; Iqbal Abdulla 5-154) by four wickets. *MoM:* Karun Nair.

Vijay Hazare Trophy

Pathiv's Gujarat ride on positivity

MANOJ NARAYAN

As a part of BCCI's intent to break free from the zonal structure, the teams for the Vijay Hazare Trophy were divided into four groups, with each group based in one city for a round-robin clash before the knockouts in Bangalore.

Suffice to say it was a shot in the arm for domestic cricket. The best players from the length and breadth of the country matched wits right from day one, rather than wait till the quarter-finals, as tended to be the case in the zonal structure. It made for some exhilarating cricket. And by the end of it all, Gujarat reigned; having won the Syed Mushtaq Ali Trophy in 2014-15, for a while, they were the limited-overs champions of the domestic circuit.

More fancied teams fell by the wayside, despite the presence of international superstars. Chief among them were Karnataka, the defending champions, whose free-fall from the Ranji Trophy campaign – which in turn meant they couldn't defend their Irani title – spilled onto the one-day tournament. They finished third in Group B, behind Jharkhand and Gujarat. Meanwhile, Delhi, the 2012-13 winners, were the favourites in the final, before Gujarat systemically dismantled them.

Horses for courses: Parthiv Patel's Gujarat weren't the most fancied side, but were helped by a positive approach. – *BCCI*

Parthiv Patel, the captain, led from the front, scoring his maiden List A century. Rujul Bhatt, one of the many promising youngsters in the set-up, scored a half-century, and the 274-run target they set for Delhi proved 139 runs too many, especially with RP Singh, the veteran professional, returning 4 for 42 to nip out Delhi's spine. The particularly pleasing bit about the triumph was that it was powered by a clear philosophy.

Parthiv was in charge of moulding a team picked fairly and transparently, the players were informed clearly of their roles, and that allowed everyone to embrace the horses for courses approach. For instance, RP Singh had not played a knockout match till the final, but when he did it was in conditions that suited him. The management took care to notify the players of why they were picked or dropped, and with the players in the loop, there was no room for miscommunication.

As enthralling as Gujarat's charge to the title was, the real zest to the tournament was provided by MS Dhoni, who simply had to put up his name for selection for Jharkhand. Having retired from Tests late in 2014, the limited-overs captain had time on his hands and knowledge to spread. He also needed to ease himself back into match fitness ahead of the Australia ODIs, and his presence added much-needed glamour to the tournament. He returned at the low-key Alur, on the outskirts of Bangalore. Despite that, a crowd of nearly 200 filled up the small venue, and were in a tizzy with everything the man did and did not do.

That said, perhaps Dhoni's biggest contribution was to his team-mates. The clamour for selfies with Dhoni among the other players in Group B was just half the story. Dhoni was obliging, and he would have been with cricketing advice as well. "The Vijay Hazare wickets were quite difficult. He advised us on how to approach such games, the thought process, the targets we should be setting; we learnt a lot from him," said Shahbaz Nadeem, the Jharkhand captain. Dhoni didn't exactly light up the tournament with his performances – his unbeaten 70 in the quarter-final against Delhi proved insufficient as Jharkhand went down by 99 runs – but his aura alone was enough.

Other senior India internationals also took the chance to stay in shape with domestic cricket, R Ashwin and M Vijay among them. Ashwin captained Tamil Nadu admirably before falling to Axar Patel and Gujarat in a closely fought semi-final. Harbhajan Singh joined Yuvraj Singh in Punjab and sat his team down in a circle on the field after the quarter-final loss to Himachal Pradesh, even as Bhuvneshwar Kumar bolstered Uttar Pradesh.

All in all, the edition was a rousing success. The format-change reaped huge dividends, the big names in Indian cricket were involved and the most deserving team surged to the title. The struggle will now be to match similar standards in the editions to follow.

Best batsman: Mandeep Singh (394 runs, 7 matches)
Best bowler: Jasprit Bumrah (21 wickets, 9 matches)

Debutants (95)
Andhra (4): Ashwin Hebbar, KV Sasikanth, K Sreekanth, Karthik Raman; **Assam (3):** Wasiqur Rahman, Jogeswar Bhumji, Bikash Chetri; **Baroda (1):** Rishi Arothe; **Bengal (6):** Aamir Gani, Sayan Ghosh, Pankay Shaw, Mukesh Kumar, Abhimanyu Easwaran, Pradipta Pramanik; **Delhi (4):** Suboth Bhati, Navdeep Saini, Himmat Singh, Rishabh Pant; **Haryana (8):** Chaitanya Bishnoi, Rahul Dagar, Mohit Hooda, Rohit Sharma, Vikram Singh, Shamsher Yadav, Umang Chugh, Poonish Mehta; **Himachal Pradesh (1):** Mayank Dagar; **Hyderabad (5):** Himalay Agarwal, Yathin Reddy, Jaweed Ali, B Anirudh, Mohammed Siraj; **Jammu & Kashmir (6):** Aamir Sofi, Pranav Gupta, Rohit Sharma, Asif Rasool, Mohsin Mufti, Nadeem Dar; **Jharkhand (2):** Ankit Dabas, Sonu Singh; **Karnataka (5):** Aniruddha Joshi, Sadiq Kirmani, Praveen Dubey, David Mathias, Abhishek Reddy; **Kerala (3):** Jafar Jamal, Mohammed Azharuddeen, Mohan Akshaya; **Madhya Pradesh (4):** Venkatesh Iyer, Rajat Patidar, Parth Sahani, Chandrakant Sakure; **Maharashtra (4):** Swapnil Gugale, Nikit Dhumal, Bharatkumar Solanki, Naushad Shaikh; **Mumbai (3):** Jay Bista, Shashank Singh, Sagar Trivedi; **Odisha (4):** Rajesh Dhuper, Shesdeep Patra, Subham Nayak, Ranjit Singh; **Punjab (2):** Karan Kaila, Pargat Singh; **Rajasthan (4):** Nathu Singh, Siddarth Dobal, Manender Singh, SF Khan; **Railways (3):** Ashish Singh, Akshat Pandey, Faiz Ahmed; **Saurashtra (3):** Deepak Punia, Vandit Jivrajani, Samarth Vyas; **Services (6):** Azaruddin Bloch, Rahul Kanujia, Sufiyan Alam, Nitin Yadav, Amit Pachhara, Kamal Passi; **Tamil Nadu (5):** Baba Indrajith, J Kousik, M Ashwin, Antony Dhas, Aswin Crist; **Tripura (2):** Chiranjit Paul, Joydeep Bhattacharjee; **Uttar Pradesh (5):** Israr Azim, Mohammed Javed, Samarth Singh, Saurabh Kumar, Shubham Chaubey; **Vidarbha (2):** Rajneesh Gurbani, Akshay Karnewar.

Group A

Rajiv Gandhi International Stadium, Uppal, Hyderabad, December 10: Assam 210 in 49.4 overs (Syed Mohammad 59, Amit Verma 24; R Ashwin 3-31, J Kousik 2-33) lost to **Tamil Nadu** 214/4 in 41.4 overs (Abhinav Mukund 104, Vijay Shankar 42) by six wickets.
Gymkhana Ground, Hyderabad, December 10: Punjab 254 in 48.1 overs (Yuvraj Singh 93, Mandeep Singh 41; Sagar Trivedi 3-21, Dhawal Kulkarni 3-41) lost to **Mumbai** 255/5 in 45.1 overs (Jay Bista 92, Abhishek Nayar 44*; Siddarth Kaul 3-58) by five wickets.
Railways Recreation Club Ground, Secunderabad, December 10: Services 230/7 in 50 overs (Yashpal Singh 75*, Nakul Verma 68; Nathu Singh 4-42) beat **Rajasthan** 167 in 41.3 overs (Puneet Yadav 52, Rajat Bhatia 36; Rajat Paliwal 2-10, Suraj Yadav 2-31) by 63 runs.
Railways Recreation Club Ground, Secunderabad, December 11: Assam 148 in 44.4 overs (Pallavkumar Das 37, Amit Sinha 27; Rajat Bhatia 5-17, Rajesh Bishnoi 2-22) lost to **Rajasthan** 149/9 in 49.3 overs (R Bhatia 68*, Arjit Gupta 27; Krishna Das 2-17, Pallavkumar Das 2-30) by one wicket.
Rajiv Gandhi International Stadium, Uppal, Hyderabad, December 11: Punjab 238 in 49.4 overs (Mayank Sidhana 64, Yuvraj Singh 36; Ravi Kiran 4-33, Chama Milind 3-62) beat **Hyderabad** 182 in 42.4 overs (K Sumanth 63*, Pagadala Naidu 35; Siddarth Kaul 5-32, Barinder Sran 3-36) by 56 runs.
Gymkhana Ground, Hyderabad, December 11: Tamil Nadu 312/7 in 50 overs (Baba Aparajith 77, Baba Indrajith 60*; Dhawal Kulkarni 3-47, Abhishek Nayar 2-56) beat **Mumbai** 286 in 45.2 overs (Akhil Herwadkar 107, Siddesh Lad 47; M Ashwin 3-38, Rahil Shah 2-55) by 26 runs.
Railways Recreation Club Ground, Secunderabad, December 13: Mumbai 198 in 49.5 overs (Shreyas Iyer 49, Suryakumar Yadav 42; Amit Verma 2-23, Syed Mohammad 2-24) beat **Assam** 102 in 35 overs (A Verma 33, Syed 25; Dhawal Kulkarni 4-19, Sagar Trivedi 3-29, Abhishek Nayar 3-37) by 96 runs.
Rajiv Gandhi International Stadium, Uppal, Hyderabad, December 13: Hyderabad 224/7 in 50 overs (Pagadala Naidu 45*, Chama Milind 42*; Azaruddin Bloch 3-34) lost to

Services 225/5 in 48.5 overs (Mumtaz Qadir 68, Rajat Paliwal 64; Ravi Kiran 2-41, C Milind 2-45) by five wickets.

Gymkhana Ground, Hyderabad, December 13: Tamil Nadu 226 in 45.3 overs (Dinesh Karthik 69, Baba Aprajith 39; Siddarth Kaul 4-17, Barinder Sran 3-37) lost to **Punjab** 230/4 in 44.5 overs (Jiwanjot Singh 85, Mayank Sidhana 67*; R Sathish 2-23) by six wickets.

Gymkhana Ground, Hyderabad, December 14: Punjab 327/4 in 50 overs (Mandeep Singh 117*, Pargat Singh 69; Amit Verma 2-61) beat **Assam** 326/8 in 50 overs (Swarupam Purkayastha 125, A Verma 71; Siddarth Kaul 3-74, Deepak Bansal 2-63) by one run.

Rajiv Gandhi International Stadium, Uppal, Hyderabad, December 14: Rajasthan 250/8 in 50 overs (Ashok Menaria 55, Manender Singh 51; Ravi Kiran 4-57) beat **Hyderabad** 148 in 39 overs (Hanuma Vihari 39, Pagadala Naidu 25*; Tanvir-ul-Haq 4-44, Nathu Singh 2-14) by 102 runs.

Railways Recreation Club Ground, Secunderabad, December 14: Services 192/8 in 50 overs (Yashpal Singh 56, Mumtaz Qadir 31; M Mohammed 5-50, R Ashwin 2-23) lost to **Tamil Nadu**193/3 in 39.4 overs (Abhinav Mukund 85, Baba Aparajith 66*; Diwesh Pathania 3-41) by seven wickets.

Gymkhana Ground, Hyderabad, December 15: Hyderabad 271/8 in 50 overs (Tanmay Agarwal 83, Hanuma Vihari 51; Arup Das 3-45, Jogeswar Bhumij 3-58) beat **Assam** 199 in 50 overs (Pallavkumar Das 54, Amit Sinha 34; Ravi Kiran 3-30, Chama Milind 3-44) by 72 runs.

Rajiv Gandhi International Stadium, Uppal, Hyderabad, December 15: Services 151 in 42.1 overs (Nakul Verma 50, Rajat Paliwal 41; Shardul Thakur 4-19, Dhawal Kulkarni 2-22) lost to **Mumbai** 156/4 in 25.2 overs (Akhil Herwadkar 46, Shreyas Iyer 35; Azaruddin Bloch 2-27) by six wickets.

Railways Recreation Club Ground, Secunderabad, December 15: Rajasthan 270/7 in 50 overs (Manender Singh 118, Puneet Yadav 43; Barinder Sran 4-60) lost to **Punjab** 273/4 in 44.4 overs (Yuvraj Singh 78*, Jiwanjot Singh 66; Siddharth Dobal 2-27) by six wickets.

Railways Recreation Club Ground, Secunderabad, December 17: Assam 261/8 in 50 overs (Amit Verma 78, Sibankar Roy 45; Diwesh Pathania 5-54, Suraj Yadav 2-49) lost to **Services** 262/4 in 45.2 overs (Amit Pachhara 75*, Soumik Chatterjee 73; Jogeswar Bhumij 2-47) by six wickets.

Rajiv Gandhi International Stadium, Uppal, Hyderabad, December 17: Hyderabad 230 in 49.2 overs (Tanmay Agarwal 105, Danny Dereck Prince 31; L Balaji 3-33, R Sathish 2-18) lost to **Tamil Nadu** 233/7 in 47.5 overs (Baba Aparajith 55, M Vijay 44; Mohammed Siraj 2-44, Ravi Kiran 2-51) by three wickets.

Gymkhana Ground, Hyderabad, December 17: Mumbai 301/9 in 50 overs (Ajinkya Rahane 114, Suryakumar Yadav 52; Pankaj Singh 4-55, Tanvir-ul-Haq 2-55) lost to **Rajasthan** 305/5 in 49 overs (Rajat Bhatia 94*, Ashok Menaria 86; Abhishek Nayar 2-28) by five wickets.

Rajiv Gandhi International Stadium, Uppal, Hyderabad, December 18: Hyderabad 217/7 in 50 overs (Hanuma Vihari 95, Jaweed Ali 44*; Shardul Thakur 2-33, Rohan Raje 2-48) lost to **Mumbai** 221/3 in 44.2 overs (Akhil Herwadkar 85, Shreyas Iyer 84) by seven wickets.

Railways Recreation Club Ground, Secunderabad, December 18: Services 323/7 in 50 overs (Nakul Verma 113, Soumya Ranjan Swain 101) lost to **Punjab** 325/7 in 49 overs (Yuvraj Singh 98, Pargat Singh 49; Ritesh Negi 3-51, Kamal Passi 2-66) by three wickets.

Gymkhana Ground, Hyderabad, December 18: Tamil Nadu 384/7 in 50 overs (Baba Aparajith 137, Dinesh Karthik 108; Tanvir-ul-Haq 3-81) beat **Rajasthan** 132 in 26.2 overs (Rajat Bhatia 29*, Manender Singh 28; Rahil Shah 6-37, Aswin Crist 2-31) by 252 runs.

Group A Points Table

Teams	M	W	L	T	N/R	Pts	NRR
Tamil Nadu	6	5	1	0	0	20	+1.254
Punjab	6	5	1	0	0	20	+0.349
Mumbai	6	4	2	0	0	16	+0.866
Services	6	3	3	0	0	12	-0.321
Rajasthan	6	3	3	0	0	12	-0.772
Hyderabad	6	1	5	0	0	4	-0.454
Assam	6	0	6	0	0	0	-0.807

Tamil Nadu and Punjab qualified for the quarter-finals

Group B

KSCA Cricket Ground (2), Alur, December 10: Jharkhand 210 in 50 overs (Ishank Jaggi 54, Kaushal Singh 53; Waseem Raza 3-31, Rohit Sharma 2-46) beat **Jammu & Kashmir** 205/7 in 50 overs (Parveez Rasool 63, Shubham Khujuria 60; Shahbaz Nadeem 3-28, Rahul Shukla 2-30) by five runs.

M Chinnaswamy Stadium, Bangalore, December 10: Karnataka 228/9 in 50 overs (Vinay Kumar 50*, Mayank Agarwal 44; Ashish Yadav 3-25, Akshat Pandey 3-45) lost to **Railways** 232/9 in 50 overs (Karn Sharma 51, Asad Pathan 50; Vinay 4-45, Aniruddha Joshi 2-31) by one wicket.

KSCA Cricket Ground, Alur, December 10: Haryana 241/7 in 50 overs (Mohit Hooda 54, Nitin Saini 52; Sandeep Warrier 2-35, Fabid Ahmed 2-35) beat **Kerala** 232 in 50 overs (Sachin Baby 95, Mohammed Azharuddeen 32; Jayant Yadav 3-21, Amit Mishra 3-35) by nine runs.

KSCA Cricket Ground (3), Alur, December 11: Jharkhand 177/7 in 47 overs (MS Dhoni 44, Ishank Jaggi 34; Axar Patel 2-30, Jasprit Bumrah 2-30) lost to **Gujarat** 179/4 in 40.5 overs (Priyank Panchal 62, Parthiv Patel 44; Shahbaz Nadeem 2-36) by six wickets.

M Chinnaswamy Stadium, Bangalore, December 11: Karnataka 242/9 in 50 overs (J Suchith 46, Vinay Kumar 41; Harshal Patel 4-62, Ashish Hooda 2-33) beat **Haryana** 204 in 46.3 overs (Rahul Dagar 96*, Rohit Sharma 46; Abhimanyu Mithun 2-26, Vinay 2-39) by 38 runs.

KSCA Cricket Ground (2), Alur, December 11: Kerala 256/8 in 50 overs (VA Jagadeesh 121, Sanju Samson 35; Anureet Singh 4-40, Krishnakant Upadhyay 2-52) beat **Railways** 196 in 43.1 overs (Saurabh Wakaskar 77, Arindam Ghosh 53; Fabid Ahmed 2-32, Sandeep Warrier 2-32) by 60 runs.

KSCA Cricket Ground (3), Alur, December 13: Railways 259/5 in 50 overs (Arindam Ghosh 96*, Mahesh Rawat 60) lost to **Gujarat** 260/6 in 49.4 overs (Axar Patel 75, Rujul Bhatt 72; Karn Sharma 2-38, Anureet Singh 2-53) by four wickets.

KSCA Cricket Ground, Alur, December 13: Jammu & Kashmir 75 in 22 overs (Bandeep Singh 24, Zahoor Sofi 20*; Harshal Patel 5-21, Amit Mishra 3-4) lost to **Haryana** 76/0 in 11 overs (Harshal 54*, Nitin Saini 20*) by ten wickets.

M Chinnaswamy Stadium, Bangalore, December 13: Kerala 236/8 in 50 overs (Sachin Baby 61, VA Jagadeesh 60; Rahul Shukla 3-47) lost to **Jharkhand** 240/5 in 47 overs (Saurabh Tiwary 87*, Kaushal Singh 48) by five wickets.

KSCA Cricket Ground, Alur, December 14: Karnataka 233/8 in 50 overs (Manish Pandey

94*, Mayank Agarwal 58; Mehul Patel 2-24, Axar Patel 2-33) beat **Gujarat** 189/8 in 44 overs (Priyank Panchal 52, Chirag Gandhi 43; J Suchith 2-25, Vinay Kumar 2-28) by 15 runs (VJD method).

KSCA Cricket (3) Ground, Alur, December 14: Haryana 133 in 33 overs (Rahul Dagar 38; Rahul Shukla 3-33, Shahbaz Nadeem 2-17) lost to **Jharkhand** 134/1 in 29.4 overs (Ishank Jaggi 62*, Kumar Deobrat 38*) by nine wickets.

KSCA Cricket Ground (2), Alur, December 14: Jammu & Kashmir 130 in 42.3 overs (Bandeep Singh 31, Zahoor Sofi 25; Fabid Ahmed 3-24, P Prasanth 2-22) lost to **Kerala** 134/3 in 29.5 overs (Nikhilesh Surendran 85*, VA Jagadeesh 20; Parveez Rasool 3-33) by seven wickets.

M Chinnaswamy Stadium, Bangalore, December 15: Gujarat 259 in 49.5 overs (Rujul Bhatt 55, Parthiv Patel 45; Amit Mishra 3-44, Ashish Hooda 2-43) beat **Haryana** 231in 49.5 overs (Poonish Mehta 57, Rahul Dagar 53; Rush Kalaria 4-37, Jasprit Bumrah 2-38) by 28 runs)

KSCA Cricket Ground, Alur, December 15: Railways 200 in 49.4 overs (Karn Sharma 60, Arindam Ghosh 36; Waseem Raza 4-31, Bandeep Singh 2-19) beat **Jammu & Kashmir** 157 in 43.5 overs (Ian Dev Singh 60, Parveez Rasool 30; Ashish Yadav 3-28, Karn 2-24) by 43 runs.

KSCA Cricket Ground (2), Alur, December 15: Jharkhand 216/8 in 50 overs (Ishank Jaggi 50, Kumar Deobrat 47*; J Suchith 4-35, Karun Nair 2-35) beat **Karnataka** 169 in 45 overs (KL Rahul 42, J Suchith 34; Shahbaz Nadeem 3-15, Sonu Singh 3-20) by 47 runs.

KSCA Cricket Ground (2), Alur, December 17: Gujarat 187 in 49.2 overs (Rujul Bhatt 66, Rohit Dahiya 27; Omar Alam 3-31, Waseem Raza 3-38) beat **Jammu & Kashmir** 151 in 47.2 overs (Parveez Rasool 65, Sandeep Singh 44; Hardik Patel 4-28, Axar Patel 2-20) by 36 runs.

KSCA Cricket Ground, Alur, December 17: Jharkhand 211/5 in 45 overs (Saurabh Tiwary 49, Kumar Deobrat 38; Avinash Yadav 2-44) beat **Railways** 96 in 37 overs (Arindam Ghosh 44; Sonu Singh 4-15, Ankit Dabas 2-20) by 115 runs.

M Chinnaswamy Stadium, Bangalore, December 17: Kerala 49 in 22 overs (Shreyas Gopal 5-19, Vinay Kumar 2-6) lost to **Karnataka** 51/1 in 5.5 overs (Karun Nair 24*) by nine wickets.

KSCA Cricket Ground (2), Alur, December 18: Kerala 102 in 43.2 overs (Sachin Baby 41; Axar Patel 3-16, Rush Kalaria 2-12) lost to **Gujarat** 103/3 in 32.5 overs (Rujul Bhatt 35*, Himalaya Barad 24; Fabid Ahmed 2-28) by seven wickets.

KSCA Cricket Ground (3), Alur, December 18: Railways 219/7 in 50 overs (Arindam Ghosh 76, Karn Sharma 29; Ashish Hooda 2-28, Jayant Hooda 2-30) beat **Haryana** 113 in 35.1 overs (Rohit Sharma 26, Nitin Saini 20; Karn 5-13, Arnab Nandi 2-12) by 106 runs.

M Chinnaswamy Stadium, Bangalore, December 18: Karnataka 349/5 in 50 overs (CM Gautam 109*, Manish Pandey 79; Zahoor Sofi 2-58, Waseem Raza 2-66) beat **Jammu & Kashmir** 142 in 27.3 overs (Bandeep Singh 42, Ian Dev Singh 35; J Suchith 3-26, S Aravind 2-23) by 207 runs.

Group B Points Table

Teams	M	W	L	T	N/R	Pts	NRR
Jharkhand	6	5	1	0	0	20	+0.860
Gujarat	6	5	1	0	0	20	+0.540
Karnataka	6	4	2	0	0	16	+1.465
Railways	6	3	3	0	0	12	-0.083
Haryana	6	2	4	0	0	8	-0.328
Kerala	6	2	4	0	0	8	-0.472
Jammu & Kashmir	6	0	6	0	0	0	-1.933

Jharkhand and Gujarat qualified for the quarter-finals

Group C

Palam B Ground, Model Sports Complex, Delhi, December 10: **Andhra** 273 in 49.3 overs (AG Pradeep 71, D Siva Kumar 51; Sanjay Majumder 2-45, Manisankar Murasingh 2-45) beat **Tripura** 215 in 45.1 overs (Nirupan Sen Chowdhary 52, Parvinder Singh 50; B Sudhakar 3-28, CV Stephen 3-41) by 58 runs.

Feroz Shah Kotla, Delhi, December 10: **Delhi** 208/7 in 50 overs (Nitish Rana 62, Pawan Negi 47*; Rishi Arothe 2-30) beat **Baroda** 177 in 46.5 overs (Deepak Hooda 50, Hardik Pandya 29; Suboth Bhati 4-17, Pradeep Sangwan 2-41) by 31 runs.

Palam A Ground, Model Sports Complex, Delhi, December 10: **Odisha** 226/9 in 50 overs (Arabind Singh 62, Biplab Samantray 37; Ravikumar Thakur 3-44, Ravi Jangid 2-34) beat **Vidarbha** 223 in 47.2 overs (R Jangid 97, Akshay Karnewar 72; Alok Sahoo 5-39, Basant Mohanty 2-27) by three runs.

Palam B Ground, Model Sports Complex, Delhi, December 11: **Baroda** 291/6 in 50 overs (Kedar Devdhar 81, Aditya Waghmode 76; B Sudhakar 2-51, CV Stephen 2-70) beat **Andhra** 202 in 43.1 overs (Jyothi Sai Krishna 59, Srikar Bharat 45; Bhargav Bhatt 6-37) by 89 runs.

Feroz Shah Kotla, Delhi, December 11: **Vidarbha** 163 in 45.2 overs (Faiz Fazal 83, Akshay Wadkar 20; Ishant Sharma 5-21, Suboth Bhati 2-21) beat **Delhi** 145 in 45.1 overs (Unmukt Chand 57, Milind Kumar 25; Akshay Wakhare 2-10, Akshay Karnewar 2-17) by 18 runs.

Palam A Ground, Model Sports Complex, Delhi, December 11: **Maharashtra** 217/8 in 50 overs (Shrikant Mundhe 50, Ankit Bawne 40; Basant Mohanty 3-40, Biplab Samantray 2-41) beat **Odisha** 177 in 43.4 overs (Govinda Poddar 74, Rajesh Dhuper 28; Shamshuzama Kazi 4-29, S Mundhe 4-35) by 40 runs.

Palam B Ground, Model Sports Complex, Delhi, December 13: **Baroda** 173 in 46 overs (Ambati Raydu 40, Yusuf Pathan 32; Ravikumar Thakur 4-27, Ravi Jangid 2-15) lost to **Vidarbha** 174/3 in 42 overs (Faiz Fazal 89, S Badrinath 47*) by seven wickets.

Feroz Shah Kotla, Delhi, December 13: **Odisha** 225/9 in 50 overs (Natraj Behera 50, Biplab Samantray 47; Manan Sharma 3-47, Pawan Negi 2-45) lost to **Delhi** 228/5 in 46.3 overs (Gautam Gambhir 67, Milind Kumar 62*; Alok Sahoo 2-58) by five wickets.

Palam A Ground, Model Sports Complex, Delhi, December 13: **Maharashtra** 294 in 49.4 overs (Kedar Jadhav 131, Harshad Khadiwale 32; Rajesh Banik 4-40, Sanjay Majumder 3-53) beat **Tripura** 183 in 49.5 overs (S Majumder 52*, Rana Dutta 26; Swapnil Gugale 4-21, Akshay Darekar 2-20) by 111 runs.

Palam B Ground, Model Sports Complex, Delhi, December 14: **Maharashtra** 241/8 in 50 overs (Kedar Jadhav 101, Ankit Bawne 100; D Siva Kumar 3-24, CV Stephen 3-54) beat **Andhra** 194 in 42.5 overs (K Sreekanth 74, AG Pradeep 28; Shamshuzama Kazi 4-36, Akshay Darekar 2-33) by 47 runs.

Palam A Ground, Model Sports Complex, Delhi, December 14: **Baroda** 225 in 50 overs (Aditya Waghmode 111, Kedar Devdhar 30; Ankit Yadav 4-44, Basant Mohanty 2-37) beat **Odisha** 169 in 46.2 overs (Natraj Behera 67*, Govinda Poddar 30; Bhargav Bhatt 2-16, Munaf Patel 2-31) by 56 runs.

Feroz Shah Kotla, Delhi, December 14: **Tripura** 100 in 39.3 overs (Parvinder Singh 20; Pawan Suyal 3-14, Pawan Negi 2-2) lost to **Delhi** 101/2 in 16 overs (Nitish Rana 67*; Rana Dutta 2-21) by eight wickets.

Palam A Ground, Model Sports Complex, Delhi, December 15: **Andhra** 261/4 in 50 overs (AG Pradeep 102*, Jyothi Sai Krishna 72, Biplab Samantray 2-43, Alok Sahoo 2-48) beat **Odisha** 206 in 48 overs (Anurag Sarangi 52, B Samantray 44; D Siva Kumar 4-37) by 55 runs.

Feroz Shah Kotla, Delhi, December 15: **Maharashtra** 176/9 in 50 overs (Rahul Tripathi 46, Harshad Khadiwale 36; Bhargav Bhatt 4-30, Rishi Arothe 2-25) lost to **Baroda** 177/2 in 39.3 overs (Aditya Waghmode 77*, Deepak Hooda 58*) by eight wickets.

Palam B Ground, Model Sports Complex, Delhi, December 15: Vidarbha 324/5 in 50 overs (Ganesh Satish 140*, Jitesh Sharma 105; Rana Dutta 2-57, Chiranjit Paul 2-64) beat **Tripura** 166 in 47.4 overs (Sanjay Majumder 39, Samrat Singha 32; Akshay Wakhare 3-29, Akshay Karnewar 2-12) by 158 runs.

Palam B Ground, Model Sports Complex, Delhi, December 17: Andhra 87 in 25.3 overs (Prasanth Kumar 38; Akshay Karnewar 4-13, Umesh Yadav 3-16) lost to **Vidarbha** 91/0 in 19.2 overs (Jiesh Sharma 47*, Faiz Fazal 44*) by ten wickets.

Palam A Ground, Model Sports Complex, Delhi, December 17: Tripura 58 in 22.2 overs (Swapnil Singh 5-25, Yusuf Pathan 3-24) lost to **Baroda** 61/4 in 6.1 overs (Ambati Raydu 31*, Chiranjit Paul 3-27) by six wickets.

Feroz Shah Kotla, Delhi, December 17: Maharashtra 194/9 in 50 overs (Kedar Jadhav 48, Swapnil Gugale 44; Manan Sharma 3-21, Pawan Negi 3-38) lost to **Delhi** 197/5 in 48.4 overs (Milind Sharma 58*, Dhruv Shorey 57; S Gugale 2-39) by five wickets.

Feroz Shah Kotla, Delhi, December 18: Andhra 183 in 49.2 overs (D Siva Kumar 38, Prasanth Kumar 33; Pawan Negi 3-29) lost to **Delhi** 184/1 in 34.1 overs (Unmukt Chand 118*, Gautam Gambhir 30) by nine wickets.

Palam B Ground, Model Sports Complex, Delhi, December 18: Maharashtra 184 in 48.2 overs (Ankit Bawne 48, Shamshuzama Kazi 40: Akshay Karnewar 4-43, Umesh Yadav 3-24) lost to **Vidarbha** 185/6 in 47 overs (Ganesh Satish 71*, Jitesh Sharma 39; S Kazi 3-45) by four wickets.

Palam A Ground, Model Sports Complex, Delhi, December 18: Tripura 206 in 49.2 overs (Parvinder Singh 65, Samrat Singha 56; Deepak Behera 2-26, Biplab Samantray 2-31) beat **Odisha** 169 in 44.3 overs (Deepak Behera 29, Arabind Singh 27; Chiranjit Paul 3-34, Rajesh Banik 3-35) by 37 runs.

Group C Points Table

Teams	M	W	L	T	N/R	Pts	NRR
Vidarbha	6	5	1	0	0	20	+1.209
Delhi	6	5	1	0	0	20	+0.860
Baroda	6	4	2	0	0	16	+1.114
Maharashtra	6	3	3	0	0	12	+0.465
Andhra	6	2	4	0	0	8	-0.844
Odisha	6	1	5	0	0	4	-0.680
Tripura	6	1	5	0	0	4	-2.407

Vidarbha and Delhi qualified for the quarter-finals

Group D

Madhavrao Scindia Cricket Ground, Rajkot, December 10: Goa 235/9 in 50 overs (Saurabh Bandekar 62, Reagan Pinto 55; Ashok Dinda 3-40, Sayan Ghosh 2-54) lost to **Bengal** 238/4 in 41.2 overs (Shreevats Goswami 70, Manoj Tiwary 62*; Darshan Misal 2-36) by six wickets.

SCA Stadium, Rajkot, December 10: Himachal Pradesh 243/8 in 50 overs (Rishi Dhawan 67*, Paras Dogra 41; Piyush Chawla 3-49, Saurabh Kumar 2-36) lost to **Uttar Pradesh** 247/3 in 47.2 overs (Eklavya Dwivedi 104*, Rinku Singh 62*) by seven wickets.

Madhavrao Scindia Cricket Ground, Rajkot, December 11: Himachal Pradesh 308/7 in 50 overs (Prashant Chopra 91, Robin Bist 84; Sayan Ghosh 3-67, Ashok Dinda 3-69) beat **Bengal** 219 in 36.3 overs (Pankaj Shaw 68, Manoj Tiwary 36; Pankaj Jaiswal 3-28, Bipul Sharma 2-39) by 89 runs.

SCA Stadium, Rajkot, December 11: Saurashtra 340/5 in 50 overs (Ravindra Jadeja 134, Sheldon Jackson 111) beat **Madhya Pradesh** 333 in 49.1 overs (Jalaj Saxena 133, Naman Ojha 58; Shaurya Sanandia 3-59, R Jadeja 2-58) by seven runs.

SCA Stadium, Rajkot, December 12: Goa 199 in 47.4 overs (Sagun Kamat 95, Swapnil Asnodkar 30; Shaurya Sanandia 3-41, Ravindra Jadeja 2-31) lost to **Saurashtra** 202/0 in 26.4 overs (Sheldon Jackson 150*, Avi Barot 49*) by ten wickets.

SCA Stadium, Rajkot, December 13: Bengal 221 in 48.3 overs (Sudip Chatterjee 97, Laxmi Ratan Shukla 32; Mohammd Javed 4-40, Piyush Chawla 3-53) lost to **Uttar Pradesh** 222/6 in 46.4 overs (Umang Sharma 73, Prashant Gupta 47; Mohammed Shami 2-52) by four wickets.

Madhavrao Scindia Cricket Ground, Rajkot, December 13: Goa 214 in 43.2 overs (Saurabh Bandekar 68, Swapnil Asnodkar 68; Jalaj Saxena 2-21, Puneet Datey 2-34) lost to **Madhya Pradesh** 215/3 in 42.2 overs (Harpreet Singh 74*, Jalaj Saxena 69; Shadab Jakati 2-49) by seven wickets.

Madhavrao Scindia Cricket Ground, Rajkot, December 14: Saurashtra 195 in 48.4 overs (Cheteshwar Pujara 73, Sheldon Jackson 32; Ronit More 3-44, Rishi Dhawan 3-46) lost to **Himachal Pradesh** 198/3 in 43.2 overs (Ankush Bains 76, Robin Bist 47; Kamlesh Makvana 2-27) by seven wickets.

SCA Stadium, Rajkot, December 14: Uttar Pradesh 211 in 46.3 overs (Akshdeep Nath 67, Umang Sharma 50; Puneet Datey 2-32, Jalaj Saxena 2-33) lost to **Madhya Pradesh** 212/2 in 39.1 overs (Naman Ojha 114*, Harpreet Singh 63*) by eight wickets.

SCA Stadium, Rajkot, December 16: Goa 184in 45.4 overs (Sagun Kamat 57, Swapnil Asnodkar 37; Pankaj Jaiswal 3-26, Nikhil Gangta 2-13) lost to **Himachal Pradesh** 187/3 in 29.2 overs (Prashant Chopra 67, Ankush Bains 36; Shadab Jakati 3-33) by seven wickets.

Madhavrao Scindia Cricket Ground, Rajkot, December 16: Saurashtra 189 in 48.5 overs (Cheteshwar Pujara 41, Arpit Vasavada 39; Piyush Chawla 3-53, Praveen Kumar 2-20) lost to **Uttar Pradesh** 191/5 in 44.4 overs (Shubham Chaubey 85*, Eklavya Dwivedi 39; Dharmendrasinh Jadeja 2-38) by five wickets.

SCA Stadium, Rajkot, December 17: Bengal 262 in 50 overs (Sayan Mondal 88, Abhimanyu Easwaran 45; Puneet Datey 2-42, Chandrakant Sakure 2-56) lost to **Madhya Pradesh** 263/5 in 46.5 overs (Harpreet Singh 71, Rajat Patidar 63; Ashok Dinda 2-35) by five wickets.

Madhavrao Scindia Cricket Ground, Rajkot, December 17: Goa 218 in 49.5 overs (Reagan Pinto 66, Sagun Kamat 57; Suresh Raina 2-32, Bhuvneshwar Kumar 2-38) lost to **Uttar Pradesh** 224/4 in 36.3 overs (Umang Sharma 85*, Rinku Singh 51*; Shadab Jakati 3-48) by six wickets.

SCA Stadium, Rajkot, December 18: Bengal 243/5 in 50 overs (Abhimanyu Easwaran 48, Manoj Tiwary 43; Dharmendrasinh Jadeja 3-46) lost to **Saurashtra** 246/4 in 46 overs (Samarth Vyas 94, Cheteshwar Pujara 50*) by six wickets.

Madhavrao Scindia Cricket Ground, Rajkot, December 18: Himachal Pradesh 295/5 in 50 overs (Rishi Dhawan 117*, Robin Bist 84) beat **Madhya Pradesh** 254 in 46.1 overs (Venkatesh Iyer 57, Parth Sahani 42; Pankaj Jaiswal 6-33) by 41 runs.

Group D Points Table

Teams	M	W	L	T	N/R	Pts	NRR
Himachal Pradesh	5	4	1	0	0	16	+1.085
Uttar Pradesh	5	4	1	0	0	16	+0.335
Saurashtra	5	3	2	0	0	12	+0.373
Madhya Pradesh	5	3	2	0	0	12	+0.305
Bengal	5	1	4	0	0	4	-0.417
Goa	5	0	5	0	0	0	-1.851

Himachal Pradesh and Uttar Pradesh qualified for the quarter-finals

1st quarter-final: Himachal Pradesh beat Punjab by five wickets

Himachal Pradesh were 77 for 3 when Robin Bist and Rishi Dhawan got together for their match-winning 102-run stand. Strike rotation was the focus of their partnership. Dhawan's wicket in the 39th over gave Punjab an opening, but Bist, who survived a few run-out chances, shifted gears. Nikhil Gangta (39 off 28) and Bipul Sharma (14* off 9) hit three fours and three sixes to complete a thrilling chase. Bist's knock overshadowed Mandeep Singh's highest List A score that came after Punjab lost Pargat Singh in the first over and Yuvraj Singh in the 15th. Mandeep had steady stands with Gurkeerat Singh Mann, Mayank Sidhana and Gitansh Khera, but the innings lacked that one big punch. Bipul's economical returns of 0 for 30 in ten overs, three scalps each for Pankaj Jaiswal and Dhawan, and two wickets in the final over proved decisive.

KSCA Cricket Ground, Alur, December 23: Punjab 263/8 in 50 overs (Mandeep Singh 119, Gurkeerat Singh Mann 35; Pankaj Jaiswal 3-50, Rishi Dhawan 3-60) lost to **Himachal Pradesh** 266/5 in 49.2 overs (Robin Bist 109*, R Dhawan 41; Siddarth Kaul 3-42) by five wickets.

2nd quarter-final: Delhi beat Jharkhand by 99 runs

MS Dhoni tried his best in a modest chase, but lacked support to rescue Jharkhand from 9 for 4. Coming in at No.5 in the fifth over, he lost partners at regular intervals as Delhi bossed their opposition. He hit five fours and four sixes to showcase his class, but his team were bundled out with 12 overs left. Asked to bat first by Varun Aaron, Delhi reached 225 because of Nitish Rana's awareness and his sixth-wicket partnership of 74 with Manan Sharma. The duo fell to Rahul Shukla in the 46th over, but Pawan Negi's unbeaten 16-ball cameo gave Delhi a good total, considering their shaky start. Navdeep Saini and Ishant Sharma dented Jharkhand's top order, and Suboth Bhati ran through the lower order to end Dhoni's first domestic stint since 2007.

M Chinnaswamy Stadium, Bangalore, December 23: Delhi 225 in 50 overs (Nitish Rana 44, Pawan Negi 38*; Rahul Shukla 3-60, Varun Aaron 2-43) beat **Jharkhand** 126 in 38 overs (MS Dhoni 70*; Suboth Bhati 4-21, Navdeep Saini 3-31) by 99 runs.

3rd quarter-final: Tamil Nadu beat Uttar Pradesh by one wicket

Tamil Nadu's fight back from 17 for 4 and then 127 for 7 to complete the job showcased their resilience. The first consolidation came through Baba Indrajith's partnerships of 64 and 37 with M Vijay and Vijay Shankar respectively after Bhuvneshwar Kumar and Praveen Kumar used the new ball to their advantage. After Indrajith became the seventh wicket to fall, Vijay Shankar and R Satish put on 35. Amid another collapse, Satish's experience made the difference. Tamil Nadu were chasing a smallish target because L Balaji exploited the early morning conditions and R Ashwin used his smarts. Aswin Crist, Vijay Shankar and Satish supported them well. Struggling at 41 for 5 in 12.4 overs, Uttar Pradesh gave them a chance because of Rinku Singh's patient 97-ball knock and his 66-run stand for the seventh wicket with Piyush Chawla.

M Chinnaswamy Stadium, Bangalore, December 24: Uttar Pradesh 168 in 48.2 overs (Rinku Singh 60, Piyush Chawla 29; L Balaji 3-32, R Ashwin 2-27) lost to **Tamil Nadu** 169/9 in 41.3 overs (Baba Indrajith 48, R Sathish 34*; Bhuvneshwar Kumar 3-25, P Chawla 3-45) by one wicket.

4th quarter-final: Gujarat beat Vidarbha by two wickets

From a well-controlled chase that was spearheaded by Parthiv Patel, Gujarat slipped to 162 for 8, thanks to some careless batting and excellent bowling by Akshay Wakhare, Ravikumar Thakur and Akshay Karnewar. It needed the calmness of Axar Patel, and his unbroken ninth-wicket partnership of 36 with Hardik Patel to take Gujarat to the semi-final. Earlier, Axar's two wickets, Jasprit Bumrah's late burst of four scalps and the run-out of Jitesh Sharma had brought Gujarat back into the game after both the Vidarbha openers made fifties. The dismissal of S Badrinath and Ravi Jangid in a space of three balls started the collapse, and despite Ganesh Satish's 47, on what was once his home ground, Vidarbha lost momentum. Bumrah gave another glimpse of his ability with the old ball, something that would make him a valuable asset in the Indian team in less than a month.

Jasprit Bumrah would soon break into the Indian side. — *Getty Images*

KSCA Cricket Ground, Alur, December 24: Vidarbha 195 in 48 overs (Faiz Fazal 52, Jitesh Sharma 51; Jasprit Bumrah 4-38, Axar Patel

2-22) lost to **Gujarat** 198/8 in 48.1 overs (Parthiv Patel 57, Axar 36*; Akshay Wakhare 3-30, Ravikumar Thakur 3-46) by two wickets.

Himachal Pradesh, Delhi, Tamil Nadu and Gujarat qualified for the semi-finals

1st semi-final: Delhi beat Himachal Pradesh by six wickets

Bipul Sharma's lusty hitting, and his ninth-wicket stand of 57 with Mayank Dagar, making his List A debut after being named in the Indian team for the Under-19 World Cup, helped Himachal Pradesh touch 200. But, it was never going to be enough against a star-studded batting line-up. Unmukt Chand's unbeaten 80 from No.3, and his partnerships of 61 with Shikhar Dhawan and unbroken 55 with Nitish Rana took Delhi to the final. Having elected to field, Delhi had Ankush Bains run out and Bist caught behind within 10.3 overs. Once Suboth Bhati accounted for Prashant Chopra, and Pawan Negi removed Rishi Dhawan and Paras Dogra in the space of two overs, Himachal Pradesh had to wait for their skipper to provide the impetus. Chand caught Bipul off the final ball of the innings to give Ishant his first wicket, and then came out and hit seven fours and two sixes.

M Chinnaswamy Stadium, Bangalore, December 26: **Himachal Pradesh** 200/9 in 50 overs (Bipul Sharma 51, Prashant Chopra 33; Nitish Rana 2-16, Suboth Bhati 2-36) lost to **Delhi** 201/4 in 41.1 overs (Unmukt Chand 80*, Shikhar Dhawan 39) by six wickets.

2nd semi-final: Gujarat beat Tamil Nadu by 31 runs

Abhinav Mukund's unbeaten century went in vain as Tamil Nadu fumbled after the opening-wicket partnership of 84 in 16 overs. The introduction of Axar triggered the turnaround as he removed the cream of Tamil Nadu's top order – Dinesh Karthik, Baba Aparajith, Baba Indrajith and M Vijay – within three overs. Abhinav reignited the spark through a sixth-wicket stand of 51 with Ashwin as the equation came down to 78 off ten overs. Axar returned to remove Ashwin and Vijay Shankar. Gujarat had a total to defend after they were 45 for 4 and 87 for 5 because of Manpreet Juneja's stands of 93 and 49 with Chirag Gandhi and Rohit Dahiya. Juneja became Ashwin's third victim in the 47th over, but by then Gujarat already had a winning total.

KSCA Cricket Ground, Alur, December 26: **Gujarat** 248/8 in 50 overs (Manpreet Juneja 74, Chirag Gandhi 71; R Ashwin 3-51, Vijay Shankar 2-36) beat **Tamil Nadu** 217 in 47.3 overs (Abhinav Mukund 104*, Dinesh Karthik 41; Axar Patel 6-43, Jasprit Bumrah 2-45) by 31 runs.

Final: Gujarat beat Delhi by 139 runs

It has long been said of cricket that it isn't always the strongest side on paper that comes away with the broadest smile. As if to emphatically drive that point home, Gujarat pulverised Delhi in the final of the all-India 50-over Vijay Hazare Trophy, their 139-run victory fashioned primarily but not only by two former internationals. Delhi seemed to have all bases covered despite a massive shake-up in personnel at the start of the season. Virender Sehwag had moved across to Haryana, several senior players including the versatile Rajat Bhatia had been shown the door, and Ajay Jadeja had quit as coach almost before he was nominated to that position. All this, combined with early elimination from the Ranji Trophy, had put Gautam Gambhir under enormous pressure, but he rallied his troops in the Hazare Trophy, and was bolstered by the availability of Shikhar Dhawan and Ishant in a rare break from international duty.

Gujarat, though, were no pushovers and had taken the tougher route to the final. Given a free hand to build and drive the team, Parthiv did an excellent job.

The final, under lights, was played on a surface with a reasonable covering of live grass, which automatically brought RP Singh back into the mix. Having sat out the two previous knockout games on sluggish tracks, he made a massive impact in the title round, his opening burst of 4 for 25 from seven overs cutting out all escape routes for Delhi after Gujarat had ridden on Parthiv's maiden List A.

Parthiv has more than a dozen years at the first-class level behind him, and put his vast experience and expertise to excellent use after Gujarat were asked to set a target. Once a predominantly off-side player, Parthiv has expanded his repertoire, and he put on a veritable exhibition against a Delhi pace attack that was admittedly a little off the boil, Ishant excepted. Parthiv lost Priyank Panchal, his opening partner, and Bhargav Merai with just 44 on the board, but found an excellent ally in Rujul Bhatt as a season-high 149 came for the third wicket.

The association wasn't built as much around a flurry of boundaries as excellent running between the wickets. It wasn't until Pawan Negi was introduced belatedly, in the 36th over, that Delhi finally broke through, triggering a mini-collapse of 4 for 21 until Chirag Gandhi made an unbeaten 44 to ensure the third-wicket association didn't go unsupported.

Gambhir had moved down to No. 4 to lend depth to the middle order, but he was forced to come in very early as RP Singh fired out Rishab Pant and Shikhar Dhawan with just 11 on the board. Using swing under lights and skid off the surface to great effect, the left-arm quick continued to give Delhi a thorough working over, leading a formidable pace attack that included Rush Kalaria and Jasprit Bumrah with aplomb.

Any distant Delhi hopes of a stirring fightback were nipped in the bud when RP Singh elicited an outside edge from Gambhir that was snapped up low at slip. And when he trapped Milind Kumar in front three deliveries later, he had all but settled the issue as a contest.

Unmukt Chand played some pleasing strokes, but as veteran RP Singh left the stage, the exciting Bumrah came on. Showcasing the skills that had already made him a vital member of the national limited-overs sides, Bumrah flummoxed the middle and lower order with his wonderful changes of pace and a yorker to die for. On another night, his 5 for 28 would have been the talking point; this time around, it was a mere glittering footnote to the Parthiv-RP Singh show. *R Kaushik*

Venue: M.Chinnaswamy Stadium, Bengaluru, India, December 28, 2015
Toss: Delhi, who chose to bowl
MoM: RP Singh (Gujarat) and Parthiv Patel (Gujarat)

Gujarat

			R	B	4s	6s	SR
Parthiv Patel* †		b Negi	105	119	10	0	88.24
Priyank Panchal		b Saini	14	20	3	0	70.00
Bhargav Merai	LBW	b Sharma	5	7	0	0	71.43
Rujul Bhatt	c † Pant	b Rana	60	74	4	1	81.08
Chirag Gandhi	Not Out	b Rana	44	39	4	0	112.82
Axar Patel		b Saini	6	5	1	0	120.00
Manpreet Juneja	c Gambhir	b Sharma	6	12	0	0	50.00
Rush Kalaria	c † Pant	b Bhati	21	20	1	1	105.00
RP Singh	c Kumar	b Bhati	0	1	0	0	0.00
Karan Patel	Run out	(Unmukt Chand)	1	2	0	0	50.00
Jasprit Bumrah	c Chand	b Negi	2	2	0	0	100.00
Extras	(0b,2lb,1nb,6w)		9				
Total	(all out, 50.0 overs)		273 (5.46 runs per over)				

Fall of wickets: 30-1 (Priyank Panchal, 6.4 ov), 44-2 (Bhargav Merai, 9.4 ov), 193-3 (Rujul Bhatt, 36.2 ov), 193-4 (Parthiv Patel, 37.1 ov), 204-5 (Axar Patel, 38.2 ov), 224-6 (Manpreet Juneja, 42.1 ov), 266-7 (Rush Kalaria, 48.4 ov), 266-8 (RP Singh, 48.5 ov), 269-9 (Karan Patel, 49.3 ov), 273-10 (Jasprit Bumrah, 49.6 ov)
Bowling: Navdeep Saini 9-0-46-2-5.11 (1 wd, 1 nb), Ishant Sharma 9-0-39-1-4.33 (3 wd), Subodh Bhati 6-0-43-2-7.17, Nitish Rana 4-0-18-1-4.50, Milind Kumar 10-0-53-0-5.30, Manan Sharma 6-0-36-1-6.00 (1 wd), Pawan Negi 6-0-36-2-6.00

Delhi

			R	B	4s	6s	SR
Rishabh Pant †		b Singh	0	1	0	0	0.00
Shikhar Dhawan	c Juneja	b Singh	5	9	1	0	55.56
Unmukt Chand		b Bumrah	33	48	6	0	68.75
Gautam Gambhir *	c Bhatt	b Singh	9	19	1	0	47.37
Milind Kumar	LBW	b Singh	0	3	0	0	0.00
Nitish Rana	c Kalaria	b Bumrah	12	35	1	0	34.29
Manan Sharma	Run out	(Jasprit Bumrah)	2	13	0	0	15.38
Pawan Negi	c Merai	b Bumrah	57	47	9	1	121.28
Subodh Bhati	LBW	b Bumrah	3	9	0	0	33.33

Ishant Sharma		b Bumrah	0	11	0	0	0.00
Navdeep Saini	Not out	b Bumrah	0	1	0	0	0.00
Extras	(0b,6lb,1nb,6w)	13					
Total	(all out, 32.3 overs)		134 (4.15 runs per over)				

Fall of wickets: 0-1 (Rishabh Pant, 0.1 ov), 11-2 (Shikhar Dhawan, 4.2 ov), 27-3 (Gautam Gambhir, 8.4 ov), 31-4 (Milind Kumar, 10.1 ov), 59-5 (Unmukt Chand, 16.3 ov), 64-6 (Manan Sharma, 19.4 ov), 70-7 (Nitish Rana, 22.1 ov), 80-8 (Subodh Bhati, 24.5 ov), 100-9 (Ishant Sharma, 28.5 ov), 134-10 (Pawan Negi, 32.3 ov)

Bowling: RP Singh 10-2-42-4-4.20 (1 wd), Rush Kalaria 6-0-21-0-3.50 (1 wd), Axar Patel 5-0-30-0-6.00 (3 wd), Jasprit Bumrah 9-1-28-5-3.11 (1 wd, 1 nb), Rujul Bhatt 2-0-7-0-3.50

Umpires: K Bharatan and Nitin Menon
TV umpire: CK Nandan
Match referee: P Roy

Deodhar Trophy

Different format, new winners

HIMANISH BHATTACHARJEE

India B beat India A by five wickets

Exceptional swing bowling from Nathu Singh and Dhawal Kulkarni, and a composed unbeaten half-century from Unmukt Chand, the captain, helped India B win the opening game of the Deodhar Trophy. The competition was played in a non-zonal format for the first time with two teams picked by the national selectors. Nathu and Kulkarni reduced India A to 29 for 5 before Stuart Binny and Pawan Negi took five wickets between them. Eight batsmen were dismissed for single-digit scores, and only the sixth-wicket partnership of 104 between Ambati Rayudu and Parveez Rasool stood out. Chand showed that the pitch carried no demons. He and Shreyas Iyer shared an opening stand of 56 before Amit Mishra had three leg before wicket decisions, including two in two, going in his favour. It made the score 78 for 4, but Chand and Dinesh Karthik had enough experience to guide the team with a 75-run partnership.

Green Park, Kanpur, January 25: India A 161 in 44.2 overs (Parveez Rasool 66, Ambati Raydu 58; Nathu Singh 3-23, Pawan Negi 3-50) lost to **India B** 162/5 in 29.2 overs (Unmukt Chand 77*, Dinesh Karthik 34; Amit Mishra 3-62) by five wickets.

India B beat Gujarat by seven runs

Unfortunately for Chirag Gandhi, his maiden List A century from No.6 came in a losing cause. Manpreet Juneja and Rujul Bhatt added 78 for the fourth wicket, but both fell in the space of 23 runs. It put the onus on Gandhi to take the team through, and he did a commendable job even though there was little support from the lower-middle order. With Gujarat 234 for 9, Gandhi gave Hardik Patel confidence to reduce the equation to 15 off the last over. A six and a single took Gandhi to 100, before Hardik, trying to get off strike, was run out with three balls left. Earlier, India B, sent in, rode on Unmukt Chand's second successive half-century and valuable contributions from Suryakumar Yadav and Stuart Binny. Dhawal Kulkarni dented Gujarat's chase early on, and the rest of the bowlers held their own.

Green Park, Kanpur, January 26: India B 280/8 in 50 overs (Unmukt Chand 63, Suryakumar Yadav 47; Mehul Patel 3-69, Santosh Shinde 2-41) beat **Gujarat** 273 in 49.3 overs (Chirag Gandhi 100*, Manpreet Juneja 50; Dhawal Kulkarni 2-21, Karn Sharma 2-56) by seven runs.

India A beat Gujarat by six wickets

Kedar Jadhav's power-packed knock, and equally crucial performances by

Rayudu and Faiz Fazal helped India A go past Gujarat by six wickets in a virtual semi-final. Parthiv Patel slammed a century, but no other batsman made 30 in the innings. That they crossed 270 was because of Santosh Shinde's three sixes and a four from No.10. Mishra and Parveez Rasool were India A's best bowlers, returning combined figures of 18.2-0-95-6. The other bowlers picked up a wicket each as Gujarat were dismissed with four balls to spare. Fazal and Rayudu had a partnership of 75 from 49 for 2 to keep the chase simple. After Fazal fell, Jadhav added 83 with Rayudu, and an unbroken 66 with Naman Ojha.

Green Park, Kanpur, January 27: Gujarat 272 in 49.2 overs (Parthiv Patel 119, Santosh Shinde 28; Parveez Rasool 3-47, Amit Mishra 3-48) lost to **India A** 273/4 in 47.2 overs (Kedar Jadhav 91*, Ambati Rayudu 75; Mehul Patel 2-53) by six wickets.

Points Table

Teams	M	W	L	T	N/R	Pts	NRR
India B	2	2	0	0	0	8	1.231
India A	2	1	1	0	0	4	-1.012
Gujarat	2	0	2	0	0	0	-0.232

India B and India A qualified for the final

Final: India A beat India B by 87 runs

A magnificent 162-run opening partnership between Fazal and M Vijay set up India A's title triumph. After Nathu dismissed Vijay, there was a stutter as India A slipped to 226 for 5. Baba Aparajith and Binny struck once each, Fazal was run out and Nathu got Sudip Chatterjee. Just when it looked like India B were in control, Jadhav hit a 39-ball 58, which included four fours and two sixes, to seize the momentum. India B's chase got off to a poor start, as they stumbled to 12 for 3 and then 54 for 5. Suryakumar Yadav and Binny tried to rebuild, but their 62-run stand was the only talking point in the innings. All of S Aravind, Krishna Das and Shardul Thakur picked up two wickets each, while Shabhaz Nadeem dismissed Binny, Negi and Nathu to finish the game with 9.2 overs still left.

Green Park, Kanpur, January 29: India A 286/7 in 50 overs (Faiz Fazal 100, M Vijay 69; Dhawal Kulkarni 2-31, Nathu Singh 2-58) beat **India B** 199 in 40.4 overs (Stuart Binny 60, Suryakumar Yadav 45; Shahbaz Nadeem 3-36, Krishna Das 2-32) by 87 runs. *MoM:* Faiz Fazal.

Best batsman: Kedar Jadhav (156 runs, 3 matches)
Best bowler: Amit Mishra (7 wickets, 3 matches)
Debutants: Gujarat (4): Dhwanil Patel, Santosh Shinde, Raxlee Taylor, Kavish Panchal
Winners: India A

Syed Mushtaq Ali Trophy

Raina delivers, Pandya sizzles

SHUBHAM MALAVIYA

Uttar Pradesh remained unbeaten throughout the tournament to lift their first title in any format since winning the 2005-06 Ranji Trophy.

The tournament was scheduled for the first time before the IPL auctions to give the players a chance to impress the franchises. That the competition was televised from the Super League onwards was an added incentive. It also allowed the national selectors more options ahead of a busy T20I season, featuring a tour of Australia, a series against Sri Lanka, the Asia Cup in Bangladesh and the World T20 at home.

While Nathu Singh's 14 wickets for Rajasthan impressed Mumbai Indians enough to dish out Rs 3.2 crore, no one made this tournament count more than Hardik Pandya. His 377 runs at a strike-rate of 130.90 and ten wickets at a strike-rate of 18.6 took Baroda to the final, almost unchallenged, and earned him a spot in the Indian team.

Pandya's capability of clearing the boundary came to the fore in a league game against Delhi where, during the course of his unbeaten 51-ball 81, he hit Akash Sudan for 34 runs in one over. Sudan conceded 39 in that over, making it the most expensive ever in T20 cricket. Gloucestershire's James Fuller, who had conceded 38 to Scott Styris in a game against Sussex in 2012, held the previous record.

Baroda's journey to the final made for a wonderful lesson on teamwork. Irfan Pathan, who was once to Indian fans what Pandya is now, led from the front to top the bowling charts and score 200 runs. Kedar Devdhar and Deepak Hooda also played their part as Baroda lost just two of their nine matches on the way to the final. In the must-win last Super League game against Mumbai, Hooda's 53 and a boundary by Bhargav Bhatt, the No.10 batsman, helped them prevail by one wicket. Mumbai, after having done almost all things right, could not hold their nerve when it mattered and slipped to second on the table.

That Baroda could not lift the title for the third time was because of Suresh Raina's masterclass under lights at the Wankhede Stadium in front of a decent turnout. It was a repeat of the 2013-14 final, but, this time, Uttar Pradesh had the final say. Raina marked his return to form with a calculated, unbeaten 37-ball 47 from No.3. Chasing 164, Baroda were done in by Kuldeep Yadav and Piyush Chawla.

With Gujarat beating Jharkhand by six wickets in the first match of the last day of the Super League stage, Uttar Pradesh needed to beat Delhi to go through to the final. They were reduced to 88 for 6 in a chase of 159, but

Unbeaten through the tournament: The Suresh Raina-led Uttar Pradesh rode on a composed knock from their captain to lift their first title since 2005-06. – *BCCI*

Eklavya Dwivedi's unbeaten 49 from 35 balls, which was studded with five fours and two sixes, proved to be the difference. His partnerships of 40 in 4.4 overs with Praveen Kumar (seventh wicket) and unbroken 31 in two overs with Amit Mishra (eighth wicket) took them home with two balls to spare.

Among other highlights, Robin Uthappa became the first batsman to reach 1000 runs in the history of the tournament, and Rahil Shah, Pathan, Shadab Jakati, Karn Sharma and CV Stephen recorded five-wicket hauls. Saurabh Wakaskar, Jitesh Sharma, Unmukt Chand and Biplab Samantray made centuries. Also, Chawla and Ishwar Pandey took hat-tricks on the same day. The last time two bowlers took a hat-trick on the same day of a competition was in the 2011 Syed Mushtaq Ali Trophy.

Best batsman: Hardik Pandya (377 runs, 10 matches)
Best bowler: Irfan Pathan (17 wickets, 10 matches)

Debutants (80)

Andhra (4): Girinath Reddy, Karan Shinde, Karthik Raman, Ajay Kumar; **Assam (5):** Krishna Das, Mrinmoy Dutta, Wasiqur Rahman, Saahil Jain, Jogeswar Bhumij; **Baroda (2):** Mrunal Devdhar, Soaeb Tai; **Bengal (3):** Pramod Chandila, Anurag Tiwari, Mukesh Kumar; **Delhi (5):** Suboth Bhati, Sarthak Ranjan, Navdeep Saini, Sarang Rawat, Akash Sudan; **Goa (3):** Snehal Kauthankar, Felix Alemno, Kashyap Bakhale; **Gujarat (3):** Raxlee Taylor, Kuldeep Ghavi, Santosh Shinde; **Haryana (6):** Rahul Dagar, Mohit Hooda, Rohit Sharma, Chaitanya Bishnoi, Poonish Mehta, Shamsher Yadav; **Hyderabad (7):** Jaweed Ali, Mohammed Siraj, Kolla Sumanth, Vishal Sharma, Annabathula Akash, Mehdi Hasan, Himalay Agarwal;**Jammu & Kashmir (3):** Rohit Sharma, Omar Alam, Jatin Wadhwan; **Jharkhand (5):** Ankit Dabas, Monu Kumar, Sumit Kumar, Shasheem Rathour, Sonu Singh; **Karnataka (1):** Mohammed

Taha; **Kerala (1):** Mohammed Azharuddeen; **Madhya Pradesh (5):** Ankit Kushwah, Ashwin Das, Ashutosh Singh, Ayan Khan, Mihir Hirwani; **Maharashtra (1):** Satyajeet Bachhav; **Mumbai (1):** Shivam Dubey; **Odisha (4):** Abhishek Yadav, Tukuna Sahoo, Manoj Barik, Rishikesh Das; **Punjab (3):** Baltej Singh, Pargat Singh, Anmol Malhotra; **Railways (3):** Karan Mahajan, Akshat Pandey, V Cheluvaraj;**Rajasthan (3):** Ajay Singh, Manender Singh, Siddharth Dobal;**Saurashtra (2):** Shaurya Sanandia, Prerak Mankad; **Services (2):** Deepak Rai, Nitin Yadav;**Tamil Nadu (4):** M Ashwin, J Kousik, Bharath Shankar, Abhishek Tanwar; **Tripura (3):** Rajat Dey, Nirupen Sen, Viki Saha; **Uttar Pradesh (3):** Saurabh Dubey, Shubham Chaubey, Saurabh Kumar; **Vidarbha (2):** Rajneesh Gurbani, Akshay Karnewar.

Group A

VCA Ground, Nagpur, January 2: Bengal 185/4 in 20 overs (Wriddhiman Saha 81, Sayan Mondal 50; Chama Milind 2-45) beat **Hyderabad** 124 in 16.2 overs (Akshath Reddy 32; Mohammed Shami 3-18, Pragyan Ojha 3-23) by 61 runs.

VCA Stadium, Jamtha, Nagpur, January 2: Gujarat 151/6 in 20 overs (Rujul Bhatt 40, Parthiv Patel 35; Akshay Chauhan 2-32) lost to **Himachal Pradesh** 152/5 in 19.3 overs (Prashant Chopra 89*, Paras Dogra 36; Rush Kalaria 2-21) by five wickets.

VCA Ground, Nagpur, January 2: Haryana 113 in 19.1 overs (Nitin Saini 50; Antony Dhas 4-10, M Ashwin 3-28) lost to **Tamil Nadu** 116/1 in 16 overs (S Anirudha 54*, Baba Aparajith 49*) by nine wickets.

VCA Ground, Nagpur, January 3: Tamil Nadu 151/8 in 20 overs (Abhinav Mukund 41, Antony Dhas 28*; Veer Pratap Singh 3-15, Mohammed Shami 2-30) beat **Bengal** 82 in 15.5 overs (Shreevats Goswami 31; Rahil Shah 5-12, M Ashwin 2-9) by 69 runs.

VCA Stadium, Jamtha, Nagpur, January 3: Gujarat 174/7 in 20 overs (Parthiv Patel 59, Manpreet Juneja 37; Ravi Jangid 2-33, Ravikumar Thakur 2-45) beat **Vidarbha** 114 in 18.4 overs (Shalabh Shrivastava 21, Jitesh Sharma 20; Jasprit Bumrah 3-16, RP Singh 3-26) by 60 runs.

VCA Stadium, Jamtha, Nagpur, January 3: Hyderabad 140/9 in 20 overs (Ashish Reddy 37, B Sandeep 29; Akshay Chauhan 4-25, Rahul Singh 2-25) beat **Himachal Pradesh** 126/9 in 20 overs (Ankush Bains 25, Nikhil Gangta 24; Chama Milind 3-34, Akash Bhandari 2-18) by 14 runs.

VCA Ground, Nagpur, January 4: Hyderabad 131/7 in 20 overs (Hanuma Vihari 32, Tanmay Agarwal 25; RP Singh 3-15, Hardik Patel 2-20) lost to **Gujarat** 134/7 in 19.3 overs (Parthiv Patel 70, Priyank Panchal 32; B Sandeep 2-14, Mohammed Siraj 2-29) by three wickets.

VCA Stadium, Jamtha, Nagpur, January 4: Haryana 136/8 in 20 overs (Mohit Hooda 65, Harshal Patel 20; Ravi Jangid 3-13, Rajneesh Gurbani 3-24) lost to **Vidarbha** 140/2 in 19.3 overs (Himanshu Joshi 61*, Faiz Fazal 37) by eight wickets.

VCA Ground, Nagpur, January 4: Bengal 154/6 in 20 overs (Pramod Chandila 70, Sudip Chatterjee 42; Pankaj Jaiswal 4-26) beat **Himachal Pradesh** 152/3 in 20 overs (Prashant Chopra 74*, Paras Dogra 52; Alok Pratap Singh 2-28) by two runs.

VCA Stadium, Jamtha, Nagpur, January 6: Bengal 101 in 19.2 overs (Ashok Dinda 22, Debabrata Das 22; Rohit Dahiya 3-14, Jasprit Bumrah 3-16) lost to **Gujarat** 104/2 in 11.5 overs (Parthiv Patel 52, Priyank Panchal 24) by eight wickets.

VCA Ground, Nagpur, January 6: Hyderabad 173/8 in 20 overs (Hanuma Vihari 44, Akshath Reddy 43; Yuzvendra Chahal 3-43, Amit Mishra 2-27) beat **Haryana** 138/7 in 20 overs (Nitin Saini 30, A Mishra 28*; H Vihari 2-13, Mohammed Siraj 2-23) by 35 runs.

VCA Stadium, Jamtha, Nagpur, January 6: Tamil Nadu 150/8 in 20 overs (Baba Aparajith 41, R Sathish 32; Ravikumar Thakur 2-22, Ravi Jangid 2-32) lost to **Vidarbha** 154/3 in 18.3 overs (Jitesh Sharma 73, Faiz Fazal 45; Rahil Shah 2-31) by seven wickets.

VCA Stadium, Jamtha, Nagpur, January 7: Bengal 147/5 in 20 overs (Abhishek Das 56,

Sayan Mondal 52; Akshay Karnewar 2-26) lost to **Vidarbha** 151/6 in 19.2 overs (Faiz Fazal 49, Apoorv Wankhade 37*; Mukesh Kumar 2-23) by four wickets.

VCA Ground, Nagpur, January 7: Gujarat 105 in 19.4 overs (Raxlee Taylor 44*; Antony Dhas 3-19, R Sathish 2-13) lost to **Tamil Nadu** 111/1 in 12.5 overs (Abhinav Mukund 67*, Baba Aparajith 30*) by nine wickets.

VCA Ground, Nagpur, January 7: Haryana 122/9 in 20 overs (Rahul Dagar 39, Harshal Patel 26; Bipul Sharma 3-20, Akshay Chauhan 3-24) lost to **Himachal Pradesh** 123/8 in 19.2 overs (Robin Bist 27; Ashish Hooda 3-15, Amit Mishra 2-26) by two wickets.

VCA Ground, Nagpur, January 9: Tamil Nadu 168/6 in 20 overs (R Sathish 41*, Bharath Shankar 41) lost to **Himachal Pradesh** 173/4 in 16.5 overs (Paras Dogra 79*, Prashant Chopra 24) by six wickets.

VCA Stadium, Jamtha, Nagpur, January 9: Hyderabad 139/7 in 20 overs (Hanuma Vihari 40, Akshath Reddy 37; Ravikumar Thakur 3-29, Akshay Karnewar 2-20) lost to **Vidarbha** 142/5 in 20 overs (Apoorv Wankhade 43*, Urvesh Patel 33; Chama Milind 2-26) by five wickets.

VCA Stadium, Jamtha, Nagpur, January 9: Haryana 127/3 in 20 overs (Nitin Saini 74*, Mohit Hooda 38) beat **Bengal** 110/8 in 20 overs (Wriddhiman Saha 32, Pramod Chandila 24; Amit Mishra 4-30, Harshal Patel 2-16) by 17 runs.

VCA Ground, Nagpur, January 10: Haryana 95 in 20 overs (Mohit Hooda 24, Chaitanya Bishnoi 21; Jasprit Bumrah 3-10, RP Singh 3-16) lost to **Gujarat** 99/1 in 6.4 overs (Parthiv Patel 51*, Rohit Dahiya 40*) by nine wickets.

VCA Ground, Nagpur, January 10: Hyderabad 140/8 in 20 overs (Jaweed Ali 35, Chama Milind 26; M Ashwin 3-18, J Kousik 3-20) lost to **Tamil Nadu** 141/6 in 18.4 overs (Dinesh Karthik 43, Abhinav Mukund 31; Akash Bhandari 2-20) by six wickets.

VCA Ground, Nagpur, January 10: Vidarbha 183/6 in 20 overs (Jitesh Sharma 106, Faiz Fazal 20; Bipul Sharma 2-23, Pankaj Jaiswal 2-40) beat **Himachal Pradesh** 156 in 19.5 overs (Bipul 58, Raghav Dhawan 43; Akshay Wakhare 4-18, Ravi Jangid 2-34) by 27 runs.

Group A Points Table

Teams	M	W	L	T	N/R	Pts	NRR
Vidarbha	6	5	1	0	0	20	+0.017
Gujarat	6	4	2	0	0	16	+1.559
Tamil Nadu	6	4	2	0	0	16	+1.136
Himachal Pradesh	6	3	3	0	0	12	-0.025
Hyderabad	6	2	4	0	0	8	-0.270
Bengal	6	2	4	0	0	8	-0.786
Haryana	6	1	5	0	0	4	-1.406

Vidarbha and Gujarat qualified for the Super League

Group B

Nehru Stadium, Kochi, January 2: Punjab 130/6 in 20 overs (Mandeep Singh 76, Gurinder Singh 29; Rajat Bhatia 2-16) lost to **Rajasthan** 133/6 in 19.4 overs (Rajesh Bishnoi 58, Dishant Yagnik 23*; Yuvraj Singh 2-16, Baltej Singh 2-29) by four wickets.

St. Paul's College Ground, Kochi, January 2: Jammu & Kashmir 126/6 in 20 overs (Bandeep Singh 37, Parveez Rasool 34*; Raiphi Gomez 2-19) lost to **Kerala** 129/5 in 18.4 overs (Rohan Prem 59*, R Gomez 22*; Mohammed Mudhasir 2-27) by five wickets.
Nehra Stadium, Kochi, January 2: Saurashtra 144/6 in 20 overs (Cheteshwar Pujara 67; Sanjay Majumder 2-22) beat **Tripura** 78 in 17.3 overs (Deepak Punia 3-19, Kamlesh Makvana 2-8) by 66 runs.
Nehra Stadium, Kochi, January 3: Jammu & Kashmir 105 in 19.3 overs (Bandeep Singh 40, Ian Dev Singh 39*; Harbhajan Singh 3-8, Baltej Singh 3-23) lost to **Punjab** 108/2 in 14.3 overs (Mandeep Singh 58*, Pargat Singh 44) by eight wickets.
Nehru Stadium, Kochi, January 3: Tripura 146/7 in 20 overs (Rajat Dev 77*; Shahbaz Nadeem 3-18, Prakash Seet 2-21) lost to **Jharkhand** 150/1 in 18.3 overs (Ishank Jaggi 75*, Virat Singh 65) by nine wickets.
St. Paul's College Ground, Kochi, January 3: Kerala 129/7 in 20 overs (Rohan Prem 38, VA Jagadeesh 28; Nathu Singh 4-13) beat **Rajasthan** 111/8 in 20 overs (Rajat Bhatia 42*; P Prasanth 3-22, Rohan Prem 2-21) by 18 runs.
Nehru Stadium, Kochi, January 4: Saurashtra 157/7 in 20 overs (Cheteshwar Pujara 81, Chirag Jani 38; Mohammed Mudhasir 2-15, Parvez Rasool 2-39) beat **Jammu & Kashmir** 84 in 17.1 overs (Ian Dev Singh 30; Dharmendrasinh Jadeja 3-19, Jaydev Unadkat 2-14) by 73 runs.
Nehru Stadium, Kochi, January 4: Rajasthan 120/9 in 20 overs (Chandrapal Singh 40, Dishant Yagnik 30; Vikash Singh 4-12) lost to **Jharkhand** 121/2 in 19.5 overs (Saurabh Tiwary 61*, Sumit Kumar 38*; Nathu Singh 2-14) by eight wickets.
St Paul's College Ground, Kochi, January 4: Tripura 111 in 19.5 overs (Udiyan Bose 35; Basil Thampi 4-15, Sandeep Warrier 2-26) lost to **Kerala** 113/2 in 16.1 overs (Sanju Samson 56*, Rohan Prem 40) by eight wickets.
Nehru Stadium, Kochi, January 6: Jharkhand 104/9 in 20 overs (Virat Singh 41; Harbhajan Singh 2-16, Siddarth Kaul 2-23) lost to **Punjab** 105/3 in 17.3 overs (Pargat Singh 60*, Gitansh Khera 22; Prakash Seet 2-31) by seven wickets.
Nehru Stadium, Kochi, January 6: Jammu & Kashmir 119 in 19.1 overs (Bandeep Singh 33, Mithun Manhas 21; Sanjay Majumder 3-17, Chiranjit Paul 2-15) lost to **Tripura** 121/6 in 18.2 overs (Samrat Singha 45, Manisankar Murasingh 23*; Parveez Rasool 3-25, Omar Alam 2-19) by four wickets.
St Paul's College Ground, Kochi, January 6: Kerala 165/9 in 20 overs (Rohan Prem 56, Sachin Baby 43; Jaydev Unadkat 3-23, Chirag Jani 2-25) beat **Saurashtra** 115/9 in 20 overs (J Unadkat 32, Cheteshwar Pujara 26; U Manukrishnan 3-11, P Prasanth 3-13) by 50 runs.
Nehru Stadium, Kochi, January 7: Jharkhand 179/4 in 20 overs (Saurabh Tiwary 57*, Shasheem Rathour 50; Rahil Sambyal 2-43) beat **Jammu & Kashmir** 103/7 in 20 overs (Ian Dev Singh 67; Sonu Singh 2-16, Shahbaz Nadeem 2-16) by 76 runs.
Nehru Stadium, Kochi, January 7: Tripura 96 in 18 overs (Samrat Singha 23; Sarabjit Ladda 3-30, Pargat Singh 2-13) lost to **Punjab** 100/2 in 15.3 overs (Anmol Malhotra 40*, Manan Vohra 35*) by eight wickets.
St Paul's College Ground, Kochi, January 7: Saurashtra 140/5 in 20 overs (Jaydev Unadkat 39*, Deepak Punia 30*; Chandrapal Singh 3-13) beat **Rajasthan** 115 in 19.3 overs (Chandrapal 36, Rajesh Bishnoi 24; Shaurya Sanandia 3-13, Prerak Mankad 2-27) by 25 runs.
Nehru Stadium, Kochi, January 9: Saurashtra 128/5 in 20 overs (Cheteshwar Pujara 54*, Chirag Jani 27; Sonu Singh 2-23) lost to **Jharkhand** 132/3 in 19.3 overs (Virat Singh 41, Shasheem Rathour 27; Shaurya Sanandia 2-22) by seven wickets.
St Paul's College Ground, Kochi, January 9: Punjab 135/7 in 20 overs (Yuvraj Singh 54, Pargat Singh 35; P Prasanth 3-11, Basil Thampi 2-30) lost to **Kerala** 139/5 in 19.5 overs (Sanju Samson 72, Mohammed Azharuddeen 25; Harbhajan Singh 2-19, Siddarth Kaul 2-24) by five wickets.
Nehru Stadium, Kochi, January 9: Rajasthan 112/9 in 20 overs (Rajat Bhatia 34; Viki Saha

2-8, Rana Dutta 2-15) lost to **Tripura** 113/9 in 20 overs (Rajat Dey 43; Nathu Singh 4-25, Chandrapal Singh 2-21) by one wicket.

Nehru Stadium, Kochi, January 10: Saurashtra 167/5 in 20 overs (Chirag Jani 39*, Sheldon Jackson 38; Jaskaran Singh 2-17) beat **Punjab** 148 in 19.2 overs (Himanshu Chawla 54, Gurinder Singh 33; Jaydev Unadkat 3-19, Dharmendrasingh Jadeja 2-26) by 19 runs.

Nehru Stadium, Kochi, January 10: Rajasthan 174/5 in 20 overs (Siddarth Dobal 71, Ankit Lamba 54; Omar Alam 2-25) beat **Jammu & Kashmir** 129/7 in 20 overs (Mithun Manhas 36, Ian Dev Singh 35; Nathu Singh 3-18, Manjeet Singh 2-31) by 45 runs.

St Paul's College Ground, Kochi, January 10: Kerala 169/6 in 20 overs (Sanju Samson 87, Rohan Prem 47; Shahbaz Nadeem 3-31, Prakash Seet 2-28) lost to **Jharkhand** 174/4 in 19 overs (Ishank Jaggi 45*, Kaushal Singh 33*; Fabid Ahmed 2-20) by six wickets.

Group B Points Table

Teams	M	W	L	T	N/R	Pts	NRR
Kerala	6	5	1	0	0	20	+0.873
Jharkhand	6	5	1	0	0	20	+0.799
Saurashtra	6	4	2	0	0	16	+1.050
Punjab	6	3	3	0	0	12	+0.528
Rajasthan	6	2	4	0	0	8	+0.034
Tripura	6	2	4	0	0	8	-1.079
J&K	6	0	6	0	0	0	-2.235

Kerala and Jharkhand qualified for the Super League

Group C

Reliance Stadium, Vadodara, January 2: Andhra 95/9 in 20 overs (Sirla Srinivas 22; Ishwar Pandey 4-20, Venkatesh Iyer 2-10) lost to **Madhya Pradesh** 96/5 in 18.2 overs (Harpreet Singh 40*, Sohraab Dhaliwal 25*; B Ayyappa 2-18) by five wickets.

Reliance Stadium, Vadodara, January 2: Baroda 165/8 in 20 overs (Kedar Devdhar 48, Deepak Hooda 48*; Syed Mohammad 2-28, Abu Nechim 2-35) beat **Assam** 116/9 in 20 overs (Syed 42*, A Nechim 20; Irfan Pathan 5-13, Swapnil Singh 2-15) by 49 runs.

Alembic Ground, Vadodara, January 2: Railways 210/2 in 20 overs (Saurabh Wakaskar 118, Asad Pathan 81*) lost to **Delhi** 214/6 in 19.2 overs (Aditya Kaushik 53, Unmukt Chand 38; Krishnakant Upadhyay 2-36, Akshat Pandey 2-41) by four wickets.

Moti Bagh Stadium, Vadodara, January 3: Goa 104/6 in 20 overs (Deepraj Gaonkar 44; Harpreet Singh 2-15) lost to **Madhya Pradesh** 106/3 in 15.5 overs (Zafar Ali 27, Jalaj Saxena 24; Shadab Jakati 2-22) by seven wickets.

Alembic Ground, Vadodara, January 3: Delhi 236/9 in 20 overs (Nitish Rana 97, Milind Singh 58; CV Stephen 5-52, B Sudhakar 2-50) beat **Andhra** 125 in 19.2 overs (K Sreekanth 37, Jyothi Sai Krishna 22; Suboth Bhati 2-13, Shivam Sharma 2-25) by 111 runs.

Moti Bagh Stadium, Vadodara, January 3: Baroda 142/5 in 20 overs (Hardik Pandya 54, Yusuf Pathan 41*; Ranjit Mali 2-21) beat **Railways** 133/6 in 20 overs (Vivek Singh 46; Deepak Hooda 3-23) by 9 runs.

Moti Bagh Stadium, Vadodara, January 4: Railways 122/9 in 20 overs (Akshat Pandey

28, Faiz Ahmed 26; CV Stephen 4-15, Girinath Reddy 2-22) beat **Andhra** 115 in 19.4 overs (Karan Shinde 28, Sirla Srinivas 24; Ranjit Mali 4-26, Anureet Singh 2-16) by seven runs.

Reliance Stadium, Vadodara, January 4: Goa 132/7 in 20 overs (Swapnil Asnodkar 24, Saurabh Bandekar 24; Syed Mohammad 2-18, Abu Nechim 2-25, Mrinmoy Dutta 2-25) lost to **Assam** 133/6 in 19.3 overs (Pallavkumar Das 44, Amit Verma 21; S Bandekar 2-16, Shadab Jakati 2-23) by four wickets.

Reliance Stadium, Vadodara, January 4: Madhya Pradesh 156/6 in 20 overs (Naman Ojha 48, Parth Sahani 36*; Pradeep Sangwan 3-22) lost to **Delhi** 160/6 in 19.5 overs (Gautam Gambhir 38, Milind Kumar 36*; Ishwar Pandey 2-23) by four wickets.

Moti Bagh Stadium, Vadodara, January 6: Baroda 154/2 in 20 overs (Irfan Pathan 49*, Kedar Devdhar 39; Darshan Misal 2-25) beat **Goa** 82 in 15.4 overs (Deepraj Gaonkar 48; Rishi Arothe 2-7, Hardik Pandya 2-14) by 72 runs.

Moti Bagh Stadium, Vadodara, January 6: Assam 44 in 12.1 overs (Suboth Bhati 4-9, Shivam Sharma 3-7) lost to **Delhi** 50/2 in 9.1 overs (Unmukt Chand 29*) by eight wickets.

Reliance Stadium, Vadodara, January 6: Railways 103 in 20 overs (Saurabh Wakaskar 28; Ashwin Das 4-10, Ishwar Pandey 2-24) lost to **Madhya Pradesh** 104/4 in 16.2 overs (Jalaj Saxena 37*, Zafar Ali 36; Karn Sharma 2-28) by six wickets.

Reliance Stadium, Vadodara, January 6: Railways 165/8 in 20 overs (Saurabh Wakaskar 39, Asad Pathan 36; Saurabh Bandekar 4-25) beat **Goa** 116/9 in 20 overs (Rituraj Singh 29*, Darshan Misal 20; Karn Sharma 5-24, Ranjit Mali 4-24) by 49 runs.

Moti Bagh Stadium, Vadodara, January 7: Andhra 117/8 in 20 overs (AG Pradeep 26; Syed Mohammad 3-15, Abu Nechim 2-14) beat **Assam** 105 in 19.3 overs (Syed 42, Amit Verma 22; CV Stephen 4-14, Sirla Srinivas 2-13) by 12 runs.

Reliance Stadium, Vadodara, January 7: Baroda 181/5 in 20 overs (Hardik Pandya 48, Mrunal Devdhar 33; Ankit Sharma 2-34) beat **Madhya Pradesh** 128 in 16.4 overs (Harpreet Singh 52; Irfan Pathan 4-34, Soaeb Tai 3-27) by 53 runs.

Reliance Stadium, Vadodara, January 9: Railways 142/8 in 20 overs (Mahesh Rawat 72*, Praveen Deshetti 25; Amit Verma 3-20, Mrinmoy Dutta 3-23) lost to **Assam** 147/5 in 18.2 overs (Pallavkumar Das 77, Syed Mohammad 36*; Ashish Yadav 2-20, Anureet Singh 2-30) by five wickets.

Moti Bagh Stadium, Vadodara, January 9: Delhi 91 in 19.2 overs (Shadab Jakati 5-17, Lakshay Garg 2-5) beat **Goa** 89/9 in 20 overs (Saurabh Bandekar 31*, Swapnil Asnodkar 21; Parvinder Awana 3-21, Akash Sudan 2-10) by two runs.

Moti Bagh Stadium, Vadodara, January 9: Andhra 91/9 in 20 overs (Srikar Bhatt 30, B Ayyappa 24; Bhargav Bhatt 2-5, Hardik Pandya 2-13) lost to **Baroda** 93/7 in 16.5 overs (Irfan Pathan 28*; B Sudhakar 3-15, Sirla Srinivas 2-18) by three wickets.

Alembic Ground, Vadodara, January 10: Andhra 97/7 in 20 overs (Sirla Srinivas 28, AG Pradeep 20; Saurabh Bandekar 2-16) lost to **Goa** 98/1 in 14.5 overs (Sagun Kamat 61*, Snehal Kauthankar 34*) by nine wickets.

Reliance Stadium, Vadodara, January 10: Assam 139/7 in 20 overs (Syed Mohammad 39, Amit Sinha 35; Ishwar Pandey 2-27, Ashwin Das 2-48) lost to **Madhya Pradesh** 140/5 in 19.4 overs (Harpreet Singh 63*, Venkatesh Iyer 44*; Mrinmoy Dutta 2-22) by five wickets.

Reliance Stadium, Vadodara, January 10: Baroda 153/6 in 20 overs (Hardik Pandya 81*, Swapnil Singh 28*; Manan Sharma 4-17, Akash Sudan 2-47) lost to **Delhi** 156/5 in 19.3 overs (Nitish Rana 53, Unmukt Chand 38; H Pandya 3-13, Swapnil 2-32) by five wickets.

Group C Points Table

Teams	M	W	L	T	N/R	Pts	NRR
Delhi	6	6	0	0	0	24	+1.936
Baroda	6	5	1	0	0	20	+1.693
MP	6	4	2	0	0	16	+0.101
Railways	6	2	4	0	0	8	-0.059
Assam	6	2	4	0	0	8	-1.050
Goa	6	1	5	0	0	4	-1.060
Andhra	6	1	5	0	0	4	-1.485

Delhi and Baroda qualified for the Super League

Group D

DRIEMS Ground, Tangi, Cuttack, January 2: Maharashtra 109/7 in 12 overs (Kedar Jadhav 52*; Piyush Chawla 4-28, Ankit Rajpoot 3-15) lost to **Uttar Pradesh** 113/3 in 11.2 overs (Prashant Gupta 35, Akshdeep Nath 34*) by seven wickets.
Barabati Stadium, Cuttack, January 2: Odisha 91 in 17.4 overs (Abhishek Yadav 33; Shardul Thakur 2-11, Dhawal Kulkarni 2-17) lost to **Mumbai** 95/4 in 15.5 overs (Aditya Tare 32, Siddhesh Lad 31*; Deepak Behera 2-14, Basant Mohanty 2-21) by six wickets.
Barabati Stadium, Cuttack, January 2: Karnataka 121/9 in 20 overs (Vinay Kumar 38, Robin Uthappa 22; Raushan Raj 3-19, Deepak Rai 2-21) lost to **Services** 122/7 in 19 overs (Anshul Gupta 27, Yashpal Singh 25; KC Cariappa 2-20) by three wickets.
DRIEMS Ground, Tangi, Cuttack, January 3: Karnataka 162 in 20 overs (Stuart Binny 38, Mohammed Taha 37; Rohan Raje 3-29, Dhawal Kulkarni 3-35) beat **Mumbai** 161 in 20 overs (Abhishek Nayar 49, Shreyas Iyer 32; Stuart Binny 2-20, S Aravind 2-32) by one run.
Barabati Stadium, Cuttack, January 3: Uttar Pradesh 150/5 in 20 overs (Prashant Gupta 53, Eklavya Dwivedi 47; Biplap Samantray 2-17, Alok Sahoo 2-23) beat **Odisha** 118/8 in 20 overs (Roshan Kumar Rao 31*, Govinda Poddar 22; Piyush Chawla 2-18, Kuldeep Yadav 2-24) by 32 runs.
Barabati Stadium, Cuttack, January 3: Maharashtra 159/8 in 20 overs (Nikhil Naik 69, Kedar Jadhav 36; Nitin Yadav 3-50, Raushan Raj 2-21) beat **Services** 128 in 18.3 overs (Soumya Ranjan Swain 27, Rajat Paliwal 25; Swapnil Gugale 3-18, Shamshuzama Kazi 3-25) by 31 runs.
DRIEMS Ground, Tangi, Cuttack, January 4: Karnataka 160/6 in 20 overs (Mohammed Taha 45, Robin Uthappa 25; Piyush Chawla 2-24) lost to **Uttar Pradesh** 161/5 in 19.1 overs (Prashant Gupta 48, Eklavya Dwivedi 29*) by five wickets.
Barabati Stadium, Cuttack, January 4: Services 127/7 in 20 overs (Yashpal Singh 40*, Rajat Paliwal 26; Shardul Thakur 2-17, Rohan Raje 2-37) lost to **Mumbai** 128/2 in 18.1 overs (Aditya Tare 49*, Akhil Herwadkar 39) by eight wickets.
Barabati Stadium, Cuttack, January 4: Odisha 183/4 in 20 overs (Biplab Samantray 102, Govinda Poddar 63; Anupam Sanklecha 2-23) lost to **Maharashtra** 184/6 in 20 overs (Ankit Bawne 49*, Prayag Bhati 44; Deepak Behera 2-32) by four wickets.
Barabati Stadium, Cuttack, January 7: Mumbai 164/6 in 20 overs (Shreyas Iyer 78, Akhil Herwadkar 28; Piyush Chawla 2-21, Ankit Rajpoot 2-27) lost to **Uttar Pradesh** 168/6 in 19.4 overs (Umang Sharma 47*, Prashant Gupta 33; Siddhesh Lad 2-27, Dhawal Kulkarni 2-31) by four wickets.

DRIEMS Ground, Tangi, Cuttack, January 7: Odisha 176/4 in 20 overs (Abhishek Yadav 52, Govinda Poddar 42*) lost to **Services** 177/6 in 19.2 overs (Nakul Verma 63, Anshul Gupta 39; Biplab Samantray 2-21, Deepak Behera 2-39) by four wickets.
Barabati Stadium, Cuttack, January 7: Maharashtra 184/8 in 20 overs (Nikhil Naik 67, Prayag Bhati 39; Vinay Kumar 3-32, Abhimanyu Mithun 2-30) beat **Karnataka** 158 in 18.3 overs (Robin Uthappa 80, Vinay Kumar 23; Anupam Sanklecha 3-23, Domnic Muthuswami 2-30) by 26 runs.
Barabati Stadium, Cuttack, January 8: Odisha 102/7 in 20 overs (Abhishek Yadav 31; Abhimanyu Mithun 2-13, KC Cariappa 2-14) lost to **Karnataka** 106/4 in 17.5 overs (Robin Uthappa 48, Stuart Binny 32*; Tukuna Sahoo 2-17) by six wickets.
DRIEMS Ground, Tangi, Cuttack, January 8: Maharashtra 155/8 in 20 overs (Prayag Bhati 36, Nikhil Naik 31; Pravin Tambe 2-24, Dhawal Kulkarni 2-28) lost to **Mumbai** 157/2 in 16.1 overs (Aditya Tare 65*, Shreyas Iyer 38) by eight wickets.
Barabati Stadium, Cuttack, January 8: Uttar Pradesh 182/6 in 20 overs (Eklavya Dwivedi 89, Prashant Gupta 43; Raushan Raj 3-42) beat **Services** 125/9 in 20 overs (Yashpal Singh 47, Vikas Hathwala 31; Ankit Rajpoot 2-11, Saurabh Kumar 2-23) by 57 runs.

Group D Points Table

Teams	M	W	L	T	N/R	Pts	NRR
Uttar Pradesh	5	5	0	0	0	20	+1.236
Mumbai	5	3	2	0	0	12	+0.621
Maharashtra	5	3	2	0	0	12	+0.152
Karnataka	5	2	3	0	0	8	-0.210
Services	5	2	3	0	0	8	-0.898
Odisha	5	0	5	0	0	0	-0.819

Uttar Pradesh and Mumbai qualified for the Super League

Super League A

Wankhede Stadium, Mumbai, January 15: Vidarbha 162/5 in 20 overs (Ganesh Satish 54, Apoorv Wankhade 40; Swapnil Singh 2-41) lost to **Baroda** 168/4 in 19 overs (Hardik Pandya 86*, Irfan Pathan 26*; Ravi Jangid 2-36) by six wickets.
Wankhede Stadium, Mumbai, January 15: Kerala 160/7 in 20 overs (Rohan Prem 69, Sachin Baby 32; Sagar Trivedi 3-34, Dhawal Kulkarni 2-29) lost to **Mumbai** 164/4 in 19.1 overs (Aditya Tare 71, Abhishek Nayar 38*; U Manukrishnan 2-36) by six wickets.
Wankhede Stadium, Mumbai, January 16: Baroda 160/6 in 20 overs (Irfan Pathan 35*, Deepak Hooda 32; P Prasanth 2-15, Sandeep Warrier 2-39) lost to **Kerala** 164/6 in 19.4 overs (Raiphi Gomez 47*, Sachin Baby 44; I Pathan 2-14) by four wickets.
Wankhede Stadium, Mumbai, January 16: Vidarbha 181/4 in 20 overs (Jitesh Sharma 56, Apoorv Wankhade 36*; Sagar Trivedi 2-44) lost to **Mumbai** 182/5 in 18.5 overs (Shreyas Iyer 86, Aditya Tare 41; Ravikumar Thakur 2-32) by five wickets.
Wankhede Stadium, Mumbai, January 18: Vidarbha 105 in 19.3 overs (Urvesh Patel 28; Nizar Niyas 3-14, U Manukrishnan 3-29) lost to **Kerala** 109/8 in 18.4 overs (Rohan Prem 34, Nikhilesh Surendran 21; Akshay Wakhare 3-26, Ravikumar Thakur 2-19) by two wickets.
Wankhede Stadium, Mumbai, January 18: Mumbai 151/5 in 20 overs (Suryakumar Yadav

57, Shashank Singh 25; Bhargav Bhatt 2-25) lost to **Baroda** 153/9 in 19 overs (Deepak Hooda 53, Hardik Pandya 28; Pravin Tambe 3-26, Dhawal Kulkarni 2-23) by one wicket.

Super League A Points Table

Teams	M	W	L	T	N/R	Pts	NRR
Baroda	3	2	1	0	0	8	+0.299
Mumbai	3	2	1	0	0	8	+0.196
Kerala	3	2	1	0	0	8	+0.172
Vidarbha	3	0	3	0	0	0	-0.657

Baroda qualified for the final

Super League B

Bandra Kurla Complex, Mumbai, January 15: Delhi 170/5 in 20 overs (Unmukt Chand 103, Aditya Kaushik 23) lost to **Gujarat** 171/2 in 17.4 overs (Priyank Kirit Panchal 69*, Parthiv Patel 42) by eight wickets.
Bandra Kurla Complex, Mumbai, January 15: Jharkhand 133/7 in 20 overs (Shasheem Rathour 40, Saurabh Tiwary 38; Amit Mishra 2-14) lost to **Uttar Pradesh** 134/1 in 16.5 overs (Samrath Singh 64, Prashant Gupta 42) by nine wickets.
Bandra Kurla Complex, Mumbai, January 16: Jharkhand 134/7 in 20 overs (Virat Singh 45, Ishank Jaggi 42; Parvinder Awana 3-28, Manan Sharma 2-28) lost to **Delhi** 138/5 in 18 overs (Nitish Rana 60*, Dhruv Shorey 30; Varun Aaron 3-27) by five wickets.
Bandra Kurla Complex, Mumbai, January 16: Gujarat 165/6 in 20 overs (Manpreet Juneja 54, Chirag Gandhi 41*; Praveen Kumar 2-32) lost to **Uttar Pradesh** 167/3 in 19 overs (Samrath Singh 65, Umang Sharma 38; Rush Kalaria 2-19) by seven wickets.
Bandra Kurla Complex, Mumbai, January 18: Jharkhand 142/6 in 20 overs (Ishank Jaggi 39, Virat Singh 29; Rush Kalaria 2-34) lost to **Gujarat** 146/4 in 14.1 overs (Priyank Panchal 35, Manpreet Juneja 33; Kaushal Singh 2-21) by six wickets.
Bandra Kurla Complex, Mumbai, January 18: Delhi 158/6 in 20 overs (Unmukt Chand 48, Pawan Negi 41*; Amit Mishra 2-25, Kuldeep Yadav 2-29) lost to **Uttar Pradesh** 159/7 in 19.4 overs (Eklavya Dwivedi 49*, Suresh Raina 22; Navdeep Saini 2-24) by three wickets.

Super League B Points Table

Teams	M	W	L	T	N/R	Pts	NRR
Uttar Pradesh	3	3	0	0	0	12	+0.688
Gujarat	3	2	1	0	0	8	+1.180
Delhi	3	1	2	0	0	4	-0.059
Jharkhand	3	0	3	0	0	0	-1.714

Uttar Pradesh qualified for the final

Final: Uttar Pradesh beat Baroda by 38 runs

• Put in, Uttar Pradesh start steadily by making 47 for 1 in the powerplay overs. • Bhargav Bhatt removes Prashant Gupta and Eklavya Dwivedi in three balls in the 13th over. • Regular wickets slow the run-rate, but Suresh Raina uses his experience to pace the innings well for a fair total. • Kedar Devdhar hits four fours, but falls in the second over as Baroda's chase receives an early dent. • Kuldeep Yadav, introduced in the eighth over, is a game-changer: He dismisses Hardik Pandya with his third ball. • Kuldeep and Piyush Chawla tighten the screws, and Ankit Rajpoot strikes regularly to give Uttar Pradesh their first title across formats since 2005-06.

Venue: Wankhede Stadium, Mumbai, India, January 20, 2016
Toss: Baroda, who bowl
MoM: Suresh Raina (Uttar Pradesh)

Uttar Pradesh

			R	*B*	*4s*	*6s*	*SR*
Ankit Rajpoot	Not Out		0	0	0	0	0.00
Kuldeep Yadav	Not Out		0	0	0	0	0.00
Prashant Gupta	LBW	b Bhatt	49	41	5	1	119.51
Samarth Singh		b Pandya	19	13	1	2	146.15
Suresh Raina*	Not Out	b Pandya	47	37	2	2	127.03
Eklavya Dwivedi †	LBW	b Bhatt	0	2	0	0	0.00
Piyush Chawla		b Ahmedbhai	17	13	1	1	130.77
Umang Sharma	Run out	(Munaf Patel)	12	6	2	0	200.00
Akshdeep Nath	Run out	(Soaeb Tai)	4	3	0	0	133.33
	c Arothe	b Pathan	3	4	0	0	75.00
Amit Mishra	Not out	b Pathan	2	2	0	0	100.00
Extras	(0b,3lb,1nb,6w)	0					
Total	(7 wkts, 20.0 overs)		163 (8.15 runs per over)				

Fall of wickets: 37-1 (Samarth Singh, 4.5 ov), 97-2 (Prashant Gupta, 12.2 ov), 97-3 (Eklavya Dwivedi, 12.4 ov), 121-4 (Piyush Chawla, 15.4 ov), 135-5 (Umang Sharma, 16.6 ov), 141-6 (Akshdeep Nath, 17.6 ov), 151-7 (, 19.1 ov)
Bowling: Irfan Pathan 4-0-44-1-11.00 (1 wd), Munaf Patel 4-0-21-0-5.25 (1 nb), Hardik Pandya 3-0-26-1-8.67, Rishi Arothe 3-0-25-0-8.33 (1 wd), Bhargav Bhatt 2-0-13-2-6.50, Soaeb Tai 4-0-31-1-7.75 (1 wd)

Baroda

			R	*B*	*4s*	*6s*	*SR*
Bhargav Bhatt	Not out	b Pathan	0	0	0	0	0.00
Munaf Patel	Not out	b Pathan	0	0	0	0	0.00
Kedar Devdhar	c Nath	b Rajpoot	19	12	4	0	158.33
Mrunal Devdhar	c † Dwivedi	b Mishra	14	15	2	0	93.33

Hardik Pandya		c & b Yadav		13	14	2	0	92.86
Deepak Hooda	c Gupta	b Yadav	15	15	0	0	100.00
Yusuf Pathan	c † Dwivedi	b Mishra	14	27	0	0	51.85
Soaeb Tai	Not out	b Mishra	26	23	3	0	113.04
Irfan Pathan*	c Sharma	b Rajpoot	10	8	1	0	125.00
Pinal Shah †	c † Dwivedi	b Rajpoot	0	1	0	0	0.00
Rishi Arothe	Not out	b Rajpoot	5	5	0	0	100.00
Extras	(1b,2lb,0nb,6w)	0					
Total	(7 wkts, 20.0 overs)		125 (6.25 runs per over)				

Fall of wickets: 20-1 (Kedar Devdhar, 1.6 ov), 48-2 (Mrunal Devdhar, 6.3 ov), 54-3 (Hardik Pandya, 7.3 ov), 71-4 (Deepak Hooda, 11.6 ov), 84-5 (Yusuf Pathan, 15.1 ov), 109-6 (Irfan Pathan, 17.3 ov), 110-7 (Pinal Shah, 17.6 ov)
Bowling: 4-0-31-0-7.75 (1 wd), Ankit Rajpoot 4-0-30-3-7.50 (1 wd), Amit Mishra 4-0-33-2-8.25, Piyush Chawla 4-0-16-0-4.00, Kuldeep Yadav 4-0-12-2-3.00

Umpires: A Nand Kishore and K Srinivasan
TV umpire: BK Ravi
Match referee: SS Raul

Winners: Uttar Pradesh

Indian Premier League

SRH seamers thwart run-machine Kohli

KARTHIK LAKSHMANAN

If you still think T20 is a batsman's game, the Indian Premier League 2016 might make you change your opinion.

The tournament, in all likelihood, will be remembered for batsmen pushing the limits of the game. Virat Kohli's season in particular will be spoken of for years to come: The Royal Challengers Bangalore captain showed that consistency is possible in the shortest format and turned run-machine, scoring 973 runs from 16 innings, averaging 81.08. It included four centuries (one of which came in a 15-overs-a-side game!) and seven half-centuries.

Not too far behind was David Warner, Kohli's counterpart at Sunrisers Hyderabad, who made 848 runs himself despite not scoring a single ton. Says it all about his consistency, doesn't it? And of course, there was AB de Villiers, smashing 687 runs at a strike-rate close to 170. Teams batting second also won 39 of the 60 matches.

But for all the exploits by the batsmen and their big bats, it was the joint might of a bowling unit that emerged victorious, with Sunrisers winning the trophy for the first time.

Hyderabad also broke the norm by banking on their pacers and letting their spinners take a backseat – something unheard of in Indian conditions. Their seam attack, led by Mustafizur Rahman and Bhuvneshwar Kumar with Ashish Nehra and Barinder Sran performing supporting roles, took 82 wickets, by far the most among all teams; their spinners took just six. Hyderabad were the only team to have an economy of less than eight runs an over, and had the best economy rate in the powerplay and the last five overs.

The strongest statement was that the Sunrisers defeated the most powerful batting unit of the IPL – on a batting paradise, the M Chinnaswamy stadium – in the final to lift the cup.

Apart from the new winner, the ninth season of the IPL was one of many firsts. It was the first of two years without the suspended Chennai Super Kings and Rajasthan Royals, which meant an opportunity for two new franchises, Gujarat Lions and Rising Pune Supergiants.

Gujarat grabbed their chance and topped the table in the league stage but two consecutive losses in the play-offs saw them fall short of making the perfect debut. Pune, on the other hand, had the worst of starts with four of their first-choice overseas players – Steven Smith, Kevin Pietersen, Mitchell Marsh and Faf du Plessis – heading home midway through injuries. It required a last-ball six from MS Dhoni in their final game to prevent a wooden spoon, which went to Kings XI Punjab. It was the first time a Dhoni-led team failed to finish in the top four.

Level playing field: Virat Kohli was in divine form, hitting four centuries and seven half-centuries, but the parsimony of the Sunrisers Hyderabad pacers, Mustafizur Rahman and Bhuvneshwar Kumar, made the difference. — *BCCI*

But even as Pune and Punjab battled to avoid the last spot, the mid-table was a cluster towards the latter stages, with the six other teams in the reckoning till the very end. In the end, Mumbai Indians, the defending champions, and Delhi Daredevils, who had an impressive season under the funky leadership group of Zaheer Khan, Rahul Dravid and Paddy Upton, made way for Gujarat, Bangalore, Hyderabad and Kolkata Knight Riders in the play-offs.

As always, the IPL also proved to be a great platform for the unknowns to make a mark for themselves. KL Rahul added a new dimension to his game and stunned many with aggressive strokeplay, Karun Nair impressed for Delhi while Yuzvendra Chahal too broke into the Indian team after a wonderful season. Another all-rounder from the Pandya household, Krunal, also grabbed his chance with impressive performances for Mumbai.

But what is an IPL season without some controversy? Mumbai and Pune couldn't play some of their home games in home venues, and Punjab had to move out of Nagpur, as the Bombay High Court ordered the shifting out of IPL matches from Maharashtra because of the drought in the state. BCCI offered to use sewage-treated water for maintenance of the grounds, contributed to the drought relief fund and pointed out that other sports continued to be played in the state. None of that, though, changed the court's mind. The games were shifted to Dharamsala, Mohali and Visakhapatnam, with the final moving to Bangalore. BCCI, unhappy with being used as a 'punching bag', threatened to shift the tournament out of the country in coming seasons.

It was not the first controversy associated with the tournament, but a minor blot in a season that saw some extraordinary cricket.

Top five draws in 2016 IPL auctions

Player	Sold for	Base price	Performance
Shane Watson (Royal Challengers Bangalore)	9.5	2	179 runs, 20 wickets (16 matches)
Pawan Negi (Delhi Daredevils)	8.5	0.3	57 runs, 1 wicket (8 matches)
Yuvraj Singh (Sunrisers Hyderabad)	7	2	236 runs, 0 wicket (10 matches)
Chris Morris (Delhi Daredevils)	7	0.5	195 runs, 13 wickets (12 matches)
Mohit Sharma (Kings XI Punjab)	6.5	1.5	32 runs, 13 wickets (14 matches)

*Value in Crores

Top performers for each franchise

Teams	Batting	Bowling
Sunrisers Hyderabad	David Warner (848runs, 17 matches)	Bhuvneshwar Kumar (23 wickets, 17 matches)
Royal Challengers Bangalore	Virat Kohli (973runs, 16 matches)	Yuzvendra Chahal (21 wickets, 13 matches)
Gujarat Lions	Suresh Raina (399runs, 15 matches)	Dhawal Kulkarni (18 wickets, 14 matches)
Kolkata Knight Riders	Gautam Gambhir (501runs, 15 matches)	Andre Russell (15 wickets, 12 matches)
Mumbai Indians	Rohit Sharma (489runs, 14 matches)	Mitchell McClenaghan (17 wickets, 14 matches)
Delhi Daredevils	Quinton de Kock (445runs, 13 matches)	Chris Morris (13 wickets, 12 matches)
Rising Pune Supergiants	Ajinkya Rahane (480runs, 14 matches)	Adam Zampa (12 wickets, 5 matches)
Kings XI Punjab	M Vijay (453runs, 14 matches)	Sandeep Sharma (15 wickets, 14 matches)

Orange Cap winner: Virat Kohli
Purple Cap winner: Bhuvneshwar Kumar

Debutants (2): Rishabh Pant (Delhi Daredevils), Shivil Kaushik (Gujarat Lions)

Review by KARUNYA KESHAV and MANOJ NARAYAN

Matches 1-11 (April 9 to 17): Winning start for former CSK players

Moving on from Chennai was emotional, MS Dhoni had admitted. But, having traded the sunshine yellow jersey for a burst of assorted pinks, purples and oranges, an opening nine-wicket win over the defending champions, Mumbai Indians would have helped him settle into a new season. Four RPS bowlers took a wicket in their first ball on a seaming Wankhede surface, while M Ashwin showed intent to validate his Rs 4.5 crore price-tag and Ajinkya Rahane wrapped up victory with two last-over sixes.

It was not a winning feeling that would last, however. In a 'CSK derby' for fans and a "Super Kings practice game" for Ravindra Jadeja, Suresh Raina got the better of his old captain. Gujarat's IPL journey began on a top-of-the-table high: Aaron Finch hit three consecutive match-winning fifties, the last of which required him to overcome cramps for a thrilling last-ball win against Mumbai, Brendon McCullum quickly overcame a duck in his first post-international retirement match, Dwayne Bravo became the first to 300 wickets in T20s and their bowlers were miserly at the death.

Beating Kohli and AB at their own game: Quinton de Kock became the youngest IPL centurion in Bangalore. – *BCCI*

Delhi threw off old habits that saw them bundled out for a paltry 98 by Kolkata's Andre Russell and Brad Hogg, with old fox Amit Mishra and young colt Quinton de Kock leading the turnaround. De Kock became the second-youngest IPL centurion, putting even Virat Kohli and AB de Villiers to shade in their Chinnaswamy home.

Batting was, of course, never an issue for Bangalore. Kohli and de Villiers (42-ball 82) combined for a 157-run second-wicket stand at over 10 an over in their opener against SRH. Mustafizur Rahman was the only bowler who was shown any respect as Shane Watson (19 in 8) and a cheeky Sarfaraz Khan (five fours, two sixes in a 10-ball 35) helped put up the first 200-plus score.

David Warner, back opening after a failed middle-order stint with Australia during the World T20, was in good touch, but an injury for Ashish Nehra was a concern for his side.

Rohit Sharma continued his romance with Eden Gardens even as Jos Buttler found his feet and dismantled Kolkata's vaunted spin attack, but there was little reason for Gautam Gambhir to panic.

Except for Bangalore's match against Hyderabad, all the others were won by the team chasing, and comfortably at that. No target was going to be too intimidating for batsmen in this ninth edition.

Wankhede Stadium, Mumbai, April 9: MI 121/8 in 20 overs (Harbhajan Singh 45*, Ambati Raydu 22; Mitchell Marsh 2-21, Ishant Sharma 2-36) lost to **RPS** 126/1 in 14.4 overs (Ajinkya Rahane 66*, Faf du Plessis 34) by nine wickets. *MoM:* Ajinkya Rahane.
Eden Gardens, Kolkata, April 10: DD 98 in 17.4 overs (Brad Hogg 3-19, Andre Russell 3-24) lost to **KKR** 99/1 in 14.1 overs (Gautam Gambhir 38*, Robin Uthappa 35) by nine wickets. *MoM:* Andre Russell.
PCA IS Bindra Stadium, Mohali, April 10: KXIP 161/6 in 20 overs (M Vijay 42, Manan Vohra 38; Dwayne Bravo 4-22, Ravindra Jadeja 2-30) lost to **GL** 162/5 in 17.4 overs (Aaron Finch 74, Dinesh Karthik 41*) by five wickets. *MoM:* Aaron Finch.
M Chinnaswamy Stadium, Bangalore, April 12: RCB 227/4 in 20 overs (AB de Villiers 82, Virat Kohli 75; Mustafizur Rahman 2-26, Bhuvneshwar Kumar2-55) beat **SRH** 182/6 in 20 overs (David Warner 58, Ashish Reddý 32; Shane Watson 2-30, Yuzvendra Chahal 2-43) by 45 runs. *MoM:* AB de Villiers.
Eden Gardens, Kolkata, April 13: KKR 187/5 in 20 overs (Gautam Gambhir 64, Manish Pandey 52; Mitchell McClenaghan 2-25) lost to **MI** 188/4 in 19.1 overs (Rohit Sharma 84*,

Jos Buttler 41) by six wickets. *MoM:* Rohit Sharma.

SCA Stadium, Rajkot, April 14: RPS 163/5 in 20 overs (Faf fu Plessis 69, Kevin Pietersen 37; Ravindra Jadeja 2-18, Pravin Tambe 2-33) lost to **GL** 164/3 in 18 overs (Aaron Finch 50, Brendon McCullum 49; M Ashwin 2-31) by seven wickets. *MoM:* Aaron Finch.

Feroz Shah Kotla, Delhi, April 15: KXIP 111/9 in 20 overs (Manan Vohra 32, Amit Mishra 4-11) lost to **DD** 113/2 in 13.3 overs (Quinton de Kock 59*, Sanju Samson 33) by eight wickets. *MoM:* Amit Mishra.

Rajiv Gandhi International Stadium, Uppal, Hyderabad, April 16: SRH 142/7 in 20 overs (Eoin Morgan 51, Naman Ojha 37; Umesh Yadav 3-28, Morne Morkel 2-35) lost to **KKR** 146/2 in 18.2 overs (Gautam Gambhir 90*, Robin Uthappa 38) by eight wickets. *MoM:* Gautam Gambhir.

Wankhede Stadium, Mumbai, April 16: MI 143/8 in 20 overs (Parthiv Patel 34, Tim Southee 25; Pravin Tambe 2-12, Dhawal Kulkarni 2-19) lost to **GL** 147/7 in 20 overs (Aaron Finch 67*, Suresh Raina 27; Mitchell McClenaghan 4-21, Jasprit Bumrah 2-32) by three wickets. *MoM:* Aaron Finch.

PCAIS Bindra Stadium, Mohali, April 17: RPS 152/7 in 20 overs (Faf du Plessis 67, Steven Smith 38; Mohit Sharma 3-23, Sandeep Sharma 2-23) lost to **KXIP** 153/4 In 18.4 overs (M Vijay 53, Manan Vohra 51; M Ashwin 3-36) by six wickets. *MoM:* Manan Vohra.

M Chinnaswamy Stadium, Bangalore, April 17: RCB 191/5 in 20 overs (Virat Kohli 79, AB de Villiers 55; Mohammed Shami 2-34) lost to **DD** 192/3 in 19.1 overs (Quinton de Kock 108, Karun Nair 57; Shane Watson 2-25) by seven wickets. *MoM:* Quinton de Kock.

Matches 12-20 (April 18 to 24): Kohli ticks a box

Even Kohli's maiden T20 hundred, off 63 balls, couldn't stave off defeat for top-heavy Bangalore against Gujarat. In a season that promised greater parity between bat and ball, Hyderabad and Kolkata best demonstrated the all-round skills it takes to win T20 matches.

The two-time champions had depth and were clinical, almost boringly so,

Innovation: MS Dhoni added the karate kick block to an already considerable arsenal, even as Virat Kohli reached new heights. – *BCCI*

in consolidating their top spot. For Hyderabad, Mustafizur's wickets were peppered with dot balls (he gave away just nine against Punjab), Bhuvneshwar Kumar was steady with his seam bowling and Barinder Sran probing in Nehra's absence. Warner was their Gibraltar at the top, rediscovering his successful partnership with Shikhar Dhawan.

Zaheer Khan, Paddy Upton and Rahul Dravid fashioned Delhi's march up, as they became only the second team to successfully defend a total. Mumbai retired their line-up experiments and with Rohit back opening and Krunal Pandya shining as a bowling all-rounder, they maintained course.

Bangalore, Pune and Punjab, though, struggled to find a winning combination. The drought that required a court-sanctioned relocation from Nagpur extended to the scorecard for Punjab with runs drying up for David Miller and Glenn Maxwell. Dhoni's karate-kick blocks were the highlight for an increasingly disparate Pune, who also had to contend with Kevin Pietersen's tournament-ending injury and an uprooting from their Maharashtra home. An out-of-form Chris Gayle's paternity leave was perhaps fortuitous as KL Rahul came in and grew into both runs and reliability, but Bangalore remained in the bottom half.

Rajiv Gandhi International Stadium, Uppal, Hyderabad, April 18: MI 142/6 in 20 overs (Ambati Raydu 54, Krunal Pandya 49*; Barinder Sran 3-28) lost to **SRH** 145/3 in 17.3 overs (David Warner 90*, Moises Henriques 20; Tim Southee 3-24) by seven wickets. *MoM:* David Warner.

PCA IS Bindra Stadium, Mohali, April 19: KXIP 138/8 in 20 overs (Shaun Marsh 56*, M Vijay 26; Sunil Narine 2-22, Morne Morkel 2-27) lost to **KKR** 141/4 in 17.1 overs (Robin Uthappa 53, Gautam Gambhir 34; Pradeep Sahu 2-18, Axar Patel 2-19) by six wickets. *MoM:* Robin Uthappa.

Wankhede Stadium, Mumbai, April 20: RCB 170/7 in 20 overs (Travis Head 37, Virat Kohli 33; Jasprit Bumrah 3-31, Krunal Pandya 2-27) lost to **MI** 171/4 in 18 overs (Rohit Sharma 62, Kieron Pollard 39*; Iqbal Abdulla 3-40) by six wickets. *MoM:* Rohit Sharma.

SCA Stadium, Rajkot, April 21: GL 135/8 in 20 overs (Suresh Raina 75, Bhuvneshwar Kumar 4-29) lost to **SRH** 137/0 in 14.5 overs (David Warner 74*, Shikhar Dhawan 53*) by ten wickets. *MoM:* Bhuvneshwar Kumar.

MCA Stadium, Pune, April 22: RCB 185/3 in 20 overs (AB de Villiers 83, Virat Kohli 80; Thisara Perera 3-34) beat **RPS** 172/8 in 20 overs (Ajinkya Rahane 60, MS Dhoni 41; Kane Richardson 3-13, Shane Watson 2-31) by 13 runs. *MoM:* AB de Villiers.

Feroz Shah Kotla, Delhi, April 23: DD 164/4 in 20 overs (Sanju Samson 60, Jean-Paul Duminy 49*; Mitchell McClenaghan 2-31) beat **MI** 154/7 in 20 overs (Rohit Sharma 65, Krunal Pandya 36; Amit Mishra 2-24) by 10 runs. *MoM:* Sanju Samson.

Rajiv Gandhi Interntional Stadium, Uppal, Hyderabad, April 23: KXIP 143/6 in 20 overs (Shaun Marsh 40, Axar Patel 36*; Mutafizur Rahman 2-9, Moises Henriques 2-33) lost to **SRH** 146/5 in 17.5 overs (David Warner 59, Shikhar Dhawan 45) by five wickets. *MoM:* Mustafizur Rahman.

SCA Stadium, Rajkot, April 24: RCB 180/2 in 20 overs (Virat Kohli 100*, KL Rahul 51*) lost to **GL** 182/4 in 19.3 overs (Dinesh Karthik 50*, Brendon McCullum 42) by six wickets. *MoM:* Virat Kohli.

MCA Stadium, Pune, April 24: 160/5 in 20 overs (Ajinkya Rahane 67, Steven Smith 31) lost to **KKR** 162/8 in 19.3 overs (Suryakumar Yadav 60, Yusuf Pathan 36; Rajat Bhatia 2-19, Thisara Perera 2-28) by two wickets. *MoM:* Suryakumar Yadav.

Matches 21-29 (April 25 to May 1): Water issue hits IPL

Chris Morris, the Rs 7 crore man, brought Delhi to within one run of a win against Gujarat. But even his manic 17-ball fifty in an unbeaten 82 off 32 couldn't undo the harm from just 22 in the powerplay overs. And with Praveen Kumar and Bravo parsimony personified, and McCullum and Dwayne Smith combining for a century stand in just nine overs, this was a thriller that lit up a flagging competition.

McCullum and Smith went on to add 93 in 8.1 overs against Pune in another last-ball affair as Gujarat made themselves comfortable at the top. The duo was only the latest to validate the trend of IPL 9 being a stage for heroics from the openers, with all of Robin Uthappa, Gambhir, Warner, Dhawan, Rahane and Rohit consistently bringing up fifties.

Punjab's opener carried the biggest burden. "We felt that David Miller's batting was suffering because of the extra responsibility of captaincy," said Sanjay Bangar announcing that M Vijay would take over. The new skipper began with a half-century against Gujarat, a comfortable win helped by the season's first hat-trick (spread across two overs) from Axar Patel.

17-ball fifty: Chris Morris, bought by Delhi for Rs 7 crore, took them to within one run of a win against Gujarat. – *BCCI*

Ashok Dinda led an inspired Pune revival and Steve Smith was set to extend it with a 54-ball 101, until the Australian joined a casualty list that included Faf du Plessis, Mitchell Marsh and Pietersen. Pune found no joy in their farewell Maharashtra derby at home on May 1 either as the teams got ready to move to Visakhapatnam.

PCA IS Bindra Stadium, Mohali, April 25: MI 189/6 in 20 overs (Parthiv Patel 81, Ambati Raydu 65; Mohit Sharma 3-38) beat **KXIP** 164/7 in 20 overs (Glenn Maxwell 56, Shaun Marsh 45; Jasprit Bumrah 3-26, Tim Southee 2-28) by 25 runs. *MoM:* Parthiv Patel.
Rajiv Gandhi International Stadium, Uppal, Hyderabad, April 26: SRH 118/8 in 20 overs (Shikhar Dhawan 56*, Bhuvneshwar Kumar 21; Ashok Dinda 3-23, Mitchell Marsh 2-14) lost to **RSP** 94/3 in 11 overs (Steven Smith 46*, Faf du Plessis 30) by 34 runs (DLS method). *MoM:* Ashok Dinda.
Feroz Shah Kotla, Delhi, April 27: GL 172/6 in 20 overs (Brendon McCullum 60, Dwayne Smith 53; Imran Tahir 3-24, Chris Morris 2-35) beat **DD** 171/5 in 20 overs (C Morris 82*, JP Duminy 48; Dhawal Kulkarni 3-19) by one run. *MoM:* Chris Morris.
Wankhede Stadium, Mumbai, April 28: KKR 174/5 in 20 overs (Gautam Gambhir 59, Rob-

in Uthappa 36; Tim Southee 2-38) lost to **MI** 178/4 in 18 overs (Rohit Sharma 68*, Kieron Pollard 51*; Sunil Narine 2-22) by six wickets. *MoM:* Rohit Sharma.

MCA Stadium, Pune, April 29: RSP 195/3 in 20 overs (Steven Smith 101, Ajinkya Rahane 53) lost to **GL** 196/7 in 20 overs (Dwayne Smith 63, Brendon McCullum 43; Ashok Dinda 2-40, Thisara Perera 2-41) by three wickets. *MoM:* Dwayne Smith.

Feroz Shah Kotla, Delhi, April 30: DD 186/8 in 20 overs (Karun Nair 68, Sam Billings 54; Andre Russell 3-26, Umesh Yadav 3-33) beat **KKR** 159 in 18.3 overs (Robin Uthappa 72, Suryakumar Yadav 21; Zaheer Khan 3-21, Carlos Brathwaite 3-47) by 27 runs. *MoM:* Carlos Brathwaite.

Rajiv Gandhi International Stadium, Uppal, Hyderabad, April 30: SRH 194/5 in 20 overs (David Warner 92, Kane Williamson 50; Kane Richardson 2-45) beat **RCB** 179/6 in 20 overs (KL Rahul 51, AB de Villiers 47) by 15 runs. *MoM:* David Warner.

SCA Stadium, Rajkot, May 1: KXIP 154 in 19.5 overs (M Vijay 55, Wriddhiman Saha 33; Shivil Kaushik 3-20, Praveen Kumar 2-25) beat **GL** 131/9 in 20 overs (James Faulkner 32, Ishan Kishan 27; Axar Patel 4-21, Mohit Sharma 3-32) by 23 runs. *MoM:* Axar Patel.

MCA Stadium, Pune, May 1: RPS 159/5 in 20 overs (Saurabh Tiwary 57, Steven Smith 45; Jasprit Bumrah 3-29) lost to **MI** 161/2 in 18.3 overs (Rohit Sharma 85*, Jos Buttler 27*) by eight wickets. *MoM:* Rohit Sharma.

Matches 30-38 (May 2 to 8): Kohli mania on the rise

Andre Russell eased into form for Kolkata, winning consecutive match awards. After bowling an economical 1 for 24 against Bangalore, he joined hands with Yusuf Pathan (60* off 29) to revive a flagging chase of 186. At one stage, Kolkata needed an unlikely 81 from six overs, but the two put on 96 for the fifth wicket, with Russell hammering a 24-ball 39. Kolkata eventually won with five balls to spare to go top of the table. Russell then contributed with the ball against Punjab, returning 4 for 20 in his four overs to stifle a dangerous chase of 165.

Pathan-Russell show: Yusuf Pathan hammered a 29-ball 60 not out in Bangalore to take Kolkata to the top of the table. – *BCCI*

Delhi were inconsistent. They saw off the power-packed Gujarat, after Rishabh Pant, at 18, became the second-youngest IPL half-centurion with his 40-ball 69. However, one day later, they succumbed to a seven-wicket loss to an injury-ravaged Pune.

Meanwhile, Kohli's hot streak showed no sign of blowing out. After his half-century in a losing cause against Kolkata, he hammered an unbeaten 58-ball 108 – his second century of the season – to chase down Pune's 192-run target with three balls to spare.

Elsewhere, Punjab, looking more effective under Vijay's stewardship, bounced back from their crushing loss against Kolkata with a nine-run win over an inconsistent Delhi. Sunrisers made it three wins in a row with an 85-run win over Mumbai, and towards the end of the week, Gujarat ensured Gambhir's men wouldn't make it a hat-trick of wins.

M Chinnaswamy Stadium, Bangalore, May 2: RCB 185/7 in 20 overs (KL Rahul 52, Virat Kohli 52; Morne Morkel 2-28, Piyush Chawla 2-32) lost to **KKR** 189/5 in 19.1 overs (Yusuf Pathan 60*, Andre Russell 39; Yuzvendra Chahal 2-27) by five wickets. *MoM:* Andre Russell.
SCA Stadium, Rajkot, May 3: GL 149/7 in 20 overs (Dinesh Karthik 53, Ravindra Jadeja 36*; Shahbaz Nadeem 2-23) lost to **DD** 150/2 in 17.2 overs (Rishabh Pant 69, Quinton de Kock 46) by eight wickets. *MoM:* Rishabh Pant.
Eden Garden, Kolkata, May 4: KKR 164/3 in 20 overs (Robin Uthappa 70, Gautam Gambhir 54) beat **KXIP** 157/9 in 20 overs (Glenn Maxwell 68, Wriddhiman Saha 24; Andre Russell 4-20, Piyush Chawla 2-27) by seven runs. *MoM:* Andre Russell.
Feroz Shah Kotla, Delhi, May 5: DD 162/7 in 20 overs (JP Duminy 34, Karun Nair 32; Rajat Bhatia 2-22, Scott Boland 2-31) lost to **RPS** 166/3 in 19.1 overs (Ajinkya Rahane 63*, Usman Khawaja 30; Imran Tahir 2-26) by seven wickets. *MoM:* Ajinkya Rahane.
Rajiv Gandhi International Stadium, Uppal, Hyderabad, May 6: GL 126/6 in 20 overs (Aaron Finch 51*, Suresh Raina 20; Mustafizur Rahman 2-17, Bhuvneshwar Kumar 2-28) lost to **SRH** 129/5 in 19 overs (Shikhar Dhawan 47*, David Warner 24; Dwayne Bravo 2-14, Dhawal Kulkarni 2-17) by five wickets. *MoM:* Bhuvneshwar Kumar.
M Chinnaswamy Stadium, Bangalore, May 7: RPS 191/6 in 20 overs (Ajinkya Rahane 74, Saurabh Tiwary 52; Shane Watson 3-24) lost to **RCB** 195/3 in 19.3 overs (Virat Kohli 108*, KL Rahul 38; Adam Zampa 2-35) by seven wickets. *MoM:* Virat Kohli.
PCA IS Bindra Stadium, Mohali, May 7: KXIP 181/5 in 20 overs (Wriddhiman Saha 52, Marcus Stoinis 52; Chris Morris 2-30) beat **DD** 172/5 in 20 overs (Quinton de Kock 52, Sanju Samson 49; M Stoinis 3-40) by nine runs. *MoM:* Marcus Stoinis.
Dr YS Rajasekhara Reddy ACA-VDCA Cricket Stadium, Visakhapatnam, May 8: SRH 177/3 in 20 overs (Shikhar Dhawan 82*, David Warner 48; Harbhajan Singh 2-29) beat **MI** 92 in 16.3 overs (Harbhajan 21*; Ashish Nehra 3-15, Mustafizur Rahman 3-16) by 85 runs. *MoM:* Ashish Nehra.
Eden Gardens, Kolkata, May 8: KKR 158/4 in 20 overs (Shakib Al-Hasan 66*, Yusuf Pathan 63*; Praveen Kumar 2-19) lost to **GL** 164/5 in 18 overs (Dinesh Karthik 51, Aaron Finch 29) by five wickets. *MoM:* Praveen Kumar.

Matches 39-47 (May 9 to 15): Kohli-de Villiers show spellbounds all

A good chunk of the highlights reel of the tournament was played out in Bangalore on May 14 with the Kohli-AB de Villiers dalliance against GL. For starters, both scored centuries: Kohli's was his third of the tournament. They added 229 runs for the second wicket: the highest partnership in the history of T20 cricket. And Bangalore's 144-run victory margin was also the largest in IPL history. Despite that, Bangalore were still plagued by inconsistency. Earlier in the week, they had secured a thrilling one-run win over Punjab, despite Vijay's gritty 57-ball 89, but that was followed by a meek six-wicket surrender to Mumbai.

Hyderabad went from strength to strength when they won their fourth match on the trot, against Pune, despite Adam Zampa's magnificent 6 for 19. It took Delhi's youngsters to snap their winning streak, with de Kock, Sanju Samson and Pant chasing down a 147-run target. Warner's men returned to winning ways soon after though, sealing a seven-wicket victory over a Punjab side who were buoyed by a comprehensive win over Mumbai heading in.

Par for the course: AB de Villiers and Virat Kohli broke their own record for the highest partnership when they added 229 against Gujarat. – BCCI

The defending champions bounced back from that drubbing, thanks to the older Pandya, Krunal, who stepped out of his brother's shadow. He first hammered a 37-ball 86, a ballistic knock comprised of seven fours and six sixes, to boost the total to 206 for 4 and followed that up with a 2 for 15 in 2.1 overs. It ensured Mumbai didn't go winless in Visakhapatnam.

PCA IS Bindra Stadium, Mohali, May 9: RCB 175/6 in 20 overs (AB de Villiers 64, KL Rahul 42; KC Cariappa 2-16, Sandeep Sharma 2-49) beat **KXIP** 174/4 in 20 overs (M Vijay 89, Marcus Stoinis 34*; Shane Watson 2-22) by one run. *MoM:* Shane Watson.

Dr YS Rajasekhara Reddy ACA-VDCA Cricket Stadium, Visakhapatnam, May 10: SRH 137/8 in 20 overs (Shikhar Dhawan 33, Kane Williamson 32; Adam Zampa 6-19) beat **RPS** 133/8 in 20 overs (George Bailey 34, MS Dhoni 30; Ashish Nehra 3-29) by four runs. *MoM:* Adam Zampa.

M Chinnaswamy Stadiun. Bangalore, May 11: RCB 151/4 in 20 overs (KL Rahul 68*, Sachin Baby 25*) lost to **MI** 153/4 in 18.4 overs (Ambati Rayudu 44, Kieron Pollard 35*; Varun Aaron 2-37) by six wickets. *MoM:* Krunal Pandya.

Rajiv Gandhi Interntional Stadium, Uppal, Hyderabad, May 12: SRH 146/8 in 20 overs (David Warner 46, Shikhar Dhawan 34; Amit Mishra 2-19, Nathan Coulter-Nile 2-25) lost to **DD** 150/3 in 18.1 overs (Quinton de Kock 44, Rishabh Pant 39; Moises Henriques 2-19) by seven wickets. *MoM:* Chris Morris.

Dr YS Rajasekhara Reddy ACA-VDCA Cricket Stadium, Visakhapatnam, May 13: MI 124/9 in 20 overs (Kieron Pollard 27, Nitish Rana 25; Marcus Stoinis 4-15, Sandeep Sharma 2-11) lost to **KXIP** 127/3 in 17 overs (Wriddhiman Saha 56, M Vijay 54*; Mitchell McClenaghan 2-24) by seven wickets. *MoM:* Marcus Stoinis.

M Chinnnaswamy Stadium, Bangalore, May 14: RCB 248/3 in 20 overs (AB de Villiers 129*, Virat Kohli 109; Praveen Kumar 2-45) beat **GL** 104 in 18.4 overs (Aaron Finch 37,

Mumbai's find of the season: Krunal Pandya stepped out of his brother's shadow, contributing to the side's wins with consistent all-round efforts. – *BCCI*

Ravindra Jadeja 21; Chris Jordan 4-11, Yuzvendra Chahal 3-19) by 144 runs. *MoM:* AB de Villiers.
Eden Gardens, Kolkata, May 14: RPS 103/6 in 17.4 overs (George Bailey 33, Usman Khawaja 21; Piyush Chawla 2-21) lost to **KKR** 66/2 in 5 overs (Yusuf Pathan 37*; R Ashwin 2-30) by eight wickets. *MoM:* Yusuf Pathan.
PCA IS Bindra Stadium, Mohali, May 15: KXIP 179/4 in 20 overs (Hashim Amla 96, Gurkeerat Singh Mann 27; Bhuvneshwar Kumar 2-32) lost to **SRH** 180/3 in 19.4 overs (David Warner 52, Yuvraj Singh 42*) by seven wickets. *MoM:* Hashim Amla.
Dr YS Rajasekhara Reddy ACA-VDCA Cricket Stadium, Visakhapatnam, May 15: MI 206/4 in 20 overs (Krunal Pandya 86, Martin Guptill 48; Chris Morris 2-34) beat **DD** 126 in 19.1 overs (Quinton de Kock 40, Rishabh Pant 23; Jasprit Bumrah 3-13, Krunal Pandya 2-15) by 80 runs. *MoM:* Krunal Pandya.

Matches 48-56 (May 16 to 22): All eyes on the table

The final week of the league phase was all about qualification scenarios. By the end of it, Gujarat sealed the top spot with a six-wicket win over Mumbai – a result that also ensured the defending champions surrendered the trophy. Bangalore, Hyderabad and Kolkata claimed the remaining play-off places on net run-rate, after all of them finished on 16 points.

Bangalore were the most impressive of the lot. They won their last three matches to secure qualification. The common factor was Kohli. His unbeaten 51-ball 75 guided their chase of 184 against Kolkata, along with Gayle's 49 and de Villiers's unbeaten 59. Then, against Punjab, he scored his fourth century of the tournament, a 50-ball 113 in a 15-overs-a-side encounter – Bangalore won that by 82 runs via the DLS method. Victory in the final clash against Delhi was imperative, and this time Kohli brought up a steady half-century, after the bowlers did well to restrict Delhi to 138 for 8. Victory and qualification were secured, as was Delhi's elimination.

M Chinnaswamy Stadium, Bangalore, May 16: KKR 183/5 in 20 overs (Gautam Gambhir 51, Manish Pandey 50; S Aravind 2-41) lost to **RCB** 186/1 in 18.4 overs (Virat Kohli 75*, AB de Villiers 59*) by nine wickets. *MoM:* Virat Kohli.

Dr YS Rajasekhara Reddy ACA-VDCA Cricket Stadium, Visakhapatnam, May 17: DD 121/6 in 20 overs (Karun Nair 41, Chris Morris 38*; Ashok Dinda 3-20, Adam Zampa 3-21) lost to **RPS** 76/1 in 11 overs (Ajinkya Rahane 42*) by 19 runs (DLS method). *MoM:* Ashok Dinda.

M Chinnaswamy Stadium, Bangalore, May 18: RCB 211/3 in 20 overs (Virat Kohli 113, Chris Gayle 73) beat **KXIP** 120/9 in 14 overs (Wriddhiman Saha 24; Yuzvendra Chahal 4-25, Shane Watson 2-7) by 82 runs (DLS method). *MoM:* Virat Kohli.

Green Park, Kanpur, May 19: KKR 124/8 in 20 overs (Yusuf Pathan 36, Robin Uthappa 25; Dwayne Smith 4-8) lost to **GL** 125/4 in 13.3 overs (Suresh Raina 53*, Aaron Finch 26) by six wickets. *MoM:* Dwayne Smith.

Shaheed Veer Narayan Singh International Stadium, Raipur, May 20: SRH 158/7 in 20 overs (David Warner 73; Carlos Brathwaite 2-27) lost to **DD** 161/4 in 20 overs (Karun Nair 83*, Rishabh Pant 32; Barinder Sran 2-34) by six wickets. *MoM:* Karun Nair.

Dr YS Rajasekhara Reddy ACA-VDCA Cricket Stadium, Visakhapatnam, May 21: KXIP 172/7 in 20 overs (M Vijay 59, Gurkeerat Singh Mann 51; R Ashwin 4-34) lost to **RPS** 173/6 in 20 overs (MS Dhoni 64*, Usman Khawaja 30; Gurkeerat Singh Mann 2-15) by four wickets. *MoM:* MS Dhoni.

Green Park, Kanpur, May 21: MI 172/8 in 20 overs (Nitish Rana 70, Jos Buttler 33; Dwayne Bravo 2-22, Praveen Kumar 2-24) lost to **GL** 173/4 in 17.5 overs (Suresh Raina 58, Brendon McCullum 45; Vinay Kumar 2-17) by six wickets. *MoM:* Suresh Raina.

Eden Gardens, Kolkata, May 22: KKR 171/6 in 20 overs (Yusuf Pathan 52*, Manish Pandey 48; Deepak Hooda 2-16, Bhuvneshwar Kumar 2-31) beat **SRH** 149/8 in 20 overs (Shikhar Dhawan 51; Sunil Narine 3-26, Kuldeep Yadav 2-28) by 22 runs. *MoM:* Yusuf Pathan.

Shaheed Veer Narayan Singh International Stadium, Raipur, May 22: DD 138/8 in 20 overs (Quinton de Kock 60, Chris Morris 27*; Yuzvendra Chahal 3-32, Chris Gayle 2-11) lost to **RCB** 139/4 in 18.1 overs (Virat Kohli 54*, KL Rahul 38) by six wickets. *MoM:* Virat Kohli.

Points Table

Teams	M	W	L	T	N/R	Pts	NRR
GL	14	9	5	0	0	18	-0.374
RCB	14	8	6	0	0	16	+0.932
SRH	14	8	6	0	0	16	+0.245
KKR	14	8	6	0	0	16	+0.106
MI	14	7	7	0	0	14	-0.146
DD	14	7	7	0	0	14	-0.155
RPS	14	5	9	0	0	10	+0.015
KXIP	14	4	10	0	0	8	-0.646

GL, RCB, SRH and KKR qualified for the play-offs

Qualifier 1: RCB beat GL by four wickets

• Gujarat have topped the table, but have the tough task of facing Bangalore at a venue where they were thrashed by 144 runs in the league stage. • Iqbal Abdulla, the left-arm spinner, strikes early: Gujarat are restricted to 9 for 3 by the fourth over. • A counter-attacking 41-ball 73 by Dwayne Smith lifts the IPL debutants to 158, even as Shane Watson ends with his first four-wicket haul. • Bangalore's chase starts terribly with Dhawal Kulkarni running through the top order, reducing them to 29 for 5 with Kohli making his first T20 duck in 51 innings. • De Villiers, though, launches a stunning fightback along with Stuart Binny (21) and then Abdulla (33*). • His unbroken 91-run stand in 8.4 overs with Abdulla takes Bangalore to the final with ten balls to spare in front a ballastic home crowd. *Karthik Lakshmanan*

M Chinnaswamy Stadium, Bangalore, May 24: GL 158 in 20 overs (Dwayne Smith 73, Dinesh Karthik 26; Shane Watson 4-29, Chris Jordan 2-26) lost to **RCB** 159/6 in 18.2 overs (AB de Villiers 79*, Iqbal Abdulla 33*; Dhawal Kulkarni 4-14, Ravindra Jadeja 2-21) by four wickets. *MoM:* AB de Villiers.

Eliminator: SRH beat KKR by 22 runs

• Openers Dhawan and Warner struggle to find any momentum after being put in by Gambhir, whose Kolkata side have mastered the chase this season. • Moises Henriques leads a brief assault until chinaman bowler Kuldeep Yadav evicts him and Warner off successive deliveries. • Yuvraj Singh plays his

The unorthodox: Chinaman bowlers Shivil Kaushik (GL) and Kuldeep Yadav (KKR) troubled batsmen in their play-off matches. — *BCCI*

most fluent knock of the competition and Hooda tees off as Hyderabad amass 53 in the last five overs to post 162 for 8. • After a frenetic start, Uthappa is dismissed by Sran, but it's Yuvraj's direct hit to run Colin Munro out that sets the cat among the pigeons. • Bolstered by excellent catching, Sunrisers pick up wickets with Bhuvneshwar and Henriques doing the bulk of the damage. • Manish Pandey's fall leaves Kolkata needing 38 off 22 with all big guns silenced, and Bhuvneshwar and Mustafizur stifle the rest. *R Kaushik*

Feroz Shah Kotla, Delhi, May 25: **SRH** 162/8 in 20 overs (Yuvraj Singh 44, Moises Henriques 31; Kuldeep Yadav 3-35, Morne Morkel 2-31) beat **KKR** 140/8 in 20 overs (Manish Pandey 36, Gautam Gambhir 28; Bhuvneshwar Kumar 3-19, M Henriques 2-17) by 22 runs. *MoM:* Moises Henriques.

Qualifier 2: SRH beat GL by four wickets

• With Mustafizur missing through a hamstring injury, Warner breaks from norm and opts to chase in the virtual semi-final. • The decision is vindicated when Gujarat lose two wickets, including skipper Raina, inside the first four overs. • McCullum and Dinesh Karthik steady the ship before Finch muscles a 31-ball 50 and Bravo slams 20 in 10 to haul their side to 162 for 7. • With Dhawan run out for his first IPL duck and the rest of the top order floundering against chinaman bowler Shivil Kaushik, Hyderabad are reduced to 117 for 6. • Unfazed by the carnage around him, Warner wages an aggressive solitary battle until he is joined by Bipul Sharma. • Bipul's 11-ball 27 and his unfinished stand of 46 off 21 with Warner (93* off 58) carry their side to a showdown in the final against RCB. *R Kaushik*

Feroz Shah Kotla, Delhi, May 27: **GL** 162/7 in 20 overs (Aaron Finch 50, Brendon McCullum 32; Ben Cutting 2-20, Bhuvneshwar Kumar 2-27) lost to **SRH** 163/6 in 19.2 overs (David Warner 93*, Bipul Sharma 27*; Shivil Kaushik 2-22, Dwayne Bravo 2-32) by four wickets. *MoM:* David Warner.

Final: SRH beat RCB by eight runs

•Despite the Chinnaswamy's reputation as a chasing ground and Bangalore's formidable top order, Warner goes for runs on the board in a cup final. • The skipper sets the tone with 69 off 38, and Yuvraj continues his recent good run as the side are braced for a final assault. • They lose 3 for 11 and seem to have left themselves short when Ben Cutting hammers 39 off 15, 40 from the last two overs contributing to a massive 208 for 7. • Faced with the highest chase in an IPL final, Bangalore make the most thrilling start with Gayle smashing eight sixes in a 38-ball 76. • His dismissal by Cutting after a 114-run stand with Kohli doesn't hurt Bangalore, but Kohli's chop-on to Sran marks the start of a stunning turnaround. • As RCB lose their nerve, and the wickets of de Villiers, Rahul and Watson, Hyderabad's celebrated bowling rises to the occasion to help complete a stirring eight-run triumph. *R Kaushik*

Captain goes for runs on the board: David Warner got Sunrisers Hyderabad to a trademark blazing start. — *BCCI*

Venue: M.Chinnaswamy Stadium, Bengaluru, India, May 29, 2016
Toss: Sunrisers Hyderabad, who bat
MoM: Ben Cutting (Sunrisers Hyderabad)
MoS: Virat Kohli (Royal Challengers Bangalore)

Sunrisers Hyderabad

			R	B	4s	6s	SR
David Warner*	c Abdulla	b Aravind	69	38	8	3	181.58
Shikhar Dhawan	c Jordan	b Chahal	28	25	3	1	112.00
Moises Henriques	c Chahal	b Jordan	4	5	0	0	80.00
Yuvraj Singh	c Watson	b Jordan	38	23	4	2	165.22
Deepak Hooda	c Kohli	b Aravind	3	6	0	0	50.00
Ben Cutting	Not out	b Aravind	39	15	3	4	260.00
Naman Ojha †	Run out	(Shane Watson)	7	4	1	0	175.00
Bipul Sharma	c Chahal	b Jordan	5	3	1	0	166.67
Bhuvneshwar Kumar	Not out	b Jordan	1	1	0	0	100.00
Extras	(1b,2lb,0nb,11w) 14						
Total	(7 wkts, 20.0 overs)		208 (10.4 runs per over)				

Fall of wickets: 63-1 (Shikhar Dhawan, 6.4 ov), 97-2 (Moises Henriques, 9.5 ov), 125-3 (David Warner, 13.3 ov), 147-4 (Deepak Hooda, 15.6 ov), 148-5 (Yuvraj Singh, 16.1 ov), 158-6 (Naman Ojha, 17.1 ov), 174-7 (Bipul Sharma, 18.4 ov)

Did not bat: Barinder Sran, Mustafizur Rahman

Bowling: S Aravind 4-0-30-2-7.50, Chris Gayle 3-0-24-0-8.00 (2 wd), Shane Watson 4-0-61-0-15.25 (2 wd), Yuzvendra Chahal 4-0-35-1-8.75, Iqbal Abdulla 1-0-10-0-10.00, Chris Jordan 4-0-45-3-11.25 (2 wd)

Royal Challengers Bangalore

			R	B	4s	6s	SR
Chris Gayle	c Sharma	b Cutting	76	38	4	8	200.00
Virat Kohli*		b Sran	54	35	5	2	154.29
AB de Villiers	c Henriques	b Sharma	5	6	0	0	83.33
KL Rahul †		b Cutting	11	9	1	0	122.22
Shane Watson	c Henriques	b Rahman	11	9	0	1	122.22
Sachin Baby	Not out	b Rahman	18	10	1	1	180.00
Stuart Binny	Run out	(Deepak Hooda, † Naman Ojha)	9	7	0	1	128.57
Chris Jordan	Run out	(† Naman Ojha)	3	4	0	0	75.00
Iqbal Abdulla	Not out	(† Naman Ojha)	4	2	1	0	200.00
Extras	(0b,5lb,0nb,4w)	9					
Total	(7 wkts, 20.0 overs)		200 (10 runs per over)				

Fall of wickets: 114-1 (Chris Gayle, 10.3 ov), 140-2 (Virat Kohli, 12.5 ov), 148-3 (AB de Villiers, 13.5 ov), 160-4 (KL Rahul, 15.3 ov), 164-5 (Shane Watson, 16.3 ov), 180-6 (Stuart Binny, 18.1 ov), 194-7 (Chris Jordan, 19.3 ov)

Did not bat: Yuzvendra Chahal, S Aravind

Bowling: Bhuvneshwar Kumar 4-0-25-0-6.25 (1 wd), Barinder Sran 3-0-41-1-13.67 (2 wd), Ben Cutting 4-0-35-2-8.75 (1 wd), Mustafizur Rahman 4-0-37-1-9.25, Moises Henriques 3-0-40-0-13.33, Bipul Sharma 2-0-17-1-8.50

Umpires: Kumar Dharmasena (Sri Lanka) and Bruce Oxenford (Australia)
TV Umpires: Anil Chaudhary (India)
Referee: Ranjan Madugalle (Sri Lanka)

Overall team records

DELHI DAREDEVILS

(P 133, W 56, L 75, A 2)
Maiden match: Beat RR by nine wickets (Delhi, 2008)
Highest team total: 231/4 v KXIP (Delhi, 2011)
Lowest team total: 80 v SRH (Hyderabad, 2013)
Highest run-getter: Virender Sehwag – 2174 in 79 matches
Highest individual score: 119 by Virender Sehwag v DC (Hyderabad, 2011)
Most 50+ scores: Virender Sehwag – 16

Highest wicket-taker: Amit Mishra – 64 in 57 matches
Best bowling: 5-17 by Amit Mishra v DC (Delhi, 2008)
Most dismissals (wicketkeeper): 45 by Dinesh Karthik in 56 matches
Most dismissals (wicketkeeper/innings): 4 by Dinesh Karthik v RR (Bloemfontein, 2009)
Most catches (fielder): Virender Sehwag – 29
Highest partnership: David Warner/Naman Ojha – 189* for second wicket v DC (Hyderabad, 2012)
Most capped player: Virender Sehwag – 79

GUJARAT LIONS

(P 16, W 9, L 7)
Maiden match: Beat KXIP by five wickets (Mohali, 2016)
Highest team total: 196/7 v RPS (Pune, 2016)
Lowest team total: 104 v RCB (Bangalore, 2016)
Highest run-getter: Suresh Raina – 399 in 15 matches
Highest individual score: 75 by Suresh Raina v SRH (Rajkot, 2016)
Most 50+ scores: Aaron Finch – 5
Highest wicket-taker: Dhawal Kulkarni – 18 in 14 matches
Best bowling: 4-8 by Dwayne Smith v KKR (Kanpur, 2016)
Most dismissals (wicketkeeper): Dinesh Karthik – 14 in 16 matches
Most dismissals (wicketkeeper/innings): 2 by Dinesh Karthik v MI (Mumbai, 2016)
Most catches (fielder): Dwayne Smith – 7
Highest partnership: Dwayne Smith/Brendon McCullum – 112 for first wicket v DD (Delhi, 2016)
Most capped player(s): Dinesh Karthik, Praveen Kumar, Brendon McCullum – 16

KINGS XI PUNJAB

(P 134, W 63, L 71)
Maiden match: Lost to CSK by 33 runs (Mohali, 2008)
Highest team total: 232/2 v RCB (Dharamsala, 2011)
Lowest team total: 88 v RCB (Bangalore, 2015)
Highest run-getter: Shaun Marsh – 2213 in 62 matches
Highest individual score: 122 by Virender Sehwag v CSK (Mumbai, 2014)
Most 50+ Scores: Shaun Marsh – 19
Highest wicket-taker: Piyush Chawla – 84 in 87 matches
Best bowling: 5-25 by Dimitri Mascarenhas v PWI (Mohali, 2012)
Most dismissals (wicketkeeper): Wriddhiman Saha – 36 in 43 matches
Most dismissals (wicketkeeper/innings): 4 by Adam Gilchrist v CSK (Dharamsala, 2012)
Most catches (fielder): David Miller – 40
Highest partnership: Adam Gilchirst/Shaun Marsh – 206 for second wicket v RCB (Dharamsala, 2011)
Most capped player: Piyush Chawla – 87

KOLKATA KNIGHT RIDERS

(P 132, W 68, L 64)
Maiden match: Beat RCB by 140 runs (Bangalore, 2008)
IPL wins (2): 2012, 2014
Highest team total: 222/3 v RCB (Bangalore, 2008)
Lowest team total: 67 v MI (Mumbai, 2008)

Highest run-getter: Gautam Gambhir – 2537 in 92 matches
Highest individual score: 158* by Brendon McCullum v RCB (Bangalore, 2008)
Most 50+ scores: Gautam Gambhir – 23
Highest wicket-taker: Sunil Narine – 85 in 66 matches
Best bowling: 5-19 by Sunil Narine v KXIP (Kolkata, 2012)
Most dismissals (wicketkeeper): Robin Uthappa – 34 in 44 matches
Most dismissals (wicketkeeper/innings): 4 by Morne van Wyk v RCB (Durban, 2009)
Most catches (fielder): Manoj Tiwary – 30
Highest partnership: Jack Kallis/Gautam Gambhir – 152* for second wicket v RR (Jaipur, 2011)
Most capped player: Gautam Gambhir – 92

MUMBAI INDIANS

(P 140, W 80, L 60)
Maiden match: Lost to RCB by five wickets (Mumbai, 2008)
IPL wins (2): 2013, 2015
Highest team total: 218/7 v DD (Delhi, 2010)
Lowest team total: 87 v KXIP (Mohali, 2011)
Highest run-getter: Rohit Sharma – 2704 in 97 matches
Highest individual score: 114* by Sanath Jayasuriya v Chennai Super Kings (Mumbai, 2008)
Most 50+ Scores: Rohit Sharma – 22
Highest wicket-taker: Lasith Malinga – 143 in 98 matches
Best bowling: 5-14 by Lasith Malinga v Delhi Daredevils (Delhi, 2011)
Most dismissals (wicketkeeper): Dinesh Karthik – 21 in 36 matches
Most dismissals (wicketkeeper/innings): 4 by Yogesh Takawale v RR (Mumbai, 2008)
Most catches (fielder): Kieron Pollard - 55
Highest partnership: Herschelle Gibbs/Rohit Sharma – 167* for second wicket v KKR (Kolkata, 2012)
Most capped player: Harbhajan Singh – 125

RISING PUNE SUPERGIANTS

(P 14, W 5, L 9)
Maiden match: Beat MI by nine wickets (Mumbai, 2016)
Highest team total: 195/3 v Gujarat Lions (Pune, 2016)
Lowest team total: 133/8 v Sunrisers Hyderabad (Vishakhapatnam, 2016)
Highest run-getter: Ajinkya Rahane - 480 runs
Highest individual score: 101 by Steven Smith v Gujarat Lions (Pune, 2016)
Most 50+ scores: Ajinkya Rahane – 6
Highest wicket-taker: Adam Zampa – 12 wickets in 5 matches
Best bowling: 6-19 by Adam Zampa v Sunrisers Hyderabad (Vishakhapatnam, 2016)
Most dismissals (wicketkeeper): MS Dhoni – 12 in 14 matches
Most dismissals (wicketkeeper/innings): 3 by MS Dhoni v SRH (Hyderabad, 2016)
Most catches (fielder): Ajinkya Rahane – 7
Highest partnership: Ajinkya Rahane/Steven Smith – 111 for second wicket v GL (Pune, 2016)
Most capped player (s): MS Dhoni, Ajinkya Rahane, R Ashwin – 14

ROYAL CHALLENGERS BANGALORE

(P 140, W 70, L 67, A 3)
Maiden match: Lost to KKR by 140 runs (Bangalore, 2008)
Highest team total: 263/5 v PWI (Bangalore, 2013)
Lowest team total: 70 v RR (Abu Dhabi, 2014)
Highest run-getter: Virat Kohli – 4110 in 139 matches
Highest individual score: 175* by Chris Gayle v PWI (Bangalore, 2013)
Most 50+ scores: Virat Kohli – 30
Highest wicket-taker: Vinay Kumar – 72 in 64 matches
Best bowling: 5-5 by Anil Kumble v RR (Cape Town, 2009)
Most dismissals (wicketkeeper): Dinesh Karthik – 18 in 16 matches
Most dismissals (wicketkeeper/innings): 3 by Parthiv Patel v KXIP (Dubai, 2014)
Most catches (fielder): Virat Kohli – 55
Highest partnership: Virat Kohli/AB de Villiers – 229 for second wicket v GL (Bangalore, 2016)
Most capped player: Virat Kohli – 139

SUNRISERS HYDERABAD

(P 62, W 34, L 28)
Maiden IPL Match: Beat PWI by 22 runs (Hyderabad, 2013)
IPL wins (1): 2016
Highest team total: 208/7 v RCB (Bangalore, 2016)
Lowest team total: 113 v MI (Hyderabad, 2015)
Highest run-getter: David Warner – 1938 in 45 matches
Highest individual score: 93* by David Warner v GL (Delhi, 2016)
Most 50+ scores: David Warner – 22
Highest wicket-taker: Bhuvneshwar Kumar - 61 in 45 matches
Best bowling: 4-14 by Bhuvneshwar Kumar v RR (Ahmedabad, 2014)
Most dismissals (wicketkeeper): Naman Ojha – 32 in 42 matches
Most dismissals (wicketkeeper/innings): 4 by Naman Ojha v MI (Vishakhapatnam, 2016)
Most catches (fielder): David Warner – 20
Highest partnership: David Warner/Shikhar Dhawan – 137 for first wicket v GL (Rajkot, 2016)
Most capped player: Shikhar Dhawan – 55

Teams that participated in earlier seasons: Chennai Super Kings* (2 wins – 2010, 2011), Rajasthan Royals* (1 win - 2008), Deccan Chargers (1 win - 2009), Kochi Tuskers Kerala, Pune Warriors India.
CSK and RR were suspended for two seasons because of the 2013 IPL spot-fixing scandal. They can return in 2018.

Deliver it your way!

Multiple options to send money to your loved ones, much faster and safer.

- Bank Transfers
- Instant Bank Transfers
- Instant Money Transfers
- Online Money Transfers

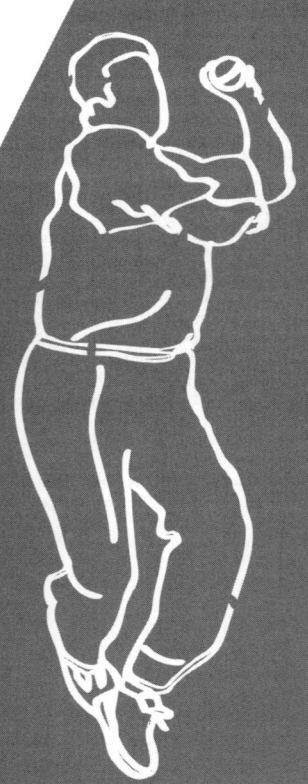

Customer Service: 600 555 550 | www.uaeexchange.com

Bista's season of plenty

HIMANISH BHATTACHARJEE

On November 26, 2015, *the Times of India* ran this headline: 'Bista: Mumbai's newest batting gun'. Thus far, Jay Gokuldas Bista, all of 19 years, had barely played two first-class matches. It was only ten days before that the opener had made his Ranji Trophy debut against Railways. Straightaway, he had big shoes to fill of Rohit Sharma, who was away on international duty after scoring a century against Uttar Pradesh.

It wasn't quite a dream debut, but his 74 set the stage for a masterful 280-run chase on the final day against Madhya Pradesh in Indore. A number of records tumbled that evening, and by the time Aditya Tare and team had sealed a quarter-final berth, journalists and enthusiasts were googling the new kid on the block.

"There was pressure, of course," Bista tells *Wisden India*, recollecting his match-winning performance at the Holkar Stadium. "But more than pressure, there was the excitement of playing for Mumbai, a team I wanted to represent at the first-class level for so many years. I knew I was given the opportunity because of the runs I had scored at age-level cricket, so I always backed my skills.

"Against Madhya Pradesh, I was a bit nervous because I hadn't done well on debut, and the pitch there was spinning right from the first day. But when my chance came in the second innings, I chose to play my natural game," he adds. "I knew if I had to score meaningful runs, I had to score them fast, because chasing 280 runs in one day was never going to be easy."

Ask Bista if any other sports ever attracted him, and he quickly says no. Growing up around Marine Drive, a stone's throw away from the Wankhede, cricket was always a big draw. Gokul, Jay's father, was a wicketkeeper-batsman who once represented Mumbai

'I backed my skills': Mumbai's Jay Bista earned a berth in the Ranji side after successful outings at the Under-19 and -23 levels. — *Wisden India*

University, and even came close to making it to the Mumbai Ranji team in the mid-1980s.

"My mom tells me that when I was a kid, I was mad about cricket. Dad didn't initially want me to become a cricketer, but he is the one who sent me to PJ Hindu Gymkhana, where I was coached for the first time, starting with tennis-ball cricket," says Bista. "When they saw me making progress, my coach and parents suggested I should join Sharadashram (Vidyamandir), because of its reputation in grooming youngsters, especially in cricket.

"When I have to leave at 6am for a match, my mom wakes up an hour before to ensure I have my breakfast," he says, grateful for the family's support. "Dad takes care of the money part and, sometimes, also helps me train by giving me knocking-practice, which often gets him late for work."

Bista, who honed his skills under Naushad Khan, father of Sarfaraz Khan, at Azad Maidan, has been scoring well at the age-group level for Mumbai since 2010. He earned a berth in the Ranji side after a successful campaign in the 2015-16 Cooch Behar Under-19 Trophy and a match-winning stint against Bengal in the subsequent CK Nayudu Under-23 Trophy, where he scored centuries in both innings.

He is the first cricketer of Nepali origin – though his family migrated to India long before his birth – to ever don the Mumbai jersey at the first-class level. Despite the illustrious stint in Indore, a couple of below-par outings led to him being dropped for the semi-final and final, which Mumbai won to clinch the Ranji Trophy for a record 41st time.

"There was a bit of disappointment (with not being part of the final), but I was on duty with the Under-23 team at that time," he says. "Winning the Ranji Trophy was important, no doubt, but we had to win the Under-23 tournament too. I knew if I perform well at any level, I would get my opportunities when the time arrives. I scored a hundred in the quarter-final and a double-hundred in the final to help my team win, so I was very happy with that."

Bista did get a hit in the Irani Cup against Rest of India later on, and the studious-looking bespectacled boy seized the opportunity to score his maiden first-class ton against a bowling attack that included the best performers in domestic cricket. If that wasn't impressive enough, there was more to come.

In the lead up to the ICC World T20, England played a practice match against an MCA XI side at Brabourne Stadium. As expected, Eoin Morgan's men, the eventual runners-up, blazed their way to 177 for 8 in 20 overs. But when MCA's chase began, Bista took on the likes of Chris Jordan, Ben Stokes, Reece Topley and Liam Plunkett to rack up 51 off 37 balls, hitting five fours and two sixes along the way, and almost capsizing the visitors' preparations.

"I did not expect to perform that well against an international side," he says. "That knock gave me the belief that I can even perform at higher levels. But in domestic cricket, people don't go so hard at each other. When I hit Ben Stokes for a four, he came up to me and said a few bad words. Instead of getting flustered by that, I chose to keep quiet and let my batting speak. But

I get it, if an international cricketer of such high repute gets hit by a small domestic player, he will obviously not like it very much."

Needless to say, his consistent performances over the past year should hold him in good stead with the selectors, but Bista is not too worried about his chances.

"I am preparing myself in my own usual way," he says. "If I get an opportunity, I will be happy, but right now, the focus is on fixing the problems I have had with my batting till now. I obviously dream to play Tests for India someday, because it is the toughest format of the game. I am not saying I don't want to play ODIs or T20Is, but I know I have to establish myself in the domestic leagues first to earn the Indian cap. I don't want to play for India just once or twice, but would rather like to make an impact and play for at least 10 to 15 years." What a story that would be!

Under-23 CK Nayudu Trophy

Devdhar's triple, Mumbai's title

NISHA SHETTY

Close on the heels of Mumbai's Ranji Trophy triumph came another piece of silverware to be added to the team's ever-growing mantelpiece: the CK Nayudu Under-23 Trophy.

The journey began in the 15-team Elite Division, Baroda and Punjab topping Group A, Madhya Pradesh and Maharashtra topping Group B, and Mumbai and Tamil Nadu topping Group C. In the 12-team Plate Division, Railways and Hyderabad won their respective semi-finals against Saurashtra and Jharkhand to join the six quarterfinalists from the Elite Division. Among them, only Madhya Pradesh and Tamil Nadu had also qualified in the previous season.

One of the highlights of the group stage games was Mrunal Devdhar's 311 in the match between Baroda and Delhi, the only triple-century in the tournament. Devdhar and Navneet Singh put on a staggering 535 runs for the second wicket – the highest partnership for any wicket this season – as Baroda went on to defeat Delhi by an innings and 194 runs. The other noteworthy performance was Jharkhand's Sonu Singh, who scalped 8 for 45 in the first innings against Odisha to secure the side a 33-run lead, before grabbing one more wicket in the second innings to clinch an 11-run thriller.

Mumbai, Maharashtra, Tamil Nadu and Madhya Pradesh then moved ahead to the semi-finals. Madhya Pradesh, aided by centuries from Venkatesh Iyer and Mukul Raghav, defeated Tamil Nadu by seven wickets to reach the final. In the other semi-final, centuries from Jay Bista, Arman Jaffer and Shivam Dube helped Mumbai pile up 697 and claim a first-innings lead against Maharashtra.

If three hundreds and one double-hundred during the season wasn't enough to grab eyeballs, 20-year-old bespectacled Bista delivered for Mumbai in the final too, scoring a magnificent 217, while Eknath Karker, the captain, chipped in with an unbeaten 102 to lift the side to 577. The gauntlet thrown for Maharashtra to try to eke out a first-innings lead, Shubham Sharma responded with 131, but it proved too tall an order as Tushar Deshpande (5 for 143) and Akash Parkar (4 for 77), Mumbai's pacers, restricted the side to 442.

Best batsman: Jay Bista (Mumbai) (1081 runs, 7 matches)
Best bowler: Satyajeet Bachhav (Maharashtra) (36 wickets, 6 matches)

Elite Group A

Reliance Cricket Stadium, Vadodara, October 10-13: Delhi 221 in 67 overs (Shivam Sharma 58*, Prashant Bhandari 50; Atit Sheth 4-53, Vikas Yadav 3-51) and 167 in 56.3 overs (Shivam 36, Himmat Singh 32; A Sheth 5-29, Kartik Kakade 2-37) lost to **Baroda** 582/4 dec in 144 overs (Mrunal Devdhar 311, Navneet Singh 224*) by an innings and 194 runs.

KD Singh Babu Stadium, Lucknow, October 10-13: Uttar Pradesh 476 in 172.3 overs (Akashdeep Nath 238, Shubham Chaubey 54; Sukhwinder Singh 3-105, Karan Kaila 2-89) drew with **Punjab** 168 in 76.5 overs (Navneet Virk 39, Anmol Malhotra 30*; Saurabh Kumar 5-46, Rajbahudur Pal 3-35) and 287/8 in 116.5 overs (f/o) (Sunny Pandey 124, A Malhotra 60; Saurabh 4-93, Mohammad Javed 2-46). Uttar Pradesh won on the basis of first-innings lead.

YS Raja Reddy Stadium, Cuddapah, October 17-18: Uttar Pradesh 89 in 29.2 overs (Rakashaan Faraz 47; Bharani Kumar 6-25) and 182 in 53.5 overs (Akashdeep Nath 67, Rishabh Mishra 21; Bharani 5-83, Sneha Kishore 4-48) lost to **Andhra** 172 in 43.3 overs (Ganesh Kumar 46, K Sreekanth 42; Vishal Choudhary 5-66, Saurabh Kumar 4-68) and 100/4 in 31.4 overs (Dharapu Naidu 35, Pranith Manyala 34*; Saurabh 3-38) by six wickets.

Sector 16 Stadium, Chandigarh, October 17-20: Punjab 341 in 125.1 overs (Prabjot Singh 73, Karan Kaila 62; Droan Chhabra 3-56, Vikas Mishra 2-61) drew with **Delhi** 178 in 86.2 overs (Hiten Dalal 42, Pratyush Singh 32; Vinay Choudhary 6-24, Sukhwinder Singh 3-45) and 457/6 in 133.5 (f/o) overs (H Dalal 133, Pratyush 103*; K Kaila 4-108). Punjab won on the basis of first-innings lead.

Moti Bagh Stadium, Vadodara, October 24-26: Andhra 96 in 31.4 overs (Kranthi Kumar 44; Rishi Arothe 5-33, Atit Sheth 5-41) and 107 in 43 overs (Pranith Manyala 36*; R Arothe 5-34, Baba Pathan 2-19) lost to **Baroda** 429 in 126.5 overs (Dhiren Mistry 110, Vishnu Solanki 94; M Rajasekhar 3-82, Sneha Kishore 3-87) by innings and 226 runs.

St. Stephen's College Ground, Delhi, October 24-27: Uttar Pradesh 236 in 71.3 overs (Himanshu Asnora 105, Saurabh Kumar 37; Shivam Sharma 3-43, Kunwar Bidhuri 2-13) and 329 in 96.2 overs (Shubham Chaubey 126, Rakashaan Faraz 54; Vikas Mishra 2-42, Vineet Kumar 2-48) lost to **Delhi** 414 in 113.5 overs (Rajesh Sharma 91, Hiten Dalal 77; Rajbahadur Pal 3-89, Mohammad Javed 3-131) and 152/2 in 41 overs (Prashant Bhandari 68*, Shivam 60*) by eight wickets.

Reliance Cricket Stadium, Vadodara, October 31-November 3: Punjab 258 in 69.4 overs (Anmol Malhotra 95*, Nikhil Choudhary 63; Kartik Kakade 4-42, Shoeb Sopariya 2-54) and 411 in 120 overs (N Choudhary 138, A Malhotra 101*; Vikas Yadav 4-109, K Kakade 2-95) drew with **Baroda** 209 in 59.1 overs (Vishnu Solanki 88, Mrunal Devdhar 54; Gurender Singh

5-63, Karan Kaila 2-24) and 389/7 in 107 overs (Dixit Patel 174, M Devdhar 93; Tajinder Singh 2-75, K Kaila 2-76). Punjab won on the basis of first-innings lead.

Feroz Shah Kotla, Delhi, October 31-November 3: Delhi 193 in 73 overs (Rajesh Sharma 77, Pratyush Singh 47; CV Stephen 6-64, Sneha Kishore 2-24) and 182 in 66.3 overs (Kunwar Bidhuri 79, Pradeep Malik 33; CV Stephen 4-37, Karthik Raman 4-64) lost to **Andhra** 201 in 84.2 overs (Sivacharan Singh 48, C Gnaneshwar 42; Vikas Mishra 5-31, Droan Chhabra 3-44) and 176/5 in 43.5 overs (Ashwin Hebbar 85, Pranith Manyala 44) by five wickets.

Moti Bagh Stadium, Vadodara, November 7-10: Uttar Pradesh 271 in 97.2 overs (Akashdeep Nath 85, Rakashaan Faraz 61; Atit Sheth 4-56, Baba Pathan 3-38) and 142/9 dec in 55.1 overs (R Faraz 29, Deepanshu Vats 25; Kartik Kakade 3-44, Mrunal Devdhar 2-1) lost to **Baroda** 391 in 137.4 overs (Rishi Arothe 79, Navneet Singh 56; Deepak Kumar 4-62, Vishal Choudhary 4-91) and 24/0 in 4 overs by ten wickets.

Sector 16 Stadium Chandigarh, November 7-9: Punjab 403/8 dec in 114.5 overs (Prabjot Singh 100, Rohan Marwaha 77; Kunnala Bhimarao 3-94, Sneha Kishore 2-108) beat **Andhra** 112 in 59 overs (Ashwin Hebbar 32; Karan Kaila 5-35, Vinay Choudhary 4-26) and 201 in 59.5 overs (f/o) (MUB Sriram 35, Pranith Manyala 35; V Choudhary 6-53, K Kaila 2-52) by an innings and 90 runs.

Elite Group A Points Table

Teams	M	W	L	D	T	A	Pts	Q
Baroda	4	3	0	1	0	0	22	2.331
Punjab	4	1	0	3	0	0	14	1.039
Andhra	4	2	2	0	0	0	12	0.663
Delhi	4	1	2	1	0	0	7	0.759
Uttar Pradesh	4	0	3	1	0	0	3	0.790

Baroda and Punjab qualified for the quarter-finals

Elite Group B

Atal Bihari Vajpayee Stadium, Amtar, October 10-13: Himachal Pradesh 293 in 127.4 overs (Arjun Sharma 76, Praveen Thakur 72; Basil Thampi 5-106, Anand Joseph 4-56) and 208 in 89.4 overs (Amit Thakur 57, Arjun 22; Abhishek Mohan 4-61, B Thampi 3-43) drew with **Kerala** 182 in 71.3 overs (A Mohan 43, Mohammed Azharuddeen 41; Vinay Galetiya 4-59, Arjun 3-9) and 149/3 in 60 overs (Vishnu Babu 56*, Atul Diamond Sowri 29). Himachal Pradesh won on the basis of first-innings lead.

MCA Stadium, Pune, October 10-13: Maharashtra 47 in 22.2 overs (Aavesh Khan 5-20, Saransh Jain 3-1) and 300/8 dec in 87.3 overs (Shamshuzama Kazi 77*, Prashant Kore 55; Aavesh 4-102, Venkatesh Iyer 2-38) lost to **Madhya Pradesh** 171 in 70.3 overs (Mukul Raghav 60, Ashutosh Singh 30; Satyajeet Bachhav 3-25, Pradeep Dadhe 3-60) and 180/3 in 55.1 overs (Ashutosh 71*, V Iyer 64*) by seven wickets.

Captain Roop Singh Stadium, Gwalior, October 17-20: Madhya Pradesh 606/9 dec in 180 overs (Rishabh Tiwari 193, Shubham Sharma 113*, Ashutosh Singh 112; Akshay Chandran 6-106) beat **Kerala** 208 in 87.5 overs (Abhishek Mohan 41, A Chandran 36; Mayank Jain 4-35, Saransh Jain 2-49) and 222 in 66.4 overs (f/o) (Basil Thampi 43, Saly Samson 41; Aavesh Khan 5-102, S Jain 2-65) by an innings and 176 runs.

VCA Stadium, Nagpur, October 17-19: Vidarbha 501 in 168.2 overs (Sanjay Ramaswamy 206, Akshay Karnewar 92; Rahul Singh 5-149, Arjun Sharma 2-144) beat **Himachal Pradesh**

106 in 47.2 overs (Ekant Sen 54; Raj Choudhury 4-11, Lalit Yadav 2-18) and 96 in 39 overs (f/o) (E Sen 35; Atharva Deshpande 5-35, R Choudhury 3-14) by an innings and 299 runs.

Atal Bihari Vajpayee Stadium, Amtar, October 24-27: Madhya Pradesh 553 in 166.5 overs (Shubham Sharma 163, Venkatesh Iyer 129; Arjun Sharma 4-187, Rahul Singh 3-158) drew with **Himachal Pradesh** 343 in 147.5 overs (Priyanshu Khanduri 94, Nakulraj Sharma 70; Saransh Jain 6-124, Palas Kochrar 2-92) and 54/1 in 26 overs (f/o) (Praveen Thakur 28*, Nakulraj 23*). Madhya Pradesh won on the basis of first-innings lead.

Pune Club Ground, October 24-27: Maharashtra 324 in 108.4 overs (Shamshuzama Kazi 103, Murtuza Trunkwala 55; Lalit Yadav 4-65, Rajneesh Gurbani 4-68) and 223 in 67 overs (M Trunkwala 45, Jay Pande 40; Atharva Deshpande 3-50, Lalit 2-13) beat **Vidarbha** 260 in 77.4 overs (Akshay Karnewar 76, Akshay Wadkar 75; Chinmay Patil 6-72, Satyajeet Bachhav 3-58) and 179 in 68.4 overs (Sachin Katariya 57, A Wadkar 35; TR Dhillon 3-61, S Bachhav 3-63) by 108 runs.

St. Xavier's College Ground, Thumba, October 31-November 3: Kerala 326 in 100.5 overs (Mohammed Azharuddeen 156, Sanju Samson 44; Satyajeet Bachhav 5-120, Pradeep Dadhe 2-65) drew with **Maharashtra** 144 in 60.3 overs (Vijay Zol 30, Jay Pande 29; Akshay Chandran 3-8, Anand Joseph 3-25, Fabid Ahmed 3-45) and 144/2 in 53 overs (f/o) (Murtuza Trunkwala 81*, Prashant Kore 39*; F Ahmed 2-49). Kerala won on the basis of first inning lead.

VCA Stadium, Nagpur, October 31-November 3: Madhya Pradesh 394 in 155 overs (Rishabh Tiwari 83, Ashutosh Singh 76; Sachin Katariya 2-31, Janmajai Acharya 2-35) beat **Vidarbha** 212 in 94.2 overs (S Katariya 112*, Sanjay Ramaswamy 28; Kulpreet Pannu 4-55, Saransh Jain 4-80) and 131 in 64.4 overs (f/o) (S Katariya 54, Atharva Manohar 25; S Jain 5-42, Parth Sahani 3-9) by an innings and 51 runs.

St. Xavier's College Ground, Thumba, November 7-10: Kerala 299 in 116.2 overs (KC Akshay 66*, Mohammed Azharuddeen 63; Akshay Karnewar 5-72, Raj Choudhury 3-68) and 112/5 in 53 overs (Nikhilesh Surendran 56, Saly Samson 22*; A Karnewar 2-23) drew with **Vidarbha** 289 in 107 overs (Sanjay Ramaswamy 103, Akshay Wadkar 74; KC Akshay 4-71, Abdul Safar 2-26). Kerala won on the basis of first-innings lead.

MCA Stadium, Pune, November 7-10: Maharashtra 472/4 dec in 118.2 overs (Nikhil Naik 164*, Murtuza Trunkwala 119, Shamshuzama Kazi 100*; Ankush Kumar 2-86, Rahul Singh 2-99) beat **Himachal Pradesh** 234 in 96.4 overs (Priyanshu Khanduri 68, Vikrant Kumar 46; Satyajeet Bachhav 5-72) and 228 in 106 overs (f/o) (Nakulraj Sharma 66, P Khanduri 54; Chinmay Patil 5-67, S Bachhav 3-43) by an innings and ten runs.

Elite Group B Points Table

Teams	M	W	L	D	T	A	Pts	Q
Madhya Pradesh	4	3	0	1	0	0	23	2.062
Maharashtra	4	2	1	1	0	0	14	1.184
Vidarbha	4	1	2	1	0	0	8	1.096
Kerala	4	0	1	3	0	0	7	0.782
Himachal Pradesh	4	0	2	2	0	0	4	0.451

Madhya Pradesh and Maharashtra qualified for the quarter-finals

Elite Group C

Jadavpur University Second Campus Ground, Kolkata, October 10-13: Karnataka 455 in 150.3 overs (KV Siddharth 117, C Karthik 99; Anurag Tiwari 4-134, Sayan Ghosh 2-81) and 157/5 in 55 overs (Abhishek Reddy 39, N Bharath 37; S Ghosh 3-53) drew with **Bengal** 368 in 137 overs (Pramod Chandila 97, Sandipan Das 84; KC Cariappa 3-111, Prateek Jain 2-36). Karnataka won on the basis of first-innings lead.

Sardar Patel Stadium B Ground, Motera, Ahmedabad, October 10-13: Gujarat 576/4 dec in 176 overs (Aditya Patel 225, Alshaaz Pathan 179; Akash Parkar 2-83) drew with **Mumbai** 560 in 171 overs (Jay Bista 201, Shivam Dubey 125; Hardik Patel 4-121, Santosh Shinde 2-81). Gujarat won on the basis of first-innings lead.

Jadavpur University Second Campus Ground, Kolkata, October 17-20: Tamil Nadu 171 in 41.5 overs (Bharath Shankar 63, Kavin Ravi 38; Pradipta Pramanik 3-49, Pritam Chakraborty 3-49) and 318 in 117.3 overs (Shahrukh Khan 138, Bharath 60; Writtick Chatterjee 4-67, P Pramanik 3-77) lost to **Bengal** 321 in 89.2 overs (Ritwik Roy Chowdhury 145, Pramod Chandila 55; Shahrukh 2-33, Mohan Abhinav 2-40) and 169/3 in 46.5 overs (P Chandila 53*, R Roy Chowdhury 36) by seven wickets.

Sachin Tendulkar Gymkhana Ground, Mumbai, October 17-20: Karnataka 316 in 89.5 overs (Abhishek Reddy 151, KC Cariappa 50; Parikshit Valsangkar 3-70, Tushar Deshpande 3-71, Dhrumil Matkar 3-90) and 234 in 70 overs (A Reddy 89, Praveen Dubey 64; D Matkar 4-62, Jay Bista 3-50) lost to **Mumbai** 478/9 dec in 169.1 overs (Eknath Kerkar 132, Vikrant Auti 121; Prateek Jain 2-77, Praveen Dubey 2-83) and 73/0 in 10.2 overs (J Bista 36*, Aakarshit Gomel 35*) by ten wickets.

Jadavpur University Second Campus Ground, Kolkata, October 24-27: Gujarat 436 in 169.3 overs (Divyang Patel 129, Raxlee Taylor 128; Writtick Chatterjee 3-83, Geet Puri 2-55) beat **Bengal** 155 in 44.1 overs (Pramod Chandila 66*, Abhishek Raman 37; Karan Patel 5-48, Santosh Shinde 3-22) and 227 in 114.3 overs (f/o) (A Raman 49, Sandipan Das 35; Chintan Gaja 3-35, Smeet Patel 2-12) by an innings and 54 runs.

India Cement Limited Guru Nanak College Ground, Chennai, October 24-27: Tamil Nadu 291 in 97.1 overs (Shahrukh Khan 91, Uthirasamy Sasidev 58; Prateek Jain 4-39, Prasidh Krishna 3-56, D Ananda 3-95) and 264 in 75 overs (Bharath Shankar 92, N Jagadeesan 65; N Bharath 4-31, KC Cariappa 3-46) beat **Karnataka** 157 in 69.3 overs (D Nischal 66, Praveen Dubey 37; DT Chandrasekar 5-61, Shahrukh Khan 3-15) and 158 in 60 overs (D Nischal 58, KV Siddarth 57; Aushik Srinivas 5-43, DT Chandrasekar 4-61) by 240 runs.

DR Bendre KSCA Stadium, Hubli, October 31-November 3: Karnataka 293 in 77.1 overs (Anurag Bajpai 98, Praveen Dubey 63; Chintan Gaja 7-74, Karan Patel 3-60) and 318/7 dec in 82 overs (D Nischal 134, N Bharath 56; Karan 3-12, Smeet Patel 2-68) drew with **Gujarat** 318 in 132 overs (Karan Viradiya 88, Raxlee Taylor 77; Bhavesh Gulecha 5-57, Prasidh Krishna 3-43) and 102/5 in 53 overs (R Taylor 38*, B Gulecha 2-20). Gujarat won on the basis of first inning lead

Bandra Kurla Complex, Mumbai, October 31-November 3: Mumbai 461/9 dec in 163.5 overs (Sachin Yadav 99, Eknath Kerkar 90*; Aushik Srinivas 3-89, B Rahul 2-41) and 185/3 dec in 49.4 overs (Aakarshit Gomel 82, Jay Bista 74; Aushik 3-43) drew with **Tamil Nadu** 344 in 119.5 overs (Shahrukh Khan 81, Bharath Shankar 67; Tushar Deshpande 4-108, J Bista 3-20) and 11/0 in 8 overs. Mumbai won on the basis of first-innings lead

Lalabai Contractor Stadium, Surat, November 7-10: Tamil Nadu 383 in 116.3 overs (Bharath Shankar 139, Shahrukh Khan 98; Hardik Patel 6-90, Karan Patel 3-76) and 226/6 dec in 43 overs (Bharath 70, Shahrukh 57; Hardik 2-59) beat **Gujarat** 313 in 117.5 overs (Karan 80, Raxlee Taylor 73; Sai Kishore 3-86, Baskaran Rahul 2-8) and 168 in 78.2 overs (Divyang Patel 50, Karan Viradiya 38; K Vignesh 5-42, S Kishore 5-53) by 128 runs.

Bandra Kurla Complex, Mumbai, November 7-10: Bengal 299 in 85 overs (Sandipan Das

109, Dipanjan Mukherjee 74; Parikshit Valsangkar 5-56, Abul Kalam 2-37) and 233 in 81.1 overs (Koushik Ghosh 100*, Abhishek Raman 34; Dhrumil Matkar 8-83) lost to **Mumbai** 323 in 88.5 overs (Jay Bista 125, Shivam Dubey 34; Anurag Tiwari 4-69, Geet Puri 3-81) and 211/3 in 51.5 overs (J Bista 130, Vikrant Auti 33*; A Tiwari 2-50) by seven wickets.

Elite Group C Points Table

Teams	M	W	L	D	T	A	Pts	Q
Mumbai	4	2	0	2	0	0	17	1.397
Tamil Nadu	4	2	1	1	0	0	13	1.024
Gujarat	4	1	1	2	0	0	13	1.138
Bengal	4	1	2	1	0	0	7	0.788
Karnataka	4	0	2	2	0	0	4	0.827

Mumbai and Tamil Nadu qualified for the quarter-finals

Plate Group A

Gymkhana Ground, Secunderabad, October 10-13: Hyderabad 362 in 143.5 overs (Yathin Reddy 88, Rohan Yadav 84; Dwaipayan Bhattacharjee 4-85, Joydeep Bhattacharjee 4-100) beat **Tripura** 106 in 58.3 overs (Subhankar Debnath 30, Joydeep Banik 24; Ravi Teja 4-23, Tanay Thyagarajan 2-18) and 91 in 34.4 overs (f/o) (T Thyagarajan 4-35, Saaketh Sairam 3-29) by an innings and 165 runs.

Sher-i-Kashmir Stadium, Srinagar, October 10-13: Jammu & Kashmir 187 in 61.1 overs (Ahmedomer Banday 44, Umar Nissar 44; Malliksab Sirur 4-20, Felix Alemao 2-20) and 376 in 123.1 overs (U Nissar 166, Pranav Gupta 103; M Sirur 5-84, Srinivas Fadte 2-69) lost to **Goa** 451/7 dec in 154 overs (Prathamesh Gawas 102, M Sirur 100; Ankush Bandral 2-46, Zahoor Khan 2-90) and 116/4 in 17.6 overs (Achit Shigwan 52, Kallal Maitra 44*; Kulwinder Singh 3-50) by six wickets.

Western Railway Ground, Rajkot, October 10-13: Saurashtra 279 in 102.1 overs (Divyaraj Chauhan 95, K Kunal 77; Ashok Singh 3-28, Ankit Lamba 2-51) and 262/5 in 85 overs (PN Mankad 87, DM Chauhan 71*; AS Singh 2-40, KD Boresa 2-63) drew with **Rajasthan** 379 in 154 overs (Mahendra Singh 103, Sidhant Dobal 64; Jay Chauhan 3-89, K Kunal 2-27). Rajasthan won on the basis of first-innings lead.

Sher-i-Kashmir Stadium, Srinagar, October 17-20: Tripura 356 in 111.3 overs (Samrat Sutradhar 113, Joydeep Bhattacharjee 46*; Aamir Ashraf 4-60, Musaib Farooq 4-96) drew with **Jammu & Kashmir** 365/5 in 98 overs (Abhinav Puri 120, Umar Nissar 74; Nabajyoti Debnath 2-9, Rajib Saha 2-85). Jammu & Kashmir won on the basis of first-innings lead

KL Saini Ground, Jaipur, October 17-19: Goa 135 in 36.2 overs (Malliksab Sirur 53, Samar Dubhashi 27; Chandrapal Chundawat 3-11, Ashok Singh 3-49) and 231 in 105.1 overs (S Dubhashi 110*, Achit Shigwan 27; Yash Kothari 3-16, Ankit Lamba 3-55) lost to **Rajasthan** 178 in 52 overs (Divyapratap Hada 52, Mahendra Singh 46; Felix Alemao 5-65, Lakshay Garg 3-46) and 191/9 in 60 overs (Mahendra 44*, RM Bihani 32; Sagar Naik 4-42, L Garg 4-61) by one wicket.

Madhavrao Scindia Cricket Ground, Rajkot, October 17-19: Saurashtra 290 in 74.5 overs (Abrar Shaikh 79, Samarth Vyas 59; Saaketh Sairam 5-93, Mohammed Siraj 3-36) and 205 in 67.2 overs (A Shaikh 66, Snell Patel 37; Tanay Thyagarajan 3-66, S Sairam 3-69) beat **Hyderabad** 180 in 72.4 overs (Yathin Reddy 54, Rohit Rayudu 37; Karamchandani Kunal

5-46, Jay Chauhan 3-47) and 267 in 73 overs (Y Reddy 87, R Rayudu 34; K Kunal 4-89, J Chauhan 3-76) by 48 runs.

Gymkhana Ground, Secunderabad, October 24-27: Hyderabad 527/9 dec in 168.3 overs (S Ravindar Reddy 123, Rohan Yadav 100; Amulaya Pandrekar 5-180, Felix Alemao 3-97) and 24/0 in 7.1 overs beat **Goa** 278 in 85.5 overs (Shriniwas Fadte 61, Lakshay Garg 34; Mohammed Siraj 3-66, Tanay Thyagarajan 3-93) and 272 in 78.1 overs (f/o) (Deepraj Gaonkar 126, Rajat Shet 39; T Thyagarajan 3-79, M Siraj 2-32) by ten wickets.

Sher-i-Kashmir Stadium, Srinagar, October 24-27: Jammu & Kashmir 360 in 139.2 overs (Aamir Ashraf 94, Abhinav Puri 79; Sidhant Dobal 3-51, Aditya Garhwal 2-34) drew with **Rajasthan** 84/3 in 27 overs (Yash Kothari 50*; Mohammad Tahir 2-20).

Madhavrao Scindia Cricket Ground, Rajkot, October 24-25: Tripura 62 in 27.2 overs (Nabajyoti Debnath 22; Yuvrajsinh Chudasama 5-21, Jay Chauhan 4-25) and 90 in 40.5 overs (Joydeep Bhattacharjee 20, Kritidipta Das 20; Y Chudasama 4-37, Prerak Mankad 3-25) lost to **Saurashtra** 360 in 91 overs (Samarth Vyas 78, Viharsinh Jadeja 57; J Bhattacharjee 5-102) by an innings and 208 runs.

KL Saini Ground, Jaipur, October 31-November 3: Hyderabad 461 in 135.5 overs (Mir Jawid Ali 120, Himalay Agarawal 90; Ankit Lamba 3-105, Sidhant Dobal 2-53) and 231/5 in 77 overs (Rohit Rayudu 71, Mir Jawid 43; Kumar Boresa 2-52) drew with **Rajasthan** 344 in 129.1 overs (S Dobal 102, Chandrapal Chunawat 42; Tanay Thyagarajan 4-80, Mohammed Siraj 3-94). Hyderabad won on the basis of first-innings lead

SCA Stadium, Rajkot, October 31-November 3: Jammu & Kashmir 377 in 118.2 overs (Jatin Wadhwan 111, Paras Sharma 74; Jay Chauhan 3-89, Karamchandani Kunal 2-59) and 180 in 103 overs (Abhinav Puri 54, Umar Nissar 40; Prerak Mankad 3-20, K Kunal 3-43) drew with **Saurashtra** 342 in 118.3 overs (P Mankad 112*, Samarth Vyas 50; Irshad Ahmad 3-47, Musaib Farooq 3-72) and 101/4 in 15 overs (S Vyas 34, J Chauhan 34; I Ahmed 2-53). Jammu & Kashmir won on the basis of first-innings lead

Tripura Institute of Technology, Agartala, October 31-November 3: Tripura 141 in 60.3 overs (Subhankar Debnath 46, Bunti Roy 36; Amulaya Pandrekar 5-41, Hrishikesh Naik 2-12) and 225 in 83.3 overs (Nabajyoti Debnath 71, Joydeep Banik 44*; Felix Alemao 5-44, H Naik 3-40) lost to **Goa** 177 in 64 overs (Achit Shigwan 36, A Pandrekar 24; Joydeep Bhattacharjee 3-34, Devnarayan Kumar 2-22) and 190/4 in 70.5 overs (Prathamesh Gawas 64, Shriniwas Fadte 50*) by six wickets.

GCA Academy Ground, Porvorim, November 7-10: Saurashtra 438 in 139.2 overs (Samarth Vyas 129, Snell Patel 105; Amulaya Pandrekar 7-120, Lakshay Garg 3-78) beat **Goa** 178 in 76.3 overs (Shriniwas Fadte 38, Prathamesh Gawas 29; Yujrajsinh Chudasama 3-20, Karamchandani Kunal 3-32) and 195 in 88.2 overs (f/o) (Samar Dubhashi 76, S Fadte 32; Y Chudasama 4-44, K-Kunal 4-54) by an innings and 65 runs.

Gymkhana Ground, Secunderabad, November 7-10: Hyderabad 626/5 dec in 173 overs (Yathin Reddy 205, Mir Jawid Ali 156*, T Ravi Teja 106*; Aamir Ashraf 3-122) drew with **Jammu & Kashmir** 181 in 82.4 overs (Umar Nissar 72, Abhinav Puri 32; Tanay Thyagarajan 7-63, Saaketh Sairam 2-39) and 230/4 in 94.5 overs (f/o) (Pranav Gupta 102*, Jatin Wadhwan 46; T Thyagarajan 2-83). Hyderabad won on the basis of first-innings lead

KL Saini Ground, Jaipur, November 7-8: Tripura 68 in 22.3 overs (Rabisankar Murasingh 23; Ankit Lamba 5-32, Nathu Singh 4-22) and 111 in 44.3 overs (Nabajyoti Debnath 29, Joydeep Banik 22; Ajay Singh 4-20, A Lamba 3-29) lost to **Rajasthan** 251 in 85.3 overs (Mahendra Singh 82, Divyapratap Hada 58; Bunti Roy 5-66, R Murasingh 2-62) by an innings and 72 runs.

Plate Group A Points Table

Teams	M	W	L	D	T	A	Pts	Q
Saurashtra	5	3	0	2	0	0	22	1.579
Hyderabad	5	2	1	2	0	0	20	1.909
Rajasthan	5	2	0	2	0	0	18	1.027
Goa	5	2	3	0	0	0	12	0.892
Jammu & Kasmir	5	0	1	3	0	0	8	0.677
Tripura	5	0	4	1	0	0	1	0.391

Saurashtra and Hyderabad qualified for the plate semi-finals

Plate Group B

Ch Bansi Lal Cricket Stadium, Lahli, Rohtak, October 10-13: Haryana 352 in 118.3 overs (RP Sarma 104, Parvesh Dahiya 79; Akshat Pandey 4-63, Sagar Mishra 4-82) and 205/7 in 97 overs (P Dahiya 73, Rohit Sharma 50; A Pandey 3-46) drew with **Railways** 310 in 129.3 overs (A Pandey 98*, Pappu Singh 52; MS Kumar 5-78, Poonish Mehta 2-59). Haryana won on the basis of first-innings lead

JSCA Ground, Ranchi, October 10-12: Assam 194 in 74 overs (Rahul Hazarika 39, Romariomomin Sharma 38; Rahul Prasad 3-37, Arun Vikash 3-37) and 217 in 50.4 overs (Rahul Hazarika 113, Romariomomin 47; Sonu Singh 4-30, A Vikash 3-39) lost to **Jharkhand** 523/4 dec in 126.1 overs (Sumit Kumar 203*, Shasheem 147) by an innings and 112 runs.

Vikas Cricket Ground, Cuttack, October 10-13: Odisha 504/6 dec in 182 overs (Ranjit Singh 209, Abhishek Yadav 66; Shubham Thakur 2-88, Ajay Mandal 2-117) and 43/2 in 15 overs drew with **Chhattisgarh** 416 in 149.5 overs (Amandeep Khare 95, Anupam Toppo 86; Priyatosh Paramanik 3-58, Ankit Yadav 3-82). Odisha won on the basis of first-innings lead

Golaghat District Sports Association Stadium, Golaghat, October 17-19: Assam 70 in 31.1 overs (Manashjyoti Gogoi 32; Satender Thakran 7-35, Sagar Mishra 3-16) and 165 in 61.3 overs (M Gogoi 37, Sunzow Brahma 32; S Mishra 4-31, Ambikeshwar Mishra 3-34) lost to **Railways** 144 in 55.2 overs (Varun Anand 46, Akash Yadav 39; Mantu Das 5-40, Romario Sharma 3-27) and 95/7 in 47.2 overs (V Anand 28, S Mishra 27; Jogeswar Bhumij 4-27, M Das 2-31) by three wickets.

Keenan Stadium, Jamshedpur, October 17-20: Chhattisgarh 313 in 133.4 overs (Anupam Toppo 103, Chhabi Jaikshatri 54; Sonu Singh 5-50, Vishal Singh 3-0) and 141 in 64 overs (C Jaikshatri 81, Ajay Mandal 26; Monu Kumar 7-29, Sonu 2-45) lost to **Jharkhand** 230 in 68.4 overs (Sumit Kumar 91, SK Mohammed Sharukh 62; Jagjot Gill 6-53, A Mandal 2-42) and 225/3 in 70.1 overs (Vishal Singh 75*, Sumit 58) by seven wickets.

Veer Surendra Sai Stadium, Sambalpur, October 17-19: Odisha 176 in 58 overs (Ranjit Singh 92, Priyatosh Paramanik 21; Poonish Mehta 4-24, Rahul Tewatia 3-42) and 171 in 62.3 overs (P Paramanik 37, Ranjit 35; R Tewatia 6-65, P Mehta 3-18) lost to **Haryana** 434 in 121.1 overs (Shamsher Yadav 130, Rohit Sharma 115; Ranjan Bhuyan 2-73, Debapriya Pattanayak 2-79) by an innings and 87 runs.

TDSA Ground, Tinsukia, October 24-27: Assam 398 in 129.1 overs (Rahul Hazarika 222*, Sohail Rahman 58; Shakeen Ahmed 3-78, Shubham Singh 3-99) and 86/3 in 35 overs (R Hazarika 43; Ajay Mandal 3-38) drew with **Chhattisgarh** 350 in 132.5 overs (Anupam Toppo 94, A Mandal 92; Mantu Das 3-75, Avoy Yadav 2-46). Assam won on the basis of first-innings lead

Ch Bansi Lal Cricket Stadium, Lahli, Rohtak, October 24-26: Haryana 201 in 84.1 overs

(RP Sharma 70, Rahul Tewatia 48; Monu Kumar 3-29, Prem Kumar 3-35, Rahul Prasad 3-52) and 127 in 44.2 overs (Ajith Chahal 23, RP Sharma 22; Prem 6-47, Monu 4-57) lost to **Jharkhand** 207 in 56 overs (Kumar Deobrat 102, Ankit Dabas 43; A Chahal 5-72, Ravi Balhara 3-38) and 123/5 in 29 overs (K Deobrat 33*, Babul Kumar 31; R Tewatia 2-25, Amit Rana 2-32) by five wickets.
Diesel Component Works Sports Stadium, Patiala, October 24-27: Odisha 281 in 120.4 overs (Ranjit Singh 109, Gaurav Mahaptra 67; Ambikeshwar Mishra 5-45, Satender Thakran 2-53) and 217 in 90.4 overs (Abhishek Yadav 74, Shantanu Mishra 51; A Mishra 6-74, Shamsul Huda 2-28) drew with **Railways** 456/7 dec in 139.3 overs (Akshat Pandey 142*, S Sudhan Sanjeevi Kandepan 74; Pappu Roy 3-95, Anurag Prusty 2-71) and 12/2 in 2 overs. Railways won on the basis of first-innings lead
JR Sharma Institute of Cricket and Technology, Barwala, October 31-November 3: Chhattisgarh 276 in 119.2 overs (Ajay Mandal 122, Shakeeb Ahmed 84; Amit Rana 4-51, Rahul Tewatia 3-69) and 260/7 in 101 overs (A Mandal 103, S Ahmed 71; Ajit Chahal 2-45) drew with **Haryana** 375 in 124.2 overs (Shamsher Yadav 164, R Tewatia 73; S Ahmed 5-66, Shahnawaz Hussain 3-89). Haryana won on the basis of first-innings lead
Gandhi Stadium, Balangir, October 31-November 2: Odisha 117 in 59.5 overs (Ranjit Singh 37, Ankit Yadav 26; Mantu Das 3-34, Sohail Rahman 3-35) and 269 in 90.5 overs (Rajkishan Patel 78, Shantanu Mishra 75; Avoy Yadav 2-45, Mantu Das 2-50) lost to **Assam** 362 in 100.3 overs (Rahul Hazarika 209, Wasiqur Rahman 110; Ankit Yadav 3-83, Priyatosh Paramanik 2-19) and 27/0 in 3.4 overs by ten wickets.
Diesel Component Works Sports Stadium, Patiala, October 31-November 3: Railways 392 in 138.1 overs (Vivek Singh 106, Amar Kala 61; Ronit Sigh 5-67, Rahul Prasad 3-86) and 242/2 in 57 overs (Ashish Sehrawat 127*, Akshat Pandey 51) drew with **Jharkhand** 269 in 127.1 overs (Shasheem 103, SK Mohammed Sharukh 48; A Pandey 4-68, Vivek 2-16). Railways won on the basis of first-innings lead
Satindra Mohan Dev Stadium, Silchar, November 7-10: Haryana 268 in 95.5 overs (Poonish Mehta 127, Amit Rana 50; Roshan Alam 4-71, Jagadwipen Das 2-37) and 158 in 58.1 overs (Shamsher Yadav 38, Lovekesh Kumar 32; Jogeswar Bhumij 5-37) lost to **Assam** 195 in 76.5 overs (Wasiqur Rahman 61*, J Das 43; Vikrant Kumar 6-34, Ajith Chahal 3-26) and 235/6 in 74.2 overs (Sunzow Brahma 61, Romariomomin Sharma 43*; RM Saini 3-74, P Mehta 2-35) by four wickets.
Bokaro Steel Limited Cricket Stadium, Bokaro, November 7-10: Jharkhand 175 in 48.4 overs (Ajat Shatru 51, Monu Kumar 39; Ankit Yadav 3-31, Tarakanta Samal 3-50) and 196 in 81.4 overs (Vishal Singh 69, A Shatru 25; Pappu Roy 3-35, T Samal 3-38) beat **Odisha** 148 in 83 overs (Debapriya Pattanayak 38, Ankit 37; Sonu Singh 8-45, Arun Vikash 2-25) and 212 in 62.5 overs (Abhishek Yadav 113, D Pattanayak 20; Monu 6-59, A Vikash 2-65) by 11 runs.
Diesel Component Works Sports Stadium, Patiala, November 7-10: Chhattisgarh 226 in 107 overs (Anuj Tiwari 46, Atul Pal 42; Akshat Pandey 3-40, Ambikeshwar Mishra 3-51, Sagar Mishra 3-63) and 240 in 90.3 overs (Shakeeb Ahmed 65, A Pal 44; A Mishra 4-50, S Mishra 3-57) lost to **Railways** 310 in 86.3 overs (Vivek Singh 83, Ashish Sehrawat 57; Vikrant Rajput 6-58, Shahnawaz Hussain 2-36) and 157/5 in 22.2 overs (Pappu Singh 68*, Sagar Mishra 29; S Hussain 2-45) by five wickets.

Plate Group B Points Table

Teams	M	W	L	D	T	A	Pts	Q
Jharkhand	5	4	0	1	0	0	26	1.322
Railways	5	2	0	3	0	0	19	1.444
Assam	5	2	2	1	0	0	16	0.910
Haryana	5	1	2	2	0	0	13	1.100
Odisha	5	0	3	2	0	0	4	0.690
Chattisgarh	5	0	2	3	0	0	3	0.731

Jharkhand and Railways qualified for the plate semi-finals

Plate semi-finals

Gymkhana Ground, Secunderabad, February 1-4: Hyderabad 461 in 180.3 overs (Gaddan Rohan Yadav 151, Akash Bhandari 123; Monu Kumar 4-65, Arun Vikash 2-58) and 114/1 in 30 overs (Mir Jawid Ali 57, Rohit Rayudu 34) drew with **Jharkhand** 359 in 129.1 overs (Vishal Singh 113, Babul Kumar 94; Mohammed Siraj 4-87, Chama Milind 2-55). Hyderabad won on the basis of first-innings lead.

Karnail Singh Stadium, Delhi, February 1-4: Saurashtra 199 in 71.1 overs (Abrar Shaikh 51, Prerak Mankad 40; Sagar Mishra 3-44, Satender Thakran 2-33) and 309 in 85.4 overs (Divyaraj Chauhan 81, Abrar Shaikh 49; S Mishra 3-49, Ambikeshwar Mishra 3-77) lost to **Railways** 429 in 140 overs (Faizahmad Hameed 168, Ashish Sehrawat 118; Yuvrajsinh Chudasama 4-63, Vivek Agath 3-69) and 83/4 in 20.4 overs (Pappu Singh 27*, F Hameed 26; P Mankad 2-13) by six wickets.

Hyderabad and Railways qualified for the quarter-finals

Plate 3rd place play-off

SCA Stadium, Rajkot, February 19-22: Saurashtra 400 in 148.2 overs (Divyaraj Chauhan 143, Harvik Desai 83; Kumar Singh 5-83, Vishal Singh 2-36) and 235/9 dec in 73.1 overs (Snell Patel 108, Jay Chauhan 44; Kumar 5-40, Vishal 2-20) beat **Jharkhand** 168 in 56.5 overs (Wilfred Beng 41, Virat Singh 40; Vivek Agath 4-43, J Chauhan 3-32) and 229 in 47.1 overs (Monu Kumar 61, Sumit Kumar 48; V Agath 4-33, J Chauhan 3-40) by 238 runs.

Quarter-finals

Moti Bagh Stadium, Vadodara, February 10-12: Baroda 177 in 66 overs (Rishi Arothe 46, Deepak Hooda 36; Tushar Deshpande 4-31, Dhrumil Matkar 2-36) and 288 in 75.4 overs (Vishnu Solanki 101, Mrunal Devdhar 58; Akash Parkar 5-33, D Matkar 4-90) lost to **Mumbai** 191 in 65.4 overs (A Parkar 55, Jay Bista 44; Vikas Yadav 4-41, R Arothe 3-61) and 279/6 in 55.3 overs (J Bista 128, Parikshit Valsangkar 44; Kartik Kakade 3-81, Vikas 3-89) by four wickets.

Gymkhana Ground, Secunderabad, February 10-13: Madhya Pradesh 442 in 147.5 overs (Shubham Sharma 182, Mukul Raghav 64; Mohammed Siraj 3-82, Akash Bhandari 3-95) and 197/3 in 58 overs (Wasim Ahmed 57, Ashutosh Singh 52*) drew with **Hyderabad** 382 in 135 overs (Yathin Reddy 116, Himalay Agarawal 93; Ashwin Das 7-92). Madhya Pradesh won on the basis of first-innings lead.

Dhruve Pandove Stadium, Patiala, February 10-11: Punjab 117 in 44.4 overs (Anmol Malhotra 39, Nikhil Chaudhary 23; Aaswin Crist 4-20, J Kousik 2-17) and 66 in 27.3 overs (J Kousik 5-8, Aushik Srinivas 2-5) lost to **Tamil Nadu** 157 in 64.5 overs (Bharath Shankar 59, Akshay Srinivasan 38; Vinay Choudhary 7-57, Sukhwinder Singh 3-28) and 27/0 in 3.3 overs by ten wickets.

Karnail Singh Stadium, Delhi, February 10-12: Maharashtra 172 in 49.5 overs (Chirag Khurana 48, Nikhil Naik 26; Karan Mahajan 3-5, Ashish Singh 2-14) and 291 in 63.4 overs (N Naik 113, Murtuza Trunkwala 102; Karan Mahajan 3-60, Ambikeshwar Mishra 3-72) beat **Railways** 165 in 75.3 overs (Faizahmad Hameed 60*, Karan Mahajan 25; Satyajeet Bachhav 5-32, C Khurana 4-42) and 168 in 48.2 overs (Akash Yadav 43, F Hameed 28; Shamshuzama Kazi 3-13, S Bachhav 2-48) by 130 runs.

Mumbai, Madhya Pradesh, Tamil Nadu and Maharashtra qualified for the semi-finals

Semi-finals

Bandra Kurla Complex, Mumbai, February 19-22: Mumbai 697 in 185.4 overs (Arman Jaffer 181, Vikrant Auti 169, Shivam Dube 114; Satyajeet Bachhav 6-193, Chinmay Patil 2-123) drew with **Maharashtra** 467 in 155 overs (Shamshuzama Kazi 98, Yassar Shaikh 77; Abdulkalam Alihusen 2-50, Parikshit Valsangkar 2-69). Mumbai won on the basis of first-innings lead

IIT Chemplast Ground, Chennai, February 19-22: Tamil Nadu 283 in 88.5 overs (Bharath Shankar 101, Baba Aparajith 67; Venkatesh Iyer 4-32, Aavesh Khan 4-56) and 319/7 dec in 46 overs (Baba Indrajith 110*, Bharath 69; Saransh Jain 3-99, Ashwin Das 2-66) lost to **Madhya Pradesh** 396 in 149.3 overs (V Iyer 109, Abhishek Bhandari 73; B Aparajith 3-43, K Vignesh 2-56) and 209/3 in 57.1 overs (Mukul Raghav 114, Shubham Sharma 30) by seven wickets.

Mumbai and Madhya Pradesh qualified for the final

Final

Holkar Stadium, Indore, February 28-March 3: Mumbai 577 in 188.5 overs (Jay Bista 217, Eknath Kerkar 102*; Venkatesh Iyer 3-118, Ashutosh Singh 2-4) drew with **Madhya Pradesh** 442 in 171.5 overs (Shubham Sharma 131, Saransh Jain 85; Tushar Deshpande 5-143, Akash Parkar 4-77). Mumbai won on the basis of first-innings lead.

Winners: Mumbai

Under-19 Vinoo Mankad Tournament

Pant, Rangi raise the bar

SIDHANTA PATNAIK

Rishab Pant, seen here turning out for Delhi Daredevils in the IPL, stood out with a strike-rate of 154.40 in the U-19 one-day games. – *BCCI*

Delhi, Uttar Pradesh and Mumbai remained unbeaten in their respective zones, while Andhra and Odisha topped the table in South and East. Rishabh Pant, Delhi's wicketkeeper-batsman, made a strong impression with a hundred and three half-centuries, maintaining an average of 90 and a strike-rate of 154.40 across four innings. Pant's 129, Himmat Singh's 130, and fifties from Sarthak Ranjan and Utkarsh Singh helped Delhi put on a massive 454 for 5 in 50 overs against Jammu & Kashmir for a 304-run win in Mohali. Apart from Pant, Himachal Pradesh's Digvijay Rangi was the only other batsman to cross the 300-run mark. He also recorded the highest individual score of the tournament, his 153 standing out in a 26-run win over Haryana. Delhi had another top performer in Yogesh Sharma, the left-arm spinner, who got his wickets at an average of 9.46. Zeeshan Ansari, the Uttar Pradesh legspinner, produced the best spell, taking 6 for 28 in a six-wicket win over Rajasthan in Bhubaneswar.

Best batsman: Rishabh Pant (Delhi) (360 runs, 4 matches)
Best bowler: Yogesh Sharma (Delhi) (15 wickets, 4 matches)

North Zone

Sector 16 Stadium, Chandigarh, October 1: Himachal Pradesh 167 in 48.5 overs (Shubham Arora 49, Nitin Sharma 25, Abhimanyu Singh 25; Yogesh Sharma 3-34, Vishvash Malik 2-23) lost to **Delhi** 169/3 in 28 overs (Rishabh Pant 91, Himmat Singh 35*; Chahat Malhotra 2-20) by seven wickets.

Dhruve Pandove Stadium, Patiala, October 1: Jammu & Kashmir 164/9 in 50 overs (Mohammad Haziq Bhat 53, Tahsin Dar 37; Prerit Dutta 3-23, Jagjit Singh 2-21) lost to **Punjab** 165/4 in 29.4 overs (Shubham Gill 74*, Anmolpreet Singh 37; Tribhuvan Singh Sambyal 2-3) by six wickets.

Sector 16 Stadium, Chandigarh, October 3: Haryana 185 in 49.3 overs (Shubham Rohilla

51, SD Dhull 50*; Yogesh Sharma 5-23, Sumit Mathur 2-28) lost to **Delhi** 186/4 in 34 overs (Rishabh Pant 62, Jonty Sidhu 52*; SD Aggarwal 3-44) by six wickets.

Dhruve Pandove Stadium, Patiala, October 3: Punjab 257/8 in 50 overs (Anmolpreet Singh 69, Sanvir Singh 53; Ayush Jamwal 2-28, Mayank Dagar 2-54) beat **Himachal Pradesh** 148 in 45 overs (Mayank Dagar 55*, Digvijay Rangi 27; Prerit Dutta 3-24, Pratap Pandove 2-32) by 109 runs.

PCA Stadium, Mohali, October 5: Haryana 288/8 in 50 overs (Shivam Chauhan 94, Mohit Hooda 52; Tribhuvan Singh Sambyal 3-48, Nair Muzaffar 3-75) beat **Jammu & Kashmir** 115 in 31.5 overs (Shubham Pundir 35, Nipun Verma 27; SD Aggarwal 4-23, Arun Bamal 2-9) by 173 runs.

Dhruve Pandove Stadium, Patiala, October 5: Punjab 144 in 40.4 overs (Anmolpreet Singh 48, Shubham Gill 22; Nitin Tanwar 5-12, Vishvash Malik 2-27) lost to **Delhi** 148/3 in 19.2 overs (Rishabh Pant 78, Sarthak Ranjan 42; Pratap Pandove 2-36) by seven wickets.

PCA IS Bindra Stadium, Mohali, October 7: Delhi 454/5 in 50 overs (Himmat Singh 130, Rishabh Pant 129; Shahbaz Ali 3-93) beat **Jammu & Kashmir** 150/9 in 50 overs (Shubham Pundir 41, Abhishek Khajuria 35; Yogesh Sharma 5-48) by 304 runs.

Sector 16 Stadium, Chandigarh, October 7: Himachal Pradesh 310/7 in 50 overs (Digvijay Rangi 153, MZ Khan 50; D Raghav 3-61, SD Dhull 2-47) beat **Haryana** 281 in 49.1 overs (Shubham Rohilla 93, Mohit Hooda 72; Mayank Dagar 4-66, Khushpal Singh 2-22) by 29 runs.

PCA IS Bindra Stadium, Mohali, October 9: Himachal Pradesh 266 in 46.1 overs (Digvijay Rangi 109, Shubham Arora 52; Momin Mansoor 3-45, Aman Sharma 2-46) beat **Jammu & Kashmir** 69 in 19.5 overs (Jagandeep Singh 26; Mayank Dagar 4-11, Ayush Jamwal 4-17) by 197 runs.

Dhruve Pandove Stadium, Patiala, October 9: Haryana 229/7 in 50 overs (SD Dhull 74*, MR Choudhary 33; Prerit Dutta 4-37) lost to **Punjab** 230/7 in 49 overs (Shubham Gill 96, Ikjot Singh Thind 27; Shubham Rohilla 3-35) by three wickets.

North Zone Points Table

Teams	M	W	L	NR	T	A	Pts	Q
Delhi	4	4	0	0	0	0	16	4.057
Punjab	4	3	1	0	0	0	12	0.386
Himachal Pradesh	4	2	2	0	0	0	8	0.095
Haryana	4	1	3	0	0	0	4	0.319
Jammu & Kashmir	4	0	4	0	0	0	0	-4.039

Central Zone

KIIT Ground, Bhubaneswar, October 1: Uttar Pradesh 288/7 in 50 overs (Rinku Singh 101, Priyam Garg 50*; Naman Dhruw 3-48, Ashish Pandey 2-56) beat **Chhattisgarh** 192 in 46.2 overs (MSS Hussain 51, Shubham Singh 35, PV Malewar 35; Shubham Mavi 3-38, Shhivam Chaudhary 2-21) by 96 runs.

ECRSA Ground, Bhubaneswar, October 1: Madhya Pradesh 253/9 in 50 overs (Yash Dubey 69, Ankush Singh 50, Abhishek Pathak 50; Vijay Singh 4-37, Yuvraj 3-31) beat **Railways** 187 in 49.4 overs (Yuvraj 65, Karan Mahajan 45*; Pawan Dhakad 3-41, Apurva Purohit 3-42) by 66 runs.

ECRSA Ground, Bhubaneswar, October 2: Vidarbha 194 in 49.5 overs (Mohit Kale 41, Ankur Wakode 38; Shubham Singh 3-29, Ashish Pandey 2-21) lost to **Chhattisgarh** 173/2 in

44 overs (Amandeep Khare 78*, PV Malewar 68*) by 21 runs (VJD method).
KIIT Ground, Bhubaneswar, October 2: Rajasthan 201/8 in 50 overs (Salman Khan 100*, Kartikeya Choudhary 23; Apurva Purohit 2-27, Ritesh Shakya 2-27) beat **Madhya Pradesh** 140/6 in 40 overs (Rahul Batham 41*, Yash Dubey 22; Mahipal Lomror 2-18) by 16 runs (VJD method).
ECRSA Ground, Bhubaneswar, October 4: Vidarbha 283/7 in 50 overs (Ankur Wakode 81, Pramod Wagh 66; AB Choudhary 3-49) beat **Railways** 131 in 37.1 overs (Saif Ali Khan 31*, S Mittal 26; Mohit Raut 3-18) by 152 runs.
KIIT Ground, Bhubaneswar, October 4: Rajasthan 153 in 48.4 overs (Salman Khan 58, Kartikeya Choudhary 28; Zeeshan Ansari 6-28) lost to **Uttar Pradesh** 155/4 in 35.5 overs (Rahul Rawat 56*, Priyam Garg 47*; Rahul Tomar 2-11) by six wickets.
KIIT Ground, Bhubaneswar, October 5: Chhattisgarh 181 in 49.1 overs (Amandeep Khare 102, Ashish Pandey 28; Shubham Sharma 3-17, Mahipal Lomror 3-37) lost to **Rajasthan** 185/2 in 41.4 overs (Kartikeya Choudhary 104*, Amit Rajera 46) by eight wickets.
ECRSA Ground, Bhubaneswar, October 5: Railways 179 in 50 overs (S Mittal 54, Yuvraj 44; Shanu Saini 4-30, Kartikey Kushwaha 2-38) lost to **Uttar Pradesh** 182/4 in 38.1 overs (Shivam Chaudhary 76, Rinku Singh 70; Yuvraj 2-27, AB Choudhary 2-52) by six wickets.
KIIT Ground, Bhubaneswar, October 7: Madhya Pradesh v **Uttar Pradesh**. Match abandoned.
ECRSA Ground, Bhubaneswar, October 7: Railways v **Chhattisgarh**. Match abandoned.
KIIT Ground, Bhubaneswar, October 8: Madhya Pradesh 207/5 in 42 overs (Yash Dubey 44, Siddharth Patidar 35; Gagandeep Singh 2-29) lost to **Chhattisgarh** 171/6 in 36 overs (Amandeep Khare 53, PV Malewar 39; Apurva Purohit 3-34, Ritesh Shakya 2-26) by 3 runs (VJD method).
ECRSA Ground, Bhubaneswar, October 8: Rajasthan 215/3 in 42 overs (Salman Khan 94*, Kartikeya Choudhary 64; Parth Rekhade 2-41) beat **Vidarbha** 147/6 in 42 overs (Pavan Parnate 41, Mohit Kale 40*; Pradeep Jakhar 4-34) by 68 runs.
ECRSA Ground, Bhubaneswar, October 10: Rajasthan 192/9 in 45 overs (Mahipal Lomror 68, Kamlesh Nagarkoti 29; Rakhan 4-27, Yuvraj 2-38) beat **Railways** 91 in 35 overs (Mahipal Lomror 2-8, Vikas Jhorar 2-12) by 101 runs.
KIIT Ground, Bhubaneswar, October 10: Vidarbha 183 in 45.4 overs (Pavan Parnate 41, Mohit Raut 31; Kartikey Kushwaha 3-24, Shubham Mavi 2-35) lost to **Uttar Pradesh** 184/3 in 41.5 overs (Madhav Kaushik 72*, Rinku Singh 60; Darshan Nalkande 2-42) by seven wickets.
ECRSA Ground, Bhubaneswar, October 11: Madhya Prdesh 220 in 47.1 overs (Abhishek Pathak 90, Yash Dubey 73; Mohit Raut 3-37, Parth Rekhade 3-38) beat **Vidarbha** 175 in 44.2 overs (Ankur Wakode 66, Siddhesh Wath 55; Ritesh Shakya 3-16, Apurva Purohit 3-28) by 45 runs.

Central Zone Points Table

Teams	M	W	L	NR	T	A	Pts	Q
Uttar Pradesh	5	4	0	0	0	1	18	1.343
Rajasthan	5	4	1	0	0	0	16	0.766
Madhya Pradesh	5	2	2	0	0	1	10	0.523
Chhattisgarh	5	2	2	0	0	1	10	-0.636
Vidarbha	5	1	4	0	0	0	4	-0.073
Railways	5	0	4	0	0	1	2	-2.013

West Zone

Sachin Tendulkar Gymkhana Ground, Mumbai, October 6: Saurashtra 213/8 in 50 overs (Harvik Desai 67, Kevin Jivrajani 25; Shubham Kothari 3-28, Paras Ratnaparkhe 2-17) lost to **Maharashtra** 214/1 in 38.4 overs (Paras Ratnaparkhe 102*, Sourabh Jagdale 86*) by nine wickets.

Bandra Kurla Complex, Mumbai, October 6: Mumbai 260 in 45 overs (Hridayesh Pawar 64, Hardik Tamore 45; Shivalik Sharma 5-35, Mistry Milan 2-44) beat **Baroda** 258/9 in 45 overs (Shivalik 78, Mitesh Patel 50; Shams Mulani 4-57, Arman Jaffer 2-33) by two runs.

Sachin Tendulkar Gymkhana Ground, Mumbai, October 7: Gujarat 281/9 in 50 overs (Raj Majithia 79, Kathan Patel 73; Dhruv Patel 4-42, Mistry Milan 2-72) beat **Baroda** 128 in 38.3 overs (Shivalik Sharma 48; Aasav Panchal 3-32, Karan Trivedi 2-3) by 153 runs.

Bandra Kurla Complex, Mumbai, October 7: Mumbai 344/6 in 50 overs (Arman Jaffer 119, Adeeb Usmani 110; Prabha Sindhav 3-84, Saurish Chakraborty 2-98) beat **Saurashtra** 99 in 30.2 overs (Niket Joshi 31, Kevin Jivrajani 25; Sidak Singh 5-9, Aditya Shinde 3-31) by 245 runs.

Bandra Kurla Complex, Mumbai, October 9: Maharashtra 185 in 41 overs (Paras Ratnaparkhe 53, Ruturaj Gaikwad 35; Jyotsnil Singh 3-7, Abbasali Momin 3-36) lost to **Baroda** 186/6 in 41.4 overs (Shivalik Sharma 47, AV Singh 39; Sunil Sonawane 2-30, Izhaan Sayed 2-40) by four wickets.

Sachin Tendulkar Gymkhana Ground, Mumbai, October 9: Gujarat 130 in 37.5 overs (Raj Majithia 50, Rahul Shah 23; Sidak Singh 4-24, Khizar Dafedar 3-15) lost to **Mumbai** 131/2 in 33.3 overs (Shams Mulani 60*, Arman Jaffer 53*) by eight wickets.

Bandra Kurla Complex, Mumbai, October 10: Saurashtra 173/7 in 50 overs (Jyortir Purohit 48, Abhal Karetha 34*; Kavish Panchal 2-34) beat **Gujarat** 172 in 46.1 overs (Rahul Shah 52, Karan Trivedi 22; Bilva Oza 3-43, Jyortir Purohit 2-10) by one run.

Sachin Tendulkar Gymkhana Ground, Mumbai, October 10: Mumbai 238/8 in 50 overs (Sairaj Patil 65*, Arman Jaffer 61; Utkarsh Agarwal 3-52, Izhaan Sayed 2-45) beat **Maharashtra** 156 in 40.3 overs (Omakar Bhawar 42, Sourabh Jagdale 30; Sidak Singh 3-12, Shams Mulani 3-29) by 82 runs.

Sachin Tendulkar Gymkhana Ground, Mumbai, October 12: Saurashtra 229/6 in 45 overs (Harvik Desai 74, Abhal Karetha 52*; Abbasali Momin 2-28, Shivalik Sharma 2-30) lost to **Baroda** 233/5 in 42.5 overs (Jyotsnil Singh 79, AV Singh 58; Mehul Chauhan 2-37) by five wickets.

Wankhede Stadium, Mumbai, October 12: Gujarat 227/7 in 50 overs (Karan Trivedi 89, Raj Majithia 51; Jaideep Bharade 3-41) beat **Maharashtra** 200 in 48 overs (Sourabh Jagdale 100, Izhaan Sayed 44; MA Hingrajia 2-22, Sumeet Gosain 2-42) by 27 runs.

West Zone Points Table

Teams	M	W	L	NR	T	A	Pts	Q
Mumbai	4	4	0	0	0	0	16	2.154
Gujarat	4	2	2	0	0	0	8	0.606
Baroda	4	2	2	0	0	0	8	-0.542
Maharashtra	4	1	3	0	0	0	4	-0.506
Saurashtra	4	1	3	0	0	0	4	-1.644

South Zone

Sanatana Dharma College Ground, Alappuzha, October 3: Tamil Nadu 141/6 in 26 overs (Vishal Vaidhya 38*, Washington Sundar 29; Karthik Raman 2-25) v **Andhra**. No result.
Rajagiri School of Engineering and Technology Ground, Ernakulam, October 3: Goa vs **Karnataka**, Match abandoned
St Paul's College Ground, Kochi, October 3: Kerala v Hyderabad. Match abandoned.
Rajagiri School of Engineering and Technology Ground, Ernakulam, October 4: Andhra vs **Goa**. Match abandoned.
Sanatana Dharma College Ground, Alappuzha, October 4: Hyderabad vs Tamil Nadu. Match abandoned
St Paul's College Ground, Kochi, October 4: Kerala v Karnataka. Match abandoned
Port Trust Golden Jubliee Stadium, Visakhapatnam, October 9: Tamil Nadu 240/5 in 50 overs (Washington Sundar 68, Suresh Lokeshwar 67; Surendra Krishna Chimata 2-51) beat **Andhra** 190 in 43.3 overs (Girinath Reddy 36, Dhruva Kumar Reddy 30; MS Sanjay 3-34, Sai Kishore 2-27) by 50 runs.
Vizzy Stadium, Vizianagram, October 9: Karnataka 243 in 43.5 overs (Devdatt Padikkal 85, BR Sharath 58; Neeraj Yadav 4-57, Suyash Prabhudessai 3-21) beat **Goa** 199 in 45.4 overs (Ishan Gadekar 88, Kashyap Bakhle 22; K Shashank 3-40, D Padikkal 2-19) by 44 runs.
Dr YS Rajasekhara Reddy ACA-VDCA Cricket Stadium, Visakhapatnam, October 9: Kerala 202 in 49.4 overs (Salman Nizar 55, Rohan Kunnummal 35; Abhirath Reddy 3-35, Vittal Anurag 2-25) beat **Hyderabad** 191 in 49.3 overs (Abhirath Reddy 49, B Rahul 41; Sijomon Joseph 5-25, SF Daryl 2-42) by 11 runs.
Dr YS Rajasekhara Reddy ACA-VDCA Cricket Stadium, Visakhapatnam, October 10: Goa 102 in 43.1 overs (Tunish Sawkar 22; Girish Karamala 3-7, Krishna Chimata 2-14) lost to **Andhra** 103/3 in 23.4 overs (D Chaitanya 35*, Karan Shinde 28*; Neeraj Yadav 2-23) by seven wickets.
Port Trust Golden Jubliee Stadium, Visakhapatnam, October 10: Hyderabad 190 in 50 overs (N Sandeep Goud 78*, Abhirath Reddy 28; MS Sanjay 4-35, Washington Sundar 3-25) lost to **Tamil Nadu** 194/2 in 43.3 overs (Washington 135*, Vishal Vaidhya 28*) by eight wickets.
Vizzy Stadium, Vizianagram, October 10: Karnataka 242/8 in 50 overs (P Vishnu 73*, Likhit Bannur 39; NP Basil 2-37, Fazil Fanoos 2-68) beat **Kerala** 222 in 47.5 overs (Maruthungal Ajinas 61, Albin Alias 60; Nikin Jose 2-27, Likhit Bannur 2-39) by 20 runs.
Dr YS Rajasekhara Reddy ACA-VDCA Cricket Stadium, Visakhapatnam, October 12: Andhra 213 in 49.2 overs (Karan Shinde 89, Dhruva Kumar Reddy 29; S Punith 3-29, Vyshak Vijaykumar 3-39) beat **Karnataka** 170 in 45.1 overs (BR Sharath 58, Nikin Jose 37; Reddy Girish Karamala 5-26, Girinath Reddy 2-29) by 43 runs.
Port Trust Golden Jubliee Stadium, Visakhapatnam, October 12: Hyedrabad 216 in 48.1 overs (Mickel Jaiswal 117, Abhirath Reddy 34; Suyash Prabhudessai 4-38, Savio Kaalko 3-53) beat **Goa** 154 in 31.2 overs (Deepraj Gaonkar 103, Ishan Gadekar 29; Rajamani Prasad 5-26, Mickel Jaiswal 3-20) by 62 runs.
Vizzy Stadium, Vizianagram, October 12: Kerala 165 in 49.5 overs (SF Daryl 36, Sijomon Joseph 28*; Suresh Aravind 5-27, Washington Sundar 2-27) lost to **Tamil Nadu** 167/8 in 45.4 overs (Vishal Vaidhya 47, Gunti Vignesh 47; SF Daryl 3-34, Fazil Fanoos 2-25) by two wickets.
Port Trust Golden Jubliee Stadium, Visakhapatnam, October 13: Andhra 312/6 in 50 overs (Maheep Kumar 70, Karan Shinde 69; Fazil Fanoos 2-59, NP Basil 2-73) beat **Kerala** 289/9 in 50 overs (SF Daryl 83, Rohan Kunnummal 78; Manish Golamaru 2-35, Girish Karamala 2-50) by 23 runs.
Dr YS Rajasekhara Reddy ACA-VDCA Cricket Stadium, Visakhapatnam, October 13: Goa 70 in 37.4 overs (Sai Kishore 4-12, Suresh Aravind 3-4) lost to **Tamil Nadu** 74/3 in 11.5 overs (Washington Sundar 51; Savio Kaalko 2-16) by seven wickets.

Vizzy Stadium, Vizianagram, October 13: Karnataka 172 in 48.2 overs (Vyshak Vijaykumar 49, Sujay Sateri 32; Mickel Jaiswal 3-36, Chandan Sahani 2-14) beat **Hyderabad** 169 in 48.4 overs (B Rahul 50, Sreecharan Edupuganty 33; Vyshak 4-29, S Chethan 4-41) by three runs.
Port Trust Golden Jubliee Stadium, Visakhapatnam, October 15: Andhra 295/9 in 50 overs (Dhruva Kumar Reddy 89, Karan Shinde 82; Mickel Jaiswal 4-54, Pabba Nilesh 3-50) beat **Hyderabad** 209 in 49.5 overs (B Rahul 55, Sreecharan Edupuganty 36; Manish Golamaru 3-29, Girish Karamala 3-43) by 86 runs.
Vizzy Stadium, Vizianagram, October 15: Goa 194/9 in 49 overs (Suyansh Prabhudessai 64, Aditya Suryawanshi 29*; SF Daryl 3-26, Vishnu Mohan 2-32) lost to **Kerala** 195/4 in 44.5 overs (Albin Alias 46, Rohan Kunnummal 43; Neeraj Yadav 2-28) by six wickets.
Dr YS Rajasekhara Reddy ACA-VDCA Cricket Stadium, Visakhapatnam, October 15: Tamil Nadu 170 in 47.3 overs (Vishal Vaidhya 54, Gunti Vignesh 42; S Chethan 3-32, Likhit Bannur 2-24) lost to **Karnataka** 173/7 in 19.2 overs (P Vishnu 70*, BR Sharath 44; MS Sanjay 4-49) by three wickets.

South Zone Points Table

Teams	M	W	L	NR	T	A	Pts	Q
Andhra	5	4	1	0	0	0	16	0.936
Karnataka	5	4	1	0	0	0	16	0.667
Tamil Nadu	5	4	1	0	0	0	16	0.611
Kerala	5	2	3	0	0	0	8	-0.138
Hyderabad	5	1	4	0	0	0	4	-0.277
Goa	5	0	5	0	0	0	0	-1.721

East Zone

Bengal Cricket Academy Ground, Kalyani, October 3: Odisha 239/9 in 50 overs (Sandeep Pattanaik 49, Preeyatam Singh 49; Mrinmoy Dutta 3-31, Avinav Choudhury 3-51) lost to **Assam** 241/3 in 46.5 overs (Sahil Jain 86*, Abhishek Thakuri 57) by seven wickets.
Jadavpur University Complex, Kolkata, October 3: Jharkhand 212/6 in 46.2 overs (Anukul Roy 62, Kumar Suraj 39; Viki Saha 2-40) vs **Tripura** Match abandoned.
Jadavpur University Complex, Kolkata, October 3: Tripura 138 in 39.4 overs (Rajat Dey 34; Mrinmoy Dutta 4-51) lost to **Assam** 142/7 in 43.3 overs (Riyan Parag 54, Subham Mandal 30; Tapash Mandal 3-33, Subham Ghosh 2-27) by three wickets.
Bengal Cricket Academy Ground, Kalyani, October 5: Odisha 218 in 49.4 overs (Soubhagya Ranjan Mishra 46, Saurabh Rawat 42; Kanishk Seth 4-35, Ishan Porel 3- 53) beat **Bengal** 186 in 47.2 overs (Agniv Pan 56*, Avijit Singh 41; Anurag Prusty 3-50, Subham Nayak 2-28) by 32 runs.
Bengal Cricket Academy Ground, Kalyani, October 7: Bengal 275/9 in 50 overs (Avijit Singh 84, Agniv Pan 81; Ayan Chaudhari 3-45, Istekhar Ahmad 2-36) beat **Jharkhand** 123 in 33.3 overs (Anukul Roy 35, Rakesh Yadav 26; Pradipta Pramanik 3-33, Kanishk Seth 2-17) by 152 runs.
Jadavpur University Complex, Kolkata, October 7: Odisha 247/9 in 50 overs (Saurabh Rawat 56, Subhranshu Senapati 38; Apurba Biswas 4-46, Arjun Debnath 2-67) beat **Tripura** 147 in 47.2 overs (Rajat Dey 41, Arjun Debnath 20, Subham Ghosh 20, Shyamshakil Gan 20; Subham Nayak 3-31, Anurag Prusty 3-34) by 100 runs.
Bengal Cricket Academy Ground, Kalyani, October 9: Jharkhand 215/9 in 50 overs (Amit

Kumar 43, Wilfred Beng 42; Mrinmoy Dutta 4-31, Avinav Choudhury 3-46) beat **Assam** 127 in 48 overs (Mrinmoy Dutta 31; Aditya Singh 3-21, Istekhar Ahmad 3-25) by 88 runs.
Jadavpur University Complex, Kolkata, October 9: Tripura 223 in 49.5 overs (Rajat Dey 104, Subham Ghosh 42; Ankit Mishra 2-39, Ananta Saha 2-45) beat **Bengal** 169 in 41 overs (Subham Saha 39, Pradipta Pramanik 34; Viki Saha 4-32, Subham Ghosh 2-22) by 54 runs.
Bengal Cricket Academy Ground, Kalyani, October 11: Assam 202/9 in 50 overs (Mujibur Ali 60, Yasir Ali 49; Pradipta Pramanik 3-30, Ananta Saha 2-39) lost to **Bengal** 206/3 in 46.5 overs (Kazi Junad Saifi 92, Arindam Ghosh 70*; Mrinmoy Dutta 2-37) by seven wickets.
Eden Gardens, Kolkata, October 11: Jharkhand 211 in 49.5 overs (Amit Kumar 65, Bhanu Anand 55; Ashutosh Das 4-45, Rajkishan Patel 3-39) lost to **Odisha** 215/4 in 44.5 overs (Sandeep Pattnaik 96*, Satyajit Sabat 36; Anand Tiwari 2-40) by six wickets.

East Zone Points Table

Teams	M	W	L	NR	T	A	Pts	Q
Odisha	4	3	1	0	0	0	12	0.729
Bengal	4	2	2	0	0	0	8	0.417
Assam	4	2	2	0	0	0	8	-0.313
Tripura	4	1	2	1	0	0	6	-0.502
Jharkhand	4	1	2	1	0	0	6	-0.600

Under-19 Vinoo Mankad Trophy Inter-Zone Tournament

Khare, Ansari keep Central spotless

SIDHANTA PATNAIK

A prolific run-getter at the age-group level, Chhattisgarh's Amandeep Khare yet again stamped his class with two hundreds and as many fifties as Central Zone won all their four matches to top the table. East Zone's Sandeep Pattnaik, the next best batsman, was over 100 runs behind at 290. Khare recorded the top two individual scores of the competition: 142 against East Zone and 139 not out against West Zone. Zeeshan Ansari, who carried his good form from the inter-state competition, supported Khare, picking up his wickets at an average of 8.21. North Zone's Mayank Dagar also picked up 14 wickets, at an average of 11.42. The best match of the tournament was on the first day when South Zone chased 200 against North Zone with just one wicket and two balls to spare.

Best batsman: Amandeep Khare (Central Zone) (404 runs, 4 matches)
Best bowler: Zeeshan Ansari (Central Zone) (14 wickets, 4 matches)

DRIEMS Ground, Tangi, Cuttack, October 17: Central Zone 310/5 in 50 overs (Amandeep Khare 139*, Shivam Chaudhary 88; SZ Mulani 2-71) beat **West Zone** 118 in 29.5 overs (AW Usmani 30, SZ Mulani 25*; Zeeshan Ansari 4-20, SKK Ahmed 2-22) by 192 runs.

Ravenshaw College Ground, Cuttack, October 17: North Zone 199 in 46.4 overs (Himmat Singh 66, Shubham Rohilla 49*; Karthik Raman 3-23, Fazil Fanoos 2-34) lost to **South Zone** 200/9 in 49.4 overs (Salman Nizar 37, K Raman 25*; Mayank Dagar 5-25, Yogesh Sharma 2-29) by one wicket.

Ravenshaw College Ground, Cuttack, October 18: Central Zone 213 in 49.1 overs (Amandeep Khare 142; Mrinmoy Dutta 4-60, Ashutosh Das 2-28) beat **East Zone** 76 in 24.4 overs (Sandeep Pattanaik 47; Zeeshan Ansari 5-16, Shubham Sharma 2-21) by 137 runs.

Prolific run-getter for Central Zone: Two hundreds and two fifties for Chhattisgarh's Amandeep Khare.
– BCCI

DRIEMS Ground, Tangi, Cuttack, October 18: North Zone 270/7 in 50 overs (Sarthak Ranjan 96, Nitin Tanwar 46; Sidak Singh 4-42) beat **West Zone** 250 in 48 overs (Raj Majithia 78, Ruturaj Gaikwad 72; Mayank Dagar 5-45, Yogesh Sharma 3-33) by 20 runs.

Ravenshaw College Ground, Cuttack, October 20: North Zone 223 in 48 overs (Sarthak Ranjan 96, Himmat Singh 34; Zeeshan Ansari 3-47, Shubham Mavi 2-34) lost to **Central Zone** 227/2 in 48.4 overs (Rinku Singh 78*, Amandeep Khare 61*; Yogesh Sharma 2-42) by eight wickets.

DRIEMS Ground, Tangi, Cuttack, October 20: East Zone 271/8 in 50 overs (Sandeep Pattanaik 79, Agniv Pan 54; Karthik Raman 3-61, MS Sanjay 2-44) beat **South Zone** 247 in 49.2 overs (Washington Sundar 55, BR Sharath 52; Viki Saha 4-43, Ashutosh Das 2-49) by 24 runs.

Ravenshaw College Ground, Cuttack, October 21: North Zone 300/6 in 50 overs (Digvijay Rangi 115, Himmat Singh 89; Kazi Junaid Saifi 3-29) beat **East Zone** 190 in 42.2 overs (Sandeep Pattanaik 62, Yasir Ali 43; Mayank Dagar 4-33, Anmolpreet Singh 3-35) by 110 runs.

DRIEMS Ground, Tangi, Cuttack, October 21: South Zone 269/5 in 50 overs (Vishal Vaidhya 85*, Washington Sundar 77; Sidak Singh 2-58) lost to **West Zone** 270/4 in 48.4 overs (AW Usmani 79, Arman Jaffer 70; R Sai Kishore 2-41, Karthik Raman 2-51) by six wickets.

Ravenshaw College Ground, Cuttack, October 23: Central Zone 301/5 in 50 overs (Mahipal Lomror 110, Amandeep Khare 62; Washington Sundar 2-63) beat **South Zone** 219/8 in 50 overs (P Vishnu 83, Salman Nizar 48; Rahul Batham 3-49, Zeeshan Ansari 2-32) by 82 runs.

DRIEMS Ground, Tangi, Cuttack, October 23: West Zone 265/8 in 50 overs (Arman Jaffer 85, Paras Ratnaparkhe 44; Subham Nayak 2-43, Mrinmoy Dutta 2-53) beat **East Zone** 238 in 47.2 overs (Sandeep Pattanaik 102, Yasir Ali 36; Sumeet Gosain 3-31, Arman Jaffer 2-17) by 27 runs.

Points table

Teams	M	W	L	T	A	Pts	Q
Central Zone	4	4	0	0	0	16	2.110
North Zone	4	2	2	0	0	8	0.589
West Zone	4	2	2	0	0	8	-0.890
South Zone	4	1	3	0	0	4	-0.557
East Zone	4	1	3	0	0	4	-1.250

Winners: Central Zone

Under-19 Challenger Trophy

Bhui leads from the front

AJAY SURESH

Ricky Bhui's match-winning 142 for India Blue against India Green in the final was the highlight of the inaugural edition of the Under-19 Challenger Trophy. The tournament was meant to facilitate team selection for the Under-19 World Cup in Bangladesh. With his team 9 for 2, Bhui, fresh off his maiden first-class century in a Ranji Trophy match for Andhra against Mumbai, built solid partnerships and took on the bowlers in the later stages. He ended as the leading run-scorer in the tournament and attributed his achievements to Rahul Dravid's advice, and the responsibility he took as captain of the team. Washington Sundar, Anmolpreet Singh, Aavesh Khan, Mahipal Lomror, Rahul Batham, Shubham Mavi and Amandeep Khare were some of the other performers who impressed the junior selection committee headed by Venkatesh Prasad.

MCA Stadium, Pune, October 28: India Blue 207/9 in 50 overs (Washington Sundar 78, Anmolpreet Singh 61; Karthik Raman 3-26, Izhaan Sayed 2-32) lost to **India Red** 208/4 in 43.3 overs (Rinku Singh 94*, Mahipal Lomror 43; Rahul Batham 3-29) by six wickets.
MCA Stadium, Pune, October 29: India Red 109 in 30.3 overs (Mayank Dagar 21; Sumeet Gosain 4-18, Aavesh Khan 4-38) lost to **India Green** 112/5 in 30.4 overs (Himmat Singh 36*, Arman Jaffer 24; Karthik Raman 2-30) by five wickets.
MCA Stadium, Pune, October 30: India Green 283/9 in 50 overs (Sarfaraz Khan 103, Rishabh Pant 41; Shubham Mavi 3-41, Mrinmoy Dutta 2-29) lost to **India Blue** 285/8 in 49.1 overs (Amandeep Khare 93, Anmolpreet Singh 75; Kanishk Seth 2-44, Aavesh Khan 2-51) by two wickets.

Best batsman: Ricky Bhui (India Blue) (176 runs, 3 matches)
Best bowler: Aavesh Khan (India Green) (10 wickets, 3 matches)

Points Table

Team	P	W	L	Pts	NRR
India Green	2	1	1	4	0.924
India Blue	2	1	1	4	-0.290
India Red	2	1	1	4	-0.564

India Green and India Blue qualified for the final

Final

MCA Stadium, Pune, October 31: India Blue 282/8 in 50 overs (Ricky Bhui 142, Washington Sundar 71; Aavesh Khan 4-60, Kanishk Seth 2-41) beat **India Green** 257/9 in 50 overs (Himmat Singh 71, Arman Jaffer 49; Rahul Batham 5-35, Yogesh Sharma 2-41) by 25 runs.

Winners: India Blue

Under-19 Cooch Behar Trophy

Arman Jaffer proves a point

AJAY SURESH

Having failed to impress the junior national selectors in the Challenger Trophy, Arman Jaffer, the nephew of Wasim Jaffer, turned heads with a massive show in the Cooch Behar Trophy. His sequence of scores read 56, 174, 224, 223, 218 not out, 83 and 40 as he aggregated 1018 runs at 169.16. He became the second batsman in the last two editions, after Anmolpreet Singh, to score more than 1000 runs. Although Mumbai failed to defend 443 against Uttar Pradesh in the final, Jaffer did enough to earn a place in the flight to Bangladesh. Uttar Pradesh rode on centuries from Madhav Kaushik, Rinku Singh and Shivam Chaudhury, the captain, to complete the job in 102.3 overs with three wickets to spare.

The mega batting show came after 24 wickets had fallen in a day in the semi-final clash between Baroda and Uttar Pradesh at the Moti Bagh Cricket Ground in Vadodara. Baroda had made it that far on the back of Ninad Rathva's 63 wickets.

Run-fest: Having conceded a first-innings lead, Uttar Pradesh came back strongly to lift the Under-19 Cooch Behar Trophy. — *BCCI*

Best batsman: Arman Jaffer (Mumbai) (1018 runs, 6 matches)
Best bowler: Ninad Rathva (Baroda) (63 wickets, 8 matches)

Group A

Alembic Ground, Vadodara, November 5-8: Baroda 347 in 108.3 overs (Ravindra Patel 86, Ninad Rathva 68*; Hridayesh Pawar 3-69, Arman Jaffer 2-7) and 283/7 in 90 overs (Jyotsnil Singh 119, Shlok Desai 51; Shams Mulani 3-70, A Jaffer 2-67) drew with **Mumbai** 682/6 dec in 159 overs (Adeeb Usmani 202, Prithvi Shaw 161, Hardik Tamore 112). Mumbai won on the basis of first-innings lead.

KSCA Ground, Alur, November 5-7: Vidarbha 126 in 53.2 overs (Mohit Kale 66, Hari 24; K Shashank 5-39, Ruchir Joshi 4-29) and 219 in 64 overs (M Kale 87*, Ankur Wakode 49; Vyshak Vijaykumar 3-55, R Joshi 3-71) lost to **Karnataka** 326 in 114.3 overs (Nikin Jose 97, Shivakumar 48; Aditya Thakare 4-43, Mohit Raut 3-60) and 21/0 in 5.1 overs by ten wickets.

DRIEMS Ground, Tangi, Cuttack, November 5-8: Madhya Pradesh 487/9 dec in 160 overs (Rahul Batham 157*, Arjun Patel 80; Anurag Prusty 3-106, Subham Nayak 3-136) beat **Odisha** 200 in 57.4 overs (Rajkishan Patel 67, Subrat Samal 53; Arshad Khan 3-48, Nikhil Sikarwar 3-50) and 169 in 90.1 overs (f/o) (Saurabh Rawat 41, S Samal 36; Pawan Dhakad 4-12, R Batham 2-9) by an innings and 118 runs.

DR Bendre KSCA Stadium, Hubli, November 14-17: Odisha 235 in 102.1 overs (Biswajit Bhuyan 60, Subhranshu Senapati 45; Likhit Bannur 5-76, K Shashank 2-36) and 341/6 dec in 116.4 overs (Subrat Samal 107, Rajkishan Patel 52*; L Bannur 2-78) drew with **Karnataka** 334 in 113.4 overs (Devdatt Padikkal 89, Nikin Jose 55; Debabrata Pradhan 4-99, Anurag Prusty 2-38) and 83/2 in 22 overs (N Jose 49*, D Padikkal 25; Gobinda Tanida 2-15). Karnataka won on the basis of first-innings lead.

MPCA Ground, Sagar, November 14-16: Madhya Pradesh 204 in 60.3 overs (Ankush Singh 42, Siddharth Patidar 37; Ninad Rathva 6-56, Shlok Desai 2-46) and 235 in 75.3 overs (Ankush 59, Krishna Soni 36; N Rathva 6-87, Shivalik Sharma 2-31) lost to **Baroda** 429 in 115.4 overs (Ravindra Patel 163, Jyotsnil Singh 99; Arshad Khan 3-63, Ritesh Shakya 3-78) and 11/0 in 3.4 overs by ten wickets.

Bandra Kurla Complex, Mumbai, November 14-16: Tripura 288 in 119.3 overs (Subham Ghosh 92*, Dipayan Debbarma 55; Minad Manjrekar 5-74, Shubham Pandey 2-23) and 71 in 22.5 overs (D Debbarma 22, Shyamshakil Gan 22; M Manjrekar 5-30, Khizar Dafedar 4-13) lost to **Mumbai** 497/9 dec in 114 overs (Arman Jaffer 174, Adeeb Usmani 102; Ajay Sarkar 5-121) by an innings and 138 runs.
Alembic Ground, Vadodara, November 21-24: Odisha 552/8 dec in 169 overs (Subhranshu Senapati 275*, Saurabh Rawat 158; Abbasali Momin 4-184, Ninad Rathva 2-122) drew with **Baroda** 553/7 in 177 overs (Mitesh Patel 228*, Dhruv Patel 83; Abinash Behera 2-90, Debabrata Pradhan 2-93). Baroda won on the basis of first-innings lead.
Maharaja Public School Ground, Rewa, November 21-24: Mumbai 677/9 in 129.1 overs (Arman Jaffer 224, Khizar Dafedar 173, Prithvi Shaw 107; Ritesh Shakya 6-152, Arshad Khan 2-106) drew with **Madhya Pradesh** 350 in 124.1 overs (Rahul Chandrol 95, Arjun Patel 72; Shams Mulani 5-68, Minad Manjrekar 4-85) and 245/2 in 86 overs (f/o) (Krishna Soni 120*, Yash Dubey 84). Mumbai won on the basis of first-innings lead.
Tripura Institute of Technology, Agartala, November 21-24: Vidarbha 429 in 155.4 overs (Siddhesh Wath 137, Hari 54; Viki Saha 6-112, Ajay Sarkar 2-87) drew with **Tripura** 214 in 96.2 overs (Rajat Dey 102, Tapash Mandal 33; Aditya Thakare 5-27, Parth Rekhade 2-54) and 266 in 103.4 overs (f/o) (R Dey 92, Dipayan Debbarma 43; Darshan Nalkande 4-36, P Rekhade 3-78, Mohit Raut 3-81). Vidarbha won on the basis of first-innings lead.
Maharaja Public School Ground, Rewa, November 28-December 1: Madhya Pradesh 170 in 52.4 overs (Ritesh Shakya 39, Arshad Khan 29; Aditya Thakare 4-36, Pramod Wagh 2-29) and 180 in 64.1 overs (Siddharth Patidar 63, R Shakya 40; A Thakare 6-48, Parth Rekhade 2-42) lost to **Vidarbha** 583 in 163.2 overs (Akshay Agarwal 98, David Shahare 79; Apruv Purohit 4-142, R Shakya 3-117) by an innings and 233 runs.
Bandra Kurla Complex, Mumbai, November 28-December 1: Odisha 248 in 109 overs (Subrat Samal 61, Biswajit Bhuyan 53; Sairaj Patil 3-34, Shams Mulani 3-39) and 283/2 in 133 overs (B Bhuyan 142*, Sandeep Pattanaik 60) drew with **Mumbai** 575/8 dec in 103.1 overs (Arman Jaffer 223, S Mulani 106; Gobinda Tandia 2-58, Debabrata Pradhan 2-104). Mumbai won on the basis of first-innings lead.
Tripura Institute of Technology, Agartala, November 28-30: Tripura 143 in 60.1 overs (Mitan Debbarma 36, Riman Saha 26; Vyshak Vijaykumar 3-52, Likhit Bannur 2-28) and 140 in 61.1 overs (M Debbarma 37, R Saha 22; Ruchir Joshi 4-24, K Shashank 2-30) lost to **Karnataka** 234 in 71.1 overs (L Bannur 48, Sujith Gowda 48; Viki Saha 4-69, Subham Ghosh 2-16) and 51/0 in 10.3 overs (BR Sharath 26*) by ten wickets.
Moti Bagh Stadium, Vadodara, December 5-7: Baroda 320 in 109 overs (Mitesh Patel 55, Jyotsnil Singh 48; Aditya Thakare 3-45, Parth Rekhade 3-84) and 20/0 in 8.5 overs beat **Vidarbha** 103 in 40.2 overs (David Shahare 49; Ninad Rathva 4-43, Dhruv Patel 2-3) and 236 in 79.4 overs (f/o) (Pramod Wagh 78, Mohit Kale 75; N Rathva 6-63, Dhruv 2-23) by ten wickets.
Srikantadatta Narasimha Raja Wadeyar Ground, Mysore, December 5-8: Karnataka 180 in 68.3 overs (Sujith Gowda 64, Likhit Bannur 38; Shubham Pandey 4-40, Arman Jaffer 3-35) and 204 in 120.5 overs (Nikin Jose 73, P Vishnu 46; Shams Mulani 4-42, Minad Manjrekar 4-59) lost to **Mumbai** 506/4 dec in 119 overs (A Jaffer 218*, S Mulani 117; L Bannur 2-101) by an innings and 122 runs.
Bhubananda Odisha School of Engineering Ground, Cuttack, December 5-8: Tripura 277 in 126.2 overs (Rajat Dey 76, Shyamshakil Gan 51; Subham Nayak 5-55, Ashutosh Das 2-34) and 200 in 77.3 overs (Dipayan Debbarma 62, Subham Ghosh 40; S Nayak 5-72, A Das 2-13) lost to **Odisha** 237 in 84.2 overs (Rajkishan Patel 78*, Subrat Samal 44; Tapash Mandal 3-58, Ajay Sarkar 2-42, JH Deb 2-42) and 241/5 in 53.5 overs (Raghunath Malla 75, Saurabh Rawat 40*; S Ghosh 2-38) by five wickets.
Alembic Ground, Vadodara, December 12-15: Baroda 436 in 119.5 overs (AV Singh 149, Mitesh Patel 94; BM Shreyas 5-121, Nikin Jose 2-12) and 147/6 in 37.5 overs (Jyotsnil Singh 49, Mitesh 30*; S Punith 3-28, Likhith Bannur 2-37) beat **Karnataka** 244 in 61.1 overs (BR

Sharath 103, Vyshak Vijaykumar 68*; Ninad Rathva 6-112) and 337 in 108.1 overs (f/o) (Devdatt Padikkal 124, N Jose 91; Shlok Desai 4-52, N Rathva 3-124) by four wickets.

Holkar Science College Ground, Indore, December 12-14: Madhya Pradesh 109 in 42.2 overs (Ashutosh Sharma 29, Rahul Chandrol 26; Viki Saha 6-53, Tapash Mandal 2-8) and 180 in 52.3 overs (Siddharth Patidar 105, R Chandrol 20; T Mandal 4-45, V Saha 3-61) beat **Tripura** 127 in 47.5 overs (Bikramjith Debnath 30, T Mandal 29; Ritesh Shakya 5-38, Kshitij Somkunwar 4-29) and 113 in 35.1 overs (Shyamshakil Gan 58; K Somkunwar 5-33, R Shakya 3-28) by 49 runs.

Bhubananda Odisha School of Engineering Ground, Cuttack, December 12-15:Odisha 146 in 58.5 overs (Sandeep Pattanaik 39, Saurabh Rawat 38; Ankur Wakode 3-9, Aditya Thakare 3-11, Parth Rekhade 3-47) and 194 in 86.1 overs (Biswajit Bhuyan 66, Subhranshu Senapati 51; P Rekhade 6-59, Parth Sagdeo 3-17) lost to **Vidarbha** 429 in 136.5 overs (Mohit Kale 148, A Wakode 148; Rajkishan Patel 4-105, Anurag Prusty 3-72) by an innings and 89 runs.

Holkar Science College Ground, Indore, December 19-22: Karnataka 160 in 76.5 overs (KG Aiyappa 34, Shivakumar 31; Kshitij Somkunwar 5-40, Ritesh Shakya 2-28) and 226 in 71.4 overs (Sujith Gowda 64, BR Sharath 36; Arshad Khan 5-49, R Shakya 2-29) lost to **Madhya Pradesh** 460/9 dec in 140.3 overs (Siddharth Patidar 100, Nikhil Sikarwar 61*; S Punith 3-131, BM Shreyas 2-97) by an innings and 74 runs.

Bandra Kurla Complex, Mumbai, December 19-21: Mumbai 318 in 89.5 overs (Shams Mulani 120, Arman Jaffer 83; Aditya Thakare 5-55, Pramod Wagh 3-32) and 222 in 56.5 overs (Sairaj Patil 60, S Mulani 43; Parth Rekhade 6-64, A Thakare 4-49) beat **Vidarbha** 269 in 67.1 overs (Mohit Kale 97, Siddhesh Wath 74; Khizar Dafedar 5-23, Minad Manjrekar 3-58) and 82 in 26.3 overs (Pavan Parnate 20*; M Manjrekar 6-26, Danish Rainy 3-50) by 189 runs.

Maharaja Bir Bikram College Stadium, Agartala, December 19-22: Baroda 370 in 123.4 overs (Ravindra Patel 80, Mitesh Patel 76; Viki Saha 5-99, Ajay Sarkar 3-78) and 215/6 dec in 61 overs (Ravindra 54, Dhruv Patel 43; A Sarkar 3-62, V Saha 2-51) beat **Tripura** 169 in 71.5 overs (Rajat Dey 56, Bikramjit Debnath 38; Ninad Rathva 5-74, Keyur Upadhyay 4-23) and 259 in 91.3 overs (R Dey 68, B Debnath 68; N Rathva 6-82, Shlok Desai 2-27) by 157 runs.

Group A Points Table

Teams	M	W	L	D	T	A	Pts	Q
Baroda	6	4	0	2	0	0	30	1.282
Mumbai	6	3	0	3	0	0	29	2.200
Madhya Pradesh	6	3	2	1	0	0	21	0.961
Vidarbha	6	2	3	1	0	0	17	1.148
Karnataka	6	2	3	1	0	0	17	0.805
Odisha	6	1	2	3	0	0	9	0.703
Tripura	6	0	5	1	0	0	1	0.590

Baroda and Mumbai qualified for the quarter-finals

Group B

Sardar Vallabhai Patel Stadium, Ahmedabad, November 5-8: Gujarat 575/6 dec in 163.2 overs (Raj Majithia 157, Kavish Panchal 140, Karan Trivedi 127; Devang Karamta 2-78) beat **Saurashtra** 143 in 65.2 overs (Mehul Chauhan 32, Niket Joshi 21; YD Kosamia 4-37, Sumeet Gosain 2-15) and 141 in 80.4 overs (f/o) (Yash Parekh 47, Priyajitsinh Chudasama 33; MA

Hingrajia 5-19, Aasav Panchal 4-39) by an innings and 291 runs.

Gandhi Memorial Science College Ground, Jammu, November 5-8: Jammu & Kashmir 178 in 63.4 overs (Sahil Lotra 59, Suryansh Raina 38; Praneeth Reddy 5-27, Nithesh Reddy 3-37) and 304 in 96 overs (Suryansh Raina 97, Mohammad Haziq Bhat 88*; Pabba Nilesh 4-39, N Reddy 2-78) lost to **Hyderabad** 201 in 57.3 overs (B Rahul 50*, N Reddy 41; Momin Mansoor 4-61, Sunil Kumar 3-16) and 287/6 in 87.5 overs (B Rahul 131*, Sai Pranay 61*; Abid Mangnoo 3-47, Auqib Nabi 2-70) by four wickets.

Dhruve Pandove Stadium, Patiala, November 5-8: Jharkhand 254 in 97.1 overs (Kumar Suraj 68*, Amit Kumar 50; Akul Pratap Pandove 5-78, Mayank Markande 3-69) and 114 in 42 overs (Anurag Sanjay 35; M Markande 3-42, Jaswinder Singh 2-12) lost to **Punjab** 366 in 133 overs (Ikjot Singh Thind 114*, Anmolpreet Singh 113; Anukul Roy 5-111, Ayan Chaudhari 3-86) and 4/0 in 0.2 overs by ten wickets.

Gymkhana Ground, Secunderabad, November 14-17: Hyderabad 290 in 103.4 overs (B Rahul 126, Nithesh Reddy 76; Anukul Roy 6-69, Ayan Chaudhari 2-49) and 178 in 94.5 overs (N Reddy 63, Abhirath Reddy 57; Himanshu Singh 5-82, Shubham Singh 3-23) lost to **Jharkhand** 505/6 dec in 126.2 overs (Kumar Suraj 239, Anurag Sanjay 91; Pabba Nilesh 2-94) by an innings and 37 runs.

Gandhi Memorial Science College Ground, Jammu, November 14-17: Punjab 310 in 89.2 overs (Ikjot Singh Thind 96, Sanvir Singh 70; Auqib Nabi 2-50, Momin Mansoor 2-55) and 209 in 74 overs (Mansab Gill 108*, IS Thind 35; Sunil Kumar 4-40, A Nabi 3-35) lost to **Jammu & Kashmir** 289 in 109.5 overs (Nipun Verma 66, A Nabi 52; Mayank Markande 5-53, Jagjit Singh 3-64) and 231/8 in 84.4 overs (Muneeb Munaf 50, Abid Mushtaq 39*; M Markande 4-76, Raman Bishnoi 3-63) by two wickets.

Madhavrao Scindia Cricket Ground, Rajkot, November 14-17: Tamil Nadu 449 in 135.4 overs (Vishal Vaidhya 150, Suresh Lokeshwar 102, Aditya Barooah 102; Devang Karamta 5-105, Prabha Sindhav 2-56) drew with **Saurashtra** 251 in 137.2 overs (Harvik Desai 93, Niket Joshi 85; Samruddh Bhat 6-40, Sai Kishore 3-65) and 198/4 in 67 overs (f/o) (H Desai 75, N Joshi 40*; S Kishore 2-49). Tamil Nadu won on the basis of first-innings lead.

Gymkhana Ground, Secunderabad, November 21-24: Saurashtra 528/8 dec in 176.5 overs (Harvik Desai 178, Niket Joshi 127, Abhal Karetha 100*; Abhirath Reddy 2-40, Pabba Nilesh 2-61) drew with **Hyderabad** 609/6 in 168.2 overs (Nithesh Reddy 238, A Reddy 141, B Rahul 121; Prabha Sindhav 2-128, Priyajitsinh Chudasama 2-133). Hyderabad won on the basis of first-innings lead.

Jethabhai Jhaverbhai College of Science Ground, Nadiad, November 21-23: Jammu & Kashmir 188 in 64.2 overs (Mohammad Haziq Bhat 92*, Nipun Verma 24; Aasav Panchal 4-49, Kavish Panchal 3-21) and 132 in 51.3 overs (Abid Mushtaq 37, MH Bhat 21; YD Kosamia 4-31, Kathan Patel 3-13) lost to **Gujarat** 247 in 83.3 overs (K Panchal 63, Rahul Shah 51; Sunil Kumar 3-51, A Mushtaq 3-64) and 76/2 in 32.4 overs (Raj Majithia 50; A Mushtaq 2-34) by eight wickets.

MA Chidambaram Stadium, Chepauk, Chennai, November 21-24: Tamil Nadu 179 in 83.3 overs (Suresh Lokeshwar 75, Suresh Aravind 52; Vinayak Vikram 4-75, Himanshu Singh 3-30) and 81/3 in 53 overs (S Aravind 29, G Vignesh 22; V Vikram 2-30) drew with **Jharkhand** 253/9 dec in 117.1 overs (Wilfred Beng 138, Anukul Roy 56; Sai Kishore 4-75, M Siddharth 3-64). Jharkhand won on the basis of first-innings lead.

Gymkhana Ground, Secunderabad, November 28-December 1: Gujarat 232 in 80.5 overs (Kavish Panchal 75, SN Thakor 60; Pabba Nilesh 3-49, Azmath Khan 2-34) and 269/7 dec in 141 overs (Rahul Shah 54, SN Thakor 44; Azmath 3-66, P Nilesh 2-52) drew with **Hyderabad** 259 in 107 overs (A Sai Pranay 42, Praneeth Reddy 41*; YD Kosamia 3-67, Kathan Patel 2-20) and 141/4 in 28 overs (B Rahul 42, Sai Pranay 27; Kathan 2-17). Hyderabad won on the basis of first-innings lead.

Dhruve Pandove Stadium, Patiala, November 28-30: Punjab 536/9 dec in 144 overs (Shubman Gill 263*, Mayank Markande 138; Jaganath Sinivas 5-79, Sai Kishore 2-137) beat **Tamil**

Nadu 71 in 45.1 overs (G Vignesh 28; Akul Pratap Pandove 5-22, Prerit Dutta 2-24) and 97 in 59.2 overs (f/o) (Suresh Lokeshwar 28; Jaswinder Singh 3-11, P Dutta 2-6) by an innings and 368 runs.

SCA Stadium, Rajkot, November 28-December 1: Saurashtra 422 in 160.5 overs (Harvik Desai 180, Priyajitsinh Chudasama 66; Sunil Kumar 4-100, Auqib Nabi 2-65) and 140/1 in 52 overs (Kevin Jivrajani 70, Yash Parekh 65*) drew with **Jammu & Kashmir** 365 in 143.3 overs (A Nabi 102, Momin Mansoor 100; Pranav Karia 6-117, Meet Dave 2-107). Saurashtra won on the basis of first-innings lead.

Sardar Vallabhai Patel Stadium, Valsad, December 5-8: Jharkhand 213 in 81 overs (Anurag Sanjay 83, Kumar Suraj 31; Aasav Panchal 3-41, Sumeet Gosain 2-38) and 208 in 90.4 overs (A Sanjay 45, Wilfred Beng 34; S Gosain 3-47, Aasav 2-40, MA Hingrajia 2-40) lost to **Gujarat** 455 in 154.1 overs (Kavish Panchal 113, Rahul Shah 82; Vinayak Vikram 3-115, Anukul Roy 2-66) by an innings and 34 runs.

Brabourne Stadium, Mumbai, December 5-8: Tamil Nadu 358 in 122.2 overs (Vishal Vaidhya 105, Jaganath Srinivas 62*; Momin Mansoor 3-67, Sunil Kumar 3-71) and 269 in 53.2 overs (Suresh Lokeshwar 73, Devendra Anchit 46; Auqib Nabi 5-81, M Mansoor 3-90) beat **Jammu & Kashmir** 374 in 101.5 overs (Shubham Pundir 178, Abid Mushtaq 58*; L Kiran Akash 5-114, MS Sanjay 2-51) and 229 in 68.1 overs (Fazil Rashid 84, S Pundir 29; Sai Kishore 5-54, Shankar Siddharth 2-7) by 24 runs.

Western Railway Ground, Rajkot, December 5-8: Saurashtra 354 in 140.4 overs (Harvik Desai 118, Niket Joshi 60; Ikjot Singh Thind 5-48, Akul Pratap Pandove 2-51) and 201/5 in 68 overs (H Desai 73, N Joshi 64*; Jagjit Singh 2-42) drew with **Punjab** 528 in 139.5 overs (Sanvir Singh 179, Karan Sharma 119; Pranav Karia 5-194, Jyotir Purohit 2-34). Punjab on won the basis of first-innings lead.

Dhruve Pandove Stadium, Patiala, December 12-13: Hyderabad 112 in 38 overs (Vikas Reddy 30, Chandan Sahani 27; Prerit Dutta 7-45) and 108 in 50.5 overs (Jaswinder Singh 4-16, P Dutta 3-24) lost to **Punjab** 211 in 57.2 overs (Ramandeep Singh 62, Pardeep Yadav 36; Vinith Reddy 4-49, Chandan Sahani 3-2) and 10/0 in 1.4 overs by ten wickets.

Western Railway Ground, Rajkot, December 12-15: Saurashtra 401 in 173 overs (Kevin Jivrajani 80, Niket Joshi 78; Himanshu Singh 4-100, Vinayak Vikram 3-105) drew with **Jharkhand** 188 in 108 overs (Amit Kumar 69, Sushant Singh 43; Meet Dave 5-50, Arjun Rathod 2-28) and 232/6 in 80 (f/o) overs (Kumar Suraj 62, Wilfred Beng 61; Devang Karamta 3-30). Saurashtra won on the basis of first-innings lead.

Kammavar Sangam College Ground, Theni, December 12-14: Gujarat 321 in 133.4 overs (Karan Trivedi 107*, Kathan Patel 49; Jaganath Srinivas 3-25, S Swaminathan 3-78) beat **Tamil Nadu** 136 in 61.3 overs (Vishal Vaidhya 63, Devendra Anchit 20; MA Hingrajia 4-45, Kathan 3-26) and 154 in 57.3 overs (f/o) (V Vaidhya 45, Shankar Siddharth 26; YD Kosamia 3-14, Kathan 2-28) by an innings and 31 runs.

Sardar Patel Stadium B Ground, Motera, Ahmedabad, December 19-22: Gujarat 304 in 107.4 overs (Kathan Patel 120, Rahul Shah 57; Ikjot Singh Thind 4-67, R Bhagat 3-61) and 425/5 in 157 overs (R Shah 207*, Kathan 144) drew with **Punjab** 276 in 79 overs (Karan Sharma 88, Mansab Gill 67; YD Kosamia 7-98, MA Hingrajia 2-32). Gujarat won the basis of first-innings lead.

Bokaro Steel Limited Cricket Stadium, Bokaro, December 19-22: Jammu & Kashmir 333 in 111.2 overs (Mohammad Haziq Bhat 88, Fazil Rashid 69; Himanshu Singh 5-85, Anukul Roy 4-53) and 148/6 in 62 overs (F Rashid 62, Abid Mushtaq 30*; Vinayak Vikram 3-49, A Roy 2-34) drew with **Jharkhand** 486/6 dec in 154.1 overs (Amit Kumar 153, Wilfred Beng 145; Faisal Fayaz 3-105). Jharkhand won the basis of first-innings lead.

PSNA College of Engineering and Technology Ground, Dindigul, December 19-22: Hyderabad 295 in 111 overs (Abhirath Reddy 86, Sai Vikas Reddy 60; Samruddh Bhat 4-73, Sai Kishore 2-50) and 165 in 65.2 overs (A Reddy 59, Nithesh Reddy 40; S Swaminathan 7-53, S Kishore 3-39) lost to **Tamil Nadu** 323 in 116.1 overs (S Swaminathan 112, M Siddharth 36*;

Mir Omer Khan 3-57, Pabba Nilesh 3-88) and 138/3 in 46.4 overs (Shankar Siddharth 64, S Swaminathan 41*) by seven wickets.

Group B Points Table

Teams	M	W	L	D	T	A	Pts	Q
Gujarat	6	4	0	2	0	0	31	2.167
Punjab	6	3	1	2	0	0	25	1.484
Tamil Nadu	6	2	2	2	0	0	16	0.735
Jharkhand	6	1	2	3	0	0	14	1.047
Hyderabad	6	1	3	2	0	0	12	0.756
Saurashtra	6	0	1	5	0	0	9	0.701
Jammu & Kashmir	6	1	3	2	0	0	8	0.754

Gujarat and Punjab qualified for the quarter-finals

Group C

Luhnu Cricket Ground, Bilaspur, November 5-8: Himachal Pradesh 357 in 107.3 overs (Mohit Dogra 67, Chahat Malhotra 62; Gagandeep Singh 3-52, Akash Saxena 3-83) and 286 in 85.3 overs (M Dogra 57, MZ Khan 52; Sanidhey Hurkat 2-23, Vishwaranjan Tripathi 2-32) drew with **Chhattisgarh** 287 in 114.4 overs (MS Hussain 117, Prateek Yadav 78; Naveen Kanwar 4-74, Ravi Sharma 2-43) and 109/3 in 39 overs (Sanidhey Hurkat 29, Amandeep Khare 26; Apporv Walia 2-24). Himachal Pradesh won on the basis of first-innings lead.

Pune Club Ground, November 5-7: Kerala 141 in 55.1 overs (Rohan Kunnummal 56, Salman Nizar 27; Utkarsh Agrawal 5-19, Ramkrishna Ghosh 2-26) and 160 in 62.4 overs (R Kunnummal 57, Albin Alias 21; Shubham Kothari 5-39, U Agrawal 3-44) lost to **Maharashtra** 433/9 dec in 123.3 overs (Ruturaj Gaikwad 120, U Agrawal 116*; Sijomon Joseph 7-108) by an innings and 132 runs.

Sawai Mansingh Stadium, Jaipur, November 5-8: Andhra 280 in 98.3 overs (Karan Shinde 98, Manish Golamaru 36; SKK Ahmed 4-69, Arafat Khan 2-37) and 288/6 in 140 overs (K Shinde 88, M Golamaru 58*; Pradeep Jakhar 3-57) drew with **Rajasthan** 313 in 100 overs (Kartikeya Choudhary 69, Mahipal Lomror 63; Sahik Mohammad Rafi 3-64, Suraj Preetam 2-50). Rajasthan won on the basis of first-innings lead.

Dr PVG RACA Sports Complex Ground, Vizianagram, November 14-17: Andhra 233 in 96.5 overs (Karan Shinde 81, C Gnaneshwar 77; Athif Bin Ashraf 5-57, Fazil Fanoos 3-71) and 145/6 in 80 overs (C Gnaneshwar 65, U Girinath 39*; Muhammed Faizal 2-30, F Fanoos 2-53) drew with **Kerala** 189 in 58.5 overs (SF Daryl 58, Suresh Subin 33; Karthik Raman 4-65, Manish Golamaru 2-14). Andhra won on the basis of first-innings lead.

Nurul Amin Stadium, Nagaon, November 14-15: Assam 106 in 32 overs (Saahil Jain 45; Shubham Sharma 4-20, Vikas Jhorar 2-25) and 128 in 62.5 overs (S Jain 38, Riyan Parag 27; Rahul Chahar 5-41, Shubham 3-29) lost to **Rajasthan** 237 in 81.5 overs (Salman Khan 78*, Ajay Gigna 39; Mrinmoy Dutta 3-69, Riyan Parag 2-6) by an innings and three runs.

Pune Club Ground, November 14-16: Chhattisgarh 155 in 72.4 overs (Sanjeet Desai 36, Sanidhey Hurkat 27; Shubham Kothari 6-35, Tejas Pawar 3-32) and 211 in 71 overs (Yash Thakur 73*, S Desai 58; Ruturaj Gaikwad 3-18, S Kothari 3-69) lost to **Maharashtra** 362 in

128 overs (Hrishikesh Motkar 87, Paras Ratnaparkhe 64; Shubham Singh 3-71, Gagandeep Singh 2-67) and 5/0 in 3.5 overs by ten wickets.

Dr PVG RACA Sports Complex Ground, Vizianagram, November 21-24: Andhra 454/8 dec in 166.5 overs (Maheep Kumar 154, Karan Shinde 110, U Girinath 109; Ruturaj Gaikwad 2-35, Tejas Pawar 2-92) and 47/0 in 11.1 overs (C Gnaneshwar 34*) beat **Maharashtra** 236 in 78.5 overs (R Gaikwad 72, KP Kothavade 54; Karthik Raman 6-82, Girinath Reddy 3-29) and 264 in 84 overs (f/o) (Hrishikesh Motkar 104*, Sourabh Jagdale 53; G Reddy 5-73, K Raman 3-85) by ten wickets.

Luhnu Cricket Ground, Bilaspur, November 21-24: Himachal Pradesh 407 in 113.2 overs (MZ Khan 98, Apporv Walia 93; Mrinmoy Dutta 3-85, Biku Borgohain 2-74) drew with **Assam** 203 in 97 overs (Yasir Ali 73, Riyan Parag 65; Ayush Jamwal 4-24, Naveen Kanwar 3-75) and 317/6 in 139 overs (f/o) (R Parag 76, Biplab Saikia 53; A Jamwal 3-60, Chahat Malhotra 2-50). Himachal Pradesh won on the basis of first-innings lead.

Conor Vyal Stadium, Thalassery, November 21-23: Kerala 143 in 58 overs (Salman Nizar 54*, Rohan Kunnummal 25; Arafat Khan 3-24, Shubham Sharma 3-26) and 115 in 39.1 overs (Albin Alias 51, Sijomon Joseph 42; Rahul Chahar 3-23, Shubham 3-31) lost to **Rajasthan** 261 in 77.1 overs (Shubham 93, Amit Rajera 52; Sijomon Joseph 6-75, Fazil Fanoos 3-70) by an innings and three runs.

Shaheed Veer Narayan Singh International Cricket Stadium, Naya Raipur, November 28-December 1: Chhattisgarh 261 in 109.2 overs (MSS Hussain 110, Ashish Pandey 37; Bikash Singh 5-53, Mrinmoy Dutta 4-94) and 221 in 62.4 overs (PV Malewar 59, Prateek Yadav 38; Mukhtar Hussain 3-65, M Dutta 3-96) drew with **Assam** 346 in 115 overs (Biplab Saikia 149, Saahil Jain 111; Vishwaranjan Tripathi 5-98, Shubham Singh 2-58) and 93/4 in 38 overs (Yasir Ali 34*, S Jain 26; V Tripathi 2-12). Assam won on the basis of first-innings lead.

Atal Bihari Vajpayee Stadium, Amtar, November 28-December 1: Himachal Pradesh 427 in 143.1 overs (Ritwij Kashyap 97, Shubham Arora 96; Sijomon Joseph 4-133, NP Basil 2-72) and 178/6 in 55 overs (R Kashyap 52*, Digvijay Rangi 43; S Joseph 3-58, NP Basil 2-47) drew with **Kerala** 588/6 dec in 159 overs (Salman Nizar 138*, Anand Krishnan 102; Khushpal Singh 2-111). Kerala won on the basis of first-innings lead.

KL Saini Ground, Jaipur, November 28-December 1: Maharashtra 135 in 49.1 overs (Mehul Patel 37, Ruturaj Gaikwad 20; Rahul Chahar 2-12, Vikas Jhorar 2-19) and 274 in 113 overs (R Gaikwad 58, OK Akhade 45*; Arafat Khan 3-48, Manish Sharma 2-40) lost to **Rajasthan** 259 in 111.4 overs (Suraj Ahuja 93, Kamalesh Nagarkoti 44; Jaideep Bharade 7-55, Ramkrishna Ghosh 3-85) and 152/3 in 52.3 overs (Kartikeya Choudhary 45, Salman Khan 36*) by seven wickets.

DSA Ground, Mangoldoi, December 5-7: Assam 122 in 52.4 overs (Bikash Singh 41, Mrinmoy Dutta 29; Jaideep Bharade 4-18, Izhaan Ashfaque Syed 3-30) and 123 in 59.3 overs (Sandip Paul Mazumdar 47; Shubham Kothari 5-33, Utkarsh Agrawal 5-41) lost to **Maharashtra** 204 in 48.2 overs (Ruturaj Gaikwad 108, U Agrawal 36; M Dutta 6-69, Riyan Parag 4-83) and 42/0 in 12.5 overs (R Gaikwad 24*) by ten wickets.

Shaheed Veer Narayan Singh International Cricket Stadium, Naya Raipur, December 5-8: Chhattisgarh 223 in 85.4 overs (VB Vaishanav 90, Prateek Yadav 35; Kamlesh Nagarkoti 3-37, Arafat Khan 2-38) and 212 in 85.1 overs (Yash Thakur 99, Sanidhev Hurkat 32; Arafat 4-32, Shubham Sharma 3-49) lost to **Rajasthan** 329 in 96.3 overs (Ajay Gigna 142*, Shubham 59; SS Agrawal 5-106, Akash Saxena 2-61) and 107/3 in 25 overs (Kartikeya Choudhary 44, Salman Khan 34*) by seven wickets.

Atal Bihari Vajpayee Stadium, Amtar, December 5-8: Himachal Pradesh 441 in 135.2 overs (Mudit Shukla 95, Apporv Walia 70; Karthik Raman 5-120, Manish Golamaru 2-102) and 277/4 dec in 44 overs (Digvijay Rangi 126, Mohit Dogra 52; M Golamaru 3-82) drew with **Andhra** 320 in 167 overs (Yudish Surapaneni 92*, Karan Shinde 54; Ayush Jamwal 7-121, D Rangi 2-27) and 18/1 in 9 overs. Himachal Pradesh won on the basis of first-innings lead.

CSR Sarma College Ground, Ongole, December 12-15: Chhattisgarh 309 in 99 overs

(MSS Hussain 90, Prateek Yadav 66; Girinath Reddy 5-64, Karthik Raman 5-95) and 195/3 in 77 overs (VB Vaishanav 107*, Sanjeet Desai 25; G Reddy 2-37) drew with **Andhra** 496/9 dec in 165 overs (U Girinath 201*, C Gnaneshwar 74; Naman Dhruw 3-64, Utkarsh Tiwari 3-153). Andhra won on the basis of first-innings lead.

Conor Vyal Stadium, Thalassery, December 12-14: Assam 255 in 97.4 overs (Sandip Paul Mazumdar 69, Yasir Ali 36; NP Basil 5-87, Athul Ravindran 3-49) and 127 in 51.4 overs (Biku Borgohain 22, Saahil Jain 20; A Ravindran 4-19, Fazil Fanoos 3-55) lost to **Kerala** 397/9 dec in 125 overs (Rohan Kunnummal 87, Arjun Aji 73; Mrinmoy Dutta 4-123, Hrishikesh Borah 2-62) by an innings and 15 runs.

MCA Stadium, Pune, December 12-15: Himachal Pradesh 334 in 91.4 overs (Shubham Arora 109, MZ Khan 56; Ramkrishna Ghosh 5-82, Utkarsh Agrawal 2-50) and 111 in 60.5 overs (MZ Khan 55; Shubham Kothari 4-18, U Agrawal 2-14) lost to **Maharashtra** 471 in 154.1 overs (Ruturaj Gaikwad 202, Paras Ratnaparkhe 88; Ayush Jamwal 5-149, Naveen Kanwar 2-31) by an innings and 26 runs.

CSR Sarma College Ground, Ongole, December 19-21: Assam 211 in 76.5 overs (Yasir Ali 94, Abhishek Thakuri 36; Manish Golamaru 3-28, Girinath Reddy 3-56, Sahik Mohammad Rafi 3-58) and 80 in 38.5 overs (Saahil Jain 25; Sahik Mohammad Rafi 4-43, G Reddy 2-0) lost to **Andhra** 228 in 74.3 overs (C Gnaneshwar 85, G Reddy 70; Mrinmoy Dutta 5-92, Biku Borgohain 2-9) and 64/2 in 17.4 overs (Karan Shinde 33*; Mukhtar Hussain 2-19) by eight wickets.

Connor Vyal Stadium, Thalassery, December 19-21: Kerala 347 in 114.3 overs (Albin Alias 86, Salman Nizar 76; Vishwaranjan Tripathi 4-86, Sanidhay Hurkat 2-51) beat **Chhattisgarh** 134 in 50 overs (VB Vaishanav 29, Sanjeet Desai 29; SF Daryl 3-36, Sijomon Joseph 2-29) and 139 in 58.2 overs (f/o) (MSS Hussain 33, Yash Thakur 31; NP Basil 7-53, SF Daryl 2-20) by an innings and 74 runs.

Sawai Mansingh Stadium, Jaipur, December 19-22: Rajasthan 351 in 126.1 overs (Kartikeya Choudhary 72, Suraj Ahuja 66; Ayush Jamwal 4-89, Nitin Sharma 3-80) and 190 in 66.3 overs (S Ahuja 60, Ajay Gigna 44; A Jamwal 4-30, Nitin 3-41) lost to **Himachal Pradesh** 195 in 53.1 overs (Nitin 60, Digvijay Rangi 43; Vikas Jhorar 3-34, Shubham Sharma 3-35) and 389 in 105 overs (f/o) (Shubham Arora 75, Ritwij Kashyap 74; V Jhorar 5-95, Amit Kumar 4-73) by 43 runs.

Group C Points Table

Teams	M	W	L	D	T	A	Pts	Q
Rajasthan	6	4	1	1	0	0	29	1.349
Maharashtra	6	4	2	0	0	0	28	1.367
Andhra	6	2	0	4	0	0	21	1.236
Kerala	6	2	2	2	0	0	18	1.082
Himachal Pradesh	6	1	1	4	0	0	16	0.906
Assam	6	0	4	2	0	0	4	0.661
Chhattisgarh	6	0	3	3	0	0	3	0.645

Rajasthan and Maharashtra qualified for the quarter-finals

Group D

St. Stephen's College Ground, Delhi, November 5-8: Delhi 265 in 83 overs (Lakshay 54, Siddhant Sharma 47, Jonty Sidhu 47; Herambh Parab 7-94, Neeraj Yadav 2-69) and 247 in 70 overs (J Sidhu 96, Sarthak Ranjan 78; H Parab 4-50, Neeraj 3-44, Vijesh Prabhudessai 3-59) lost to **Goa** 233 in 90 overs (Kashyap Bakhle 76, Tunish Sawkar 59; Ahlawat 5-66, Vishvash Malik 3-51) and 282/6 in 61.5 overs (Deepraj Gaonkar 99*, Ishan Gadekar 65; Ahlawat 2-60) by four wickets.

TERI Oval, Gurgaon, November 5-8: Haryana 248 in 69.4 overs (Mohit Hooda 67*, Shubham Rohilla 66; Karan Mahajan 6-69, AB Choudhary 2-48) and 281 in 103 overs (M Hooda 107, SD Dhull 60; K Mahajan 7-111) beat **Railways** 153 in 70.3 overs (Vikas Meena 32, VB Choudhary 20; Yashu Sharma 4-27, DS Raghav 2-26) and 200 in 62.5 overs (Annu Ram 74, Yuvraj 42; SD Dhull 5-42, KP Yadav 2-43) by 176 runs.

Bhamashah Stadium, Meerut, November 5-8: Bengal 247 in 94.4 overs (Kanishk Seth 56, Shahbaz 53; Shanu Saini 4-54, Zeeshan Ansari 3-50) and 247/9 dec in 86.5 overs (Agniv Pan 71, K Seth 52*; Z Ansari 4-83, Shubham Mavi 3-41) drew with **Uttar Pradesh** 229 in 98.5 overs (Shivam Chaudhary 55, S Saini 49; K Seth 3-56, Ishan Porel 2-41) and 21/0 in 5 overs. Bengal won on the basis of first-innings lead.

St. Stephen's College Ground, Delhi, November 14-17: Bengal 341 in 90 overs (Avijit Singh 155, Agniv Pan 54; Yogesh Sharma 4-93, Ahlawat 2-50) and 110/4 in 30.1 overs (SK Asif Hossain 33*, Sudip Kumar Gharami 27; Ahlawat 2-23) beat **Delhi** 190 in 75.5 overs (Manjot Kalra 47, Vishvash Malik 33*; AK Asif Hossain 3-22, Ankit Mishra 3-55) and 260 in 110.4 overs (f/o) (Nitin Tanwar 85, Sarthak Ranjan 41; Ishan Porel 5-53, Ananta Saha 2-53) by six wickets.

Karnail Singh Stadium, Delhi, November 14-17: Goa 458 in 135.5 overs (Kashyap Bakhle 159, Deepraj Gaonkar 120; Saif Ali Khan 5-83, Rakhan 3-78) beat **Railways** 118 in 63.1 overs (Annu Ram 31, Vikas Meena 25; Y Dheeraj 5-43) and 267 in 88.2 overs (f/o) (Karan Mahajan 56, A Ram 45; Y Dheeraj 3-67, Vaibhav Govekar 3-73) by an innings and 73 runs.

Bhamashah Stadium, Meerut, November 14-17: Uttar Pradesh 524/8 dec in 134.5 overs (Priyam Garg 223*, Sandeep Kumar 110; SD Aggarwal 5-153) and 206/3 dec in 40 overs (Sandeep Kumar 102*, Madhav Kaushik 52; SD Dhull 3-56) drew with **Haryana** 402 in 132 overs (Shubham Rohilla 80, SD Aggarwal 73*; Shanu Saini 4-79, Vineet Panwar 3-87) and 156/4 in 42.3 overs (Yashu Sharma 55*, Shivam Chauhan 53; S Saini 2-46). Uttar Pradesh won on the basis of first-innings lead.

St. Stephen's College Ground, Delhi, November 21-24: Delhi 537/7 dec in 138.4 overs (Jonty Sidhu 117, Manjot Kalra 109; DS Raghav 2-76, PK Kumar 2-99) beat **Haryana** 276 in 90.2 overs (SD Dhull 70*, Shivam Chauhan 50; Nitin Tanwar 3-41, Vishvash Malik 3-48, Sumit Mathur 3-63) and 128 in 42.2 overs (f/o) (S Chauhan 68; V Malik 5-25, Ahlawat 2-9) by an innings and 133 runs.

GCA Academy Ground, Porvorim, November 21-24: Goa 215 in 99.3 overs (Ishan Gadekar 56, Tunish Sawkar 44; Ishan Porel 3-33, SK Asif Hussain 2-24, Sandipan Das 2-24) and 135 in 55.4 overs (Kashyap Bakhle 41, Vaibhav Govekar 32; Kaustubh Singh 6-41, Ankit Mishra 2-52) lost to **Bengal** 210 in 67.1 overs (Irfan Ansari 73, Arindam Ghosh 62; Saurav Shetgaonkar 4-54, Y Dheeraj 4-80) and 142/6 in 46.3 overs (A Ghosh 56*, Agniv Pan 35*; Y Dheeraj 4-65, Neeraj Yadav 2-19) by four wickets.

Chaudhary Charan Singh Sports Stadium, Muzaffarnagar, November 21-24: Uttar Pradesh 455 in 111.5 overs (Madhav Kaushik 219*, Sandeep Kumar 46; V Dhaka 3-82, Karan Mahajan 2-145) and 63/1 in 15.5 overs (Rinku Singh 37*) beat **Railways** 171 in 61.2 overs (VB Choudhary 62, V Dhaka 42; Vineet Panwar 3-31, Shanu Saini 3-61) and 341 in 124.5 overs (f/o) (Yuvraj 90, Mohit Pal 65; S Saini 3-125, V Panwar 2-40) by nine wickets.

Karnail Singh Stadium, Delhi, November 28-December 1: Railways 195 in 102.4 overs (VB Choudhary 59, Karan Mahajan 33; SK Asif Hossain 4-18, Ankit Mishra 3-61) and 151 in 60.5 overs (V Dhaka 37, Yuvraj 29; Ankit Mishra 5-59, Asif Hossain 2-22) lost to **Bengal**

134 in 50.3 overs (Agniv Pan 46*, Irfan Ansari 36; K Mahajan 7-38) and 216/7 in 76.1 overs (Arindam Ghosh 56, Avijit Singh 36; K Mahajan 4-75) by three wickets.

Bhamashah Stadium, Meerut, November 28-29: Uttar Pradesh 143 in 64.1 overs (Upendra Yadav 39, Kartikey Kushwaha 37; Sumit Mathur 6-26, Nitin Tanwar 4-59) and 106 in 43 overs (Sandeep Kumar 27, Rinku Singh 24; S Mathur 5-48, N Tanwar 3-50) lost to **Delhi** 276 in 75.1 overs (Manjot Kalra 87, Sarthak Ranjan 68; K Kushwaha 4-35, Trishal Vijay Trivedi 4-74) by an innings and 27 runs.

Dr Rajendra Prasad Stadium, Margao, November 28-December 1: Haryana 544/6 dec in 141 overs (Shivam Chauhan 198, Shubham Rohilla 108; Neeraj Yadav 2-109) drew with **Goa** 354 in 138.1 overs (Suyash Prabhudessai 134, Kashyap Bakhle 81; DS Raghav 4-60, PK Kumar 3-65) and 245/5 in 70 overs (f/o) (Deepraj Gaonkar 99, K Bakhle 40; Utkarsh Bhukkal 2-73). Haryana won on the basis of first-innings lead.

Karnail Singh Stadium, Delhi, December 5-8: Railways 235 in 89.1 overs (Annu Ram 74, Yuvraj 48; Susheel 4-59, Ahlawat 3-76) and 257 in 77 overs (V Dhaka 60, Karan Mahajan 51; Vishvash Malik 3-54, Sumit Mathur 2-17) beat **Delhi** 297 in 68.4 overs (Sarthak Ranjan 112, Lakshay 55; K Mahajan 4-98, Rakhan 2-40) and 140 in 47.4 overs (S Ranjan 44, S Mathur 36; K Mahajan 4-39, Vikas Singh 4-46) by 55 runs.

Dr Rajendra Prasad Stadium, Margao, December 5-7: Uttar Pradesh 470 in 129.4 overs (Rinku Singh 158, Rinku Chaudhary 104; Suyash Prabhudessai 5-84, Y Dheeraj 2-112) beat **Goa** 179 in 63.3 overs (Vaibhav Govekar 42, S Prabhudessai 28; Trishal Vijay Trivedi 6-55, Vineet Panwar 2-33) and 205 in 77 overs (f/o) (Tunish Sawkar 43*, Deepraj Gaonkar 40; TV Trivedi 5-67, Shanu Saini 2-64) by an innings and 86 runs.

Ch Bansi Lal Cricket Stadium, Lahli, Rohtak, December 5-8: Haryana 241 in 112.4 overs (Shubham Rohilla 85, Abhimanyu Tanwar 38; Pradipta Pramanik 4-61, Ananta Saha 3-59) and 170/2 in 61.2 overs (Shivam Chauhan 103*, Lakshay Dalal 62) drew with **Bengal** 394 in 141.3 overs (Agniv Pan 142, Arindam Ghosh 60; SD Aggarwal 5-99, DS Raghav 3-89). Bengal won on the basis of first-innings lead.

Group D Points Table

Teams	M	W	L	D	T	A	Pts	Q
Bengal	5	3	0	2	0	0	24	1.219
Uttar Pradesh	5	2	1	2	0	0	17	1.334
Delhi	5	2	3	0	0	0	14	1.225
Goa	5	2	2	1	0	0	14	0.906
Haryana	5	1	1	3	0	0	11	0.819
Railways	5	1	4	0	0	0	6	0.711

Bengal and Uttar Pradesh qualified for the quarter-finals

Quarter-finals

Bengal Cricket Academy Ground, Kalyani, January 2-5: Bengal 347 in 121.4 overs (Shahbaz 108, Pradipta Pramanik 95; Sairaj Patil 2-37, Shams Mulani 2-71) and 238/6 dec in 46 overs (Irfan Ansari 100, Shahbaz 87; Sidak Singh 4-52) drew with **Mumbai** 354 in 115.2 overs (Hardik Tamore 170, Prithvi Shaw 45; Ishan Porel 4-83, Saurabh Singh 3-30) and 174/3 in 57 overs (P Shaw 100, Abeeb Usmani 37; P Pramanik 2-36). Mumbai won on the basis of

first-innings lead.
MCA Stadium, Pune, January 2-5: Gujarat 474 in 156.1 overs (Kavish Panchal 148, YD Kosamia 74; Ramkrishna Ghosh 4-103, Jaideep Bharade 2-63) and 162/3 in 69 overs (Kathan Patel 71*, Abhishek Nair 53; Utkarsh Agrawal 2-43) drew with **Maharashtra** 403 in 117.4 overs (Ruturaj Gaikwad 198, Izhaan Sayed 48*; Sumeet Gosain 5-80, YD Kosamia 4-148). Gujarat won on the basis of first-innings lead.
Wankhede Stadium, Mumbai, January 2-5: Punjab 429 in 138.4 overs (Mansab Gill 161, Shubman Gill 80; Vineet Panwar 4-78, Harshvardhan 3-99) and 260/2 in 65 overs (S Gill 77*, M Gill 68*; Trishal Vijay Trivedi 2-65) drew with **Uttar Pradesh** 583 in 141.5 overs (Rinku Singh 235, Shivam Chaudhary 183; Jaswinder Singh 7-161, Mayank Markande 2-77). Uttar Pradesh won on the basis of first-innings lead
Sawai Mansingh Stadium, Jaipur, January 2-4: Rajasthan 259 in 78.3 overs (Arafat Khan 95, Kartikeya Choudhary 39; Ninad Rathva 4-73, Mistry Milan 3-56) and 175 in 58.5 overs (Salman Khan 73, Vikas Jhorar 25; N Rathva 4-72, Shlok Desai 3-36) lost to **Baroda** 306 in 94.1 overs (Jyotsnil Singh 98, Dhruv Patel 64; Shubham Sharma 4-64, Rahul Chahar 4-93) and 129/4 in 40 overs (Ravindra Patel 61, Jyotsnil 27; R Chahar 2-45, Shubham 2-57) by six wickets.

Mumbai, Gujarat, Uttar Pradesh, Baroda qualified for the semi-finals

Semi-finals
Moti Bagh Stadium, Vadodara, January 11-12: Baroda 127 in 45.5 overs (Dhruv Patel 29, Ravindra Patel 26; Shivam Chaudhary 5-18, Shanu Saini 3-36) and 78 in 29.3 overs (Jyotsnil Singh 27, AV Singh 23; S Saini 6-28, Trishal Vijay Trivedi 3-24) lost to **Uttar Pradesh** 67 in 21.3 overs (Ninad Rathva 7-29, Shlok Desai 3-28) and 142/4 in 26.5 overs (S Chaudhary 49, Sandeep Kumar 44*; N Rathva 3-52) by six wickets.
Sardar Vallabhai Patel Stadium, Valsad, January 11-14: Mumbai 511 in 134.4 overs (Sairaj Patel 183*, Shams Mulani 80; YD Kosamia 5-150, Aasav Panchal 2-126) and 201/3 in 38 overs (Prithvi Shaw 83, Rudra Dhanday 38*) drew with **Gujarat** 433 in 170.1 overs (MA Hingrajia 130*, Karan Trivedi 103; Minad Manjrekar 3-79, S Mulani 3-128). Mumbai won on the basis of first-innings lead.

Uttar Pradesh and Mumbai qualified for the final

Final
Sachin Tendulkar Gymkhana Ground, Mumbai, January 19-22: Mumbai 289 in 75.5 overs (Hardik Tamore 76, Shams Mulani 56; Harshvardhan 3-53, Trishal Vijay Trivedi 3-75) and 359 in 93.1 overs (Onkar Jadhav 130, Rudra Dhanday 122; Shanu Saini 6-108, TV Trivedi 3-129) lost to **Uttar Pradesh** 205 in 69.2 overs (Shivam Chaudhary 54, Upendra Yadav 34; S Mulani 5-70, Sidak Singh 3-57) and 446/7 in 102.3 overs (Madhav Kaushik 136, Rinku Singh 130, S Chaudhary 121) by three wickets.

Winners: Uttar Pradesh

Under-16 Vijay Merchant Trophy

Abhishek Sharma races ahead

SHUBHAM MALAVIYA

Son of Raj Kumar Sharma, the former Punjab spinner, Abhishek Sharma made heads turn with his all-round performance. He led from the front, topping the batting and bowling charts to help Punjab retain the title. The 16-year-old's six centuries, three fifties, eight five-wicket hauls and two match-hauls of ten wickets gave him a batting average of 109 and a bowling average of 10.56. Himachal Pradesh were the first team to witness the teenager's potential when he made 102 and then finished with innings returns of 9 for 7. In the final against Mumbai in Alur, Abhishek made 66 and 123, and took five wickets in the first innings as Punjab took the lead.

Best batsman: Abhishek Sharma (Punjab) (1200 runs, 7 matches)
Best bowler: Abhishek Sharma (Punjab) (57 wickets, 7 matches)

North Zone

Ch Bansi Lal Cricket Stadium, Lahli, Rohtak, December 1-3: Haryana 209 in 84 overs (AB Joon 67, RS Saini 50; Tanwar 5-71, Ayush Badoni 3-30) and 139 in 59.2 overs (RS Saini 38, SK Panchal 34*; Mayank Malhotra 4-21, Nav Pabreja 2-33) drew with **Delhi** 205 in 86.5 overs (A Badoni 62, Vaibhav Kandpal 57; Ashok Sandhu 3-44, Neeraj Rathee 2-33) and 57/5 in 25 overs (Vikas Solanki 25). Haryana won on the basis of first-innings lead.
Luhnu Cricket Ground, Bilaspur, December 1-3: Punjab 321 in 113.2 overs (Abhishek Sharma 102, Jagjit Singh Sandhu 52; Vikram Thakur 4-34, Prashant Bakshi 3-60) beat **Himachal Pradesh** 59 in 40.4 overs (Abhishek 9-7) and 99 in 67.4 overs (f/o) (Purab Singh 38; Abhishek 6-12, Nehal Wadhera 2-6) by an innings and 163 runs.
Luhnu Cricket Ground, Bilaspur, December 6-8: Himachal Pradesh 288 in 97 overs (Shorya Garg 89, Harsh Jamwal 52; Ayush Badoni 4-35, Rishab Negi 4-70) and 65/1 in 14 overs (Vaibhav Sharma 36, H Jamwal 29*) drew with **Delhi** 364 in 108 overs (Rishab Drall 210, Tanwar 95; Vaibhav 3-45, S Garg 2-59). Delhi won on the basis of first-innings lead.
Dhruve Pandove Stadium, Patiala, December 6-7: Punjab 551/5 dec in 101 overs (Abhishek Sharma 226*, Naman Shir 126; Mujtaba Yousuf 3-133) beat **Jammu & Kashmir** 36 in 24 overs (Jagjit Singh Sandhu 7-16, Abhishek 2-6) and 164 in 57.2 overs (f/o) (Abdul Samad 47, Qamran Iqbal 32; Abhishek 5-55, Abhishek Verma 2-47) by an innings and 351 runs.
St. Stephen's College Ground, Delhi, December 11-13: Punjab 424 in 103.5 overs (Abhishek Sharma 152, Nehal Wadhera 110; Tanwar 4-60, Vikas Solanki 3-69) and 338/5 in 50 overs (Prabhsimran Singh 150, Abhishek 95; Rishab Drall 2-66, V Solanki 2-84) drew with **Delhi** 275 in 103.1 overs (Ayush Badoni 117, Vaibhav Kandpal 44; Abhishek 5-91, Kulwinder Singh 2-33). Punjab won on the basis of first-innings lead.
Ch Bansi Lal Cricket Stadium, Lahli, Rohtak, December 11-13: Jammu & Kashmir 104 in 56.3 overs (Qamran Iqbal 45; Ashok Sandhu 5-35, MS Makhija 2-10) and 171 in 88 overs (Q Iqbal 63, Muneer Zulf 26; A Sandhu 6-53, Treyaksh Bali 2-22) lost to **Haryana** 324/6 dec in 80.2 overs (Sachin Choudhary 149*, Arun Kumar 110; Aditya Chib 4-46, Muneer Zulf 2-60) by an innings and 49 runs.

Ch Bansi Lal Cricket Stadium, Lahli, Rohtak, December 16-18: Himachal Pradesh 293 in 153.1 overs (Vaibhav Sharma 127, Siddharth Metha 61*; Ashok Sandhu 4-62, MS Makhija 2-51) and 63/2 dec in 32 overs (Vaibhav 23*) drew with **Haryana** 157 in 95.1 overs (Arun Kumar 68, RS Saini 25; Shorya Garg 5-40, Vaibhav 2-28) and 120/6 in 24 overs (SK Panchal 65*, Treyaksh Bali 20; Shivam Sharma 2-16, Vaibhav 2-48). Himachal Pradesh won on the basis of first-innings lead.

Gandhi Memorial Science College Ground, Jammu, December 16-17: Jammu & Kashmir 170 in 45.3 overs (Muneer Zulf 72; Ayush Badoni 5-48, Rishab Drall 3-21) and 134 in 60.4 overs (Abdul Samad 38, Qamran Iqbal 29; Satyarth Singh 3-22, A Badoni 3-36, Vikas Solanki 3-37) lost to **Delhi** 503/6 dec in 83 overs (A Badoni 209, R Drall 204; Javid Ahmad 3-102, Aditya Chib 2-93) by an innings and 199 runs.

Gandhi Memorial Science College Ground, Jammu, December 20-22: Himachal Pradesh 144 in 38.2 overs (Purab Singh 29*, Shorya Garg 22; Javid Ahmad 4-40, Aditya Chib 2-19) and 353/5 dec in 71 overs (Rohit Narang 140*, S Garg 72; Aryan Gandral 2-39, J Ahmad 2-101) beat **Jammu & Kashmir** 69 in 35.2 overs (Owais Ahmad 31; S Garg 7-31, Shivam Sharma 2-20) and 212 in 68.3 overs (Qamran Iqbal 141, Aryan Dogra 24; Shivam 6-48, S Garg 3-65) by 216 runs.

Dhruve Pandove Stadium, Patiala, December 20-22: Punjab 407 in 103.4 overs (Abhishek Sharma 128, Naman Dhir 105; Suraj Sahuwas 3-44, AB Joon 2-42) and 193/7 in 67 overs (Abhishek 63, Prabhsimran Singh 31; AB Joon 2-37, S Sahuwas 2-39) drew with **Haryana** 303 in 98.4 overs (Sachin Choudhary 113, RS Saini 101; Abhishek 5-62, Sumit Sharma 3-41). Punjab won on the basis of first-innings lead.

North Zone Points Table

Teams	M	W	L	D	T	A	Pts	Q
Punjab	4	2	0	2	0	0	20	3.047
Delhi	4	1	0	3	0	0	12	1.279
Haryana	4	1	0	3	0	0	12	1.032
Himachal Pradesh	4	1	1	2	0	0	10	1.060
Jammu & Kashmir	4	0	4	0	0	0	0	0.226

Punjab and Delhi qualified for the knockouts

Central Zone

MPCA Ground, Sagar, December 1-3: Madhya Pradesh 273 in 98 overs (Rishabh Chouhan 118, Sani Patel 39; Kartik Tyagi 3-52, Mohit Jangra 2-35) and 207/6 dec in 57 overs (Sani 81, Rishabh Chouhan 40*; Tejashwa Raj 4-31) drew with **Uttar Pradesh** 126 in 45.2 overs (Aryan Juyal 38; R Chouhan 4-24, Sagar Solanki 3-20, Adheer Pratap Singh 3-37) and 180/5 in 68 overs (Aabhishek Pandey 49, Prabhnoor Singh 45*; Adheer Pratap 4-50). Madhya Pradesh won on the basis of first-innings lead.

VCA Stadium, Nagpur, December 1-2: Vidarbha 287 in 103.1 overs (Yash Rathod 119, Prerit Agrawal 31; Narayan Sahu 4-82, Piyush Pillai 2-21) beat **Chhattisgarh** 72 in 34.1 overs (Rishi Sharma 20; KP Datey 6-22, Yash Kadam 2-2) and 88 in 36.5 overs (f/o) (KP Datey 6-8, NR Chavan 2-13) by an innings and 127 runs.

MPCA Ground, Sagar, December 6-8: Vidarbha 112 in 55.4 overs (NR Chavan 38, Prerit Agrawal 29; Rishabh Chouhan 5-18, Adheer Pratap Singh 3-39) and 146 in 80.4 overs (Mandar Mahale 45, Yash Rathod 30; Adheer Pratap 4-34, R Chouhan 3-52) lost to **Madhya**

Pradesh 316 in 99.3 overs (Nikhil Singh 86, Chanchal Rathore 79; Yash Kadam 6-64) by an innings and 58 runs.

Madan Mohan Malaviya Stadium, Allahabad, December 6-8: Rajasthan 288 in 109 overs (AN Garhwal 72, SS Ahmad 44; Kartik Tyagi 5-47, Tejashwa Raj 3-46) and 121/3 in 41.2 overs (DR Gajraj 88, SS Ahmad 27; Pratham Mishra 2-17) drew with **Uttar Pradesh** 256 in 105 overs (Aryan Juyal 148, Prabhnoor Singh 45; AS Indoriya 5-50, NR Shukla 3-72). Rajasthan won on the basis of first-innings lead.

Sawai Mansingh Stadium, Jaipur, December 11-13: Madhya Pradesh 278 in 96.1 overs (Rishabh Chouhan 120, Sagar Solanki 39; NR Shukla 5-74, AM Mathur 3-76) and 61/2 in 37 overs (S Raghuvanshi 29*; NR Shukla 2-21) drew with **Rajasthan** 227 in 133.1 overs (NR Shukla 60, VS Menaria 58; Adheer Pratap Singh 3-27, Ajay Mishra 3-57, R Chouhan 3-67). Madhya Pradesh won on the basis of first-innings lead.

Aligarh Muslim University Ground, December 11-13: Uttar Pradesh 244 in 77.4 overs (Aabhishek Pandey 114, Aryan Jyal 48; RT Taank 5-97, Narayan Sahu 3-41) and 142/5 dec in 33 overs (A Pandey 50, Om Saini 34; RT Taank 3-57) beat **Chhattisgarh** 125 in 65.5 overs (Alok Sahu 32, Yogendra Patil 26; Harshit Paliwal 5-44, Tejashwa Raj 2-16) and 140 in 74.4 overs (Vedvyas Sahu 32, Alok Sahu 23; H Paliwal 4-69, T Raj 3-30) by 121 runs.

Shaheed Veer Narayan Singh International Cricket Stadium, Naya Raipur, December 16-18: Madhya Pradesh 217 in 110.1 overs (Chanchal Rathore 63, Devsharan Barnale 41; Narayan Sahu 5-65, RT Taank 3-56) and 130/9 dec in 45.4 overs (Rishabh Chouhan 45, Sani Patel 42; Piyush Pillai 4-39, Parivesh Dhar 3-25) drew with **Chhattisgarh** 94 in 31.1 overs (Sagar Solanki 6-34, Adheer Pratap Singh 2-7) and 75/6 in 75 overs (Rishi Sharma 28, Adheer Pratap 2-15). Madhya Pradesh won on the basis of first-innings lead.

VCA Stadium, Nagpur, December 16-18: Rajasthan 228 in 87.2 overs (Amit Rajera 66, SS Ahmad 55; Rohit Dattatraya 5-58, Prerit Agrawal 2-20) and 144/8 in 82 overs (NR Shukla 32, VS Menaria 31, AS Indoriya 31*; Rohit Dattatraya 4-41, Dushyant Tekan 2-6) drew with **Vidarbha** 329/7 dec in 111.2 overs (Yash Rathod 180, Yash Kadam 63; AS Indoriya 6-96). Vidarbha won on the basis of first-innings lead.

KL Saini Ground, Jaipur, December 21-23: Chhattisgarh 316 in 132.1 overs (Vedvyas Sahu 67, Alok Sahu 64; AN Garhwal 3-48, AS Indoriya 2-57) drew with **Rajasthan** 143 in 71.4 overs (Hitesh Patel 58, SS Ahmad 43; RT Taank 7-37, Piyush Pillai 2-41) and 120/2 in 49 overs (f/o) (SS Ahmad 53*, JA Watts 34). Chhattisgarh won on the basis of first-innings lead.

VCA Stadium, Nagpur, December 21-23: Uttar Pradesh 400 in 124.2 overs (Aabhishek Pandey 75, Arya Sethi 64; Prerit Agrawal 4-46, Yash Kadam 2-54) beat **Vidarbha** 93 in 38.4 overs (Yash Rathod 30, Sanket Khedkar 30*; Harshit Paliwal 3-20, Om Saini 2-3) and 193 in 87 overs (f/o) (Y Kadam 87*, NR Chavan 2; Kartik Tyagi 2-13, Mohit Jangra 2-33) by an innings and 114 runs.

Central Zone Points Table

Teams	M	W	L	D	T	A	Pts	Q
Madhya Pradesh	4	1	0	3	0	0	16	1.652
Uttar Pradesh	4	2	0	2	0	0	15	1.292
Vidarbha	4	1	2	1	0	0	10	0.946
Rajasthan	4	0	0	4	0	0	6	0.754
Chhattisgarh	4	0	2	2	0	0	4	0.602

Madhya Pradesh and Uttar Pradesh qualified for the knockout

West Zone

Reliance Cricket Stadium, Vadodara, December 1-3: Baroda 126 in 65.3 overs (Atharv Karulkar 31, Jay Abhale 25; Vignesh Solanki 3-19, Arjun Tendulkar 2-18) and 200 in 91.4 overs (Vasudev Patil 77, Parth Patel 42; Mukund Sardar 3-25, Atharva Ankolekar 3-44) lost to **Mumbai** 320 in 102 overs (Tanvish 63*, A Ankolekar 56; Manav Mehta 5-103, Yash Yadav 3-86) and 8/0 in 1.3 overs by ten wickets.

SCA Stadium, Rajkot, December 1-3: Gujarat 431/8 dec in 136.5 overs (Sunpreet Bagga 100*, Tanush Gusain 82; Parshwarajsinh Rana 3-141, Pavan Parmar 2-63) and 82/0 in 18 overs (T Gusain 60*, LM Kocher 21*) drew with **Saurashtra** 255 in 102 overs (P Parmar 56, Karan Malmadi 52; Siddarth Desai 6-51, Akash Pandey 2-68). Gujarat won on the basis of first-innings lead.

Bandra Kurla Complex, Mumbai, December 6-8: Mumbai 366 in 118.4 overs (Satyalakshya Jain 93, Yashasvi Jaiswal 92; Omkar Mohite 5-104, YS Dongre 3-45) drew with **Maharashtra** 144 in 82.4 overs (Vinay Patil 50, KB More 41; Vignesh Solanki 4-41, Atharva Ankolekar 3-25) and 158/2 in 70 overs (f/o) (Siddesh Veer 54*, OM Bhosale 44*). Mumbai won on the basis of first-innings lead.

SCA Stadium, Rajkot, December 6-8: Saurashtra 279 in 107.5 overs (Parshwarajsinh Rana 75*, Jitendra Gyanchandani 54; Aditya Rangwani 3-55, Siddharth Marvania 3-55) and 77/1 in 23 overs (Siddhant Rana 45*, Digvijay Vala 27) drew with **Baroda** 404/7 dec in 122 overs (Vasudev Patil 252, Atharv Karulkar 38; Pavan Parmar 2-48, P Rana 2-90). Baroda won on the basis of first-innings lead.

Lalabhai Contractor Stadium, Surat, December 11-13: Gujarat 275 in 122 overs (Sunpreet Bagga 95*, SS Patel 56; Vignesh Solanki 5-60, Tanvish 2-26) drew with **Mumbai** 117 in 65.5 overs (Suved Parkar 39, Satyalakshya Jain 30; Siddharth Desai 5-40, Suraj Suryal 3-17) and 188/4 in 91 overs (f/o) (S Parkar 68*, Shreeraj Gharat 50; S Suryal 2-49). Gujarat won on the basis of first-innings lead.

MCA Stadium, Pune, December 11-13: Maharashtra 428/8 dec in 109.3 overs (Atharva Kale 144, KB More 107, OM Bhosale 100; Ashutosh Das 2-62, Aditya Rangwani 2-67) drew with **Baroda** 160 in 81.4 overs (Jay Abhale 33*, Parth Patel 26; Omkar Mohite 7-33) and 182/1 in 62.2 overs (f/o) (Vasudev Patil 101*, Swapnil Ugle 52*). Maharashtra won on the basis of first-innings lead.

Moti Bagh Stadium, Vadodara, December 16-18: Gujarat 122 in 46.2 overs (Suraj Suryal 42; Manav Mehta 6-58, Ashutosh Das 2-34) and 245/2 in 81.1 overs (SS Patel 106*, Umang Kumar 52*) drew with **Baroda** 284/7 dec in 134.3 overs (Jay Abhale 95, Kush Marathe 51; DA Patel 2-32, NB Bhuyan 2-58). Baroda won on the basis of first-innings lead

MCA Stadium, Pune, December 16-18: Saurashtra 244 in 82 overs (Pavan Parmar 70, Jaynil Dadhaniya 47; AR Pore 4-36, Omkar Mohite 3-61) and 145/4 in 56 overs (Digvijay Vala 48*, Parshwarajsinh Rana 37*; AR Pore 2-25) drew with **Maharashtra** 370/6 dec in 123.1 overs (Siddesh Veer 100*, KB More 96; Karan Malmadi 4-101). Maharashtra won on the basis of first-innings lead

Sardar Vallabhai Patel Stadium, Valsad, December 21-23: Maharashtra 149 in 72.3 overs (OM Bhosale 84, Atharva Kale 24; Siddharth Desai 3-25, DA Patel 2-8) and 233/6 dec in 47.1 overs (OM Bhosale 73, YS Dongre 64; Suraj Suryal 2-47, DA Patel 2-58) drew with **Gujarat** 239 in 121.4 overs (Sunpreet Bagga 80, SS Patel 62; AR Pore 5-84, Omkar Mohite 3-36) and 52/2 in 25 overs (Umang Kumar 28*). Gujarat won on the basis of first-innings lead

Sachin Tendulkar Gymkhana Ground, Mumbai, December 21-23: Mumbai 429/6 dec in 131.3 overs (Divyansh Saxena 136, Suved Parkar 132; Parshwarajsinh Rana 3-115) and 148/2 in 42 overs (D Saxena 67*, Omkar Ghule 63*) drew with **Saurashtra** 181 in 83.3 overs (Pavan Parmar 61, P Rana 35; Mukund Sardar 4-60, Atharva Akolekar 3-41). Mumbai won on the basis of first-innings lead.

West Zone Points Table

Teams	M	W	L	D	T	A	Pts	Q
Mumbai	4	1	0	3	0	0	14	1.800
Gujarat	4	0	0	4	0	0	10	1.320
Maharashtra	4	0	0	4	0	0	8	1.195
Baroda	4	0	1	3	0	0	7	0.835
Saurashtra	4	0	0	4	0	0	4	0.408

Mumbai and Gujarat qualified for the knockout

South Zone

ECIL Ground, Hyderabad, December 1-3: Tamil Nadu 110 in 48.4 overs (TD Lokesh Raj 26, S Kishan Kumar 21; KP Sai Rahul 3-18, K Saiteja 3-35) and 205/9 dec in 66 overs (Abishiek Selvakumar 53, S Kishan 42; B Satvik 5-55, Dinesh Chandra 2-53) beat **Andhra** 118 in 51.4 overs (Y Sandeep 29, PBVS Yaswanth 28; KD Lingesh 6-39, S Kishan 3-27) and 109 in 47.5 overs (M Ramprasad 38*; S Kishan 4-50, KD Lingesh 2-9) by 88 runs.

Railways Recreation Club Ground, Secunderabad, December 1-2: Karnataka 328 in 91.3 overs (SS Luvnith 77, Jeswanth Acharya 71; Balkrishna Kanekar 3-78, Devdatt Chodankar 2-22) beat **Goa** 48 in 31.2 overs (Shubhang Hegde 3-7, Tanish Mahesh 3-8) and 171 in 55 overs (f/o) (Rahul Mehta 83, Alam Khan 60; S Hegde 4-51, Gaurav Narayan 3-45) by an innings and 109 runs.

Nuclear Fuel Complex Ground, Secunderabad, December 1-3: Hyderabad 413/6 dec in 121 overs (A Varun Goud 154, Pragnay Reddy 68; Adithya Mohan 3-89) and 28/0 in 6 overs (M Pratyush Kumar 23*) drew with **Kerala** 283 in 131.4 overs (Anil Amal 113, Akshay Manohar 43; Ajay Dev Goud 4-68, Rathan Teja 2-61). Hyderabad won on the basis of first-innings lead.

Railways Recreation Club Ground, Secunderabad, December 5-7: Andhra 410/4 dec in 106.4 overs (Saivardhan 189, Y Sandeep 145; Sachin Mishra 2-79) beat **Goa** 156 in 61 overs (Rahul Mehta 45, Sachin Mishra 29; D Kadharvali 3-12, KP Sai Rahul 2-18) and 194 in 70.5 overs (f/o) (Umang Gosavi 67, Alam Khan 59; Y Sandeep 4-38, D Kadharvali 2-23) by an innings and 60 runs.

Nuclear Fuel Complex Ground, Secunderabad, December 5-7: Tamil Nadu 343 in 107 overs (S Kishan Kumar 77, S Aakash 62; Hitesh Yadav 5-76, Ajay Dev Gound 2-76) drew with **Hyderabad** 360/8 in 158 overs (B Revanth 108, Pragnay Reddy 79; Yazh Arunmozhi 2-44). Hyderabad won on the basis of first-innings lead.

ECIL Ground, Hyderabad, December 5-7: Karnataka 406 in 97.5 overs (SS Sudhanshu 124, SS Luvnith 102; S Midhun 5-115, Ashwin Anand 3-78) drew with **Kerala** 134 in 62 overs (Anil Amal 31, Akshay Manohar 29; Shubhang Hegde 4-37, Rohan Nayakar 2-3) and 209/6 in 110 overs (f/o) (A Manohar 52, T Nikhil 50; Anirudh Kulkarni 3-58, S Hegde 2-54). Karnataka won on the basis of first-innings lead.

Railways Recreation Club Ground, Secunderabad, December 10-12: Karnataka 431/8 dec in 126.2 overs (Aadarsh Prajwal 112, Sai Prajwal Reddy 100*; Dinesh Chandra 4-96, B Satvik 2-110) drew with **Andhra** 143 in 68.4 overs (Y Sandeep 41, J Durga Kumar 34*; Rohan Nayakar 4-14, Shubhang Hegde 3-36) and 170/7 in 77 overs (f/o) (Y Sandeep 61, M Ramprasad 47; Anirudh Kulkarni 4-49, S Hegde 2-63). Karnataka won on the basis of first-innings lead.

Nuclear Fuel Complex Ground, Secunderbabad, December 10-11: Goa 76 in 36.2 overs

(Triroy 26, Alam Khan 22; Aniketh Reddy 4-14, Ajay Dev Goud 4-16) and 101 in 42.5 overs (Rahul Mehta 62; A Reddy 5-33, A Dev Goud 4-23) lost to **Hyderabad** 369/6 dec in 85.1 overs (A Varun Goud 134, B Revanth 74; Ruthvik Naik 2-85) by an innings and 192 runs.

ECIL Ground, Hyderabad, December 10-12: Kerala 394 in 126.3 overs (T Nikhil 135, Akshay Bhat 62; Pradosh Ranjan Paul 2-15, TD Lokesh Raj 2-51) drew with **Tamil Nadu** 505 in 142.3 overs (Nidhish Rajagopal 200, PR Paul 95; Umashankar Adhwaidh 2-68, Adithya Mohan 2-77). Tamil Nadu won on the basis of first-innings lead.

ECIL Ground, Hyderabad, December 14-16: Kerala 93 in 41 overs (J Ananthakrishnan 26; B Satvik 5-22, Y Sandeep 2-20) and 166 in 82.4 overs (Anil Amal 86*; B Satvik 3-36, Dinesh Chandra 3-45) lost to **Andhra** 335 in 99 overs (J Durga Kumar 82*, KP Sai Rahul 46; S Midhun 3-87, Ashwin Anand 2-42) by an innings and 76 runs.

Nuclear Fuel Complex Ground, Secunderbabad, December 14-16: Goa 73 in 49 overs (S Kishan Kumar 4-22, TD Lokesh Raj 2-8) and 281 in 115.5 overs (Alam Khan 67, Rahul Mehta 51; N Harishh 4-57, S Kishan 2-52) lost to **Tamil Nadu** 346/9 dec in 88 overs (Pradosh Ranjan Paul 114, TD Lokesh Raj 60*; Umang Gosavi 3-32, Ruthvik Naik 2-60) and 12/0 in 7.1 overs by ten wickets.

Railways Recreation Club Ground, Secunderbabad, December 14-16: Karnataka 191 in 59.1 overs (Sai Prajwal Reddy 73, Aadarsh Prajwal 40; Aniketh Reddy 6-36, E Sanketh 3-22) and 98/2 in 41 overs (Rohan Nayakar 51, Jeswanth Acharya 40*; Hitesh Yadav 2-19) drew with **Hyderabad** 342/9 dec in 157.5 overs (A Varun Goud 110, B Revanth 73; Rohan Nayakar 4-51, Danish Shariff 3-70). Hyderabad won on the basis of first-innings lead.

Railways Recreation Club Ground, Secunderbabad, December 19-21: Kerala 265 in 126 overs (J Ananthakrishnan 103, S Midhun 42*; Ruthvik Naik 4-61) and 105/1 in 32 overs (Anil Amal 50*, Aslam Thoufeek 29*) drew with **Goa** 228 in 99 overs (Umang Gosavi 51, R Naik 32; K Adithya Krishnan 3-42, J Ananthakrishnan 2-16). Kerala won on the basis of first-innings lead.

ECIL Ground, Hyderabad, December 19-21: Andhra 193 in 105.2 overs (Y Sandeep 78, D Kadharvali 26; Ajay Dev Goud 6-36) drew with **Hyderabad** 353/8 dec in 150 overs (Pragnay Reddy 123, Aniketh Reddy 60; Dinesh Chandra 3-81, Y Sandeep 2-70). Hyderabad won on the basis of first-innings lead.

Nuclear Fuel Complex Ground, Secunderbabad, December 19-21: Karnataka 366/8 dec in 90 overs (Devdatt Padikkal 188*, Sai Prajwal Reddy 60; Yazh Arunmozhi 5-106) and 198/3 dec in 32 overs (Nikin Jose 104*, SP Reddy 52*) drew with **Tamil Nadu** 413 in 130.5 overs (S Kishan Kumar 166, Nidhish Rajagopal 59; Shubhang Hegde 3-110, D Padikkal 2-14) and 60/3 in 18 overs (Abishiek Selvakumar 23; Anirudh Kulkarni 3-19). Tamil Nadu won on the basis of first-innings lead.

South Zone Points Table

Teams	M	W	L	D	T	A	Pts	Q
Tamil Nadu	5	2	0	3	0	0	20	1.188
Hyderabad	5	1	0	4	0	0	19	2.432
Andhra	5	2	1	2	0	0	16	1.064
Karnataka	5	1	0	4	0	0	15	1.733
Kerala	5	0	1	4	0	0	6	0.600
Goa	5	0	4	1	0	0	1	0.322

Tamil Nadu and Hyderabad qualified for the knockout

East Zone

Bengal Cricket Academy Ground, Kalyani, December 1-3: Jharkhand 186 in 146 overs (Harshit Namdev 59, Shrisht Sagar 39; Sourav Mandal 4-33, Kaushik Maity 2-39) and 114/3 in 43 overs (S Sagar 50*, Dibyanshu Raj 43) drew with **Bengal** 170 in 94 overs (Sharnik Banerjee 49, Sayan Kumar Biswas 41; Shlok 5-42, Pankaj Yadav 2-37). Jharkhand won on the basis of first-innings lead.

Bidanasi Ground, Cuttack, December 1-3: Tripura 186 in 49 overs (RN Chakma 75, Bikram Ghosh 25; Rajesh Mohanty 6-54, Sahil Raza 2-45) and 248/5 dec in 89 overs (Bikramkumar Das 168, RN Chakma 63; R Mohanty 3-63) drew with **Odisha** 248 in 104.4 overs (Aakash Nayak 57, Rajat Das 53; Sankar Paul 5-57, Saruk Hossain 2-26) and 25/0 in 10 overs. Odisha won on the basis of first-innings lead.

DSA Outdoor Stadium, Dibrugarh, December 7-9: Odisha 162 in 71.1 overs (Rajat Das 53, Aakash Nayak 39; Akash Sengupta 5-25, Bishal Das 3-40) and 123 in 53.3 overs (Kshyamasagar Bal 36, Swastik Samal 23; Rituraj Biswas 5-27, Bibhakar Nag 3-21) lost to **Assam** 169 in 90.2 overs (A Sengupta 65; Binit Mohanty 4-23, Pritam Jena 4-45) and 119/6 in 42.1 overs (Sambhav Jain 41, Amlanjyoti Das 30; B Mohanty 2-34) by four wickets.

Bengal Cricket AcademyGround, Kalyani, December 7-9: Bengal 352/4 dec in 117 overs (Indrajit Orang 121, Debojyoti Ghosh 90; Subha Sinha 2-63) and 131/2 in 47 overs (I Orang 54 retd. hurt, Arnab Bhattacharjee 40*) drew with **Tripura** 245 in 89.5 overs (Bikramkumar Das 120, TP Majumder 47; D Ghosh 5-58, Tribrit Roy 5-78). Bengal won on the basis of first-innings lead.

Birsa Munda Cricket Stadium, Chaibasa, December 13-14: Jharkhand 268 in 68.1 overs (Aditya Narayan 160, Apurva Anand 64; Jitumoni Kalita 3-62, Amlanjyoti Das 2-15) beat **Assam** 103 in 49 overs (Abdul Ajij Kuraishi 32, Subhashish Dutta 28; Pankaj Yadav 7-40) and 151 in 63.3 overs (f/o) (Bibhakar Nag 31, Nasir Ullah 24; A Anand 4-24, Pankaj 3-82) by an innings and 14 runs.

Sunshine Ground, Cuttack, December 13-15: Bengal 338/9 dec in 101.1 overs (Ankit Chakraborthy 84, Debojyoti Ghosh 74; Kshyamasagar Bal 5-39) and 44/5 in 22 overs (Sai Prasad Acharya 2-7) drew with **Odisha** 349 in 126.3 overs (Rajat Das 115*, Swastik Samal 72; Tribrit Roy 5-109, D Ghosh 2-52). Odisha won on the basis of first-innings lead.

Keenan Stadium, Jamshedpur, December 19-21: Odisha 264 in 103 overs (Rajat Das 73, Pritam Jena 41; Avinash Kumar 2-14, Pankaj Yadav 2-56) and 90/7 in 29.2 overs (Swastik Samal 34; Pankaj 2-11, Sushant Mishra 2-29) drew with **Jharkhand** 186 in 103.1 overs (Harshit Namdev 65*, Aditya Narayan 33; P Jena 5-37, Pratyush Mahapatra 2-17) and 75/5 in 42 overs (Rajat Das 2-10, Soumya Kumar 2-26). Odisha won on the basis of first-innings lead.

Tripura Institute of Technology, Agartala, December 19-21: Assam 354 in 102 overs (Riyan Parag 144, Amlanjyoti Das 67*; Saruk Hossain 4-57, Sankar Paul 3-89) and 23/1 in 4.5 overs beat **Tripura** 112 in 38.5 overs (Bikramkumar Das 41, S Paul 20; Riyan Parag 4-32, Akash Sengupta 3-48) and 261 in 99.3 overs (f/o) (S Paul 67, RN Chakma 64; Jitumoni Kalita 4-39, R Parag 3-66) by nine wickets.

BDSA Ground, Bokakhat, December 25-27: Bengal 200 in 91.5 overs (Ankit Chakraborthy 72, Kaushik Maity 29; Rituraj Biswas 5-30, Akash Sengupta 2-40) and 100 in 56.3 overs (K Maity 50; Gunjandeka 5-26, R Biswas 2-12) drew with **Assam** 169 in 94 overs (Riyan Parag 55, Abdul Ajij Kuraishi 31; K Maity 4-25, Tribrit Roy 2-65) and 106/7 in 37 overs (R Parag 23, Jitumoni Kalita 22; T Roy 3-24, K Maity 3-27). Bengal won on the basis of first-innings lead.

Tripura Institute of Technology, Agartala, December 25-27: Tripura 127 in 51.4 overs (Bikram Ghosh 39, Bikram Debnath 23; Apurva Anand 5-35, Sushant Mishra 2-28) and 106 in 58.1 overs (Pankaj Yadav 4-28, A Anand 2-34) lost to **Jharkhand** 85 in 38.2 overs (Sankar Paul 4-18, Krishna Kant Singh 4-23) and 150/4 in 49 overs (Shrisht Sagar 55*, Aditya Narayan 35; Subha Sinha 2-35) by six wickets.

East Zone Points Table

Teams	M	W	L	D	T	A	Pts	Q
Jharkhand	4	2	0	2	0	0	17	1.356
Assam	4	2	1	1	0	0	13	1.065
Odisha	4	0	1	3	0	0	9	0.972
Bengal	4	0	0	4	0	0	8	1.142
Tripura	4	0	2	2	0	0	2	0.592

Jharkhand and Assam qualified for the knockout

Pre-quarter-finals

KSCA Ground No. 2, Alur, January 3-6: Gujarat 173 in 85.3 overs (Suraj Suryal 50, NM Jadhav 27; S Kishan Kumar 5-45, N Harissh 3-42) and 334 in 169.5 overs (NM Jadhav 81, Supreet Bagga 66; Yazh Arunmozhi 5-92, S Kishan 4-118) drew with **Tamil Nadu** 148 in 89.4 overs (Nidhish Rajagopal 58, S Aakash 26; Siddharth Desai 4-42, DA Patel 3-18). Gujarat won on the basis of first-innings lead.

KSCA Ground No. 3, Alur, January 3-6: Hyderabad 310 in 134.4 overs (B Revanth 102, A Varun Goud 89; Tanvish 3-32, Atharva Ankolekar 3-80, Mukund Sardar 3-100) and 189/3 in 76 overs (N Suryateja 73*, AV Goud 62*) drew with **Mumbai** 336 in 162.2 overs (Suved Parkar 150, A Ankolekar 71; Hitesh Yadav 4-65, Aniketh Reddy 2-113). Mumbai won on the basis of first-innings lead.

Gujarat and Mumbai qualified for the quarter-finals

Quarter-finals

KSCA Ground, Alur, January 9-12: Uttar Pradesh 150 in 56.5 overs (Mohit Jangra 35*, Arya Sethi 26; Jitumoni Kalita 6-35, Akash Sengupta 2-30) and 413 in 192.3 overs (Aryan Sharma 124*, Aabhishek Pandey 80; J Kalita 5-144, A Sengupta 2-52) drew with **Assam** 128 in 69.4 overs (Riyan Parag 63, Nihar Deka 20; Tejashwa Raj 4-33, Kartik Tyagi 3-45) and 128/1 in 34 overs (R Parag 97, Nasir Ullah 24). Uttar Pradesh won on the basis of first-innings lead.

KSCA Ground No. 3, Alur, January 9-12: Gujarat 323 in 133.3 overs (Sunpreet Bagga 130*, NM Jadhav 47; Abhishek Sharma 4-68, Madhav Singh Pathania 3-31) and 251 in 86.4 overs (SS Patel 55, Mihir Vaccheta 51; Abhishek 8-81) lost to **Punjab** 163 in 56.1 overs (Shubman Gill 39, Abhishek 31; Siddharth Desai 5-69, DA Patel 3-29) and 412/5 in 69.5 overs (S Gill 186, Abhishek 174; S Desai 3-119) by five wickets.

KSCA Ground No. 2, Alur, January 9-12: Haryana 264 in 115.5 overs (RS Saini 163, Sachin Choudhary 30; Shlok 4-72, Apurva Anand 3-83) and 196 in 65.3 overs (RS Saini 43, Arun Kumar 38; Pankaj Yadav 5-61, A Anand 4-60) beat **Jharkhand** 179 in 100.4 overs (Shrisht Sagar 55*, Ram Raushan Sharan 26; Ashok Sandhu 5-30, Neeraj Rathee 2-21) and 96 in 46.5 overs (Harshit Namdev 28*; Neeraj Rathee 3-9, Treyaksh Bali 3-24, Divanshu Singla 3-32) by 185 runs.

Rajinder Insititute Ground, Bangalore, January 9-12: Mumbai 475 in 204.3 overs (Sheeraj Gharat 160, Yashasvi Jaiswal 98; Fateh Ullah Khan 6-109, Adheer Pratap Singh 2-100) and 8/0 in 7 overs drew with **Madhya Pradesh** 431 in 143.4 overs (Rishabh Chouhan 106, Devsharan Barnale 94; Atharva Ankolekar 4-119, Vignesh Solanki 3-75). Mumbai won on the basis of first-innings lead.

Uttar Pradesh, Punjab Haryana and Mumbai
qualified for the semi-finals

Semi-finals

KSCA Ground No. 2, Alur, January 15-18: Mumbai 293 in 134.4 overs (Divyansh Saxena 95, Satyalakshya Jain 70*; Treyaksh Bali 2-56, Divanshu Singla 2-57) and 213 in 92.4 overs (Suved Parkar 111, Atharva Ankolekar 39; D Singla 3-45, T Bali 3-45, Neeraj Rathee 3-58) beat **Haryana** 159 in 46.2 overs (SR Singroha 41, Ashok Sandhu 33; Vignesh Solanki 5-38, Tanvish 2-17) and 152 in 56.1 overs (RS Saini 34, Arun Kumar 33; Mukund Sardar 4-23, V Solanki 4-41) by 195 runs.

KSCA Ground No. 3, Alur, January 15-17: Punjab 242 in 61.4 overs (Shubman Gill 86, Prabhsimran Singh 40; Tejashwa Raj 5-84, Mohit Jangra 4-94) and 239 in 80.1 overs (S Gill 52, Abhishek Sharma 40; M Jangra 5-68, T Raj 4-93) beat **Uttar Pradesh** 158 in 67.2 overs (Aryan Sharma 47, T Raj 27*; Sumit Sharma 3-26, Abhishek 3-57) and 169 in 48.3 overs (M Jangra 48*, Aabhishek Pandey 43; Abhishek 5-68, Naman Dhir 2-15) by 154 runs.

Mumbai and Punjab qualified for the final

Final

KSCA Ground, Alur, January 21-24: Punjab 311 in 94 overs (Deepin Chitkara 69, Abhishek Sharma 66; Atharva Ankolekar 6-105) and 514 in 127.3 overs (Abhishek 123, D Chitkara 123; Vignesh Solanki 8-173, A Ankolekar 2-138) drew with **Mumbai** 174 in 85 overs (Divyansh Saxena 109*, Suved Parkar 23; Abhishek 5-59, Naman Dhir 3-18) and 220/5 in 65 overs (Suved Parkar 91, Yashasvi Jaiswal 41*; Madhav Singh Pathania 2-24, Kulwinder Singh 2-34). Punjab won on the basis of first-innings lead.

Winners: Punjab

Vizzy Trophy (Inter-Zonal University)

Chandela's 318 gives North title

SIDHANTA PATNAIK

Kunal Chandela's triple-century and Saleem Ansari's 102 helped North Zone Universities beat West Zone Universities, the defending champions, in the final on first-innings lead and claim the title for the first time since 2007-08. Apart from Chandela and Ansari, North had contributors in Karan Dagar, Rohan Rathi, Amit Verma, who made 201 against East Zone Universities in the semi-final, and Tahmeed Ahmed.

Best batsman: Kunal Chandela (North Zone Universities) (378 runs, 2 matches)
Best bowler: Karan Dagar (North Zone Universities) (7 wickets, 2 matches)

Semi-finals

Jamia Millia Cricket Ground, Delhi, March 29-31: North Zone Universities 225 in 68.2 overs (Rohan Rathi 50, Saleem Ansari 48; Rishav Kathri 3-37, Ravi Kumar 2-34) and 524 in 150.2 overs (Amit Verma 201, Tahmeed Ahmad 88; Atul Kumar 5-193) drew with **East Zone Universities** 108 in 51.2 overs (Sanjay Mohanty 28, Atul 21*; Karan Dagar 4-28, Mohd Sultan 2-16). North Zone Universities won on the basis of first-innings lead.

St. Stephen's College Ground, Delhi, March 29-31: West Zone Universities 615/6 dec in 160 overs (Akash Anand 176, Vikrant Auti 148, Gandhar Bhatawadekar 130*; P Ajith Kumar 4-167, V Vyshak 2-116) drew with **South Zone Universities** 316 in 82.3 overs (Amith Sidharth 124, KL Shrijith 54; Aditya Dhumal 5-92, Shubham Shukla 4-47) and 69/1 in 9.3 overs (f/o) (Kolla Sumanth 39*, Rohith Gowda 24). West Zone Universities won on the basis of first-innings lead.

North Zone Universities and West Zone Universities qualified for the final

Final

Jamia Millia Cricket Ground, Delhi, April 2-5: West Zone Universities 603 in 191.5 overs (Sandeep Jagbirsingh Mor 174, Gandhar Bhatawadekar 146, Vikrant Auti 115; Karan Dagar 3-189, Rohan Rathi 2-40) drew with **North Zone Universities** 604/6 in 168 overs (Kunal Chandela 318, Saleem Ansari 102; Puneet Tripathi 3-123). North Zone Universities won on the basis of first-innings lead.

Winners: North Zone Universities

WOMEN'S CRICKET

All too easy for Railways, yet again

ANANYA UPENDRAN

March of dominance: The Railways side, packed with India internationals and led by Mithali Raj, won their ninth national title. — *Special arrangement*

Inter-State One-Day Competition

Keeping with tradition, Mithali Raj's Railways swept aside the competition in the Elite Group to register their ninth national title, while Madhya Pradesh grabbed the honours in the Plate Division beating Baroda in the final. In a low-scoring competition, Raj and team-mate MD Thirushkamini, and MP's Varsha Choudhary were the only batters to cross the 200-run mark; while Smriti Mandhana, the Maharashtra captain who missed the initial part of the season with illness, smashed 193 runs in only four innings. The spinners dominated the bowling, with only three medium-pacers featuring in the top ten wicket-takers. Ekta Bisht, the wily left-arm spinner from Railways, finished at the top of that list with 15 wickets at an astonishing average of 5.73.

Best Batter: Mithali Raj (Railways) (264 runs in 7 matches)
Best Bowler: Ekta Bisht (Railways) (15 wickets in 7 matches)

Elite Group A

Western Railway Ground, Rajkot, November 15: Punjab 165/9 in 50 overs (Jasia Akhtar 80, Reva Arora 22; Humaira Kazi 3-19, Fatima Jaffer 2-30) beat **Mumbai** 129 in 47.3 overs (Jemimah Rodrigues 37, Sunetra Paranjape 21; Mehak Kesar 3-31, Sunita Rani 2-27) by 36 runs.

Saurashtra University Ground, Rajkot, November 15: Odisha 87 in 41.1 overs (Madhusmita Behera 31; Ekta Bisht 4-5, Kavita Patil 3-21) lost to **Railways** 91/1 in 15.2 overs (MD Thirushkamini 41*, Mithali Raj 37*) by nine wickets.

Saurashtra University Ground, Rajkot, November 17: Punjab 171/5 in 50 overs (Reva Arora 62*, Neelam Bisht 34*; Priyanka Priyadarshini 2/11) beat **Odisha** 164/9 in 50 overs (Sarita Meher 31, Swagatika Rath 29; Mehak Kesar 2-20, Bharti Bawa 2-22) by seven runs.

Western Railway Ground, Rajkot, November 17: Andhra 132/7 in 50 overs (R Kalpana 35, Chandra Lekha 28; Ekta Bisht 3-15) lost to **Railways** 138/2 in 40.4 overs (Mithali Raj 72*, Punam Raut 34) by eight wickets.

Saurashtra University Ground, Rajkot, November 19: Mumbai 194/8 in 50 overs (Mugdha Joshi 47, Sulakshana Naik 38; C Jhansi Lakshmi 3-27, M Bhavana 2-27) beat **Andhra** 169/9 in 50 overs (Meghana Sabbineni 71, K Anjali Sarvani 26; Manali Dakshini 2-11, Prakashika Naik 2-33) by 25 runs.

Western Railway Ground, Rajkot, November 19: Railways 199/5 in 50 overs (Veda Krishnamurthy 45, Niranjana Nagarajan 43*; Mehak Kesar 2-47) beat **Punjab** 45 in 28.2 overs (Reva Arora 22; Ekta Bist 2-0, Kavita Patil 2-3) by 144 runs.

Saurashtra University Ground, Rajkot, November 21: Punjab 147/8 in 50 overs (Reva Arora 42, Anureet Kaur 39; Saranya Gadwal 3-35, Salma Banu 2-27) lost to **Andhra** 148/7 in 46.4 overs (N Anusha 53, C Jhansi Lakshmi 41; Neelam Bisht 3-27, Mehak Kesar 3-37) by three wickets.

Western Railway Ground, Rajkot, November 21: Odisha 70 in 42.2 overs (Swagatika Rath 26; Manali Dakshini 4-13, Prakashika Naik 3-9) lost to **Mumbai** 71/3 in 27.3 overs (Sunetra Paranjape 35*, Mugdha Joshi 22) by seven wickets.

Western Railway Ground, Rajkot, November 23: Andhra 172/8 in 50 overs (R Kalpana 42, N Anusha 34; Rajasree Swain 3-35) lost to **Odisha** 175/6 in 49 overs (Madhusmita Behera 76*, Kadambini Mohakhud 41; M Bhavana 3-18, Meghana Sabbineni 2-23) by four wickets.

Saurashtra University Ground, Rajkot, November 23: Railways 208/8 in 50 overs (MD Thirushkamini 96, Mithali Raj 63; Fatima Jaffer 3-27, Humaira Kazi 2-35) beat **Mumbai** 99/9 in 50 overs (Jemimah Rodrigues 45; Ekta Bisht 3-18, Sneh Rana 3-20) by 109 runs.

Elite Group A Points Table

Team	M	W	L	T	N/R	Pts	NRR
Railways	4	4	0	0	0	16	+2.262
Mumbai	4	2	2	0	0	8	-0.283
Punjab	4	2	2	0	0	8	-0.614
Andhra	4	1	3	0	0	4	-0.291
Haryana	4	1	3	0	0	4	-1.043

Railways and Mumbai qualified for the Super League

Elite Group B

Bhausaheb Bandodkar Ground, Panaji, November 15: Hyderabad 133 in 45.2 overs (Sneha Morey 48, D Ramya 30; Saika Ishaque 5-30, Tanusree Sarkar 2-26) beat **Bengal** 83 in 39.2 overs (Sravanthi Naidu 3-12, Ananya Upendran 3-13) by 50 runs.

Dr Rajendra Prasad Stadium, Margao, November 15: Maharashtra 145/9 in 50 overs (Anuja Patil 32, Shweta Mane 25; Babita Negi 4-31) beat **Delhi** 68 in 41.2 overs (Shweta Mane 3-17) by 77 runs.

Bhausaheb Bandodkar Ground, Panaji, November 17: Bengal 121/9 in 50 overs (Jhulan Goswami 40; Lalita Sharma 2-21, Soni Yadav 2-23) beat **Delhi** 55 in 36.1 overs (J Goswami 4-7, Tanusree Sarkar 2-13) by 66 runs.

Dr Rajendra Prasad Stadium, Margao, November 17: Maharashtra 135/9 in 50 overs (Devika Vaidya 52*, Tejal Hasabnis 30; Shikha Pandey 3-16, Rupali Chavan 2-18) beat **Goa** 133/9 in 50 overs (Sunanda Yetrekar 56*; T Hasabnis 3-29) by two runs.

Dr Rajendra Prasad Stadium, Margao, November 19: Bengal 99 in 37.1 overs (Mandira Mahapatra 32; Devika Vaidya 4-8, Tejal Hasabnis 2-21) lost to **Maharashtra** 100/3 in 35.3 overs (Snehal Jadhav 41, Anuja Patil 22*, D Vaidya 22*) by seven wickets.

Bhausaheb Bandodkar Ground, Panaji, November 19: Goa 82 in 48.3 overs (Santoshi Rane 39; Sravanthi Naidu 3-19, Arundhati Reddy 2-7) lost to **Hyderabad** 83/4 in 33.4 overs (VM Kavya 25*, M Shalini 20) by six wickets.

Bhausaheb Bandodkar Ground, Panaji, November 21: Hyderabad 62 in 43 overs (Reema Malhotra 2-12) lost to **Delhi** 63/5 in 25.1 overs (Latika Kumari 23; Arundhati Reddy 2-8, M Shalini 2-8) by five wickets.

Dr Rajendra Prasad Stadium, Margao, November 21: Bengal 96 in 39 overs (Priyanka Roy 40*; Shikha Pandey 5-21, Sunanda Yetrekar 2-12) lost to **Goa** 97/4 in 36.4 overs (S Yetrekar 29*, S Pandey 25*; Jhulan Goswami 2-14) by six wickets.

Dr Rajendra Prasad Stadium, Margao, November 23: Goa 102 in 47.1 overs (Sanjula Naik 46; Shashi Malik 2-4, Lalita Sharma 2-11) lost to **Delhi** 104/5 in 40.2 overs (Latika Kumari 25, S Malik 24; Santoshi Rane 2-24) by five wickets.

Bhausaheb Bandodkar Ground, Panaji, November 23: Maharashtra 101 in 50 overs (Shweta Mane 25; Gouher Sultana 3-16, Arundhati Reddy 2-12) lost to **Hyderabad** 86/5 in 35 overs (VM Kavya 50*; S Mane 3-21) by five wickets (VJD method).

Elite Group B Points Table

Team	M	W	L	T	N/R	Pts	NRR
Maharashtra	4	3	1	0	0	12	+0.724
Hyderabad	4	3	1	0	0	12	+0.338
Delhi	4	2	2	0	0	8	-0.398
Goa	4	1	3	0	0	4	-0.184
Bengal	4	1	3	0	0	4	-0.241

Maharashtra and Hyderabad qualified for the Super League

Plate Group A

JSCA Oval Ground, Ranchi, November 15: Jharkhand 180/6 in 50 overs (Niharika Prasad 41, Rasmi 36*) beat **Assam** 123/9 in 50 overs (Mamatha Kanojia 56*; Kavita Roy 3-16, Ritu Kumari 2-26) by 57 runs.

JSCA Stadium Complex, Ranchi, November 15: Uttar Pradesh 126/9 in 50 overs (Bhawana Tomar 27, Aditi Sharma 26; C Pratyusha 3-19, K Rakshita 2-21) lost to **Karnataka** 127/2 in 40 overs (Karuna Jain 55*, G Divya 26) by eight wickets.

MECON Limited Sail Stadium, Ranchi, November 15: Saurashtra 88 in 48.3 overs (Mamta Sharma 2-7) lost to **Madhya Pradesh** 89/4 in 31.5 overs (Nuzhat Parween 29, Varsha Choudhary 27*) by six wickets.

JSCA Stadium Complex, Ranchi, November 17: Assam 135/9 in 50 overs (Monikha Das 29, Genevie Pando 20; Nidhi Buley 3-35) lost to **Madhya Pradesh** 136/7 in 47.4 overs (N Buley 31*, Nuzhat Parween 31; G Pando 2-21) by three wickets.

MECON Sail Stadium, Ranchi, November 17: Jharkhand 126 in 49.1 overs (Priyanka Sawaiyan 27, Seema Singh 27; Zeenat Firdos 3-16, Aditi Sharma 2-20) lost to **Uttar Pradesh** 127/7 in 45 overs (Deepti Sharma 57; Rinni Burman 3-33, Roshni Kannojia 2-22) by three wickets.

JSCA Oval Ground, Ranchi, November 17: Saurashtra 117 in 41.3 overs (Neha Chavda 39; Debasmita Dutta 4-29) lost to **Karnataka** 118/6 in 45.2 overs (Karuna Jain 34, VR Vanitha 26; Reena Dabhi 3-16) by four wickets.

MECON Limited Sail Stadium, Ranchi, November 19: Assam 179/8 in 50 overs (Rumeli Dhar 64, Mamatha Kanojia 51; Deepti Sharma 2-37) beat **Uttar Pradesh** 160 in 48.3 overs (Shashi Singh 65, Neetu Singh 51; Nirupama Bora 4-20) by 19 runs.

JSCA Stadium Complex, Ranchi, November 19: Jharkhand 112 in 49.3 overs (Ritu Kumari 38; Mridula Jadeja 2-18, Neha Chavda 2-19) beat **Saurashtra** 94 in 48 overs (Jayshreeba Jadeja 26; Kanaka Lata 2-5, Kavita Roy 2-13) by 18 runs.

JSCA Oval Ground, Ranchi, November 19: Madhya Pradesh 150 in 49 overs (Varsha Choudhary 34, Ruchita Buley 29; C Pratyusha 5-42, Akanksha Kohli 2-9) lost to **Karnataka** 153/5 in 46.1 overs (Karuna Jain 68*, Pushpa Kiresur 22; V Choudhary 2-31) by five wickets.

MECON Limited Sail Stadium, Ranchi, November 21: Saurashtra 63 in 38 overs (Rashmi Dey 2-4, Nirupama Baro 2-7) lost to **Assam** 67/7 in 21.4 overs (Neha Chavda 3-21, Nirali Oza 2-14) by three wickets.

Bokaro Steel Limited Cricket Stadium, November 21: Jharkhand 131/7 in 50 overs (Shobha Kumari 41, Kavita Roy 36; Sahana Pawar 2-14) lost to **Karnataka** 132/5 in 48.1 overs (K Rakshita 44, Pushpa Kiresur 29*; Kanaka Lata 2-13) by five wickets.

JSCA Oval Ground, Ranchi, November 21: Madhya Pradesh 160/8 in 50 overs (Varsha Choudhary 60, Neha Badwaik 29; Pallavi Bharadwaj 2-19, Shivangiraj Singh 2-24) beat **Uttar Pradesh** 105 in 45.4 overs (Shashi Singh 31, Aditi Sharma 21*; Ruchita Bhuley 3-10, Mamta Sharma 3-11) by 55 runs.

Bokaro Steel Limited Cricket Stadium, November 23: Assam 167/7 in 50 overs (Mamatha Kanojia 56*, Rekharani Bora 37; Sahana Pawar 2-27, Debasmitha Dutta 2-32) lost to **Karnataka** 168/8 in 47.5 overs (VR Vanitha 95; Nirupama Baro 3-20, Rashmi Dey 2-26) by two wickets.

MECON Limited Sail Stadium, Ranchi, November 23: Madhya Pradesh 116 in 48.3 overs (Varsha Choudhary 49, Pooja Vastrakar 24; Niharika Prasad 4-19, RachanaKumari 2-7) beat **Jharkhand** 56 in 36.4 overs (Nidhi Buley 2-4, Ruchita Buley 2-6) by 60 runs.

JSCA Oval Ground, Ranchi, November 23: Uttar Pradesh 184/8 in 50 overs (Deepti Sharma 56, Shivangiraj Singh 47*; Pooja Nimavat 4-25, Neha Chavda 2-35) beat **Saurashtra** 107/8 in 50 overs (Jayshree Jadeja 51; Deepti 4-8, Shivangiraj 2-11) by 77 runs.

Plate Group A Points Table

Team	M	W	L	T	N/R	Pts	NRR
Karnataka	5	5	0	0	0	20	+0.304
Madhya Pradesh	5	4	1	0	0	16	+0.655
Assam	5	2	3	0	0	8	+0.147
Jharkhand	5	2	3	0	0	8	-0.015
Uttar Pradesh	5	2	3	0	0	8	-0.047
Saurashtra	5	0	5	0	0	0	-0.991

Karnataka and Madhya Pradesh qualified for the Plate Knockout

Plate Group B

Sardar Patel Stadium C Ground, Motera, Ahmedabad, November 15: Jammu & Kashmir 54 in 27.4 overs (Seema Pujare 3-5, Falguni Chauhan 2-16) lost to **Gujarat** 55/1 in 20.5 overs (Renuka Chaudhari 21*) by nine wickets.

Sardar Patel Stadium B Ground, Motera, Ahmedabad, November 15: Haryana 135/7 in 50 overs (Sonia Khatri 48, Suman Gulia 42; Nikita Chauhan 2-25) beat **Himachal Pradesh** 97/9 in 50 overs (Vandna Rana 21; Mansi Joshi 3-22, Shiva Prajapati 2-13) by 38 runs.

Sardar Patel Stadium B Ground, Motera, Ahmedabad, November 17: Haryana 174/8 in 50 overs (Sonia Khatri 56, Mansi Joshi 33; Priyanka Acharjee 2-22) beat **Tripura** 73 in 40.3 overs (Shiva Prajapati 2-11, Nirupma Tanwar 2-15) by 101 runs.

Sardar Patel Stadium C Ground, Motera, Ahmedabad, November 17: Himachal Pradesh 209/8 in 50 overs (Harleen Deol 85, Neena Choudhary 45; Sheerazah Banoo 4-41, Sandhya Balkar 3-37) beat **Jammu & Kashmir** 85 in 32.5 overs (Sarla Devi 35; H Deol 4-19, Susmitha Kumari 3-7) by 124 runs.

Sardar Patel Stadium B Ground, Motera, Ahmedabad, November 19: Gujarat 112 in 50 overs (Falguni Chauhan 26; Reema Chakraborty 2-13, Suravi Roy 2-25) beat **Tripura** 77 in 37 overs (Mouchaity Debnath 31, Rizu Saha 20; Darshan Rajput 4-15, Deepa Patel 2-2) by 35 runs.

Sardar Patel Stadium C Ground, Motera, Ahmedabad, November 19: Haryana 167/6 in 50 overs (Suman Gulia 49, Anju Tomar 28*; Sandhya Balkar 2-29) beat **Jammu & Kashmir** 87/8 in 50 overs (Rubia Syed 29; Preeti Bose 3-7) by 80 runs.

Sardar Patel Stadium B Ground, Motera, Ahmedabad, November 21: Gujarat 119 in 49.5 overs (Renuka Chaudhari 36; Susmitha Kumari 2-18, Nikita Chauhan 2-24) lost to **Himachal Pradesh** 123/5 in 42.4 overs (Neena Choudhary 62*, Vandna Rana 24) by five wickets.

Sardar Patel Stadium C Ground, Motera, Ahmedabad, November 21: Tripura 212/8 in 50 overs (Reema Chakraborty 77, Rizu Saha 58; Sarla Devi 2-28) beat **Jammu & Kashmir** 146/9 in 50 overs (Payal Choudhary 47, Anju Devi 31; Reema Charaborty 2-28, Annapurna Das 2-31) by 66 runs.

Sardar Patel Stadium B Ground, Motera, Ahmedabad, November 23: Gujarat 140/6 in 50 overs (Archana Das 45*, Darshan Rajput 45; Shiva Prajapati 3-19) beat **Haryana** 118/9 in 50 overs (Sonia Khatri 44; Darshan Rajput 3-29, Krutika Chaudhari 2-21) by 22 runs.

Sardar Patel Stadium C Ground, Motera, Ahmedabad, November 23: Himachal Pradesh 151/9 in 50 overs (Harleen Deol 38, Tanuja Kanwar 36; Annapurna Das 3-22, Suravi Roy 3-27) beat **Tripura** 88 in 36.5 overs (Rizu Saha 25, Mouchaity Debnath 24; H Deol 3-9, Anisha Ansari 2-15) by 63 runs.

Plate Group B Points Table

Team	M	W	L	T	N/R	Pts	NRR
Haryana	4	3	1	0	0	12	+0.985
Himachal Pradesh	4	3	1	0	0	12	+0.875
Gujarat	4	3	1	0	0	12	+0.563
Tripura	4	1	3	0	0	4	-0.665
Jammu & Kashmir	4	0	4	0	0	0	-1.904

Haryana and Himachal Pradesh qualified for the Plate Knockout

Plate Group C

St Paul's College Ground, Kochi, November 15: Tamil Nadu 66 in 34.5 overs (S Asha 5-10, S Sajana 2-5) lost to **Kerala** 67/0 in 18.2 overs (T Shani 33*, Mariya Benny 28*) by ten wickets.

Rajagiri School of Engineering and Technology Ground, Ernakulam, November 15: Rajasthan 107 in 47.1 overs (JU Bijarnya 34; Bharati Fulmali 4-8, Kalyani Chawarkar 2-17) lost to **Vidarbha** 112/2 in 33.4 overs (Vaishnavi Khandkar 36, Neha Dabli 34) by eight wickets.

Rajagiri School of Engineering and Technology Ground, Ernakulam, November 17: Baroda 111 in 38.3 overs (Tarannum Pathan 38, Palak Patel 22; CV Swetha 3-36, Shyla Alam 2-13) lost to **Tamil Nadu** 114/9 in 46 overs (M Shailaja 35, CV Swetha 21*; Nancy Patel 3-29, Radha Yadav 2-11) by one wicket.

St Paul's College Ground, Kochi, November 17: Kerala 153/7 in 50 overs (A Akshaya 38*, Jincy George 35*; Jyoti Bhagat 2-12, Nupur Kohale 2-19) beat **Vidarbha** 57 in 32 overs (T Shani 5-3, VS Mridhula 2-4) by 96 runs.

St Paul's College Ground, Kochi, November 19: Rajasthan 54 in 34.5 overs (Nancy Patel 4-10, Radha Yadav 3-9) lost to **Baroda** 55/4 in 26 overs (Renu Yadav 2-11) by six wickets.

Rajagiri School of Engineering and Technology Ground, Ernakulam, November 19: Vidarbha 159/8 in 47 overs (Neha Dabli 86) lost to **Tamil Nadu** 70/3 in 25.2 overs (V Vilasini 28; Kalyani Chawarkar 3-7) by two runs (VJD method).

Rajagiri School of Engineering and Technology Ground, Ernakulam, November 21: Vidarbha 87 in 40.3 overs (Bharati Fulmali 31; Radha Yadav 2-2, Shalini Sharma 2-12) lost to **Baroda** 88/0 in 19.3 overs (Palak Patel 45*, Heena Patel 40*) by ten wickets.

St Paul's College Ground, Kochi, November 21: Rajasthan 99 in 46.2 overs (Ayushi Garg 20; S Asha 2-14, S Sajana 2-18) lost to **Kerala** 101/3 in 32.5 overs (T Shani 45, S Asha 34*; Sofi Sidhu 2-38) by seven wickets.

St Paul's College Ground, Kochi, November 23: Kerala 107 in 49.5 overs (S Asha 22, Anjana Thomas 22; Radha Yadav 2-9, Tarannum Pathan 2-10) lost to **Baroda** 108/4 in 43 overs (Palak Patel 39, T Pathan 27; T Shani 2-21) by six wickets.

Rajagiri School of Engineering and Technology Ground, Ernakulam, November 23: Rajasthan 136 in 49.3 overs (Ayushi Garg 55, Renu Yadav 20; Hemalatha Dayalan 3-29, Nethra Iyer 3-29) lost to **Tamil Nadu** 137/4 in 43 overs (Hemalatha Dayalan 72*; Suman Meena 2-17, Rinku Tank 2-34) by six wickets.

Plate Group C Points Table

Team	M	W	L	T	N/R	Pts	NRR
Kerala	4	3	1	0	0	12	+1.121
Baroda	4	3	1	0	0	12	+0.767
Tamil Nadu	4	3	1	0	0	12	-0.304
Vidarbha	4	1	3	0	0	4	-0.848
Rajasthan	4	0	4	0	0	0	-1.009

Kerala and Baroda qualified for the Plate Knockout

Plate Group Knockout

1st Quarter-Final: Santosh Garj Cricket Stadium, Una, December 1: Madhya Pradesh 128/8 in 50 overs (Nuzhat Parween 28, Nidhi Buley 24; Suman Gulia 2-13, Preeti Bose 2-19) beat **Haryana** 75 in 43.4 overs (Mamta Sharma 4-11) by 53 runs.

2nd Quarter-Final: Indira Gandhi Stadium, Una, December 1: Himachal Pradesh 91 in 40.4 overs (Neena Choudhary 50; Jaya Mohite 3-23, Shalini Sharma 2-11) lost to **Baroda** 94/2 in 22.2 overs (Palak Patel 43, Tanuja Kanwar 2-39) by eight wickets.

1st Semi-Final: Indira Gandhi Stadium, Una, December 3: Karnataka 104 in 41.3 overs (C Pratyusha 35*, Akanksha Kohli 26; Zulekha Yakubwala 3-25, Nancy Patel 2-8) lost to **Baroda** 105/6 in 44.3 overs (Yastika Bhatia 26; Sahana Pawar 2-5, A Kohli 2-16) by four wickets.

2nd Semi-Final: Santosh Garj Cricket Stadium, Una, December 3: Kerala 74 in 42.4 overs (K Jincy George 23*, Pooja Vastrakar 4-12, Nidhi Buley 3-16) lost to **Madhya Pradesh** 75/5 in 31.5 overs (Varsha Choudhary 26*; V Mridhula 2-28, Aswathy Mol 2-17) by five wickets.

Final: Gandhi Stadium, Una, December 5: Baroda 112 in 49.5 overs (Heena Patel 43; Nidhi Buley 3-14, Ruchita Buley 2-13) lost to **Madhya Pradesh** 113/5 in 37.3 overs (Pallavi Bharadwaj 23, Gayatri Naik 2-20) by five wickets.

Winners: Madhya Pradesh

Elite Group Super League

Railways Recreation Club Ground, Secunderabad, December 1: Hyderabad 60 in 37.4 overs (Kavita Patil 3-15, Rajeshwari Gayakwad 2-4) lost to **Railways** 61/2 in 24.4 overs (Punam Raut 33*) by eight wickets.

Vijayanand Gardens Ground, Hyderabad, December 1: Mumbai 150 in 50 overs (Sheral Rozario 51*, Bhakti Tamore 22; Shweta Mane 3-37, Anuja Patil 2-22) lost to **Maharashtra** 151/2 in 43.2 overs (Smriti Mandhana 84*, Snehal Jadhav 24) by eight wickets.

Vijayanand Gardens Ground, Hyderabad, December 3: Mumbai 114 in 49.1 overs (Mugdha Joshi 30, Prajakta Shirwadkar 20; Sneh Rana 4-20, Kavita Patil 2-22) lost to **Railways** 108/1 in 34.3 overs (MD Thirushkamini 65*, Punam Raut 35) by nine wickets (VJD method).

Gymkhana Ground, Hyderabad, December 3: Maharashtra 134/7 in 50 overs (Shweta Mane 34*, Anuja Patil 25) lost to **Hyderabad** 135/4 in 42.1 overs (M Shalini 44, Diana David 35*; Shweta Mane 2-22) by six wickets.

Gymkhana Ground, Hyderabad, December 4: Mumbai 155/7 in 50 overs (Bhakti Tamore 34, Mugdha Joshi 31; Gouher Sultana 3-33, VM Kavya 2-15) beat **Hyderabad** 94 in 35 overs

(Arundhati Reddy 38; Sunetra Paranjape 3-9, Humaira Kazi 3-16, Sheral Rozario 3-30) by 61 runs.
Vijayanand Gardens Ground, Hyderabad, December 4: Railways 218/6 in 50 overs (Mithali Raj 68, Niranjana Nagarajan 53; Anuja Patil 3-35) beat **Maharashtra** 161/9 in 50 overs (Smriti Mandhana 78, Shweta Mane 36; Harmanpreet Kaur 2-22, Sneh Rana 2-29) by 57 runs.

Elite Group Super League Points Table

Team	M	W	L	T	N/R	Pts	NRR
Railways	3	3	0	0	0	12	1.486
Mumbai	3	1	2	0	0	4	-0.077
Maharashtra	3	1	2	0	0	4	-0.426
Hyderabad	3	1	2	0	0	4	-0.775

Winners: Railways

Inter-State T20 Competition

Mandhana gives Railways a scare

Mithali Raj's Railways recovered from an early loss against Maharashtra in the first round to successfully defend their T20 crown. They maintained a clean slate in the super league games, televised for the first time, defeating Odisha and Maharashtra, and overcoming Goa in a nail-biting encounter. Smriti Mandhana, Maharashtra's captain, topped the batting charts; her trademark flicks through square leg and punches off the back foot on full display. Sunetra Paranjape-led Mumbai took the honours in the Plate Division, beating a spirited Uttar Pradesh in the final. Among other individual performances, Devika Vaidya, the 18-year-old leg-spinner from Maharashtra, scalped a hat-trick against Odisha, while Renu Yadav of Rajasthan finished with 5 for 5, the only five-wicket haul of the tournament, against Gujarat.

Best Batter: Smriti Mandhana (Maharashtra) (224 runs, 7 matches)
Best Bowler: Rupali Chavan (Goa) (13 wickets, 7 matches)

Elite Group A
Jagarlamudi Kuppuswamy Choudary College, Guntur, January 2: Punjab 104/6 in 20 overs (Jasia Akhtar 43, Taniya Bhatia 23; Ruchita Buley 2-12) lost to **Madhya Pradesh** 107/8 in 19.4 overs (Nidhi Buley 28*, Pooja Vastrakar 25; Priyanka Guleria 3-21, Mehak Kesar 2-18) by two wickets.
Jagarlamudi Kuppuswamy Choudary College, Guntur, January 2: Odisha 110/7 in 20

Goa were unbeaten in the first round of the Elite group and went on to give defending champions Railways a tough fight. — *Special arrangement*

overs (Madhuri Meheta 30, Kadambini Mohakhud 27; T Shani 3-17) beat **Kerala** 81/9 in 20 overs (S Asha 33; Ritu Singh 2-6, Sushree Pradhan 2-13) by 29 runs.

Jagarlamudi Kuppuswamy Choudary College, Guntur, January 3: Punjab 75/9 in 20 overs (Parveen Khan 32; Shikha Pandey 2-7, Rupali Chavan 2-17) lost to **Goa** 77/2 in 16.2 overs (Sunanda Yetrekar 43*, Shikha Pandey 20*) by eight wickets.

Jagarlamudi Kuppuswamy Choudary College, Guntur, January 3: Odisha 125/3 in 20 overs (Madhusmita Behera 50, Madhuri Meheta 34; Nidhi Buley 2-24) tied with **Madhya Pradesh** 125/7 in 20 overs (Varsh Choudhary 32, Pooja Choudhary 28; M Behara 2-23). Super Over: Madhya Pradesh 6/0 in 1 over lost to Odisha 7/0 in 1 over.

Jagarlamudi Kuppuswamy Choudary College, Guntur, January 4: Kerala 64 in 19.5 overs (Rupali Chavan 3-8, Shikha Pandey 2-10) lost to **Goa** 68/7 in 18.5 overs (Santoshi Rane 25*; S Sajana 4-10, VS Mridhula 2-11) by three wickets.

Jagarlamudi Kuppuswamy Choudary College, Guntur, January 4: Punjab 92/9 in 20 overs (Parveen Khan 30; Priyanka Priyadarshini 4-13) lost to **Odisha** 93/2 in 17.5 overs (Madhusmita Behera 40*, Pragyanparamita Mohanty 23*) by eight wickets.

Jagarlamudi Kuppuswamy Choudary College, Guntur, January 5: Kerala 62/8 in 20 overs (Varsha Choudhary 3-14) lost to **Madhya Pradesh** 63/0 in 15.3 overs (V Choudhary 29*, Nuzhat Parween 28*) by ten wickets.

Jagarlamudi Kuppuswamy Choudary College, Guntur, January 5: Odisha 69 in 17.5 overs (Pragyan Mohanty 29; Sunanda Yetrekar 2-9, Sonali Gaunder 2-14) lost to **Goa** 72/2 in 18.3 overs (Shikha Pandey 35*, Sunanda Yetrekar 24*) by eight wickets.

Jagarlamudi Kuppuswamy Choudary College, Guntur, January 6: Punjab 106/3 in 20 overs (Reva Arora 38*, Jasia Akhtar 32) lost to **Kerala** 107/3 in 20 overs (S Sajana 31*, S Asha 27) by seven wickets.

Jagarlamudi Kuppuswamy Choudary College, Guntur, January 6: Madhya Pradesh 86/9 in 20 overs (Pooja Choudhary 36; Rupali Chavan 3-10, Santoshi Rane 2-11) lost to **Goa** 88/4 in 17 overs (Sanjula Naik 50; Pooja Vastrakar 2-15) by six wickets.

Elite Group A Points Table

Teams	M	W	L	T	N/R	Pts	NRR
Goa	4	4	0	0	0	16	+0.641
Odisha	4	3	1	0	0	12	+0.387
Madhya Pradesh	4	2	2	0	0	8	+0.147
Kerala	4	1	3	0	0	4	-0.743
Punjab	4	0	4	0	0	0	-0.488

Goa and Odisha qualified for the Elite Super League

Elite Group B

Jadavpur University Complex, Kolkata, January 2: Delhi 71/9 in 20 overs (Gouher Sultana 2-2, VM Kavya 2-10) lost to **Hyderabad** 72/3 in 14.4 overs (Sneha Morey 28) by seven wickets.

Jadavpur University Complex, Kolkata, January 2: Railways 92/5 in 20 overs (Veda Krishnamurthy 35*, Niranjana Nagarajan 27; Shweta Mane 2-19) lost to **Maharashtra** 93/3 in 20 overs (Snehal Jadhav 41, Smriti Mandhana 30) by seven wickets.

Jadavpur University Complex, Kolkata, January 3: Bengal 101/7 in 20 overs (Priyanka Roy 42, Dipali Shaw 20) beat **Maharashtra** 72 in 17.3 overs (Tanusree Sarkar 3-13, Jhulan Goswami 2-2) by 29 runs.

Jadavpur University Complex, Kolkata, January 3: Railways 103/7 in 20 overs (Anagha Deshpande 38, MD Thirushkamini 38; Lalita Sharma 3-19) beat **Delhi** 60/9 in 20 overs (Shubhlakshmi Sharma 3-10, Ekta Bisht 2-7) by 43 runs.

Eden Gardens, Kolkata, January 4: Bengal 82 in 20 overs (Gouher Sultana 2-8) lost to **Hyderabad** 83/3 in 19.2 overs (M Shalini 24, Sukanya Parida 3-12, Priya Pandey 2-10) by two wickets.

Eden Gardens, Kolkata, January 4: Maharashtra 108/6 in 20 overs (Smriti Mandhana 45, Snehal Jadhav 29) beat **Delhi** 86/6 in 20 overs (Priya Punia 32, Latika Kumari 25; Shweta Mane 2-20) by 22 runs.

Eden Gardens, Kolkata, January 5: Railways 103/3 in 20 overs (Mithali Raj 41*, Veda Krishnamurthy 36*; VM Kavya 2-10) beat **Hyderabad** 76/8 in 20 overs (VM Kavya 20, Poonam Yadav 3-17, Ekta Bisht 2-14) by 27 runs.

Eden Gardens, Kolkata, January 5: Bengal 98/9 in 20 overs (Jhulan Goswami 47; Babita Negi 3-16, Soni Yadav 2-22) beat **Delhi** 95/4 in 20 overs (Priya Punia 38, Latika Kumari 31; Jhulan Goswami 2-22) by three runs.

Eden Gardens, Kolkata, January 6: Hyderabad 92 in 20 overs (Anuja Patil 3-15, Devika Vaidya 3-10) lost to **Maharashtra** 93/8 in 19.3 overs (A Patil 37, Mukta Magre 20; Ananya Upendran 3-14) by two wickets.

Eden Gardens, Kolkata, January 6: Railways 145/3 in 20 overs (MD Thirushkamini 61, Harmanpreet Kaur 49*; Saiqa Ishaque 2-32) beat **Bengal** 85/5 in 20 overs (Priyanka Roy 38*; Rajeshwari Gayakwad 2-18) by 60 runs.

Elite Group B Points Table

Teams	M	W	L	T	N/R	Pts	NRR
Railways	4	3	1	0	0	12	+1.613
Maharashtra	4	3	1	0	0	12	-0.034
Hyderabad	4	2	2	0	0	8	-0.025
Bengal	4	2	2	0	0	8	-0.404
Delhi	4	0	4	0	0	0	-1.203

Railways and Maharashtra qualified for the Elite Super League

Plate Group A

JSCA Oval Ground, Ranchi, January 2: Assam 137/8 in 20 overs (Rumeli Dhar 48, Mamatha Kanojia 41; Krutika Chaudhari 3-28) beat **Gujarat** 100/4 in 20 overs (Darshan Rajput 47, Renuka Chaudhari 27; Shanti Rai 3-14) by 37 runs.

JSCA Oval Ground, Ranchi, January 2: Rajasthan 86/7 in 20 overs (Niresh Kumari 34; Tanuja Kanwar 2-6) lost to **Himachal Pradesh** 88/1 in 18.2 overs (Neena Choudhari 41*, Shivani Sharma 26*) by nine wickets.

JSCA Oval Ground, Ranchi, January 2: Jammu & Kashmir 49 in 18 overs (Radha Yadav 3-11, Tarannum Pathan 2-3) lost to **Baroda** 51/1 in 10 overs (Palak Patel 22*) by nine wickets.

JSCA Oval Ground, Ranchi, January 3: Himachal Pradesh 101/6 in 20 overs (Shivani Sharma 28, Nikita Chauhan 24; Nirupama Baro 2-10) beat **Assam** 90/7 in 20 overs (Monika Das 24, N Chauhan 2-17) by 11 runs.

JSCA Cricket Stadium Complex, Ranchi, January 3: Rajasthan 120/6 in 20 overs (Babita Meena 30*, Sangeeta Kumawat 27; Bushra Ashraf 2-21) beat **Jammu & Kashmir** 73/9 in 20 overs (Rubia Syed 22; S Kumawat 2-5, Renu Yadav 2-15) by 47 runs.

JSCA Oval Ground, Ranchi, January 3: Baroda 123/6 in 20 overs (Yastika Bhatia 44, Palak Patel 23; Pragna Chaudhari 2-23) beat **Gujarat** 70/7 in 20 overs (Tarannum Pathan 3-6, Jaya Mohite 2-9) by 53 runs.

JSCA Stadium Complex, Ranchi, January 4: Rajasthan 90/6 in 20 overs (Shweta Bishnoi 27; Debashree Konwar 3-19) lost to **Assam** 91/6 in 19.2 overs (Rumeli Dhar 49, Mamatha Kanojia 20; Rinku Tank 2-8) by four wickets.

JSCA Oval Ground, Ranchi, January 4: Baroda 125/8 in 20 overs (Radha Yadav 32*, Binaisha Surti 28; Renuka Singh 2-12, Tanuja Kanwar 2-25) lost to **Himachal Pradesh** 126/6 in 19.4 overs (Neena Choudhary 47, Vandna Rana 33; Tarannum Pathan 2-17) by four wickets.

JSCA Stadium Complex, Ranchi, January 4: Jammu & Kashmir 87 in 20 overs (Ankita Jalla 31, Rubia Syed 21; Seema Pujare 2-22) lost to **Gujarat** 88/0 in 12.2 overs (Renuka Chaudhari 51*, Darshan Rajpur 29*) by ten wickets.

JSCA Oval Ground, Ranchi, January 5: Baroda 112/6 in 20 overs (Yastika Bhatia 36, Binaisha Surti 23; Kakoli Saikia 2-24, Rumeli Dhar 2-25) beat **Assam** 37 in 17.3 overs (Radha Yadav 3-5, Nancy Patel 3-6) by 75 runs.

JSCA Stadium Complex, Ranchi, January 5: Rajasthan 100/9 in 20 overs (Shweta Bishnoi 48, Sangeeta Kumawat 25; Seema Pujare 4-7, Krutika Chaudhari 2-14) beat **Gujarat** 80 in 19.2 overs (Archana 22, Renu Yadav 5-5) by 20 runs.

JSCA Oval Ground, Ranchi, January 5: Jammu & Kashmir 63/6 in 20 overs (Ankita Jalla 35; Tanuja Kanwar 2-13) lost to **Himachal Pradesh** 64/2 in 13.5 overs (Harleen Deol 42*) by eight wickets.

JSCA Oval Ground, Ranchi, January 6: Jammu & Kashmir 92/5 in 20 overs (Rubia Syed 57) lost to **Assam** 93/2 in 16.3 overs (Rumeli Dhar 38, Mamatha Kanojia 29*) by eight wickets.

JSCA Oval Ground, Ranchi, January 6: Rajasthan 85/7 in 20 overs (Niresh Kumari 29*; Tarannum Pathan 3-11) lost to **Baroda** 88/5 in 16.2 overs (Binaisha Surti 41, Palak Patel 37; Babita Meena 3-17) by five wickets.

JSCA Oval Ground, Ranchi, January 6: Gujarat 72/7 in 20 overs (Archana Das 31) lost to **Himachal Pradesh** 73/4 in 16.3 overs (Vandna Rana 28*) by six wickets.

Plate Group A Points Table

Teams	M	W	L	T	N/R	Pts	NRR
Himachal Pradesh	5	5	0	0	0	20	+0.757
Baroda	5	4	1	0	0	16	+2.098
Assam	5	3	2	0	0	12	-0.275
Rajasthan	5	2	3	0	0	8	+0.342
Gujarat	5	1	4	0	0	4	-0.948
Jammu & Kashmir	5	0	5	0	0	0	-2.085

Himachal Pradesh and Baroda qualified for the Plate Knockout

Plate Group B

Dr Akhilesh Das Stadium, Lucknow, January 2: Mumbai 122/3 in 20 overs (Sunetra Paranjape 38, Jemimah Rodrigues 36*) beat **Saurashtra** 62 in 19.5 overs (Humaira Kazi 3-12, Fatima Jaffer 2-7) by 60 runs.

Dr Akhilesh Das Stadium, Lucknow, January 2: Vidarbha 70/5 in 20 overs (Bharati Fulmali 22, Mona Meshram 21; Shefali Sahu 2-10) lost to **Uttar Pradesh** 71/4 in 17 overs (Shashi Singh 23) by six wickets.

Dr Akhilesh Das Stadium, Lucknow, January 3: Tripura 80/7 in 20 overs (Manali Dakshini 3-15, Fatima Jaffer 2-11) lost to **Mumbai** 81/3 in 14.3 overs (Mugdha Joshi 29*, Sunetra Paranjpe 20) by seven wickets.

Dr Akhilesh Das Stadium, Lucknow, January 3: Saurashtra 61/9 in 20 overs (Jayshree Jadeja 33; Deepti Sharma 4-9) lost to **Uttar Pradesh** 65/4 in 15.1 overs (Deepti 34*) by six wickets.

Dr Akhilesh Das Stadium, Lucknow, January 4: Tripura 97/8 in 20 overs (Jhumki Debanth 29, Mouchaity Debanth 25; Nupur Kohale 3-13, Kalyani Chawarkar 3-19) lost to **Vidarbha** 103/2 in 18.2 overs (Bharati Fulmali 54*) by eight wickets.

Dr Akhilesh Das Stadium, Lucknow, January 4: Mumbai 102/9 in 20 overs (Sulakshana Naik 28, Humaira Kazi 27*; Shivangi Raj Singh 3-9, Deepti Sharma 2-10) beat **Uttar Pradesh** 65/7 in 20 overs by 37 runs.

Dr Akhilesh Das Stadium, Lucknow, January 5: Saurashtra 85/9 in 20 overs (Jayshreeba Jadeja 28; Kalyani Chawarkar 3-16, Reena Paul 2-8) beat **Vidarbha** 66/9 in 20 overs (Reena Dabhi 3-11, Drasti Somaiya 2-12) by 19 runs.

Dr Akhilesh Das Stadium, Lucknow, January 5: Uttar Pradesh 112/8 in 20 overs (Deepti Sharma 47, Aditi Sharma 27; Moutushi Dey 4-16, Suravi Roy 2-11) beat **Tripura** 92/7 in 20 overs (Rizu Saha 26, Annapurna Das 24; Deepti 3-22, Zeenat Firdos 2-15) by 20 runs.

Dr Akhilesh Das Stadium, Lucknow, January 6: Mumbai 96/8 in 20 overs (Sheral Rozario

38, Bhakti Tamore 31*; Komal Zanzad 3-12, Kalyani Chawarkar 2-18) beat **Vidarbha** 89/2 in 20 overs (Mona Meshram 43*, Bharati Fulmali 28) by 7 runs.
Dr Akhilesh Das Stadium, Lucknow, January 6: Saurashtra 102/5 in 20 overs (Bhakti Shastri 43) beat **Tripura** 89/7 in 20 overs (Mouchaity Debnath 34, Jhumki Debnath 20; Neha Chavda 4-10, Reena Dabhi 2-19) by 13 runs.

Plate Group B Points Table

Teams	M	W	L	T	N/R	Pts	NRR
Mumbai	4	4	0	0	0	16	+1.683
Uttar Pradesh	4	3	1	0	0	12	+0.275
Saurashtra	4	2	2	0	0	8	-0.675
Vidarbha	4	1	3	0	0	4	-0.345
Tripura	4	0	4	0	0	0	-0.990

Mumbai and Uttar Pradesh qualified for the Plate Knockout

Plate Group C

CH Bansi Lal Cricket Stadium, Lahli, Rohtak, January 2: Haryana 92/5 in 20 overs (Pooja Sharma 25, Sonia Khatri 21) beat **Karnataka** 80/7 in 20 overs (K Rakshita 29*; Savita Malik 2-16) by 12 runs.
CH Bansi Lal Cricket Stadium, Lahli, Rohtak, January 2: Andhra 74/9 in 20 overs (Anusha Prabhakaran 4-17, Anusha Sundaresan 2-8) beat **Tamil Nadu** 52 in 19.5 overs (Vilasini Nair 21; M Bhavana 2-6, Meghana Sabbineni 2-10) by 22 runs.
CH Bansi Lal Cricket Stadium, Lahli, Rohtak, January 3: Jharkhand 54 in 19.3 overs (K Rakshita 4-17, Akanksha Kohli 2-7) beat **Karnataka** 53 in 20 overs (Kavita Roy 2-5, Kanaka Lata 2-7) by one run.
CH Bansi Lal Cricket Stadium, Lahli, Rohtak, January 3: Andhra 75/4 in 20 overs (N Anusha 33; Preeti Bose 2-13) lost to **Haryana** 76/6 in 18.5 overs (Bhawna Ohlan 27, Mansi Joshi 21; M Bhavana 3-17) by four wickets.
CH Bansi Lal Cricket Stadium, Lahli, Rohtak, January 4: Jharkhand 83/6 in 20 overs (Priyanka Sawaiyan 25; Hemalatha Dayalan 2-13) beat **Tamil Nadu** 71/7 in 20 overs (Namita Ojha 20; Roshni Kannojia 4-3) by 12 runs.
CH Bansi Lal Cricket Stadium, Lahli, Rohtak, January 4: Andhra 80/8 in 20 overs (C Jhansi Lakshmi 21; Akanksha Kohli 2-16, Sahana Pawar 2-19) beat **Karnataka** 47 in 19.2 overs (C Jhansi Lakshmi 2-5) by 33 runs.
CH Bansi Lal Cricket Stadium, Lahli, Rohtak, January 5: Tamil Nadu 80/6 in 20 overs (Namita Ojha 25; Mansi Joshi 2-4) beat **Haryana** 61/9 in 20 overs (Mansi Joshi 22; Anusha Prabhakaran 2-7, SB Keerthana 2-9) by 19 runs.
CH Bansi Lal Cricket Stadium, Lahli, Rohtak, January 5: Jharkhand 68/9 in 20 overs (C Jhansi Lakshmi 3-6) lost to **Andhra** 69/4 in 17.4 overs (Meghana Sabbineni 25*, C Jhansi Lakshmi 21; Roshni Kannojia 2-13) by six wickets.
CH Bansi Lal Cricket Stadium, Lahli, Rohtak, January 6: Tamil Nadu 108/4 in 20 overs (Hemalatha Dayalan 69*; Rameshwari Gayakwad 2-11) lost to **Karnataka** 111/4 in 19.1 overs (G Divya 36, Karuna Jain 28*) by six wickets.
CH Bansi Lal Cricket Stadium, Lahli, Rohtak, January 6: Jharkhand 62/7 in 20 overs (Preeti Bose 4-12) lost to **Haryana** 63/2 in 17.4 overs (Mansi Joshi 28) by eight wickets.

Plate Group C Points Table

Teams	M	W	L	T	N/R	Pts	NRR
Andhra	4	3	1	0	0	12	+0.754
Haryana	4	3	1	0	0	12	+0.104
Jharkhand	4	2	2	0	0	8	-0.061
Tamil Nadu	4	1	3	0	0	4	-0.268
Karnataka	4	1	3	0	0	4	-0.499

Andhra and Haryana qualified for the Plate Knockout

Plate Knockout

1st quarter-final: JSCA Oval Ground, Ranchi, January 11: Haryana 109/6 in 20 overs (Mansi Joshi 51, Sonia Khatri 31*; Fatima Jaffer 3-7) lost to **Mumbai** 112/5 in 19.3 overs (Sulakshana Naik 47, Sunetra Paranjape 41; Preeti Bose 2-10) by five wickets.

2nd quarter-final: JSCA Oval Ground, Ranchi, January 11: Baroda 104/6 in 20 overs (Binaisha Surti 28, Palak Patel 22; Zeenat Firdos 2-15) lost to **Uttar Pradesh** 105/7 in 18.3 overs (Deepti Sharma 41, Shefali Sahu 37*) by three wickets.

1st semi-final: JSCA Oval Ground, Ranchi, January 13: Mumbai 126/7 in 20 overs (Sulakshana Naik 55, Jemimah Rodrigues 25; Tanuja Kanwar 3-21) beat **Himachal Pradesh** 100/9 in 20 overs (T Kanwar 27, Susmitha Kumari 20; Nancy Daruwalla 2-22) by 26 runs.

2nd semi-final: JSCA Oval Ground, Ranchi, January 13: Uttar Pradesh 123/6 in 20 overs (Deepti Sharma 44, Muskan Malik 23; Saranya Gadwal 2-18, M Bhavana 2-25) beat **Andhra** 80/9 in 20 overs (N Anusha 29, C Jhansi Lakshmi 20; Suamya Singh 4-13, Deepti Sharma 2-13) by 43 runs.

Final: JSCA Oval Ground, Ranchi, January 15: Uttar Pradesh 64 in 18.2 overs (Sheral Rozario 2-11, Sunetra Paranjape 2-11) lost to **Mumbai** 65/2 in 17.2 overs (Jemimah Rodrigues 30*) by eight wickets.

Winners: Mumbai

Elite Group Super League

Holkar Stadium, Indore, January 11: Railways 134/3 in 20 overs (Mithali Raj 74, MD Thirushkamini 39) beat **Odisha** 80/2 in 20 overs (Madhuri Meheta 40*, Madhusmita Behera 21; Poonam Yadav 2-9) by 54 runs.

Holkar Stadium, Indore, January 11: Maharashtra 132/1 in 20 overs (Smriti Mandhana 69*, Anuja Patil 42*) beat **Goa** 100/7 in 20 overs (Sunanda Yetrekar 42, Shikha Pandey 21; Shweta Mane 3-20) by 32 runs.

Holkar Stadium, Indore, January 12: Odisha 89/6 in 20 overs (Sushree Pradhan 33*; Sunanda Yetrekar 2-18) lost to **Goa** 90/2 in 17.5 overs (Sunanda Yetrekar 32*, Sanjula Naik 26) by eight wickets.

Holkar Stadium, Indore, January 12: Railways 131/6 in 20 overs (Niranjana Nagarajan 55, MD Thirushkamini 24; Tejal Hasabnis 2-16) beat **Maharashtra** 87/8 in 20 overs (Smriti Mandhana 29, Tejal Hasabnis 25*) by 44 runs.

Holkar Stadium, Indore, January 14: Railways 76/9 in 20 overs (Sonali Gaunder 3-20, Santoshi Rane 2-13) beat **Goa** 73/8 in 20 overs (Sunanda Yetrekar 24; Sneh Rana 3-17) by three runs.

Holkar Stadium, Indore, January 14: Odisha 80/8 in 20 overs (Sarita Meher 23; Devika Vaidya 4-14) lost to **Maharashtra** 81/5 in 16 overs (Smriti Mandhana 31; Sushree Pradhan 3-20) by five wickets.

Elite Group Super League Points Table

Teams	M	W	L	T	N/R	Pts	NRR
Railways	3	3	0	0	0	12	+1.683
Maharashtra	3	2	1	0	0	8	+0.174
Goa	3	1	2	0	0	4	-0.402
Odisha	3	0	3	0	0	0	-1.516

Winners: Railways

Inter-Zonal Three-Day Competition

Meshram, Sultana shine; Central wins

Gouher Sultana, who had represented Central Zone in previous seasons, turned out for South. – *File photo*

The senior women's inter-zonal tournament was changed from a two-day format to a three-day format, but that did not alter the result as Central Zone retained the title. Mona Meshram, the right-hand batter, led Central's campaign scoring 490 runs in four matches. Her tally included knocks of 96 against East Zone, 193 against North Zone and 201 against West Zone. Central grabbed top honours thanks to their innings-and-57-run win over North Zone – the only outright win in the competition. Apart from Meshram, Meghana Sabbineni of South Zone was the only other centurion. Gouher Sultana, who turned out for South Zone this year having represented Central for the previous three seasons, stole the limelight with the ball. The left-arm spinner's tally of 18 wickets included two five-wicket hauls and came at an impressive average of 10.22. Her heroics, however, went in vain as South finished in third place.

Best batter: Mona Mehsram (Central Zone) (490 runs in 4 matches)
Best bowler: Gouher Sultana (South Zone) (18 wickets in 4 matches)

SGVR ACA Stadium, Perecherla, February 26-28: East Zone 268 in 140.5 overs (Priyanka Roy 94, Tanusree Sarkar 73; Reema Malhotra 4-48, Preeti Bose 3-39) and 27/1 in 12 overs drew with **North Zone** 195 in 101.4 overs (Taniya Bhatia 34, Priya Punia 33; Reema Chakroborty 3-4, P Roy 3-27). East Zone won on the basis of first-innings lead.

Jagarlamudi Kuppuswamy Choudary College, Guntur, February 26-28: South Zone 147 in 71 overs (Hemalatha Dayalan 26, Sunanda Yetrekar 26; Sheral Rozario 2-19, Devika Vaidya 2-31) and 246/8 in 91.4 overs (S Yetrekar 52*, T Shani 33; S Rozario 3-40, D Vaidya 3-81) drew with **West Zone** 240 in 113.1 overs (Sulakshana Naik 99, Heena Patel 47; Gouher Sultana 5-41, S Asha 3-31). West Zone won on the basis of first-innings lead.

SGVR ACA Stadium, Perecherla, March 2-4: Central Zone 262 in 129 overs (Mona Meshram 96, Sneh Rana 45; Priyanka Roy 2-47, Sushree Pradhan 2-48) drew with **East Zone** 192 in 144.5 overs (Madhuri Meheta 56, S Pradhan 30; Nidhi Buley 4-28, Sneh Rana 4-69). Central Zone won on the basis of first-innings lead.

Jagarlamudi Kuppuswamy Choudary College, Guntur, March 2-4: South Zone 323/9 decl. in 107.3 overs (Meghana Sabbineni 133, Hemalatha Dayalan 55; Mansi Joshi 3-53, Soni Yadab 2-55) and 85/4 in 34 overs (M Sabbineni 28, K Rakshita 28; Soni Yadav 2-32) drew with **North Zone** 181 in 112.5 overs (Harleen Deol 57, Latika Kumari 32; Gouher Sultana 4-48, S Asha 3-37). South Zone won on the basis of first-innings lead.

Jagarlamudi Kuppuswamy Choudary College, Guntur, March 6-8: North Zone 158 in 68 overs (Reema Malhotra 51*, Priya Punia 40; Sheral Rozario 3-14, Devika Vaidya 3-61) and 291/6 decl. in 88.4 overs (Taniya Bhatia 85*, Reema Malhotra 53; D Vaidya 2-69) drew with **West Zone** 293 in 116.1 overs (D Vaidya 72, Mugdha Joshi 70; Mansi Joshi 3-43, Preeti Bose 3-79). West Zone won on the basis of first-innings lead.

SGVR ACA Stadium, Perecherla, March 6-8: South Zone 215 in 103 overs (Meghana Sabbineni 48, Sunanda Yetrekar 45; Nidhi Buley 5-72, Kavita Patil 3-42) and 134/7 in 65 overs (M Sabbineni 41, N Anush 32; Sneh Rana 5-58) drew with **Central Zone** 168 in 111.2 overs (Shweta Bishnoi 38, Punam Raut 33; Gouher Sultana 6-46; T Shani 2-12). South Zone won on the basis of first-innings lead.

SGVR ACA Stadium, Perecherla, March 10-12: Central Zone 277 in 114.2 overs (Mona Meshram 193; Preeti Bose 4-59, Neena Choudhary 2-17) beat **North Zone** 124 in 77.1 overs (Taniya Bhatia 45, Priya Punia 22; Sneh Rana 3-39, Nidhi Buley 2-18) and 96 in 63.4 overs (Harleen Deol 41; N Buley 3-30, Kavita Patil 2-7) by an innings and 57 runs.

Jagarlamudi Kuppuswamy Choudary College, Guntur, March 10-12: East Zone 270 in 139.1 overs (Madhuri Meheta 82, Tanusree Sarkar 75; Devika Vaidya 3-79, Tejal Hasabnis 2-21) and 20/0 in 4 overs drew with **West Zone** 212 in 110.5 overs (Sulakshana Naik 68, Palak Patel 52; Sukanya Parida 3-30, Priyanka Roy 3-44). East Zone won on the basis of first-innings lead.

Jagarlamudi Kuppuswamy Choudary College, Guntur, March 14-16: Central Zone 398/5 decl in 128.5 overs (Mona Meshram 201, Punam Raut 66; Radha Yadav 3-79) drew with **West Zone** 207 in 91.3 overs (Sulakshana Naik 47, Mugdha Joshi 32; Shivangiraj Singh 4-40, Kavita Patil 3-27) and 120/6 in 40 overs (M Joshi 62*; Pooja Vastrakar 2-32). Central Zone won on the basis of first-innings lead.

SGVR ACA Stadium, Perecherla, March 14-16: East Zone 299 in 152.3 overs (Madhusmita Behera 88, Priyanka Roy 55; Gouher Sultana 3-49, Sunanda Yetrekar 3-58) and 44/2 in 9 overs (Swagatika Rath 33*) drew with **South Zone** 206 in 92.2 overs (Hemalatha Dayalan 52, Karuna Jain 41; Sushree Pradhan 2-25, Sukanya Parida 2-36). East Zone won on the basis of first-innings lead.

Points Table

Team	M	W	L	D	T	A	Pts	Q
Central Zone	4	1	0	3	0	0	14	1.828
East Zone	4	0	0	4	0	0	10	1.191
South Zone	4	0	0	4	0	0	8	1.054
West Zone	4	0	0	4	0	0	8	0.746
North Zone	4	0	1	3	0	0	3	0.645

Winners: Central Zone

Inter-State Under-23 One-Day Competition

Nine tons lights up new tourney

The maiden Under-23 tournament, introduced to provide fringe cricketers with more game time, began with nine centuries scored across all five zones. Meghana Sabbineni, Andhra captain, was the standout among the batters, smashing two hundreds in her team's march to the South Zone title. Her astounding average of 128.66 was only bettered by her team-mate N Anusha, who managed 151. The duo's team-mate K Dhatri, the leg-spinner, continued her impressive form from the Under-19s to finish at the top of the wicket-takers list. Devika Vaidya, who led Maharashtra in the absence of Smriti Mandhana (away on international duty), showcased her all-round ability, scoring 258 runs to add to her nine wickets. Himachal Pradesh, Madhya Pradesh, Andhra and Bengal were unbeaten in their respective zones.

Best batter: Meghana Sabbineni (Andhra) (386 runs in 5 matches)
Best bowler: K Dhatri (Andhra) (15 wickets in 5 matches)

North Zone
St Stephen's College Ground, Delhi, February 4: Himachal Pradesh 151 in 47.1 overs (N Chauhan 50, Kashish Verma 40; Neha Chhillar 3-14, Kirti Arya 2-21) beat **Delhi** 103 in 42.4 overs (Susmitha Kumari 3-16, Anisha Ansari 2-20) by 48 runs.
Bharat Nagar Sports Complex, Delhi, February 4: Jammu & Kashmir 87 in 38.3 overs (Rajni Devi 5-19, Priyanka Guleria 2-21) lost to **Punjab** 90/0 in 18 overs (Taniya Bhatia 53*, Ramandeep Kaur 24*) by ten wickets.
St Stephen's College Ground, Delhi, February 6: Haryana 230/4 in 50 overs (Mansi Joshi 92, Bhawna Ohlan 77) beat **Delhi** 160 in 45.5 overs (Priya Punia 86; Priyanka Sharma 2-13, Shiva Prajapati 2-29) by 70 runs.
Bharat Nagar Sports Complex, Delhi, February 6: Punjab 83 in 30.3 overs (Neelam Bisht 35; Susmitha Kumari 3-15, Renuka Singh 3-17) lost to **Himachal Pradesh** 84/4 in 20.5 overs (Harleen Deol 44*, Kashish Verma 20; Rajni Devi 2-23) by six wickets.

Bharat Nagar Sports Complex, Delhi, February 8: Delhi 148/9 in 50 overs (Priya Punia 38, Vaishali Mathur 28; Sunita Rani 3-28, Mehak Kesar 2-20) beat **Punjab** 120 in 38.1 overs (Amarpaul Kaur 22; Soni Yadav 3-29, Neha Chhillar 2-16) by 28 runs.

St Stephen's College Ground, Delhi, February 8: Haryana 211/6 in 50 overs (Sonia Khatri 106*, Sheetal Rana 41; Sarla Devi 3-23, Rubia Syed 2-47) beat **Jammu & Kashmir** 94/9 in 50 overs (Ruksara Akhter 34; Rabita Bhadu 2-3, Savita Malik 2-7) by 117 runs.

Bharat Nagar Sports Complex, Delhi, February 10: Delhi 76 in 32.3 overs (Qounsar Jabeen 4-8, Sarla Devi 3-21) beat **Jammu & Kashmir** 38 in 29.3 overs (Vaishali Mathur 4-9, Soni Yadav 3-7) by 38 runs.

St Stephen's College Ground, Delhi, February 10: Himachal Pradesh 186/8 in 50 overs (Kashish Verma 66, Monika Devi 37; Shiva Prajapati 2-22, Diksha Sharma 2-36) beat **Haryana** 144/9 in 50 overs (Sonia Khatri 40, Mansi Joshi 39; Renuka Singh 3-25, Susmitha Kumari 2-12) by 42 runs.

St Stephen's College Ground, Delhi, February 12: Haryana 114/9 in 50 overs (Sonia Khatri 41, Sheetal Rana 28; Neelam Bisht 4-19, Sunita Rani 3-13) lost to **Punjab** 115/7 in 46.5 overs (Taniya Bhatia 54; P Sharma 2-23) by three wickets.

Bharat Nagar Sports Complex, Delhi, February 12: Jammu & Kashmir 51 in 25.5 overs (T Kanwer 3-7, Prachi Chauhan 3-13) lost to **Himachal Pradesh** 52/1 in 10 overs (Monika Devi 22*) by nine wickets.

North Zone Points Table

Teams	M	W	L	T	N/R	Pts	NRR
Himachal Pradesh	4	4	0	0	0	16	+1.710
Haryana	4	2	2	0	0	8	+0.675
Punjab	4	2	2	0	0	8	-0.059
Delhi	4	2	2	0	0	8	-0.260
Jammu & Kashmir	4	0	4	0	0	0	-2.002

Central Zone

Kamla Club Sports Ground, Kanpur, February 2: Railways 191/4 in 50 overs (Paramita Roy 55, S Hima Bindu 38) beat **Vidarbha** 115/8 in 50 overs (Disha Kasat 47, Vaishnavi Khandkar 20; Swati Thapliyal 3-19) by 76 runs.

Modi Stadium, Kanpur, February 2: Uttar Pradesh 131 in 43.1 overs (Aditi Sharma 63*, Shobha Devi 31; Tarang Jha 5-23, Pooja Vastrakar 3-32) lost to **Madhya Pradesh** 132/6 in 42.4 overs (Neha Badwaik 53; Shefali Sahu 3-27, Tanu Kala 2-35) by four wickets.

Kamla Club Sports Ground, Kanpur, February 3: Rajasthan 277/3 in 50 overs (Shweta Bishnoi 78, J Bijarnya 66*) beat **Chhattisgarh** 49 in 36.3 overs (Zkiya Dilshad 3-9, Babita Meena 2-13) by 228 runs.

Modi Stadium, Kanpur, February 3: Vidarbha 118 in 49.2 overs (Vaishnavi Khandkar 29, Sapna Meshram 22; Tanu Kala 3-14, Shefali Sahu 3-32) beat **Uttar Pradesh** 85 in 34 overs (Shobha Devi 29; Dhanashree Parekh 4-12, GargiWankar 2-16) by 33 runs.

Kamla Club Sports Ground, Kanpur, February 4: Railways 232/6 in 50 overs (S Hima Bindu 88, Ritu Dhrub 53; Kajal Meshram 2-49) beat **Chhattisgarh** 43 in 17.3 overs (Meghna Singh 5-15, Suchi Kaushik 3-12) by 189 runs.

Modi Stadium, Kanpur, February 4: Rajasthan 105 in 41.2 overs (Babita Meena 26; Tarang Jha 3-26, Pooja Vastrakar 2-34) lost to **Madhya Pradesh** 108/6 in 45.3 overs (Pooja Choudhary 31, Charu Joshi 24; Babita Meena 2-22) by four wickets.

Kamla Club Sports Ground, Kanpur, February 5: Madhya Pradesh 234/5 in 50 overs (Charu Joshi 55, Pooja Vastrakar 40*) beat **Vidarbha** 124 in 48.2 overs (Vaishnavi Khandkar 20, Disha Kasat 20; C Joshi 4-23) by 110 runs.
Modi Stadium, Kanpur, February 5: Railways 158/8 in 50 overs (Sarika Koli 37, Komal Hora 32; Aditi Sharma 3-23, Tanu Kala 2-30) lost to **Uttar Pradesh** 161/5 in 45.3 overs (Deepti Sharma 89*, Shivpriya Pandey 22; Rajni Lodhi 2-16) by five wickets.
Modi Stadium, Kanpur, February 7: Vidarbha 215/8 in 50 overs (Bharati Fulmali 106, Sapna Meshram 40; Shweta Bishnoi 2-32) beat **Rajasthan** 201/7 in 50 overs (Babita Meena 56, J Bijarnya 38; Dhanashree Parekh 2-40) by 14 runs.
Kamla Club Sports Ground, Kanpur, February 7: Chhattisgarh 57 in 45.5 overs (Alka Singh 4-10, Aditi Sharma 2-3) lost to **Uttar Pradesh** 59/1 in 12.1 overs (Deepti Sharma 25*, Ekta Singh 24) by nine wickets.
Modi Stadium, Kanpur, February 8: Chhattisgarh 81/7 in 50 overs (Charu Joshi 2-12) lost to **Madhya Pradesh** 82/3 in 28.1 overs (Tamanna Nigam 33*, C Joshi 21) by seven wickets.
Kamla Club Sports Ground, Kanpur, February 8: Railways 183/8 in 50 overs (Paramita Roy 51, Rajni Lodhi 38; Suman Meena 2-28) beat **Rajasthan** 131 in 46.4 overs (Shweta Bishnoi 40, J Bijarnya 24; Sarika Koli 3-15, Anita Lodhi 3-21) by 52 runs.
Modi Stadium, Kanpur, February 9: Madhya Pradesh 174 in 49.1 overs (Nuzhat Parween 41, Pooja Choudhary 35; S Hima Bindu 2-18, Swati Thapliyal 2-37) beat **Railways** 151 in 42.4 overs (Komal Hora 38, Sapna Choudhary 24; Priti Yadav 6-28, Charu Joshi 2-34) by 23 runs.
Modi Stadium, Kanpur, February 10: Chhattisgarh 57 in 32 overs (Krutika Pophali 5-33, Vaishnavi Khandkar 3-1) lost to **Vidarbha** 60/3 in 11.3 overs (Krutika Pophali 20) by seven wickets.
Kamla Club Sports Ground, Kanpur, February 10: Rajasthan 193/5 in 50 overs (Babita Meena 63, Sangeeta Kumawat 56*; Shefali Sahu 2-40) beat **Uttar Pradesh** 184/7 in 50 overs (Aditi Sharma 48*, Ekta Singh 31; Babita Meena 2-28, Suman Meena 2-48) by 9 runs.

Central Zone Points Table

Teams	M	W	L	T	N/R	Pts	NRR
Madhya Pradesh	5	5	0	0	0	20	+1.006
Railways	5	3	2	0	0	12	+1.118
Vidarbha	5	3	2	0	0	12	-0.084
Rajasthan	5	2	3	0	0	8	+0.618
Uttar Pradesh	5	2	3	0	0	8	+0.274
Chhattisgarh	5	0	5	0	0	0	-3.528

West Zone

Bandra Kurla Complex, Mumbai, February 2: Baroda 221/7 in 50 overs (Yastika Bhatia 74, Tarannum Pathan 71; Khushboo Patel 5-52) beat **Gujarat** 73 in 34.4 overs (Radha Yadav 3-5, T Pathan 3-8) by 148 runs.
Sachin Tendulkar Gymkhana Ground, Mumbai, February 2: Mumbai 189 in 50 overs (Hemali Borwankar 57, Vrushali Bhagat 43; Tanya Rao 2-23, Pooja Nimavat 2-36) beat **Saurashtra** 81 in 33.4 overs (Bhakti Shastri 41; Jemimah Rodrigues 3-7, Sayali Satghare 2-17) by 108 runs.
Sachin Tendulkar Gymkhana Ground, Mumbai, February 3: Maharashtra 216/8 in 50 overs (Devika Vaidya 75, Tejal Hasabnis 53; Pragna Chaudhari 3-37, Harpriyaben Patel 3-44)

beat **Gujarat** 130/7 in 50 overs (Renuka Chaudhari 40, Krutika Chaudhari 26; D Vaidya 3-9) by 86 runs.

Bandra Kurla Complex, Mumbai, February 3: Mumbai 231/8 in 50 overs (Humaira Kazi 64, Shweta Haranhalli 57; Gayatri Naik 2-35, Nancy Patel 2-42) beat **Baroda** 145 in 41.1 overs (Palak Patel 51, Tarannum Pathan 48; Fatima Jaffer 2-21, Manali Dakshini 2-26) by 86 runs.

Sachin Tendulkar Gymkhana Ground, Mumbai, February 5: Maharashtra 136 in 49.5 overs (Devika Vaidya 34, Priyanka Garkhede 29; Shalini Sharma 3-27, Pragya Rawat 2-22) lost to **Baroda** 137/7 in 40.3 overs (Yastika Bhatia 30, Tanvir Shaikh 29; Tejal Hasabnis 2-22, D Vaidya 2-47) by three wickets.

Bandra Kurla Complex, Mumbai, February 5: Gujarat 122 in 45 overs (Krutika Chaudhari 30; Pooja Nimavat 3-12, Reena Dabhi 3-26) beat **Saurashtra** 88 in 31.1 overs (Neha Chavda 20; Khushboo Patel 4-20, Pragna Chaudhari 2-20) by 34 runs.

Sachin Tendulkar Gymkhana Ground, Mumbai, February 6: Baroda 251/5 in 50 overs (Palak Patel 125, Yastika Bhatia 61; Pooja Nimavat 2-44) beat **Saurashtra** 98 in 43.5 overs (Shalini Sharma 3-15, Radha Yadav 3-25) by 153 runs.

Bandra Kurla Complex, Mumbai, February 6: Mumbai 211 in 49.4 overs (Hemali Borwankar 79, Mugdha Joshi 36; Devika Vaidya 4-32, Tejal Hasabnis 2-44) lost to **Maharashtra** 212/5 in 44.2 overs (D Vaidya 109*; Tejal Hasabnis 26; Humaira Kazi 2-40) by five wickets.

Bandra Kurla Complex, Mumbai, February 8: Saurashtra 114/6 in 50 overs (Bhakti Shastri 33, Neha Chavda 24; Tejal Hasabnis 2-20) lost to **Maharashtra** 115/6 in 20.4 overs (Devika Vaidya 40; Ritu Dabhi 4-27, N Chavda 2-29) by four wickets.

Sachin Tendulkar Gymkhana Ground, Mumbai, February 8: Mumbai 327/4 in 50 overs (Hemali Borwankar 116, Jemimah Rodrigues 101; Anjali Patel 2-55) beat **Gujarat** 97 in 41.2 overs (Renuka Chaudhari 20; S Thakor 4-15, J Rodrigues 3-19) by 230 runs.

West Zone Points Table

Teams	M	W	L	T	N/R	Pts	NRR
Mumbai	4	3	1	0	0	12	+2.037
Baroda	4	3	1	0	0	12	+1.268
Maharashtra	4	3	1	0	0	12	+1.008
Gujarat	4	1	3	0	0	4	-2.150
Saurashtra	4	0	4	0	0	0	-2.062

South Zone

Nuclear Fuel Complex Ground, Secunderabad, February 2: Tamil Nadu 147 in 49.1 overs (Hemalatha Dayalan 53; Saranya Gadwal 4-38, K Dhatri 2-29) lost to **Andhra** 148/0 in 30.1 overs (Meghana Sabbineni 98*, C Jhansi Lakshmi 42*) by ten wickets.

Electronic Corporation of India Limited, Hyderabad, February 2: Karnataka 160/7 in 50 overs (Debasmita Dutta 33, G Divya 32; Sanjula Naik 2-28, Teju 2-28) beat **Goa** 134 in 43.3 overs (Pratiksha Gadekar 34; V Chandu 2-21) by 26 runs.

Rajiv Gandhi International Stadium, Uppal, Hyderabad, February 2: Kerala 62 in 30.2 overs (Jilu George 25; Rachna Kumar 5-9, VM Kavya 4-2) lost to **Hyderabad** 63/3 in 17.5 overs (Sneha More 36; S Sajana 2-16) by seven wickets.

Electronic Corporation of India Limited, Hyderabad, February 3: Goa 164 in 49.4 overs (Sugandha Ghadi 29, Nikita Malik 29; C Jhansi Lakshmi 4-28, Saranya Gadwal 2-27) lost to **Andhra** 167/1 in 36 overs (C Jhansi Lakshmi 66*, N Anusha 51*) by nine wickets.

Rajiv Gandhi International Stadium, Uppal, Hyderabad, February 3: Tamil Nadu 141/6 in 50 overs (Hemalatha Dayalan 39, SB Keerthana 39; Rachna Kumar 2-24, B Shravani 2-25)

beat **Hyderabad** 139 in 46.2 overs (VM Kavya 28, G Pranathi Reddy 27*; SB Keerthna 3-22, K Ramyashri 2-19) by two runs.
Nuclear Fuel Complex Ground, Secunderabad, February 3: Karnataka 142/8 in 50 overs (G Divya 38, Simren Henry 30*; Keerthi James 4-17, S Mrudhula 2-23) beat **Kerala** 78 in 35.3 overs (Aswaty Babu 30; Sahana Pawar 5-9, C Pratyusha 2-19) by 64 runs.
Electronic Corporation of India Limited, Hyderabad, February 5: Andhra 244/5 in 50 overs (Meghana Sabbineni 105, V Sneha Deepthi 75*; V Chandu 2-42) beat **Karnataka** 127 in 48.3 overs (Simren Henry 52, G Divya 41; K Dhatri 4-18, M Bhavana 3-24) by 117 runs.
Nuclear Fuel Complex Ground, Secunderabad, February 5: Goa 175 in 49.1 overs (Sanjula Naik 38, Vinavi Gurav 38; VM Kavya 3-21, B Shravani 2-30) lost to **Hyderabad** 178/3 in 40 overs (Himani Yadav 50, VM Kavya 45*) by seven wickets.
Rajiv Gandhi International Stadium, Uppal, Hyderabad, February 5: Tamil Nadu 123 in 48.2 overs (L Nethra Iyer 34, S Anusha 22; S Sajana 3-18, Keerthi James 2-24) lost to **Kerala** 124/4 in 48.3 overs (Minnu Mani 38*, Aswathy Babu 30) by six wickets.
Gymkhana Ground, Secunderabad, February 6: Kerala 99 in 33.2 overs (Arathy Jayapal 22; K Dhatri 6-26, Saranya Gadwal 2-20) lost to **Andhra** 100/2 in 18.4 overs (V Sneha Deepthi 58, C Jhansi Lakshmi 31) by eight wickets.
Nuclear Fuel Complex Ground, Secunderabad, February 6: Tamil Nadu 203/5 in 50 overs (L Nethra Iyer 69*, Hemalatha Dayalan 66; Diksha Gawde 3-35) v **Goa** 203/8 in 50 overs (Nikita Malik 46, Sanjula Naik 35; S Anusha 5-23). Match tied.
Electronic Corporation of India Limited, Hyderabad, February 6: Karnataka 68 in 34.4 overs (VM Kavya 3-10, Arundhati Reddy 2-26) lost to **Hyderabad** 71/2 in 19.5 overs (Trisha Poojitha 28, Sneha More 25) by eight wickets.
Nuclear Fuel Complex Ground, Secunderabad, February 8: Goa 176 in 47.1 overs (Sanjula Naik 57, Nikita Malik 34; Minnu Mani 3-27, VS Mrudhula 2-35) beat **Kerala** 112 in 39 overs (S Sajana 40; Rakshanda Pilankar 4-25, Snehal Shet 2-20) by 64 runs.
Gymkhana Ground, Secunderabad, February 8: Andhra 260/2 in 50 overs (Meghana Sabbineni 143, N Anusha 100*) beat **Hyderabad** 81 in 41.1 overs (VM Kavya 22; C Jhansi Lakshmi 4-13, Mallika Thalluri 3-4) by 179 runs.
Electronic Corporation of India Limited, Hyderabad, February 8: Karnataka 176/6 in 50 overs (C Pratyusha 52, G Divya 28; D Nisha 2-27, L Nethra Iyer 2-30) beat **Tamil Nadu** 119 in 47.5 overs (Hemalatha Dayalan 27; Debasmita Dutta 4-18, C Pratyusha 3-24) by 57 runs.

South Zone Points Table

Teams	M	W	L	T	N/R	Pts	NRR
Andhra	5	5	0	0	0	20	+2.500
Hyderabad	5	3	2	0	0	12	+0.170
Karnataka	5	3	2	0	0	12	-0.247
Goa	5	1	3	1	0	6	-0.220
Tamil Nadu	5	1	3	1	0	6	-0.523
Kerala	5	1	4	0	0	4	-1.327

East Zone

Nimpur Sports and Cricket Club Ground, Cuttack, February 2: Bengal 145 in 48.3 overs (Tanusree Sarkar 48; Rachana Kumari 3-12, Ritu Kumari 2-18) beat **Jharkhand** 73 in 33.5 overs (Priyanka Sawaiyan 24; Saiqa Ishaque 4-11, Priya Pandey 2-10) by 72 runs.
Ravenshaw College Ground, Cuttack, February 2: Assam 85 in 39.1 overs (Kalpana

Shoutal 21; Sarojini Giri 4-10, Sushree Pradhan 2-15) lost to **Odisha** 86/6 in 43 overs (S Dibyadarshini 27, Anjali Singh 21; Kakoli Saikia 2-4, Rashmi Dey 2-17) by four wickets.

Ravenshaw College Ground, Cuttack, February 4: Assam 113 in 49.4 overs (Rekharani Bora 37*, Kalpana Shoutal 26; Ritu Kumari 2-19, Ekta Mondal 2-24) lost to **Jharkhand** 114/2 in 38.3 overs (Monika Murmu 64*, Priyanka Sawaiyan 21*) by eight wickets.

Nimpur Sports and Cricket Club Ground, Cuttack, February 4: Odisha 173 in 50 overs (Pragyan Mohanty 56, Sunita Murmu 40; Rita Debbarma 4-39, Ritu Malakar 2-23) beat **Tripura** 113 in 44.3 overs (R Debbarma 30; Sushree Pradhan 4-20, Sarojini Giri 2-18) by 60 runs.

Ravenshaw College Ground, Cuttack, February 6: Tripura 92 in 48.1 overs (Reema Chakraborty 39, Rizu Saha 23; Priya Pandey 3-27, Tanusree Sarkar 2-21) lost to **Bengal** 95/2 in 32.1 overs (Ambika Guha 36*, Tanusree Sarkar 32*) by eight wickets.

Nimpur Sports and Cricket Club Ground, Cuttack, February 6: Odisha 76 in 44.5 overs (Rachana Kumari 2-14, Roshni 2-15) lost to **Jharkhand** 78/3 in 26.5 overs (Sonia 24*; Sarojini Giri 2-17) by seven wickets.

Nimpur Sports and Cricket Club Ground, Cuttack, February 8: Bengal 201/8 in 50 overs (Tanusree Sarkar 99, Saiqa Ishaque 44; Nirupama Baro 2-18) beat **Assam** 54 in 25.1 overs (Sukanya Parida 5-12, Sabana Khatoon 3-29) by 147 runs.

Ravenshaw College Ground, Cuttack, February 8: Tripura 191/4 in 50 overs (Nikita Debnath 66*, Reema Chakraborty 48; Kanchan Nagwani 2-15) beat **Jharkhand** 130 in 46.2 overs (Nilam Yadav 37, Kanchan Nagwani 28; Rita Debbarma 2-14, Suravi Roy 2-25) by 61 runs.

Nimpur Sports and Cricket Club Ground, Cuttack, February 10: Tripura 114 in 49.5 overs (Reema Chakraborty 49; Rekharani Bora 2-12, Konwar 2-31) beat **Assam** 62 in 36.4 overs (R Chakraborty 3-8, Sweety Sinha 3-16) by 52 runs.

Ravenshaw College Ground, Cuttack, February 10: Odisha 149/7 in 50 overs (Pragyan Mohanty 43, Ritu Singh 38; Saiqa Ishaque 2-15) lost to **Bengal** 150/0 in 33.3 overs (Priyanka Bala 72*, Ambika Guha 58*) by ten wickets.

East Zone Points Table

Teams	M	W	L	T	N/R	Pts	NRR
Bengal	4	4	0	0	0	16	+1.727
Tripura	4	2	2	0	0	8	+0.025
Odisha	4	2	2	0	0	8	-0.149
Jharkhand	4	2	2	0	0	8	-0.236
Assam	4	0	4	0	0	0	-1.267

Inter-Zonal Under-23 One-Day Competition

South Zone claim inaugural title

Barring a heartbreaking five-run loss to Central Zone, South Zone were untroubled as they emerged victorious in the inaugural Under-23 Inter-Zonal Championship. Meghana Sabbineni, South vice-captain, kept up her good run, amassing 208 runs at an average of 52, while also scoring the only century of the tournament. In a series where most batters struggled and the spinners wreaked havoc, the right-hander's powerful strokeplay kept her well ahead of the pack. All of the top ten wicket-takers were spinners, Devika Vaidya, West Zone captain, leading the way. Vaidya's impressive showing meant her team finished runners-up thanks to a superior run-rate over Central and East Zone who had also secured eight points.

Best batter: Meghana Sabbineni (South Zone) (208 runs in 4 matches)
Best bowler: Devika Vaidya (West Zone) (8 wickets in 4 matches)

Shaheed Veer Narayan Singh International Cricket Stadium, Naya Raipur, February 16: East Zone 186/5 in 50 overs (Reema Chakraborty 48*, Pragyan Mohanty 46) beat **North Zone** 126 in 46.1 overs (Mansi Joshi 50, Priya Punia 32; Tanusree Sarkar 4-28, Sushree Pradhan 3-21) by 60 runs.
University Stadium, Raipur, February 16: West Zone 177 in 49 overs (Tejal Hasabnis 42*, Manali Dakshini 26; Hemalatha Dayalan 4-26, Arundhati Reddy 2-33) lost to **South Zone** 178/8 in 49.2 overs (G Divya 47, H Dayalan 38; Devika Vaidya 3-29, Tarannum Pathan 2-24) by two wickets.
Shaheed Veer Narayan Singh International Cricket Stadium, Naya Raipur, February 17: Central Zone 185/9 in 50 overs (Shweta Bishnoi 39, Anita Lodhi 31; Priya Pandey 2-15, Saiqa Ishaque 2-26) beat **East Zone** 128 in 41.3 overs (S Ishaque 35, Sushree Pradhan 27; Priti Yadav 4-23, Suchi Kaushik 2-20) by 57 runs.
University Stadium, Raipur, February 17: South Zone 216/9 in 50 overs (Meghana Sabbineni 76, N Anusha 44; Rani 2-27, Harleen Deol 2-36) beat **North Zone** 128 in 47.4 overs (Taniya Bhatia 41, Mansi Joshi 38*; VM Kavya 4-20, Hemalatha Dayalan 2-22) by 88 runs.
Shaheed Veer Narayan Singh International Cricket Stadium, Naya Raipur, February 19: Central Zone 123 in 47.1 overs (Nuzhat Parween 47; C Pratyusha 2-22, Rameshwari Gayakwad 2-29) beat **South Zone** 118 in 41.5 overs (Hemalatha Dayalan 46; Sarika Koli 2-12, Aditi Sharma 2-18) by 5 runs.
University Stadium, Raipur, February 19: North Zone 113 in 47.1 overs (Taniya Bhatia 25; Devika Vaidya 4-17, P Chaudhari 2-16) lost to **West Zone** 115/1 in 32.5 overs (Yastika Bhatia 59*, Jemimah Rodrigues 40) by nine wickets.
University Stadium, Raipur, February 20: North Zone 118 in 50 overs (Sonia Khatri 25, Bhawna Ohlan 25; Sarika Koli 3-15, Anita Lodhi 2-13) beat **Central Zone** 104 in 47.2 overs (Aditi Sharma 27*; Harleen Deol 4-17, Sunita Rani 3-9) by 14 runs.
Shaheed Veer Narayan Singh International Cricket Stadium, Naya Raipur, February 20: West Zone 133 in 42.2 overs (Devika Vaidya 41, Tarannum Pathan 21; Saiqa Ishaque 6-26, Sushree Pradhan 2-27) lost to **East Zone** 134/8 in 42.4 overs (Pragyan Mohanty 46; T Pathan 2-8) by two wickets.
Shaheed Veer Narayan Singh International Cricket Stadium, Naya Raipur, February 21: Central Zone 111 in 50 overs (Sarika Koli 21; Manali Dakshini 3-9, Pragya Rawat 2-20) lost to **West Zone** 112/2 in 29.4 overs (Jemimah Rodrigues 71*) by eight wickets.
University Stadium, Raipur, February 21: South Zone 206/8 in 50 overs (Meghana Sabbineni 110, G Divya 33; Tanusree Sarkar 3-36, Sushree Pradhan 3-40) beat **East Zone** 161/9 in 50 overs (S Pradhan 28, T Sarkar 25; C Pratyusha 4-31, Rameshwari Gayakwad 2-29) by 45 runs.

Points Table

Teams	M	W	L	T	N/R	Pts	NRR
South Zone	4	3	1	0	0	12	+0.657
West Zone	4	2	2	0	0	8	+0.513
Central Zone	4	2	2	0	0	8	-0.034
East Zone	4	2	2	0	0	8	-0.089
North Zone	4	1	3	0	0	4	-0.972

Winners: South Zone

Inter-State Under-19 One-Day Competition

Andhra break jinx

Andhra broke a nine-year jinx to become the first team from the south to lift the Inter-State Women's Under-19 One-Day title when they beat Uttar Pradesh in the final by six wickets. Apart from a loss against Bengal in the Super League stages, the champions were clinical. K Dhatri, the leg-spinner, and N Anusha, the opening batter, were Andhra's standout performers. While Dhatri took 25 wickets, Anusha scored 431 runs, including a highest of 168 not out against Tamil Nadu. In a tournament where low-scores were the norm, as many as eight centuries were scored, the most in any year so far. The best performance came from Deepti Sharma, the Uttar Pradesh captain, when she made 175 and picked up five wickets against Chhattisgarh. Other notable performances include Delhi's 317-run win over Jammu & Kashmir, and K Kavya's two six-wicket hauls for Kerala.

Best Batter: Deepti Sharma (Uttar Pradesh) (499 runs in 10 matches)
Best Bowler: K Dhathri (Andhra) (25 wickets in 11 matches)

North Zone

Jawaharlal NavodayVidhyalay Stadium, Una, September 22: Delhi 148 in 46.1 overs (Arushi Goel 40, Ayushi Soni 28*; Harleen Deol 3-30) beat **Himachal Pradesh** 64 in 38.1 overs (Ritu Singh 5-10, Vandana Chaturvedi 2-10) by 84 runs.
Indira Gandhi Stadium, Una, September 22: Jammu & Kashmir 38 in 14.3 overs (Komalpreet Kaur 4-10, Monika Pandey 3-4, Nandni Sharma 3-17) lost to **Punjab** 39/0 in 2.3 overs (Ramandeep Kaur 20*) by ten wickets.
Indira Gandhi Stadium, Una, September 24: Delhi 99 in 39.3 overs (Ayushi Soni 33; Suman Gulia 4-14, Sheetal Rana 3-15) lost to **Haryana** 100/0 (S Gulia 50*, Bhawna Ohlan 28*) by ten wickets.
Santoshi Garj Cricket Stadium, Una, September 24: Himachal Pradesh 96 in 44 overs (Harleen Deol 31; Rajni Devi 6-14) lost to **Punjab** 97/4 in 44 overs (Ramandeep Kaur 36,

Ending a long wait for the south: A six-wicket win in the final gave Andhra the Inter-State Under-19 title. — *Special arrangement*

Ridhima Aggarwal 21*; N Chauhan 3-20) by six wickets.
Santoshi Garj Cricket Stadium, Una, September 26: Punjab 78 in 36.5 overs (Ridhima Agarwal 22; Vandana Chaturvedi 3-6, Kirti Arya 3-6) lost to **Delhi** 79/4 in 37.2 overs (Arushi Goel 28, Lakshmi Yadav 22; Rajni Devi 2-22) by six wickets.
Indira Gandhi Stadium, Una, September 26: Jammu & Kashmir 46 in 21.4 overs (Diksha Sharma 6-19) lost to **Haryana** 47/0 in 4 overs (Suman Gulia 28*) by ten wickets.
Indira Gandhi Stadium, Una, September 28: Delhi 327/2 in 50 overs (Arushi Goel 136*, Ayushi Soni 117*) beat **Jammu & Kashmir** 10 in 21.1 overs (Vandana Chaturvedi 4-2, Kajal 3-0) by 317 runs.
Santoshi Garj Cricket Stadium, Una, September 28: Himachal Pradesh 129/9 in 50 overs (Harleen Deol 40, Kashish Verma 26; S Kumari 3-13, Diksha Sharma 3-24) lost to **Haryana** 130/2 in 31.3 overs (Bhawna Ohlan 60*, Suman Gulia 42) by eight wickets.
Santoshi Garj Cricket Stadium, Una, September 30: Punjab 69 in 35.4 overs (Priya Kumari 40; Sheetal Rana 4-10) lost to **Haryana** 70/0 in 13 overs (Bhawna Ohlan 34*, Suman Gulia 30*) by ten wickets.
Jawaharlal NavodayVidhyalay Stadium, Una, September 30: Himachal Pradesh 205 in 37.5 overs (Kashish Verma 55, Shivani Thakur 23; Nadiya Batloo 3-49, Aditi Aryan 2-42) beat **Jammu & Kashmir** 36 in 15.5 overs (Prachi Chauhan 4-10, Harleen Deol 3-9) by 169 runs.

North Zone Points Table

Team	M	W	L	T	N/R	Pts	NRR
Haryana	4	4	0	0	0	16	+2.974
Delhi	4	3	1	0	0	12	+2.050
Punjab	4	2	2	0	0	8	+0.049
Himachal Pradesh	4	1	3	0	0	4	+0.128
Jammu & Kashmir	4	0	4	0	0	0	-5.153

Haryana and Delhi qualified for the Super League

Central Zone

Kasiga School Ground, Dehradun, September 20: Chhattisgarh 55 in 41.1 overs (Anshula Rao 2-3, Poonam Soni 2-7) lost to **Madhya Pradesh** 58/0 in 13.1 overs (Nuzhat Parween 30*, Yashi Pandey 22*) by ten wickets.

Abhimanyu Cricket Academy Ground, Dehradun, September 20: Vidarbha 57 in 48.1 overs (Kajal 3-7, Tanu Kala 3-8) lost to **Uttar Pradesh** 58/0 in 18.3 overs (Deepti Sharma 30*, Ekta Singh 20*) by ten wickets.

Kasiga School Ground, Dehradun, September 21: Vidarbha 164/3 in 50 overs (Rohini More 70*, Disha Kasat 37) beat **Rajasthan** 146 in 47.2 overs (Sangeeta Kumawat 28, Rinku Tank 22*; Gargi Wankar 2-24, D Kasat 2-29) by 18 runs.

Abhimanyu Cricket Academy Ground, Dehradun, September 21: Uttar Pradesh 182/8 in 50 overs (Deepti Sharma 60, Ekta Singh 27; Yashi Pandey 2-11, Payal Balmik 2-23) lost to **Madhya Pradesh** 185/5 in 49.1 overs (Nuzhat Parween 52, Pooja Vastrakar 42; Kajal 2-21, Anjali 2-39) by five wickets.

Abhimanyu Cricket Academy Ground, Dehradun, September 22: Rajasthan 249/9 in 50 overs (A Garg 73, Sangeeta Kumawat 45; Shraddha Vaishnava 2-24, Sanjana Pardi 2-34) beat **Chhattisgarh** 55 in 33.4 overs (Danielle Sharma 2-8, Ruby Choudary 2-11) by 194 runs.

Kasiga School Ground, Dehradun, September 23: Vidarbha 67 in 45.4 overs (Poonam Soni 2-3, Nikita Singh 2-9) lost to **Madhya Pradesh** 69/4 in 23.4 overs (Nupur Kohale 3-18) by six wickets.

Abhimanyu Cricket Academy Ground, Dehradun, September 23: Uttar Pradesh 331/3 in 50 overs (Deepti Sharma 175, Kshama 63*) beat **Chhattisgarh** 26 in 31 overs (Deepti 5-5, Tanu Kala 2-5) by 305 runs.

Abhimanyu Cricket Academy Ground, Dehradun, September 24: Rajasthan 126/9 in 50 overs (T Vaishnav 29, A Garg 29; Poonam Soni 2-17, Pooja Vastrakar 2-24) lost to **Madhya Pradesh** 127/1 in 31 overs (Nuzhat Parween 54*, Yashi Pandey 43) by nine wickets.

Kasiga School Ground, Dehradun, September 25: Chhattisgarh 78 in 40.3 overs (Vidya Verma 22; S Thorat 3-11, L Inamdar 2-6) lost to **Vidarbha** 79/7 in 31 overs (Manpreet Kaur 4-4) by three wickets.

Abhimanyu Cricket Academy Ground, Dehradun, September 25: Rajasthan 88 in 49 overs (J Choudhary 26; Anjali 3-3, Kajal 2-6) lost to **Uttar Pradesh** 89/4 in 27 overs (Kshama 38, Deepti Sharma 28*; Rinku Tank 3-34) by six wickets.

Central Zone Points Table

Team	M	W	L	T	N/R	Pts	NRR
Madhya Pradesh	4	4	0	0	0	16	+1.602
Uttar Pradesh	4	3	1	0	0	12	+2.749
Vidarbha	4	2	2	0	0	8	-0.441
Team Rajasthan	4	1	3	0	0	4	+0.292
Chhattisgarh	4	0	4	0	0	0	-3.903

Madhya Pradesh and Uttar Pradesh qualified for the Super League

West Zone

Madhavrao Scindia Cricket Ground, Rajkot, September 20: Gujarat v **Mumbai**. No result.

Western Railway Ground, Rajkot, September 20: Saurashtra v **Baroda**. No result.

Madhavrao Scindia Cricket Ground, Rajkot, September 22: Maharashtra 96/5 in 20 overs (Nikita Bhor 21*; Jaya Mohite 2-22) beat **Baroda** 59 in 18.5 overs (Jaya Mohite 20; Maya Sonawane 4-8, N Bhor 2-5) by 37 runs.
SCA Stadium, Rajkot, September 22: Gujarat 112 in 40.5 overs (Renuka Chaudhari 33, Hani Patel 27; Reena Savasadiya 3-15, Tanya Rao 3-26) beat **Saurashtra** 94/9 in 50 overs (Tanya Rao 23*, Drasti Somaiya 22; Krutika Chaudhari 3-7, R Chaudhari 2-23) by·18 runs.
SCA Stadium, Rajkot, September 23: Mumbai 109 in 44.5 overs (Sayali Satghare 24; Kesha 3-23) beat **Baroda** 72 in 35.5 overs (Prakashika Naik 5-7) by 37 runs.
Madhavrao Scindia Cricket Ground, Rajkot, September 23: Saurashtra 54 in 35.3 overs (Aditi Gaikwad 4-19, Maya Sonawane 3-19) lost to **Maharashtra** 55/3 in 15.2 overs by seven wickets.
Madhavrao Scindia Cricket Ground, Rajkot, September 24: Mumbai 179/6 in 50 overs (Prakashika Naik 52*, Riya Chaudhari 40; Sujan Sama 2-33, Tanya Rao 2-44) beat **Saurashtra** 56 in 30.5 overs (Fatima Jaffer 3-4, A Narvekar 2-1) by 123 runs.
Madhavrao Scindia Cricket Ground, Rajkot, September 25: Baroda 166/4 in 50 overs (Jaya Mohite 68, Yastika Bhatia 55) beat **Gujarat** 86 in 40.4 overs (J Mohite 4-19, Kesha Patel 2-16) by 80 runs.
SCA Stadium, Rajkot, September 25: Maharashtra 103 in 48 overs (Aditi Gaikwad 22; Fatima Jaffer 5-26, Manjiri Gawde 2-22) beat **Mumbai** 64 in 47 overs (M Solao 4-15, Nikita Bhor 3-6) by 39 runs.

West Zone Points Table

Team	M	W	L	T	N/R	Pts	NRR
Maharashtra	4	4	0	0	0	16	+1.365
Mumbai	4	2	1	0	1	10	+0.807
Baroda	4	1	2	0	1	6	+0.050
Gujarat	4	1	2	0	1	6	-0.726
Saurashtra	4	0	3	0	1	2	-1.640

Maharashtra and Mumbai qualified for the Super League

South Zone

SGVR ACA Stadium, Perecherla, September 20: Andhra 302/0 in 50 overs (N Anusha 168*, M Durga 100*) beat **Tamil Nadu** 73 in 32.3 overs (E Padmaja 3-17, Saranya Gadwal 2-10) by 229 runs.
Jagarlamudi Kuppuswamy Choudary College, Guntur, September 20: Goa 133/9 in 49 overs (Sanjula Naik 63, Shreya Parab 20; C Pratyusha 3-13, S Shubha 2-9) beat **Karnataka** 129/5 in 48.5 overs (Simren Henry 36, S Shubha 36; Vanita Bhandari 2-13, Pooja Bharati 2-26) by four runs.
Rayapati VenkataRangarao and Jagarlamudi Chandramouli College of Engineering Ground, Guntur, September 20: Hyderabad 139/8 in 50 overs (D Ramya 100; Aneena Mathews 3-26, Minnu Mani 2-22) beat **Kerala** 115 in 45.4 overs (A Akshaya 52, Keerthi James 22; Pranathi Reddy 3-9, Pooja Vanka 3-16) by 24 runs.
SGVR ACA Stadium, Perecherla, September 21: Goa 54 in 31.5 overs (K Dhatri 4-12) lost to **Andhra** 58/0 in 14 overs (N Anusha 43*) by ten wickets.
Jagarlamudi Kuppuswamy Choudary College, Guntur, September 21: Hyderabad 206/9

in 50 overs (Anuradha Nayak 57*, Lakshmi Prasanna 33; Belinda Ann 3-42, SB Keerthana 2-28) beat **Tamil Nadu** 143/9 in 50 overs (SB Keerthana 48; Harleen Kaur 3-29, Geethanjali Bomma 2-13) by 63 runs.

Rayapati Venkata Rangarao and Jagarlamudi Chandramouli College of Engineering Ground, Guntur, September 21: Karnataka 138 in 49.4 overs (S Shubha 54; K Kavya 6-17) lost to **Kerala** 139/9 in 49.4 overs (Keerthi James 25; S Shubha 4-27, C Pratyusha 2-21) by one wicket.

Jagarlamudi Kuppuswamy Choudary College, Guntur, September 23: Andhra 192/5 in 50 overs (G Sneha 104*, M Durga 27; C Pratyusha 2-38) beat **Karnataka** 77 in 38 overs (S Shubha 29; K Dhatri 3-30, Saranya Gadwal 2-5) by 115 runs.

Rayapati Venkata Rangarao and Jagarlamudi Chandramouli College of Engineering Ground, Guntur, September 23: Hyderabad 218/6 in 50 overs (D Ramya 100*, Pranathi Reddy 59) beat **Goa** 190/7 in 50 overs (Sanjula Naik 38, Suganda Ghadi 27; Pooja Vanka 2-28, Lakshmi Prasanna 2-34) by 28 runs.

SGVR ACA Stadium, Perecherla, September 23: Tamil Nadu 63 in 49.2 overs (Aneena Mathews 3-11, A Akshaya 2-8) lost to **Kerala** 64/2 in 23.4 overs (Jilu George 27) by eight wickets.

Jagarlamudi Kuppuswamy Choudary College, Guntur, September 24: Andhra 131 in 48.1 overs (N Anusha 37, C Jhansi Lakshmi 21; K Kavya 6-24) beat **Kerala** 72 in 36.5 overs (Anjali Sarvani 3-21, Saranya Gadwal 2-8) by 59 runs.

Rayapati Venkata Rangarao and Jagarlamudi Chandramouli College of Engineering Ground, Guntur, September 24: Goa 155 in 46 overs (Sanjula Naik 63, Shreya Parab 26; Gomathi Rajam 3-24, K Ramyashri 3-29) beat **Tamil Nadu** 46 in 32.2 overs (Rakshanda Pilankar 3-6, Vanita Bhandari 3-14) by 109 runs.

SGVR ACA Stadium, Perecherla, September 24: Karnataka 186/7 in 50 overs (S Shubha 63, C Pratyusha 39; Keerthi Reddy 3-31) beat **Hyderabad** 63/5 in 23 overs (S Shubha 2-9, Sahana Pawar 2-15) by 44 runs (VJD method).

Jagarlamudi Kuppuswamy Choudary College, Guntur, September 26: Andhra 249/4 in 50 overs (C Jhansi Lakshmi 89*, E Padmaja 78) beat **Hyderabad** 142 in 42 overs (D Ramya 62, Anuradha Nayak 28; Saranya Gadwal 4-35, CJ Lakshmi 2-20) by 107 runs.

SGVR ACA Stadium, Perecherla, September 26: Goa 69 in 32.1 overs (A Akshaya 6-16) lost to **Kerala** 70/4 in 36 overs (A Akshaya 21*) by six wickets.

Rayapati Venkata Rangarao and Jagarlamudi Chandramouli College of Engineering Ground, Guntur, September 26: Tamil Nadu 45 in 32.4 overs (C Pratyusha 3-8, Sahana Pawar 2-5) lost to **Karnataka** 46/3 in 26.2 overs (Sanjana Batni 22; K Ramyashri 2-12) by seven wickets.

South Zone Points Table

Team	M	W	L	T	N/R	Pts	NRR
Andhra	5	5	0	0	0	20	+2.683
Kerala	5	3	2	0	0	12	+0.037
Hyderabad	5	3	2	0	0	12	-0.161
Karnataka	5	2	3	0	0	8	-0.075
Goa	5	2	3	0	0	8	-0.204
Tamil Nadu	5	0	5	0	0	0	-2.385

Andhra and Kerala qualified for the Super League

East Zone

Tata Digwadi Stadium, Jamadoba, September 20: Assam 143 in 49.5 overs (Ruhina Pegu 30; Shiuli Chakraborthy 2-26, PHK Das 2-29) beat **Tripura** 117/9 in 50 overs (Suravi Roy 31, Jhumki Debnath 26; Kakoli Saikia 3-10, Sanchari Roy 2-22) by 26 runs.

Jawaharlal Nehru Stadium, Dhanbad, September 20: Bengal 123 in 49.4 overs (Tanusree Sarkar 33, Pama Paul 20; Banalata Mallick 3-18, Sushree Pradhan 3-23) lost to **Odisha** 124/4 in 43.3 overs (Sasmita Mahalik 33, Anjali Singh 28) by six wickets.

Jawaharlal Nehru Stadium, Dhanbad, September 22: Odisha 40/8 in 19 overs (Nirupama Baro 4-3) v **Assam**. No result.

Tata Digwadi Stadium, Jamadoba, September 22: Jharkhand 80/9 in 33 overs (Priti Saha 4-14) v **Bengal** 23/1 in 8 overs. No result.

Jawaharlal Nehru Stadium, Dhanbad, September 24: Bengal 124/9 in 50 overs (Rupa Dutta 34, Indrani Roy 33; Suravi Roy 2-18) beat **Tripura** 79 in 43.3 overs (S Roy 35; Shreyansh Aich 5-22, P Choudhary 2-9) by 45 runs.

Tata Digwadi Stadium, Jamadoba, September 24: Jharkhand 134 in 43.5 overs (Rasmi 30, Kumari Mahato 20; Sarojini Giri 3/23, Anjali Singh 2-8) lost to **Odisha** 138/8 in 49 overs (Sushree Pradhan 39, Sumitra Sahoo 28; Roshni Kannojia 2-17, Devyani Prasad 2-17) by two wickets.

Jawaharlal Nehru Stadium, Dhanbad, September 26: Assam 76 in 48.3 (Devyani Prasad 3-7, Roshni Kannojia 3-13) lost to **Jharkhand** 80/3 in 36.1 overs (Shivani Kandeyang 24*; Nirupama Baro 2-18) by seven wickets.

Tata Digwadi Stadium, Jamadoba, September 26: Odisha 222/6 in 50 overs (Anjali Singh 60, Sushree Pradhan 58; Suravi Roy 2-33) beat **Tripura** 73 in 43.2 overs (Jhumki Debnath 23; S Pradhan 3-5, Janaki Reddy 2-11) by 149 runs.

Tata Digwadi Stadium, Jamadoba, September 28: Bengal 120 in 46.4 (Indrani Roy 31; K Saikia 3-20) beat **Assam** 48 in 34 overs (Shreyansh Aich 2-8, Prativa Rana 2-11) by 72 runs.

Jawaharlal Nehru Stadium, Dhanbad, September 28: Tripura 81 in 37.5 overs (Shannti Kumari 3-12, Ritu Kumari 2-10) lost to **Jharkhand** 82/4 in 30 overs (Sonia 38*; Ritu Malakar 2-17) by six wickets.

East Zone Points Table

Team	M	W	L	T	N/R	Pts	NRR
Odisha	4	3	0	0	1	14	+1.196
Bengal	4	2	1	0	1	10	+0.698
Jharkhand	4	2	1	0	1	10	+0.568
Assam	4	1	2	0	1	6	-0.548
Tripura	4	0	4	0	0	0	-1.422

Odisha and Bengal qualified for the Super League

Group A Super League

Rayapati Venkata Rangarao and Jagarlamudi Chandramouli College of Engineering Ground, Guntur, October 5: Haryana 193/8 in 50 overs (Bhawna Ohlan 99, Suman Gulia 55; Minnu Mani 2-35) beat **Kerala** 118/8 in 50 overs (M Mani 25, Keerthy James 21; Shweta Sharma 3-21, Diksha Sharma 3-22) by 75 runs.

SGVR ACA Stadium, Perecherla, October 5: Odisha 124 in 48.5 overs (Sangeeta Khadia 31, Kuni Badara 23; Sayali Satghare 3-12, Fatima Jaffer 2-21) lost to **Mumbai** 126/4 in 45 overs (Jemimah Rodrigues 37, Vrushali Bhagat 28; Sushree Pradhan 3-16) by six wickets.

SGVR ACA Stadium, Perecherla, October 7: Mumbai 144/9 in 50 overs (Jemimah Rodrigues 30, Manali Dakshini 26; Simran 5-18) beat **Haryana** 116 in 45.5 overs (Sheetal Rana 52, Bhawna Ohlan 24; Manji Gawade 2-20, Fatima Jaffer 2-28) by 28 runs.

Rayapati Venkata Rangarao and Jagarlamudi Chandramouli College of Engineering Ground, Guntur, October 7: Odisha 146/9 in 50 overs (Sushree Pradhan 61, Sumitra Sahoo 25; Nikita Singh 2-19, Pooja Vastrakar 2-27) lost to **Madhya Pradesh** 147/7 in 47.4 overs (Saleena Dwivedi 59, Nikita 38*; Janaki Reddy 2-15) by three wickets.

SGVR ACA Stadium, Perecherla, October 9: Odisha100 in 49.4 overs (Shweta Sharma 3-20, Sheetal Rana 3-20) lost to **Haryana** 101/5 in 40.1 overs (Suman Gulia 59) by five wickets.

Rayapati Venkata Rangarao and Jagarlamudi Chandramouli College of Engineering Ground, Guntur, October 9: Madhya Pradesh 205/5 in 50 overs (Shivi Pandey 67, Nuzhat Parween 66; Keerthy James 3-38) beat **Kerala** 96/6 in 50 overs (K James 27*; Khushboo Verma 2-5) by 109 runs.

SGVR ACA Stadium, Perecherla, October 10: Kerala 77 in 46.5 overs (Sarojini Giri 3-9, Janaki Reddy 2-7) beat **Odisha** 75 in 33.4 overs (Keerthy James 3-8, Minnu Mani 3-26) by two runs.

Rayapati Venkata Rangarao and Jagarlamudi Chandramouli College of Engineering Ground, Guntur, October 10: Mumbai 76 in 44.1 overs (Pooja Yadav 26; Poonam Soni 3-13, Khushboo Verma 2-12) lost to **Madhya Pradesh** 80/4 in 27.2 overs (Nuzhat Parween 44; Fatima Jaffer 3-18) by six wickets.

Rayapati Venkata Rangarao and Jagarlamudi Chandramouli College of Engineering Ground, Guntur, October 12: Madhya Pradesh 102/8 in 50 overs (Nuzhat Parween 28, Soniya Sharma 20; Diksha Sharma 2-19, Shweta Sharma 2-25) beat **Haryana** 56 in 45.5 overs (Preeti Bhatiwal 21; Nikita Singh 2-4) by 46 runs.

SGVR ACA Stadium, Perecherla, October 12: Mumbai 216/7 in 50 overs (Jemimah Rodrigues 88, Vrushali Bhagat 56; Aneena Mathews 2-24, Minnu Mani 2-29) beat **Kerala** 101/7 in 50 overs (Jilu George 21; Fatima Jaffer 2-20) by 115 runs.

Super League Group A Points Table

Team	M	W	L	T	N/R	Pts	NRR
Madhya Pradesh	4	4	0	0	0	16	+1.181
Mumbai	4	3	1	0	0	12	+0.508
Haryana	4	2	2	0	0	8	+0.130
Kerala	4	1	3	0	0	4	-1.485
Odisha	4	0	4	0	0	0	-0.242

Madhya Pradesh and Mumbai qualified for the semi-finals

Group B Super League

Ravenshaw College Ground, Cuttack, October 5: Delhi 93 in 47.1 overs (Laxmi Yadav 36, Vandana Chaturvedi 21; Saranya Gadwal 3-6, Anjali Sarvani 2-11) lost to **Andhra** 96/2 in 29.2 overs (N Anusha 46, M Durga 21) by eight wickets.

Nimpur Sports and Cricket Club Ground, Cuttack, October 5: Maharashtra 135 in 44.3 overs (Tejal Hasabnis 88; Shreyansh Aich 3-23, Prativa Rana 2-21) beat **Bengal** 112 in 44.5 overs (P Rana 24; Aditi Gaikwad 3-23, Maya Sonawane 2-22) by 23 runs.

Ravenshaw College Ground, Cuttack, October 7: Uttar Pradesh 89/5 in 32.2 overs (Deepti

Sharma 27, Shobha Devi 20; Tanusree Sarkar 2-11) beat **Bengal** 82 in 21.3 overs (Deepti 3-12, Anjali 2-14) by eight runs.
Nimpur Sports and Cricket Club Ground, Cuttack, October 7: Maharashtra 86/3 in 36 overs (Tejal Hasabnis 33, Maya Sonawane 22; Vandana Chaturvedi 2-11) beat **Delhi** 61/7 in 25 overs (Aditi Gaikwad 2-11, M Sonawane 2-23) by 43 runs (VJD method).
Ravenshaw College Ground, Cuttack, October 9: Andhra 113 in 49.3 overs (Saranya Gadwal 27, N Anusha 23) beat **Uttar Pradesh** 82 in 43 overs (M Bhavana 5-17, K Dhathri 3-22) by 31 runs.
Nimpur Sports and Cricket Club Ground, Cuttack, October 9: Bengal 130/7 in 50 overs (Rupa Dutta 33, Indrani Roy 32*; Neha Bhargava 3-23, Nidhi Dabas 2-12) beat **Delhi** 67 in 47.3 overs (Tanusree Sarkar 4-6, Shreyansh Aich 3-17) by 63 runs.
Nimpur Sports and Cricket Club Ground, Cuttack, October 10: Andhra 85 in 50 overs (N Anusha 21; S Adhikary 2-14, Shreyansh Aich 2-22) lost to **Bengal** 89/8 in 47.4 overs (K Dhathri 3-15, M Bhavana 2-14) by two wickets.
Ravenshaw College Ground, Cuttack, October 10: Uttar Pradesh 88 in 38.3 overs (Aditi Gaikwad 3-24, Utkarsha Pawar 2-15) beat **Maharashtra** 35 in 25.5 overs (Anju Rani 4-7, Tanu Kala 2-4) by 53 runs.
Nimpur Sports and Cricket Club Ground, Cuttack, October 12: Andhra 100 in 41.3 overs (N Anusha 29; M Solao 3-19, Nikita Bhor 2-15) beat **Maharashtra** 77 in 38.4 overs (K Dhathri 4-20, M Bhavana 3-13) by 23 runs.
Ravenshaw College Ground, Cuttack, October 12: Delhi 70 in 44 overs (Laxmi Yadav 36*; Rashi Kanojiya 3-9, Kajal 2-7) lost to **Uttar Pradesh** 71/2 in 32.3 overs (Ekta Singh 22*; Kirti Arya 2-20) by eight wickets.

Super League Group B Points Table

Team	M	W	L	T	N/R	Pts	NRR
Uttar Pradesh	4	3	1	0	0	12	+0.504
Andhra	4	3	1	0	0	12	+0.472
Bengal	4	2	2	0	0	8	+0.286
Maharashtra	4	2	2	0	0	8	-0.057
Delhi	4	0	4	0	0	0	-1.268

Andhra and Uttar Pradesh qualified for the semi-finals

1st Semi-Final: Nimpur Sports and Cricket Club Ground, Cuttack, October 16: Andhra 139/9 in 50 overs (C Jhansi Lakshmi 53, G Sneha 27; Manji Gawade 4-35, Fatima Jaffer 2-32) beat **Mumbai** 76/9 in 50 overs (F Jaffer 25*; K Dhathri 3-15, M Bhavana 2-8) by 63 runs.
2nd Semi-Final: Ravenshaw College Ground, Cuttack, October 16: Uttar Pradesh 165/3 in 50 overs (Deepti Sharma 83, Ekta Singh 45*) beat **Madhya Pradesh** 127 in 47.4 overs (Pooja Vastrakar 58*, Soniya Sharma 23; Kajal 3-18, Rashi Kanojiya 2-18) by 38 runs.

Andhra and Uttar Pradesh qualified for the final

Final: Nimpur Sports and Cricket Club Ground, Cuttack, October 19: Uttar Pradesh 112/9 in 50 overs (Deepti Sharma 56; E Padmaja 3-25, M Bhavana 2-9) lost to **Andhra** 113/4 in 40.5 overs (E Padmaja 36*, C Jhansi Lakshmi 23; Tanu Kala 2-27) by six wickets.

Winners: Andhra

Inter-Zonal Under-19 Two-Day Competition

Sushree, Tanushree script East's success

The off-spin pair of Sushree Pradhan, the captain, and Tanusree Sarkar spun a web around the opposition batters with their loop and sharp turn, picking up 31 wickets between them as East Zone took the title. They also scored 157 runs apiece – Sarkar's tally including a century to steal the show. South Zone, led by C Pratyusha, finished runners up with some consistent performances as well. As many as three centuries were scored in the tournament, but even then, Disha Kasat of Central Zone and Harleen Deol of North Zone were the only batters to cross the 200-run mark. Pradhan's match-haul of 10 for 66 against North Zone was particularly remarkable, as it gave East the only outright win of the competition. Fatima Jaffer, nephew of Wasim Jaffer, also caught the eye, bagging 14 wickets with her left-arm spin for West Zone.

Sushree Pradhan led East Zone to success. – *File photo*

Best Batter: Disha Kasat (Central Zone) (216 runs, 4 matches)
Best Bowler: Sushree Pradhan (East Zone) (19 wickets, 4 matches)

JSCA Stadium Complex, Ranchi, January 17-18: East Zone 229 in 90.5 overs (Tanusree Sarkar 107, Sushree Pradhan 36; Komalpreet Kour 2-8, Suman Gulia 2-37) beat **North Zone** 29 in 33.1 overs (Sarojini Giri 4-0, S Pradhan 4-13) and 166 in 67.3 overs (Harleen Deol 116; S Pradhan 6-53) by an innings and 34 runs.
JSCA Oval Ground, Ranchi, January 17-18: South Zone 245 in 64.4 overs (E Padmaja 44, S Shubha 41; Fatima Jaffer 4-87, Jaya Mohite 2-12) drew with **West Zone** 125 in 54 overs (F Jaffer 40, Renuka Chaudhari 28; Sahana Pawar 4-43, C Jhansi Lakshmi 2-14) and 122/1 in 48 overs (Jemimah Rodrigues 51, Yastika Bhatia 48*). South Zone won on the basis of first-innings lead.
JSCA Oval Ground, Ranchi, January 20-21: Central Zone 232/8 dec in 83 overs (Nuzhat Parween 67, Sangeeta Kumawat 51; Sushree Pradhan 4-74, Sarojini Giri 2-20) drew with **East Zone** 189/8 in 88 overs (Indrani Roy 91*, Tanusree Sarkar 23; Yashi Pandey 2-22, Pooja Vastrakar 2-43).
JSCA Stadium Complex, Ranchi, January 20-21: South Zone 235/9 dec in 93 overs (E Padmaja 90, C Pratyusha 44; Harleen Deol 3-45, Komalpreet Kour 2-41) and 23/0 in 10 overs drew with **North Zone** 138 in 62.4 overs (Ayush Soni 22; C Pratyusha 4-36, M Bhavana 2-14). South Zone won on the basis of first-innings lead.

JSCA Stadium Complex, Ranchi, January 23-24: Central Zone 248/9 dec in 111.5 overs (Disha Kasat 116, Sangeeta Kumawat 26; C Pratyusha 2-40, C Jhansi Lakshmi 2-63) drew with **South Zone** 199/9 in 83 overs (N Anusha 59, S Shubha 36; Poonam Soni 4-39, Tanu Kala 3-45).

JSCA Oval Ground, Ranchi, January 23-24: West Zone 149 in 59.5 overs (Tejal Hasabnis 54, Renuka Chaudhari 53; Harleen Deol 5-39, Vandana Chaturvedi 3-38) and 101/1 in 39 overs (Jemimah Rodrigues 45, Yastika Bhatia 43*) drew with **North Zone** 210 in 76.3 overs (H Deol 47, Suman Gulai 34; T Hasabnis 4-36, J Rodrigues 2-16). North Zone won on the basis of first-innings lead.

JSCA Oval Ground, Ranchi, January 26-27: North Zone 213 in 107.5 overs (Sheetal Rana 53, Laxmi Yadav 33; Tanu Kala 3-42, Poonam Soni 2-19) drew with **Central Zone** 162/7 in 99 overs (Nuzhat Parween 51, Ekta Singh 43; S Rana 5-36).

JSCA Stadium Complex, Ranchi, January 26-27: East Zone 168 in 91.5 overs (Sushree Pradhan 60, Sasmita Mahalik 26; Fatima Jaffer 6-59, Tejal Hasabnis 2-45) and 62/5 in 44 overs (Sumitra Sahoo 22; Jaya Mohite 2-13, Prakashika Naik 2-16) drew with **West Zone** 74 in 48.5 overs (Vrushali Bhagat 20; Tanusree Sarkar 4-11, S Pradhan 3-13). East Zone won on the basis of first-innings lead.

JSCA Stadium Complex, Ranchi, January 29-30: Central Zone 187 in 91.5 overs (Ekta Singh 53, Yashi Pandey 43*; Jaya Mohite 4-46, Fatima Jaffer 3-35) and 68/3 in 34 overs (Nuzhat Parween 22, Disha Kasat 20; Prakashika Naik 3-21) drew with **West Zone** 133 in 80 overs (Vushali Bhagat 24, Renuka Chaudhari 24; Tanu Kala 4-34, Rashi Kanojiya 3-47). Central Zone won on the basis of first-innings lead.

JSCA Oval Ground, Ranchi, January 29-30: South Zone 229 in 70.5 overs (Sanjula Naik 86, C Pratyusha 50; Tanusree Sarkar 4-59, Nirupama Baro 2-23) and 51/3 dec in 9 overs (G Sneha 35; Nirupama Baro 2-22) drew with **East Zone** 135 in 85.5 overs (Anjali Singh 42, Sushree Pradhan 33; S Naik 4-10, M Bhavana 2-11) and 31/3 in 22 overs (K Kavya 2-8). South Zone won on the basis of first-innings lead.

Points Table

Teams	M	W	L	D	T	A	Pts	Q
East Zone	4	1	0	3	0	0	12	1.156
South Zone	4	0	0	4	0	0	10	1.289
Central Zone	4	0	0	4	0	0	6	1.222
North Zone	4	0	1	3	0	0	5	0.622
West Zone	4	0	0	4	0	0	4	0.856

Winners: East Zone

Shashank Manohar, then BCCI president, presenting the CK Nayudu Lifetime Achievement Award to Syed Kirmani. — *BCCI*

BCCI Awards 2015-16 (Winners of 2014-15 season)

CK Nayudu Lifetime Achievement Award: Syed Kirmani
Polly Umrigar award for best Indian cricketer of the year: Virat Kohli
Madhavrao Scindia award for most runs in Ranji Trophy: Robin Uthappa (Karnataka)
Madhavrao Scindia award for most wickets in Ranji Trophy: Vinay Kumar (Karnataka)/Shardul Thakur (Mumbai)
Lala Amarnath award for the best all-rounder in Ranji Trophy: Jalaj Saxena (Madhya Pradesh)
Lala Amarnath award for the best all-rounder in limited-overs cricket: Deepak Hooda (Baroda)
MA Chidambaram award for the best Under-23 cricketer: Almas Shaukat (Uttar Pradesh)
MA Chidambaram award for the best Under-19 cricketer: Anmolpreet Singh (Punjab)
MA Chidambaram award for the best Under-16 cricketer: Shubham Gill (Punjab)
MA Chidambaram award for the best Woman cricketer: Mithali Raj (Railways)
MA Chidambaram award for best junior Woman cricketer: Devika Vaidya (Maharashtra)
Best umpire in domestic cricket: CK Nandan (Karnataka)
Best association: Karnataka State Cricket Association

Period: October 1, 2014, to September 30, 2015

PAKISTAN CRICKET

PSL takes birth in UAE

MAZHER ARSHAD

Quaid-e-Azam Trophy

Pakistan Cricket Board revamped the format of the country's premier first-class tournament for the third time in four years notwithstanding the announcement they made in 2014 that the format wouldn't be changed for at least three years. The Quaid-e-Azam Trophy, which in the previous season was contested by 26 teams, was this time reduced to a 16-team tournament. Of those, 12 – six departments and six regions – gained automatic qualification and four through a qualifying round of 14. Strangely, the qualifying round, despite having four-day matches, was not given first-class status. It left teams such as State Bank of Pakistan (SBP), Zarai Taraqiati Bank Limited (ZTBL), Pakistan International Airlines (PIA), Faisalabad and Sialkot among those without any first-class cricket in the season.

The inter-department qualifying tournament saw the return of Mohammad Amir to four-day cricket. He finished as their best bowler – 34 wickets at 9.79 including two ten-fors – helping Sui Southern Gas Corporation (SSGC) reach the main round.

History was made in the inter-region qualifying tournament when a team from Federally Administered Tribal Areas (FATA) made it to a first-class tournament for the first time, ahead of Karachi Blues, Faisalabad and Abbottabad. FATA, a remote region of the country, had been given full regional status only in 2013. In the main round, however, they ended with the wooden spoon. Against Rawalpindi, they became the first first-class team in Pakistan to lose four wickets without a run on board. Surprisingly, they still won.

Taj Wali, Peshawar's seamer, took four wickets in four balls against Port Qasim Authority (PQA), becoming just the sixth bowler to do so in the country's first-class cricket.

Sui Northern Gas Pipelines Limited (SNGPL) led by Pakistan's Test captain Misbah-ul-Haq defeated United Bank Limited (UBL) by six wickets in the final in Karachi, which was played under lights with a pink ball. It was SNGPL's fourth consecutive win. They had Bilawal Bhatti to thank for that: his 8 for 56 in the second innings were the best in a final.

Best batsman: Asif Zakir (Sui Southern Gas Corporation) (791 runs, 10 matches)
Best bowler: Mohammad Abbas (Khan Research Laboratories) (61 wickets, 10 matches)

Winners: Sui Northern Gas Pipelines Limited

National One-day Cup

Sixteen teams – eight departments and eight regions – participated in the National One-day Cup, which featured 59 matches in January. United Bank Limited (UBL) and Islamabad from Pool A, and Khan Research Laboratories (KRL) and National Bank of Pakistan (NBP) from Pool B made it to the semi-final.

NBP and Islamabad shared the trophy after the final in Lahore was washed out. This was the third time in four years that a one-day final ended in a no-result due to fog or rain in Punjab during the winter.

Salman Butt and Mohammad Asif returned to competitive cricket after serving their five-year bans for fixing. Butt surprised everyone with 135 off 143 for WAPDA against FATA in his first match, while his team-mate Asif grabbed two wickets for 22 in six overs. Butt finished second on the runs chart: 536 at 107.20 in seven games.

The best innings came from Mohammad Nawaz, the 22-year-old NBP all-rounder, who made 187 off 157 balls against Karachi Whites.

Best batsman: Kamran Akmal (National Bank of Pakistan) (576 runs, 8 matches)
Best bowler: Sadaf Hussain (Khan Research Laboratories) (20 wickets, 8 matches)

Winners: National Bank of Pakistan and Islamabad (shared)

Pakistan Super League

The idea of Pakistan's own T20 league was first mooted in 2008 and it finally materialised in 2016. PCB hosted the 24-match Pakistan Super League in the UAE in February. The five franchises that would later be named Karachi Kings ($26million), Lahore Qalandars ($25m), Peshawar Zalmi ($16m), Islamabad United ($15m) and Quetta Gladiators ($11m) were sold for a combined sum of $93m for ten years.

The draft in Lahore in December had 98 players, including 29 foreigners, being picked by the five franchises. Each franchise had a purse of $1.1m and could pick 15 players. Shahid Afridi, Shoaib Malik, Shane Watson, Kevin Pietersen and Chris Gayle were the five icon players snapped up by Peshawar, Karachi, Islamabad, Quetta and Lahore respectively for $200,000 each.

The bizarre format meant just one of the five teams got knocked out at the end of league stage. Lahore, hampered by injury to Mustafizur Rahman, a ban on Yasir Shah for taking illegal drugs and the poor form of Gayle, finished last after winning just two games. Karachi also won just two, but since their wins came against Lahore – one of them engineered by a Mohammad Amir hat-trick – they made it to the play-offs, where they lost the eliminator to Islamabad. Peshawar topped the points table, but lost to Quetta and Islamabad in the play-offs. Islamabad, led by Misbah-ul-Haq, overcame a poor start to win five straight games and lift the title before a full house in Dubai.

Quetta set Islamabad 175 to win the final courtesy Ahmed Shehzad's 64 and Kumar Sangakkara's 55. Dwayne Smith (73) and Brad Haddin (61*) ensured a smooth chase.

The find of the tournament was Quetta's Mohammad Nawaz, the off-spinner, who took 13 wickets and scored 120 runs. The tournament's only hundred was by Sharjeel Khan, earning him a call to Pakistan's World T20 squad.

Best batsman: Umar Akmal (Lahore Qalandars) (335 runs, 7 matches)
Best bowler: Andre Russell (Islamabad United) (16 wickets, 10 matches)

Winners: Islamabad United

Pakistan Cup (One-Day)

PCB changed the name of Pentangular Cup, a one-day competition between the four provinces and the capital Islamabad, to Pakistan Cup. The tournament, staged in April in Faisalabad, was played in a round-robin format with the top two qualifying for the final. The captains, Shoaib Malik (Punjab), Sarfraz Ahmed (Sindh), Azhar Ali (Balochistan), Misbah-ul-Haq (Islamabad) and Younis Khan (Khyber Pakhtunkhwa), selected a 15-man squad from a draft of 150 players.

KPK, the defending champions, topped the group stage before comprehensively beating Punjab by 151 runs in the final: Fakhar Zaman's 115 had helped them put up 311.

Khalid Latif (168* for Sindh) and Ahmed Shehzad (143 for KPK) both made hundreds in the same match, with Latif ending on the losing side. Khurram Manzoor (Sindh) scored back-to-back hundreds, while Mohammad

Weathering the storm: Younis Khan put behind him the umpiring controversy to lead Khyber Pakhtunkhwa to victory in the Pakistan Cup. – *PCB*

Amir (Sindh) took the only five-wicket haul in the tournament – his first in a one-day game.

There was controversy when Younis withdrew from the tournament to protest against umpiring decisions. He was issued a show cause notice and fined, and returned to lead his side in the final.

Best batsman: Ahmed Shehzad (Khyber Pakhtunkhwa) (372 runs, 5 matches)
Best bowler: Mohammad Amir (Sindh) (11 wickets, 5 matches)

Winners: Khyber Pakhtunkhwa

The National T20 Cup

The PCB held a T20 tournament between the eight teams that qualified for the next Quaid-e-Azam Trophy, a first-class tournament, instead of the eight from the previous national T20 championship. As a result, established T20 teams such as Sialkot and Multan missed out.

Karachi Whites, Karachi Blues, Lahore Whites, Lahore Blues, Peshawar, Islamabad, Rawalpindi and FATA picked players through a draft, which meant many could not represent their home teams.

Umar Akmal's 43-ball hundred for Lahore Whites against Rawalpindi was the joint-fastest in T20 cricket in Pakistan, and included 34 off an over by Yasir Arafat. Salman Butt (Lahore Whites), with 350 runs at 70, strengthened his case for a national comeback after serving the spot-fixing ban.

The final was a Karachi derby. The Blues created history by becoming the first team from the city to win a T20 championship. Mohammad Nawaz took 4 for 26 and defended 11 in the last over to keep Whites to 179, four runs short. Earlier, Blues' 182 had been built on Khurram Manzoor's 70 off 42 and Fawad Alam's unbeaten 44-ball 67.

Best batsman: Umar Akmal (Lahore Whites) (363 runs, 8 matches)
Best bowler: Saeed Ajmal (Karachi Blues) (20 wickets, 9 matches)

Winners: Karachi Blues

Shaheed Mohtarma Benazir Bhutto Women's Challenge Trophy

Zarai Taraqiati Bank Limited put a strong opening stand of 110 runs through Nahida Khan and Javeria Khan after asked to bat first in the final

Pakistan internationals to the fore: ZTBL, with several national team players in their midst, lifted the T20 title. — PCB

against State Bank of Pakistan in Lahore. Chasing 159 for the national T20 title, SBP had no answer to Sana Mir, Almas Akram and Diana Baig, all of whom picked up two wickets to restrict the opponent to 88 for 7.

Best batter: Javeria Khan (Zarai Taraqiati Bank Limited) (654 runs, 7 matches)
Best bowler: Sana Mir (Zarai Taraqiati Bank Limited) (18 wickets, 8 matches)

Winners: Zarai Taraqiati Bank Limited

Mohtarma Fatima Jinnah National Women's Championship

In a repeat of the T20 final, Nahida Khan and Javeria Khan made half-centuries and put on an opening stand of 116 to help Zarai Taraqiati Bank Limited chase down 180 against State Bank of Pakistan in Rawalpindi. Bismah Maroof and Nain Abidi did their bit to get the job done in 34.1 overs with eight wickets in hand. Aimen Anwar was the team's bowling star with returns of 3 for 25.

Best batter: Javeria Khan (Zarai Taraqiati Bank Limited) (654 runs, 7 matches)
Best bowler: Sana Mir (Zarai Taraqiati Bank Limited) (18 wickets, 8 matches)

Winners: Zarai Taraqiati Bank Limited

Mazher Arshad (@MazherArshad) is a journalist based in Lahore.

SRI LANKA CRICKET

Success for Tamil Union after six decades

ANDREW FERNANDO

Premier League Tournament

Tamil Union Cricket and Athletic Club is tucked away by a canal in one of Colombo's shabbier neighbourhoods, but for decades has produced cricket and cricketers that transcend the surrounds. On the home honours boards are names like Mahadevan Sathasivam, who is widely held to be Sri Lanka's greatest pre-Test batsman, and Muttiah Muralitharan, who played for Tamil Union right through that storied career.

The P Saravanamuttu Oval itself can lay claim to a little glory. Donald Bradman's 1948 Invincibles played there en route to England. In 1982, the ground hosted Sri Lanka's inaugural Test. And in the decades since, the P Sara's bouncy track has forged itself a reputation as one of the most reliable result-pitches in the world.

Yet, for all the history, Tamil Union owned one of Sri Lankan cricket's more puzzling records. The club had won a domestic cricket title in 1950-51, but no Tamil Union side had lifted the trophy since. It took two pairs of old hands combining with one of Sri Lanka's brightest young talents to shake up the team's cricket, and end a 64-year-drought.

At the helm of this triumphant season was Sri Lanka fast bowler Suranga Lakmal, who only played four matches, but claimed 19 wickets at an average of 17.84. At No. 3, former Sri Lanka opener Tharanga Paranavitana provided the campaign its substance – reeling off three hundred and five fifties to top the batting chart with 953 runs at an average of 79.41.

But it was Dhananjaya de Silva, the 24-year-old allrounder, who gave the team their edge. In 17 innings, he struck 824 runs at an average of 54.25 and a strike-rate of 73. That made him

The all-rounder's edge: 824 runs and 34 wickets for Dhananjaya de Silva.
– *Getty Images*

Tamil Union's second-highest run-scorer, and fifth overall, but he was also the club's most successful bowler: his off-spin brought 34 wickets at 14.23.

These three players coming together in the second innings of the final match of the season secured their team the title. Having given up a 148-run first-innings lead to Galle Cricket Club, Lakmal blasted out the opposition middle order, to take 4 for 20 while Galle CC collapsed to 126 all out. With 279 needed in the fourth innings, de Silva stroked a 131-ball 124 from the top of the order, and Paranavitana 67 not out to guide the team to victory, sparking much relief and jubilation.

Almost as incredible as the release of six-and-a-half decades of frustration, was the rate of Port Authority Cricket Club's decline. They had won the previous year's title but through alleged mismanagement, had seen a mass exodus of their best players, including de Silva. They found themselves relegated from the first-class competition next season.

Best batsman: Tharanga Paranavitana (Tamil Union) (953 runs, 10 matches)
Best bowler: Lakshan Sandakan (Colombo Cricket Club) (52 wickets, 10 matches)

Winners: Tamil Union Cricket and Athletic Club

Premier Limited Over Tournament

On the one-day front, Nondescripts Cricket Club defeated Colts Cricket Club in the televised final, to win a rain-affected tournament. The weather only allowed NCC to complete two of their six group games, but they scored enough points in those matches to move to the final four. They then beat Sinhalese Sports Club by 121 runs in the semi-final, before triumphing by 77 runs in the final.

Farveez Maharoof's 16 wickets at an average of 6.31 was the basis for NCC's victory, particularly as he claimed three wickets for two runs in the final, before leaving the field through injury.

Best batsman: Danushka Gunathilaka (Sinhalese Sports Club) (270 runs, 5 matches)
Best bowler: Farveez Maharoof (Nondescripts Cricket Club) (16 wickets, 5 matches)

Winners: Nondescripts Cricket Club

Premier T20 Tournament

SLC organised two T20 tournaments ahead of the World T20 in March and April. Sri Lanka Army won the club-based Premier T20 tournament, defeating Tamil Union in the final, as Asela Gunaratna struck an unbeaten 65 off 43 balls to run down a target of 165. This tournament had earlier been lit up by Dasun Shanaka, who hit a Sri Lankan record 16 sixes for SSC, in a match against Saracens Sports Club. That innings of 123 off 46 balls was Shanaka's second blitz in a week, after he had also struck 131 off 48 against Galle Cricket Club.

Best batsman: Dasun Shanaka (Sinhalese Sports Club) (348 runs, 7 matches)
Best bowler: Thilan Thushara (Colombo Cricket Club) (13 wickets, 6 matches)

Winners: Sri Lanka Army

Super T20 Provincial Tournament

The 11-day Super T20 Provincial Tournament, featuring five teams, comprised of the best players from the Premier T20 competition. It was won by the Colombo Commandos, which was led by Milinda Siriwardana.

Best batsman: Dhananjaya de Silva (Colombo Commandos) (234 runs, 6 matches)
Best bowler: Shaminda Eranga (Colombo Commandos) (14 wickets, 6 matches)

Winners: Colombo Commandos

Women's T20 Tournament – Division 1

Sudeepa Athukorala, the left-arm medium pacer, returned sensational figures of 4-0-9-5 as Sri Lanka Air Force Sports Club beat Sri Lanka Army Sports Club by 75 runs in the final of the national T20 competition. Put in to bat, Air Force rode on Yasoda Mendis's 36 to post 108 for 6. Army were never in with a chance as they lost regular wickets to be dismissed for 33 in 10.5 overs.

Winners: Sri Lanka Air Force Sports Club

Andrew Fernando (@andrewffernando) is ESPNcricinfo's Sri Lanka correspondent.

BANGLADESH CRICKET

Mosaddek's star turn

QUAZI ZULQUARNAIN ISLAM

National Cricket League

Khulna Division wrapped up their fourth title with a six-point lead. Unlike the previous season, where they narrowly missed out on the first-class title on the last day, this time a draw against Rangpur in the final game was enough for them to pick up the seven points necessary to pip Dhaka Metropolis to the honours. They were driven by two spinners at opposite ends of their careers: the wily Abdur Razzak, who took 28 wickets in six matches, and Mehedi Hasan, a young off-spinner who took 30 in just five games at an astonishing average of 16.43. Imrul Kayes struck two centuries for them, while Nurul Hasan had 384 runs at 64 on average.

Both, however, were well down the list of highest scorers. That accolade belonged to Test discard Shahriar Nafees, who plundered 715 at an average of close to 80. The young Mosaddek Hossain scored an unbeaten double-century, but he was still dwarfed by Mominul Haque. Mominul's 239 for Chittagong was the highest individual score of the season.

Best batsman: Shahriar Nafees (Barisal Division) (715 runs, 6 matches)
Best bowler: Sunzamul Islam (Rajshahi Division) (39 wickets, 6 matches)

Winners: Khulna Division

All-format hero: Young Mosaddek has the "brains of a 45-year-old cricketer", said Tamim Iqbal, his captain at Abahani Limited. – *BCB*

Dhaka Premier League

The 50-over tournament was dogged by controversies. Victoria players complained about not being paid, Suhrawadi Shuvo was hospitalised after a bouncer struck him, and Tamim Iqbal's outburst directed at the umpires earned him a BDT1lakh ($1270) fine and an incomplete match. The umpires walked out, and after much deliberation, a no-result was called that gave Abahani Limited the one point they needed to finish on top of the table. They were crowned champions over Prime Doleshwar – amid mutterings of favouritism.

This took away from an otherwise enthralling and tight season. Abahani, who last won the title in 2010-11, started with three wins in four games, but were in danger of missing out on a place in the Super League after three consecutive losses. A four game streak to coincide with the arrival of a typically belligerent Shakib Al Hasan after his IPL stint took them over the line. Captain Tamim was all praise for Mosaddek Hossain: "He has the brains of a 45-year-old cricketer." He finished with three Man of the Match awards, 15 wickets and a batting average of 77.

Best batsman: Raqibul Hasan (Prime Doleshwar Sporting Club) (719 runs, 16 matches)
Best bowler: PC de Silva (Victoria Sporting Club) (30 wickets, 14 matches)

Winners: Abahani Limited

Bangladesh Premier League

With no payment hassles and fewer flash points this time, the BPL, which was held in November and December to help players prepare for the Asia Cup and ICC World T20, passed off controversy-free. Comilla Victorians claimed a maiden title triumph over Barisal Bulls off the last ball. Their win was scripted by Alok Kapali's 39, which included five fours off the last eight balls of the game. It was perhaps just reward for the professionally managed Comilla Victorians, under the inspirational leadership of Mashrafe bin Mortaza. The limited-overs captain played part of the competition with a torn hamstring, restricted to standing at cover or midwicket.

Ashar Zaidi, Imrul Kayes and Abu Hider were the standout performers. Zaidi won the tournament honours for his 215 runs and 17 wickets, almost all of which came as crucial match-winning interventions.

Best batsman: Kumar Sangakkara (Dhaka Dynamites) (349 runs, 10 matches)
Best bowler: Kevon Cooper (Barisal Bulls) (22 wickets, 9 matches)

Winners: Comilla Victorians

Quazi Zulquarnain Islam (@nondeplume) is a senior sports writer for the Daily Star.

THE UNITED ARAB EMIRATES CRICKET

UAE has competition

PAUL RADLEY

Ever since Abdul Rahman Bukhatir, the Emirati business magnate, birthed Sharjah cricket in the early 1980s, the UAE has enjoyed a monopoly on the sport in the Middle East. Peerless in infrastructure, contacts and performance amongst Gulf countries, the Emirates can consider itself the region's lone cricket power.

It would be a push to suggest their neighbours have overtaken them this year. But some of the countries with which they share a border did at least agitate to get noticed.

Oman, in particular, gained most ground on the field. The team enjoyed their finest moment in the sport to date when they marked their debut at an ICC tournament by beating Associate trendsetters Ireland at the World T20.

The thrilling two-wicket win in Dharamsala, secured with two balls to spare, left some indelible memories. Within five months, the ICC upload of Zeeshan Maqsood's diving catch to dismiss Irish opener Paul Stirling had been viewed over 120,000 times.

Off the field, too, other Gulf nations were making moves towards greater upward mobility in cricket. Saudi Arabia became the 39th Associate member of the ICC in June.

According to a 2014 census, Saudi has 4350 cricketers and 80 cricket facilities. And, impressed by a three-year deal penned by Saudi Cricket Centre (SCC) with MoneyGram, the ICC agreed to upgrade their status from the Affiliate level they had held since 2003, after an inspection in March.

"I hope [SCC] will continue to play its positive and active role in promoting and developing the game in its territory," said Shashank Manohar, the ICC chairman.

Although Qatar has yet to stage an international series of note, the Pakistan Cricket Board did use a new relationship with Doha to leverage a deal out of the Emirates Cricket Board for their new T20 league.

The ECB had pre-booked the Masters Champions League, a troubled venture for "retired" international players, for their stadia in Dubai and Sharjah. Organisers of the Pakistan Super League threatened to move their debut competition to Qatar, in order to squeeze Emirates cricket bosses in shifting the MCL away from the dates they wanted. In the end, the tournaments overlapped, and the crowds at the PSL were far larger.

The UAE's national team were conspicuous absentees from the World T20. They have facilities the envy of many Test nations, let alone their peers in the Associate sphere. Good enough, of course, to make Pakistan feel at home away from home for so long.

They have a relatively vast player base, plucked from the sizable subcontinental expatriate workforce. And, under the stewardship of Aaqib Javed, they had been to the previous two ICC tournaments.

However, a side in transition had played pitifully in the qualifying competition, and were beaten to a place in India by, amongst others, Oman. Superficially, the UAE's status as Gulf cricket's power was eroded by missing out on the trip to India. Realistically, though, they remain far ahead in the Middle East on most barometers.

Aaqib left in June to take up a role with Lahore Qalanders, the PSL franchise, after four years in Dubai. He was the longest serving and most successful UAE coach ever.

The team's ascent was inexorable for the first three years under the former Pakistan seamer. The fourth, though, was tough, particularly after a winless World Cup. Reaching it was the pinnacle of UAE cricket achievement, but they went into a tailspin thereafter.

At least Aaqib managed to go out on a high. His team ended a dismal 12 months by gaining a first win over Ireland in 15 years in February.

That was a warm-up match for the Asia Cup, where the UAE further inverted the form guide by laying waste to Hong Kong, Afghanistan, and Oman to qualify with unforeseen ease to play Asia's Big Four.

They even impressed for half the games against Sri Lanka, Bangladesh and Pakistan, thanks to fine bowling by Mohammed Naveed, Amjad Javed and Ahmed Raza. Muddled batting meant they failed to register a win, but the optimism engendered was a major boost after a tough year.

It even prompted Paul Franks, Aaqib's short-term assistant in Bangladesh, to return to take up the role of interim UAE head coach in July.

"The next two years looks better now for Associate cricket," Franks said after succeeding Aaqib. "Opportunities will be there. Now is a good time to be in the UAE team, performing well. If you do, there is a very, very clear future for you."

Franks might have been moved to review that sentiment, though, after a winless spell in temporary charge in Scotland in August 2016. The UAE lost both World Cricket League matches, to remain bottom of the table, and a washout in the Intercontinental Cup meant they were left in a similar position in the four-day league, too.

Paul Radley (@PaulRadley) is a journalist with The National.

WINNERS AROUND THE GLOBE
AUSTRALIA

Rebel WBBL breaks new ground

Sheffield Shield: Victoria

Travis Dean and Peter Handscomb made three centuries each in Victoria's title defence. — *Getty Images*

Travis Dean, the Sheffield Shield player of the year, and Peter Handscomb made three centuries each to front-end a strong batting performance by Victoria, who defended the title. They scored more than 1500 runs between them to finish among the season's top three run-getters. In the final against South Australia, Dean and Handscomb made 111 and 112 in the first innings respectively to put the team in a commanding position. Jon Holland's five-wicket haul in South Australia's second innings gave Victoria a target of 193. Dean (54), Marcus Stoinis (72) and Handscomb (61*) engineered a seven-wicket win. Victoria's success lost a bit of shine as Mick Lewis, the bowling coach, was fined $A2226 for ball tampering on the third day of the final.

Among other highlights, South Australia's Callum Ferguson and Jake Lehmann made double-centuries and put on a fourth-wicket stand of 378 in a 302-run win over Tasmania in a league game.

Best batsman: Ben Dunk (Tasmania) (837 runs, 10 matches)
Best bowler: Joe Mennie (South Australia) (51 wickets, 11 matches)

Matador BBQs One-Day Cup: New South Wales

Steve Smith and Mitchell Starc starred with bat and ball as New South Wales won six of their seven matches to lift the trophy after a decade. They had finished runners-up in the last two seasons. They rode on an unbroken 165-run partnership between Ed Cowan and Smith to beat South Australia by nine wickets in the final. Incidentally, they had beaten South Australia in the 2005-06 final also. Starc, who finished with figures of 3 for 39 in the final, got good company from Josh Hazlewood in the second half of South Australia's innings as the batting team went from being 191 for 3 to 221 all out. Starc had started the tournament with a six-wicket haul against Cricket Australia XI, who were making their tournament debut.

In other developments, Victoria suspended Glenn Maxwell twice in two seasons because of disciplinary issues and Travis Head became the third Australian to score a List A double-century.

Best batsman: Steven Smith (New South Wales) (435 runs, 6 matches)
Best bowler: Mitchell Starc (New South Wales) (26 wickets, 6 matches)

Big Bash League: Sydney Thunder

Chris Gayle's controversial "don't blush, baby" comment to Mel McLaughlin on air in what could be his final Big Bash League was the biggest blip in what was otherwise a wonderful tournament. In his last appearance for Melbourne Renegades, Gayle equalled Yuvraj Singh's fastest T20 fifty off 12 balls but Adelaide Strikers prevailed to make it to the knockouts.

In the final, Kevin Pietersen's 39-ball 74 for Melbourne Stars was overshadowed by Usman Khawaja's 40-ball 70 for Sydney Thunder. Khawaja was the only batsman to score two hundreds in the tournament. Thunder stayed calm in a tense run chase of 181 to win by three wickets with three balls left and lift their maiden title. Paddy Upton, the coach, acknowledged the inputs of *Wisden India's Impact Index* team for their success.

Best batsman: Chris Lynn (Brisbane Heat) (378 runs, 8 matches)
Best bowler: Clint McKay (Sydney Thunder) (18 wickets, 10 matches)

Women's National Cricket League: South Australia

Sarah Taylor's 110 and her second-wicket stand of 181 runs with Bridget Patterson (74) took South Australia to 264 for 7 in the final against New South Wales. After that all the six bowlers picked up at least a wicket each to give the team a 54-run win. New South Wales's Ellyse Perry was the only batter to cross 400 runs in the tournament.

Best batter: Ellyse Perry (New South Wales) (403 runs, 7 matches)
Best bowler: Amanda-Jade Wellington (South Australia) (13 wickets, 7 matches)

Women's Big Bash League: Sydney Thunder

The inaugural edition was widely acknowledged as a success, with good crowds turning up and even better television audiences tuning in. A thrilling final was befitting the occasion, with Sydney Thunder, the most consistent side of the tournament, lifting the title.

Chasing 116 against Sydney Sixers, Sydney Thunder started strongly be-

The pioneers: Claire Koski and Lauren Cheatle celebrate the Sydney Thunder victory against Ellyse Perry's Sydney Sixers. — *Getty Images*

fore a collapse reduced them to 109 for 6 in 18.4 overs. Another wicket fell in the final over, but Sixers missed run-out chances as Thunder romped home by three wickets with three balls to spare. Meg Lanning of Melbourne Stars was the player of the tournament for hitting five fifties and having the best average of 56.00.

Best batter: Meg Lanning (Melbourne Stars) (560 runs, 14 matches)
Best bowler: Rene Farrell (Sydney Thunder) (26 wickets, 16 matches)

ENGLAND

Thrilling end to 'no toss' season

Championship Division One: Middlesex

England Cricket Board broke an age-old tradition by doing away with mandatory toss and giving the visitors the option to decide whether to field first. The move was aimed at encouraging the development of spinners. In a season as pioneering as this, Toby Ronald-Jones's dramatic match-ending hat-trick at Lord's in the dying hours of the final day helped Middlesex beat Yorkshire, the double-defending champions, by 61 runs and lift the title for the first time since 1993. Middlesex, the season's only unbeaten team, Yorkshire and Somerset were all in the running for the title till then. Somerset, who revived their campaign in spectacular fashion after early losses, fell short of their maiden title yet again as Middlesex and Yorkshire agreed upon a fourth-innings chase of 240 in 40 overs.

Durham finished fourth, but were relegated, along with Nottinghamshire, with a 48-point penalty for receiving a £3.8m bailout from ECB during the season. Jeetan Patel's rich-haul could not take Warwickshire to the top, but earned him a recall into the New Zealand Test squad after more than three years.

Best batsman: Keaton Jennings (Durham) (1548 runs, 16 matches)
Best bowler: Jeetan Patel (Warwickshire) (69 wickets, 16 matches)

Championship Division Two: Essex

Kent finished second on the table with 212 points, behind Essex's tally of 235, but ECB denied them a promotion to Division One. The county had thought that they would earn a place as Durham were relegated, but ECB retained Hampshire in Division 1.

Essex, meanwhile, rode on 1000-plus runs from Tom Westley, captain Ryan ten Doeschate and Nick Browne, and Graham Napier's 63 wickets in his farewell season to earn promotion after a long gap. Ben Duckett's batting for Northamptonshire was one of the talking points of the season.

Best batsman: Ben Duckett (Northamptonshire) (1338 runs, 14 matches)
Best bowler: Joe Leach (Worcestershire) (65 wickets, 15 matches)

Royal London One-Day Cup: Warwickshire

Sam Hain and Jonathan Trott, who returned for his final season of cricket, topped the batting charts, and Jeetan Patel took 22 wickets at an average of 20.31 to front-end Warwickshire's title finish. In the final, Chris Woakes, Ateeq Javid, Oliver Hannon-Dalby and Patel took two wickets each as Surrey, who had Kumar Sangakkara with them, were dismissed for 136 in 40.1 overs. Trott's unbeaten 82 saw through the chase for Warwickshire, who prevailed by eight wickets with 118 balls to spare.

Best batsman: Sam Hain (Warwickshire) (540 runs, 10 matches)
Best bowler: Matt Coles (Kent) (24 wickets, 9 matches)

Another trophy for Edwards: Charlotte Edwards, the former England Women captain, had a point to prove with Southern Vipers. – *Getty Images*

NatWest T20 Blast: Northamptonshire

Ben Duckett's 47-ball 84 for Northamptonshire in the semi-final against a Nottinghamshire attack consisting of Andre Russell, Stuart Broad, Samit Patel and Jake Ball was the highlight of finals day. In the other semi-final, Mark Wood's career-best 4 for 25, after an injury that kept him out of action for long, derailed Yorkshire just when they looked set to chase down 157. Riding on Ben Sanderson's 3 for 31, Josh Cobb's 48-ball 80 and Alex Wakley's 43, Northamptonshire beat Durham by four wickets in the final.

Best batsman: Michael Klinger (Gloucestershire) (548 runs, 15 matches)
Best bowler: Benny Howell (Gloucestershire) (24 wickets, 15 matches)

Royal London Women's One-Day Cup: Kent

Kent won seven of their eight games to notch up 133 points in Division One and win the title. Tammy Beaumont, the women's player of the summer, was Kent's star. She made 292 runs in eight matches to finish third on the run charts. She was well supported by Megan Belt, Tash Farrant and Charlotte Pape. They picked up 45 wickets between them to finish among the best five bowlers.

Best batter: Aylish Cranstone (Devon) (327 runs, 7 matches)
Best bowler: Samantha Betts (Hampshire) (18 wickets, 7 matches)

Women's Cricket Super League: Southern Vipers

Having retired from international cricket, Charlotte Edwards proved a point by leading Southern Vipers to the inaugural title. Inspired by WBBL, the competition was a success but made little noise outside of England. As league toppers, Vipers made it to the final directly. Western Storm beat Loughborough Lightning by five wickets in the first game on the final day to book the second spot. In the final, Suzie Bates, who took two wickets and made 52, and Edwards had an opening stand of 78 to shape the chase of 141. Fittingly, Lyda Greenway, another recent England retiree, was at the middle when the winning runs were hit.

Best batter: Stafanie Taylor (Western Storm) (289 runs, 7 matches)
Best bowler: Stafanie Taylor (Western Storm) (11 wickets, 7 matches)

NEW ZEALAND

Auckland's season of plenty

Plunket Shield: Auckland

Having lost the title in 2014-15 because of some smart play by Canterbury, Auckland covered all their bases to top the table with 132 points in 2015-16. They were the only team to win six of their ten matches. It came on the back of five centuries and six fifties between Michael Guptill-Bunce and Jeet Raval, and Tarun Nethula's 39-wicket season. It was their first Plunket Shield title since 2008-09. Auckland's character was best displayed in a home game against Central Districts where they conceded the first-innings lead but won by 47 runs because of Nethula's match-haul of 11 and second-innings centuries by Raval and Robert O'Donnell.

Canterbury, who had defended the title successfully last season, finished second with 117 points. Central District's Ben Smith and George Worker, and Raval made double-centuries. Raval was rewarded with a call-up to the Test squad.

Breakthrough season: Auckland's Jeet Raval was rewarded with a call-up to the national side. — *Getty Images*

Best batsman: Bharat Popli (Northern Districts) (1149 runs, 7 matches)
Best bowler: Ajaz Patel (Central Districts) (43 wickets, 8 matches)

The Ford Trophy: Central Districts

George Worker's 159, and half-centuries from Jesse Ryder, Will Young and Tom Bruce set the foundation for Central Districts against Canterbury in the final as they raced off to 405 for 6 after winning the toss. Bevan Small and Seth Rance picked up five wickets between them to dismiss Canterbury for 249 in 37.4 overs. Central District's successful title defence was built on teamwork as they won four matches in the league stages to finish second on the table and make it to the final. Ryder (506 runs) and Worker (431) were their key contributors with the bat. Small and rest of the nine bowlers who bowled at least ten overs in the tournament provided adequate support to Rance to pick up his wickets at an average of 13.78.

Best batsman: Neil Broom (Otago) (508 runs, 9 matches)
Best bowler: Seth Rance (Central Districts) (19 wickets, 9 matches)

George Pie Super Smash: Auckland

Runners-up last season, Auckland went a step further to make it a season of double silverware. Colin Munro (366 runs), Rob Nicol (279 runs and 13 wickets), Mitchell McClenaghan (15 wickets) and Donovan Grobbelaar (14 wickets) were the chief architects of their fourth T20 title. In the final against Otago, Nicol made 77, and McClenaghan and Grobbelaar picked up three wickets each in a 20-run win. Mark Chapman, who plays for Hong Kong, also claimed a scalp in the big match.

Mahela Jayawardene's 59-ball 97 for Central Districts against Northern Districts was the highest score of the tournament, and returns of 5 for 9 for Canterbury's Andrew Ellis against Northern Districts was the best bowling performance. Wellington, the champions last season, took the wooden spoon with three wins in ten games.

Best batsman: Colin Munro (Auckland) (366 runs, 11 matches)
Best bowler: Mitchell McClenaghan (Auckland) (15 wickets, 9 matches)

Women's One-Day Competition: Auckland

Rachel Priest made 107 in the final, but the next highest score for Wellington was 13. Rosalind McNeil and Holly Huddleston picked up seven wickets between them to bowl the opposition out for 146 in 45.2 overs. After that, Auckalnd rode on the opening stand of 134 runs between Lauren Down (63) and Samantha Curtis (65 not out) to win by eight wickets in 43 overs.

Best batter: Amy Satterthwaite (Canterbury) (512 runs, 9 matches)
Best bowler: Frances Mackay (Canterbury) (17 wickets, 9 matches)

Women's T20 Competition: Canterbury

Having stood out with the ball in the 50-over competition, Frances Mackay made her opportunities with the bat count in the T20 competition. She also picked up seven wickets for Canterbury. They beat Central Districts by nine wickets in the final. Amy Satterthwaite picked up three wickets to restrict Central Districts to 92 for 9. After that, she and Mackay put on 73 for the first wicket.

Best batter: Frances Mackay (Canterbury) (190 runs, 5 matches)
Best bowler: Deanna Doughty (Wellington) (7 wickets, 5 matches)

SOUTH AFRICA

Twin triumph for Titans

Sunfoil Series: Titans

Titans defended 136 on the third day of their game against Cape Cobras to finish at the top of the table with 133.2 points. Bowled out for 164 and 256 in their two innings, Titans relied on Rowan Richards's 7 for 40 to clinch a thrilling ten-run win and reclaim the title after three seasons. Heino Kuhn, the only batsman to cross 1000 runs in the season, and Tabraiz Shamsi's 41 wickets, had been instrumental in their run till them. Shamsi took 12 for 85 in a ten-wicket win over Cobras.

Lions gave Titans a good run through the competition, but were bowled out for 68 in their final game against Warriors and settled for second after the innings loss.

JP Duminy and Dane Vilas made double-centuries and shared an unbroken stand of 393 for the fourth wicket for Cobras against Lions.

Best batsman: Heino Kuhn (Titans) (1126 runs, 10 matches)
Best bowler: Hardus Viljoen (Lions) (47 wickets, 9 matches)

Momentum One-Day Cup: Lions

Even as his action was under scrutiny, Aaron Phangiso produced a solid spell of left-arm spin in the final against Cape Cobras to finish with figures of 3 for 33 as Lions won the title. Pumelela Matshikwe also picked up three wickets as Cobras were dismissed for 169 in 42 overs. Lions built their successful chase through a second-wicket stand of 96 between Stephen Cook

(77 not out), the captain, and Alviro Petersen (55). Petersen was the best batsman of the competition by some distance. He hit five hundreds and a fifty, and was ahead of the second-placed Cook on the batting charts by 222 runs. Eddie Leie, who took 12 wickets with his leg spin, played his part.

Best batsman: Alviro Petersen (Lions) (726 runs, 12 matches)
Best bowler: Malusi Siboto (Knights) (19 wickets, 10 matches)

Ram Slam T20 Challenge: Titans

Mangaliso Mosehle made a 39-ball 87, which included six fours and seven sixes, to help Titans chase down 160 against Dolphins in the final in Centurion. Their seven-wicket win also had other contributors in David Wiese (two wickets) and Henry Davids (35). Dolphins' chances were severly dented early in the game after Kevin Pietersen, the second-highest run-getter of the tournament, perished in the tenth over. Dwayne Bravo made 53, but lacked support from the rest. Quinton de Kock and Chris Morris were the most consistent performers and it reflected in the success of Titans.

Best batsman: Quinton de Kock (Titans) (437 runs, 11 matches)
Best bowler: Chris Morris (Titans) (18 wickets, 11 matches)

Women's Provincial League: Western Province

Laura Wolvaardt made 46 as Western Province recovered from 14 for 2 to post 181 in 49.3 overs against Gauteng in the final in Bloemfontein. After that, Robyn Appels, Shandre Fritz and Lara Goodall took two wickets each as Gauteng were bowled out for 83 in 40.2 overs. The 98-run win gave Western Province the title.

Best batter: Alicia Smith (Boland) (468 runs, 10 matches)
Best bowler: Yolandi Potgieter (Boland, Free State) (19 wickets, 10 matches)

Women's Provincial T20 Competition: Western Province

Western Province won four of their five matches to top the table in the Top 6 competition. Shandre Fritz was their best batter with 114 runs, with a highest of 34 not out.

Best batter: Angelique Taai (Border) (163 runs, 4 matches)
Best bowler: N Tayi (Border) (14 wickets, 4 matches)

Winning knock by Darren Bravo: Trinidad & Tobago beat Barbados by 72 runs in the final to defend their Super50 title. – *WICB*

WEST INDIES

Gayle's Tallawahs celebrate

Regional Four-Day Competition: Guyana

Guyana won eight of their ten matches and collected 149 points to finish seven points clear of Barbados. The 1500-plus runs between Leon Johnson and Vishaul Singh, and 40 wickets each for Gudakesh Motie and Veerasamy Permaul were vital in their run to the top. The father-son duo of Shivnarine and Tagenarine Chanderpaul finished as Guyana's fourth and fifth-highest run-getters. Nikita Miller (Barbados) and Jon-Russ Jaggesar (Trinidad & Tobago) were the only bowlers to take eight wickets in an innings, and Barbados's Shai Hope produced the best knock of the league, making 162 in an innings win over Windward Island. West Indies's lack of batting depth was exposed, as Vishaul was the only other batsman to make 150 in an innings.

Best batsman: Leon Johnson (Guyana) (807 runs, 10 matches)
Best bowler: Nikita Miller (Jamaica) (65 wickets, 9 matches)

Nagico Super50: Trinidad & Tobago

Darren Bravo's 97 and Ryad Emrit's three-wicket haul helped Trinidad & Tobago beat Barbados by 72 runs in the final to defend the title. Bravo had useful partnerships for the fourth, fifth and sixth wickets to help his team to 270 for 7. Barbados were reduced to 31 for 4 in their chase, and never recovered, despite the efforts of Shai Hope (50) and Carlos Brathwaite (46).

Bravo made three fifties in the three matches he was available for. Apart from him, only Guyana's Assad Fudadin showed some consistency with an average of 51.80 across seven innings.

Delorn Johnson, the left-arm fast bowler from Windward Island, took 6 for 37 against Combined Campuses and Colleges. That Windward failed to chase 158 was because Chemar Holder finished with 5 for 22. Ignored for the Under-19 World Cup, this performance earned him a place as a replacement player in time to play decisive roles in the semi-final and final.

Best batsman: Darren Bravo (Trinidad & Tobago) (274 runs, 3 matches)
Best bowler: Sulieman Benn (Barbados) (15 wickets, 7 matches)

Caribbean Premier League: Jamaica Tallawahs

Imad Wasim's 3 for 21 and Chris Gayle's 54, with three fours and six sixes, stood out in the final as Jamaica Tallawahs beat Guyana Amazon Warriors for their second title. There was more to the entertaining tournament than Gayle, who hit more than 35 sixes, and his boys. Matches were played in Florida, there were thrilling encounters, and Dwayne Bravo and Sohail Tanvir were the only ones to pick up 20 or more wickets. Gayle, Colin Munro and Andre Russell struck a century each.

Best batsman: Chris Lynn (Guyana Amazon Warriors) (454 runs, 12 matches)
Best bowler: Dwayne Bravo (Trinbago Knight Riders) (21 wickets, 12 matches)

WICB Regional Women's Championship: Trinidad & Tobago

The final between Trinidad & Tobago and Barbados in Georgetown was abandoned without a ball bowled. Trinidad & Tobago were named champions because of their better performance in the league stages. They had topped the table with 12 points, while Barbados finished third with 11.

WICB Regional Women's T20 Championship: Trinidad & Tobago

In a thrilling final at the Guyana National Stadium, Trinidad & Tobago chased down 101 against Barbados to win by two wickets with two balls to spare. The unbroken ninth-wicket stand of 11 runs between Selene O'Neil and Shenelle Lord got the job done.

ZIMBABWE

Clean sweep for Eagles

Logan Cup: Mashonaland Eagles

Mashonaland Eagles won four matches to top the table in a thrilling four-day competition, where Matabeleland Tuskers and Mountaineers were also in contention. Tuskers benefitted from Craig Ervine, who scored his runs at an average of 95.40. Eagles' campaign was built around Regis Chakabva's 381 runs and Tanyaradzwa Munyaradzi's 24 wickets.

Best batsman: Craig Ervine (Matabeleland Tuskers) (477 runs, 3 matches)
Best bowler: Shingi Masakadza (Mountaineers) (25 wickets, 6 matches)

Pro50 Championship: Mashonaland Eagles

Mashonaland Eagles won five of their six games to secure 25 points and retain the 50-over title. Eagles had Regis Chakabva, who made 245 runs in four games including one of the three centuries of the tournament. His unbeaten 106 against Matabeleland Tuskers overshadowed Bonaparte Mujuru's 107 not out.

Best batsman: Prince Masvaure (Mid West Rhinos) (250 runs, 5 matches)
Best bowler: Tawanda Mupariwa (Matabeleland Tuskers) (13 wickets, 6 matches)

Domestic T20 Competition: Mashonaland Eagles

The domestic T20 competition returned to the calendar after a gap of two seasons, and it produced the most thrilling game of the season. Hamilton Masakadza's 66 took Mountaineers to 167 for 6. In their chase, Mashonaland Eagles depended on Cephas Zhuwao's 71 to level the score. Eagles then prevailed in the Super Over by one run to complete a clean sweep in the season.

Men's champions

Country	First-Class	List A	T20
Australia	Victoria	New South Wales	Sydney Thunder
Bangladesh	Khulna Division	Abahani Limited	Comilla Victorians
England	Middlesex	Warwickshire	Northamptonshire
India	Mumbai	Gujarat	Uttar Pradesh Sunrisers Hyderabad
New Zealand	Auckland	Central Districts	Auckland
Pakistan	SNGPL	NBP/Islamabad Khyber Pakhtunkhwa	Islamabad United Karachi Blues
South Africa	Titans	Lions	Titans
Sri Lanka	Tamil Union	Nondescripts CC	Sri Lanka Army Colombo Commandos
West Indies	Guyana	Trinidad & Tobago	Jamaica Tallawahs
Zimbabwe	Mashonaland Eagles	Mashonaland Eagles	Mashonaland Eagles

Women's champions

Country	50-overs	T20
Australia	South Australia	Sydney Thunder
Bangladesh	-	-
England	Kent	Southern Vipers
India	Railways	Railways
New Zealand	Auckland	Canterbury
Pakistan	ZTBL	ZTBL
South Africa	Western Province	Western Province
Sri Lanka	-	Sri Lanka Air Force SC
West Indies	Trinidad & Tobago	Trinidad & Tobago
Zimbabwe	-	-

PART FOUR
International

High-impact Ashwin raises the bar

IMPACT INDEX

The list of highest impact players in the period October 1, 2015, to September 30, 2016, will throw up a few surprises. For starters, Australia's Adam Voges, who averaged nearly 91 in this period and hit four centuries, does not even feature among the top 15 Test batsmen. One of his two high-impact performances was against a weak West Indies. In general, he scored in high-scoring matches. On the other hand, Josh Hazlewood, whose bowling average in ODIs is not even in the top 20, is among the five highest impact bowlers.

The key word here is 'context', which is what Impact Index offers by measuring each performance relative to other performances in the same match, and in the context of the series. Impact numbers here are on a scale 0 to 100, with the maximum assigned to the highest impact performer and the others scaled relative to that.

This year, the qualification criteria for Tests and ODIs have been lowered, as the World T20 meant fewer matches were played in the longer formats.

Highest Impact Test batsmen
Misbah-ul-Haq (100), **Asad Shafiq** (90), **Dinesh Chandimal** (76), **Younis Khan** (73) and **Kusal Mendis** (64) (minimum qualification: 6 matches)

Misbah-ul-Haq's average was only 12th in the period under consideration, but that masked his big-match temperament. No batsman scored more runs under pressure than Misbah and his ability to build partnerships was the best in the world. All his seven Tests were against England, a formidable team, and he failed in only one. In fact, his consistency rate of 86% was also the best. Misbah started the season with a series-defining performance (SD: a high-impact performance that helped win the series or draw level; or when a player dominates in two or more matches in a series) against England in the UAE and ended as captain of the No.1 Test side.

One of three Pakistanis on this list, **Asad Shafiq** capped a memorable year with an SD performance in the final Test against England at The Oval, where he scored 109 in his only innings and helped Pakistan level the series 2-2. Shafiq was only 13th in batting averages, but his Runs Tally Impact (proportion of runs scored in a match) was third after Kane Williamson and Misbah. His ability to handle pressure was also among the five best. In fact, since 2010, Shafiq has been the highest impact and most consistent batsman from No.6. Talk about being underrated.

Dinesh Chandimal's landmark 162 against India at Galle in 2015 was the second-highest impact batting performance ever in Tests. He followed that up in 2016 with an SD performance against the then No.1 Test team, Australia. For the second straight year, he had the highest Pressure Impact (ability to absorb the pressure of falling wickets).

Conventionally, **Younis Khan** had the 11th-best aver-

Under pressure: Asad Shafiq's series-defining knock came at The Oval to help Pakistan draw level and become the No.1 Test side. – *Getty Images*

age. But, like Shafiq, he produced his highest impact performance at The Oval with a 218. His consistency rate was only 57%, but he stepped up when his team needed it.

Much like Chandimal, **Kusal Mendis**'s consistency rate (56%) wasn't much, but in his debut season, he showed a penchant for producing match-changing knocks under pressure. Bowled out for 117 in the first innings and trailing by 86, Sri Lanka were 6 for 2 in their second innings in the First Test against Australia when Mendis hit 176 off 254 balls to turn the match, and the series, on its head. He followed that up with scores of 86 and 7 in the next Test to earn an SD for the series.

Notable mentions: Kane Williamson (62), Steve Smith (53), Usman Khawaja (51), Jonny Bairstow (50), Alastair Cook (50)
Highest Runs Tally Impact: Kane Williamson, Misbah-ul-Haq, Asad Shafiq
Highest Pressure Impact: Dinesh Chandimal, Misbah-ul-Haq, Mohammad Hafeez

Highest Impact Test bowlers
R Ashwin (100), **Mitchell Starc** (62), **Rangana Herath** (59), **Neil Wagner** (59) and **Yasir Shah** (51) (minimum qualification: 6 matches)

In recent years, **R Ashwin**'s Test performances have been on another level. He is the fifth-highest wicket-taker after Rangana Herath, James Anderson, Stuart Broad and Nathan Lyon, but his wickets have come in significantly fewer Tests. His bowling average is the best, and he didn't fail in any of the six completed Tests. His SD effort came at home against South Africa, where he had 31 victims in four Tests.

Mitchell Starc had the second-best bowling average and a 100% consistency rate. He picked up the second-most proportion of top/middle-order wickets (after Ashwin). He showed his mettle in subcontinental conditions as well. Had Australia won or even drawn the Sri Lanka series, his would have been an SD performance.

Rangana Herath had mediocre returns in New Zealand and England, as seen in a consistency rate of only 50%. But that changed when Australia toured Sri Lanka. He picked up 28 wickets in three matches for an SD effort. He also had the highest Economy Impact in the period.

Neil Wagner, the New Zealand pacer, had the fourth-best average after Ashwin, Starc and Anderson. He didn't fail in any of his six Tests and was third in picking up top/middle-order wickets.

Yasir Shah failed in only one of the six Tests he played. His 6 for 72 and 4 for 69 in the First Test at Lord's was his highest impact performance.

Notable mentions: Morne Morkel (46), Chris Woakes (46), Nathan Lyon (45), Kagiso Rabada (44)
Highest Top/Middle-order Wickets Tally Impact: R Ashwin, Mitchell Starc, Yasir Shah
Highest Pressure-building Impact (taking wickets in quick succession): R Ashwin, Yasir Shah, Chris Woakes

Highest Impact ODI batsmen
Martin Guptill (100), **AB de Villiers** (64), **Quinton de Kock** (63), **Joe Root** (59), **Jos Buttler** (55) (minimum qualification: 8 matches)

Martin Guptill had a stellar run, scoring 604 runs in ten innings. The New Zealander had the highest Runs Tally Impact, the highest Strike-rate Impact and the third-highest Partnership-building Impact (after Joe Root and Virat Kohli). His 78% consistency rate was second only to Afghanistan's Mohammad Shahzad. He produced two SD performances in only nine ODIs, and New Zealand didn't lose any of their three series.

Conventionally, **AB de Villiers** slots in sixth in batting averages, but was higher on Impact charts, as one of only two batsmen to have two SD performances: South Africa's ODI captain bludgeoned 119 off only 61 balls in the decider in Mumbai, while his unbeaten 101 off 97 balls in the fifth ODI against England ensured another series triumph.

Quinton de Kock scored the most number of runs and did so at an average of almost 66, the fifth best. His only SD performance came against India where he scored 109 runs off 87 balls in the series decider in Mumbai.

Joe Root was second on the list of run-scorers and had the highest Partnership-Building Impact. Even though he had a relatively poor Strike-Rate Impact, he made up for it with his consistency rate of 76% (third after Shahzad and Guptill). The Englishman's only SD performance came against Pakistan at home where he posted scores of 61, 89, 85, 30 and 9.

As a non-specialist batsman without a fixed batting position, it is not surprising that **Jos Buttler**'s consistency rate is only 50%, but he produced four very high impact performances in seven innings. His SD performance came against Pakistan in the UAE where his scores read 1, 11, 49*, and 116*.

Notable mentions: George Bailey (54), Faf du Plessis (51), Rohit Sharma (50), Virat Kohli (48)
Highest Runs Tally Impact: Martin Guptill, Rohit Sharma, Virat Kohli
Highest Strike-rate Impact: Martin Guptill, Mohammad Shahzad, Jos Buttler

Highest Impact ODI bowlers

Matt Henry (100), **Kagiso Rabada** (89), **Mitchell Starc** (66), **Josh Hazlewood** (60), **Kyle Abbott** (58) (minimum qualification: 8 matches)

Matt Henry, the New Zealand pacer, was the best bowler of the year, both conventionally and through the Impact Index prism. He had the best bowling average (16), the best bowling strike-rate (19), picked up the highest proportion of top/middle-order wickets and was the most restrictive. He produced three high-impact performances in just eight innings – all in a single series at home against Sri Lanka in 2015-16.

Kagiso Rabada's big-match temperament stood out. He was the only bowler with two SD performances: 4 for 41 (three top/middle-order wickets) against India in Mumbai and 3 for 34 (all top/middle-order wickets) against England in the decider in Cape Town. His five high impact performances in 20 appearances for South Africa is also the highest by any bowler.

Starc's bowling average of 20 is third after Henry and Afghanistan's Amir Hamza. His ability to pick top/middle-order wickets is second only to Henry's. With a consistency rate of 89%, he stands behind Mashrafe Mortaza and Rashid Khan.

Josh Hazlewood is not even in the top 20 in bowling averages, but had an SD performance (5 for 50) in the tri-series final against West Indies.

Kyle Abbott was also not in the top 10, but ranks high on impact for picking up the highest proportion of top/middle-order wickets after Henry and Starc, and being among the five most restrictive bowlers. His consistency rate of 89% too ranks high.

Notable mentions: Dale Steyn (57), John Hastings (52), Sunil Narine (50), Imran Tahir (45), Adil Rashid (44), Adam Zampa (42), Chris Woakes (41), Mitchell Marsh (40)
Highest Economy Impact: Matt Henry (100), Sunil Narine (72), Mashrafe Mortaza (50)

Highest Impact in T20Is

Batsmen: Virat Kohli (100), Martin Guptill (83), Colin Munro (71), Kane Williamson (68), Jos Buttler (67)
Bowlers: Imran Tahir (100), Samuel Badree (94), Mitchell Santner (83), Dwayne Bravo (79), Mustafizur Rahman (77)
(minimum qualification: 7 matches)

Soham Sarkhel (@Sarkhailovic) and Nikhil Narain (@nikhil8483) are part of Impact Index, a cricket statistics and analytics system.

Series scoreline

The home team's name is mentioned first. The scoreline reflects their performance

Series	Tests	ODIs	T20Is	Page
India Internationals				
India v South Africa	3-0 (4)	2-3 (5)	0-2 (3)	491
Australia v India	-	4-1 (5)	0-3 (3)	513
India v Sri Lanka	-	-	2-1 (3)	519
Zimbabwe v India	-	0-3 (3)	1-2 (3)	522
West Indies v India	0-2 (4)	-	1-0 (2)	528
Multi-nation tournaments				
Asia Cup	India beat Bangladesh in the final			547
ICC World T20 2016	West Indies beat England in the final			556
Other internationals				
Pakistan v England in UAE	2-0 (3)	1-3 (4)	0-3 (3)	600
Zimbabwe v Ireland	-	2-1 (3)	-	610
Zimbabwe v Afghanistan	-	2-3 (5)	0-2 (2)	611
Sri Lanka v West Indies	2-0 (2)	3-0 (3)	1-1 (2)	614
Australia v New Zealand	2-0 (3)	-	-	620
Bangladesh v Zimbabwe	-	3-0 (3)	-	628
Australia v West Indies	2-0 (3)	-	-	630
New Zealand v Sri Lanka	2-0 (2)	3-1 (5)	2-0 (2)	635
South Africa v England	1-2 (4)	3-2 (5)	2-0 (2)	642
Afghanistan v Zimbabwe in UAE	-	3-2 (5)	2-0 (2)	651
New Zealand v Pakistan	-	2-0 (3)	1-2 (3)	653
Bangladesh v Zimbabwe	-	-	2-2	655
New Zealand v Australia	0-2 (2)	2-1 (3)	-	657
South Africa v Australia	-	-	1-2 (3)	663
England v Sri Lanka	2-0 (3)	3-0 (4)	1-0 (1)	665
Ireland v Sri Lanka	-	0-2 (2)	-	
Tri-nation series in the West Indies	Australia beat West Indies in the final			676
England v Pakistan	2-2 (4)	4-1 (5)	0-1 (1)	679
Ireland v Pakistan	-	0-1 (2)	-	

Sri Lanka v Australia	3-0 (3)	1-4 (5)	0-2 (2)	692
Zimbabwe v New Zealand	0-2 (2)			702
South Africa v New Zealand	1-0 (2)	-	-	704
Bangladesh v Afghanistan	-	2-1 (3)	-	706
South Africa v Ireland	-	1-0 (1)	-	708
Australia v Ireland in South Africa	-	1-0 (1)	-	
South Africa v Australia	-	5-0 (5)	-	

Debutants (October 1, 2015-September 30, 2016)

Tests (28)

Player	Cap	Date	Opponent	Venue
Australia (1)				
Jon Holland	444	August 4	Sri Lanka	Galle
England (4)				
Adil Rashid	668	October 13	Pakistan	Abu Dhabi
Alex Hales	669	December 26	South Africa	Durban
James Vince	670	May 19	Sri Lanka	Leeds
Jake Ball	671	July 14	Pakistan	Lord's, London
New Zealand (2)				
Mitchell Santner	268	November 27	Australia	Adelaide
Henry Nicholls	269	February 12	Australia	Wellington
Pakistan (1)				
Iftikhar Ahmed	221	August 11	England	Oval, London
South Africa (4)				
Kagiso Rabada	323	November 5	India	Mohali
Chris Morris	324	January 2	England	Cape Town
Hardus Viljoen	325	January 14	England	Johannesburg
Simon Cook	326	January 22	England	Centurion
Sri Lanka (7)				
Milinda Siriwardana	131	October 14	West Indies	Galle
Kusal Mendis	132	October 22	West Indies	PSS, Colombo

Udara Jayasundera	133	December 10	New Zealand	Dunedin
Dasun Shanaka	134	May 19	England	Leeds
Dhananjaya de Silva	135	July 26	Australia	Pallekele
Lakshan Sandakan	136	July 26	Australia	Pallekele
Vishwa Fernando	137	August 4	Australia	Galle
West Indies (5)				
Jomel Warrican	305	October 22	Sri Lanka	PSS, Colombo
Carlos Brathwaite	306	December 26	Australia	Melbourne
Roston Chase	307	July 21	India	North Sound
Miguel Cummins	308	July 30	India	Kingston
Alzarri Joseph	309	August 9	India	Gros Islet
Zimbabwe (4)				
Chamu Chibhabha	96	July 28	New Zealand	Bulawayo
Michael Chinouya	97	July 28	New Zealand	Bulawayo
Prince Masvaure	98	July 28	New Zealand	Bulawayo
Peter Moor	99	August 6	New Zealand	Bulawayo

One-Day Internationals (70)

Australia (8: 209-216): Marcus Stoinis, Scott Boland, Joel Paris, Adam Zampa, Travis Head, Daniel Worrall, Joe Mennie, Chris Tremain; **Bangladesh (1: 119):** Mosaddek Hossain; **England (1: 244):** Liam Dawson; **India (8: 207-214):** Barinder Sran, Rishi Dhawan, Gurkeera Singh Mann, Jasprit Bumrah, Yuzvendra Chahal, Karun Nair, KL Rahul, Faiz Fazal; **New Zealand (1: 189):** Henry Nicholls; **Pakistan (4: 207-210):** Iftikhar Ahmed, Zafar Gohar, Hasan Ali, Mohammad Nawaz; **South Africa (4: 116-119):** Tabraiz Shamsi, Temba Bavuma, Andile Phehlukwayo, Dwaine Pretorius; **Sri Lanka (10: 166-175):** Danushka Gunathilaka, Shehan Jayasuriya, Jeffrey Vandersay, Dhananjaya de Silva, Kusal Mendis, Dasun Shanaka, Chaminda Bandara, Amila Aponso, Lakshan Sandakan, Avishka Fernando; **West Indies (2: 170-171):** Jermaine Blackwood, Shannon Gabriel; **Zimbabwe (3: 127-129):** Wellington Masakadza, Taurai Muzarabani, Tendai Chisoro; **Afghanistan (4: 36-39):** Rashid Khan, Yamin Ahmadzai, Rokhan Barakzai, Naveen-ul-Haq; **Hong Kong (7: 31-37):** Christopher Carter, Mark Chapman, Waqas Khan, Ishtiaq Muhammad, Ehsan Khan, Shahid Wasif, Tanveer Ahmed; **Ireland (2: 49-50):** Barry McCarthy, Sean Terry; **Scotland (5: 57-61):** Brad Wheal, Con de Lange, Ruaidhiri Smith, Chris Sole, Mark Watt; **United Arab Emirates (10: 57-66):** Abdul Shakoor, Asif Iqbal, Yodhin Punja, Laxman Sreekumar, Umair Ali, Zaheer Maqsood, Qadeer Ahmed, Usman Mushtaq, Muhammad Usman, Rameez Shahzad.

Twenty20 Internationals (93)

Australia (9: 75-83): Travis Head, Scott Boland, Nathan Lyon, Andrew Tye, Cameron Bancroft, Usman Khawaja, Peter Nevill, Adam Zampa, Ashton Agar; **Bangladesh (8: 48-55):** Jubair Hossain, Nurul Hasan, Shuvagata Hom, Abu Hider, Mohammad Shahid, Mossadek Hossain, Muktar Ali, Saqlain Sajib; **England (3: 75-77):** James Vince, Liam Dawson, Tymal Mills; **India (11: 56-66):** S Aravind, Jasprit Bumrah, Hardik Pandya, Pawan Negi, Yuzvendra Chahal, Rishi Dhawan, Mandeep Singh, KL Rahul, Jaydev Unadkat, Dhawal Kulkarni, Barinder Sran; **New Zealand (2: 68-69):** Todd Astle, Henry Nicholls; **Pakistan (7: 65-71):** Rafatullah Mohammad, Aamer Yamin, Khurram Manzoor, Mohammad Nawaz, Iftikhar Ahmed, Babar Azam, Hasan Ali; **Sri Lanka (9: 59-67):** Dushmantha Chameera, Danushka

Gunathilaka, Niroshan Dickwella, Kasun Rajitha, Asela Gunaratne, Chaminda Bandara, Nuwan Pradeep, Kusal Mendis, Sachith Pathirana; **West Indies (1: 63):** Evin Lewis; **Zimbabwe (4: 42-45):** Tendai Chisoro, Wellington Masakadza, Peter Moor, Donald Tiripano; **Afghanistan (6: 27-32):** Rashid Khan, Usman Ghani, Mohammed Baras, Rokhan Barakzai, Sayed Shinzad, Yamin Ahmadzai; **Hong Kong (6: 18-23):** Christopher Carter, Adil Mehmood, Tanveer Ahmed, Ryan Campbell, Ehsan Khan, Shahid Wasif; **Ireland (5: 36-40):** Joshua Little, Jacob Mulder, Greg Thompson, Lorcan Tucker; **Netherlands (2: 36-37):** Sikander Zulfiqar, Vivian Kingma; **Oman (6: 12-17):** Aaqib Sulehri, Adnan Ilyas, Bilal Khan, Ajay Lalcheta, Sufyan Mehmood, Vaibhav Wategaonkar; **Papua New Guinea (4: 14-17):** Sese Bau, Hiri Hiri, Nosaina Pokana, Pipi Raho; **Scotland (1: 43):** Brad Wheal; **United Arab Emirates (9: 21-29):** Amjad Gul, Qadeer Ahmed, Zaheer Maqsood, Fahad Tariq, Usman Mushtaq, Muhamaad Kaleem, Muhammad Usman, Saqlain Hyder, Usman Mushtaq.

India Women

ODI (1: 115): Preeti Bose
T20I (1: 50): Deepti Sharma.

Some shine in the rough

VANEISA BAKSH

If one were to have searched for the story of West Indies cricket over the past couple of decades, it might have been easiest to type in the keyword 'afflicted' – such had been its state. Yet, despite the various maladies, it managed to come up with some spectacular moments in 2015-16.

In Sri Lanka in October 2015, the senior men's side lost the two Tests, the three ODIs and drew 1-1 in the T20I matches. This was uncomfortably followed in Australia in December with two Test defeats. The women's team, meanwhile, kept their chins up to beat Pakistan in the West Indies in October, winning three of the four ODIs and the three T20Is.

Luck turned in the new year, as in February, the junior team, led by Shimron Hetmyer won the ICC Under-19 Cricket World Cup, bowling out India for 145 runs to bring home that title for the first time. Two of the players were among the top five for the tournament: Shamar Springer with 285 runs, and Alzarri Joseph with 13 wickets. The Antiguan fast bowler made his Test debut against India, playing in the Third Test and picking up 3 for 69, making it even more curious that he had not been played in the previous match.

He, along with players like Evin Lewis, Kraigg Brathwaite, Nicholas Pooran, Rovman Powell and Roston Chase are the players to watch, especially after performances at the Caribbean Premier League 2016. In its fourth year, the tournament was the biggest cricket event in the Caribbean, even venturing to Fort Lauderdale in Florida for one segment.

But before that tournament began, there was the biggest celebration. In April, Stafanie Taylor's side won the ICC Women's World T20. Later that fateful day, Darren Sammy led the men to their own title: Carlos Brathwaite striking four consecutive sixes in the final over, bringing Ben Stokes to his knees and 66,000 spectators at Eden Gardens to their feet.

The impact on the Caribbean was electrifying. But the moments of bliss turned bittersweet when the obviously frustrated Sammy could not summon his trademark composure at the post-match interview and lambasted the West Indies Cricket Board for its lack of support. His comments were incendiary straws on an already broken camel's back. "We had a lot of issues, we felt disrespected by our board. Mark Nicholas described our team as a team with no brains," he said, explaining how it brought the team together. He went on to thank the heads of CARICOM (the political grouping known as the Caribbean Community). "[T]hroughout this tournament they have been supporting the team. We've got emails, we've got phone calls, Prime Minister Mitchell (of Grenada), he sent a very inspiring email for the team this morning… and I'm yet to hear from our own cricket board. That is very disappointing."

Three on three: Despite the off-field chaos, Darren Sammy, Stafanie Taylor and Shimron Hetmyer led the West Indies senior men's, women's and Under-19 sides respectively to global success. — *ICC/Getty Images*

A month later, in an interview with Andrew Miller, Sammy referred to a gathering of West Indian cricket legends in April to call for the dissolution of the WICB. The movement had been triggered by a CARICOM review, whose recommendations caused the WICB, led by Dave Cameron, to dig in its obstinate heels. "I listened to Sir Garry (Sobers) speak and it brought tears to my eyes," said Sammy. "The same thing he went through, playing 50 years ago, it is still happening. To watch a legend that I look up to, speak with such passion and hurt, it's sad. The people in charge of West Indies cricket have to make it better, swallow their pride and ego – and some of us players too – and work for the betterment of West Indies cricket."

The hurt he witnessed and felt had been echoed for years by Tony Cozier, who died on May 11, still writing columns outlining the ills that plagued West Indies cricket and calling for reform.

The Cameron administration at the WICB remained unmoved by the on-line petition and the calls from citizens, cricketers and governments. Just before the WT20, Cameron had sought to take credit for improved team performances by saying it was the reward for the board's investment in developing their cricket plans. He stunned the cricket world with his confident assertions that his relationship with the players was fine.

Players like Kieron Pollard, Dwayne Bravo and Chris Gayle had already questioned selection policies, claiming arbitrary inclusions and exclusions. For the ODI tri-series with Australia and South Africa in June, Bravo, Sammy and Gayle wondered how Kieron Pollard and Sunil Narine had been named for the squad when they had not played in the domestic 50-over competition. Pollard, for his part, seemed equally baffled.

And then the CPL came to town, proving again that T20 is the form of the game with the most appeal in the Caribbean. Matches were well attended, the atmosphere was festive, camaraderie was evident and the performances were spectacular.

A bizarre end to the India series, when, after 22 overs had been bowled in the Fourth Test, the match had to be called off for rain, despite blistering sunshine for the better part of four days proved an embarrassment. The lumpy outfield was too hazardous, said the officials. So, every day players and a handful of spectators waited until the umpires announced no play and then went away disgruntled. Queen's Park Oval officials and the Trinidad and Tobago Cricket Board were asked to provide a report on how such a maintenance nightmare could have happened.

Then, when the teams moved to sunny Florida for the two T20I matches, the second was abandoned after a torrential shower. Upsettingly, it was discovered that the match had been delayed by 40 minutes to accommodate the television broadcasters' technical difficulties, and that lost time prevented a result. It was all an embarrassing time for cricket in the region.

Where is West Indies cricket to go from here? At the top in its T20 incarnation, it is still languishing near the bottom of the Test table and should a two-tier system be considered, it will no doubt be in the lower bunk. In the meantime, the incorrigible WICB continues to resist all efforts at reform and the immediate future looks like more rain than sunshine.

Vaneisa Baksh is a writer based in Trinidad and the editor of UWI Today.

Big boys play at night

DILEEP PREMACHANDRAN

It remains one of cricket's iconic photographs from a time when the stark beauty of black-and-white photography was giving way to rainbow hues. Zaheer Abbas is biting down on a finger with his elbow resting on Imran Khan's shoulder. Imran, his tousled mane protected by a floppy sun hat, is wearing a T-shirt that says "Big boys play at night". The 'I' in 'night' is the World Series Cricket logo.

What Kerry Packer initially intended as a poke in the cricket establishment's eye after being denied telecast rights to Australian cricket went on to become something far bigger, an endeavour that would transform the sport and especially its finances. The matches played under floodlights – many of them woefully inadequate for the purpose – also helped bring in a new audience, those that wanted a dollop of razzmatazz to go with sporting excellence.

International cricket, however, was slow to embrace matches that began at lunchtime and stretched on past sundown. For almost five years, the Sydney Cricket Ground was the only venue that hosted such games. That changed when New Delhi's Jawaharlal Nehru Stadium – built for the Asian Games in 1982 – saw India and Australia battle it out under lights in 1984, with some fours beating the fielders across the athletics track.

Thereafter, 50-over cricket under lights became mainstream. By November 27, 2015, as many as 1411 of the 3826 ODIs played had been under lights, with the white ball. Cricket's newest format, T20, was almost exclusively played in the evening, except for a World T20 in the Caribbean (2010) that saw day games to accommodate the millions watching on the subcontinent.

But Test cricket, the grand old dame, stayed stubbornly immune to the charms of cricket after dusk. Matches continued to start between 9 and 11am, with stumps drawn before sunset, just as the vast majority of office-goers were getting ready to leave for home. Attendances have been in decline for years, except in England where the stadiums are small enough for demand to exceed supply when it comes to marquee series.

Melbourne Cricket Ground still attracts upward of 60,000 most years on Boxing Day, but even Australian venues are noticeably empty for series not involving England or India. In the subcontinent, the picture is grimmer. The smaller Indian stadiums – like Kanpur and Indore against New Zealand at the start of the 13-Test 2016-17 home season – still attract raucous crowds, but other centres like Mohali and Nagpur are notable mostly for the sounds of silence and sporadic applause.

That's not to say that Test cricket is on life support. Millions still follow

Evening plans: There were few empty seats at the Adelaide Oval for the inaugural pink-ball Test, with 1,23,736 people attending over three days. — *Getty Images*

the format, thanks to the wonders of online ball-by-ball commentary and social media. Petitions are signed in the thousands to widen the Test pool by including the likes of Ireland, and niche movies like *Death of a Gentleman* are watched and shared across continents.

But empty seats and a lack of atmosphere don't make for good television. In that regard, Test cricket has had a problem for over a decade now, even in India. Unless matches are scheduled around holidays like Diwali, it's hard for those that work or study to watch the action live. The Indian Premier League and 50-over cricket, with matches going on well past sundown, give passionate cricket fans the luxury of popping across once the day's tasks are done. Test cricket has done them no such favours.

That finally changed in November 2015. In previous seasons, Cricket Australia had experimented with cricket balls of shades ranging from orange to pink in Sheffield Shield matches, and with little spectator interest in Tests not involving the other two members of cricket's financial Big Three, the Adelaide Oval became the venue for the collision between a 138-year-old tradition and a brave new world under lights.

If you were in Adelaide in the days leading up to the game, it was impossible to miss the anticipation in the air. For all the talk of a trans-Tasman rivalry, these matches don't usually get a fraction of the attention that the Rugby Union contest for the Bledisloe Cup does. But in Adelaide, most seemed to know that a Test was imminent and that it was going to be the first of its kind.

In the build-up, there were a few hat tips in the direction of nostalgia. Nearly 38 years earlier, Australia's Lenny Pascoe had bowled the first ball under lights to the Rest of the World's Barry Richards. In keeping with Pascoe's wild and woolly reputation, it was both a no-ball and a wide. On November 24, three days before the start of the Test and as evening cast its shadows, both men met in the middle of the Adelaide Oval to recreate that scene from long ago.

This time, Pascoe, 65, was bowling to the 70-year-old Richards off a couple of paces. The ball just about reached him, but Richards couldn't put it away. There was also another difference from 1978. The ball was pink.

Day one featured both festivities and solemnity. By a quirk of scheduling fate, November 27 marked 36 years since the first official ODI had been played under lights in Australia. It also marked a year since the tragic passing of Phillip Hughes. His family didn't want a minute's silence, but at the tea interval – which had taken the place of the traditional lunch break – there was a moving retrospective on the giant screen.

The ground was more than half-full by the time New Zealand's openers came out to bat, and by the time stumps were drawn after 9pm local time, as many as 47,441 had come through the turnstiles. There was similar enthusiasm on the second day, with 43,272 making their way along River Torrens to one of the most picturesque venues in sport. And on the Sunday, with the match rushing to its denouement, another 33,923 marked their attendance, taking the grand total to 1,23,736.

On the field, the batsmen were confused. They had just come from Perth, home of the once-feared WACA pitch, where Ross Taylor had made 290 and David Warner 253 in a match marked by mammoth totals. In Adelaide, renowned for being a batsmen's paradise over the first three days, they found 8mm of grass cover on the pitch.

Before the match began, Greg Chappell, who had been part of those early white-ball experiments, had told *The Advertiser* about the challenges of batting in the evening before the lights shone bright. "The hardest part was the twilight," he said. "Until the lights took over, you were playing in bad light. That's what it was."

On the opening day, New Zealand slipped from a relatively healthy 80 for 2 to 173 for 7 in the session between tea and dinner. But on subsequent days, with the grassy surface giving plenty of assistance, it was hard to fathom which was the best session for batting. Australia lost six wickets for 62 in the opening session on day two, and in the final one on day three, they lost four before crossing the line in a tense finish.

Low-scoring game or not, the crowd loved it. There was plenty of colour and noise, and no little appreciation for an engrossing contest between bat and ball. And it wasn't only those inside the Oval that were captivated. The TV audience in Australia for each of the first two days nudged two million. For the climax, there were as many as 3.19 million watching, just a few thousand less than had tuned in to the World Cup semi-final between India and Australia in March 2015.

Others watched from continents away and hoped that their administrators would also follow Cricket Australia's lead. Apart from India's epic series against Australia in 2001 and the equally thrilling Ashes series of 2005, it's hard to think of a long-form contest that drew in so many neutrals, even if it was for only three days.

Since this contest, Pakistan and West Indies have featured in the second day-night Test, in Dubai, which went into an intriguing five days, and South Africa became the second team to experience the pink ball in Australia. England have said they'll embrace the concept at Edgbaston when West Indies come visiting in the 2017 summer, while India have experimented in domestic games.

The conditions will vary drastically from country to country, and even between venues in the same one. In future, curators may think of leaving a little less grass on the pitch. But once you get past the hidebound notion that five-day cricket can only be played with a red balls and in whites, it's not hard to see the attraction of day-night Test cricket.

Bowlers and batsmen alike will need to adapt to conditions they don't usually encounter in a Test match, but if the crowds keep flocking in, it gives them a massive incentive to perform. It is one thing to talk about the primacy of Test cricket, and quite another to have it watched by two old men in a deckchair. Day-night Tests give the game an opportunity to reconnect with working-class fans. Cricket would be foolish to spurn it.

Stephen Fry, one of the very few who remain pithily articulate even in the turbulent environs of Twitter, put it best when he said: "Sitting with Julia Gillard and watching the pink ball swing. Wickets tumbling. Fine S. Australian wine slipping down. It's all just lovely."

Dileep Premachandran (@spiceboxofearth) is editor-in-chief of Wisden India*.*

Captain Kohli's coronation: The South African capitulation gave the young Test captain his first series win at home. – *BCCI*

INDIA INTERNATIONALS
South Africa in India

Top travellers unstuck by spin

SAURABH SOMANI

The T20Is had a bottle-throwing incident in one stadium and a washout due to a water-logged outfield in the next. The ODIs had a young gun getting the better of one of the game's greats to begin with, and India's team director allegedly spewing choice words at the curator for the final game. But the abiding memories of South Africa's tour of India in late 2015 will be of the dethroning of the team that had been first among mostly unequals in the Test arena.

It was not quite Ashes to Ashes, but the dust to dust part held true, with pitches tailor-made for spinners. A skilled Indian spin contingent then employed a bagful of tricks, and the minds of the South African batsmen amplified those to make them seem like an avalanche. South Africa had come into the Tests with the proud record of not having lost away for nine years and 15 series. It took three days of cricket in the First Test and three days in the Third to end that streak, India winning each of those matches by more than 100 runs. The last match in Delhi had the visiting side putting up their most dogged fight; but it was telling that the resistance was one built on time rather than runs, because although the Test went into its final session, India were victors by 337 runs – their biggest run-margin ever. Virat Kohli got to celebrate his first home series win as captain. If anything, the 3-0 margin did a slight disservice to India, who were in control of the Bangalore Test – AB de Villiers's 100th – before it was washed out.

The pitches did come in for scrutiny, with the one in Nagpur getting a 'poor' rating from the ICC in a match where the highest individual score across four innings was M Vijay's 40. In Mohali, the surface was a spinner-friendly one without coming even close to being diabolical. Delhi played easier than Mohali, though it still offered purchase and varying bounce at times. Ironically, the washed out match in Bangalore had perhaps the most balanced surface of all. But far more than the demons in the pitch, the South Africans were undone by the demons in their minds. No small credit for that goes to R Ashwin, who staked further claim to being among the foremost spinners of his era with a second Man of the Series performance on the trot, soon after his star turn in India's away win in Sri Lanka. Ashwin's 31 wickets were more than double what any South African bowler managed. The niggardly Ravindra Jadeja – he of the straight ball that became the deadliest weapon on turning pitches – had 23 scalps. Between the two, they sent down more than 300 overs combined in seven innings, almost two-thirds of the overs India bowled and ample indication of the load they shouldered as well as the conditions on offer.

Beating Dhoni: Kagiso Rabada, all of 20 years old, defended 11 in the final over against the India captain in Kanpur. — *Hindustan Times/Getty Images*

Twin centuries in Delhi marked Ajinkya Rahane out as the standout batsman on either side, though his series tally of 266 runs was only marginally ahead of de Villiers's 258. But where Rahane had six other batsmen in his side who topped three figures and three – Vijay, Cheteshwar Pujara and Virat

Kohli – who hit 200, only two South Africans apart from de Villiers made at least 100 runs and none made more than 150.

Outgunned while batting and outspun in the bowling, South Africa's fall from their No.1 Test ranking was swift, and pushed a successful limited-overs series completely to the background.

South Africa had won the T20Is by a 2-0 margin, hunting down a 200-run target in the first match and shooting India out for 92 in the second in a dominant show.

The ODIs were more closely contested. The gathering debate about MS Dhoni's ability as one of the greatest finishers the game came to a head in the very first match in Kanpur. Kagiso Rabada, all of 20 years old, was entrusted with bowling the final over to Dhoni with only 11 runs to defend, and came out the comprehensive winner.

The fourth match in Chennai on a low, slow pitch, was an ominous portent for the Test series debacle to follow. Chasing 300, the visitors were kept in the game solely by the will and skill of a remarkable de Villiers, the only South African batsman to master the conditions. More than the victory that kept them alive in the series, though, India had taken note of how the South African line-up came unstuck in conditions that aided the slower men.

The Indian think-tank thought another slow turner at the Wankhede would be ideal, but were served up with a batting paradise, which led to the alleged exchange of unpleasantries between Ravi Shastri, the team director, and Sudhir Naik, the Wankhede curator. The South Africans plundered 438 for 4 at the Wankhede Stadium to add the ODI trophy to their T20I one, de Villiers having hit a scarcely believable three ODI hundreds in a five-match series.

India may have lost the battle on that front, but the strategy for winning the war was clear. South Africa did end with two out of three trophies at the end of a 72-day long tour, but the spoils went to India.

Tour match

Palam A Ground, Delhi, September 29: South Africa 189/3 in 20 overs (JP Duminy 68*, Faf du Plessis 42) lost to **India A** 193/2 in 19.4 overs (Mayank Agarwal 87, Manan Vohra 56) by eight wickets.

T20I series (3): South Africa 2 India 0 (1 cancelled)

1st T20I: South Africa win by seven wickets

• Put in on a flat track, India lose Shikhar Dhawan early but Rohit Sharma looks dangerous. • Rohit is the second Indian to make a T20I century, while Virat Kohli becomes the fastest to 1000 runs in the format, as the duo puts on 138 in the country's best stand. • The hosts' 126 runs in boundaries is nearly matched by the visitors' 122; the 20 sixes hit are the most in India. • Hashim Amla and AB de Villiers add a blazing 77 for the opening wicket but losing their top three in a heap with the score yet to hit 100 is a setback. • JP Duminy brings up his fifty in 28 balls and fends off the spinners to ease

Rohit Sharma became the second Indian to make a T20 international century but it wasn't enough for a win in Dharamsala. — *Hindustan Times/Getty Images*

run-rate pressure with help from Farhaan Behardien. • R Ashwin is the only Indian bowler to concede fewer than 10 runs an over. *Roshan Thyagarajan*

HPCA Stadium, Dharamsala, October 2: India 199/5 in 20 overs (Rohit Sharma 106, Virat Kohli 43; Kyle Abbott 2-29) lost to **South Africa** 200/3 in 19.4 overs (JP Duminy 68*, AB de Villiers 51) by seven wickets. *MoM*: JP Duminy.

2nd T20I: South Africa win by six wickets

• A full house is dancing to popular Odia songs almost three hours before the venue's first T20I. • Put in on a pitch with uneven bounce, India wobble as the in-form pair of Rohit and Kohli is spectacularly run out early. • South Africa bowl 50 dot balls, Imran Tahir picks up two wickets, and the end is near when Suresh Raina, MS Dhoni and Harbhajan Singh fall in the space of three runs. • Albie Morkel, a replacement for the injured David Wiese, finishes with career-best figures in his first international game in over 18 months as India are dismissed for their then lowest score at home. • Ashwin responds to Dhoni's attacking field setting with three wickets, but it is only of academic interest. • Spectators from two galleries throw bottles to stop play twice before South Africa complete their first limited-overs series win in India. *Sidhanta Patnaik*

Barabati Stadium, Cuttack, October 5: India 92 in 17.2 overs (Rohit Sharma 22, Suresh Raina 22; Albie Morkel 3-12, Chris Morris 2-16) lost to **South Africa** 96/4 in 17.1 overs (JP Duminy 30*; R Ashwin 3-24) by six wickets. *MoM*: Albie Morkel.

3rd T20I: Match cancelled

• The first international fixture at Eden Gardens after the death of Jagmohan Dalmiya is marred by controversy. • Despite three super soppers being pressed into service and no drizzle after 4pm, play is called off after four inspections. • It turns out the groundstaff had not covered the entire ground before the first spell of rain despite the forecast. • Prabir Mukherjee, the venue's octogenarian curator, who passes away less than a year later, comes in for criticism, even as doubts are raised about the venue's preparedness for the World T20. *Sidhanta Patnaik*

Eden Gardens, Kolkata, October 8: India v South Africa. Match cancelled without a ball bowled. *MoS*: JP Duminy.

ODI series (5): South Africa 3 India 2

1st ODI: South Africa win by five runs

It would have been a tale of centuries from de Villiers and Rohit, with Kagiso Rabada's final over not in the script. The five-run win didn't just help the visitors take a 1-0 lead, it also signalled the arrival of South Africa's latest pace gem. India needed 11 runs, and with Dhoni on strike, they looked set to go all the way. Rabada, 20, showed immense steel though, giving away just five while scalping Dhoni and Stuart Binny to spark wild celebrations.

Earlier, de Villiers's 73-ball 104 took South Africa past 300, the total helped along by Faf du Plessis's half-century and Ashwin's side strain, which restricted him to 4.4 overs. Rohit then hammered a scintillating 133-ball 150 to propel the chase, but Tahir's 47th over, in which he accounted for both Rohit and Raina, tilted the balance in South Africa's favour before *that* Rabada over. *Manoj Narayan*

Green Park, Kanpur, October 11: South Africa 303/5 in 50 overs (AB de Villiers 104*, Faf du Plessis 62; Amit Mishra 2-47, Umesh Yadav 2-71) beat **India** 298/7 in 50 overs (Rohit Sharma 150, Ajinkya Rahane 60; Imran Tahir 2-57, Kagiso Rabada 2-58) by five runs. *MoM*: AB de Villiers.

2nd ODI: India win by 22 runs

Dhoni rode the pressure in his 86-ball unbeaten 92 that helped India draw level 1-1. On a pitch touted as a batting track, India were reduced to 124

Cool knock under pressure: MS Dhoni put on crucial partnerships in his 86-ball 92*.
– *Hindustan Times/Getty Images*

for 6 after opting to bat, with only Ajinkya Rahane's 63-ball 51 a knock of note. Dhoni then batted with the tail and displayed excellent knowledge of his team-mates' strengths. He put on partnerships of 41 and 56 with Bhuvneshwar Kumar and Harbhajan, pacing his innings shrewdly.

The bowlers, without the injured Ashwin, ensured their captain's knock wouldn't go in vain. Axar Patel had du Plessis and Duminy dismissed in successive overs to induce a collapse. India sensed victory when de Villiers was dismissed with 81 runs left to score, and the tail was wiped out.

Manoj Narayan

Holkar Cricket Stadium, Indore, October 14: India 247/9 in 50 overs (MS Dhoni 92*, Ajinkya Rahane 51; Dale Steyn 3-49, Morne Morkel 2-42, Imran Tahir 2-42) beat **South Africa** 225 in 43.4 overs (Faf du Plessis 51, JP Duminy 36; Axar Patel 3-39, Bhuvneshwar Kumar 3-41) by 22 runs. *MoM*: MS Dhoni.

3rd ODI: South Africa win by 18 runs

After Quinton de Kock's century took South Africa to what was thought to be no more than a par score, Morne Morkel fashioned an excellent comeback to help them go 2-1 up. Rohit got going with his half-century, after which a sedate Kohli and Dhoni had India's chase in control. An attempt to accelerate, however, was foiled by South Africa bowling short at the body and packing the on-side field. Morkel snuffed out Dhoni, Kohli and Rahane late in the innings to seal the fate of the game. India's bowlers had similarly thwarted South Africa. De Kock roared back into form as India missed four opportunities to end his 118-run third-wicket stand with du Plessis. The duo set up a platform from which the side looked good for more, but quick wickets put paid to that. It took a smart cameo from Farhaan Behardien to score the runs that made the difference.

Akshay Gopalakrishnan

SCA Stadium, Rajkot, October 18: South Africa 270/7 in 50 overs (Quinton de Kock 103, Faf du Plessis 60; Mohit Sharma 2-62) beat **India** 252/6 in 50 overs (Virat Kohli 77, Rohit Sharma 65; Morne Morkel 4-39) by 18 runs. *MoM*: Morne Morkel.

4th ODI: India win by 35 runs

Kohli's 140-ball 138 trumped de Villiers's 112 off 107, as India kept the series alive. Batting first, India lost Dhawan and Rohit, their openers, to pace within the powerplay, but a calculated knock from Kohli and contributions from Rahane (45) and Raina powered them to just short of 300 on a tough surface. Amla fell cheaply but de Kock gave South Africa a quick start before India's spinners, led by Harbhajan, took control. Harbhajan, Amit Mishra and Axar combined to reduce South Africa to 144 for 5 even as de Villiers kept them in the game. His departure in the 45th over ended their hopes and India squared the series 2-2. *Karthik Lakshmanan*

MA Chidambaram Stadium, Chepauk, Chennai, October 22: India 299/8 in 50 overs (Virat Kohli 138, Suresh Raina 53; Kagiso Rabada 3-54, Dale Steyn 3-61) beat **South Africa** 264/9 in 50 overs (AB de Villiers 112, Quinton de Kock 43; Bhuvneshwar Kumar 3-68, Harbhajan Singh 2-50) by 35 runs. *MoM*: Virat Kohli.

5th ODI: South Africa win by 214 runs

South Africa sealed their first bilateral ODI series win on Indian soil with a stunning win. They were powered to the highest ODI score in India by centuries from de Kock, du Plessis and de Villiers on a flat batting track before their bowlers shot out India in 36 overs. It was the fifth instance in the series of the team choosing to bat and going on to win the match. Amla fell early but de Kock set the platform with an 87-ball 109 before passing on the baton to du Plessis (133 off 115) and de Villiers (119 off 61). South Africa scored a whopping 38 fours and 20 sixes – 11 of them from de Villiers – to bat India out of the game.

Karthik Lakshmanan

Highest ODI score in India: Two of three centuries on the day came from Quinton de Kock and Daf du Plessis.
– Hindustan Times/Getty Images

Wankhede Stadium, Mumbai, October 25: South Africa 438/4 in 50 overs (Faf du Plessis 133, AB de Villiers 119, Quinton de Kock 109) beat **India** 224 in 50 overs (Ajinkya Rahane 87, Shikhar Dhawan 60; Kagiso Rabada 4-41, Dale Steyn 3-38) by 214 runs. *MoM*: Quinton de Kock. *MoS*: AB de Villiers.

Tour match
Brabourne Stadium, Mumbai, October 30-31: Indian Board President's XI 296 in 78.5 overs (KL Rahul 72, Naman Ojha 52; Simon Harmer 3-41, Dale Steyn 3-46) and 92/0 in 30 overs (Cheteshwar Pujara 49*, Rahul 43*) drew with **South Africans** 302 in 69.2 overs (AB de Villiers 112, Dane Vilas 54; Shardul Thakur 4-70, Kuldeep Yadav 2-24).

Test series (4): India 3 South Africa 0

1st Test: India win by 108 runs

Having travelled the world playing Test cricket exclusively overseas for the preceding 23 months, India finally had the luxury of home comfort when South Africa came calling for a four-match series.

Much had changed in the interim. India's last home Test before the First Test in Mohali had been Sachin Tendulkar's 200th and final appearance in November 2013. A little over a year after that, Dhoni had retired from Test cricket and the mantle of captaincy had fallen on the broad shoulders of Kohli. The Mohali game would be Kohli's first as Test skipper on home patch, but he was leading a buoyant team out, what with India having completed their first series win in Sri Lanka in 22 years just two months earlier.

South Africa have historically been the most accomplished and adaptable travellers, and have invariably acquitted themselves well in Indian conditions. With the irrepressible de Villiers and the master of swing Dale Steyn in the forefront, Amla had a wealth of talent at his disposal, several of them at home in India following their IPL forays.

Cricket in the subcontinent, however, isn't just about talent and skill. It requires nerve and character, especially on surfaces that bear little resemblance to the ones on which you have been raised. The pitch at the PCA Stadium was far from diabolical, but from the time they sighted the 22 yards, South Africa allowed gremlins in their minds. Long before the toss, they had lost the battle.

It wasn't as if India were the overwhelmingly dominant force in their own backyard. Not for the first time was their fallibility against quality spin laid threadbare. If it had been Moeen Ali in England, Nathan Lyon in Australia and Rangana Herath in Sri Lanka, then the unlikely figure of Dean Elgar rocked them in the first innings in Mohali, before the more regular spinners, Tahir and Simon Harmer, spun them to their doom in the second.

If, despite losing 15 wickets to spin and mustering totals of just 201 and 200, India still trooped out victors by the princely margin of 108 runs, it was largely because Ashwin and Ravindra Jadeja, in his first Test in 15 months, masterfully exploited both assistance from the track and the diffidence of the South African batsmen. Ashwin, fresh off a Man-of-the-Series performance in Sri Lanka, was a delight to watch, teasing and probing with his flight, loop, pace, turn, drift and bounce. His five-for in the first innings was his fourth in five previous Tests. Jadeja is a far less complicated bowler, his greatest virtue his remarkable consistency and the slight turn that he procures that is more than a handful on helpful pitches. Amit Mishra, the leg-spinner, had only one wicket to show in each innings, but not many can claim to have hoodwinked de Villiers twice in the same match.

South Africa's problems had started long before Amla called wrong at the toss, the experienced pair of Duminy and Morkel both ruled out through injury, though Morkel's injury did hasten the initiation into Test cricket of the

Spin demons: South Africa's capitulation was as much because of the gremlins in their minds as the skill of R Ashwin, Ranvindra Jadeja and Amit Mishra. – *BCCI*

exciting Rabada. To exacerbate matters, Steyn could not bowl in the second innings – he would go on to miss the rest of the series with a groin strain – a huge blow considering his success on Indian soil in preceding tours.

Despite the margin of victory, it was far from a convincing batting performance from the home team. Only M Vijay, outstanding in his judgment and committed in both defence and attack, and Cheteshwar Pujara, back at his favoured No. 3 position after being preferred to Rohit, showed the patience, the soft hands and a propensity to play close to the body. They accounted for more than 57% of the 401 runs mustered by India. Particularly galling for the hosts was losing 8 for 39 in the second innings to hurtle from 161 for 2 to 200 all out. Had Amla introduced the leg-spin of Tahir earlier in the first innings – he didn't come on until the 44th over – there might have been another twist in a game full of twists.

South Africa's capitulation in the final hour of the third day, made this the fourth consecutive three-day finish to a Test match in India. It wasn't to be the last of the series, either. *R Kaushik*

Venue: Punjab Cricket Association IS Bindra Stadium, Mohali, India, November 5, 2015
Toss: India, who chose to bat
MoM: Ravindra Jadeja

India

		R		*R*
Murali Vijay	LBW b Harmer	75	c Bavuma b Tahir	47
Shikhar Dhawan	c Amla b Philander	0	c de Villiers b Philander	0
Cheteshwar Pujara	LBW b Elgar	31	c Amla b Tahir	77
Virat Kohli*	c Elgar b Rabada	1	c † Vilas b van Zyl	29
Ajinkya Rahane	c Amla b Elgar	15	c Bavuma b Harmer	2
Wriddhiman Saha †	c Amla b Elgar	0	c † Vilas b Tahir	20
Ravindra Jadeja	LBW b Philander	38	LBW b Harmer	8
Amit Mishra	c Steyn b Elgar	6	c du Plessis b Harmer	2
R Ashwin	Not out	20	c Amla b Tahir	3
Umesh Yadav	b Tahir	5	b Harmer	1
Varun Aaron	b Tahir	0	Not out	1
Extras	(6b,11b,3nb,0w)	0	(9b,11b,0nb,0w)	0
Total	(all out, 68.0 overs, 2.96 runs per over)	201	(all out, 75.3 overs, 2.66 runs per over)	200

Fall of wickets: 1st innings: 0-1 (Shikhar Dhawan, 1.4 ov), 63-2 (Cheteshwar Pujara, 21.4 ov), 65-3 (Virat Kohli, 22.2 ov), 102-4 (Ajinkya Rahane, 37.6 ov), 102-5 (Wriddhiman Saha, 39.1 ov), 140-6 (Murali Vijay, 46.4 ov), 154-7 (Amit Mishra, 50.5 ov), 196-8 (Ravindra Jadeja, 66.2 ov), 201-9 (Umesh Yadav, 67.3 ov), 201-10 (Varun Aaron, 67.6 ov)

2nd innings: 9-1 (Shikhar Dhawan, 2.3 ov), 95-2 (Murali Vijay, 33.1 ov), 161-3 (Virat Kohli, 55.5 ov), 164-4 (Cheteshwar Pujara, 57.1 ov), 164-5 (Ajinkya Rahane, 58.3 ov), 178-6 (Ravindra Jadeja, 64.6 ov), 182-7 (Amit Mishra, 66.4 ov), 185-8 (R Ashwin, 69.1 ov), 188-9 (Umesh Yadav, 70.2 ov), 200-10 (Wriddhiman Saha, 75.3 ov)

Bowling: 1st innings: Dale Steyn 11-3-30-0-2.73, Vernon Philander 15-5-38-2-2.53, Simon Harmer 14-1-51-1-3.64, Kagiso Rabada 10-0-30-1-3.00 (3 nb), Dean Elgar 8-1-22-4-2.75, Imran Tahir 10-3-23-2-2.30

2nd innings: Vernon Philander 12-3-23-1-1.92, Simon Harmer 24-5-61-4-2.54, Dean Elgar 7-1-34-0-4.86, Imran Tahir 16-1-48-4-3.00, Kagiso Rabada 12-7-19-0-1.58, Stiaan van Zyl 4-1-5-1-1.25

South Africa

		R		*R*
Dean Elgar	c Jadeja b Ashwin	37	c Kohli b Aaron	16
Stiaan van Zyl	LBW b Ashwin	5	c Rahane b Ashwin	36
Faf du Plessis	b Jadeja	0	c Rahane b Ashwin	1
Hashim Amla*	st † Saha b Ashwin	43	b Jadeja	0
AB de Villiers	b Mishra	63	b Mishra	16
Dane Vilas †	c Jadeja b Ashwin	1	b Jadeja	7
Vernon Philander	c Rahane b Jadeja	3	LBW b Jadeja	1
Simon Harmer	LBW b Mishra	7	c Rahane b Jadeja	11

Dale Steyn	st † Saha b Jadeja	6	c Vijay b Ashwin	2
Kagiso Rabada	Not out	1	Not out	1
Imran Tahir	c Pujara b Ashwin	4	LBW b Jadeja	4
Extras	(6b,7lb,1nb,0w)	0	(8b,5lb,0nb,1w)	0
Total	(all out, 68.0 overs, 2.71 runs per over)	184	(all out, 39.5 overs, 2.76 runs per over)	109

Fall of wickets: 1st innings: 9-1 (Stiaan van Zyl, 6.4 ov), 9-2 (Faf du Plessis, 8.2 ov), 85-3 (Dean Elgar, 37.4 ov), 105-4 (Hashim Amla, 45.2 ov), 107-5 (Dane Vilas, 45.6 ov), 136-6 (Vernon Philander, 54.3 ov), 170-7 (Simon Harmer, 62.4 ov), 179-8 (Dale Steyn, 65.5 ov), 179-9 (AB de Villiers, 66.3 ov), 184-10 (Imran Tahir, 67.6 ov)
2nd innings: 8-1 (Vernon Philander, 1.1 ov), 9-2 (Faf du Plessis, 2.2 ov), 10-3 (Hashim Amla, 3.5 ov), 32-4 (AB de Villiers, 9.5 ov), 45-5 (Dean Elgar, 16.4 ov), 60-6 (Dane Vilas, 23.6 ov), 102-7 (Simon Harmer, 35.1 ov), 102-8 (Stiaan van Zyl, 36.2 ov), 105-9 (Dale Steyn, 38.2 ov), 109-10 (Imran Tahir, 39.5 ov)

Bowling: 1st innings: R Ashwin 24-5-51-5-2.13, Umesh Yadav 6-1-12-0-2.00, Varun Aaron 8-1-18-0-2.25, Ravindra Jadeja 18-0-55-3-3.06 (1 nb), Amit Mishra 12-3-35-2-2.92
2nd innings: R Ashwin 14-5-39-3-2.79, Ravindra Jadeja 11-4-21-5-1.91, Amit Mishra 8-0-26-1-3.25, Varun Aaron 3-0-3-1-1.00 (1 wd), Umesh Yadav 3-0-7-0-2.33

Umpires: Kumar Dharmasena (Sri Lanka) and Richard Kettleborough (England)
TV umpire: Vineet Kulkarni
Match referee: Jeff Crowe (New Zealand)

2nd Test: Match drawn

When India had to be content with a drawn Test in Bangladesh in June 2016 due to wet weather in spite of making the home team follow on, Kohli had advanced the opinion that an extra day for rain-affected Test matches might not be remiss. Even an extra day however, would not have been enough to save the Second Test, which began full of promise and ended with moods mirroring skies: grey and dull. It was the perfect setting for the match, a city that had always had a good turnout for the longest format playing host to the 100th Test of one of its adopted sons, and the foremost batsman of his era, in de Villiers.

Day one lived up to the hype: the Indian spin duo of Ashwin and Jadeja wreaking havoc while only de Villiers stood tall. Stepping lightly on his feet when moving forward, moving back to play late with assurance, manipulating the angles of the Chinnaswamy just like he does for Royal Challengers Bangalore, de Villiers alone contributed 40% of his team's total. He had walked in to the crease to an ovation that would have done Sachin Tendulkar or Kohli proud, and had his parents, wife and baby son watching from the stands. But just how little the majority of South Africa's batsmen had done became apparent when Vijay and Dhawan raced to 80 without loss by the close of the first day's play.

But a match set up so tantalisingly ended in bleak frustration with not a single ball bowled for any of the remaining four days. Even a temporary wedding *shamiana* of sorts assembled above the pitch couldn't ensure action beyond the 81 overs bowled – the second-fewest for a match in India. The visiting side escaped with a draw, but the Test reinforced the idea that the current South African line-up had not yet come to grips with high-quality spinners operating in friendly conditions.
Saurabh Somani

Venue: M Chinnaswamy Stadium, Bengaluru, India, November 14, 2015
Toss: India, who chose to bowl

South Africa

		R
Stiaan van Zyl	LBW b Ashwin	10
Dean Elgar	b Jadeja	38
Faf du Plessis	c Pujara b Ashwin	0
Hashim Amla*	b Aaron	7
AB de Villiers	c † Saha b Jadeja	85
JP Duminy	c Rahane b Ashwin	15
Dane Vilas †	c & b Jadeja	15
Kyle Abbott	Run out (Dhawan/ † Saha)	14
Kagiso Rabada	c Pujara b Jadeja	0
Morne Morkel	c Binny b Ashwin	22
Imran Tahir	Not out	0
Extras	(0b,2lb,6nb,0w)	0
Total	(all out, 59.0 overs, 3.63 runs per over)	214

Fall of wickets: 1st innings: 15-1 (Stiaan van Zyl, 7.2 ov), 15-2 (Faf du Plessis, 7.5 ov), 45-3 (Hashim Amla, 14.6 ov), 78-4 (Dean Elgar, 24.2 ov), 120-5 (JP Duminy, 34.6 ov), 159-6 (Dane Vilas, 45.4 ov), 177-7 (AB de Villiers, 51.3 ov), 177-8 (Kagiso Rabada, 51.5 ov), 214-9 (Morne Morkel, 58.5 ov), 214-10 (Kyle Abbott, 58.6 ov)

Bowling: 1st innings: Ishant Sharma 13-3-40-0-3.08 (4 nb), Stuart Binny 3-2-1-0-0.33, R Ashwin 18-2-70-4-3.89, Varun Aaron 9-0-51-1-5.67 (2 nb), Ravindra Jadeja 16-2-50-4-3.13

India

		R
Murali Vijay	Not out	28
Shikhar Dhawan	Not out	45
Extras	(4b,0lb,3nb,0w)	0
Total	(22.0 overs, 3.64 runs per over)	80

Did not bat: Virat Kohli, Wriddhiman Saha, Cheteshwar Pujara, Ajinkya Rahane, Stuart

Binny, Ravindra Jadeja, Varun Aaron, Ishant Sharma
Bowling: 1st innings: Morne Morkel 7-1-23-0-3.29 (3 nb), Kyle Abbott 6-1-18-0-3.00, Kagiso Rabada 5-1-17-0-3.40, JP Duminy 2-0-9-0-4.50, Imran Tahir 2-0-9-0-4.50

Umpires: Ian Gould (England) and Richard Kettleborough (England)
TV umpire: C Shamshuddin
Match referee: Jeff Crowe (New Zealand)

3rd Test: India win by 124 runs

South Africa knew exactly what they were in for when they arrived in Nagpur trailing 0-1, taking on India on a pitch that looked more like a fifth-day surface than a virgin one. Before the toss could happen, wise heads in the commentary boxes were rescheduling return flights for as early as the evening of the third day. And those that did so were spot on.

Batting first, or, more importantly, giving themselves the pleasure of bowling last, India were wise enough to realise that cashing in on the loose balls was the only way forward as crease occupation was unlikely to be easy. Vijay and Dhawan pounced on anything they could get away in an opening stand of 50 that would prove to be the highest of the day. Vijay made 40, the top score in India's 215 on a day when no batsman could say he was truly set. That Jadeja with 34 was the second-most successful batsman was telling as few players know how to make the most of a turning track as he.

South Africa were 11 for 2 when the day ended, Stiaan van Zyl's nightmare against Ashwin replaying with an air of inevitability. The second day, however, was worse than the stuff of bad dreams. It began with Amla and

The year of Ashwin: The off-spinner picked up his 15th five-wicket haul in South Africa's second innings in Nagpur; it was his 31st Test. – *BCCI*

Elgar being at the crease and ended with the same pair in harness, the small matter of 20 wickets having fallen in between.

Ashwin and Jadeja reduced South Africa to 12 for 5 in the first innings, with binary scores being the most popular, and only a counter-attacking Duminy allowed South Africa to get to 79 all out, five runs shy of their previous lowest score against India. In their second dig, India appeared to be debunking the theory that this pitch was unplayable, reaching 97 for 2 before Tahir was pressed into service as late as the 24th over. Tahir preyed on the batsmen's need to not miss out on a single scoring opportunity, collecting five as India were bowled out for 173.

Set a notional target of 309, one that has never been chased down by a visiting team in India, South Africa reprised their first-innings early effort, van Zyl falling to Ashwin a fifth time in as many innings and nightwatchman Tahir not lasting long enough to trouble anyone.

On the third, and final day of the Test, South Africa registered their first loss in an away series in nine years, Ashwin ending the batsmen's agony on 185, with match figures of 12 for 98. The only passage when the game was a contest was when Amla and Faf du Plessis batted 404 balls between them for 68 runs. But, India had three spinners to call on, and there was little chance South Africa could resist. Despite players from both teams doing their best to deflect attention from the pitch, it was subsequently censured as "poor" by the International Cricket Council, and Amla conceded that these were the toughest three days of his life.

Anand Vasu

> South Africa's first-innings total of 79 was their lowest since readmission in 1992. It is also the lowest total by any team against India. The series loss was their first overseas since they lost 2-0 to Sri Lanka in 2006, and it ended their unbeaten steak from 15 away series.

Venue: Vidarbha Cricket Association Ground, Nagpur, India, November 25, 2015
Toss: India, who chose to bat
MoM: R Ashwin

India

		R		*R*
Murali Vijay	LBW b Morkel	40	c Amla b Morkel	5
Shikhar Dhawan	c & b Elgar	12	c † Vilas b Tahir	39
Cheteshwar Pujara	LBW b Harmer	21	b Duminy	31
Virat Kohli*	c † Vilas b Morkel	22	c du Plessis b Tahir	16
Ajinkya Rahane	b Morkel	13	c Duminy b Tahir	9
Rohit Sharma	c de Villiers b Harmer	2	c Elgar b Morkel	23
Wriddhiman Saha †	c Duminy b Harmer	32	c Amla b Tahir	7
Ravindra Jadeja	b Rabada	34	b Harmer	5

South Africa in India

R Ashwin	b Tahir	15	LBW b Morkel	7
Amit Mishra	LBW b Harmer	3	b Tahir	14
Ishant Sharma	Not out	0	Not out	1
Extras	(15b,3lb,1nb,2w)	21	(8b,5lb,3nb,0w)	16
Total	(all out, 78.2 overs, 2.75 runs per over)	215	(all out, 46.3 overs, 3.74 runs per over)	173

Fall of wickets: 1st innings: 50-1 (Shikhar Dhawan, 13.6 ov), 69-2 (Murali Vijay, 21.2 ov), 94-3 (Cheteshwar Pujara, 30.1 ov), 115-4 (Ajinkya Rahane, 37.2 ov), 116-5 (Virat Kohli, 39.2 ov), 125-6 (Rohit Sharma, 46.2 ov), 173-7 (Ravindra Jadeja, 63.6 ov), 201-8 (Wriddhiman Saha, 72.6 ov), 215-9 (R Ashwin, 77.6 ov), 215-10 (Amit Mishra, 78.2 ov).
2nd innings: 8-1 (Murali Vijay, 4.2 ov), 52-2 (Cheteshwar Pujara, 17.3 ov), 97-3 (Shikhar Dhawan, 26.5 ov), 102-4 (Virat Kohli, 28.1 ov), 108-5 (Ajinkya Rahane, 30.3 ov), 122-6 (Wriddhiman Saha, 34.1 ov), 128-7 (Ravindra Jadeja, 35.3 ov), 150-8 (R Ashwin, 41.4 ov), 171-9 (Rohit Sharma, 45.4 ov), 173-10 (Amit Mishra, 46.3 ov)

Bowling: 1st innings: Morne Morkel 16-7-35-3-2.19 (1 nb), Kagiso Rabada 17-8-30-1-1.76 (2 wd), Simon Harmer 27-2-78-4-2.89, Dean Elgar 4-0-7-1-1.75, Imran Tahir 12-4-41-1-3.42, JP Duminy 1-0-6-0-6.00
2nd innings: Morne Morkel 10-5-19-3-1.90, Simon Harmer 18-3-64-1-3.56, Kagiso Rabada 5-1-15-0-3.00 (1 nb), JP Duminy 2-0-24-1-12.00 (1 nb), Imran Tahir 11-2-38-5-3.45 (1 nb)

South Africa

		R		*R*
Dean Elgar	b Ashwin	7	c Pujara b Ashwin	18
Stiaan van Zyl	c Rahane b Ashwin	0	c Sharma b Ashwin	5
Imran Tahir	b Jadeja	4	LBW b Mishra	8
Hashim Amla*	c Rahane b Ashwin	1	c Kohli b Mishra	39
AB de Villiers	c & b Jadeja	0	LBW b Ashwin	9
Faf du Plessis	b Jadeja	10	b Mishra	39
JP Duminy	LBW b Mishra	35	LBW b Ashwin	19
Dane Vilas †	b Jadeja	1	c † Saha b Ashwin	12
Simon Harmer	b Ashwin	13	Not out	8
Kagiso Rabada	Not out	6	c Kohli b Ashwin	6
Morne Morkel	c & b Ashwin	1	b Ashwin	4
Extras	(0b,1lb,0nb,0w)	1	(9b,5lb,4nb,0w)	18
Total	(all out, 33.1 overs, 2.39 runs per over)	79	(all out, 89.5 overs, 2.07 runs per over)	185

Fall of wickets: 1st innings: 4-1 (Stiaan van Zyl, 3.1 ov), 9-2 (Imran Tahir, 6.5 ov), 11-3 (Dean Elgar, 9.5 ov), 12-4 (Hashim Amla, 11.1 ov), 12-5 (AB de Villiers, 12.3 ov), 35-6 (Faf du Plessis, 16.6 ov), 47-7 (Dane Vilas, 22.2 ov), 66-8 (Simon Harmer, 27.2 ov), 76-9 (JP Duminy, 32.1 ov), 79-10 (Morne Morkel, 33.1 ov).
2nd innings: 17-1 (Stiaan van Zyl, 7.4 ov), 29-2 (Imran Tahir, 11.1 ov), 40-3 (Dean Elgar, 17.5 ov), 58-4 (AB de Villiers, 23.4 ov), 130-5 (Hashim Amla, 69.6 ov), 135-6 (Faf du

Plessis, 71.5 ov), 164-7 (JP Duminy, 81.1 ov), 167-8 (Dane Vilas, 81.6 ov), 177-9 (Kagiso Rabada, 87.4 ov), 185-10 (Morne Morkel, 89.5 ov)

Bowling: 1st innings: Ishant Sharma 2-1-4-0-2.00, R Ashwin 16-6-32-5-2.00, Ravindra Jadeja 12-3-33-4-2.75, Amit Mishra 3-0-9-1-3.00
2nd innings: Ishant Sharma 15-6-20-0-1.33 (4 nb), R Ashwin 29-7-66-7-2.28, Ravindra Jadeja 25-12-34-0-1.36, Amit Mishra 20-2-51-3-2.55

Umpires: Ian Gould (England) and Bruce Oxenford (Australia)
TV umpire: Anil Chaudhary
Match referee: Jeff Crowe (New Zealand)

4th Test: India win by 337 runs

After the debacle in central India, South Africa travelled north to the capital, the Delhi and District Cricket Administration managing to hang on to hosting rights for the final Test by the skin of their dentures after serious wrangling with several governmental agencies. The forecast was for turn, and misery for batsmen, but the typically lifeless nature of the Feroz Shah Kotla pitch allowed this Test to go the distance, even if the result was depressingly familiar for the visitors.

India won yet another important toss and had the kind of first day that reflected hard graft that this Test would be characterised by. India managed to get up to 231, after being 139 for 6, Rahane getting to an invaluable 89 not out when stumps were drawn. It was the kind of day that left both teams reasonably happy, but neither with a good night's sleep.

As it turned out, it was India who managed to take the game forward, Rahane scoring a century and Ashwin making 56 at No. 9 to go past 300. South Africa batted with all the determination of weary travellers who had their boarding passes for the return flight home in their back pockets. Temba Bavuma, playing in place of van Zyl, was the one bright spot, toughing it out for 22 in a 36-run opening stand, but that was a false dawn as the team were bundled out for only 121.

For a change, it was not Ashwin who hogged the headlines, but Jadeja, whose pin-point accurate left-arm spin yielded five for him. There was a general sense of panic in the South African batting, characterised by poor shot selection and a lack of an overall strategy.

When India batted a second time, declining to enforce the most unlikely of follow-ons, Rahane comprehensively erased the memories of his forgettable debut at the Kotla, adding an even 100 not out to his first-innings century. Kohli's 88 meant that India could declare at 267 for 5, setting South Africa 481 for victory.

By this stage, the pitch had gone into deep slumber, slow and low, offering nothing to either slow or fast bowlers. South Africa settled for the siege, deploying all their skill and technical expertise in blocking the ball. There wasn't even a token attempt to score runs. Bavuma consumed 117 balls for

Back in the reckoning: Ravindra Jadeja backed up Ashwin's 31 wickets for the series with 23 of his own at an average of 10.82. – *BCCI*

Blockathon: AB de Villiers's 297-ball 43 in Delhi was part of the South African attempt to play out time. – *BCCI*

34, Amla 244 for 25, de Villiers 297 for 43, du Plessis 97 for 10 but they could only delay the inevitable. Ashwin was as irresistible as ever, taking 5 for 61, but it was Umesh Yadav who bowled the spell of his life, marrying genuine pace with late, tailing reverse swing to end with the stunning figures of 21-16-9-3. India's will to win comfortably trumped South Africa's ability to survive and the series was sealed 3-0. *Anand Vasu*

Venue: Feroz Shah Kotla, Delhi, India, December 3, 2015
Toss: India, who chose to bat
MoM: Ajinkya Rahane (India)
MoS: R Ashwin (India)
Series result: India won the four-match series 3-0

India

		R		*R*
Murali Vijay	c Amla b Piedt	12	c † Vilas b Morkel	3
Shikhar Dhawan	LBW b Piedt	33	b Morkel	21
Cheteshwar Pujara	b Abbott	14	b Tahir	28
Virat Kohli*	c † Vilas b Piedt	44	LBW b Abbott	88
Ajinkya Rahane	c de Villiers b Tahir	127	Not out	100
Rohit Sharma	c Tahir b Piedt	1	b Morkel	0
Wriddhiman Saha †	b Abbott	1	Not out	23
Ravindra Jadeja	c Elgar b Abbott	24		
R Ashwin	c de Villiers b Abbott	56		
Umesh Yadav	Not out	10		
Ishant Sharma	LBW b Abbott	0		
Extras	(8b, 0lb, 3nb, 1w)	12	(0b, 4lb, 2nb, 0w)	6
Total	(all out, 117.5 overs, 2.84 runs per over)	334	(5 wkts, 100.1 overs, 2.67 runs per over)	267

South Africa in India

Fall of wickets: 1st innings: 30-1 (Murali Vijay, 16.2 ov), 62-2 (Shikhar Dhawan, 28.5 ov), 66-3 (Cheteshwar Pujara, 29.6 ov), 136-4 (Virat Kohli, 46.6 ov), 138-5 (Rohit Sharma, 50.1 ov), 139-6 (Wriddhiman Saha, 53.5 ov), 198-7 (Ravindra Jadeja, 72.4 ov), 296-8 (Ajinkya Rahane, 104.5 ov), 334-9 (R Ashwin, 117.3 ov), 334-10 (Ishant Sharma, 117.5 ov)
2nd innings: 4-1 (Murali Vijay, 4.6 ov), 8-2 (Rohit Sharma, 6.1 ov), 53-3 (Shikhar Dhawan, 28.6 ov), 57-4 (Cheteshwar Pujara, 31.1 ov), 211-5 (Virat Kohli, 85.4 ov)

Bowling: 1st innings: Morne Morkel 24-5-58-0-2.42 (1 wd, 1 nb), Kyle Abbott 24-7-40-5-1.67 (1 nb), Dane Piedt 38-6-117-4-3.08 (1 nb), Imran Tahir 16-2-66-1-4.13, Dean Elgar 11-0-33-0-3.00, JP Duminy 4-0-12-0-3.00
2nd innings: Morne Morkel 21-6-51-3-2.43 (1 nb), Kyle Abbott 22-9-47-1-2.14, Dane Piedt 18-1-53-0-2.94, Imran Tahir 26-4-74-1-2.85 (1 nb), Dean Elgar 13-1-40-0-3.08

South Africa

		R		R
Dean Elgar	c † Saha b Yadav	17	c Rahane b Ashwin	4
Temba Bavuma	b Jadeja	22	b Ashwin	34
Hashim Amla*	c † Saha b Jadeja	3	b Jadeja	25
AB de Villiers	c Sharma b Jadeja	42	c Jadeja b Ashwin	43
Faf du Plessis	c Rahane b Jadeja	0	LBW b Jadeja	10
JP Duminy	b Yadav	1	LBW b Ashwin	0
Dane Vilas †	b Sharma	11	b Yadav	13
Kyle Abbott	LBW b Ashwin	4	b Yadav	0
Dane Piedt	c Rahane b Jadeja	5	c Saha b Yadav	1
Morne Morkel	Not out	9	b Ashwin	2
Imran Tahir	c Rahul b Ashwin	1	Not out	0
Extras	(5b,0lb,1nb,0w)	6	(8b,3lb,0nb,0w)	11
Total	(all out, 49.3 overs, 2.45 runs per over)	121	(all out, 143.1 overs, 1 runs per over)	143

Fall of wickets: 1st innings: 36-1 (Dean Elgar, 14.3 ov), 40-2 (Temba Bavuma, 19.6 ov), 56-3 (Hashim Amla, 25.6 ov), 62-4 (Faf du Plessis, 27.6 ov), 65-5 (JP Duminy, 30.6 ov), 79-6 (Dane Vilas, 36.4 ov), 84-7 (Kyle Abbott, 37.5 ov), 103-8 (Dane Piedt, 42.5 ov), 118-9 (AB de Villiers, 46.6 ov), 121-10 (Imran Tahir, 49.3 ov)
2nd innings: 5-1 (Dean Elgar, 3.6 ov), 49-2 (Temba Bavuma, 42.4 ov), 76-3 (Hashim Amla, 84.5 ov), 111-4 (Faf du Plessis, 119.6 ov), 112-5 (JP Duminy, 124.2 ov), 136-6 (Dane Vilas, 138.5 ov), 136-7 (AB de Villiers, 139.1 ov), 140-8 (Kyle Abbott, 140.6 ov), 143-9 (Dane Piedt, 142.5 ov), 143-10 (Morne Morkel, 143.1 ov)

Bowling: 1st innings: Ishant Sharma 12-5-28-1-2.33 (1 nb), Umesh Yadav 12-3-32-2-2.67, R Ashwin 13-5-26-2-2.00, Ravindra Jadeja 12-2-30-5-2.50
2nd innings: Ishant Sharma 20-12-23-0-1.15, R Ashwin 49-26-61-5-1.24, Ravindra Jadeja 46-33-26-2-0.57, Umesh Yadav 21-16-9-3-0.43, Shikhar Dhawan 3-1-9-0-3.00, Murali Vijay 2-0-2-0-1.00, Virat Kohli 1-1-0-0-0.00, Cheteshwar Pujara 1-0-2-0-2.00

Umpires: Kumar Dharmasena (Sri Lanka) and Bruce Oxenford (Australia)
TV umpires: CK Nandan
Referee: Jeff Crowe (New Zealand)

	Tests	**ODIs**	**T20Is**
Best batsman	Ajinkya Rahane (266 runs, 4 matches)	AB de Villiers (358 runs, 5 matches)	Rohit Sharma (128 runs, 2 matches)
Best bowler	R Ashwin (31 wickets, 4 matches)	Kagiso Rabada (10 wickets, 5 matches)	R Ashwin (4 wickets, 2 matches)

Series Averages

India

Batting

Player	M	I	NO	R	HS	Ave	100s/50s
A Rahane	4	6	1	266	127	53.20	2/0
M Vijay	4	7	1	210	75	35.00	0/1
C Pujara	4	6	0	202	77	33.66	0/1
V Kohli	4	6	0	200	88	33.33	0/1
R Ashwin	4	5	1	101	56	25.25	0/1
S Dhawan	4	7	1	150	45*	25.00	0/0
R Jadeja	4	5	0	109	38	21.80	0/0
W Saha	4	6	1	83	32	16.60	0/0
U Yadav	2	3	1	16	10*	8.00	0/0
R Sharma	2	4	0	26	23	6.50	0/0
A Mishra	2	4	0	25	14	6.25	0/0
V Aaron	2	2	1	1	1*	1.00	0/0
I Sharma	3	3	2	1	1*	1.00	0/0
S Binny	1	-	-	-	-	-	-/-

Bowling and Fielding

Player	M	W	R	BBI	BBM	Ave	5wI/10wM	Ct/St
R Jadeja	4	23	249	5-21	8-76	10.82	2/0	5/-
R Ashwin	4	31	345	7-66	12-98	11.12	4/1	1/-
UT Yadav	2	5	60	3-9	5-41	12	0/0	0/-

A Mishra	2	7	121	3-51	4-60	17.28	0/0	0/-
V Aaron	2	2	72	1-3	1-21	36	0/0	0/-
I Sharma	3	1	115	1-28	1-51	115	0/0	1/-
V Kohli	4	0	0	-	-	-	0/0	3/-
S Binny	1	0	1	-	-	-	0/0	1/-
C Pujara	4	0	2	-	-	-	0/0	3/-
M Vijay	4	0	2	-	-	-	0/0	1/-
S Dhawan	4	0	9	-	-	-	0/0	0/-
A Rahane	4	-	-	-	-	-	0/0	10/-
W Saha	4	-	-	-	-	-	0/0	5/2
R Sharma	2	-	-	-	-	-	0/0	1/-

South Africa

Batting

Player	M	I	NO	R	HS	Ave	100s/50s
AB de Villiers	4	7	0	258	85	36.85	0/2
T Bavuma	1	2	0	56	34	28.00	0/0
D Elgar	4	7	0	137	38	19.57	0/0
H Amla	4	7	0	118	43	16.85	0/0
JP Duminy	3	5	0	70	35	14.00	0/0
S Harmer	2	4	1	39	13	13.00	0/0
S van Zyl	3	5	0	56	36	11.20	0/0
M Morkel	3	5	1	38	22	9.50	0/0
F du Plessis	4	7	0	60	39	8.57	0/0
D Vilas	4	7	0	60	15	8.57	0/0
K Rabada	3	5	3	14	6*	7.00	0/0
K Abbott	2	3	0	18	14	6.00	0/0
I Tahir	4	7	2	21	8	4.20	0/0
D Steyn	1	2	0	8	6	4.00	0/0
D Piedt	1	2	0	6	5	3.00	0/0
V Philander	1	2	0	4	3	2.00	0/0

Bowling and Fielding

Player	M	W	R	BBI	BBM	Ave	5wI/10wM	Ct/S
S van Zyl	3	1	5	1-5	1-5	5.00	0/0	0/-
K Abbott	2	6	105	5-40	6-87	17.50	1/0	0/-
V Philander	1	3	61	2-38	3-61	20.33	0/0	0/-
M Morkel	3	9	186	3-19	6-54	20.66	0/0	0/-
I Tahir	4	14	299	5-38	6-71	21.35	1/0	1/-
S Harmer	2	10	254	4-61	5-112	25.40	0/0	0/-
D Elgar	4	5	136	4-22	4-56	27.20	0/0	4/-
D Piedt	1	4	170	4-117	4-170	42.50	0/0	0/-
JP Duminy	3	1	51	1-24	1-30	51.00	0/0	2/-
K Rabada	3	2	111	1-30	1-45	55.50	0/0	0/-
D Steyn	1	0	30	-	-	-	0/0	1/-
H Amla	4	-	-	-	-	-	-/-	8/-
T Bavuma	1	-	-	-	-	-	-/-	0/-
AB de Villiers	4	-	-	-	-	-	-/-	4/-
F du Plessis	4	-	-	-	-	-	-/-	2/-
D Vilas	4	-	-	-	-	-	-/-	6/0

Squads

India: Virat Kohli (capt), Ajinkya Rahane, M Vijay, Shikhar Dhawan, R Ashwin, Cheteshwar Pujara, Ravindra Jadeja, Amit Mishra, Umesh Yadav, Ishant Sharma, Wriddhiman Saha (wk), Bhuvneshwar Kumar, Rohit Sharma, Varun Aaron, Stuart Binny, KL Rahul, Gurkeerat Singh Mann.

South Africa: Hasim Amla (capt), AB de Villiers, Faf du Plessis, Dale Steyn, Morne Morkel, Kyle Abbott, Imran Tahir, Dean Elgar, Temba Bavuma, Dane Vilas (wk), JP Duminy, Marchant de Lange, Simon Harmer, Dane Piedt, Kagiso Rabada, Stiaan van Zyl, Vernon Philander.

The rookie and the veteran: Jasprit Bumrah and the returning Ashish Nehra nailed their variations and yorkers in the T20Is in Australia. — *Getty Images*

India in Australia

Bumrah, batsmen change into T20 gear

SAURABH SOMANI

India ended their visit to Australia in January 2016 as the happier side, even though both teams had won four matches each. That in itself seemed unthinkable at the halfway stage, when the Indians were on the wrong end of a 4-0 scoreline.

The visitors, though, knew it could have well read at least 2-2, if not been completely reversed. Their turnaround from almost winning to actually crossing the line began in the fifth and final ODI. A rejuvenated team then benefitted from some specialist T20 additions to sweep the T20I series 3-0, creating history by becoming the first Indian team to whitewash Australia in Australia – in any format.

The tour was to serve as the first stop in a long T20 international season that would culminate with the World T20 2016 in March-April. Both teams aimed to identify personnel for key roles, and India quickly coalesced into a combination that gave the team batting depth, bowling options in pace and spin, and verve in fielding without sacrificing experience. The versatility of all-round players they lacked in the ODIs they found in the T20Is with Suresh Raina, Hardik Pandya and Yuvraj Singh. And where the pace bowlers could find neither the right lengths nor speeds to bowl, in the 20-over games, the returning Ashish Nehra and rookie Jasprit Bumrah nailed their variations and yorkers.

It was of course debatable if beginning preparations for a subcontinental event in far-off Australia – with its different climate, pitches, ground dynamics and atmosphere – was ideal. However, considering modern commercial realities of the big teams playing one another for lucrative returns, it was also inevitable that this tour materialised merely a year after India had spent a good four months Down Under playing a Test series, an ODI tri-series and the 2015 World Cup. Given that, the format of the tour was the best one could have got, though the pitches ensured that it was a bat versus bat contest across innings. The traditionally pace and seam friendly WACA and the Gabba saw 300-plus targets chased down, and the help for spinners at the historic MCG and SCG seemed to be a thing of the past. The lowest total came at the third ODI in Melbourne, where Australia chased down India's 295 for 6 with seven balls to spare.

The main batsmen all prospered, none more so than Virat Kohli, whose bat only had a middle. Rohit Sharma was not far behind while Shikhar Dhawan shrugged off a poor start with scintillating strokeplay. Australia's top order had more shuffling with players rested, but the batsmen had a uniformly good time of it in the ODIs. Shane Watson's century in the final T20I was also a key moment, the veteran showing he could still serve his country well.

Overall, it was not a happy series in which to be a bowler, much less one making a debut. In the ODIs, Barinder Sran showed some spark, but Rishi Dhawan, Joel Paris and Scott Boland all had tough initiations. Australia didn't have a full-strength attack for the series, Mitchell Starc being the towering absence, but John Hastings stepped into the breach of attack leader with aplomb, bowling the most sustained testing spells and finding the energy to hurry batsmen even on placid tracks.

For MS Dhoni, Bumrah was "the find of the tour". Originally not part of either the ODI or T20I squads, he was called up for the 20-over games in place of an injured Mohammed Shami. A longer route to Adelaide, venue of the first T20I, meant he travelled directly to Sydney ahead of the final ODI. He ended up making his debut there because of another injury, this time to Bhuvneshwar Kumar. A split webbing in Ajinkya Rahane's hand opened up a spot in the batting too, and the Bumrah-Manish Pandey duo ended up the standout performers. The bowler's quirky action and ability to nail toe-crushers was a godsend for India, while the batsman's nerveless calm in the face of a pressure chase a welcome sign.

Victory in that final ODI brought relief to a beleaguered team that had seen winning moments slip out of its grasp the four previous matches. How well that belief was capitalised upon was evident in the T20I sweep that followed.

Tour matches

WACA Ground, Perth, January 8: Indians 192/4 in 20 overs (Virat Kohli 74, Shikhar Dhawan 74) beat **Western Australia XI** 118/6 in 20 overs (Travis Birt 74*; Axar Patel 2-13, Ravindra Jadeja 2-13) by 74 runs.

WACA Ground, Perth, January 9: Indians 249 in 50 overs (Rohit Sharma 67, Manish Pandey 58; Drew Porter 5-37, James Muirhead 2-55) beat **Western Australia XI** 185 in 49.2 overs (Jaron Morgan 50, Jake Carder 45; Rishi Dhawan 2-28, Axar Patel 2-29) by 64 runs.

ODI series (5): Australia 4 India 1

1st ODI: Australia win by five wickets

Rohit Sharma went past Viv Richards to hit the highest score against Australia in Australia, but the home team etched a record of its own with the highest successful chase at the WACA. The opening match of a short, sharp limited-overs series featured three debutant pacers as well as three centurions – not to forget Virat Kohli's 91 – and set the stage for the series to follow. Barinder Sran, who comfortably outshone fellow debutants Joel Paris and Scott Boland, had Australia in some early trouble, but an expertly helmed chase by Steve Smith and George Bailey put India's effort in the shade. Rohit had shown his growing mastery of ODI cricket, but the Smith and Bailey show was more impressive in how they soaked up pressure, grabbed momentum and set the pace with a settling in period followed by targeted acceleration against spinners.

WACA Ground, Perth, January 12: India 309/3 in 50 overs (Rohit Sharma 171, Virat Kohli 91; James Faulkner 2-60) lost to **Australia** 310/5 in 50 overs (Steve Smith 149, George Bailey 112; Barinder Sran 3-56, R Ashwin 2-68) by five wickets. *MoM*: Steve Smith.

Setting the pace: George Bailey played a crucial role in the first two chases, giving Australia a 2-0 lead in the series. – *Getty Images*

2nd ODI: Australia win by seven wickets

The second ODI followed the pattern of the first, in that Rohit hit a century and India crossed 300 – but Australia won the key moments and the match, with Bailey central to the chase once again. India were let down in the field, dropping Shaun Marsh four times, and suffering two run-outs during their own innings. Rohit's was unfortunate, coming at the non-striker's end after the bowler got a hand to a straight drive; Kohli's came because the in-form vice-captain went for a non-existent second run. India thus didn't have the final-overs ballast needed, which proved crucial. Australia's top order clicked in unison, Smith's 46 the lowest score among batsmen dismissed. Bailey, sporting a new stance with back leg out and body more side on, picked runs off at a T20 pace without ever appearing in a hurry, to seal victory.

Brisbane Cricket Ground, Woolloongabba, January 15: India 308/8 in 50 overs (Rohit Sharma 124, Ajinkya Rahane 89; James Faulkner 2-64) lost to **Australia** 309/3 in 49 overs (George Bailey 76, Aaron Finch 71) by seven wickets. *MoM*: Rohit Sharma.

3rd ODI: Australia win by three wickets

Kohli made the century he had been threatening to all series long and the Indian bowlers put in a much better show – but once again Australia found a man for the moment. Glenn Maxwell played one of his finest ODI innings yet to give the home team a series win. With the Australian middle order under pressure for the first time in the series, Maxwell blended consolidation with his aggressive instincts, showcasing Australia's depth in batting and his own mental chops. Dhawan's laboured innings at the top ate up valuable overs, but Kohli's mastery and a Dhoni cameo pushed India near 300 again. Australia's chase could have been more difficult had India not dropped Ashwin on a pitch that had something for spinners. With Ravindra Jadeja the best bowler, the decision seemed all the more perplexing.

Melbourne Cricket Ground, January 17: India 295/6 in 50 overs (Virat Kohli 117, Shikhar Dhawan 68; John Hastings 4-58) lost to **Australia** 296/7 in 48.5 overs (Glenn Maxwell 96, Shaun Marsh 62; Ravindra Jadeja 2-49, Ishant Sharma 2-53) by three wickets. *MoM*: Glenn Maxwell.

4th ODI: Australia win by 25 runs

India had been competitive in the first two ODIs, could have won the third, and should have won the fourth. However, a spectacular collapse derailed what had been a magnificent run-chase till then, India losing their way from 277 for 1 when only 72 were required from 76. Australia had been driven to an imposing total courtesy big knocks from the openers, Aaron Finch and David Warner, and an end-overs blast from Smith and Maxwell. But India had it well in hand; Kohli, the master of chases, became the fastest to 25 ODI hundreds (in 162 innings) and Dhawan returned to form with a century of his own. But Kane Richardson's five-wicket haul, including a second spell of 4 for 16, meant it all unravelled quickly.

Manuka Oval, Canberra, January 20: Australia 348/8 in 50 overs (Aaron Finch 107, David Warner 93; Ishant Sharma 4-77, Umesh Yadav 3-67) beat **India** 323 in 49.2 overs (Shikhar Dhawan 126, Virat Kohli 106; Kane Richardson 5-68, John Hastings 2-50) by 25 runs. *MoM*: Kane Richardson.

5th ODI: India win by six wickets

In a series that had seen five individual hundreds by India, it was the sixth – by a man playing only his fourth ODI – that finally resulted in victory. Manish Pandey's unbeaten 104 was the third three-figure knock of the day, following Warner and Mitchell Marsh's efforts, but he stole the show with a nerveless knock under mounting pressure. Australia had an imposing total once again, though in handing Jasprit Bumrah a debut, India hit gold. A rollicking opening stand set the base, but with Kohli's first failure in the series – hemmed in by fielders against short bowling – and Dhoni struggling for touch, India looked to go down the 'so close yet so far' route again. Fortunately for them, Pandey kept his cool in a tight finish to deny Australia a series whitewash.

Manish Pandey gave India their first win of the series. – *Getty Images*

Sydney Cricket Ground, January 23: Australia 330/7 in 50 overs (David Warner 122, Mitchell Marsh 102*; Jasprit Bumrah 2-40, Ishant Sharma 2-60) lost to **India** 331/4 in 49.4 overs (Manish Pandey 104*, Rohit Sharma 99; John Hastings 3-61) by six wickets. *MoM*: *Manish Pandey*. *MoS*: *Rohit Sharma*.

T20I series (3): India 3 Australia 0

1st T20I: India win by 37 runs

• Shaun Tait returns, but more with a wild fling than as the Wild Thing, with Rohit especially punishing early on. • Kohli walks in after 4.1 overs but hits his zone immediately, his timing impeccable. • His love affair with the Adelaide Oval almost results in another century; he is only denied because overs run out. • Finch, Warner and Smith give Australia a robust start; Hardik Pandya has a horror debut, conceding 19 in his first T20I over, including five wides. • Jadeja and Ashwin engineer a collapse in the second half of Australia's innings. • Bumrah, on T20I debut, takes the final wicket to end with the best figures.

Adelaide Oval, January 26: India 188/3 in 20 overs (Virat Kohli 90*, Suresh Raina 41;

Shane Watson 2-24) beat **Australia** 151 in 19.3 overs (Aaron Finch 44, Steve Smith 21; Jasprit Bumrah 3-23, Ravindra Jadeja 2-21) by 37 runs. *MoM*: Virat Kohli.

2nd T20I: India win by 27 runs

• Rohit and Dhawan make a quiet start before exploding to life. • Both men are dismissed against the run of play, but Kohli assumes command once again. • Without any noticeable slogging, Kohli ups the ante to give India a formidable score. • Finch takes the lead in the chase, starting aggressively. • He injures his hamstring mid-innings, while other batsmen fall around him. • All bowlers chip in at vital times, and backed by Dhoni's quicksilver keeping – he overtakes Kumar Sangakkara for most stumpings with 140 to his credit – India take a series-winning lead.

Melbourne Cricket Ground, January 29: India 184/3 in 20 overs (Rohit Sharma 60, Virat Kohli 59*) beat **Australia** 157/8 in 20 overs (Aaron Finch 74, Shaun Marsh 23; Ravindra Jadeja 2-32 Jasprit Bumrah 2-37) by 27 runs. *MoM*: Virat Kohli.

3rd T20I: India win by seven wickets

• Shane Watson becomes the first man to captain Australia in all three formats, taking over from an injured Finch. • He also becomes the only Australian with centuries in all three formats: coming out to open, he adroitly farms the strike and connects the big shots. • Dhawan ignites the Indian reply with a 24-run over off Tait, before Rohit and Kohli come together. • Cameron Boyce gets both set batsmen with his leg spin, but a missed stumping of Raina off his bowling proves costly. • Watson seems to be everywhere on the field, taking a wicket and a catch. • Yuvraj Singh shrugs off his initial struggles, smashing a six and four in the final over before Raina steers the winning runs off the last ball.

Sydney Cricket Ground, January 31: Australia 197/5 in 20 overs (Shane Watson 124, Travis Head 26) lost to **India** 200/3 in 20 overs (Rohit Sharma 52, Virat Kohli 50; Cameron Boyce 2-28) by seven wickets. *MoM*: Shane Watson. *MoS*: Virat Kohli.

	T20Is	ODIs
Best batsman	Virat Kohli (199 runs, 3 matches)	Rohit Sharma (441 runs, 5 matches)
Best bowler	Jasprit Bumrah (6 wickets, 3 matches)	John Hastings (10 wickets, 4 matches)

Sri Lanka in India

Experience thwarts youthful challenge

KARTHIK LAKSHMANAN

T20I series (3): India 2 Sri Lanka 1

1st T20I: Sri Lanka win by five wickets

• A young and inexperienced Sri Lankan side takes on a strong, in-form India at home in a series crucial to World T20 preparations. • After Sri Lanka opt to bowl, Kasun Rajitha, the debutant, and Dasun Shanaka pick up three wickets each as Sri Lanka's pacers run riot. • Only three Indian batsmen manage double-digit scores, with the highest coming from the No. 9. • Ashish Nehra removes Niroshan Dickwella and Danushka Gunathilaka early to reduce Sri Lanka to 23 for 2. • Dinesh Chandimal and Chamara Kapugedera steady the innings with some sturdy batting. • Suresh Raina and R Ashwin get rid of them but it's too late for India as Sri Lanka romp home.

MCA Stadium, Pune, February 9: India 101 in 18.5 overs (R Ashwin 31, Suresh Raina 20; Dasun Shanaka 3-16, Kasun Rajitha 3-29) lost to **Sri Lanka** 105/5 in 18 overs (Dinesh Chandimal 35, Chamara Kapugedera 25; R Ashwin 2-13, Ashish Nehra 2-21) by five wickets. *MoM*: Kasun Rajitha.

2nd T20I: India win by 69 runs

• Sri Lanka again field but India's openers, Rohit Sharma and Shikhar Dhawan, start strongly with a 75-run stand. • Dhawan gets out for a 25-ball 51 but Rohit and Ajinkya Rahane (25) keep India going. • Raina (30 off 19) and Hardik Pandya (27 off 12) play cameos, even as Thisara Perera bags a late hat-trick. • Sri Lanka lose Tillakaratne Dilshan first ball to Ashwin before Nehra reduces them to 16 for 3. • Chandimal, Kapugedera, Milinda Siriwardana and Shanaka keep Sri Lanka going. • Ashwin and Ravindra Jadeja quell any challenge as India square the series.

JSCA International Stadium, Ranchi, February 12: India 196/6 in 20 overs (Shikhar Dhawan 51, Rohit Sharma 43; Thisara Perera 3-33, Dushmantha Chameera 2-38) beat **Sri Lanka** 127/9 in 20 overs (Chamara Kapugedera 32, Dinesh Chandimal 31; R Ashwin 3-14, Jasprit Bumrah 2-17) by 69 runs. *MoM*: Shikhar Dhawan.

3rd T20I: India win by nine wickets

• With the convincing win in Ranchi, India go into the deciding match as the clear favourites. • Fielding first, they begin on a terrific note with Ashwin going through a dream spell of 4-1-8-4 as Sri Lanka are reduced to 21 for 5. • Only Shanaka (19) and Perera (12) manage double-digit scores as Sri Lanka

Among the wickets: Suresh Raina made contributions with both bat and ball through the series, finishing with 2-6 in the third T20I. – BCCI

are skittled out. • Chameera removes Rohit within the powerplay. • Dhawan and Rahane ensure Sri Lanka don't find a way back with a steady, unbeaten 55-run partnership. • India race home in 13.5 overs, the win leading to a 2-1 series victory.

Dr YS Rajasekhara Reddy ACA-VDCA Cricket Stadium, Visakhapatnam, February 14: Sri Lanka 82 in 18 overs (R Ashwin 4-8, Suresh Raina 2-6) lost to **India** 84/1 in 13.5 overs (Shikhar Dhawan 46*, Ajinkya Rahane 22*) by nine wickets. *MoM*: R Ashwin. *MoS*: R Ashwin.

Best batsman: Shikhar Dhawan (106 runs, 3 matches)
Best bowler: R Ashwin (9 wickets, 3 matches)

Imagine money reaching its destination bank account even before the fielder could complete a diving catch.

FLASHremit
Real-time Remittance

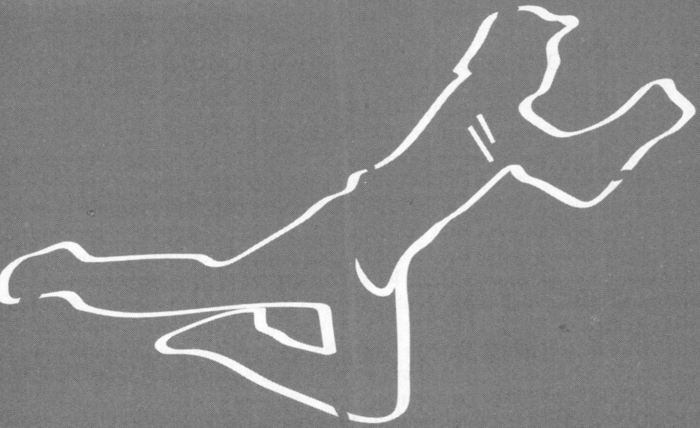

Customer Service: 600 555 550 | www.uaeexchange.com

A different Dhoni: The India captain, who last played in Zimbabwe in 2005, returned to the country in 2016 leading a team of hopefuls. — *AFP/Getty Images*

India in Zimbabwe

Dhoni breaks ice with Generation Y

BHARAT SUNDARESAN

MS Dhoni last came to Zimbabwe in 2005. He was a rookie sporting a rustic *mehendi* brown-coloured mane in the midst of a galaxy of stars. As he landed in Harare 11 years later, his hair was fashionably cropped in a quiff but flecked with grey, showing the effects of a life more or less spent living out of suitcases and leading the most sought-after cricket team in the world. More importantly, he was the lone star surrounded by a plethora of young upstarts and middle-aged second-stringers desperate to make a mark in his presence.

Like most recent Zimbabwe tours, this one too was built up to be a platform of sorts for the bench to make a mark; it was also a chance for Dhoni to prove that he remained relevant.

On a personal level, he didn't quite set the stage on fire, despite even the Zimbabweans cheering him on to do so. It was here on his last tour that Dhoni earned the reputation of being the cricketing Houdini by getting India over the line from improbable scenarios. But while all his batting stints during the ODI series were restricted to the nets, he looked a shadow of his brutal self in the T20Is. He couldn't finish the first T20I off with four required off the last ball, and he was dismissed cheaply in his only other outing, getting struck in the eye by a rogue bail in the process.

Dhoni the captain, though, was rejuvenated and more involved than ever before, and that was true both on and off the field. His hotel room was the hub of all non-cricketing activities, from FIFA games on PlayStation to communal takeaway dinners and tête-à-têtes. He spent copious amounts of time during practice sessions playing mentor, from helping Jayant Yadav, the young off-spinner, master his doosra to recommending techniques of stepping out of the crease to the batsmen. During matches, he never missed a chance to put an arm around a bowler's shoulder, but was quick to give them an earful whenever they let him down. His hands-on leadership came to the fore in the third T20 as he overcame slighted vision to guide young Barinder Sran through a tempestuous final over. Being the high-profile star on the low-profile tour, he could have easily shut himself up and counted down the days, but instead he was right in the mix, showing that his passion for the game was still burning bright. You had to see him seething with disgust post the first T20 loss to know how much it meant to him.

A number of younger names blossomed as a result. Jasprit Bumrah showed why he's fast emerging as India's No.1 wicket-taking option in limited overs cricket along with being his captain's most trusted ally in a fight. Sran and Dhawal Kulkarni too had their moments, with Yuzvendra Chahal providing the right dollop of fillip that this team needed with his wily leg-spin and infectious attitude. Axar Patel was the most economical bowler on show while KL Rahul and Ambati Rayudu were consistent with the bat.

Zimbabwe cricket was just on the verge of slipping into the mire the last time Dhoni was here. And by the time he left, most certainly never to return here as an active cricketer, it seemed to have sunk deeper in it than ever before. The series started on a sour note with the sacking of coach Dav Whatmore, and Makhaya Ntini, the stand-in coach, promising to sweep the Indians under the carpet.

With each collapse, their woes just got worse, and though Elton Chigumbura and his team did put a few smiles on the faces of their often-fickle-but-forever-partisan fans, they didn't last long. The newer faces in the team looked out of depth while the senior pros didn't

Demand for reform: Zimbabwe cricket fans weren't happy with cricketers or officials, and made it known. – *Wisden India*

always seem happy to be out there. Zimbabwe cricket will face its moment of truth in 2017 as it fights to keep both its ODI and Test status alive. As far as Dhoni's future goes, there wasn't much of a giveaway, just the inevitable suspense. He at least didn't look like someone in a hurry to leave. But as we've learnt the hard way so often with Dhoni and his career, you make predictions at your own peril.

ODI series (3): India 3 Zimbabwe 0

1st ODI: India win by nine wickets

Reputations can hang around your neck like an unyielding albatross in international cricket. And despite a path-breaking IPL 9, KL Rahul hadn't quite shed the tag of being a slight misfit in the wham bam era. That was before he hit it out of the park, quite literally, with a last-ball six to become the first Indian to score a century on ODI debut. His nicely paced unbeaten 100, and a steady hand from Ambati Rayudu, helped India chase down 169 and cruise to a comfortable win. The Zimbabweans put up a candid display of why their cricket is staring down the barrel. Their batsmen looked inept against Barinder Sran's sharp in-coming deliveries with the new ball and timidly succumbed to the wiles of Jasprit Bumrah, who despite playing only his second ODI seemed a ubiquitous presence in India colours.

Harare Sports Club, June 11: Zimbabwe 168 in 49.5 overs (Elton Chigumbura 41, Sikandar Raza 23; Jasprit Bumrah 4-28, Dhawal Kulkarni 2-42, Barinder Sran 2-42) lost to **India** 173/1 in 42.3 overs (KL Rahul 100*, Ambati Rayudu 62*) by nine wickets. *MoM*: KL Rahul.

2nd ODI: India win by eight wickets

Another day, another Zimbabwe collapse. This one was so abominable that it prompted Makhaya Ntini to go looking for a tomato tree to hang himself, or so he claimed. At 106 for 3, Vusi Sibanda and Sikandar Raza had given the hosts a semblance of stability on a flat pitch. But Raza's needless and fatal attempt to clear long-on off Yuzvendra Chahal switched on the self-destruct button in the Zimbabwe camp. It also set off a crowd revolt with some spectators demanding that their players be "arrested for treason". Their remaining six wickets fell for 20 runs as Chahal, the former chess prodigy, checkmated the home team with his crafty bag of tricks and almost snared a hat-trick for good measure. The Karnataka opening pair of Karun Nair and Rahul set off cautiously, but it was Ambati Rayudu, on his third straight trip to Zimbabwe, who sealed India's first bilateral ODI series win since November 2014.

Harare Sports Club, June 13: Zimbabwe 126 in 34.3 overs (Vusi Sibanda 53, Chamu Chibhabha 21; Yuzvendra Chahal 3-25, Barinder Sran 2-17) lost to **India** 129/2 in 26.5 overs (Ambati Rayudu 41*, Karun Nair 39) by eight wickets. *MoM*: Yuzvendra Chahal.

KL Rahul (right) proved his limited-overs credentials while Ambati Rayudu played a steady hand. — *AFP/Getty Images*

3rd ODI: India win by ten wickets

When Graeme Cremer won the toss for a change, it looked like finally the series would witness a contest. For, obviously the Zimbabwe captain would give his fast bowlers a go at the young Indian top-order when there was swing in the chilly Harare morning air. Inexplicably, he chose to bat. And the batsmen put on a show that was as masochistic as their skipper's decision, at one point losing four wickets at the same score: 104 for 3 to 104 for 7. The run-chase, which finished with a ten-wicket win for India in a series where they lost only three wickets overall, had a touch of cricketing romance with 30-year-old Faiz Fazal marking his unexpected ODI debut with a sparkling unbeaten half-century. A month earlier he had been freezing away at Hetton-le-Hole in north-east London, sure that the dream of playing for India had slipped away, but there he was, living it out in Harare.

Harare Sports Club, June 15: Zimbabwe 123 in 42.2 overs (Vusi Sibanda 38, Chamu Chibhabha 27; Jasprit Bumrah 4-22, Yuzvendra Chahal 2-25) lost to **India** 126/0 in 21.5 overs (KL Rahul 63*, Faiz Fazal 55*) by ten wickets. *MoM*: KL Rahul. *MoS*: KL Rahul.

T20I series (3): India 2 Zimbabwe 1

1st T20I: Zimbabwe win by two runs

• Bumrah's entry puts the shackles on Zimbabwe, who are flying at 33 for no loss in four overs courtesy Hamilton Masakadza's three sixes. • Elton Chigumbura, called "useless" during the ODIs, is back to being the fans' hero when he smashes seven sixes in his match-turning 26-ball 54, taking a special liking for Jaydev Unadkat. • A week after his century on ODI debut, Rahul is out first ball in his maiden T20I. • Manish Pandey throws away his wicket after a well-compiled 35-ball 48, while Rishi Dhawan has a day to forget. • Dhawan fails to connect with attempted lap-sweeps despite Dhoni pushing him for a single. • Neville Madziva defends eight in the last over, denying Dhoni a boundary off the last ball.

Harare Sports Club, June 18: Zimbabwe 170/6 in 20 overs (Elton Chigumbura 54*, Malcolm Waller 30; Jasprit Bumrah 2-24) beat **India** 168/6 in 20 overs (Manish Pandey 48, Mandeep Singh 31; Chamu Chibhabha 2-13, Taurai Muzarabani 2-31) by two runs. *MoM*: Elton Chigumbura.

2nd T20I: India win by ten wickets

• Stunned by the loss, India bring back Sran and Kulkarni, and it makes an immediate difference. • By his third over, Sran has 4 for 9, three wickets coming in one over and his in-coming deliveries a particular scourge. • Zimbabwe are wary of Chahal, who holds up one end in the middle before Bumrah sends down a burst in the death, removing the well-set PJ Moor. • Mandeep Singh made the most of his promotion from regular A side appearances to outscore Rahul in their unbeaten opening stand. • Cremer, the Zimbabwe captain, doesn't just fail to inspire, he is also their biggest dud with the ball, invariably letting the pressure slip. • Rahul continues to prove he could well be the all-season, all-format opener that India seek, showcasing again his ability to score quickly without comprising on basics and aesthetics.

Harare Sports Club, June 20: Zimbabwe 99/9 in 20 overs (Peter Moor 31; Barinder Sran 4-10, Jasprit Bumrah 3-11) lost to **India** 103/0 in 13.1 overs (Mandeep Singh 52*, KL Rahul 47*) by ten wickets. *MoM*: Barinder Sran.

3rd T20I: India win by three runs

• In his first game of the series, it is mighty impressive for Tendai Chatara to open with a maiden over to the in-form Rahul. Incidentally, Sran would return the favour in the Zimbabwe innings. • Donald Tiripano puts India under the cosh – he would have three crucial strikes, including that of Dhoni – as India are 27 for 3. • Kedar Jadhav, who has played 11 of his 12 games for India at this venue, finds the boundary on a tricky surface to help add a crucial 43 runs in the last three overs. • Axar Patel's lusty hitting could come in handy for the first-choice Indian squad someday, as it did here with his 11-ball 20. • Axar also puts the brakes on in the middle overs of the Zimbabwe chase, before Kulkarni bowls a brilliant 18th, giving away only three. • With 21 required off Sran's last, Timycen Maruma launches the first ball over deep midwicket, before Sran responds with a chest-high full-toss, which is called a no-ball and goes for four. But gathering his wits, Sran sends down wide yorkers with precision and denies Chigumbura a four off the last ball.

Harare Sports Club, June 22: India 138/6 in 20 overs (Kedar Jadhav 58, KL Rahul 22; Donald Tiripano 3-20) beat **Zimbabwe** 135/6 in 20 overs (Vusi Sibanda 28, Peter Moor 26; Dhawal Kulkarni 2-23, Barinder Sran 2-31) by 3 runs. *MoM*: Kedar Jadhav. *MoS*: Barinder Sran.

	ODIs	T20Is
Best batsman	KL Rahul (196 runs, 3 matches)	Mandeep Singh (87 runs, 3 matches)
Best bowler	Jasprit Bumrah (9 wickets, 3 matches)	Barinder Sran (6 wickets, 2 matches)

Bharat Sundaresan (@beastieboy07) is a cricket writer at the Indian Express.

Two hundreds, 17 wickets: R Ashwin proved he could be a match-winner overseas as well, tormenting West Indies with bat and ball alike. – *WICB*

India in the West Indies and USA

Emphatic welcome for Kumble

ANAND VASU

Indian teams of the past have arrived on Caribbean shores weak-kneed and anxious, bracing themselves for a battering from a four-pronged pace attack that feasted on subcontinental batsmen on hard and bouncy pitches. But, those days of dominance are a thing of the past and young Indian cricketers today strut their stuff as if they fear nothing in the world.

When Virat Kohli's men arrived in the West Indies in 2016, with new coach Anil Kumble in harness, the expectation was that they would win the series. West Indies are a team perpetually in transition and the best players in the islands are too busy hopping from one T20 extravaganza to another to play Test cricket on a regular basis.

That being said, India would not have expected to win as easily as they did, two crushing wins sealing the series and rain playing a major part in two Test matches ending in draws. Truth be told, West Indies managed just one good day's cricket in the entire series, on the final day in Kingston when Roston Chase sealed his end up for an unbeaten 137.

But, India will not focus on the fallibilities of the opposition, for they can only compete against the XI put up against them. Instead, they will look at the serious gains made on the tour in multiple departments.

The brightest was the emergence of R Ashwin as a match-winner overseas. While he has tormented batsmen at home, Ashwin has been unable to replicate this success overseas. To be fair to him, he did not feature regularly enough in the playing XI in England or South Africa or Australia to get into any sort of rhythm and the 2016 version of the off-spinner is a much matured version of the one who embarked on early tours.

Ashwin picked up 17 wickets at 23.17 and made the most of his promotion to No. 6, scoring two centuries. Emerging as a solid all-round prospect that allowed Kohli to tailor his bowling attack or batting composition based on the conditions, Ashwin comfortably walked away with the series award.

The transition of KL Rahul from stand-in opener to indispensible member of the XI was the other major gain from the tour. A stunning 158 in the Second Test meant that Rahul kept his place in the XI even when the injured M Vijay regained fitness. Since then, as Shikhar Dhawan's form has dipped, Rahul has edged ahead in the queue.

Kohli's captaincy also showed signs of improving with experience. Where he once believed in attack at all costs, Kohli was now choosing his moments better. When the occasion called for it, he still went for the kill, but the approach was more calculated. The fact that he scored his maiden first-class double-century early in the tour can only have helped his confidence.

Also of note was India's ability to find ways to pick up 20 wickets even when the conditions were not loaded in favour of the bowlers. The bounce of Ishant Sharma, swing of Bhuvneshwar Kumar and seam of Mohammed Shami all played a part at different times, giving Kohli multiple options.

The opposition may not have given them the stiffest of fights, but a 2-0 win in the West Indies is something no previous Indian team had achieved. That in itself will be a matter of lasting pride for the class of 2016.

Tour matches

Warner Park, Basseterre, St Kitts, July 9-10: Indians 258/6 dec in 93 overs (Rohit Sharma 54*, Shikhar Dhawan 51 retd. out; Jomel Warrican 2-61) drew with **West Indies Cricket Board President's XI** 281/7 in 87 overs (Shai Hope 118*, Rajendra Chandrika 69; Amit Mishra 4-67).

Warner Park, Basseterre, St Kitts, July 14-16: West Indies Cricket Board President's XI 180 in 62.5 overs (Rahkeem Cornwall 41, Jermaine Blackwood 36; Ravindra Jadeja 3-16, R Ashwin 3-62) and 223/6 in 86 overs (J Blackwood 51, Montcin Hodge 39*; R Ashwin 3-59) drew with **Indians** 364 in 105.4 overs (KL Rahul 64 retd. out, R Jadeja 56; R Cornwall 5-118).

Test series (4): India 2 West Indies 0

1st Test: India win by an innings and 92 runs

Pitting boxers of different weight categories against each other is never a good idea and when India took on West Indies at the Sir Vivian Richards Stadium in Antigua, the result was a battering.

After calling right at the toss, Kohli did not put a foot wrong in a Test match that would set the tone for the four-Test series. Dhawan silenced the voices doubting his place in the team with 84, but it was Kohli who stole the limelight, scoring his maiden first-class double-century. On a sluggish pitch where batsmen struggled for fluency, Kohli was a class apart, picking off the spinners and pacemen alike with precision and timing. The hallmark of Kohli's innings was his ability to hit good balls to the fence, and West Indies simply did not have the ammunition to counter this.

Kohli enjoyed a 168-run stand with Ashwin, promoted to No. 6 for the first time in his career. Ashwin, who loves batting almost as much as he does picking up wickets, scored 113, his third Test century, all of which had come against West Indies.

With the pressure of the scoreboard weighing heavily, an inexperienced West Indies batting line-up provided feeble resistance. Kraigg Brathwaite was rock solid at the top of the order, applying himself with caution and determination to occupy the crease for almost five hours, reaching 74, but his was largely a lone battle. None of the other batsmen from the top six got going, as Shami, returning to the Test team after more than a year, ran amok. He bowled with ever improving rhythm and pace, seaming the ball both ways to rip out the heart of the West Indies batting. Brathwaite aside, the only bright spot in the innings was the manner in which Shane Dowrich, the young wicketkeeper, handled India's spinners. Using his feet well, deploying

First double-century by an Indian captain away from home: Virat Kohli was a class apart on a sluggish pitch. — *WICB*

supple wrists, Dowrich made an unbeaten 57 at No. 7 as West Indies folded for 243.

Having needed only 90.2 overs to bowl West Indies out, with no bowler overused, Kohli enforced the follow-on. There was an air of resignation in the West Indies camp as spin began to play a part and Ashwin came to the fore. Following his century with a seven-for, Ashwin locked up the match award.

It was India's first win by an innings in the West Indies, and only their fourth outside Asia. In two innings combined, West Indies had fallen 92 short of India's effort.

> Ashwin's 7-83 is the third-best figures for an Indian spinner outside Asia, after Erapalli Prasanna (8-76 v New Zealand, Auckland, 1976) and Anil Kumble (8-141 v Australia, Sydney, 2004).
> With his 113, he became one of only three Indian players – after Vinoo Mankad and Polly Umrigar – to make a century and take at least five wickets in an innings; and the only one to have done so twice.

Venue: Sir Vivian Richards Stadium, Antigua, West Indies, July 21, 2016
Toss: India, who chose to bat
MoM: R Ashwin

India

		R
Murali Vijay	c Brathwaite b Gabriel	7
Shikhar Dhawan	LBW b Bishoo	84
Cheteshwar Pujara	c Brathwaite b Bishoo	16
Virat Kohli*	b Gabriel	200
Ajinkya Rahane	c Bravo b Bishoo	22
R Ashwin	c Gabriel b Brathwaite	113
Wriddhiman Saha †	st † Dowrich b Brathwaite	40
Amit Mishra	c Holder b Brathwaite	53
Mohammed Shami	Not out	17
Extras	(6b,2lb,6nb,0w)	14
Total	(8 wkts dec, 161.5 overs, 3.5 runs per over)	566

Fall of wickets: 1st innings: 14-1 (Murali Vijay, 6.2 ov), 74-2 (Cheteshwar Pujara, 27.4 ov), 179-3 (Shikhar Dhawan, 54.5 ov), 236-4 (Ajinkya Rahane, 67.2 ov), 404-5 (Virat Kohli, 119.2 ov), 475-6 (Wriddhiman Saha, 143.6 ov), 526-7 (R Ashwin, 157.3 ov), 566-8 (Amit Mishra, 161.5 ov)

Did not bat: 1st innings: Ishant Sharma, Umesh Yadav, **2nd innings:** Virat Kohli, Ajinkya

Rahane, Wriddhiman Saha, Amit Mishra, Cheteshwar Pujara, Ishant Sharma, Mohammed Shami, Murali Vijay, R Ashwin, Shikhar Dhawan, Umesh Yadav

Bowling: 1st innings: Shannon Gabriel 21-5-65-2-3.10 (4 nb), Jason Holder 24-4-83-0-3.46 (2 nb), Carlos Brathwaite 25-5-80-0-3.20, Roston Chase 34-3-102-0-3.00, Devendra Bishoo 43-1-163-3-3.79, Kraigg Brathwaite 14.5-1-65-3-4.38

West Indies

		R			*R*
Kraigg Brathwaite	c † Saha b Yadav	74	LBW b Sharma		2
Rajindra Chandrika	c † Saha b Shami	16	c † Saha b Ashwin		31
Devendra Bishoo	st † Saha b Mishra	12	c Pujara b Ashwin		45
Darren Bravo	c † Saha b Shami	11	c Rahane b Yadav		10
Marlon Samuels	c † Saha b Shami	1	b Ashwin		50
Jermaine Blackwood	c Rahane b Shami	0	c Kohli b Ashwin		0
Roston Chase	c Kohli b Yadav	23	c sub (Rahul) b Ashwin		8
Shane Dowrich †	Not out	57	LBW b Mishra		9
Jason Holder*	c Saha b Yadav	36	b Ashwin		16
Carlos Brathwaite	b Yadav	0	Not out		51
Shannon Gabriel	b Mishra	2	b Ashwin		4
Extras	(4b,2lb,3nb,2w)	11	(0b,0lb,5nb,0w)		5
Total	(all out, 90.2 overs, 2.69 runs per over)	243	(all out, 78.0 overs, 2.96 runs per over)		231

Fall of wickets: 1st innings: 30-1 (Rajindra Chandrika, 14.2 ov), 68-2 (Devendra Bishoo, 32.1 ov), 90-3 (Darren Bravo, 42.3 ov), 92-4 (Marlon Samuels, 48.2 ov), 92-5 (Jermaine Blackwood, 48.6 ov), 139-6 (Roston Chase, 65.4 ov), 144-7 (Kraigg Brathwaite, 67.3 ov), 213-8 (Jason Holder, 85.2 ov), 213-9 (Carlos Brathwaite, 85.3 ov), 243-10 (Shannon Gabriel, 90.2 ov).
2nd innings: 2-1 (Kraigg Brathwaite, 0.5 ov), 21-2 (Darren Bravo, 13.5 ov), 88-3 (Rajindra Chandrika, 35.5 ov), 92-4 (Jermaine Blackwood, 37.5 ov), 101-5 (Marlon Samuels, 41.5 ov), 106-6 (Roston Chase, 45.4 ov), 120-7 (Shane Dowrich, 48.6 ov), 132-8 (Jason Holder, 53.2 ov), 227-9 (Devendra Bishoo, 77.3 ov), 231-10 (Shannon Gabriel, 77.6 ov)

Bowling: 1st innings: Ishant Sharma 20-7-44-0-2.20 (3 nb), Umesh Yadav 18-8-41-4-2.28, Mohammed Shami 20-4-66-4-3.30 (2 wd), R Ashwin 17-5-43-0-2.53, Amit Mishra 15.2-4-43-2-2.80
2nd innings: Ishant Sharma 11-2-27-1-2.45 (3 nb), Mohammed Shami 10-3-26-0-2.60 (1 nb), Umesh Yadav 13-4-34-1-2.62, R Ashwin 25-8-83-7-3.32, Amit Mishra 19-3-61-1-3.21 (1 nb)

Umpires: Aleem Dar (Pakistan) and Ian Gould (England)
TV umpire: Gregory Brathwaite (Barbados)
Referee: Ranjan Madugalle (Sri Lanka)

2nd Test: Match drawn

At the storied Sabina Park, a West Indian star was born. Roston Chase, playing only his second Test, showed that all hope was not lost for West Indian cricket with a defiant innings that earned West Indies a hard-fought draw.

In cricket, players often speak about the importance of momentum, and this Test was a classic example of that. After Jason Holder made the curious choice of batting first on a damp pitch, India's bowlers were all over West Indies like a rash. Ishant, bowling fuller than he has for the best part of his career, picked up wickets off successive balls to reduce West Indies to 4 for 2. Shami continued his impressive upward trajectory and West Indies found themselves at 88 for 4 before Ashwin, India's most dangerous bowler, even got on the scoreboard.

When he did get going, however, Ashwin was unstoppable, picking up yet another five-wicket haul as West Indies were bowled out for only 196.

India were impressive with the bat once more, as Rahul, stepping in to open the innings in place of Vijay, who was nursing a sore thumb, made a polished 158. Rahul's strokeplay was pure and his temperament came to the fore as he delicately took apart the West Indian bowling. Ajinkya Rahane added to his bouquet of overseas centuries and India strode to 500 for 9, with plenty of time left in the game. As they considered a declaration, tropical storm Earl swept through Jamaica, and though Kingston was not the epicentre, there was enough precipitation to wash out the final session of the third day.

Roston Chase achieved the double of a century and five wickets in just his second match. – WICB

Declaring overnight, India were right on top of the game, reducing West Indies to 48 for 4 in 15.5 overs before the rain came down once more, causing the best part of the fourth day to be washed out.

On the final day, however, the sun was out, and India took the field realistically expecting to close out the game at the earliest. But, the break in play allowed West Indies to regroup, and how.

Jermaine Blackwood took the attack to the Indian bowlers, favouring the straight boundary against the seamers, clattering two sixes and nine fours in a stunning counter-attack that yielded 63 from only 54 balls. Mood suitably lifted, Chase then put his head down and found an able ally in Shane Dowrich. All of a sudden, the ball was meeting the middle of the bat and the pitch offered little for the bowlers as Chase batted through the whole day for an unbeaten 137. Dowrich might have still been at the crease as well, so assured was his batting, had an umpiring error not cut his innings short on 74, a thick inside edge being ignored as Amit Mishra won an lbw appeal. Where previously wickets had tumbled in heaps, India managed just two scalps from 90 overs as West Indies ended on 388 for 6 and clung on for dear life to secure the draw.

Venue: Sabina Park, Kingston - Jamaica, West Indies, July 30, 2016
Toss: West Indies, who bat
MoM: Roston Chase

West Indies

		R		*R*
Rajindra Chandrika	c Rahul b Shami	5	b Sharma	1
Kraigg Brathwaite	c Pujara b Sharma	1	c Rahul b Mishra	23
Darren Bravo	c Kohli b Sharma	0	c Rahul b Shami	20
Marlon Samuels	c Rahul b Ashwin	37	b Shami	0
Jermaine Blackwood	LBW b Ashwin	62	c Pujara b Ashwin	63
Roston Chase	c Dhawan b Shami	10	Not out	137
Shane Dowrich †	c † Saha b Ashwin	5	LBW b Mishra	74
Jason Holder*	c Rahul b Ashwin	13	Not out	64
Devendra Bishoo	c Dhawan b Ashwin	12		
Miguel Cummins	Not out	24		
Shannon Gabriel	c Kohli b Mishra	15		
Extras	(0b,0lb,10nb,2w)	12	(0b,2lb,3nb,1w)	6
Total	(all out, 52.3 overs, 3.73 runs per over)	196	(6 wkts, 104.0 overs, 3.73 runs per over)	388

Fall of wickets: 1st innings: 4-1 (Kraigg Brathwaite, 2.4 ov), 4-2 (Darren Bravo, 2.5 ov), 7-3 (Rajindra Chandrika, 5.1 ov), 88-4 (Jermaine Blackwood, 25.3 ov), 115-5 (Marlon Samuels, 29.3 ov), 127-6 (Shane Dowrich, 35.1 ov), 131-7 (Roston Chase, 36.4 ov), 151-8 (Devendra Bishoo, 43.3 ov), 158-9 (Jason Holder, 45.5 ov), 196-10 (Shannon Gabriel, 52.3 ov)
2nd innings: 5-1 (Rajindra Chandrika, 2.3 ov), 41-2 (Kraigg Brathwaite, 12.6 ov), 41-3 (Marlon Samuels, 13.5 ov), 48-4 (Darren Bravo, 15.5 ov), 141-5 (Jermaine Blackwood, 33.3 ov), 285-6 (Shane Dowrich, 71.4 ov)
Did not bat (2nd innings): Devendra Bishoo, Shannon Gabriel, Miguel Cummins

Bowling: 1st innings: Ishant Sharma 10-1-53-2-5.30 (7 nb), Mohammed Shami 10-3-23-2-2.30 (1 wd, 1 nb), R Ashwin 16-2-52-5-3.25, Umesh Yadav 6-1-30-0-5.00 (1 wd), Amit Mishra 10.3-3-38-1-3.62 (2 nb)
2nd innings: Ishant Sharma 18-3-56-1-3.11 (2 nb), Mohammed Shami 19-3-82-2-4.32, Amit Mishra 25-6-90-2-3.60 (1 nb), Umesh Yadav 12-2-44-0-3.67 (1 wd), R Ashwin 30-4-114-1-3.80

India

		R
KL Rahul	c † Dowrich b Gabriel	158
Shikhar Dhawan	c Bravo b Chase	27
Cheteshwar Pujara	Run out (Chase)	46
Virat Kohli*	c Chandrika b Chase	44
Ajinkya Rahane	Not out	108
R Ashwin	LBW b Bishoo	3
Wriddhiman Saha †	LBW b Holder	47
Amit Mishra	c Chandrika b Chase	21
Mohammed Shami	b Chase	0
Umesh Yadav	c Holder b Chase	19
Extras	(8b, 3lb, 10nb, 6w)	27
Total	(9 wkts dec, 171.1 overs, 2.92 runs per over)	500

Fall of wickets: 1st innings: 87-1 (Shikhar Dhawan, 19.3 ov), 208-2 (Cheteshwar Pujara, 72.2 ov), 277-3 (KL Rahul, 95.4 ov), 310-4 (Virat Kohli, 103.3 ov), 327-5 (R Ashwin, 112.1 ov), 425-6 (Wriddhiman Saha, 151.4 ov), 458-7 (Amit Mishra, 163.4 ov), 458-8 (Mohammed Shami, 163.5 ov), 500-9 (Umesh Yadav, 171.1 ov)
Did not bat: 1st innings: Ishant Sharma; **2nd innings:** Virat Kohli, Ajinkya Rahane, Wriddhiman Saha, Amit Mishra, Cheteshwar Pujara, Ishant Sharma, KL Rahul, Mohammed Shami, R Ashwin, Shikhar Dhawan, Umesh Yadav

Bowling: 1st innings: Shannon Gabriel 28-8-62-1-2.21 (7 nb), Miguel Cummins 26.4-4-87-0-3.26 (1 wd), Jason Holder 34.2-12-72-1-2.10 (1 wd, 2 nb), Roston Chase 36.1-4-121-5-3.35, Devendra Bishoo 35-5-107-1-3.06, Kraigg Brathwaite 11-0-40-0-3.64

Umpires: Aleem Dar (Pakistan) and Ian Gould (England)
TV umpire: Nigel Duguid
Referee: Ranjan Madugalle (Sri Lanka)

3rd Test: India win by 237 runs

If West Indies were inspired by Roston Chase in Kingston, India were back with a bang in St Lucia. Choosing to leave out Vijay for Rahul, fresh from a century, and picking Rohit Sharma ahead of Cheteshwar Pujara were unusual moves to say the least, but the decision to bring Bhuvneshwar Kumar back from the cold was one that nobody could argue with.

Batting first, India were in more than a spot of bother, reduced to 87 for 4 by some energetic bowling from Shannon Gabriel and Alzarri Joseph, the young debutant. But, once pace gave way to part-time offerings, Ashwin and Wriddhiman Saha began the rescue act. Ashwin was perfectly comfortable against this West Indian attack and Saha curbed his natural strokemaking tendencies. They piled on 213 for the sixth wicket and though India only

R Ashwin's second century of the tour was followed by a sensational burst from Bhuvneshwar Kumar. – *WICB*

managed 353, it was far in excess of what they might have reasonably expected to reach when the top order imploded.

West Indies showed the stomach for battle, reaching 129 for 1 and then 202 for 3. It wasn't until after lunch on the fourth day – the whole of the third day was washed out by rain – that India found their answer. Bhuvneshwar, seemingly out of nowhere, got the ball to swing, and his ability to mix up incoming and outgoing deliveries left the batsmen flummoxed. In a spell that read 23.4-10-33-5, he turned the game on its head, knocking West Indies over for only 225. India then added to their lead of 128, setting West Indies an improbable 346 for victory.

It should not have been beyond West Indies to bat out time, but they put together their worst performance of the series, lasting just 47.3 overs. Every bowler Kohli turned to found success, and only Darren Bravo managed more than a dozen runs, scoring 59.

The 237-run win gave India an unassailable 2-0 lead, and created history. India had never won two Tests on a single Caribbean tour, and the state of disarray of the opposition raised hopes of the hat-trick being completed.

Venue: Darren Sammy National Cricket Stadium, St Lucia, West Indies, August 9, 2016
Toss: West Indies, who chose to bowl
MoM: R Ashwin (India)

India

		R		*R*
KL Rahul	c Brathwaite b Chase	50	c Brathwaite b Cummins	28
Shikhar Dhawan	c † Dowrich b Gabriel	1	LBW b Chase	26

Virat Kohli*	c Bravo b Joseph	3	LBW b Cummins	4
Ajinkya Rahane	b Chase	35	Not out	78
Rohit Sharma	c † Dowrich b Joseph	9	LBW b Cummins	41
R Ashwin	c Blackwood b Cummins	118	c Brathwaite b Cummins	1
Wriddhiman Saha †	c † Dowrich b Joseph	104	c † Dowrich b Cummins	14
Ravindra Jadeja	c † Dowrich b Cummins	6	c Samuels b Cummins	16
Bhuvneshwar Kumar	c Johnson b Gabriel	0		
Mohammed Shami	Not out	0		
Ishant Sharma	c Johnson b Cummins	0		
Extras	(7b,8lb,10nb,2w)	27	(1b,2lb,6nb,0w)	9
Total	(all out, 129.4 overs, 2.72 runs per over)	353	(7 wkts dec, 48.0 overs, 4.52 runs per over)	217

Fall of wickets: 1st innings: 9-1 (Shikhar Dhawan, 2.3 ov), 19-2 (Virat Kohli, 5.3 ov), 77-3 (KL Rahul, 19.3 ov), 87-4 (Rohit Sharma, 25.6 ov), 126-5 (Ajinkya Rahane, 49.3 ov), 339-6 (Wriddhiman Saha, 121.5 ov), 351-7 (Ravindra Jadeja, 127.1 ov), 353-8 (Bhuvneshwar Kumar, 128.6 ov), 353-9 (R Ashwin, 129.1 ov), 353-10 (Ishant Sharma, 129.4 ov)
2nd innings: 49-1 (KL Rahul, 7.3 ov), 58-2 (Virat Kohli, 11.6 ov), 72-3 (Shikhar Dhawan, 16.3 ov), 157-4 (Rohit Sharma, 39.2 ov), 181-5 (Wriddhiman Saha, 43.3 ov), 213-6 (Ravindra Jadeja, 47.2 ov), 217-7 (R Ashwin, 47.6 ov)

Did not bat: 2nd innings: Bhuvneshwar Kumar, Ishant Sharma, Mohammed Shami

Bowling: 1st innings: Shannon Gabriel 23-4-84-2-3.65 (1 wd, 7 nb), Alzarri Joseph 24-6-69-3-2.88, Miguel Cummins 21.4-8-54-3-2.49 (1 wd), Jason Holder 19-7-34-0-1.79 (1 nb), Roston Chase 33-9-70-2-2.12, Kraigg Brathwaite 9-1-27-0-3.00
2nd innings: Shannon Gabriel 3-0-19-0-6.33 (1 nb), Alzarri Joseph 4-0-23-0-5.75 (2 nb), Miguel Cummins 11-1-48-6-4.36 (3 nb), Jason Holder 9-1-50-0-5.56, Roston Chase 11-1-41-1-3.73, Kraigg Brathwaite 10-1-33-0-3.30

West Indies

		R		R
Kraigg Brathwaite	c Saha b Ashwin	64	LBW b Kumar	4
Leon Johnson	Run out (Rahul)	23	c Sharma b Shami	0
Darren Bravo	c Jadeja b Sharma	29	c Sharma b Shami	59
Marlon Samuels	b Kumar	48	b Sharma	12
Jermaine Blackwood	c Kohli b Kumar	20	st Saha b Jadeja	1
Roston Chase	c Rahane b Jadeja	2	b Sharma	10
Shane Dowrich	c Dhawan b Kumar	18	c Kohli b Shami	5
Jason Holder	LBW b Kumar	2	Run out (Ashwin)	1
Alzarri Joseph	c Rahul b Kumar	0	c Shami b Ashwin	0
Miguel Cummins	c Saha b Ashwin	0	Not out	2
Shannon Gabriel	Not out	0	c Kumar b Jadeja	11
Extras	(13b,2lb,2nb,2w)	19	(0b,2lb,1nb,0w)	3

Total	(all out, 103.4 overs, 2.17 runs per over)	225	(all out, 47.3 overs, 2.27 runs per over)	108

Fall of wickets: 1st Innings: 59-1 (Leon Johnson, 23.6 ov), 129-2 (Darren Bravo, 55.4 ov), 135-3 (Kraigg Brathwaite, 58.1 ov), 202-4 (Jermaine Blackwood, 87.2 ov), 203-5 (Marlon Samuels, 89.5 ov), 205-6 (Roston Chase, 90.5 ov), 212-7 (Jason Holder, 93.5 ov), 212-8 (Alzarri Joseph, 95.4 ov), 221-9 (Miguel Cummins, 102.3 ov), 225-10 (Shane Dowrich, 103.4 ov)
2nd Innings: 4-1 (Leon Johnson, 3.5 ov), 4-2 (Kraigg Brathwaite, 4.2 ov), 35-3 (Marlon Samuels, 13.2 ov), 64-4 (Roston Chase, 25.2 ov), 68-5 (Jermaine Blackwood, 29.1 ov), 84-6 (Shane Dowrich, 37.1 ov), 88-7 (Jason Holder, 39.5 ov), 95-8 (Darren Bravo, 41.4 ov), 95-9 (Alzarri Joseph, 42.1 ov), 108-10 (Shannon Gabriel, 47.3 ov)

Bowling: 1st Innings: Bhuvneshwar Kumar 23.4-10-33-5-1.39 (2 wd), Mohammed Shami 17-3-58-0-3.41, R Ashwin 26-7-52-2-2.00, Ishant Sharma 13-2-40-1-3.08 (2 nb), Ravindra Jadeja 24-9-27-1-1.13
2nd Innings: Bhuvneshwar Kumar 12-6-13-1-1.08, Mohammed Shami 11-2-15-3-1.36, Ishant Sharma 7-0-30-2-4.29 (1 nb), R Ashwin 12-2-28-1-2.33, Ravindra Jadeja 5.3-1-20-2-3.64

Umpires: Nigel Llong (England) and Rodney Tucker (Australia)
TV umpires: Gregory Brathwaite (Barbados)
Referee: Ranjan Madugalle (Sri Lanka)

4th Test: Match drawn

The Queen's Park Cricket Club, home to some of West Indies' finest players, was celebrating its 125th birthday along with the fourth India-West Indies Test, but the shambles that followed attracted universal criticism.

After only 22.2 overs on the first day, with West Indies on 62 for 2, the rain that followed the Indian team all around the islands came down with typical tropical intensity. It was quickly clear that there would be no further play on that day.

Fortunately, the second day dawned bright and sunny, raising hopes of a restart. Repeated inspections of the outfield, however, put paid to such thoughts. The drainage at the ground was clogged, leaving the outfield a swamp and the lack of SuperSoppers did not help. In a depressing pattern that would follow for next three days, the umpires inspected, the ground staff toiled, but play was called off on each occasion without a ball being bowled. Following the second day, the Indian team did not even make the trip to the ground, instead settling for telephonic reports.

Soon after the game the International Cricket Council censured the authorities running the ground, calling the outfield for the Test "poor."

Venue: Queen's Park Oval (Trinidad), Trinidad, West Indies, August 18 2016
Toss: West Indies, who chose to bat
MoS: R Ashwin (India)
Series result: India won the four-match series 2-0

West Indies

		R
Kraigg Brathwaite	Not out	32
Leon Johnson	c Sharma b Sharma	9
Darren Bravo	b Ashwin	10
Marlon Samuels	Not out	4
Extras	(0b,6lb,1nb,0w)	7
Total	(2 wkts, 22.0 overs, 2.82 runs per over)	62

Fall of wickets: 1st innings: 31-1 (Leon Johnson, 11.1 ov), 48-2 (Darren Bravo, 14.4 ov)

Did not bat: 1st innings: Jason Holder, Devendra Bishoo, Jermaine Blackwood, Roston Chase, Shane Dowrich, Shannon Gabriel, Miguel Cummins
2nd innings: Jason Holder, Kraigg Brathwaite, Darren Bravo, Devendra Bishoo, Jermaine Blackwood, Leon Johnson, Marlon Samuels, Roston Chase, Shane Dowrich, Shannon Gabriel, Miguel Cummins

Bowling: 1st innings: Bhuvneshwar Kumar 6-1-13-0-2.17, Mohammed Shami 6-2-14-0-2.33 (1 nb), Ishant Sharma 5-3-7-1-1.40, R Ashwin 5-1-22-1-4.40

India, did not bat: Virat Kohli, Ajinkya Rahane, Wriddhiman Saha, Bhuvneshwar Kumar, Cheteshwar Pujara, Ishant Sharma, KL Rahul, Mohammed Shami, Murali Vijay, R Ashwin, Rohit Sharma

Umpires: Nigel Llong (England) and Rodney Tucker (Australia)
TV umpire: Nigel Duguid (Guyana)
Referee: Ranjan Madugalle (Sri Lanka)

T20I (2): West Indies 1 India 0

1st T20I: West Indies win by one run

• A hastily organised series, but the first foray of the Indian team to the US generates goodwill and promises an exciting future. • Put in, Johnson Charles and Evin Lewis, making a comeback because of Chris Gayle's injury, are off to a flier, adding 126 for the opening wicket. • Lewis smashes a 49-ball 100, which includes 32 off a Stuart Binny over. • India are in top gear in their chase of 246, Rahul's unbeaten 51-ball 110 leading the way. • He becomes the third Indian with centuries in three international formats, and his 107-run partnership with MS Dhoni leaves India needing two off the last ball from Dwayne Bravo. • The Indian captain, though, is caught at short third-man as his former Chennai Super Kings team-mate breaks into the 'Champion' dance. *Sidhanta Patnaik*

Central Broward Regional Park Stadium Turf Ground, Lauderhill, August 27: West Indies 245/6 in 20 overs (Evin Lewis 100, Johnson Charles 79; Ravindra Jadeja 2-39, Jasprit

India's finisher is thwarted: Dwayne Bravo allowed MS Dhoni and KL Rahul just six runs off his last over, when eight were needed. – *WICB*

Bumrah 2-47) beat **India** 244/4 in 20 overs (KL Rahul 110*, Rohit Sharma 62; Dwayne Bravo 2-37) by one run. *MoM:* Evin Lewis.

2nd T20I: No result

• Play begins 40 minutes after the scheduled start because of a "technical" delay caused by broadcast issues. • The Indian bowlers rectify their length to put up a dominant show. • Amit Mishra, coming in in place of Binny, produces career-best figures and three other bowlers take two wickets each as West Indies fail to play out their quota of overs. • India start steadily but are able to bat for only two overs before rain stops play. • Wet outfield and bad drainage means West Indies take the series. Brathwaite calls the outfield "unsafe", but Dhoni says he has played in far worse conditions. • Barring complaints about overpriced tickets and focus being on television audiences rather than fans at the ground, the venture seems to have checked enough boxes to keep BCCI interested. *Sidhanta Patnaik*

Central Broward Regional Park Stadium Turf Ground, Lauderhill, August 28: West Indies 143 in 19.4 overs (Johnson Charles 43; Amit Mishra 3-24, R Ashwin 2-11) v **India** 15/0 in 2 overs. No result.

	Tests	T20Is
Best batsman	Virat Kohli (251 runs, 4 matches)	Johnson Charles (122 runs, 2 matches)
Best bowler	R Ashwin (17 wickets, 4 matches)	Jasprit Bumrah (4 wickets, 2 matches)

Series averages

West Indies

Batting

Player	M	I	NO	R	HS	Ave	100s/50s
C Brathwaite	1	2	1	51	51*	51	0/1
R Chase	4	6	1	190	137*	38	1/0
S Dowrich	4	6	1	168	74	33.6	0/2
K Brathwaite	4	7	1	200	74	33.33	0/2
J Holder	4	6	1	132	64*	26.4	0/1
M Cummins	3	3	2	26	24*	26	0/0
M Samuels	4	7	1	152	50	25.33	0/1
J Blackwood	4	6	0	146	63	24.33	0/2
D Bishoo	3	3	0	69	45	23	0/0
D Bravo	4	7	0	139	59	19.85	0/1
R Chandrika	2	4	0	53	31	13.25	0/0
L Johnson	2	3	0	32	23	10.66	0/0
S Gabriel	4	5	1	32	15	8	0/0
A Joseph	1	2	0	0	0	0	0/0

Bowling and Fielding

Player	M	W	R	BBI	BBM	Ave	5wI/10wM	Ct/St
M Cummins	3	9	189	5-33	6-46	21.00	1/0	0/-
A Joseph	1	3	92	2-20	3-47	30.66	0/0	0/-
R Chase	4	8	334	7-83	7-126	41.75	2/0	0/-
S Gabriel	4	5	230	4-66	4-66	46.00	0/0	1/-
K Brathwaite	4	3	165	4-41	4-41	55.00	0/0	5/-

Player								
D Bishoo	3	4	270	2-30	2-30	67.50	0/0	0/-
J Holder	4	1	239	2-43	2-43	239.00	0/0	2/-
C Brathwaite	1	0	80	-	-	-	0/0	0/-
J Blackwood	4	-	-	-	-	-		1/-
D Bravo	4	-	-	-	-	-		3/-
R Chandrika	2	-	-	-	-	-		2/-
S Dowrich	4	-	-	-	-	-		6/1
L Johnson	2	-	-	-	-	-		2/-
M Samuels	4	-	-	-	-	-		1/-

India

Batting

Player	M	I	NO	R	HS	Ave	100s/50s
A Rahane	4	4	2	243	108*	121.5	1/1
KL Rahul	3	3	0	236	158	78.66	1/1
V Kohli	4	4	0	251	200	62.75	1/0
R Ashwin	4	4	0	235	118	58.75	2/0
W Saha	4	4	0	205	104	51.25	1/0
A Mishra	2	2	0	74	53	37	0/1
S Dhawan	3	4	0	138	84	34.5	0/1
C Pujara	3	2	0	62	46	31	0/0
R Sharma	2	2	0	50	41	25	0/0
U Yadav	2	1	0	19	19	19	0/0
M Shami	4	3	2	17	17*	17	0/0
R Jadeja	1	2	0	22	16	11	0/0
M Vijay	2	1	0	7	7	7	0/0
B Kumar	2	1	0	0	0	0	0/0
I Sharma	4	1	0	0	0	0	0/0

Bowling and Fielding

Player	M	W	R	BBI	BBM	Ave	5wI/10wM	Ct/St
B Kumar	2	6	59	5-33	6-46	9.83	1/0	1/-
R Jadeja	1	3	47	2-20	3-47	15.66	0/0	1/-
R Ashwin	4	17	394	7-83	7-126	23.17	2/0	0/-
M Shami	4	11	284	4-66	4-92	25.81	0/0	1/-
U Yadav	2	5	149	4-41	5-75	29.80	0/0	0/-
I Sharma	4	8	257	2-30	3-70	32.12	0/0	0/-
A Mishra	2	6	232	2-43	3-104	38.66	0/0	0/-
S Dhawan	3	-	-	-	-	-	-	3/-
V Kohli	4	-	-	-	-	-	-	6/-
C Pujara	3	-	-	-	-	-	-	3/-
A Rahane	4	-	-	-	-	-	-	3/-
KL Rahul	3	-	-	-	-	-	-	6/-
W Saha	4	-	-	-	-	-	-	9/2
R Sharma	2	-	-	-	-	-	-	3/-
M Vijay	2	-	-	-	-	-	-	0/-

Squads

West Indies: Jason Holder (capt), Kraigg Brathwaite, Roston Chase, Marlon Samuels, Darren Bravo, Alzarri Joseph, Jermaine Blackwood, Miguel Cummins, Shane Dowrich (wk), Rajendra Chandrika, Devendra Bishoo, Shannon Gabriel, Carlos Brathwaite, Leon Johnson, Shai Hope.

India: Virat Kohli (capt), Ajinkya Rahane, M Vijay, KL Rahul, Shikhar Dhawan, Cheteshwar Pujara, R Ashwin, Wriddhiman Saha (wk), Ravindra Jadeja, Amit Mishra, Rohit Sharma, Umesh Yadav, Mohammed Shami, Bhuvneshwar Kumar, Ishant Sharma, Stuart Binny, Shardul Thakur.

Anand Vasu (@anandvasu) is joint editor-in-chief of Wisden India.

India's overall Test averages from October 1, 2015, to September 21, 2016

Batting

Player	M	I	NO	R	HS	Ave	100s/50s
KL Rahul	3	3	0	236	158	78.66	1/1
A Rahane	8	10	3	509	127	72.71	3/1
V Kohli	8	10	0	451	200	45.1	1/1
R Ashwin	8	9	1	336	118	42	2/1
C Pujara	7	8	0	264	77	33	0/1
W Saha	8	10	1	288	104	32	1/0
M Vijay	6	8	1	217	75	31	0/1
S Dhawan	7	11	1	288	84	28.8	0/1
R Jadeja	5	7	0	131	38	18.71	0/0
M Shami	4	3	2	17	17*	17	0/0
A Mishra	4	6	0	99	53	16.5	0/1
R Sharma	4	6	0	76	41	12.66	0/0
U Yadav	4	4	1	35	19	11.66	0/0
V Aaron	2	2	1	1	1*	1	0/0
I Sharma	7	4	2	1	1*	0.5	0/0
B Kumar	2	1	0	0	0	0	0/0
S Binny	1	-	-	-	-	-	0/0

Bowling and fielding

Player	M	W	R	BBI	BBM	Ave	5wI/10wM	Ct/St
B Kumar	2	6	59	5-33	6-46	9.83	1/0	1/-
R Jadeja	5	26	296	5-21	8-76	11.38	2/0	6/-
R Ashwin	8	48	739	7-66	12-98	15.39	6/1	1/-
U Yadav	4	10	209	4-41	5-41	20.9	0/0	0/-
M Shami	4	11	284	4-66	4-92	25.81	0/0	1/-
A Mishra	4	13	353	3-51	4-60	27.15	0/0	0/-
V Aaron	2	2	72	1-3	1-21	36.00	0/0	0/-
I Sharma	7	9	372	2-30	3-70	41.33	0/0	1/-

S Binny	1	0	1	-	-	-	0/0	1/-
S Dhawan	7	0	9	-	-	-	0/0	3/-
V Kohli	8	0	0	-	-	-	0/0	9/-
C Pujara	7	0	2	-	-	-	0/0	6/-
M Vijay	6	0	2	-	-	-	0/0	1/-
A Rahane	8	-	-	-	-	-	-	13/-
KL Rahul	3	-	-	-	-	-	-	6/-
W Saha	8	-	-	-	-	-	-	14/4
R Sharma	4	-	-	-	-	-	-	4/-

MULTI-NATION TOURNAMENT

ASIA CUP

Bangladesh's rising T20 stock

SHAMYA DASGUPTA

This year, the Asia Cup was rendered a T20 tournament. The reason: Context. The World T20 was up next, so why pitter-patter for 100 overs in Mirpur?

Over the past few years, cricket administrators as well as analysts have been looking for context in every competition, whether bilateral or multilateral. Context, they say, will attract more viewers, on the field and in front of TV sets, while raising the level of performance. Tough to argue with that. But the 2016 Asia Cup showcased both the best and the worst of what context could mean for a multi-team event.

More than once during the tournament, players stressed on the importance of looking beyond. It's not about winning the Asia Cup, they said in different ways. It's about trying to find the best combination, get form-checks done and that sort of thing for the bigger prize. So far not so good.

The Sher-e-Bangla National Stadium in Mirpur, on the outskirts of Dhaka, provided another reason to quibble: sluggish pitches with a decent covering of grass. Run scoring was tough, and pacers, whether medium or Mohammad Amir, had plenty of fun.

Balance between bat and ball redressed then? But in T20 cricket? Shouldn't it be about 160-plus runs in 20 overs and last-ball finishes? Only five times did the team totals cross 140, and 160 only once. And only thrice did matches go into the last over. It made for fascinating viewing, mind you, because teams struggled to get going at the early stages almost each time, the ball moved around nicely, and the lack of maximums gave the games a more competitive feel. But, then again, 'context': It was a T20 event as preparation for the World T20 – were the pitches right? Probably not.

As for the smaller-picture stories, oh, there were plenty, none more than the return of Amir. But there was also the establishment of the old-and-new firm of Ashish Nehra and Jasprit Bumrah, Bangladesh's emergence as a T20 force – at least at home – and the fact that Sri Lanka and Pakistan severely underperformed.

Not to forget UAE, who were in it for a bit of exposure really. They had come through the qualifying rounds knowing that they had no place in the World T20, having failed to make the cut for it. More than once, UAE created ripples in the opposition ranks, especially against Sri Lanka and Pakistan, and Amjad Javed, the captain who bowls medium-pace, and Ahmed Raza,

Losing wasn't an option: Virat Kohli was in top form and the Nehra-Bumrah duo worked in tandem as India lifted the Asia Cup title. — *AFP/Getty Images*

the left-arm spinner, were very, very good. But the Asia Cup wasn't for them.

Yes, it was at home, and yes, the pitches were perfect for their medium and fast-medium bowlers, but that Bangladesh managed to make the final was impressive. Mustafizur Rahman and Taskin Ahmed turned it on, and Al-Amin Hossain picked up wickets almost each time, as did the spin duo of Shakib Al Hasan and Mahmudullah, who also made a name for himself as a very calm customer under pressure, knocking off runs at the death almost as a habit. It came apart for them in the end against India, but it wasn't for lack of will, intent or skill.

The most exciting passage of play, across the 11 games of the tournament, was India's chase of a meagre 84 against Pakistan. In the space of four balls, Amir had fired out Rohit Sharma and Ajinkya Rahane, both beaten for pace and swing, and soon after, he had the measure of Suresh Raina, swing again doing the trick, helped by Raina's ineptitude. It was heady stuff – not very T20, but still! It took Virat Kohli to put on a masterclass in chasing and Amir running out of overs for India to cruise home. But Amir was back, and how!

Sri Lanka, meanwhile, lost Lasith Malinga after a four-wicket burst in their first match – against UAE, the only one they won – and lost their way altogether after that, finishing nowhere on the points table. Their crash since the exit of Kumar Sangakkara and Mahela Jayawardene has been distressing, and there seem to be few signs of recovery.

"India losing the final is a bigger headline than India winning a final," said MS Dhoni before the final against Bangladesh. "You're supposed to win."

He didn't say it, but in the subcontinent, with Bangladesh as opposition, losing in the final was not an option. Thankfully for Dhoni & co., it worked out fine. Not unexpected, considering their run of form. Just before the Asia Cup, after poor performances against South Africa, India won five of six games (losing only once to Sri Lanka, then beating them twice and blanking Australia in Australia). They ended the Asia Cup with ten wins in 11 games.

Everything wasn't perfect, but Kohli – 153 runs in four innings at 76.5 – was. And that helped the team mask the little cracks, like the form of Shikhar Dhawan and Yuvraj Singh. Both of them were smashing it by the end, a tribute to the team's faith in and persistence with them. The bowling, meanwhile, was on autopilot, everyone doing what they were supposed to, with Bumrah doing a bit more, at the start and at the death.

Dhaka might not be everyone's favourite holiday destination, but if cricket, or any sport, exists chiefly for the spectators, there is no crowd more fanatical than the Dhaka folk. There are the star fans – the Tigers – and there are the rest, as passionate, but not as ridiculously attired. Not always is it pleasant, especially when tickets run out, but there are about as many people outside the ground as there are inside when there's an international game on, and not only if Bangladesh are playing, though that helps. The atmosphere has to be seen to be believed.

This was the third straight Asia Cup in Bangladesh and, really, that's where it should stay. Whether 50-50 or 20-20, it's fair to say that nowhere else will the tournament be received as warmly. For that reason alone, the Asia Cup was a success.

Best batsman: Sabbir Rahman (Bangladesh) (176 runs, 5 matches)
Best bowler: Al-Amin Hossain (Bangladesh) (11 wickets, 5 matches)

Qualifying group

United Arab Emirates beat Afghanistan by 16 runs
Khan Shaheb Osman Ali Stadium, Fatullah, February 19: United Arab Emirates 176/4 in 20 overs (Rohan Mustafa 77, Mohammad Shahzad 25*; Rashid Khan 3-25) beat **Afghanistan** 160 in 19.5 overs (Karim Sadiq 72, Mohammad Nabi 23; Rohan Mustafa 3-19, Farhan Ahmed 2-28) by 16 runs.

Oman beat Hong Kong by five runs
Khan Shaheb Osman Ali Stadium, Fatullah, February 19: Oman 180/5 in 20 overs (Jatinder Singh 42, Amir Ali 32*; Nadeem Ahmed 3-27) beat **Hong Kong** 175/7 in 20 overs (Babar Hayat 122) by five runs.

Afghanistan beat Oman by three wickets
Khan Shaheb Osman Ali Stadium, Fatullah, February 20: Oman 165/4 in 20 overs (Adnan Ilyas 54, Zeeshan Maqsood 52; Gulbadin Naib 2-24) lost to **Afghanistan** 168/7 in 19.3 overs (Noor Ali Zadran 63, Asghar Stanikzai 34; Mehran Khan 3-18, Bilal Khan 3-33) by three wickets.

United Arab Emirates beat Hong Kong by six wickets
Khan Shaheb Osman Ali Stadium, Fatullah, February 21: Hong Kong 146/7 in 20 overs (Babar Hayat 54, Mark Chapman 29; Mohammad Naveed 3-14, Amjad Javed 2-21) lost to

United Arab Emirates 147/4 in 18.3 overs (Mohammad Shahzad 52, Muhammad Usman 41) by six wickets.

Afghanistan beat Hong Kong by 66 runs

Sher Bangla National Stadium, Mirpur, February 22: Afghanistan 178/7 in 20 overs (Najibullah Zadran 60*, Asghar Stanikzai 49; Aizaz Khan 3-38) beat **Hong Kong** 112 in 17.1 overs (Anshuman Rath 41, Kinchit Shah 29; Mohammad Nabi 4-17, Rashid Khan 2-10) by 66 runs.

United Arab Emirates beat Oman by 71 runs

Sher Bangla National Stadium, Mirpur, February 22: United Arab Emirates 172/6 in 20 overs (Muhammad Kaleem 50, Muhammad Usman 46; Aamir Kaleem 4-36) beat **Oman** 101/8 in 20 overs (Zeeshan Maqsood 46; Mohammad Naveed 2-14, Qadeer Ahmed 2-25) by 71 runs.

Qualifying group points table

Teams	M	W	L	T	N/R	Pts	NRR
United Arab Emirates	3	3	0	0	0	6	1.678
Afghanistan	3	2	1	0	0	4	0.954
Oman	3	1	2	0	0	2	-1.222
Hong Kong	3	0	3	0	0	0	-1.416

United Arab Emirates qualified for the main round

India beat Bangladesh by 45 runs

• Shikhar Dhawan and Virat Kohli fall quickly after India are put in, and Suresh Raina follows soon after. • Rohit Sharma finds the right partner in Yuvraj Singh, who hangs in there as Rohit steps it up. • Yuvraj falls after a 55-run stand but Hardik Pandya joins Rohit and smashes an 18-ball 31 to push India ahead. • Rohit adds a brilliant 83 in 55 balls with seven fours and three sixes. • Ashish Nehra and Jasprit Bumrah strike early as Bangladesh struggle to get going. • There is resistance, and Sabbir Rahman looks good with a 32-ball 44, but Nehra stops Bangladesh short.

Sher-e-Bangla National Stadium, Mirpur, February 24: India 166/6 in 20 overs (Rohit Sharma 83, Hardik Pandya 31; Al-Amin Hossain 3-37) beat **Bangladesh** 121/7 in 20 overs (Sabbir Rahman 44; Ashish Nehra 3-23) by 45 runs. *MoM:* Rohit Sharma.

Sri Lanka beat United Arab Emirates by 14 runs

• The UAE medium-pacers can't break through, but keep things reasonably tight after asking Sri Lanka to bat. • On a tricky pitch, Dinesh Chandimal and Tillakaratne Dilshan put up 68 runs in 9.1 overs. • Chandimal scores 50 in 39 balls, but Amjad Javed leads the way in reining them in. • Lasith Malinga and Nuwan Kulasekara rock UAE early with a clutch of wickets to have them 16 for 4. • There is no let up for UAE even though Swapnil Patil

Mohammad Amir's (top) bowling against India was one of the finest moments of the tournament, while Sabbir Rahman led Bangladesh's charge. — *AFP/Getty Images*

is stubborn. • The target is, however, within striking distance when Malinga comes back to finish off the match.

Sher-e-Bangla National Stadium, Mirpur, February 25: Sri Lanka 129/8 in 20 overs (Dinesh Chandimal 50, Tillakaratne Dilshan 27; Amjad Javed 3-25, Mohammad Shahzad 2-27) beat **United Arab Emirates** 115/9 in 20 overs (Swapnil Patel 37, Lasith Malinga 4-26, Nuwan Kulasekara 3-10) by 14 runs. *MoM:* Lasith Malinga.

Bangladesh beat United Arab Emirates by 51 runs

• Having put bangladesh in, UAE's pacers find the going tough against Mohammad Mithun and Soumya Sarkar. • Mohammad Shahzad sends back Sarkar after a 46-run stand, and wickets fall quickly after that as UAE fight back. • Mahmudullah props up the innings, but the miserly Ahmed Raza keeps Bangladesh in check. • Al-Amin Hossain, Mashrafe Mortaza, Mustafizur Rahman and Taskin Ahmed, the Bangladesh pacers, are on the money. • The pacers reduce UAE to 34 for 5 and then 46 for 7 soon after. • Shakib Al Hasan and Mahmudullah, the spinners, are also among the wickets as UAE are bowled out for just 82.

Sher-e-Bangla National Stadium, Mirpur, February 26: Bangladesh 133/8 in 20 overs (Mohammad Mithun 47, Mahmudullah 36*; Mohammad Naveed 2-12, Amjad Javed 2-34) beat **United Arab Emirates** 82 in 17.4 overs (Muhammad Usman 30; Mahmudullah 2-5, Mashrafe Mortaza 2-12) by 51 runs. *MoM:* Mahmudullah.

India beat Pakistan by five wickets

• Nehra and Bumrah strike early as Pakistan are down at 32 for 3 in the powerplay after being put in. • The resistance, very little of it, takes its time coming. • Sarfraz Ahmed looks good, but with Hardik Pandya leading the way, Pakistan are shot out for 83. • The target appears larger than it is when Mohammad Amir swings it around at the start, leaving India at 8 for 3. • Kohli and Yuvraj get together, see Amir out, and build a stand on singles and the occasional four. • Kohli masters the chase, scoring 49 in 51 balls before falling with the target just eight runs away. • Yuvraj (14 not out in 32 balls) hangs in there as MS Dhoni walks in and finishes it off with a four off Wahab Riaz.

Sher-e-Bangla National Stadium, Mirpur, February 27: Pakistan 83 in 17.3 overs (Sarfraz Ahmed 25; Hardik Pandya 3-8, Ravindra Jadeja 2-11) lost to **India** 85/5 in 15.3 overs (Virat Kohli 49; Mohammad Amir 3-18, Mohammad Sami 2-16) by five wickets. *MoM:* Virat Kohli.

Bangladesh beat Sri Lanka by 23 runs

• Angelo Mathews and Kulasekara strike early, leaving Bangladesh at 2 for 2. • Mushfiqur Rahim doesn't last long, but Sabbir and Shakib add 82. • Sabbir's 54-ball 80, Shakib's 32 in 34 balls and Mahmudullah's unbeaten 23 in 12 prop up Bangladesh. • Sri Lanka lose Dilshan early in the chase, but get a 56-run stand between Chandimal and Shehan Jayasuriya. • Once Mahmudullah and Shakib send them back in consecutive overs, however, the chase goes off the rails. • Al-Amin Hossain picks up three wickets as his side earn their first T20I win against Sri Lanka.

Sher-e-Bangla National Stadium, Mirpur, February 28: Bangladesh 147/7 in 20 overs (Sabbir Rahman 80, Shakib Al Hasan 32; Dushmantha Chameera 3-30) beat **Sri Lanka** 124/8 in 20 overs (Dinesh Chandimal 37, Shehan Jayasuriya 26; Al-Amin Hossain 3-34, Shakib 2-21) by 23 runs. *MoM:* Sabbir Rahman.

Pakistan beat United Arab Emirates by seven wickets

• With this their 100th T20I, Pakistan have played more matches in the format than any other nation. • UAE are left floundering at 12 for 3 after the three Mohammads – Sami, Amir and Irfan – strike early. • Shaiman Anwar, quiet in the tournament prior to this game, shores up the innings. • Mohammad Usman and Javed score quickly towards the end to lift UAE. • Javed creates a flutter when he sends back Sharjeel Khan, Mohammad Hafeez and Khurram Manzoor early. • Once he runs through his quota, though, it is comfortable going for Umar Akmal and Shoaib Malik in an unbeaten 114-run stand, a record for the fourth wicket at the time.

Sher-e-Bangla National Stadium, Mirpur, February 29: United Arab Emirates 129/6 in 20 overs (Shaiman Anwar 46, Amjad Javed 27*; Mohammad Amir 2-6, Mohammad Irfan 2-30) lost to **Pakistan** 131/3 in 18.4 overs (Shoaib Malik 63, Umar Akmal 50; A Javed 3-36) by seven wickets. *MoM:* Shoaib Malik.

India beat Sri Lanka by five wickets

• Nehra and Bumrah are at it again after India send Sri Lanka in. • A number of Sri Lankans get starts, but the Indian bowlers fire as one to keep their team ahead. • Kapugedara does the early running, while Thisara Perera and Kulasekara hit out at the end. • Kulasekara returns to send back the Indian openers, but Kohli and Raina take control of the chase. • After Raina falls, Yuvraj smashes the ball around in an entertaining 18-ball 35 with three sixes and three fours. • Kohli is again instrumental in pulling off the chase, staying till the end as India go through.

Sher-e-Bangla National Stadium, Mirpur, March 1: Sri Lanka 138/9 in 20 overs (Chamara Kapugedera 30, Milinda Siriwardana 22; R Ashwin 2-26, Hardik Pandya 2-26) lost to **India** 142/5 in 19.2 overs (Virat Kohli 56, Yuvraj Singh 35; Nuwan Kulasekara 2-21) by five wickets. *MoM:* Virat Kohli.

Bangladesh beat Pakistan by five wickets

• In keeping with the trend in the series, Pakistan start badly, slipping to 18 for 3 in the fifth over after opting to bat. • Akmal doesn't last long, but Sarfraz and Malik string together a stand of 70. • Sarfraz completes his half-century and remains unbeaten even as Al-Amin strikes. • Sarkar takes charge of the chase, stroking his way to a run-a-ball 48 to keep Bangladesh ahead of the rate. • Wickets fall on either side of his effort, and when he departs in the 14th over, it still needs work to take his team home. • Mahmudullah provids the finishing touches, scoring 22 not out in 15 balls to seal Bangladesh's place in the final.

Sher-e-Bangla National Stadium, Mirpur, March 2: Pakistan 129/7 in 20 overs (Sarfraz Ahmed 58, Shoaib Malik 41; Al-Amin Hossain 3-25, Arafat Sunny 2-35) lost to **Bangladesh** 131/5 in 19.1 overs (Soumya Sarkar 48, Mahmudullah 22*; Mohammad Amir 2-26) by five wickets. *MoM:* Soumya Sarkar.

India beat United Arab Emirates by nine wickets

• India, already in the final, make a number of changes, but still reduce UAE to 25 for 3 early on. • Anwar makes an impact, with Rohan Mustafa (11 in 22 balls) the only other double-digiter. • Bhuvneshwar Kumar leads the way as all the Indian bowlers pick up wickets. • Rohit provides the early impetus, scoring 39 in 28 balls in an opening stand of 43 with Dhawan. • Dhawan, going through a lean patch, stays till the end, scoring a 20-ball 16 with three hits to the fence. • Yuvraj Singh, who comes in at No. 3, hits an unbeaten 14-ball 25 to take India to their biggest T20I win in terms of balls remaining.

Shere Bangla National Stadium, Mirpur, March 3: United Arab Emirates 81/9 in 20 overs (Shaiman Anwar 43; Bhuvneshwar Kumar 2-8) lost to **India** 82/1 in 10.1 overs (Rohit Sharma 39, Yuvraj Singh 25*) by nine wickets. *MoM:* Rohit Sharma.

Pakistan beat Sri Lanka by six wickets

• This is a zero-sum game, with India and Bangladesh already in the final. • Sri Lanka do well, with Chandimal (58 in 49 balls) and Tillakaratne Dilshan putting together 110 runs. • Dilshan stays till the end, unbeaten on a 56-ball 75. • Pakistan start well too, with Sharjeel, Hafeez and Sarfraz keeping them abreast of the rate. • Once they depart, Akmal takes charge, scoring 48 in 37 balls, with four fours and two sixes. •Akmal falls with scores level, but Pakistan go over the line without any fuss.

Sher-e-Bangla National Stadium, Mirpur, March 4: Sri Lanka 150/4 in 20 overs (Tillakaratne Dilshan 75*, Dinesh Chandimal 58; Mohammad Irfan 2-18) lost to **Pakistan** 151/4 in 19.2 overs (Umar Akmal 48, Sarfraz Ahmed 38) by six wickets. *MoM:* Umar Akmal.

Points Table

Teams	M	W	L	T	N/R	Pts	NRR
India	4	4	0	0	0	8	2.020
Bangladesh	4	3	1	0	0	6	0.458
Pakistan	4	2	2	0	0	4	-0.296
Sri Lanka	4	1	3	0	0	2	-0.293
United Arab Emirates	4	0	4	0	0	0	-1.813

Final: India beat Bangladesh by eight wickets

• India win a crucial toss and break through early courtesy Nehra and Bumrah. • Sabbir (32 not out in 29 balls) and Shakib (21 in 16 balls) keep Bangladesh going, albeit slowly. • Mahmudullah comes in and slams an unbeaten 33 in 13 balls in the 15-overs-a-side match. • Rohit falls early in the chase, but Dhawan and Kohli put up 94 for the second wicket. • Taskin gets Dhawan at

60 in 44 balls, but by then India are at the doorstep of victory. • Kohli, with an unbeaten 41 in 28 balls, and Dhoni (20 not out in 6 balls with two sixes and a four) take India to the title.

Sher-e-Bangla National Stadium, Mirpur, March 6: Bangladesh 120/5 in 15 overs (Mahmudullah 33*, Sabbir Rahman 32*) lost to **India** 122/2 in 13.5 overs (Shikhar Dhawan 60, Virat Kohli 41*) by eight wickets. *MoM:* Shikhar Dhawan. *MoS:* Sabbir Rahman.

ICC WORLD T20

Kingdom and coronation

TIM WIGMORE

As an Englishman preparing to explore India properly for the first time – before the World Twenty20 2016 I had been only to Bangalore, for two nights, and Goa – you are inundated with advice. Immerse yourself in it. Don't apply Western cultural norms. Make sure you see the Taj Mahal. And, whatever else you do, for god's sake, don't eat any prawns. No one ever says: Visit Nagpur.

But that was where my month in India began; I spent the first ten days in Nagpur, the calm before the hurly-burly of near-daily driving or flying between cities began. Besides the scorching heat, Nagpur is almost the antithesis of what you are told India will be. It is relatively tranquil, and, well, dull. I only ventured away from the hotel or the ground a couple of times, although that was more than most journalists and players mustered. I expected something unforgettable, for good or bad. I was left with neither – but I did have a hard-won local mobile and SIM card. After several attempts to purchase one, which failed on account of not being a resident of the state, I was eventually allowed to do so using a taxi driver's address. That was about as dramatic as the city got. If Nagpur has an English twin, perhaps it is Milton Keynes: orderly enough, but with no real soul, nothing invigorating about it.

Still, I had nothing to complain about compared to the Scottish fans I encountered a few days later. While their match with Zimbabwe had begun, they were marooned outside the stadium in Nagpur, unable to get in. They had been promised complimentary tickets by Cricket Scotland's team manager, but the tickets, left in a hotel, had been picked up by another group. Having come all this way, the Scots were not about to be deterred from seeing their team in action; fortunately for them, virtually the entire stadium was empty, and tickets to the game could be bought for as little as Rs 100. The trouble was they could only be bought at the old stadium, some 18km away. So while the World T20 played out with 40,000 empty seats inside – projecting a terrible image of the tournament to broadcasters and fans around the world – fans desperate to get in were actively locked out. A few overs and many fraught phone calls later, the coterie of Scots were reunited with the manager, who helped them get in.

This embarrassing incident was just an example of the BCCI's appalling organisation of the tournament.

One hundred days before the event in India, we knew the venues that were being used in the 2019 World Cup, just not those for the 2016 WT20.

And then there was the fiasco over the India-Pakistan match. To award the match to Dharamsala was a decision that touched the confines of lunacy. It

"See the Taj Mahal, they said": England cricketers took some time off from training for the World T20 2016 to do a spot of touristing. – *ICC*

might have a picturesque stadium, but Dharamsala is too remote, too small and too isolated to host a match of such magnitude and security concerns. This was a triumph for politicking over common sense.

The game was eventually moved at a week's notice, and Eden Gardens managed the match superbly. By then, though, the tournament had already been undermined by awarding Dharamsala, which had only hosted three previous internationals, World T20 matches. The first stage was utterly devalued, ruined by persistent rain and the perverse lack of a reserve day. The elements eliminated the Netherlands, who had come through an arduous eight-game qualification campaign the year before. The Dutch played just one game – and that an agonising eight-run defeat to Bangladesh. The sight of Peter Borren, the captain, in his own words "emotional and pretty devastated" and resembling a dishevelled puppy, embodied the ICC's myopic treatment of the associate world.

There was a sharp divergence in how Indian journalists reacted to these fiascos. To this outsider there was an iron law among the Indian media: The younger they were, the more jingoistic and the less willing they were to criticise the BCCI.

I was surprised by how many journalists took to loudly applauding each hard-run two from Virat Kohli during India's tense victory over Australia. At one point, after MS Dhoni had professed himself "average" in comparison to Kohli in a press conference, a fawning journalist rushed after Dhoni, assuring him, "You are not average".

Did this show the impact of Narendra Modi's tub-thumping brand of Hindu nationalism upon India? Or was it, in fact, nothing to do with high politics at all, but simply a young generation aware of India's increasing importance in the world, who considered the orthodoxies of press box etiquette archaic?

***

A few weeks into the tournament, a friend from England emailed to say that it felt "like the most important cricket tournament in years".

I think he was right. The World T20 was a homecoming – the T20 World Cup finally being taken to the land of the IPL, the country that had done more than any other to popularise T20. It was also a point of no return: a tournament that both embodied, and sped along, the inexorable rise of T20.

It was another riposte, too, to those who still sneer at the quality of the sport, considering it a game for unrefined sloggers. It is now manifestly clear that T20 has as many intricacies as Test cricket.

That was showcased by a happy by-product of the BCCI's politicking. Normally the World T20 is played across three, perhaps four, grounds. Here it was played across seven. From stodgy Nagpur to batting nirvana Mumbai, each pitch had a distinct character, showcasing the variety of tactics that can be used to win T20 matches and compelling teams to shuffle their squads.

I visited all but one: Dharamsala. For a freelance journalist, it was a good one to miss. No one wants to pay someone to write about rain, no matter how stunning the backdrop. Besides, the other six – Kolkata, by turns magical and grimly penurious; Delhi, nearly a ghost city during the holi festival; Mumbai, all-consuming and suffocatingly hot; Nagpur, with my elusive local mobile; Bangalore, eminently liveable but a city made for residents not tourists; and Mohali, which I will remember most for one of the worst views of any press box in international cricket – offered plenty, even if there was precious little time to see as much of India as I'd hoped.

The cricket was all-consuming. And the more of it I saw, the more it became clear that the format is as distinct from Tests as rugby sevens is from rugby union.

"T20 cricket is a completely different sport," R Ashwin declared in an interview to *ESPNcricinfo* shortly after the tournament. "I basically think that six well-constructed bad balls could be the way to go forward in T20 cricket... Probably the best ball is not any more the best ball now. Probably a short, wide and shit ball could be the best ball to bowl from now on."

While Ashwin had an underwhelming tournament, his words were not just frustration, but also emblematic of how high-skilled Test bowlers were struggling to adapt to T20 cricket. Dale Steyn, the world's top Test bowler, was even dropped by South Africa.

All the while, a part-time PE teacher was showing the virtues of specialising in T20. Samuel Badree arrived in India as a prematurely balding 35-year-old, an antidote to the razzmatazz of the West Indies side. He left the tour-

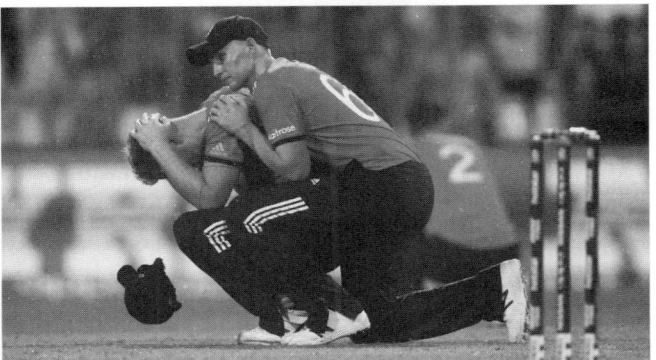

6,6,6,6 - the mark of the best: Carlos Brathwaite's four final-over sixes made history, while Ben Stokes, the bowler, was left unconsolable. — *Getty Images*

nament having confirmed his reputation as not merely the preeminent T20I bowler today, but the best there has ever been.

He has done it all without ever being selected for the West Indies' Test or ODI teams; indeed, Badree's last first-class game was in 2009. He is a leg-spinner made for the T20 age, delivering the ball with accuracy, pace and bounce. Even his lack of spin is arguably an advantage in T20, rendering it harder for batsmen to open up angles.

More than anything, Badree is a player who has mastered his role. In each of his first 28 T20Is, Badree opened the bowling, normally bowling three overs during the powerplay. He did just that in the final, dismissing Jason Roy with a slider and taking 2 for 16 from four frugal overs: a distillation of all Badree's T20 qualities.

By the day's end, this admirable effort had been completely usurped by Carlos Brathwaite's remarkable heist, plundering four consecutive sixes off Ben Stokes. The blows did far more than seal the title for West Indies: They also vindicated their approach to T20 batting, derided as "short of brains" by Mark Nicholas before the tournament.

In a sense Nicholas had a point: The West Indies approach was in defiance of conventional wisdom about T20 batting. They batted with contempt for the notion of minimising dot balls, knowing that they could make up for them by pummelling the ball over the ropes.

In their magnificent run chase against India in Mumbai, where they waltzed to 193, their batsmen played 50 dot balls, 23 more than India allowed, and ran just 44 between the wickets, while India ran 95. But it did not matter: 146 runs came in boundaries, including 11 sixes leaving Caribbean bats like fireworks released into the night sky. By the evening's end, disconsolate Indian fans slouched against the fences separating the supporters from the outfield, unable to quite comprehend what they had witnessed.

The West Indies approach seemed diametrically opposed to that of Joe Root and Virat Kohli, classical Test batsmen who built their innings upon minimising dot balls: Root faced only four in 44 balls against South Africa. Kohli, caressing the ball into gaps and harrying between the wickets, scored four twos in five balls during India's run chase against Australia, only breaking up the sequence by flicking a delivery through the long-on boundary. If Ashwin's words hinted at uncertainty over how bowlers would respond in T20, the future of T20 batting seemed clear: to marry the certainties of Kohli's game with the power of Brathwaite and Co. And Kohli soon took it upon himself to do just that, hitting four centuries during the IPL.

***

A month after the tournament, an ICC press release praised India's hosting of the event. Seldom has one press release so neatly encapsulated where cricket's balance of power lies.

Yet, more significant was another ICC press release later, confirming that the World T20 would return in 2018. So great was interest in this tournament – there were 750 million views for online videos featuring match footage of the tournament, compared to 250 million during the 2015 50-over World Cup; over 80 million Indians watched their matches with Australia, Pakistan and West Indies on television, and many millions more online; and the closing stages of the final attracted more viewers in the UK than any cricket game ever on pay TV – that to leave a four-year hiatus until the next edition would be madness. Especially considering that the tournament generated $250 million.

This was the real legacy of the 2016 World T20: a tournament so popular it compelled the ICC to recognise the shape of the future.

Tim Wigmore (@timwig) is a freelance cricket writer and co-author of Second XI: Cricket in its Outposts.

First round

Group A

Bangladesh beat the Netherlands by eight runs

• In form and much improved, Bangladesh take on the Netherlands in their opening World T20 game barely days after the Asia Cup final. • Put in, Bangladesh are off to a solid start as Tamim Iqbal ends a T20I run drought to score a measured half-century. • The Netherlands strike at regular intervals but Tamim remains unbeaten on a 58-ball 83. • The Netherlands lose Wesley Barresi early but Stephan Myburg and Peter Borren keep them in the hunt. • Shakib Al Hasan takes two wickets to derail the chase in the middle overs. • The Netherlands need 42 from four overs, but with only one six in their innings and terrific death bowling by Mashrafe Mortaza (1 for 14) and Taskin Ahmed, their challenge is curtailed. *Karthik Lakshmanan*

HPCA Stadium, Dharamsala, March 9: Bangladesh 153/7 in 20 overs (Tamim Iqbal 83*; Timm Van Der Gugten 3-21, Paul Van Meekeren 2-17) beat **Netherlands** 145/7 in 20 overs (Peter Borren 30, Stephan Myburgh 29; Al-Amin Hossain 2-24, Shakib Al Hassan 2-29) by eight runs. *MoM:* Tamim Iqbal.

Oman beat Ireland by two wickets

• It is a historic occasion for Oman, who are making their first appearance in an ICC event; it ends with more history made as they pull off a stunning win over Ireland. • Ireland begin well with their top order getting starts, taking them to 112 for 2 in 15 overs. • Munees Ansari fashions a fightback with three wickets, and is backed up by disciplined bowling. • Zeeshan Maqsood and Khawar Ali play with freedom, adding 69 for the opening wicket by the

Oman make history: The Associate nation have their first win in their first appearance at a top-flight ICC event. – *ICC*

ninth over of the chase. • Oman's inexperience shows in the middle, as they slip to 90 for 5 in 14. • Amir Ali, the No. 7, making his debut at 37, launches a blazing counterattack, his 17-ball 32 sealing a thrilling win and triggering manic celebrations.
Karthik Lakshmanan

HPCA Stadium, Dharamsala, March 9: Ireland 154/5 in 20 overs (Gary Wilson 38, Paul Stirling 29; Munis Ansari 3-37) lost to **Oman** 157/8 in 19.4 overs (Zeeshan Maqsood 38, Khawar Ali 34; Andy McBrine 2-15, Kevin O'Brien 2-25) by two wickets. *MoM:* Amir Ali.

Netherlands v Oman: Match abandoned

• The Netherlands need a win to stay alive in the competition. • However, the game is abandoned after the toss without a ball being bowled due to incessant rain. • The Netherlands are knocked out having played just one match, and Borren, their captain, is devastated: "We've won a lot of games (over the year), and an eight-run loss to Bangladesh, and we're gone. It's hard to take."
Karthik Lakshmanan

HPCA Stadium, Dharamsala, March 11: Netherlands v **Oman**. Match abandoned with a toss.

Bangladesh v Ireland: No result

• The format of the tournament is called into question by another Associate, as Ireland become the second team to be knocked out after just one game and a washout. • The skies clear enough for Bangladesh to start well courtesy Tamim after they are put in. • However, it starts to pour – and doesn't stop – with them 94 for 2 after eight overs. • "That is why the ICC has the tournament in two phases, because they will lose a lot of revenue if one of the 'top nations' go out to any of us in the early rounds," fumes William Porterfield, the Irish captain. *Karthik Lakshmanan*

HPCA Stadium, Dharamsala, March 11: Bangladesh 94/2 in 8 overs (Tamim Iqbal 47, Soumya Sarkar 20) v **Ireland**. No result.

The Netherlands beat Ireland by 12 runs

• The Netherlands and Ireland face off in a dead rubber, their last match of the World T20. • The match is reduced to six overs a side due to rain that comes after Ireland opt to field. • George Dockrell strikes thrice in his two overs but Myburgh ensures Ireland will need to go at ten runs an over to win. • It proves too tall an ask as Paul van Meekeren runs through the Irish batting line-up. • Paul Stirling, who started well with a seven-ball 15, is the only one to get into double digits. • Ireland end their campaign well short and the Netherlands sign off with a consolation win. *Karthik Lakshmanan*

HPCA Stadium, Dharamsala, March 13: Netherlands 59/5 in 6 overs (Stephan Myburgh 27; George Dockrell 3-7) beat **Ireland** 47/7 in 6 overs (Paul Van Meekeren 4-11, Roelof van der Merwe 2-3) by 12 runs. *MoM:* Paul van Meekeren.

Bangladesh beat Oman by 54 runs (DLS method)

• Bangladesh and Oman know the winner will qualify for the Super 10 stage. • Oman field in overcast conditions, but Tamim continues his good form. • He takes time to settle down before smashing his maiden T20I ton (103 not out off 63) and the first by a Bangladesh batsman. • The 181 target is revised to 120 from 12 overs after a rain interruption. • When play resumes, Shakib runs through Oman's inexperienced line-up for his best T20I haul. • Another spell of rain leaves them needing 75 off 22, which proves too steep, and Bangladesh make it to the next stage.

Karthik Lakshmanan

HPCA Stadium, Dharamsala, March 13: Bangladesh 180/2 in 20 overs (Tamim Iqbal 103*, Sabbir Rahman 44) beat **Oman** 65/9 in 12 overs (Jatinder Singh 25; Shakib Al Hasan 4-15) by 54 runs (DLS method). *MoM:* Tamim Iqbal.

Tamim Iqbal led the scoring for Bangladesh. – *ICC*

Group A Points Table

Teams	M	W	L	T	N/R	Pts	NRR
Bangladesh	3	2	0	0	1	5	1.938
Netherlands	3	1	1	0	1	3	0.154
Oman	3	1	1	0	1	3	-1.521
Ireland	3	0	2	0	1	1	-0.685

Group B

Zimbabwe beat Hong Kong by 14 runs

• Hong Kong mark a low-key start to the tournament before a small crowd by electing to chase on a turgid wicket. • Ryan Campbell makes Hong Kong debut at 44, 13 years after his two ODIs for Australia, and becomes the oldest T20I player. • Hamilton Masakadza launches Zimbabwe with crisp hitting down the ground off the wayward Haseeb Amjad, only to fall run-out because both his bat and foot are in the air. • Vusi Sibanda holds Zimbabwe together, but they need three huge straight sixes from Elton Chigumbura to get respectable. • Hong Kong crawl to 48 for 2 in ten overs, Campbell contributing a meek nine from 19. • Jamie Atkinson plunders a fifty and Tanwir Afzal adds late-order pyrotechnics, but, after Chapman is caught off a full toss, Zimbabwe are in control. *Tim Wigmore*

VCA Stadium, Jamtha, Nagpur, March 8: Zimbabwe 158/8 in 20 overs (Vusi Sibanda 59, Elton Chigumbura 30*; Tanwir Afzal 2-19, Aizaz Khan 2-33) beat **Hong Kong** 144/6 in 12 overs (Jamie Atkinson 53, T Afzal 31*; Donald Tiripano 2-27, Tendai Chatara 2-28) by 14 runs. *MoM:* Vusi Sibanda.

Afghanistan beat Scotland by 14 runs

• Mohammad Shahzad narrowly avoids a golden duck; it was "a bit hot" to make a century, he says later. • Mark Watt impresses with his left-arm spin, delivered from unusually wide of the crease, in his first match in an ICC global event. • A measured half-century from Asghar Stanikzai and three wides in the final over help Afghanistan. • Scotland's openers bristle with intent: Kyle Coetzer hits a sumptuous six over cover off Amir Hamza, while George Munsey freely hits the ball over the infield and is ruthless against anything on his legs. • When their stand of 84 in 8.5 overs ends, the new batsmen struggle: just six boundaries in 15 overs of spin. • Needing 63 from 44, Matt Machan and Preston Mommsen score just one boundary in 50 balls between them. *Tim Wigmore*

VCA Stadium, Jamtha, Nagpur, March 8: **Afghanistan** 170/5 in 20 overs (Mohammad Shahzad 61, Asghar Stanikzai 55*) beat **Scotland** 156/5 in 12 overs (George Munsey 41, Kyle Coetzer 40; Rashid Khan 2-28) by 14 runs. *MoM:* Mohammad Shahzad.

Zimbabwe beat Scotland by 11 runs

• Masakadza again throws away a sprightly start. Some Scottish fans miss the early wickets, unable to buy tickets at the gate. • Zimbabwe's innings has a disjointed feel, but they are again indebted to Sean Williams. • Cutters and yorkers restrict Zimbabwe to 19 from the final three. • Munsey falls in the opening over, stumped after hitting two reverse sweeps for four and Scotland's top order seem gripped by panic. • From 43 for 5, Mommsen joins Richie Berrington in an alliance of 51 in 6.3. • When Mommsen goes, leaving Scotland needing 55 in 34 balls, Josh Davey picks up the baton, hitting two straight sixes, but the death bowling is too accurate. *Tim Wigmore*

VCA Stadium, Jamtha, Nagpur, March 10: Zimbabwe 147/7 in 20 overs (Sean Williams 53, Elton Chigumbura 20; Mark Watt 2-21, Alasdair Evans 2-30) beat **Scotland** 136 in 19.4 overs (Richie Berrington 36, Preston Mommsen 31; Wellington Masakadza 4-28, Donald Tiripano 2-20) by 11 runs. *MoM:* Wellington Masakadza.

Afghanistan beat Hong Kong by six wickets

• Campbell flourishes briefly, carving five boundaries through the off side before top-edging a delivery onto his helmet and onto the stumps. • Only three boundaries follow in the rest of the innings as Hong Kong are becalmed by Mohammad Nabi and his flat off-spin. • A target of 117 never threatens and Shahzad leads Afghanistan's waltz to victory. • When Shahzad thrashes a delivery to the hands of long off, it gives Campbell, who kept wicket in his two ODIs for Australia, the first wicket of his international career. • Afghanistan shuffle their batting in preparation for sterner challenges. *Tim Wigmore*

VCA Stadium, Jamtha, Nagpur, March 10: Hong Kong 116/6 in 20 overs (Anshuman Rath 28*, Ryan Campbell 27; Mohammad Nabi 4-20) lost to **Afghanistan** 119/4 in 18 overs (Mohammad Shahzad 41, Noor Ali Zadran 35; Ryan Campbell 2-28) by six wickets. *MoM:* Mohammad Nabi.

Afghanistan beat Zimbabwe by 59 runs

• Shahzad begins with customary swagger, thumping 40 from 23. • He falls reverse-sweeping Williams and a collapse of 4 for 14 ensues. • Nabi and Samiullah Shenwari add 98 in 10.4, moving seamlessly from unobtrusive consolidation to acceleration. • Afghanistan heave 77 from the final five, the best by an Associate nation at the death. • After Hamid Hassan castles Masakadza with a trademark yorker, Zimbabwe never threaten. • Rashid Khan shows off his googly in taking three wickets, and qualification ensured, Afghanistan's players embrace coach Inzamam-ul-Haq. *Tim Wigmore*

VCA Stadium, Jamtha, Nagpur, March 12: Afghanistan 186/6 in 20 overs (Mohammad Nabi 52, Samiullah Shenwari 43; Tinashe Panyangara 3-32) beat **Zimbabwe** 127 in 19.4 overs (Rashid Khan 3-11, Hamid Hassan 2-11) by 59 runs. *MoM:* Mohammad Nabi.

The wait ends: Scotland got their first victory in a global ICC event when they defeated Hong Kong. – *ICC*

Scotland beat Hong Kong by eight wickets (DLS method)

• Campbell slashes Gavin Main's first delivery to third man, his much-anticipated international comeback ending with 36 in three innings. • Scotland's spin trio records 4 for 66, conceding only three boundaries, two of which are consecutive sixes by Nizakat Khan in the 19th over. • Mark Chapman oozes assurance as he holds Hong Kong together, though 15 of his 41 are dot balls. • Rain looms as the largest threat to Scotland's inaugural win in an ICC global event, after 19 consecutive defeats over 16 years. • The top four all come good, and Scotland's moment of history is sealed with a six, when Machan slog-sweeps Nadeem Ahmed over midwicket. *Tim Wigmore*

VCA Stadium, Jamtha, Nagpur, March 12: Hong Kong 127/7 in 20 overs (Mark Chapman 40, Anshuman Rath 21; Matt Machan 2-26) lost to **Scotland** 78/2 in 8 overs (Matthew Cross 22, Kyle Coetzer 20*) by eight wickets (DLS method). *MoM:* Matt Machan.

Group B Points Table

Teams	M	W	L	T	N/R	Pts	NRR
Afghanistan	3	3	0	0	0	6	1.540
Zimbabwe	3	2	1	0	0	4	-0.567
Scotland	3	1	2	0	0	2	-0.132
Hong Kong	3	0	3	0	0	0	-1.017

Bangladesh and Afghanistan qualified for Super 10s

Super 10

Group 1

West Indies beat England by six wickets

• Jason Roy and Alex Hales add 37 from just 27 balls to give England a fast start. • Suliemann Benn concedes just nine in his first two overs to stem the tide. • Eoin Morgan, Jos Buttler and Ben Stokes all score at better than nine an over to build on Joe Root's 36-ball 48. • Marlon Samuels strokes 37 from 27 as West Indies make 55 in the powerplay. • Chris Jordan is the only bowler to escape serious punishment – four overs for 24 – as Chris Gayle cuts loose after Samuels's dismissal. • Gayle hits five fours and 11 sixes, taking just 27 balls for his half-century, and only a further 20 for the fastest World T20 hundred. *Dileep Premachandran*

Wankhede Stadium, Mumbai, March 16: England 182/6 in 20 overs (Joe Root 48, Jos Buttler 30; Andre Russell 2-36, Dwayne Bravo 2-41) lost to **West Indies** 183/4 in 18.1 overs (Chris Gayle 100*, Marlon Samuels 37) by six wickets. *MoM:* Chris Gayle.

Sri Lanka beat Afghanistan by six wickets

• Afghanistan batsmen find runs hard to come by, with the spinners proving difficult to handle. • They are 51 for 4 in 11 overs when Stanikzai shifts gears with consecutive sixes in the 13th over and adds 61 for the fifth wicket with Shenwari. • Thisara Perera has Stanikzai dismissed in the 19th for his third wicket, but Afghanistan have accumulated a defendable total. • Dinesh Chandimal and Tillakaratne Dilshan start the chase well, putting on 41 without being troubled by the pacers. • Spin brings Afghanistan right back in it as Nabi and Rashid restrict runs and run through the middle order. • Dilshan works the gaps for his half-century and adds 42 with Angelo Mathews to get the defending champions off to a winning start. *Manoj Narayan*

Eden Gardens, Kolkata, March 17: Afghanistan 153/7 in 20 overs (Asghar Stanikzai 62, Samiullah Shenwari 31; Thisara Perera 3-33, Rangana Herath 2-24) lost to **Sri Lanka** 155/4 in 18.5 overs (Tillakaratne Dilshan 83*, Angelo Mathews 21*) by six wickets. *MoM:* Tillakaratne Dilshan.

England beat South Africa by two wickets

• After taking just two from David Willey's opening over, South Africa finish the powerplay with 83. • Quentin de Kock leads the way with a 21-ball 50, and there are sprightly half-centuries for Hashim Amla (25 balls) and JP Duminy (26 balls) as well. • Moeen Ali and Adil Rashid have 3 for 69 from their eight overs, even as the pace bowlers take fearful punishment. • The Durban-born Roy smashes 43 from 16 balls, taking England past 50 in just 17 balls. • Root and Buttler build on the whopping 89 that England make in the powerplay with a 75-run partnership off just 36 balls. • Despite Imran

England's top-order pyrotechnics: Joe Root 's 44-ball 83 against South Africa was studded with four sixes. — *Getty Images*

Tahir's 1 for 28, Root's 44-ball 83, studded with four sixes, proves decisive as England chase down 230 with two balls to spare. *Dileep Premachandran*

Wankhede Stadium, Mumbai, March 18: South Africa 229/4 in 20 overs (Hashim Amla 58, JP Duminy 54*; Moeen Ali 2-34) lost to **England** 230/8 in 19.4 overs (Joe Root 83, Jason Roy 43; Kyle Abbott 3-41, Kagiso Rabada 2-50) by two wickets. *MoM:* Joe Root.

South Africa beat Afghanistan by 37 runs
• De Kock and du Plessis cruise on a wicket that adds to Mumbai's reputation as the best surface in the tournament. • Afghanistan restrict South Africa to 138 for 3 after 16 overs, a total that seems under par, before AB de Villiers takes command, heaving 29 in a Rashid over, including two sixes apiece straight and over midwicket. • Shahzad, undeterred by a chase of 210, hoicks

his second ball over third man for six, and then three times harrumphs Kyle Abbott over the leg-side boundary before late-cutting the last ball for four. • After Shahzad's pyrotechnics are ended by a Chris Morris yorker, Gulbadin Naib and Zadran help Afghanistan pass 100 in the tenth over, but the new batsmen cannot maintain the assault. • South Africa's pace heavy attack is vindicated: they deliver 16 overs of pace against Afghanistan's six. • Even in defeat Afghanistan make a record for an Associate against a top nine Test side.
Tim Wigmore

Wankhede Stadium, Mumbai, March 20: South Africa 209/5 in 20 overs (AB de Villiers 64, Quinton de Kock 45) beat **Afghanistan** 172 in 20 overs (Mohammad Shahzad 44, Gulbadin Naib 26; Chris Morris 4-27, Imran Tahir 2-24) by 37 runs. *MoM*: Chris Morris.

West Indies beat Sri Lanka by seven wickets

• Carlos Brathwaite accounts for Dilshan, while Chandimal is run out in a poor Sri Lankan start. • Samuel Badree strikes thrice on a turning pitch, reducing Sri Lanka to 47 for 5 in 8.4 overs. • Big hits from Perera (40 in 29 balls) saves Sri Lanka some pain despite Dwayne Bravo's late wickets. • Gayle, injured while fielding, doesn't bat, leaving his 'home' crowd in Bangalore disappointed. • Andre Fletcher, opening in his place, bosses the Sri Lankans, taking Mathews for a four and a six first over. • Spin troubles the other batsmen, with Johnson Charles, Samuels and Denesh Ramdin falling cheaply. • Gayle is set to come in with 51 needed from 43 balls, but the umpires are having none of it; Andre Russell and Fletcher make sure he is not missed.
Shamya Dasgupta

M Chinnaswamy Stadium, Bangalore, March 20: Sri Lanka 122/9 in 20 overs (Thisara Perera 40, Angelo Mathews 20; Samuel Badree 3-12, Dwayne Bravo 2-20) lost to **West Indies** 127/3 in 18.2 overs (Andre Fletcher 84*, Andre Russell 20*; Milinda Siriwardana 2-33) by seven wickets. *MoM*: Andre Fletcher.

England beat Afghanistan by 15 runs

• Afghanistan choke the flow of runs with spin from the first over. • Morgan and James Vince keep England going, pushing the score to 41 for 1. • Nabi scalps them off consecutive balls and Root is run out off the final ball of the sixth over to leave England reeling at 42 for 4. • Moeen and Willey add 57 in an unbroken eighth-wicket stand to rescue England from the depths of 50 for 5. • Willey strikes twice early in Afghanistan's innings and gets good support at the other end. • At 39 for 5, the chase is as good as over, but Shafiqullah fights at No. 9 to reduce the margin of defeat.
Anand Vasu

Feroz Shah Kotla, Delhi, March 23: England 142/7 in 20 overs (Moeen Ali 41*, James Vince 22; Mohammad Nabi 2-17, Rashid Khan 2-17) beat **Afghanistan** 127/9 in 20 overs (Shafiqullah 35*, Samiullah Shenwari 22; Adil Rashid 2-18, David Willey 2-23) by 15 runs. *MoM*: Moeen Ali.

West Indies beat South Africa by three wickets

• Expecting a de Villiers and Gayle show, the stadium is packed; it is the highest attendance for a non-India match at the World T20. • South Africa's batsmen don't adapt to the sluggish pitch quickly enough. • De Villiers's cheap dismissal buries hopes of an above-average total, with only de Kock mastering the slowness. • There is no Gayle show either: the Jamaican ends the match with more success with ball than bat. • Samuels keeps one end tight, as the West Indies batsmen build small partnerships that are crucial in the context of a low chase. • Brathwaite wins the battle of the young guns against Kagiso Rabada, a final-over six sealing a semi-final spot for West Indies. *Saurabh Somani*

VCA Stadium, Jamtha, Nagpur, March 25: South Africa 122/8 in 20 overs (Quinton de Kock 47, David Wiese 28; Chris Gayle 2-17, Dwayne Bravo 2-20) lost to **West Indies** 123/7 in 19.4 overs (Marlon Samuels 43, Johnson Charles 32; Imran Tahir 2-13) by three wickets. *MoM:* Marlon Samuels.

England beat Sri Lanka by 10 runs

• In a must-win match, England begin with caution, putting only 65 on the board in the first ten overs. • With wickets in hand, a fierce assault is launched, Buttler hitting eight fours and two sixes in a 37-ball 66 that pushes England to 171 for 4. • Jordan and Willey cut into the top order, reducing Sri Lanka to 15 for 4. • Mathews, almost unable to run because of a hamstring injury, keeps his end up, striking towering sixes just often enough to keep Sri Lanka in the game. • He and Chamara Kapugedera add 80 for the fifth wicket leaving Sri Lanka needing 22 off the last two overs and 15 off the final one. • Mathews swings hard but just cannot connect cleanly enough to add to his five sixes and is disconsolate as Sri Lanka are knocked out. *Anand Vasu*

Feroz Shah Kotla, Delhi, March 26: England 171/4 in 20 overs (Jos Buttler 66*, Jason Roy 42; Jeffrey Vandersay 2-26) beat **Sri Lanka** 161/8 in 20 overs (Angelo Mathews 73*, Chamara Kapugedera 30; Chris Jordan 4-28, David Willey 2-26) by 10 runs. *MoM:* Jos Buttler.

Afghanistan beat West Indies by six runs

• Shahzad begins the first international match between these two sides with customary flair before losing the contest against Badree. • Afghanistan are stifled in the middle overs, until Najibullah provides vital impetus at the end. • Nabi's dismissal is the high point of the fielding, with Darren Sammy palming a hard hit in the covers for Samuels to complete the catch at mid-off. • West Indies begin aggressively, but are tied down by Afghanistan's spinners. • Najibullah puts his body on the line to catch Brathwaite at the midwicket boundary in the final over, swinging the game. • Gayle, rested for this match, sportingly comes out to join an ecstatic Associate side in the Champion dance after a historic win against the table toppers. *Saurabh Somani*

Flair and fire: Celebrations were manic when an inspired Afghanistan upset the table-toppers in Nagpur. — *Getty Images*

VCA Stadium, Jamtha, Nagpur, March 27: Afghanistan 123/7 in 20 overs (Najibullah Zadran 48*, Mohammad Shahzad 24; Samuel Badree 3-14, Andre Russell 2-23) beat **West Indies** 117/8 in 20 overs (Dwayne Bravo 28, Johnson Charles 22; Mohammad Nabi 2-26, Rashid Khan 2-26) by 6 runs. *MoM:* Najibullah Zadran.

South Africa beat Sri Lanka by eight wickets

• Chandimal and Dilshan make a breezy start until Aaron Phangiso's intervention: he removes Chandimal with a non-turning delivery and then Thirimanne, first ball, with one that turns in through the gate. • Sri Lanka's batting frailties are again exposed, not helped by a becalmed Dilshan taking 30 balls over his last 19 runs; 21 of his 40 balls are dots. • Abbott ends his strong tournament with another display oozing vim, and Sri Lanka suffer the ignominy of being bowled out. • Despite Dilshan running out de Kock with a direct hit from point, South Africa saunter towards their target, with Amla typically nonchalant. • Over 16,000 have come to the dead rubber largely to watch de Villiers bat and chants of 'AB! AB!' are a common refrain. He hits a six over long on to secure South Africa's facile win. *Tim Wigmore*

Feroz Shah Kotla, Delhi, March 28: Sri Lanka 120 in 19.3 overs (Tillakaratne Dilshan 36, Dinesh Chandimal 21; Kyle Abbott 2-14, Farhaan Behardien 2-15) lost to **South Africa** 122/2 in 17.4 overs (Hashim Amla 56*, Faf du Plessis 31) by eight wickets. *MoM:* Aaron Phangiso.

Group 1 Points Table

Teams	M	W	L	T	N/R	Pts	NRR
West Indies	4	3	1	0	0	6	0.359
England	4	3	1	0	0	6	0.145
South Africa	4	2	2	0	0	4	0.651
Sri Lanka	4	1	3	0	0	2	-0.461
Afghanistan	4	1	3	0	0	2	-0.715

West Indies and England qualified for the semifinals

Group 2

New Zealand beat India by 47 runs

• Kane Williamson wins an important toss and promptly opts to bat on a square turner as New Zealand leave out Trent Boult and Tim Southee to bolster spin resources. • An eventful first over from R Ashwin produces two sixes and Martin Guptill's scalp, showcasing New Zealand's desire to attack from the get-go. • India claw back, even as Luke Ronchi takes 15 off the last over from Ashish Nehra. • A tricky run-chase with the ball turning, jumping and scooting through becomes gargantuan once Mitchell Santner strikes twice in his first over to leave India floundering at 12 for 3. • Ish Sodhi has Virat Kohli caught at slip with his first ball, a ripping leg break. • The spin trio of Santner, Sodhi and Nathan McCullum accounts for nine wickets as India capitulate to their second-lowest T20I score. *R Kaushik*

VCA Stadium, Jamtha, Nagpur, March 15: New Zealand 126/7 in 20 overs (Corey Anderson 34, Luke Ronchi 21*) beat **India** 79 in 18.1 overs (MS Dhoni 30, Virat Kohli 23; Mitchell Santner 4-11, Ish Sodhi 3-18) by 47 runs. *MoM:* Mitchell Santner.

Pakistan beat Bangladesh by 55 runs

• Mohammad Hafeez and Ahmed Shehzad get Pakistan off to a ballistic start, their second-wicket stand of 95 aided by loose bowling. • Shehzad holes out attempting a helicopter, but Shahid Afridi, having promoted himself, continues pillaging bowlers with typically unorthodox bating. • Afridi picks 18 runs off a Mortaza over and has reached a 19-ball 49 when Sarkar rides the boundary line to pull off a stunning catch. • Mohammad Amir runs through Sarkar early in the Bangladesh chase, but Tamim and Sabbir steady the innings. • Afridi chips in with the ball, dismissing both batsmen in successive overs. • Shakib scores an unbeaten 40-ball 50, but the rest of the line-up struggles to mount a challenge. *Manoj Narayan*

Eden Gardens, Kolkata, March 16: Pakistan 201/5 in 20 overs (Mohammad Hafeez 64, Ahmed Shehzad 52; Taskin Ahmed 2-32, Arafat Sunny 2-34) beat **Bangladesh** 146/6 in 20

Horses for courses: Picking Mitchell Santner and Mitchell McClenaghan proved to be inspired choices as New Zealand won their first two games. — *Getty Images*

overs (Shakib Al Hasan 50*, Sabbir Rahman 25; Shahid Afridi 2-27, Mohammad Amir 2-27) by 55 runs. *MoM:* Shahid Afridi.

New Zealand beat Australia by eight runs

• Australia boost their spin strength with Ashton Agar and Adam Zampa, but both bowl only one over each, Agar immediately taken for three sixes. • New Zealand's opening stand of 61 in 7.1 overs is their best of the match as batsmen fail to build on starts, but their total would be tricky on a slowing surface. • Usman Khawaja is timing the ball well, but Australia miss the power of Aaron Finch at the top. • Mitchell McClenaghan, drafted in for the game, and Santner make inroads, while New Zealand's slower bowlers stem the flow of runs. • From 42 for no loss after five overs, Australia are 66 for 4 in a little after ten. • Agar, sent in before James Faulkner, can't get the big hits, and is one of two wickets for McClenaghan in the 19th, before Corey Anderson takes two more in the last to deny their trans-Tasman rivals.

HPCA Stadium, Dharamsala, March 18: New Zealand 142/8 in 20 overs (Martin Guptill 39, Grant Elliot 27; James Faulkner 2-18, Glenn Maxwell 2-18) beat **Australia** 134/9 in 20 overs (Usman Khawaja 38, Mitchell Marsh 24; Mitchell McClenaghan 3-17, Corey Anderson 2-29) by 8 runs. *MoM:* Mitchell McClenaghan.

India beat Pakistan by six wickets

• Sharp showers leading up to the scheduled start render the clash – which has been relocated from Dharamsala – an 18-over affair. • Both teams fortify

Record maintained: Virat Kohli acknowledged Sachin Tendulkar, who was in the crowd, when he got to his fifty against Pakistan in Eden Gardens. — *Getty Images*

pace resources, but once play begins and Pakistan are stuck in, it is obvious that both have misread the surface. • Despite a steady start, Pakistan fail to find any momentum, with India's spinners finding purchase from the damp strip. • Amir and Mohammad Sami make 118 for 5 appear a mountain, triggering a top-order collapse to leave India on 23 for 3. • Kohli steps up to the plate with the first of many memorable knocks, first steadying the ship in Yuvraj Singh's company and then stepping into overdrive. • He steers India home as the hosts maintain World Cup hegemony over Pakistan. *R Kaushik*

Eden Gardens, Kolkata, March 19: Pakistan 118/5 in 18 overs (Shoaib Malik 26, Ahmed Shehzad 25) lost to **India** 119/4 in 15.5 overs (Virat Kohli 55*, Yuvraj Singh 24; Mohammad Sami 2-17) by six wickets. *MoM:* Virat Kohli.

Australia beat Bangladesh by three wickets

• After Soumya Sarkar thrashes a rank Shane Watson delivery straight to point, Bangladesh start lamely. • Adam Zampa claims a wicket with a long-hop second ball, and then delivers a spell of wicket-to-wicket leg-spin with canny variations, like the flipper that accounts for Shuvagata Hom. • The nimble Shakib gives Bangladesh impetus, but it falls to Mahmudullah to lift Bangladesh over 150, pulling his fifth ball emphatically for six and then carving four boundaries through backward point. • Khawaja clips his fourth ball for a straight six and looks serene in compiling his maiden T20I half-century. • Australia end the powerplay on 51 for no loss, and even wondrous cutters from Mustafizur cannot deny them a routine victory. • Mustafizur manages the rare feat of bowling Steve Smith around his legs, flummoxes Mitchell Marsh with a delivery that holds up in the pitch and has Watson dropped, but it isn't enough. *Tim Wigmore*

M Chinnaswamy Stadium, Bangalore, March 21: Bangladesh 156/5 in 20 overs (Mahmudullah 49*, Shakib Al Hasan 33; Adam Zampa 3-23, Shane Watson 2-31) lost to **Australia** 157/7 in 18.3 overs (Usman Khawaja 58, Glenn Maxwell 26; Shakib Al Hasan 3-27, Mustafizur Rahman 2-30) by three wickets. *MoM:* Adam Zampa.

New Zealand beat Pakistan by 22 runs

• With a semi-final spot one win away, New Zealand start strongly through Guptill, who prefers the long-on boundary for three sixes during his 48-ball knock. • His partnerships of 62 with Williamson (first-wicket) and 53 with Corey Anderson (third-wicket) push New Zealand ahead. • Swift bowling changes by Afridi bring Pakistan back as they concede only three fours and two sixes in the last five overs. • New Zealand bowlers target the wrong length and Sharjeel Khan makes them pay with a brisk 47. • Williamson introduces Sodhi, the legspinner playing his first game in the state where he was born, in the eighth over and that is the turning point. • Pakistan fail to find the boundary in the last 31 balls of their innings, and the batting unit's inability is criticised by Waqar Younis, the coach, in the post-match press conference. *Sidhanta Patnaik*

PCA IS Bindra Stadium, Mohali, Chandigarh, March 22: New Zealand 180/5 in 20 overs (Martin Guptill 80, Ross Taylor 36*; Mohammad Sami 2-23, Shahid Afridi 2-40) beat **Pakistan** 158/5 in 20 overs (Sharjeel Khan 47, Ahmed Shehzad 30; Adam Milne 2-26, Mitchell Santner 2-29) by 22 runs. *MoM:* Martin Guptill.

India beat Bangladesh by one run

• Put in on a third successive sluggish surface, India make their best start through a 42-run opening stand between Shikhar Dhawan and Rohit Sharma. • Kohli and the enterprising Suresh Raina build on that with a 50-run association for the third wicket. • Once the ball gets softer, however, stroke-making becomes difficult and India struggle for impetus, adding just 34 in the last five overs. • Ashwin cleans up Mohammad Mithun but Bangladesh kick on through Tamim, Sabbir and Shakib. • With 11 needed off the final over from Hardik Pandya, Bangladesh bring the equation down to two off three following consecutive boundaries from Mushfiqur. • Mushfiqur and Mahmudullah are caught in the deep off successive deliveries going for glory, and Mustafizur is outsprinted and run out by MS Dhoni, as India fashion a narrow win out of nowhere. *R Kaushik*

M Chinnaswamy Stadium, Bangalore, March 23: India 146/7 in 20 overs (Suresh Raina 30, Virat Kohli 24; Mustafizur Rahman 2-34, Al-Amin Hossain 2-37) beat **Bangladesh** 145/9 in 20 overs (Tamim Iqbal 35, Sabbir Rahman 26; R Ashwin 2-20, Ravindra Jadeja 2-22) by one run. *MoM:* R Ashwin.

Manic last over: Bangladesh brought the equation down to two required off three deliveries before they went into meltdown. — *Getty Images*

Australia beat Pakistan by 21 runs

• A day before the must-win clash for both teams, Watson makes it official that the World T20 is his last international assignment. • The announcement possibly frees him up as, batting at No.6 for only the third time in his career, he hits four fours and three sixes in his 21-ball knock. • The fourth-wicket stand of 62 between Smith and Glenn Maxwell, and the unbroken fifth-wicket association of 74 between Smith and Watson nullifies the good work of Wahab Riaz and Imad Wasim. • Regular wickets hamper Pakistan's progress in the chase. • Afridi, in what could be his last innings for Pakistan, hits a six off Zampa before being stumped as Pakistan slide further. • James Faulkner, Player of the Match in the World Cup final, rises to the occasion again with career-best figures, keeping Watson in international cricket for at least one more night. *Sidhanta Patnaik*

PCA IS Bindra Stadium, Mohali, March 23: Australia 193/4 in 20 overs (Steven Smith 61*, Shane Watson 44*; Imad Wasim 2-31, Wahab Riaz 2-35) beat **Pakistan** 172/8 in 20 overs (Khalid Latif 46, Shoaib Malik 40*; James Faulkner 5-27, Adam Zampa 2-32) by 21 runs. *MoM:* James Faulkner.

New Zealand beat Bangladesh by 75 runs

• On a slow and dry Kolkata surface, Mustafizur picks up his maiden five-for, but where the New Zealand batsmen are watchful, their Bangladesh counterparts succumb to Grant Elliott's cutters and Sodhi's leg-spin. • The Williamson-Mustafizur battle is an intriguing one, the young Bangladesh left-armer toying with the well-set New Zealand captain and setting him up to be bowled around the legs. • Colin Munro, pacing his innings wisely, holds fort with Ross Taylor. • Mustafizur misses out on a hat-trick even as no batsman after No. 4 gets into double-figures. • A 25-run stand for the second wicket is the only partnership of note for Bangladesh. • Unable to make even half of what New Zealand managed, they are bowled out for their lowest T20I total and finish the Super 10 stage winless. *Karunya Keshav*

Eden Gardens, Kolkata, March 26: New Zealand 145/8 in 20 overs (Kane Williamson 42, Colin Munro 35; Mustafizur Rahman 5-22, Al-Amin Hossain 2-27) beat **Bangladesh** 70 in 15.4 overs (Grant Elliott 3-12, Ish Sodhi 3-21) by 75 runs. *MoM:* Kane Williamson.

India beat Australia by six wickets

• In a virtual quarterfinal, Australia make a frenetic start through Khawaja and Finch, the first four overs producing 53, 22 of those coming from one Ashwin over. • Nehra has Khawaja caught behind, an event that puts a remarkable brake on the scoring rate. • Australia manage just 107 runs in the last 16 overs, Nehra the standout with 1 for 20 from four. • Not even the vastly improved batting conditions inspire the Indian top order as the hosts are left gasping at 49 for 3. • Kohli does his reputation as chase-master no harm, arresting the slide alongside Yuvraj through a stand of 45. • India need 59 off the last five overs and Kohli seals a semi-final berth with five balls to share, totally overshadowing Dhoni in a fifth-wicket stand of 67 in just 31 balls. *R Kaushik*

PCA IS Bindra Stadium, Mohali, March 27: Australia 160/6 in 20 overs (Aaron Finch 43, Glenn Maxwell 31; Hardik Pandya 2-36) lost to **India** 161/4 in 19.1 overs (Virat Kohli 82*, Yuvraj Singh 21; Shane Watson 2-23) by six wickets. *MoM:* Virat Kohli.

Group 1 Points Table

Teams	M	W	L	T	N/R	Pts	NRR
New Zealand	4	4	0	0	0	8	1.900
India	4	3	1	0	0	6	-0.305
Australia	4	2	2	0	0	4	0.233
Pakistan	4	1	3	0	0	2	-0.093
Bangladesh	4	0	4	0	0	0	-1.805

New Zealand and India qualified for the semi-finals

1st semi-final: England beat New Zealand by seven wickets

• Munro thrashes England with impunity while virtually ignoring the offside: between the wicketkeeper and long-off, he only scores 11 runs, ten of which come from switch hits. • New Zealand rapidly lose impetus from 89 for 1 off ten overs as England concede only 20 in the last four overs, their most frugal performance in a T20I. • While Jordan is an expert practitioner of the wide yorker, Stokes gets two wickets in consecutive balls with full tosses. • Roy crunches four boundaries from the opening over of the chase and launches an unbridled assault on New Zealand; he alone has 49 runs before the powerplay is up, and marries power, orthodoxy and impudence in his 78. • New Zealand lose control in the field for the first time in the tournament, and Sodhi's wickets in consecutive balls come far too late. They have now lost eight of nine semi-finals across the World Cup and WT20. • Buttler races to victory with three sixes in four balls, embodying England's uninhibited spirit.

Tim Wigmore

Feroz Shah Kotla, Delhi, March 30: New Zealand 153/8 in 20 overs (Colin Munro 46, Kane Williamson 32; Ben Stokes 3-26) lost to **England** 159/3 in 17.1 overs (Jason Roy 78, Jos Buttler 32*; Ish Sodhi 2-42) by seven wickets. *MoM:* Jason Roy.

2nd semi-final: West Indies beat India by seven wickets

• The new opening pair of Rohit Sharma and Ajinkya Rahane put on 62 to lay the perfect base after India are stuck in by Sammy. • Both men fall in their 40s, but Kohli continues his breathtaking run with another sensational innings. • Clearly the dominant partner in a third-wicket stand of 64 in 27 deliveries with Dhoni, Kohli smashes an unbeaten 47-ball 89. • West Indies lose Gayle and Samuels inside the first three overs as a capacity crowd senses a famous home victory. • Lendl Simmons, a last-minute replacement for Fletcher, capitalises on being caught off no balls when 18 and 50 to take India to the cleaners alongside Johnson Charles. • Russell justifies his elevation to No. 5 with a 20-ball 43 as India's campaign runs out of steam. *R Kaushik*

Wankhede Stadium, Mumbai, March 31: India 192/2 in 20 overs (Virat Kohli 89*, Rohit Sharma 43) lost to **West Indies** 196/3 in 19.4 overs (Lendl Simmons 82*, Johnson Charles 52) by seven wickets. *MoM:* Lendl Simmons.

Final: West Indies beat England by four wickets

• In a repeat of the opening league tie for both teams, West Indies do the early running through Badree, the No. 1 T20I bowler in the world. • Root and Buttler briefly boss the bowling with Sulieman Benn going for 40 in three overs as England are primed for a final flourish. • Brathwaite makes his first impression on the final by evicting both set batsmen. • Gayle fails for a third time on the trot and is quickly joined by Charles and Simmons as England grab the initiative at 11 for 3. • West Indies rebuild steadily until Samuels lashes out in the last quarter of the chase, leaving Ben Stokes 19 to defend in the last over against Brathwaite. • 6, 6, 6, 6. Carlos Brathwaite has emerged a

The first two-time champions: Darren Sammy's West Indians were spurred on by off-field slights in their charge to the title. — *Getty Images*

match-winner, leaving Stokes battered, England beaten and 2012 titlists West Indies the first repeat champions at the World T20. *R Kaushik*

Venue: Eden Gardens, Kolkata, India, April 3, 2016
Toss: West Indies, who chose to bowl
MoM: Marlon Samuels (West Indies)
MoS: Virat Kohli (India)

England

			R	*B*	*4s*	*6s*	*SR*
Jason Roy		b Badree	0	2	0	0	0.00
Alex Hales	c Badree	b Russell	1	3	0	0	33.33
Joe Root	c Benn	b Brathwaite	54	36	7	0	150.00
Eoin Morgan	c Gayle	b Badree	5	12	1	0	41.67
Jos Buttler	c Bravo	b Brathwaite	36	22	1	3	163.64
Ben Stokes	c Simmons	b Bravo	13	8	1	0	162.50
Moeen Ali	c Ramdin	b Bravo	0	2	0	0	0.00
Chris Jordan	Not out	b Bravo	12	13	1	0	92.31
David Willey	c Charles	b Brathwaite	21	14	1	2	150.00
Liam Plunkett	c Badree	b Bravo	4	4	0	0	100.00
Adil Rashid	Not out	b Bravo	4	4	0	0	100.00

Extras	(0b,4lb,0nb,1w)	5					
Total	(9 wkts, 20.0 overs)		155 (7.75 runs per over)				

Fall of wickets: 0-1 (Jason Roy, 0.2 ov), 8-2 (Alex Hales, 1.5 ov), 23-3 (Eoin Morgan, 4.4 ov), 84-4 (Jos Buttler, 11.2 ov), 110-5 (Ben Stokes, 13.4 ov), 110-6 (Moeen Ali, 13.6 ov), 111-7 (Joe Root, 14.1 ov), 136-8 (David Willey, 17.3 ov), 142-9 (Liam Plunkett, 18.3 ov)

Bowling: Samuel Badree 4-1-16-2-4.00, Andre Russell 4-0-21-1-5.25, Sulieman Benn 3-0-40-0-13.33, Dwayne Bravo 4-0-37-3-9.25, Carlos Brathwaite 4-0-23-3-5.75 (1 wd), Darren Sammy 1-0-14-0-14.00

West Indies

			R	*B*	*4s*	*6s*	*SR*
Johnson Charles	c Stokes	b Root	1	7	0	0	14.29
Chris Gayle	c Stokes	b Root	4	2	1	0	200.00
Marlon Samuels	Not out	b Root	85	66	9	2	128.79
Lendl Simmons	LBW	b Willey	0	1	0	0	0.00
Dwayne Bravo	c Root	b Rashid	25	27	1	1	92.59
Andre Russell	c Stokes	b Willey	1	3	0	0	33.33
Darren Sammy	c Hales	b Willey	2	2	0	0	100.00
Carlos Brathwaite	Not out	b Willey	34	10	1	4	340.00
Extras	(0b,3lb,0nb,6w)	9					
Total	(6 wkts, 19.4 overs)		161 (8.19 runs per over)				

Fall of wickets: 1-1 (Johnson Charles, 1.1 ov), 5-2 (Chris Gayle, 1.3 ov), 11-3 (Lendl Simmons, 2.3 ov), 86-4 (Dwayne Bravo, 13.6 ov), 104-5 (Andre Russell, 15.1 ov), 107-6 (Darren Sammy, 15.3 ov)
Did Not Bat: Denesh Ramdin, Samuel Badree, Sulieman Benn

Bowling: David Willey 4-0-20-3-5.00 (2 wd), Joe Root 1-0-9-2-9.00, Chris Jordan 4-0-36-0-9.00 (1 wd), Liam Plunkett 4-0-29-0-7.25 (1 wd), Adil Rashid 4-0-23-1-5.75, Ben Stokes 2.4-0-41-0-15.38 (2 wd)

Umpires: Kumar Dharmasena (Sri Lanka) and Rodney Tucker (Australia)
TV umpires: Marais Erasmus (South Africa)
Referee: Ranjan Madugalle (Sri Lanka)

Winners: West Indies

Best batsman: Tamim Iqbal (Bangladesh) (295 runs, 6 matches)
Best bowler: Mohammad Nabi (Afghanistan) (12 wickets, 7 matches)

World T20 winners

Year (Venue)	Result
2007 (South Africa)	India beat Pakistan by 5 runs
2009 (England)	Pakistan beat Sri Lanka by eight wickets
2010 (West Indies)	England beat Australia by seven wickets
2012 (Sri Lanka)	West Indies beat Sri Lanka by 36 runs
2014 (Bangladesh)	Sri Lanka beat India by six wickets
2016 (India)	West Indies beat England by four wickets

West Indies: 2, **India:** 1, **Pakistan**: 1, **England:** 1, **Sri Lanka**: 1

Play it, from the pavilion.

Bowl out inconveniences by sending money online from wherever you are, in just a few clicks.

- Competitive rates
- Hassle-free transactions

Customer Service: 600 555 550 | www.uaeexchange.co

INDIA'S OTHER INTERNATIONALS
Under-19 Triangular Series in Kolkata

Winning start for Dravid's boys

DISHA SHETTY

Rahul Dravid made a successful debut as India's Under-19 coach as his side began their preparation for the U-19 World Cup by hosting Afghanistan and Bangladesh in Kolkata. The hosts put up a dominant show throughout the double round-robin stage, winning all four group matches before storming into the final where they beat Bangladesh by seven wickets.

With new focus on the side given their high-profile coach, Rishabh Pant, Washington Sundar, Sarfaraz Khan and Ricky Bhui, the captain, impressed on the batting front; Avesh Khan starred with the new ball. In the final, India's bowlers, led by Mayank Dagar, the left-arm spinner, bundled out Bangladesh for 116 in 36.5 overs. Sarfaraz then struck an unbeaten half-century to wrap up the chase in just 13.3 overs. Pant, who topped the run charts with a ton and two half-centuries from four matches, was adjudged the Man of the Series.

Bangladesh, who won half their group matches, suffered because of lack of substantial partnerships. Mehedi Hasan Miraz, their captain, led by example with handy all-round contributions, but found little support. Rashid Khan's all-round show against India was a silver lining in Afghanistan's winless campaign.

Best batsman: Rishabh Pant (282 runs, 4 matches)
Best bowler: Saleh Ahmed Shawon (12 wickets, 5 matches)

Jadavpur University Complex, Kolkata, November 20: India 158 in 45.3 overs (Washington Sundar 34, Zeeshan Ansari 34; Mehedi Hasan Miraz 3-31, Abdul Halim 2-24) beat **Bangladesh** 76 in 22 overs (Shafiul Hayet 26; Avesh Khan 4-4, Z Ansari 2-1) by 82 runs.

Jadavpur University Complex, Kolkata, November 21: India 236 in 50 overs (Rishabh Pant 87, Mahipal Lomror 43; Rashid Khan 4-47, Muslim Musa 2-32) beat **Afghanistan** 203 in 47.3 overs (Rashid 43, Mohammad Sardar 33; Khaleel Ahmed 4-41, M Lomror 2-31) by 33 runs.

Jadavpur University Complex, Kolkata, November 22: Afghanistan 85 in 30.4 overs (Hazratullah 32; Saleh Ahmed Shawon 6-10, Mehedi Hasan Miraz 2-19) lost to **Bangladesh** 89/6 in 14.4 overs (Saif Hasan 32; Zia-ur-Rehman 2-20, Karim Janat 2-23) by four wickets.

Jadavpur University Complex, Kolkata, November 24: Bangladesh 222/7 in 50 overs (Mehedi Hasan Miraz 87, Saif Hasan 33; Washington Sundar 2-25) lost to **India** 223/6 in 48.4 overs (Rishabh Pant 51, Washington 50; MH Miraz 2-50) by four wickets.

Jadavpur University Complex, Kolkata, November 25: Afghanistan 99 in 26.2 overs (Tariq Stanikzai 27; Saeed Sarkar 3-6, Saleh Ahmed Shawon 3-32) lost to **Bangladesh** 101/2 in 24.3 overs (Nazmul Hossain Shanto 38*, Mehedi Hasan Miraz 37*) by eight wickets.

Jadavpur University Complex, Kolkata, November 27: India 266/7 in 50 overs (Rishabh

Pant 118, Virat Singh 71; Muslim Musa 2-38, Mohammad Zahir 2-40) beat **Afghanistan** 162 in 28 overs (Naveed Obaid 63, Tariq Stanikzai 26; Zeeshan Ansari 5-37, Sarfaraz Khan 2-15) by 104 runs.

India and Bangladesh qualified for the final

Points Table

Teams	M	W	L	T	N/R	Pts	NRR
India	4	4	0	0	0	14	1.130
Bangladesh	4	2	2	0	0	14	0.222
Afghanistan	4	0	4	0	0	0	-1.603

Final: Jadavpur University Complex, Kolkata, November 29: Bangladesh 116 in 36.5 overs (Nazmul Hossain Shanto 45, Joyraz Sheik 28; Mayank Dagar 3-32, Mahipal Lomror 2-11) lost to **India** 117/2 in 13.3 overs (Sarfaraz Khan 59, Rishabh Pant 26) by seven wickets.

Winners: India

Under-19 Triangular Series in Colombo

Easy work for Indians

DISHA SHETTY

India extended their winning run when they travelled to Sri Lanka for a tri-series against the hosts and England. They won all their round-robin matches, and also secured a comprehensive five-wicket win in the final. Avesh Khan and Khaleel Ahmed formed a potent new-ball pair, and it was Ahmed's 3 for 29 in nine overs that restricted Sri Lanka to 148 in the final.

While Sri Lanka couldn't make the most of their home advantage against a spirited Indian side, they rode on captain Charith Asalanka's 48 to beat England in the round-robin stage. Rain marred the teams' second encounter where the home side was in pole position throughout. For England, Dan Lawrence starred with 132 runs in four matches, including two half-centuries. Although they failed to win a match, the tri-series was a vital experience of subcontinental conditions prior to the U-19 World Cup in Bangladesh.

Best batsman: Washington Sundar (208 runs, 4 matches)
Best bowler: Khaleel Ahmed (7 wickets, 2 matches)

R Premadasa Stadium, Colombo, December 11: India 254/7 in 34 overs (Sarfaraz Khan 84, Anmolpreet Singh 56; Ben Green 3-28, Hugh Bernard 2-46) beat **England** 159/9 in 29 overs (Dan Lawrence 55, B Green 23*; Mahipal Lomror 4-10, Kanishk Seth 2-17) by 86 runs (D/L method).

R Premadasa Stadium, Colombo, December 12: India 284/7 in 50 overs (Amandeep Khare 102, Washington Sundar 77; Asitha Fernando 3-54) beat **Sri Lanka** 250/5 in 47 overs (Avishka Fernando 75, Charith Asalanka 74; Rahul Batham 2-32) by four runs (D/L method).

R Premadasa Stadium, Colombo, December 14: Sri Lanka 191 in 49.1 overs (Charith Asalanka 48, Shammu Ashan 38; Brad Taylor 4-34, Ben Green 2-20) beat **England** 139 in 38.3 overs (Jack Burnham 32, Ryan Davies 28; Wanidu Hasaranga 2-22, Damitha Silva 2-38) by 52 runs.

R Premadasa Stadium, Colombo, December 15: India 261 in 50 overs (Rishabh Pant 71, Himanshu Rana 50; Mason Crane 3-51, Dan Lawrence 2-30) beat **England** 241 in 49.3 overs (George Bartlett 70, D-Lawrence 55; Rahul Batham 3-24, Mayank Dagar 3-27) by 20 runs.

R Premadasa Stadium, Colombo, December 17: Sri Lanka 221/9 in 50 overs (Kaveen Bandara 74, Kamindu Mendis 65; Khaleel Ahmed 4-55) lost to **India** 223/6 in 47.5 overs (Washington Sundar 61, Virat Singh 60*; Lahiru Kumara 2-33) by four wickets.

R Premadasa Stadium, Colombo, December 18: Sri Lanka 227 in 45 overs (Kamindu Mendis 52, Kaveen Bandara 36; Sam Curran 4-52, Mason Crane 2-49) v **England** 41/2 in 10 overs. No result.

Points Table

Teams	M	W	L	T	N/R	Pts	NRR
India	4	4	0	0	0	17	0.706
Sri Lanka	4	1	2	0	1	7	0.250
England	4	0	3	0	1	2	-1.225

India and Sri Lanka qualified for the final

Final: R Premadasa Stadium, Colombo, December 21: Sri Lanka 158 in 47.2 overs (Vishad Randika 58, Damitha Silva 23; Khaleel Ahmed 3-29, Avesh Khan 2-24, Mayank Dagar 2-24) lost to **India** 159/5 in 33.5 overs (Washington Sundar 56, Rishabh Pant 35; D Silva 3-18) by five wickets.

Winners: India

ICC Under-19 World Cup

The new generation West Indies

MANOJ NARAYAN

For its teenage participants, the Under-19 World Cup has always been a three-week microcosm of what a career in cricket could be: glory, but also pressure, controversy and heartbreak.

There is no saying that many of those who featured in the event in Bangladesh would continue in cricket. The controversies and disappointments might have proved too much for some of them. It can't have been easy, being locked up in a hotel or going to and from the grounds, always flanked by RAB forces, the spectre of a security threat throughout. But irrespective of the path they choose, they would have returned with invaluable lessons.

That statement holds particularly true for the champions from the West Indies. In a must-win group game against Zimbabwe, needing a wicket to win and with Zimbabwe just three runs away from victory, Keemo Paul mankaded Richard Ngarava. The batsman didn't appear to intend to steal an advantage, but he had strayed and was ruled out according to the laws of the game. The 'Spirit of the Game' argument, of course, saw much criticism directed at the youngsters from the Caribbean, and the management did well to shield the side from the backlash.

Instead, they instilled a siege mentality. It strengthened the bond within the team, and in the victories that followed, against Pakistan in the quarter-final, home favourite Bangladesh in the semis and heavyweights India in the final, the all-round qualities of the team came to the fore. They showed they could dominate, as in the five-wicket victory over Pakistan. They were capable of absorbing pressure and digging themselves in, as against Bangladesh. And they wouldn't be fazed in decisive moments, remaining calm and composed to seal victory against India with just three balls remaining.

In all that, Shimron Hetmyer displayed excellent leadership to go with some fine performances when it mattered the most in the knockouts. Alzarri Joseph, with his raw pace, and Chemar Holder, with wily movement of the ball, formed a bowling duo that nipped out the best of the opposition. And around them, the likes of Gidron Pope, Keacy Carty, Shamar Springer – who also introduced the world to the chest roll – and Paul himself made it a fine team. It didn't take long after they lifted the trophy for some quarters to suggest the future of West Indies cricket was in safe hands.

While West Indies were definitely the story of the tournament, every other team contributed to making it the success it was. Up till the final, India, the favourites, enthralled viewers with dominant displays and fine individual feats, all under the guidance of Rahul Dravid, who typically shied away from the limelight whenever he could. Even Canada, who finished 15th, had a memorable tale to tell of Dravid, the legend going out of his way to comfort the boys after India beat them by 372 runs in a warm-up.

Bangladesh, led by the excellent Mehedi Hasan Miraz – the Player of the Tournament – played attractive cricket and found fans beyond their loyal home support. And further down, the likes of Namibia, Nepal and Afghanistan suggested the gap between Associates and Full Members was reducing every day.

That the tournament went off smoothly was credit to the host nation. Bangladesh had been under pressure to oversee an eventless youth world cup the moment Cricket Australia withdrew, citing security concerns. To widespread relief, it passed without incident. The facilities were fine, and the crowds turned up despite minimal advertisement.

West Indies' Shimron Hetmyer displayed excellent leadership. – ICC

ICC though, had some questions to answer about the very structure of the tournament. For starters, the relevance of the Plate League, contested by teams failing to make the quarterfinals, was questioned, especially after it became evident just how skewed the system was against Associate and Affiliate sides. Namibia and Nepal beat South Africa and New Zealand respectively en route to the quarterfinals. They finished seventh and eighth, above ninth-placed Afghanistan, who won the Plate Championship by beating another Full Member side in Zimbabwe. However, apart from Namibia, who qualified for the 2018 tournament by being the highest-placed Associate side, the other two will have to wade through the qualifiers again, while South Africa and New Zealand, who finished 11th and 12th respectively, will automatically qualify on account of being Full Members.

Something just isn't right there, especially when you consider the fact that the top three wicket-takers of the tournament – Fritz Coetzee from Namibia, Sandeep Lamichhane from Nepal and Rory Anders from Ireland – are all from Associate sides.

The other question asked of the ICC was about the age verification process, after Nepal's Raju Rijal was alleged to be overage. Kaustubh Pawar, the 25-year-old Mumbai cricketer claimed Rijal was actually Raju Sharma, with whom he had played age-group cricket years ago. "The trouble is that the medical experts tell you that there is very little we can do to test the age of someone in a reliable fashion," ICC's David Richardson later said. "We've

The favourites: India found future stars in the likes of Sarfaraz Khan and Anmolpreet Singh, who drove the team into the final. – *ICC*

to rely quite heavily on documentation that is available and the honesty and integrity of the player."

These will be matters for the ICC to consider ahead of the next edition in New Zealand. The class of 2016, meanwhile, will have other priorities. They started the tournament as boys. Three weeks later, they were still boys, of course, but were stronger and wiser for the experience. It's up to them now to make the most of it.

Best batsman: Jack Burnham (420 runs, 6 matches)
Best bowler: Fritz Coetzee (15 wickets, 4 matches)

Group A

Zahur Ahmed Chowdhury Stadium, Chittagong, January 27: Bangladesh 240/7 in 50 overs (Nazmul Hossain Shanto 73, Joyraz Sheik 46; Wiaan Mulder 3-42) beat **South Africa** 197 in 48.4 overs (Liam Smith 100, Dayyaan Galiem 22; Mohammad Saifuddin 3-30, Mehedi Hasan Miraz 3-37) by 43 runs. *MoM*: Nazmul Hossain Shanto.
Sheikh Kamal International Cricket Stadium, Cox's Bazar, January 29: Scotland 159 in 36.3 overs (Owais Shah 39, Haris Aslam 31; Michael van Lingen 3-19, SJ Loftie-Eaton 2-13) lost to **Namibia** 162/1 in 26 overs (SJ Loftie-Eaton 67*, Niko Davin 52) by nine wickets. *MoM*: SJ Loftie-Eaton.
Sheikh Kamal International Cricket Stadium, Cox's Bazar, January 31: Bangladesh 256/6 in 50 overs (Nazmul Hossain Shanto 113*, Mehedi Hasan Miraz 51; Mohammad Ghaffar 4-60) beat **Scotland** 142 in 47.2 overs (Azeem Dar 50, Neil Flack 28; Mohammad Saifuddin 3-17, Saleh Ahmed Shawon 3-27) by 114 runs. *MoM*: Nazmul Hossain Shanto.
Sheikh Kamal International Cricket Stadium Academy Ground, Cox's Bazar, January

31: South Africa 136/9 in 50 overs (Willem Ludick 42; Michael van Lingen 4-24, Fritz Coetzee 3-16) lost to **Namibia** 137/8 in 39.4 overs (Lohan Louwrens 58*, Charl Brits 27, Ziyaad Abrahams 2-18, Sean Whitehead 2-27) by two wickets. *MoM*: Michael van Lingen.
Sheikh Kamal International Cricket Stadium, Cox's Bazar, February 2: Namibia 65 in 32.5 overs (Ariful Islam 2-9, Saleh Ahmed Shawon 2-10) lost to **Bangladesh** 66/2 in 16 overs (Joyraz Sheik 34*; Fritz Coetzee 2-20) by eight wickets. *MoM*: Saleh Ahmed Shawon.
Sheikh Kamal International Cricket Stadium Academy Ground, Cox's Bazar, February 2: Scotland 127 in 45.4 overs (Harris Carnegie 29*, Finlay McCreath 24; Wiaan Mulder 2-16, Dayyaan Galiem 2-16, Sean Whitehead 2-16) lost to **South Africa** 129/0 in 29 overs (Liam Smith 64*, Kyle Verreynne 64*) by ten wickets. *MoM*: Kyle Verreynne.

Group A Points Table

Teams	M	W	L	T	N/R	Pts	NRR
Bangladesh	3	3	0	0	0	6	2.151
Namibia	3	2	1	0	0	4	0.035
South Africa	3	1	2	0	0	2	-0.027
Scotland	3	0	3	0	0	0	-2.356

Bangladesh and Namibia qualified for the quarter-finals

Group B

Sylhet International Cricket Stadium, January 28: Afghanistan 126 in 41.2 overs (Tariq Stanikzai 53, Karim Janat 27; Shadab Khan 4-9, Hasan Mohsin 3-24) lost to **Pakistan** 129/4 in 31.3 overs (Zeeshan Malik 29, H Mohsin 28*; Zia-ur-Rehman 2-31) by six wickets. *MoM*: Hasan Mohsin.
Sylhet District Stadium, January 28: Sri Lanka 315/6 in 50 overs (Charith Asalanka 76, Shammu Ashan 74*; Abdul Haseeb 2-65) beat **Canada** 119 in 39.2 overs (Arslan Khan 42*, Bhavindu Adhihetty 22; Damitha Silva 2-16, Thilan Nimesh 2-19, Asitha Fernando 2-19) by 196 runs. *MoM*: Charith Asalanka.
Sylhet International Cricket Stadium, January 30: Sri Lanka 184 in 48.1 overs (Charith Asalanka 71, Avishka Fernando 30; Shamsurrahman 3-19, Zahir Khan 2-36) beat **Afghanistan** 151 in 44.5 overs (Waheedullah Shafaq 47, Karim Janat 40; Kamindu Mendis 3-36, C Asalanka 2-18) by 196 runs. *MoM*: Charith Asalanka.
Sylhet District Stadium, January 30: Canada 178 in 48.3 overs (Bhavindu Adhihetty 51, Abraash Khan 44; Hasan Khan 3-36, Shadab Khan 2-44) lost to **Pakistan** 180/3 in 40.5 overs (Zeeshan Malik 89*, Saif Badar 44) by seven wickets. *MoM*: Zeeshan Malik.
Sylhet International Cricket Stadium, February 1: Canada 147 in 50 overs (Arslan Khan 38, Abraash Khan 33; Shamsurrahman 3-21, Muslim Musa 3-31) lost to **Afghanistan** 149/6 in 24.1 overs (Tariq Stanikzai 56, Ihsanullah 31; Miraj Patel 3-17, Shlok Patel 2-31) by four wickets. *MoM*: Tariq Stanikzai.
Sher-e-Bangla National Stadium, Mirpur, February 3: Pakistan 212 in 48.4 overs (Hasan Mohsin 86, Salman Fayyaz 33; Wanidu Hasaranga 2-30, Thilan Nimesh 2-38) beat **Sri Lanka** 189 in 46.4 overs (Kamindu Mendis 68, Vishad Randika 46; Shadab Khan 3-31, Ahmad Shafiq 2-23) by 23 runs. *MoM*: Hasan Mohsin.

Group B Points Table

Teams	M	W	L	T	N/R	Pts	NRR
Pakistan	3	3	0	0	0	6	0.972
Sri Lanka	3	2	1	0	0	4	1.373
Afghanistan	3	1	2	0	0	2	-0.067
Canada	3	0	3	0	0	0	-2.640

Pakistan and Sri Lanka qualified for the quarter-finals

Group C

MA Aziz Stadium, Chittagong, January 27: England 371/3 in 50 overs (Dan Lawrence 174, Jack Burnham 148) beat **Fiji** 72 in 27.3 overs (Peni Vuniwaqa 36; Saqib Mahmood 3-2, Sam Curran 3-22) by 299 runs. *MoM*: Dan Lawrence.

Zahur Ahmed Chowdhury Stadium, Chittagong, January 29: England 282/7 in 50 overs (Callum Taylor 59, Dan Lawrence 55; Gidron Pope 2-45) beat **West Indies** 221 in 43.4 overs (Keemo Paul 65, G Pope 60; Saqib Mahmood 4-42, Sam Curran 2-23) by 61 runs. *MoM*: Dan Lawrence.

MA Aziz Stadium, Chittagong, January 29: Fiji 81 in 27.4 overs (Wesley Madhevere 5-24, Brandon Mavuta 3-13) lost to **Zimbabwe** 84/3 in 18.5 overs (Brendan Sly 29*, Jeremy Ives 23; Josaia Baleicikoibia 2-19) by seven wickets. *MoM*: Wesley Madhevere.

Zahur Ahmed Chowdhury Stadium, Chittagong, January 31: England 288/4 in 50 overs (Jack Burnham 106*, Dan Lawrence 59; Rugare Magarira 2-36) beat **Zimbabwe** 159 in 43.4 overs (Jeremy Ives 91; Saqib Mahmood 4-39, Callum Taylor 3-14) by 129 runs. *MoM*: Jack Burnham.

MA Aziz Stadium, Chittagong, January 31: West Indies 340/7 in 50 overs (Shamar Springer 106, Gidron Pope 76; Cakacaka Tikoisuva 6-59) beat **Fiji** 78 in 27.3 overs (Peni Vuniwaqa 29; G Pope 4-24, Alzarri Joseph 3-15) by 262 runs. *MoM*: Gidron Pope.

Zahur Ahmed Chowdhury Stadium, Chittagong, February 2: West Indies 226/9 in 50 overs (Shamar Springer 61, Tevin Imlach 31; Rugare Magarira 3-28, Wesley Madhevere 2-48) beat **Zimbabwe** 224 in 49 overs (Shaun Snyder 52, Adam Keefe 43; Alzarri Joseph 4-30, S Springer 2-16) by two runs. *MoM*: Alzarri Joseph.

Group C Points Table

Teams	M	W	L	T	N/R	Pts	NRR
England	3	3	0	0	0	6	3.260
West Indies	3	2	1	0	0	4	1.353
Zimbabwe	3	1	2	0	0	2	-0.037
Fiji	3	0	3	0	0	0	-5.150

England and West Indies qualified for the quarter-finals

Group D

Sher-e-Bangla National Stadium, Mirpur, January 28: India 268/9 in 50 overs (Sarfaraz Khan 74, Washington Sundar 62; Rory Anders 3-35, Joshua Little 3-52) beat **Ireland** 189 in 49.1 overs (William McClintock 58, Lorcan Tucker 57; Rahul Batham 3-15, Avesh Khan 2-24) by 79 runs. *MoM*: Sarfaraz Khan.
Khan Shaheb Osman Ali Stadium, Fatullah, January 28: Nepal 238/7 in 50 overs (Raju Rijal 48, Sandeep Sunar 39, Aarif Sheikh 39; Nathan Smith 3-58) beat **New Zealand** 206 in 47.1 overs (Glenn Phillips 52, Dale Phillips 41; Dipendra Singh Airee 3-24, Prem Tamang 2-38) by 32 runs. *MoM*: Raju Rijal.
Sher-e-Bangla National Stadium, Mirpur, January 30: India 258/8 in 50 overs (Sarfaraz Khan 74, Rishabh Pant 57; Zak Gibson 3-50, Nathan Smith 2-39) beat **New Zealand** 138 in 31.3 overs (Christian Leopard 40, Finn Allen 29, Talor Scott 29; Mahipal Lomror 5-47, Avesh Khan 4-32) by 120 runs. *MoM*: Avesh Khan.
Khan Shaheb Osman Ali Stadium, Fatullah, January 30: Ireland 131/9 in 50 overs (Harry Tector 30*, Jack Tector 27; Sandeep Lamichhane 5-27, Dipendra Singh Airee 2-18) lost to **Nepal** 132/2 in 25.3 overs (Yogendra Singh Karki 61*, Aarif Sheikh 31*) by eight wickets. *MoM*: Sandeep Lamichhane.
Sher-e-Bangla National Stadium, Mirpur, February 1: Nepal 169/8 in 48 overs (Sandeep Sunar 37, Rajbir Singh 35; Avesh Khan 3-34, Washington Sundar 2-20) lost to **India** 175/3 in 18.1 overs (Rishabh Pant 78, Ishan Kishan 52; Prem Tamang 2-41) by seven wickets. *MoM*: Rishabh Pant.
Khan Shaheb Osman Ali Stadium, Fatullah, February 1: Ireland 212 in 47.5 overs (Jack Tector 56, Adam Dennison 46; Josh Finnie 3-30, Rachin Ravindra 3-36) lost to **New Zealand** 213/6 in 40.1 overs (Finn Allen 97, Dale Phillips 58; Rory Anders 4-32, Fiachra Tucker 2-26) by four wickets. *MoM*: Finn Allen.

Points Table

Teams	M	W	L	T	N/R	Pts	NRR
India	3	3	0	0	0	6	2.581
Nepal	3	2	1	0	0	4	0.032
New Zealand	3	1	2	0	0	2	-0.810
Ireland	3	0	3	0	0	0	-1.705

Plate League

9th Place Play-off Quarter-Final: Sheikh Kamal International Cricket Stadium, Cox's Bazar, February 4: Ireland 185/7 in 50 overs (Lorcan Tucker 77*, Fiachra Tucker 20; Dayyaan Galiem 2-22, Willem Ludick 2-43) lost to **South Africa** 187/2 in 46 overs (Kyle Verreynne 77, Liam Smith 49) by eight wickets. *MoM*: Kyle Verreynne.
9th Place Play-off Quarter-Final: Sheikh Kamal International Cricket Stadium Academy Ground, Cox's Bazar, February 4: Scotland 181/9 in 50 overs (Owais Shah 32, Jack Waller 24; Ross ter Braak 3-34, Felix Murray 2-31) lost to **New Zealand** 185/3 in 27 overs (Glenn Phillips 89, Finn Allen 31*; Haris Aslam 2-37) by seven wickets. *MoM*: Glenn Phillips.
9th Place Play-off Quarter-Final: Sheikh Kamal International Cricket Stadium, Cox's Bazar, February 5: Afghanistan 340/9 in 50 overs (Karim Janat 156, Perwez Malakzai 74; Peni Vuniwaqa 3-41, T Veitacini 2-49) beat **Fiji** 114 in 31.2 overs (Josaia Baleicikoibia 29, Malakai Cokovaki 25; Nijat Masood 3-6, Rashid Khan 3-16) by 226 runs. *MoM*: Karim Janat.
9th Place Play-off Quarter-Final: Sheikh Kamal International Cricket Stadium Academy

Ground, Cox's Bazar, February 5: Canada 186/8 in 50 overs (Amish Taploo 37, Abraash Khan 32; Jeremy Ives 3-30) lost to **Zimbabwe** 190/4 in 31.4 overs (Shaun Snyder 56, J Ives 43*; Bhavindu Adhihetty 2-23, Shlok Patel 2-62) by six wickets. *MoM*: Jeremy Ives.

13th Place Play-off Semi-Final: Sheikh Kamal International Cricket Stadium, Cox's Bazar, February 7: Canada 139 in 48.2 overs (Arslan Khan 47, Prushoth Wijayaraj 26; Rory Anders 4-21, Fiachra Anders 2-21) lost to **Ireland** 142/4 in 34.3 overs (Stephan Doheny 33, Jack Tector 33; Bhavindu Adhihetty 3-25) by six wickets. *MoM*: Gary McClintock.

13th Place Play-off Semi-Final: Sheikh Kamal International Cricket Stadium Academy Ground, Cox's Bazar, February 8: Scotland 225 in 48.1 overs (Finlay McCreath 60, Owais Shah 39; Cakacaka Tikoisuva 4-46, Josaia Baleicikoibia 2-37) beat **Fiji** 149 in 42.2 overs (Peni Vuniwaqa 80, J Baleicikoibia 27; Cameron Sloman 3-30, F McCreath 3-48) by 76 runs. *MoM*: Finlay McCreath.

9th Place Play-off Semi-Final: Sheikh Kamal International Cricket Stadium, Cox's Bazar, February 8: South Africa 91 in 39.5 overs (Rivaldo Moonsamy 32; Richard Ngarava 4-10, Rugare Magarira 2-11) lost to **Zimbabwe** 94/2 in 22 overs (Jeremy Ives 34*, Ryan Murray 26*) by eight wickets. *MoM*: Richard Ngarava.

9th Place Play-off Semi-Final: Sheikh Kamal International Cricket Stadium Academy Ground, Cox's Bazar, February 8: New Zealand Under-19 135 in 44.5 overs (Aniket Parikh 48, Josh Clarkson 25; Rashid Khan 3-30, Shamsurrahman 3-37) lost to **Afghanistan** 137/2 in 27.3 overs (Tariq Stanikzai 50*, Ihsanullah 47; Aniket Parikh 2-50) by eight wickets. *MoM*: Tariq Stanikzai.

13th Place Play-off: Sheikh Kamal International Cricket Stadium, Cox's Bazar, February 10: Ireland 235/7 in 50 overs (William McClintock 69, Lorcan Tucker 59; Mohammad Ghaffar 3-49) beat **Scotland** 140 in 44 overs (Harry Tector 4-28, Fiachra Tucker 3-29) by 95 runs. *MoM*: William McClintock.

15th Place Play-off: Sheikh Kamal International Cricket Stadium Academy Ground, Cox's Bazar, February 11: Fiji 83 in 28 overs (Miraj Patel 4-16, Shlok Patel 3-18) lost to **Canada** 84/2 in 20 overs (Akash Gill 38*) by eight wickets. *MoM*: Miraj Patel.

11th Place Play-off: Sheikh Kamal International Cricket Stadium Academy Ground, Cox's Bazar, February 12: South Africa 288/6 in 50 overs (Dean Foxcroft 117, Rivaldo Moonsamy 51; Aniket Parikh 2-33) beat **New Zealand** 150 in 38.4 overs (Finn Allen 40, Rachin Ravindra 39; Wiaan Mulder 4-14, Ziyaad Abrahams 2-37) by 138 runs. *MoM*: Dean Foxcroft.

Plate Final: Sheikh Kamal International Cricket Stadium, Cox's Bazar, February 12: Zimbabwe 216/9 in 50 overs (William Mashinge 66, Ryan Murray 53; Zia-ur-Rehman 3-33, Muslim Musa 3-38) lost to **Afghanistan** 218/5 in 46.5 overs (Tariq Stanikzai 106*, Rashid Khan 55*; Jeremy Ives 2-36) by five wickets. *MoM*: Tariq Stanikzai.

Afghanistan won the Plate League

Quarter-finals

1st Quarter-final: Sher-e-Bangla National Stadium, Mirpur, February 5: Nepal 211/9 in 50 overs (Raju Rijal 72, Sunil Dhamala 25; Mohammad Saifuddin 2-38) lost to **Bangladesh** 215/4 in 48.2 overs (Zakir Hasan 75*, Mehedi Hasan Miraz 55*; S Dhamala 2-33) by six wickets. *MoM*: Mehedi Hasan Miraz.

2nd Quarter-final: Khan Shaheb Osman Ali Stadium, Fatullah, February 6: India 349/6 in 50 overs (Rishabh Pant 111, Sarfaraz Khan 76; Fritz Coetzee 3-78) beat **Namibia** 152 in 39 overs (Niko Davin 37, Zane Green 27; Mayank Dagar 3-25, Anmolpreet Singh 3-27) by 197 runs. *MoM*: Rishabh Pant.

3rd Quarter-final: Sher-e-Bangla National Stadium, Mirpur, February 7: England 184 in 49.2 overs (Callum Taylor 42, Ben Green 26; Wanidu Hasaranga 3-34, Asitha Fernando 2-16) lost to **Sri Lanka** 186/4 in 35.4 overs (Avishka Fernando 95, Charith Asalanka 34) by six wickets. *MoM*: Avishka Fernando.

4th Quarter-final: Khan Shaheb Osman Ali Stadium, Fatullah, February 8: Pakistan 227/6 in 50 overs (Umair Masood 113, Salman Fayyaz 58*; Chemar Holder 2-26) lost to **West Indies** 229/5 in 40 overs (Tevin Imlach 54, Shimron Hetmyer 52) by five wickets. *MoM*: Umair Masood.

Bangladesh, India, Sri Lanka and West Indies qualified for the semi-finals

5th place play-offs

5th place play-off semi-final: Khan Shaheb Osman Ali Stadium, Fatullah, February 9: **Pakistan** 258/8 in 50 overs (Hasan Mohsin 117, Saif Badar 88; Sandeep Lamichhane 3-53, Aarif Sheikh 2-22) beat **Nepal** 136 in 43.5 overs (Prem Tamang 65*; H Mohsin 4-42, Saif Ali 2-9) by 122 runs. *MoM*: Hasan Mohsin.

5th place play-off semi-final: Khan Shaheb Osman Ali Stadium, Fatullah, February 10: **England** 286/9 in 48 overs (Jack Burnham 109, Tom Moores 85; Fritz Coetzee 3-72, Burton Jacobs 2-58) beat **Namibia** 83 in 25.2 overs (Lohan Louwrens 24; Mason Crane 3-3, Dan Lawrence 2-7) by 203 runs. *MoM*: Jack Burnham.

7th place play-off: Khan Shaheb Osman Ali Stadium, Fatullah, February 11: **Namibia** 225/9 in 45 overs (Lohan Louwrens 59, Michael van Lingen 58; Sandeep Lamichhane 3-35, Sushil Kandel 2-30) beat **Nepal** 210 in 44.2 overs (Sunil Dhamala 59, Yogendra Singh Karki 35; M van Lingen 4-24, Fritz Coetzee 3-34) by 15 runs. *MoM*: Michael van Lingen.

5th place play-off: Khan Shaheb Osman Ali Stadium, Fatullah, February 12: England 264/7 in 50 overs (Sam Curran 83, Tom Moores 47; Saif Ali 2-37, Sameen Gul 2-42) lost to **Pakistan** 265/3 in 43.1 overs (Zeeshan Malik 93, Saif Badar 75*) by seven wickets. *MoM*: Zeeshan Malik.

Semi-finals

1st semi-final: Sher-e-Bangla National Stadium, Mirpur, February 9: India 267/9 in 50 overs (Anmolpreet Singh 72, Sarfaraz Khan 59; Asitha Fernando 4-43, Thilan Nimesh 2-50, Lahiru Kumara 2-50) beat **Sri Lanka** 170 in 42.4 overs (Kamindu Mendis 39, Shammu Ashan 38; Mayank Dagar 3-21, Avesh Khan 2-41) by 97 runs. *MoM*: Anmolpreet Singh.

2nd semi-final: Sher-e-Bangla National Stadium, Mirpur, February 11: Bangladesh 226 in 50 overs (Mehedi Hasan Miraz 60, Mohammad Saifuddin 36; Keemo Paul 3-20, Shamar Springer 2-36, Chemar K Holder 2-36) lost to **West Indies** 230/7 in 48.4 overs (S Springer 62*, Shimron Hetmyer 60; Saleh Ahmed Shawon 3-37, M Saifuddin 2-46) by three wickets. *MoM*: Shamar Springer.

India and West Indies qualified for the final

3rd place play-off

3rd place play-off: Khan Shaheb Osman Ali Stadium, Fatullah, February 13: Sri Lanka 214 in 48.5 overs (Charith Asalanka 76, Salindu Ushan 34; Mehedi Hasan Miraz 3-28, Abdul Halim 2-26) lost to **Bangladesh** 218/7 in 49.3 overs (MH Miraz 53, Nazmul Hossain Shanto 40; Shammu Ashan 2-39) by three wickets. *MoM*: Mehedi Hasan Miraz.

Final: West Indies beat India by five wickets

The scoreboard will suggest it was a low-scoring match in which West Indies comfortably strolled through with a five-wicket win. Reality was far from it. India rued the fact that West Indies were the sharper side off the blocks on the day. That much was evident four balls in when Tevin Imlach, the West Indies wicketkeeper, had Rishabh Pant stumped off Alzarri Joseph, the express paceman, after Pant had strayed from the crease. The pacemen then dominated the Indians and had them bowled out for 145, thanks largely to Sarfaraz Khan's 89-ball 51.

India rallied. West Indies were reduced to 28 for 2, and Mayank Dagar, the left-arm spinner, ran through the middle order, returning 3 for 25. However, Keacy Carty and Keemo Paul ground it out, and their unbroken 69-run stand tested their resolve as much as that of India's. They nurdled their way past the target with three balls to spare, and the scenes of elation that followed were only matched in drama by India's tears.

Final: Sher-e-Bangla National Stadium, Mirpur, February 13: India 145 in 45.1 overs (Sarfaraz Khan 51, Rahul Batham 21; Ryan John 3-38, Alzarri Joseph 3-39) lost to **West Indies** 146/5 in 49.3 overs (Keacy Carty 52*, Keemo Paul 40*; Mayank Dagar 3-25) by five wickets. *MoM*: Keacy Carty. *MoS*: Mehedi Hasan Miraz.

Winners: West Indies

Under-19 World Cup winners

Year (Venue)	Result
1988 (Australia)	Australia beat Pakistan by five wickets
1998 (South Africa)	England beat New Zealand by seven wickets
2000 (Sri Lanka)	India beat Sri Lanka by six wickets
2002 (New Zealand)	Australia beat South Africa by seven wickets
2004 (Bangladesh)	Pakistan beat West Indies by 25 runs
2006 (Sri Lanka)	Pakistan beat India by 38 runs
2008 (Malaysia)	India beat South Africa by 12 runs (D/L method)
2010 (New Zealand)	Australia beat Pakistan by 25 runs
2012 (Australia)	India beat Australia by six wickets
2014 (United Arab Emirates)	South Africa beat Pakistan by six wickets
2016 (Bangladesh)	West Indies beat India by five wickets

Australia: 3, **India**: 3, **Pakistan**: 2, **England**: 1, **South Africa**: 1, **West Indies**: 1

Manoj Narayan (@ojerson8) is a senior staff writer at Wisden India.

India A in Australia

Pandey, Mandeep engineer comeback

MANOJ NARAYAN

It's supposed to be the age of professionalism. The BCCI, however, slipped up on this occasion, making a mess of announcing the squads for the quadrangular series and two four-day games away against Australia A in August-September 2016. Naman Ojha was initially named captain of both limited-overs and four-day teams. However, the squad for the limited-overs games was then considerably changed, with Manish Pandey named captain.

Pandey's side, despite a poor start, surged to the title in the quadrangular series also featuring Australia A, South Africa A and an NPS XI, but the Indians were then blanked 1-0 in the two four-day matches.

India were bundled out for 55 in their tour opener against Australia A in the quadrangular, with pacemen Chris Tremain and Daniel Worrall, both of whom were later called up to the Australia ODI squad for the tour of South Africa, taking nine wickets between them. Axar Patel was India's highest scorer with 15, as Australia won by eight wickets.

That was an aberration, however. India bounced right back, beating South Africa A by three wickets, and followed that up with comprehensive wins against NPS. They lost a thriller to Australia again, the hosts winning by

Mandeep Singh's 95 in the quadrangular final and his captain Manish Pandey's consistency were some of the highlights of the tour for India A. — CA

a run after India lost two wickets in the last two deliveries, but the tables turned in the final.

India's unit clicked when it mattered. Mandeep Singh's 95 and sizeable hands from Shreyas Iyer (41) and Pandey (61) set Australia a target of 267. Yuzvendra Chahal, the leg-spinner, starred with 4 for 34 as the home side were bowled out for 209.

Pandey, the highest scorer of the tournament with centuries against Australia and South Africa, excelled in the role of skipper. He was rewarded with a call-up to the ODI squad to face New Zealand, along with Kedar Jadhav.

In the four-dayers, a second-innings collapse for 156 meant Australia needed just 159 to win the first match. They reached the target with three wickets to spare, with Cameron Bancroft, the opener, scoring an unbeaten 58. With the second match washed out, India had no chance to draw level. There were still several positives: Akhil Herwadkar, who scored an unbeaten 82 before the washout, was the top-scorer of the series with 148. Shardul Thakur, the paceman, and Jayant Yadav, the off-spinner, led the wicket-taking charts with 16 between them. Thakur took nine wickets in two matches, and would have been particularly pleased with his display, having travelled with the Test side to West Indies only to warm the benches.

Quadrangular Series

Tony Ireland Stadium, Townsville, August 13: National Performance Squad 243/8 in 50 overs (Sam Heazlett 101, Arjun Nair 40; Aaron Phangiso 2-46, Andile Phehlukwayo 2-49) beat **South AfricaA** 226 in 48.4 overs (Qaasim Adams 78, Sisanda Magala 35; David Grant 4-31, David Moody 3-44) by 17 runs. *MoM:* Sam Heazlett.

Tony Ireland Stadium, Townsville, August 14: India A 55 in 15.4 overs (Chris Tremain 5-25, Daniel Worrall 4-26) lost to **Australia A** 56/2 in 17.1 overs (Kurtis Patterson 23*) by eight wickets. *MoM:* Chris Tremain.

Tony Ireland Stadium, Townsville, August 16: National Performance Squad 231/9 in 49 overs (Hilton Cartwright 81, Sean Abbott 44; Chris Tremain 5-47, Marcus Stoinis 2-25) beat **AustraliaA** 177/7 in 28 overs (Chris Lynn 42, Marcus Stoinis 42; Hilton Cartwright 3-26, Sean Abbott 2-32) by 12 runs (D/L method). *MoM:* Hilton Cartwright.

Tony Ireland Stadium, Townsville, August 17: South AfricaA 230/8 in 50 overs (David Miller 90, Qaasim Adams 52; Dhawal Kulkarni 4-37, Jaydev Unadkat 2-42) lost to **India A** 234/7 in 48.4 overs (Manish Pandey 100*, Kedar Jadhav 26; Qaasim Adams 2-16, Andile Phehlukwayo 2-32) by three wickets. *MoM:* Manish Pandey.

Tony Ireland Stadium, Townsville, August 20: Australia A 107 in 37.2 overs (Kane Richardson 34*; Dane Paterson 3-13, Tabraiz Shamsi 3-25) lost to **South Africa A** 108/2 in 21 overs (Theunis de Bruyn 57*, David Miller 20*; Joe Mennie 2-25) by eight wickets. *MoM:* Dane Paterson.

Tony Ireland Stadium, Townsville, August 21: India A 304/7 in 50 overs (Karun Nair 72, Sanju Samson 54; Tom O'Donnell 2-46, Michael Neser 2-65) beat **National Performance Squad** 218 in 46 overs (Hilton Cartwright 65, Sam Heazlett 60; Dhawal Kulkarni 3-38, Jaydev Unadkat 3-43) by 86 runs. *MoM:* Sanju Samson.

Ray Mitchell Oval, Harrup Park, Mackay, August 24: Australia A vs **National Performance Squad**. Match abandoned without a ball bowled.

Ray Mitchell Oval, Harrup Park, Mackay, August 25: India A 140/4 in 35.2 overs (Manish Pandey 47, Kedar Jadhav 41*; Andile Phehlukwayo 2-23) vs **South Africa A**. No Result.

Ray Mitchell Oval, Harrup Park, Mackay, August 27: National Performance Squad 207/8 in 50 overs (Sam Harper 72, Clint Hinchliffe 43; Varun Aaron 3-58) lost **India A** 208/4 in 38.2 overs (Kedar Jadhav 93*, Shreyas Iyer 62; Tom O'Donnell 4-28) by six wickets. *MoM:* Kedar Jadhav.
Ray Mitchell Oval, Harrup Park, Mackay, August 28: South Africa A 134 in 42.1 overs (Khaya Zondo 40, Qaasim Adams 27; Cameron Boyce 4-21, Kane Richardson 2-11) lost to **Australia A** 136/2 in 18.5 overs (Chris Lynn 56*, Glenn Maxwell 46*) by eight wickets. *MoM:* Glenn Maxwell.
Ray Mitchell Oval, Harrup Park, Mackay, August 30: Australia A 322/6 in 50 overs (Nic Maddinson 118, Kurtis Patterson 115; Shradul Thakur 2-50) beat **India A** 321/8 in 50 overs (Manish Pandey 110, Sanju Samson 87; Daniel Worrall 2-57, Cameron Boyce 2-72) by one run. *MoM:* Nic Maddinson.
Ray Mitchell Oval, Harrup Park, Mackay, August 31: National Performance Squad 287/7 in 50 overs (Sam Heazlett 73, Caleb Jewell 62; Tabraiz Shamsi 2-68) lost to **South Africa A** 288/5 in 46.3 overs (David Miller 124*, Dane Vilas 45*; Matthew Short 2-49, Kyle Gardiner 2-57) by five wickets. *MoM:* David Miller.

Points Table

Teams	M	W	L	T	N/R	Pts	NRR
Australia A	6	3	2	0	1	16	+0.811
India A	6	3	2	0	1	16	-0.023
South Africa A	6	2	3	0	1	11	-0.097
National Performance Squad	6	2	3	0	1	10	-0.635

Australia A and India A qualified for the final

3rd place play-off: South Africa beat National Performance Squad by nine wickets

Ray Mitchell Oval, Harrup Park, Mackay, September 3: National Performance Squad 207 in 48.3 overs (Matthew Short 70, Sam Harper 60; Dwaine Pretorius 2-20, Andile Phehlukwayo 2-27) lost to **South Africa A** 209/1 in 38.2 overs (Theunis de Bruyn 90*, David Miller 72*) by five wickets. *MoM:* Theunis de Bruyn.

Final: India beat Australia by 57 runs

Ray Mitchell Oval, Harrup Park, Mackay, September 4: India A 266/4 in 50 overs (Mandeep Singh 95, Manish Pandey 61) beat **Australia A** 209 in 44.5 overs (Peter Handscomb 43, Alex Ross 34; Yuzvendra Chahal 4-34, Dhawal Kulkarni 2-22) by 57 runs. *MoM:* Mandeep Singh.

Unofficial Test series (2): Australia A 1 India A 0

1st unofficial Test: Australia A win by three wickets

Allan Border Field, Brisbane, September 8-11: India A 230 in 81.3 overs (Manish Pandey 77, Faiz Fazal 48; Mitchell Swepson 4-78, David Moody 3-26) and 156 in 48 overs (Jayant Yadav 46, Shreyas Iyer 26; Chadd Sayers 3-21, Daniel Worrall 3-43, D Moody 3-64) lost to

Australia A 228 in 63.3 overs (Peter Handscomb 87, Joe Burns 78; Varun Aaron 3-41, Jayant 3-44) and 161/7 in 57.3 overs (Cameron Bancroft 58*, Beau Webster 30; Shardul Thakur 3-42, V Aaron 2-52) by three wickets. *MoM*: Peter Handscomb.

2nd unofficial Test: Match drawn

Allan Border Field, Brisbane, September 15-18: India A 169 in 66.4 overs (Hardik Pandya 79, Jayant Yadav 28; Kane Richardson 4-37, Jackson Bird 3-53) and 158/4 in 60 overs (Akhil Herwadkar 82*, Sanju Samson 34*; Jon Holland 3-59) drew with **Australia A** 435 in 124.1 overs (Hilton Cartwright 117, Nic Maddinson 81; Shardul Thakur 5-101, Jayant 3-95). *MoM*: Hilton Cartwright.

	List A	First-class
Best batsman	Manish Pandey (India) (359 runs, 7 matches)	Akhil Herwadkar (148 runs, 2 matches)
Best bowler	Chris Tremain (Australia) (13 wickets, 5 matches)	Shardul Thakur (9 wickets, 2 matches)

Alert. Vigilant. Prepared.

A bit more for you - customers, is what made UAE Exchange the most preferred brand. This penchant for excellence has helped us in protecting your identity and safeguarding trust, thus ensuring safe and secure transactions.

Customer Service: 600 555 550 | www.uaeexchange.com

OTHER INTERNATIONALS
Pakistan v England in UAE

A tour of two halves

JOHN ETHERIDGE

Defeat in the Tests was followed by limited-overs dominance, making England's second visit to the United Arab Emirates to play Pakistan truly a tour of two halves. Familiar issues with spin – bowling it and batting against it – characterised their 2-0 Test loss, before a new-found confidence in the shorter formats illuminated six wins out of seven, the last of them, a T20 game in Sharjah, courtesy of their first super over.

The Test scoreline probably flattered Pakistan. England would have won the Abu Dhabi game had the light allowed another few overs; they were 39 balls from saving the Second Test in Dubai after an astonishing rearguard; and they gained a first-innings lead of 72 in Sharjah. The truth, however, was that once leg-spinner Yasir Shah – the most dangerous bowler on either side – was fit (he had missed the First Test after injuring his back the day before the game), Pakistan were much the stronger. By the end, they were still to lose a Test series in the UAE since it became their home in 2010-11. England, meanwhile, had won only one away Test in 15 since winning in Kolkata three winters earlier.

Yasir bowled with a pace and potency that England's spinners could not equal. The failure of Adil Rashid in particular, and to a lesser extent Moeen Ali and Samit Patel, to trouble the Pakistan batsmen caused much hand-wringing about the lack of slow bowlers in English cricket. Within weeks the ECB had decided to allow the away team in County Championship matches the choice of bowling first, without the need for a toss, mainly in the hope that groundsmen wouldn't simply produce greentops to favour the home seamers.

The Pakistan batsmen's plan, with Misbah-ul-Haq its most ruthless exponent, was clear: block the seamers, attack the spinners. Not even a visit from Shane Warne helped England. Warne spent 90 minutes offering Rashid advice on the eve of the Third Test, encouraging him to straighten his run-up and drive through his action, and discussed field-settings with Cook.

Warne also had a session with Yasir, who took 15 wickets in two Tests – taking him to 76 in his first 12. When Yasir failed a drugs test in December, it felt like a blow to the world game.

The task of containment fell instead to England's seamers. On dry, unhelpful pitches, and with little conventional swing, James Anderson produced a string of masterclasses, featuring a mixture of reverse swing, slower balls, cutters, bouncers and even spinners, conceding just 1.87 runs

Head and shoulders above: Yasir Shah bowled with a pace and potency that England's spinners could not equal. – *Getty Images*

an over. Shan Masood, the opener, found Anderson especially unplayable, falling to him four times in 17 balls before being dropped. Stuart Broad took only seven wickets, but was hardly less economical, costing just above two an over; neither had enjoyed a thriftier Test series.

England's cause was not helped by Alastair Cook losing all three tosses, though he did his best to make up for it by scoring 450 runs; he also completed a Test hundred in all nine countries in which he has played (ten if you separate England and Wales).

Five players scored centuries for Pakistan and, in Dubai, Misbah became the oldest since Bob Simpson in 1977-78 to do so in a Test, at the age of 41 years 147 days. Shoaib Malik scored 245 in Abu Dhabi, then announced his retirement from Test cricket mid-game at Sharjah. Younis Khan was persuaded to continue in one-day cricket but, bizarrely, then announced that the first game would be his last.

England grew in confidence with the white ball. Jos Buttler struggled to find a method and tempo in five-day cricket, but had few such problems in one-day cricket, and finished the 50-over series with an astonishing 46-ball century, easily beating his own record as the fastest for England. And, with the selectors looking to cover all bases ahead of the World T20, he also captained them for the first time, in the second T20 game.

Tour matches

Sharjah Cricket Stadium, October 5-6: England XI 286/5 dec in 90 overs (Jonny Bairstow 66*, Joe Root 59 retd. not out; Zafar Gohar 3-72) drew with **Pakistan A** 216/5 in 90 overs (Iftikhar Ahmed 92*, Fawad Alam 55; Moeen Ali 3-41)

Sharjah Cricket Stadium, October 8-9: Pakistan A 192/12 dec in 87.5 overs (Adnan Akmal 74*, Sami Aslam 43; Steven Finn 4-16, Adil Rashid 3-53) drew with **England XI** 198 in 78 overs (James Taylor 61, Ian Bell 53; Mir Hamza 4-34, Junaid Khan 2-28).

Test series (3): Pakistan 2 England 0

1st Test: Match drawn

Two monumental innings dominated the scorecard. Shoaib Malik, in his first Test for more than five years, hit 245 – a unique score in Tests – in 639 minutes on a slow surface, and was put on a drip in the dressing-room to rehydrate. He was trumped by Alastair Cook, whose minor medical condition allowed him to retain liquid where others sweated profusely. He knuckled down to play the longest Test innings by an England batsman, and the third-longest by anyone. For 836 minutes – four short of 14 hours – he exercised supreme skill and concentration to make 263, the second-highest of his career and, like Shoaib's, an unprecedented Test score. It left only 229, 238 and 252 unclaimed among scores below 264. His 28th Test hundred was his eighth in Asia, matching Jacques Kallis's record for a non-subcontinental batsman.

Moeen Ali became Cook's seventh opening partner since 2012, while Ian Bell overcame a nervous start to help add 165, taking 134 deliveries over his fifty. Joe Root and Ben Stokes were more fluent. Spin finally secured a wicket with its 1,021st ball of the game for Pakistan.

Cook's feat of endurance almost set up the most unlikely success. After England had declared with a first-innings lead of 75, James Anderson made inroads with an exacting new-ball spell. Then, after tea, panic spread through the Pakistan ranks. Only 16 wickets had fallen on the first four days; now

Final waltz: A unique 245 in his first Test in five years and a career-best 7 for 59 in his last wasn't a bad way for Shoaib Malik to bow out. – *Getty Images*

they were all falling at once. Pakistan lost their last seven wickets for 60 in 16.5 overs to the turning ball. Having suffered the most expensive wicketless innings figures by any debutant earlier in the game, Rashid now claimed the first five-wicket haul by an England leggie in Asia.

And so, from contemplating early handshakes, England needed 99 to win from a theoretical 19 overs – though they knew the light would allow little more than an hour, and Pakistan would slow things down. England promoted the hitters, while Pakistan relied on the spin of Shoaib and Zulfiqar Babar to take pace off the ball. The floodlights were switched on around 5.20, but made only a brief impact before Paul Reiffel and Bruce Oxenford called time at 5.46. After four and a half days of tedium, a positive finish had been denied, despite floodlights and batsmen sensing glory rather than danger. And people wonder why cricket has never taken off in America. *Richard Hobson*

Sheikh Zayed Stadium, Abu Dhabi, October 13-17: Pakistan 523/8 dec in 151.1 overs (Shoaib Malik 245, Asad Shafiq 107; Ben Stokes 4-57, James Anderson 2-42) and 173 in 57.5 overs (Misbah-ul-Haq 51, Younis Khan 45; Adil Rashid 5-64, Moeen Ali 2-28) drew with **England** 598/9 dec in 206 overs (Alastair Cook 263, Joe Root 85; Wahab Riaz 3-125, Imran Khan 2-74) and 74/4 in 11 overs (J Root 33*; S Malik 2-25, Zulfiqar Babar 2-27) *MoM*: Alastair Cook.

2nd Test: Pakistan win by 178 runs

England began the third morning upright and calm, and ended horizontal and frazzled, having lost their last seven wickets for 36 in 18 overs – and their best chance of claiming the series. That they ultimately came so close to recovering from this kick in the guts, almost saving the Test on a delicious slow-burner of a final day, was proof of their progress and potential. Rashid so nearly became a national hero. But they had simply left themselves too much to do.

The causes of their first-innings collapse, after an exemplary performance by Root, were familiar: extreme pace at one end, quality leg-spin at the other. Wahab Riaz and Yasir Shah took six of those seven wickets. Wahab took the lead role in an unbroken nine-over spell that was as remarkable for its duration as for the pace he maintained – an average of nearly 88mph. His reward was three wickets, all caught behind by Sarfraz Ahmed, all reversing away. The big one was Root. The spell consigned England to a wholly inadequate total. Round these parts, once a team concedes a lead as big as 136, it is almost impossible to plot a way back.

The first day had belonged to Misbah-ul-Haq, who made his seventh Test century as captain, equalling the Pakistan record of Inzamam-ul-Haq. Coming in at 85 for 3, Misbah settled down with Younis. Their approach was straightforward: fasting against the seamers, feasting off the spinners. Misbah scored 26 runs from 125 balls of pace, but 76 off 72 from Moeen and Rashid; Younis managed 20 from 28 bowled by the spinners, and a more sedate 36 off 87 from the seamers.

In their second hit, Younis worked his way to his 31st Test hundred, his tenth in 24 matches in the UAE, and an innings he had been threatening to play all series. He was inevitably partnered by Misbah. Pakistan declared half an hour after lunch on the fourth day, leaving England to bat out just under five sessions or 144 overs, rather than entertain thoughts of chasing down 491.

Twice on the final day, a Pakistan triumph looked a formality: first when Root, having passed 3000 Test runs, fell after another accomplished fifty; then, after Broad was eighth out, bowled by Wahab, with 41 overs left. Yet, in cahoots with Mark Wood, Rashid got his head down. On a fifth-day pitch, they batted for 29.2 overs, a Test record for the ninth wicket in the fourth innings. When the resistance ended after four hours with 39 balls left, Cook – still stung by his side's first-innings surrender – admitted they probably hadn't deserved "to get out of jail". *Osman Samiuddin*

Dubai International Cricket Stadium, October 22-26: Pakistan 378 in 118.5 overs (Misbah-ul-Haq 102, Asad Shafiq 83; Mark Wood 3-39, Moeen Ali 3-108) and 354/6 dec in 95 overs (Younis Khan 118, Misbah 87; James Anderson 2-22, Mark Wood 2-44) beat **England** 242 in 75.2 overs (Joe Root 88, Alastair Cook 65; Wahab Riaz 4-66, Yasir Shah 4-93) and 312 in 137.3 overs (J Root 71, Adil Rashid 61; Y Shah 4-87, Zulfiqar Babar 3-53) by 178 runs. *MoM*: Wahab Riaz.

3rd Test: Pakistan win by 127 runs

Though England refused to feel sorry for themselves, their hard-luck narrative – deprived of victory in Abu Dhabi and of a draw in Dubai – took further sustenance from a series-clinching century by Mohammad Hafeez. Early in Pakistan's second innings, he was given out caught behind off Anderson for two, only to be saved by a review. He survived a stumping chance and went on to an accomplished 151, before England folded with *fin de series* decadence.

As during the first two Tests, it was the difference between the teams' spinners that took its toll. While Yasir, Babar and Shoaib managed 17 wickets for 313 and conceded only 2.34 runs an over between them, Moeen, Rashid and Samit Patel took 7 for 423 and leaked 3.66. Most galling for England was the manner in which their batsmen allowed Shoaib, with only 25 wickets from 34 Tests, to harvest career-best match figures of 7 for 59.

The seamers gave England a chance. Anderson drew level with Shaun Pollock on 421 Test wickets – joint-eighth in the all-time list – when he had Azhar Ali caught behind, and would finish a triumphant first day with 15.1–7–17–4. Thirteen overs from Broad, who at one stage sent down 48 successive dot balls, yielded an equally miserly 2 for 13. Without Misbah's typically quirky 71 (of which 62 came from the spinners), Pakistan would not have scraped even 234, though a slow outfield disguised the total's worth.

England's response contained more grunt work than panache. James Taylor, back in Tests for the first time since 2012, and Jonny Bairstow shepherded the batting, before Ben Stokes's plucky emergence at No. 11 after injuring his right shoulder could extend the lead only to 72.

Hafeez, so often outshone by Younis and Misbah, dominated a fifth-wicket stand of 93 with his captain, and had made 151 out of 257 by the time he launched Moeen to long-on. Again, England had a glimmer: 185 behind, four wickets to take. But Pakistan knew how to stay ahead: the diligent Shafiq and the energetic Sarfraz ensured the final reckoning would be 284 in 112 overs, 75 more than England had ever made in the fourth innings to win a Test in Asia. Hope evaporated: England lost six for 25, the eight runs contributed by Nos. 3 to 7 equalling England's worst such effort. *Laurence Booth*

Sharjah Cricket Stadium, November 1-5: Pakistan 234 in 85.1 overs (Misbah-ul-Haq 71, Sarfraz Ahmed 39; James Anderson 4-17, Stuart Broad 2-13) and 355 in 118.2 overs (Mohammad Hafeez 151, Asad Shafiq 46; Stuart Broad 3-44, J Anderson 2-52) beat **England** 306 in 126.5 overs (James Taylor 76, Alastair Cook 49; Shoaib Malik 4-33, Yasir Shah 3-99) and 156 in 60.3 overs (A Cook 63, Moeen Ali 22; Y Shah 4-44, S Malik 3-26) by 127 runs*MoM*: Mohammad Hafeez. *MoS*: Yasir Shah.

Tour match
Sheikh Zayed Stadium Nursery 1, Abu Dhabi, November 8: England XI 342/8 in 50 overs (Moeen Ali 76, Alex Hales 67; Tanwir Afzal 2-40, Nadeem Ahmed 2-58) beat **Hong Kong** 181 in 43 overs (Babar Hayat 78, Christopher Carter 34; David Willey 4-43, Reece Topley 2-18) by 161 runs.

ODI series (4): England 3 Pakistan 1

1st ODI: Pakistan win by six wickets

England's recently revamped side began the series eager to maintain the white-ball momentum they had gained during the summer, but were perhaps a little over-eager at first. After being undone by spin in the Tests, they found themselves surprised by Pakistan's seamers, and never fully recovered from losing three wickets in the first 19 deliveries. From 14 for 3, Eoin Morgan and Taylor forged a restorative stand of 133. But both fell in a second cluster of wickets, this time four in 32 balls.

Topley, in his second ODI, gave England brief hope, swinging the new ball to take three early wickets, including Younis in his last ODI for nine. But Hafeez, continuing his form from the Tests, went on to reach his 11th ODI hundred – and first against England – while Babar Azam confirmed his promise with a sparky unbeaten half-century. An ultimately straightforward win. *John Westerby*

Sheikh Zayed Stadium, Abu Dhabi, November 11: England 216 in 49.4 overs (Eoin Morgan 76, James Taylor 60; Mohammad Irfan 3-35, Anwar Ali 2-32) lost to **Pakistan** 217/4 in 43.4 overs (Mohammad Hafeez 102*, Babar Azam 62; Reece Topley 3-26) by six wickets. *MoM*: Mohammad Hafeez.

2nd ODI: England win by 95 runs

Alex Hales made his first ODI hundred to help England square the series. They had clearly heeded the lessons from the first game, as the

White ball spark: Jos Buttler rediscovered his touch in the limited-overs games, sealing the series with a 46-ball century. – *Getty Images*

batsmen permitted themselves more time to calibrate their strokeplay to the demands of another slow pitch. Hales began as the junior partner in a measured opening stand of 102 inside 18 overs with Jason Roy, then put on 114 with Root. England looked primed for a big score, but it did not quite happen, partly because of some excellent death bowling from Riaz and Mohammad Irfan. But the Friday crowd was soon disappointed: David Willey swung one back into Babar Azam, and pushed another across Hafeez. Pakistan's middle order subsided, a slump typified by Shoaib's careless pull to short midwicket. That was one of four scalps for Woakes, who had gone wicketless in his previous six ODIs. *John Westerby*

Sheikh Zayed Stadium, Abu Dhabi, November 13: England283/5 in 50 overs (Alex Hales 109, Joe Root 63; Wahab Riaz 3-43) beat **Pakistan**188 in 45.5 overs (Sarfraz Ahmed 64, Anwar Ali 23; Chris Woakes 4-33, David Willey 3-25) by 95 runs. *MoM*: Alex Hales.

3rd ODI: England win by six wickets

Taylor's skill against spin was once again in evidence as England claimed a 2-1 lead on a turning pitch. He and Jos Buttler, who returned to form in an unbroken fifth-wicket stand of 117, rescued them from a perilous 93 for 4. Irfan had bowled a hostile opening spell to account for Roy, and Taylor and Buttler came together when Shoaib and Zafar Gohar, the debutant left-arm spinner, were turning the ball sharply. But Sarfraz missed a stumping off Shoaib before Buttler had scored; Pakistan would not get another opportunity.

Their own innings had featured an extraordinary collapse from 132 for 2. Three of the top six fell to absurd run-outs, and five others provided catches on the boundary. Woakes finished with another haul of four as the last eight wickets tumbled for 76. *John Westerby*

Sharjah Cricket Stadium, Abu Dhabi, November 17: Pakistan 208 in 49.5 overs

(Mohammad Hafeez 45, Azhar Ali 36; Chris Woakes 4-40) lost to **England** 210/4 in 41 overs (James Taylor 67*, Jos Buttler 49*; Zafar Gohar 2-54) by six wickets. *MoM*: James Taylor.

4th ODI: England win by 84 runs

The fickleness of form had seldom been more starkly illustrated than in Buttler's fortunes on this tour. Dropped from the Test team a couple of weeks earlier, he rediscovered his touch in spectacular fashion, paving the way for England's 3-1 series win with an imperious 46-ball century. He sliced a full 15 deliveries off his own record for the fastest one-day hundred for England, set against Sri Lanka at Lord's 18 months earlier. Roy hit a century too, his first in international cricket, and 355 for 5 was England's highest total overseas. Buttler's final tally of 116 not out from 52 balls included eight sixes, the most by an England batsman in a one-day innings. But even the statistics did scant justice to his strokeplay. He seemed to make use of all 360 degrees, with powerful drives back over the bowler's head, ramps over his own, and sweeps of every description. Pakistan raced off in reply and, while Shoaib was compiling a 31-ball half-century, an unlikely pursuit remained alive. But a superb diving catch from Hales ended his flurry, and the spinners did the rest. *John Westerby*

Dubai International Cricket Stadium, November 20: England 355/5 in 50 overs (Jos Buttler 116*, Jason Roy 102; Azhar Ali 2-26, Mohammad Irfan 2-64) beat **Pakistan** 271 in 40.4 overs (Shoaib Malik 52, Babar Azam 51; Moeen Ali 3-53, Adil Rashid 3-78) by 84 runs. *MoM*: Jos Buttler. *MoS*: Jos Buttler.

Tour match
Sheikh Zayed Stadium, Abu Dhabi, November 23: England XI 174/6 in 20 overs (Jason Roy 59, Alex Hales 40; Imran Haider 2-23) beat **United Arab Emirates** 95/9 in 20 overs (Fahad Tariq 23; Moeen Ali 4-11, Chris Jordan 2-14) by 79 runs.

T20I series (3): England 3 Pakistan 0

1st T20I: England win by 14 runs

• England slip to 19 for 3, but, in the absence of the rested Buttler and Root, are rescued by debutant James Vince and Morgan. • With one eye on the World T20, England adopt a rotation policy and Sam Billings is among the fringe candidates who most advances his case. • Employing strong wrists to good effect, he flicks Sohail Tanvir through midwicket and scoops Riaz over fine leg for six, reaching his maiden international fifty from 24 balls. • Rafatullah Mohmand, a 39-year-old opening batsman on his debut, is one of two early wickets for Liam Plunkett, who bowls rapidly in his first meaningful game of a long tour. • Pakistan slump to 75 for 7; their collapse includes a comical run-out, with Umar Akmal and Sohaib Maqsood racing each other to the bowler's end before Maqsood's longer reach prevails. • Reece Topley then nips Wahab's late fightback in the bud. *John Westerby*

Dubai International Cricket Stadium, November 26: England 160/5 in 20 overs (Sam

Calm at the finish: Chris Jordan reined it in at the death to deliver six precise yorkers in the super over. — *Getty Images*

Billings 53, Eoin Morgan 45*; Sohail Tanwir 2-31) beat **Pakistan** 146 in 20 overs (Sohail Tanvir 25*, Sohaib Maqsood 24; Liam Plunkett 3-21, Reece Topley 3-24) by 14 runs. *MoM*: Sam Billings.

2nd T20I: England win by three runs

• England clinch the series when Woakes holds his nerve with the last ball, which Anwar Ali needed to hit for four; they ensure Pakistan's late surge, inspired by Shahid Afridi, is in vain. • The frantic final stages are a test for Buttler, captaining England for the first time while Morgan sits out. • When Afridi comes in, Pakistan are 120 for 6 following a tidy spell from Rashid, and still require 53 from 20 balls. • But, in front of an adoring full house, he blasts Woakes for three sixes in five deliveries – the third of them a no-ball on height – during the 18th over, only to fall to the sixth. • Pakistan want 11 from the last over and though Sohail Tanvir swings the second ball through square leg for four, Woakes proves equal to the task. • Earlier, Vince top-scores for England, before becoming one of three victims for Afridi. *John Westerby*

Dubai International Cricket Stadium, November 27: England 172/8 in 20 overs (James Vince 38, Jos Buttler 33; Shahid Afridi 3-15, Anwar Ali 2-27) beat **Pakistan** 169/8 in 20 overs (Ahmed Shehzad 28, Shoaib Malik 26; Liam Plunkett 3-33, Adil Rashid 2-18) by three runs. *MoM*: Liam Plunkett.

3rd T20I: England beat Pakistan in one-over eliminator

• Neither Chris Jordan nor England has been involved in a super over before, yet the response to the tie-breaker is magnificent. • Jordan delivers six precise yorkers, restricting Afridi and Akmal to two leg-byes and a single. • It means Morgan and Buttler can pace themselves against Afridi's leg-spin, leaving England with five T20 wins out of five in 2015. • That the scores finish level after 20 overs apiece is thanks to another skilful piece of death bowling by Woakes, who limits Pakistan to two runs from the last four balls and takes the wicket of the enterprising Shoaib. • In England's innings, Aamer Yamin, a bustling seamer, produces a sharp nip-backer to remove Roy with his first ball in T20Is. • Root sparkles briefly while Woakes hits a valuable 37 from 24 before he intervenes with the ball as England finish their tour on a high.

John Westerby

Sharjah Cricket Stadium, November 30: England 154/8 in 20 overs (James Vince 46, Chris Woakes 37; Shahid Afridi 2-19, Sohail Tanwir 2-36) tied with **Pakistan** 154/7 in 20 overs (Shoaib Malik 75, S Afridi 29; David Willey 3-36). One-over eliminator: **Pakistan** 3/1 in 1 over lost to **England** 4/0 in 0.5 overs by two wickets. *MoM*: Shoaib Malik. *MoS*: James Vince.

	Tests	ODIs	T20Is
Best batsman	Alastair Cook (450 runs, 3 matches)	Mohammad Hafeez (184 runs, 4 matches)	James Vince (125 runs, 3 matches)
Best bowler	Yasir Shah (15 wickets, 2 matches)	Chris Woakes (4 wickets, 8 matches)	Liam Plunkett (6 wickets, 2 matches)

John Etheridge (@JohnSunCricket) is a journalist at News UK.

Ireland in Zimbabwe

Ervine presses home advantage

Zimbabwe overcame injury concerns and a busy schedule to save crucial ODI points against Ireland. They exploited their home advantage for a series victory that was sweeter given their deflating loss at the hands of the same opponent in the 2015 World Cup.

Both teams had their moments in the one-dayers: there were six half-centuries for the visitors, while the hosts had five scores of fifty and above, including a century for Craig Ervine, and both sets of spinners made the most of a tired Harare surface. But both were also as liable to come undone under pressure. The hosts perhaps proved a shade better in finding a batsman or two to soak in the demands of the chase. Sikandar Raza rallied the tail in the opening win; in the next, Ervine found support from Sean Williams and the middle order during his series-winning ton from No. 3. Gary Wilson and Paul Stirling stood out, and Stuart Poynter brought up his maiden hundred in the four-day game, but Ireland would have benefitted most from Tim Murtagh's consistency ahead of the Intercontinental Cup clash against Namibia.

Best batsman: Craig Ervine (161 runs, 2 matches)
Best bowler: Tim Murtagh (6 wickets, 3 matches)

ODI series (3): Zimbabwe 2 Ireland 1

1st ODI: Zimbabwe win by two wickets
Harare Sports Club, October 9: Ireland 219/8 in 50 overs (Gary Wilson 70*, Ed Joyce 53; John Nyumbu 2-35, Wellington Masakadza 2-45) lost to **Zimbabwe** 222/8 in 49 overs (Sikandar Raza 60*, Craig Ervine 60; George Dockrell 2-29, Andy McBrine 2-53) by two wickets. *MoM*: Sikandar Raza.

2nd ODI: Zimbabwe win by five wickets
Harare Sports Club, October 11: Ireland 268/7 in 50 overs (Paul Stirling 72, Gary Wilson 65; Sikandar Raza 3-49) lost to **Zimbabwe** 270/5 in 48.3 overs (Craig Ervine 101*, Sean Williams 43; Kevin O'Brien 2-46) by five wickets. *MoM*: Craig Ervine.

3rd ODI: Ireland win by two wickets
Harare Sports Club, October 13: Zimbabwe 187 in 49.2 overs (Sean Williams 51, Sikandar Raza 50; Tim Murtagh 4-32) lost to **Ireland** 189/8 in 46.5 overs (Paul Stirling 50, Andy Balbirnie 24; Wellington Masakadza 2-31, Tinotenda Mutombodzi 2-33) by two wickets. *MoM*: Tim Murtagh. *MoS*: Sikandar Raza.

Tour match
Harare Sports Club, October 17-20: Zimbabwe A 392 in 102.3 overs (Malcolm Waller 138, Regis Chakabva 104; John Mooney 4-74, Craig Young 4-107) & 346/6 dec in 71 overs (M Waller 118, R Chakabva 101; Kevin O'Brien 2-34, George Dockrell 2-75) drew with **Ireland** 353 in 95.4 overs (Stuart Poynter 125, Gary Wilson 47; Trevor Garwe 4-61, Brian Vitori 3-63) & 271/5 in 81.5 overs (J Mooney 65*, K O'Brien 56*; B Vitori 2-51, Tatenda Mupunga 2-52).

Afghanistan's march upwards: It was the first time an Associate Member beat a Test-playing nation. — *Zimbabwe Cricket*

Afghanistan in Zimbabwe

History made in Bulawayo

It was the early days of one of the biggest developing rivalries of our times. One that got no little boost when, for the first time, an Associate Member beat a Test-playing nation in a bilateral series – and went on to make it two multi-format series win for good measure.

Afghanistan's 2014 tour of Zimbabwe had ended in a deadlock, the ODIs level at 2-2 and the T20Is 1-1. The following year, under new coach Inzamam-ul-Haq and with a renewed sense of purpose, they returned to be comprehensive winners. They twice found themselves behind, and twice fought back, winning the last two ODIs and not letting up the celebrations in the two T20Is that followed.

Zimbabwe, in the middle of a suddenly busy few months, began the 50-over games well. Wellington Mazakadza, in his second series, claimed 4 for 21, while fellow left-arm spinner Tendai Chisoro on debut and Luke Jongwe took three each to keep the visitors to 122. Afghanistan's batsmen bounced back right away though, Mohammad Nabi vindicating a move up to No. 3 with his maiden ODI hundred. His big hitting, which included six sixes, resulted in a considerably more flattering total of 271; Mazakadza, the star of the previous match, was battered straight down the ground, the ball nearly clearing a three-storeyed building. Another batting collapse in the third was quickly compensated for by Mohammad Shahzad in the fourth, before an all-round performance – Dawalt Zadran's 4 for 22 perhaps the showpiece – sealed the series for them.

In a series where spinners featured prominently among the wicket takers, Rashid Khan, then all of 17, stood out as one to watch.

Sean Williams, returning from injury midway through the series, made nearly 60% of his team's 172 in the final game, and smashed Zimbabwe's fastest fifty in the deciding T20I, but both came in losing causes. Afghanistan's top order had finally come together, with the middle stepping up when it counted as well.

Tour matches

Bulawayo Athletic Club, October 8: Afghanistan 356/5 in 50 overs (Noor Ali Zadran 98, Mohammad Shahzad 78; Tendai Chisoro 3-48) beat **Zimbabwe Chairman's XI** 286 in 48.1 overs (Kevin Kasuza 80, Peter Moor 43; Nawroz Mangal 2-22, Amir Hamza 2-30) by 70 runs.
Bulawayo Athletic Club, October 10: Afghanistan 226 in 49 overs (Mohammad Shahzad 72, Asghar Stanikzai 36; Tapiwa Mufudza 3-57, Tendai Chisoro 2-29) beat **Zimbabwe Chairman's XI** 204 in 44.1 overs (T Chisoro 63, Donald Tiripano 44*; Amir Hamza 2-12, Dawlat Zadran 2-26) by 22 runs.
Bulawayo Athletic Club, October 12: Zimbabwe Chairman's XI 215 in 49 overs (Regis Chakabva 92, Joylord Gumbie 32; Fareed Ahmad 3-27, Shapoor Zadran 2-28) beat **Afghanistan** 181 in 45.3 overs (Samiullah Shenwari 57, Mohammad Shahzad 31, Asghar Stanikzai 31; Donald Tiripano 3-15, Tendai Chisoro 3-43) by 34 runs.

ODI series (5): Afghanistan 3 Zimbabwe 2

1st ODI: Zimbabwe win by eight wickets
Queens Sports Club, Bulawayo, October 16: Afghanistan 122 in 34.1 overs (Najibullah Zadran 25, Dawlat Zadran 25; Wellington Masakadza 4-21, Tendai Chisoro 3-16) lost to **Zimbabwe** 126/2 in 23.2 overs (Chamu Chibhabha 58, Richmond Mutumbami 30) by eight wickets. *MoM*: Wellington Masakadza.

2nd ODI: Afghanistan win by 58 runs
Queens Sports Club, Bulawayo, October 18: Afghanistan 271/6 in 50 overs (Mohammad Nabi 116, Noor Ali Zadran 60; Tinotenda Mutombodzi 2-40, Tinashe Panyangara 2-43) beat **Zimbabwe** 213 in 46.4 overs (Luke Jongwe 46, Craig Ervine 43; Samiullah Shenwari 2-23, Dawlat Zadran 2-25) by 58 runs. *MoM*: Mohammad Nabi.

3rd ODI: Zimbabwe win by six wickets
Queens Sports Club, Bulawayo, October 20: Afghanistan 223/6 in 50 overs (Noor Ali Zadran 56, Mohammad Nabi 42; Tendai Chisoro 2-40, Sean Williams 2-52) lost to **Zimbabwe** 229/4 in 49.4 overs (Richmond Mutumbami 74, Elton Chigumbura 49*; Amir Hamza 3-47) by six wickets. *MoM*: Richmond Mutumbami.

4th ODI: Afghanistan win by three wickets
Queens Sports Club, Bulawayo, October 22: Zimbabwe 184/8 in 50 overs (Sikandar Raza 86, Chamu Chibhabha 26; Dawlat Zadran 3-37, Rashid Khan 2-37) lost to **Afghanistan** 185/7 in 46.4 overs (Mohammad Shahzad 80, Asghar Stanikzai 32; Tendai Chisoro 3-38, Sean Williams 2-31) by three wickets. *MoM*: Mohammad Shahzad.

5th ODI: Afghanistan win by 73 runs
Queens Sports Club, Bulawayo, October 24: Afghanistan 245/9 in 50 overs (Noor Ali Zadran 54, Mohammad Nabi 53; Wellington Masakadza 3-31, Sikandar Raza 3-40) beat **Zimbabwe** 172 in 44.1 overs (Sean Williams 102; Dawlat Zadran 4-22, Amir Hamza 3-41) by 73 runs. *MoM*: Dawlat Zadran and Sean Williams. *MoS*: Mohammad Nabi.

T20I series (2): Afghanistan 2 Zimbabwe 0

1st T20I: Afghanistan win by six wickets
Queens Sports Club, Bulawayo, October 26: Zimbabwe 153/5 in 20 overs (Sikandar Raza 59, Chamu Chibhabha 54; Dawlat Zadran 3-29) lost to **Afghanistan** 154/4 in 19.1 overs (Najibullah Zadran 37*, Mohammad Shahzad 34) by six wickets. *MoM*: Dawlat Zadran.

2nd T20I: Afghanistan win by five wickets
Queens Sports Club, Bulawayo, October 28: Zimbabwe 190/7 in 20 overs (Sean Williams 54, Richmond Mutumbami 43; Dawlat Zadran 2-24, Amir Hamza 2-26) lost to **Afghanistan** 191/5 in 19.5 overs (Usman Ghani 65, Gulbadin Naib 56*; Chamu Chibhabha 2-37) by five wickets. *MoM*: Gulbadin Naib.

	T20Is	ODIs
Best batsman	Sikandar Raza (80 runs, 2 matches)	Mohammad Nabi (223 runs, 5 matches)
Best bowler	Dawlat Zadran (5 wickets, 2 matches)	Wellington Masakadza (10 wickets, 5 matches)

West Indies in Sri Lanka

Struggling visitors narrowly avoid sweep

SA'ADI THAWFEEQ

After successive home defeats by Pakistan and India, the Sri Lankans kicked off a new era – their first series without both Mahela Jayawardene and Kumar Sangakkara – by winning their two Tests against West Indies. They swept the one-day internationals, too, before West Indies salvaged something from a miserable tour with victory in the second T20 game.

It was a tough assignment for 23-year-old Jason Holder, who had replaced Denesh Ramdin as the Test captain. As ever, West Indies were in a state of flux: This was their first tour for years without the steadying influence of Shivnarine Chanderpaul, while Chris Gayle was not sighted at all after undergoing surgery on his troublesome back in August. Dwayne Bravo and Kieron Pollard were selected only for the T20 leg, angering the new coach Phil Simmons, who had wanted them for the 50-over games as well. He blamed their absence on "too much interference from outside in the selection", comments which meant he was suspended by the West Indian board; Eldine Baptiste took temporary charge.

Sri Lanka were also under new command, following Marvan Atapattu's surprise resignation early in September after the India series: Jerome Jayaratne, who had a modest first-class career as an all-rounder in the 1990s, took over as interim coach, and presided over such a happy atmosphere in the dressing-room that the players asked the board to keep him on.

As so often in Sri Lanka, spin was the visitors' undoing. Rangana Herath claimed ten wickets in the innings victory at Galle, and five more in the Second Test, to take him close to 300 overall. He had promising support from Milinda Siriwardana, another slow left-armer and, at 29, a latecomer to Test cricket. But there was a setback for off-spinner Tharindu Kaushal, a prolific do-

Old-school force: The West Indies batsmen yielded to Rangana Herath's spin. – *WICB*

mestic wicket-taker, who managed only one expensive scalp at Galle. He had been reported for a suspect action after the series against India, which seemed to affect his confidence.

The West Indian batsmen struggled in both Tests – their highest total in four attempts was 251 – and managed only three half-centuries, two of them by Darren Bravo. The bowling was equally uninspiring, though Jomel Warrican on debut and part-time off-spinner Kraigg Brathwaite set up an outside chance of victory in the Second Test.

Sri Lanka's 2-0 victory made them the first holders of a new trophy between the sides, named after Garry Sobers and Michael Tissera, a Sri Lankan captain from pre-Test days. Sobers flew in for the Second Test, and gave a tearful speech: "My whole obligation was to West Indies cricket. I never made a run for me. I always played for the West Indies teams. Records meant nothing. I don't think we have that kind of person today."

Tour match
Sinhalese Sports Club Ground, Colombo, October 9-11: West Indies 209 in 65.3 overs (Carlos Brathwaite 54, Kraigg Brathwaite 46; Suraj Randiv 5-73, Suranga Lakmal 3-26) drew with **Sri Lanka Board President's XI** 455/7 in 107 overs (Udara Jayasundera 142, Milinda Siriwardana 105*, Minod Bhanuka 101; Jason Holder 2-54, Kemar Roach 2-58).

Test series (2): Sri Lanka 2 West Indies 0

1st Test: Sri Lanka win by an innings and six runs

Sri Lanka were easy winners, running up a huge total, then letting their spinners loose on the ever-helpful Galle pitch. But it might have been different had West Indies not dropped five catches – two of them off Dinesh Chandimal, who went on to make 151.

Dimuth Karunaratne, the cautious left-hander, and the more adventurous Chandimal batted through heat and humidity to complete the first 200 partnership by either side in this fixture. Karunaratne compiled a career-best 186 in 482 minutes, before the last seven wickets tumbled for 59, Devendra Bishoo taking three in 12 balls.

It wasn't long before Sri Lanka's spinners got stuck in. Darren Bravo – who had scored 58 on Test debut at Galle five years previously – made another studied half-century, but no one else could make much headway. Rangana Herath finished with his eighth five-for at the ground.

Angelo Mathews enforced the follow-on, and this time it was the other slow left-armer, the debutant Milinda Siriwardana, who made the breakthrough. Marlon Samuels failed again – a miserable match got worse when his bowling action was reported for the third time in his career – and West Indies were sinking fast at 88 for 5. Jermaine Blackwood counter-attacked, hitting three sixes on his way to 92, but only delayed the inevitable. He was last out, midway through the fourth day, as Sri Lanka completed the ninth win in 14 Tests at Galle since July 2009.

Cool customer: Dinesh Chandimal made the most of the chances given to him to bring up a century. – *WICB*

Galle International Stadium, October 14-17: Sri Lanka 484 in 152.3 overs (Dimuth Karunaratne 186, Dinesh Chandimal 151; Devendra Bishoo 4-143, Jerome Taylor 2-65) beat **West Indies** 251 in 82 overs (Darren Bravo 50, J Taylor 31; Rangana Herath 6-68, Dhammika Prasad 2-38) and 227 in 68.3 overs (f/o) (Jermaine Blackwood 92, Kraigg Brathwaite 34; R Herath 4-79, D Prasad 2-28) by 6 runs. *MoM*: Rangana Herath.

2nd Test: Sri Lanka win by 72 runs

In front of Sir Garfield Sobers, and hordes of schoolchildren admitted free, West Indies twice threatened to square the series, only for their batsmen to fall short again. They owed the chance of their first Test win in 11 attempts in Sri Lanka to two unheralded bowlers: Jomel Warrican, a slow left-armer from Barbados making his debut, took four wickets on the opening day. Then, Kraigg Brathwaite, whose rarely seen off-breaks had claimed a solitary wicket in 23 previous Tests, polished off the second innings with a six-for.

However, West Indies' batting would have made Sobers wince. It was a team effort by Sri Lanka's bowlers: Herath, Siriwardana, and Dhammika Prasad, the paceman, took five wickets apiece, while Dilruwan Perera, the off-spinner, claimed four.

Siriwardana also starred with the bat, his maiden Test half-century in the first innings the highest score of the match after Sri Lanka had slipped to 90 for 5. Sri Lanka then tried to build on their slender lead of 37, and Mathews and Siriwardana took Sri Lanka 188 in front – only for the unsung Brathwaite to up-end the innings with six cheap wickets for his rusty off-breaks as the hosts collapsed in a heap.

With West Indies needing 244, rain wiped out the fourth day. Shai Hope and Bravo took the total to 80 when play resumed on the fifth morning. But then, the wheels fell off.

P Sara Oval, Colombo, October 22-26: Sri Lanka 200 in 66 overs (Milinda Siriwardana 68, Rangana Herath 26*; Jomel Warrican 4-67, Jason Holder 2-22) and 206 in 75.3 overs (Angelo Mathews 46, M Siriwardana 42; Kraigg Brathwaite 6-29, Jerome Taylor 2-26) beat **West Indies** 163 in 64.2 overs (K Brathwaite 47, J Holder 21; Dhammika Prasad 4-34, Dilruwan Perera 3-28) and 171 in 65.5 overs (Darren Bravo 61, Shai Hope 35; R Herath 4-56, M Siriwardana 3-25) by 72. *MoM*: Milinda Siriwardana. *MoS*: Rangana Herath.

Tour match
Colts Cricket Club Ground, Colombo, October 29: West Indies 318 in 48.4 overs (Carlos Brathwaite 113, Andre Russell 89; Binura Fernando 3-71, Seekkuge Prasanna 2-60) beat **Sri Lanka Board President's XI** 103/3 in 21 overs (Lahiru Thirimanne 41, Kusal Mendis 32) by 43 runs (D/L Method).

ODI series (3): Sri Lanka 3 West Indies 0

1st ODI: Sri Lanka win by one wicket (DLS method)

Sri Lanka's last pair pinched a close game, after coming together with 11 needed from 14 balls to overhaul a revised target of 163 in 26 overs. A leg injury to Andre Russell meant West Indies were a bowler short. Jason Holder entrusted the penultimate over to the medium-pace of Johnson Charles, who had never bowled in 32 previous one-day appearances. After conceding three from his first four balls, Charles overstepped – and Ajantha Mendis smashed the free hit over the long-on boundary to win the match. It was tough on Sunil Narine, who took 3 for 21 in his first international for more than a year. Earlier, West Indies had been floundering at 42 for 4, before Russell clouted 41 from 24 balls, and Holder 36 from 13; both hit three sixes. Tillakaratne Dilshan gave the chase an explosive start with 59 from 32. Holder was suspended from the next match for a slow over-rate.

R Premadasa Stadium, Colombo, November 1: West Indies 159/8 in 26 overs (Andre Russell 41, Darren Bravo 38; Suranga Lakmal 3-15, Ajantha Mendis 2-46) lost to **Sri Lanka** 164/9 in 24.5 overs (Tillakaratne Dilshan 59, A Mendis 21*; Sunil Narine 3-21, Jonathan Carter 2-14) by one wicket. *MoM*: Tillakaratne Dilshan.

2nd ODI: Sri Lanka win by eight wickets (DLS method)

Charles did his best with the bat to atone for his first-match bowling, but a rainbreak in the 27th over, which lopped 12 off each innings, was untimely for West Indies, who then lost 6 for 65 in 11 – four of them to silly run-outs. After a worrying time with injuries, Lasith Malinga looked back to full fitness. Kusal Perera and Lahiru Thirimanne piled on 156 for the second wicket, taking Sri Lanka close to their revised target of 225 in 38 overs. Stand-in captain Samuels should not have been permitted to bowl, as the 14-day grace period since his action was reported had run out. But West Indies had chosen

Picking up the baton: Kusal Perera narrowly missed out on a century, finishing the ODIs with two fifties. – *WICB*

their team after being incorrectly advised by the ICC that Samuels could bowl.

R Premadasa Stadium, Colombo, November 4: West Indies 214 in 37.4 overs (Johnson Charles 83, Marlon Samuels 63; Milinda Siriwardana 2-27, Lasith Malinga 2-43) lost to **Sri Lanka** 225/2 in 36.3 overs (Kusal Perera 99, Lahiru Thirimanne 81) by eight wickets. *MoM*: Kusal Perera.

3rd ODI: Sri Lanka win by 19 runs (DLS method)

Rain again played spoilsport, interrupting West Indies' innings twice, then making a final appearance late on with Sri Lanka ahead of the par score of 161. West Indies had nosedived to 18 for 4 in the sixth over, and were indebted to Samuels's ninth century in ODIs. But his team-mates mustered only 74 between them. Sri Lanka stayed in front, reaching 100 in the 18th over, and the rain finally ended proceedings in the 33rd. There was more bad news for West Indies after the match: Narine's action was reported again, and he was banned from bowling in international cricket three weeks later.

Pallekele International Cricket Stadium, November 7: West Indies 206/9 in 36 overs (Marlon Samuels 110; Dushmantha Chameera 2-39, Suranga Lakmal 2-40) lost to **Sri Lanka** 180/5 in 32.3 overs (Kusal Perera 50, Angelo Mathews 27*; Jason Holder 2-44) by 19 runs. *MoM*: Marlon Samuels. *MoS*: Kusal Perera.

T20I series (2): Sri Lanka 1 West Indies 1

1st T20I: Sri Lanka win by 30 runs

• Sri Lanka go along at more than ten an over, and pass 200 for the first time in a home T20I. • Perera and Dilshan put on 91 in 9.4, Shehan Jayasuriya chips in, and Chandimal and Mathews keep swinging. • In all, 84 come from the last five. • West Indies lose Charles to Malinga's second delivery, but Fletcher clobbers six sixes to keep his side in the hunt. • West Indies sniff a chance when Dwayne Bravo and Kieron Pollard – restored to the side for the shortest format – put on 51. • But both fall in the space of four balls, before the dangerous pair of Darren Sammy and Holder succumbs to successive deliveries from Sachithra Senanayake.

Pallekele International Cricket Stadium, November 9: Sri Lanka 215/3 in 20 overs (Tillakaratne Dilshan 56, Dinesh Chandimal 40*; Kieron Pollard 2-42) beat **West Indies** 185 in 19.5

overs (Andre Fletcher 57, K Pollard 26; Sachithra Senanayake 4-46, Lasith Malinga 2-19) by 30 runs. *MoM*: Sachithra Senanayake.

2nd T20I: West Indies win by 23 runs

• West Indies break their international duck for the tour at the last gasp, thanks to Dwayne Bravo, who follows a run-a-ball 31 with four wickets. • Sri Lanka, at one stage 93 for 1, lose their last nine for 46. • Fletcher and Charles start the match with 62 in 6.2 overs, then the unsung Ramdin's brisk unbeaten 34 pushes his side well past 150. • Dilshan begins in typically belligerent fashion, and puts on 70 with Jayasuriya. • After that, only Siriwardana can manage double figures. • West Indies' fielding finally hits the heights: Russell sprints to his left from long-on to cling on superbly to Jayasuriya's lofted drive.

R Premadasa Stadium, Colombo, November 11: West Indies 162/6 in 20 overs (Denesh Ramdin 34*, Johnson Charles 34; Lasith Malinga 2-16, Milinda Siriwardana 2-17) beat **Sri Lanka** 139 in 20 overs (Tillakaratne Dilshan 52, Shehan Jayasuriya 30; Dwayne Bravo 4-28, Ravi Rampaul 3-20) by 23 runs. *MoM*: Dwayne Bravo. *MoS*: Tillakaratne Dilshan.

	Tests	ODIs	T20Is
Best batsman	Dimuth Karunaratne (199 runs, 2 matches)	Marlon Samuels (175 runs, 3 matches)	Tillakaratne Dilshan (108 runs, 2 matches)
Best bowler	Rangana Herath (15 wickets, 2 matches)	Suranga Lakmal (6 wickets, 3 matches)	Lasith Malinga (4 wickets, 2 matches)

Sa'adi Thawfeeq (@SThawfeeq) is a cricket writer based in Colombo.

New Zealand in Australia

Hosts take honours on pink ball debut

GEOFF LEMON

This series will be remembered as the birth of day-night Test cricket, so newly delivered as to feel slick with caul. Its infant health proved sufficiently robust to avoid abandonment on a hillside, but, depending on your perspective, the weanling could grow up to be either cricket's saviour or the monster that devours it. Either scenario places a lot of responsibility on a newborn.

Destruction, at least, won't be attributable to the format's pink ball. The lurid Kookaburra with the pine-green stitching stood up staunchly to everything asked of it on its first Test outing, during the third match, in Adelaide. The grassy pitch designed to preserve the ball's condition also helped preserve the sanity of onlookers, providing a more balanced contest after the Perth Test was dominated by the bat. As for concerns about visibility, ask the fan who pulled off a spectacular catch from the first pink-ball six, at deep square leg, at dusk.

When this series had first been scheduled, New Zealand's Test side were so weak they were designated as the warm-up act for the touring clown show that is the modern West Indies. But Brendon McCullum had overseen New Zealand's resurgence. Australia had lost badly in the UAE and England over

Test cricket in the shadows: Are day-night Test matches cricket's saviour or the monster that devours it? — *Getty Images*

the previous 13 months, while the New Zealanders had fought creditably in both countries for 1-1 draws.

Yet, as it turned out, their new breed retained a mental block. They were barely present for the First Test, nor for the opening day of the Second, and with that the chance of a series win was gone. While they fought back in Perth to draw, and were denied a potentially match-winning lead in Adelaide by an error from third umpire Nigel Llong, it was the first time since their tour of England in 2013, eight series earlier, that New Zealand had tasted overall defeat.

Even so, there was plenty to cheer. As his Test average marched towards 50, Kane Williamson filled one of the few remaining holes in his resume by taking a hundred – in fact two – off the Australians, to finish the series with 428 runs at 85. Ross Taylor's Perth 290, meanwhile, was the highest Test score by a visiting batsman in Australia. Doug Bracewell bowled impressive spells, and Trent Boult came close to winning the Third Test with 5 for 60. McCullum was admired, and his every dismissal – in what turned out to be his final overseas series – cheered with a tinge of relief.

For Australia the series was about renewal. Two seasons earlier, 11 Australians surged through the 2013-14 Ashes whitewash unchanged. Only three were ever-present then and now. Against England, Steve Smith, David Warner and Nathan Lyon had been junior parties. Now they were captain, vice-captain and the 'GOAT' – designated mirthfully by team-mates as the Greatest Of All Time after becoming the nation's most prolific off-spinner.

Warner embraced responsibility, making three consecutive centuries for the second time in his career, including his first double and his two longest innings. He finished with 592 runs; only Graham Gooch (752), Brian Lara (688) and Mohammad Yousuf (665) had compiled more in a series of three Tests. Usman Khawaja scored two tons on his return to the side before tweaking his hamstring, while newly anointed opener Joe Burns also hit a maiden hundred, in the First Test. Adam Voges proved his worth as a late-blooming selection with 285 runs at 71. The sensible and economical choice of Peter Siddle had been forced on the selectors come Adelaide, where Mitchell Starc's injured ankle allowed Josh Hazlewood a turn as attack leader.

Best batsman: David Warner (592 runs, 3 matches)
Best bowler: Mitchell Starc (13 wickets, 3 matches)

Tour matches

Manuka Oval, Canberra, October 23: New Zealanders 307/8 in 50 overs (Tom Latham 131, Martin Guptill 94; Jason Behrendorff 3-56) beat **Prime Minister's XI** 205 in 45.2 overs (Ryan Carters 74, Adam Voges 55; James Neesham 3-23, Trent Boult 3-27) by 102 runs.
Manuka Oval, Canberra, October 24-25: Cricket Australia XI 325/4 in 90 overs (Usman Khawaja 111*, Joe Burns 102) drew with **New Zealanders** 368/8 in 82 overs (Kane Williamson 68, Mark Craig 60).
Blacktown International Sportspark, Sydney, October 29-31: Cricket Australia XI 503/1 dec in 121.1 overs (Aaron Finch 288*, Ryan Carters 209) drew with **New Zealanders**.

Study in styles: David Warner struck centuries in both innings in Brisbane, while Kane Williamson's ton was typically immaculate. — *Getty Images*

Test series (3): Australia 2 New Zealand 0

1st Test: Australia win by 208 runs

You could understand why people fancied New Zealand. Australia's new opener Joe Burns had boshed a few one-day runs in the build-up. Steve Smith, their sole success at first drop since Ricky Ponting, was forced down to No. 4 by the return of Usman Khawaja, a previous failure, which in turn placed extra pressure on Khawaja himself. Adam Voges was lucky to have made it to seven Tests. And Mitchell Marsh had not proved himself more than a bowling slogger. Arrayed against this disorder were Tim Southee and Trent Boult, both of whom had spent most of the World Cup hooping the white ball into the stumps of defenceless batsmen. A muggy tropical morning, you imagined, and they might cause havoc. That remained in the imagination. For the first 20 minutes Southee bent a few, including one just past Burns's off stump. But, once that brief shadow passed, the pattern of so many Gabba Tests was imposed once more, as Australia chugged relentlessly to 556 for 4, and New Zealand delivered lengths that made scoring simple.

For the third home season in a row, David Warner struck a century in Australia's opening match. And, for the second season in a row, he did it in both innings, joining Ponting and Sunil Gavaskar as the only batsmen to make twin Test tons on three occasions. Khawaja's maiden century came to generous home-ground applause; when he fell on the second day, it provoked

Smith's declaration. Williamson provided the only resistance after the long drag in the field. His 140 out of 317 was a Test knock of the finest standard, especially when the three below him mustered nine runs between them; it made him the first to pass 2000 international runs in 2015. It was his work through cover and point that thrilled the most, the immaculate timing of each cut, late cut and drive, the way the ball flew from his bat to the fence. He made nearly a century in boundaries alone, and was caught behind only when the need to shield No. 11 Boult from Starc disrupted his rhythm.

With a lead of 239 and liberty to swing, Burns and Warner became the first Australian openers to put on 100 in each innings of a Test. Burns reached his first century in Tests with two sixes in three balls off Mark Craig under stormy skies; Warner followed in a blaze of shots.

Set 504 on the fourth morning, New Zealand could opt only for a go-slow. Tom Latham stonewalled for more than an hour and a half, and Martin Guptill for more than three. But they were prised out and, while Williamson batted as fluidly as his first attempt and Brendon McCullum entertained, you couldn't help feeling flat at the contest that never materialised.

Brisbane Cricket Ground, Woolloongabba, November 5-9: Australia 556/4 dec in 130.2 overs (Usman Khawaja 174, David Warner 163) and 264/4 in 42 overs (Joe Burns 129, D Warner 116; Mark Craig 3-78) beat **New Zealand** 317 in 82.2 overs (Kane Williamson 140, Tom Latham 47; Mitchell Starc 4-57, Mitchell Johnson 3-105) and 295 in 88.3 overs (Brendon McCullum 80, K Williamson 59; Nathan Lyon 3-63, Mitchell Marsh 2-25) by 208 runs. *MoM*: David Warner.

2nd Test: Match drawn

It is Perthian pre-match tradition to talk things up. This, we are told every year, will be a return to the old WACA pitch: pace, carry, bounce, lightning, nostalgia. But, as so often, looking to the past leads to disappointment. The 2015 edition was more kitchen sponge than trampoline. Nicks, even in the opening overs, didn't carry. Runs were plonked at will. The bowlers couldn't work on swing because the ball kept going out of shape. "Things fall apart; the centre cannot hold," warned WB Yeats. And so the icons fell: the WACA dead, the Kookaburra plucked and, some time on the third day, Australia's fourth-highest wicket-taker looked around and asked, "What's the point?"

Again, Smith won the toss; again, New Zealand bowled poorly. This time, Warner went bigger, scoring more runs on the first day of a Test – 244 – than anyone bar Don Bradman, who made 309 in Leeds in 1930 (and 244 himself at The Oval in 1934). His innings of 253 was measured and controlled, balancing risk against reward. Until Ross Taylor trumped him, it was the WACA's second-highest Test score, after Matthew Hayden's then world-record 380 against Zimbabwe in 2003-04. Khawaja added a century of his own, but he would injure a hamstring in the field the following day and take no further part in the series.

New Zealand fought back admirably on the second day, bowling tighter lines to a side looking to push on, and defying the conditions to take 7 for

143, but Smith's declaration denied them the satisfaction of bowling his side out.

Deep into the fifth session of the match, New Zealand's batsmen could easily have fallen over. Guptill went fifth ball and Latham for 36, but this time Williamson found support in Taylor for a partnership that would reach 265 before Williamson miscued Josh Hazlewood halfway through the third day.

Starc unleashed a terrifically fast new-ball spell, the speed gun alleging 160.4kph (99.66mph), but Taylor fought fire with fire, slashing six boundaries in Starc's six-over burst. He passed Martin Crowe's 188 in 1985-86 to reach the highest New Zealand score against Australia, and started his third day of batting on 235. He finished with 290 – including 43 fours – the highest by an overseas batsman in Australia, passing Englishman Tip Foster's 287, set in Sydney on his debut way back in 1903-04.

With 624, New Zealand had a 65-run lead. It was during this batathon that Johnson found himself, ball in hand, wondering why he was still doing this. If ever a pitch was going to prompt an existential crisis, this was it. Only a mighty collapse would produce a result. Instead, Smith and Voges made centuries in a stand of 224, and Johnson announced his retirement on the final morning.

Australia batted until after lunch, before setting a nominal 321. The sparse crowd could only cheer Johnson's last few boundaries with the bat, and his final wickets as he removed New Zealand's openers with two farewell bouncers. But then it was back to Taylor and Williamson, condemning Johnson's last outing to a conclusion as flat as the pitch that hosted it.

WACA Ground, Perth, November 13-17: Australia 559/9 dec in 133 overs (David Warner 253, Usman Khawaja 121; Mark Craig 3-123, Doug Bracewell 2-81) and 385/7 dec in 103 overs (Steven Smith 138, Alex Voges 119; Tim Southee 4-97, Trent Boult 2-77) drew with **New Zealand** 624 in 153.5 overs (Ross Taylor 290, Kane Williamson 166; Mitchell Starc 4-119, Nathan Lyon 3-107) and 104/2 in 28 overs (Ross Taylor 36*, Kane Williamson 32*; Mitchell Johnson 2-20). *MoM*: Ross Taylor.

Tour match

WACA Ground, Perth, November 21-22: Western Australia XI 345/13 in 90 overs (Sam Whiteman 117, William Bosisto 78; Neil Wagner 5-62, Mitchell Santner 4-62) drew with **New Zealanders** 426/11 in 89.2 overs (Martin Guptill 103, BJ Watling 81; Andrew Tye 4-40, Joel Paris 3-31).

3rd Test: Australia win by three wickets

It's not often that an umpiring blooper overshadows a match of such historical significance. But that was what happened at Adelaide Oval in the first Test match to be played under lights. Australia won by three wickets, more comfortably than the margin suggests, but it was Nigel Llong's reprieve of Nathan Lyon on the second evening that dominated discussions long after the last ball was bowled.

Australia had bowled with tremendous discipline to dismiss New Zealand

Keeping up the pressure: New Zealand pushed the Australians hard on the third evening in Adelaide, but the hosts' lower middle order held on to wrap up the Test and the series. – *Getty Images*

Errors and consequences: Nigel Llong ruled Nathan Lyon not out based on wrong replays and the spinner went on to save the match. — *Getty Images*

for 202 soon after dinner on the opening day. Starc and Hazlewood took three wickets apiece, but it was Peter Siddle that stemmed New Zealand's early momentum with a marvellously restrictive spell to the in-form Williamson. And despite losing Warner and Burns early, Smith and Voges ensured it was emphatically Australia's day in front of a huge crowd of 47,441.

That home-team dominance didn't extend into day two. No one New Zealand bowler stood out, but they performed impeccably as a unit. By tea, now the first interval of the day, Australia had slumped to 116 for 8, with only Smith putting up any resistance. And moments after play resumed, it should have been 118 for 9.

Lyon looked to sweep Mitchell Santner, the left-arm spinner who was making his debut, and the ball leapt off the back of the bat on to his shoulder. From there, it lobbed to Williamson at second slip. S Ravi, the umpire, said not out, but New Zealand's decision to review was immediate. Hot Spot showed a mark as clear as the pink blush on the back of Lyon's bat, and he was halfway to the pavilion by the time Llong, the third umpire, was going through the replays.

After a farcical sequence of events that lasted five minutes and included the wrong replay being viewed, the absence of a Snickometer spike convinced Llong that the Hot Spot evidence "could have come from anywhere". A sheepish Lyon resumed his innings and added an invaluable 74 with Peter Nevill, whose punchy 66 was the highest score of the game.

Instead of a sizeable deficit, Australia finished with a 22-run lead. And by stumps, with the pink ball zipping around on an unusually well-grassed Adelaide pitch, New Zealand had slipped to 116 for 5. Santner's all-round quality and some lower-order biffing from Doug Bracewell allowed them to eke past 200, but a target of 187 was never likely to be enough once Warner stroked his way to 35 from just 37 balls.

Boult finally found his rhythm to give Australia a real scare, but the much-maligned Shaun Marsh made 49, adding 46 with Mitchell, his younger brother. There were more stutters after dinner, but Siddle and Starc, two of the bowling heroes, finished things off, even as the third of the pace trio, Hazlewood, won match honours for his 6 for 70 in the second innings.

For once, Adelaide hadn't delivered a batting beauty, but the 123,736 that

came through the turnstiles lapped up the three-day Test. Blood-orange skies provided the backdrop for one of cricket's prettiest venues, but it was the bright pink ball that was the cynosure of most eyes. The batsmen didn't enjoy the experience as much as the bowlers, but the Test that started a year to the day after Phillip Hughes's tragic passing felt very much like the gateway to a brave new world.
Dileep Premachandran

Adelaide Oval, November 27-29: New Zealand 202 in 65.2 overs (Tom Latham 50, Mitchell Santner 31; Mitchell Starc 3-24, Josh Hazlewood 3-66) and 208 in 62.5 overs (M Santner 45, Ross Taylor 32; J Hazlewood 6-70, Mitchell Marsh 3-59) lost to **Australia** 224 in 72.1 overs (Peter Nevill 66, Steven Smith 53; Doug Bracewell 3-18, Trent Boult 2-41) and 187/7 in 51 overs (Shaun Marsh 49, David Warner 35; T Boult 5-60) by three wickets. *MoM*: Josh Hazlewood. *MoS*: David Warner.

Geoff Lemon (@GeoffLemonSport.) is a writer and broadcaster for The Guardian *and* The Roar.

Zimbabwe in Bangladesh

Slighted hosts extend home run

NEIL MANTHORP

The cancellation by Australia of their two-Test series because of security fears had created a window in Bangladesh's calendar. It needed to be filled, for commercial as much as philanthropic reasons, in a nation whose passionate supporters had finally begun to see their team beating the world's top sides. One-day victories over Pakistan, India and South Africa had led to a belief that, 15 years after Test admission, Bangladesh's cricketers were finally doing their country justice. The Australian tour was going to be a test of their worth. The disappointment was palpable when security reports suggested the visit would be unsafe.

The gap was filled by the ever-eager Zimbabweans, who had also been willing to tour Pakistan five months earlier, despite security advice to the contrary. Safety was just about the last concern for a team who had grown almost as familiar with Dhaka as they had with Harare or Bulawayo.

Bangladesh grabbed the opportunity to confirm they had moved on, and left the sides' recent rivalry behind. For their part, Zimbabwe had a chance to show that their busiest international home season had improved their game. As always, they played fine shots, bowled good balls and held excellent catches. But they could also slog wildly, deliver a pie every over and drop dollies. Most worrying was their naivety in match situations that most club teams would recognise and understand better. Thanks to Malcolm Waller and Neville Madziva, who saw off the 18 they needed in the last over, they did at least round off the tour with a win, which squared the T20 series after a 50-over whitewash.

Bangladesh looked clinical and complete. Soft of hand and quick of foot, Mushfiqur Rahim set up their first win with a calm hundred, his fourth in ODIs. The slippery Mustafizur Rahman again showed his class – and there were several nods of appreciation and shakes of the head from the batsmen who survived him.

The fact that their unprecedented five series wins were all at home was not their fault; rather it was an indictment of the embarrassment that passes for an international schedule. The major nations say Bangladesh tours lose money, so they don't invite them. That may have been the case in the past, but the current team, more than any other, deserves a chance to prove its worth overseas.

Tour match
Khan Saheb Osman Ali Stadium, Fatullah, November 5: Bangladesh Cricket Board XI
277/8 in 50 overs (Mushfiqur Rahim 81*, Imrul Kayes 56; Luke Jongwe 3-20, Graeme Cremer

3-21) lost to **Zimbabwe** 281/3 in 46.4 overs (Craig Ervine 95, Elton Chigumbura 64; Sunzamul Islam 2-70) by seven wickets.

ODI series (3): Bangladesh 3 Zimbabwe 0

1st ODI: Bangladesh win by 145 runs
Shere Bangla National Stadium, Mirpur, November 7: Bangladesh 273/9 in 50 overs (Mushfiqur Rahim 107, Sabbir Rahman 57; Sikandar Raza 2-47, Taurai Muzarabani 2-64) beat **Zimbabwe** 128 in 36.1 overs (Elton Chigumbura 41, Luke Jongwe 39; Shakib Al Hasan 5-47, Mashrafe Mortaza 2-13) by 145 runs. *MoM*: Mushfiqur Rahim.

2nd ODI: Bangladesh win by 58 runs
Shere Bangla National Stadium, Mirpur, November 9: Bangladesh 241/9 in 50 overs (Imrul Kayes 76, Nasir Hossain 41; Tinashe Panyangara 3-41, Taurai Muzarabani 2-32) beat **Zimbabwe** 183 in 43.2 overs (Elton Chigumbura 47, Sikandar Raza 33; Mustafizur Rahman 3-33, Al-Amin Hossain 2-22) by 58 runs. *MoM*: Imrul Kayes.

3rd ODI: Bangladesh win by 61 runs
Shere Bangla National Stadium, Mirpur, November 11: Bangladesh 276/9 in 50 overs (Imrul Kayes 73, Tamim Iqbal 73; Luke Jongwe 2-50, Graeme Cremer 2-53) beat **Zimbabwe** 215 in 43.3 overs (Sean Williams 64, Elton Chigumbura 45; Mustafizur Rahman 5-34) by 61 runs. *MoM*: Tamim Iqbal. *MoS*: Mustafizur Rahman.

T20I series (2): Bangladesh 1 Zimbabwe 1

1st T20I: Bangladesh win by four wickets
Shere Bangla National Stadium, Mirpur, November 13: Zimbabwe 131 in 19.3 overs (Malcolm Waller 68, Craig Ervine 20; Mustafizur Rahman 2-16, Al-Amin Hossain 2-20, Mashrafe Mortaza 2-20) lost to **Bangladesh** 136/6 in 17.4 overs (Tamim Iqbal 31, Mahmudullah 22*, Graeme Cremer 3-29, Tendai Chisoro 2-15) by four wickets. *MoM*: Malcolm Waller.

2nd T20I: Zimbabwe win by three wickets
Shere Bangla National Stadium, Mirpur, November 15: Bangladesh 135/9 in 20 overs (Anamul Haque 47, Tamim Iqbal 21; Tinashe Panyangara 3-30, Graeme Cremer 2-21) lost to **Zimbabwe** 136/7 in 19.5 overs (Malcolm Waller 40, Luke Jongwe 34; Al-Amin Hossain 3-20) by three wickets. *MoM*: Neville Madziva. *MoS*: Malcolm Waller.

	T20Is	ODIs
Best batsman	Malcolm Waller (108 runs, 2 matches)	Mushfiqur Rahim (156 runs, 3 matches)
Best bowler	Al-Amin Hossain (5 wickets, 2 matches)	Mustafizur Rahman (8 wickets, 3 matches)

Neil Manthorp (@NeilManthorp) is a cricket writer and broadcaster based in Cape Town.

West Indies in Australia

Holder's men wilt under spotlight

ADAM COLLINS

It is said that to hang a lantern on your problems is to begin solving them. The solution may be distant, but West Indies cricket had the biggest, brightest floodlights trained on its troubles, as the side was annihilated in the premier time slot of the Australian summer. Across three Test matches, the tourists served as glorified bowling machines – and their batting fared little better.

As usual, West Indies were, for various reasons, missing some of their strongest players, not least the trio of Chris Gayle, Dwayne Bravo and Andre Russell, all enjoying themselves in Australia's Big Bash League while the Test team wilted.

The statistics were no less absurd. Adam Voges lifted his average against West Indies to 542 in five Tests (and his overall figure to 85). In a welcome counter-attack in Hobart, Kraigg Brathwaite briefly threatened Charles Bannerman's record for the highest proportion of runs in a completed innings (67.34%), dating back to the very first Test match in 1877; he had to settle for fourth on the list, having made 94 out of West Indies' 148 all out – or 63.51%. In Melbourne, four Australians made centuries in an innings for the

Driving force: Adam Voges lifted his average against the West Indies to an absurd 542 in five Tests. – *Getty Images*

third time. And only a promotion up the order on the final day of the Third Test saved wicketkeeper Peter Nevill from registering a "did not bat" through an entire series. In all, Australia scored 1489 runs for the loss of 12 wickets, to West Indies' 1254 for 48.

This isn't to say the series didn't matter to individuals. An understated story was the elevation of 31-year-old slow left-armer Stephen O'Keefe to the Australian team for the Third Test, in which he looked the part, and put himself in contention for the second spinner's role for the tour of Sri Lanka in 2016.

On the batting front, the Australian selectors made a tough – but justified – decision to drop Shaun Marsh after his 182 at Hobart. Instead, they kept faith with Usman Khawaja, returning from a hamstring injury, and Joe Burns, both of whom had been picked against New Zealand at the start of the summer; each made a century in Melbourne.

West Indies did, though, have one or two bright spots. Darren Bravo's refusal to accept the status quo in Melbourne, where he made a dogged 81, was as impressive as his classy century in Hobart. Kraigg Brathwaite looked up to the task of being a Test opener, while his unrelated namesake Carlos added much-needed spunk as a big-hitting all-rounder down the order. Jason Holder, the captain, showed himself to be a capable cricketer with visible determination, speaking with eloquence and purpose. He bowled better than his numbers suggested, and his batting may demand a promotion to bolster a fragile middle order in which Marlon Samuels registered 35 runs, and about as many hapless half-attempts in the field.

But we could laud green shoots for the rest of our lives. It's more serious than that now. A fight for the very survival of Test cricket in the Caribbean awaits. It's not going to be pretty.

Best batsman: Adam Voges (375 runs, 3 matches)
Best bowler: James Pattinson (13 wickets, 3 matches)

Tour match
Allan Border Field, Brisbane, December 2-5: West Indians 243 in 90.5 overs (Darren Bravo 51, Carlos Brathwaite 47; Simon Milenko 5-76, James Bazley 2-37) and 210 in 58.2 overs (Jason Holder 65, Kemar Roach 36; Cameron Boyce 4-84, Ryan Lees 3-68) lost to **Cricket Australia XI** 444 in 104.2 overs (Mathew Short 76, Jimmy Peirson 64; J Holder 4-76, C Brathwaite 2-93) and 13/0 in 2.5 overs by ten wickets.

Test series (3): Australia 2 West Indies 0

1st Test: Australia win by an innings and 212 runs

Twelve West Indian wickets fell on the third day to complete a hiding in half the allotted time. The visitors had talked up their fast bowlers, but there were 16 boundaries in the opening hour, and David Warner raised his fifty from 40 deliveries. To their credit, West Indies fought back to have Australia three down by lunch, with the key wickets of Warner and Steve Smith falling to Jomel Warrican, a 23-year-old left-arm spinner playing only his second Test. This brought together Adam Voges and Shaun Marsh.

Initially restrained, Voges broke free with four boundaries in an over from Warrican. Feasting on the wayward Jerome Taylor, he made his third Test century a formality. Marsh was content to watch and accumulate, raising his own third Test hundred. By the time Marsh slog-swept Warrican for 182 (a first-class best), their alliance was worth 449. It was the highest fourth wicket stand in Tests (beating 437 between Mahela Jayawardene and Thilan Samaraweera for Sri Lanka against Pakistan at Karachi in 2008-09), the highest for any wicket in Australia (beating 405 between Sid Barnes and Don Bradman for the fifth, against England at Sydney in 1946-47) and the highest against West Indies (beating 411 between Peter May and Colin Cowdrey at Edgbaston in 1957). Over lunch, Voges – who had already surpassed Doug Walters's 242 at Sydney in 1968-69 as the highest score for Australia against West Indies – sportingly agreed to forego the chance of a triple-century, allowing Smith to declare and unleash his bowlers.

Josh Hazlewood made the initial incision, but the wickets really started to tumble after Nathan Lyon came on. Darren Bravo showed the responsibility and class missing from the rest of the top order and reached his seventh Test hundred, including 20 boundaries.

James Pattinson, returning to the Test team after 21 injury-blighted months, had been wicketless and expensive. But, the follow-on enforced, he responded with a burst of four wickets in his first four overs to set off an even more spectacular collapse. Kraigg Brathwaite hit out with enterprise, but when his stumps were bent back by Hazlewood before tea on the third day, West Indies were condemned to their heaviest defeat by Australia for almost 85 years.

Bellerive Oval, Hobart, December 10-12: Australia 583/4 dec in 114 overs (Adam Voges 269*, Shaun Marsh 182; Jomel Warrican 3-158) beat **West Indies** 223 in 70 overs (Darren Bravo 108, Kemar Roach 31; Josh Hazlewood 4-45, Nathan Lyon 3-43) and 148 in 36.3 overs (f/o) (Kraigg Brathwaite 94; James Pattinson 5-27, J Hazlewood 3-33) by an innings and 212 runs. *MoM*: Adam Voges.

Tour match

Simonds Stadium, South Geelong, Victoria, December 19-20: West Indians 303/8 dec in 90 overs (Kraigg Brathwaite 78, Jermaine Blackwood 69; Jeremy Hart 4-93) drew with **Victoria XI** 169/3 in 58 overs (Jake Hancock 80*, Tom Donnell 34; Devendra Bishoo 2-60).

2nd Test: Australia win by 177 runs

Put in, Warner struck five of his first eight deliveries, from Kemar Roach and Taylor, for four: Merry Christmas! He holed out soon after, but the point had been made.

Usman Khawaja, returning from a hamstring tear, and Joe Burns, preferred to the unlucky Shaun Marsh, each had plenty to play for, and neither hurried. A rhythm more in keeping with Test cricket prevailed until lunch, before both batsmen shifted gears with limited risk in a stand of 258. Smith was

Catalyst for a collapse: Nathan Lyon finished with 48 wickets in 13 matches in 2015, putting him third among spinners, behind R Ashwin and Yasir Shah. – *Getty Images*

desperate to join in the run-fest after missing out at Hobart, while Voges was too savvy to pass up an opportunity against shrunken bowlers. Smith's sixth century in 2015, and his fifth in eight Tests as captain, meant he would finish the year with more runs (1474) than anyone. Voges joined him on three figures – making it four hundreds from the top five for only the third time in a Test innings – before Australia declared.

It felt like Hobart all over again. As before, Lyon's early introduction was the catalyst for another batting debacle. Once more Bravo was watching it all unfold from the other end. Finally, on the third day, he received help in the big, determined shape of Barbadian debutant Carlos Brathwaite.

Khawaja and Smith enjoyed a game of target practice for a session before Australia declared for the third innings in succession, setting West Indies 460 to win or, more to the point, two days to survive. Rajendra Chandrika embodied a more committed effort and there followed a spirited stand of 100 between Holder and Denesh Ramdin; for a moment, it seemed possible Australia would be deprived of their day off. It was not to be. Mitchell Marsh, who had barely featured in the series until now, bowled with genuine pace to dismiss both en route to a Test-best 4 for 61, as the tail fell in a flurry. For the 11th time in a row, the Frank Worrell Trophy was Australia's.

Melbourne Cricket Ground, December 26-29: Australia 551/3 dec in 135 overs (Usman Khawaja 144, Steven Smith 134*, Joe Burns 128, Adam Voges 106*; Jerome Taylor 2-97) and 179/3 dec in 32 overs (S Smith 70*, U Khawaja 56; Jason Holder 2-49) beat **West Indies** 271 in 100.3 overs (Darren Bravo 81, Carlos Brathwaite 59; Nathan Lyon 4-66, James Pattinson 4-72) and 282 in 88.3 overs (J Holder 68, Denesh Ramdin 59; Mitchell Marsh 4-61, N Lyon 3-85) by 177 runs. *MoM*: Nathan Lyon.

3rd Test: Match drawn

Torrents of rain not seen at a Sydney Test for a quarter of a century denied Australia the chance of a series sweep. There was improvement in the visitors' batting, but too often wickets were lost just as a partnership was blossoming. It was Kraigg Brathwaite's turn to be the trunk of the innings while the branches snapped off around him; Samuels's comical run-out, stranded after Brathwaite dropped his bat mid-pitch and then returned to safety, summed up his tour and the frustration for those around him.

Big-hitting all-rounder: Carlos Brathwaite added much-needed spunk down the order. – *Getty Images*

Only 11.2 overs were possible on the second day. After the third and fourth days were washed out, Smith suggested a mix of forfeited innings and declaration bowling, but Holder was keen for his side to pass 300 for the first time in the series. And so they did, guided by Ramdin's 62, an innings that spanned all five days. Warner had been the only member of Australia's top five yet to notch a century in the series, but he made amends with a hundred from 82 balls, the fastest in Tests at the SCG.

A damp, limp match to end the dampest, limpest series felt about right.

Sydney Cricket Ground, January 3-7: West Indies 330 in 112.1 overs (Kraigg Brathwaite 85, Carlos Brathwaite 69; Steve O'Keefe 3-63, Nathan Lyon 3-120) drew with **Australia** 176/2 in 38 overs (David Warner 122*, Joe Burns 26; Jomel Warrican 2-62) *MoM*: David Warner. *MoS*: Adam Voges.

Adam Collins (@collinsadam) is a writer and broadcaster.

Sri Lanka in New Zealand

Munro, Guptill scale fresh peaks

MARK GEENTY

By the time Sri Lanka's weary, wounded cricketers departed in mid-January, they had spent more than 100 days in New Zealand over the previous 13 months, across two tours and a World Cup. This was no ticket to success: in fact, familiarity very nearly bred contempt. A solitary victory from nine internationals was the tourists' lot on their latest visit, and by the final T20 game in Auckland, there was minimal resistance from a team who looked as if they couldn't wait for the plane home.

It always looked a tough task against a New Zealand side that had not lost a home Test since March 2012. Even before a ball was bowled in Dunedin, Kusal Perera, the wicketkeeper-batsman, was sent home after he tested positive for an unspecified banned substance, while Dammika Prasad, the seamer, suffered a back injury in the warm-up and was ruled out of the tour.

None of the visiting batsmen managed a century. The one shining light was Dushmantha Chameera, the wiry fast bowler, who, but for a horror second-innings batting collapse, might have bowled Sri Lanka to a Test victory in Hamilton.

New Zealand's Martin Guptill was the standout figure, reaching 50 seven

Record flow: Martin Guptill averaged 63 in the Tests and 82 in the one-dayers. Then he blasted 121 off 59 deliveries in two T20I innings. – *Getty Images*

times in 11 innings, and averaging 63 in the Tests and 82 in the one-dayers. Then he blasted 121 off 59 deliveries in two T20 innings, including a national-record 19-ball half-century in Auckland. That stood for barely 20 minutes before Colin Munro bettered it – or battered it – by five. Kane Williamson wasn't far behind. Following his match-winning century in Hamilton, he ate his Christmas dinner as the world's top-ranked Test batsman.

Life after Brendon McCullum also loomed into view. He led them to victory in both Tests, then confirmed he would be retiring after the home series against Australia in February.

Tour match

Queenstown Events Centre, December 3-5: Sri Lankans 193 in 72.5 overs (Dimuth Karunaratne 93, Rangana Herath 34; Tim Johnston 4-43, Neil Wagner 3-31) and 226/6 in 71 overs (Udara Jayasundera 63, Kithuruwan Vithanage 61; James Baker 2-21) drew with **New Zealand Board President's XI** 399/8 in 84.3 overs (Ben Smith 81, Shawn Hicks 79*; Dushmantha Chameera 4-57, Dilruwan Perera 2-31).

Test series (2): New Zealand 2 Sri Lanka 0

1st Test: New Zealand win by 122 runs

As Angelo Mathews found out, a thick covering of grass didn't automatically mean a seamer's haven. The pitch in cold Dunedin has always been slow and lifeless, needing grass cover to add some zing, but it remained sluggish, with worryingly variable bounce. Martin Guptill's second-innings dismissal to Rangana Herath – bowled by one that shot along the ground – was a concern for a venue whose Test credentials were under scrutiny.

New Zealand were in control from the first morning. Guptill reached his third Test century – the first for 41 innings – during a stand of 173 with Kane Williamson, then watched Brendon McCullum conduct a typical late-afternoon assault of 75 from 57 balls.

The hosts had chosen four pacemen, with Neil Wagner recalled for his first Test in almost a year, alongside the inexperienced spinner Mitchell Santner. And all of them had to put in the hard yards in the victory push – only interrupted by hailstones that cascaded onto the outfield on the final day. BJ Watling, the reliable wicketkeeper, was the central figure in the hosts' slow march towards all 20 wickets. He would catch nine of them, to equal the national record shared by him and McCullum.

Before that, Latham extended the lead with his third Test century. McCullum's brief innings occupied only six balls, but included two sixes – the second of which was his 100th in Tests, to equal Adam Gilchrist's record. "It's the only record of mine Kane Williamson won't break," he joked.

University Oval, Dunedin, December 10-14: New Zealand 431 in 96.1 overs (Martin Guptill 156, Kane Williamson 88; Nuwan Pradeep 4-112, Suranga Lakmal 2-69) and 267/3 dec in 65.4 overs (Tom Latham 109*, K Williamson 71; Rangana Herath 2-62) beat **Sri Lanka** 294 in 117.1 overs (Dimuth Karunaratne 84, Dinesh Chandimal 83; Tim Southee 3-71, Neil Wagner

3-87) and 282 in 95.2 overs (D Chandimal 58, Kusal Mendis 46; T Southee 3-52, Mitchell Santner 2-53) by 122 runs. *MoM*: Martin Guptill.

Most sixes in Test career			
Player	Matches	Innings	6s
Brendon McCullum	101	176	107
Adam Gilchrist	96	137	100
Chris Gayle	103	182	98
Jacques Kallis	166	280	97
Virender Sehwag	104	180	88

2nd Test: New Zealand win by five wickets

Two years previously, New Zealand had been alarmed to find the Seddon Park pitch dry, and providing help to West Indies' spinners. There was no such problem this time: Mike Hesson's pre-series call for green surfaces had been heard loud and clear. It didn't offer as much seam movement as the verdancy suggested, but the new track – relaid the previous year – still ensured a spicy time for batsmen. Steep bounce was their greatest enemy, prompting spectacular collapses and sore fingers on both sides. But Williamson's class told, as he coolly guided New Zealand home, despite a fine display from the speedy Chameera.

Kusal Mendis, in only his third Test, had an exciting time, Dinesh Chandimal scored a breezy 47, and Mathews and Milinda Siriwardana tucked in as Wagner overdid the short stuff. In reply, Guptill and Tom Latham put on 81, helped by Mathews's mysterious reluctance to try Chameera. The pacer eventually came on as third change, immediately after lunch, and had Latham caught at leg gully in his second over. Williamson followed in his next, skying a pull, and Taylor edged a fizzer in the one after that. With Herath removing Guptill in between, New Zealand had lost four for eight.

In his 99th Test – all consecutive from debut, breaking AB de Villiers's record – McCullum buckled down, surviving 80 minutes for 18; the prom-

Eye on the ball: Kane Williamson offered a batting masterclass in tricky conditions. — *Getty Images*

Giving Sri Lanka a shot at victory: Dushmantha Chameera's was a fine display of speed and skill, his nine wickets taking the visitors close. — *Getty Images*

ising Santner followed suit and Bracewell hung around too, but Sri Lanka took a lead of 55, and sniffed a chance of squaring the series.

Chameera's success, however, had shown New Zealand what to do, and the Sri Lankans were subjected to a short-pitched barrage on the springy surface. The hosts eyed a target of 189 to maintain their unbeaten home Test record since losing to South Africa in March 2012.

Chameera was given the new ball this time, and by the end of his third over had removed both openers. It was game on. Williamson, though, was equal to the task: He had learned from his brief first innings, and now shelved the pull or hook when Chameera dropped short. In tricky conditions, with the match on the line, it was another batting masterclass – driving, cutting, deflecting. This innings briefly took him to the top of the ICC rankings for Test batsmen, having scored 1172 Test runs, eight more than McCullum's national record from the year before.

Seddon Park, Hamilton, December 18-21: Sri Lanka 292 in 80.1 overs (Angelo Mathews 77, Milinda Siriwardana 62; Tim Southee 3-63, Trent Boult 2-51) and 133 in 36.3 overs (Kusal Mendis 46, Dimuth Karunaratne 27; T Southee 4-26, Neil Wagner 3-40) lost to **New Zealand** 237 in 79.4 overs (Martin Guptill 50, Mitchell Santner 38; Dushmantha Chameera 5-47, Nuwan Pradeep 2-39) and 189/5 in 54.3 overs (Kane Williamson 108*, Ross Taylor 35; D Chameera 4-68) by five wickets. *MoM*: Kane Williamson.

ODI series (5): New Zealand 3 Sri Lanka 1

1st ODI: New Zealand win by seven wickets

Ten months on from the World Cup opener, the two combatants from that chilly, giddy afternoon reconvened at the same venue. New Zealand won again, even more emphatically. With Trent Boult and Tim Southee both rested, Mathews opted to bat first – but the young tearaways did the damage. Bowling full and shaping the ball away, Matt Henry, whose opening spell on his home ground was 7-1-26-4, and Adam Milne reduced Sri Lanka to 27 for 5. There was no way back, although Siriwardana and Nuwan Kulasekara put on 98. In reply, 108 came from the first ten overs. Guptill hit four sixes in his 79 from 56 balls, while McCullum slammed a trademark 55 off 25, with 50 in boundaries. It was left to Henry Nicholls, the local left-hander on international debut, to finish things off with successive fours off Ajantha Mendis, and 29 overs to spare.

Hagley Oval, Christchurch, December 26: Sri Lanka 188 in 47 overs (Milinda Siriwardana 66, Nuwan Kulasekara 58; Matt Henry 4-49, Doug Bracewell 3-37) lost to **New Zealand** 191/3 in 21 overs (Martin Guptill 79, Brendon McCullum 55; M Siriwardana 2-45) by seven wickets. *MoM*: Matt Henry.

2nd ODI: New Zealand win by ten wickets

If Boxing Day had been a stroll in the park for New Zealand, this was a sleepwalk. Henry again haunted the top order, before Guptill monstered the bowling. The batsman Guptill scorched to his half-century in 17 balls, one short of the world record, clouting eight sixes and nine fours in his unbeaten 93 from 30. His strike-rate of 310 had been bettered only by de Villiers (338, in his 149 from 44 against West Indies in Johannesburg, 2014-15) in an innings of 25 balls or more. Jeffrey Vandersay, Sri Lanka's debutant leg-spinner, had a cruel introduction, conceding 34 from his two overs. The caterers had to rustle up an early lunch, as the entire match lasted 36 overs.

Hagley Oval, Christchurch, December 28: Sri Lanka 117 in 27.4 overs (Matt Henry 4-33, Mitchell McClenaghan 3-32) lost to **New Zealand** 118/0 in 8.2 overs (Martin Guptill 93) by ten wickets. *MoM*: Martin Guptill.

3rd ODI: Sri Lanka win by eight wickets

Sri Lanka finally found some semblance of form, and rescued the tour from disaster with a fine batting display. Williamson returned for New Zealand after missing the previous two matches with a knee niggle, and took over as captain from McCullum, who had aggravated a back injury trying to prevent a boundary in the previous game. He top-scored with 59, but Saxton Oval had been a batting paradise during the World Cup, and New Zealand's total – with Chameera outstanding and Vandersay applying the brakes after his nightmare debut – looked underwhelming. Still, the verve with which Sri Lanka took on the challenge was refreshing. Danushka Gunathilaka started with four sixes in his 65 from 45 balls, putting on 98 with Tillakaratne Dilshan, who kept the rate under control with a run-a-ball 91. He added 111 with Lahiru Thirimanne, who calmly collected the rest with Chandimal. New Zealand missed Henry, strangely sent back to domestic cricket.

Saxton Oval, Nelson, December 31: New Zealand 276/8 in 50 overs (Kane Williamson 59,

Tom Latham 42; Dushmantha Chameera 2-38, Nuwan Pradeep 2-55, Jeffrey Vandersay 2-55) lost to **Sri Lanka** 277/2 in 46.2 overs (Tillakaratne Dilshan 91, Lahiru Thirimanne 87*) by eight wickets. *MoM*: Danushka Gunathilaka.

4th ODI: No result

Nelson boasts some of the highest sunshine hours in New Zealand, but couldn't rustle up two bright days for its New Year double-header. Early rain had already shortened this one to a 24-over match, which was interestingly poised when another downpour forced the players off for good. There was time for Guptill to wallop three sixes off Chameera in an over costing 26.

Saxton Oval, Nelson, January 2: **New Zealand** 75/3 in 9 overs (Martin Guptill 27, Ross Taylor 20*) v **Sri Lanka**. No result.

5th ODI: New Zealand win by 36 runs

Sri Lanka still had a chance to level the series, but were thwarted again by Henry. Restored after missing the first Nelson test, he sliced through the order to finish with 13 wickets in the series at nine apiece. After Dilshan sent a trademark scoop straight to the wicketkeeper, Henry got going with the scalps of Thirimanne and Gunathilaka. A stand of 93 between Chandimal and Mathews was broken by the rusty Boult, then Henry returned at the death to claim three more wickets, the key one being Mathews, who hooked to deep square, where Nicholls took a good high catch that would have carried for six. Earlier, Guptill's tenth ODI century was the backbone of New Zealand's substantial innings, helped by 61s from Williamson and Taylor.

Bay Oval, Mount Maunganui, January 5: **New Zealand** 294/5 in 50 overs (Martin Guptill 102, Ross Taylor 61; Nuwan Kulasekara 3-53) beat **Sri Lanka** 258 in 47.1 overs (Angelo Mathews 95, Dinesh Chandimal 50; Matt Henry 5-40, Trent Boult 3-43) by 36 runs. *MoM*: Matt Henry.

T20I series (2): New Zealand 2 Sri Lanka 0

1st T20I: New Zealand win by three runs

• New Zealand are ranked a lowly eighth in the format, while Sri Lanka are first. • The hosts are lifted by an opening stand of 101 between Guptill and Williamson, although the later batsmen fail to capitalise. • Henry and Boult reduce Sri Lanka to 42 for 4 after five overs. • But Gunathilaka and Siriwardana blaze away. • It boils down to 13 off the last over, which is entrusted to Grant Elliott, making an international comeback after breaking his arm in the nets in November. • Kulasekara slogs the third ball to deep midwicket, Chamara Kapugedera is run out, and New Zealand hang on.

Bay Oval, Mount Maunganui, January 7: **New Zealand** 182/4 in 20 overs (Martin Guptill 58, Kane Williamson 53; Nuwan Kulasekara 2-26) beat **Sri Lanka** 179/9 in 20 overs (Danushka Gunathilaka 46, Milinda Siriwardana 42; Trent Boult 3-21, Matt Henry 3-44) by three runs. *MoM*: Trent Boult.

2nd T20I: New Zealand win by nine wickets

• Sri Lanka's dispiriting tour ends with another shellacking from New Zealand's batsmen, to the delight of a crowd of 17,000. • Mathews, unbeaten on 81 from 49, is the lone star. • He then has to watch helplessly as Guptill zooms to his half-century in 19 balls, breaking by four the national record he shared with Aaron Redmond. • Guptill owns the record for about 20 minutes, as Munro slams a fifty from just 14 deliveries. • He wins the match with his seventh six, from the last ball of the tenth over. • "I'm not sure what these two had for breakfast," says Williamson. "But it was unbelievable to watch."

Eden Park, Auckland, January 10: Sri Lanka 142/8 in 20 overs (Angelo Mathews 81*, Tillakaratne Dilshan 28; Grant Elliot 4-22, Mitchell Santner 2-24) lost to **New Zealand** 147/1 in 10 overs (Martin Guptill 63, Colin Munro 50*) by nine wickets. *MoM*: Colin Munro.

Fastest T20I fifties

Balls	Player	Match	Venue	Date
12	Yuvraj Singh	India v England	Durban	Sept 19, 2007
14	**Colin Munro**	**New Zealand v Sri Lanka**	**Auckland**	**Jan 10, 2016**
17	Paul Stirling	Ireland v Afghanistan	Dubai	Mar 24, 2012
17	Stephan Myburgh	Netherlands v Ireland	Sylhet	Mar 21, 2014
17	Chris Gayle	West Indies v South Africa	Cape Town	Jan 9, 2015
18	David Warner	Australia v West Indies	Sydney	Feb 23, 2010
18	Glenn Maxwell	Australia v Pakistan	Mirpur	Mar 23, 2014
18	**Glenn Maxwell**	**Australia v Sri Lanka**	**Colombo**	**Sept 9, 2016**
19	David Warner	Australia v South Africa	Melbourne	Jan 11, 2009
19	Gautam Gambhir	India v Sri Lanka	Nagpur	Dec 9, 2009
19	**Martin Guptill**	**New Zealand v Sri Lanka**	**Auckland**	**Jan 10, 2016**

	Tests	ODIs	T20
Best batsman	Kane Williamson (268 runs, 2 matches)	Martin Guptill (331 runs, 5 matches)	Martin Guptill (121 runs, 2 matches)
Best bowler	Tim Southee (13 wickets, 2 matches)	Matt Henry (13 wickets, 4 matches)	Grant Elliot (5 wickets, 2 matches)

Mark Geenty (@mark_geenty) is a sports writer for Fairfaz based in New Zealand.

Post Flintoff all-rounder: With his 411 runs and 18 wickets, this was a coming of age for Ben Stokes. – *Getty Images*

England in South Africa

Stokes, Broad knock hosts off perch

STEPHEN BRENKLEY

Few Test series have everything, but the four matches between South Africa and England came mighty close. They contained imperishable, sometimes record-breaking, individual performances, a dramatic resignation, the emergence of two black players who may yet change the course of the game in their country, and an unexpected 2-1 triumph for the tourists.

South Africa had the leading run-scorer in Hashim Amla – revitalised, even freed, by his decision to give up the captaincy halfway through the series – the leading wicket-taker in Kagiso Rabada, and the leading outfield catcher in Dean Elgar. They had more centuries (six to three) and five-wicket hauls (four to one). Yet England, despite some obvious weaknesses – especially in their batting and catching – thoroughly deserved victory, which removed their opponents from the No. 1 spot in the rankings. Only a late meltdown in the limited-overs matches robbed their tour of some of its gloss.

Ben Stokes, who scored England's fastest double-hundred, and shared a Test-record sixth-wicket stand of 399 with Jonny Bairstow in the drawn Second Test, was Man of the Series. Consistently dazzling with the bat – his strike-rate was a one-day-like 109 – he was increasingly impressive with the ball. He was the first to score 400 runs and take ten wickets in a series for

England since Andrew Flintoff during the 2005 Ashes. These seven weeks may come to be seen as Stokes's coming of age as an all-rounder of the highest calibre.

If England began as underdogs, South Africa had their own difficulties, having recently returned from a 3-0 mauling in India. The injuries to the new-ball partners Dale Steyn, who played only the first game, and Vernon Philander, unfit throughout, exacerbated the selectoral muddle. Players were added match by match, and 17 used in all – four of them only once, and four twice. England, by contrast, needed only 12, with Chris Woakes's presence in the first and last games prompted by injuries.

Yet, Temba Bavuma and Rabada, playing together in a Test for the first time, gave a nation hope for the future. At one hotel on the final morning of the series, the (mostly black) reception staff were excited about impending victory: "We're gonna win today, we're gonna win!" That would not have happened even ten years ago.

South Africa won both the limited-overs series that followed. If this put into perspective the progress England had made in both formats in recent months, they could – and perhaps should – have won the one-day series.

Victories in the first two matches, with the sort of uninhibited strokeplay that had marked their renaissance, suggested a team full of conviction. Alex Hales, Joe Root and Jos Buttler were at the top of their game. Freed from the confused approach that plagued his batting in the Tests, Hales looked as if he knew once more what he was supposed to do. He finished the 50-over series with a century and four fifties, including 99 to anchor the chase in Port Elizabeth.

England's strategy appeared plain and simple: Make big totals at a rapid lick to ease the burden on the bowlers. In the series opener in Bloemfontein, they reached 399, comfortably their highest score overseas, with Buttler butchering a 73-ball hundred. The trouble occurred when it started to go awry and South Africa rediscovered their own reserves of self-belief.

Eoin Morgan's team had one golden chance to take an unassailable lead in the ODI series. At 2-1 ahead, they reduced South Africa to 211 for 8 in the fourth match at the Wanderers, still requiring 52 when Adil Rashid put down a steepling catch in the deep off Chris Morris. England lost the

A new South Africa: Temba Bavuma (left) and Kagiso Rabada playing together gave a nation hope for the future. – *Getty Images*

plot a little thereafter. South Africa's batsmen, not least AB de Villiers, found their range.

In the first T20 game, the visitors missed the chance to force a super over when Reece Topley fumbled Root's over-the-stumps return. The limitations of their bowling were also exposed, with the new ball and at the death: de Villiers hit South Africa's fastest 20-over half-century, from 21 deliveries, and Amla got there from 27. The tour ended in a humbling defeat at the Wanderers – a few weeks earlier the scene of one of their most memorable Test victories.

Tour matches

Senwes Park, Potchefstroom, December 15-17: England XI 470/7 in 88 overs (Ben Stokes 158, James Taylor 114, Thandolwethu Mnyaka 3-66) and 190 in 52.4 overs (Joe Root 39, Alastair Cook 37; Junior Dala 5-34, Andile Phehlukwayo 3-36) drew with **South African Invitation XI** 188 in 57.1 overs (Heinrich Klaasen 48, Qaasim Adams 34; Stuart Broad 3-18, B Stokes 2-25) and 5/0 in 2 overs.

City Oval, Pietermaritzburg, December 20-22: South Africa A 136 in 56 overs (Stephen Cook 53*, Chris Morris 21; Steven Finn 4-34, Ben Stokes 3-25) and 187 in 42.5 overs (Quinton de Kock 53, Rilee Rossouw 32; Moeen Ali 6-77, Steven Finn 2-30) lost to **England XI** 414/6 dec in 97.5 overs (Alastair Cook 126, Joe Root 117; Keshav Maharaj 4-129) by an inning and 91 runs.

Test series (4): England 2 South Africa 1

1st Test: England win by 241 runs

A match robbed of its sharpest arrows – a shoulder strain limited Dale Steyn to 29 overs, while James Anderson was ruled out altogether with a calf problem – changed the perceptions and perspectives of those still standing. In England's case, it allowed Chris Woakes to earn his fifth cap, and gave Stuart Broad the choice of ends. For South Africa, unsettlingly, it was deja vu: Steyn had not bowled after the first innings of the First Test in India, where they were thumped 3-0.

The surface suited the bloody-mindedness of both Dean Elgar, who scored his fourth century, an innings made up of equal parts steadiness and scrapping, and Nick Compton, who, in the city of his birth, made 85 and 49 on his return to Test cricket after a two-and-a-half-year absence. The understated off-spin of Moeen Ali, meanwhile, earned him his first match award in Tests.

England were righted by a fourth-wicket stand of 125 between a cautious Compton and James Taylor. When Compton finally bottom-edged a pull off Morne Morkel through to AB de Villiers – who had been asked nicely to keep wicket again, even while rumours swirled about his future – it was as if all South African supporters had been put out of their misery.

The South Africans took England's last seven wickets for 129 in a total of 303. For the first time since they beat West Indies at home in January 2015, they looked like a team with places to go and things to do – none more than Steyn and Morkel, who claimed eight between them. But, they soon reverted

Uneasy lies the head: Hashim Amla stepped down as Test captain midway through the series, though it could hardly be said he wasn't in good touch. — *Getty Images*

to recent type. Broad did most of the wrecking, with superb control of line and length, while Moeen bamboozled four lower down and Steven Finn took the last two in the same over. Elgar carried his bat, contributing 55% of his side's total.

Root passed 50 for the 13th time in Tests in 2015 to equal the world record. But it was Jonny Bairstow's purposeful 79 off 76 balls that lifted England to their eventual lead of 415. And when South Africa's middle order collapsed in a heap, with seven lost for 38 inside 25 overs, England surged to a comprehensive victory. *Telford Vice*

Kingsmead, Durban, December 26-30: England 303 in 100.1 overs (Nick Compton 85, James Taylor 70; Dale Steyn 4-70, Morne Morkel 4-76) and 326 in 102.1 overs (Jonny Bairstow 79, Joe Root 73; Dane Piedt 5-153, Stiaan van Zyl 3-20) beat **South Africa** 214 in 81.4 overs (Dean Elgar 118*, AB de Villiers 49; Stuart Broad 4-25, Moeen Ali 4-69) and 174 in 71 overs (D Elgar 40, AB de Villiers 37; Steven Finn 4-42, M Ali 3-47) by 241 runs. *MoM*: Moeen Ali.

2nd Test: Match drawn

There were only a few periods when an outright result looked even remotely on the cards. But this was a Test that will burn brightly in the memory of anyone who witnessed it. It produced four hundreds, of which two were doubles, and one by Temba Bavuma, the first for South Africa by a member of the majority black African population in 127 years of Test cricket.

No sooner had the game been called off with 31 overs remaining after a halt for rain, than Cricket South Africa announced Amla was stepping down as Test captain, and handing the reins to de Villiers. As Amla had just batted

11 and three-quarter hours for 201 to keep his side in the contest, it could hardly be said the job was affecting his form. But it was clearly a role he found uncomfortable.

Ben Stokes's murderous assault on South Africa's bowlers, which brought him 258 runs from 198 balls, including 30 fours and 11 sixes, would have driven many captains to distraction. If Amla had a plan for either Stokes or Jonny Bairstow, who assisted him in a Test-record sixth-wicket partnership of 399 in 346 balls, the fastest above 200 in Tests, it was not altogether divinable. Stokes's double-century, from 163 balls, was the second-fastest in Tests, and his 250, from 196, the fastest.

Cook called an end to the mayhem at 629 for 6. England had made their biggest score under his captaincy. By scoring so fast, they had created plenty of time to dismiss South Africa twice. As they were to discover, they had also created time for their own position to become vulnerable.

Amla and de Villiers put on South Africa's first century partnership since 2014, before Amla and du Plessis added 171. Three wickets in five overs for Broad and Anderson with the third new ball revived England, but Bavuma restore equanimity in the home dressing-room. He batted beautifully: organised, yet adventurous when the chance arose. When Amla imaginatively declared, two runs behind, shortly before stumps on the fourth day, South Africa had recorded their biggest home score against England. *Simon Wilde*

Newlands, Cape Town, January 2-6: England 629/6 dec in 125.5 overs (Ben Stokes 258, Jonny Bairstow 150*; Kagiso Rabada 3-175) and 159/6 in 65 overs (J Bairstow 30*, Joe Root 29; Dane Piedt 3-38) drew with **South Africa** 627/7 dec in 211 overs (Hashim Amla 201, Temba Bavuma 102*; Stuart Broad 2-94, Steven Finn 2-132). *MoM*: Ben Stokes.

3rd Test: England win by seven wickets

On a riotous third afternoon at Wanderers, South Africa were torn apart by England's seam attack across 33 overs of unchecked mayhem. The passage sealed England's first overseas series win since December 2012. It was Broad who flicked the switch, claiming five or more wickets in a single Test spell for the seventh time. His six wickets here included a spell of 5 for 1 in 31 balls – and four successive wicket maidens.

Broad's brilliance was buttressed by insistent fast bowling at the other end, and inspired close catching. In snapping up Amla's wicket, for example, from connection to catch, which Taylor – standing slightly deeper at short leg because of the extra bounce – took down by his bootlaces, just 0.41 seconds had elapsed.

Trevor Bayliss, England's routinely taciturn head coach, had chosen the lunch break on the third day to administer what Cook called a "kick up the arse". The game was on a knife-edge: South Africa were six runs ahead, with all ten second-innings wickets in hand; by tea, they were 71 for 8.

All out for 83, it was their second-lowest total since readmission, behind 79 against India in Nagpur seven weeks earlier.

Spells of brilliance: Stuart Broad's six wickets at Wanderers included a spell of 5 for 1 in 31 balls, and four successive wicket maidens. – *Getty Images*

A hapless scene echoed the chaos that had engulfed their preparations. On the eve of the match, Quinton de Kock had twisted his knee walking his Jack Russells, necessitating a call-up for Dane Vilas; he arrived halfway through the opening session. Other, more sinister stories were doing the rounds. It's impossible to say whether the rumours surfacing about match-fixing in South Africa's domestic Ram Slam T20 Challenge affected the Test team's state of mind, but a sense of self-inflicted collapse was in the air.

Yet, led by Kagiso Rabada's preternatural brilliance, the home side scented blood halfway through the game. Stokes had joined Root with their team in strife, and in less than 16 overs of oddly inevitable bedlam, they had added 111. Root had cantered to a run-a-ball three figures, crowned with another of those immaculate drives through the covers. But thanks to Rabada, with the hosts only ten behind on first innings, the narrative was set. Until Broad improvised to steal the show. *Phil Walker*

New Wanderers Stadium, Johannesburg, January 14-16: South Africa 313 in 99.3 overs (Dean Elgar 46, Hashim Amla 40; Ben Stokes 3-53, Steven Finn 2-50) and 83 in 33.1 overs (Stuart Broad 6-17, B Stokes 2-24) lost to **England** 323 in 76.1 overs (Joe Root 110, B Stokes 58; Kagiso Rabada 5-78, Morne Morkel 3-76) and 74/3 in 22.4 overs (Alastair Cook 43; D Elgar 2-10) by seven wickets. *MoM:* Stuart Broad.

4th Test: South Africa win by 280 runs

Rabada placed a broad and much-needed smile on the face of South African cricket with a remarkable match haul of 13 for 144 to gloss over their series defeat. The only bowler younger than him to take at least 13 wickets

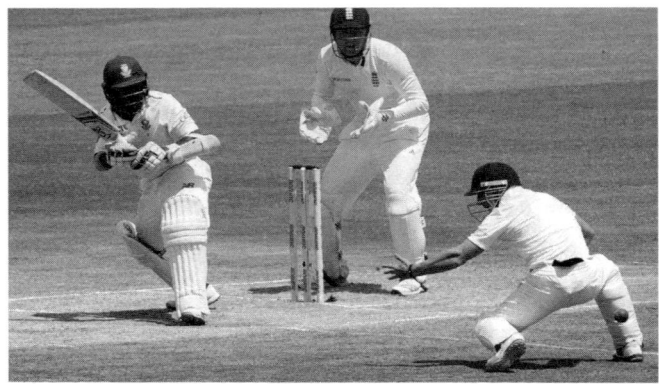

Close-in technique: England's bowlers had plenty to thank James Taylor for after his stunning fielding at short leg. — *Getty Images*

in a Test was Indian leg-spinner Narendra Hirwani, who was 19 years 89 days when he claimed 16 for 136 on debut against West Indies in Madras in 1987-88.

England were made to pay for a dreadful bowling performance in the first two sessions, and an embarrassing capitulation on the final morning, when they lost 7 for 43 in 65 deliveries. Following events at The Oval five months earlier, it seemed dead games were not for them. South Africa won the decisive moments, capitalising on the tourists' poor start, adding 139 for their final three wickets, then dismissing Cook and Root when both looked set.

A first-innings advantage of 133 was always likely to be crucial on a surface full of character, which cracked and deteriorated at the perfect rate. The contrasting natures of Amla's 109 – his 25th Test hundred – and 96 perfectly illustrated the change in conditions.

Despite Amla's artistry, it was Stephen Cook, 33, who had dominated the initial exchanges on his debut. A heavy scorer at domestic level, his demeanour commanded Test membership from the start, when he left the ball expertly, through to the time he spent in the nineties, unfazed by England's tactics.

De Kock, one of five changes, was positive from the outset. He looked to score from every ball, despite defensive fields and negative bowling, and often jumped outside off stump to take advantage of the spaces on the leg side. His maiden Test century came from just 104 deliveries.

England's reply to South Africa's 475 never delivered on its promise. Anderson finally made an impact, removing South Africa's first three with only 49 on the board – including de Villiers. Having endured just four ducks in his first 173 innings, South Africa's new captain now had three in a row.

But Bavuma removed any doubts about South Africa's superiority with an unbeaten 78, which showed a level of courage and skill not required during his ground-breaking century at Newlands. An hour's rain after tea on the fourth afternoon hastened the declaration, leaving England 21 overs and a day to make 382. It was never on the cards. *Neil Manthorp*

SuperSport Park, Centurion, January 22-26: South Africa 475 in 132 overs (Quinton de Kock 129*, Stephen Cook 115, Hashim Amla 109; Ben Stckes 4-86, Stuart Broad 2-91) and 248/5 dec in 83.2 overs (H Amla 96, Temba Bavuma 78*; James Anderson 3-47) beat **England** 342 in 104.2 overs (Joe Root 76, Alastair Cook 76; Kagiso Rabada 7-112, Morne Morkel 2-73) and 101 in 34.4 overs (James Taylor 24, J Root 20; K Rabada 6-32, M Morkel 3-36) by 280 runs. *MoM*: Kagiso Rabada. *MoS*: Ben Stokes.

Tour match
Diamond Oval, Kimberley, January 30: England XI 368/7 in 50 overs (James Taylor 116, Jonny Bairstow 58; Marchant de Lange 2-69, David Wiese 2-73) beat **South Africa A** 205 in 30.5 overs (Theunis de Bruyn 73*, Dane Vilas 40; Reece Topley 3-38, Chris Jordan 3-48, Adil Rashid 3-55) by 163 runs.

ODI series (5): South Africa 3 England 2

1st ODI: England win by 39 runs (D/L Method)
Mangaung Oval, Bloemfontein, February 3: England 399/9 in 50 overs (Jos Buttler 105, Ben Stokes 57; Chris Morris 3-74, Imran Tahir 2-71) beat **South Africa** 250/5 in 33.3 overs (Quinton de Kock 138*, Faf du Plessis 55; Moeen Ali 3-43) by 39 runs (D/L method). *MoM*: Quinton de Kock.

2nd ODI: England win by five wickets
St George's Park, Port Elizabeth, February 6: South Africa 262/7 in 50 overs (AB de Villiers 73, JP Duminy 47; Reece Topley 4-50; Ben Stokes 2-54) lost to **England** 263/5 in 46.2 overs (Alex Hales 99, Jos Buttler 48*; Kyle Abbott 3-58, Morne Morkel 2-31) by five wickets. *MoM*: Alex Hales.

3rd ODI: South Africa win by seven wickets
SuperSport Park, Centurion, February 9: England 318/8 in 50 overs (Joe Root 125, Alex Hales 65; Kyle Abbott 2-50, Kagiso Rabada 2-65) lost to **South Africa** 319/3 in 46.2 overs (Quinton de Kock 135, Hashim Amla 127) by seven wickets. *MoM*: Quinton de Kock.

4th ODI: South Africa win by one wicket
New Wanderers Stadium, Johannesburg, February 12: England 262 in 47.5 overs (Joe Root 109, Alex Hales 50; Kagiso Rabada 4-45, Imran Tahir 3-46) lost to **South Africa** 266/9 in 47.2 overs (Chris Morris 62, Farhaan Behardien 38; Adil Rashid 2-38, Reece Topley 2-39) by one wicket. *MoM*: Chris Morris.

5th ODI: South Africa win by five wickets
Newlands, Cape Town, February 14: England 236 in 45 overs (Alex Hales 112, Ben Stokes 29; Kagiso Rabada 3-34, David Wiese 3-50, Imran Tahir 3-53) lost to **South Africa** 237/5 in 44 overs (AB de Villiers 101*, Hashim Amla 59; Reece Topley 3-41) by five wickets. *MoM*: AB de Villiers. *MoS*: Alex Hales.

Tour match
Boland Park, Paarl, February 17: England XI 202/6 in 20 overs (Alex Hales 78, Eoin Morgan 42; Wayne Parnell 3-26, Andile Phehlukwayo 2-32) beat **South Africa A** 158/8 in 20 overs (Theunis de Bruyn 56, Morne van Wyk 32; Reece Topley 3-29, Adil Rashid 2-27) by 44 runs.

T20I series (2): South Africa 2 England 0

1st T20I: South Africa win by three wickets
Newlands, Cape Town, February 19: England 134/8 in 20 overs (Jos Buttler 32*, Alex Hales 27; Imran Tahir 4-21, Kyle Abbott 2-31) lost to **South Africa** 135/7 in 20 overs (Faf du Plessis 25, JP Duminy 23; Chris Morris 3-23, Moeen Ali 2-22) by three wickets. *MoM*: Imran Tahir.

2nd T20I: South Africa win by nine wickets
New Wanderers Stadium, Johannesburg, February 21: England 171 in 19.4 overs (Jos Buttler 54, Eoin Morgan 38; Kyle Abbott 3-26, Kagiso Rabada 2-28) lost to **South Africa** 172/1 in 14.4 overs (AB de Villiers 71, Hashim Amla 69*) by nine wickets. *MoM*: AB de Villiers. *MoS*: Imran Tahir.

	Tests	ODIs	T20Is
Best batsman	Hashim Amla (470 runs, 4 matches)	Alex Hales (383 runs, 5 matches)	Hashim Amla (91 runs, 2 matches)
Best bowler	Kagiso Rabada (22 wickets, 3 matches)	Reece Topley (10 wickets, 5 matches)	Imran Tahir (5 wickets, 2 matches)

Stephen Brenkley (@stephenbrenkley) is a cricket correspondent of The Independent.

Afghanistan v Zimbabwe in UAE

Afghans rise up the charts

It wasn't quite 'home' for Afghanistan, but it was as close as it would get, as they kept up their commendable international run and extended their edge over Zimbabwe, both on the field and on the limited-overs ranking charts.

The visitors, having conceded series to Afghanistan (home) and Bangladesh (away) within the previous three months, came to Sharjah with considerable batting concerns. They immediately felt the absence of Sean Williams, who missed the tour with injury, as they crashed to 82 all out in what couldn't have been a very merry Christmas. And, 2-0 down in the series and 47 for 7 in the third in the new year, it seemed their maladies were chronic.

But Hamilton Masakadza, PJ Moor, Craig Ervine, Graeme Cremer and Chamu Chibhabha all worked on making amends. Masakadza, who earned his way back into the team through strong A side performances, averaged 66.5; he made a match-saving fifty in that third game and gave his team a good shot at a series win with his 111-ball 110 in the decider.

Unfortunately, their bowlers stumbled under pressure. Gulbadin Naib, returning to the side after nearly a year, expertly shepherded Afghanistan's chase. Coming together with young Rashid Khan with 104 needed off 93 balls, he steadily knocked off the runs, especially severe on Neville Madziva, whom he took for 16 in the 46th. Naib's celebration might have been premature, but when the end came, with a six over the deep backward square leg boundary, it was well earned.

The Associate nation, though, would have been kicking themselves for letting the contest to go down to the wire. Mohammad Shahzad recorded the highest score for his team in ODIs, unbeaten on 131 off 133 in the second match, making more than half the runs his team needed. He would go on to temper his characteristic belligerence with maturity when his side needed it.

There was no holding him back in the T20Is. His 67-ball 118 not out in the second and final match included eight lusty sixes and ten fours. It was a ferocious exhibition of hitting, and the most made by an Associate batsman in T20Is; the next-best in the total of 215 was Nabi's 22.

Zimbabwe would have felt their efforts deserved better. The defining moment in the shortest format, perhaps, was the frenetic final over of the first contest. Chasing 188, Zimbabwe needed 21 with five wickets in hand in the final over bowled by Dawlat Zadran. It had a wide/waist-high no-ball, a run-out off a free hit, another waist-high no-ball that to the Zimbabweans' consternation didn't get the bowler sent off, a six, a four and a wide that wasn't called.

ODI series (5): Afghanistan 3 Zimbabwe 2

1st ODI: Afghanistan win by 49 runs
Sharjah Cricket Stadium, December 25: Afghanistan 131 in 38.5 overs (Noor Ali Zadran 63; Graeme Cremer 5-20) beat **Zimbabwe** 82 in 30.5 overs (Elton Chigumbura 28, Peter Moor 21; Amir Hamza 4-17, Mohammad Nabi 3-15) by 49 runs. *MoM*: Amir Hamza.

2nd ODI: Afghanistan win by four wickets
Sharjah Cricket Stadium, December 29: Zimbabwe 253/7 in 50 overs (Craig Ervine 73, Peter Moor 50; Dawlat Zadran 3-57, Rokhan Barakzai 2-45) lost to **Afghanistan** 254/6 in 47.4 overs (Mohammad Shahzad 131*, Mohammad Nabi 33; Elton Chigumbura 3-32) by four wickets. *MoM*: Mohammad Shahzad.

3rd ODI: Zimbabwe win by 117 runs
Sharjah Cricket Stadium, January 2: Zimbabwe 175 in 48.3 overs (Hamilton Masakadza 83, Graeme Cremer 58; Mirwais Ashraf 3-20, Dawlat Zadran 2-25) beat **Afghanistan** 58 in 16.1 overs (Mohammad Shahzad 31*; Luke Jongwe 5-6, Neville Madziva 3-27) by 117 runs. *MoM*: Hamilton Masakadza.

4th ODI: Zimbabwe win by 65 runs
Sharjah Cricket Stadium, January 4: Zimbabwe 226 in 49.1 overs (Chamu Chibhabha 53, Peter Moor 52; Dawlat Zadran 3-54, Rashid Khan 3-43) beat **Afghanistan** 161 in 45 overs (Mohammad Shahzad 45, Hashmatullah Shahidi 31; C Chibhabha 4-25, Neville Madziva 2-22, Luke Jongwe 2-22) by 65 runs. *MoM*: Chamu Chibhabha.

5th ODI: Afghanistan win by two wickets
Sharjah Cricket Stadium, January 6: Zimbabwe 248 in 49.5 overs (Hamilton Masakadza 110, Peter Moor 42; Amir Hamza 3-41, Mohammad Nabi 2-23) lost to **Afghanistan** 254/8 in 49.4 overs (Gulbadin Naib 82*, Hashmatullah Shahidi 32; Luke Jongwe 3-50, Sikandar Raza 2-37) by two wickets. *MoM*: Gulbadin Naib. *MoS*: Mohammad Shahzad.

T20I series (2): Afghanistan 2 Zimbabwe 0

1st T20I: Afghanistan win by five runs
Sharjah Cricket Stadium, January 8: Afghanistan 187/7 in 20 overs (Usman Ghani 42, Gulbadin Naib 37; Graeme Cremer 3-17) beat **Zimbabwe** 182/7 in 20 overs (Malcolm Waller 49*, Hamilton Masakadza 33; Dawlat Zadran 3-32) by five runs. *MoM*: Gulbadin Naib.

2nd T20I: Afghanistan win by 81 runs
Sharjah Cricket Stadium, January 10: Afghanistan 215/6 in 20 overs (Mohammad Shahzad 118*, Mohammad Nabi 22) beat **Zimbabwe** 134 in 18.1 overs (Hamilton Masakadza 63, Peter Moor 35; Amir Hamza 2-15, Dawlat Zadran 2-21) by 81 runs. *MoM*: Mohammad Shahzad. *MoS*: Mohammad Shahzad.

	T20Is	ODIs
Best batsman	Mohammad Shahzad (151 runs, 2 matches)	Hamilton Masakadza (266 runs, 5 matches)
Best bowler	Dawlat Zadran (5 wickets, 2 matches)	Amir Hamza (11 wickets, 5 matches)

The boy grows up: Mohammad Amir showed he still had the pace and skill to trouble batsmen. — *Getty Images*

Pakistan in New Zealand

Amir returns to duty

Would he or wouldn't he. The potential return of one of the game's most exciting young talents after a five-year ban for his role in one of the game's most shameful episodes triggered several rounds of introspection and almost no consensus among stakeholders. Mohammad Amir was among the 26 selected for a conditioning camp before the tour of New Zealand, but Azhar Ali, Pakistan's ODI captain, and Mohammad Hafeez weren't on board with Amir's 'reintegration', choosing to stay away from the camp until the board chairman mended fences. There were questions, too, if Amir would even get a visa, but soon the path was cleared for that most debated comeback.

Amir 2.0 went for 31 runs in his first four overs and picked up a late wicket – promisingly for Pakistan, the pace and raw skill were still there – as the visiting bowlers all pitched in to open with a win. But after that, it was all New Zealand, who had plenty to feel confident about going into the World T20 soon after.

The in-form Martin Guptill and Kane Williamson combined for a 171-run stand, the highest T20I chase without losing a wicket. Corey Anderson then played through injury for two wickets to add to his match-defining 42-ball 82 not out to seal the series.

Henry Nicholls led the ODI revival after they slumped to 99 for 6, adding 79 for the seventh wicket with Mitchell Santner, while Matt Henry and Mitchell McClenaghan (who would miss the rest of the series with a fracture from a bouncer that hit him through his helmet) contributed 73 in an attacking unbroken ninth. Rain denied the visitors a chance to get even, and then came into play again as the returning Brendon McCullum lifted the trophy after a tense finish. Hafeez, Babar Azam and Sarfraz Ahmed were the pillars on whom Pakistan's batting hopes rested, but there was more work to be done ahead of the T20 extravaganza.

T20I series (3): New Zealand 2 Pakistan 1

1st T20I: Pakistan win by 16 runs
Eden Park, Auckland, January 15: Pakistan 171/8 in 20 overs (Mohammad Hafeez 61, Umar Akmal 24; Adam Milne 4-37, Mitchell Santner 2-14) beat **New Zealand** 155 in 20 overs (Kane Williamson 70, Colin Munro 56; Wahab Riaz 3-34, Shahid Afridi 2-26) by 16 runs. *MoM*: Shahid Afridi.

2nd T20I: New Zealand win by ten wickets
Seddon Park, Hamilton, January 17: Pakistan 168/7 in 20 overs (Umar Akmal 56*, Shoaib Malik 39; Mitchell McClenaghan 2-23) lost to **New Zealand** 171/0 in 17.4 overs (Martin Guptill 87*, Kane Williamson 72*) by ten wickets. *MoM*: Martin Guptill.

3rd T20I: New Zealand win by 95 runs
Westpac Stadium, Wellington, January 22: New Zealand 196/5 in 20 overs (Corey Anderson 82*, Martin Guptill 42; Wahab Riaz 2-43) beat **Pakistan** 101 in 16.1 overs (Sarfraz Ahmed 41; Grant Elliott 3-7, Adam Milne 3-8) by 95 runs. *MoM*: Corey Anderson.

ODI series (3): New Zealand 2 Pakistan 0

1st ODI: New Zealand win by 70 runs
Basin Reserve, Wellington, January 25: New Zealand 280/8 in 50 overs (Henry Nicholls 82, Matt Henry 48*; Mohammad Amir 3-28, Anwar Ali 3-66) beat **Pakistan** 210 in 46 overs (Babar Azam 62, Mohammad Hafeez 42; Trent Boult 4-40, Grant Elliott 3-43) by 70 runs. *MoM*: Henry Nicholls.

2nd ODI: Match abandoned
McLean Park, Napier, January 28: New Zealand v **Pakistan**. Match abandoned without a ball bowled.

3rd ODI: New Zealand win by three wickets (D/L method)
Eden Park, Auckland, January 31: Pakistan 290 in 47.3 overs (Babar Azam 83, Mohammad Hafeez 76; Adam Milne 3-49, Matt Henry 2-44) lost to **New Zealand** 265/7 in 42.3 overs (Kane Williamson 84, Martin Guptill 82; Azhar Ali 2-37, Mohammad Amir 2-39) by three wickets (D/L method). *MoM*: Martin Guptill.

	T20Is	ODIs
Best batsman	Kane Williamson (175 runs, 3 matches)	Babar Azam (145 runs, 2 matches)
Best bowler	Adam Milne (8 wickets, 3 matches)	Trent Boult (6 wickets, 2 matches)

Zimbabwe in Bangladesh

Masakadza fires up World T20 warm-up

Just two months after they played three ODIs and two T20Is in Bangladesh, Zimbabwe were back in the nation. With the 20-over world cup looming, they arrived with intentions clear: they would play four T20Is, a proposal to include a Test was kept on hold. As in November, the teams were evenly matched, sharing the honours.

Injuries and pre-world tournament experimenting meant the sides were rarely settled. Vusi Sibanda's comeback was a happy one, first adding a Zimbabwe record 101 for the opening wicket with Hamilton Masakadza, and following that up with two more strong first-wicket stands as their side came from behind to draw level. Malcolm Waller and Neville Madziva, the visitors' stars from their previous visit, came good again, Waller providing consistent, vital late hitting and Madziva scalping four in the decider to dismantle the hosts' chase. The batting revolved around Masakadza, though: While his 53-ball 79 in the first game couldn't ensure a win after the middle order collapsed, he took no chances in the fourth, remaining unbeaten on 93 from 58 as Zimbabwe posted a competitive 180 for 4. Graeme Cremer led their spinners, turning the screws on the hosts, who obliged with scrappy batting and collapses of their own.

Zimbabwe's mainstay: Hamilton Masakadza's attacking play at the top allowed the visitors to draw level.
– *AFP/Getty Images*

Sabbir Rahman's all-round show in the first two matches was the biggest positive for Mashrafe Mortaza, while Mustafizur Rahman proved reliable as ever until his injury. The constant shuffling, however – there were four debutants in the third game – meant a gulf between intention and execution that would cost them.

Best batsman: Hamilton Masakadza (222 runs, 4 matches)
Best bowler: Graeme Cremer (6 wickets, 4 matches)

T20I series (4): Bangladesh 2 Zimbabwe 2

1st T20I: Bangladesh win by four wickets
Sheikh Abu Naser Stadium, Khulna, January 15: Zimbabwe 163/7 in 20 overs (Hamilton Masakadza 79, Vusi Sibanda 46; Mustafizur Rahman 2-18, Al-Amin Hossain 2-24) lost to **Bangladesh** 166/6 in 18.4 overs (Sabbir Rahman 46, Tamim Iqbal 29; Graeme Cremer 2-32) by four wickets. *MoM*: Hamilton Masakadza.

2nd T20I: Bangladesh win by 42 runs
Sheikh Abu Naser Stadium, Khulna, January 17: Bangladesh 167/3 in 20 overs (Sabbir Rahman 43*, Soumya Sarkar 43) beat **Zimbabwe** 125/8 in 20 overs (Hamilton Masakadza 30, Malcolm Waller 29; S Rahman 3-11, Mustafizur Rahman 2-19) by 42 runs. *MoM*: Sabbir Rahman.

3rd T20I: Zimbabwe win by 31 runs
Sheikh Abu Naser Stadium, Khulna, January 20: Zimbabwe 187/6 in 20 overs (Malcolm Waller 49, Vusi Sibanda 44; Shakib Al Hasan 3-32, Abu Hider 2-40) beat **Bangladesh** 156/6 in 20 overs (Sabbir Rahman 50, Nurul Hasan 30*; Graeme Cremer 3-18, Sikandar Raza 2-7) by 31 runs. *MoM*: Malcolm Waller.

4th T20I: Zimbabwe win by 18 runs
Sheikh Abu Naser Stadium, Khulna, January 22: Zimbabwe 180/4 in 20 overs (Hamilton Masakadza 93*, Malcolm Waller 36) beat **Bangladesh** 162 in 19 overs (Mahmudullah 54, Mashrafe Mortaza 22; Neville Madziva 4-34, Tendai Chisoro 3-17) by 18 runs. *MoM*: Hamilton Masakadza. *MoS*: Hamilton Masakadza.

Test mace in the tropy cabinet: Steve Smith's men claimed the No.1 ranking in Tests, ending South Africa's three-year run. — *Getty Images*

Australia in New Zealand

Mixed farewell for McCullum

GEOFF LEMON

For New Zealanders, a February visit from Australia was all about farewelling their captain and talisman Brendon McCullum, who intended to sign off first with his 260th ODI, then his 101st Test match. For Australia, the focus was on one thing: surviving green seaming wickets away from home. Behind this preoccupation was the prior humiliation that such conditions had wrought at Edgbaston and Trent Bridge in the 2015 Ashes. With its perceived similarities, the land across the Tasman was seen as a useful proving ground.

The ODI series was a belter, with a tense comeback win for New Zealand in the third and final match to see McCullum exit his signature format in style. The man himself got each innings off to a flyer, Martin Guptill backed up that early work, Matt Henry bowled heat and took wickets. Spin all-rounder Mitchell Santner played outstanding hands with bat and ball in the first two matches, then was injured. His replacement for the decider, leg-spinner Ish Sodhi, twirled New Zealand to victory.

All of that suggested the Test series would be a contest, but the home side never kept up. New Zealand had blazed to the 2015 World Cup final against Australia before falling flat, then key lapses cost a chance to win the inaugural day-night Test later that year in Adelaide. That time, a possible 1-1 series draw slipped to a 2-0 defeat; in this return series, high expectations once more fell short.

It was an outstanding series for the Australians, individually and as a team. The much-discussed seaming wickets never really eventuated, bar a couple of lively hours on each first day that the visiting batsmen avoided and the bowlers exploited by winning both tosses. Afterwards the pitches flattened and slowed, and Australia were better able to adapt with more disciplined batting and pack bowling.

Only six Australians used the ball over two Tests, each delivering at least one important innings. New Zealand used nine bowlers, with averages in the 50s or 60s for frontliners Trent Boult, Tim Southee, Mark Craig, Doug Bracewell and Corey Anderson, while Henry would have averaged 134 had he taken a wicket. Only Neil Wagner was flattered, but his stubborn innings of 6 for 106 in his only match couldn't stop Australia passing 500.

The batting was as lopsided: Adam Voges, Steve Smith, Joe Burns and Usman Khawaja each made a century, totalled over 200 runs and averaged between 69.66 and 154.50, while the best series return for New Zealand was McCullum's 180, most of them in one knock, and the best average was his 45.00.

For New Zealanders though, both results vanish behind the memory of McCullum's feat in the second Test. It was his final match, on his home ground in Christchurch, packed with fans and trembling with adoration, when he walked out on the first morning with his team in trouble and responded with the fastest century in Test history. This freewheeling carnage took 54 balls to hit the milestone, two fewer than the previous record shared by the unlikely pair of Vivian Richards and Misbah-ul-Haq. McCullum finished on 145 from 79, as breath returned to the crowd. Individual brilliance left the lasting impression, but overall the tour reflected New Zealand's history against Australia: enough success to contend, not enough collective assurance when the moments arrived.

Turning it around: Trent Boult had a disappointing Test series, but had been immediately effective in the one-dayers. – *Getty Images*

ODI series (3): New Zealand 2 Australia 1

1st ODI: New Zealand win by 159 runs

Eden Park, Auckland, February 3: New Zealand 307/8 in 50 overs (Martin Guptill 90, Henry Nicholls 61; Mitchell Marsh 2-35, James Faulkner 2-67) beat **Australia** 148 in 24.2 overs (Matthew Wade 37, James Faulkner 36; Trent Boult 3-38, Matt Henry 3-41) by 159 runs. *MoM*: Martin Guptill.

2nd ODI: Australia win by four wickets

Westpac Stadium, Wellington, February 6: New Zealand 281/9 in 50 overs (Kane Williamson 60, Mitchell Santner 45*; Josh Hazlewood 3-61, Mitchell Marsh 2-30) lost to **Australia** 283/6 in 46.3 overs (David Warner 98, M Marsh 69; M Santner 3-47, Matt Henry 2-57) by four wickets. *MoM*: Mitchell Marsh.

3rd ODI: New Zealand win by 55 runs

Seddon Park, Hamilton, February 8: New Zealand 246 in 45.3 overs (Martin Guptill 59, Grant Elliot 50; Mitchell Marsh 3-34, John Hastings 2-42) beat **Australia** 191 in 43.4 overs (Usman Khawaja 44, M Marsh 41; Matt Henry 3-60, Corey Anderson 2-16) by 55 runs. *MoM*: Ish Sodhi.

Test series (2): Australia 2 New Zealand 0

1st Test: Australia win by an innings and 52 runs

A perfect New Zealand summer and the picturesque Basin Reserve made the Wellington Test an aesthetic pleasure for spectators. It wasn't a pretty picture for the home side though, as New Zealand's time in the gentle sunshine was shortened from five days to three and a half. A first-morning collapse left few paths back into the match, then Voges's double-century walled off any byways.

Josh Hazlewood's tight lines had Tom Latham caught behind thanks to a DRS appeal, Guptill taken at second slip, then McCullum edging via his pad to third for a duck in his 100th Test. Either side of the captain's dismissal, Peter Siddle took the key wicket of Williamson thanks to a brilliant Peter Nevill catch from an inside edge, then drew Nicholls, on debut, into a nick. Five down within 12 overs for 51 runs.

BJ Watling made it to lunch but was out soon afterwards. Southee followed quickly, while Anderson wasted a patient 87-ball stay holing out against Nathan Lyon. Boult and Mark Craig bashed the highest partnership of the innings with 46, but a total of 183 looked far too slender.

Things could still have got interesting: Southee knocked off Australia's openers, Smith fell to Craig for 71 after being dropped by him on 18, then Voges was bowled leaving a ball in the last over of day one. At that stage it would have been 146 for 4, a deficit of 37, but Richard Illingworth, the umpire, inexplicably called a no-ball despite Doug Bracewell's heel being entirely behind the line. The live signal meant there was no way to reverse the error, and Voges cashed in his reprieve for a further 232 runs.

The West Australian accumulated throughout the second day, then opened up on the third. By the time he was last man out before lunch, his two prior innings meant that he had made a world record 614 runs and batted 110 minutes between dismissals. He had also briefly raised his Test average above 100.

New Zealand batted better second time around, but a deficit of 379 still meant an innings defeat. Young guns Nicholls and Latham made good fifties, Southee broke the career record for sixes scored from No.10, and Boult followed suit from No.11, but in the end their efforts served only as pretty summer entertainment.

Basin Reserve, Wellington, February 12-15: New Zealand 183 in 48 overs (Mark Craig 41*, Corey Anderson 38; Josh Hazlewood 4-42, Nathan Lyon 3-32) and 327 in 104.3 overs (Tom Latham 63, Henry Nicholls 59; N Lyon 4-91, Mitchell Marsh 3-73) lost to **Australia** 562 in 154.2 overs (Adam Voges 239, Usman Khawaja 140; C Anderson 2-79, Tim Southee 2-87) by an innings and 52 runs. *MoM*: Adam Voges.

2nd Test: Australia win by seven wickets

Christchurch was centre stage for the Second Test: the fifth anniversary of its devastating earthquakes was during lunch on the third day, the only time that the ringing sounds of construction work stopped echoing across the town centre. Hagley Oval, the city's new cricket home after Lancaster Park was destroyed, sat amid lavish central parkland. Here the New Zealand captain and hometown hero would bring an admired international career to an end.

Siddle missed out with an ankle injury, raising speculation that his Test career may have finished on 208 wickets. His absence meant that Jackson Bird kept a spot with James Pattinson returning, and with the pitch juiced and jumping, that pair and Hazlewood dropped New Zealand to 32 for 3.

Out came McCullum, beaten by his first ball, slashing his second over slip. With the pitch as it was, he wanted Australia batting on the first day. That meant scoring as fast as possible before being bowled out. He took 21 runs from a Marsh over, went to lunch at 37 from 18, then was caught at gully from a Pattinson no-ball soon after the break. His fifty came via an outrageous leaping forehand over long-on for six. Hazlewood went for 21 from an over, 18 from the next, and the century was up from a record 54 balls.

Devastating shots were sandwiched between miscues and edges. So many boundaries came from the top edge that Australia employed a long-stop behind the wicketkeeper. It didn't matter. As per the *Wisden India* report on the day, McCullum "had rubbed the gold Buddha's belly until it glowed like lamplight. He had fired the right joss sticks, lopped off the pertinent parts of animals, thrown a saltshaker over his shoulder while picking unusual specimens of vegetation as recommended. All luck was his."

Anderson offered 72 from 66. The pair's 179 at 9.76 an over was the fastest Test partnership worth more than 120. Far less exhilarating, Burns and Smith made patient hundreds that took Australia's lead to 135, despite Wagner's

Hometown hero: Before an adoring Christchurch crowd, Brendon McCullum played the only way he knew how to, bringing up a century from 54 balls. — *Getty Images*

relentless short-ball attack. Bird came to the fore second time around, his maiden five-for removing the key scorers in Williamson and Anderson as well as the clouting Henry, keeping New Zealand's lead to 200, which was comfortably chased on day five. Nonetheless, the lasting memory was McCullum leaving the way he had played: uncompromising, fearless, a gamble whose final hand paid off in spades.

Hagley Oval, Christchurch, February 20-24: New Zealand 370 in 65.4 overs (Brendon McCullum 145, Corey Anderson 72; Nathan Lyon 3-61, Jackson Bird 2-66) and 335 in 111. overs (Kane Williamson 97, Matt Henry 66; Jackson Bird 5-59, James Pattinson 4-77) lost to **Australia** 505 in 153.1 overs (Joe Burns 170, Steven Smith 138; Neil Wagner 6-106, Trent Boult 2-108) and 201/3 in 54 overs (J Burns 65, S Smith 53*) by seven wickets. *MoM*: Joe Burns.

	Tests	ODIs
Best batsman	Adam Voges (309 runs, 2 matches)	Martin Guptill (180 runs, 3 matches)
Best bowler	Nathan Lyon (10 wickets, 2 matches)	Matt Henry (8 wickets, 3 matches)

Australia in South Africa

Teams warm up for India

Australia's schedule over six previous months had been packed with the longest format. In their only acknowledgement of the 20-over game, the visiting Indians had swept them 3-0. In fact, since the 2014 World T20, they had played just eight T20I, of which they won three. So, with the ICC World T20 2016 around the corner, they leapt at the chance to get in as much practice in the format. South Africa obliged – although how much of a lead-in to a subcontinental challenge the three-match series would be was debatable.

Steve Smith was handed the reins of the T20I team as well after the India thrashing and entrusted with the responsibility of ensuring continuity in leadership and settling on a winning XI. Despite a series win, however, they were no closer to a complete answer. Combinations of Usman Khawaja, Shane Watson and Aaron Finch all took turns opening, while David Warner lost out on a spot he was a natural at – though that didn't stop his 40-ball 77 and 33 from 27 from No.4 in their two wins.

Imran Tahir struck regularly for the hosts, but leaked runs: he went for 47 in the second match as Glenn Maxwell and Warner overhauled South Africa's 204 at the last gasp. It was Australia's spinners, though, led by Adam Zampa in his debut series, who had the final say, negating Hasim Amla's career-best 97 not out to seal the series.

Aaron Phangiso, South Africa's left-arm spinner, missed out on the series

Australia's spinners, led by Adam Zampa in his debut series, negated Hashim Amla's career-best 97 not out in the decider. – *Getty Images*

after his action was reported in a domestic game and found illegal. He was cleared to bowl on the eve of the final game, but was left out as he worked on his bowling ahead of the global tournament.

Best batsman: David Warner (130 runs, 3 matches)
Best bowler: Nathan Coulter-Nile (5 wickets, 2 matches)

T20I series: Australia 2 South Africa 1

1st T20I: South Africa win by three wickets
Kingsmead, Durban, March 4: Australia 157/9 in 20 overs (Aaron Finch 40, Mitchell Marsh 35; Imran Tahir 3-21, David Wiese 2-16) lost to **South Africa** 158/7 in 19.2 overs (David Miller 53*, Faf du Plessis 40; Nathan Coulter-Nile 3-29) by three wickets. *MoM*: David Miller.

2nd T20I: Australia win by five wickets
New Wanderers Stadium, Johannesburg, March 6: South Africa 204/7 in 20 overs (Faf du Plessis 79, Quinton de Kock 44; James Faulkner 3-28, John Hastings 2-42) lost to **Australia** 205/5 in 20 overs (David Warner 77, Glenn Maxwell 75; Kagiso Rabada 2-25, Dale Steyn 2-32) by five wickets. *MoM*: David Warner.

3rd T20I: Australia win by six wickets
Newlands, Cape Town, March 9: South Africa 178/4 in 20 overs (Hashim Amla 97*, David Miller 30; Nathan Coulter-Nile 2-36) lost to **Australia** 181/4 in 19.2 overs (Shane Watson 42, Steven Smith 44; Imran Tahir 2-38) by six wickets. *MoM*: Hashim Amla. *MoS*: David Warner.

Balm for the hearbreak of 2014: Round 1 went comfortably to Alastair Cook's men, before England's limited-overs sides kept up their fearless cricket. – *Getty Images*

Sri Lanka in England and Ireland

Visitors' struggles derail points trial

GARY NAYLOR

When the tourists conceded 412 for 4 in 100 overs to Division Two's Essex in their opening warm-up match, the writing was on the wall. Since their visit two years previously, when they won the Test series, the ODI series and T20I match in a magnificent clean sweep, they had lost their two icons, Kumar Sangakkara and Mahela Jayawardene. Besides, Angelo Mathews, their inspirational captain, did not look in peak condition physically or mentally, having played a lot of cricket during the intervening years.

And so it proved, the visitors failing to win a match on tour and failing to provide a useful pilot for the Andrew Strauss-approved multi-format points system, with an overall winner decided across the three formats of the game. A draw in the Third Test, a tie in the first ODI and a no result in the third hardly provided the ebb and flow across a tour's fixtures that the new system sought to reflect, nor was anyone in any doubt as to which was the better team. Whether points deciding the 'winners' of a tour is an idea that will stick like neutral umpires or fade like replacing a batsman with a bowler halfway through ODIs, remains to be seen, but the general consensus appeared to be that the game had invented a solution for a problem that didn't exist.

After the rare tie in the first ODI, England outclassed Sri Lanka in the next four matches. The visitors were left looking for the right blend, especially with the ball, while Eoin Morgan's men played with the fearlessness they have embraced since the tame World Cup exit two years ago. In picking Tymal Mills for his T20 debut, they also showed a willingness to back not just a T20 specialist at international level, but also at domestic level as the young left-arm quick is restricted by injury to the game's shortest form.

Sri Lanka searched for consistency, but, in Dinesh Chandimal and the emerging Kusal Mendis, they have talent with the bat. They desperately need Angelo Mathews to rediscover his mojo with the ball (running in would be a start) and get him the support required to take wickets and restrict run-rates when opponents line them up and tee off.

Next time they tour, it might be most interesting if the Lankans are given three Tests again, but not so far north, and three ODIs and three T20Is, a balance that would be more fun for everyone and less likely to be rain affected.

Tour matches

County Ground, Chelmsford, May 8-10: Sri Lankans 254 in 63 overs (Kusal Mendis 66, Niroshan Dickwella 53; Aaron Beard 4-62, Thomas Moore 3-48) and 42/2 in 13 overs drew with **Essex** 412/4 dec in 100 overs (Jaik Mickleburgh 109, Tom Westley 108; Dhammika Prasad 2-78).

Grace Road, Leicester, May 13-15: Sri Lankans 367 in 97.1 overs (Dasun Shanaka 112, Kusal Mendis 65; Rob Sayer 2-41, Rob Taylor 2-55) and 200/4 dec in 50.2 overs (Dimuth Karunaratne 100 retd. out, Kaushal Silva 43) drew with **Leicestershire** 375/5 dec in 100 overs (Michael Burgess 98, Tom Wells 87*; Rangana Herath 2-39, Milinda Siriwardana 2-57).

Test series (3): England 2 Sri Lanka 0

1st Test: England win by an innings and 88 runs

England sent their visitors to their northern outposts in mid-May into environments as alien to those who grew up on the teardrop island as cricket can provide. If it were a tactic (as opposed to the result of financial bids and beancounters' algorithms) it worked, with the series secured before a ball was bowled at Lord's.

Sri Lanka invited England to bat, with new cap James Vince to come in at No. 5. But it was the Lankans' debutant who made the bigger impact: Dasun Shanaka, picked for his batting, shot out England captain Alastair Cook, out-of-sorts Nick Compton and gun batsman Joe Root in his first three overs. Shanaka had two more wickets than runs against his name and England were 51 for 3. It was as good as things would get for Sri Lanka, though.

Enter Jonny Bairstow at No. 7, on his home ground, full of confidence after a maiden century in South Africa, to join Alex Hales, the opener, who had toughed it out for 31 overs. After a little look, Bairstow used his baseball stance to hit boundaries and raised his fifty from just 60 balls. The Yorkshire wicketkeeper passed his partner early on the second day and was in the 90s when Hales went after Rangana Herath and holed out. Bairstow was eventually ninth out for 140, almost half of England's 298 all out, a score that looked handy rather than match-winning.

England's seamers had other ideas, the old mates James Anderson and Stuart Broad combining to shoot out Sri Lanka for less than 100, the visitors unable to deal with the moving ball in helpful bowling conditions.

England's best: James Anderson's 10-45 at Headingley was his career's third ten-wicket haul. – *Getty Images*

In an increasingly rare move in Test cricket, Cook stuck the Lankans in again, for more examination of technique by the peerless Anderson. Only Kusal Mendis, the 21-year-old playing his first Test in England and giving a glimpse of what looks like the next great Sri Lankan batsman, could deal with England, his 53 the third-highest score of the match. It wasn't enough to save his team, defeat coming in three days of cricket that taught the visitors how hard it can be up north to bat against a ball that swings and seams.

Anderson's 10 for 45 was his career's third ten-wicket haul and, coming at an average of 4.5, was the best by an Englishman against Sri Lanka. There were finally smiles for him at the ground after the Headingley heartbreak of 2014 that left him in tears, his brave last-wicket resistance ending in the 55th ball he faced and the penultimate one of the match.

Headingley, Leeds, May 19-21: England 298 in 90.3 overs (Jonny Bairstow 140, Alex Hales 86; Dasun Shanaka 3-46, Dushmantha Chameera 3-64) beat **Sri Lanka** 91 in 36.4 overs (Angelo Mathews 34, Lahiru Thirimanne 22; James Anderson 5-16, Stuart Broad 4-21) and 119 in 35.3 overs (f/o) (Kusal Mendis 53; J Anderson 5-29, Steven Finn 3-26) by an innings and 88 runs. *MoM*: Jonny Bairstow.

2nd Test: England win by nine wickets

With just a few days to recover from their First Test mauling, Sri Lanka lost the toss at Chester-le-Street and prepared for some hard yards in the field. Cook, on the other hand, prepared to celebrate his 10,000th Test match run, but he was kept waiting longer than he expected by a Sri Lankan side that finally got a foothold in the series in the second innings – by which time it was too late to salvage much.

While Cook had gone for a disappointing 15 first time round, Hales crossed 80 for a second consecutive innings. England found another centurion down the order: an imperious Moeen Ali at No. 7. When Cook eventually declared two short of 500, Anderson took off his pads and, sharing the wickets with Broad and Chris Woakes (in for the injured Ben Stokes) swept aside the visitors.

Sitting on a lead just shy of 400, Cook invited Angelo Mathews to have another go and this time the Lankans made a much better fist of it. Mathews brought up a fifty while Dinesh Chandimal showed his undoubted class with a century. Captain and vice-captain got useful support from Kaushal Silva, whose 60 at the top occupied almost four hours and even Herath, who showed a hitherto unseen willingness to get into line and defend and ge inside the line and carve as he made 61 in a couple of hours that everyone except England's bowlers enjoyed immensely. Anderson was again the pick of the bowlers, with another five wickets in 27 probing overs, but Moeen not for the first time nor the last, was attacked by the batsman going at a tick under five an over with just the wicket of Lahiru Thirimanne to show for it.

If a target of 200 might have proved tricky with Herath opening the bowling and hitting a consistent line and length for the first time on tour, 79 was never going to trouble the hosts. In fact, it was just enough for Cook to cross the 10,000-run landmark and shake off a monkey that had been on this back for far too long.

Although the series was lost, the Lankans showed fight and, in batting through the third day losing just seven wickets, gave notice that in a side with just two men with over 27 Tests to their names (Mathews and Herath), they had plenty to work with in the future. England were just happy to get some revenge for the narrow series defeat of two years earlier.

Alastair Cook became the 12th batsman to reach 10,000 Test runs, and did so in 229 innings. At 31 years and 157 days, he was also the youngest to reach the milestone, getting there five months earlier than Sachin Tendulkar, who did so at 31 years and 326 days. Tendulkar, however, needed just 195 innings.

Riverside Ground, Chester-le-Street, May 27-30: England 498/9 dec in 132 overs (Moeen Ali 155*, Alex Hales 83; Nuwan Pradeep 4-107, Milinda Siriwardana 2-35) and 80/1 in 23.2 overs (Alastair Cook 47*, Nick Compton 22*) beat **Sri Lanka** 101 in 43.3 overs (Kusal Men-

Man of the series: Jonny Bairstow proved invaluable as a batsman, stepping up when his team needed him, but his glovework was exposed. – *Getty Images*

dis 35; Stuart Broad 4-40, Chris Woakes 3-9, James Anderson 3-36) and 475 in 128.2 overs (f/o) (Dinesh Chandimal 126, Angelo Mathews 80; J Anderson 5-58, C Woakes 2-103) by nine wickets. *MoM*: James Anderson.

3rd Test: Match drawn

Lord's was as immaculately presented as ever, as May gave way to June and the egg and tomato shades of the MCC provided a traditional backdrop for Test cricket.

England, not for the first time, were in a bit of trouble at 84 for 4. Compton and Vince had continued their poor series before the captain found an ally in Bairstow, in the form of his life with the bat if still unconvincing on the other side of the wickets. Cook was disappointed to throw away a century, out for 85 when trapped in front by Nuwan Pradeep, but Bairstow batted on and on. He was helped by an increasingly confident Woakes, who made 66. Herath was the pick of the bowlers, his left-arm spin never quite there to hit.

By the end of the second day, the visitors had advanced the score to 162 for 1 with Silva continuing his good form and Dimuth Karunaratne registering his first fifty of the series. For the first time, Sri Lanka looked like they might construct a platform, if not to win the match, then certainly to be competitive. Broad and Woakes, though, got into them at the start of the third day and three wickets fell in just over half an hour. England's seamers shared the ten wickets between them and the hosts, if not their incapacitated captain, were soon batting again, with a lead of 128.

Cook reappeared at No. 7 to steady the ship with the score 120 for 5, while Hales finished an impressive series with another important knock. He had survived having his off stump knocked back by Pradeep as umpire Rod Tucker had called no-ball, though replays suggested otherwise. But what Test series does not have a television inspired controversy these days?

With Sri Lanka going into the fifth day needing 330 and England ten wickets, all four results were in play, but the rain that had necessitated a delayed start on the fourth day returned and hands were shaken with the scoreboard showing 78 for 1.

Although the three Tests schedule was more satisfactory than the Lankans' two Tests itinerary of 2014, it was a shame that the visitors never had time to hit their best form. But they could go into the white ball phase of the tour with growing confidence.

Lord's, London, June 9-13: **England** 416 in 128.4 overs (Jonny Bairstow 167*, Alastair Cook 85; Rangana Herath 4-81, Suranga Lakmal 3-90) and 233/7 dec in 71 overs (Alex Hales 94, A Cook 49*; Nuwan Pradeep 3-37, Shaminda Eranga 3-58) drew with **Sri Lanka** 288 in 95.1 overs (Kaushal Silva 79, Dimuth Karunaratne 50; Chris Woakes 3-31, Steven Finn 3-59) and 78/1 in 24.2 overs (D Karunaratne 37*). *MoM*: Jonny Bairstow. *MoS*: Jonny Bairstow and Kaushal Silva.

ODI series (Ireland v Sri Lanka): Sri Lanka 2 Ireland 0

1st ODI: Sri Lanka win by 76 runs (DLS method)

Ireland have made no secret of their cricketing ambitions and facing a chastened Sri Lanka seemed a good way to start an unusually busy season. With Boyd Rankin returning to the side after four years and debutant Barry McCarthy sending back Sri Lanka's openers for 47, they were on track. But the visitors, who had just about found their feet in British shores, dug in.

Great expectations: Dasun Shanaka, seen here in action against England, became only the 12th bowler to take five wickets on ODI debut, in Sri Lanka's clash against Ireland. – *Getty Images*

Chandimal chose persistence over big-hitting in his first ODI hundred in five years, building vital partnerships with debutant Mendis and Mathews (49), while Shanaka, also on debut, smashed 42 off 19. Mathews turned to Shanaka to break a dangerous opening stand between William Porterfield and Paul Stirling. As a bonus, he also sent back Ed Joyce and John Anderson for single-digit scores, and later cleaned up the middle order for his five-for. A rain interruption left Ireland needing an adjusted 293 from 47 overs, and Kevin O'Brien swung his bat, but with little support on offer, the hosts crumbled.

The Village, Malahide, Dublin, June 16: Sri Lanka 303/7 in 50 overs (Dinesh Chandimal 100*, Kusal Mendis 51; Byod Rankin 2-45, Barry McCarthy 2-69) beat Ireland 216 in 40.4 overs (William Porterfield 73, Kevin O'Brien 64; Dasun Shanaka 5-43, Angelo Mathews 2-37) by 76 runs (DLS method).

2nd ODI: Sri Lanka win by 136 runs

A comprehensive win in which more records fell than wickets gave Sri Lanka confidence to carry into their limited-overs leg in England. The visitors' 377 for 8 was built on two main partnerships: 147 for the first wicket between Kusal Perera and Danushka Gunathilaka, and 161 for the second-wicket pair of Perera and Seekkuge Prasanna going at 10.5 an over. Prasanna was one six away from a century and beating Sanath Jayasuriya's long-standing national record of a 48-ball hundred; he had hit nine sixes and five fours before being bowled by Tim Murtagh. John Bracewell, Ireland's coach, described his side's bowling as "unforgivable", suggesting their failure to put to use data about the batsmen was down to "arrogance, or ignorance or stubbornness". With Suranga Lakmal tearing through the Irish top order and their highest score coming from Andy McBrine at No.8, the humiliation was complete.

The Village, Malahide, Dublin, June 18: Sri Lanka 377/8 in 50 overs (Kusal Perera 135, Seekkuge Prasanna 95; Tim Murtagh 3-66, Barry McCarthy 2-52) beat Ireland 241 in 45 overs (Andy McBrine 79, Stuart Poynter 36; Suranga Lakmal 4-38, S Prasanna 2-32) by 136 runs. MoS: Dasun Shanaka.

ODI series: England 3 Sri Lanka 0

1st ODI: Match tied

Sri Lanka had shown by the end of the Test series that they were an emerging side with much to learn but had the determination and skills to improve. More than any other match on tour, the opening ODI bore out that opinion. On the longest day of the year, Mathews led the batting effort, starting in the first ten overs and finishing in the last five. He got good support from Prasanna, whose 59 off 28 added vital impetus. When England were 82 for 6, the target looked distant, but Jos Buttler made a responsible 93, Woakes a superb 95 off 92 to leave No. 10 Liam Plunkett to score a six off Pradeep's last ball to tie. Amazingly, he did!

All-round influence: Chris Woakes's 95 off 92 and a 138-run stand for the seventh wicket with Jos Buttler was crucial as England tied the first ODI. — *Getty Images*

Trent Bridge, Nottingham, June 21: Sri Lanka 286/9 in 50 overs (Angelo Mathews 73 Seekkuge Prasanna 59; Chris Woakes 2-56, David Willey 2-56) tied with **England** 286/8 in 50 overs (C Woakes 95*, Jos Buttler 93; A Mathews 2-22, Nuwan Pradeep 2-64). *MoM*: Chris Woakes.

2nd ODI: England win by ten wickets

After the thrills and spills of the series opener, much was expected of the second ODI at Edgbaston, home of the T20 Blast Finals Day and England's most raucous ground. The Lankans batted first again, this time of their own volition, but their progress was stymied by regular wickets whenever they tried to accelerate. Adil Rashid had been the pick of the bowlers, his leg breaks and googlies yielding just 36 runs from his full allocation and the wickets of the danger men, Mathews and Prasanna. What looked like a score 30 or 40 under par was soon made to look 130 or 140 under par as England's opening pair took the visitors' attack apart. After a circumspect start, all the bowling came as one to Jason Roy and Hales, the target overhauled in the 35th over. It was England's highest partnership for any wicket, and a world record for the highest successful chase without losing a wicket.

Edgbaston, Birmingham, June 24: Sri Lanka 254/7 in 50 overs (Upul Tharanga 53*, Dinesh Chandimal 52; Adil Rashid 2-34, Liam Plunkett 2-49) lost to **England** 256/0 in 34.1 overs (Alex Hales 133*, Jason Roy 112*) by ten wickets. *MoM*: Jason Roy.

> England's chase of 256 was the highest by any side without losing a wicket. The previous highest chase for a 10-wicket win was by New Zealand, who easily overhauled Zimbabwe's 235for 9 at the Harare Sports Club on August 4, 2015. Martin Guptill and Tom Latham had brought up centuries and wrapped up the game with 46 balls to spare.

	England's highest partnerships				
Players	Wicket	Runs	Opposition	Venue	Date
Alex Hales Jason Roy	1	256*	Sri Lanka	Birmingham	Jun 24, 2016
Andrew Strauss Jonathan Trott	2	250	Bangladesh	Birmngham	Jul 12, 2010
Alex Hales Joe Root	2	248	Pakistan	Nottingham	Aug 30, 2016

3rd ODI: No result

The caravan headed west to Bristol, this one played in natural light in front of a decent Sunday crowd. Mindful of the forecast, England inserted the Lankans preferring to manage any Duckworth/Lewis/Stern calculations with bat and not ball. The Lankans had a decent platform at the start of the 36th over with the score 165 for 3 and Mathews and Chandimal both well set, but Woakes snared Chandimal and the Lankans were able to score just two fours and one six in the last 15 overs as just 83 were added. England would have fancied their chances even with a bit of rain around – but there was a lot of rain around and the match was abandoned.

County Ground, Bristol, June 26: **Sri Lanka** 248/9 in 50 overs (Dinesh Chandimal 62, Angelo Mathews 56; Chris Woakes 3-34, Liam Plunkett 3-46) v **England** 16/1 in 4 overs. No result.

4th ODI: England win by six wickets (DLS method)

In a rain-affected day-nighter, Gunathilaka, Mendis, Chandimal and Mathews all cashed in with half-centuries with only Gunathilaka going at a strike-rate under 120. DLS converted Sri Lanka's 305 off 42 overs into a target of 308 from the same number of overs, which looked, if not quite daunting, then certainly stiff. But it was merely the red rag to Roy's bull, the England opener, on his home ground, smashing the ball all round as he racked up England's second-highest ODI score. He fell with the victory target just 27 runs away. Root had supported him with a fine fifty and England's two wicketkeepers, red ball's Bairstow and white ball's Buttler ensured there were no scares. That win secured the series and underlined the big change in white ball culture since Trevor Bayliss took on the coaching job after England's World Cup debacle.

Kennington Oval, London, June 29: **Sri Lanka** 305/5 in 42 overs (Kusal Mendis 77, Angelo Mathews 67*; Adil Rashid 2-57, David Willey 2-58) lost to **England** 309/4 in 40.1 overs (Jason Roy 162, Joe Root 65; Nuwan Pradeep 2-78) by six wickets (DLS method). *MoM*: Jason Roy.

5th ODI: England win by 122 runs

England went west again for the final ODI, but found better weather in Cardiff than they had in Bristol six days earlier. Mathews, possibly thinking that his strength lay in batting, took the dangerous step of inserting a batting unit brimming with confidence and then could do little as England piled up the runs. 324 is not an enormous score these days, but a decent one in English (well, Welsh) conditions. Root anchored the innings while Buttler's explosive 70 off 45 balls turned a good score into a very good score. England then employed the old maxim of 'You miss, I hit' with five of the top six Lankans lbw or bowled as the visitors wilted in the face of David Willey's aggression, Plunkett's pace and Rashid's variations. The three Yorkshire players shared nine wickets with the other run out by another county teammate, Bairstow.

In familiar territory: On his home ground in London, Jason Roy brought up England's second-highest ODI score. – *Getty Images*

Sophia Gardens, Cardiff, July 2: England 324/7 in 50 overs (Joe Root 93, Jos Buttler 70, Danushka Gunathilaka 3-48) beat **Sri Lanka** 202 in 42.4 overs (Dinesh Chandimal 53, D Gunathilaka 48; David Willey 4-34, Liam Plunkett 3-44) by 122 runs. *MoM*: Jos Buttler. *MoS*: Jason Roy.

Only T20I: England win by eight wickets

• England take another step towards T20 specialisation by giving a debut to Tymal Mills, a left-armer quick, whose rapid four overs cost just 22 runs. • On his home ground, Chris Jordan shows his value as a death bowler conceding just six runs from the 18th and 20th overs while picking up three wickets. • The absence of a Sri Lankan batsman who can go on limits the target to useful rather than challenging. • England play three wicketkeepers by trade, Bairstow, Buttler and Billings, whose ultra-aggressive batting suits their new culture, but it means Eoin Morgan is limited in his bowling options. • Buttler, whose boundary hitting is intimidating and his shot selection good enough to avoid flaming out, keeps the required rate below 8, never mind the dangerous 10. • Morgan's cool head has a role to play in white ball cricket, letting the tearaways loose but knocking it around himself as required.

The Rose Bowl, Southampton, July 5: Sri Lanka 140 in 20 overs (Danushka Gunathilaka 26, Dinesh Chandimal 23; Liam Dawson 3-27, Chris Jordan 3-29) lost to **England** 144/2 in 17.3 overs (Jos Buttler 73*, Eoin Morgan 47*; Angelo Mathews 2-27) by eight wickets. *PoM:* Jos Buttler

Multi-format Points Table

Teams	M	W	L	T	D	Aban.	Pts
England	9	6	0	1	1	1	20
Sri Lanka	9	0	6	1	1	1	4

Test match win: 4 points, ODI/T20I win: 2 points, Tie: 2 points, Draw/Aban.: 1 point

	Tests	ODIs	T20I
Best batsman	Jonny Bairstow (387 runs, 3 matches)	Jason Roy (316 runs, 5 matches)	Jos Buttler (73 runs, 1 match)
Best bowler	James Anderson (21 wickets, 3 matches)	David Willey (10 wickets, 5 matches)	Liam Dawson (3 wickets, 1 match)

Best batsman v Ireland: Kusal Perera (167 runs, 2 matches)
Best bowler v Ireland: Dasun Shanaka (6 wickets, 2 matches)

Gary Naylor (@garynaylor999) is a writer and broadcaster in the UK.

In an Australian success built on team effort, captain Steve Smith led the batting charts while Mitchell Marsh (right) proved his worth as an all-rounder. – *WICB*

Tri-nation series in West Indies

Australia seize key moments

AJAY SURESH

West Indies lost their third successive triangular series at home but played with flair to mark a comeback of sorts in ODIs, taking baby steps to earn a direct qualification for the 2019 World Cup. They were without the services of Andre Russell, Chris Gayle, Dwayne Bravo and Darren Sammy, all of whom were crucial to their World T20 triumph in India a few months earlier, but performed commendably against Australia – they lost to the No.1 ODI side by 58 runs in the final – and South Africa, the third-ranked team.

Sunil Narine and Kieron Pollard made a statement on their international comebacks in the first game of the series, against South Africa. Narine, bowling with a reworked action, returned career-best figures of 6 for 27, and Pollard, having recovered from an injury that kept him out of the World T20, made 67 in a four-wicket win.

West Indies were also helped by Marlon Samuels, one of the four centurions in the tournament and the second-highest run-getter. While Samuels kept West Indies in the hunt, it was Darren Bravo's 102 in the last league game against South Africa that took the home team to the final.

A total of 11 South African players came to the series on the back of some heavy workload at the Indian Premier League, but that was no excuse for their defeat in yet another knockout game.

On pitches that were not ideal for batting, Australia used their bowling resources the best, even though Imran Tahir headed the wickets column. The combination of Josh Hazlewood, Adam Zampa, Mitchell Starc, who was making a comeback since being injured in November 2015, Nathan Coulter-Nile, Mitchell Marsh, who took his status as an all-rounder to the next level, and Nathan Lyon bowled well as a unit. It made up for the absence of David Warner, who played just three matches before breaking his finger. Not to be forgotten was the guts displayed by the batting unit. Steve Smith, the captain, was the only batsman to average more than 50 in the series, Marsh's 79 not out in a thrilling win against West Indies in a league game took Australia to the final, and Matthew Wade's unbeaten 57 from No.7 in the title clash was worth gold dust.

Best batsman: Steven Smith (Australia) (264 runs, 7 matches)
Best bowler: Imran Tahir (South Africa) (13 wickets, 6 matches)

1st ODI: West Indies beat South Africa by four wickets
Providence Stadium, Guyana, June 3: South Africa 188 in 46.5 overs (Rilee Rossouw 61, AB de Villiers 31; Sunil Narine 6-27, Carlos Brathwaite 2-35) lost to **West Indies** 191/6 in 48.1 overs (Kieron Pollard 67*, Johnson Charles 31; Aaron Phangiso 3-40, Imran Tahir 2-41) by four wickets. *MoM*: Sunil Narine.

2nd ODI: Australia beat West Indies by six wickets
Providence Stadium, Guyana, June 5: West Indies 116 in 32.3 overs (Johnson Charles 22, Carlos Brathwaite 21; Adam Zampa 3-16, Nathan Lyon 3-39) lost to **Australia** 117/4 in 25.4 overs (David Warner 55*, Usman Khawaja 27; Sunil Narine 2-36) by six wickets. *MoM*: Nathan Lyon.

3rd ODI: South Africa beat Australia by 47 runs
Providence Stadium, Guyana, June 7: South Africa 189/9 in 50 overs (Farhaan Behardien 62, Hashim Amla 35; Glenn Maxwell 2-15, Josh Hazlewood 2-20) beat **Australia** 142 in 34.2 overs (Aaron Finch 72, Nathan Lyon 30; Kagiso Rabada 3-13, Wayne Parnell 2-23) by 47 runs. *MoM*: Farhaan Behardien.

4th ODI: Australia beat South Africa by 36 runs
Warner Park, Basseterre, St Kitts, June 11: Australia 288/6 in 50 overs (David Warner 109, Usman Khawaja 59; Imran Tahir 2-45) beat **South Africa** 252 in 47.4 overs (Faf du Plessis 63, Hashim Amla 60; Mitchell Starc 3-43, Josh Hazlewood 3-52, Adam Zampa 3-52) by 36 runs. *MoM*: David Warner.

5th ODI: West Indies beat Australia by four wickets
Warner Park, Basseterre, St Kitts, June 13: Australia 265/7 in 50 overs (Usman Khawaja 98, Steven Smith 74; Kieron Pollard 2-32, Jason Holder 2-44) lost to **West Indies** 266/6 in 45.4 overs (Marlon Samuels 92, Johnson Charles 48; Adam Zampa 2-60, Nathan Coulter-Nile 2-67) by four wickets. *MoM*: Marlon Samuels.

6th ODI: South Africa beat West Indies by 139 runs
Warner Park, Basseterre, St Kitts, June 15: South Africa 343/4 in 50 overs (Hashim Amla 110, Faf du Plessis 73*; Kieron Pollard 2-64) beat **West Indies** 204 in 38 overs (Johnson Charles 49, Marlon Samuels 24; Imran Tahir 7-45, Tabraiz Shamsi 2-41) by 139 runs. *MoM*: Imran Tahir.

7th ODI: No result
Kensington Oval, Bridgetown, Barbados, June 19: South Africa 8/0 in 1 over v **Australia**. No result.

8th ODI: Australia beat West Indies by six wickets
Kensington Oval, Bridgetown, Barbados, June 21: West Indies 282/8 in 50 overs (Marlon Samuels 125, Denesh Ramdin 91; Mitchell Starc 3-51, James Faulkner 2-56) lost to **Australia** 283/4 in 48.4 overs (Mitchell Marsh 79*, Steven Smith 78) by six wickets. *MoM*: Marlon Samuels.

9th ODI: West Indies beat South Africa by 100 runs
Kensington Oval, Bridgetown, Barbados, June 24: West Indies 285 in 49.5 overs (Darren Bravo 102, Kieron Pollard 62; Kagiso Rabada 3-31, Chris Morris 3-63) beat **South Africa** 185 in 46 overs (Farhaan Behardien 35, Morne Morkel 32*; Shannon Gabriel 3-17, Sunil Narine 3-28) by 100 runs. *MoM*: Darren Bravo.

Points Table

Teams	M	W	L	T	N/R	Pts	NRR
Australia	6	3	2	0	1	15	0.383
West Indies	6	3	3	0	0	13	-0.460
South Africa	6	2	3	0	1	12	0.155

Final: Australia beat West Indies by 58 runs

Usman Khawaja and Aaron Finch began with six boundaries in the first four overs, before they led a procession of Australian batsmen who failed to capitalise on good starts. Wade put behind him recent struggles with his form, marshalling the lower order with a timely half-century on a slowing pitch. Marsh was able to keep the batsmen guessing and extract extra bounce during a three-wicket burst that saw off Johnson Charles, Bravo and Samuels for ten runs. West Indies found themselves 72 for 4 soon after 20 overs. Denesh Ramdin and Jason Holder (34) kept up the fight, but Hazlewood had little trouble mopping up the tail.

It was a credible showing for Hazlewood all through on what Justin Langer, the stand-in coach, described as "lifeless wickets" made to help spinners. "There is so much fast-bowling talent here," he rued. "They run in and bowl fast and they keep bowling all day, but I don't understand why they play on such dead, low, lifeless wickets."

Kensington Oval, Bridgetown, Barbados, June 26: Australia 270/9 in 50 overs (Matthew Wade 57*, Aaron Finch 47; Jason Holder 2-51, Shannon Gabriel 2-58) beat **West Indies** 212 in 45.4 overs (Johnson Charles 45, Denesh Ramdin 40; Josh Hazlewood 5-50, Mitchell Marsh 3-32) by 58 runs. *MoM*: Mitchell Marsh. *MoS*: Josh Hazlewood.

Winners: Australia

Ever the statesman: Under the inspiring Misbah-ul-Haq, Pakistan climbed to No.1 in Tests for the first time, never having played at home since 2009. – *Getty Images*

Pakistan in England and Ireland

Red-ball ascent away from home

LAWRENCE BOOTH

Rarely can a draw have felt so much like a victory. After a momentous win in the First Test at Lord's, Pakistan lost feebly at Old Trafford, then again – despite a three-figure first-innings lead – at Edgbaston. Before the finale at The Oval, pundits agreed that 3-1 was the likeliest outcome; England wouldn't foul it up twice.

Instead, they were stunned by the tourists' Khan-do attitude: Sohail claimed a second successive five-for and Younis, until now a bewilderingly spare part, hit a sparkling 218. The final scoreline of 2-2 left fans craving a decider, and meant the Pakistanis could take their 4-1 defeat in the subsequent 50-over series on the chin. That was a problem for another day.

It helped that, by the time the white-ball cricket began, Misbah-ul-Haq's team had for the first time reached No. 1 in Test rankings. If their ascent relied to a degree on results and poor weather elsewhere, then there could be no denying the size of their achievement, for not since 2009 and the terrorist attack in Lahore had they played a Test at home. As ever, Pakistan hogged the best storylines.

Misbah, at 42 every inch the elder statesman, was an inspiration. With new coach Mickey Arthur, he spread calm, discipline, even a splash of fun. The

A team re-energised: Following their captain's example, Younis Khan led the victorious Pakistanis in press-ups and salutes on the Lord's outfield, a nod to the army's role in their pre-tour training camp. – *Getty Images*

Pakistanis had arrived for their first tour of England since the disastrous 2010 visit, determined to remake friends and influence people, even hiring a PR man to pull a few strings.

More to the point, they were determined to come away with a result. A boot camp in Abbottabad with the Pakistan army was followed by a skills camp in Lahore. They then used Southampton as a pre-tour base, the better to get used to English conditions. By the First Test, they also had first-class matches against Somerset and Sussex under their belt. They were ready – and it showed.

Neither were they distracted by the Test return of Mohammad Amir, at the venue where his deliberate no-balls six years earlier had earned him a spell in a British prison. There were tedious cries of "no-ball" during the two non-London Tests, but little aggravation besides.

Misbah led the way with a century at Lord's and celebrated with ten press-ups, a nod to the army and the tour's leitmotif. Other batsmen followed. Although Pakistan suffered a collective meltdown in Manchester, where they succumbed to Joe Root's brilliant 254, Azhar Ali made 139 at Edgbaston and Asad Shafiq kept Younis company at The Oval with 109.

Their bowlers had their moments, too. Yasir Shah, the leg-spinner, looked set to dominate England's batsmen after taking ten wickets at Lord's, only for them to play him straighter and neutralise him altogether in the Second and Third Tests; overall, his 19 wickets cost over 40 each. Sohail Khan took two five-fors in his first Tests for five years, and Wahab Riaz relished the battle. Amir was badly served by his fielders: 12 wickets at 42 didn't tell his story.

Yasir Shah: Cricketer of the Year

p 146

For the hosts, Chris Woakes was an unlikely star. His 26 wickets at 16 apiece were a record for England in a series against Pakistan, and his 11-for at Lord's deserved better. But there were too many holes in the batting to secure the Test series.

Alex Hales averaged 19, a disappointment only partly assuaged by his national-record 171 during England's one-day world-record score of 444 for 3 at Trent Bridge. James Vince kept edging elegant drives and Gary Ballance made a lone half-century.

All too often, the burden fell on Alastair Cook, who batted more fluently than ever, Root, the ever-pugnacious Jonny Bairstow and the ever-watchable Moeen Ali. In both London Tests, that fragility cost them dear.

But if anything summed up a happy tour that avoided the bickering so common to previous encounters between these sides, it was the sight of a sold-out Old Trafford, awash with Pakistani green, during the one-off T20I.

Pakistan won at a canter, turning Manchester into a happy cauldron of horns and cheers, and encouraging the thought that England v Pakistan was no longer an excuse merely to air old prejudices. Finally, some games of cricket had broken out.

Tour matches

County Ground, Taunton, July 3-5: Pakistanis 359/8 dec in 100 overs (Younis Khan 104, Asad Shafiq 80; Paul van Meekeren 3-78, Tim Groenewald 2-24) and 236/4 dec in 59.4 overs (Azhar Ali 101*, A Shafiq 69*; Jack Leach 2-61) drew with **Somerset** 128 in 34.1 overs (James Hildreth 47*, Peter Trego 23; Sohail Khan 3-26, Mohammad Amir 3-36) and 258/8 in 73 overs (Marcus Trescothick 106, J Hildreth 48; Yasir Shah 4-107, Rahat Ali 2-30).

County Ground, Hove, July 8-10: Pakistanis 363/5 dec in 99 overs (Azhar Ali 145, Misbh-ul-Haq 68; Jofra Archer 4-49) and 71/1 in 24 overs (Shan Masood 38*, Mohammad Hafeez 23) drew with **Sussex** 291/5 dec in 63.5 overs (Harry Finch 103, Luke Wells 93; Imran Khan 2-60, Wahab Riaz 2-62).

Test series (4): England 2 Pakistan 2

1st Test: Pakistan win by 75 runs

Pakistan's first win at Lord's in 20 years was a riotous affair. Inspired by ten wickets for the leg-spin of Yasir Shah, it culminated in the sight of the entire squad – led by senior batsman Younis Khan – doing press-ups and salutes on the outfield. This was a tribute to the Pakistani soldiers in Abbottabad, and to the galvanising qualities of captain Misbah-ul-Haq, who had marked his first-day century with ten press-ups of his own. The gesture went viral.

England, meanwhile, seemed infected by another kind of contagion. In reply to Pakistan's 339 – which would have been more had Chris Woakes not intervened with a Test-best six-wicket haul – they had moved to 118 for 1 on the second afternoon when Joe Root made a hash of a slog-sweep and was caught off Yasir just short of a fifty. By stumps, they were 253 for 7, and Yasir had five, benefiting from England's ill-considered obsession with hitting him square of the wicket.

First win at Lord's: Picking up from where he left off in UAE, Yasir Shah continued to torment the England batsmen as he got himself on the honours board. – *Getty Images*

He made it six next morning as Pakistan grabbed a lead of 86. On a plumb Lord's track, only Alastair Cook had made it past 50 before edging a drive against Mohammad Amir onto his stumps. For Amir, making his return to Test cricket at the scene of his no-balling crime six years earlier, it was third time lucky: twice, on 22 and 55, Cook had edged him; twice he had been dropped.

Woakes picked up five more as Pakistan showed their batting was almost as fragile. England had the best part of two days to chase 283, one more than they had ever managed in the fourth innings to win a Test at Lord's. The hill quickly became a mountain, as the unheralded Rahat Ali, one of three Pakistani left-arm seamers on show, picked up three early wickets, including that of Root, who shovelled incautiously to deep backward square. James Vince fell on the drive shortly after lunch, before Yasir resumed his role as tormentor-in-chief. First, Gary Ballance went too far across his stumps and was bowled round his legs. Then Moeen Ali charged at his fourth ball and was bowled. Gary Bairstow and Woakes resisted for more than 30 overs, until Bairstow missed a pull at Yasir, at which point the tail folded. Symbolically, perhaps, the final wicket fell to Amir, who bowled debutant Jake Ball and wheeled away in joy, the memories of 2010 receding into the evening sunshine.

Lord's, London, July 14-17: Pakistan 339 in 99.2 overs (Misbah-ul-Haq 114, Asad Shafiq 73; Chris Woakes 6-70, Stuart Broad 3-71) and 215 in 79.1 overs (A Shafiq 49, Sarfraz Ahmed 45; C Woakes 5-32, S Broad 3-38) beat **England** 272 in 79.1 overs (Alastair Cook 81, Joe Root 48; Yasir Shah 6-72) and 207 in 75.5 overs (Jonny Bairstow 48, Gary Ballance 43; Y Shah 4-69, Rahat Ali 3-47) by 75 runs. *MoM:* Yasir Shah.

2nd Test: England win by 330 runs

From the moment Cook won his first toss against Misbah in five attempts, the result of this game seemed strangely ordained. While Cook himself and Root set about making up for England's batting failures at Lord's almost on their own, Pakistan looked barely more threatening than the Sri Lankans had earlier in the summer. It was the kind of turnaround that gives momentum a bad name.

The tone was set on the opening day by a second-wicket stand of 185 between England's two premier batsmen, during which Yasir was played with a common sense bordering on disdain. Gone were the cross-batted hacks that had helped earn him ten wickets at Lord's. Instead, England played it straight. The pitch offered Yasir little by way of consolation. By the end of the Test, he had figures of 1 for 266 – comfortably the most expensive in Old Trafford's history.

Cook was bowled by Amir on the stroke of tea, though not before he had secured his 29th Test hundred. But Root shrugged off the loss of Vince and Ballance before stumps to move on next day to a majestic career-best 254, compiled in ten-and-a-quarter hours of awe-inspiring concentration, during

New milestones: Cook secured his 29th Test hundred while Joe Root had a career-best 254. — *Getty Images*

which he resolved to drive at almost nothing slanted across him by Pakistan's left-arm seamers.

Woakes, a high-class nightwatchman, and Bairstow both made 58, and England's declaration allowed them 24 overs at Pakistan before stumps on the second evening. The visitors caved in to 57 for 4, with Woakes striking twice. That was soon 119 for 8 next day, and it needed Misbah's steady hand and some lower-order frolics from Wahab Riaz to get them to 198, trailing by a demoralising 391.

Nearly seven sessions remained when Cook – to the derision of many former pros in the commentary box, some of whom fancied a day-off and a round of golf – chose to bat again. Alex Hales went cheaply once more, but the captain and Root combined for their second century stand of the match, taking their aggregate to 503 for twice out.

With showers around, Pakistan were set a purely notional 565 in the best part of two days, but were unable to extend matters into a fifth. James Anderson continued his mastery over Shan Masood, Moeen persuaded Younis to slog to long-on and Woakes continued to chip away. Not even a calf injury to Ben Stokes could remove the gloss from an England win so comprehensive it was as if Lord's had been an aberration.

Old Trafford, Manchester, July 22-25: England 589/8 dec in 152.2 overs (Joe Root 254, Alastair Cook 105; Wahab Riaz 3-106, Mohammad Amir 2-89) and 173/1 dec in 30 overs (A Cook 76*, J Root 71*) beat **Pakistan** 198 in 63.4 overs (Misbah-ul-Haq 52, Wahab Riaz 39; Chris Woakes 4-67, Ben Stokes 2-39) and 234 in 70.3 overs (Mohammad Hafeez 42, Asad Shafiq 39; James Anderson 3-41, Chris Woakes 3-41, Moeen Ali 3-88) by 330 runs. *MoM*: Joe Root.

Tour match
County Ground, New Road, Worcester, July 29-30: Pakistanis 261/3 dec in 80 overs (Azhar Ali 81, Shan Masood 67) drew with **Worcestershire** 260/6 in 76 overs (Tom Kohler-Cadmore 73, Joe Clarke 58; Rahat Ali 2-29).

3rd Test: England win by 141 runs

England's 500th home Test was among their most dramatic. At 79 for 1 on the final afternoon, Pakistan seemed set for the draw that would have set up a decider at The Oval. Instead, with the ball starting to reverse – not prolifically, but just enough – England reduced them to 151 for 9. Not even a doughty last-wicket stand of 50 could sugar-coat the truth: After claiming a first-innings lead of 103, Pakistan had blown it.

Edgbaston has always been one of English cricket's most trusted friends. No Asian team has won here, and the crowd are reliably raucous. Yet England's first-day subsidence to 297 hinted at complacency. In his first Test for five years, Sohail Khan – in for Riaz – joyously claimed 5 for 96, and only sensible half-centuries from Ballance and Moeen kept the innings afloat.

Then, with one ball to go on day two, Pakistan were a painstaking 257 for 2. So England were thrilled when Azhar lost focus and edged Woakes to Cook at first slip. The wicket gave England hope. Next day, they hurried Pakistan out for 400, the deficit troublesome but not terminal; by stumps, Cook and Hales had eased them into a small lead. The game was shifting on its axis.

Unlikely star: Chris Woakes shared the series award with Misbah for his all-round effort. – *Getty Images*

But both openers fell inside 20 minutes on the fourth morning, and it needed circumspection from Root and Vince to keep Pakistan at bay. Had Mohammad Hafeez held on at first slip when Root had 25, things might have been different. Though wickets fell, however, the closest the tourists got to dragging themselves back into it came when England found themselves 282 for 5, a lead of 179.

Jonny Bairstow and Moeen now set about ensuring only one team could win, putting on an energetic 152, and allowing Cook to declare on the final morning and set Pakistan an improbable 343 in 84 overs. Almost immediately, Hafeez top-edged Stuart Broad to long leg, but Sami Aslam – who had replaced Masood – settled down for his second substantial innings of the match, and Azhar joined in.

A draw began to look inevitable, only for Azhar to edge Moeen, and Anderson – the ball now reversing – to induce a nick from Younis Khan. But the real damage was wrought by Steven Finn and Woakes. In 23 balls, they claimed four wickets for one run, including that of Aslam. The end came a couple of overs into the final hour, leaving England to breathe again, and Pakistan to wonder how they had let it slip.

Edgbaston, Birmingham, August 3-7: England 297 in 86 overs (Gary Ballance 70, Moeen Ali 63; Sohail Khan 5-96, Mohammad Amir 2-53) and 445/6 dec in 129 overs (Moeen Ali 86*, Jonny Bairstow 83; M Amir 2-75, Sohail 2-111) beat **Pakistan** 400 in 136 overs (Azhar Ali

139, Sami Aslam 82; Chris Woakes 3-79, Stuart Broad 3-83) and 201 in 70.5 overs (S Aslam 70, Azhar Ali 38; S Broad 2-24, James Anderson 2-31) by 141 runs. *MoM:* Moeen Ali.

4th Test: Pakistan win by ten wickets

This was the Test in which Younis finally woke up – and England didn't know what hit them. Until now, he had been a fidgety presence at the crease, kicking up his back leg like a 1920s flapper girl. But, on the advice of Mohammad Azharuddin, of all people, Younis resolved to stand taller, stay deep in his crease and play the ball late. The result was a blistering double-hundred, which put England's first-innings 328 into harsh perspective and set Pakistan up for a memorable, series-squaring, ten-wicket win.

For a while, it looked as if England might reprise their come-from-behind win in Birmingham. A lovely century from Moeen – after being dropped on nine by Azhar at third slip – had transformed their first innings from the rags of 110 for 5 to the relative riches of 328. And three late wickets on the second day left Pakistan six down and only 12 ahead. But Younis, 101 overnight after his 32nd Test century, was not in the mood to relive the Third Test. After losing Sarfraz Ahmed for a typically punchy 44, he supervised stands of 37 with Riaz and 97 with Amir. By the time he was given out lbw to Anderson, Younis had hit 31 fours and four sixes (all off Moeen). He had passed Zaheer Abbas's 215 against India in Lahore in 1982-83 to make the highest score by a Pakistan No. 5. Some of his driving was out of this world.

England resumed on the third afternoon battered, bruised and 214 behind. And, in 31 overs that evening, their plight worsened. Cook was caught at slip off Wahab – the liveliest seamer in the match – before Yasir claimed 3 for 4 in 22 balls, including Root. A match-winner at Lord's, but a non-entity in Manchester and Birmingham, Yasir now had the scoreboard pressure he craved.

Next morning, after Sohail built on his first-innings five-for with the wicket of Ballance, carving to the keeper, Yasir had Moeen caught behind shortly before lunch, then completed a five-wicket haul of his own when Broad reverse-swept to slip. In between, only the impressive Bairstow held Pakistan up, though a last-wicket flurry obliged them to bat again. It merely allowed Misbah's men to finish with a flourish of their own: Azhar Ali's straight six off Moeen was triumphant punctuation mark to a wonderful series.

Kennington Oval, London, August 11-14: England 328 in 76.4 overs (Moeen Ali 108, Jonny Bairstow 55; Sohail Khan 5-68, Wahab Riaz 3-93) and 253 in 79.2 overs (J Bairstow 81, Joe Root 39; Yasir Shah 5-71, W Riaz 2-48) lost to **Pakistan** 542 in 146 overs (Younis Khan 218, Asad Shafiq 109; Chris Woakes 3-82, Steven Finn 3-110) and 42/0 in 13.1 overs (Azhar Ali 30*) by ten wickets. *MoM:* Younis Khan. *MoS*: Misbah-ul-Haq, Chris Woakes.

ODI series (2): Pakistan 1 Ireland 0

1st ODI: Pakistan win by 255 runs

Just as Ireland were getting more opportunities than ever before to play the top teams, they were facing their most challenging period. Having failed to contain the Pakistan batsmen under cloudy skies, they crashed to their lowest total at home, giving Pakistan their biggest ODI win in terms of runs. Sharjeel Khan needed just 86 balls for his 152 – his was the fourth-fastest century by a Pakistani, after Shahid Afridi – dominating stands of 90 with Mohammad Hafeez and 94 with Babar Azam. Fifties from Shoaib Malik and debutant Mohammad Nawaz took the score past 330. Barry McCarthy's was among the wickets again, but his strikes were eventually cosmetic. Pace and swing proved the hosts' undoing, Mohammad Amir and Umar Gul ripping through the top order before Imad Wasim wrapped things up.

The Village, Malahide, Dublin, August 18: Pakistan 337/6 in 47 overs (Sharjeel Khan 152, Shoaib Malik 57*; Barry McCarthy 4-62) beat **Ireland** 82 in 23.4 overs (Gary Wilson 21; Imad Wasim 5-14, Umar Gul 3-23) by 255 runs.

2nd ODI: Match abandoned

The Village, Malahide, Dublin, August 20: **Pakistan** v **Ireland**. Match abandoned without a ball bowled.

ODI series (5): England 4 Pakistan 1

1st ODI: England win by 44 runs (DLS method)

England cantered to a rain-affected victory thanks to a tidy bowling display and sixties from Jason Roy and Root. Pakistan's total of 260 for 6 felt neither here nor there, an ambivalence embodied by captain Azhar Ali's laborious 82 from 110 balls. Azam (40 from 42) and Sarfraz (55 from 58) were sprightlier, but England – boosted by the return of Mark Wood – retained control, conceding only 82 after Azhar fell in the 36th over. Hales's poor sequence against the Pakistanis continued when he edged Gul to slip, but Roy – after a dizzy spell brought on by low blood-sugar levels – was in late-summer form. Although fortunate to survive on 24, when Sarfraz made a hash of a skyer, he showed touches of genius in his 56-ball 65. Eoin Morgan's hairy call for a single cost Root his wicket, but England were well ahead when the weather intervened with more than 15 overs left.

The Rose Bowl, Southampton, August 24: Pakistan 260/6 in 50 overs (Azhar Ali 82, Sarfraz Ahmed 55; Adil Rashid 2-51) lost to **England** 194/3 in 34.3 overs (Jason Roy 65, Joe Root 61) by 44 runs. (DLS method). *MoM:* Jason Roy

2nd ODI: England win by four wickets

Another effortless display from Root confirmed the suspicion that Pakistan's batting was ill-suited to the demands of modern 50-over cricket. He fell for 89, having broken the back of England's pursuit of a modest 252 and added 112 for the third wicket with Morgan, who made his first international half-century in 24 innings. Stokes's 30-ball 42 hurried the game towards a conclusion that had felt inevitable from the moment Pakistan slipped to 2 for 3 in the fourth over. Sarfraz responded with a defiant hundred, his country's first in an ODI at Lord's, and Wasim ensured respectability with a career-best unbeaten 63. But, like an ageing umpire, the Pakistan innings was too heavy around the middle: Nos. 1-3 and 8-11 managed 13 between them, as England's seamers – Wood, Woakes and Liam Plunkett – shared eight wickets.

Lord's, London, August 27: Pakistan 251 in 49.5 overs (Sarfraz Ahmed 105, Imad Wasim 63*; Chris Woakes 3-42, Mark Wood 3-46) lost to **England** 255/6 in 47.3 overs (Joe Root 89, Eoin Morgan 68; Imad Wasim 2-38) by four wickets. *MoM:* Joe Root.

3rd ODI: England win by 169 runs

England battered their way into the record books, slamming a world-record 444 for 3 to beat Sri Lanka's 443 for 9 against the Netherlands in 2006. Landmarks fell like confetti. Hales made 171 from 122 balls, England's highest score in the format, surpassing Robin Smith's 167 not out against Australia at Edgbaston 23 years earlier, and launched four of England's 16 sixes – another national best. With Root – who registered his fifth successive half-century – he added 248, the highest partnership for any wicket against Pakistan. Then Jos Buttler and Morgan took over, putting on a scintillating 161 at more than 13 an over. It was carnage: Buttler racked up seven sixes in his 51-ball 90, Morgan five in his 27-ball 57. Riaz, who was twice denied a wicket after overstepping, finished with none for 110, the second-most expensive analysis in ODI history. Pakistan needed a miracle to avoid going 3-0 down, but stood more chance of bumping into Robin Hood. Woakes quickly removed the top three, and only Amir's 28-ball 58 – the first ODI half-century by a No. 11 – held England up. To call it men against boys did not do the chasm justice.

Going, going, gone: Alex Hales's 171 from 122 balls at Trent Bridge is England's highest individual score in the format. – *Getty Images*

Trent Bridge, Nottingham, August 30: England 444/3 in 50 overs (Alex Hales 171, Jos Buttler 90*; Hasan Ali 2-74) beat **Pakistan** 275 in 42.4 overs (Mohammad Amir 58, Sharjeel Khan 58; Chris Woakes 4-41, Adil Rashid 2-73) by 169 runs. *MoM:* Alex Hales.

	Records set at Trent Bridge
444/3	The highest ODI total ever. England broke the record of 443 set by Sri Lanka v the Netherlands in 2006.
171 for Hales	The highest ODI score by an Englishman. Alex Hales easily went ahead of Robin Smith's 167* v Australia at Edgbaston in 1993.
22-ball 50 for Buttler	The fastest by an England player. Eoin Morgan took 24 balls to get to his fifty, joint second with Paul Collingwood from 2008 v New Zealand.
248-run stand	England's third-highest partnership for any wicket. This second-wicket stand between Hales and Root is the highest against Pakistan.
16 sixes	The most by England in an ODI.
58 for Amir	The only 50-plus score by a No.11 batsman.
0-110 for Riaz	The second-worst bowling figures in ODIs. Australia's Mike Lewis conceded 113 v South Africa at the Wanderers in 2006.

4th ODI: England win by four wickets

When England slipped to 72 for 4 in pursuit of 248, a consolation win for Pakistan looked possible. But Stokes was joined by Bairstow – a late inclusion after Buttler tweaked a quad muscle – and the pair added 103. England were helped when Mohammad Irfan, who had removed both openers in his first game of the series, walked off with cramp, and Moeen completed the job with two sixes in an over from Azhar. Earlier, Pakistan had been restricted to another middling total by the spin of Rashid and Moeen, who claimed five for 86 between them. Azhar made a steady 80, but it needed an unbeaten 57 from 41 balls by the combative Wasim to ensure Pakistan stayed even remotely competitive. Roy and Hales went cheaply, Root fell 20 short of a sixth successive ODI fifty, and Morgan fiddled carelessly at Gul. But England's batting depth won the day – and clinched the Super Series.

Headingley, Leeds, September 1: Pakistan 247/8 in 50 overs (Azhar Ali 80, Imad Wasim 57*; Adil Rashid 3-47, Moeen Ali 2-39) lost to **England** 252/6 in 48 overs (Ben Stokes 69, Jonny Bairstow 61; Mohammad Irfan 2-26) by four wickets. *MoM:* Jonny Bairstow.

5th ODI: Pakistan win by four wickets

Pakistan avoided becoming the first team to lose a one-day series 5-0 in England, thanks to a rollicking stand of 163 in 24 overs between Shoaib and Sarfraz. Both players took toll of Liam Dawson's left-arm spin, Dawson con-

Face-saver: A century in the second game was followed up by a match-winning 90 in Cardiff for Sarfraz Ahmed. — *Getty Images*

ceding 70 in eight overs – the most expensive return by a debutant England bowler. He eventually removed both, but the damage was done, and Pakistan completed their first 300-plus chase outside Asia with ten balls to spare. It was only their second 50-over win against England in 14 attempts. England should have scored more after Roy and Stokes thrashed fifties, but the last ten overs yielded only 58 against Pakistan's best bowling performance of the series. Two wickets in three balls for Wood then reduced the tourists to 77 for 3, only for Shoaib – with his first international half-century in England in 35 innings – and Sarfraz to respond in style.

Sophia Gardens, Cardiff, September 4: England 302/9 in 50 overs (Jason Roy 87, Ben Stokes 75; Hasan Ali 4-60, Mohammad Amir 3-50) lost to **Pakistan** 304/6 in 48.2 overs (Sarfraz Ahmed 90, Shoaib Malik 77; Mark Wood 2-56, Liam Dawson 2-70) by four wickets. *MoM:* Sarfraz Ahmed. *MoS:* Joe Root

Only T20I: Pakistan win by nine wickets

• England's openers begin by adding 56 in 6.4 overs, with only left-arm spinner Wasim escaping punishment. • But, to the delight of a strong Pakistan contingent, the tourists hit back, mixing up their pace and lengths. • After the openers, only Buttler and David Willey find the boundary, as England limp to 135 for 7, their lowest home T20 total for four years after batting first. • With dew starting to take effect, a skiddy ball presents Pakistan's openers with more scoring opportunities, as Sharjeel races to a half-century in 30 deliveries. • By the time he skyes Rashid to cover, he and Khalid Latif have put on 107 in 11.1 overs. • Pakistan race home with nine wickets and 31 balls to spare, to end their tour on a raucous high.

Old Trafford, Manchester, September 7: England 135/7 in 20 overs (Alex Hales 37, Jason Roy 21; Wahab Riaz 3-18, Imad Wasim 2-17) lost to **Pakistan** 139/1 in 14.5 overs (Khalid Latif 59*, Sharjeel Khan 59) by nine wickets. *MoM:* Wahab Riaz.

	Tests	ODI	T20
Best batsman	Joe Root (512 runs, 4 matches)	Sarfraz Ahmed (300 runs, 5 matches)	Khalid Latif (59 runs, 1 match)
Best bowler	Chris Woakes (26 wickets, 4 matches)	Chris Woakes (9 wickets, 4 matches)	Wahab Riaz (3 wickets, 1 match)

Ireland v Pakistan
Best batsman: Sharjeel Khan (152 runs, 1 match)
Best bowler: Imad Wasim (5 wickets, 1 match)

Lawrence Booth (@the_topspin) is editor of Wisden Cricketers' Almanack *and cricket writer for the* Daily Mail.

Constant threat: An Australian side hapless against the turning ball gave Rangana Herath 28 wickets, including a hat-trick, the biggest tally by any left-arm bowler in a three-Test series. — *AFP/Getty Images*

Australia in Sri Lanka

No.1 Test side humbled by spin

GEOFF LEMON

If anyone says they expected Sri Lanka to win this Test series, offer a raised eyebrow. If they expected a whitewash, offer a polygraph test. Or a financial check. Few predicted anything but an Australian procession.

This was down to a winning history against and in Sri Lanka, whether by the stars of 2004 or the earthly mob of 2011; the sole headache was self-induced, when Steve Waugh and Jason Gillespie hospitalised each other with their 1999 version of Kandy Krush. Sri Lanka's only Test win over Australia came in that nine-man game. By 2016, a team of youth and mid-tier players missing retired stars struggled through a poor England tour and a disastrous World T20.

Suddenly, that new lot found ferocity. Local pessimism was best represented by the board: With Australia to be awarded the No. 1 Test ranking trophy before the series, Sri Lanka Cricket requested a private ceremony to avoid dispiriting home fans. Steven Smith was handed the mace like a brown paper parcel in a dockside car. Three weeks later, he was handing it to Pakistan.

The chief inverter was Rangana Herath, 38-year-old finger spinner, he of the late-career renaissance. An Australian side hapless against the turning ball gave him 28 wickets, including a hat-trick, at 12.75 runs apiece; the

100 Test wickets for the speedster: Mitchell Starc finished with 24 wickets for Australia, nearly double that taken by all other seamers combined.
– *AFP/Getty Images*

biggest tally by any left-arm bowler in a three-Test series. Around him rallied the young in age or experience. In the World T20, captain Angelo Mathews had carried his team. Now he gave the odd direction while kicking back in a sedan chair.

Kusal Mendis was the catalyst, a 21-year-old with six Tests to his name. His fearless 176 was the second-highest score by a Sri Lankan against Australia, and reversed a parlous position in the First Test. He was key again at Galle, on the most difficult pitch, then third-gamer Dhananjaya de Silva took the baton with a hundred that rescued the side in Colombo.

Lakshan Sandakan, the rare left-arm wrist-spinner, made a decisive contribution on debut; top-up off-breaker Dilruwan Perera grabbed ten wickets and a cheerful half-century at Galle; Herath did the business in Colombo. Kusal Perera made versatile batting contributions and subbed admirably with the gloves. Kaushal Silva redeemed his miserable series with a hundred at his last attempt.

This lessened reliance on Dinesh Chandimal, who offered low-key support in key partnerships and eventually unlocked a century. Mathews put Herath on at one end, made good DRS referrals and organised the celebrations. He called Suranga Lakmal's injury in Pallekele "a blessing in disguise", leaving no option but to play three spinners. The winning strategy was born.

Mitchell Starc was immense for the visitors with 24 wickets, nearly double the 13 taken by every other seamer combined. His left-arm pace with an old ball on low pitches was a sight to behold. Smith fought hard with a century and a fifty, while Shaun Marsh made a ton in his comeback match in Colombo. Highlights were otherwise scarce for the visitors: Nathan Lyon won't recall the context of his 200th wicket with any fondness.

The one-day series to follow saw Australian batsmen make strides against packed spin attacks. They chased in all five matches, and hit the target in four. The second T20 had the same pattern. In the first, the only time on tour that Australia batted first, Glenn Maxwell's century carried his side to the highest score in T20 internationals. Nonetheless, the tour was largely about elation for the Sri Lankans, and in the longest format, Australia went home with no visible progress playing in Asia.

P Saravanamuttu Stadium, Colombo, July 18-20: Sri Lankan XI 229 in 57.2 overs (Asela Gunaratne 58, Milinda Siriwardana 53; Steve O'Keefe 5-43, Jackson Bird 2-26) and 83 in 20.5 overs (Shehan Jayasurriya 29, A Gunaratne 23; S O'Keefe 5-21, Nathan Lyon 2-14) lost to **Australia** 474 in 132.3 overs (S O'Keefe 78*, Joe Burns 72; S Jayasuriya 5-110, Vimukthi Perera 2-45) by an innings and 162 runs.

Test series (3): Sri Lanka 3 Australia 0

1st Test: Sri Lanka win by 106 runs

It was all going so well for Australia. Mitchell Starc and Josh Hazlewood demolished the top order, new spinner Steve O'Keefe got an early booster, then Nathan Lyon snatched three wickets in three overs. Toss-winners Sri Lanka were done for 117 halfway through the first day, and the reply was serenely 69 for 2 by stumps.

Next morning, Rangana Herath twisted the door handle and Lakshan Sandakan barged through it. The veteran shook off Steve Smith and Usman Khawaja in consecutive overs, exposing the middle order to the debutant, whose standard wrist-spinner turned sharply and whose googly was as yet unidentified. Adam Voges resisted longest but fell to pace, and the hosts were still in the game.

That's when Kusal Mendis arrived. The topmost four batsmen around him perished for single figures, but the youngest player in the match was unperturbed. Briskly and cleanly he scored 75 of his team's first hundred runs, and would add 101 more by the third morning. It was an innings of precise cuts, flicks and sweeps, including a six off Lyon for the century.

Support for Mendis came from Dinesh Chandimal, then Dhananjaya de Silva, the second debutant, who had scored his first Test runs in the first innings with a six from O'Keefe. When those three departed, Herath marshalled a lower-order swing-fest that frustrated the Australians and swelled their required chase. When O'Keefe tore a hamstring while chasing a ball, the damage was compounded.

In the fourth innings, it remained anyone's game. Joe Burns was off to a good clouting start until Sandakan produced the ball of the series, shredding from a yard or more beyond off stump to crash into middle. Smith meanwhile built a determined half-century, until at 139 for 4, Herath and Sandakan toppled him, Marsh and Starc in four overs for two runs. Suddenly Australia's

Fearless: The 21-year-old Kusal Mendis was unperturbed during a vital innings of precise cuts, flicks and sweeps. — *AFP/Getty Images*

hope turned from victory to escape, via the regular afternoon rain that had pushed play into the fifth day.

Peter Nevill and the hobbled O'Keefe put together an admirable rearguard through the second-last session: 29.4 stubborn overs with one scoring shot, while the scoreboard rusted at 161 for 8, the clouds roiled and gathered above, the air darkened, and the tension grew. But on this day alone, the elements did not intervene, and eventually it ended with Herath, taking his fifth wicket for the innings with O'Keefe's 98th ball, and raising both arms to the sky as though calling down lightning at last.

Pallekele Interntional Cricket Stadium, July 26-30: Sri Lanka 117 in 34.2 overs (Dhananjaya de Silva 24, Kusal Perera 20; Nathan Lyon 3-12, Josh Hazlewood 3-21) and 353 in 93.4 overs (Kusal Mendis 176, Dinesh Chandimal 42; Mitchell Starc 4-84, J Hazlewood 2-59) beat **Australia** 203 in 79.2 overs (Adam Voges 47, Mitchell Marsh 31; Rangana Herath 4-49, Lakshan Sandakan 4-58) and 161 in 88.3 overs (Steve Smith 55, Joe Burns 29; R Herath 5-54, L Sandakan 3-49) by 106 runs. *MoM:* Kusal Mendis.

2nd Test: Sri Lanka win by 229 runs

Heading into the Second Test, no one could decide if the first had been an anomalous Sri Lankan escape or a display of Australian frailty. The pitch at Galle looked dry and crumbly, the home side batted anyway, and again the openers fell to pace – Starc taking Dimuth Karunaratne with the first ball of the match. Mendis counterattacked with an urgency to collect runs on a pitch that would only worsen. Two early sixes dented Lyon, after which Mendis swept the spinners and drove the quicks.

He couldn't reach another century, but gave one to Starc: the bowler's 100th Test wicket via reverse swing and movement off the pitch to take the edge with tremendous skill. Kusal Perera had helped shift the momentum, after which Mathews and de Silva carried it on. Replacement spinner Jon Holland was ineffective on debut, and though Starc ended up with five wickets, Sri Lanka's 281 was both brisk and substantial.

Australia made another good start at 54 for 1, but David Warner edged to slip defending the last over of the day. Khawaja didn't add to his overnight score before Dilruwan Perera came round the wicket to the left-hander, who played a straight bat for the off-break only for it to skid on with the angle. The batsman looked lost, and that feeling pervaded the innings: Smith fell to a similar ball, before Voges, Nevill, and Starc made up Herath's hat-trick, the last thanks to a well-timed DRS review.

Having started the day two down, Australia were bowled out before lunch after facing fewer than 20 morning overs. The collapse was 9 for 52, all to spin, and while debutant paceman Vishwa Fernando had dismissed Burns with his second ball in Tests, he would end up bowling two overs for the match.

With the game all but decided, Sri Lanka swung merrily, and again Australia couldn't finish them off: Herath had another frolic and Dilruwan bludgeoned the top score. Starc did all he could with 6 for 50, a fine exhibition on a pitch offering nothing, but his team-mates offered the same.

Trailing by 412 on day two, the Australians were mentally shot and technically incapable. Khawaja got the same delivery as his first innings and didn't offer a shot, bowled by the same bowler twice the same day within seven balls for no run. From 10 for 3, even increased stodge by the middle order dragged things just past lunch on the third day. The series was gone, and Sri Lanka held the Warne-Muralitharan trophy for the first time.

Galle Interntional Stadium, August 4-6: Sri Lanka 281 in 73.1 overs (Kusal Mendis 86, Angelo Mathews 54; Mitchell Starc 5-44, Nathan Lyon 2-78) and 237 in 59.3 overs (Dilruwan Perera 64, A Mathews 47; M Starc 6-50, N Lyon 2-80) beat **Australia** 106 in 33.2 overs (David Warner 42, Mitchell Marsh 27; D Perera 4-29, Rangana Herath 4-35) and 183 in 50.1 overs (D Warner 41, Steve Smith 30; D Perera 6-70, R Herath 2-74) by 229 runs. *MoM*: Dilruwan Perera.

3rd Test: Sri Lanka win by 163 runs

For Australia the final Test wasn't just about pride, it was about prising any positives from the tour. For Sri Lanka it was all about pride, a chance to whitewash a team that before this series they had only beaten once.

Australia's selection hinted at panic: Marsh as opener made some sense, spare all-rounder Moises Henriques plonked at No.5 made none. Initially, Australia's bowlers brought the fire, Starc and Lyon knocking Sri Lanka down to 26 for 5. Then, inexorably and inevitably, Sri Lanka did what they had done all series.

The architect was de Silva, who after four starts was primed to go bigger. Reprieved by DRS on 5, he first went after the bowling, then settled in to occupation, as Chandimal was doing in support.

The pair batted from the first morning to the second, defending for long stretches while staying alert to scoring chances. De Silva's 129 came at a strike-rate of 46 but had 18 boundaries, an ideal mix of attack and defence for the circumstances, while Chandimal's 132 was a model of discipline. Herath batted productively until struck in the box by Hazlewood, having to retire hurt, but 355 was an outrageous comeback.

Marsh and Smith replied with Australia's best partnership of the series, 246 runs across 78.5 overs. For once Australian batsmen looked in control of the conditions, but the illusion was brief. Herath had been hampered by his injury, bowling without his usual zip, but by the third day he found it. After 22 overs returning 0 for 48 he suddenly took 6 for 33, Australia lost 9 for 112, and a potentially decisive lead sputtered out at 24.

Kaushal Silva's series had given him five single-figure scores in his book and six stitches in his hand, but he managed a workmanlike hundred at the last to set a target. Again Australia couldn't get through the tail, and Sri Lanka declared early on the last day.

Australia looked briefly in the chase for 324, with a fast opening stand of 77 driven by a courageous and controlled attack from Warner, but Marsh fell just before lunch, Smith just after it, and the usual collapse followed. Dilruwan foxed Warner behind his legs, Henriques was done by quick thinking at slip, and Herath hoovered up the rest to ensure this was his most prolific series.

Sinhalese Sports Club Ground, August 13-17: Sri Lanka 355 in 141.1 overs (Dinesh Chandimal 132, Dhananjaya de Silva 129; Mitchell Starc 5-63, Nathan Lyon 3-110) and 347/8 dec in 99.3 overs (Kaushal Silva 115, D de Silva 65*; N Lyon 4-123, Jon Holland 2-72, M Starc 2-72) beat **Australia** 379 in 125.1 overs (Shaun Marsh 130, Steve Smith 119; Rangana Herath 6-81, Dilruwan Perera 2-129) and 160 in 44.1 overs (David Warner 68, M Starc 23; R Herath 7-64, D Perera 2-71) by 163 runs. *MoM:* Rangana Herath.

ODI series (5): Sri Lanka 1 Australia 4

1st ODI: Australia win by three wickets

Australia's first morale boost came in a tricky chase on a pitch offering turn and occasional bounce. The visiting seamers used the latter, Starc striking in the first over before becoming the fastest bowler to 100 ODI wickets, in one game fewer than Saqlain Mushtaq's 53. James Faulkner's change-ups, meanwhile, were effective. Chandimal was forced to bat cautiously as wickets fell around him. With timing difficult, the final overs brought no rush of runs.

Aaron Finch did though, the Australian opener smacking two sixes in a fast fifty after deciding that the new ball offered the best chance to score. That gave Smith, Matthew Wade and George Bailey breathing space even as the pitch turned more sharply and Amila Aponso, the debut spinner, gave nothing away. Late wickets made the chase look closer than it was, but Australia's pace-heavy attack had worked, while Sri Lanka's two specialist bowlers plus a raft of all-rounders had not.

R Premadasa Stadium, Colombo, August 21: Sri Lanka 227/8 in 50 overs (Dinesh Chandimal 80*, Kusal Mendis 67, James Faulkner 4-38, Mitchell Starc 3-32) lost to **Australia** 228/7 in 46.5 overs (Steve Smith 58, Aaron Finch 56; Dilruwan Perera 3-48, Lakshan Sandakan 2-33) by three wickets. *MoM:* James Faulkner.

2nd ODI: Sri Lanka win by 82 runs

Sri Lanka's best batting performance of the series produced three half-centuries through the middle order, while Chandimal just missed another, also missing the chance to join the half-dozen batsmen to have made six ODI fifties in a row.

Mendis offered style, Mathews muscle, while Kusal Perera adapted after dropping down to accommodate Danushka Gunathalika, who only helped Starc maintain his habit of taking early wickets. Lyon took one as well, opening the bowling and performing solidly, but it would be his only limited-overs match on tour. Adam Zampa combined economy and threat through the middle, while Faulkner nabbed a late hat-trick, but their good work was undone as part-timers Travis Head and Henriques were savaged.

Both openers and Smith fell early, leaving Bailey, Wade, and Head sandbagging on a slope too steep, while Aponso's run-rate of 1.92 an over offered nothing to build with. Australia subsided, the series was level.

R Premadasa Stadium, Colombo, August 24: Sri Lanka 288 in 48.5 overs (Kusal Mendis 69, Angelo Mathews 57; Adam Zampa 3-42, James Faulkner 3-45, Mitchell Starc 3-53) beat **Australia** 206 in 47.2 overs (Matthew Wade 76, Travis Head 31; Amila Aponso 4-18, Thisara Perera 3-33) by 82 runs. *MoM:* Angelo Mathews.

3rd ODI: Australia win by two wickets

Sri Lanka went back to stutter speed as Chandimal was again forced to buckle down. His fourth and slowest ODI century was backed up only by Tillakaratne Dilshan in what would be the veteran opener's last ODI innings, having abruptly announced his retirement to give younger players a chance before the 2019 World Cup.

It was also Warner's first international as captain, after Smith headed home for a rest. Marsh came in, broke a finger fielding and followed Smith home. Lyon was ditched for Hazlewood, while John Hastings was abruptly elevated from the T20 squad to replace the ineffective Henriques.

Hastings was immediately effective, Zampa was the pick once more, Faulkner maintained his run and Starc hit the stumps in the first over yet again. Bailey's 70 was the core of the chase, with Wade and Head in support after another quick start from Finch. Late wickets provided some alarm, slipping from 204 for 5 to 222 for 8, but the target was within reach.

Rangiri Dambulla International Stadium, August 28: **Sri Lanka** 226 in 49.2 overs (Dinesh Chandimal 102, Tillakaratne Dilshan 42; Adam Zampa 3-38, John Hastings 2-41) lost to **Australia** 227/8 in 46 overs (George Bailey 70, Matthew Wade 42; Angelo Mathews 2-30, Amila Aponso 2-44) by two wickets. *MoM:* George Bailey.

4th ODI: Australia win by six wickets

No more close finishes, as Finch and Bailey blitzed past 212 in 31 overs. Finch could have equalled AB de Villiers's fastest ODI fifty from 16 balls, but settled for matching the Australian record of 18. Bailey lashed 20 from his first five, then built an unbeaten 90. Australia had never reached 100 faster: it took 49 balls.

Sri Lanka's poor total was thanks to Hastings, his 6 for 45 the eighth best Australian ODI figures. Scott Boland followed Hastings in elevation from the T20I squad and hit the spot right away. The only brightness for Sri Lanka was de Silva as Dilshan's replacement, carrying across his confidence from the Test series. Mathews limped off with a calf injury and returned to be last out. Avishka Fernando replaced Gunathilaka, and the 18-year-old who had never played domestic cricket unsurprisingly became Starc's ritual first-over victim. The rest did little better, five single-figure scores among the top seven. Easy does it, series won.

Rangiri Dambulla International Stadium, August 31: **Sri Lanka** 212 in 50 overs (Dhananjaya de Silva 76, Angelo Mathews 40; John Hastings 6-45) lost to **Australia** 217/4 in 31 overs (George Bailey 90*, Aaron Finch 55; Sachith Pathirana 3-37) by six wickets. *MoM:* John Hastings.

5th ODI: Australia win by five wickets

Sri Lanka's team shuffled further, with stand-in captain Chandimal overseeing a mass exodus of Pereras: Dilruwan, Thisara and Angelo all out, Shanaka, Lakmal and Tharanga in. Australia played unchanged, though Finch became the latest to break a finger fielding.

The formula was unchanged too, five of Australia's six bowlers going for less than 4.5 an over, wickets shared between them. Gunathilaka returned, and a 73-run opening stand with de Silva deserved a better follow-up, but the innings fell away to the lowest score of the series. Wade departed early as a makeshift opener, Khawaja followed, but Warner and Bailey put on a controlled partnership of 132 despite genuine turn. Warner pushed on to end a century drought that had extended over his whole tour, taking his team within 11 runs of victory, while Bailey was Player of the Series with 270 runs at 67.50.

Pallekele International Cricket Stadium, September 1: **Sri Lanka** 195 in 40.2 overs (Danushka Gunathilaka 39, Dhananjaya de Silva 34; Mitchell Starc 3-40, Travis Head 2-22) lost to **Australia** 199/5 in 43 overs (David Warner 106, George Bailey 44; Dilruwan Perera 3-51, D de Silva 2-35) by five wickets. *MoM:* David Warner. *MoS:* George Bailey.

First T20I century: Opening the innings, Glenn Maxwell ended unbeaten on 145, just 11 short of the highest individual T20I score. — *AFP/Getty Images*

T20Is (2): Sri Lanka 0 Australia 2

1st T20I: Australia win by 85 runs

• Glenn Maxwell's unbeaten 145 takes Australia to the highest score in T20Is, beating Sri Lanka's 260 for 6 against Kenya, and equals the highest score in any professional T20. • Maxwell only opens the innings because of Finch's injury, and ends up 11 runs short of Finch's record for the highest individual T20I score. • It is Maxwell's first century in any T20, having made four 90s. • Sri Lanka's principal bowlers go for between 11.25 and 15.33 runs per over; the most economical is de Silva, who bowls one over for eight. • Australia use four batsmen, three of whom score faster than all XI Sri Lankans. The fourth, Khawaja, scores faster than nine opponents. • Starc again takes a wicket in the first over, bowling Dilshan, and half of his deliveries are not scored from.

Highest T20 totals				
Team	**Total**	**Opposition**	**Venue**	**Date**
RCB	263/5	Warriors	Bangalore	Apr 23, 2013
Australia	**263/3**	**Sri Lanka**	**Pallekele**	**Sept 6, 2016**
Sri Lanka	260/6	Kenya	Johannesburg	Sept 14, 2007

Pallekele International Cricket Stadium, September 6: **Australia** 263/3 in 20 overs (Glenn Maxwell 145*, Travis Head 45) beat **Sri Lanka** 178/9 in 20 overs (Dinesh Chandimal 58, Chamara Kapugedera 43; Mitchell Starc 3-26, Scott Boland 3-26) by 85 runs. *MoM:* George Bailey.

2nd T20I: Australia win by four wickets

• Dilshan plays his last international, and while he fails with the bat, he creates late excitement with the ball. • Sri Lanka's batsmen produce nine single-figure scores en route to 128, with Faulkner, Zampa and Hastings able to suffocate scoring once again. • In contrast, Australia's openers pile on 84 from their first 42 balls, in a partnership eventually worth 93. • Maxwell is Player of the Match again, equalling his own and his partner Warner's Australian record for the fastest T20I fifty from 18 balls. • With both playing switch-hits, it is hard to tell who is right-handed and who is left. • Dilshan takes two late wickets in two overs to compound a collapse and give hope of an upset, but even at six wickets down, an equation of nine runs from 18 balls is easily solved by Nevill and Head.

R Premadasa Stadium, Colombo, September 9: **Sri Lanka** 128/9 in 20 overs (Dhananjaya de Silva 62, Kusal Perera 22; Adam Zampa 3-16, James Faulkner 3-19) lost to **Australia 130/6 in 17.5 overs (Glenn Maxwell 66, David Warner 25; Tillakaratne Dilshan 2-8, Sachith Pathirana 2-23)** by four wickets. *MoM:* Glenn Maxwell. *MoS:* Glenn Maxwell.

	Tests	ODI	T20
Best batsman	Dhananjaya de Silva (325 runs, 3 matches)	George Bailey (270 runs, 5 matches)	Glenn Maxwell (211 runs, 2 matches)
Best bowler	Rangana Herath (28 wickets, 3 matches)	Mitchell Starc (12 wickets, 5 matches)	Adam Zampa (4 wickets, 2 matches)

New Zealand in Zimbabwe

Winning start to Williamson's captaincy

When top teams play Zimbabwe in Tests these days, the result is often a foregone conclusion – such has been the decline of cricket in Zimbabwe over the past decade or so. It was no different when New Zealand stopped by for a two-Test exchange ahead of the more significant series in South Africa.

Zimbabwe were led by Graeme Cremer, the 30-year-old leg-spinner who had played 11 Tests prior to the series with a bowling average of well over 50. It was also Kane Williamson's first series as Test captain following Brendon McCullum's goodbye. That said, this most certainly was not a proper test of his credentials.

The gulf in class being what it was, it wasn't a surprise that Neil Wagner ran through Zimbabwe in the first innings of the first Test, returning a career-best 6 for 41. Tom Latham (105), Ross Taylor (173 not out) and BJ Watling (107) then hit centuries and Trent Boult (4 for 52) led the demolition in the second innings for an innings-and-117-run win, despite Sean Williams's 119 late in the piece. Williams fought through the flu on his Test comeback of sorts for his maiden century in the five-day game. Latham's century came 24 years after his father Rod's hundred in Bulawayo.

"When you don't play enough cricket, you can come into a Test match and

Brave comeback: Despite having limited Test experience and having been low by the flu, Sean Williams stepped up for Zimbabwe with his maiden ton. — *AFP/Getty Images*

be shell-shocked and that's what happened," Ceremer would say later about the first-innings collapse. "[But] I knew guys were going to fight back."

If it was Williams displaying the fighting spirit in the First Test, it was Craig Ervine in the next, standing out for Zimbabwe with 146 in the first innings. But things mostly went New Zealand's way again. Latham (136), Williamson (113) and Ross Taylor (124 not out) slammed centuries in the first innings and it was all downhill thereafter for Zimbabwe. They lost by 254 runs, chasing 387. Williamson, who ticked off another column in a flattering resume by scoring hundreds against all Test nations, got his captaincy career off to a fine start.

Best batter: Ross Taylor (364 runs, 2 matches)
Best bowler: Neil Wagner (11 wickets, 2 matches)

Tour match

Harare Sports Club, July 22-24: New Zealanders 345/7 dec in 90 overs (Martin Guptill 74, BJ Watling 61 retd.out; Gerald Aliseni 2-31) and 201/7 dec in 51.5 overs (Mitchell Santner 51 retd. out, Kane Williamson 49 retd.out) beat **Zimbabwe A** 114 in 49.5 overs (Sean Williams 55, Sikandar Raza 27; Ish Sodhi 4-18, Tim Southee 2-31) and 173 in 61.5 overs (Regis Chakabva 48, S Williams 46; T Southee 2-15, Neil Wagner 2-19) by 259 runs.

Test series (2): New Zealand 2 Zimbabwe 0

1st Test: New Zealand win by an innings and 117 runs

Queen Sports Club, Bulawayo, July 28-31: Zimbabwe 164 in 77.5 overs (Donald Tiripano 49*, Prince Masvaure 42; Neil Wagner 6-41, Mitchell Santner 2-16) and 295 in 79 overs (Sean Williams 119, Craig Ervine 50; Trent Boult 4-52, N Wagner 2-62) lost to **New Zealand** 576/6 dec in 166.5 overs (Ross Taylor 173*, BJ Walting 107, Tom Latham 105) by an innings and 117 runs. *MoM*: Ross Taylor.

2nd Test: New Zealand win by 254 runs

Queen Sports Club, Bulawayo, July 28-31: New Zealand 582/4 dec in 150 overs (Tom Latham 136, Ross Taylor 124*, Kane Williamson 113) and 166/2 dec in 36 overs (K Williamson 68*, R Taylor 67*) beat **Zimbabwe** 362 in 143.4 overs (Craig Ervine 146, Peter Moor 71; Ish Sodhi 4-60, Neil Wagner 2-61) and 132 in 68.4 overs (Tino Mawoyo 35, C Ervine 27) by 254 runs. *MoM*: Kane Williamson. *MoS*: Neil Wagner.

New Zealand in South Africa

Durban put under notice

A short two-Test series was shoehorned into the calendar for South Africa and New Zealand before their longer exchanges with Australia and India respectively, but more than the teams, the cricket world gauged the Durban outfield in the First Test, and it wasn't pleasing.

After opting to bat, South Africa put up 263 in just under 90 overs with Trent Boult and Neil Wagner picking up three wickets each. However, New Zealand were restricted to all of 12 overs, in which Dale Steyn had them at a sorry 15 for 2. That was it as rain first and then a wet outfield left Kingsmead in a shambles.

Andy Pycroft, the match referee, rated the outfield 'poor' and it received a warning from ICC.

Proper Test cricket took place in the second game, in Centurion, making it Kane Williamson's first major Test as captain against top opposition, following New Zealand's whitewash of Zimbabwe prior to this series. Williamson had a tough time though as New Zealand went down by 204 runs within four days. In the first innings, Wagner's 5 for 86 was offset by a century from Faf du Plessis – leading in the absence of an injured AB de Villiers – at No. 5. All four men before du Plessis got half-centuries: Quinton de Kock underscored his long-format ability with quick knocks of 82 and 50 in the two innings, to go with the six dismissals he effected. Williamson's 77 was the standout performance in the New Zealand response, even though it did little to swing the game his team's way.

Steyn rolled back the years to return a match-haul of 8 for 99, continuing his affair with Centurion. And with the other pacemen faring well, it was 1-0 to South Africa as they kept up their record of not having lost a Test series to New Zealand. "We almost played the perfect Test," said du Plessis, insisting his side had rediscovered the passion that would help them climb the team charts again.

For Williamson's men, it was not the best preparation for the three-Test series in India.

Test series (2): South Africa 1 New Zealand 0

1st Test: Match drawn
ingsmead, Durban, August 19-23: **South Africa** 263 in 87.4 overs (Hashim Amla 53, Temba Bavuma 46; Neil Wagner 3-47, Trent Boult 3-52) drew with **New Zealand** 15/2 in 12overs (Dale Steyn 2-3).

Passion rediscovered: Faf du Plessis may have been without the services of AB de Villiers, but had a fired-up Dale Steyn by his side at Centurion. — *Getty Images*

2nd Test: South Africa win by 204 runs

SuperSport Park, Centurion, August 27-30: South Africa 481/8 dec in 154 overs (Faf du Plessis 112*, JP Duminy 88; Neil Wagner 5-86) and 132/7 dec in 47 overs (Quinton de Kock 50, Temba Bavuma 40*; Tim Southee 3-46, Trent Boult 2-44) beat **New Zealand** 214 in 58.3 overs (Kane Williamson 77, Henry Nicholls 36; Kagiso Rabada 3-62, Dale Steyn 3-66) and 195 in 58.2 overs (H Nicholls 76, BJ Watling 32; D Steyn 5-33, Vernon Philander 2-34) by 204 runs. *MoM:* Quinton de Kock.

Best batsman: Quinton de Kock (165 runs, 2 matches)
Best bowler: Dale Steyn (10 wickets, 2 matches)

Afghanistan in Bangladesh

Thriller goes hosts' way

Bangladesh might have scripted an unstoppable run at home in one-day cricket, but Afghanistan are a strong, well-knit unit, as tough as they come. So when a three-match ODI series was arranged, Bangladesh knew they would be pushed almost as much as they would against any top team, more so without the services of the zesty paceman Mustafizur Rahman.

And so it proved. Afghanistan needed 27 off 18 balls in the first ODI, chasing Bangladesh's 265 with five wickets in hand. But Taskin Ahmed, returning after suspension for a faulty action, made the difference in the 48th over, nipping out Mohammad Nabi and Asghar Stanikzai to end with 4 for 59. Afghanistan fell seven runs short.

Disappointed but not disheartened, Afghanistan bounced right back in the second game. They restricted Bangladesh to 208 as the spinners, Mohammad Nabi and Rashid Khan, picked up five wickets between them. They nearly lost their way again in the high-pressure situations, but managed to scrape through for a two-wicket win, Stanikzai top-scoring with a 95-ball 57.

Both matches could have gone either way and 1-1 was a fair reflection of each side's abilities. However, Bangladesh's relative experience came through in the decider. They rode on Tamim Iqbal's run-a-ball 118 at the top of the order before Mosharraf Hossain's 3 for 24 helped bundle out Afghanistan for just 138 in chase of 280, Bangladesh winning by 141 runs.

The 2-1 win would have come as a relief for Bangladesh, their domination in ODIs at home being stretched. As for Afghanistan, there was no disgrace despite the margin of defeat in the last game; they had made a fine statement.

Bragging rights in the rivalry: Mosharraf Hossain's 3-24 set up Bangladesh's big win. — *AFP/Getty Images*

Tour match
Khan Shaheb Osman Ali Stadium, Fatullah, September 23: Afghanistan 233 in 49.2 overs (Hashmatullah Shahidi 69, Mirwais Ashraf 32*; Alauddin Babu 3-32, Mehedi Hasan Miraz

3-48) beat **Bangladesh Cricket Board XI** 167 in 38.1 overs (Mosaddek Hossain 76, Shuvagata Hom 34; Mohammad Nabi 4-24, Fareed Ahmad 2-19) by 66 runs.

ODI series (3): Bangladesh 2 Afghanistan 1

1st ODI: Bangladesh win by seven runs

Shere Bangla National Stadium, Mirpur, September 25: **Bangladesh** 265 in 50 overs (Tamim Iqbal 80, Mahmudullah 62; Dawlat Zadran 4-73, Rashid Khan 2-37) beat **Afghanistan** 258 in 50 overs (Hashmatullah Shahidi 72, Rahmat Shah 71; Taskin Ahmed 4-59, Shakib Al Hasan 2-26) by 7 runs. *MoM*: Shakib Al Hasan.

2nd ODI: Afghanistan win by two wickets

Shere Bangla National Stadium, Mirpur, September 28: **Bangladesh** 208 in 49.2 overs (Mosaddek Hossain 45*, Mushfiqur Rahim 38; Rashid Khan 3-35, Mohammad Nabi 2-16) lost to **Afghanistan** 212/8 in 49.4 overs (Asghar Stanikzai 57, Mohammad Nabi 49; Shakib Al Hasan 4-47, Mosaddek Hossain 2-30) by two wickets. *MoM*: Mohammad Nabi.

3rd ODI: Bangladesh win by 141 runs

Shere Bangla National Stadium, Mirpur, October 1: **Bangladesh** 279/8 in 50 overs (Tamim Iqbal 118, Sabbir Rahman 65; Rashid Khan 2-39, Mohammad Nabi 2-41) beat **Afghanistan** 138 in 33.5 overs (Rahmat Shah 36, Nawroz Mangal 33; Mosharraf Hossain 3-24, Taskin Ahmed 2-31) by 141 runs. *MoM*: Tamim Iqbal. *MoS*: Tamim Iqbal.

Best batsman: Tamim Iqbal (218 runs, 3 matches)
Best bowler: Rashid Khan (7 wickets, 3 matches)

Ireland and Australia in South Africa

Australia handed rare whitewash

When Ireland bagged an ODI each against South Africa and Australia – appetisers before the five-match series between the big boys – in Benoni, it was a chance for them to create a buzz. Not necessarily by winning the matches, but by pushing the home side and the world champions hard, throwing in a few, strong individual performances.

Unfortunately, there wasn't much evidence of either, as Ireland's disappointing run against the top teams continued. Temba Bavuma, on ODI debut, helped South Africa beat Ireland by 206 runs in the first game. Then Australia, despite a second-string bowling attack that would later come unstuck against South Africa, bowled Ireland out for 198 before cantering to victory by nine wickets in 30.1 overs.

Over to the main course then, but in the end, it was as one-sided as the games against Ireland were.

It started with a Quinton de Kock-engineered romp in the first game. Australia put up a decent 294 for 9 and would have expected a close match in the absence of AB de Villiers, recuperating after shoulder surgery, and Hashim Amla, who was unwell. But against a bowling attack missing Mitchell Starc, Josh Hazlewood and James Faulkner for different reasons, all it took South Africa to overhaul the target was 36.2 overs. De Kock smashed 178 in 113 balls.

That set the tone, and it never changed.

Rilee Rossouw, stepping in to fill the Amla void, scored 75 and Faf du Plessis, leading in de Villiers's absence, hit 111 as the second match was won by 142 runs. The third, a run-fest to match the best of them, went away from Australia even though David Warner and Steve Smith hit centuries to take the visitors to 371 for 6. This time, David Miller made the difference with an unbeaten 79-ball 118. And then came the series sweep with two more facile wins, Warner's scintillating 136-ball 173 in the final game proving insufficient to prevent the first whitewash inflicted on Australia ever in a bilateral five-match series.

South Africa found stars everywhere, with JP Duminy and Andile Phehlukwayo, who made his debut in the Ireland match, among them. Australia found none, apart from Warner, and suffered mainly because of their depleted bowling resources and a lack of consistency with the bat.

South Africa beat Ireland by 206 runs in one-off ODI

Willowmoore Park, Benoni, September 25: South Africa 354/5 in 50 overs (Temba Bavuma 113, Quinton de Kock 82; Craig Young 3-81, Kevin O'Brien 2-66) beat **Ireland** 148 in 30.5 overs (K O'Brien 41, Paul Stirling 40; JP Duminy 4-16, Aaron Phangiso 2-33) by 206 runs. *MoM*: Temba Bavuma.

South Africa found stars everywhere: They chased down tall totals and handed Australia their first ever whitewash in a five-match bilateral series. — *Getty Images*

Australia beat Ireland by nine wickets in one-off ODI
Willowmoore Park, Benoni, September 27: Ireland 198 in 43.5 overs (John Anderson 39, Paul Stirling 30; Adam Zampa 3-37, John Hastings 2-31) lost to **Australia** 199/1 in 30.1 overs (Usman Khawaja 82*, Steven Smith 59*) by nine wickets. *MoM*: Usman Khawaja.

ODI series (5): South Africa 5 Australia 0

1st ODI: South Africa win by six wickets
SuperSport Park, Centurion, September 30: Australia 294/9 in 50 overs (George Bailey 74, John Hastings 51; Andile Phehlukwayo 4-44, Dale Steyn 2-65) lost to **South Africa** 295/4 in 36.2 overs (Quinton de Kock 178, Rilee Rossouw 63; Scott Boland 3-67) by six wickets. *MoM*: Quinton de Kock.

2nd ODI: South Africa win by six wickets
New Wanderers Stadium, Johannesburg, October 2: South Africa 361/6 in 50 overs (Faf du Plessis 111, JP Duminy 82; John Hastings 3-57, Mitchell Marsh 2-68) beat **Australia** 219 in 37.4 overs (Travis Head 51, David Warner 50; Wayne Parnell 3-40, Kagiso Rabada 2-31) by six wickets. *MoM*: Faf du Plessis.

3rd ODI: South Africa win by four wickets
Kingsmead, Durban, October 5: Australia 371/6 in 50 overs (David Warner 117, Steven Smith 108; Imran Tahir 2-54, Dale Steyn 2-96) lost to **South Africa** 372/6 in 49.2 overs (David Miller 118*, Quinton de Kock 70; John Hastings 2-79) by four wickets. *MoM*: David Miller.

4th ODI: South Africa win by six wickets
St George's Park, Port Elizabeth, October 9: Australia 167 in 36.4 overs (Matthew Wade 52, Mitchell Marsh 50; Kyle Abbott 4-40, Tabraiz Shamsi 3-36) lost to **South Africa** 168/4 in 35.3 overs (Faf du Plessis 69, Rilee Rossouw 33*; Chris Tremain 2-48) by six wickets. *MoM*: Kyle Abbott.

5th ODI: South Africa win by 31 runs
Newlands, Cape Town, October 12: South Africa 327/8 in 50 overs (Rilee Rossouw 122, JP Duminy 73; Joe Mennie 3-49, Chris Tremain 3-64) beat **Australia** 296 in 48.2 overs (David Warner 173, Mitchell Marsh 35; Imran Tahir 2-42, Kyle Abbott 2-48) by 31 runs. *MoM*: David Warner. *MoS*: Rilee Rossouw.

Best batsman: David Warner (386 runs, 5 matches)
Best bowler: Andile Phehlukwayo (8 wickets, 5 matches)

BEYOND THE TEST NATIONS

Hong Kong v Oman in UAE

T20I series (3): Oman 2 Hong Kong 1

1st T20I: Oman win by six wickets
Sheikh Zayed Stadium, Abu Dhabi, November 21: Hong Kong 106/9 in 20 overs (Bilal Khan 3-29, Mehran Khan 2-20) lost to **Oman** 107/4 in 18.3 overs (Sultan Ahmed 37*, Zeeshan Siddiqui 33*; Tanwir Afzal 2-22) by six wickets.

2nd T20I: Oman win by four runs
Sheikh Zayed Stadium, Abu Dhabi, November 25: Oman 131/6 in 20 overs (Aamir Kaleem 42*, Adnan Ilyas 37; Aizaz Khan 3-22) beat **Hong Kong** 127 in 19.5 overs (Nizakat Khan 29, Babar Hayat 27; Bilal Khan 4-20, Zeeshan Maqsood 3-22) by four runs.

3rd T20I: Hong Kong win by eight wickets
Sheikh Zayed Stadium, Abu Dhabi, November 26: Oman 149/4 in 20 overs (Adnan Ilyas 49, Aamir Kaleem 46*; Aizaz Khan 2-15, Haseeb Amjad 2-52) lost to **Hong Kong** 155/2 in 18.3 overs (Babar Hayat 65*, Mark Chapman 63*) by eight wickets.

Best batsman: Babar Hayat (108 runs, 3 matches)
Best bowler: Bilal Khan (7 wickets, 3 matches)

Landmark tour: Fifties for Babar Hayat and Mark Chapman gave Hong Kong a consolation win against Oman. It was one of two wins for them on the multi-format tour of UAE, which included games against Afghanistan, UAE and Pakistan. – *HKCA*

United Arab Emirates v Oman

UAE beat Oman by seven wickets in the one-off T20I
Sheikh Zayed Stadium, Abu Dhabi, November 22: **Oman** 133/8 in 20 overs (Zeeshan Maqsood 44, Adnan Ilyas 22; Rohan Mustafa 3-9, Manjula Guruge 2-22) lost to **United Arab Emirates** 134/3 in 18.2 overs (Shaiman Anwar 54, R Mustafa 41) by seven wickets.

Best batsman: Shaiman Anwar (54 runs, 1 match)
Best bowler: Rohan Mustafa (3 wickets, 1 match)

Afghanistan v Hong Kong

Hong Kong beat Afghanistan by four wickets in the one-off T20I
Sheikh Zayed Stadium, Abu Dhabi, November 28: **Afghanistan** 162/6 in 20 overs (Asghar Stanikzai 51, Samiullah Shenwari 34) lost to **Hong Kong** 166/6 in 19.4 overs (Tanwir Afzal 42, Babar Hayat 35; Karim Sadiq 2-20, Rokhan Barakzai 2-32) by four wickets.

Best Batsman: Asghar Stanikzai (51 runs, 1 match)
Best Bowler: KarimSadiq (2 wickets, 1 match)

Afghanistan v Oman

T20I series (2): Afghanistan 2 Oman 0

1st T20I: Afghansitan win by 27 runs
Sheikh Zayed Stadium, Abu Dhabi, November 29: **Afghanistan** 159/8 in 20 overs (Usman Ghani 69, Karim Sadiq 26; Mehran Khan 3-30) beat **Oman** 132 in 18.1 overs (Adnan Ilyas 34, Sultan Ahmed 27; Sayed Shirzad 3-16, Rokhan Barakzai 2-22) by 27 runs.

2nd T20I: Afghansitan win by 12 runs
Sheikh Zayed Stadium, Abu Dhabi, November 30: **Afghanistan** 160/4 in 20 overs (Mohammad Shahzad 60, Shafiqullah 32*; Zeeshan Maqsood 2-20, Bilal Khan 2-24) beat **Oman** 148/8 in 20 overs (Khawar Ali 38, Jatinder Singh 28; Yamin Ahmadzai 3-34, Rokhan Barakzai 2-21) by 12 runs.

Best batsman: Usman Ghani (74 runs, 2 matches)
Best bowler: Sayed Shirzad (5 wickets, 2 matches)

Scotland in Hong Kong

T20I series (2): Hong Kong 1 Scotland1

1st T20I: Hong Kong win by nine wickets
Mission Road Ground, Mong Kok, Hong Kong, January 30: **Scotland** 66/7 in 10 overs lost to **Hong Kong** 72/1 in 6.2 overs (Babar Hayat 26*, Jamie Atkinson 20) by nine wickets. *MoM*: Babar Hayat.

2nd T20I: Scotland win by 37 runs
Sheikh Zayed Stadium, Abu Dhabi, January 31: Scotland 161/9 in 20 overs (Kyle Coetzer 70, Matthew Cross 27; Haseeb Amjad 3-21, Nadeem Ahmed 3-23) beat **Hong Kong** 124 in 18.4 overs (Tanwir Afzal 56, Aizaz Khan 20; Brad Wheal 3-20, Richie Berrington 3-22) by 37 runs. *MoM*: Kyle Coetzer.

Best batsman: Kyle Coetzer (70 runs, 2 matches)
Best bowler: Haseeb Amjad (4 wickets, 2 matches)

Netherlands in United Arab Emirates

Netherlands beat UAE by 84 runs in the one-off T20I
ICC Academy, Dubai, February 3: Netherlands 157/5 in 20 overs (Wesley Barresi 48, Peter Borren 43; Rohan Mustafa 2-19) beat **United Arab Emirates** 73 in 16.4 overs (Muhammad Usman 49*; Mudassar Bukhari 4-7, Michael Rippon 3-8) by 84 runs. *MoM:* Mudassar Bukhari.

Best batsman: Muhammad Usman (49 runs, 1 match)
Best bowler: Mudassar Bukhari (4 wickets, 1 match)

Netherlands v Scotland in United Arab Emirates

Scotland beat Netherlands by 37 runs in one-off T20I
ICC Academy, Dubai, February 5: Scotland 140/5 in 20 overs (Matt Machan 43, Richie Berrington 42) beat **Netherlands** 103 in 18.2 overs (Ben Cooper 32, Michael Swart 26; Mark Watt 5-27) by 37 runs. *MoM:* Mark Watt.

Best batsman: Matt Machan (43 runs, 1 match)
Best bowler: Mark Watt (5 wickets, 1 match)

Ireland v Papua New Guinea in Australia

T20I series (3): Ireland 2 Papua New Guinea 1

1st T20I: Ireland win by five wickets
Tony Ireland Stadium, Townsville, February 6: Papua New Guinea 92/9 in 20 overs (Sese Bau 22, Charles Amini 21; Kevin O'Brien 2-10, Craig Young 2-15) lost to **Ireland** 97/5 in 12.1 overs (Gary Wilson 45; Norman Vanua 3-26) by five wickets.

2nd T20I: Ireland win by seven runs (D/L method)
Tony Ireland Stadium, Townsville, February 7: Ireland 96/5 in 11 overs (Stuart Poynter 35, William Porterfield 30; Pipi Raho 3-11, Assad Vala 2-19) beat **Papua New Guinea** 89/9 in 11 overs (Norman Vanua 26*, A Vala 25; Max Sorensen 3-17, George Dockrell 3-18) by seven runs (D/L method).

New rivalries: Ireland got the better of PNG in three low-scoring T20Is held after their ICC Intercontinental Cup match. — *Cricket PNG*

3rd T20I: Papua New Guinea win by 11 runs

Tony Ireland Stadium, Townsville, February 9: Papua New Guinea 116/8 in 20 overs (Sese Bau 25, Charles Amini 24; Tim Murtagh 3-23, George Dockrell 2-15) beat **Ireland** 105 in 19.1 overs (Niall O'Brien 27; Chad Soper 3-13, C Amini 2-13) by 11 runs.

Best batsman: Gary Wilson (73 runs, 3 match)
Best bowler: George Dockrell (6 wickets, 3 match)

Ireland in United Arab Emirates

T20I series (2): Ireland 1 United Arab Emirates 1

1st T20I: Ireland win by 34 runs

Sheikh Zayed Stadium, Abu Dhabi, February 14: Ireland 134/8 in 20 overs (Niall O'Brien 38, Max Sorensen 26; Amjad Javed 3-41) beat **United Arab Emirates** 100 in 19.2 overs (Shaiman Anwar 24; Kevin O'Brien 3-14, Boyd Rankin 2-16) by 34 runs.

2nd T20I: United Arab Emirates win by five runs

Sheikh Zayed Stadium, Abu Dhabi, February 16: United Arab Emirates 133/7 in 20 overs (Swapnil Patil 31, Mohammad Shahzad 22; Boyd Rankin 3-17, Max Sorensen 2-16) beat **Ireland** 128/9 in 20 overs (William Porterfield 72, Paul Stirling 28; M Shahzad 2-10, Mohammad Naveed 2-16) by 5 runs.

Best batsman: William Porterfield (80 runs, 2 match)
Best bowler: Boyd Rankin (5 wickets, 2 match)

ICC Intercontinental Cup

Ireland in strong position

Ireland won all their first four matches to strengthen their position at the top of the I-Cup table with 80 points. They take on Afghanistan, who are second with 61 points in four games, in Noida in March 2017, in what will be a decisive match. The 2015-17 tournament, which has eight teams participating, will decide who plays the tenth-ranked Test side for the ultimate prize of securing Test status. In the last game before going to print, Asad Vala's unbeaten 144 helped Papua New Guinea beat Namibia by 199 runs to go fourth on the table and record their maiden first-class win at home. Vala is the only batsman to score three hundreds in the tournament so far.

Best batsman: Ed Joyce (Ireland) (592 runs, 4 matches)
Best bowler: Zahir Khan (Afghanistan) (19 wickets, 3 matches)

Points Table

Teams	M	W	L	D	T	A	Pts	Q
Ireland	4	4	0	0	0	0	80	1.873
Afghanistan	4	3	0	1	0	0	61	1.590
Netherlands	4	2	2	0	0	0	46	0.861
Papua New Guinea	4	2	2	0	0	0	40	0.925
Hong Kong	4	1	2	0	0	1	30	0.980
Scotland	4	0	1	2	0	1	30	0.896
Namibia	4	1	3	0	0	0	20	0.652
United Arab Emirates	4	0	3	1	0	0	7	0.664

*As on October 25, 2016. Points table will be updated in Wisden India Almanack 2018.

Afghanistan in Scotland, Ireland and Netherlands
ODI series (2): Afghanistan 1 Scotland 0

1st ODI: No result
GCC Ground, Raeburn Place, Edinburgh, July 4: Afghanistan 283/4 in 47.2 overs (Rahmat Shah 100*, Najibullah Zadran 89*; Brad Wheal 2-51) v **Scotland**. No Result.

2nd ODI: Afghanistan win by 78 runs (DLS method)
GCC Ground, Raeburn Place, Edinburgh, July 6: Afghanistan 178/6 in 37.2 overs (Mo-

hammad Shahzad 84, Rahmat Shah 26; Brad Wheal 2-31, Alasdair Evans 2-34) beat **Scotland** 132 in 27.1 overs (Craig Wallace 33, Matthew Cross 24; Mohammad Nabi 3-26, Rashid Khan 2-19) by 78 runs. (DLS method)

Best batsman: Rahmat Shah (126 runs, 2 matches)
Best bowler: Brad Wheal (4 wickets, 2 matches)

ODI series (5): Afghanistan 2 Ireland 2

1st ODI: Match abandoned
Civil Service Cricket Club, Stormont, Belfast, July 10: Ireland vs **Afghanistan**.Match abandoned without a ball bowled.

2nd ODI: Afghanistan win by 39 runs
Civil Service Cricket Club, Stormont, Belfast, July 12: **Afghanistan** 250 in 49.2 overs (Mohammad Shahzad 66, Najibullah Zadran 59; Kevin O'Brien 4-45, Barry McCarthy 4-59) beat **Ireland** 211 in 48.2 overs (Ed Joyce 62, K O'Brien 35; Rashid Khan 3-28, Mohammad Nabi 3-45) by 39 runs.

3rd ODI: Ireland win by six wickets
Civil Service Cricket Club, Stormont, Belfast, July 14: **Afghanistan** 236 in 49.1 overs (Mohammad Shahzad 81, Mohammad Nabi 40; Kevin O'Brien 3-28, Barry McCarthy 3-57) lost to **Ireland** 237/4 in 47.3 overs (Ed Joyce 105*, K O'Brien 75; Hamid Hassan 2-21) by six wickets.

4th ODI: Afghanistan win by 79 runs
Civil Service Cricket Club, Stormont, Belfast, July 17: **Afghanistan** 229/7 in 50 overs (Rashid Khan 60*, Mohammad Nabi 50; Andy McBrine 2-29, Peter Chase 2-52) beat **Ireland** 150 in 41 overs (Kevin O'Brien 34, Paul Stirling 31; Rashid Khan 4-21, Rahmat Shah 2-30) by 79 runs.

5th ODI: Ireland win by 12 runs
Civil Service Cricket Club, Stormont, Belfast, July 19: **Ireland** 265/5 in 50 overs (Ed Joyce 160*, Gary Wilson 58; Dawlat Zadran 2-49) beat **Afghanistan** 253/9 in 50 overs (Najibullah Zadran 54, Rashid Khan 40; Kevin O'Brien 3-57, Barry McCarthy 2-21) by 12 runs.

Best batsman: Ed Joyce (339 runs, 4 matches)
Best bowler: Kevin O'Brien (10 wickets, 4 matches)

Afghanistan beat Netherlands by an innings and 36 runs in the one-off first-class match

Sportspark Westvliet, Voorburg, July 29-30: **Netherlands** 117 in 39.4 overs (Pieter Seelaar 38*, Michael Rippon 24; Yamin Ahmadzai 5-29, Dawlat Zadran 4-32) and 159 in 43.1 overs (M Rippon 80, Stephan Myburgh 23; Zahir Khan 4-29, D Zadran 3-45) lost to **Afghanistan** 312 in 102.2 overs (Hashmatullah Shahidi 83, Rahmat Shah 51; M Rippon 5-79, Vivian Kingma 2-41) by an innings and 36 runs.

ICC World Cricket League

PNG rise to the top

Papua New Guinea won six of their first eight matches to go joint top of the WCL table with the Netherlands as on October 25. The Netherlands have won five, with two no results. Roelof van der Merwe, the former South African all-rounder who was eligible to play for the Netherlands by birth, led their campaign. After the completion of the double round robin-based tournament, the top two sides will progress to the World Cup qualifier in Bangladesh in 2018, for a chance to qualify for the 2019 World Cup.

Points Table

Teams	M	W	L	T	N/R	Pts	NRR
Papua New Guinea	8	6	2	0	0	12	+0.037
Netherlands	8	5	1	0	2	12	+1.557
Scotland	8	4	1	0	3	11	+0.245
Hong Kong	6	4	1	0	1	9	+1.604
Kenya	6	3	3	0	0	6	+0.123
Nepal	8	3	5	0	0	6	-0.505
Namibia	8	1	7	0	0	2	-0.507
United Arab Emirates	8	1	7	0	0	2	-1.319

*As on October 25, 2016. Points table will be updated in *Wisden India Almanack 2018*.

Your call: Our priority.

Address all your queries at our
24 X 7 customer service centre.
We are happy to serve you.

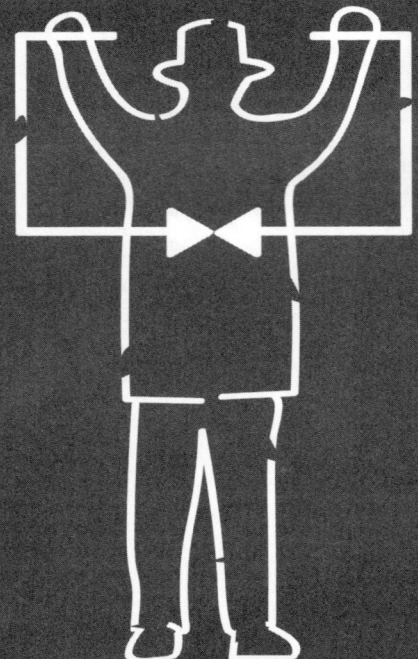

Customer Service: 600 555 550 | www.uaeexchange.co

Coming of age of the youth brigade: Where Jhulan Goswami and Mithali Raj continued to set the standards, the younger bunch proved they too could win matches. – *Getty Images*

WOMEN'S CRICKET

India Internationals

Much promise, yet much ground to cover

SHASHANK KISHORE

Thirty thousand fans. Chants of 'India, India!' Virat Kohli and Yuvraj Singh coaxed the crowd into cheering some more. There was a spark of excitement as Jhulan Goswami biffed one into the stands. India's chase was back into the realms of possibility. A World T20 2016 semi-final berth, something that the team didn't come close to in the last two editions, was being talked about. Then there was a run-out. Stunned silence. India Women lost to eventual champions West Indies, but a peek into the future – this was India's first men's and women's double-header – pointed to endless possibilities if promoted well.

India's World T20 campaign promised much, but ended in disappointment again after the group stage exit. The points table would indicate one win in four matches, against relative novices Bangladesh. What it won't indicate is the fight, the spirit and admirable energy with which the team fought, be it in their defence of a lowly 96 against Pakistan or 90 against England.

But, as well as they fought, their inability to conquer spin resulted in their undoing.

To say expectations on the team were high would be an understatement, given their exploits in the run-up to the tournament. A historic maiden series win in Australia – they won the T20 internationals 2-1 – was highlighted by the coming-of-age of their youth brigade. Harmanpreet Kaur, the team's vice-captain, led the charge to script the side's highest T20I run-chase in Adelaide. Veda Krishnamurthy, Smriti Mandhana, Poonam Yadav and Rajeshwari Gayakwad all contributed at different times.

Such was the freshness to the approach that Alyssa Healy, Australia's wicketkeeper, would later say, "India taught us how to chase." A member of the India's men's team on tour in Australia remarked how the performance of the women's team inspired them to resurrect their tour after losing the ODIs 4-1.

Compliments such as these have been rare, partly because performances like these have been few and far between, and because performances like these haven't had the visibility – India Women's historic Test triumph in England after eight years was given a pass by Indian broadcasters. Now, the players were professionals, coming under central contracts from November 2015. They were now accountable.

Two comprehensive losses in ICC Women's Championship ODIs raised old questions of the team's inability to sustain momentum, so the three ODIs against Sri Lanka in Ranchi were by no means unimportant. With India far from the automatic qualification zone for the 2017 World Cup, nothing short of a whitewash would do. Credit to them that they ran roughshod over a side that had left mental scars on them, most notably in the final league game of the 2013 World Cup that resulted in their ouster.

Away from the 22 yards, BCCI giving the players clearance to participation in foreign leagues was another step in the right direction. The timing of it, coming after the final list of players for the inaugural Women's Super League in England was announced, unfortunately meant those in the fray missed out valuable match time in England, venue for the 2017 World Cup.

Harmanpreet's signing by Sydney Thunder, the Women's Big Bash League champions, and Mandhana's by Brisbane Heat, were path-breakers. An opportunity to play alongside the best from Australia, England, West Indies, New Zealand and South Africa would stand them in good stead.

Signings apart, the BCCI also took another small step towards parity by declaring equal daily allowances for all national and A teams – men's and women's.

At the time of writing, India are scheduled to play Pakistan and West Indies to complete their round of championship matches. Raj has been vocal

India in Australia

Visitors' youthful spark kindles history

SAURABH SOMANI

Before the India women's team landed in Australia for a T20I and ODI series comprising three matches each, Mithali Raj thought the chances of her side beating the formidable Australia Women in their own den was about "20%, Australia 80%". Their only warm-up match before the tour was washed out after just four overs, and landing up cold in the first T20I, they saw Alyssa Healy smack 41 not out off 15 balls to take Australia to a commanding total of 140 for 5. From the start of the chase though, India were assured. Veda Krishnmurthy was confident and aggressive in her strokeplay, while Harmanpreet Kaur marshalled the middle order with an innings that had punch and chutzpah. If taking the lead against the world champions was commendable, the Indians went one better in the next match.

All three women's T20Is were played as double-headers with the men's matches. While this had the advantage of getting in bigger numbers, with enthusiastic audiences across Adelaide, Melbourne and Sydney providing for a good atmosphere, it also meant that there wasn't much leeway in terms of delays. But neither the rain gods nor the schedule could stop the Indians from taking a historic series-winning lead in Melbourne. Fittingly, it was Raj who hit the boundary that brought up victory, the first win for India Women against Australia Women in any bilateral series.

Ellyse Perry, the winner of the Belinda Clarke medal, showed just why she was rated among the best players with a superb all-round show that gave Australia a 2-1 scoreline, but over the course of the T20Is, it was undoubtedly the Indians who had been the better team.

The script was reversed for the ODIs, with Australia winning 2-1. But for the India women, parity felt like victory, since they had landed in the country with Australia the overwhelming favourites.

The BCCI awarding them contracts played its part in instilling a more secure environment in the team and mentally freeing the players, a fact Raj

Next generation: (clockwise from top) Harmanpreet Kaur took the lead with an innings of chutzpah in the first T20I; Rajeshwari Gayakwad and Anuja Patil went from strength to strength; Smriti Mandhana brought up her first ODI hundred in Hobart.
– *Getty Images*

acknowledged: "I'm very happy that we actually proved that we are worth it and deserve them. I'm sure it will be a motivation for the other players back home."

While Raj and Jhulan Goswami, the veterans, were reliable as ever, the stepping up of Smriti Mandhana as an opener of elegance and substance – she brought up her first ODI hundred – the continuing evolution of Harmanpreet Kaur as the team lynchpin and Shikha Pandey stepping up as a wicket-taking bowler gave the team a core that the future could be built around.

India in Australia 723

Tour match
Drummoyne Oval, Sydney, January 22: **Australia** Governor-General's XI 19/1 in 4 overs **India**. No result.

T20I series (3): India 2 Australia 1

1st T20I: India win by five wickets
Adelaide Oval, January 26: **Australia** 140/5 in 20 overs (Alyssa Healy 41*, Beth Mooney 36; Poonam Yadav 2-26) lost to **India** 141/5 in 18.4 overs (Harmanpreet Kaur 46, Veda Krishnamurthy 35; Megan Schutt 2-23, Jess Jonassen 2-24) by five wickets. *PoM:* Harmanpreet Kaur.

2nd T20I: India win by ten wickets (DLS method)
Melbourne Cricket Ground, January 29: **Australia** 125/8 in 18 overs (Meg Lanning 49, Jess Jonassen 27; Jhulan Goswami 2-16, Rajeshwari Gayakwad 2-27) lost to **India** 69/0 in 9.1 overs (Mithali Raj 37*, Smriti Mandhana 22*) by ten wickets (D/L method). *PoM:* Jhulan Goswami.

3rd T20I: Australia win by 15 runs
Sydney Cricket Ground, January 31: **Australia** 136/5 in 20 overs (Ellyse Perry 55*, Beth Mooney 34; Rajeshwari Gayakwad 2-36) beat **India** 121/8 in 20 overs (VR Vanitha 28, Harmanpreet Kaur 24; E Perry 4-12, Rene Farrell 2-18) by 15 runs. *PoM:* Ellyse Perry. *PoS:* Jhulan Goswami.

ODI series (3): Australia 2 India 1

1st ODI: Australia win by 101 runs
Manuka Oval, Canberra, February 2: **Australia** 276/6 in 50 overs (Alex Blackwell 114, Ellyse Perry 90; Shikha Pandey 3-32) beat **India** 175 in 46.5 overs (Harmanpreet Kaur 42, Jhulan Goswami 25; E Perry 4-45) by 101 runs. *PoM:* Alex Blackwell.

2nd ODI: Australia win by six wickets
Bellerive Oval, Hobart, February 5: **India** 252/8 in 50 overs (Smriti Mandhana 102, Mithali Raj 58; Ellyse Perry 3-54, Megan Schutt 2-35) lost to **Australia** 253/4 in 46.4 overs (Nicole Bolton 77, Meg Lanning 61; Rajeshwari Gayakwad 2-42, Shikha Pandey 2-50) by six wickets. *PoM:* Smriti Mandhana.

3rd ODI: India win by five wickets
Bellerive Oval, Hobart, February 7: **Australia** 231/7 in 50 overs (Alex Blackwell 60, Ellyse Perry 50; Shikha Pandey 3-50, Rajeshwari Gayakwad 2-41) lost to **India** 234/5 in 47 overs (Mithali Raj 89, Smriti Mandhana 55; E Perry 2-50) by five wickets. *PoM:* Mithali Raj.

	ODIs	T20Is
Best batter	Alex Blackwell (193 runs, 3 matches)	Meg Lanning (87 runs, 3 matches)
Best bowler	Ellyse Perry (9 wickets, 3 matches)	Ellyse Perry (4 wickets, 3 matches)

Sri Lanka in India

Hosts gain pace before World T20

ANANYA UPENDRAN

High on confidence after their successful tour of Australia, India carried that momentum into their limited overs home series against Sri Lanka in Ranchi. Neither a lack of rest nor a dangerous outfield could dampen the spirits of Mithali Raj's team, as they quashed the challenge without much fuss.

Smriti Mandhana, Harmanpreet Kaur and Veda Krishnamurthy continued their run-scoring ways, while the Indian spinners made best use of helpful conditions. For India, every match brought forth a new hero, but it was Deepti Sharma, the off-spinner, who stole the show. Her haul of 12 wickets in the three ODIs included six in the final match. Playing only her seventh ODI, the 18-year-old became the first Indian spinner and the third Indian bowler to claim six wickets in a match. Her figures of 6 for 20 are also the best in the ICC Women's Championship so far.

Deepti Sharma: The first Indian spinner to claim six wickets in a match. — *Wisden India*

Sri Lanka finished the tour without a win. Only Dilani Manodara, the diminutive wicketkeeper, and Prasadani Weerakkody showed some resistance with the bat. Manodara was particularly impressive with her endless array of sweep shots and her energy between the wickets.

Anuja Patil's unbeaten 22 and three-wicket burst with the new ball in the first T20I was a reminder of how effective an all-rounder she can be. India also managed to test the depth in their squad, resting Jhulan Goswami and Kaur at different points of the series, and handing Preeti Bose, the left-arm spinner, her ODI debut.

ODI series (3): India 3 Sri Lanka 0

1st ODI: India win by 107 runs

JSCA International Stadium Complex, Ranchi, February 15: **India** 245/6 in 50 overs (Smriti Mandhana 55, Harmanpreet Kaur 50; Shashikala Siriwardene 2-31, Udeshika Prabodhani 2-38) beat **Sri Lanka** 138 in 45.2 overs (Prasadani Weerakkody 69; Poonam Yadav 4-22, Deepti Sharma 2-20) by 107 runs. *PoM:* Smriti Mandhana.

2nd ODI: India win by six wickets

JSCA International Stadium Complex, Ranchi, February 17: Sri Lanka 178/9 in 50 overs (Dilani Manodara 43, Prasadani Weerakkody 37; Deepti Sharma 4-23) lost to **India** 179/4 in 43.1 overs (Mithali Raj 53*, Smriti Mandhana 46; Sugandika Kumari 4-39) by six wickets. *PoM:* Deepti Sharma.

3rd ODI: India win by seven wickets

JSCA International Stadium Complex, Ranchi, February 19: Sri Lanka 112 in 38.2 overs (Dilani Manodara 23; Deepti Sharma 6-20, Preeti Bose 2-8) lost to **India** 114/3 in 29.3 overs (Veda Krishnamurthy 61*, Deepti 28) by seven wickets. *PoM:* Deepti Sharma.

T20I series (3): India 3 Sri Lanka 0

1st T20I: India win by 34 runs

JSCA International Stadium Complex, Ranchi, February 22: **India** 130/6 in 20 overs (Harmanpreet Kaur 36, Smriti Mandhana 35; Sugandika Kumari 3-28, Eshani Lokusuriyage 2-19) beat **Sri Lanka** 96/7 in 20 overs (Dilani Manodara 41*; Anuja Patil 3-14, Deepti Sharma 2-23) by 34 runs. *PoM:* Anuja Patil.

2nd T20: India win by five wickets

JSCA International Stadium Complex, Ranchi, February 24: Sri Lanka 107/8 in 20 overs (Dilani Manodara 27, Shashikala Siriwardene 26; Poonam Yadav 3-17, Ekta Bisht 3-22) lost to **India** 108/5 in 19 overs (Mithali Raj 51*, Anuja Patil 34; Inoka Ranaweera 3-10) by five wickets. *PoM:* Mithali Raj.

3rd T20I: India win by nine wickets

JSCA International Stadium Complex, Ranchi, February 26: Sri Lanka 89/9 in 20 overs (Eshani Lokusuriyage 25*, Chamari Atapattu 21; Ekta Bisht 3-17, Anuja Patil 2-19) lost to **India** 91/1 in 13.5 overs (Smriti Mandhana 43*, VR Vanitha 34) by nine wickets. *PoM:* Smriti Mandhana.

	ODIs	T20Is
Best batter	Prasadani Weerakkody (125 runs, 3 matches)	Smriti Mandhana (83 runs, 3 matches)
Best bowler	Deepti Sharma (12 wickets, 3 matches)	Ekta Bisht (7 wickets, 3 matches)

ICC Women's World T20 Qualifier

Ireland, Bangladesh book tickets to India

KARUNYA KESHAV

Ireland Women faced rain, the loss of late wickets, a count of eight required off six balls and an attempted Mankading – the umpires reversed their original run-out decision to a dead ball – before completing a frenetic last-ball two-wicket win against Bangladesh to lift the ICC Women's World T20 2016 Qualifier trophy in Thailand. Bangladesh could take solace in that they had, by being a finalist, ensured a trip to India in a few months and found in Rumana Ahmed – player of tournament with 14 wickets – a canny spin-bowling all-rounder. Zimbabwe edged Scotland and PNG for third, while China celebrated their first two wins in international cricket, over Thailand and the Netherlands.

Ireland edged Bangladesh in a close final, but the Asian side found in Rumana Ahmed a canny spin-bowling all-rounder. – *ICC*

Best batter: Cecelia Joyce (152 runs, 5 matches)
Best bowler: Rumana Ahmed (14 wickets, 5 matches)

Final: Ireland beat Bangladesh by two wickets

Terdthai Cricket Ground, Bangkok, December 5: Bangladesh 105/3 in 20 overs (Nigar Sultana 41, Rumana Ahmed 38*; Ciara Metcalfe 3-14) lost to **Ireland** 106/8 in 20 overs (Cecelia Joyce 32, Laura Delany 26*; Rumana 2-16, Nahida Akter 2-18) by two wickets. *PoM*: Rumana Ahmed. *PoS*: Rumana Ahmed.

Ireland and Bangladesh qualified for the World Twenty20

ICC Women's World T20

Fearless West Indies ride tectonic shift

KARUNYA KESHAV

The signs of change couldn't have been more visible if they came with blinking neon lights. This way to the end of Australian domination, they said. In the months leading up to the ICC Women's World T20 2016, India, newly contracted but scarcely regarded, shook off T20 rust to complete a record chase and humbled world champions Australia in their own backyard. A few weeks later, New Zealand helped strip away more of the Southern Stars' aura.

Away in South Africa, the hosts won their first T20 international against England and kept West Indies honest. The world tournament had perhaps never before seen such an even field.

But when the final line-up read Australia v West Indies, and a 'four-peat' most likely for the defending champions against maiden finalists, the change seemed more incremental than tectonic.

Until, of course, Stafanie Taylor's girls, underawed even if nobody else was, announced the coming of a brave new world. Taylor was in tears after their penultimate group match, which they lost last ball to England. At Eden Gardens on that final Sunday, she kept her promise – to herself, to play "fearless" cricket, and to Dwayne Bravo, to lead the girls in a jubilant rendition of his 'champions dance'.

"We're not intimidated at all. If anything, they should be," she had warned the Australians – with good reason. She and 18-year-old Hayley Matthews were audacious in their strokeplay, soaking up the pressure of a 149-run chase through big hits and quick running.

The earliest winds blew at the inaugural Women's Big Bash League at the turn of the year. It was no coincidence that all four World T20 semifinalists had players in the breakthrough Australian tournament, rubbing shoulders with the best and testing themselves against every rising standards. Add that to greater use of analytics and TV coverage, and there was no place for players to hide. As Meg Lanning, the Australia captain, said, "There are no easy games in women's cricket any more."

Most exposed were the home team. India had no players at the WBBL, and paid for it as they crumbled in the group stage under pressure and poor fitness. They were on the wrong side of close contests against West Indies, England and, most infuriatingly for them, Pakistan, when rain stymied a late comeback. Their batters lost the spark that lit their recent successes, the fielding was patchy and the side was wanting in big-match awareness.

Those most hurting would be New Zealand. The White Ferns were a pink-and-black flurry of positivity. Their top order was on fire, their spinners were

Much to celebrate: (clockwise from top) New Zealand were a pink-and-black flurry of positivity; South Africa's Sune Luus had the only five-wicket haul; Pakistan inspired with their dignity and drive; Bangladesh were led admirably by Jahanara Alam; Charlotte Edwards was at the forefront of England's last-gasp wins. – *ICC/Getty Images*

miserly, their fielders did the work of twice as many. A 12-hour journey before a big game against Australia too couldn't shake their skill or smiles. In fact, that unblemished run through group A only halted in the semifinal by an all-round West Indies might have hurt them. Where they never before had to chase more than 111, they were left scrapping to get to 144. And ended with another knockout ghost to haunt them.

That, however, should take nothing away from their spin trio of Leigh Kasperek, Erin Bermingham and Morna Nielsen, off-spinner, leg-spinner and left-arm spinner respectively, who bowled 43.3 overs and took 17 wickets at an economy rate of 3.83. On slow pitches and no pace on the ball to work with, opposition batters struggled against them – at least until Taylor and co. negated that threat.

England, the fourth semifinalist, had less reason for anguish: They had, after all, made it to the semifinal despite – not because of – how they played. They were over-reliant on Charlotte Edwards and their top-place finish in group B hid the stories of poor application, antithetical to the 360-degree batting they aimed for.

As for the others, Ireland and Bangladesh didn't achieve the upset they craved – the European side especially undone by the conditions – but brought to the competition refreshing young talent. Sri Lanka recovered from the early loss of their captain, while a disappointing South Africa had the widest gulf between promise and performance.

And Pakistan. And Pakistan! With Sana Mir proving to be an incomparable statesman, they did what their men couldn't: not just in defeating arch rivals India, but in inspiring a country with their dignity and drive.

The revolution was supposed to be televised. And it was. Sort of. For 13 games, which was more than ever, but still ten games less than all, and an opportunity missed. Crowd numbers were mixed, but surely disappointing for a world event. And while there's something to be said for the sight of Virat Kohli and a stadium of blue sharing the disappointment of Raj's side, and Darren Sammy racing to the field to share in the exultation of the women, there is readiness for the women to stand alone next edition.

The nearly non-existent marketing for the women's event didn't help. Nor did the unusually slow pitches. Make no mistake: a better balance between bat and ball made for thrilling contests, but as an introduction to the women's game – and it would have been for many viewers – it wasn't the T20 fare of boundaries and big hitting that, say, the IPL crowd was used to.

The echoes were felt even months after the tournament. Edwards was forced into retirement by a tough-talking Mark Robinson. Mir, Isobel Joyce (Ireland) and Mignon du Preez (South Africa) had more graceful exits from some or all forms of captaincy after landmark stints, leaving behind sides that had, win or lose, grown in self-belief. It was to their credit: When change blows so strongly and there's a new path to follow, it might be wise to have a fresh pair of eyes reading the signs.

Best batter: Stafanie Taylor (West Indies - 246 runs, 6 matches)
Best bowler: Leigh Kasperek and Sophie Devine (New Zealand - 9 wickets, 5 matches)

Pool A

Feroz Shah Kotla, Delhi, March 15: Sri Lanka 110/8 in 20 overs (Dilani Manodara 37, Yasoda Mendis 30; Leigh Kasperek 2-19) lost to **New Zealand** 111/3 in 15.5 overs (Suzie Bates 37, Rachel Priest 28) by seven wickets. *PoM:* Suzie Bates.

PCA IS Bindra Stadium, Mohali, March 18: **New Zealand** 177/3 in 20 overs (Suzie Bates 82, Sophie Devine 47) beat **Ireland** 84/5 in 20 overs (Isobel Joyce 28; Erin Bermingham 2-17) by 93 runs. *PoM:* Suzie Bates.

VCA Stadium, Jamtha, Nagpur, March 18: South Africa 102/6 in 20 overs (Dane van Niekerk 45, Trisha Chetty 34; Lauren Cheatle 2-13, Ellyse Perry 2-13) lost to **Australia** 105/4 in 18.3 overs (Alex Blackwell 42*, Meg Lanning 30*; Shabnim Ismail 2-15) by six wickets. *PoM:* Meg Lanning.

PCA IS Bindra Stadium, Mohali, March 20: Sri Lanka 129/7 in 20 overs (Eshani Lokusuriyage 35*, Chamari Atapattu 34; Ciara Metcalfe 4-15) beat **Ireland** 115/8 in 20 overs (Cecilia Joyce 29, Laura Delany 29; Sugandika Kumari 3-24) by 14 runs. *PoM:* Ciara Metcalfe.

Attacking play: Suzie Bates gave New Zealand blazing starts at the top. — *ICC/Getty Images*

VCA Stadium, Jamtha, Nagpur, March 20: Australia 103/8 in 20 overs (Ellyse Perry 42, Jess Jonassen 23; Leigh Kasperek 3-13, Erin Bermingham 2-23) lost to **New Zealand** 104/4 in 16.2 overs (Rachel Priest 34, Suzie Bates 23) by six wickets. *PoM:* Leigh Kasperek.

MA Chidambaram Stadium, Chepauk, Chennai, March 23: South Africa 156/5 in 20 overs (Trisha Chetty 35, Lizelle Lee 30*; Kim Garth 2-26) beat **Ireland** 89/9 in 20 overs (Clare Shillington 34, Isobel Joyce 22; Sune Luus 5-8) by 67 runs. *PoM:* Sune Luus.

Feroz Shah Kotla, Delhi, March 24: Sri Lanka 123/8 in 20 overs (Chamari Atapattu 38, Dilani Manodara 38; Megan Schutt 2-25, Kristen Beams 2-25) lost to **Australia** 125/1 in 17.4 overs (Meg Lanning 56*, Elyse Villani 53*) by nine wickets. *PoM:* Elyse Villani.

Feroz Shah Kotla, Delhi, March 26: Ireland 91/7 in 20 overs (Kim Garth 27, Cecilia Joyce 23; Megan Schutt 3-29, Rene Farrell 2-11) lost to **Australia** 92/3 in 13.2 overs (Elyse Villani 43*, Ellyse Perry 29*; K Garth 2-24) by seven wickets. *PoM:* Megan Schutt.

M Chinnaswamy Stadium, Bangalore, March 26: South Africa 99 in 19.3 overs (Marizanne Kapp 22; Sophie Devine 3-16, Leigh Kasperek 3-19) lost to **New Zealand** 100/3 in 14.3 overs (Suzie Bates 29, Rachel Priest 28) by seven wickets. *PoM:* Sophie Devine.

M Chinnaswamy Stadium, Bangalore, March 28: Sri Lanka 114/7 in 20 overs (Chamari Atapattu 52; Marizanne Kapp 2-17, Sune Luus 2-20) beat **South Africa** 104/7 in 20 overs (Trisha Chetty 26, Dane van Niekerk 24; Udeshika Prabodhani 2-13, Sugandika Kumari 2-24) by 10 runs. *PoM:* Chamari Atapattu.

Points Table

Teams	M	W	L	T	N/R	Pts	NRR
New Zealand	4	4	0	0	0	8	+2.430
Australia	4	3	1	0	0	6	+0.613
Sri Lanka	4	2	2	0	0	4	-0.240
South Africa	4	1	3	0	0	2	+0.173
Ireland	4	0	4	0	0	0	-2.817

New Zealand and Australia qualified for the semifinals

Pool B

M Chinnaswamy Stadium, Bangalore, March 15: **India** 163/5 in 20 overs (Mithali Raj 42, Harmanpreet Kaur 34; Fahima Khatun 2-31, Rumana Ahmed 2-35) beat **Bangladesh** 91/5 in 20 overs (Nigar Sultana 27*, Sharmin Akhter 21; Anuja Patil 2-16, Poonam Yadav 2-17) by 72 runs. *PoM:* Harmanpreet Kaur.

MA Chidambaram Stadium, Chepauk, Chennai, March 16: **West Indies** 103/8 in 20 overs (Stafanie Taylor 40; Anam Amin 4-16, Sadia Yousuf 2-14) beat **Pakistan** 99/5 in 20 overs (Bismah Maroof 22, Sidra Ameen 20; Anisa Mohammed 3-25) by four runs. *PoM:* Anam Amin.

M Chinnaswamy Stadium, Bangalore, March 17: **England** 153/7 in 20 overs (Charlotte Edwards 60, Natalie Sciver 27; Jahanara Alam 3-32) beat **Bangladesh** 117/6 in 20 overs (Nigar Sultana 35, Salma Khatun 32*; Anya Shrubsole 2-27) by 36 runs. *PoM:* Charlotte Edwards.

Feroz Shah Kotla, Delhi, March 19: India 96/7 in 20 overs (Veda Krishnamurthy 24) lost to **Pakistan** 77/6 in 16 overs (Sidra Ameen 26) by two runs (D/L method). *PoM:* Anam Amin.

Deandra Dottin confirmed West Indies' spot in the knockout.
— *ICC/Getty Images*

MA Chidambaram Stadium, Chepauk, Chennai, March 20: **West Indies** 148/4 in 20 overs (Haley Matthews 41, Stafanie Taylor 40; Nahida Akter 3-27) beat **Bangladesh** 99 in 18.3 overs (Nigar Sultana 27; S Taylor 3-13, H Matthews 2-16) by 49 runs. *PoM:* Stafanie Taylor.

HPCA Stadium, Dharamsala, March 22: **India** 90/8 in 20 overs (Harmanpreet Kaur 26, Mithali Raj 20; Heather Knight 3-15, Anya Shrubsole 2-12) lost to **England** 92/8 in 19 overs (Tammy Beaumont 20; Ekta Bisht 4-21, H Kaur 2-22) by two wickets. *PoM:* Heather Knight.

HPCA Stadium, Dharamsala, March 24: **West Indies** 108/4 in 20 overs (Stafanie Taylor 35, Shaquana Quintyne 29) lost to **England** 109/9 in 20 overs (Tammy Beaumont 31, Charlotte Edwards 30; Afy Fletcher 3-12, S Quintyne 3-19) by one wicket. *PoM:* Tammy Beaumont.

Feroz Shah Kotla, Delhi, March 24: **Bangladesh** 113/9 in 20 overs (Fargana Hoque 36; Anam Amin 2-12, Asmavia Iqbal 2-30) lost to **Pakistan** 114/1 in 16.3 overs (Sidra Ameen 53*, Bismah Maroof 43*) by nine wickets. *PoM:* Sidra Ameen.

PCA IS Bindra Stadium, Mohali, Chandigarh, March 27: **West Indies** 114/8 in 20 overs

(Stafanie Taylor 47, Deandra Dottin 45; Harmanpreet Kaur 4-23, Anuja Patil 3-16) beat **India** 111/9 in 20 overs (A Patil 26, Jhulan Goswami 25; D Dottin 3-16, Afy Fletcher 2-15) by three runs. *PoM:* Deandra Dottin.
MA Chidambaram Stadium, Chepauk, Chennai, March 27: **England** 148/5 in 20 overs (Charlotte Edwards 77*, Tammy Beaumont 37; Nida Dar 3-21, Asmavia Iqbal 2-18) beat **Pakistan** 80 in 17.5 overs (Laura Marsh 3-12, Georgia Elwiss 2-9) by 68 runs. *PoM:* Charlotte Edwards.

England and West Indies qualified for the semifinals

Points Table

Teams	M	W	L	T	N/R	Pts	NRR
England	4	4	0	0	0	8	+1.417
West Indies	4	3	1	0	0	6	+0.688
Pakistan	4	2	2	0	0	4	-0.673
India	4	1	3	0	0	2	+0.790
Bangladesh	4	0	4	0	0	0	-2.306

Knockout

1st semi-final: Australia beat England by five runs

• England have been their own biggest enemy so far, and prove as much when they implode, allowing a clinical Australia to win a battle of nerves and a shot at a fourth World T20 title. • Put in, Australia add 47 in the powerplay, Alyssa Healy leading the attack until Elyse Villani joins in with three fours off an Anya Shrubsole over. • Natalie Sciver fights back with the wickets of Healy and Ellyse Perry, but Meg Lanning plays smart cricket in bringing up her fifty. • Charlotte Edwards and Tammy Beaumont are a combination of elegance and muscle, their first-wicket stand worth 67 in ten overs. • England are on track at 89 for 1 in the 14th over, but the pressure gets to the middle order as Australia's spinners throttle them. • They lose six wickets for 28 – coach Mark Robinson would later criticise their poor application and running – and Rene Farrell defends 12 in the last over. *Karunya Keshav*

Feroz Shah Kotla, Delhi, March 30: **Australia** 132/6 in 20 overs (Meg Lanning 55, Alyssa Healy 25; Natalie Sciver 2-22) beat **England** 127/7 in 20 overs (Tammy Beaumont 32, Charlotte Edwards 31; Megan Schutt 2-15) by five runs. *PoM:* Meg Lanning.

2nd semi-final: West Indies beat New Zealand by 6 runs

• Stafanie Taylor assumes the role of anchor, while Britney Cooper, promoted up the order, chooses an opportune time to score her maiden T20I fifty. • Cooper's innings is marked by power hitting straight down the ground, as in the two consecutive sixes she bludgeons off Leigh Kasperek, New Zealand's best bowler in the group stages. • Sophie Devine takes three wickets with

slower balls in a spell of cunning wicket-to-wicket bowling at the death. •
Devine looks serene until being dismissed by a direct hit from Deandra Dottin at cover; New Zealand are floundering at 49 for 3. • Sara McGlashan and
Amy Satterthwaite bring the equation to 37 needed from the last four overs,
one fewer than West Indies scored, but Taylor has both set batters caught in
the deep off consecutive balls. • West Indies had lost their previous three
WT20 semi-finals, but on the large outfield, their extra power is decisive:
they hit 60 runs in boundaries to New Zealand's 44. *Tim Wigmore*

Wankhede Stadium, Mumbai, March 31: **West Indies** 143/6 in 20 overs (Britney Cooper
51, Stafanie Taylor 25; Sophie Devine 4-22) beat **New Zealand** 137/8 in 20 overs (Sara McGlashan 38, Amy Satterthwaite 24; S Taylor 3-26) by six runs. *PoM:* Britney Cooper.

Final: West Indies beat Australia by eight wickets

• Villani begins Australia's hunt for their fourth title with a 34-ball half-century as the defending champions make 54 in the powerplay and 76 from
the first ten overs. • Lanning buttresses Villani's effort with a 45-ball 50 that
gives Australia the perfect launchpad. • After Anisa Mohammed takes 1 for
19 from four tidy overs, Dottin – who has gone for 32 in her first three –
concedes just one in the final over. • West Indies match Australia's halfway
score of 76 without losing a wicket, as 18-year-old Hayley Matthews scores a
sparkling 45-ball 66, featuring six fours and three sixes. • Taylor anchors the
innings with 59 off 57 as the opening pair adds 120 in 94 deliveries. • Dottin's
rapid cameo finishes things off, with West Indies doing the Champion dance
after three consecutive semi-final exits. *Dileep Premachandran*
Venue: Eden Gardens, Kolkata, India,

Big-match batting: Fifties by Meg Lanning and Elyse Villani were put in the shade by Hayley Matthews. – *ICC/Getty Images*

Date: April 3, 2016
Result: West Indies Women won by eight wickets
MoM: Hayley Matthews (West Indies Women)
MoS: Stafanie Taylor (West Indies Women)
Series result: West Indies Women won the 2016 Women's World T20

Australia Women

			R	*B*	*4s*	*6s*	*SR*
Alyssa Healy		c & b Matthews	4	5	0	0	80.00
Elyse Villani	c Taylor	b Dottin	52	37	9	0	140.54
Meghann Lanning	LBW	b Mohammed	52	49	8	0	106.12
Ellyse Perry	LBW	b Dottin	28	23	0	2	121.74
Alex Blackwell	Not Out	b Dottin	3	5	0	0	60.00
Erin Osborne	Run Out	(Stacy-Ann King)	0	1	0	0	0.00
Jess Jonassen	Not Out	(Stacy-Ann King)	0	0	0	0	0.00
Extras	(4b,2lb,0nb,3w)	9					
Total	(5 wkts, 20.0 overs)		148 (7.4 runs per over)				

Fall of wickets: 15-1 (Alyssa Healy, 1.6 ov), 92-2 (Elyse Villani, 11.6 ov), 134-3 (Meghann Lanning, 17.4 ov), 147-4 (Ellyse Perry, 19.4 ov), 147-5 (Erin Osborne, 19.5 ov)

Did not bat: Kristen Beams, Megan Schutt, Rene Farrell, Beth Mooney

Bowling: Shamilia Connell 2-0-15-0-7.50 (1 wd), Hayley Matthews 2-0-13-1-6.50, Stafanie Taylor 3-0-26-0-8.67, Deandra Dottin 4-0-33-2-8.25 (1 wd), Afy Fletcher 1-0-9-0-9.00, Anisa Mohammed 4-0-19-1-4.75, Shaquana Quintyne 4-0-27-0-6.75 (1 wd)

West Indies Women

			R	*B*	*4s*	*6s*	*SR*
Hayley Matthews	c Blackwell	b Beams	66	45	6	3	146.67
Stafanie Taylor	c Jonassen	b Farrell	59	57	6	0	103.51
Deandra Dottin	Not Out	b Farrell	18	12	2	0	150.00
Britney Cooper	Not Out	b Farrell	3	3	0	0	100.00
Extras	(0b,2lb,0nb,1w)	3					
Total	(2 wkts, 19.3 overs)		149 (7.64 runs per over)				

Fall of wickets: 120-1 (Hayley Matthews, 15.4 ov), 144-2 (Stafanie Taylor, 18.4 ov)

Did not bat: Merissa Aguilleira, Afy Fletcher, Anisa Mohammed, Shamilia Connell, Shaquana Quintyne, Shemaine Campbelle, Stacy-Ann King

Bowling: Jess Jonassen 4-0-26-0-6.50, Ellyse Perry 3.3-0-27-0-7.71, Megan Schutt 3-0-26-0-8.67 (1 wd), Rene Farrell 4-0-35-1-8.75, Kristen Beams 4-0-27-1-6.75, Erin Osborne 1-0-6-0-6.00

Umpires: Aleem Dar (Pakistan) and Richard Illingworth (England)

TV umpire: Nigel Llong (England)
Referee: Sundaram Ravi (India)

Women's World T20 Winners

Year	Venue	Result
2009	England	England beat New Zealand by six wickets
2010	West Indies	Australia beat New Zealand by three runs
2012	Sri Lanka	Australia beat England by four runs
2014	Bangladesh	Australia beat England by six wickets
2016	India	West Indies beat Australia by eight wikets

Australia: 3, **England:** 1, **West Indies:** 1

OTHER INTERNATIONALS
Pakistan in West Indies

Taylor, Dottin show all-round class

Stafanie Taylor's reign as West Indies captain began on a victorious note, as West Indies crushed Pakistan in both the ODI and T20I series at home. Taylor and Deandra Dottin, the hard-hitting all-rounder, dominated the series, both playing vital roles with bat and ball. To their credit, the visitors did show some fight – Javeria Khan's 90 helped them win the opening ODI – but they couldn't carry the momentum. In the T20Is too, the Pakistani batters found it hard to match the power of the West Indians, at best scoring at five runs per over. They did however manage to tie the final T20I before the hosts won the one-over eliminator.

ODI series (4): West Indies 3 Pakistan 1

1st ODI: Pakistan win by six wickets
Beausejour Stadium, Gros Islet, St. Lucia, October 16: **West Indies** 222/9 in 50 overs (Merissa Aguilleira 67*, Britney Cooper 37; Anam Amin 2-33, Nida Dar 2-34) lost to **Pakistan** 225/4 in 48.1 overs (Javeria Khan 90, Nain Abidi 31; Deandra Dottin 2-44) by six wickets. *PoM:* Javeria Khan.

2nd ODI: West Indies win by three wickets
Beausejour Stadium, Gros Islet, St. Lucia, October 18: **Pakistan** 149 in 46.1 overs (Nain

Victorious start to captaincy: Stafanie Taylor dominated the Pakistan bowlers. – *WICB*

Abidi 48, Bismah Maroof 28 retd. hurt; Haley Matthews 2-22, Anisa Mohammed 2-24) lost to **West Indies** 150/7 in 46.5 overs (Stafanie Taylor 49, Kyshona Knight 28*; Anam Amin 4-27, Asmavia Iqbal 2-17) by three wickets. *PoM:* Anisa Mohammed.

3rd ODI: West Indies win by 109 runs

Beausejour Stadium, Gros Islet, St. Lucia, October 21: West Indies 281/5 in 50 overs (Stafanie Taylor 98*, Merissa Aguilleira 68; Anam Amin 2-50) beat **Pakistan** 172/9 in 50 overs (Javeria Khan 73*; S Taylor 3-26, Shamilia Connell 2-28) by 109 runs. *PoM:* Stafanie Taylor.

4th ODI: West Indies win by six wickets

Beausejour Stadium, Gros Islet, St. Lucia, October 24: Pakistan 182/5 in 50 overs (Asmavia Iqbal 44*, Bismah Maroof 41; Shamilia Connell 3-32, Anisa Mohammed 2-30) lost to **West Indies** 183/4 in 42.2 overs (Stafanie Taylor 87*, Merissa Aguilleira 37) by six wickets. *PoM:* Stafanie Taylor. *PoS:* Stafanie Taylor.

T20I series (3): West Indies 3 Pakistan 0

1st T20I: West Indies win by eight wickets
National Cricket Stadium, St. George's, Grenada, October 29: Pakistan 74/9 in 20 overs (Deandra Dottin 2-10, Tremayne Smartt 2-13) lost to **West Indies** 78/2 in 16.2 overs (D Dottin 38*) by eight wickets. *PoM:* Deandra Dottin.

2nd T20I: West Indies win by 11 runs (DLS method)
National Cricket Stadium, St. George's, Grenada, October 31: Pakistan 95/7 in 20 overs (Nain Abidi 35, Bismah Maroof 25; Deandra Dottin 3-20) lost to **West Indies** 91/3 in 17.4 overs (Stafanie Taylor 48*; Nida Dar 2-12) by 11 runs (DLS method). *PoM:* Stafanie Taylor.

3rd T20I: Match tied; West Indies won in eliminator
National Cricket Stadium, St. George's, Grenada, November 1: West Indies 88 in 19.5 overs (Kycia Knight 49; Sana Mir 4-14, Anam Amin 2-10) tied with **Pakistan** 77/7 in 17 overs (Bismah Maroof 30, S Mir 22) (DLS method). Pakistan 3/2 in 1 over lost to **West Indies** 6/1 in 1 over in the One-Over Elimintaor. *PoM:* Sana Mir. *PoS:* Deandra Dottin.

Tour matches
Brian Piccolo Park, Cooper City, Fort Lauderdale, November 4: United States of America 56/8 in 20 overs (Bismah Maroof 2-5, Sumaiya Siddiqi 2-14) lost to **Pakistan** 57/0 in 5 overs (Nain Abidi 27*, Javeria Khan 27*) by ten wickets.

Brian Piccolo Park, Cooper City, Fort Lauderdale, November 4: Pakistan 233/4 in 20 overs (Aliya Riaz 106*, Ayesha Zafar 55; Zeenat Kauser 2-36) beat **United States of America** 49/5 in 17 overs (Nida Dar 2-2, Sumaiya Sidiqqi 2-9) by 142 runs (D/L method).

	ODIs	T20Is
Best batter	Stafanie Taylor (261 runs, 4 matches)	Deandra Dottin (65 runs, 3 matches)
Best bowler	Anam Amin (9 wickets, 4 matches)	Deandra Dottin (6 wickets, 3 matches)

Sri Lanka in New Zealand

Bates, Priest hammer Sri Lanka

For New Zealand, the limited overs clean sweep against Sri Lanka at home was a series of many firsts. Rachel Priest, the veteran wicketkeeper-batter, scored her maiden ODI century in the first match of the series, only to better that in the third ODI when she smashed a 146-ball 157, her third consecutive score of fifty. Morna Nielsen, the left-arm spinner, scalped her first five-for with 5 for 21 in the fourth ODI, while Erin Bermingham also managed career-best figures of 4 for 16 in the final game. In every match, New Zealand found a new hero, while Sri Lanka's over-reliance on Chamari Atapattu, Shashikala Siriwardene and Dilani Manodara was exposed. The three-match T20I series was an equally one-sided affair, with Suzie Bates, the New Zealand skipper, taking centre stage.

Power play: Rachel Priest followed up her maiden ODI ton with another soon after. – *Getty Images*

Tour match
Bert Sutcliffe Oval, Lincoln, November 1: **Sri Lanka** 204/9 in 50 overs (Dilani Manodara 41, Chamari Atapattu 35; Frances Nackay 3-30, Thamsyn Newton 3-30) lost to **New Zealand A** 205/4 in 44.3 overs (Sam Curtis 93*, Suzie McDonald 33*) by six wickets.

ODI series (5): New Zealand 5 Sri Lanka 0

1st ODI: New Zealand win by 96 runs
Bert Sutcliffe Oval, Lincoln, November 3: **New Zealand** 283/9 in 50 overs (Rachel Priest 108, Amy Satterthwaite 69; Inoka Ranaweera 4-53, Shashikala Siriwardene 2-50) beat **Sri Lanka** 187/9 in 50 overs (Chamari Atapattu 75; Leigh Kasperek 4-27) by 96 runs. *PoM:* Rachel Priest.

2nd ODI: New Zealand win by ten wickets
Bert Sutcliffe Oval, Lincoln, November 5: **Sri Lanka** 126 in 46.5 overs (Chamari Polgampola 35, Dilani Manodara 31; Suzie Bates 3-27, Sophie Devine 2-17) lost to **New Zealand** 130/0 in 14.3 overs (S Bates 70*, Rachel Priest 51*) by ten wickets. *PoM:* Suzie Bates.

3rd ODI: New Zealand win by 188 runs
Bert Sutcliffe Oval, Lincoln, November 7: **New Zealand** 326/5 in 50 overs (Rachel Priest 157, Suzie Bates 80; Ama Kanchana 2-54) beat **Sri Lanka** 138 in 41.5 overs (A Kanchana 28*; Erin Bermingham 3-26, Amy Satterthwaite 2-5) by 188 runs. *PoM:* Rachel Priest.

4th ODI: New Zealand win by ten wickets
Bert Sutcliffe Oval, Lincoln, November 10: Sri Lanka 126 in 46.2 overs (Chamari Atapattu 56, Ama Kanchana 31; Morna Nielsen 5-21, Sophie Devine 2-30) lost to **New Zealand** 127/0 in 18.3 overs (Suzie Bates 70*, Amy Satterthwaite 49*) by ten wickets. *PoM:* Morna Nielsen.

5th ODI: New Zealand win by eight wickets
Hagley Oval, Christchurch, November 13: Sri Lanka 99 in 47.5 overs (Prasadani Weerakkody 27; Erin Bermingham 4-16, Suzie Bates 2-8) lost to **New Zealand** 102/2 in 17.3 overs (Sara McGlashan 39, Katie Perkins 29*) by eight wickets. *PoM:* Erin Bermingham.

T20I series (3): New Zealand 3 Sri Lanka 0

1st T20I: New Zealand win by 102 runs
Hagley Oval, Christchurch, November 15: **New Zealand** 188/3 in 20 overs (Sophie Devine 54, Rachel Priest 49) beat **Sri Lanka** 86/6 in 20 overs (Oshadi Ranasinghe 34*; Lea Tahuhu 2-10) by 102 runs. *PoM:* Sophie Devine.

2nd T20I: New Zealand win by 11 runs
Saxton Oval, Nelson, November 20: **New Zealand** 114/7 in 20 overs (Suzie Bates 69; Ama Kanchana 3-22) beat **Sri Lanka** 103/8 in 20 overs (Chamari Atapattu 47, Prasadani Weerakkody 21; Leigh Kasperek 3-7, S Bates 3-23) by 11 runs. *PoM:* Suzie Bates.

3rd T20I: New Zealand win by nine wickets
Saxton Oval, Nelson, November 22: Sri Lanka 86/9 in 20 overs (Dilani Manodara 23; Thamsyn Newton 3-9, Leigh Kasperek 2-7) lost to **New Zealand** 90/1 in 9.2 overs (Rachel Priest 37*, Amy Satterthwaite 33) by nine wickets. *PoM:* Thamsyn Newton. *PoS:* Suzie Bates.

	ODIs	T20Is
Best batter	Rachel Priest (316 runs, 5 matches)	Suzie Bates (105 runs, 3 matches)
Best bowler	Erin Bermingham (10 wickets, 5 matches)	Leigh Kasperek (5 wickets, 2 matches)

Zimbabwe in Bangladesh

Jahanara leads from the front

Rumana Ahmed and Jahanara Alam, the new skipper, registered three-wicket hauls in the first and second T20I respectively to help Bangladesh complete a clean sweep over Zimbabwe. Ayasha Rahman was impressive among the batters, recording the sole half-century of the series. For Zimbabwe, it was useful match practice on their way to Thailand for the Women's World T20 2016 Qualifier.

Best batter: Ayasha Rahman (78 runs, 2 matches)
Best bowler: Rumana Ahmed, Jahanara Alam (3 wickets, 2 matches)

T20I series (2): Bangladesh 2 Zimbabwe 0

1st T20I: Bangladesh win by 35 runs

Sheikh Kamal International Cricket Stadium, Cox's Bazar, November 17: Bangladesh 125/3 in 20 overs (Ayasha Rahman 50, Sharmin Akhter 35) beat **Zimbabwe** 90/8 in 20 overs (Sharne Mayers 29; Rumana Ahmed 3-11, Salma Khatun 2-18) by 35 runs. *PoM*: Ayasha Rahman.

2nd T20I: Bangladesh win by eight wickets

Sheikh Kamal International Cricket Stadium, Cox's Bazar, November 19: Zimbabwe 69/6 in 20 overs (Sharne Mayers 21; Jahanara Alam 3-11) lost to **Bangladesh** 70/2 in 11.5 overs (Ayasha Rahman 28, Shaila Sharmin 23*) by eight wickets. *PoM*: Jahanara Alam.

England in South Africa

Hosts make history, visitors take series

England, who ahead of this ODI series were fifth on the ICC Women's Championship – one position behind the hosts – came into it desperate for a whitewash. Their expectations were not unrealistic: South Africa hadn't tasted success against them since 2004. Having won the opening match rather easily, the visitors were in for a shock in the second game. Powered by a rapid 112-run partnership between Lizelle Lee and Marizanne Kapp, the hosts overcame a target of 263 to level the series, only for England to fight back in the final ODI. The T20I series too, was closely fought. Dane van Niekerk's splendid all-round show in the second T20I gave South Africa their first T20I victory over England, before Sarah Taylor's third consecutive T20I fifty sealed the deal in England's favour. It perhaps helped England that South Africa were short of match practice after the tour of Bangladesh was cancelled for security reasons.

Tour matches

LC de Villiers Oval, Pretoria, February 2: **England** 337/8 in 50 overs (Lauren Winfield 81, Jenny Gunn 62; Michelle Burt 3-63, Lauren Booysen 2-49) beat **South Africa Emerging Players** 193 in 49.1 overs (Danielle Wyatt 62, Tammy Beaumont 28; Katherine Brunt 4-20, Rebecca Grundy 2-39) by 144 runs.

Mamelodi Oval, Pretoria, February 4: **South Africa Emerging Players** 62 in 28.2 overs (Danielle Wyatt 3-7, Anya Shrubsole 2-15) lost to **England** 63/1 in 10.1 overs (Amy Jones 44*) by nine wickets.

Array of shots: South Africa managed their first T20I victory over England, but Sarah Taylor's third consecutive fifty confirmed a series win for the visitors. – *Getty Images*

ODI series (3): England 2 South Africa 1

1st ODI: England win by seven wickets (DLS method)
Willowmoore Park, Benoni, February 7: **South Africa** 196 in 49.2 overs (Trisha Chetty 90, Mignon du Preez 38; Anya Shrubsole 4-29, Jenny Gunn 2-25) lost to **England** 150/3 in 28.3 overs (Sarah Taylor 41*, Amy Jones 34) by seven wickets (D/L method). *PoM:* Anya Shrubsole.

2nd ODI: South Africa win by five wickets
SuperSport Park, Centurion, February 12: **England** 262/9 in 50 overs (Heather Knight 61, Charlotte Edwards 45; Shabnim Ismail 3-32, Sune Luus 2-33) lost to **South Africa** 265/5 in 48.5 overs (Lizelle Lee 69, Trisha Chetty 66; Danielle Hazell 2-34, H Knight 2-63) by five wickets. *PoM:* Lizelle Lee.

3rd ODI: England win by five wickets
New Wanderers Stadium, Johannesburg, February 14: **South Africa** 196/9 in 50 overs (Lizelle Lee 74, Trisha Chetty 31; Anya Shrubsole 3-35, Heather Knight 2-36) lost to **England** 198/5 in 43.5 overs (H Knight 67*, Georgia Elwiss 61; Chloe Tryon 2-28, Shabnim Ismail 2-35) by five wickets. *PoM:* Heather Knight.

T20I series (3): England 2 South Africa 1

1st T20I: England win by 15 runs
Boland Park, Paarl, February 18: **England** 147/7 in 20 overs (Sarah Taylor 74*; Moseline Daniels 2-20, Dane van Niekerk 2-26) beat **South Africa** 132/6 in 20 overs (D van Niekerk 52, Trisha Chetty 46; Anya Shrubsole 3-25, Jenny Gunn 2-28) by 15 runs. *PoM:* Sarah Taylor.

2nd T20I: South Africa win by 17 runs (DLS method)
Newlands, Cape Town, February 19: **England** 156/6 in 20 overs (Sarah Taylor 66, Charlotte

Edwards 34; Sune Luus 2-26) lost to **South Africa** 145/3 in 17.2 overs (Dane van Niekerk 63, Mignon du Preez 47*) by 17 runs (DLS method). *PoM:* Dane van Niekerk.

3rd T20I: England win by four wickets
New Wanderers Stadium, Johannesburg, February 21: **South Africa** 131/4 in 20 overs (Lizelle Lee 69*, Mignon du Preez 39; Anya Shrubsole 2-28) lost to **England** 133/6 in 15.3 overs (Sarah Taylor 60, Heather Knight 25; Shabnim Ismail 3-27) by four wickets. *PoM:* Sarah Taylor. *PoS:* Sarah Taylor.

	ODIs	T20Is
Best batter	Trisha Chetty (187 runs, 3 matches)	Sarah Taylor (200 runs, 3 matches)
Best bowler	Anya Shrubsole (7 wickets, 3 matches)	Anya Shrubsole (5 wickets, 3 matches)

Australia in New Zealand

Bates, Lanning headline Rose Bowl clash

Suzie Bates and Meg Lanning became the first pair of captains to score centuries in a women's ODI when they smashed 110 and 127 respectively, in the third and final ODI of the series. It was Lanning who finished on the winning side as Australia, who after losing the opening match bounced back through the efforts of Jess Jonassen, Ellyse Perry and the captain herself, extended their 17-year hold on the Rose Bowl trophy. Bates's good run of form continued into the T20I series as she scored two half-centuries and inspired her team to a series victory ahead of the World T20. Leigh Kasperek bowled impressively, picking up seven wickets, including career-best figures of 4 for 7 in the first T20I.

ODI series (3): Australia 2 New Zealand 1

1st ODI: New Zealand win by nine runs
Bay Oval, Mount Maunganui, February 20: **New Zealand** 202/9 in 50 overs (Amy Satterthwaite 72, Suzie Bates 43; Grace Harris 3-32, Jess Jonassen 3-32) beat **Australia** 193 in 49.4 overs (Beth Mooney 53, Ellyse Perry 51; Lea Tahuhu 3-34, Erin Bermingham 3-38) by nine runs. *PoM:* Amy Satterthwaite.

2nd ODI: Australia win by eight wickets
Bay Oval, Mount Maunganui, February 22: **New Zealand** 206/9 in 50 overs (Sophie Devine 67, Suzie Bates 61; Jess Jonassen 5-50, Megan Schutt 2-25) lost to **Australia** 210/2 in 41 overs (Meg Lanning 114*, Ellyse Perry 64*) by eight wickets. *PoM:* Meg Lanning.

3rd ODI: Australia win by six wickets
Bay Oval, Mount Maunganui, February 24: New Zealand 243/5 in 50 overs (Suzie Bates 110, Sara McGlashan 46) lost to **Australia** 244/4 in 48.4 overs (Meg Lanning 127, Alex Blackwell 50*; Leigh Kasperek 2-37) by six wickets. *PoM:* Meg Lanning.

T20I series (3): New Zealand 2 Australia 1

1st T20I: New Zealand win by four wickets
Basin Reserve, Wellington, February 28: Australia 113/7 in 20 overs (Meg Lanning 30; Leigh Kasperek 4-7) lost to **New Zealand** 114/6 in 18.3 overs (Suzie Bates 33, Sara McGlashan 22; Megan Schutt 2-11, Lauren Cheatle 2-36) by four wickets. *PoM:* Leigh Kasperek.

2nd T20I: New Zealand win by five wickets
Basin Reserve, Wellington, March 1: Australia 116/6 in 20 overs (Ellyse Perry 55*, Alyssa Healy 23; Leigh Kasperek 3-26, Morna Nielsen 2-12) lost to **New Zealand** 117/5 in 19.3 overs (Suzie Bates 54, Amy Satterthwaite 34; Meg Lanning 2-17, Rene Farrell 2-23) by five wickets. *PoM:* Suzie Bates.

3rd T20I: Australia win by 17 runs
Pukekura Park, New Plymouth, March 4: **Australia** 145/7 in 20 overs (Ellyse Perry 43, Alex Blackwell 27; Thamsyn Newton 2-16) beat New Zealand 128/8 in 20 overs (Suzie Bates 54, Sara McGlashan 35; E Perry 2-15, Megan Schutt 2-19) by 17 runs. *PoM:* Ellyse Perry.

	ODIs	T20Is
Best batter	Meg Lanning (246 runs, 3 matches)	Suzie Bates (141 runs, 3 matches)
Best bowler	Jess Jonassen (9 wickets, 3 matches)	Leigh Kasperek (7 wickets, 3 matches)

West Indies in South Africa

Onwards and upwards for du Preez's girls

Having given England a run for their money only a few weeks earlier, Mignon du Preez's South African team showed West Indies too how much they had improved. Although the visitors took the ODI series quite comfortably, they survived a scare in the very first match, where Deandra Dottin's maiden five-wicket haul pulled them out of trouble. South Africa grabbed a consolation win in the final ODI and carried that winning momentum into the T20I series where they rode on Shabnim Ismail's fiery opening burst to record their first T20I victory over West Indies. Heroics from Ismail and Lizelle Lee in the deciding T20I saw the hosts through to a historic series victory.

ODI series (3): West Indies 2 South Africa 1

1st ODI: West Indies win by 16 runs
Buffalo Park, East London, February 24: **West Indies** 214/7 in 50 overs (Haley Matthews 56, Britney Cooper 55*; Dane van Niekerk 2-25, Shabnim Ismail 2-40) beat **South Africa** 198 in 48.5 overs (Marizanne Kapp 69*, Trisha Chetty 47; Deandra Dottin 5-34, Shaquana Quintyne 2-15) by 16 runs. *PoM:* Deandra Dottin.

2nd ODI: West Indies win by 57 runs
Buffalo Park, East London, February 27:**West Indies** 232 in 49.1 overs (Stafanie Taylor 79, Deandra Dottin 61; Sune Luus 3-34, Marizanne Kapp 2-38) beat **South Africa** 175 in 45.3 overs (Trisha Chetty 51, Mignon du Preez 24; Haley Matthews 2-18, Shaquana Quintyne 2-20) by 57 runs. *PoM:* Stafanie Taylor.

3rd ODI: South Africa win by 35 runs
Buffalo Park, East London, February 29: **South Africa** 235/6 in 50 overs (Trisha Chetty 55, Dane van Niekerk 55) beat **West Indies** 200/8 in 50 overs (Shaquana Quintyne 40, Merissa Aguilleira 40; Sune Luus 2-30, Masabata Klaas 2-33) by 35 runs. *PoM:* Trisha Chetty.

T20I series (3): South Africa 2 West Indies 1

1st T20I: South Africa win by 11 runs
Kingsmead, Durban, March 4: **South Africa** 125/6 in 20 overs (Lizelle Lee 35, Dane van Niekerk 22; Anisa Mohammed 2-23, Haley Matthews 2-24) beat **West Indies** 114/6 in 20 overs (Deandra Dottin 40, Stacy-Ann King 29; Shabnim Ismail 3-12, D van Niekerk 2-19) by 11 runs. *PoM:* Shabnim Ismail.

2nd T20I: West Indies win by 45 runs
New Wanderers Stadium, Johannesburg, March 6: **West Indies** 143/6 in 20 overs (Stafanie Taylor 63, Stacy-Ann King 24; Shabnim Ismail 3-25) beat **South Africa** 98 in 18.4 overs (Anisa Mohammed 2-12, Hayley Matthews 2-17) by 45 runs. *PoM:* Stafanie Taylor.

3rd T20I: South Africa win by four runs
Newlands, Cape Town, March 9: **South Africa** 119/3 in 20 overs (Lizelle Lee 33*, Mignon du Preez 32) beat **West Indies** 115/8 in 20 overs (Haley Matthews 24, Deandra Dottin 24; Yolani Fourie 2-20) by four runs. *PoM:* Lizelle Lee. *PoS:* Stafanie Taylor.

	ODIs	T20Is
Best batter	Trisha Chetty (153 runs, 3 matches)	Stafanie Taylor (88 runs, 3 matches)
Best bowler	Deandra Dottin (7 wickets, 3 matches)	Shabnim Ismail (7 wickets, 3 matches)

New era: Heather Knight became the first woman to take a five-for and score a fifty in the same match, before leading England to a win in a record-breaking series.
— *Getty Images*

Pakistan in England

Beaumont, England rewrite record books

Ahead of their home series against Pakistan, England were thought to be vulnerable. They were without the services of Charlotte Edwards, their marquee captain who had retired from international cricket just before the series, and Sarah Taylor, easily one of the best wicketkeeper-batters in the world, who had taken a break from the game. Heather Knight stepped into the role of captain, and her England team proceeded to smash the record books. She led the way in the first ODI becoming the first woman to take a five-for and score a fifty in the same match. The next encounter saw the hosts record their highest ever ODI total (378 for 5) as Tammy Beaumont and Lauren Winfield scored their maiden international centuries and Natalie Sciver (80 off 33 balls) blasted a 22-ball fifty, the fastest in ODIs. Beaumont bettered her effort in the final ODI (168*), thus setting a record for the most number of runs (342) in a three-match series. The T20Is were no different: England once again posted their highest total (187 for 5) in the format with a 147-run stand – another England record – between Beaumont and Winfield in the first match. The visitors were never really in the contest, as Knight's England team announced the start of a new era with utmost authority.

Tour match

Haslegrave Ground, Loughborough, June 18: **Loughborough Lightning** 123/8 in 25 overs (Georgia Boyce 23, Paige Schofield 22; Nida Dar 3-16, Anam Amin 2-3) lost to **Pakistan** 124/5 in 24.1 overs (Sidra Ameen 51, Javeria Khan 29; Kirstie Gordon 3-28, Sonia Odedra 2-19) by five wickets.

ODI series (3): England 3 Pakistan 0

1st ODI: England win by seven wickets
Grace Road, Leicester, June 21: Pakistan 165 in 45.4 overs (Sidra Ameen 52, Asmavia Iqbal 22; Heather Knight 5-26, Katherine Brunt 2-24) lost to England 166/3 in 31.5 overs (Tammy Beaumont 70, H Knight 50*; A Iqbal 2-49) by seven wickets. *PoM:* Heather Knight.

2nd ODI: England win by 212 runs
County Ground, New Road, Worcester, June 22: England 378/5 in 50 overs (Lauren Winfield 123, Tammy Beaumont 104; Maham Tariq 2-63) beat Pakistan 166 in 47.4 overs (Bismah Maroof 61, Javeria Khan 26; Anya Shrubsole 4-19, Natalie Sciver 2-12) by 212 runs. *PoM:* Tammy Beaumont & Lauren Winfield.

3rd ODI: England win by 202 runs
County Ground, Taunton, June 27: England 366/4 in 50 overs (Tammy Beaumont 168*, Georgia Elwiss 77; Sana Mir, 2-69) beat Pakistan 164 in 44.5 overs (Sidra Nawaz 47, Bismah Maroof 33; Katherine Brunt 5-30, Laura Marsh 3-29) by 202 runs. *PoM:* Tammy Beaumont.

Tour match
North Parade, Bath, June 30: England Academy 109 in 19.5 overs (Aiman Anwer 2-17, Sania Khan 2-18) lost to **Pakistan** 110/4 in 18.5 overs (Javeria Khan 50, Bismah Maroof 27) by six wickets.

T20I series (3): England 3 Pakistan 0

1st T20I: England win by 68 runs
County Ground, Bristol, July 3: England 187/5 in 20 overs (Tammy Beaumont 82, Lauren Winfield 74; Nida Dar 2-28) beat Pakistan 119/7 in 20 overs (Asmavia Iqbal 35, Nain Abidi 24; Danielle Hazell 2-18, Jennu Gunn 2-22) by 68 runs. *PoM:* Tammy Beaumont.

2nd T20I: England win by 35 runs
The Rose Bowl, Southampton, July 5: England 138/7 in 20 overs (Fran Wilson 43*, Lauren Winfield 29; Bismah Maroof 2-19, Sadia Yousuf 2-31) beat Pakistan 103 in 19.4 overs (Javeria Khan 23, Nida Dar 22; Jenny Gunn 2-7, Natalie Sciver 2-16) by 35 runs. *PoM:* Fran Wilson.

3rd T20I: England win by 57 runs
County Ground, Chelmsford, July 7: England 170/5 in 20 overs (Lauren Winfield 63, Tammy Beaumont 55; Nida Dar 2-23) beat Pakistan 113/7 in 20 overs (Bismah Marrof 35, Javeria Khan 23; Alex Hartley 2-19) by 57 runs. *PoM:* Lauren Winfield.

	ODIs	T20Is
Best batter	Tammy Beaumont (342 runs, 3 matches)	Lauren Winfield (166 runs, 3 matches)
Best bowler	Katherine Brunt (9 wickets, 3 matches)	Jenny Gunn (5 wickets, 3 matches)

South Africa in Ireland

Memorable start for Delany

Ireland tasted their first success ever against South Africa, albeit an under strength side, in both the ODI and T20I formats, but unfortunately for Laura Delany, they were unable to clinch a series victory in her first outing as skipper. The visitors, led by Dinesha Devnarain, were without the services of Dane van Niekerk, their newly appointed captain, Marizanne Kapp, Shabnim Ismail and Lizelle Lee, all of whom were taking part in the Kia Super League in England. They survived a scare in the first T20I, to win off the final ball, courtesy a panicked overthrow from Ireland, but the hosts came back in the second match to square the series 1-1. In the ODIs, the South Africans lifted their game significantly to clinch the series 3-1. Sune Luus emulated Heather Knight's efforts against Pakistan to become only the second woman to score a fifty and scalp five wickets in the same match. Mignon du Preez smashed the second highest score by a South African (116*) in the second match, while Laura Wolfvaardt, the 17-year-old, became the youngest South African, male or female, to score a century in international cricket, in the third. Having conceded the series, Ireland managed another memorable win in a low-scoring game. Kim Garth and Isobel Joyce were particularly impressive for them.

T20I series (2): Ireland 1 South Africa 1

1st T20I: South Africa win by four wickets
YMCA Cricket Club, Dublin, August 1: Ireland 140/4 in 20 overs (Isobel Joyce 31*, Kim Garth 30*; Sune Luus 2-24) lost to **South Africa** 144/6 in 20 overs (Mignon du Preez 55, Laura Wolvaardt 24; K Garth 2-30) by four wickets.

2nd T20I: Ireland win by 20 runs
YMCA Cricket Club, Dublin, August 3: Ireland 115/7 in 20 overs (Clare Shillington 48, Gaby Lewis 26; Marcia Letsoalo 2-17) beat **South Africa** 95 in 19.3 overs (Trisha Chetty 27; Kim Garth 2-12) by 20 runs.

ODI series (4): South Africa 3 Ireland 1

1st ODI: South Africa win by 89 runs
Merrion Cricket Club Ground, Dublin, August 5: South Africa 283/7 in 50 overs (Chloe Tryon 92, Laura Wolvaardt 55; Kim Garth 3-61) beat **Ireland** 194 in 44.5 overs (K Garth 72*, Clare Shillington 27; Sune Luus 6-36, Masabata Klaas 2-38) by 89 runs.

2nd ODI: South Africa win by 68 runs
YMCA Cricket Club, Dublin, August 7: South Africa 272/6 in 50 overs (Mignon du Preez 116*, Chloe Tryon 52; Ciara Metcalfe 2-40, Lucy O'Reilly 2-65) beat **Ireland** 204 in 48.2 overs (Mary Waldron 42, Clare Shillington 41; Masabata Klaas 2-6, Sune Luus 2-47) by 68 runs.

3rd ODI: South Africa win by 67 runs
The Village, Malahide, Dublin, August 9: South Africa 260/6 in 50 overs (Laura Wolvaardt 105, Trisha Chetty 95; Ciara Metcalfe 2-37) beat **Ireland** 193 in 45 overs (Isobel Joyce 57, Kim Garth 51*; Sune Luus 5-32, Ayabonga Khaka 2-31) by 67 runs.

4th ODI: Ireland win by seven wickets
The Hills Cricket Club Ground, Dublin, August 11: South Africa 143 in 46.4 overs (Andrie Steyn 43, Chloe Tryon 30; Ciara Metcalfe 3-23, Kim Garth 3-27) lost to **Ireland** 146/3 in 36.1 overs (Isobel Joyce 62*, Clare Shillington 28) by seven wickets. *PoS:* Sune Luus

	ODIs	T20Is
Best batter	Laura Wolvaardt (215 runs, 4 matches)	Clare Shillington (78 runs, 2 matches)
Best bowler	Sune Luus (14 wickets, 4 matches)	Kim Garth (4 wickets, 2 matches)

Bangladesh in Ireland

Weather denies teams vital game time

Rumana Ahmed: First hat-trick by a Bangladesh woman. – *ICC*

Bangladesh's first international assignment since the World T20 in India was marred by the Irish weather, with only two of the scheduled five matches completed. The visitors, without the services of their senior-most player Salma Khatun, who missed the trip with a shoulder injury, had only one day to prepare in alien conditions. Their rustiness showed as they lost the first T20I, thus conceding the series 1-0. After the first two ODIs were washed out, Rumana Ahmed, the leg-spinner, led the visitors' charge, picking up a hat-trick – the first by a Bangladesh woman in international cricket – to seal the win in a low-scoring encounter.

T20I series (2): Ireland 1 Bangladesh 0

1st T20I: Ireland win by six runs
Bready Cricket Club, Magheramason, Bready, September 5: Ireland 54/8 in 10 overs (Clare Shillington 26; Kadija Tul Kubra 3-5) beat **Bangladesh** 48/6 in 10 overs (Fargana Hoque 24; Lucy O'Reilly 2-5) by six runs.

Driven: The Virat Kohli Story
Author: Vijay Lokapally
ISBN: 978-93-85936-26-5

What makes Virat Kohli the undisputed monarch of the cricket world today is not his iconic status in the sports hierarchy but that the highest praise comes from the opposition camp and past greats.

Widely travelled sports journalist Vijay Lokapally goes on to recount happier times on the journey of Virat's rapid rise to international stardom, an account punctuated with little-known stories by his fellow players, coaches and intimates.

Cricket World Cup: The Indian Challenge
Author: Ashis Ray
ISBN: 978-93-84898-19-9

This is an eye-witness history of the Cricket World Cup from an Indian perspective. It highlights the turning point for India at Berbice; has reports and scores on all India matches in World Cup competition as well as on every semi-final and final, including India's triumphs in 1983 and 2011. It also projects the Indian victory in the World Championship of Cricket in 1985; and previews the 2015 World Cup.

ISBN: 978-93-82951-80-3 ISBN: 978-93-84898-47-2 ISBN: 978-93-84898-30-4

For orders e-mail: india@bloomsbury.com   Ph: +91-11-40574954/7

 BLOOMSBURY INDIA

2nd T20I: Match abandoned
Bready Cricket Club, Magheramason, Bready, September 6: Bangladesh v Ireland.
Match abandoned without a ball bowled.

ODI series (3): Bangladesh 1 Ireland 0

1st ODI: Match abandoned
Bready Cricket Club, Magheramason, Bready, September 8: Bangladesh v Ireland.
Match abandoned without a ball bowled.

2nd ODI: No result
Instonians Cricket Club, Shaw's Bridge Lower Ground, Belfast, September 9: Ireland 68/0 in 18 overs (Cecelia Joyce 37*, Meg Kendal 26*) v **Bangladesh**. No result.

3rd ODI: Bangladesh win by 10 runs
Instonians Cricket Club, Shaw's Bridge Lower Ground, Belfast, September 10: Bangladesh 106 in 40.1 overs (Sanjida Islam 33; Amy Kenealy 4-32, Kim Garth 2-24) beat **Ireland** 96 in 37.5 overs (Cecelia Joyce 35, Laura Delany 26; Rumana Ahmed 3-20, Fahima Khatun 2-13) by 10 runs. *PoS:* Rumana Ahmed.

	ODIs	T20Is
Best batter	Cecelia Joyce (72 runs, 2 matches)	Clare Shillington (26 runs, 1 match)
Best bowler	Amy Kenealy (4 wickets, 2 matches)	Khadija Tul Kubra (3 wickets, 1 match)

Australia in Sri Lanka

Beams drives Australia to World Cup

Australia became the first team to secure direct entry into the 2017 ICC Women's World Cup in England thanks to their 4-0 victory in the ODI series over Sri Lanka. Kristen Beams, the leg-spinner, took full advantage of helpful sub-continent conditions, taking 13 wickets in the ODI series, including career-best figures of 4 for 15 in the second match. She followed it up with figures of 3 for 11 in the one-off T20I – also a career best – to headline Australia's ten-wicket win that came with 71 balls to spare – a women's record.

Nicole Bolton, Australia's left-handed opener, also played a crucial role in the series, scoring her second ODI century in the final match to add to a crucial half-century that came earlier in match two.

In the second ODI, Alex Blackwell became the third Australian, after Beinda Clark and Karen Rolton, and ninth batter overall, to score 3000 career runs.

The hosts were unable to challenge Australia's dominance as they struggled with both bat and ball. In the opening fixture, five of their top six fell for ducks, with the No. 4 making 1 run. Chamari Polgampola played their only knock of substance in the second ODI scoring an unbeaten 68, while Inoka Ranaweera's 3 for 20 in the first match gave the visitors somewhat of a scare. Overall, Meg Lanning's side sailed through.

ODI series (4): Australia 4 Sri Lanka 0

1st ODI: Australia win by four wickets
Ranagiri Dambulla International Stadium, September 18: Sri Lanka 76 in 24.5 overs (Inoka Ranaweera 32*; Holly Ferling 3-4, Kristen Beams 3-16) lost to **Australia** 79/6 in 15.4 overs (Meg Lanning 27; I Ranaweera 3-20) by four wickets. *PoM:* Holly Ferling.

Kristen Beams: The off-spinner made good use of subcontinental conditions. – *Getty Images*

2nd ODI: Australia win by 78 runs
Ranagiri Dambulla International Stadium, September 20: **Australia** 254/8 in 50 overs (Nicole Bolton 64, Alex Blackwell 54*; Chamari Atapattu 3-31, Sugandika Kumari 2-54) beat **Sri Lanka** 176/9 in 50 overs (Chamari Polgampola 68*, Eshani Lokusuriyage 20; Kristen Beams 4-15, Ellyse Perry 2-28) by 78 runs. *PoM:* Kristen Beams.

3rd ODI: Australia win by nine wickets
R Premadasa Stadium, Colombo, September 23: Sri Lanka 102 in 36.5 overs (Prasadai Weerakkody 31, Nipuni Hansika 23; Jessica Jonassen 3-1, Kristen Beams 2-20) lost to **Australia** 104/1 in 27.3 overs (Elyse Villani 48*, Nicole Bolton 35) by nine wickets. *PoM:* Jess Jonassen.

4th ODI: Australia win by 137 runs
R Premadasa Stadium, Colombo, September 25: **Australia** 268/3 in 50 overs (Nicole Bolton 113, Ellyse Perry 77*; Chamari Atapattu 2-48) beat **Sri Lanka** 131 in 45.5 overs (Prasadani Weerakkody 33, C Atapattu 26; Kristen Beams 4-26, Rene Farrell 3-17) by 137 runs. *PoM:* Nicole Bolton.

Australia win the one-off T20I by ten wickets
Sinhalese Sports Club Ground, Colombo, September 27: Sri Lanka 59/8 in 20 overs (Kristen Beams 3-11) lost to **Australia** 63/0 in 8.1 overs (Elyse Villani 34*, Beth Mooney 29*) by ten wickets. *PoM:* Kristen Beams.

	ODIs	T20Is
Best Batter	Nicole Bolton (231 runs, 4 matches)	Elyse Villani (34 runs, 1 match)
Best Bowler	Kristen Beams (13 wickets, 4 matches)	Kristen Beams (3 wickets, 1 match)

ICC Women's Championship 2014-2017

Points Table

Teams	M	W	L	T	N/R	Pts	NRR
Australia	18	15	3	0	0	30	+0.994
West Indies	15	10	5	0	0	20	+0.497
England	15	9	5	0	1	19	+0.754
New Zealand	15	8	7	0	0	16	+0.232
South Africa	15	7	7	0	1	15	-0.069
India	15	6	8	0	1	13	+0.008
Pakistan	15	4	11	0	0	8	-1.030
Sri Lanka	18	2	15	0	1	5	-1.339

Points as on September 30, 2016.

PART FIVE
Reviews and Records

CRICKET BOOKS

ZENODOTUS

The best books on cricket are written with passion; they are quirky, personal, tease out life lessons from the ordinary and the commonplace, and could be written by anybody if they had the range of knowledge and the breadth of vision possessed by Scyld Berry. Or Gideon Haigh.

Both these chroniclers of the game, who would have been among the best in any era, published books that made almost everything else that appeared on the stands a little less erudite and a little more ordinary.

On page 234 of **Cricket: The Game of Life**, Berry says, "Words can add up to fine writing, and fine writing makes an additional source of pleasure for those who follow the game, almost a reason in itself."

Berry wasn't speaking about his own work, but he might well have been. In 1981-82, England played a six-Test series in India which was one of the dullest, most boring on Indian (or any other) soil. Five Tests were drawn; at one stage India let the over-rate slip to ten an hour and England retaliated by bowling slower still. India won the First Test and proceeded to sit on the lead.

Yet Berry's tour book, *Cricketwallah,* remains one of the best. Through the boredom, the dust and the grime and the defensive mindset of Indian cricket then, Berry foresaw a future dominated by India both on and off the field.

His latest book might fall under the heading of "unclassifiable", which is its charm. It is as much about the game, its history and its idiosyncrasies, as it is about his own history and idiosyncrasies.

There is a section on David (and not just the one by Michelangelo in Florence) and his relation to beauty in cricket that alone is worth the price of the book. What is the connection between David and Walter Hammond in action? Berry tells us. A painting by Castagno is compared to the Australian fast bowler Ted McDonald bowling in the 1921 Ashes series, a sculpture by Donatello and another by Bernini captures not just David but the aesthetics of modern batsmanship. Berry's touch is as light as his knowledge is deep, and it makes for reading that is at once relaxing and thought-provoking.

It is a combination that applies equally

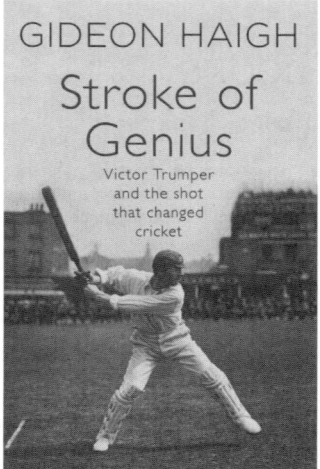

to Gideon Haigh's **Stroke of Genius: Victor Trumper and the Shot That Changed Cricket.**

The picture of Trumper jumping out to drive, leaving the safety of the crease, bat held high is an iconic one. Photographed by George Beldam, it captures the player, his time, his attitude, his impact.

As Haigh explains, this is not a biography of Trumper. "It is instead, for want of a better word, an iconography, a study of Trumper's valence in cricket's mythology and imagery." It is too a study in the development of photography, social commentary, cricket technique, Beldam's obsession to find out how great players did their stuff, an effort to cancel out some of the air brushing indulged in by the few biographies of Trumper, a sideways look at the Golden Age of cricket and a study in the art of presenting profound research with a casual, chatty air. Haigh pulls all these threads together and colours them with the richness of his prose.

What adds to the Trumper aura for us is the air of mystery fostered by the lack of information about him. We don't know when he was born, where and to whom. His childhood is a sealed book. There is little for the biographer to go by, although at least two other Australian cricketers, Jack Fingleton and Ashley Mallett, have written biographies, some of it based on Trumper's diary of the 1902 tour of England. But that diary, in Haigh's words, is "almost comically succinct". For example, here's a roundup of a full day's events: "Thursday 1 May: Practice all day. Went to Ben-Hur at night – Drury Lane." That summer, Trumper made 2570 runs in first-class cricket!

Haigh's history of sports action photography is fascinating in itself. Allied to the instinct for putting elements back into the Trumper story respectfully airbrushed by others makes this a rare coming together in the annals of cricket writing. The specificity and technical depth of the story of photography meshes well with the necessarily incomplete and thus interpretative story of the batsman who like all romantic heroes died young. There are parallels to the Bradman story too that are quite remarkable.

That 1902 season, says Haigh, is the "gateway myth of the Trumper legend", because there were no action photographs, no purple prose in the newspapers, and much of the legend came off the pen of Neville Cardus, who was 14 in 1902 but watched Trumper three or four times. "Given his admitted tendency to write what was 'true to character' rather than true to fact, whether

Cardus was at the Old Trafford at all (in 1902, when Trumper made a century before lunch) may be open to some doubt," says Haigh wryly.

It wasn't Cardus but CB Fry who made the telling comment about Trumper: "He has no style, yet he is all style."

For its boldness of concept, its easy and unexpected linking of disparate elements of the game and its personalities, for its reflection of Fry's tribute to Trumper, for its passion and for it being a jolly good read, *Stroke of Genius* is *Wisden India Almanack*'s Book of the Year.

Trumper, for all his innovation, would have been amazed at the manner in which modern batsmen, in particular AB de Villiers, the 360-degree man, play the game.

There has always been the temptation to see South Africa's all-round batsman de Villiers as a Renaissance man. After all, he was shortlisted for the South African national hockey squad and their football squad, he captained the national junior team in rugby and continues to hold six national schools swimming records. He ran the fastest 100-metres among juniors in his country, and was a member of the junior Davis Cup team and the Under-19 badminton champion. He is a scratch golfer too. And to top it all he had received a medal from Nelson Mandela for his science project.

All wonderful stories, and all untrue, according to **AB: The Autobiography**. "These are the facts," says the player, "decent at golf, useful at rugby and tennis when I was young, and enjoying cricket ever since. The errors will doubtless remain on the internet and people will continue to believe I was some kind of prodigy at all those different sports, but the truth will hopefully somehow endure."

This is merely an example of the honesty which runs like a golden thread through the autobiography. Early in his career, de Villiers decided that it "wasn't going to be enough for me to be just another run-of-the-mill international batsman with an average in the mid 30s". He promised himself he "would become the best batsman in the world". It was a three-pronged strategy: give up his partying lifestyle, organise his technique and get professional. He got himself an agent, a financial advisor and a personal assistant. The template for the successful modern sportsman was thus set.

"ABD", the cry rents the air wherever de Villiers plays in India, even for South Africa, and not just for his IPL team. "I had been inspired by India," he writes, "this great country that has provided me with so many opportunities and has become so important in my career." De Villiers singing Bollywood songs are a great hit on YouTube. The love between a player and his public is special, and when it is a two-way street, it is extra special. There is a childlike quality to the writing that could be said to reflect the player himself.

The Autobiography is a book full of sunshine and joy, of god and gratitude. There are passing references to South Africa at World Cups – de Villiers has a recurring dream in which he takes a catch at cover to win South Africa the World Cup final – but nothing controversial.

Cricket is a useful prism through which to view society, as Shehan Karunatilaka (*Chinaman*) and Joseph O'Neill (*Netherland*), have shown recently. In India, however, cricket is mostly in the Bollywood rags-to-riches format. Arvind Adiga's **Selection Day** subverts that. Although a novel on cricket, it is not a cricket novel. Adiga has a message, so characters and situations are cut to fit.

Cricket is usually seen in India like boxing was in America: a vehicle for social mobility and class advancement. But is it really, asks the author. Does cricket erase caste marks or merely reinforce them?

The surface story is simple enough. Talented schoolboys Radha and Manju, pushed hard by their father Mohan Kumar and marked out as the future of Indian cricket, are put through their paces by coach Tommy Sir, who convinces businessman Anand Mehta to sponsor them in return for a percentage of future earnings. The mixture of boyish innocence, parental ambition and business acumen is thus established early. Soon so is the homoerotic relationship between Manju and Javed Ansari, another talented batsman in a minority twice over for his religion and his sexuality. This relationship alone has some warmth and understanding in this largely male-dominated book.

Selection Day is more subtle than Booker-winning *The White Tiger*, but Adiga continues to philosophise with a hammer. There are references to Sachin Tendulkar and Vinod Kambli, and the suggestion that it was not lack of talent but being born lower down on the social scale that limited the latter.

Kunal Purandare's **Ramakant Achrekar: Master Blaster's Master** tells the story of how India's best-known cricket coach produced international players for at least three decades starting with Ramnath Parkar, who opened India's batting with Sunil Gavaskar in 1972-73 against England. The line-up is impressive: Parkar, Lalchand Rajput, Kambli, Tendulkar, Pravin Amre, Chandrakant Pandit, Ajit Agarkar, Sanjay Bangar, Sameer Dighe, Balwinder Singh Sandhu, Ramesh Powar. This is from among his wards who make up an exciting XI.

Achrekar was more than coach or mentor. He once adopted a promising player legally so the boy could watch international cricket from behind the bowler's arm at the stadium. This and other stories of his passion and dedication make the slim biography a treasure.

Cricket books

There is an intensity about Virat Kohli that is at once apparent when you see him on the field, and emerges with a lack of complication in Vijay Lokapally's biography **Driven: The Virat Kohli Story**. "That Virat was destined to serve Indian cricket was never doubted by his coach," writes Lokapally, and then continues with charming honesty: "However, I would be lying if I claimed to have foreseen Virat's growth." Yet few journalists have watched Kohli grow from a promising lad under 15 to one of the leading batsmen in the world.

In some ways, the author was repeating a feeling that was prevalent in cricket circles in India, which believed that Kohli was talented, but lacked the temperament to succeed at the highest level. Even his India colleague Yuvraj Singh, no shrinking violet himself in his time, took to the media to warn Kohli that he might be on the path to devastation and destruction. It was all a bit unfair since Kohli was just a teenager when he came into national prominence as captain of India's World Cup-winning Under-19 team, and teenagers who get there quickly should be given time to settle down.

Kohli has indeed settled down, and how! As India captain, he invites comparison with Tiger Pataudi; as the side's leading batsman, he carries the responsibility for not just ten others but about a billion others beyond the boundary ropes.

Lokapally traces the growth of the player and the man from the early days with empathy and understanding. The facts of the life are well recorded, but there are anecdotes that describe the man just as surely as the statistics describe the batsman.

On the morning of Teachers' Day in 2014, Kohli's coach Raj Kumar Sharma was woken up by a ring at the door. Virat was away in the US, but his brother Vikas stood on the doorstep. On entering the house, he gave his phone to the coach who heard Virat wish him. He then stepped outside and discovered that his ward had presented him a Skoda Rapid. The book has many such stories.

That serious books are being written about the IPL, about to enter its tenth season, is a good sign. For too long have we had marketing gimmicks and self-promotion that pass off for books. **Not Out: The Incredible Story of the Indian Premier League** by Desh Gaurav Sekhri, a sports attorney, asks the kind of question and takes you to the regions where these other manuals do not go. "The IPL has taken all of Indian society, thrown it into a blender, shaken it with some olives, and served it as a heady cocktail of intrigue, sport, controversy and general entertainment," says the author.

Yet of the original teams, only the Mumbai Indians and the Kolkata Knight Riders have not undergone change of ownership, been suspended or terminated, been in the market to be sold or flirted with insolvency. With the novelty having long disappeared, the league may have reached a turning point. Following the spot-fixing scandal of 2013 and the entry of the Supreme Court necessitated by the cricket board's ham-handed manner of handling it, the IPL has lost some sparkle. "The future needn't have been this uncertain," says Sekhri, in this fine analysis of the rise, fall and stagnation of one of the most exciting sporting properties in the world.

Fixed: Cash and Corruption in Cricket by Shantanu Guha Ray takes a look at the underbelly of cricket in India, and while speculation might occasionally override documented fact in some areas, it still asks a lot of questions that ought to worry the average cricket lover. "We were all pushed into spot-fixing by the mafia, the betting syndicates. We had no option," Danish Kaneira, the banned leg-spinner, tells Guha Ray at one point. "The ICC needs to understand the way these syndicates operate and how lethal they can be if their offers are turned down."

The question is not asked so often these days: Does fixing continue to exist in cricket? Ray tells us the history of the recent cases, talks to players and more importantly, unnamed sources and concludes: "No matter the nature of the investigations, guilty cricketers remain bold, and unfettered by laws and regulations." That is disturbing. The Lodha Committee suggested that betting be made legal in India. But human greed cannot be legislated against.

Additional reviews by Duncan Hamilton

To endure life, rather than enjoy it, is a tragedy for anyone. But that, it appears, is what happened to Peter Roebuck. Contentment seems to have been a fleeting companion. That's because wrapped around Roebuck's considerable talent – first as a cricketer, then as a writer – was the labyrinthine nature of his personality. He emerges from **Chasing Shadows** as a Chinese box of a man; a box, moreover, that was armour-plated to ward off intruders. Written by Tim Lane and Elliot Cartledge, it is the saddest cricket story I have ever read. Indeed, there were times – a lot of them – when I wished I wasn't reading it at all. The book is disturbing, but grimly gripping. I never met Roebuck. Something in me regrets that very much. Something else is relieved.

The title is plucked from a piece of advice his mother offers the authors: "You'll never know Peter until you look back. You'll be chasing shadows." The subtitle – *The Life and Death of Peter Roebuck* – reinforces the point. Lane and Cartledge think only the former can explain what led to the latter: his fall, aged 55, from the sixth floor of Cape Town's Southern Sun hotel, where police had gone to arrest him in November 2011 following a claim of sexual assault on a 26-year-old Zimbabwean man. Roebuck's death was declared as suicide. The book investigates whether that verdict was accurate, whether the procedures to determine it were correctly carried out and whether alternative possibilities have credence.

Reopening his case means re-examining his character. The authors – Lane worked alongside Roebuck at the Australian Broadcasting Corporation – call him a "cerebral loner" who was an "eccentric [and] sometimes shambolic figure". He is described as "strangely detached from life's normal polite transactions". This is putting it kindly. Depression, which could descend on him like a shelf cloud, doesn't completely explain behaviour that, over several decades, was extremely odd and often troubling. After one game, for Somerset at Sussex, he stopped his car at traffic lights, tossed the keys to a travelling companion and declared that he was going to walk from Worthing to Taunton; he spent that night at a B&B in Salisbury. During another match, as captain of Devon, he bowled three balls, then sat on the pitch yelling: "What's the point of life?" (Within an hour he'd taken 9 for 12.)

Chasing Shadows is as comprehensive as it can be in the circumstances, except in one crucial aspect. It lacks a lyrical appreciation of the books and journalism that defined Roebuck for readers who knew little of his unfathomable nature. There are scores of things we don't know about him. What we do know is this: He was one of the best cricket correspondents of his and most other generations, a prose stylist with the writerly sensibilities of a poet. Someone needs to stitch together an anthology of his work before we forget.

In **The Strange Death of English Leg Spin,** Justin Parkinson nabs his title from George Dangerfield's seminal political work, *The Strange Death of Liberal England.* In truth there is nothing strange here. A combination of factors sent it to the embalmer: climate, pitches, the change in the lbw law, prejudice, impatience and the bone-weary slog of becoming even half-proficient at the job.

Whether Parkinson is raking over the development of leg-spin, or tracking the characters who dominated it – such as Bosanquet, "Father" Marriott and Freeman – he does so with brio. He's good on Ian Peebles and the suicide of his mentor, Aubrey Faulkner. He's good on the naysayers of leg-spin: Archie MacLaren despised the googly, thinking preposterously that it killed the "beauty of high-class batting". He is good, too, on the tribulations of the modern-day leggie.

Parkinson thinks England "developed a national inferiority complex about leg-spin" after Shane Warne showed how it should be done. He also thinks youngsters ought to be encouraged to play twisti-twosti, a table-top game beloved of Bosanquet, which necessitates contortions of the wrist to spin a ball. Parkinson lives in hope of a revival, and dedicates his book in part to Richie Benaud.

We all miss him, especially when a commentator goes into blabbering rapture to describe something Benaud would have summed up in a sentence short enough to fit on a first-class stamp. "The art of commentary is sometimes to let what happened speak for itself," writes Michael Parkinson, using Benaud-like concision to capture his gift in **Remembering Richie**, a collection of his writing for Hodder & Stoughton, a Darby and Joan publishing marriage that lasted more than 55 years. It is one book in an honour guard of titles. **Benaud in Wisden**, edited by Rob Smyth, contains some lovely lines, perfectly weighted, from Dileep Premachandran: "Benaud never made the commentary about him. He could have if he wanted to. After all, he had been one of the great all-rounders of his era... But he wore that greatness as lightly as a cream linen suit." Paul Connolly's **Richie Benaud 1930–2015, Those Summers of Cricket** is heavily illustrated. My favourite photograph shows Benaud leaning back on a padded bench, one booted foot resting on a rail, as he talks to Don Bradman during the tied Test in Brisbane in 1960-61. Bradman wears a dark suit, inappropriately pale socks and a pair of sunglasses. With his hair swept slickly back, he's the spit of Tony Soprano's Uncle Junior, about to condemn someone to a concrete overcoat and eternity with the fishes.

The cure for admiring Ted McDonald was surely to have met him. He was a duplicitous rake. Even RC Robertson-Glasgow, who saw the best in everyone, conceded that McDonald "fell into ways... that somehow foreshadowed tragedy". Nick Richardson's **The Silk Express**, a compelling book about a complicated figure, articulates what Robertson-Glasgow was too polite to say explicitly. McDonald's achievements in the 1920s coincided with the end of Jack Gregory's career and the bloom of Harold Larwood's. He appeared in only 11 Tests for Australia, preferring to play in England, where he eventually became Nelson's pro in the Lancashire League. History has consequently marginalised him, even though he took almost 1400 first-class wickets. He claimed 205 of them for Lancashire in 1925, the prelude to their four Championship wins in five high summers.

For almost a decade, McDonald's scary pace, achieved with a supremely gorgeous action, made him the highest-paid cricketer. Nelson lured him with wages and perks that are the equivalent of a lottery win today: £500 per season, plus talent money and free accommodation. But successes were constantly interrupted by calamities, usually self-inflicted, which make both his life and his career seem like a string of comebacks. He liked to get drunk with society's underbelly. This was a minor vice compared with his chief one – crazy gambling. If two flies were buzzing around a room, McDonald would put a wad on which of them flew out of the window first. When he died at the age of 46, following a freak road accident in 1937, his estate was worth a mere £300. He embodied that ancient Greek belief about a man's character determining his fate.

Stephen Chalke's **Summer's Crown** will be reread until the pages drop out. Sumptuously produced and written in window-clear prose, Chalke's history of the 125-year-old Championship makes you wish the world's physicists weren't dawdling over the invention of a time machine, enabling us to pop back and see for ourselves what he describes.

The standard nuts and bolts – the Championship's awkward birth and repeated tinkering with the points system – never obscure the characters, each spotlighted through quotation, anecdote and portraiture.

Two of the best are locked together to illustrate what Chalke calls the "no-nonsense hardness" of the postwar era. Warwickshire's Tom Dollery fought in Africa. On his return, hearing a team-mate complain of thirst and asking for a drinks break, he is aghast: "Drinks? What do you want drinks for? In the desert we had two pints of water a day – and that was for you *and* your vehicle." George Emmett, of Gloucestershire, bore a passing resemblance to Prince Philip and could be just as cantankerous. Anyone applauding a catch too loudly was quickly rebuked: "There's enough exhibitionism in cricket without your adding to it." A third vignette has Derek Randall answering the door in his pads during a snowy January. "I'm breaking them in for the summer," he explains to his bemused caller, before escorting him into the lounge, where Mrs Randall is breaking in a second pair.

Simon Lister waits until the last page of **Fire in Babylon** before quoting CLR James's most resonant line: "What do they know of cricket...?" He should have planted it on the first page because he answers the question just as comprehensively as James did, and also gives it a modern relevance.

Books usually inspire films. In flipping that process, Lister's important work does more than merely complement Stevan Riley's 2010 documentary, which explained how West Indies, unleashing fast bowlers like some nuclear attack, pummelled everyone into submission from the mid-1970s. The staging posts of that process are familiar. But what Lister does in print, with Jamesian scholarship, is something Riley couldn't have done on screen without making his film longer than *Apocalypse Now*. He adds depth and breadth, and places the story in the wider context of social history, genealogy and race. He explains why cricket in the 1970s was so welded to identity and status in the disparate Caribbean islands, and also why the thunderous success of the team mattered to first- and second-generation West Indians in Britain (especially during the racial tensions of the early 1980s).

Lister's dignified central character is Clive Lloyd, the subject of his earlier biography, *Supercat*. "Those who say Lloyd was a limited captain... understand little of cricket, less of leadership and nothing of the West Indies," snorts Lister with a peppery brusqueness. Lloyd made a splintered dressing-room whole again through judicious man-management, and rid it of the "detested" sobriquet "calypso cricketers", a euphemism for sparkly entertainers lacking substance. Lister is even-handed. He gives a fair shout to critics who complained about intimidatory tactics. Geoffrey Boycott is then summoned to the witness box to point out the bleeding obvious: "Any human being who tries to tell me he wouldn't have played four fast bowlers because they were winning Test matches is a liar," he says. "We'd all have done it." I finished *Fire in Babylon* certain that CLR James would have greatly admired it.

I confess prejudice towards WG Grace. The more I read about his shenanigans, the less I like him. In **Wisden on Grace**, edited by Jonathan Rice, Geoffrey Moorhouse's opinion of his character chimes with my own. "He has never been a hero of mine," writes Moorhouse, recalling the moment he discovered Grace was "sometimes a shameless cheat" and not a "particularly attractive" personality. Not much he wasn't. He was violently bad-tempered, dictatorial, vindictive, thin-skinned, snobby and colossally arrogant. As a cricketer, he was stellar; as a human being, he was not. Nowadays the shamateur would hardly be a candidate for MCC's Spirit of Cricket Lecture at Lord's – he might not even be al-

Richard Tomlinson's **Amazing Grace**, marking the centenary of WG's death, runs into some speculative cul-de-sacs. Even someone as mega-famous as Grace left mysteries behind, which means observations often have to be prefaced with "possibly" or "probably". There's a further quandary for Tomlinson: How many anecdotes were wishful thinking or deliberate fabrications designed to enhance the reputation of the teller? As Tomlinson points out, MCC's *Memorial Biography* was sanitised to satisfy Mrs Grace's desire to immortalise her husband as "bluff, genial and boyish". Grace's memoirs are as unreliable as some of the eyewitness testimony and Tomlinson also says that bandwagon-jumpers "exaggerated their familiarity" with him. Chief among them was that terrible fraud Pelham Warner who, while never a member of Grace's inner circle, imagined enough "personal reminiscences" to con the BBC into making a programme about them.

Tomlinson's brief afterword, going into detail about his research, ought really to be read first, because you learn how Grace's public persona was initially shaped and subsequently preserved. In it you glimpse what *Amazing Grace* could have been if Tomlinson had freed himself from the corset of conventional biography. The best bits aren't descriptions of events or the regurgitation of established facts – recorded in a yard of other books – but his interpretation of them. His WG is an innovator in tactics and technique. He portrays Grace as a relatively impecunious and socially inferior chap whose stupendous talent enabled him to soar above the hypocrisies of the class system. Tomlinson thinks his grab for money – Grace was a financial incompetent, soon parted from what he earned – stemmed from the nagging fear of being without it. This wasn't the most darkly troubling of his psychological burdens. Food and drink were consumed gluttonously, first for solace, then as a dependency, finally as a compulsive disorder. Despite his swagger, Grace was as vulnerable and insecure as anyone. I still didn't warm to him. I did, however, warm to Tomlinson, a good and insightful writer.

David Frith has spent almost half a century chasing WG's contemporary, AE Stoddart, which makes Boswell's shadowing of Dr Johnson seem like a recreational pursuit. **Stoddy: England's Finest Sportsman** is the product of a magnificent obsession. It is his third book about him, each surpassing the last. Stoddart tears through the pages like a fictional character in an improbable yarn. He was born in South Shields and spoke with the "faintest" Geordie accent, but looked like a Home Counties gent. He behaved like one, too, even when shooting himself in 1915. The reasons for his suicide were manifold: money worries, bad mental and physical health, a lacklustre marriage. Incompetence, stupidity or malice had also led MCC to refuse an application to reactivate his lapsed membership. Frith is incandescent that nothing publicly – such as an English Heritage blue plaque – commemorates Stoddart's feats. He shouldn't worry. With words, he builds his monument high.

The vast proportion of ghosted autobiographies are bland, self-justifying and bereft of insight or wit. As a rule, you'll find more literary merit in the *Argos Catalogue*. Here are three exceptions. The fabulous opening chapter of David Lloyd's **Last in the Tin Bath** is a bit like Tony Capstick's "They Dunt Know They're Born Today". Anyone under 40 won't recognise the boyhood Lloyd describes. Anyone under 20 will assume he once shook hands with Queen Victoria. But anyone of roughly the same generation, from a working-class background, will see their past unspool in front of them: the rows of terraced housing without central heating; the outside lavatory; the extended family everywhere in the town; the stumps chalked roughly on walls. It offers a new definition of earthy Northern Soul.

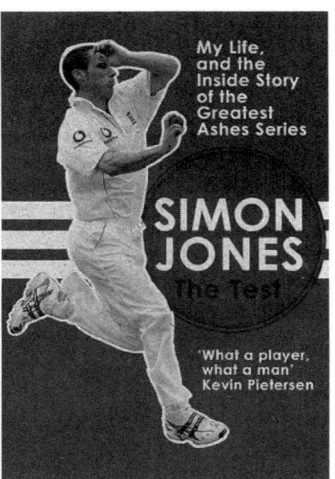

Andrew Flintoff's **Second Innings** reminds us that the best of men – even superheroes are only men at best. It separates the Flintoff we know from the Flintoff we don't. Developing a split personality, a mask for his fame, macho Fred, the ultra-confident showman, coexists with Andrew, the timid introvert. Flintoff likens his career peak to "being in a soap opera and gradually turning into the character you're acting". He is frank about the bouts of depression that grew from it, which will help a lot of people suffering in silence.

Simon Jones's **The Test** is exceptional. Along with Marcus Trescothick's revelatory *Coming Back to Me*, published in 2008, it has succeeded in renewing my faith in the genre.

Jones weaves his life story around the 2005 Ashes. Making the series freshly relevant is a feat in itself. We couldn't start the last Ashes without first celebrating the tenth anniversary of that belting summer, the scenes from which ran on a perpetual loop. It was nostalgia overkill, suggesting we were taking refuge in old memories because we didn't fancy our chances of matching them. But everything about 2005 had been said or seen so often that, soon, nothing about it carried any emotional charge.

Jones restores it by personalising the journey from Lord's to The Oval. The best sports books are never about sport alone, but the human condition. Jones shares his fears, failings and fallibilities. He discusses his hell-bent ambition and the business of bowling brutally fast, likening it to the possession of a 'superpower". None of this would have been possible without Jon Hotten, his literary ventriloquist, who helps give him such a distinctive voice. The style and rhythm of the early chapters are reminiscent of a mud-and-grit David Peace novel in which the first-person narrator becomes luminously aware of being caught up in something much bigger than himself.

FILM REVIEW

The miscue and the slog

RAKESH RAMAMOORTHY

The Indian cricket film is a strange entity in that it barely exists. Considering the Indian public's passion for cricket and popular cinema, one would expect filmmakers to exploit the sport's inherent drama and spectacle. The release of *Lagaan*, a delightfully well-researched cricket tale, could have been a watershed moment; but a decade and a half downstream, we have only had a narrow trickle of well-made cricket films: *Iqbal* and *Kai Po Che* in Hindi, *1983* in Malayalam, and *Chennai 600028* and *Jeeva* in Tamil. The two biopics, *Azhar and MS Dhoni: The Untold Story,* do not upset this trend. *Azhar* is an unmitigated disaster, while *MS Dhoni* is engaging without being exceptional.

Most disconcerting about *Azhar* is its blatant attempt to establish that Mohammad Azharuddin is innocent of the charges of match-fixing, all while claiming that the film is a fictional narrative merely inspired by a few events in Azharuddin's life. The crude strategy of referring to cricketers by their first names to evade lawsuits might have been acceptable if it were a gripping narrative, but in *Azhar* they merely add to the woes of a movie that offers neither the insight of a factual account nor the fanciful delights of a fictitious one.

As a revelatory narrative, the movie could also have been a nostalgic account, providing a glimpse into the cricket of the 1980s and '90s. Azharuddin's long career coincides with several memorable moments of Indian cricket: the cricket carnivals of Sharjah, the emergence of Sachin Tendulkar, the traumatic 1996 World Cup semi-final. Alternatively, the filmmaker could have taken refuge in fiction – a well-crafted story that dispenses with real names, and charts the rise and fall of a reticent, stylish cricketer from a minority comnunity, cleared of all charges and triumphantly returning to play his hundredth Test match.

One can't help questioning the movie's assumption that the cricket or film audiences of today would be emotionally invested in the truth behind the allegations. As the former captain himself remarked at one of the promotional events, he has few fans left. A plot that exploits the pathos inherent in the Azharuddin story – the tragic tale of an incredibly talented yet flawed personality, who falls from the heights of fame and glory – might have been more effective in reinstating the once popular batsman in the public imagination.

The movie does have rare flashes of brilliance: The humiliating experience of the great batsman being coaxed to demonstrate his wristy shots at a gym opening would move most cricket fans. The motif of the opposing lawyer being a former fan could have been interesting. Sachin's straight drive is adeptly re-enacted, as is Azhar's batting style in the climactic cricket sequence. Yet, other cricketing scenes fail to impress. The presentation of one of the biggest achievements of Azharuddin's career, him scoring centuries in his first three Tests, is rather tame.

Where *Azhar* is a squandered opportunity, *MS Dhoni: The Untold Story* is a thoroughly enjoyable film with a relatable rise-of-the-underdog narrative. The story of a young boy from Ranchi becoming one of the most loved cricketers of his time is one that needs little embellishment, and the movie's success lies in playing to the strengths of this source material. Pan Singh Dhoni's quest for job security and his son's despair at being stuck in the daily routine of a ticket collector were bound to strike a chord. And by revealing that Dhoni's signature helicopter shot was invented by his friend Santosh, the film acknowledges the contribution of a talented cricketer who never made it to the top.

The movie successfully evokes two vital aspects of Indian cricket fandom: the visual pleasure derived from the game and the partisan joy of backing one's national side. Apart from the striking casting of a young Yuvraj Singh, also notable is the performance of the lead actor, Sushant Singh Rajput, whose imitation of Dhoni's mannerisms is uncanny. The cricketing sequences are well executed, and movie Dhoni's characteristic gait, flamboyant strokeplay and unorthodox style evoke the cricketer the Indian public has come to know and love. The spectacle loses its sheen in some parts of the second half where, instead of re-creating cricket matches, Rajput has been inserted into the original footage of the match. But it is obvious that the makers of the film have sensed the pulse of Indian cricket fans, who relished the opportunity to relive the triumphs of 2007 and 2011.

But for all its virtues, *MS Dhoni: The Untold Story* is not a masterpiece of the genre. It is consistently hagiographic, and the controversies that have plagued his career are all omitted. There is no reference to the nepotism and corruption that plagues Indian cricket.

Fans will love the feel-good tale of *MS Dhoni*, and love to hate *Azhar*. However, the wait for that perfect cricket film, one that is as frank and insightful as it is entertaining, continues.

Rakesh Ramamoorthy teaches at the Department of English, St John's College, Kerala, and his doctoral research is on South Asian Cricket Narratives.

OBITUARIES

AKHTAR, JAVED, who died on July 8, aged 75, was a Pakistani cricketer and umpire who was born in Delhi and played one Test match, against England at Headingley in 1962. He officiated in 18 Tests and 40 ODIs. The last of those was between England and India in the 1999 World Cup in Birmingham, where his decision to uphold a Javagal Srinath appeal for lbw against Graham Thorpe led to quite a bit of chatter. His penultimate Test as an official – the game between England and South Africa at Headingley in 1998 – was marred by controversy as well when he was charged with bias in favour of England after he gave eight questionable decisions against South Africa in what was the series decider.

"[L]ast man (Makhaya) Ntini was hit on the pad by (Darren) Gough and Pakistani umpire Javed Akhtar made the last and easiest of the decisions that had brought him four days of painful notoriety," reported the Wisden Cricketers' Almanack.

He officiated in one more Test – against Australia in Rawalpindi – before retiring in 1999. But in 2000, Dr Ali Bacher alleged that Akhtar was involved in match-fixing, hinting at the umpire's conduct in that Headingley Test. *The Telegraph*, at the time, reported that Bacher had claimed Akhtar was "on the payroll of a Pakistani bookmaker" for the game that England won by 23 runs.

Akthar rubbished the claims and sued Bacher, but the South African did not turn up for the hearing, and the Justice Karamat Nazir Bhandari Commission in Pakistan subsequently cleared Akhtar (in 2002) of any wrongdoing.

Javed Akhtar: Played one Test, officiated in 18. – *Getty Images*

As a cricketer, Akthar finished with 187 wickets and 835 runs in 51 first-class matches. He represented Rawalpindi and Services between 1959-60 and 1975-76.

ALLIN, TIM died on January 4, aged 28, after falling from the Torridge Bridge in Bideford, north Devon. Allin was a fast bowler who played for Warwickshire. He took a break from representative cricket in 2014, concentrating on earning a living away from the pro game, before settling back into the club game with North Devon CC. He had also worked as a professional

"Last man Ntini was hit on the pad by Gough and Pakistani umpire Javed Akhtar made the last and easiest of the decisions that had brought him four days of painful notoriety." — *Getty Images*

cricket coach. "He was a great lad who always had a smile on his face," said England's Chris Woakes.

BANERJEE, SUBRATA was an international umpire who died on August 19, aged 71. Banerjee had a 15-year career at the international level, where he officiated in 13 ODIs and one women's Test. He made his international debut in November 1983, in an ODI between India and West Indies in Baroda. His last international appearance came in May 1998, in a match between India and Kenya in Gwalior.

Banerjee, son of Sunil Banerjee, the former Test umpire, also stood in 64 first-class matches, besides serving as a television umpire in ODIs, and a reserve umpire in a Test between India and England in Mohali in 2001.

BANNISTER, JOHN DAVID 'JACK', who died on January 23, aged 85, was a medium-pacer who took 1198 first-class wickets. His figures of 10 for 41 against Combined Services in 1959 remain the best innings figures by a Warwickshire bowler. While still a player, he began a career in journalism, writing for the *Birmingham Post*.

His most significant contribution came when he set up the Professional Cricketers' Association of which he was secretary, and then chairman and president. He helped establish a standard employment contract and minimum wage for cricketers, and set to work establishing their first pension system. Later, he helped negotiate a solution when some counties were keen to ban players who had appeared in Packer's World Series. The roots of better salries, freedom of movement and more equitable terms and conditions for players all grew from there.

He was chairman of the Cricket Writers' Club between 1994 and 1996. According to George Dobell, Bannister referred to Richie Benaud as his "best friend in life" and, every week from 1987 – when Bannister joined Benaud in the BBC TV commentary box – to three weeks before Benaud's death in April 2015, the pair exchanged racing tips. Golf was another passion they shared.

BANNON, JOHN, who died on December 13, aged 72, was South Australia's longest-serving premier and a Cricket Australia director. He served on the board of CA for 15 years from 2000. David Peever, CA chairman, said: "John bravely battled illness over many years, but never did it dampen his passion for cricket or his home state of South Australia. We will miss John's stature, his knowledge and his wisdom. He provided the Board with astute judgment and decades of experience navigating complex and challenging issues."

BARUAH, HEMANGA, who died of liver failure on November 14 aged 49, was a medium-pacer who took 50 wickets in 20 Ranji Trophy matches for Assam, with a best of 5 for 38 against Tripura in Guwahati in 1991-92. In March 1985, he played an Under-19 'Test' in Patna, sharing the new ball with Jaspal Singh and dismissing Tom Moody and Dean Reynolds, the Australian captain.

BANSAL, JASPAL SINGH, who died of cancer on November 12, aged 47, was a brisk opening bowler who started with Delhi in the Ranji Trophy, but had more success with Punjab, taking 6 for 87 against Jammu & Kashmir in November 1989. He was also a handy batsman, spanking 78 against Haryana in the next match. When West Indies toured in 1987-88, Jaspal played for India Under-25 in Chandigarh, and encountered an in-form Viv Richards: "My captain Sanjay Manjrekar asked me not to pitch the ball on the leg side after I had been hit for a couple of boundaries through midwicket – but I was actually bowling outside off stump!" Richards escaped him (he retired after making 138), but Jaspal dismissed Richie Richardson and Roger Harper, and later scored 70. In 2000 he moved to Australia, where he turned out for Dubbo. His older brother, Gurusharan Singh, played one Test for India in 1989-90.

BURROWS, ALFRED, who died on August 16, 2015, aged 61, had a peculiar career in Indian domestic cricket, scoring 193 – his fourth first-class century – in what turned out to be his final match, for Railways against Vidarbha in December 1985. A stylish batsman, born into an Anglo-Indian family in Chennai, Burrows had twice been selected for Central Zone, including against the 1983-84 West Indian tourists; he made 31 against an attack spearheaded by Michael Holding and Wayne Daniel. He later took up coaching and umpiring, and stood in the first two seasons of the unauthorised Indian Cricket League. Four years before his death he emigrated to Western Australia.

CAMACHO, GEORGE STEPHEN, died on October 2, aged 69. Steve Camacho was the longest-serving chief executive of the West Indies Cricket Board, and the last Test cricketer to hold the position. Appointed the first executive secretary in 1982, he operated virtually on his own from a small office at Kensington Oval in Bridgetown. He was upgraded to CEO when the board moved their headquarters to Antigua, but stood down in 2000 after the first signs of the cancer that eventually killed him. During his 18 years in charge he also served as manager, assistant manager and selector of West Indies teams, and was a member of the ICC's chief executives' committee.

A Guyanese of Portuguese descent, he was one of their last white Test players. A patient, technically correct opener who batted in glasses, Camacho played 11 Tests for West Indies and 35 times for his native Guyana between 1964-65 and 1978-79. His modest averages – 29 in Tests and 34 in first-class cricket – did little justice to his talent, which was first evident in an innings of 157 for Guyana Colts against the Australian tourists in 1964-65 at Bourda, where he had developed his passion for the game. Camacho's 87 against England at Port-of-Spain in his debut series in 1967-68 remained his highest Test score: "He played hitherto unrevealed strokes all round the wicket," reported *Wisden*. He struggled in Australia in 1968-69, but retained his place for the tour of England that followed, where he topped the Test averages with 46. But an unremarkable home series against India in 1970-71 proved his last. An unexpected opportunity to revive his Test career in England in 1973 was cut short by a crushing blow to the face from Andy Roberts in the tour game against Hampshire. He continued playing for Guyana, latterly as captain, until he turned to administration in 1979.

Donald Carr: England captain and administrator. – *Getty Images*

CARR, DONALD BRYCE, who died on June 11, aged 89, was an England captain and administrator. Carr played two Tests, both on the 1951-52 tour of India. He captained in the absence of the injured Nigel Howard in the Fifth Test in Madras, where India registered their first ever Test win.

A right-hand batsman and left-arm spinner, Carr made 19,257 first-class runs and grabbed 327 wickets in a 23-year career. He led Derbyshire between 1955 and 1962 and was named Wisden Cricketer of the Year in 1960.

In Asia, Carr is best known as the leader of the expedition that 'kidnapped' Idris Baig, the Pakistani umpire, during an MCC tour there, and gave him the 'water treatment', dunking the umpire with buckets of water in a misplaced sense of jollity that would have earned the players (seven were involved, according to reports) bans today.

Carr served as secretary of the Test and County Cricket Board, the forerunner of the current England and Wales Cricket Board. He was also an assistant secretary of MCC, managed three England overseas tours and later became an International Cricket Council match referee. Carr's son, John, also became a first-class cricketer, with Middlesex, and later followed his father into cricket administration.

CHAKRABARTI, SAMIR, who died on December 11, aged 72, was a medium-pacer who played Ranji Trophy cricket for Services and Bengal. In 41 first-class matches, he claimed 139 wickets.

COZIER, TONY, the voice of West Indies cricket, died on May 11, aged 75. Having begun writing about cricket as a teenager, he didn't stop till his last days, with his work over the past couple of years reflecting his anguish at the state of affairs of cricket in his beloved Caribbean.

"He was not just a great journalist, but also a great ambassador. He represented West Indies wherever he went. He educated people around the world about our cricket, our people, our culture and who we are," said the West Indies Cricket Board in its tribute. *(Obit by Vaneisa Baksh on page 776.)*

CROWE, MARTIN died on March 3, aged 53, after a long battle with cancer. Making his debut for New Zealand at 19, against Australia, he grew to be one of his country's best batsmen – and an even better captain. His attacking tactics saw them sailing through the league stages of the 1992 World Cup before they were thwarted by Inzamam-ul-Haq in the semi-final.

"Wasim Akram reminded me just the other day that Martin was the greatest batsman he ever bowled to – no higher praise than that," said Jeff Crowe, his brother and ICC match referee.

Crowe had 5444 Test runs from 77 matches at 45.36 and 4704 from 143 ODIs. He retired with New Zealand records for the most Test runs, highest Test score (299), most half-centuries (35) and most hundreds (17) – the last of which still stands.

Crowe devised a format that would set the foundation for the T20 game. He became a mentor for several New Zealand players, including Martin Guptill and Ross Taylor, whom he described as "the two sons I never had". Having announced that the lymphoma he had battled in 2012-13 had returned a year later, he became a rallying factor in New Zealand's remarkable

Voice in the Windies

VANEISA BAKSH

When Tony Cozier died on May 11, 2016, it felt like a rock of ages had been yanked from the foundation of West Indian cricket. For more than fifty years he had been its soundtrack: a joyful aria that had segued into more of a dirge as he narrated its decline.

He was inextricably connected to the fortunes of the game he loved with a deep and obsessive passion from childhood. A memory of West Indies cricket does not resonate without Tony Cozier in the background, and sometimes playing a starring role.

Winston Anthony Lloyd Cozier was deeply influenced by his father's passions. He was brought up in an environment of reading, writing and cricket. His father, Edward Lloyd Cozier, wrote books, edited newspapers and magazines across the Caribbean and gave him his first full-time newspaper job in the Barbadian *Daily News*, where he began writing about cricket. As a teenager, he covered a Test match in 1955 for the *St Lucian Voice* when his father was editor there. He studied journalism at Carleton University in Canada.

A memory of West Indies cricket does not resonate without Tony Cozier in the background. — *Getty Images*

He did his first radio Test match commentary in 1965, and television came with Kerry Packer's World Series Cricket on Channel Nine in Australia in the late seventies. With commentary he found the voice that became wildly popular around the world because of its distinctive Barbadian lilt, his wit, his sense of humour and, above all, his insightful coverage of the game.

He was a pioneer in a field that had hitherto been dominated by English voices and he brought a Caribbean perspective. Like CLR James, he analysed cricket nd cricketers within the context of their roots and culture, deepening the understanding of what had been deemed a distinctive West Indian style of play. His presence offered West Indians a marker with which they could measure, and feel, their significance in the broader world of cricket.

Over time, Tony developed a phenomenal encyclopaedic knowledge, which he wove into his commentary at a time when statistics and records were not readily available to broadcast teams. In 1970, he began publishing the West Indian Cricket Annual, which ran for over two decades.

After his death, it was evident in the hundreds of comments on social media that he had touched many lives – spectators and fans, journalists and commentators, cricketers and other athletes – for he was not just a trove of cricket information, he was also a keen follower of sports. He played for the Barbados national hockey team as well as cricket clubs Vanderers and Carlton. In his unassuming way, he generously shared information and advice.

In Barbados, the media centre at Kensington Oval carries his name, and he has been widely celebrated throughout the world, even with honorary life membership at the Marylebone Cricket Club for his contribution to cricket.

Born to Maggie Cozier in Barbados on July 10, 1940, he inhabited the Caribbean with the intimacy of one who has lived inside its nooks and histories. He spent long periods in the various islands as his father moved around editing different newspapers over time. Later through his own broadcast career (which spanned over the BBC, Sky, Channel Nine, the Caribbean Broadcasting Corporation, the Associated Press and *The Independent*) he tasted freely of what every territory had to offer, and shared it with his various audiences, whether through radio, television or the weekly newspaper columns that he continued to write right up to the very end.

Those final columns were bitter and almost despairing as he watched the game being brought to its knees by maladministration that had also trained its guns on him. He had been watching its decline for more than 25 years. At least he saw some sun shine on West Indies cricket in its triple World T20 victories in 2016.

The rotund figure with the hat and the microphone the cricket world had met fifty years ago had become gaunt and angular though illness, but never did he lose his spirit or passion for the game he loved and represented.

He is survived by children Craig and Natalie.

Lasting legacy: Martin Crowe retired with a host of New Zealand records and went on to mentor several of those who followed in his footsteps. – *Getty Images*

run to the 2015 final when the World Cup returned to the Antipodes. *(Obit by Greg Chappell on page 104.)*

DESAI, KANTHILAL RANCHODJI, who died on July 23, aged 84, played 19 matches for Gujarat as a batsman in the 1960s. His 795 runs in 19 matches included the top score of 117.

FERNANDES, ANTHONY LONGINUS, died on December 19, aged 70. Tony Fernandes was a tall, nippy swing bowler who took exactly 100 first-

...ss wickets, mainly for Baroda, with a best of 6 for 41 against Maharashtra 1968-69. And he was a handy batsman, who hit ten first-class fifties. Fernandes also represented West Zone, appearing in three Duleep Trophy finals and against the 1969-70 Australian tourists, when he dismissed Ian Chappell. His brother Leslie, a wicketkeeper, also played for Baroda; they combined have Sunil Gavaskar caught behind in a Ranji Trophy match in 1972-73.

GANTEAUME, ANDREW GORDON, who died on February 17, aged 95, was a West Indies wicketkeeper-batsman who holds the record for the highest Test average, having made 112 in his only Test innings. He shared an opening stand worth 173 with George Carew but took four and a half hours over his century in the drawn Test against England at Queen's Park Oval in 1948.

He was criticised for taking too long to score his runs, with Gerry Gomez, the captain, sending a note to Ganteaume and his batting partner Frank Worrell saying, "I want you to push on now. We are behind the clock and need to score more quickly." In his autobiography, Ganteaume echoed his supporters who believed he was a victim of "establishment" politics. While he was named on the 1957 tour of England at the age of 36, he did not get to play a game. He featured in 50 first-class games for Trinidad and Tobago, making 1785 runs at an average of 34.81.

On Ganteaume's 95th birthday on January 22, Dave Cameron, West Indies Cricket Board president, paid tribute to West Indies' oldest Test cricketer: "He is one of the stalwarts in Trinidad and Tobago and West Indies cricket ... His most memorable performance on the field will forever be a famous performance in our history. Andy has also contributed a lot off the field as well, especially with the development of our cricket."

GARUDACHAR B K, who died on February 26, aged 99, was an all-rounder who was Karnataka's first star player and one who was largely responsible for the team gaining respectability on the Ranji circuit in the 1940s. He scored 1126 runs from 27 matches and claimed 100 wickets. "He was one of the finest cricketers not to have played for India but I never saw any bitterness in him," said Gundappa Viswanath. "He was known for his batting when he began but turned out to be a very good bowler as well – he could bowl off-breaks, leg-breaks, googlies and medium-pace."

In the 1941-42 season, Garudachar took a then-record 34 wickets in four matches. In Karnataka's run to the final, he had 6 for 46 when Hyderabad were bowled out for 69, top-scored with 56 in the second innings, and picked up 5 for 78 as they won by 111 runs. Against Tamil Nadu, he top-scored again, with 57 out of 147, picked up 6 for 56, including MJ Gopalan in the first innings, and followed it up with 8 for 99 in the second. In the final, Karnataka lost to Mumbai. Garudachar had the wickets of Madhav Mantri, Vijay Merchant and Khandu Rangnekar.

Garudachar, who also played for United Provinces and Mumbai, led Kar-

Grand old man of Karnataka cricket: BK Garudachar was one of the finest cricketers not to play for India, said Gundappa Viswanath. – *Wisden India*

nataka in the 1946 semi-final against Holkar, a match known for Holkar' record score of 912 for 8.

"In 1946, out of the blue, I got a telegram asking me to lead Karnataka in that game in Indore," he said. "When I joined the team at the Mumbai railway station, I was shocked to see that apart from B Frank and YS Ramaswamy, the rest were all kids who spent the entire train ride studying for their university exams!

"The match was played at the Yeshwant Club ground where the wicket was at a higher level than the outfield. There was not a blade of grass on the ground. If you touched the ball, it would go for four. When Holkar scored 900-plus, it was probably equal to 400 runs,"

Holkar's 912 had five centuries, including one from skipper CK Nayudu. Mysore were shot out for 190 with Chandu Sarwate, one of the centurions, picking up 9 for 61. Following on, Mysore gave a better account of themselves making 509 for 6, Garudachar scoring his only century: 164.

During his innings, Nayudu asked if it was true that Garudachar played tennis. When Garudachar told him of his early days as champion in Benares, Nayudu reportedly said: "There are a couple of national doubles champions here. If you have the stamina, let's teach them a lesson." The match began after the day's play ended. Nayudu and Garudachar came back from a set down to level the score before dusk gave way to darkness and the game had to be called off.

Born and raised in the coffee country of Chikmagalur, Garudachar was gifted student, who spent four years earning a degree at the Benares University. While this led to his representing United Provinces, it also allowed him to play tennis, and he was the university champion for his entire tenure.

Garudachar lost what might have been his best years to the Second World War, when his expertise with metals was of more use to the nation than his ability to take wickets or score runs. As an inspector with the office of the Director General of Munitions in Bombay, Garudachar found himself in a critical role. "My job was to inspect the steel produced in India, and also that which was extracted from German ships seized in the high seas as good enough to go to the defence forces' factories to make arms," he once said.

Garudachar was a rare old-timer who thought that the game had changed for the better. "There is a tremendous improvement in cricket values and cricket standards since my days," he said.

In his final years, he immersed himself in classical music and reading ancient works of literature. His collection included the complete works of *Kalidasa* in Sanskrit from which he could reel off verses at will.

GOVINDAN, I VELAYUDHAN, who died on March 18, 2015, aged about 80, was a medium-paced all-rounder who played 15 Ranji Trophy matches for Kerala from 1957-58. He was ignored for five seasons after 1960-61 but, recalled in November 1966, made an undefeated 102 from No. 9 against Andhra at Vijayawada. However, in the next two games, he fell for ducks to two Test bowlers – Syed Abid Ali and BS Chandrasekhar – and was dropped again, this time for good.

GRAVENEY, JOHN KENNETH RICHARD, who died on October 25, aged 90, was a fast-medium swing bowler who mixed great skill with wholehearted commitment, until his career was curtailed by a back injury. Older brother of Tom, and father of David, Ken was the founder of Gloucestershire's Graveney dynasty, and served the county as captain, chairman and president, sometimes in fractious times.

GRAVENEY, THOMAS WILLIAM died on November 3, aged 88, nine days after his brother Ken. When it came to earning marks for artistic impression, or inspiring lines of poetic enchantment, few England batsmen have ranked higher than Tom Graveney. Not everyone was keen to rhapsodise: Many of cricket's more pragmatic minds – Len Hutton and Peter May among them – remained immune to his charms, and doubted his temperament for Test cricket. Like David Gower, Graveney became the subject of anguished national debate.

Perhaps only in England could a player of such natural talent have been treated with suspicion: Richie Benaud, Ian Johnson and Frank Worrell insisted he would have been an automatic selection in their sides. It was hard to argue with his weight of runs. In a career lasting more than 20 years, he scored nearly 48,000 at almost 45, including 122 centuries. Of English players since

In a career lasting more than 20 years, Tom Graveney scored nearly 48,000 at almost 45, including 122 centuries. — *Popperfoto/Getty Images*

the war, only Geoff Boycott has been more prolific. And, in a fragmented Test career that began 1951 and ended in 1969 he scored almost 5000 at 44, with 11 hundreds. These were hardly the figures of a dilettante.

What was not up for debate was his easy grace. He had a long reach and high backlift, and his off side play was a study in elegance. Through leg he was less orthodox, hooking off the front foot, but he was never flustered. If cricket were destroyed and only Graveney survived, wrote Neville Cardus, it could be reconstructed "from his way of batting, from the man himself". He relied on his top hand, allowing the bat to swing through the stroke like a pendulum. But, while he might have conveyed the impression that he was naturally gifted, he trained assiduously, always arriving first at the ground. "He would not miss his morning practice for anything," said Ron Headley, a future team-mate at Worcestershire. "He liked to have a bat in his hand every day."

Graveney approached nets like an innings, batting defensively at first, then easing into a more attacking mode. His talent extended to his fielding, and he was a magnificent golfer.

His public persona was of an affable West Countryman who took top-flight sport in his stride. The reality was different. Born in Northumberland, he retained a propensity for plain speaking. "He was his own man and would tell you exactly what he thought," said Frank McHugh, his Gloucestershire team-mate. His single-mindedness shone through in two major controversies. In 1960, when he lost the Gloucestershire captaincy, he left immediately and spent a year playing Second XI and club cricket while qualifying for Worcestershire. And, nine years later, his international career was cut short when he appeared in a benefit match during a Test, and was suspended.

A first England call-up came against South Africa at Old Trafford in 1951.

he was afflicted by nerves and his technique was tested on a damp pitch; but though he made only 15, he created a good impression. "Full of cultured promise," said John Arlott on the radio. Graveney scored more than 2000 runs at 48 that summer to earn a place in an understrength England team to tour the subcontinent. In the Second Test in Bombay he compiled 175 in eight hours, one of six centuries on a productive trip.

He played in all four Tests against India at home in 1952, but with a best of only 73. In county cricket, however, he was in imperious form.

By his own admission, he was fortunate to keep his place throughout the 1953 Ashes, his one significant contribution a first-innings 78 at Lord's. He and Hutton were in command against a tiring attack on the second evening when, an hour from the close, the captain ordered: "Right, that's it for tonight." Graveney retreated into his shell, and was bowled by Ray Lindwall next morning without addition.

In the Caribbean that winter, Graveney hit two fours in an over on a day of funereal scoring. "We don't want any of that," said Hutton. "We've got to grind it out." Graveney was convinced Hutton did not entirely trust any player with rosy cheeks.

The 1957 home series against West Indies might have represented his last chance. He made a duck at Lord's, but in the Third Test at Trent Bridge he survived an early scare, glancing perilously close to Sobers at leg slip, to make a glorious 258. He did not rate it his best Test innings, but it was probably the most important. He followed it with 164 at The Oval.

Despite his habitual modesty, Graveney felt he was the best batsman in the country during his years out of the Test arena. Eventually the clamour for a return could not be ignored. In 1966, surfing waves of goodwill, he made 96 on his comeback, against West Indies at Lord's, followed by centuries at Trent Bridge and The Oval, where his brilliant counter-attacking partnership of 217 with John Murray turned the match. He scored heavily again the next summer, against India and Pakistan, and rated his 151 against Bishan Singh Bedi, Erapalli Prasanna and BS Chandrasekhar on a turning Lord's pitch as his finest Test innings. In the 1968 Ashes, he stood in as emergency captain in Colin Cowdrey's absence during the drawn Fourth Test at Headingley. His final Test century came against Pakistan in Karachi in 1968-69, more than 17 years after his first.

Graveney had been vindicated in his second coming as a Test batsman, but he knew it could not last. His benefit year was in 1969, and a businessman offered him £1000 to play in a Sunday charity match at Luton – on the rest day of the First Test against West Indies at Old Trafford. What happened next was forever disputed. Graveney insisted he called Alec Bedser, the chairman of selectors, explaining the situation; when he was refused permission to play in the benefit game, he asked to be left out of the Test squad. When his name was included, he assumed Bedser had agreed to his absence. It was only as he soaked in the bath on 56 not out at the end of the first day in Manchester that he was told the ban remained. Determined to collect his fee, Graveney took a desultory part in the match at Luton, but retribution was swift. Next day, while he was in the field, the Old Trafford PA announced he had been summoned to a disciplinary hearing at Lord's later that week. It was his 42nd birthday; he knew his international career was over. He was officially banned from the next three Tests, and never chosen again.

His job as an ICC match referee ended when he was appointed in 1994 to a West Indies-Pakistan series, and the Pakistan Cricket Board excavated some injudicious remarks he had made in the wake of the Shakoor Rana affair: "They've been cheating us for 37 years." His greatest honour came in 2004, when he was the first former professional cricketer to be named president of MCC.

GREEN, DAVID MICHAEL, who died on March 19, aged 76, was a Gloucester stalwart and one of county cricket's great entertainers, whether on the field for Lancashire and Gloucestershire or in the press boxes after his retirement. In 1969, he was named one of *Wisden*'s five Cricketers of the Year. The *Almanack*'s judgment was: "David Green is undoubtedly the sort of player the game demands – aggressive, talented and entertaining."

"Perhaps his conviction that professional cricket was about camaraderie as well as victory meant that he did not entirely achieve his potential, but the game – and many who followed it – was richer for his presence," wrote David Hopps.

He was regarded as a teenage prodigy at Manchester Grammar School and won his cricket Blue at Oxford University, where he studied history, for three seasons from 1959. He made his Lancashire debut in the first of those and passed 1000 runs for the first of seven times. It was here, too, according to India's Tiger Pataudi, that he gave the young Nawab the image of a sexy blue blood, an image Pataudi said he could never live up to.

GUDGE, SUNIL CHANDRAKANT, who died on May 3, aged 56, was a leg-spinner who played Ranji Trophy for Maharashtra. He died following a heart attack while watching TV at home. Born on the last day of 1959, Gudge, also a handy lower-order batsman, played 55 first-class matches during a career lasting a decade and a half.

He was an integral part of the strong Maharashtra teams of the 1980s led by Rajendra Bhalekar, Milind Gunjal and Surendra Bhave, taking 110 wickets with best figures of 5 for 46. He scored 1033 runs from 61 innings with a century.

Gudge was part of the India Under-22 side that played against the visiting England side in Pune in 1981-82. He also played for the Board President's XI against the touring Sri Lanka and West Indies teams of 86-87 and 87-88 in Gwalior and Visakhapatnam respectively.

HAMZA ALI, who died on June 9 aged 20 played for Hampshire. He drowned in the River Avon. Ali had also played trial games for the MCC

Young Cricketers. Charlie Freeston, head of player development at Hampshire Cricket, said: "Hamza had formed a very important part of the 2nd XI team since making his debut against Kent last season. He was an incredibly committed and enthusiastic cricketer who always gave 100% ."

HANIF MOHAMMAD, known as 'the Little Master' died on August 11, aged 81. He was, in the words of Scyld Berry, "the first star of Pakistan cricket, who played the longest innings in Test history – his 970-minute 337 against West Indies in Bridgetown in 1957-58 – then followed it a year later with the highest first-class innings to that point, 499 run out. With such feats, broadcast on radio, he turned cricket in Pakistan from the preserve of the Lahore educated elite into the mass sport it is today. Although famous for his immaculate defence and never hitting the ball in the air, Hanif could also attack, and was probably the originator of the reverse-sweep." In 55 Tests, he made 3915 runs at an average of nearly 44.

"They found captains after Kardar, they found bowlers after Fazal. Never found another Hanif," wrote Osman Samiuddin. *(obit by Ayaz Memon on page 50)*

Hanif Mohammad: Never another like the original Little Master. – *Getty Images*

HARRIS, NORMAN HILLIER, who collapsed and died in a London street on November 20, aged 75, was perhaps the most original cricket journalist of his generation. He was also well known as an athletics writer and founding father of the fun run sponsored by his then newspaper, the *Sunday Times*, which was a major event in the early days of the keep-fit craze. He may even deserve the credit for rescuing the word "jogging" from disuse before would-be joggers felt obliged either to run properly or stay on the sofa. But he was also fond of cricket, and as a teenager in his native New Zealand was manning the Hamilton scoreboard in 1958-59 when MCC came to town and Colin Cowdrey was out for a duck. He joined the *Sunday Times* in 1969, and one of his earliest exclusives was an explanation for a plague of misshapen balls in that summer's county matches: Harris tracked the fault down to a production error by an assistant in the ball factory. It was a classic Harris story, of the kind he would keep giving the paper for the next 20 years. "He had a curiosity for the bits of cricket nobody else was interested in," said its former deputy sports editor, Nick Mason.

HASAN JAMIL ALVI, who died on October 7, aged 63, was a left-handed all-rounder who played six ODIs for Pakistan, all at home. He took 3 for 18 at Sahiwal to set up victory over India in October 1978, which helped win a place in the squad for the 1979 World Cup – but he did not appear in any of the matches in England. He was a consistent performer over a 15-year career in domestic cricket, scoring four first-class hundreds – the highest 172 for PIA against Dawood Industries in 1975-76 – and also taking 204 wickets with a best of 5 for 38 for Pakistan Universities against Railways in 1973-74.

HIGGS, KENNETH, a medium-pacer of stamina and accuracy, died on September 7 aged 72. He played only 15 Tests for England, which was strange given both his economy rate (2.14) and average (20.74). For Lancashire (where he opened the bowling with Brian Statham) he claimed more than 1000 first class wickets. He was renowned for getting out top-order batsmen and his most successful series for England saw him take 24 wickets against West Indies in 1966.

Higgs took 7 for 36 on his Championship debut and claimed more than 100 wickets in a season on five occasions. He was named one of *Wisden*'s Five Cricketers of the Year in 1968.

He won his first England cap in 1965, in Statham's last Test, and took eight wickets against South Africa. Alongside a knack for wicket-taking and a parsimonious economy rate, he produced a memorable contribution with the bat to help England win the deciding Test at The Oval against West Indies in 1966, putting on 128 – two runs shy of the world record – for the last wicket with John Snow.

"Higgs was dour and undemonstrative, and though well-liked and respected by his peers, he was unimpressed by figures of authority. Opposing batsmen knew how good he was, however: Higgs wasn't fast, but he was one of those who, by bowling a fuller length than most seamers of his pace, hit the splice persistently and jarred the hands. The ratio be-

Kenneth Higgs: Wisden Cricketer of the Year in 1968. – *Getty Images*

ween specialist batsmen and tailenders among his 71 England victims was astounding," wrote John Thicknesse.

Higgs left Lancashire in 1969, to be the cricket professional at Rishton and run a boarding house in Blackpool, but was talked out of retirement and moved to play for Leicestershire from 1972. He took 4 for 10, including a hat-trick, in the 1974 Benson & Hedges Cup final – although Leicestershire lost – and a few years later scored 98 batting a No. 11, during what remains a club record partnership of 228 with Ray Illingworth.

HILTON, COLIN, who died on October 30, aged 78, was for a few short summers in the late 1950s and early '60s one of the most feared fast bowlers on the county circuit. He joined Lancashire in 1957 via Atherton, his home club, and Ribblesdale Wanderers, and was identified as the long-term successor to Statham. But, as the new decade wore on and Statham showed few signs of decline, Hilton became a victim of the competition for places created by the presence of Higgs and Peter Lever.

He was no more than average height, but broad across the shoulders, and muscular. While his run-up was not especially long, his formidable strength and athleticism generated real pace. A book about his career was called *The White Flash: The story of the fastest English bowler of his time*, yet he had more than just speed. On a helpful pitch he found seam movement and, blessed with long fingers, mastered the subtleties of cutting the ball. He was, however, prone to nerves. The Lancashire captain Bob Barber recalled a match at Trent Bridge against Nottinghamshire, who included Reg Simpson, then in his forties. "He bowled a couple of beamers at Reg, who just moved out of the way as they went whistling past. I said: 'What's going on?' Colin replied: 'Sweaty fingers.' He showed me his hands and they were sweaty. His nervousness was genuine."

HOBDEN, MATTHEW died on January 2 while celebrating the new year with friends in Scotland. He was 22.
The Sussex medium-pacer fell to his death after falling asleep on the roof of the building where he had gone to look at the stars.

Hobden played 18 first-class matches for 48 wickets at 39.35. He had been a regular in the ECB Potential England Performance Programme for two seasons and was touted as a possible future international for the country.

"Matt was a young cricketer with huge potential, and he is going to be missed so badly by all the guys. He made you smile every time you saw him, because he was so excited to be there and wanted to be the best he could," said Kevin Shine, ECB's lead fast bowling coach.

IQBAL HUSSAIN SHEIKH died on January 9, aged 80. Iqbal Sheikh was a Karachi doctor who fitted in 22 first-class matches in Pakistan around his medical duties. A batsman and occasional leg-spinner, he scored 91 for Hyderabad against Khairpur in the Ayub Trophy in 1965-66.

Matthew Hobden: A young cricketer with huge potential. — *Getty Images*

ISRAR ALI, who died on February aged 88, following a bout of pneumo nia had been Pakistan's oldest crick eter since January 2011. He playe in his country's inaugural Test. I all he played four Tests as a left-arm medium-pacer. Five wickets agains Australia in two Tests at home too his international tally to six. That wa to be his last outing for his country and he remained convinced that a dif ference of opinion with Abdul Hafee: Kardar, his captain during the India tour, brought an early end to his inter national career.

Israr claimed 114 wickets at a average of 22.63 from 40 first-class matches, even as he notched up 113(runs. An accident forced his retire ment, but he continued to be involved in the game as an administrator. He was a member of Pakistan's selection committee in 1983 and 1984 and a beneficiary of the Cricketers Benefit Fund Series played in Sharjah.

JADEJA, LALUBHA RAMSINHJI, who died on July 19, 2015, aged 93, played 31 matches, mainly for Saurashtra, over a long career that stretched until 1962-63. A medium- pacer, he took 7 for 61 (and 11 for 137 in the match) against Maharashtra at Rajkot in 1958-59. Three seasons later, by now 39, he claimed successive five-fors against Maharashtra and Baroda. His early matches were for Nawanagar, though he was not a member of their princely Jadeja family, which included Ranjitsinhji and Duleepsinhji.

JOSHI, BHANU, who died on April 17, aged 26, had collided with two other fielders, who were also trying to catch the ball. He succumbed to his injuries in the hospital following a liver rapture and a serious head injury. Bhanu, who used to bat well for his team of Chanderia village, was fielding at mid-on in the match against Chittorgarh in Hokampura village in Rajasthan. "He played every Sunday. He got married two months ago and was work ing in a private company earning Rs 5000 a month. He had done a diploma in mechanical engineering from a polytechnic college in Chittorgarh," said Pooja Sharma, Bhanu's sister, to the *Times of India*.

KANITKAR, HEMANT SHAMSUNDER, who died on June 9, 2015, aged

72, was a compact batsman, noted for the late cut and an inside-out lofted drive. "He could hit a six over extra cover on demand," remembered Milind Gunjal, a former team-mate. He was also a serviceable wicketkeeper. Kanitkar piled up more than 3500 Ranji Trophy runs for Maharashtra, beginning with 151 not out on debut, against Saurashtra in Poona in 1963-64. His dozen centuries for Maharashtra included 250 against Rajasthan in 1970-71; the following season he made 168 for the Rest against an Indian XI. A belated call to national colours came in 1974-75, when he was nearly 32, for the First Test against West Indies in Bangalore. He started by top-scoring with 65, but three failures followed, and he was jettisoned for good. Kanitkar later turned to coaching, and was a state selector. "He had an astute cricketing brain," said his state colleague Yajurvindra Singh. "He was a fabulous captain to play under, never ruffled. He had an expressionless demeanour that stood him well, especially when we played cards." His son, Hrishikesh, also played two Tests for India, in Australia in 1999-2000.

KARIA, PANKIL DHIRAJILAL, died on March 29, 2015, aged 48, of a presumed heart attack while watching the World Cup final on television. A bowler who won two Under-19 one-day caps for India against Australia in 1984-85, Karia also played twice for Saurashtra.

KLINE, LINDSAY FRANCIS, who died on October 2, aged 81, faced the last delivery of one of the most famous of all matches – the tied Test between Australia and West Indies in Brisbane in December 1960. With the scores level, last man Kline nudged the ball, from Wes Hall, towards square leg, and set off for the winning run – but his partner, Ian Meckiff, was run out when Joe Solomon hit the stumps from side-on.

In the famous photograph of that frenzied finale, Kline is running to the safety of the bowler's end, looking over his shoulder to see whether Meckiff has made it. In the heat of the moment, the batsmen were confused: "There was me running for a win," said Kline, "and him running for a tie." Meckiff thought Australia had lost, and was inconsolable until Kline assured him they hadn't.

Although he missed the next two matches, Kline's part in an exciting see-saw series wasn't quite over. He was recalled for the Fourth Test in Adelaide, where West Indies seemed set to take a 2-1 lead when Australia's ninth wicket fell with nearly two hours remaining. A left-arm wrist-spinner with few pretensions to batting, Kline had prepared by having a net against Australia's part-time bowlers, who confounded him repeatedly. A female spectator lamented that it was hardly worth sending him out to the middle, and Kline was forced to agree. But somehow he survived everything the West Indians could muster for 109 minutes, and an unlikely draw was secured when Ken 'Slasher' Mackay chested away Hall's final thunderbolt.

Kline's unbeaten 15 was his highest score, but that was the last of his 13 Tests, after 34 wickets at 22, around five runs cheaper than his overall first-

Australia's Lindsay Kline faced the last delivery of the first tied Test in 1960. Seen here are West Indies and Australian cricketers who played that game at an event to mark its anniversary. — *Getty Images*

class average. He did tour England later in 1961, but there were few opportunities for another slow bowler in a side captained by leg-spinner Richie Benaud. Kline nonetheless took 54 wickets in the county games, including 5 for 16 against Nottinghamshire. He retired from first-class cricket after one more season at home.

Born in 1934 in Camberwell, east Melbourne, Kline was playing for the prestigious Melbourne Cricket Club by 1952-53. A tall man, with a kangaroo-like hop just before delivery, he was unusually accurate for a bowler of his type. He did not turn his stock ball prodigiously, but had a well-disguised variant – the left-arm wrist-spinner's googly.

Early in 1957, Australia's recently retired Test captain Ian Johnson wrote that Kline's wrong'un was "fast becoming the most dangerous and successful ball in Australian cricket", and he was selected to tour South Africa. After going wicketless on debut, he wrapped up the Second Test in Cape Town with a hat-trick – the last to date in any Test in South Africa (since then, there have been 28 elsewhere). Kline had Eddie Fuller caught at short leg, trapped Hugh Tayfield lbw – "It must have been close," said Kline, "because they were South African umpires!" – then had last man Neil Adcock well caught by Bob Simpson at slip.

Kline took 15 wickets in the series, but was overshadowed by Benaud, who reaped 106 wickets in all on the tour, and never looked back. Next season he took over as Australia's captain, which meant Kline – an inferior batsman and fielder – was likely to play only on spin-friendly pitches. On one, at Lahore in November 1959, he claimed a career-best 7 for 75 as Australia completed their first series victory in Pakistan.

In the previous match, on a matting wicket in Dacca (now Dhaka), Kline had an important role, even though he wasn't actually playing. He was deputed to travel to the ground early each morning, to ensure the groundstaff stretched out the coir mat as taut as possible before nailing it down. "Those of us on the tour," wrote Benaud, "will never forget stepping off the bus and hearing the ringing cries of 'Pull, you bastards, pull!' floating across the ground. Not politically correct, but effective!"

Lindsay Kline with West Indies' Wes Hall - tied together in history because of the Brisbane Test of 1960. – *Getty Images*

KRISHNA, T VAMSHI, died after being hit by a cork ball on a school playground in Vanasthalipuram, near Hyderabad in India, on April 24, 2015. Although aged only six, he was fielding close in, and was struck on the chest by a powerful shot from a 12-year-old.

KRISHNAPRASAD V, who died on 27 November, aged 69, was a leg-spinner who represented Karnataka in one Ranji Trophy match. He was one of three brothers who played for the state, Ramdas being the third, who also played one Ranji match. V Subramanian was the best known and most successful cricketer in the family, having led Karnataka in the Ranji Trophy and turned out in nine Tests for India.

KUMAR, VIKRANT, a junior cricketer from Himachal Pradesh, died on September 28 following an accident in Una four days after his 23rd birthday. His car was involved in a head-on collision with a truck. Vikrant, an all-rounder, bowled off-spin and was a regular on the circuit since making his debut for Himachal Pradesh Under-15 in the 2007-08 Polly Umrigar Trophy. He made 34 and took five wickets on his debut against Jammu & Kashmir, and ended the tournament with 144 runs and six wickets.

He graduated to the Under-16 level the next season and made his Under-19 debut in 2011-12. On debut in the Under-23 CK Nayudu Trophy, his 509 runs at 56.55 included two centuries and three fifties. He played a big role in Himachal's march to the final.

LEE, ALAN PETER, who died suddenly on December 19, aged 61, was cricket correspondent of *The Times* from 1988 to 1999. Among his col-

Vikrant Kumar: A junior cricketer from Himachal Pradesh, he took his state to the final of the Under-23 CK Nayudu Trophy. — *HPCA*

leagues, he was perhaps the most respected sports journalist of his generation. Sports desks loved the fact that, when they asked for however many words at whenever o'clock, Lee would deliver precisely. His fellow writers were fearful that, whatever was going on behind the scenes, Lee probably had more information than they did.

He was a born journalist, writing football reports as a nine-year-old, joining the *Watford Observer* at 16 and moving on to the boot camp of Hayter's sports agency, where tyros had to work fast and furiously. Still only 24, he went to Australia to report the Kerry Packer-led breakaway and produced a remarkably mature book, *A Pitch in Both Camps*. He later freelanced before becoming cricket correspondent of the *Mail on Sunday*, then edged out Christopher Martin-Jenkins to succeed John Woodcock at *The Times*. All the while, he would produce biographies, ghosted autobiographies and other books at a matchless pace (Greig, Gower, Gooch, Dexter, Willis, etc.), without ever neglecting the day job. Surrounded by press-box chaos, he was always orderly and focused. "Eff-all's happened and they still want 800 words," wailed Martin Johnson of *The Independent* one rained-off day. "I've written three stories already," replied Lee.

No colleague could recall him having a day's illness until he was rushed to hospital last summer for a major coronary operation, and he was on the brink of returning to work when he had a heart attack. Divorced, he had a long-term relationship with the former England cricketer Sarah Potter.

MADDOCKS, LEONARD VICTOR, who died on September 1, aged 90, will be remembered as the man Jim Laker trapped leg-before to complete his famous ten-for at Old Trafford in 1956. A photograph of the dismissal seems to indicate that Maddocks walked even before the umpire had raised his finger. "I knew I was plumb," he said later, thus becoming the counter-example for those who claimed that Australians never walked.

Maddocks was a wicketkeeper and after retirement became a prominent figure in the administration of Australian cricket. Slightly built, he played his cricket with a smile on his face. He first played for Victoria in 1946, and made his Test debut against England in the Third Test of the 1954-55 series after the first-choice keeper Gil Langley was injured during a Shefield Shield match. He did well, top-scoring in the first-innings with 47 against Statham and Frank Tyson, and retained his place for the remainder of that series as well as the First Test of the next rubber against West Indies in the Caribbean. However, Langley's superior glove work soon won him back his position, and Maddocks played only four more Tests. He was unlucky to be in an era when Australia were blessed with so many fine technicians between the stumps, with Langley, Don Tallon and Wally Grout all around, but was probably a little out of his depth in such company.

Len Maddocks: The wicketkeeper was a counter-example for those who claimed Australians never walked. – *Getty Images*

MENDIS, LIONEL, who died on October 9, aged 80, was a celebrated coach in Sri Lanka. He supervised the strong Ananda College team for many years, bringing on the future national captain Arjuna Ranatunga, and had run a coaching school at Colombo's Nondescripts CC since 1986. Mahela Jayawardene, one of his charges there, called him "the best teacher I had". In 2000, Mendis wrote *Cricket Huruwa*, the first coaching manual in the Sinhala language.

MUKHERJEE, PRABIR, who died on May 31, aged 86, was the legendary chief curator of the Cricket Association of Bengal. He was in charge of Eden Gardens for nearly 25 years after retiring as an accounts officer with South Eastern Railway.

"(He was) a man who dedicated his heart and soul to the great Eden Gardens," commented India cricketer Ambati Rayudu.

Mukherjee's last wish was that his body should not be taken to the CAB premises for people to pay their last respects – a tradition of sorts in the city's cricket community for its distinguished members. This, a family member explained, was because he was displeased with the way the CAB administration treated him on many occasions over the years, culminating in his bosses laying the blame on him for the washed-out third and final T20I between India and South Africa in October 2015.

Prior to that setback, he had been in the eye of a storm for going against the demand of MS Dhoni, the then Indian Test captain, for a turning track to be prepared for the Test against England in December 2012. Mukherjee took

Prabir Mukherjee: An Eden Gardens institution. The legendary curator is seen here with umpire Steve Davis in 2010.
— Gallo/Getty Images

exception, spoke at length to sections of the local and national media, and then went on sick leave in protest before returning and preparing a straightforward Eden Gardens pitch, with a bit of grass and decent bounce on the first day. England went on to win the Test by seven wickets on their way to a 2-1 series win.

Mukherjee, a fast bowler as well as a football goalkeeper in the 1940s, became involved with cricket in 1952 after his playing days ended following a road accident. Kartik Bose, the then chief coach of the CAB, introduced him to pitch-making. After starting out at Suburban Club, in 1964 he was elected secretary of Bengal National Railways Club.

He became a part of the CAB in 1979, going on to become the manager of the Bengal as well as the East Zone teams soon after, and started working on pitches by the mid-1980s.

MUNRO, ANTHONY JOHN, who died on April 23, aged 52, had suffered a stroke earlier from which he didn't recover. He covered Associate and Affiliate cricket for more than a decade with *ESPNcricinfo*. He also edited the Cricket Round the World section of *Wisden Cricketers' Almanack* from the mid-2000s to 2011.

Munro, who was born with dwarfism, had suffered health complications throughout his life, including a previous stroke in 2008. "It was very hard for him, but he loved sports journalism and what he did was with some great difficulty," his older brother Scott said.

Munro was spectacular at finding stories about cricket in low-profile locations such as the Falkland Islands in the Atlantic Ocean or Nauru in the South Pacific. For a regular interview feature titled, 'Totally Homegrown', he profiled indigenous players in emerging nations to demonstrate the game's growth was not solely reliant upon expatriate talent.

"He used to run up massive international phone bills," Scott said. "At the time he was doing it, international calls were very expensive. The smaller and more remote, the juicier it was for him."

PAL, CHANDRAVATI, who died on April 17, aged 40, played for Bengal. She was riding pillion on her way to the Calcutta Parsi Club where she was coaching when she was hit by a bus from behind. A top-order batter, Chandravati represented Bengal for 15 years and also played for East Zone. She coached Combined District Team for two years and was coach of Howrah District.

PATEL, JAYANTHIBAI C, who died on November 21, aged 86 was a left-arm spinner who played Ranji cricket for Tamil Nadu. He was also a gritty batman, who, in the words of team-mate VV Kumar, "was a lively person who had great enthusiasm for the game". It was this passion that kept the all-rounder playing club cricket into his 60s. The Surat-born Patel first represented Baroda before settling down in Tamil Nadu. In all, he made 1248 runs in 41 first-class matches at 21.15. Patel also claimed 54 wickets at 22.57. Former India stumper Bharat Reddy said: "He was a versatile cricketer. He could bowl slow medium-pace with the new ball and brought the delivery in. He was also a fun-loving personality. In all, his contribution to the Madras Cricket Club was immense."

PATHMANATHAN, BAVALAN, died on July 7, 2015, two days after being struck on the chest while batting in a club game in Long Ditton in Surrey. He was 24. Playing for Hersham's Manipay Parish in the British Tamil League, Pathmanathan collapsed at the crease after being hit by a rising delivery. He was taken to Kingston Hospital by air ambulance, but never recovered.

PEIRIS, IAN, who died on January 1, aged 82, served as president of Sri Lanka Cricket for two sessions. His first term, in 1989, lasted just four months and the second, in 1990, for one year. In his first term, Pieris did not see eye to eye with the board's executive committee on the need to follow the instructions of Nanda Mathew, the sports minister, and subsequently resigned on principle. During his second term, Pieris, along with secretary S Skandakumar, did a lot of groundwork to get international tours to Sri Lanka.

Pieris also had a distinguished cricket career playing as a top-order batsman for St Thomas' College, Mt Lavinia, and as a right-arm opening bowler for Singhalese Sports Club, Cambridge University and All-Ceylon (as the national team was then known). While at school, Pieris made his international debut when he was picked to play against Lindsay Hassett's Australia team in 1953.

PRIDEAUX, RUTH, who died on April 7, aged 85, was England's wicket-keeper-batter and became England Women's first permanent head coach in 1988. She guided them to the 1993 World Cup.

Prideaux (née Westbrook) earned 11 Test caps between 1957 and 1963, scoring 476 runs at 31.73, with a top score of 87 against South Africa in Cape Town. However, it was for her off-field role that she would be best remembered. She was acknowledged as having helped England become leaders in the women's game during the early 1990s – bringing in backroom staff that included nutritionists and physios – which had its crowning moment at Lord's in 1993 when they defeated New Zealand.

She is survived by her husband, Roger Prideaux, who played three Tests for England between 1968 and 1969.

RAGHUNATH, PONNAMBATH MAMBALLY KRISHNAN who died on January 14 played first-class cricket for Kerala as a medium-pacer. He was born in Mahe. In nine matches, he claimed 11 wickets, with a best of 3 for 66.

RAMPRASAD, BAJINA who died on March 30, aged 75, played for Andhra in the Ranji Trophy as a wicketkeeper. His batting was important for a team that usually trailed the Big Three of South Zone – Karnataka, Tamil Nadu, Hyderabad – in the 1960s and 1970s when he was active. Ramprasad's 2240 runs in 59 matches included two centuries and seven fifties.

RAMPRASAD, KALADEVANHALLI MURUDEVAGOWDA, who died on November 23, aged 81, was president of the Karnataka State Cricket Association from 1998 to 2007, and had also been a vice-president of the BCCI. He played four games for the state (then known as Mysore) as a medium-pacer, including the 1959-60 Ranji Trophy final defeat by Bombay; against Kerala in October 1961 he took 6 for 26. He managed the Indian team at the Champions Trophy in Sri Lanka in 2002, when the Sourav Ganguly-led side emerged joint winners alongside the host nation. It was during his time as president of the association that Karnataka won the Ranji Trophy title for a third time in four years in the 1998-99 season. Alongside Brijesh Patel, who became the secretary of the KSCA also in 1998, Ramprasad struck up an excellent administrative tandem. It was during Ramprasad's presidency that the KSCA acquired a 30-acre property at Alur on the outskirts of Bangalore, a facility that now hosts three grounds and a practice area with 22 pitches. Once work at Alur was completed in 2013, Ramprasad was invited to inaugurate the pavilion.

ROBINSON, IAN DAVID, who died of lung cancer on April 3, aged 69, umpired in Zimbabwe's inaugural Test. Born in Oxford, Robinson was a wicketkeeper-batsman who turned out for Hatfield Sports Club. He officiated in 28 Tests, 90 ODIs and three World Cups

Ian Robinson: Umpire in Zimbabwe's inaugural Test. – *Getty Images*

– 1992, 1996 and 1999. He began his umpiring career in 1975 and was appointed to Zimbabwe's first-class panel in 1978. In 2004, he was sacked by the Zimbabwe Cricket Union without being given a reason.

Apart from his umpiring duties, Robinson served as a ZCU board member for 14 years and an employee of the board for nine. He also served as the board's international cricket manager. Robinson was appointed to the first international panel of umpires established by the ICC in 1994.

RANA, AZMAT who died on May 30, 2015, aged 63, played one Test for Pakistan against Australia in his native Lahore in 1979-80, scoring 49 in his only innings of a high-scoring draw. A left-hander who cut and drove well, he had already played two one-day internationals, against India, but never appeared again, despite amassing over 6000 runs in first-class cricket, with 16 centuries – the highest 206 not out for Punjab Greens against North West Frontier Province in Peshawar in 1977-78. He had also toured England, in 1971 – but was unable to shrug off malaria – and New Zealand in 1972-73, without much success. Azmat was a member of a prominent cricketing family: His brother Shafqat Rana and two nephews also represented Pakistan, while the umpire Shakoor Rana was another brother.

RYAN, MELVILLE, who died on November 16, aged 82, was a tall, physically imposing seamer who won four County Championship titles with the formidable Yorkshire team of the late 1950s and '60s – a useful strike-rate for a player who made just 150 first-class appearances. Ryan, usually known as Mel, made his debut in 1954, but had to wait seven years to become a regular.

He had, in the words of team-mate Bob Platt, a "busy and effective run-up", and bowled at a lively pace. "He did not bowl bouncers. His main thing was line and length." In 1959, when Yorkshire won the Championship under Ronnie Burnet, he took 21 wickets in five appearances. He was a more regular presence in later title-winning sides, taking 37 wickets in 1960, then 73 in 1962 and 57 in 1963. Ryan's final season was 1965, and he retired with 413 wickets at just under 23. "He was a great bowler, straight-talking, and a kindly and generous man," said team-mate Ken Taylor.

Ryan loved opening the bowling with Fred Trueman, but recalled: "He had the best end. It was uphill and against the wind for the rest of us. The only time it would change was if we were getting wickets and he wasn't. I would say 390 of my wickets were batsmen one to six. I would probably have taken another 100 if I'd been able to bowl at nine, ten and eleven, and from the right end. And no question, I would have been more successful if Fred hadn't been at the other."

SETH, KAPIL died on July 2 following an attack of Hepatitis B. He was 36. Seth, who bowled medium-pace, represented Madhya Pradesh in only one first-class and List A game in the 2000-01 season. He made his sole Ranji Trophy appearance against Vidarbha in November 2000 and scored an unbeaten 125 at No. 10. His century, along with Ankit Srivastava's 204, helped Madhya Pradesh rally from 276 for 8 to 552 for 8 declared, and the side eventually beat Vidarbha by an innings and 176 runs.

He did not bat in his only List A match – also against Vidarbha, in the Ranji Trophy One Day competition – but had figures of 1 for 27 in the match.

SHODHAN ROSHAN HARSHADLAL 'DEEPAK', the second Indian to make a century in his debut innings, died on May 16 aged 87. He was, at the time, India's oldest living Test cricketer. Shodhan succumbed to lung cancer.

An attractive left-hand batsman who bowled left-arm pace as well, Shodhan was given his first India cap at 25, against Pakistan at Eden Gardens in 1952, and made an immediate impact. He walked in at No. 8, with the score on 179 for 6 and no specialist batsmen left, and he walked out with 110 against his name. India claimed a lead of 140 runs, but the match ended in a draw.

"I was in the reserves for the series against Pakistan in 1952-53, the historic first Test series between our two newly independent nations," Shodhan had said. "In the final Test match, at Calcutta, I was drafted into the playing XI after our captain Vijay Hazare pulled out unwell. It was Lala Amarnath, who was captaining India in Vijay Hazare's absence, who asked for me to be brought in – 'that tall Gujarati boy who had done so well in the trials and other matches'."

Despite that bright start, Shodhan played only two more Tests, on a tour of West Indies in 1953. The team had journeyed to the Caribbean by a small boat, which kept tossing and turning. Everyone got sick and Shodhan remembered being the last man standing. Having made 45 and 11 in the first Test at Port of Spain, he did not play the next three and was taken ill when he returned for the fifth in Jamaica. That didn't stop him from walking out at No. 10, after West Indies had taken a 264-run lead, to try and salvage a draw. Madhav Apte, the 83-year-old former opening batsman who was part of that series, recollected Shodhan's bravery.

Deepak Shodhan: The second Indian to make a century on debut. — *Wisden India*

"He was down with flu and was admitted to the hospital and did not bat in the first innings. [In the second innings] we needed someone to waste time and delay the West Indies batting. Deepak managed to just do that and consumed enough time to help India draw that match."

Shodhan had a long domestic career, playing for Gujarat and Baroda in the Ranji Trophy and was a title-winner in 1957-58.

it has remained a mystery why Shodhan played only three Tests, despite having an average above 60.

Years later, he gave a hint, saying, "When I got into the Indian team, Vinoo Mankad asked me whether I chose to support him or Vijay Hazare. I told him I support India and the team. That ticked him off. After the West Indies tour, our manager, C Ramaswamy, is supposed to have written against me in his report. I have never held anything against him, Mankad or anyone else for not having played more for India."

SHUKLA, ANAND, who died on February 2, 2015, aged 74, scored more than 4000 runs and took nearly 400 wickets in Indian domestic cricket with his leg-breaks, chiefly for Bihar and neighbouring Uttar Pradesh. His career started in 1959-60, and ended with the Ranji Trophy final in April 1978. Shukla was unlucky to be plying his trade in the golden era of Indian slow bowling: One giant obstacle to Test selection was BS Chandrasekhar. Shukla took 7 for 91 in his third match, for Uttar Pradesh against Vidarbha in January 1960, and the following season allied ten wickets in the match against Rajasthan to an undefeated 168. In 1969-70 he took 42 wickets at 16, including a career-best 8 for 50 in the Moin-ud-Dowlah Cup. Although he could be devastating against the weaker teams – he took 71 Ranji Trophy wickets against Assam and 69 against Orissa, both at under 11 apiece – he was less of a force against stronger opposition, and in the Duleep Trophy zonal tournament his wickets cost around 35. And so a national call never came, even though Shukla was a much better batsman than his rivals.

He hit nine first-class centuries, the highest 242 not out for Bihar against Orissa at Cuttack in December 1967, after taking 5 for 68 in the first innings. His younger brother Rakesh Shukla, another leg-spinner, played one Test for India in 1982-83.

SINGH, CHARRAN KAMKARAN, who died on November 19, eight days short of his 80th birthday, was a left-arm spinner from Trinidad whose Test debut, against England at Port of Spain in 1959-60, was marred by the first serious crowd disturbance at a match in the West Indies. England had made 382 and West Indies had struggled to 98 for 7 in reply before Singh was run out for a duck. Angered mainly by the batting failure, many of the estimated 30,000 crowd – the largest for any sporting event in the Caribbean at the time – started throwing bottles, then streamed onto the ground. The riot squad and the fire brigade were summoned, and play was abandoned for the day. Cricket resumed next morning, as England rolled on to win by 256 runs, the only outright result of the series.

Singh's fleeting Test career ended after his second match, at Georgetown; his five wickets overall included Colin Cowdrey, Ted Dexter and Peter May. He had been selected after five-fors in his first two matches for Trinidad, against Jamaica in October 1959 and the England tourists the following January. "A 21-year-old messenger on the Aranguez Estates, Singh bowled 34 overs on a perfect batting pitch to take 5 for 57," wrote Alan Ross of the second game. "He has a gently curving flight with some late dip, though no evident sharpness of spin."

SMART, LAWRENCE MAXWELL, AM, died on October 13, aged 87. A seam-bowling all-rounder (and a state baseball pitcher) Lawrie Smart played five matches for South Australia in the 1950s, split by a seven-year absence in Britain doing postgraduate studies in dentistry. He became a Member of the Order of Australia in January 2015 for "significant service to dentistry in the field of clinical orthodontics".

St JOHN, ADRIAN, who died on April 12, aged 22, was shot dead during an armed robbery while holidaying in Trinidad. St John, who worked as a recruitment consultant in London, was captain of the Chris Gayle Academy. He also played for Alleyn Cricket Club in south London and for his university squad at the University of Hertfordshire. Local media reported the armed robbery took place in Mt D'Or in the north of the island, as St John stopped his car to pick up the daughter of a female passenger. Police said that two men robbed the passengers and then ordered St John to drive off but fired a gun after the car, hitting him.

TUCKETT, LINDSAY, died in Bloemfontein on September 5, aged 97. He was the oldest surviving Test cricketer at the time. Tuckett featured in nine Test matches for South Africa – all against England – between June 1947, when cricket resumed after the Second World War, and March 1949. A right-arm medium-fast bowler, Tuckett picked up 19 wickets, with career-best figures of 5 for 68 on his debut at Trent Bridge. He followed that up with his second and last five-for at Lord's and a four-wicket haul in Manchester. Hampered by a groin injury, he went wicketless in the last two games to finish the series with 15 scalps at an average of 44.26. He was South Africa's joint-highest wicket-taker in that series along with Tufty Mann, the left-arm spinner.

He famously bowled the final eight-ball over of the Durban Test during that series when England won by two wickets. "With three balls left any one of four results remained possible. Before Bedser brought the scores level with a single from Tuckett off the sixth delivery of the last over, a draw or a tie could be visualised as easily as a victory for either side," wrote *Wisden*. "Gladwin hit at but missed the seventh ball. Then in a mid-wicket conference about the last ball he and Bedser decided to run in any event except the wicket being hit.

"Few of their England colleagues in the pavilion could bear the strain of watching as Tuckett began his run-up," added the *Almanack*. "As he did so the fieldsmen started to run in like sprinters towards the wicket to prevent the single, which would win the match. Gladwin went into his stumps, swung his bat, but again missed his stroke. The ball struck his thigh and bounced a yard or two in front of him. From short-leg Mann pounced on the ball, but both batsmen galloped to safety."

Lindsay's father Len Tuckett and uncle Joe Cox also played Test cricket for South Africa.

VAN SCHOOR, RAYMOND, died on November 20, aged 25, five days after collapsing during Namibia's match against Free State at Windhoek in the South African one-day competition. Namibia were 16 short of their eventual victory when, on 15 not out, van Schoor fell into the arms of his batting partner, Nicolaas Scholtz, and was rushed to hospital. He had suffered a stroke.

A batsman who often kept wicket, van Schoor had played a record 265 matches for Namibia in all formats since his debut at 17 in 2007, appearing five times alongside his father Melt. "He was a sensational fielder and could basically do anything," said Doug Watson, the former national coach. "If you asked him to play wicky, he'd probably be the best wicketkeeper in Namibia. He was just as brilliant in the slips as he was at backward point."

Van Schoor was the player of the tournament in the World T20 Qualifier early in 2012, scoring 323 runs as Namibia won all seven of their group games. He hit five first-class centuries, including 157 during an opening stand of 348 with Ewald Steenkamp against Bermuda in the ICC Intercontinental Shield at Windhoek in April 2010.

WALKER, MAXWELL HENRY NORMAN, who died on September 28 a few days after his 68th birthday, was a medium-pacer who bowled into the wind while Dennis Lillee and Jeff Thomson bowled with the wind in memorable summers in the mid-1970s.

"Just as Lindwall and Miller were complemented by Bill Johnston, during their salad days Lillee and Thomson had the unflagging support of Max Walker, a strapping paceman whose convoluted wrong-footed action inspired the nickname 'Tangles' and was imitated in backyard games across the country. He was capable of leading Australia's attack at a pinch, as he did during their 1972-73 tour of the West Indies and when he obtained 8 for 143 in the Sixth Test of the 1974-75 Ashes series with both Thomson and Lillee hors de combat," wrote Gideon Haigh.

Walker, who played 34 Tests for 138 wickets was among the breakaway group of players who took part in Kerry Packer's World Series Cricket from 1977 to 1979. Hailing from west Hobart, where he lived until recruited to the Melbourne Football Club by the legendary coach Norm Smith, Walker became an instantly recognisable figure for his handlebar moustache and toothy grin. Later in life those features helped him become a popular commentator and entertainer, publishing a string of comedic books and hosting *Wide World of Sports*.

James Sutherland, the Cricket Australia chief executive, paid tribute to Walker. "Max was an outstanding cricketer who played an important role in the emergence of successful Australian cricket teams in the 1970s," he

Instantly recognisable for his handlebar moustache and toothy grin, Australia's Max Walker (R) went on to present the 'Wide World of Sports' show on TV. He's seen here with Ken Sutcliffe. — *Fairfax Media/Getty Images*

said. "It was a golden era of Test Cricket under the captaincy of Ian and Greg Chappell, and Max's medium-fast bowling and his unmistakeable bowling action were a feature of those teams, and then in the late 1970s when he joined World Series Cricket.

Tony Dodemaide, CEO of Cricket Victoria, spoke of Walker's contribution. "Max was a positive and jovial character and devoted much of his life to playing and serving the game, during what many would call a revolutionary period for cricket," he said. "At the completion of his playing career, Max charmed many on our TV screens as he built his career in the entertainment industry."

WARR, JOHN JAMES, who died on May 9, aged 88, played two Tests for England as a medium-pacer against Australia on the 1950-51 Ashes tour. He was also a writer for *Sunday Telegraph* and president of MCC. His Test career was recalled when his debut figures of 0 for 142 in Sydney were overtaken as the worst by an England player in their first Test by Adil Rashid's 0 for 163 in his first innings against Pakistan in Abu Dhabi. For Middlesex, Warr claimed 956 first-class wickets at 22.79.

WESTAWAY, COLIN EDWARD, died on October 15, aged 79. A leg-spinner who took 6 for 88 against New South Wales at the Gabba in 1960-61 – his victims included Brian Booth, Neil Harvey and Grahame Thomas – Col Westaway was poorly treated by Queensland's selectors, who cast him aside for good two years later. He was a member of a cricket-playing family who owned a pineapple farm at Moggill, near Brisbane.

WIGHT, PETER BERNARD, who died on December 31, aged 85, was one of the most attractive batsmen in English county cricket in the late 1950s and early '60s, his runs a vital part of a Somerset revival that followed four successive years at the foot of the Championship table.

With Scottish and Portuguese ancestry, he was part of a large sporting family in Georgetown, British Guiana (now Guyana). His cousin Vibart was vice-captain of the West Indies team that toured England in 1928; his brother Leslie played one Test, at Georgetown in 1952-53; and other family members represented British Guiana at cricket, hockey, tennis and football.

In March 1951, the 20-year-old Wight made his debut, against Jamaica, scoring 39 before being given caught behind, to his annoyance. It was his only match in the West Indies: Within days he was on a cargo boat to England, linking up with fellow countryman Bruce Pairaudeau at Burnley. He planned to become an engineer, but England did not impress him – the cold, the rationing, the outside toilets – and his employer refused to give him time off for his night-school exams. However, his cricket prospered in the Lancashire League, and he met his future wife Joyce.

"Why don't you play for Somerset?" his sister's husband suggested when he visited them in Bridgwater in 1953. "They've got no players." Next day they were on the bus to Taunton and soon enough he was making his debut against the touring Australians. Out for a duck, and feeling low during a skittles evening, he was consoled by Richie Benaud: "Don't worry, you'll get a century in the second innings." And he did.

A waif-like figure, Wight gained a reputation for hypochondria. "I kept fit running down the chemist for him," one twelfth man recalled. But, with a bat in his hands, he was no weakling. "His perfect timing," wrote John Arlott, "invests his most delicate strokes with a power remarkable for one so slightly built." His team-mate Graham Atkinson recalled: "There was always a lovely ring to his bat. I used to stand at the other end and drool."

His way of playing the quicks – backing away and freeing up his arms – gained him an unwarranted reputation for being vulnerable against pace. Yet at Blackpool in 1959 he made a fine 106 against Statham; and, at The Oval in 1956, when Peter Loader skittled Somerset for 159 and 196, he hit 62 and 128, both unbeaten. Only Trueman consistently got the better of him. When in 1962 the Yorkshire captain Vic Wilson dropped Trueman for arriving late at Taunton, Wight celebrated with the second double-century of his career. In all, he hit 16,965 first-class runs for Somerset, a total exceeded only by Harold Gimblett. He also enjoyed occasional success as an off-spinner, most notably at Chesterfield in 1957 when, on as fifth change, he won the match with 6 for 29.

After his retirement he set up a cricket school in Bath, where he spent his winters coaching. He became an umpire, standing for 30 summers until 1995, but never in an international; in fact he never saw an international day's cricket in his life. His total of first-class appearances in England (328 as player, 567 as umpire) is a post-war record.

WILLIAMS, ALVADON BASIL, died on October 25, aged 65. Known as 'Shotgun' for his approach to opening the batting for Jamaica and West Indies, Williams played seven Tests in the absence of those signed up by Kerry Packer for World Series Cricket. He started superbly, with a rapid 100 in the second innings of his debut, against Australia at Georgetown in April 1978. He added a more sedate 111 against India in Calcutta in December, and averaged 39 overall – but had to make way on the return of Gordon Greenidge and Desmond Haynes when WSC was disbanded the following year.

That 118-ball 100 at Bourda typified his attitude. "A fascinating duel between [Jeff] Thomson and Williams held the crowd's attention," reported the *West Indies Cricket Annual*. "Although beaten several times for pace, Williams kept on going for his shots, cutting and driving with relish and having 11 fours in 60 when stumps were drawn on the second day." He collected eight more boundaries within an hour on the third morning to reach his hundred, then hooked the next ball, from Wayne Clark, straight to fine leg.

Strong off the back foot and an especially ferocious cutter, Williams made five first-class centuries, the highest 126 not out against Karnataka on the 1978-79 Indian tour. After retirement he became a Jamaican selector, board member and team manager. One of his sons, Germaine, became an entertainer in a different sphere in the United States, as the popular rap artist Canibus.

WYATT, JOHN LEONARD, died on January 29, aged 95. Len Wyatt was part of the first Northern Districts side to compete in New Zealand's Plunket Shield, in 1956-57, and was their oldest surviving player. His four matches all came that season, which he rounded off with 54, opening against a Wellington side containing several Test players. Wyatt played club cricket until he was 59, and claimed to have scored 42,175 runs, with 128 centuries, and taken 1,165 wickets. His brother, Ivan, played first-class cricket for Auckland.

YAWAR SAEED, who died on October 21, aged 80, was the manager of Pakistan's troubled tour of England in 2010, which was tarnished by the spot-fixing controversy involving Mohammad Asif, Mohammad Amir and their captain Salman Butt. Yawar saw the tour out, but stepped down shortly afterwards, ending a career in cricket administration that had featured long stints as a board member and selector, and managing overseas tours. He was manager of the only Pakistan team to win the annual triangular one-day series in Australia, in 1996-97.

Yawar's father, Mian Mohammad Saeed, had been the first captain of independent Pakistan, skippering them in unofficial Tests – but he was sidelined by the autocratic Abdul Hafeez Kardar, who may have stymied Yawar's international career too.

A handy medium-pacer, he had two seasons with Somerset. According to Peter Roebuck's county history, "Yawar was apt to ask colleagues, 'Don't you think I'm quick?' but wisely he rarely waited for the answer." He took 76 ickets for them, including a career-best 5 for 61 against the 1955 South African tourists. The previous year he had played against the Pakistan team on their first Test tour of England. He took five wickets in the match at Taunton, but was upset his compatriots did not speak to him, apparently under orders from Kardar, their captain. It might not have helped that Pakistan's star bowler Fazal Mahmood, with whom Kardar had an uneasy relationship, was his brother-in-law.

Yawar played only nine first-class matches at home in Pakistan, although he did claim 5 for 133 for Punjab against the 1955-56 MCC A team, and 5 for 89 the following season to help Punjab beat Karachi Whites in the Quaid-i-Azam Trophy final.

ZAFAR ALTAF, who died on December 5, aged 74, was secretary of the Board of Control for Cricket in Pakistan between 1972 and 1975, and later the board's chairman and a national selector. He was assistant manager during Pakistan's tour of England in 1974, and manager in 1999, when they reached the World Cup final. He was also a fine batsman, scoring 99 in his third match and 111 in the fourth, in 1958-59; two years later he toured India under Fazal Mahmood's captaincy, but did not play a Test. For Lahore Greens against Bahawalpur in the Ayub Trophy in 1965-66, Zafar scored 268 and shared a stand of 346 with Majid Khan, who made 241. An economist, he joined Pakistan's civil service and was the Federal Secretary for Agriculture for ten years.

ZEESHAN MOHAMMED, who was 18, died after he was struck by the ball in a club game in Pakistan on January 25, 2015. "He was hit in the chest by a fast bowler while batting and collapsed on the pitch," said a doctor at the Orangi Town hospital near Karachi.

CHRONICLES

(Stories from media sources around the world)

Prime Minister McCullum
Given the huge draw that cricket is in India, it was no surprise that Brendon McCullum was part of New Zealand prime minister John Key's trade delegation during a visit to the country. But did the presence of the inspirational captain create too much of an impression? At an event to promote New Zealand tourism, in New Delhi, India's minister of culture Mahesh Sharma made a gaffe by addressing Key as "his excellency Prime Minister McCullum". Perhaps it was in the air: Bollywood star Sidharth Malhotra, who was also in attendance, later failed to recall Sharma's name while addressing the audience. Wonder if being referred to "his excellency" might tempt McCullum to take a shot.

Rwanda nets a record
By the time he played the final ball of his session, bowled by his wife in front of a large crowd in Rwanda's capital, Kigali, Eric Dusingizimana had batted for 51 successive hours, setting a new Guinness world record for the longest individual net session. Despite having batted for more than two days, he still had energy to pull off an unusual celebration: a headstand. Dusingizimana, the Rwanda cricket team captain, beat the record set by India's Virag Mare of Pune (50 hours, five minutes and 51 seconds), and did it with the aim of raising money for the Rwanda Cricket Stadium Foundation, which was set up to help fund the country's first international cricket ground. He began batting on May 11 and was allowed a five-minute break in every hour of his batting session, giving the player time to undergo health checks and eat. By the time he completed his session, Dusingizimana had faced throwdowns from former British Prime Minister Tony Blair, the British High Commissioner to Rwanda William Gelling and Miss Rwanda. The *Independent* newspaper reported that Dusingizimana had batted approximately five-and-a-half hours longer than the entire Australian cricket team in the 2015 Ashes.

Dhoni is no Vishnu
A local court in Andhra Pradesh's district of Anantapur issued a non-bailable warrant against India's limited-overs captain MS Dhoni. The case related to a morphed picture of Dhoni that appeared on the cover of a magazine in April 2013, which depicted him as a Hindu deity endorsing a lot of products,

including a shoe. The headline said, "God of big deals". The summons was a result of the petition filed by a local Vishwa Hindu Parishad (VHP) leader who saw the portrayal of Dhoni as the deity as hurtful to Hindu sentiments. The Supreme Court quashed criminal proceedings against the player.

Mundhe makes it
Colwyn Bay cricketer Shrikant Mundhe made history by becoming the first Liverpool Competition Premier League bowler to take 10 wickets in an innings when he destroyed Birkenhead Park's batting at Penrhyn Avenue. Indian ace Mundhe is only the 17th league player dating back to 1920 to claim a full house and just the fifth since the standardisation of fixtures in 1949. However, he is the sole man to achieve the feat since the Premier Division was formed in 1999.

On too long
A Victorian Premier Cricket match between St Kilda and Footscray-Edgewater ended in farce after it was discovered that the pitch they were playing on was eight feet too long. The true length of the strip at the Harry Trott Oval in Melbourne's Albert Park was only discovered after the match when the umpires ran a measuring tape over it. Glenn Lalor, St Kilda's coach, admitted his team had had their doubts throughout the game. "I bowled slow enough, mate. I didn't need an extra eight feet. I would have been bowling backwards," he told *the Caulfield Glen Eira Leader*. Footscray won the match by six wickets after chasing down St Kilda's total of 197, but not before two of their batsman, Matt Underwood and Dylan Kight, had been run out on the extra-long surface.

Out and six
Clitheroe's Sri Lankan pro Janaka Gunaratne became the first player in the 122-year history of the Ribblesdale League to hit six sixes in an over, and lost four balls in the process. But furious Ribblesdale Wanderers players believed he should have been out for a duck. Ian Britcliffe, who conceded the sixes, said Gunaratne had actually been bowled second ball, but the square-leg umpire believed it had bounced back off the keeper.

Cowdrey's reality
Colin Cowdrey's grandson became the latest star of *Made in Chelsea*, the hugely popular, if somewhat vapid, British 'constructed reality' TV show. Julius Cowdrey is the son of former England captain Chris and brother of current Kent batsman Fabian. Cowdrey, a 23-year-old singer-songwriter, attended Tonbridge School and has played in the past for Sevenoaks Vine Cricket Club.

Cork hazard

Spectators at Lord's have been warned to desist from the time-honoured tradition of firing their champagne corks onto the field of play, because they risk causing a "hazard" to the players. Lord's is the only international cricket ground at which spectators are still allowed to bring in their own alcohol, but in a newsletter, Marylebone Cricket Club admitted that concerns had been "formally raised" by visiting players who have been in the firing line.

Nasser's catch

At 48, former England captain Nasser Hussain still has it when it comes to catching a cricket ball. Armed with one white and red wicketkeeping glove, and one black and yellow one, he settled under a drone at Lord's and caught his way into the Guinness Book of World Records. The drone dropped the ball from a height of 150 feet, the ball reached estimated speeds of 74mph on its descent, it swirled around a bit, but none of it was too much for Nasser.

"It was great fun to spend the morning attempting to catch cricket balls dropped from a drone at the home of cricket – something I never thought I would do," he said after his record-setter, according to the Guinness Book of World Records website. "But I am looking forward to giving my hands a rest and getting back to the commentary box." Nasser attempted one more: a monster 400-feet drop – the highest the drone could go. The wind displacement, as expected, proved too much on that one, blowing the ball well out of his reach.

A selfie too far

What happens when a Gujarat Lion goes to visit actual lions? Trouble. Ravindra Jadeja was taking a guided tour of Gir National Park, a wildlife sanctuary in Gujarat when he reportedly got out of the vehicle to take pictures with the lions. That, however, is against the rules. A park official told *Times of India* that "the dos and don'ts clearly mention that getting down from the Jeep or even smoking inside the forest is an offense, and in this case Jadeja has taken photographs in the vicinity of the lions".

Fast food, slow money

Shahid Afridi and Ahmed Shehzad walked into a fast food outlet at the Auckland airport but discovered they didn't have any local currency. Waqas, a Pakistani living in New Zealand, saved them much embarrassment by stepping in and paying for their food. "It is a good feeling to have my local team, Pakistan's team, over here," Waqas said. "I am going to support them all."

Mid-pitch parking

A cricket match in Queensland was interrupted by a pitch invasion. The unusual four-wheeled protest was a result of a taxi driver having his windshield cracked by a six and then deciding to express his anger by parking up mid-pitch. The fixture between Macgregor and Griffith University was held up for an hour until the police intervened. The car's window was reportedly broken by a straight six from Macgregor player Nigel Sherborne. The Warehouse Cricket Association Queensland posted on Facebook: "Weird events at cricket. This cabbie had his front windscreen damaged by a cricket ball today at DM Henderson Park, unhappy with the outcome he decided to park on the middle of pitch, he stayed for an hour and had to be moved on by the Queensland Police Service."

Five reasons to continue

Mick Massey, 82, took 5 for 38 for the Hatherleigh CC midweek team against the Englefield Green touring side. This increased his determination to continue for another season. His captain, David Manning, said: "I'm 68, but I can't even think of packing up when Mick's doing so well."

No rooms, no match

The weather. Stadium issues. General elections… The reasons for shifting the venue of a cricket match are many, but rarely a laughing matter. Not so in the case of the Uttar Pradesh's Ranji Trophy game against Baroda. "The venue of the UP v Baroda Ranji Trophy match scheduled to be held in Kanpur from December 1 to December 4, 2015, is shifted to Greater Noida Cricket Stadium," the Uttar Pradesh Cricket Association said in a statement. But why? Well, because of all the weddings in Kanpur at the time. The hotels were all booked out by wedding guests, leaving no space for the visiting cricketers. On the upside, the players were not tempted to ditch their diets by the wedding feasts all around.

Sachin's service

The 1895 residents of a remote village in Andhra Pradesh have had their lives transformed since they were "adopted" by Sachin Tendulkar a year ago under a national scheme whereby MPs and VIPs help a poor village. The Ministry of Rural Development named the village, Puttamrajuvari Kandriga, among the top three villages of the 300 involved as an example of what can be done. The villagers have gained paved roads, footpaths, drainage, power, drinking water, sanitation, a hall, a school and a sports ground.

Secretary hits 50

Roy Thorne, the last surviving founder member of Dinder and Croscombe

CC, Somerset, has retired as the club's honorary secretary after 50 years. Thorne, 83, has held almost every other post in the club since it began in 1948. Though he often opened the batting, his highest score was 26. "I'm more gifted in organising things," he said.

A boar-ing story
Yorkley Star CC, on the edge of the Forest of Dean in Gloucestershire, is to close after more than 130 years because the pitch, at Cut and Fry Green, is being destroyed by wild boar. In 2014, Yorkley were top of their league until the ground was churned up by the boar and their season had to be abandoned. The club paid for the ground to be relaid, but the beasts struck again. Trustee Alec Kear, 80, said: "The forest is overrun with these things. The ground is like a war zone. It's unbelievable. Nothing has stopped play before. We were going all the way through the war, but we just can't cope with this."

Looping leggies
Thomas Wrigglesworth, aged ten, took 5 for 9 with his "looping leggies" in a Victorian senior fourth-grade match for Sale against Stratford. It was his second senior appearance, but the first time he had attempted leg-spin in a match. "He was a wicketkeeper last year," said his father Ian, who played for Victoria in the 1990s. "And he's just decided the leggies were worth a try, and pestered everyone enough to the point where he was given a bowl." He refused to be drawn about the chances of his son following him into first-class cricket: "We were more inclined to talk about the duck he made in the morning. We're not going to pump him up."

Cricket bats for POWs
New research has revealed how British intelligence officers helped some of the most daring escapes by wartime POWs. Maps were concealed in gifts sent out to prisoners, such as hollowed-out chess sets, Christmas crackers – and the handles of cricket bats.

Bar none
The prison authorities in Pune rejected a request from the BCCI to provide two iron bars to create the Freedom Trophy for Tests between India and South Africa. The trophy honours Mahatma Gandhi and Nelson Mandela, and the bars were to come from the cells where they were held. However, prison official BK Upadhyay said: "The cell where Gandhi was kept is declared as 'heritage', and the rods of the heritage cannot be removed."

Sachin fans upset
After Sachin Tendulkar complained to British Airways about poor service

and what he called a "don't care" attitude from staff, the airline responded by apologising – and asking for his full name and address. This enraged Tendulkar's fan army, who declared social-media war on the airline for not recognising him. Some called for the Indian prime minister to cancel his visit to the UK. Other posts included: "How dare you ask his full name, you swines," and, more subtly, "Try Sachin Ramesh Tendulkar, India. I'm sure this is enough."

Finn's folly
Steven Finn, England's 6ft 7in opening bowler, gashed his head on a street sign while trying to walk and text simultaneously.

Glass ceiling
Street cricket has become the latest battleground for a growing women's rights movement in Pakistan. Women and girls are posting photos of themselves taking part in traditionally male pursuits such as cricket, hanging out at the beach, climbing trees and eating in roadside cafes known as *dhabas*. "Most of us could narrate instances of childhood where we were either told by the boys playing street cricket that we can't play with them or were discouraged or not allowed by parents," said Sadia Khatri, one of the movement's founders. "Cricket on the streets is something girls aren't supposed to do, so it seemed like a natural next step to take."

The bribe
In-demand teachers are being offered extra days off to attend events such as cricket during school hours in a bid to lure them into jobs, according to Ben Thompson, the head of Trinity Academy in south London, an area where it has been difficult to recruit. Maths, English and physics teachers are currently hard to find, particularly in inner cities.

Sachin's first question
Three years after he was first nominated to the Rajya Sabha, India's upper house, Sachin Tendulkar asked his first question: about the zoning system used on suburban railways in India's four main cities.

Cricket at the Bar
One of the purest gold nuggets ever found, the Maitland Bar, has been unwittingly used for years by New South Wales Treasury officials as a wicket. The bar, NSW Premier Mike Baird explained, had been entrusted to the Treasury some years ago: "Someone studiously decided they'd place it in a box. The problem was they forgot to tell anyone, and that box became used for hallway cricket." The bar has a gold content of 8.87kg. "My good friends

in Treasury – I love them dearly, but that was not their finest moment," Mr Baird sighed.

No betting

Angela Reakes, who plays for the ACT Meteors in the Australian Women's League, has been given a two-year suspended ban for placing five bets, totalling nine dollars, on the match award for the men's World Cup final. The chief of Cricket Australia's integrity unit said: "All elite cricketers are reminded regularly that betting on any form of cricket is strictly prohibited."

Nine wickets and a run out

A Harris Shield match between two Mumbai schools turned to farce after 14-year-old left-arm spinner Daksh Agarwal of Vibgyor High took the first nine wickets against St Joseph's Secondary. With the last pair still 71 short Agarwal's team-mates devoted themselves to ensuring he got all ten. Their efforts included the wicketkeeper standing with the ball by the stumps as the batsmen ran nine, and intentionally bad bowling from the other end. Finally Agarwal ended the nonsense by effecting a run-out off his own bowling for a 51-run win. "I am not disappointed," he said. "I have an all-ten. My team won. So what if my tenth wicket is a run-out? I am proud."

TEST MATCHES

BATTING

Highest individual innings

Score	Player	For/Against	Venue	Season
400*	Brian Lara	WI v Eng	St John's	2003-04
380	Matthew Hayden	Aus v Zim	Perth	2003-04
375	Brian Lara	WI v Eng	St John's	1993-94

Triple hundred and hundred in a Test

1st Inn	2nd Inn	Player	For/Against	Venue	Season
333	123	Graham Gooch	Eng v Ind	Lord's	1990
319	105	Kumar Sangakkara	Ban v SL	Chittagong	2013-14

Double hundred and hundred in a Test

1st Inn	2nd Inn	Player	For/Against	Venue	Season
242	103	Doug Walters	Aus v WI	Sydney	1968-69
124	220	Sunil Gavaskar	Ind v WI	Port of Spain	1970-71
214	100*	Lawrence Rowe	WI v NZ	Kingston	1971-72
247*	133	Greg Chappell	Aus v NZ	Wellington	1973-74
221	130	Brian Lara	WI v SL	Colombo (SSC)	2001-02

*Lawrence Rowe achieved this on his Test debut.

Highest Aggregates

Player	Team	M	I	NO	R	HS	Avg	100s/50s
Sachin Tendulkar	Ind	200	329	33	15921	248*	53.78	51/68
Ricky Ponting	Aus	168	287	29	13378	257	51.85	41/62
Jacques Kallis	SA/ICC	166	280	40	13289	224	55.37	45/58

Most Ducks

Ducks	Player	Team
43	Courtney Walsh	WI
36	Chris Martin	NZ
35	Glenn McGrath	Aus
34	Shane Warne	Aus
33	Muttiah Muralitharan	SL/ICC

900 runs in a series

Player	M	I	NO	R	HS	100s	Avg	For/Against	Season
Don Bradman	5	7	0	974	334	4	139.14	Aus v Eng	1930
Wally Hammond	5	9	1	905	251	4	113.12	Eng v Aus	1928-29

1500 runs in a calendar year

Player	Team	T	I	NO	Runs	HS	100s	Avg	Year
Mohammad Yousuf	Pak	11	19	1	1,788	202	9	99.33	2006
Viv Richards	WI	11	19	0	1,710	291	7	90.00	1976
Graeme Smith	ICC/SA	15	25	2	1,656	232	6	72.00	2008
Michael Clarke	Aus	11	18	3	1,595	329*	5	106.33	2012
Sachin Tendulkar	Ind	14	23	3	1,562	214	7	78.10	2010
Sunil Gavaskar	Ind	18	27	1	1,555	221	5	59.80	1979
Ricky Ponting	Aus	15	28	5	1,544	207	6	67.13	2005
Ricky Ponting	Aus	11	18	3	1,503	257	6	100.20	2003

Highest percentage of team's runs over Test career (Qualification – 20 matches)

Player	Team	Tests	Runs	Team Runs	% Of Team Runs
Don Bradman	Aus	52	6,996	28,810	24.28
George Headley	WI	22	2,190	10,239	21.38
Brian Lara	WI	131	11,953	63,328	18.87

*The percentage shows the proportion of a team's runs scored by that player in all Tests in which he played, including team runs in innings in which he did not bat.

Fastest 50s (Minutes)

Minutes	Player	For/Against	Venue	Season
24	Misbah-ul-Haq	Pak v Aus	Abu Dhabi	2014-15
27	Mohammad Ashraful	Ban v Ind	Mirpur	2007
28	John Brown	Eng v Aus	Melbourne	1894-95

Fastest 50s (Balls)

Balls	Player	For/Against	Venue	Season
21	Misbah-ul-Haq	Pak v Aus	Abu Dhabi	2014-15
24	Jacque Kallis	SA v Zim	Cape Town	2004-05
25	Shane Shillingford	WI v NZ	Kingston	2014

Fastest 100s (Minutes)

Minutes	Player	For/Against	Venue	Season
	Jack Gregory	Aus v SA	Johannesburg	1921-22
	Misbah-ul-Haq	Pak v Aus	Abu Dhabi	2014-15
	Gilbert Jessop	Eng v Aus	The Oval	1902

Fastest 100s (Balls)

Balls	Player	For/Against	Venue	Season
4	Brendon McCullum	NZ v AUS	Christchurch	2015/16
5	Viv Richards	WI v Eng	St John's	1985-86
5	Misbah-ul-Haq	Pak v Aus	Abu Dhabi	2014-15

Fastest 200s (Minutes)

Minutes	Player	For/Against	Venue	Season
14	Don Bradman	Aus v Eng	Leeds	1930
17	Nathan Astle	NZ v Eng	Christchurch	2001-02
23	Stan McCabe	Aus v Eng	Nottingham	1938

Fastest 200s (Balls)

Balls	Player	For/Against	Venue	Season
53	Nathan Astle	NZ v Eng	Christchurch	2001-02
63	Ben Stokes	Eng v SA	Cape Town	2015-16
68	Virender Sehwag	Ind v SL	Mumbai	2009-10

Fastest 300s (Minutes)

Minutes	Player	For/Against	Venue	Season
288	Wally Hammond	Eng v NZ	Auckland	1932-33
336	Don Bradman	Aus v Eng	Leeds	1930
425	Don Bradman	Aus v Eng	Leeds	1934

Fastest 300s (Balls)

Balls	Player	For/Against	Venue	Season
278	Virender Sehwag	Ind v SA	Chennai	2007-08
362	Mathew Hayden	Aus v Zim	Perth	2003-04
364	Virender Sehwag	Ind v Pak	Multan	2003-04

Most runs in one over

Runs	Batsman	Details	Bowler	For/Against	Venue	Season
28	Brian Lara	(466444)	Robin Peterson	WI v SA	Johannesburg	2003-0
28	George Bailey	(462466)	James Anderson	Aus v Eng	Perth	2013-1
27	Shahid Afridi	(666621)	Harbhajan Singh	Pak v Ind	Lahore	2005-0

Most runs in a day

Runs	Player	For/Against	Venue	Season
309	Don Bradman	Aus v Eng	Leeds	1930
295	Wally Hammond	Eng v NZ	Auckland	1932-33
284	Virender Sehwag	Ind v SL	Mumbai	2009-10

Slowest individual batting

Runs	Minutes	Player	For/Against	Venue	Season
0	101	Geoff Allott	NZ v SA	Auckland	1998-99
4*	110	Abdul Razzaq	Pak v Aus	Melbourne	2004-05
6	137	Stuart Broad	Eng v NZ	Auckland	2012-13

Slowest hundreds (Minutes)

Minutes	Player	For/Against	Venue	Season
557	Mudassar Nazar	Pak v Eng	Lahore	1977-78
545	Jackie McGlew	SA v Aus	Durban	1957-58
535	Asanka Gurusinha	SL v Zim	Harare	1994-95

Slowest hundreds (Balls)

Balls	Player	For/Against	Venue	Season
419	Mudassar Nazar	Pak v Eng	Lahore	1977-78
397	Sanjay Manjrekar	Ind v Zim	Harare	1992-93
396	Clive Radley	Eng v NZ	Auckland	1977-78

Highest partnerships for each wicket

Wicket	Runs	Batsmen	For/Against	Venue	Season
1st	415	Neil McKenzie (226) & Graeme Smith (232)	SA v Ban	Chittagong	2007-08
2nd	576	Sanath Jayasuriya (340) & Roshan Mahanama (225)	SL v Ind	Colombo (RPS)	1997
3rd	624	Kumar Sangakkara (287) & Mahela Jayawardene (374)	SL v SA	Colombo (SSC)	2006

449	Adam Voges (269*) & Shaun Marsh (182)	Aus v WI	Hobart	2015-16
405	Sydney Barnes (234) & Don Bradman (234)	Aus v Eng	Sydney	1946-47
399	Ben Stokes (258) & Jonathan Bairstow (150*)	Eng v SA	Cape Town	2015-16
347	Denis Atkinson (219) & Clairmonte Depeiaza (122)	WI v Aus	Bridgetown	1954-55
332	Jonathan Trott (184) & Stuart Broad (169)	Eng v Pak	Lord's	2010
195	Mark Boucher (78) & Pat Symcox (108)	SA v Pak	Johannesburg	1997-98
198	Joe Root (154*) & James Anderson (81)	Eng v Ind	Nottingham	2014

Unusual dismissals

Handled the ball

Player	For/Against	Venue	Season
Russell Endean	SA v Eng	Cape Town	1956-57
Andrew Hilditch	Aus v Pak	Perth	1978-79
Mohsin Khan	Pak v Aus	Karachi	1982-83
Desmond Haynes	WI v Ind	Mumbai	1983-84
Graham Gooch	Eng v Aus	Manchester	1993
Steve Waugh	Aus v Ind	Chennai	2000-01
Michael Vaughan	Eng v Ind	Bangalore	2001-02

Obstructing the field

Batsman	For/Against	Venue	Season
Len Hutton	Eng v SA	The Oval	1951

BOWLING

Most wickets

Player	Team	W	Balls	R	BBI	BBM	Avg	5wI	10wM
Muttiah Muralitharan	SL/ICC	800	44,039	18,180	9-51	16-220	22.72	67	22
Shane Warne	Aus	708	40,705	17,995	8-71	12-128	25.41	37	10
Anil Kumble	Ind	619	40,850	18,355	10-74	14-149	29.65	35	8

Most wickets in an innings

Figures	Player	For/Against	Venue	Season
10-53	Jim Laker	Eng v Aus	Manchester	1956
10-74	Anil Kumble	Ind v Pak	Delhi	1998-99
9-28	George Lohmann	Eng v SA	Johannesburg	1895-96

Four wickets in five balls

Player	For/Against	Venue	Season
Maurice Allom	Eng v NZ	Christchurch	1929-30
Christopher Old	Eng v Pak	Birmingham	1978
Wasim Akram	Pak v WI	Lahore	1990-91

Most wickets in a Test

Match Figures	Innings Figures	Player	For/Against	Venue	Season
19-90	(9-37, 10-53)	Jim Laker	Eng v Aus	Manchester	1956
17-159	(8-56, 9-103)	Sydney Barnes	Eng v SA	Johannesburg	1913-14
16-136	(8-61, 8-75)	Narendra Hirwani	Ind v WI	Chennai	1987-88

Most balls bowled in a Test

Balls	Player	For/Against	Venue	Season
774	Sonny Ramadhin	WI v Eng	Birmingham	1957
766	Hedley Verity	Eng v SA	Durban	1938-39
749	Jack White	Eng v Aus	Adelaide	1928-29

Most wickets in a series

Player	M	W	R	BBI	BBM	For/Against	Season
Sydney Barnes	4	49	536	9/103	17/159	Eng v SA	1913-14
Jim Laker	5	46	442	10/53	19/90	Eng v Aus	1956
Clarrie Grimmett	5	44	642	7/40	13/173	Aus v SA	1935-36

Most wickets in a calendar year

Player	Team	Year	Matches	Wickets	Runs	BBI	BBM
Shane Warne	Aus	2005	15	96	2114	6/46	12/246
Muttiah Muralitharan	SL	2006	11	90	1521	8/70	12/225
Dennis Lillee	Aus	1981	13	85	1781	7/83	11/159

Best career averages (Qualification – 75 wickets)

Player	Team	Balls	M	R	W	Avg
George Lohmann	Eng	3,830	364	1,205	112	10.75
Sydney Barnes	Eng	7,873	356	3,106	189	16.43
Charlie Turner	Aus	5,179	457	1,670	101	16.53

Best career strike rates (Qualification – 75 wickets)

Player	Team	SR	Balls	M	R	W	5wI	10wM
George Lohmann	Eng	34.19	3,830	364	1,205	112	9	5
Shane Bond	NZ	38.75	3,372	114	1,922	87	5	1
Dale Steyn	SA	41.37	17,210	619	9,252	416	26	5

Highest percentage of team's wickets over Test career (Qualification – 20 matches)

Player	Team	Matches	Wickets	Team Wkts	% Of Team Wickets
Muttiah Muralitharan	SL	133	800	2,070	38.64
Sydney Barnes	Eng	27	189	494	38.25
Richard Hadlee	NZ	86	431	1,255	34.34

ALL-ROUND

Century and 10 wickets in a Test

Player	Batting	Bowling	For/Against	Venue	Season
Ian Botham	114	6-58 7-48	Eng v Ind	Mumbai	1979-80
Imran Khan	117	6-98 5-82	Pak v Ind	Faisalabad	1982-83
Shakib Al Hasan	137	5-80 5-44	Ban v Zim	Khulna	2014-15

3000 runs and 300 wickets

Player	Team	M	R	Bat Avg	W	Bowl Avg
Kapil Dev	Ind	131	5248	31.05	434	29.64
Ian Botham	Eng	102	5200	33.54	383	28.40
Daniel Vettori	NZ/ICC	113	4531	30.00	362	34.36
Imran Khan	Pak	88	3807	37.69	362	22.81
Shaun Pollock	SA	108	3781	32.31	421	23.11
Shane Warne	Aus	145	3154	17.32	708	25.41

Richard Hadlee	NZ	86	3124	27.16	431	22.29
Chaminda Vaas	SL	111	3089	24.32	355	29.58

WICKETKEEPING

Most dismissals in an innings

Dismissal	Ct.	St.	Player	For/Against	Venue	Season
7	7	0	Wasim Bari	Pak v NZ	Auckland	1978-79
7	7	0	Bob Taylor	Eng v Ind	Mumbai	1979-80
7	7	0	Ian Smith	NZ v SL	Hamilton	1990-91
7	7	0	Ridley Jacobs	WI v Aus	Melbourne	2000-01

Most dismissals in a Test

Dismissal	Ct.	St.	Player	For/Against	Venue	Season
11	11	0	Jack Russell	Eng v SA	Johannesburg	1995-96
11	11	0	AB de Villiers	SA v Pak	Johannesburg	2012-13

Most dismissals in a series

Player	M	Inn	Dismissal	Ct.	St.	Dism./Inn	For/Against	Season
Brad Haddin	5	10	29	29	0	2.900	Aus v Eng	2013-14
Rod Marsh	5	10	28	28	0	2.800	Aus v Eng	1982-83
Jack Russell	5	7	27	25	2	3.857	Eng v SA	1995-96
Ian Healy	6	12	27	25	2	2.250	Aus v Eng	1997

Most dismissals in a career

Dismissals	Player	Team	M	Ct.	St.
555	Mark Boucher	South Africa/ICC	147	532	23
416	Adam Gilchrist	Australia	96	379	37
395	Ian Healy	Australia	119	366	29

FIELDING

Most catches in a Test

Ct.	Player	For/Against	Venue	Season
8	Ajinkya Rahane	Ind v SL	Galle	2015

Most catches in a series

Ct.	Player	Matches	For/Against	Season
15	Jack Gregory	5	Aus v Eng	1920-21
14	Greg Chappell	6	Aus v Eng	1974-75

Most catches in a career

Ct.	M	Player	Team
210	164	Rahul Dravid	India/ICC
205	149	Mahela Jayawardene	Sri Lanka
200	166	Jacques Kallis	South Africa/ICC

TEAM TOTALS

Highest innings totals

Score	For/Against	Venue	Season
952-6d	SL v Ind	Colombo (RPS)	1997
903-7d	Eng v Aus	The Oval	1938
849	Eng v WI	Kingston	1929-30

Highest fourth innings totals

Category	Score	For/Against	Venue	Season
To Draw	654-5	Eng v SA	Durban	1938-39
To Lose	451	NZ v Eng	Christchurch	2001-02
To Draw	450-7	SA v Ind	Johannesburg	2013-14
To Lose	445	Ind v Aus	Adelaide	1977/78

Most runs in a day by both sides

Total	Day	Team 1	Score	Team 2	Score	Venue	Season
588	2	England	(398-6)	India	(190-0)	Manchester	1936
522	2	England	(503-2)	South Africa	(19-0)	Lord's	1924
509	2	Sri Lanka	(509-9)	Bangladesh		Colombo (PSS)	2002

Most wickets in a day

Team 1	Team 2	Day	Runs	Wickets	Venue	Date
Eng	Aus	2	157	27	Lord's	16 Jul 1888
Aus	Eng	1	221	25	Melbourne	1 Jan 1902
Eng	Aus	2	255	24	The Oval	10 Aug 1896

Lowest innings total

Score	For/Against	Venue	Season
26	NZ v Eng	Auckland	1954-55
30	SA v Eng	Port Elizabeth	1895-96
30	SA v Eng	Birmingham	1924

Fewest runs in a full day's play

Runs	Teams/Scores	Day, Time	Venue	Season
95	Aus (80) v Pak (15-2)	1st day, 5½ hours	Karachi	1956-57
104	Pak (104-5) v Aus	4th day, 5½ hours	Karachi	1959-60
106	Eng (92-2 to 198) v Aus	4th day, 5 hours	Brisbane	1958-59

Lowest aggregates in a completed Test

Runs	Teams	Venue	Season
234	Aus v SA	Melbourne	1931-32
291	Eng v Aus	Lord's	1888
295	NZ v Aus	Wellington	1945-46

Largest victories (by an innings)

Margin	Teams	Venue	Season
Innings and 579 runs	Eng beat Aus	The Oval	1938
Innings and 360 runs	Aus beat SA	Johannesburg	2001-02
Innings and 336 runs	WI beat Ind	Kolkata	1958-59

Largest victories (by runs)

Margin	Teams	Venue	Season
675 runs	Eng beat Aus	Brisbane	1928-29
562 runs	Aus beat Eng	The Oval	1934
530 runs	Aus beat SA	Melbourne	1910-11

Tied Tests

Teams and Score	Venue	Season
Aus (505 & 232) v WI (453 & 284)	Brisbane	1960-61
Ind (397 & 347) v Aus (574-7d & 170-5d)	Chennai	1986-87

Most consecutive Test victories

Matches	Team	Duration	
16	Aus	1999/00	2000/01
16	Aus	2005/06	2007/08
11	WI	1983/84	1984/85

Most consecutive Tests without a win

Matches	Team	Duration	
44	NZ	1929/30	1955/56
34	Ban	2000/01	2004/05
31	Ind	1981/82	1984/85

Whitewashes

Teams	Season
Five Test Series	
Australia beat England	1920-21
Australia beat South Africa	1931-32
England beat India	1959
West Indies beat India	1961-62
West Indies beat England	1984
West Indies beat England	1985-86
South Africa beat West Indies	1998-99
Australia beat West Indies	2000-01
Australia beat England	2006-07
Australia beat England	2013-14
Four Test Series	
Australia beat India	1967-68
South Africa beat Australia	1969-70
England beat West Indies	2004
England beat India	2011
Australia beat India	2011-12
India beat Australia	2012-13
Three Test Series	
England beat Australia	1886
England beat South Africa	1895-96
England beat South Africa	1912
England beat West Indies	1928
England beat New Zealand	1962-63

England beat New Zealand	1965
England beat India	1967
Australia beat Pakistan	1972-73
England beat India	1974
England beat New Zealand	1978
Australia beat England	1979-80
Pakistan beat Australia	1982-83
Pakistan beat New Zealand	1990-91
India beat England	1992-93
India beat Sri Lanka	1993-94
Australia beat Sri Lanka	1995-96
Pakistan beat West Indies	1997-98
Australia beat Pakistan	1999-00
Australia beat India	1999-00
Australia beat New Zealand	1999-00
Sri Lanka beat West Indies	2001-02
Australia beat South Africa	2001-02
Sri Lanka beat Zimbabwe	2001-02
Australia beat Pakistan	2002-03
Pakistan beat Bangladesh	2003-04
Australia beat Sri Lanka	2003-04
England beat New Zealand	2004
Australia beat Pakistan	2004-05
Australia beat West Indies	2005-06
Australia beat South Africa	2005-06
Sri Lanka beat Bangladesh	2007
Australia beat Pakistan	2009-10
Pakistan beat England	2011-12
Australia beat Sri Lanka	2012-13
South Africa beat Pakistan	2012-13
Bangladesh beat Zimbabwe	2014-15
Sri Lanka beat Australia	2016
India beat New Zealand	2016-17

PLAYERS

Most capped players

Matches	Player	For
200	Sachin Tendulkar	Ind
168	Ricky Ponting	Aus
168	Steve Waugh	Aus

Youngest Test players

Age	Player	For/Against	Venue	Season
14 y 227 d	Hasan Raza	Pak v Zim	Faisalabad	1996-97
15 y 124 d	Mushtaq Mohammad	Pak v WI	Lahore	1958-59
16 y 189 d	Aaqib Javed	Pak v NZ	Wellington	1988-89

Oldest players on debut

Age	Player	For/Against	Venue	Season
49 y 119 d	James Southerton	Eng v Aus	Melbourne	1876-77
47 y 284 d	Miran Bakhsh	Pak v Ind	Lahore	1954-55
46 y 253 d	Don Blackie	Aus v Eng	Sydney	1928-29

Oldest Test players

Age	Player	For/Against	Venue	Season
52 y 165 d	Wilfred Rhodes	Eng v WI	Kingston	1929-30
50 y 327 d	Bert Ironmonger	Aus v Eng	Sydney	1932-33
50 y 320 d	WG Grace	Eng v Aus	Nottingham	1899

Most consecutive Test appearances

Matches	Player	Team	Duration	
153	Allan Border	Aus	March 1979	March 1994
133	Alastair Cook	Eng	May 2006	October 2016
107	Mark Waugh	Aus	June 1993	October 2002

Most Tests as captain

Matches	Won	Player	Team
109	53	Graeme Smith	SA/ICC
93	32	Allan Border	Aus
80	28	Stephen Fleming	NZ

UMPIRES

Most Tests

Tests	Umpire	Country	Duration	
128	Steve Bucknor	WI	1988/89	2008/09
108	Rudi Koertzen	SA	1992/93	2010
105	Aleem Dar	Pak	2003/04	2016

ONE-DAY INTERNATIONALS

BATTING

Highest Aggregates

Player	Team	R	M	Inn	NO	HS	Avg	100s/50
Sachin Tendulkar	Ind	18,426	463	452	41	200*	44.83	49/96
Kumar Sangakkara	SL/Asia/ICC	14,234	404	380	41	169	41.98	25/93
Ricky Ponting	Aus/ICC	13,704	375	365	39	164	42.03	30/82

Highest Individual innings

Score	Player	For/Against	Venue	Season
264	Rohit Sharma	Ind v SL	Kolkata	2014-15
237*	Martin Guptill	NZ v WI	Wellington	2014-15
219	Virender Sehwag	Ind v WI	Indore	2011-12

Fastest 50s

Balls	Player	For/Against	Venue	Season
16	AB de Villiers	SA v WI	Johannesburg	2014-15
17	Sanath Jayasuriya	SL v Pak	Singapore	1995-96
17	Kusal Perera	SL v Pak	Pallekele	2015

Fastest 100s

Balls	Player	For/Against	Venue	Season
31	AB de Villiers	SA v WI	Johannesburg	2014-15
36	Corey Anderson	NZ v WI	Queenstown	2013-14
37	Shahid Afridi	Pak v SL	Nairobi	1996-97

Highest partnerships for each wicket

Wicket	Runs	Batsmen	For/Against	Venue	Season
1st	286	Upul Tharanga & Sanath Jayasuriya	SL v Eng	Leeds	2006
2nd	372	Chris Gayle & Marlon Samuels	WI v Zim	Canberra	2014-15
3rd	258	Darren Bravo & Denesh Ramdin	WI v Ban	Basseterre	2014
4th	275*	Mohammad Azharuddin & Ajay Jadeja	Ind v Zim	Cuttack	1997-98
5th	256*	David Miller & JP Duminy	SA v Zim	Hamilton	2014-15
6th	267*	Grant Elliott & Luke Ronchi	NZ v SL	Dunedin	2014-15
7th	177	Jos Buttler & Adil Rashid	Eng v NZ	Harare	2015
8th	138*	Justin Kemp & Andrew Hall	SA v Ind	Cape Town	2006-07
9th	132	Angelo Mathews & Lasith Malinga	SL v Aus	Melbourne	2010-11
10th	106*	Vivian Richards & Michael Holding	WI v Eng	Manchester	1984

BOWLING

Most wickets

Player	Team	W	Balls	R	BB	Avg	5w
Muttiah Muralitharan	SL/ICC/Asia	534	18,811	12,326	7-30	23.08	10
Wasim Akram	Pak	502	18,186	11,812	5-15	23.52	6
Waqar Younis	Pak	416	12,698	9,919	7-36	23.84	13

Best bowling analysis

Figures	Player	For/Against	Venue	Season
8-19	Chaminda Vaas	SL v Zim	Colombo (SSC)	2001-02
7-12	Shahid Afridi	Pak v WI	Providence	2013
7-15	Glenn McGrath	Aus v Nam	Potchefstroom	2002-03

Best career strike rates (Qualification – 1500 balls bowled)

Player	Team	SR	Balls	R	W	BB	5w
Mitchell Starc	Aus	24.60	2,707	2,158	110	6-28	5
Mohammed Shami	Ind	26.95	2,345	2,166	87	4-35	-
Hamid Hassan	Afg	27.10	1,518	1,153	56	5-45	1

WICKETKEEPING

Most dismissals in an innings

Dismissals	Ct.	St.	Player	For/Against	Venue	Season
6	6	0	Adam Gilchrist	Aus v SA	Cape Town	1999-00
6	6	0	Alec Stewart	Eng v Zim	Manchester	2000
6	5	1	Ridley Jacobs	WI v SL	Colombo (RPS)	2001-02
6	5	1	Adam Gilchrist	Aus v Eng	Sydney	2002-03
6	6	0	Adam Gilchrist	Aus v Nam	Potchefstroom	2002-03
6	6	0	Adam Gilchrist	Aus v SL	Colombo (RPS)	2003-04
6	6	0	Mark Boucher	SA v Pak	Cape Town	2006-07
6	5	1	MS Dhoni	Ind v Eng	Leeds	2007
6	6	0	Adam Gilchrist	Aus v Ind	Vadodara	2007-08
6	5	1	Adam Gilchrist	Aus v Ind	Sydney	2007-08
6	6	0	Matt Prior	Eng v SA	Nottingham	2008
6	6	0	Jos Butler	Eng v SA	The Oval	2013
6	6	0	Matthew Cross	Sco v Can	Christchurch	2013-14
6	5	1	Quinton de Kock	SA v NZ	Mount Maunganui	2014-15
6	6	0	Sarfraz Ahmed	Pak v SA	Auckland	2014-15

Most dismissals in career

Dismissals	Player	Team	Matches	Ct.	St.
482	Kumar Sangakkara	SL/Asia/ICC	404	384	98
472	Adam Gilchrist	Aus/ICC	287	417	55
424	Mark Boucher	SA/Africa	295	402	22

FIELDING

Most catches in an innings

Ct.	Player	For/Against	Venue	Season
5	Jonty Rhodes	SA v WI	Mumbai	1993-94

Most catches in a career

Ct.	Matches	Player	Team
218	448	Mahela Jayawardene	SL/Asia
160	375	Ricky Ponting	Australia/ICC
156	334	Mohammad Azharuddin	Ind

TEAM

Highest totals

Score	Overs	For/Against	Venue	Season
444-3	50	Eng v Pak	Nottingham	2016
443-9	50	SL v Net	Amstelveen	2006
439-2	50	SA v WI	Wanderers	2014-15

Highest totals batting second

Score	Overs	For/Against	Venue	Season
438-9	49.5	SA v Aus	Johannesburg	2005-06
411-8	50	SL v Ind	Rajkot	2009-10
372-6	49.2	SA v Aus	Durban	2016-17

Highest match aggregates

Runs	Wickets	Overs	Teams	Venue	Season
872	13	99.5	SA v Aus	Johannesburg	2005-06
825	15	100	Ind v SL	Rajkot	2009-10
763	14	96	Eng v NZ	The Oval	2015

Lowest totals

Score	Overs	For/Against	Venue	Season
35	18	Zim v SL	Harare	2004
36	18.4	Can v SL	Paarl	2002-03
38	15.4	Zim v SL	Colombo (SSC)	2001-02

Largest victories (By runs)

Margin	For/Against	Venue	Season
290	NZ beat Ire	Aberdeen	2008
275	Aus beat Afg	Perth	2014-15
272	SA beat Zim	Benoni	2010-11

PLAYER

Most matches as captain

Matches	Won	Player	Team
230	165	Ricky Ponting	Aus/ICC
218	98	Stephen Fleming	NZ

199	110	MS Dhoni	IND

Most capped cricketers

Matches	Player	Team
463	Sachin Tendulkar	Ind
448	Mahela Jayawardene	SL/Asia
445	Sanath Jayasuriya	SL/Asia

T20 INTERNATIONALS

BATTING

Highest Aggregates

Player	Team	Runs	M	Inn	NO	HS	Avg	100s/50
Brendon McCullum	NZ	2,140	71	70	10	123	35.66	2/13
Tillakaratne Dilshan	SL	1889	80	79	12	104*	28.19	1/13
Martin Guptill	NZ	1806	61	59	7	101*	34.73	1/10

Highest Individual Innings

Runs	Player	For/Against	Venue	Season
156	Aaron Finch	Aus v Eng	Southampton	2013
145*	Glenn Maxwell	Aus v SL	Pallekele	2016
124*	Shane Watson	Aus v Ind	Sydney	2015-16

Highest partnerships for each wicket

Wicket	Runs	Batsmen	For/Against	Venue	Season
1st	171*	Martin Guptill & Kane Williamson	NZ v Pak	Hamilton	2015-16
2nd	166	Mahela Jayawardene & Kumar Sangakkara	SL v WI	Bridgetown	2010
3rd	152	Alex Hales & Eoin Morgan	Eng v SL	Chittagong	2013-14
4th	161	David Warner & Glenn Maxwell	Aus v SA	Johannesburg	2015-16
5th	119*	Shoaib Malik & Misbah-ul-Haq	Pak v Aus	Johannesburg	2007-08
6th	101*	Cameron White & Michael Hussey	Aus v SL	Bridgetown	2010
7th	91	Paul Collingwood & Michael Yardy	Eng v WI	The Oval	2007
8th	80	Preston Mommsen & Safyaan Sharif	Sco v Net	Edinburgh	2015
9th	66	Dwayne Bravo & Jerome Taylor	WI v Pak	Dubai	2016-17
10th	31*	Wahab Riaz & Shoaib Akhtar	Pak v NZ	Auckland	2010-11

BOWLING

Most wickets

Player	Team	W	Balls	R	BB	Avg	4w
Shahid Afridi	Pak	97	2,144	2,362	4-11	24.35	3
Umar Gul	Pak	85	1,203	1,443	5-6	16.97	4
Saeed Ajmal	Pak	85	1,430	1,516	4-19	17.83	4

Best bowling analysis

Figures	Player	For/Against	Venue	Season
6-8	Ajantha Mendis	SL v Zim	Hambantota	2012-13
6-16	Ajantha Mendis	SL v Aus	Pallekele	2011
5-3	Rangana Herath	SL v NZ	Chittagong	2013-14

WICKETKEEPING

Most dismissals in an innings

Dismissals	Ct.	St.	Player	For/Against	Venue	Season
5	3	2	Mohammad Shahzad	Afg v Oman	Abu Dhabi	2015-16
4	4	0	Adam Gilchrist	Aus v Zim	Cape Town	2007-08
4	4	0	Matt Prior	Eng v SA	Cape Town	2007-08
4	4	0	Adam Gilchrist	Aus v NZ	Perth	2007-08
4	0	4	Kamran Akmal	Pak v Net	Lord's	2009
4	3	1	Neil O'Brien	Ire v SL	Lord's	2009
4	4	0	MS Dhoni	Ind v Afg	Gros Islet	2010
4	2	2	AB de Villiers	SA v WI	North Sound	2010
4	3	1	Gary Wilson	Ire v Ken	Dubai	2011-12
4	4	0	AB de Villiers	SA v Zim	Hambantota	2012-13
4	4	0	MS Dhoni	Ind v Pak	Colombo	2012-13
4	2	2	Quinton de Kock	SA v Pak	Dubai	2013-14
4	4	0	Wesley Barresi	Net v Ken	Dubai	2013-14
4	0	4	Denesh Ramdin	WI v Pak	Mirpur	2013-14
4	1	3	Richmond Mutumbami	Zim v Sco	Nagpur	2015-16
4	3	1	Quinton de Kock	SA v Afg	Mumbai	2015-16

Most dismissals in a career

Dismissals	Player	Team	Matches	Ct.	St.
63	MS Dhoni	Ind	73	41	22
60	Kamran Akmal	Pak	53	28	32
51	Denesh Ramdin	WI	58	32	19

FIELDING

Most catches in career

Ct.	Matches	Player	Team
42	73	Ross Taylor	NZ
40	71	AB de Villiers	SA
38	82	Umar Akmal	Pak

TEAM

Highest Team totals

Score	Overs	For/Against	Venue	Season
263-3	20	Aus v SL	Pallekele	2016
260-6	20	SL v Ken	Johannesburg	2007-08
248-6	20	Aus v Eng	Southampton	2013

Lowest Team totals

Score	Overs	For/Against	Venue	Season
39	10.3	Ned v SL	Chittagong	2013-14
53	14.3	Npl v Ire	Belfast	2015-16
56	18.4	Ken v Afg	Sharjah	2013-14

FIRST-CLASS

BATTING

Highest Aggregates

Player	Runs	M	Inns	NO	HS	Avg	100s/50s
Jack Hobbs	61760	834	1325	107	316*	50.70	199/273
Frank Woolley	58,959	978	1,530	84	305*	40.77	145/295
Patsy Hendren	57,611	833	1,300	166	301*	50.80	170/272

Highest individual innings

Score	Player	For/Against	Venue	Season
501*	Brian Lara	Warwickshire v Durham	Birmingham	1994
499	Hanif Mohammad	Karachi v Bahawalpur	Karachi	1958-59
452*	Don Bradman	New South Wales v Queensland	Sydney	1929-30

Two double hundreds in a match

1st Inn	2nd Inn	Player	For/Against	Venue	Season
244	202*	Arthur Edward Fagg	Kent v Essex	Colchester	1938

Most double-hundreds in a career

200s	Player
37	Don Bradman
36	Wally Hammond
22	Elias Henry Hendren

Most hundreds in a career

100s	Player
199	Jack Hobbs
170	Elias Henry Hendren
167	Wally Hammond

Highest career averages (Qualification 10,000 Runs)

Player	M	Inn	NO	R	HS	Avg	100s/50s
Don Bradman	234	338	43	28,067	452*	95.14	117/69
Vijay Merchant	150	234	46	13,470	359*	71.64	45/52
Ajay Sharma	129	166	16	10,120	259*	67.46	38/36

Highest season aggregates in Asia

Country - League	Player	Team	M	I	NO	R	HS	100s	Avg	Season
Bangladesh – National Cricket League	Minhazul Abedin	Chittagong Division	9	15	1	1,012	210	3	126.50	2001-02
India – Ranji Trophy	VVS Laxman	Hyderabad	9	14	1	1,415	353	8	176.87	1999-00

Pakistan – Quaid-e-Azam Trophy	Saadat Ali	House Building Finance Corporation	9	18	1	1,217	208	3	152.12 1983-84
Sri Lanka – Club Championship	Russell Arnold	Nondescripts Cricket Club	14	21	3	1,430	217*	5	130.00 1995-96

Most runs in a day by one batsman

Runs	Player	For/Against	Venue	Season
390	Brian Lara	Warwickshire v Durham	Birmingham	1994
345	Charles Macartney	Australians v Nottinghamshire	Nottingham	1921
334	Bill Ponsford	Victoria v New South Wales	Melbourne	1926-27

Longest innings

Duration	Player	Score	For/Against	Venue	Season
16h 55m	Rajeev Nayyar	271	Himachal Pradesh v Jammu & Kashmir	Chamba	1999-00
16h 10m	Hanif Mohammad	337	Pakistan v West Indies	Bridgetown	1957-58
15h 7m	Vineet Saxena	257	Rajasthan v Tamil Nadu	Chennai	2011-12

36 runs in one over

Batsman	Bowler	For/Against	Venue	Season
Garry Sobers	Malcolm Nash	Nottinghamshire v Glamorgan	Swansea	1968
Ravi Shastri	Tilak Raj	Bombay v Baroda	Mumbai	1984-85

Most 6s in a match

6s	Player	For/Against	Venue	Season
23	Colin Munro	Auckland v Central District	Napier	2014-15
20	Andrew Symonds	Gloucestershire v Glamorgan	Abergavenny	1995

Highest partnerships for each wicket

Wicket	Runs	Batsmen	For/Against	Venue	Season
1st	561	Waheed Mirza (324) & Mansoor Akhtar (224*)	Karachi Whites v Quetta	Karachi	1976-77
2nd	580	Rafatullah Mohmand (302*) & Aamer Sajjad (289)	Water and Power Development Authority v Sui Southern Gas Corporation	Sheikhupura	2009-10

	624	Kumar Sangakkara (287) & Mahela Jayawardene (374)	Sri Lanka v South Africa	Colombo (SSC)	2006
	577	Vijay Hazare (288) & Gul Mahomed (319)	Baroda v Holkar	Vadodara	1946-47
	520*	Cheteshwar Pujara (302*) & Ravindra Jadeja (232*)	Saurashtra v Orissa	Rajkot	2008-09
	487*	George Headley (344*) & Charles Passailaigue (261*)	Jamaica v Lord Tennyson's XI	Kingston	1931-32
	460	Bhupinder Singh jun. (297) & Pankaj Dharmani (202*)	Punjab v Delhi	Delhi	1994-95
	433	Arthur Sims (184*) & Victor Trumper (293)	Australians v Canterbury	Christchurch	1913-14
	283	Arnold Warren (123) & John Chapman (165)	Derbyshire v Warwickshire	Blackwell	1910
10th	307	Alan Kippax (260*) & Hal Hooker (62)	New South Wales v Victoria	Melbourne	1928-29

BOWLING

Most wickets in career

Player	W	B	R	BBI	Avg	5wI	10wM
Wilfred Rhodes	4,204	185,742	70,322	9-24	16.72	287	68
Tich Freeman	3,776	154,658	69,577	10-53	18.42	386	140
Charlie Parker	3,278	157,059	63,817	10-79	19.46	277	91

Most wickets in an innings

Figures	Player	For/Against	Venue	Season
10-10	Hedley Verity	Yorkshire v Nottinghamshire	Leeds	1932
10-18	George Geary	Leicestershire v Glamorgan	Pontypridd	1929
10-20	Premangsu Chatterjee	Bengal v Assam	Jorhat	1956-57

*A total of 80 times bowlers have taken 10 wickets in an innings.

Most wickets in a match

Match Figures	Innings Figures	Player	For/Against	Venue	Season
19-90	(9-37, 10-53)	Jim Laker	Eng v Aus	Manchester	1956
18-96	(9-43, 9-53)	Henry Arkwright	Gentlemen of MCC v Gentlemen of Kent	Canterbury	1861

| 17-46 | (9-27, 8-19) | John Wisden | United England XI v Yorkshire | Sheffield | 1853 |

WICKETKEEPING

Most dismissals in an innings

Dismissals	Ct.	St.	Player	For/Against	Venue	Season
9	8	1	Tahir Rashid	Habib Bank Limited v Pakistan Automobiles Corporation	Gujranwala	1992-93
9	7	2	Wayne James	Matabeleland v Mashonaland Country Districts	Bulawayo	1995-96

Most dismissals in a match

Dismissals	Ct.	St.	Player	For/Against	Venue	Season
14	11	3	Ibrahim Khaleel	Hyderabad v Assam	Guwahati	2011-12
13	11	2	Wayne James	Matabeleland v Mashonaland Country Districts	Bulawayo	1995-96

Most dismissals in career

Dismissal	Player	Matches	Ct.	St.
1649	Bob Taylor	639	1,473	176
1,518	John Murray	635	1268	259
1,495	Bert Strudwick	674	1237	258

The record for Bob Taylor excludes 3 catches in 3 matches as a fielder.
The record for John Murray excludes 11 catches in 19 matches as a fielder.
The record for Bert Strudwick excludes 1 catch in 2 matches as a fielder.

FIELDING

Most catches in an innings

Ct.	Player	For/Against	Venue	Season
7	Micky Stewart	Surrey v Northamptonshire	Northampton	1957
7	Tony Brown	Gloucestershire v Nottinghamshire	Nottingham	1966
7	Rikki Clarke	Warwickshire v Lancashire	Liverpool	2011

Most catches in a match

Ct.	Player	For/Against	Venue	Season
10	Wally Hammond	Gloucestershire v Surrey	Cheltenham	1928
9	Rikki Clarke	Warwickshire v Lancashire	Liverpool	2011

Most catches in career

Ct.	Matches	Player
1,018	979	Frank Woolley
887	879	WG Grace
830	654	Tony Lock

The record for WG Grace excludes 1 catch as wicketkeeper but includes 7 catches in 48 matches in which it is not known whether he kept wicket.

TEAM

Highest innings totals

Score	For/Against	Venue	Season
1,107	Victoria v New South Wales	Melbourne	1926-27
1,059	Victoria v Tasmania	Melbourne	1922-23
952-6d	Sri Lanka v India	Colombo (RPS)	1997

Highest fourth innings totals

Score	For/Against	Venue	Season
654-5	England v South Africa	Durban	1938-39
604	Maharashtra v Bombay	Pune	1948-49
576-8	Trinidad v Barbados	Port-of-Spain	1945-46

Most runs in a day by both sides

Total	Day	Team 1	Score	Team 2	Score	Venue	Season
721	1	Australians	(721)	Essex		Southend-On-Sea	1948
685	2	North	(169-8 & 255-7)	South	(261-8d)	Blackpool	1961
666	2	Surrey	(607-4)	Northamptonshire	(59-2)	Northampton	1920

Highest match aggregate

Runs	Wickets	Teams	Venue	Season
2,376	37	Maharashtra v Bombay	Pune	1948-49
2,078	40	Bombay v Holkar	Mumbai	1944-45
1,981	35	South Africa v England	Durban	1938-39

Lowest innings totals

Total	For/Against	Venue	Season
12	Oxford University v Marylebone Cricket Club	Oxford	1877
12	Northamptonshire v Gloucestershire	Gloucester	1907
13	Auckland v Canterbury	Auckland	1877-78
13	Nottinghamshire v Yorkshire	Nottingham	1901

Lowest totals in a match

Total	For/Against	Venue	Season
34	Border v Natal	East London	1959-60
41	Quetta v Rawalpindi	Islamabad	2008-09
42	Northamptonshire v Yorkshire	Northampton	1908

Lowest aggregate in a completed match

Total	Teams	Venue	Season
85	Quetta v Rawalpindi	Islamabad	2008-09
105	Marylebone Cricket Club v Australians	Lord's	1878

Largest victories (by an innings)

Margin	Teams	Venue	Season
Innings and 851 runs	Railways beat Dera Ismail Khan	Lahore	1964-65
Innings and 666 runs	Victoria beat Tasmania	Melbourne	1922-23
Innings and 656 runs	Victoria beat New South Wales	Melbourne	1926-27

Largest victories (by runs)

Margin	Teams	Venue	Season
685 runs	New South Wales beat Queensland	Sydney	1929-30
675 runs	England beat Australia	Brisbane	1928-29
638 runs	New South Wales beat South Australia	Adelaide	1920-21

RANJI TROPHY

BATTING

Highest Aggregates

Player	R	M	Inn	NO	HS	Avg	100s/50s
Wasim Jaffer	10,143	129	201	23	314*	56.98	35/41

...mol Muzumdar	9,202	136	200	21	260	51.40	28/45
...evendra Bundela	8,549	134	214	28	167*	45.96	23/46

Highest Individual Innings

Runs	Player	For/Against	Venue	Season
443*	Bhausaheb Nimbalkar	Maharashtra v Kathiawar	Pune	1948-49
377	Sanjay Manjrekar	Bombay v Hyderabad	Mumbai	1990-91
366	MV Sridhar	Hyderabad v Andhra	Secunderabad	1993-94

Most Centuries

100s	Player
35	Wasim Jaffer
31	Ajay Sharma
28	Hrishikesh Kanitkar
28	Amol Muzumdar

Highest partnerships for each wicket

Wicket	Runs	Players	For/Against	Venue	Season
1st	464	Ravi Sehgal & Raman Lamba	Delhi v Himachal Pradesh	Delhi	1994-95
2nd	475	Zahir Alam & Lalchand Rajput	Assam v Tripura	Guwahati	1991-92
3rd	594*	Swapnil Gugale & Ankit Bawne	Maharashtra v Delhi	Mumbai	2016-17
4th	577	Vijay Hazare & Gul Mahomed	Baroda v Holkar	Vadodara	1946-47
5th	520*	Cheteshwar Pujara & Ravindra Jadeja	Saurashtra v Orissa	Rajkot	2008-09
6th	417	Wriddhiman Saha & Laxmi Ratan Shukla	Bengal v Assam	Kolkata	2010-11
7th	460	Bhupinder Singh, jun. & Pankaj Dharmani	Punjab v Delhi	Delhi	1994-95
8th	392	Amit Mishra & Jayant Yadav	Haryana v Karnataka	Hubli	2012-13
9th	249*	Amkit Srivastava & Kapil Seth	Madhya Pradesh v Vidarbha	Indore	2000-01
10th	233	Ajay Sharma & Maninder Singh	Delhi v Bombay	Mumbai	1991-92

BOWLING

Most wickets in career

Bowler	W	B	R	BBI	Avg	5wI	10wI
Rajinder Goel	637	31,945	11,010	8-55	17.28	53	17
S Venkataraghavan	530	26,775	9,658	7-42	18.22	45	11
Sunil Joshi	479	28,884	11,139	7-29	23.25	27	5

Most wickets in an innings

Figures	Player	For/Against	Venue	Season
10-20	Premangsu Chatterjee	Bengal v Assam	Jorhat	1956-57
10-78	Pradeep Sunderam	Rajasthan v Vidarbha	Jodhpur	1985-86
9-23	Ankeet Chavan	Mumbai v Punjab	Mumbai	2012-13

Most wickets in a match

Match Figures	Innings Figures	Player	For/Against	Venue	Season
16-99	(8-58, 8-41)	Anil Kumble	Karnataka v Kerala	Thalassery	1994-9
16-154	(10-78, 6-76)	Pradeep Sunderam	Rajasthan v Vidarbha	Jodhpur	1985-8
15-154	(8-96, 8-54)	Jalaj Saxena	Madhya Pradesh v Railways	Gwalior	2015-1

WICKETKEEPING

Most dismissals in a match

Dismissals	Ct.	St.	Player	For/Against	Venue	Season
14	11	3	Ibrahim Khaleel	Hyderabad v Assam	Guwahati	2011-12
11	10	1	Samarjit Nath	Assam v Tripura	Guwahati	2001-02
11	9	2	Manvinder Bisla	Himachal Pradesh v Saurashtra	Dharmasala	2004-05

Most dismissals in career

Dismissals	Player	Matches	Ct.	St.
335	Vinayak Samant	94	298	37
299	Naman Ojha	94	270	29
293	Sagar Jogiyani	94	255	38

FIELDING

Most catches in a match

Catches	Player	For/Against	Venue	Season
	Shaukat Dukanwala	Baroda v Saurashtra	Bhavnagar	1981-82
	Pradeep Khanna	Bihar v Assam	Jamshedpur	1987-88
	K. Bhaskar Pillai	Delhi v Services	Delhi	1990-91
	S. Abbas Ali	Madhya Pradesh v Orissa	Cuttack	1996-97
	Sunil Oasis	Kerala v Andhra	Kozhikode	1999-00
	Balachandra Akhil	Karnataka v Andhra	Anantapur	2006-07

Most catches in career

Catches	Matches	Player
173	129	Wasim Jaffer
128	136	Amol Muzumdar
127	125	Sanjay Bangar

TEAM

Highest Team Total

Score	For/Against	Venue	Season
944-6d	Hyderabad v Andhra	Secunderabad	1993-94
912-8d	Holkar v Mysore	Indore	1945-46
912-6d	Tamil Nadu v Goa	Panaji	1988-89

Lowest Team Total

Score	For/Against	Venue	Season
21	Hyderabad v Rajasthan	Jaipur	2010-11
22	Southern Punjab v Northern India	Amritsar	1934-35
23	Sind v Southern Punjab	Patiala	1938-39
23	Jammu and Kashmir v Delhi	Srinagar	1960-61
23	Jammu and Kashmir v Haryana	Rai	1977-78

Largest victories (by an innings)

Margin	Teams	Venue	Season
Innings and 472 runs	Assam beat Tripura	Guwahati	1991-92
Innings and 453 runs	Bombay beat Sind	Mumbai	1947-48
Innings and 413 runs	Bengal beat Assam	Kolkata	1951-52

Largest victories (by runs)

Margin	Teams	Venue	Season
540 runs	Bengal beat Orissa	Cuttack	1953-54
531 runs	Bombay beat Holkar	Mumbai	1951-52
489 runs	Maharashtra beat Nawanagar	Pune	1944-45

Most-capped cricketers

Matches	Player	Teams
136	Amol Muzumdar	Mumbai, Assam, Andhra
134	Devendra Bundela	Madhya Pradesh
134	Mithun Manhas	Delhi, Jammu & Kashmir

All records are updated till November 4, 2016.

M - Matches, **T** – Tests, **I** - Innings, **NO** – Not Out, **R** - Runs, **HS** – Highest Score, **Avg** – Average, **W** – Wickets, **BBI** – Best Bowling in an Innings, **BBM** – Best Bowling in a Match, **5wI** –Five wickets in an innings, **10wM** – 10 wickets in a match, **SR** – Strike Rate, **Econ** – Economy Rate, **Ct.** – Catches, **St.** – Stumpings, **Dism./Inn** – Dismissal/Innings, **BB** – Best Bowling.

INDIA'S OVERALL TEST RECORD

Australia
(P 90, W 24, L 40, T 1, D 25)
Maiden match: Australia won by an innings and 226 runs
(Brisbane, November 28-December 4, 1947)

	India	Australia
Highest team total	705/7 dec (Sydney, 2004)	674 (Adelaide, 1948)
Lowest team total	58 (Brisbane, 1947)	83 (Melbourne, 1981)
Highest run-getter	Sachin Tendulkar (3630, 39 matches)	Ricky Ponting (2555, 29 matches)
Highest individual score	281 – VVS Laxman (Kolkata, 2001)	329* – Michael Clarke (Sydney, 2012)
Most hundreds	11 – Sachin Tendulkar	8 – Ricky Ponting
Highest wicket taker	Anil Kumble (111, 20 matches)	Brett Lee (53, 12 matches)
Best bowling (innings)	9-69 – Jasu Patel (Kanpur, 1959)	8-215 – Jason Kreza (Nagpur, 2008)
Best bowling (match)	15-217 – Harbhajan Singh (Chennai, 2001)	12-124 – Alan Davidson (Kanpur, 1959)
Highest wicket taker in a series	32 – Harbhajan Singh (2001)	31 – Craig McDermott (1991-92)
Most dismissals (wicketkeeper)	71 – MS Dhoni (19 matches)	75 – Adam Gilchrist (18 matches)
Most dismissals (wicketkeeper/innings)	5 – MS Dhoni (Perth, 2008)	6 – Brad Haddin (Brisbane, 2014)
Most catches (fielder)	46 – Rahul Dravid (32 matches)	36 – Ricky Ponting (29 matches)
Highest partnership	Rahul Dravid / VVS Laxman 376 for 5th wicket (Kolkata, 2001)	Michael Clarke / Ricky Ponting 386 for 4th wicket (Adelaide, 2012)
Most capped player	Sachin Tendulkar – 39	Ricky Ponting – 29

Bangladesh
(P 8, W 6, L 0, T 0, D 2)
Maiden match: India won by nine wickets (Dhaka, November 10-13, 2000)

	India	Bangladesh
Highest team total	610/3 dec (Mirpur, 2007)	400 (Dhaka, 2000)
Lowest team total	243 (Chittagong, 2010)	91 (Dhaka, 2000)
Highest run-getter	Sachin Tendulkar (820, 7 matches)	Mohammad Ashraful (386 runs, 6 matches)
Highest individual score	248* – Sachin Tendulkar (Dhaka, 2004)	158* – Mohammad Ashraful (Chittagong, 2004)

Most hundreds	5 – Sachin Tendulkar	1 – (Aminul Islam, Mohammad Ashraful, Mushfiqur Rahim, Tamim Iqbal)
Highest wicket taker	Zaheer Khan (31, 7 matches)	Mohammad Rafique (15, 5 matches)
Best bowling (innings)	7-87 – Zaheer Khan (Dhaka, 2010)	6-132 – Naimur Rahman (Dhaka, 2000)
Best bowling (match)	11-96 – Irfan Pathan (Dhaka, 2004)	7-174 – Shakib Al Hasan (Chittagong, 2010)
Highest wicket taker in a series	18 – Irfan Pathan (2004)	9 – Shakib Al Hasan (2010)
Most dismissals (wicketkeeper)	15 – MS Dhoni (3 matches)	8 – Mushfiqur Rahim (2 matches)
Most dismissals (wicket-keeper/innings)	5 – MS Dhoni (Dhaka, 2010)	5 – Mushfiqur Rahim (Dhaka, 2010)
Most catches (fielder)	13 – Rahul Dravid (7 matches)	4 – Habibul Bashar (5 matches)
Highest partnership	M Vijay/Shikhar Dhawan 283 for 1st wicket (Fatullah, 2015)	Junaid Siddique/Tamim Iqbal 200 for 2nd wicket (Dhaka, 2010)
Most capped player	Rahul Dravid, Sachin Tendulkar, Zaheer Khan – 7	Mohammad Ashraful – 6

England
(P 112, W 21, L 43, T 0, D 48)
Maiden match: England won by 158 runs (June 25-28, 1932)

	India	England
Highest team total	664 (The Oval, 2007)	710/7 dec (Birmingham, 2011)
Lowest team total	42 (Lord's, 1974)	101 (The Oval, 1971)
Highest run-getter	Sachin Tendulkar (2535, 32 matches)	Alastair Cook (1735, 20 matches)
Highest individual score	224 – Vinod Kambli (Mumbai, 1993)	333 – Graham Gooch (Lord's, 1990)
Most hundreds	7 – Rahul Dravid (21 matches)	6 – Kevin Pietersen (16 matches)
Highest wicket taker	Bhagwath Chandrasekhar (95, 23 matches)	James Anderson (82, 19 matches)
Best bowling (innings)	8-55 – Vinoo Mankad (Chennai, 1952)	8-31 – Fred Trueman (Manchester, 1952)
Best bowling (match)	12-108 – Vinoo Mankad (Chennai, 1952)	13-106 – Ian Botham (Mumbai, 1980)
Highest wicket taker in a series	35 – Bhagwath Chandrasekhar (1972-73)	29 – Fred Trueman (1952), Derek Underwood (1976-77)

Most dismissals (wicketkeeper)	67 – MS Dhoni (21 matches)	54 – Alan Knott (16 matches)
Most dismissals (wicketkeeper/innings)	5 – Budhi Kunderan (Mumbai (BS), 1961)	7 – Bob Taylor (Mumbai, 1980)
Most catches (fielder)	35 – Sunil Gavaskar (38 matches)	22 – Alastair Cook (20 matches)
Highest partnership	Gundappa Viswanath/Yashpal Sharma – 316 for 3rd wicket (Chennai, 1982)	Ian Bell/Kevin Pietersen – 350 for 3rd wicket (The Oval, 2011)
Most capped player	Sunil Gavaskar – 38	David Gower – 24

New Zealand
(P 57, W 21, L 10, T 0, D 26)

Maiden match: Drawn (Hyderabad, November 19-24, 1955)

	India	New Zealand
Highest team total	583/7 dec (Ahmedabad, 1999)	680/8 dec (Wellington, 2014)
Lowest team total	81 (Wellington, 1976)	94 (Hamilton, 2002)
Highest run-getter	Rahul Dravid (1659, 15 matches)	Brendon McCullum (1224, 10 matches)
Highest individual score	231 – Vinoo Mankad (Chennai, 1956)	302 – Brendon McCullum (Wellington, 2014)
Most hundreds	6 – Rahul Dravid (15 matches)	4 – Brendon McCullum (10 matches)
Highest wicket taker	Bishan Bedi (57, 12 matches)	Richard Hadlee (65 wickets, 14 matches)
Best bowling (innings)	8-72 – S Venkataraghavan (Delhi, 1965)	7-23 by Richard Hadlee (Wellington, 1976)
Best bowling (match)	13-140 – R Ashwin (Indore, 2016)	11-58 – Richard Hadlee (Wellington, 1976)
Highest wicket taker in a series	34 – Subhash Gupte (1955-56)	18 – Richard Hadlee (1988-89)
Most dismissals (wicketkeeper)	33 – MS Dhoni (9 matches)	29 – Ian Smith (9 matches)
Most dismissals (wicketkeeper/innings)	6 – Syed Kirmani (Christchurch, 1976) & MS Dhoni (Wellington, 2009)	6 – BJ Watling (Auckland, 2014)
Most catches (fielder)	17 – Rahul Dravid (15 matches)	20 – Stephen Fleming (13 matches)
Highest partnership	Vinoo Mankad/Pankaj Roy – 413 for 1st wicket (Chennai, 1956)	Brendon McCullum/BJ Watling – 352 for 6th wicket (Wellington, 2014)
Most capped player	Sachin Tendulkar – 24	Daniel Vettori – 15

Pakistan
(P 59, W 9, L 12, T 0, D 38)

Maiden match: India won by an innings and 70 runs (October 16-18, 1952)

	India	Pakistan
Highest team total	675/5 dec (Multan, 2004)	699/5 (Lahore, 1989)
Lowest team total	106 (Lucknow, 1952)	116 (Bangalore, 1987)
Highest run-getter	Sunil Gavaskar (2089, 24 matches)	Javed Miandad (2228, 28 matches)
Highest individual score	309 – Virender Sehwag (Multan, 2004)	280* – Javed Miandad (Hyderabad (Sind), 1983)
Most hundreds	5 – Rahul Dravid (15), Sunil Gavaskar (24), Polly Umrigar (15)	6 – Mudassar Nazar (18), Zaheer Abbas (19)
Highest wicket taker	Kapil Dev (99 in 29 matches)	Imran Khan (94 in 23 matches)
Best bowling (innings)	10-74 – Anil Kumble (Delhi, 1999)	8-60 – Imran Khan (Karachi, 1982)
Best bowling (match)	14-149 – Anil Kumble (Delhi, 1999)	12-94 – Fazal Mahmood (Lucknow, 1952)
Highest wicket taker in a series	32 – Kapil Dev (1979-80)	40 – Imran Khan (1982-83)
Most dismissals (wicketkeeper)	50 – Syed Kirmani (20 matches)	55 – Wasim Bari (18 matches)
Most dismissals (wicketkeeper/innings)	5 – Syed Kirmani (Faisalabad, 1983) & Nayan Mongia (Kolkata, 1999)	4 – Wasim Bari (Karachi 1978; Mumbai 1979; Lahore 1982; Karachi 1983; Jalandhar 1983), Saleem Yousuf (Chennai, 1987) & Kamran Akmal (Faisalabad 2006; Karachi 2006)
Most catches (fielder)	19 – Rahul Dravid (15) & Sunil Gavaskar (24)	18 – Iqbal Qasim (15) & Javed Miandad (28)
Highest partnership	Rahul Dravid/Virender Sehwag – 410 for 1st wicket (Lahore, 2006)	Javed Miandad/Mudassar Nazar – 451 for 3rd wicket (Hyderabad (Sind), 1983)
Most capped player	Kapil Dev – 29	Javed Miandad – 28

South Africa
(P 33, W 10, L 13, T 0, D 10)

Maiden match: Drawn (Durban, November 13-17, 1992)

	India	South Africa
Highest team total	643/6 dec (Kolkata, 2010)	620/4 dec (Centurion, 2010)
Lowest team total	66 (Durban, 1996)	79 (Nagpur, 2015)

ghest run-getter	Sachin Tendulkar (1741, 25 matches)	Jacques Kallis (1734, 18 matches)
ghest individual score	319 – Virender Sehwag (Chennai, 2008)	253* – Hashim Amla (Nagpur, 2010)
ost hundreds	7 – Sachin Tendulkar (25 matches)	7 – Jacques Kallis (18 matches)
ghest wicket taker	Anil Kumble (84, 21 matches)	Dale Steyn (63, 13 matches)
est bowling (innings)	7-66 – R Ashwin (Nagpur, 2015)	8-64 – Lance Klusener (Kolkata, 1996)
est bowling (match)	12-98 – R Ashwin (Nagpur, 2015)	12-139 – Allan Donald (Port Elizabeth, 1992)
ighest wicket taker a series	31 – R Ashwin (2015-16)	21 – Dale Steyn (2010-11)
ost dismissals vicketkeeper)	28 – MS Dhoni (12 matches)	60 – Mark Boucher (14 matches)
ost dismissals vicketkeeper/innings)	5 – Nayan Mongia (Durban, 1996) & MS Dhoni (Cape Town, 2011)	5 – David Richardson (Port Elizabeth, 1992), Mark Boucher (Mumbai, 2000; Durban, 2010) & AB de Villiers (Durban, 2013)
ost catches (fielder)	21 – Rahul Dravid (21 matches)	23 – Jacques Kallis (18 matches)
ighest partnership	Rahul Dravid/Virender Sehwag – 268 for 2nd wicket (Chennai, 2008)	Hashim Amla/ Jacques Kallis – 340 for 3rd wicket (Nagpur, 2010)
Most capped player	Sachin Tendulkar – 25	Hashim Amla & Jacques Kallis – 18

Sri Lanka
(P 38, W 16, L 7, T 0, D 15)

Maiden match: Drawn (Chennai, September 17-22, 1982)

	India	Sri Lanka
Highest team total	726/9 dec (Mumbai, 2009)	952/6 dec (Colombo, 1997)
Lowest team total	112 (Galle, 2015)	82 (Chandigarh, 1990)
Highest run-getter	Sachin Tendulkar (1995, 25 matches)	Mahela Jayawardene (1822, 18 matches)
Highest individual score	293 – Virender Sehwag (Mumbai, 2009)	340 – Sanath Jayasuriya (Colombo, 1997)
Most hundreds	9 – Sachin Tendulkar (25 matches)	6 – Mahela Jayawardene (18 matches)
Highest wicket taker	Anil Kumble (74, 18 matches)	Muttiah Muralitharan (105, 22 matches)
Best bowling (innings)	7-51 – Maninder Singh (Nagpur in 1986)	8-87 – Muttiah Muralitharan (Colombo, 2001)

Best bowling (match)	11-125 – Venkatapathy Raju (Ahmedabad, 1994)	11-110 – Muttiah Muralitharan (Colombo, 2008)
Highest wicket taker in a series	21 – R Ashwin (2015-16)	26 – Ajantha Mendis (2008-09)
Most dismissals (wicketkeeper)	22 – MS Dhoni (9 matches)	22 – Amal Silva (3 matches)
Most dismissals (wicketkeeper/innings)	4 – Sadanand Viswanath (Kandy, 1985) & MS Dhoni (Mumbai, 2009)	6 – Amal Silva (Colombo, 1985)
Most catches (fielder)	27 – Mohammad Azharuddin (17 matches)	22 – Mahela Jayawardene (18 matches)
Highest partnership	Mohammad Azharuddin/ Kapil Dev – 272 for 6th wicket (Kanpur, 1986)	Sanath Jayasuriya/Mahanama – 576 for 2nd wicket (Colombo, 1997)
Most capped player	Sachin Tendulkar – 25 matches	Muttiah Muralitharan – 22 matches

West Indies
(P 94, W 18, L 30, T 0, D 46)
Maiden match: Drawn (Delhi, November 10-14, 1948)

	India	West Indies
Highest team total	644/7 dec (Kanpur, 1979)	644/8 dec (Delhi, 1959)
Lowest team total	75 (Delhi, 1987)	103 (Kingston, 2003)
Highest run-getter	Sunil Gavaskar (2749, 27 matches)	Clive Llyod (2344, 28 matches)
Highest individual score	236 – Sunil Gavaskar (Chennai, 1983)	256 – Rohan Kanhai (Kolkata, 1958)
Most hundreds	13 – Sunil Gavaskar (27 matches)	8 – Viv Richards (28), Garry Sobers (18)
Highest wicket taker	Kapil Dev (89, 25 matches)	Malcom Marshall (76, 17 matches)
Best bowling (innings)	9-83 – Kapil Dev (Ahmedabad, 1983)	9-95 – Jack Noreiga (Port of Spain, 1971)
Best bowling (match)	16-136 – Narendra Hirwani (Chennai, 1988)	12-121 – Andy Roberts (Chennai, 1975)
Highest wicket taker in a series	29 – Kapil Dev (1983-84)	33 – Malcom Marshall (1983-84)
Most dismissals (wicketkeeper)	48 – MS Dhoni (12 matches)	60 – Jeff Dujon (19 matches)
Most dismissals (wicketkeeper/innings)	6 – Wriddhiman Saha (North Sound, 2016)	5 – David Murray (Delhi, 1979), Jeff Dujon (Kingston, 1983) & Ridley Jacobs (Mumbai, 2002)
Most catches (fielder)	26 – Rahul Dravid (23 matches)	39 – Viv Richards (28 matches)

Highest partnership	Sunil Gavaskar/ Dilip Vengsarkar– 344* for 2nd wicket (Kolkata, 1978)	Gordon Greenidge/ Desmond Haynes– 296 for 1st wicket (St John's, 1983)
Most capped player	Sunil Gavaskar – 27	Clive Lloyd & Viv Richards – 28

Zimbabwe
(P 11, W 7, L 2, T 0, D 2)
Maiden match: Drawn (Harare, October 18-22, 1992)

	India	Zimbabwe
Highest team total	609/6 dec (Nagpur, 2000)	503/6 (Nagpur, 2000)
Lowest team total	173 (Harare, 1998)	146 (Delhi, 2002)
Highest run-getter	Rahul Dravid (979, 9 matches)	Andy Flower (1138, 9 matches)
Highest individual score	227 – Vinod Kambli (Delhi, 1993)	232* – Andy Flower (Nagpur, 2000)
Most hundreds	3 – Rahul Dravid (9) & Sachin Tendulkar (9)	3 – Andy Flower (9 matches)
Highest wicket taker	Anil Kumble (38, 7 matches)	Heath Streak (30, 9 matches)
Best bowling (innings)	7-59 – Irfan Pathan (Harare, 2005)	6-73 – Heath Streak (Harare, 2005)
Best bowling (match)	12-126 – Irfan Pathan (Harare, 2005)	7-115 – Heath Streak (Harare, 2001)
Highest wicket taker in a series	21 – Irfan Pathan (2005-06)	10 – Heath Streak & Ray Price (2001-02)
Most dismissals (wicketkeeper)	6 – Vijay Dahiya (2) & Dinesh Karthik (2)	17 – Andy Flower (7 matches)
Most dismissals (wicketkeeper/innings)	3 – Vijay Dahiya (Nagpur, 2000), Sameer Dighe, (Bulawayo, 2001), Dinesh Karthik (Harare, 2005)	4 – Andy Flower (Harare, 2001) & Tatenda Taibu (Harare, 2005)
Most catches (fielder)	21 – Rahul Dravid (9 matches)	5 – Grant Flower (8 matches)
Highest partnership	Rahul Dravid/Sachin Tendulkar– 249 for 3rd wicket (Nagpur, 2000)	Alistair Campbell/ Andy Flower– 209 for 4th wicket (Nagpur, 2000)
Most capped player	Rahul Dravid, Saurav Ganguly & Sachin Tendulkar – 9	Alistair Campbell, Andy Flower & Heath Streak – 9

Test record

Played: 502; **Won:** 132; **Lost:** 157; **Tied:** 1; **Drawn:** 212

Won series: 57
Drawn series: 32
Lost series: 62

Series results

1932: India in England 0-1; **1933-34:** England in India 0-2 (3); **1936:** India in England 0-2 (3); **1946:** India in England 0-1 (3); **1947-48:** India in Australia 0-4 (5); **1948-49:** West Indies in India 0-1 (5); **1951-52:** England in India 1-1 (5); **1952:** India in England 0-3 (4); **1952-53:** Pakistan in India 2-1 (5), India in West Indies 0-1 (5); **1954-55:** India in Pakistan 0-0 (5); **1955-56:** New Zealand in India 2-0 (5); **1956-57:** Australia in India 0-2 (3); **1958-5** West Indies in India 0-3 (5); **1959:** India in England 0-5 (5); **1959-60:** Australia in India 1-2 (5); **1960-61:** Pakistan in India 0-0 (5); **1961-62:** England in India 2-0 (5), India in West Indies 0-5 (5); **1963-64:** England in India 0-0 (5); **1964-65:** Australia in India 1-1 (3), New Zealand in India 1-0 (4); **1966-67:** West Indies in India 0-2 (3); **1967:** India in England 0-3 (3); **1967-68:** India in Australia 0-4 (4), India in New Zealand 3-1 (4); **1969-70:** New Zealand in India 1-1 (3), Australia in India 1-3 (5), **1970-71:** India in West Indies 1-0 (5); **1971:** India in England 1-0 (3); **1972-73:** England in India 2-1 (5); **1974:** India in England 0-3 (3); **1974-75:** West Indies in India 2-3 (5); **1975-76:** India in New Zealand 1-1 (3), India in West Indies 1-2 (4); **1976-77:** New Zealand in India 2-0 (3), England in India 1-3 (5); **1977-78:** India in Australia 2-3 (5); **1978-79:** India in Pakistan 0-2 (3), West Indies in India 1-0 (6); **1979:** India in England 0-1 (4); **1979-80:** Australia in India 2-0 (6), Pakistan in India 2-0 (6), England in India (Golden Jubilee Test) 0-1 (1); **1980-81:** India in Australia 1-1 (3); India in New Zealand 0-1 (3); **1981-82:** England in India 1-0 (6); **1982:** India in England 0-1 (3); **1982-83:** Sri Lanka in India 0-0 (1), India in Pakistan 0-3 (6); India in West Indies 0-2 (5); **1983-84:** Pakistan in India 0-0 (3), West Indies in India 0-3 (6); **1984-85:** India in Pakistan 0-0 (2), England in India 1-2 (5); **1985:** India in Sri Lanka 0-1 (3); **1985-86:** India in Australia 0-0 (3); **1986:** India in England 2-0 (3); **1986-87:** Australia in India 0-0 (3), Sri Lanka in India 2-0 (3), Pakistan in India 0-1 (5); **1987-88:** West Indies in India 1-1 (4); **1988-89:** New Zealand in India 2-1 (3), India in West Indies 0-3 (4); **1989-90:** India in Pakistan 0-0 (4), India in New Zealand 0-1 (3); **1990:** India in England 0-1 (3); **1990-91:** Sri Lanka in India 1-0 (1); **1991-92:** India in Australia 0-4 (5); **1992-93:** India in Zimbabwe 0-0 (1), India in South Africa 0-1 (4), England in India 3-0 (3), Zimbabwe in India 1-0 (1); **1993:** India in Sri Lanka 1-0 (3); **1993-94:** Sri Lanka in India 3-0 (3), India in New Zealand 0-0 (1); **1994-95:** West Indies in India 1-1 (3); **1995-96:** New Zealand in India 1-0 (3); **1996:** India in England 0-1 (3); **1996-97:** Australia in India 1-0 (1), South Africa in India 2-1 (3), India in South Africa 0-2 (3), India in West Indies 0-1 (5); **1997:** India in Sri Lanka 0-0 (2); **1997-98:** Sri Lanka in India 0-0 (3), Australia in India 2-1 (3); **1998-99:** India in Zimbabwe 0-1 (1), India in New Zealand 0-1 (2), Pakistan in India 1-1 (2), Asian Test Championship – Pakistan; **1999-00:** New Zealand in India 1-0 (3), India in Australia 0-3 (3), South Africa in India 0-2 (2); **2000-01:** India in Bangladesh 1-0 (1); Zimbabwe in India 1-0 (2), Australia in India 2-1 (3); **2001:** India in Zimbabwe 1-1 (2), India in Sri Lanka 1-2 (3); **2001-02:** India in South Africa 0-1 (2), England in India 1-0 (3), Zimbabwe in India 2-0 (2); **2002:** India in West Indies 1-2 (5), India in England 1-1 (4); **2002-03:** West Indies in India 2-0 (3), India in New Zealand 0-2 (2); **2003-04:** New Zealand in India 0-0 (2), India in Australia 1-1 (4), India in Pakistan 2-1 (3); **2004-05:** Australia in India 1-2 (4), South Africa in India 1-0 (2), India in Bangladesh 2-0 (2), Pakistan in India 1-1 (3); **2005:** India in Zimbabwe 2-0 (2); **2005-06:** Sri Lanka in India 2-0 (3), India in Pakistan 0-1 (3), England in India 1-1 (3); **2006:** India in West Indies 1-0 (4); **2006-07:** India in South Africa 1-2 (3); **2007:** India in Bangladesh 1-0 (2), India in England 1-0 (3); **2007-08:** Pakistan in India 1-0 (3), India in Australia 1-2 (4), outh Africa in India 1-1 (3); **2008:** India in Sri Lanka 1-2 (3); **2008-09:** Australia in India -0 (4), England in India 1-0 (2), India in New Zealand 1-0 (3); **2009-10:** Sri Lanka in India -0 (3), India in Bangladesh 2-0 (2), South Africa in India 1-1 (2); **2010:** India in Sri Lanka -1 (3); **2010-11:** Australia in India 2-0 (2), New Zealand in India 1-0 (3), India in South frica 1-1 (3); **2011:** India in West Indies 1-0 (3), India in England 0-4 (4); **2011-12:** West dies in India 2-0 (3), India in Australia 0-4 (4); **2012:** New Zealand in India 2-0 (2); **2012- 3:** England in India 1-2 (4), Australia in India 4-0 (4); **2013-14:** West Indies in India 2-0 (2), dia in South Africa 0-1 (2), India in New Zealand 0-1 (2); **2014:** India in England 1-3 (5); **014-15:** India in Australia 0-2 (4); **2015:** India in Bangladesh 0-0 (1), India in Sri Lanka 2-1); **2015-16:** South Africa in India 3-0 (4); **2016:** India in West Indies 2-0 (4). **2016-17:** New ealand in India 3-0 (3).

Test cricketers (285 in 502 Tests)

Amar Singh • Sorabji Colah • Jahangir Khan • Lall Singh • Naoomal Jaoomal • Janardan avle • **CK Nayudu** • Syed Nazir Ali • Mohammad Nissar • Phiroze Palia • Syed Wazir Ali • **ala Amarnath** • LP Jai • Rustomji Jamshedji • Vijay Merchant • L Ramji • Dilawar Hussain MJ Gopalan • Syed Mushtaq Ali • CS Nayudu • Yuvraj of Patiala • Dattaram Hindlekar • **izianagaram** • Khershed Meherhomji • Cotar Ramaswami • M Baqa Jilani • Gul Mohammad **Vijay Hazare** • Abdul Hafeez Kardar • **Vinoo Mankad** • Rusi Modi • **IAK Pataudi** • Sadhu hinde • Chandu Sarwate • Ranga Sohoni • **Hemu Adhikari** • Jenni Irani • G Kishenchand Khandu Rangnekar • Amir Elahi • Dattu Phadkar • K Rai Singh • Khokhan Sen • CR Ran- achari • KC Ibrahim • Keki Tarapore • **Polly Umrigar** • Mantu Banerjee • **Ghulam Ahmed** • Nirode Chowdhury • Madhusudan Rege • Shute Banerjee • Nana Joshi • **Pankaj Roy** • CD opinath • Madhav Mantri • Ramesh Divecha • Subhash Gupte • Vijay Manjrekar • **Datta Gaekwad** • **Gulabrai Ramchand** • Hiralal Gaekwad • S Nyalchand • Madhav Apte • Bal Dani • V Rajindernath • Ebrahim Maka • Deepak Shodhan • Chandrasekhar Gadkari • JM horpade • Pananmal Punjabi • Naren Tamhane • Prakash Bhandari • Jasu Patel • AG Kripal Singh • VN Swamy • **Nari Contractor** • Vijay Mehra • Sadashiv Patil • Bapu Nadkarni • GR Sunderam • Chandrakant Patankar • **Chandu Borde** • Ghulam Guard • Manohar Hardikar • Vasant Ranjane • Ramnath Kenny • Surendranath • Apoorva Sengupta • Ramakant Desai • ML Jaisimha • Arvind Apte • Abbas Ali Baig • VM Muddiah • Salim Durrani • Budhi Kunderan • AG Milkha Singh • Manmohan Sood • Rusi Surti • Balu Gupte • VV Kumar • Farokh Engineer • Dillip Sardesai • **MAK Pataudi** • Erapalli Prasanna • Bhagwat Chandrasekhar • Rajinder Pal • Hanumant Singh • KS Indrajitsinhji • **S Venkataraghavan** • V Subramanya • **Ajit Wadekar** • **Bishan Singh Bedi** • Subrata Guha • Ramesh Saxena • Syed Abid Ali • Umesh Kulkarni • Chetan Chauhan • Ashok Mankad • Ajit Pai • Ambar Roy • Ashok Gandotra • Eknath Solkar • **Gundappa Viswanath** • Mohinder Amarnath • Kenia Jayantilal • P Krishnamurthy • **Sunil Gavaskar** • Ramnath Parkar • Madan Lal • Brijesh Patel • Sudhir Naik • Hemant Kanitkar • Parthasarthi Sharma • Aunshuman Gaekwad • Karsan Ghavri • Surinder Amarnath • Syed Kirmani • **Dillip Vengsarkar** • Yajurvindra Singh • **Kapil Dev** • MV Narasimha Rao • Dhiraj Parsana • Bharath Reddy • Yashpal Sharma • Dillip Doshi • Shivlal Yadav • Roger Binny • Sandeep Patil • Kirti Azad • **Ravi Shastri** • Yograj Singh • TE Srinivasan • **K Srikkanth** • Ashok Malhotra • Pranab Roy • Ghulam Parkar • Suru Nayak • Arun Lal • Rakesh Shukla • Maninder Singh • Balwinder Singh Sandhu • TA Sekhar • L Sivaramakrishnan • Raghuram Bhat • NS Sidhu • Chetan Sharma • Manoj Prabhakar • **Mohammad Azharuddin** • Gopal Sharma • Lalchand Rajput • Sadanand Viswanath • Kiran More • Chandrakant Pandit • Raju Kulkarni • B Arun • Raman Lamba • Arshad Ayub • Sanjay Manjrekar • Narendra Hirwani • WV Raman • Ajay Sharma • Rashid Patel • Sanjeev Sharma • M Venkataramana • Salil Ankola • **Sachin Tendulkar** • Vivek Razdan • Venkatapathy Raju • Atul Wassan • Gursharan Singh • **Anil Kumble** • Javagal Srinath • Subroto Banerjee • Pravin Amre • Ajay Jadeja • Rajesh Chauhan • Vinod Kambli • Vijay Yadav • Nayan Mongia • Ashish Kapoor • Sunil Joshi •

Paras Mhambrey • Venkatesh Prasad • Vikram Rathour • **Rahul Dravid** • **Sourav Ganguly** • David Johnson • VVS Laxman • Dodda Ganesh • Abey Kuruvilla • Nilesh Kulkarni • Debas Mohanty • Harvinder Singh • Harbhajan Singh • Ajit Agarkar • Robin Singh • Robin Singh j • S Ramesh • Ashish Nehra • Devang Gandhi • MSK Prasad • Vijay Bharadwaj • Hrishikes Kanitkar • Wasim Jaffer • Murali Kartik • Nikhil Chopra • Mohammad Kaif • Shiv Sunder D • Syed Saba Karim • Zaheer Khan • Vijay Dahiya • Sarandeep Singh • Rahul Sanghvi • Sair Bahutule • Samir Dighe • Hemang Badani • Deep Dasgupta • **Virender Sehwag** • Sanjay Ba gar • Iqbal Siddiqui • Tinu Yohannan • Ajay Ratra • Parthiv Patel • L Balaji • Aakash Chopra Yuvraj Singh • Irfan Pathan • Gautam Gambhir • Dinesh Karthik • **MS Dhoni** • RP Singh Sreesanth • Piyush Chawla • Munaf Patel • VRV Singh • Ramesh Powar • Ishant Sharma • Am Mishra • M Vijay • Pragyan Ojha • S Badrinath • Wriddhiman Saha • Abhimanyu Mithun Suresh Raina • Cheteshwar Pujara • Jaydev Unadkat • **Virat Kohli** • Praveen Kumar • Abhina Mukund • R Ashwin • Umesh Yadav • Varun Aaron • R Vinay Kumar • Ravindra Jadeja • Bhu vneshwar Kumar • Shikhar Dhawan • Ajinkya Rahane • Mohammed Shami • Rohit Sharma Stuart Binny • Pankaj Singh • Karn Sharma • KL Rahul • Naman Ojha.

The names of those who have captained India are in bold
Records as on November 9, 2016

SELECTION FROM WISDEN INDIA WEBSITE

From war-torn Rwanda to cricket in South Africa, Sebareme's walk to remember
Himanish Bhattacharjee
When asked if a youngster like him has to be over-cautious about not bending his arm beyond the permissible 15-degree limit, there is an awkward silence, before he hesitantly replies: "But I do not throw…"
Clearly, there's some miscommunication there. Upon reiteration, the young man almost lets out a sigh of relief. "Oh ok, yes, I do have to work very hard on my shape."

Getting inside the mind of R Ashwin, the spin-scientist
R Kaushik
"I was very confident that the slowness could fetch me a caught-and-bowled if the batsman wanted to go through the covers because I was very, very sure about where I was landing the ball. That control, I am actually able to execute my plans and actually toy around with my fields because of that control."

How Dalmiya won Calcutta over with his people skills
Shamya Dasgupta
And, oh, was he accessible! If I felt I had some sort of special access to him, so did every other journalist in Kolkata. He knew everyone by name, everyone could call him, or push him into holding impromptu press conferences, even ask for improved food in the Eden Gardens press box – he never said no; the food didn't always improve.
Yes, it was easy to like Mr Dalmiya.

Inspired by the Mahatma, driven by Madiba
Karunya Keshav
The only way there could be more concentration of good in one place would be if Gandhi, Mandela and the Dalai Lama were at a tea party organised by Mother Teresa and Martin Luther King surprised them with cake.
Funnily enough, this is a story of a kind of party – there definitely was celebration. Where Mother Teresa did make an appearance.

The coming of age of Kagiso Rabada
Manoj Narayan
It was a youngster showing he's more than just raw talent. It was a moment

that significantly strengthened South Africa's hopes of having unearthed their next great paceman. He wasn't just a boy who could go places. He was already going places.

Aleem Dar, a victim of someone else's making
Anand Vasu

The fact that a group of thugs – and their behaviour leaves no other description possible – can put a spoke in perfectly legitimate activity, shines a light on just what a pass things have come to. That the president of the BCCI cannot discharge his duties in his own office without being subjected to the coarsest slang, reflects as poorly as possible on a country that loudly claims to love cricket to the point of calling it a religion.

Gavaskar in a fever, and memories of 1987
Manoj Narayan

These days, if you sit yourself at the VCA stadium and squint your eyes hard enough, you can still see Gavaskar swinging through his lines and a vociferous crowd erupting in his wake.

Shreyas Iyer, the thoroughbred for the long haul
Sidhanta Patnaik

"On the match day, I forgot my whites. Pravin sir was unhappy. I took Shardul's t-shirt, pant and sweater. In my brain it was going on, if I don't score runs in this match, I will be bombarded from all sides."

Sunny Days: Talking technique and temperament with Sunil Gavaskar
R Kaushik

Astonishing, really: 264 deliveries, eight fours, hours of stolid, solid stonewalling, and all he remembers is two deliveries? How do you get into that state of mind?

Ranji reporter turned lone ranger in Lahli
Karthik Lakshmanan

Conflicting thoughts ran through my idle mind as I watched the proceedings, sitting all alone with only an internet connection from the 1980s for company. Frankly, watching diligently wasn't the easiest of things to do (especially after all the paneer-loaded lunches) and a part of me tried to convince myself not to bother concentrating too hard - nobody else would know what exactly happened anyway. (To those who read the reports, and to my bosses, trust me, this part of me didn't win.)

The building blocks of Assam's success
Sidhanta Patnaik

For the people of Assam – where the Indian team last played almost five years ago – the success of their state team is the gateway to acknowledgement. For Gokul and Krishna, a quarterfinal berth means the scope of being seen on television, which would percolate to a loftier status in the neighbourhood. For Arup, it might be a promotion at his job, while for Hazarika, it might be an opening for employment with the state government.

Pradeep Sangwan travels the path from dark to light
Roshan Thyagarajan

"When people heard that I was banned for doing drugs, they thought I was doing cocaine and ganja. When someone says 'caught for doping', usually people think of these things. They don't think of supplements or medicines."

Father-son, coach-protege, life and passion – cricket spills over for Hirwanis
Saurabh Somani

When later asked about how he separated the dad from the coach, Narendra would say, "To tell you the absolute truth, 80 to 90% I speak to him like a coach more than a father." That drew an immediate quip from Mihir. "It's 95%!"

Prakash Munda: Blazing an indigenous trail
Disha Shetty

The fairly small-framed 24-year-old garnered a lot of attention during the 2015-16 Ranji Trophy quarterfinal against Mumbai, not so much for his skills as his appearance. Surprisingly, quite a few from the Mumbai camp mistook him for a member of Jharkhand's support staff, of Caribbean origin.

Mr Viswanath, Hero No. 1.01
R Kaushik

He smiled sweetly – can he in any other manner? – as he gently prised the tightly-held little book out of my hand, affixed his signature, put his right hand out for a priceless handshake, and then handed the book back to me. Hero No. 2 had just become Hero No. 1.5. Maybe even 1.1. And, almost spookily, even though the first page was blank, he had chosen to sign on the second!

The exuberance, resilience and brotherhood of Oman cricket
Karthik Lakshmanan

Everything about Oman cricket is driven by joint Indo-Pak ventures. They listen to Bollywood songs, gather regularly for dinners during the off-season. Aamer Ali and Aamir Kaleem, who hail from Pakistan, work at an Indian restaurant named Passage to India.

Never before, never since – the magic of Eden 2001
Shamya Dasgupta
As a young boy and man, Kapil Dev was the first Eden hero and then there was Mohammad Azharuddin. That day on, Laxman and Harbhajan joined the club. There are no honours boards at Eden, but in the hearts of the Kolkata cricket fan, the two men made permanent nests. Oh, what a celebration was! No Thursday will ever match up.

An Irish blend that smells like team spirit
Karunya Keshav
Speaking to the ladies of the Irish women's cricket team at the ICC World T20 2016 is an education – into cricket records and currency exchange rates from back in 1997, as well as Chris Brown's party jam and thea cappella abilities of Anna Kendrick – and a challenge to preconceived notions of age and accomplishment and friendships.

Ian Bishop on Mankading: 'What fairness in different rules for non-striker?'
Ian Bishop
Why is it that the non-striker plays by a different set of rules from the striker? What is special about him/her? Why do I need to deliver the courtesy of warning him that I will dismiss him if he breaks the rules. To be gentlemanly? Who decided it was gentlemanly? Is the non-striker being "gentlemanly" or "civilized" in trying to win the game from an advantageous position?

Virat Kohli: The artistry, the audacious engineering
Saurabh Somani
The dominant question when Kohli was building India's run-chase was not 'if' or 'when' he would get there, but 'how' he would choose to do it this time. The how became 'How??!!!' in a matter of minutes. How did he do that? Yes it was a given he would, but still, how??!!! It's an entirely plausible, and completely irrelevant question. Virat Kohli does what he does. Like the Light Brigade, ours is not to question why. Unlike them, ours is to watch and sigh.

Overseeing DDCA among the toughest challenges I've faced: Mudgal
Anand Vasu
"In particular, the proxy system is like a cancer. The person who controls the

ost proxies runs his writs at the DDCA. It's not that the DDCA does not
ve good people. But these good people, who are very interested in cricket,
e forced to succumb to the pressures of proxies. Even the good people get
bmerged in the DDCA."

pen letter to James Taylor: One step back, three steps forward
idhanta Patnaik

s you start living your second innings, you will no more be bothered about
ow many likes your Facebook status message or tweet has got. The positivity within you will culminate in new doors opening and it will take you to
laces you would have never imagined.

n immortal among us mice – Muhammad Ali, forever The Greatest
'hamya Dasgupta

Iow much must I have spoken about him – born 34 years before me in a
own far, far away, his career done and dusted before I was old enough to follow it – that some friends actually messaged me their condolences? Everyone
.new, I felt, that I had lost someone.

he Ghost of Antigua – Kumble relives a painful, stirring memory
Anand Vasu

"I remember it was a Saturday. Once I was out and in the dressing room, an
announcement was made on the PA system asking if there was a doctor in
the house," recalled Kumble. Of course there was, but the good doctor in
question was enjoying his day off, and showed up in the dressing room pint
in hand, jammy shorts and flowery shirt doing little to hide his festive mood.

On with the butter – the story of cricket in Iceland
Nisha Shetty

Don't tell anyone in Iceland that something isn't practical.
They won't listen to you anyway.
That's why there even exists a cricket team in the land of fire and ice.

Peter O'Toole: Lawrence of Arabia, Lazarus of cricket
Nisha Shetty

Yet, O'Toole still squeezed time for cricket, playing games in the middle of
the desert with Omar Sharif while filming *Lawrence of Arabia* and in the
middle of a lounge while in character in *What's New Pussycat?* If somebody
said they didn't understand cricket, he would take it as a challenge and teach
them just as he taught Katherine Hepburn the basics on set in *The Lion in
Winter*.

Stay back, play it late – the Azhar advice that changed Younis's game
R Kaushik

Azhar's suggestion to bat inside the crease stemmed from experience and straightforward logic. "A lot of people stand outside the crease in a bid to counter swing," pointed out Azhar. "When you stand outside the crease, you reduce the distance between yourself and the ball, so the ball comes quicker on to you. Also, you are playing the ball when it is still swinging, which maximises the chances of getting beaten or nicking off."

Oh for another India-Pakistan Test!
Dileep Premachandran

An India-Pakistan Test match got me my first job. The Chennai Test, the first between the two countries since 1989, was to start the following day. "I want you to do a preview that takes in the history and politics of the rivalry," my editor told me. "I have no interest in who's batting at No. 3, or who will open the bowling. Tell me what this means to both countries. Set the stage for our readers. You have two hours."

Bumrah eager for a slice of the Test pie
Hardik Worah

Players like Malinga, Chanderpaul and Sehwag have proved that you can be successful in international circuit with unorthodox ingredients. "People have only seen me bowling in shorter formats but I have also played Ranji matches and first-class cricket, and done well there," points out Bumrah. "I do know how Test cricket works."

Wisden India Honours Board

ar	Hall of Fame	Cricketers of The Year	Book of The Year	Beyond the Boundary
13	MAK Pataudi Kapil Dev Sunil Gavaskar	Rahul Dravid Virat Kohli Umesh Yadav Saeed Ajmal Kumar Sangakkara Shakib Al Hasan	Out of the Blue by Aakash Chopra	
14	CK Nayudu Anil Kumble	MS Dhoni Ravindra Jadeja Cheteshwar Pujara Misbah-ul-Haq Rangana Herath Mushfiqur Rahim	On Warne by Gideon Haigh	
15	Vijay Hazare Bishan Singh Bedi	Ajinkya Rahane Mithali Raj Rishi Dhawan Umar Akmal Angelo Mathews Mominul Haque	Wounded Tiger: A History of Cricket in Pakistan by Peter Oborne	
016	Vijay Merchant BS Chandrasekhar	R Ashwin R Vinay Kumar Younis Khan Dhammika Prasad Mashrafe Mortaza Joe Root	The Unquiet Ones: A History of Pakistan Cricket by Osman Samiuddin	Mukul Mudgal
017	Vinoo Mankad Sourav Ganguly	Virat Kohli Shreyas Iyer Yasir Shah Kusal Mendis Mustafizur Rahman David Warner	Stroke of Genius: Victor Trumper and the Shot that Changed Cricket by Gideon Haigh	Rajendra Mal Lodha

Contributors over five editions

Aakash Chopra
Abhishek Nayar
Aditya Iyer
Ahmer Naqvi
Ajay Suresh
Ajit Wadekar
Akash Sarkar
Akshay G
Alagappan Muthu
Alan Gardner
Amol Muzumdar
Amol Rajan
Anand Vasu
Ananya Upendran
Andrew Alderson
Andrew Fernando
Andrew McGlashan
Andrew Miller
Andrew Wu
Andy Bull
Angus Fraser
Anil Kumble
AT Sayeeduzzaman
Ayaz Memon
Badri Seshadri
Bishan Bedi
Brydon Coverdale
Chandu Borde
CK Nayudu
Clayton Murzello
Daniel Brettig
Daniel Harris
David Papineau
DB Deodhar
D Premachandran
Disha Shetty
D Sanzgiri
Ed Smith
Firdose Moonda
Fraser Stewart
G Bhattacharya
Geoff Lemon
Gideon Haigh
Gopal Hegde
Graham Hardcastle
Greg Chappell
Haresh Pandya
Harsha Bhogle
H Bhattacharjee
Ian Chappell
Isa Guha
J Arun Kumar
Jack Hobbs
Jaideep Verma
James Willoughby
Jarrod Kimber
Javagal Srinath
Jayanth Kodkani
Jeff Murimbechi
John Wright
Justice Mudgal
Kamila Shamsie
Kanishkaa B
Karthik L
Karunya Keshav
KC Vijaya Kumar
Ken Borland
Kevin Pile
KN Prabhu
Kritika Naidu
KR Nayar
KV Gopala Ratnam
Lawrence Booth
Lisa Sthalekar
Madhav Apte
M Jayawardene
M Waingankar
Manoj Narayan
Manu Joseph
Mazher Arshad
Mark Geenty
Michael Holding
Mike Coward
Mike Marqusee
Mike Selvey
Mithali Raj
Mohammad Isam
Mohandas Menon
Mudar Patherya
Murali Kartik
Mushtaq Ali
Narendar Pani
Nari Contractor
Naseeruddin Shah
Neil Manthorp
Nikhil Narain
Nisha Shetty
NS Ramaswami
Osman Samiuddin
Paddy Upton
Paul Radley
Pete Lalor
Pico Iyer
Prashant Kidambi
PR Mansingh
P Mukhopadhyay
Purnima Rau
QZ Islam
R Kaushik
R Mohan
Raf Nicholson
Rahul Bhattacharya
Rajdeep Sardesai
Raju Bharatan
Ramachandra Guha
Ray Monk
Rex Clementine
Richard Hadlee
Richard Sydenham
R Thyagarajan
Ruchir Joshi
Sa'adi Thawfeeq
Sambit Bal
Samir Chopra
Sandeep Dwivedi
Sanjay Manjrekar
Satya Nadella
Saurabh Somani
Shailesh Chaturvedi
S Chakrabarty
Shamya Dasgupta
S Karunatilaka
S Amarasinghe
Shantha R
Sharda Ugra
Shashank Kishore
Shashi Tharoor
Shubham Malaviya
Shubhangi Kulkarni
S Vaidyanathan
Sidharth Monga
Sidhanta Patnaik
Simon Barnes
Snehal Pradhan
Soham Sarkhel
S Bhattacharya
Sourav Ganguly
Sriram Veera
Stephen Brenkley
Subash Jayaraman
Sunil Gavaskar
Suresh Menon
Syed Kirmani
Tariq Ali
Telford Vice
Tim Albone
Tim Wigmore
TM Krishna
Tom Alter
Tony Cozier
Tristan Holme
Tunku Varadaraja
Utpal Shuvro
V Ramnarayan
Vaneisa Baksh
Vasant Raiji
Vedam Jaishankar
Vic Marks
Vidya Subramania
Vijay Lokapally
Vijay Merchant
Virat Kohli
VR Ferose
VVS Laxman
WV Raman

)+ direct offices
ountries
 million+ customers
)0+ employees representing
+ nationalities

e Brand

Customer Service: 600 555 550 | www.uaeexchange.com